THE MARTHA STEWART LIVING COOKBOOK

The Original Classics

THE MARTHA STEWART LIVING COOKBOOK

The Original Classics

By the Editors of Martha Stewart Living

CLARKSON POTTER • PUBLISHERS • NEW YORK

PUBLISHED IN THE UNITED STATES BY CLARKSON POTTER/PUBLISHERS,
AN IMPRINT OF THE CROWN PUBLISHING GROUP, A DIVISION OF RANDOM HOUSE, INC., NEW YORK.
WWW.CROWNPUBLISHING.COM
WWW.CLARKSONPOTTER.COM

WWW.MARTHASTEWART.COM

CLARKSON N. POTTER IS A TRADEMARK AND POTTER AND COLOPHON
ARE REGISTERED TRADEMARKS OF RANDOM HOUSE, INC.

THE RECIPES AND PHOTOGRAPHS IN THIS BOOK HAVE BEEN PREVIOUSLY PUBLISHED
IN SLIGHTLY DIFFERENT FORM IN *MARTHA STEWART LIVING* MAGAZINE.

LIBRARY OF CONGRESS CATALOGING-IN-PUBLICATION DATA
THE MARTHA STEWART LIVING COOKBOOK: THE ORIGINAL CLASSICS / MARTHA STEWART LIVING
MAGAZINE.—REV. AND UPDATED. EARLIER ED.: THE MARTHA STEWART LIVING COOKBOOK, 2000. INCLUDES INDEX.
1. COOKERY.   I. MARTHA STEWART LIVING COOKBOOK.
II. MARTHA STEWART LIVING.   III. TITLE.
TX714.M346 2007
641.5—DC22   2007006085

ISBN 978-0-307-39382-1

PRINTED IN THE UNITED STATES OF AMERICA

DESIGN BY AMBER BLAKESLEY, MARY JANE CALLISTER, AND MATT PAPA

10 9 8 7 6 5 4 3 2 1

contents

acknowledgments

THE RECIPES IN THIS book represent the creativity and extraordinary talents of the many food editors, recipe developers, and testers who worked in the *Martha Stewart Living* kitchens, largely under the direction of Susan Spungen and Frances Boswell, from the magazine's first issue in 1990 through 2000. I remain grateful to each of them for having created such a remarkable and timeless body of work.

For updating this book, I'd like thank Amy Conway and Ellen Morrissey, who thought up ways to make the original edition even more useful, and Evelyn Battaglia for her culinary and editorial knowledge as she implemented those changes impeccably. Under the expert guidance of William van Roden, Amber Blakesley designed a stunning cover, and Mary Jane Callister and Matt Papa made sure the recipes are easy to read and use.

Current food editors Jennifer Aaronson and Sarah Carey, two invaluable members of Lucinda Scala Quinn's talented team, lent their considerable expertise. Robb Riedel and Denise Clappi kept the project on track along the way, and Emily Burns and Lori Key took care of countless details.

Heartfelt thanks also to the photographers whose work appears in this book (see their names on page 656), along with our photo archive manager, Alison Vanek Devine, and the photo editors, art directors, and stylists who collaborated in the creation of the images.

As always, our executive team of Gael Towey, Lauren Podlach Stanich, Margaret Roach, and Eric A. Pike lent valuable support to the project. And thanks to our colleagues at Clarkson Potter: Jenny Frost, Lauren Shakely, Doris Cooper, Jane Treuhaft, Amy Boorstein, Mark McCauslin, and Derek Gullino.

introduction

When *The Martha Stewart Living Cookbook* was published several years ago, I was so gratified by the response of our many longtime readers. They let us know how delighted they were to have well over a thousand recipes from *Martha Stewart Living* magazine's first ten years in a single convenient volume. (I know I reach for it all the time.) And new readers were happy to have a cookbook with such depth and breadth.

  When we started talking about revising this book, the question we asked ourselves was how to make a good thing even better. The answer: Make it more useful and inspiring for today's cooks. So in this updated edition, you'll find beautiful new color images of some of our favorite dishes. And throughout, there are informative sidebars and how-to photographs to walk you through essential culinary techniques, such as trimming an artichoke and poaching salmon, step-by-step. (If you've never made pizza from scratch, don't wait any longer. See pages 177–79.)

To reflect the continuing evolution in the world of food, we've also updated the Pantry and Equipment sections of the book. And because so many people—myself included—are more interested than ever in a healthful diet, we have included nutritional analyses for what we call our "Fit to Eat" recipes, making it easier for you to plan wholesome meals for yourself and your family. While you're planning, don't forget to see our new menu section, too, in which we've suggested combinations of recipes that make up great meals. I think you'll find this especially helpful when you're entertaining, but there are quick and easy meals for any day of the week as well. By the way, we didn't cut a single recipe from the original edition to make room for all of this—we didn't want anyone to miss a favorite. *Martha Stewart*

P.S. The exceptionally talented food editors at Martha Stewart Living *are always coming up with excellent new recipes—you might want to save space on your shelf for another book:* The Martha Stewart Living Cookbook—The New Classics. *It contains more than a thousand recipes published in the magazine between 2001 and 2007.*

pantry

ANCHOVIES These tiny salt-cured fish are a staple of the cuisines of France, Spain, and Italy, where they are used to impart depth of flavor to sauces, such as salsa verde and bagna cauda, as well as to many meat, poultry, and vegetable dishes. When possible, buy anchovies that are salt-packed and sold in jars rather than those packed in oil and sold in tins. To tame their saltiness, rinse anchovies briefly under cold running water before using. Avoid overcooking, or cooking in oil that is too hot, as they will fry and harden instead of dissolving; mashing them first helps them blend quickly. Keep unopened tins at room temperature; once opened, transfer the fillets to an airtight container, cover with oil, and refrigerate for up to a month. Salt-packed anchovies have a much longer shelf life, and will keep for up to a year at room temperature (even after opening).

BEANS Black beans, cannellini beans, and chickpeas are versatile—add them to salads or combine them with rice or pasta for hearty side dishes or meatless main courses. Before using, rinse canned beans under cold running water and allow them to drain thoroughly. Once opened, transfer beans to an airtight container and refrigerate for up to a week.

CANNED MILK (EVAPORATED MILK AND SWEETENED CONDENSED MILK) Both products are made by removing about half the water from fresh milk, but sweetened condensed milk has sugar added while evaporated milk does not. They are not interchangeable. Evaporated milk lends creaminess to sauces and desserts; it can be mixed with an equal amount of water and used in place of fresh milk in a pinch. Sweetened condensed milk has a very sweet, distinctive flavor, and is used in pies, candies, and other desserts; it is the only milk used in dulce de leche, a creamy Spanish sauce with a caramel flavor, and one of three milks in Pastel Tres Leches, a classic Mexican cake. Canned milk can be kept in the pantry for months; once opened, the milk should be refrigerated in an airtight container and used within several days.

CANNED TOMATOES You can find tomatoes in many forms (diced, crushed, seasoned, and so on), but whole tomatoes (in juice, not puree) are the most versatile. The tomatoes will break down over long, slow cooking, making them ideal for stews, braises, and meat sauces. They can also be cut with kitchen scissors or crushed with your hands for use in quick-cooking sauces and dishes or pureed for a smooth consistency (instead of using canned tomato sauce).

CANNED TUNA Oil-packed tuna from Italy, particularly Sicily, has the best flavor. The cans will keep, unopened, for up to a year; after opening, transfer the tuna to a tightly sealed container and use within a few days.

CAPERS Capers are the salt-processed, unopened flower buds of a trailing shrub that thrives in the arid climate along the shores of the Mediterranean. Tangy and pungent, with a slight astringency, capers are an essential ingredient in many well-known dishes such as caponata, pasta puttanesca, and salad Niçoise, as well as classic sauces such as rémoulade. Nonpareils, the tiniest capers, are the most expensive but have the most delicate flavor. Capers are either packed in brine or salt; since they are rinsed and drained before using, the salt-packed type actually have a less salty taste. Capers keep indefinitely in unopened jars. Once opened, they are best used within a year; refrigerate brine-packed capers and keep salt-packed capers at room temperature (in a well-sealed jar).

CHUTNEYS Chutneys, a broad category of relishes with roots in India, often have a chunky texture and can be made with chiles, herbs, spices, fruits, and vegetables (mango is the most widely known, but tomato, cranberry, and others are also common). Pair them with grilled meats or cheeses, add to chicken salad, or blend with mayonnaise for a flavorful sandwich spread. Chutneys should be refrigerated and used within a few months after opening.

COCONUT MILK Canned coconut milk, made from coconut meat that is steeped in boiling water and then strained to form a creamy liquid, is widely used in Eastern and Caribbean cooking. It should not be confused with coconut cream, which is made the same way but with less water, or with sweetened cream of coconut, generally used to make blended cocktails. Before opening, shake the can to mix the coconut milk thoroughly. Unopened cans will keep for up to eighteen months; transfer the contents of opened cans to an airtight container and refrigerate for up to a week.

COUSCOUS A staple of North African cuisine, couscous is a tiny pasta made from hard-wheat flour (durum) or precooked semolina. The larger pearls of Israeli couscous are lightly oven-dried, giving them a faintly golden color and toasted flavor (it is often labeled "toasted"). The large pearls also have a more toothsome texture. Keep couscous in the original container until opened, then store it in an airtight container for up to a year.

DIJON MUSTARD Dijon is a general term for a French-style mustard, which is prized for its clean, sharp flavor. It's made from brown or black mustard seeds, white wine, must (unfermented grape juice), and seasonings. It can be used on sandwiches and in sauces, vinaigrettes, and other salad dressings.

DRIED HERBS AND SPICES Most spices will lose their potency after about a year, but their flavor will deteriorate faster if stored improperly. Keep them in airtight containers, away from heat or direct sunlight; label them with the date of purchase so you'll know when it's time to replenish. For the freshest flavor, buy whole spices when possible and then grind just what you need in a spice or coffee grinder (or with a mortar and pestle).

DRIED PASTA Stock an assortment of shapes for different sauces, such as spaghetti, bucatini, and perciatelli for tomato sauces; linguine for clam sauce; capellini for light, delicate sauces (or no sauce at all); penne, rigatoni, and pappardelle for meaty ragus; and fusilli, farfalle, and fettucine for cream sauces. Whole-wheat pastas offer more nutritional benefits (and a slightly chewier texture). Dried pasta can be stored in its original package until opened, then transferred to airtight containers; for best results, use within a year.

GRAINS Except as noted, the following items can be stored in the pantry for up to one year; transfer to airtight containers after opening.

barley Of the various types of barley available, pearl barley is the easiest to find and to use. It comes in three sizes: coarse, medium, and fine. Barley adds substance and flavor to soups (beef barley is a classic), stews, pilafs, and other side dishes. Its earthy flavor pairs well with mushrooms, and is enhanced by a brief toasting before cooking in water or broth.

cornmeal Cornmeal is made from dried corn kernels that are steel-ground, a process by which the hull and germ of the kernel are removed. Cornmeal is typically white or yellow, depending on the variety of corn used; the taste is virtually the same. It is sold in three varieties: fine (also known as corn flour), medium (the most common), and coarse. Fine and medium cornmeal are used frequently in baking; coarse cornmeal is used to make polenta. Stone-ground cornmeal, a coarser relative of cornmeal, is water-ground; this process results in the meal retaining some of the hull and germ, giving foods a deeper flavor and rougher texture. Store stone-ground cornmeal in the freezer for up to a year.

lentils These tiny, round legumes grow in small pods. When ripe, the pods are picked, dried, and smashed to release the seeds, which are then dried further and left whole or split. The most common form is brown, but they are also available in green (also called French, or *lentilles de Puy*) as well as red, black, and yellow (used primarily in Indian cooking). Because they lose moisture over time, older lentils will take longer to cook than fresher ones. Before using, sort through lentils to remove any shriveled ones and small stones and twigs, and then rinse well.

oats Rolled oats, also called old-fashioned oats, are whole oats that have been steamed and flattened to make them more tender; they cook in about 15 minutes. Quick-cooking oats have been cut into smaller pieces before steaming and then rolled even thinner; they cook in about 5 minutes. It is generally acceptable to substitute one for the other in most recipes, but never substitute instant oatmeal. Steel-cut oats or Irish oatmeal, which are not rolled, take longer to cook, but have a pleasantly chewy texture.

HOISIN SAUCE Although ingredients vary by brand, this thick, dark brown sauce is generally made with soybeans, chiles, and spices. It is widely used in Chinese cooking as a condiment as well as in marinades, glazes, sauces, and other dishes. Bottled hoisin will keep almost indefinitely in the refrigerator.

NUTS AND DRIED FRUIT These staples can be used in a wide array of dishes and cooking, both sweet and savory, so stock at least a few of the following: walnut and pecan halves, almonds (whole and sliced), hazelnuts, raisins (dark and golden), currants, dates, apricots, and figs. Nuts can turn rancid easily, so store them in the freezer for up to six months. Dried fruit can be kept at room temperature for up to a year; keep them well sealed to preserve freshness and prevent stickiness.

OILS Store vegetable oils in their original bottles, in a cool, dark place, for up to six months. Nut oils should be refrigerated and used within three months. There are three types to keep in your pantry:

neutral-tasting oils These flavorless oils are good to use when you don't want to affect the taste of a dish. They also have high smoke points (the temperature at which the oil will cause foods to burn), making them ideal for sautéing, frying, and other high-temperature cooking. Good choices include canola oil, corn oil, peanut oil, and vegetable oil.

nut and seed oils Flavorful nut oils, such as walnut and hazelnut, are generally not used in cooking, but as condiments. Drizzle them onto salads, vegetables, and rice and pasta dishes. There are two basic types of sesame oil to look for: regular (light-colored) and toasted (dark). Regular sesame oil, which has a mild nutty taste and a high smoke point, is the most versatile and is more commonly used in cooking, especially frying. Toasted sesame oil has a richer, more assertive flavor; it is used sparingly in marinades and salad dressings, and can be drizzled over cooked dishes just before serving. It can also be combined with a neutral vegetable oil for stir-frying.

olive oils These oils can be used to impart flavor as well as for cooking. Extra-virgin olive oil is perfect for lower-temperature sautéing, for salads and marinades, and for drizzling over pasta and rice dishes. Light and extra-light olive oils have been cut with vegetable oils so they are light in flavor but not in fat. Grapeseed oil is a good alternative to olive oil; with its mildly nutty flavor, it can be used in salad dressings and marinades, while its high smoke point makes it perfect for all types of cooking.

ORZO *Orzo* means "barley" in Italian, but it's actually a type of pasta. It looks like rice and makes a fine substitute as a side or in salads and soups. Toasting orzo before cooking will give it a deeper flavor.

PANTRY VEGETABLES These essential ingredients are part of any well-stocked kitchen, and are sturdy enough to keep in a cupboard or other cool, dark, dry spot, but not the refrigerator. Garlic, onions, shallots, and potatoes will generally keep for about a month. Dried mushrooms, such as porcini or shiitake, can be kept in a well-sealed container for several months.

PEPPERCORNS There are three basic types of peppercorns: black, white, and green. The black kind is picked when the berry is slightly underripe, then dried until black and shriveled; it has a slightly hot flavor. The green type is also picked when underripe

and then either preserved in brine or sold dried; it is tart, slightly fruity, and especially good in chutneys and mustards. The white variety is a fully ripened berry that has had its skin removed before being dried; it is slightly milder tasting than black pepper and is often used instead of black pepper to preserve the appearance of a light-colored dish. The pink peppercorn is not a peppercorn at all, but a dried berry from the Baies rose plant; it is mild and slightly sweet. Peppercorns are available whole, cracked, or ground. For the freshest flavor, buy them whole and then grind just what you need at a time. Like all spices, peppercorns should be stored in tightly sealed containers, away from heat or light.

RICE It helps to keep a variety of rices in your pantry at all times, as they make an easy side dish and are used in many types of cooking across the world. Keep rice in its original packaging until opening, then store it in an airtight container at room temperature. Martha likes to write cooking instructions for each and affix them to the lid of the container for handy reference (for example, "combine 1 cup water, ½ cup rice, and ½ teaspoon salt; cook 25 minutes"). For best results, use within a year.

arborio rice: When properly prepared, this short-grain Italian rice develops a creamy texture and a chewy center and has an exceptional ability to absorb flavors, making it ideal for risotto. Carnaroli is similar in starch content.

basmati rice: With its slender long grains, basmati is prized for its delicate nutty aroma. It is an essential element of Indian cooking.

brown rice (medium- to long-grain) is the entire grain of rice with only the inedible husk removed. The nutritious, high-fiber bran coating gives it its light tan color. When cooked, brown rice has a strong, nutty flavor and chewy texture. Medium-grain brown rice is starchier than the long-grain variety.

jasmine rice: This long-grain rice has the aroma of basmati but the softer, starchier texture of medium-grain rice. It is ideal for serving with Thai curries.

sushi rice: Japanese sushi rice is a short-grained, glutinous white rice that becomes moist, firm, and sticky when cooked. If you can't find Japanese sushi rice, substitute short-grained white rice (called pearl).

white rice (medium- to long-grain), which has been stripped of the husk and bran, has a mild flavor and firm texture, making it a versatile vehicle for carrying the flavor of other ingredients. Medium-grain is a little stickier than the long-grain variety. Converted white rice, which is made by soaking, pressure-steaming, and then drying unhulled grains, takes slightly longer to cook than unconverted white rice; it also has a pale tan color. Instant or quick white rice has been fully or partially cooked before being dehydrated and packaged; this should not be substituted in recipes.

white rice (short-grain, or pearl): The fat, almost round grains of short-grain white rice have a higher starch content than medium- and long-grain rice. They become moist and viscous when cooked, causing the grains to stick together. Also called glutinous rice (even though it is gluten-free), this variety is most often used in Asian cooking.

wild rice is actually the seed of a grass found in the Great Lakes region of the United States. It is harvested by hand and it has a nutty flavor and chewy texture, making it particularly good in rice salads and stuffings. Although wild rice can take up to an hour to cook, it is important to watch it carefully toward the end; overcooking produces starchy results.

SALT The two most common types are kosher (coarse) salt and table (iodized) salt. Kosher salt is a good choice for cooking (and brining) and for use at the table. Since coarse salt does not contain any additives or iodine, it has a cleaner flavor and is not as strong or sharply acidic as table salt; it also dissolves quickly in cold water. When seasoning foods, the larger grain of coarse salt make it easier to control the amount you use (and the saltiness of the dish). In most recipes, these salts can generally be used interchangeably, without altering amounts, though you may prefer to use table salt for baking.

If you want to add a more distinctive accent to dishes, consider one of the many types of sea salts. Fleur de sel, one of the rarest and most prized of sea salts, comes from the Brittany region of France; it has a mild salty taste and is best used as a condiment, sprinkled over salads, egg dishes, fish, and other foods at the table. Gray salt also hails from Brittany, and has a stronger saltiness. Maldon, an English sea salt, consists of small white crystalline flakes that can easily be crushed with your fingers and added to dishes as they cook or once they are at the table. Sun-dried sea salts also come from Sicily and Maine; they are perfect for garnishing the rims of cocktail glasses.

SOY SAUCE Soy sauce is traditionally made by fermenting whole boiled soybeans with wheat or barley. Varieties can range from dark to light in color and thick to thin in texture. Light soy sauce is generally saltier and thinner than dark and is used when the flavor of the sauce is desired but the color is not. Dark soy sauce is less salty and provides a richer flavor and hue to a dish, due to the addition of caramel color. Tamari, a similar sauce, is brewed from whole soybeans but contains no wheat; it has a more pronounced flavor and is often used to season long-cooking dishes such as soups and stews. Both types are very versatile and can be used in marinades and dressings and as a table condiment. Soy sauce will keep indefinitely in a cool pantry.

SUN-DRIED TOMATOES Sun-dried tomatoes are available dry-packed or oil-packed. Dry ones need to be softened by soaking in water or another liquid before using, while oil-packed tomatoes can be used right out of the jar and often have a more consistently chewy texture (the oil can be used to flavor sauces and salad dressings). Use sun-dried tomatoes throughout the year to make sandwiches, pizza, salads, and pasta dishes. The dry-packed tomatoes will keep almost indefinitely in a well-sealed bag; oil-packed tomatoes should be refrigerated after opening and used within a month or so.

TOMATO PASTE Tomato paste is highly concentrated and generally used as a thickener and flavor enhancer in soups, stews, and tomato-based sauces. A little paste goes a long way; many recipes often call for just one or two tablespoons. The rest should be transferred to an airtight container and can be refrigerated for several weeks. Or it can be frozen for up to six months: Drop 1 tablespoon of tomato paste into each section of an ice-cube tray and freeze until solid, then pop frozen cubes into a resealable plastic bag and return to the freezer until ready to use.

VINEGARS Because they add brightness to everything from salad dressings to sauces, vinegars are pantry essentials. Experiment with different types; those made with wine and sherry are the most versatile. For the longest shelf life (up to a year), store bottles in a cool spot, away from direct sunlight.

balsamic vinegar is made from the boiled-down must of white grapes. With its sweetness and intense flavor, balsamic should be used sparingly. It is delicious in vinaigrettes (often in combination with other vinegars) or drizzled over strawberries. When used in cooking, add balsamic vinegar only at the end or just before serving to retain its flavor.

cider vinegar is derived from fermented apple cider. Mild-tasting and slightly sweet, it is what gives coleslaws and sauerkraut their familiar tang. You can also use it instead of lemon juice to enhance the flavor of apples in pies and other desserts.

red-wine and white-wine vinegars are made from fermented wines. They are most frequently used in salad dressings and marinades and as last-minute additions to sauces and stews.

rice-wine vinegar, made from fermented rice wine, is much milder and faintly sweeter than other wine-based vinegars. Look for unseasoned rice-wine vinegar (seasoned vinegars are clearly labeled as such).

sherry vinegar, produced in Spain from fermented fino sherry, is prized for its concentrated, balanced flavor. It is essential in gazpacho and wonderful in vinaigrettes, but it can also be used sparingly in cooking to give dishes depth of flavor.

WORCESTERSHIRE SAUCE This dark, piquant sauce is usually made from garlic, soy sauce, tamarind, onions, molasses, anchovies, vinegar, and seasonings. It can be used at the table or to flavor meats, marinades, soups, and salad dressings. There is also a light-colored version for use with fish and poultry. It will keep almost indefinitely in a cool spot.

BAKING NEEDS

BAKING POWDER Baking powder combines the leavening action of baking soda with a premixed acidic agent. When mixed with water or other liquid, baking powder releases carbon dioxide gas bubbles that cause a bread or cake to rise. Before buying, check the date on the bottom of the canister; it loses its potency over time, and usually needs to be replaced after one year. To test if your baking powder is still active, mix 1 teaspoon powder with ⅓ cup hot water; it should bubble instantly.

BAKING SODA Baking soda is another type of leavener. When used with an acidic ingredient, such as buttermilk or yogurt, baking soda produces gas bubbles, causing bread or cakes to rise. It should be mixed with the other dry ingredients before a liquid is added, as baking soda reacts immediately when moistened. Keep it in a cool spot and check the expiration date on the bottom of the box. It's also good as a household cleaner, and an open box in the refrigerator will help eliminate any odors (buy one specifically for this purpose; do not use it in recipes).

CHOCOLATE Keeping chocolate bars and chips on hand is a must for spur-of-the-moment desserts. Semisweet is the most commonly called for, but some people prefer the taste of bittersweet. Unsweetened chocolate is used in some recipes and cannot be swapped for the others. If you prefer a richer flavor, explore the higher-quality brands such as Callebaut and Scharffen Berger. Unopened packages should be stored in a cool, dry, dark spot for up to a year; once they've been opened, wrap the packages in plastic or foil, or place in a resealable plastic bag. Don't worry if a grayish-white bloom develops on the chocolate; it doesn't affect the flavor and can be scraped off.

COCOA POWDER Cocoa powder is unsweetened chocolate with most of the cocoa butter removed. Dutch-processed cocoa, which is treated with alkali, a mineral salt that helps to neutralize cocoa's natural acidity, is richer, darker, and less bitter than regular unsweetened cocoa; it is also more powdery and does not dissolve readily in cold milk. Although the two types can often be used interchangeably, it's a good idea to use what is called for in a recipe.

CORN SYRUP Because corn syrup prevents crystallization, it's an important ingredient in some candies, jams, jellies, frostings, and glazes. It is also used in pie fillings, including pecan. There are two types to choose from: light corn syrup, which has been stripped of all color and cloudiness and has a purer flavor, and dark corn syrup, with added caramel flavor and coloring. Store syrup at room temperature in its original container for up to a year.

CORNSTARCH Dense, powdery cornstarch comes from the endosperm, or white heart, of the corn kernel. It is commonly used instead of flour as a thickening agent for pie fillings and custards; it is also added to gravies, soups, and savory sauces (especially in Chinese cooking). Because it tends to form lumps, cornstarch should be blended with a small amount of cold or room-temperature liquid to form a slurry, or paste, before being stirred into a hot mixture. Keep in a cool spot, tightly sealed, and use within a year.

CREAM OF TARTAR This powder is tartaric acid derived from fermented grapes. It increases the stability and volume of whipped egg whites in meringues or angel food cake. It is also used to give some candy and frostings a creamier consistency. Cream of tartar will keep for a year or longer in a cool spot.

FLOUR Different flours have different amounts of protein, which will affect the way each behaves in a recipe: The protein in flour forms an elastic network that helps contain the gases that make doughs and batters rise as they bake. It is only necessary to sift flour if a recipe specifically calls for it, but you may want to run a whisk through it before measuring to break up any clumps. Store in airtight containers at room temperature for up to a year; choose containers with wide mouths for easy scooping.

all-purpose flour is made from a blend of high-protein hard wheat and low-protein soft wheat; use it to make piecrusts, cookies, pancakes, waffles, and biscuits. Look for the unbleached variety.

bread flour, with its high protein content, is appropriate for making yeast breads and popovers.

cake, or pastry, flour is a fine-textured, low-protein flour best used for cakes, pastries, and quick breads, where a tender crumb is desired. Most recipes call for cake flour that is not self-rising (meaning baking powder and salt have been added), so be sure to check the label before buying.

wheat flour: Unlike white flour, wheat flour contains the bran and germ of the wheat berry. It has higher fiber, nutritional, and fat content than white flour. Many recipes call for a combination of white and wheat flour for improved flavor and texture, as using all wheat flour can give very chewy results.

GELATIN There are two forms of gelatin: granulated, which is easiest to find, and sheet (or leaf), available at gourmet and baking supply shops. Granulated gelatin must always be softened first by soaking in cold water for several minutes; sheet gelatin must be soaked a bit longer, but it is preferred by many professional bakers for the creamier texture it develops. Four sheets of gelatin equals one package of powdered. Check for expiration dates on packets of powdered gelatin; sheet gelatin will keep for about ten months at room temperature. Besides making jelled desserts, gelatin can be used to stabilize mousses, whipped creams, and dessert sauces.

MOLASSES Molasses is made from the juice extracted from cane sugar during the refining process; the juice is boiled, then sugar crystals are removed from the resulting liquid, leaving behind the thick syrup that is molasses. Light molasses is made by boiling the juice once; for dark molasses, it's boiled twice. The light version has a subtle sweetness and is most often used for pancakes and waffles. Dark molasses, which is less sweet and has a deeper taste, is preferred for

baking. Both light and dark are sold in two forms: sulfured (which has been processed with sulfur as a preservative and is sweeter and thicker) and unsulfured, often preferred for its sharper, more pronounced taste. If a recipe calls for unsulfured molasses, you can use sulfured, but the outcome might be slightly different; adding a bit less sugar might help balance the flavor. Blackstrap molasses, created by boiling sugarcane juice three times, is very dense and bitter tasting and should not be substituted for other types of molasses. Stored in a cool, dark place, molasses will keep for up to a year.

SUGAR Besides sweetness, sugar adds tenderness to doughs, stability to meringues, and a golden-brown hue to the surface of almost any baked good. Humidity can make sugars lumpy, so keep them in well-sealed containers in a cool, dry spot. Double-wrap brown sugars to keep them moist.

brown sugar, a combination of granulated sugar and molasses, has a softer texture, darker color, and distinctive flavor. Light brown sugar has a more delicate taste than dark; they can usually be used interchangeably. If your brown sugar has hardened, there are a couple of ways to soften it. To use it right away, place a half pound in a microwaveable bowl, drape with a damp paper towel, and cover with plastic wrap; heat at ten-second intervals, just until it becomes soft, then break apart the lumps with a fork. If you have more time, place an apple or bread slice in the bag overnight (no longer), which will return the sugar to its optimal consistency.

confectioners' sugar, also called powdered sugar, is made by grinding granulated sugar to a fine powder, then sifting and adding a small amount of cornstarch to prevent caking. It dissolves easily in icings and candies, and can be dusted over finished desserts.

granulated sugar has a fine grain that makes it perfect as a table sweetener and cooking ingredient.

superfine sugar has finer crystals than granulated sugar (though not as fine as confectioners'), and is often used to make meringues or fine-textured cakes, such as angel food. Because it dissolves quickly, superfine is good for sweetening cold drinks.

turbinado sugar is made by steaming raw sugar to remove impurities. The caramel-colored coarse crystals are slightly crunchy and have a mild molasses flavor. Sprinkle it on cereal or stir it into hot drinks.

VANILLA BEANS AND EXTRACT The thin black fruit of an orchid, vanilla beans are actually pods that are picked when green, then cured and fermented. To preserve the flavor and aroma of vanilla beans, store them carefully: Wrap tightly in plastic, then put them in an airtight container and keep in a cool, dark place for six months to a year. Vanilla extract is made by steeping chopped vanilla pods in alcohol and water and then aging the strained liquid. Always buy extract that is labeled "pure" (imitation vanilla offers little flavor and a bitter aftertaste); Mexican and Tahitian extracts are worth the extra cost. Tightly sealed, vanilla extract will last indefinitely at room temperature.

VEGETABLE SHORTENING Shortening is made by hydrogenating vegetable oils to make them solid. It is virtually flavorless and used for making tender piecrusts and other baked goods. Store shortening at room temperature for up to a year.

REFRIGERATED GOODS

BACON Besides being delicious on its own, bacon lends incomparable flavor to many dishes, such as chowders and other soups, baked beans and collard greens, and savory custards and tarts. There are many types; look for bacon that is free of nitrates and other artificial ingredients. Thick-sliced bacon, along with its melted fat, provides not only flavor but also a hot dressing for wilting spinach or other greens. The subtler flavor of Canadian bacon (which is also lower in fat and calories than American-style bacon), is an essential component of eggs Benedict. Pancetta, a traditional Italian bacon, is cured but not smoked; it is highly flavorful and slightly salty, and a small amount is all it takes to flavor pasta sauces and other dishes. All bacon can be tightly wrapped and kept for up to three weeks in the refrigerator or three months in the freezer.

BUTTER Unsalted butter has the purest flavor. It is ideal for all types of cooking, especially baking. European-style butters are also good for baking, especially pastries and shortbread, as well as for spreading at the table. They have a higher percentage of butterfat (typically 83 percent compared to 80 percent) and a richer, more distinctive taste.

CHEESE Of all the many types of cheese available, the following are among the more versatile. Of course, it's also nice to keep a supply of favorites, such as Cheddar and Muenster, for making grilled cheese or for quickly putting together an appetizer to share with unexpected guests.

fontina cheese is a cow's milk cheese with a mildly sweet, nutty, buttery flavor. Smooth and shot through with tiny holes, fontina is a very good melting cheese and is excellent on pizza and in hot sandwiches.

goat cheese Made from goat's milk, this soft and creamy cheese is usually sold in logs or disks; French goat cheeses are often called chèvre. Goat cheese is particularly good in egg dishes, salads, sandwiches, and savory tarts, as well as paired with fresh fruit as a light snack or dessert. Aged goat cheeses are more pungent and often have a rind; they are harder in texture and not generally a good substitute for fresh in recipes (but they are delicious as a snacking cheese). Keep fresh goat cheese, loosely wrapped, in the least cold part of the refrigerator. It should not be frozen, but you may want to pop it in the freezer for five or ten minutes to make it easier to slice.

gruyère is another wonderful melting cheese, and is traditionally used in making croque-monsieurs.

parmesan This popular cheese is a hard, dry cheese made from skimmed or partially skimmed cow's milk. The finest of the many kinds of Parmesan is Parmigiano-Reggiano (the name should be printed on the perimeter of the rind), produced in the Emilia-Romagna region of Italy. Known for its sumptuous flavor, this cheese can appear at any point of the meal, from hors d'oeuvres to dessert. A good alternative is Pecorino Romano. For the best flavor, buy wedges of cheese (instead of already grated) and grate just before using or serving. To keep Parmesan, wrap it in parchment paper and then plastic, and store it on the bottom shelf (or in the cheese bin) of the refrigerator.

EGGS Eggs come in many sizes; large is the most common and the size most often used in our recipes. Shell color has nothing to do with flavor or nutritional value, but is determined by the breed of the hen. When buying eggs, check to make sure the eggs are clean and free of cracks, and look on the carton for an expiration date. To store, refrigerate eggs in their original carton; it will help protect the delicate, porous shells from cracking and absorbing odors. Eggs are freshest within a week of purchase, but will keep longer (up to a month).

FRESH HERBS Fresh herbs have a singular ability to brighten any dish. To store, wrap them in damp paper towels, then place in a resealable plastic bag; keep them in the refrigerator's vegetable bin. Leafy herbs, such as basil, will keep for up to a week; sturdier herbs such as thyme and rosemary will keep a bit longer. Wash leafy herbs as soon as you bring them home, before storing.

FRESH GINGER Fresh ginger adds brightness to many dishes, making vegetables taste fresher and giving bite to seafood. The fine sharpness cuts through rich sauces and meats, such as duck or pork, and is a key note in many chutneys, curries, and pickling brines. When buying ginger, look for roots that are hard and seem swollen. The skin should be smooth; wrinkling is a sign of age. Unpeeled ginger keeps for up to three weeks when wrapped in a paper towel or placed in a paper bag, and then refrigerated in an airtight container. Freezing can preserve the flavor and makes it easier to grate.

LEMONS AND LIMES A squeeze of lemon or lime juice makes fish, vegetables, fruit salad, and many other foods taste better. The juice and zest are also flavorful components of many dishes and baked goods. Keep fruit in a plastic bag in the fruit or vegetable bin of the refrigerator for up to two weeks.

MILK Although you can sometimes substitute one type of milk for another, it's best to use what is called for in a recipe. Whole milk, for instance, will produce a much creamier texture than skim. However, if a recipe calls for heavy cream and you don't have any, whole milk can often be used instead. Keep buttermilk on hand for making salad dressings, biscuits, pancakes, and some cakes and quick breads. You can make your own buttermilk in a pinch: add a tablespoon of white vinegar or lemon juice for each cup of regular milk called for, and let sit for ten minutes before using in a recipe.

OLIVES Olives can be used in salads, sandwiches, pasta dishes, pizza toppings, and more. Purplish kalamata are meaty and tangy (and easy to pit); other common varieties include Niçoise, Gaeta, and picholine, which have a slightly salty, nutty flavor and are ideal as appetizers. When possible, buy olives in bulk instead of in jars or cans. They will keep for several months, as long as they are submerged in oil or brine, and stored in a sealed container.

SPECIALTY ITEMS

ASIAN FISH SAUCE This dark brown sauce is made from fermented fish (often anchovies) and has a pungent aroma and a subtle, salty taste. It is a popular condiment in Southeast Asia, particularly Thailand (where it's known as nam pla) and Vietnam (nuoc nam). Nam pla is also added during cooking, often with soy sauce, tamarind, or other seasonings. Opened bottles should be refrigerated, where they will keep almost indefinitely.

ASIAN NOODLES Here are the most common types of Asian noodles; as with Italian pasta, it is a good idea to have a few types on hand at all times for making soups, salads, and other dishes. Unopened, they can be kept in their original packages almost indefinitely. Once opened, store in a tightly sealed bag or container and use within a year.

cellophane noodles, also known as bean threads or glass noodles, are made from processed mung beans. They are opaque in their dried form, but once they have been soaked in hot water, they become clear and gelatinous. These noodles are generally prized for their texture, since they have very little flavor. Capellini or vermicelli can often be substituted.

chinese egg noodles, made from wheat flour and whole eggs or egg whites, come in various widths. They are usually sold in small tangled nests that are meant to be dropped into hot soups (without prior cooking). Fresh egg noodles can also be found in the refrigerated section of many supermarkets.

rice noodles, also known as rice-stick noodles and rice vermicelli (slightly thinner strands), are made from rice flour. There are two shapes: round and flat. The extra-thin rice vermicelli are also known as mi fen (Chinese), bun (Vietnamese), and sen mee (Thai). They are usually soaked to soften in hot water before eating. Rice sticks are the flat version. Medium-size sticks are called pho. The slightly wider Thai version is called jantaboon.

soba noodles, made from buckwheat flour, have a nutty flavor and are rich in fiber and protein. These noodles are extremely versatile, and can be served hot or cold in soups, salads, and stir-fries.

somen noodles, the most prized of all Japanese noodles, have a delicate flavor and texture. They are made from wheat flour and a little oil and are always packaged in small bundles. The difference between somen and other Japanese noodles is the way they are made: Somen are made by pulling; other noodles are made by rolling and cutting.

udon These thick, white, slippery Japanese noodles are made from wheat or corn flour. Udon may be round, square, or flat. Their neutral flavor makes them the ideal addition to robust flavored soups and sauces. Udon can be found in both fresh and dried forms at Asian markets.

ASIAN WRAPPERS

dumpling wrappers Most supermarkets carry at least one or two types of frozen dumpling wrappers, usually wonton or shao mai skins. You can find more of a variety of fresh and frozen wrappers at Asian markets; if you have access to one, buy an assortment of wrappers and store them, well wrapped, in the freezer, where they'll keep for up to six months. Fresh wrappers will last for up to a month in the refrigerator; frozen ones defrost fully in about an hour. Paper-thin yet durable spring-roll skins are sold only frozen and can be thawed and frozen repeatedly without any deterioration in quality. When making dumplings, fill one at a time and keep the remaining wrappers covered with a damp paper towel so they do not dry out. Once formed, dumplings can be steamed, boiled, or fried. Besides their traditional use in making Asian-style dumplings, some wrappers (especially wonton) are a convenient substitute for fresh pasta when making ravioli and other filled shapes.

rice-paper wrappers These round or triangular wrappers are made from a mixture of rice flour, water, and salt, which is machine-rolled paper thin, then dried in the sun on bamboo mats, the weave of which gives them their unique texture and pattern. They are brittle, so moisten them with water before using and keep them covered with a damp paper towel while you work. These wrappers can be used uncooked, as when making summer rolls. They are also sturdy enough for steaming or deep-frying.

BUCKWHEAT FLOUR Buckwheat flour is the ground seeds of the buckwheat plant, which is not a grain but actually an herb. Because it is rather dense, buckwheat flour is generally combined with another flour in a three-to-one ratio to achieve an appealing texture without sacrificing its deep, pleasantly sour flavor. Perhaps the most familiar food made with buckwheat is blini; soba noodles are another. Store the flour in an airtight container at room temperature for up to a year.

BULGUR WHEAT Popular in Middle Eastern dishes, such as tabbouleh, bulgur wheat is steamed, dried, and crushed wheat kernels. It has a tender, chewy texture and comes in coarse, medium, and fine grinds. Store in a cool, dark spot for up to a year.

CAVIAR Caviar is the roe, or egg mass, of sturgeon, the best of which is generally considered to come from female sturgeon caught in the Caspian Sea. Three species of sturgeon swim in this sea: beluga, the largest; midsize osetra; and sevruga, the smallest. Beluga roe varies in color from pale to dark gray and is the most delicately flavored caviar: subtle, buttery, and creamy. Though smaller than beluga, osetra eggs have a more assertive taste: nutty and voluptuous. Their color ranges from gold (very rare) to dark brown. Sevruga eggs are tiny, nearly black, and sweet—almost fruity. The general rule for serving caviar is to purchase one to two ounces per guest and buy the best you can afford. Beluga is the priciest, sevruga the least expensive. Serve the caviar in its tin on a bed of ice. Store in the coldest part of the refrigerator for up to two weeks. Once opened, a tin should not be resealed.

CHILE OIL Used extensively in Chinese cooking, chile oil is made by steeping dried red chiles in flavorless vegetable oil. Chile oil will keep almost indefinitely when stored in a cool, dark place.

CHILE PASTE Made of a pungent mixture of ground chiles, oil, salt, and sometimes garlic, chile paste is used in cooking as well as at the table. The flavor is intensely concentrated and ranges from mild to very hot, depending on the types of chiles included. Heat it along with the oil when making stir-fries, or serve it as an accompaniment to grilled or roasted meat or fish. It should keep indefinitely in the refrigerator.

CHILE PEPPERS, DRIED Because the drying process concentrates their heat, dried chiles are hotter than fresh. They vary in size, which generally indicates how hot they are: The larger the chile, the milder it will be. Larger chiles can be chopped and sprinkled into sauces for subtle heat. Smaller chiles should be used sparingly and prepared with caution; handle the seeds carefully, since they harbor much of the heat. (If you prefer, wear gloves when working with them.) Look for dried chiles that are shiny, pliable, and evenly colored. Keep them in a tightly sealed container at room temperature; they are best used within a year of purchase.

CHIPOTLE CHILES Chipotle chiles are smoked jalapeños with a complex flavor that is hot, smoky, and sweet. They're typically sold canned, packed in adobo—a spicy, vinegary, tomato-based sauce. Both the chiles and the sauce are used in a wide variety of dishes. Once opened, transfer the contents to an airtight container and refrigerate, for up to several months. Also look for dried chipotles, which can be used in similar ways to other dried chiles (above), and chipotle powder, both sold at Mexican groceries and many supermarkets.

COCONUT Packaged coconut is available in several forms. Sweetened shredded coconut and unsweetened flaked coconut are primarily used in making desserts. Dessicated coconut, which is dried, shredded, and unsweetened, is a fine substitute for fresh; it is commonly called for in Thai and Indian cooking. Be careful about substituting sweetened for the unsweetened varieties, as you may need to adjust the amount of sugar or other ingredients. Unopened packages can be kept for up to six months; opened bags should be refrigerated (tightly sealed) and used within a month. If flaked or shredded coconut becomes too dry, soak it in milk for thirty minutes, then drain well and pat dry.

FILÉ POWDER Made from the dried leaves of the sassafras tree, filé powder is an earthy seasoning used in Creole cooking. Use it for thickening gumbos, but be sure to add it at the end of cooking to avoid a gluey consistency. Keep it with other spices in your kitchen, preferably in a cool, dark place.

FIVE-SPICE POWDER Composed of an equal mixture of cinnamon, cloves, fennel seed, star anise, and Szechuan peppercorns, five-spice powder imparts a fragrant, sweet, and spicy flavor to dishes.

GALANGAL This Indian root has a strong, spicy taste similar to ginger, and is usually combined with ginger and lemongrass in Thai and Southeast Asian cooking. The whole root form is generally found only at Asian markets; grate it or, for more subtle flavor, steep it in hot soups and sauces (and then discard). The powdered form is more readily available, and will last for six months when kept in a tightly sealed container in a cool, dark spot.

GARAM MASALA A blend of cumin, pepper, cardamom, cinnamon, and other spices gives garam masala a spicy heat. It is a staple of northern Indian cooking, where it adds depth of flavor to curries and other traditional dishes. It should be added near the end of cooking time, and stored in a cool, dark place.

HARISSA PASTE This peppery North African relish is a mix of dried red chiles, garlic, tomato puree, olive oil, salt, and ground cumin, coriander, and caraway seeds. It is commonly added to couscous, stews, sauces, and marinades, either during cooking or at the table; because it is so fiery, start with a little and then add more to taste. Imported from Tunisia, harissa is sold in tubes in specialty-food stores. Once opened, refrigerate for up to a year.

HERBES DE PROVENCE This classic blend of dried herbs, frequently used in southern French cooking, typically includes thyme, basil, fennel, savory, sage, rosemary, tarragon, and lavender, although other herbs can be found in some versions. You can make your own (using equal parts of the herbs) or buy it in the spice section of most supermarkets. Keep it on hand for seasoning sauces, soups, and a variety of other dishes; it is especially delicious with roasted chicken, rack of lamb, and vegetables.

KAFFIR LIME LEAVES These lime leaves have a citrus aroma and flavor and are primarily used in Thai cooking. Frozen lime leaves are a good substitute for fresh; dried leaves are much less flavorful, so use up to twice as many as a recipe calls for if substituting for fresh (but don't chop them; use them like bay leaves and discard before serving). If you can't find lime leaves, substitute 1 teaspoon of grated lime or lemon zest for each leaf.

LEMONGRASS Lemongrass is an herb that grows in long stalks; it has a citrusy flavor and fragrance and is a staple of Southeast Asian cooking. Use only the lower, fleshy portion for cooking, as the flavor is more highly concentrated there than in the flattened blades. First, remove any dry or tough outer layers; then, if you like, bruise the stalks with the back of a knife to help release the flavor. The stalks can be used whole or cut into slices; they can also be dried and either ground into a powder (one teaspoon of dried lemongrass is as potent as one fresh stalk) or reconstituted by soaking in water for two hours. Keep the stalks, tightly wrapped in paper towels, for up to three weeks in the refrigerator. Or seal them in plastic storage bags and freeze for several months.

MIRIN This slightly syrupy, sweet rice wine is highly prized in Japanese cuisine for its ability to add a delicate sweetness to foods and to impart depth of flavor; it is commonly added to sushi rice. Made from fermented, glutinous rice, mirin is generally used only for cooking, although some finer varieties can be sipped. Mirin is sold in most supermarkets, where it is sometimes labeled "rice wine." It will keep indefinitely in a cool pantry.

PANKO Made from wheat flour and honey, these large and flaky Japanese breadcrumbs are most commonly used to coat foods before deep-frying. They create a wonderful crispy texture and maintain it long after frying. Store panko in an airtight container at room temperature for up to a year.

PEPITAS Pepitas, which are pumpkin seeds, are very popular in Mexican cooking; they are sold raw or roasted at many health-food stores and supermarkets. Peptitas can be sprinkled on salads or on a variety of dishes as a garnish, or ground into a paste and stirred into soups and sauces (where they will also act as a thickener). Like all seeds, pepitas should be stored in an airtight container in the refrigerator or freezer and used within several months.

QUINOA There are more than 1,800 varieties of this protein-rich grain in a range of hues; the quinoa (pronounced keen-wah) most readily available in the grocery store is generally the color of toasted nuts. The tiny, bead-shaped grains are cooked like rice but require only half the cooking time and can be used in place of rice in many dishes. Quinoa will keep in the cupboard in a well-sealed container for up to a year.

SESAME SEEDS Sesame seeds are available in many colors, but white, tan, and black are the most common. Tan and black seeds are similar in flavor, while the white seeds are more delicate; toasting the seeds intensifies their nutty taste. They have a slightly sweet flavor that enhances bread, pastry, cookies, and other baked goods as well as many savory preparations. Sesame seeds have a high oil content and tend to turn rancid rather quickly; store them in the refrigerator in an airtight container for up to six months, or in the freezer for up to a year.

STAR ANISE This small eight-pointed fruit pod looks like a star and tastes like licorice (or anise seed). It is used to flavor custards, dessert sauces, and sorbets and many savory dishes, including stews and braised meats. Use a clean coffee grinder (or spice mill) to grind star anise to a powder, or break off points from the pod, bundle in cheesecloth, and add to the cooking liquid as foods simmer or braise.

TAHINI This thick, creamy paste, made from ground and toasted sesame seeds, is a staple in Middle Eastern cooking, where it's used to make hummus and baba ghanoush as well as halvah. Much like natural peanut butter, tahini separates as it sits. To reincorporate the oil, transfer the contents to a large bowl and stir vigorously. Return the unused portion to the original container, and store in the refrigerator for up to three months.

TAMARIND The tamarind is the fruit of a tall evergreen tree native to Africa. Intensely tart, tamarind is essential in Indian cooking, and is an important ingredient in many curry dishes and chutneys (as well as Worcestershire sauce). Try adding it to a marinade, grilling glaze, or any number of richly flavored meat dishes. It is sold in powder, paste, or bottled forms. Powdered tamarind must be dissolved in hot water before use; the other types can be used straight from the container. Store the powder as you would other spices; the paste and bottled forms are more perishable, so check the label for expiration dates. If you cannot find tamarind, substitute lemon juice with a touch of brown sugar for a similar flavor.

TURMERIC Turmeric is the root of a tropical plant related to ginger, and is primarily grown in India and the Caribbean. Because it has a biting, pungent flavor, turmeric is more commonly used for its bright yellow-orange color. Powdered turmeric is widely available; store in a cool, dark place for no more than a year.

WASABI Also known as Japanese horseradish, wasabi is the root of a perennial Asian plant. It has a distinctively sharp flavor and is used as a condiment, often with sushi. Wasabi is available fresh, powdered, or as a paste; the powdered form is easiest to find and keeps indefinitely in a cool, dry place. Powdered wasabi can be reconstituted with water to make a paste. Mix the paste with soy sauce when making a dipping sauce for sushi and dumplings, or with mayonnaise for a spicy sandwich spread.

equipment

SMALL APPLIANCES

BLENDER Even if you reserve it for a few purposes—making smoothies and pureeing soups, for instance—a blender should be powerful (at least 500 watts). Besides being the best tool for giving sauces a velvety consistency, a blender is essential for making margaritas and other blended cocktails. An immersion (or stick) blender is a convenient alternative to a standard blender, especially for pureeing soups and sauces; you use this wand-style tool by inserting it right into the pot.

COFFEE/SPICE GRINDERS Whenever possible, we recommend using freshly ground spices for their superior flavor. Although you can buy a hand-cranked spice grinder (similar to a pepper mill), an electric coffee grinder is a nice alternative. The steel blades can grind whole spices into fine powder in just a few seconds. Buy two: one to use for spices, the other for coffee beans. It's a good idea to clean the bowl after each use; process a few tablespoons of uncooked rice grains or small bits of bread for several seconds.

ELECTRIC JUICER Nothing can chop, shred, and spin the pulp of fruits and vegetables to extract every bit of juice the way an electric juicer can. If you like to make your own vegetable and fruit juices, either to drink or to use in cooking, this tool is a good (and not particularly substantial) investment, especially given the cost of juices purchased from a store.

FOOD PROCESSOR A food processor is an enormous help with many common, time-consuming tasks, including chopping, slicing, and shredding vegetables and other ingredients; grinding nuts; and making purees and breadcrumbs. It also offers an efficient way to mix dough for pastry and bread. Processors range in size, but one with a 7-cup bowl will suffice for most home cooks. Most come equipped with a multipurpose blade and two disks for shredding and slicing. Special dough blades are also available.

ICE CREAM MACHINE There are many versions available in a range of sizes and prices; the compact ones (with a 1.5-quart capacity) have a metal canister that can handily tuck into your freezer (allowing you to make ice cream on the spur of the moment). Choose among old-fashioned hand-cranked machines or the newer electronic ones that allow you to prepare a batch of ice cream, frozen yogurt, gelato, or sorbet in about thirty minutes.

MINI FOOD PROCESSOR (MINI CHOPPER OR MINI PREP) Some kitchen chores, such as chopping nuts and mincing herbs, do not require the power or heft of the standard-size processor. A 3-cup version is the perfect size for making small batches of sauces, spreads, pesto, and dips.

MIXERS A sturdy standing mixer with paddle, whisk, and dough-hook attachments is a must for the avid baker. You can use it to mix cake batters and cookie dough, whip buttercream and other frostings, and even blend and knead bread dough. A hand mixer is a convenient alternative for some easy tasks, like whipping cream or egg whites.

POTS AND PANS

Every kitchen should have these essential items: a 10-inch skillet, a 2-quart saucepan, a 4-quart saucepan, and a large (8-quart) stockpot. A roasting pan is also necessary for cooking meats, poultry, fish, and vegetables; look for a pan with a fitted rack. A nonstick 10-inch skillet is perfect for making omelets, a covered sauté pan for braising meat. Always look for thick, heavy pans, as they tend to be durable and the best distributors of heat. Those made of aluminum (preferably anodized to make them harder) or stainless steel are good options for everyday use.

As your needs expand, you may want to add some of the following pieces.

DOUBLE BOILER A double boiler, essentially two pans in one, provides gentle, indirect heat: The bottom pan holds simmering water, which becomes the heat source for the top pan. (You can improvise by setting an appropriately sized heatproof mixing bowl over a pot of simmering water.) Do not allow the water to touch the bottom of the top pot (or bowl), or the mixture may scorch. A double boiler is often preferred when melting chocolate or preparing custards and delicate cream sauces.

DUTCH OVEN The shape and design of this heavy pot is ideal for long, slow cooking methods, such as braising. The thick bottom and sides evenly distribute heat and prevent hot spots; a tight-fitting lid traps in moisture. A 5- to 6-quart Dutch oven is best for braising meats and vegetables as well as making stews, casseroles, and pot roasts. Dutch ovens are ovenproof, so you can start by browning meat and other ingredients on the stove, then cover and transfer to the oven for even cooking.

GRILL PAN Since they are used on top of the stove, these pans are a practical substitute for an outdoor grill. During cooking, the raised ridges give foods the characteristic grill marks (preheat the pan until very hot); they also allow the fat to drip below the food as it cooks. If you buy a cast-iron pan, be sure to season it before the first use; after that, avoid washing with soap, as it will remove the seasoned finish.

WOK Originally from China, the wok is designed to cook food rapidly, its round-bottomed shape evenly spreading heat across its surface. Besides being especially suited for stir-frying, the wok can be used for steaming, deep-frying, and making stews.

TOOLS AND GADGETS

CITRUS REAMER Using an old-fashioned wooden reamer is a great way to quickly juice lemons and limes. The ridged, teardrop-shaped head is about the size of an egg and has a pointed tip that penetrates the fruit. To extract the most juice possible, roll the fruit on a work surface to soften it before halving, and then twist the reamer back and forth into the flesh, over a bowl. Strain the juice before using.

COLANDER A colander is invaluable for draining pasta and vegetables. Most are footed, so they can stand in the sink, and have handles for easy transport. They come in many sizes, and are made of plastic, stainless steel, or porcelain ceramic.

CUTTING BOARDS Whether you prefer plastic or wood boards, you may want to consider buying at least two to avoid cross-contamination: use one for raw meat and another for produce. It's also helpful to have one large and one small board. To keep boards from slipping as you work, place a damp paper towel underneath.

FOOD MILL Although you can use a food processor or blender to puree food, a food mill gives you greater control over the texture. Most models have three interchangeable disks, each perforated with fine, medium, or coarse holes for making purees of different thickness. Food mills also strain out seeds, skins, and other fibrous bits, so they are especially

helpful for making applesauce as well as the smoothest sauces and soups. Fitted with the coarse disk, the food mill will produce mashed potatoes that are wonderfully fluffy.

GRATERS

box grater A box grater is versatile and convenient. Use it for grating cheese, citrus zest, raw fruits and vegetables, and whole nutmeg. Three sides offer different-size holes for grating; the slicing blades on the fourth side create thin, uniform pieces.

citrus zester This tool is designed to remove only the flavorful outer zest from citrus fruit in long, thin strips, leaving the bitter white pith behind. Use it to make colorful garnishes from carrots, cucumbers, beets, and other vegetables, too.

rasp-style grater The tiny, razorlike holes of this ruler-shaped grater (Microplane is one brand) make quick, efficient work of removing the outer zest of whole fruit; the unique design creates the finest, fluffiest zest. This tool can also be used to grate chocolate, whole nutmeg, and hard cheeses.

KNIVES If properly cared for, good knives will last a lifetime. Before buying one, try it out; a knife should feel like an extension of your hand, the blade and the handle balanced. Look for knives made of carbon or stainless steel. Always wash and dry knives by hand, and store them carefully, preferably in a drawer tray with slits that isolate each blade, or in a felt-lined drawer that is wide enough to accommodate the width of each knife. Be sure to use a steel regularly to hone the blade's edges, and a stone every few months to sharpen it. Although it seems there is a knife for every job, a basic set of the following five knives (plus kitchen shears) are really all you need.

boning knife The narrow blade of a 5- to 6-inch boning knife can reach between meat and bones, allowing you to easily trim off fat, tendons, and cartilage. A stiff blade is good for boning cuts of beef; a flexible one is better for poultry.

chef's knife The broad, substantial blade with a curved bottom is specially designed to be rocked back and forth. Although often considered an all-purpose knife, it is ideally suited for chopping and slicing firm vegetables and mincing (or cutting into fine julienne) delicate herbs without bruising. Use the flat side of the blade to smash garlic cloves (for easy peeling), to crush herbs, or to crack peppercorns and other whole spices. Chef's knives are available with either an 8- or 10-inch blade; choose the one you are comfortable working with.

kitchen shears Use shears when a knife won't do, such as for snipping herbs, trimming vegetables, and cutting through the twine of a trussed bird.

paring knife With a 3-inch or shorter blade, this knife is flexible enough to handle small jobs, such as trimming, coring, and peeling.

serrated knife Also called a bread knife, a serrated knife has a scalloped blade (or serrated edge) that can cut through foods that are hard and crisp on the outside and tender inside (such as bread). Using a sawing motion allows you to cut soft fruits and vegetables, such as peaches and tomatoes, as well as cakes and delicate pastries, which might otherwise be crushed or torn by the pressure of a slicing knife. This is also the knife to use for chopping bar chocolate. Be sure to buy a knife with at least an 8-inch blade, or longer if you like larger loaves of bread.

slicing knife Marked by its long, flexible blade, a slicing knife is perfectly designed for carving roasts, evenly slicing meat and poultry, and filleting fish.

MANDOLINE This tool makes it possible to quickly and easily slice vegetables and potatoes paper thin; it can also be adjusted to create julienne or waffle-patterned pieces. If you do a lot of slicing, you may want to invest in a high-quality stainless-steel French model. Otherwise, look for the plastic Japanese mandoline (such as the Benriner), which is significantly smaller and less expensive, making it convenient for the home kitchen.

MEASURING CUPS AND SPOONS These are basics that each kitchen needs: a glass measuring cup for liquids (or a few in different sizes); a nesting set of cups for dry measures; and a nesting set of spoons. Stainless steel is a good choice for nesting cups and spoons, as it is long lasting and easy to clean.

MEAT MALLET (OR MEAT POUNDER) The waffled side is used for tenderizing beef; the flat side, for pounding and flattening cuts of meat and poultry, such as when making medallions or paillards.

MELON BALLER This simple tool can do more than scoop a melon into uniform balls. Use it to seed a halved cucumber or core a halved apple or pear; when making hors d'oeuvres, use it to hollow out cherry tomatoes or form soft cheese into little orbs.

MIXING BOWLS A set of wide stainless-steel nesting bowls will be able to handle almost any task in the kitchen. Those with a generous width are helpful for prepping, folding, and whipping. Get at least five different sizes so you can do more than one job at a time.

PIZZA PEEL This shovel-like flat wooden board with tapered edges and a long handle is used to slip pizza in and out of a hot oven and onto a pizza stone. When the peel is lightly dusted with semolina or cornmeal, the pizza may be formed directly on it.

PIZZA STONE Essentially a heavy round or square slab of stone, this simple piece of equipment can dramatically improve the quality of home-baked breads and pizza crusts. When bread is placed directly on the stone, heat is distributed evenly, from the bottom; this is essential for heating the dough quickly and encouraging a light, airy loaf. The porous texture helps absorb excess moisture, creating very crisp crusts. To use the stone, set it on the lowest shelf, then preheat the oven with the stone in place. Pizza stones vary in size, so be sure to measure the width and depth of your oven rack before purchasing one.

PIZZA WHEEL Besides being the perfect tool for slicing through pizza and flatbreads, a pizza wheel can be used to cut pie or pastry dough into strips or other shapes and to trim the edges of rolled-out pie or cookie dough. It is also great for cutting homemade pasta dough to make ravioli.

SIEVES Sieves are available in fine, medium, and coarse mesh, as well as in several sizes, so you may want to buy an assortment. Use a fine-meshed sieve for sifting dry ingredients and dusting cakes and other sweets with cocoa or confectioners' sugar; use others for straining soups or sauces.

SPATULAS Silicone spatulas are great for folding cake batters or transferring them from bowl to baking pan. They are heatproof up to 800° F., won't pick up or impart flavors from other foods, and are safe to use on nonstick pots and pans. A set of three (1-, 2-, and 3-inch) silicone spatulas is ideal. Metal spatulas are useful for other purposes: Choose at least one thin, flexible spatula for flipping pancakes or patties and removing cookies from baking sheets; a long, wide spatula is ideal for lifting fish out of a pan or for transferring a cake to and from a turntable or stand. Offset spatulas, which have angled handles for easy maneuvering, are good for icing cakes and spreading batters in pans.

STEAMERS Collapsible metal baskets are fine for steaming a batch of vegetables. The larger, 10-inch baskets will allow vegetables enough room to cook evenly, without becoming soggy.

Because they can be stacked, Chinese bamboo steamers are terrific for steaming different types of food at one time. Before using, soak a new bamboo steamer for at least 20 minutes in cool water to rid it of its bamboo odor. To prevent the food from sticking to the bamboo during cooking, line the basket with lettuce leaves or a ceramic plate.

THERMOMETERS

candy This is an indispensable tool for making candy, syrup, jams, and jellies. Choose a model that is easy to read, with an adjustable clip on the back for use with pans of different depths. Since it measures temperatures up to 400° F, a candy thermometer can generally be used for deep frying (when the oil needs to be maintained at 350° F), but we recommend buying a separate one for each purpose.

meat A meat thermometer allows you to determine whether a roast is ready to come out of the oven, without having to cut into the meat and lose precious juices. There are several models: some are inserted into the meat before it goes into the oven; others, called instant-read or rapid-response thermometers, are inserted near the end of cooking time (resulting in fewer juices being lost).

TONGS Kitchen tongs enable you to grasp foods that might otherwise slip off a spatula or spoon. They are ideal for turning meat and chicken when browning or roasting, lifting vegetables out of boiling water, and for cooking on the grill.

VEGETABLE PEELER A U-shaped (or harp-shaped) peeler has a wide blade that can tackle even thick-skinned produce, such as butternut squash and fresh ginger. Besides peeling fruit (even citrus) and vegetables, use it to shave cheese, cut zucchini and cucumbers into ribbons, and make chocolate curls.

WHISKS These multitasking tools handle myriad tasks, including beating egg whites, making roux, and stirring together dry ingredients when preparing batters and dough. The most versatile whisk measures from 3 to 3½ inches across at the widest point and is more elongated than a balloon whisk. A small whisk (8 inches long and about 1½ inches at its widest point) is handy for mixing glazes, marinades, and vinaigrettes; a flat whisk (12 inches long) reaches into the corners of pans to keep custards and puddings from scorching during cooking.

WOODEN SPOONS Though they come in many sizes and shapes, you really need just two wooden spoons. They should have long handles for stirring all the way to the bottom of deep pots. Reserve one for savory, the other for sweet. You might also want to buy two flat wooden spoons for scraping across the bottom of pans when cooking custards and thick sauces; those with angled edges will reach into the corners.

BAKING EQUIPMENT

BAKING SHEETS There are two basic types of baking sheets: rimmed baking sheets (also called jelly-roll pans or sheet pans) and baking sheets that are either flat or have a raised lip (also called cookie sheets). For both types, look for ones made of heavy-duty aluminum; they won't warp and buckle over time and will ensure even cooking. Large ones can be more efficient than smaller sheets, but make sure they are at least two inches smaller than the inside of your oven to allow proper air circulation. There's no need to buy sheets with nonstick coating; line them with parchment paper or a baking mat such as Silpat instead. Use rimmed baking sheets for items such as nuts, which can easily roll off when sliding the pan in and out of the oven, or for food that releases juices. Flat baking sheets allow cookies to brown more evenly. If you like cookies that are crisp, avoid insulated sheets.

BENCH SCRAPER If you are a frequent baker, you will reach for this tool again and again. When rolling out pie dough, run the flat edge under the edges of the dough prevent sticking. When kneading bread dough, use it to loosen the bits of dough from the surface. Use the scraper to neatly divide mounds of dough in half, such as when making pâte brisée, or into uniform triangles, as when making scones.

BOWL SCRAPER With its rounded edge, this inexpensive plastic tool is designed to scrape dough and batter from mixing bowls when transferring them to a work surface or baking pan.

BUNDT PAN The edges of this ring-shaped pan make distinguished pound cakes and coffee cakes. Choose one made of professional-grade aluminum.

CAKE PANS It's a good idea to have a variety of shapes and sizes on hand. A standard 9-inch (2-inch deep) round cake pan is compatible with most recipes for layer cakes (buy two); there are also "professional" cake pans that are 3 inches deep. An 8- or 9-inch square pan will handle brownies and other bar cookies, as well as some cakes. A 13 × 9-inch pan is a must for sheet cakes (and can also accommodate lasagna and other savory dishes).

MUFFIN TINS If you enjoy baking muffins and cupcakes, you'll want to have a combination of sizes: two or three standard 12-cup pans, two jumbo pans, and two mini muffin pans.

NONSTICK BAKING MATS Made of rubberized silicone, these mats (Silpat is a common brand) are great for baking items such as cookies or meringues that might stick to an unlined cookie sheet. They are well worth the initial cost, since, unlike parchment paper, they are extremely long lasting, and can be used over and over. Silicone mats can withstand extremely high oven temperatures and are easy to clean. Don't put the mats in the dishwasher; wipe them with a sponge and dry them flat so they retain their shape.

OFFSET SPATULA The handle of this spatula is set at an angle so your hand is raised away from the work surface, making for more even spreading of frostings and batters, and easier flipping of crêpes and blini. An offset spatula with a 4-inch blade is a good multipurpose size; smaller ones are better for more delicate jobs, such as decorating cupcakes and cookies.

PARCHMENT PAPER Naturally nonstick, parchment is ideal for lining baking sheets and pans. The baked goods will be easy to remove and the pans easy to clean. Roll a small piece of parchment into a cone, snip the pointed tip, and you have a disposable piping bag for royal icing and melted chocolate.

PASTRY BAG Pastry bags range in size from 8 to 24 inches long. Smaller ones are perfect for decorating cakes and cookies, larger ones for piping dough and batters, as when making puffs or gougeres. The 16-inch bag is a good multipurpose length. Look for reusable vinyl-coated cotton bags, which shouldn't absorb odors and are easy to clean.

PASTRY BRUSHES Two basic pastry brushes, one with nylon bristles, the other with natural, are essential. Durable nylon bristles are best for brushing melted butter on muffin tins and other baking pans; they are also great for brushing glazes and sauces onto meats and vegetables. Natural bristles are softer than nylon; use them to apply glazes to pies, cakes, and tarts. Though not essential, a third brush, reserved and labeled as a "dry brush," is very helpful for sweeping away excess flour from dough when rolling it out as well as excess crumbs from cakes before frosting.

PASTRY TIPS Pastry tips allow you to create decorative toppings on everything from hors d'oeuvres to birthday cakes and holiday cookies. They can be purchased individually or in sets; the sets provide a variety of options as well as a convenient storage case. Most sets also come with a plastic coupler, which has two parts: a piece that fits inside the pastry bag (where the tip usually goes) and a ring that screws on the outside, allowing you to lock the pastry tip in place. The coupler allows you to use the same pastry bag to pipe different decorations.

PIE DISHES Because metals can react with some acidic fruits, your best bet is to buy glass or ceramic pie dishes. A 9-inch pan is the most commonly called for, but 8- or 10-inch ones are versatile options. If you bake frequently, consider buying a deep-dish pan.

RAMEKINS Traditionally used for baking pots de crème and crème brûlées, these small ovenproof dishes also enable you to make individual-size cakes, custards, soufflés, puddings, and frozen mousses. They can help you organize your ingredients as you get started, too; for example, measure spices into one dish, lemon zest into another.

ROLLING PINS There are two types of pins: one with handles on both ends, called a baker's pin, and one without, called a French pin. When choosing a baker's pin, look for one that rotates around an axis attached to the handles (rather than handles that are stationary); those with ball bearings inside roll particularly smoothly. Most baker's pins are made of wood; marble is also a good choice for rolling out pastry dough, since it stays cool. French pins, constructed of solid wood, are lighter and longer than baker's pins. They allow you to distribute pressure evenly, and to roll out large pieces of dough.

ROTATING CAKE STAND A turntable is essential for decorating cakes. It elevates the cake, making it easier to reach and more comfortable to work on. It also allows the cake to rotate as you work, making it easier to apply frosting and pipe decorations.

SOUFFLÉ DISH A 2-quart dish made of porcelain, with straight, ridged sides and a flat bottom, will work for most soufflé recipes. It can also be used for baking casseroles and other savory dishes.

SPRINGFORM PAN Cheesecakes and other dense, moist cakes (such as tortes) call for this type of pan, which features a spring-loaded clamp allowing the side of the pan to be removed when the cake is ready to be unmolded. Invest in a heavy-duty nonreactive pan with a protruding lip, which keeps thin batter from leaking through. (If you are setting the pan in a water bath during cooking, wrap the bottom and side with heavy-duty aluminum foil to prevent water from seeping into the pan.) Because of its removable sides, a springform pan can also double as a tart pan.

TART AND TARTLET PANS These pans have removable bottoms and come in a wide range of sizes; some have fluted edges, others straight. The smaller pans are ideal for hors d'oeuvres as well as individual tarts. Flan rings, essentially bottomless tartlet pans that are set on a baking sheet, can often be used instead.

menus

SPRING BUFFET
SERVES 12

sautéed mushroom in phyllo crisps · 68

spring-greens soup · 109

fresh ham 101 with green-herb paste · 242

rhubarb pickle · 621

butter bean and sugar snap pea salad · 143

artichoke bottoms au gratin · 327

roasted garlic and sage parker house rolls · 556

fresh apricot almond tart · 454

coconut cream pie · 451

VEGETARIAN DINNER
SERVES 6

portobello mushrooms stuffed with
gratinéed potatoes · 345

sorrel and onion tart · 174

chickpea, asparagus, and herbed orzo
salad with feta dressing · 155

spring greens with herb vinaigrette · 161

black-currant sorbet with vanilla tuiles · 398, 512

SUNDAY BRUNCH WITH FRIENDS
SERVES 6

freshly squeezed orange juice

frozen bloody mary · 601

french toast with strawberry ginger
compote · 578

cherry tomato and ricotta omelets
in toast cups · 568

spring vegetable hash · 591

sopressata skillet rolls · 557

MOTHER'S DAY LUNCH
SERVES 4 TO 6

sweet-pea soup with crushed mint ice · 105

roast rack of lamb and mint · 236

mashed potatoes and fava beans · 365

carrot-ginger layer cake · 481

PASSOVER SEDER
SERVES 8

spiced nuts · 100

matzo ball soup · 114

spice-rubbed hens
(double the recipe) · 279

brisket of beef · 225

baked stuffed onions · 346

boiled beets with sautéed beet greens · 334

oven-roasted asparagus and leeks
(double the recipe) · 328

tzimmes · 366

mandarin fruit sundaes
(double the recipe) · 404

macaroons (plain/chocolate chunk) · 510

almond crisps · 510

EASTER BRUNCH
SERVES 4 TO 6

gravlax with cucumber slaw on black bread · 91

layered spring omelet · 567

celery root, potato, and leek home fries · 590

coconut layer cake · 482

MEALS IN ABOUT AN HOUR
EACH SERVES 4

baby artichokes with warm vinaigrette · 326

spaetzle with butter and parsley · 206

spring chicken ragout · 263

blueberry upside-down cake · 470

flageolet and frisée salad · 136

baked oven frites · 363

boiled shrimp with tarragon mayonnaise · 76

blueberry upside-down cake · 470

SUMMER

DINNER ON THE BEACH
SERVES 6

campfired potatoes · 590

slow-roasted tomatoes · 352

grilled chicken with cilantro mint rub · 260

corn on the grill · 339

five-bean salad · 145

shortbread fruit tart · 462

SUMMER GARDEN PARTY
SERVES 6 TO 8

curried parchment bread with mango and
fresh pepper chutney · 551, 609

curried lamb in cucumber cornucopias · 74

assorted satays (beef, chicken, and shrimp)
with peanut dipping sauce · 82

crab salad with noodles and spicy
carrot sauce · 158

chickpea salad with green mango · 145

kulfi cake (traditional Indian molded
ice cream dessert) · 413

mango lassi · 597

kiwi-honeydew limeade · 595

SPANISH SUMMER SUPPER
SERVES 10 TO 12

cerignola olives with hot pepper garlic oil · 97

gazpacho with shrimp and mussels · 125

roasted artichoke hearts with red pepper relish · 73

seafood paella · 304

grilled asparagus · 328

almond torte with peach sauce · 472

chocolate cookies · 532

COCKTAILS AT DUSK
SERVES 10 TO 12

fresh goat cheese wrapped in grape leaves · 93

corn cakes with smoky tomato coulis · 86

crab salad canapés · 90

grilled butterflied leg of lamb · 236

citrus marinated quail · 279

grilled peach salsa · 606

lime meltaways · 529

pink grapefruit "margaritas" · 597

blue parrot · 599

FARMSTAND DINNER
SERVES 4

summer corn chowder · 103

grilled swordfish steaks with
olive pesto · 294

grilled leeks vinaigrette · 344

mixed greens with yellow tomato
vinaigrette · 162

summer fruit tart · 461

peach ice cream · 391

AWAY FOR THE WEEKEND
breakfast
SERVES 6

skillet scones with cherry preserves · 582, 615

homemade granola · 581

brown sugar glazed bacon · 592

fresh fruit and juices

picnic lunch
SERVES 6 TO 8

hard-boiled eggs · 571

caesar salad sandwiches · 166

mediterranean melt · 167

new potatoes with gremolata · 152

fruit crumb bars · 516

pecan sandies · 531

blueberry-mint lemonade · 594

dinner
SERVES 8

baked white bean purée with pita bread
and raw vegetables · 613

fig pizzas · 181

seared scallops niçoise · 307

garden vegetable couscous · 211

plum crumb pie · 447

SUMMER

A SUMMER HOUSEWARMING PARTY
SERVES 8

mint juleps · 601

chilled bloody mary soup with crabmeat · 126

maquechoux oysters with red pepper
mayonnaise · 301

pecan-crusted catfish with wilted greens
and tomato chutney · 289

red bean and rice salad · 213

banana cake · 477

LAKESIDE COOKOUT
SERVES 8 TO 10

herb-scented flatbread · 553

summer slaw with poppy-seed dressing · 148

individual corn puddings · 340

cedar-planked salmon · 292

minted peach and tomato salad · 142

blackberry and blueberry cobbler · 384

SUMMER HARVEST LUNCH PARTY
SERVES 8

cherry lemonade · 594

dig-deep layered summer salad · 155

skillet cornbread · 562

grilled chicken with spicy barbecue sauce · 259

peach-raspberry pie · 448

lemon-blueberry tart · 459

POOLSIDE BIRTHDAY PARTY
SERVES 8 TO 10 AS PART OF A BUFFET

sausage profiteroles · 69

smoked trout brandade · 90

steak au poivre · 228

swordfish kebabs · 295

grilled corn on the cob · 339

potato waffle chips · 100

chocolate cupcakes · 487

burnt-sugar ice cream · 392

NEW ENGLAND LOBSTER DINNER
SERVES 12

boiled maine lobster · 297

corn on the cob with herbed butter · 339

rosemary shallot popovers · 560

bacon, lettuce, and tomato salad · 129

potato salad with crème fraîche dressing · 150

roasted beets and shallots · 334

blueberry pie · 444

WEEKEND IN THE COUNTRY WITH FRIENDS
SERVES 12 TO 14

fingerling potatoes with goat
cheese fondue · 94

mixed greens with shallot vinaigrette · 163

grilled tuna with balsamic glaze · 295

mixed grill of spring onions, white eggplant,
and baby lamb chops · 239

parmesan risotto · 216

ricotta gelato with fresh berries · 394

hazelnut biscotti · 520

MEALS IN ABOUT AN HOUR
EACH SERVES 4

pappa al pomodoro · 109

chicken saltimbocca · 268

potatoes and green beans with mint pesto or
new potatoes with gremolata · 152, 153

roasted peaches with pecan shortbread · 377, 517

chilled cucumber soup · 102

orecchiette with raw tomato sauce · 192

seared tuna steaks with caper butter · 296

baked stuffed apricots · 375

herb salad · 130

pan bagnat · 167

baked oven frites · 363

roasted plums with crème fraîche · 379

A CLASSIC AMERICAN THANKSGIVING
SERVES 8 TO 10

butternut squash soup · 107

roast turkey with chestnut stuffing · 269, 368

brussels sprouts with vinegar-glazed
red onions · 335

cranberry-orange relish · 611

roasted fall vegetables · 357

sweet-potato hash browns · 591

classic greenmarket apple pie · 442

autumn parfaits · 434

chocolate black-pepper icebox cookies · 528

FALL DINNER WITH FRIENDS
SERVES 10

vegetable barley soup · 110

cider-braised pork loin and ribs · 245

green tomato chutney · 608

polenta triangles · 222

deepest-dish apple pie · 442

CALIFORNIA GARDEN PARTY
SERVES 8

campari cooler · 602

radishes with flavored salts and butter · 95

goat cheese and lima bean bruschetta · 88

green tomato and leek frittata · 573

lamb medallions with black-olive
wine sauce · 240

chopped-tomato salads · 142

grilled mediterranean potato salad · 151

fig tart with cornmeal crust · 458

MEXICAN LUNCH BUFFET
SERVES 8

caramelized corn, zucchini, and
vidalia quesadilla · 85–86

chunky avocado salad · 132

grilled flank-steak tostada · 231

jumbo shrimp with cilantro stuffing · 303

black bean and grilled corn salsa · 607

mango ice cream · 390

limeade · 594

TEXAS BARBECUE
SERVES 12 TO 14

avocado enchiladas · 318

grilled quail and rib-eye steak or beef tacos
with pico de gallo · 232, 233

barbecued pork ribs with maple rub · 246

hot cheddar grits · 579

jícama slaw · 149

west texas baked beans · 332

chocolate pecan pie with chocolate crust
with homemade vanilla ice cream · 390, 453

PUMPKIN CARVING PARTY
SERVES 8

hot cinnamon-thyme tea · 604

roasted pumpkin seeds · 100

oat scones with assorted flavored butters
(herb, chile, and curry) · 581

potato and root vegetable tarts · 173

white bean and sausage stew in
pumpkin shells · 120

mixed beans with crisp rosemary
and sage leaves · 332

molasses drop cookies · 509

cornmeal-pecan biscuits · 530

apple-butter hand pies · 444

FALL

ORCHARD HARVEST PARTY
SERVES 8 TO 10

winter squash salad with goat
cheese "truffles" · 138

grilled game sausage and pears over
cabbage · 252

roast poussin with prunes and thyme · 256

mixed greens with pumpkin vinaigrette · 161

thin pear tart · 457

caramelized apple galette · 455

plum-frangipane tart · 464

VEGETARIAN DINNER PARTY
SERVES 4 TO 6

marinated bocconcini · 92

whole-wheat onion focaccia · 552

raw artichoke salad · 133

perciatelli with garlic, walnuts, and
tomatoes · 189

stuffed swiss chard rolls · 314

hazelnut gelato · 396

pears poached in red wine with black
pepper and vanilla · 378

double-chocolate biscotti · 521

LATE-NIGHT SUPPER FOR FOUR
SERVES 4

warm goat cheese with walnuts and toast · 92

endive and warm pear salad · 129

pasta with caramelized garlic and shallots · 195

oven-roasted apples with cider sabayon · 370

MEALS IN ABOUT AN HOUR
EACH SERVES 4

tarragon marinated mushrooms · 69

braised fennel with chestnuts and shallots · 343

butternut squash risotto · 217

warm brownie cups · 421

grilled figs with goat cheese and prosciutto
or eggplant ragoût · 94, 341

sicilian rigatoni (with cauliflower, raisins,
and saffron) · 196

shaved fennel salad · 134

blood orange cheesecake · 490

WINTER

QUICK HORS D'OEUVRES
SERVES 10 TO 12

smoked salmon and caramelized onion
stuffed celery stalks · 78

olive tapenade and goat cheese crostini · 89

chickpea pimiento crostini · 89

cherry tomato and avocado canapés · 90

radishes with flavored salts and butter · 95

twice-baked cheese strudel · 80

basic quesadillas · 85

pear pecan toasts · 90

FANCY CHRISTMAS DINNER
SERVES 10

blood-orange champagne cocktails · 602

chilled oysters on the halfshell · 75

gougères · 96

louisiana crab salad with lemon vinaigrette
(double the recipe) · 158

boeuf bourguignon with golden mashed
potato crust · 228

braised fennel with chestnuts and shallots · 343

haricots verts with hazelnuts · 331

golden caramels · 534

chocolate pots de crème
(make two batches) · 421

FAMILY NEW YEAR'S
SERVES 10 TO 12

grapefruit and avocado salad with spicy
lime vinaigrette · 137

roasted pork tenderloins with bacon
and herbs · 247

creamed swiss chard · 352

caramelized roasted parsnips · 348

wild mushroom ragoût · 345

caramelized apple galette · 455

shortbread wedges · 517

rich chocolate tart · 464

HOLIDAY FAMILY BREAKFAST
SERVES 6 TO 8

cornmeal pancakes with maple butter and
chunky fruit syrup · 576, 578, 617

chicken and apple sausage patties · 592

bacon and egg pie · 572

winter salad · 130

CHINESE NEW YEAR BUFFET
SERVES 8 AS PART OF A BUFFET

tea tofu · 320

crisp spring rolls · 79

stir-fried fava beans · 330

steamed shrimp · 302

shrimp and fennel noodle soup · 126

braised flounder with chinese cabbage · 282

spicy stir-fried chicken and vegetables · 265

steamed eggplant with black bean sauce · 342

chunky ginger ice cream · 393

VALENTINE'S DINNER
SERVES 2

artichokes à la barigoule · 327

shaved beet salad · 132

chicken stuffed with savory duxelles · 259

perfect mashed potatoes · 365

haricots verts with hazelnuts · 331

warm chocolate cakes · 485

VEGETARIAN VALENTINE'S DINNER
SERVES 2

rosemary flatbread with
spicy squash dip · 550, 614

wild mushroom ragu with polenta · 321

asparagus panzanella · 154

roasted-strawberry napoleon · 498

WINTER

AFTER-SKI DINNER
SERVES 8

spinach, egg, and bacon salad · 130

seafood pot au feu · 299

winter fruit crisp · 382

ginger cookies · 529

ICE-SKATING PARTY
SERVES 8

the best hot chocolate · 603

twice-baked cheese strudel · 80

creamy tomato soup · 108

classic oatmeal cookies
(with chocolate chunks) · 507

blondies · 519

MEALS IN ABOUT AN HOUR
EACH SERVES 4

winter crudité salad · 136

halibut with puttanesca sauce · 287

caramelized onion and fennel mashed
potatoes · 365

chocolate turnovers · 500

sausage with sautéed red onions and
thyme · 249

fennel and celeriac gratin · 343

sautéed broccoli rabe · 335

baked pears with cream · 378

shrimp and scallop stew · 124

couscous pilaf · 206

winter salad · 130

banana bread puddings · 439

beef tenderloin with shallots and
red wine glaze · 224

endive slaw · 148

lemon roasted potatoes · 360

no-bake chocolate-crust cheesecake · 489

cheese coins with jalapeño jelly PAGE 98

creamy tomato soup PAGE 108 · *(opposite) vietnamese fisherman's soup* PAGE 121

beet, endive, and orange salad PAGE 133

classic caesar salad PAGE 131   *warm plum salad with prosciutto and arugula* PAGE 139

shaved beet salad PAGE 132

chunky avocado salad PAGE 132

summer shrimp salad PAGE 160

open-face turkey sandwiches
with mushroom gravy PAGE 170

(opposite) cherry tomato "pie" with
gruyère crust PAGE 171

41

whole poached salmon PAGE 290

(clockwise from top left)

braised cod with plum tomatoes PAGE 286

mustard-rubbed pork
with blackberry-mustard sauce PAGE 246

curried shrimp skewers
with rice salad PAGE 303

roast chicken PAGE 254

*roasted mushrooms with asparagus
and parmesan* PAGE 317

fried chicken PAGE 257

prime rib roast PAGE 226

pasta with roasted chestnuts and hazelnuts PAGE 185

wild mushroom and spinach lasagna PAGE 312

garden linguine with ricotta PAGE 190

(opposite) macaroni and cheese PAGE 196

gnocchi with brown butter and sage PAGE 204

grilled leeks vinaigrette PAGE 344

(opposite) latkes PAGE 363

mashed potatoes PAGE 364

haricots verts with hazelnuts PAGE 331

twice-baked butternut squash PAGE 350

stuffed artichokes PAGE 326

lemon curd tarts PAGE 460

(opposite) rainbow sorbet cake PAGE 416

56

(clockwise from right)

chocolate macadamia-nut tart PAGE 465

coconut bonbons PAGE 408

frozen tiramisù PAGE 412

fig and berry trifle PAGE 479

1-2-3-4 lemon cake PAGE 473

ginger-pecan cake PAGE 480

pposite) shortbread with dried plum petals PAGE 462

angel food swirl cake PAGE 472 · *(opposite)* *grandma's sugar cookies* PAGE 533

three variations of
cherry preserves PAGE 615

starters

....

deviled eggs

MAKES 16

We've updated deviled eggs, a staple of child-hood picnics and family reunions. These modern versions are tasty alternatives to the mayonnaise-and-paprika standby. Serve them on a bed of leafy greens or fresh sprouts.

- 8 hard-boiled eggs (see page 571)
  Kosher salt and freshly ground black pepper

for basil deviled eggs

- ½ cup fresh basil leaves, roughly chopped
- 3 tablespoons Homemade Mayonnaise (page 632) or prepared

for crème fraîche deviled eggs

- 3 tablespoons crème fraîche
- 2 teaspoons Dijon mustard
- 4 cornichons, minced (about 1 tablespoon)

1. Peel the hard-boiled eggs, and cut lengthwise. Carefully remove the yolks; place 4 yolks in 2 separate bowls. Set the whites aside. Mash each bowl of yolks with a fork.

2. For the basil eggs: Place the basil and mayonnaise in the bowl of a food processor; blend about 2 minutes. Add the mayonnaise mixture to one bowl of yolks; mix. Season with salt and pepper.

3. For the crème fraîche eggs: Add the crème fraîche, mustard, and cornichons to the second bowl of yolks; mix. Season with salt and pepper.

4. Fill 8 reserved egg-white halves with each filling; serve. The prepared eggs may be made up to 2 hours ahead and kept refrigerated, covered with plastic wrap.

cucumber tapa

SERVES 4

- 2 seedless cucumbers (about 1 pound each), peeled if waxy
- 2 tablespoons extra-virgin olive oil
- 1 teaspoon sherry vinegar
- 2 ounces feta cheese, diced
- ¼ teaspoon kosher salt
  Pinch of freshly ground black pepper
- 1 tablespoon fresh oregano leaves, chopped

1. Slice the cucumbers lengthwise, and remove any small seeds. Cut 1 cucumber half into ¼-inch dice, and transfer to a small bowl. Add the olive oil, vinegar, feta cheese, salt, and pepper, and toss well to combine. Add the oregano, and toss again.

2. Use a vegetable peeler to remove 1 or 2 long strips of the peel (if the cucumbers are already peeled, remove a strip of the flesh) from the underside of each of the remaining 3 cucumber halves so they will sit without tipping. Spoon the cucumber-and-feta mixture into the long trough of each half.

3. Slice cucumbers crosswise on a slight diagonal into 1½-inch pieces, and serve immediately.

endive boats with marinated vegetables

MAKES 3 DOZEN

Long, elegant endive spears are perfect for cradling grated or finely chopped vegetables.

- 1 small (about 3 ounces) beet
- ¾ teaspoon kosher salt
- 1 medium carrot
- ½ fennel bulb, trimmed
- 1 tablespoon white-wine vinegar
- 2 teaspoons extra-virgin olive oil
- ⅛ teaspoon freshly ground black pepper
- 1¼ pounds (5 large heads) Belgian endive
- 2 tablespoons salmon roe, optional
- 2 teaspoons chopped fresh chervil or flat-leaf parsley leaves

1. Place the beet and ½ teaspoon salt in a saucepan of water; cover and bring to a boil. Reduce heat to medium; boil until the beet is tender when pierced with the tip of a knife, about 30 minutes. Drain, and peel the beet; grate on the large holes of a box grater, and place in a bowl. Grate the carrot; add to the beets.

2. Cut the fennel into very thin, ½-inch-long slivers; add to the beets and carrots.

3. Whisk together the vinegar, olive oil, pepper, and ¼ teaspoon salt. Toss with the vegetables. Refrigerate for 1 hour.

4. Trim the endive, separating the leaves. Reserve the large leaves for another use. Fill the lower half of the small leaves with 1½ teaspoons of the vegetable mixture. Top with ⅛ teaspoon of the salmon roe, if using; garnish with the chervil. Serve.

roasted stuffed new potatoes
MAKES 3 DOZEN

- 22   very small red potatoes
- ½   cup low-fat cottage cheese,
     or 4 ounces low-fat goat cheese
- 1   tablespoon fresh lemon juice
- ½   teaspoon kosher salt
- ⅛   teaspoon freshly ground black pepper
- 1   large egg white, lightly beaten
- 1½   teaspoons snipped chives,
     plus 1 teaspoon for garnish

1. Preheat the oven to 425°F. On a baking sheet, roast the potatoes until tender when pierced with the tip of a knife, turning two to three times, 20 to 30 minutes. Let cool.

2. Halve 18 potatoes. Cut a sliver off the bottom of each. Using a small melon baller or teaspoon, scoop the flesh from the potato halves into a bowl, leaving a shell ¼ inch thick. Peel the remaining potatoes; add to the potato flesh. Mash coarsely with a fork. Mix in the cheese, lemon juice, salt, and pepper. Mix in the egg white and chives.

3. Spoon the filling into the potato shells. Place on a baking sheet. Bake until golden, about 15 minutes. Garnish with the remaining chives. Serve hot.

fried peppers
MAKES 16

Small peppers weighing less than half an ounce, such as jalapeños or serranos, cook quickly and work best for this recipe.

- 16   small fresh jalapeño or serrano
     chile peppers
- 8   ounces queso blanco or
     mozzarella cheese
- 1   cup yellow cornmeal
- 4   large eggs
- ½   teaspoon kosher salt
- 2   cups peanut oil

1. Slice off the top ⅛ inch of each pepper, including the stem, and reserve. Remove the seeds from inside the peppers. (Use thin plastic gloves if you have sensitive skin.)

2. Cut the cheese into slivers to fit inside the peppers. Insert the cheese into the peppers. Carefully fit the tops back onto each pepper, tucking the edges into the rim of the peppers. Secure with a toothpick if needed.

3. Place the cornmeal in a medium bowl. Place the eggs in another medium bowl, add the salt, and whisk well. Heat the oil in a 10-inch skillet over medium heat. Place half the peppers in the egg mixture, and coat. Transfer the coated peppers to the cornmeal, and turn to coat evenly. When the oil registers 365°F on a deep-frying thermometer, or is hot but not smoking, carefully slip in the 8 coated peppers. Turn as needed, and fry until evenly browned, 2 to 3 minutes. Remove with a slotted spoon; set on paper towels to drain. Repeat with the remaining peppers. Serve warm.

sautéed mushrooms in phyllo crisps

MAKES 3 DOZEN

Select small mushroom varieties that will fit in the phyllo cups, such as yellow oyster, yellow foot, and cultivated enokis, or cut large mushrooms to fit. Use a mini-muffin tin that has 2-inch-wide and 1-inch-deep cups (see Equipment Sources, page 650).

- 11 tablespoons unsalted butter
- 2 tablespoons plus 1½ teaspoons finely chopped fresh thyme, plus more for garnish
- 12 sheets frozen phyllo dough, thawed
- 2 shallots, minced
- 8 ounces assorted fresh mushrooms, wiped clean
- ½ teaspoon kosher salt
- ¼ teaspoon freshly ground black pepper
- 4 ounces fresh goat cheese

1. Preheat the oven to 350°F with a rack in the center. Melt 8 tablespoons butter, and set aside. Set aside 2 tablespoons thyme. Brush a mini-muffin tin with melted butter, and set the tin aside.

2. Place 1 sheet of the phyllo dough on a clean, dry surface; brush the entire surface generously with melted butter. Sprinkle lightly with some of the reserved thyme. Place another sheet of phyllo on top, brush with melted butter, and sprinkle with thyme. Repeat with 2 more sheets of phyllo. Cut the stack into twelve 3-inch squares. Gently press each square into a muffin-tin cup. Bake until the edges are just golden brown, 8 to 10 minutes.

3. Repeat step 2 with 4 more sheets of phyllo dough, melted butter, and thyme. Repeat again, for a total of 36 crisps. (The crisps may be made 1 day ahead and kept in an airtight container.)

4. In a large skillet, melt the remaining 3 tablespoons butter over medium heat. Add the shallots, and cook, stirring occasionally, until soft, 3 to 5 minutes. Stir in the mushrooms, salt, pepper, and the remaining thyme. Continue cooking, stirring often,

until the mushrooms have released some liquid and have cooked through, about 5 minutes.

5. Place ¼ teaspoon goat cheese in the bottom of each phyllo crisp, and place 1 heaping teaspoon of the mushroom mixture on top of the goat cheese. Transfer the filled cups to a baking sheet. Bake until heated through, about 3 minutes. Garnish with more thyme, and serve warm.

cannellini-stuffed mushrooms

MAKES 3 DOZEN

- 1 15-ounce can cannellini or white kidney beans, drained and rinsed
- 3 tablespoons finely chopped red onion
- ½ teaspoon chopped fresh thyme
- ½ teaspoon finely chopped fresh rosemary
- 1 teaspoon chopped fresh flat-leaf parsley
- ½ teaspoon kosher salt
- ¼ teaspoon freshly ground black pepper
- 36 small white-button mushrooms, wiped clean, stemmed
   Olive oil, for brushing

1. Preheat the broiler. In a large bowl, mash the beans to a coarse purée with a fork. Mix in the onion, thyme, rosemary, parsley, ¼ teaspoon salt, and ⅛ teaspoon pepper.

2. Using a melon baller, scoop out some of each mushroom cap from the bottom, stem side. Lightly brush the mushroom caps with oil; place on a baking sheet, trimmed-side up. Sprinkle with the remaining salt and pepper.

3. Fill each mushroom with about 1½ teaspoons of the bean mixture. Broil until tender and browned, about 4 minutes. Serve hot.

tarragon marinated mushrooms

SERVES 4

Serve these with a rustic loaf of bread and cheese.

- 12 ounces small white-button mushrooms
- 3 tablespoons fresh lemon juice
- 3 tablespoons coarsely chopped fresh tarragon leaves
- 2 tablespoons white-wine vinegar
- 3 tablespoons extra-virgin olive oil
- ¾ teaspoon kosher salt
- ⅛ teaspoon freshly ground black pepper

Using a damp towel, gently wipe the dirt from the mushrooms. Trim the stems flush with the caps; discard stems. Place the mushrooms in a medium bowl, and add the lemon juice, tarragon, vinegar, oil, salt, and pepper. Toss to combine. Set the mushrooms aside at room temperature, stirring occasionally, to marinate, at least 20 minutes or up to 4 hours. Serve at room temperature.

sausage profiteroles

MAKES ABOUT 2½ DOZEN

Pork sausage can be substituted for the chicken, turkey, or veal.

- 1½ tablespoons olive oil
- ½ cup finely chopped onion
- 1 garlic clove, minced
- 8 ounces chicken, turkey, or veal sausage, casings removed
  Choux Pastry Puffs (page 638)
- 1 roasted red bell pepper (see page 645), cut in ½-inch squares
- ¼ cup fresh flat-leaf parsley leaves

1. Preheat the oven to 350°F. Heat the olive oil in a medium skillet over medium-high heat. Add the onion and garlic, and cook until translucent, about 8 minutes. Add the sausage, breaking the meat into small pieces with a spoon. Cook until the sausage is cooked through, about 8 minutes.

2. Slice the pastry puffs crosswise. Spoon about 1 teaspoon sausage filling into the bottom half of each, add a piece of red pepper, then replace the top half. Transfer the profiteroles to a baking sheet, and bake until warm, about 2 minutes. Garnish each with a parsley leaf, and serve immediately.

beef-and-asparagus negamaki

MAKES 2 DOZEN

The classic Japanese negamaki is made with beef and scallions only. We have added crisp asparagus tips to this version.

- Kosher salt
- 24 thin stalks asparagus, or 12 thick stalks sliced in half lengthwise
- ½ cup soy sauce
- ¼ cup sugar
- 1 bunch scallions, green parts only
- 1½ pounds beef tenderloin
  Freshly ground black pepper

1. Heat a grill or a grill pan until hot, or preheat the broiler. Prepare an ice-water bath. Cover and bring a medium saucepan of salted water to a boil. Trim the asparagus to 3½-inch lengths from the tip. Transfer the asparagus to the boiling water; cook until bright green but still crunchy, about 1 minute. Drain; transfer to the ice-water bath to stop the cooking. Drain in a colander, and set aside.

2. Whisk together the soy sauce and sugar in a small bowl until dissolved; set aside. Cut the scallion greens into 3½-inch lengths, and julienne lengthwise; set aside.

3. Slice the tenderloin into ¼-inch-thick pieces. Place one slice between two pieces of plastic; pound lightly to an even thickness. Remove the plastic; trim into 2 x 5-inch rectangles. Repeat.

4. Dip a piece of beef in the soy-sauce mixture, and place on a clean surface. Season with the salt and pepper. Place 1 piece of the scallion and 2 asparagus tips across one end of the beef, so the vegetables extend over the edges; roll. Set aside. Repeat with the remaining beef and vegetables.

5. Grill or broil the negamaki, brushing with the sauce and turning, until slightly charred and medium rare, about 2 minutes. Serve.

pork and vegetable dumplings

MAKES 2½ TO 3 DOZEN

- 2 pounds bok choy
- 8 ounces ground pork
- 1 large egg
- 1 teaspoon cornstarch, plus more for dusting
- 1 tablespoon canola oil
- ½ cup plus 1 tablespoon soy sauce
- 1 teaspoon freshly grated ginger
- 2 teaspoons Asian fish sauce (nam pla), optional
- ½ teaspoon kosher salt
- ¼ teaspoon freshly ground black pepper
- 1 12-ounce package round dumpling wrappers
- 2½ teaspoons sugar
- 1½ tablespoons dark sesame oil
- 2 tablespoons thinly sliced scallion greens

1. Cover and bring a large saucepan of water to a boil. Prepare an ice-water bath. Add the whole heads of bok choy to the pan, and gently boil until tender, about 3 minutes. Using a slotted spoon, remove the bok choy from saucepan, and plunge into the ice-water bath. Drain, discarding the liquid, and finely chop. Place the bok choy in a clean kitchen towel or a double thickness of cheesecloth, and squeeze out all of the water. Transfer to a bowl, and set aside.

2. In a medium bowl, combine the pork, egg, cornstarch, oil, 1 tablespoon soy sauce, the ginger, the fish sauce if using, salt, and pepper. Add the chopped bok choy, and mix well.

3. Lightly dust a baking sheet with cornstarch. Make dumplings (see box, page 72). Place completed dumplings on the baking sheet; cover with a damp towel.

4. Cover and bring a large pot of water to a boil. Add as many dumplings as will fit without crowding. Gently stir them up from the bottom to prevent sticking, cover, and return to a boil, about 1 minute. Uncover, add ¼ cup cold water, replace the cover, and return the water to a boil. Boil for about 2 minutes more. Remove dumplings with a slotted spoon, and keep warm. Continue until all the dumplings are cooked.

5. Make the dipping sauce by combining the remaining soy sauce, sugar, sesame oil, and scallion. Mix well, transfer to small serving dishes, and serve with the warm dumplings.

broccoli rabe dumplings

MAKES 3 DOZEN

- Kosher salt
- 1 bunch (about 1 pound) broccoli rabe
- 1½ tablespoons olive oil
- 1 tablespoon minced garlic
- ½ cup pine nuts, toasted (see page 644), finely chopped
- Freshly ground black pepper
- Cornstarch, for dusting
- 36 dumpling wrappers
- Olive oil, for brushing
- Parsley Oil (recipe, right)
- 1 tablespoon small fresh flat-leaf parsley leaves

1. Cover and bring a large stockpot of salted water to a boil. Prepare an ice-water bath. Trim and discard the stems of the broccoli rabe. Place the broccoli rabe in the boiling water; cook until tender and bright green, about 2 minutes. Drain, and transfer to the ice-water bath to stop the cooking. Drain again. Finely chop, and set aside.

2. Heat the oil in a medium skillet over low heat. Add the garlic; cook 1 to 2 minutes. Raise heat to medium. Add the broccoli rabe and the nuts. Season with salt and pepper; cook 5 minutes. Transfer to the bowl of a food processor. Pulse until finely chopped but not puréed, about 15 pulses.

3. Lightly dust a baking sheet with cornstarch. Make dumplings (see box, page 72). Place completed dumplings on the baking sheet; cover with a damp towel.

4. Fill a wok or a high-sided saucepan with water; cover and bring to a boil. Reduce heat to medium, and bring the water to a simmer. Using a pastry brush, generously brush the top and bottom compartments of a large bamboo steamer basket with oil. Brush any excess cornstarch from the dumplings; loosely arrange in the steamer. Assemble the steamer, cover, and place over the simmering water. Steam until the wrappers are soft and the filling is heated through, about 8 minutes, switching the top and bottom compartments halfway through steaming.

5. Drizzle the parsley oil over the warm dumplings, garnish with a parsley leaf, and serve.

parsley oil

MAKES ABOUT ½ CUP

The oil may be made up to 1 day ahead and kept in an airtight container in the refrigerator; let return to room temperature before using.

 Kosher salt
2 large bunches fresh flat-leaf parsley
¼ cup extra-virgin olive oil

1. Cover and bring a medium saucepan of salted water to a boil; prepare an ice-water bath. Use tongs to immerse the parsley in the boiling water; cook until bright green, about 20 seconds. Drain, and transfer to the ice-water bath to stop the cooking.

2. Transfer the parsley to the bowl of a food processor, and process until puréed. Transfer the purée to a double thickness of cheesecloth; squeeze out all the bright-green juice into a small bowl. Discard the leaves. Whisk in the olive oil; season with salt.

....

BUYING DUMPLING WRAPPERS

Dumpling wrappers can be found in the produce or refrigerated sections of some supermarkets and in Asian markets, or ordered by mail (see Food Sources, page 648).

....

vegetable dumplings

MAKES 2½ DOZEN

2 tablespoons dark sesame oil
1 tablespoon chopped garlic
2 medium leeks, white and pale-green parts, thinly sliced, well washed (see page 646)
1½ cups finely diced carrots
¾ cup chopped wood-ear or shiitake mushrooms
2 cups shredded bok choy
½ cup chopped garlic chives or regular chives
2 tablespoons chopped fresh ginger
 Kosher salt and freshly ground black pepper
 Dash of soy sauce
1 large egg white
 Cornstarch, for dusting
30 round wonton wrappers

1. In a heavy skillet, heat sesame oil over medium heat. Add garlic; cook until lightly colored. Add leeks and carrots; cook, stirring often, until soft, 5 to 10 minutes.

2. Add mushrooms and bok choy; cook until wilted. Add garlic chives and ginger; cook 2 to 3 minutes. Season with salt, pepper, and soy sauce. Let cool; mix in the egg white. Filling can be made up to this point 1 to 2 days ahead and chilled.

3. Lightly dust a baking sheet with cornstarch. Make dumplings (see box, page 72). Place completed dumplings on the baking sheet; cover with a damp towel.

4. Set a bamboo steamer in a wok; add water to within 1 inch of steamer bottom. Bring to a boil, place dumplings on steamer rack, cover, and steam 15 minutes. Alternatively, dumplings can be boiled: Cover and boil a large pot of water. Add as many dumplings as will fit without crowding. Gently stir to prevent sticking; cover. Return to a boil, about 1 minute. Uncover, add ¼ cup cold water, replace cover, and return to a boil. Boil about 2 minutes more. Remove with a slotted spoon; keep warm. Repeat with remaining dumplings. Serve.

shrimp potstickers

MAKES ABOUT 2½ DOZEN

Legend has it that potstickers were created accidentally when the water boiled away from a pot of dumplings, causing them to stick to the bottom of the pot and creating the delicious browned crust on one side.

for the potstickers

    2 tablespoons fresh cilantro leaves
    8 ounces large shrimp, peeled and deveined
    1 large egg white
 1½ teaspoons chile oil, or 1½ teaspoons olive oil mixed with a pinch of cayenne pepper
 1½ teaspoons sesame oil
    2 teaspoons low-sodium soy sauce
    1 medium carrot, grated
  ¾ cup (about 2 ounces) finely chopped Napa cabbage
  ½ teaspoon freshly grated ginger
    2 small scallions, finely chopped
    1 small shallot, minced
  ½ teaspoon kosher salt
  ⅛ teaspoon freshly ground black pepper
        Cornstarch, for dusting
  30 round dumpling wrappers
    3 tablespoons canola oil

for the dipping sauce

  ¼ cup low-sodium soy sauce
    1 tablespoon dark sesame oil
    1 teaspoon rice-wine vinegar
    1 scallion, white and green parts, sliced thin

1. Finely chop 1 tablespoon cilantro. Set aside. Coarsely chop half the shrimp by hand; set aside. In the bowl of a food processor, combine remaining shrimp, egg white, chile oil, sesame oil, and soy sauce. Purée into a smooth paste. Transfer to a bowl; add cilantro, reserved chopped shrimp, carrot, cabbage, ginger, scallions, shallot, salt, and pepper; mix well.

2. Lightly dust a baking sheet with cornstarch. Place 1 teaspoon of filling on a wrapper. Make dumplings (see box below). Place completed dumplings on baking sheet; cover with a damp towel.

3. In a small serving bowl, whisk together soy sauce, sesame oil, vinegar, and scallion.

4. Heat 1½ tablespoons canola oil in a well-seasoned, 11-inch cast-iron skillet over medium-high heat for 1 to 2 minutes. Arrange half of the dumplings tightly together in the hot skillet, and cook until deep golden brown, shaking the pan once or twice, about 1 to 2 minutes. Add 1 cup hot water; partially cover. Steam for 4 to 5 minutes.

5. Reduce heat to medium, and cook until the bottoms of the dumplings are very crisp, and all the water has evaporated, about 5 minutes more. Slide a spatula under the dumplings to loosen them from the pan. Serve this batch of dumplings immediately, or place them on a baking sheet, cover loosely with aluminum foil, and keep warm in a 250°F oven. Wash the skillet, and repeat the process with the remaining dumplings. Transfer to a plate, garnish with the remaining cilantro leaves, and serve with the dipping sauce on the side.

....

MAKING DUMPLINGS

To fill dumplings, place a wrapper in one hand, and spoon about 1 tablespoon of the filling into the middle of the wrapper. Moisten the edges with water. Fold to form a crescent shape around filling. There are two ways to shape dumplings: For a smooth edge, tightly pinch the edges closed. For a pleated edge, pinch the edges together only in the top center to seal. Pinch 6 small pleats (3 on either side of the sealed center point) along the top layer. Seal dumplings by pressing pleated and unpleated edges together.

....

caramelized onion tartlets

MAKES TWELVE 2-INCH TARTS; SERVES 6

Cipollini onions are perfect for these tarts because they are small and flat. Shallots can be substituted. You will need a mini-muffin tin with 2-inch openings (see Equipment Sources, page 650).

- 12 cipollini onions
  - All-purpose flour, for dusting
  - Martha's Perfect Pâte Brisée (page 634)
- 3 tablespoons unsalted butter
- ¼ cup plus 2 tablespoons sugar
  - Kosher salt and freshly ground black pepper
- 1 tablespoon balsamic vinegar
- 2 sprigs fresh thyme

1. Cover and bring a large saucepan of water to a boil. Cook the onions in the boiling water for 2 minutes. Drain; let cool. Carefully peel the onions, leaving the root and stem ends intact. Set aside.

2. On a lightly floured surface, roll pâte brisée to an ⅛-inch thickness. Using a 2-inch-round biscuit cutter, cut out 12 circles. Transfer to a parchment-lined baking sheet, and refrigerate until needed.

3. Melt the butter in a heavy skillet over medium heat. Sprinkle sugar over butter; cook, stirring, until sugar melts and starts to turn amber in color.

4. Halve onions crosswise. Season with salt and pepper. Arrange in a single layer, cut-side down, in the skillet. Cook over medium-low heat, without turning, until caramelized sugar bubbles up, about 15 minutes. Remove from heat.

5. Using a slotted spoon or spatula to keep onions intact, transfer them to mini-muffin tins, placing half an onion, cut-side down, in each cup (leave sugar syrup in pan). Return the skillet to low heat. Stir in the balsamic vinegar, season with salt and pepper, and top with a few leaves of fresh thyme.

6. Preheat the oven to 425°F. Quickly, before the sugar cools, spoon a generous teaspoon of the sugar mixture into each muffin tin. Drape the chilled pastry rounds over each onion, and, using your fingers, press to secure. The onions should be swaddled in the pastry. Transfer the muffin tin to the oven; bake

until the pastry is golden brown and the sugar bubbles up over the pastry, about 20 minutes. Remove from the oven. Immediately set the baking sheet over the muffin tin; invert, being careful of the hot caramel that might drip from the tin. Once you invert the tin, the tarts will be right-side up; serve garnished with fresh thyme leaves. Serve warm or at room temperature.

roasted artichoke hearts with red pepper relish

MAKES 3 DOZEN

- 3 lemons, cut in half
- 6 artichokes (8 ounces each)
- 2 teaspoons olive oil
- 1 teaspoon kosher salt
- ¼ teaspoon freshly ground black pepper
- 2 large roasted red bell peppers (see page 645), cut in ⅛-inch pieces
- 2½ teaspoons balsamic vinegar
- 1 teaspoon minced garlic
- 14 large fresh basil leaves, cut into thin strips, plus more for garnish

1. Preheat the oven to 450°F. Setting 2 teaspoons juice aside, squeeze the 3 lemons' juice into a bowl of water. Add the lemon halves to the water. Trim the artichoke stems to ½ inch, and cut 2 inches off the tops of the artichokes. Peel away the leaves until the smaller, yellow leaves are exposed. Using a paring knife, trim the base, and peel the stem. Cut the hearts in sixths. Cut away the bristly chokes, placing the artichoke hearts in the lemon water as you cut them.

2. Drain the artichokes; place in a medium bowl, and toss with the olive oil, ¾ teaspoon salt, ⅛ teaspoon pepper, and the reserved lemon juice. Transfer to a baking pan, add ¼ cup water, cover with aluminum foil, and roast 8 minutes. Remove the foil, and roast until browned, about 5 minutes more.

3. In a large bowl, combine the roasted peppers, vinegar, garlic, basil strips, and the remaining salt and pepper; toss. Fill each artichoke heart section with 1½ teaspoons of the pepper relish, and garnish with basil. Serve.

curried lamb in cucumber cornucopias

MAKES 3 DOZEN

- 1 large seedless cucumber
- 1 tablespoon olive oil
- 1 medium onion, finely diced
- 6 ounces lean ground leg of lamb
- 2 tablespoons currants
- 2¼ teaspoons Curry Powder (page 633) or prepared
- ¼ teaspoon ground cinnamon
- ½ teaspoon kosher salt
- ⅛ teaspoon freshly ground black pepper
- 1½ teaspoons chopped fresh mint, plus 36 leaves for garnish
- 1 tablespoon plus 2 teaspoons plain low-fat yogurt

1. Slice cucumber widthwise into 3½-inch-long sections. Using a vegetable peeler or a mandoline, slice lengthwise as thin as possible, yielding flat rectangular slices. Discard slices with seeds.

2. Heat the oil in a large skillet over medium heat. Add the onion, and cook until translucent, about 8 minutes. Add the lamb, currants, curry powder, cinnamon, salt, and pepper; raise heat to medium high, and cook until the meat is browned and cooked through, 10 to 20 minutes. Remove from the heat, and stir in the chopped mint and yogurt.

3. Form a cucumber slice into a cone shape. (When the cucumber is sliced very thin, the moist edges stick together to form a cone.) Fill with 1 to 1½ teaspoons of the meat mixture, and garnish with a mint leaf. Repeat the process, using all the cucumber slices and the lamb mixture, and serve.

FIT TO EAT RECIPE PER PIECE: 14 CALORIES, TRACE OF FAT, 4 MG CHOLESTEROL, 1 G CARBOHYDRATE, 34 MG SODIUM, 2 G PROTEIN, 0 G DIETARY FIBER

calamari filled with couscous

SERVES 10 TO 12

Ask the fishmonger for unbroken pieces of calamari.

- 2 cups couscous
- 1½ tablespoons olive oil
- 1 red bell pepper, seeds and ribs removed, finely diced
- 1 yellow bell pepper, seeds and ribs removed, finely diced
- 2 shallots, minced
- 1 large garlic clove, minced
- 1½ pounds very small calamari
     Kosher salt and freshly ground black pepper
- 2 tablespoons finely chopped fresh flat-leaf parsley
- 2 tablespoons fresh lemon juice
- ¼ cup plus 2 tablespoons currants

1. Place the couscous in a medium heat-proof bowl. Pour 2 cups boiling water over it. Cover and let sit until slightly cooled, about 10 minutes. Fluff with a fork. Set aside to cool.

2. Heat a grill or a grill pan until hot. In a large skillet over medium heat, heat the oil. Add the red and yellow bell peppers, shallots, and garlic; cook until softened, about 5 minutes.

3. Rinse the calamari under cold running water, discarding any debris. Finely chop the tentacles; stir into the vegetable mixture. Cook, stirring, 2 minutes. Season with salt and pepper. Transfer to a large bowl; add the parsley, lemon juice, and currants.

4. Fill a pastry or plastic freezer bag one-third full with the vegetable mixture. (If using a plastic bag, snip of the bottom corner to use as a piping bag.) Without using a pastry tip, insert the bag into the open end of a calamari body, and loosely stuff each calamari (the calamari will shrink while grilling).

5. Grill the calamari, turning often, until the flesh becomes opaque and cooked through, about 5 minutes. Let stand 1 to 2 minutes. Slice on an angle into 1-inch-thick pieces. Serve immediately.

mussels remoulade

The mussels can be cooked 1 day in advance.

½ bunch fresh tarragon
½ bunch fresh flat-leaf parsley
1 750-ml bottle dry white wine
3 tablespoons fresh lemon juice
2 shallots, sliced
20 whole black peppercorns
2 tablespoons kosher salt
5 pounds mussels, scrubbed, debearded, and washed clean
1 large roasted red bell pepper (see page 645)
 Rémoulade Sauce (page 630)
 Chopped fresh flat-leaf parsley, for garnish

1. Tie the tarragon and parsley in a small piece of cheesecloth to make a bouquet garni. Set aside.

2. Combine the wine, 2½ cups water, lemon juice, shallots, peppercorns, salt, and bouquet garni in a stockpot with a tight-fitting lid. Bring to a boil; reduce to a simmer over low heat for 15 minutes.

3. Add the mussels, and cover. Increase heat to medium high, and cook, shaking occasionally, until all the mussels are open, about 5 minutes.

4. Using a slotted spoon, remove the mussels from the broth, and cool both separately. Discard any unopened shells as well as the half shell to which the mussel isn't attached. When cool, put the mussels back into the broth, cover, and chill until ready to serve. This can be done 1 day before serving.

5. Cut the roasted pepper into ½-inch-wide strips, then into diamonds. Set aside.

6. Loosen the mussels from the shells with a paring knife. Pour a little rémoulade sauce in each shell, and garnish with the chopped parsley and a red-pepper diamond. Pass on a tray with toothpicks or wooden cocktail forks.

chilled oysters on the halfshell

 Crushed ice
4 dozen fresh oysters
 Lemon wedges

Arrange crushed ice on a large platter. Open oysters, and place on ice. Serve with lemon wedges.

barbecued oysters

Shucking oysters before grilling them is optional. Serve with Hogwash or Red Oyster Sauce (page 76).

4 dozen fresh oysters, scrubbed

Heat a grill until very hot. Place the oysters on the grill. When the shells open, after about 3 minutes, use an oyster knife to detach oysters from top shells. Loosen the top shells, and discard. Serve.

three sauces for oysters

Plan to serve between 3 and 6 oysters per person for a first-course serving, and between 8 and 12 for a main-course serving.

black-pepper ponzu mignonette

This recipe is an Asian version of the classic mignonette sauce of red-wine vinegar, shallots, and fresh lemon juice. They both include fresh black pepper. This makes enough for 1 to 2 dozen oysters.

¼ cup rice-wine vinegar
1 teaspoon sugar
1 tablespoon fresh lemon juice
2 tablespoons soy sauce
¼ teaspoon freshly ground black pepper

In a small bowl, whisk together the rice-wine vinegar, sugar, lemon juice, soy sauce, and black pepper. Serve with raw oysters.

hogwash for oysters

MAKES 1 1/2 CUPS

The two vinegars in this recipe contrast perfectly: Seasoned rice vinegar (see Food Sources, page 648) is sweet; natural rice vinegar is sour. This makes enough for 3 to 4 dozen oysters.

- ½ cup rice-wine vinegar
- ½ cup seasoned rice vinegar
- 2 shallots, minced
- 3 tablespoons fresh lime juice
- 1 small jalapeño pepper, seeds and ribs removed, minced
- 1 small bunch fresh cilantro leaves, roughly chopped

Combine both vinegars, shallots, lime juice, jalapeño, and cilantro in a medium bowl. Refrigerate at least 1 hour before using. Serve with raw or grilled oysters.

red oyster sauce

MAKES 1 CUP

Thai red-curry paste (see Food Sources, page 648) usually comes in a 14-ounce bucket and can be bought at most Asian markets.

- 4 tablespoons unsalted butter
- ½ cup extra-virgin olive oil
- 1 large garlic clove, minced
- ¼ cup sun-dried-tomato paste
- ¼ teaspoon Thai red-curry paste
- 10 fresh basil leaves

Melt butter in a medium saucepan over medium-low heat. Add olive oil, garlic, tomato paste, and red-curry paste, and simmer until the butter is brown, about 15 minutes. Roughly chop the basil, and add to the sauce. Serve warm with raw oysters.

boiled shrimp

SERVES 8

A large bowl of steaming boiled shrimp is an instant crowd-pleaser for a casual dinner.

- 3 dried or fresh bay leaves
- 6 to 8 whole black peppercorns
- 2 pounds (about 72) medium shrimp, heads and shells left on

Fill a large pot with water; add the bay leaves and peppercorns. Cover and bring to a boil over high heat. Reduce heat; simmer for 10 minutes. Add the shrimp, and cook until they are bright pink and cooked through, 8 to 10 minutes. Drain, and serve.

three sauces for shrimp

The chefs at Balthazar, a popular French brasserie in New York City, like to serve all of these sauces with the restaurant's famed plateau de fruits de mer. Allow about 1 cup of sauce for eight people. All three sauces can be made a day in advance and refrigerated until needed. Serve the sauces with Boiled Shrimp (recipe above), Steamed Shrimp (page 302), cracked crab claws, Boiled Maine Lobster (page 297), or other fresh shellfish.

mignonette sauce

MAKES 1 1/2 CUPS

- ½ cup red-wine vinegar
- ½ cup sherry vinegar
- 2 shallots, minced
  Kosher salt and freshly ground black pepper

In a small bowl, combine the red-wine vinegar, sherry vinegar, and shallots; whisk to combine well. Season with salt and pepper. Serve.

cocktail sauce

MAKES 1 CUP

¾ cup chili sauce

1 tablespoon Worcestershire sauce

¼ teaspoon hot red-pepper sauce

3 tablespoons brandy, optional

1 tablespoon red-wine vinegar

3 tablespoons fresh lemon juice

1 to 2 tablespoons Fresh Horseradish (page 633) or prepared

Kosher salt

In a small bowl, combine the chili sauce; Worcestershire sauce; pepper sauce; brandy, if using; the red-wine vinegar; lemon juice; and grated horseradish. Whisk to combine well. Season with salt. Serve.

tarragon mayonnaise

MAKES 1¾ CUPS

If you don't want to use brandy, add 2 more tablespoons of fresh lemon juice to the mayonnaise.

½ cup Homemade Mayonnaise (page 632) or prepared

2 tablespoons ketchup

½ tablespoon hot red-pepper sauce

2 tablespoons brandy

1 tablespoon fresh lemon juice

Pinch of cayenne pepper

2 tablespoons fresh tarragon, finely chopped

Kosher salt

In a small bowl, combine the mayonnaise; ketchup; pepper sauce; brandy, if using; the lemon juice; cayenne; and tarragon. Whisk to combine. Season with salt. Serve.

grilled shrimp cocktail with orange horseradish sauce

SERVES 8; MAKES 1⅓ CUPS SAUCE

Grated zest of 1 orange

½ cup fresh orange juice (2 oranges)

1 cup sour cream

2 tablespoons red-wine vinegar

3 tablespoons Fresh Horseradish (page 633) or prepared

Kosher salt and freshly ground black pepper

2 pounds (about 48) large shrimp, peeled and deveined

1 tablespoon olive oil

1. In a medium bowl, mix the orange zest, orange juice, sour cream, vinegar, and horseradish; stir to combine. Season with salt and pepper. Cover the orange-horseradish sauce, and chill in the refrigerator, covered, at least 1 hour, or overnight.

2. Heat a grill or a grill pan to medium hot. Drizzle the shrimp with the olive oil, and toss to coat. Arrange the shrimp on the grill, working in batches if necessary. Grill until pink and developing golden-brown marks, about 2½ minutes per side. Remove from the heat. Serve the shrimp with the orange-horseradish sauce.

. . . .

HOW TO PEEL AND DEVEIN SHRIMP

1. Hold the shrimp with the legs facing up. Using your thumb and forefinger, peel the shell away from the head of the shrimp on the inside curve in two or three sections.

2. To expose the vein that runs along the back of the shrimp, use a small paring knife to make a shallow cut just above the vein from the head to the tail. Remove the vein with the tip of the knife or with your fingers. Alternatively, small kitchen scissors can be used to cut down the length of the back of the shrimp from head to tail, cracking open the shell and making it easier to remove in one piece. The vein will already be exposed and can be lifted out with your fingers.

. . . .

smoked salmon and caramelized onion stuffed celery stalks

SERVES 10 TO 12

- 1 tablespoon olive oil
- 1 medium red onion, thinly sliced
- 2 teaspoons sugar
- 8 ounces whipped cream cheese
- ¼ cup plus 1 tablespoon Fresh Horseradish (page 633) or prepared
- 5 ounces smoked salmon
- 1 tablespoon finely snipped dill, plus small tips for garnish
- 9 celery stalks, strings removed, cut into 2-inch lengths

1. In a skillet, heat the olive oil over medium heat. Add the onion slices; reduce heat to low. Cook, stirring occasionally, until very soft and melting, about 15 minutes. Add the sugar. Cook over very low heat, stirring occasionally, until the onion slices are caramelized, about 30 minutes more. Remove from the heat; set aside.

2. In a medium bowl, combine the cream cheese and horseradish; divide the mixture between two bowls. Coarsely chop one-quarter of the salmon, and add to half the cheese mixture; add the dill, and mix. Cut the remaining salmon into thin slivers; set aside. Fill half the celery with the salmon-cream-cheese mixture. Garnish each with a sliver of salmon and a dill sprig. Fill remaining celery with remaining cheese mixture; garnish with reserved caramelized onions, and serve.

smoked snappers

SERVES 8 TO 10

The classic combination of salmon, dill, and cream cheese is assembled to look like the party "snappers" that can be pulled apart from both ends to reveal a surprise inside. Choose smoked salmon that is not too salty, and ask to have it sliced evenly and thinly. Seedless cucumbers may still contain a few seeds; remove them if necessary.

- ½ cup whipped cream cheese
- ½ ounce (about 7 halves) sun-dried tomatoes, cut into ⅛-inch dice
- 1 tablespoon finely snipped dill
  Kosher salt and freshly ground black pepper
- ½ seedless cucumber, peeled
- 8 ounces smoked salmon, thinly sliced
- ¼ bunch frisée (1 cup picked leaves) or other small lettuce

1. In a medium bowl, combine the cream cheese, tomatoes, and dill. Season with salt and pepper. Transfer the cream-cheese mixture to a pastry bag fitted with a plain #12 Ateco round tip, and set aside.

2. Cut the cucumber into ¼ x 1¼-inch matchsticks, and set aside. Cut the salmon into 1¼ x 2¼-inch rectangles, and place on a clean work surface. Pipe a line of the cream-cheese mixture across the bottom edge of salmon, place a cucumber baton on top, and roll. Insert a small piece of the frisée at each end, and transfer to a tray lined with parchment paper. Repeat the process until all the salmon slices and filling are used. Wrap with plastic wrap, and place in the refrigerator until ready to serve. Serve chilled. May be made up to 1 day ahead.

crab and mango summer rolls

MAKES 10 ROLLS OR 40 PIECES

These rolls can be made several hours in advance and stored at room temperature in an airtight container lined with dampened cheesecloth. Do not refrigerate, or the rice paper will toughen.

- 1 pound king crab legs or 8 ounces lump crabmeat, shells and cartilage removed
- 1 large mango, peeled, pit removed (see page 647)
- 10 leaves Boston lettuce
- 3 scallions, white and green parts
  Kosher salt
- 2 ounces rice vermicelli noodles
- 10 8½-inch round rice-paper wrappers
- 1 cup tightly packed fresh cilantro leaves
- 1 cup tightly packed fresh mint leaves
  Citrus Dipping Sauce (page 630)

1. Using a mallet or small hammer, and your fingers, crack open the crab legs, and remove the meat from each. Slice in thin strips 5 inches long, cover, and refrigerate.

2. Cut the mango into ½ x 2½-inch strips. Cut the lettuce leaves in half, discarding the center ribs. Trim each scallion into two 5-inch lengths; slice lengthwise into very thin strips.

3. Cover and bring a large pot of salted water to a boil. Add the rice vermicelli, and cook until tender, 2 to 3 minutes. Drain, and rinse under cold running water.

4. Fill a pan large enough to hold the rice paper with hot water. Dampen a kitchen towel with water; spread it out on a clean surface. Immerse 1 sheet of the rice paper in the hot water until softened and flexible, about 1 minute. Transfer to the dampened towel, and smooth out.

5. Across the bottom third of the rice paper, place 2 pieces of lettuce, 4 cilantro leaves, 4 mint leaves, 1 piece of crab (if using lump crabmeat, 2 tablespoons), 2 pieces of mango (end to end), and ¼ cup vermicelli. Cover with 4 strips of scallion, 4 cilantro leaves, and 4 mint leaves. Roll the rice paper into a cylinder, stopping halfway. Fold the left and right sides into the middle; finish rolling.

6. Place the roll on a baking sheet lined with plastic wrap; cover. Repeat the entire process, making 10 rolls. To serve, trim the ends with a sharp knife, and cut each roll into 4 pieces. Serve with the dipping sauce on the side.

crisp spring rolls
MAKES ABOUT 3 DOZEN

Serve the lettuce and herbs on a platter, and use them to wrap around the spring rolls. See Food Sources (page 648) for the dried tree-ear and wood-ear mushrooms.

- 1   ounce green bean-thread vermicelli or other vermicelli
- 1   tablespoon dried tree-ear or wood-ear mushrooms
- ½   cup finely chopped onion
- 1   cup finely grated carrots
- ¼   cup thinly sliced scallions
- 2   large eggs
- 2   tablespoons Asian fish sauce (nam pla)
- 1½ teaspoons minced garlic
- 2   teaspoons sugar
- ¼   teaspoon kosher salt
- ½   teaspoon freshly ground black pepper
- 8   ounces ground skinless chicken breast
- 8   ounces ground pork
- 1   tablespoon cornstarch
- 36 8-inch square fresh or frozen spring-roll wrappers, thawed
- 3   cups peanut oil
- 1   small head red-leaf lettuce, leaves separated
- 1   bunch fresh basil, leaves only
- 1   bunch fresh mint, leaves only
- 1   bunch fresh cilantro, leaves only
     Vietnamese Dipping Sauce (page 630)

1. Place the vermicelli in a large bowl. Cover with hot water; soak 30 minutes, then drain. Cut into ½-inch lengths. Place the mushrooms in a small bowl, and cover with very hot water. Let stand until the mushrooms are soft, about 20 minutes. Drain, and roughly chop the mushrooms; add to the vermicelli along with the onion, carrots, and scallions.

2. Whisk together the eggs, fish sauce, garlic, sugar, salt, and pepper. Using a fork, mix the chicken and pork into the egg mixture. Add the noodle mixture; mix just until combined.

3. In a small saucepan over medium heat, whisk the cornstarch and ¼ cup plus 1 tablespoon water until the mixture comes to a boil and looks like a smooth porridge, 1 to 2 minutes; remove the cornstarch paste from the heat.

4. Line a baking sheet with parchment paper. Place the wrappers in a neat stack; cut in half into 4 x 8-inch rectangles. Loosely cover with plastic wrap. Place 1 wrapper on a clean surface with the narrow edge facing you. Place 1 tablespoon of the filling ½ inch in from the narrow edge. Fold about ½ inch of the right and left sides over the filling, and roll the wrapper to form a cylinder. Use your finger to smear the cornstarch paste along the end of the wrapper; gently press to seal. Transfer rolls to the prepared baking sheet, keeping the completed rolls covered with plastic wrap. Repeat, using all the wrappers and filling.

5. Heat the oil (there should be enough to cover the spring rolls) in a wok or large saucepan over medium-high heat until a deep-frying thermometer registers 375°F. (If using a wok, turn the burner grate over; place the wok directly on the grate so it is as close to the flame as possible.) Carefully transfer as many spring rolls as will fit comfortably in the oil. Fry, turning often, until golden and crisp, about 3 minutes. Using a slotted spoon, transfer the spring rolls to paper towels to drain. Repeat until all the rolls are cooked. Serve immediately. To eat, sprinkle the inside of a lettuce leaf with the herb leaves, wrap around a spring roll, and dip in the dipping sauce.

twice-baked cheese strudel

SERVES 10 TO 12

Keep the phyllo dough pliable and moist by covering it with damp paper towels.

- *7 sheets phyllo dough*
- *8 tablespoons (1 stick) unsalted butter, melted*
- *10 tablespoons finely grated Asiago cheese*
- *12 tablespoons finely grated Parmesan cheese*
- *10 tablespoons finely grated Pecorino Romano cheese*
- *¼ cup plus 1½ tablespoons poppy seeds, plus more for topping*

1. Preheat the oven to 350°F. Place one sheet of phyllo on a clean surface, and brush evenly with the butter. Repeat with two more sheets of phyllo. Sprinkle a third layer of buttered phyllo evenly with 2 tablespoons of each cheese and 1 tablespoon of the poppy seeds. Add four more layers with cheeses and seeds, for a total of two layers that only have butter and five layers with cheeses and seeds.

2. Carefully roll up the pastry and filling lengthwise so it is compact. The roll should measure 1½ to 2 inches in diameter. Brush the outside of the roll with

butter, and sprinkle with the remaining 2 tablespoons Parmesan cheese and the remaining ½ tablespoon of poppy seeds. Cut the roll in half, and transfer to a parchment-lined baking pan. (Alternatively, wrap each half in plastic wrap and freeze for up to 1 month. When ready to bake, remove the plastic; bake on a parchment-lined baking pan.)

3. Bake until deep golden, 20 to 25 minutes. Remove from the oven, and transfer to a wire rack until cool enough to handle.

4. Using a serrated knife, carefully slice the roll into ½-inch-thick slices, and return to the baking pan, cut-side down. Bake until golden throughout, about 10 minutes. Remove from the oven, and serve warm or at room temperature.

potato croquettes

MAKES ABOUT 2 DOZEN

The batter should taste a little salty, but once you fry the croquettes the seasoning will be perfect.

- *4 slices white bread, crusts removed*
- *2 cups cold leftover mashed potatoes*
- *¼ cup plus 2 tablespoons chopped mixed fresh herbs, such as flat-leaf parsley, cilantro, or chives*
- *1 large egg, lightly beaten*
- *¼ cup all-purpose flour*
   Kosher salt and freshly ground black pepper
- *2 cups canola oil*

1. Place the bread in the bowl of a food processor. Process until crumbs form, about 10 seconds. Transfer the crumbs to a medium bowl; set aside. Line one baking sheet with parchment paper and another one with a double thickness of paper towels; set both aside.

2. In a small bowl, combine the potatoes, herbs, egg, and flour using a fork or spoon. Season with salt and pepper. Using a spoon, scoop the mixture into an egg-shaped piece. Using a second spoon, push the shape into the bowl of bread crumbs. Roll to coat, and transfer to the parchment-lined baking sheet. Repeat with the remaining potato mixture.

3. Place the oil in a small deep saucepan. Heat over medium heat until a deep-frying thermometer registers 350°F. Using a slotted spoon, place 5 croquettes in the oil. Cook until golden and puffed, turning once, about 5 minutes. Transfer to the paper-towel-lined baking sheet. Repeat with the remaining croquettes. Serve hot.

individual cauliflower soufflés over baby greens

SERVES 6

for the soufflés

- 2 tablespoons unsalted butter, plus more for ramekins
- ½ ounce Parmesan cheese, grated on the small holes of a box grater
- 1 1½-pound head cauliflower
- 3 tablespoons all-purpose flour
- 1 cup hot milk
- 4 large egg yolks
- 2½ ounces Maytag or other blue cheese, crumbled to yield ½ cup
- ½ teaspoon kosher salt
- ⅛ teaspoon paprika
- ¼ teaspoon freshly ground black pepper
- ¼ teaspoon ground nutmeg
- 1 teaspoon minced fresh flat-leaf parsley
- 5 large egg whites

for the salad

- 2 tablespoons sherry or red-wine vinegar
- ¼ cup plus 2 tablespoons extra-virgin olive oil

  Kosher salt and freshly ground black pepper
- 5 ounces baby salad greens

1. Preheat the oven to 400°F with a rack in the center. Butter six 5-ounce ovenproof ramekins. Sprinkle the inside of each with the Parmesan. Arrange the ramekins, evenly spaced, in a baking pan.

2. Cut the cauliflower into quarters; remove the center core and leaves. Thinly slice about 30 cauliflower florets vertically. Mince the remaining cauliflower to yield about 1 cup. Set aside.

3. In a medium saucepan over medium heat, melt 2 tablespoons butter. Whisk in the flour until it is cooked but not brown, about 2 minutes. Whisk in the hot milk until fully incorporated; let cook 3 minutes. Whisk in the egg yolks, one at a time, until fully incorporated. Using a wooden spoon, stir in the cheese, salt, paprika, pepper, and nutmeg, stirring constantly. Once the cheese has melted, stir in the reserved minced cauliflower and the parsley. Cook 2 minutes more. Transfer the mixture to a large mixing bowl. Set aside.

4. In the bowl of an electric mixer fitted with the whisk attachment, beat the egg whites on low speed until frothy, about 2 minutes. Increase speed to medium, and beat 1 minute more. When the egg whites are foamy, increase speed to high, and beat just until they hold soft peaks; do not overbeat the egg whites. Using a large rubber spatula, lightly mix a third of the whites into the cheese mixture to lighten it. Fold in the remaining whites, until just combined.

5. Fill each ramekin with ½ cup soufflé mixture; smooth the tops. Insert 4 or 5 of the thin cauliflower florets around the edges of each ramekin, poking the florets into the soufflé mixture with the ruffled edge up. Bake until the tops are golden brown and the mixture is set, 20 to 25 minutes.

6. Meanwhile, place the vinegar in a small bowl, and slowly whisk in the olive oil until combined. Season with salt and pepper. Toss the salad greens with the vinaigrette. Just before serving, divide the salad evenly among six plates. Remove the soufflés from the oven. Use a kitchen towel to hold the ramekins, and invert the soufflés onto your hand, and then bottom-side down onto the plates with the salad. Serve warm.

beef or chicken satay

MAKES 3 TO 4 DOZEN

For satays, you'll need bamboo or wooden skewers; soak them in water for at least 20 minutes before using to prevent charring during cooking. Sambal is an Indonesian chili paste (see Food Sources, page 648).

- 1 tablespoon chopped fresh ginger
- 1 onion, cut into chunks
- 3 garlic cloves
- 1 cup soy sauce
- 1 teaspoon sambal or 1 hot red chile pepper
- Juice of 1 lemon
- 1 tablespoon sugar
- ½ teaspoon ground cumin
- 2 tablespoons sesame oil
- 1½ pounds filet of beef or 4 boneless, skinless chicken-breast halves
- Peanut Dipping Sauce (recipe follows)

1. Combine the ginger, onion, garlic, soy sauce, sambal, lemon juice, sugar, cumin, and sesame oil in a blender, and purée until smooth. Set aside.

2. Trim the fat from the beef or chicken. Cut into strips about 3 inches long and ½ inch thick, and transfer to a large bowl. Pour the reserved sauce over the meat, and mix to coat evenly. Cover with plastic wrap, and marinate in the refrigerator at least 1 hour or overnight.

3. Heat a grill or a grill pan until hot. Thread a piece of meat lengthwise on each skewer, and grill on each side until grill marks appear and meat is cooked through, about 3 minutes per side. Baste occasionally with the marinade during cooking. Discard any remaining marinade. Serve immediately with the peanut sauce.

peanut dipping sauce

MAKES 1½ CUPS

- 1 cup smooth peanut butter
- 2 tablespoons dark sesame oil
- 3 tablespoons soy sauce
- 1 garlic clove
- 1 teaspoon sambal
- 1 tablespoon sugar
- Fresh lemon juice
- Coconut milk or water to thin
- 1 scallion, white and pale-green parts, thinly sliced

1. In a blender or a food processor, combine peanut butter, oil, soy sauce, garlic, sambal, and sugar until smooth. Add lemon juice to taste.

2. With the machine running, add coconut milk until sauce reaches desired consistency. Garnish with scallion slices. Serve. Sauce may be made up to 2 days in advance; refrigerate in an airtight container. Return to room temperature before serving.

shrimp satay

MAKES 4 DOZEN

You'll need about 48 bamboo skewers, soaked in water for at least 20 minutes before using, for this dish. Red hot chile peppers are fine substitutes for sambal, an Indonesian chili paste (see Food Sources, page 648).

- 48 jumbo (about 3 pounds) shrimp, peeled and deveined
- 2 onions, cut into chunks
- 4 garlic cloves
- ¾ cup low-sodium soy sauce
- 4 lemongrass stalks, bottom 2½ inches only
- 1 tablespoon sugar
- ¼ cup peanut oil
- 1½ cups coconut milk
- 2 teaspoons sambal or 2 hot red chile peppers
- Juice of 2 lemons
- Peanut Dipping Sauce (recipe above)

1. Place the shrimp in a large bowl. Combine the remaining ingredients (except the peanut dipping sauce) in a blender, and purée until smooth. Pour over the shrimp, and mix to coat evenly. Marinate 1 hour.

2. Heat a grill or a grill pan until hot. Thread a shrimp lengthwise on each skewer, and grill until opaque, 2 to 3 minutes per side. Baste occasionally with the marinade while cooking. Serve immediately with the peanut sauce.

carambola with papaya, crabmeat, and avocado

MAKES 20

Carambola, also known as star fruit, provides a decorative base for this hors d'oeuvre.

- 8 ounces jumbo lump crabmeat, shells and cartilage removed
- ½ large avocado, peeled, pitted (see page 647), cut into ¼-inch cubes
- 1 1½-pound red or yellow papaya, peeled and seeded, cut into ¼-inch cubes
- 2 tablespoons fresh lime juice
- ¼ cup loosely packed fresh cilantro leaves, finely chopped
- ½ jalapeño pepper, seeds and ribs removed, minced
- ¼ teaspoon kosher salt
  Freshly ground black pepper
- 3 large (about 4 ounces each) ripe carambola, sliced ½ inch thick

1. Shred the crabmeat, and place in a medium bowl. Add the avocado, papaya, lime juice, cilantro, jalapeño, salt, and black pepper to taste; toss. Adjust seasoning.

2. Spoon a heaping teaspoon of the crab mixture over each carambola slice. Arrange on a serving platter, and serve immediately.

shrimp and grit cakes with seven-pepper jelly

MAKES 2 DOZEN

The grits can be cooked and the cakes assembled in advance and refrigerated. If the shrimp loosen from the cakes as they cook, press them back into the patties.

- 12 medium shrimp
- 2½ cups grits, preferably stoneground
- 2 cups (5 ounces) grated Cheddar cheese
- 1 tablespoon ground cumin
- ½ teaspoon cayenne pepper
- 2 teaspoons kosher salt
- 1½ teaspoons ground white pepper
- 2 bunches scallions, white and pale-green parts, minced to equal ½ cup (reserve dark greens for garnish)
- 2 tablespoons butter, plus more for pan
- ½ cup all-purpose flour
- ½ cup yellow cornmeal
- 2 tablespoons canola oil
- ½ cup seven-pepper jelly

1. Cover and bring a medium saucepan of water to a boil. Prepare an ice-water bath. Cook the shrimp until opaque and cooked through, 1 to 2 minutes. Transfer the shrimp to the ice-water bath to cool. When cool, peel and cut in half lengthwise along the vein. Discard the vein; set aside the shrimp.

2. Bring 1 quart plus 2 cups water to a boil in a medium saucepan. Slowly sprinkle the grits into the boiling water, stirring constantly with a whisk. Reduce heat to medium, and stir constantly until the mixture is thick, about 5 minutes. Remove the pan from the heat, and stir in the Cheddar, cumin, cayenne, salt, white pepper, and scallions.

3. Pour mixture into a buttered 10 x 15-inch jelly-roll pan; smooth to a ½-inch-thick layer. Using a 2½-inch round cookie cutter, lightly press 24 circles in grits. Press 1 halved shrimp into each circle, flat-side down. Cover with plastic wrap, press lightly to smooth, and chill until set, 1 to 2 hours.

4. Combine the flour and cornmeal in a small bowl. Using the cookie cutter, cut the grits along the marked lines into rounds, keeping the shrimp centered in each circle. Heat 2 teaspoons butter and 2 teaspoons oil in a large skillet over medium-high heat. Dredge cakes in flour mixture; cook, 8 at a time, until golden brown, 1 to 2 minutes per side. Wipe skillet; repeat, adding butter and oil, until all the cakes are cooked. Transfer to a baking sheet or a paper-towel-lined plate. Top with a teaspoon of pepper jelly and scallion greens and serve.

shrimp salad rolls

MAKES 2 DOZEN

Look for the smallest, sweetest shrimp available.

- 1 pound small shrimp, peeled and deveined
- 1 tablespoon unsalted butter
  Kosher salt and freshly ground black pepper
- 3 tablespoons fresh lemon juice, plus more for seasoning
- ¾ cup Homemade Mayonnaise (page 632) or prepared
- 1 scallion, white and pale-green parts, finely chopped
- 24 small prepared rolls, such as Parker House
- 1 small head Bibb lettuce, washed and trimmed

1. Rinse the shrimp under cold running water, and pat dry. Heat the butter in a large skillet over medium heat. Add the shrimp; season with salt and pepper. Cook the shrimp until bright pink and opaque, about 2 minutes per side. Add the lemon juice; remove from the heat.

2. When the shrimp has cooled, cut into ½-inch pieces. In a large bowl, combine the shrimp, mayonnaise, and scallion; toss to coat. Season the shrimp salad with salt, pepper, and lemon juice, if desired. Chill.

3. Split open the rolls. Gently press a lettuce leaf into each roll, and fill with a heaping teaspoon of the shrimp salad. Serve.

tuna carpaccio on orange slices

SERVES 10 TO 12

Before preparing the tuna, freeze it for about 3 hours—until almost frozen—so it will slice thinly.

- ½ cup Homemade Mayonnaise (page 632) or prepared
- 1 tablespoon Black Pepper Ponzu (recipe follows)
- 12 ounces sushi-quality tuna
- 4 small navel or juice oranges, cut into ¼-inch-thick slices
- 3 tablespoons capers, drained
- ½ bunch fresh cilantro, leaves only

1. In a small bowl, whisk together the mayonnaise and ponzu sauce, and set aside.

2. Remove the tuna from the freezer; slice into ⅛-inch-thick, 1½ x 2¼-inch rectangles. Arrange a slice of tuna on top of an orange slice. Drizzle with ¼ teaspoon of the mayonnaise mixture; garnish with several capers and the cilantro. Repeat with the remaining ingredients. Serve immediately.

black pepper ponzu

MAKES ½ CUP

- ¼ cup rice-wine vinegar
- 1 teaspoon sugar
- 1 tablespoon fresh lemon juice
- 2 tablespoons soy sauce
- ¼ teaspoon freshly ground black pepper

In a bowl, whisk together all the ingredients.

melon ribbons with bresaola

SERVES 8

Bresaola, air-dried beef that has been aged for about 2 months, is available in Italian groceries and specialty food shops (see Food Sources, page 648). Ask the butcher to slice it very thinly. Prosciutto or other dry-cured ham or beef can be used as well. Choose melons that are just beginning to ripen for best results.

- 1 cantaloupe, cut in half crosswise, rind and seeds removed
- 1 honeydew melon, cut in half crosswise, rind and seeds removed
- 1 Crenshaw melon, cut in half crosswise, rind and seeds removed
- 3 tablespoons fresh lemon juice
- ¼ teaspoon kosher salt
- ¼ teaspoon freshly ground black pepper
- ½ cup fresh mint leaves, coarsely chopped
- 4 ounces bresaola, sliced paper thin

1. Using a vegetable peeler, shave along the cut edge of each melon half to make long, thin, flat strips. Carefully lift melon strips into a bowl.

2. Sprinkle the lemon juice, salt, pepper, and half the mint over the melon strips; toss gently.

3. Divide the melon strips among serving plates and arrange the bresaola slices over each. Garnish with the remaining mint, and serve.

mini frittatas

MAKES 4 DOZEN

Martha loves these easy, colorful hors d'oeuvres, which pack all the flavor of a large frittata into just one or two bites. For mini-muffin tins, see Equipment Sources, page 650.

- Olive oil, for tins
- 1 medium zucchini
- 6 white-button mushrooms, wiped clean
- 16 large eggs
- 2 teaspoons kosher salt
- ¾ teaspoon freshly ground black pepper
- 1 tablespoon snipped chives

- 1 red bell pepper, seeds and ribs removed, cut in ⅛-inch dice
- 1 yellow bell pepper, seeds and ribs removed, cut in ⅛-inch dice
- ½ cup finely grated Gruyère or fontina cheese

1. Lightly brush two 24-mini-muffin tins with oil. Slice the zucchini into ⅛-inch rounds. Slice the mushrooms lengthwise into ⅛-inch-thick pieces.

2. Preheat the oven to 400°F. In a large mixing bowl, whisk the eggs, salt, pepper, and chives, and set aside. Arrange the cut zucchini, mushrooms, and peppers in each muffin tin. Ladle the egg mixture into each tin, just even with the rim, and sprinkle with the cheese. Bake until the frittatas are set, about 10 minutes. Serve warm.

basic quesadillas

MAKES 4

If you are using corn tortillas, you may need to increase the amount of oil; corn tortillas tend to absorb more liquid than the flour variety.

- 1 tablespoon plus 1 teaspoon canola oil, or more as needed
- 8 6- to 8-inch flour or corn tortillas
- 2 cups grated cheese, such as Monterey Jack, manchego, or mozzarella
- 1 cup filling (recipes follow), room temperature, optional

1. Heat a heavy skillet over medium heat; add ½ teaspoon oil. When hot, place 1 tortilla in the pan; sprinkle with ¼ cup grated cheese, ¼ cup filling, if using, and top with another ¼ cup grated cheese.

2. Top with a second tortilla; cook until the cheese is melting and the bottom tortilla is golden brown. Using a metal spatula, flip; cook until golden on both sides, the cheese is melted, and the filling is hot. Cut into wedges. Repeat with remaining ingredients; serve hot.

caramelized corn, zucchini, and vidalia filling

MAKES ABOUT 3 CUPS

Make filling no more than 3 hours before using.

- 1 teaspoon olive oil
- 1 large garlic clove, minced
- 1 Vidalia or other sweet onion, thinly sliced lengthwise into slivers
- 3 ears fresh corn, kernels shaved from the cob
- 8 ounces baby or regular zucchini, cut into ¼-inch-thick rounds

    Kosher salt and freshly ground black pepper

Heat the oil in a medium skillet over medium heat. Add garlic and onion; cook until translucent, about 8 minutes. Add the corn, zucchini, and ¼ to ½ cup water, and cook, stirring occasionally, until the vegetables are tender and caramelized, about 10 minutes. Season with salt and pepper.

orange-braised pork filling

MAKES ABOUT 2 CUPS

This filling can be made up to 1 day in advance and frozen for up to 1 month.

- 8 ounces center-cut pork loin

    Kosher salt and freshly ground black pepper

- 1 tablespoon canola oil
- 1 small onion, thinly sliced lengthwise

    Zest and juice of 1 orange

- ¼ cup golden raisins
- 2 cups Homemade Chicken Stock (page 624), or low-sodium store-bought chicken broth, skimmed of fat
- 1 tablespoon white-wine vinegar
- 1 tablespoon honey
- ¼ teaspoon fresh thyme leaves
- ¼ teaspoon ground cumin

1. Season the pork with salt and pepper. Heat the oil in a saucepan over medium-high heat. When the oil is very hot, add the pork; brown on all sides.

2. Add the onion, orange zest and juice, raisins, stock, vinegar, honey, thyme, and cumin. Cover, and simmer over medium-low heat until the pork is tender, about 30 minutes.

3. Remove the pork, let cool, shred, and return to the pan. Simmer until the liquid is reduced to a thick sauce, 10 to 15 minutes.

....

SIMPLE QUESADILLA FILLINGS

Roasted poblano peppers (see page 645)

Caramelized onions (see page 646)

Boiled or roasted red potatoes

Roasted or grilled vegetables

Chorizo sausage

Flank steak or leftover stew meats

Grilled chicken

....

corn cakes with smoky tomato coulis

MAKES TWENTY 2½-INCH CAKES

- 4 ears fresh yellow or white corn, kernels shaved from the cob
- ½ cup yellow or blue cornmeal
- ½ cup all-purpose flour
- 1 teaspoon kosher salt
- 1 teaspoon sugar
- ½ teaspoon baking powder
- ¼ teaspoon cayenne pepper
- 1 large egg, beaten
- ¾ cup buttermilk
- 3 tablespoons unsalted butter, melted and cooled
- 2 scallions, white and green parts, finely chopped

    Canola oil, for frying

    Smoky Tomato Coulis (recipe follows)

- 1 cup sour cream

    Fresh chives, for garnish

1. Cover and bring a medium pot of water to a boil. Blanch the corn briefly, about 1 minute, and drain. Mash lightly with a fork to break up some of the kernels; set aside.

2. In a small bowl, combine the cornmeal, flour, salt, sugar, baking powder, and cayenne pepper.

3. In another bowl, whisk together the egg, buttermilk, and butter. Add to the dry ingredients, and stir just until mixed. Fold in the scallions and corn.

4. Heat the oil in a skillet or on a griddle over medium heat. Place heaping tablespoons of the batter in the skillet, and cook until golden, 1 to 2 minutes per side. Serve immediately with the tomato coulis and sour cream, garnished with chives.

smoky tomato coulis
MAKES 2 CUPS

Chipotle peppers are dried, smoked jalapeños (see Food Sources, page 648). Extra ground chipotle pepper or chili powder may be added to taste.

- 8 tomatoes
- 2 garlic cloves, thinly sliced
- 2 shallots, thinly sliced
- 2 sun-dried tomatoes
- ¾ teaspoon ground chipotle pepper
- ¼ teaspoon chili powder
  Kosher salt

1. Roast the tomatoes over a gas flame or on a grill until the skins are charred and blackened.

2. In a saucepan, combine the roasted tomatoes with the skins, garlic, shallots, and sun-dried tomatoes. Cook over medium heat for about 40 minutes, stirring occasionally. Add the ground chipotle pepper and chili powder; cook for 40 minutes more. Strain the mixture through a fine sieve or cheesecloth-lined strainer, pressing on the solids, or put through a food mill fitted with a fine disc. Discard the solids. If necessary, return to the pot, and reduce over medium heat until desired thickness is reached. Season with salt, and adjust the spices. Cool, and serve. Coulis will keep, refrigerated in an airtight container, for up to 3 days or frozen for up to 3 months.

tomato ice with sugared basil leaves
SERVES 8

- 4 pounds large very ripe red tomatoes
- ½ cup plus 2 tablespoons granulated sugar
- ¼ cup fresh lemon juice
- 8 fresh basil leaves
- 1 large egg white
- ¼ cup superfine sugar

1. Line a large bowl with two layers of cheesecloth, with about a 2-inch overhang. Set aside. Cut the tomatoes into quarters, and place in the bowl of a food processor. Process the tomatoes until completely puréed. Transfer to the prepared bowl. With kitchen twine, tie up the cheesecloth to enclose all of the tomato purée, and tie the cheesecloth to a large wooden spoon. Rest the spoon on two tall jars or stacks of books, and allow the juices to drip into a large glass measuring cup or glass bowl. Let the tomatoes drip, without squeezing, overnight or until they have released 3 cups of tomato water. If the tomatoes have not released enough water, gently squeeze the cheesecloth. If necessary, repeat with additional tomatoes.

2. Place the granulated sugar in a small saucepan with ½ cup water. Bring to a simmer, and stir until all the sugar is dissolved. Set aside to cool.

3. In a large glass measuring cup or glass bowl, combine 3 cups of the tomato water with the lemon juice and the reserved cooled sugar syrup. Pour the mixture into an 8- or 9-inch square glass baking dish; place in the freezer. After 1 hour, stir the ice with a fork, and return the pan to the freezer. Repeat this every hour until the mixture is frozen into granulated clumps.

4. Meanwhile, sugar the basil leaves: Mix the egg white and 1 teaspoon water in small bowl. Brush each leaf with the egg-white mixture; blot almost dry with a paper towel. Sprinkle the fronts and backs with superfine sugar, and let dry on a wire rack. To serve, spoon the tomato ice into bowls, and garnish each serving with a sugared basil sprig.

squash and portobello bruschetta

MAKES 2½ DOZEN

Olive oil, for pan and drizzling

1¾   pounds butternut or other orange-flesh winter squash

12   ounces portobello mushrooms, wiped clean, stems removed

4   garlic cloves

Kosher salt and freshly ground black pepper

1   tablespoon chopped fresh oregano, plus more for garnish

1   tablespoon chopped fresh rosemary, plus more for garnish

2   tablespoons balsamic vinegar

¼   cup Homemade Chicken Stock (page 624), or low-sodium store-bought chicken broth, skimmed of fat

¼   cup soft goat cheese

6   slices whole-wheat country bread, cut in small pieces

1. Preheat the oven to 425°F with a rack in the center. Brush a roasting pan with olive oil. Cut squash in half lengthwise. Remove seeds and fibers, and peel. Cut the squash into ½-inch pieces. Cut portobellos into ½-inch pieces. Transfer squash and mushrooms to the pan, keeping each separate. Add the garlic. Drizzle with olive oil, and season with salt and pepper and half the oregano and rosemary.

2. Cook until the portobellos are tender when pierced with the tip of a knife, 15 to 20 minutes; remove the portobellos. Spread out the squash in the pan, turning with a spatula. Raise heat to 450°F. Cook until squash is just tender and garlic is soft, about 15 minutes more. Remove from the oven. Remove the garlic cloves, and reserve.

3. Return the portobellos to the pan, and place over medium-high heat on the stove. Add the vinegar, chicken stock, and the remaining oregano and rosemary, and scrape along the bottom of the pan to remove any cooked-on pieces. Cook, stirring often, until the liquid has been reduced to a glaze, 2 to 3 minutes. Transfer the mixture to a large bowl. Let cool slightly.

4. Remove about one-third of the squash cubes from the mixture, and transfer to a medium bowl. Squeeze the soft garlic from the cloves, and add to the bowl. Add the goat cheese. Use a fork to mash the ingredients to a paste. Set aside. Lightly toast the bread slices on a grill pan or under the broiler. Spread each with the squash paste. Top each with the squash-and-portobello mixture. Garnish with oregano and rosemary. Serve.

goat cheese and lima bean bruschetta

MAKES ABOUT 2½ DOZEN

1   baguette, sliced on the diagonal ½ inch thick

5   ounces soft goat cheese

Kosher salt

1½   pounds fresh or frozen lima beans, shelled

1   teaspoon fresh thyme leaves

Freshly ground black pepper

1. Preheat the oven to 350°F. Place the bread slices in a baking pan. Toast until the tops are golden brown, about 8 minutes. Turn and toast until golden brown on other side, 8 minutes more.

2. Remove the baking pan from the oven. Spread the goat cheese over each slice of bread.

3. Cover and bring a small pot of salted water to a boil, and prepare an ice-water bath. Add the lima beans to the boiling water, and cook until bright green, about 2 minutes. Using a slotted spoon, transfer the beans to the ice-water bath, and let cool. Drain the beans in a colander.

4. Arrange the beans on the bruschetta. Sprinkle with the thyme, salt, and pepper; serve.

chickpea pimiento crostini

MAKES 2½ DOZEN

1 large garlic clove

1 15½-ounce can chickpeas, drained
   and rinsed

3 tablespoons pimientos, finely chopped,
   plus more sliced for garnish

¼ cup extra-virgin olive oil

¾ teaspoon ground cumin

1 tablespoon finely chopped fresh flat-leaf
   parsley, plus leaves for garnish

   Kosher salt and freshly ground
   black pepper

   Crostini (recipe, right)

Process the garlic in the bowl of a food processor until finely chopped. Add the chickpeas, then pulse until crushed but not puréed, 7 to 8 pulses. Transfer to a small bowl. Add chopped pimientos, olive oil, cumin, and parsley; stir to combine. Season with salt and pepper. Place about 1 tablespoon of the mixture on top of each crostini. Garnish with a parsley leaf and a slice of pimiento, and serve.

olive tapenade and goat cheese crostini

MAKES 2½ DOZEN

To make your own tapenade, chop black or green pitted olives; add salt and olive oil to bind the mixture.

¾ cup green- or black-olive tapenade

3 tablespoons fresh thyme leaves, roughly
   chopped, plus sprig tips for garnish

¼ cup plus 1 tablespoon finely
   chopped walnuts

¼ cup dried currants

5 ounces soft goat cheese

   Crostini (recipe, right)

In a small bowl, combine the tapenade, thyme leaves, walnuts, and currants. Spread 1 to 2 teaspoons of the goat cheese onto each crostini. Place 1 to 2 teaspoons of the olive mixture on top, and garnish each with thyme. Serve.

avocado crostini with green sauce

MAKES 2½ DOZEN

If you like a more textured green sauce, chop the parsley, basil, and garlic by hand, then whisk in the olive oil, vinegar, salt, and pepper.

1 small garlic clove

¾ cup packed fresh flat-leaf parsley leaves,
   plus more for garnish

¾ cup packed fresh basil leaves

¼ cup plus 2 tablespoons
   extra-virgin olive oil

1½ teaspoons red-wine vinegar

   Kosher salt and freshly ground
   black pepper

2 avocados, peeled and pitted
   (see page 647)

1 tablespoon fresh lemon juice

   Crostini (recipe follows)

1. Place the garlic in the bowl of a food processor, and pulse. Add the parsley, basil, 5 tablespoons olive oil, and vinegar, and season with salt and pepper; purée. Set the sauce aside.

2. Cut the avocados into ½-inch chunks. Toss with the lemon juice and the remaining olive oil.

3. Spread the green sauce on each crostini. Arrange the avocado chunks on top, sprinkle with a pinch of ground pepper, and garnish with the parsley. Serve immediately.

crostini

MAKES 2½ DOZEN

Crostini can be made 1 to 2 days in advance and stored in an airtight container.

1 5- to 6-ounce baguette (at least 12 inches
   long), sliced on the diagonal, ¼ inch thick

2 tablespoons extra-virgin olive oil

Preheat the oven to 350°F. Brush each bread slice lightly on both sides with the olive oil. Place on a baking sheet; toast until lightly golden, 5 to 6 minutes per side. Remove from the oven, and transfer to a wire rack to cool.

smoked trout brandade

MAKES 2½ DOZEN

Smoked whitefish can be substituted for the trout in this recipe.

- 8 ounces smoked boneless trout, skin removed
- 1 tablespoon finely chopped shallots
- ½ cup plus 1 tablespoon heavy cream
- 2 teaspoons Fresh Horseradish (page 633) or prepared
  Pinch of freshly ground black pepper
  Crostini (page 89)
- 30 small fresh chervil or parsley leaves, for garnish

Place the trout, shallots, cream, horseradish, and pepper in the bowl of a food processor, and purée. Spread about ½ tablespoon of the trout purée onto each crostini. Garnish each with a small sprig of chervil, and serve immediately.

pear pecan toasts

MAKES 2½ DOZEN

- 10 ounces Roquefort cheese
- ¼ cup plus 1 tablespoon heavy cream
- 15 slices thin white sandwich bread, crusts removed
- 2 Bartlett pears, thinly sliced into wedges
- ⅓ cup pecan halves, thinly sliced crosswise

1. Preheat the oven to 350°F. Place the cheese and the heavy cream in a small bowl. Using a fork or wooden spoon, combine until the mixture is soft enough to spread but not too runny; set aside.

2. Cut the bread in half crosswise, making rectangles that are about 3 x 1½ inches. Transfer the rectangles to a baking sheet; toast in the oven until light golden on each side, about 15 minutes. Remove from the oven.

3. Spread 1 heaping teaspoon of cheese mixture on each piece of bread. Top with a pear slice; garnish with pecan slices. Serve at room temperature.

cherry tomato and avocado canapés

MAKES 2½ DOZEN

Prepare the ingredients and assemble the sandwiches as close to serving time as possible to prevent the tomatoes from making the bread soggy.

- 1 avocado, peeled and pitted (see page 647)
- 2 teaspoons fresh lime juice
- ½ cup fresh ricotta cheese
- 16 slices white bread, cut in half, crusts removed
- 1 pint cherry tomatoes, thinly sliced
  Kosher salt and freshly ground black pepper

1. Scrape the avocado flesh into small bowl. Add the lime juice, and mash together with a fork. Add the ricotta; mash with the avocado to make a purée.

2. Spread the avocado-ricotta purée on each piece of bread, and top with the tomato slices. Sprinkle the sandwiches with salt and pepper, and serve.

crab salad canapés

MAKES 1 DOZEN

Use yellow or red bell peppers instead of orange if you wish to vary the color. French for "string," a *ficelle* is a very thin baguette, usually shorter than the traditional baguette.

- 4 tablespoons unsalted butter, room temperature
- 2 teaspoons whole-grain mustard
- 2 teaspoons Dijon mustard
- ½ baguette or ficelle, cut into ¼-inch-thick pieces
- 4 ounces jumbo lump crabmeat, shells and cartilage removed
- ½ celery stalk, strings removed, cut into ⅛-inch-thick slices
- ½ small carrot, cut into ½-inch-long matchsticks
- ½ teaspoon ground cumin
- ¼ teaspoon ground coriander

2 teaspoons extra-virgin olive oil

1 tablespoon white-wine vinegar

   Kosher salt and freshly ground black pepper

1 roasted orange bell pepper (see page 645), cut in large diamonds

1 tablespoon fresh marjoram or oregano leaves, for garnish

1. Using a wooden spoon, mix together the butter and the two mustards in a small bowl until well combined. Spread a generous dollop of the mustard butter on each slice of the bread.

2. Place the crabmeat, celery, carrot, cumin, coriander, oil, and vinegar in a medium bowl, and toss to combine. Season with salt and pepper. Place a pepper diamond on each piece of bread, and top with a mound of the crab salad. Garnish each canapé with several marjoram leaves, and serve.

....

TEA SANDWICHES AND CANAPÉS

There are several different breads you can use to make tea sandwiches and canapés; large pullman loaves or any soft, artisan breads made by a local baker are some of our favorites. Ask your baker to slice the bread for you on a machine set on melba or thin slice, for delicate and uniform slices. Or you can use the small party loaves that are pre-sliced and found in the bread or deli section of most grocery stores. Sandwiches and canapés, single slices of bread topped with a spread, meat, or cheese, should be filled or topped before cutting into the desired shapes (triangles, circles, or any cookie-cutter shape) for more neat-looking hors d'oeuvres. For a less formal look, the bread can be cut ahead of time and the fillings arranged loosely on top. Since thin slices of bread will dry out quickly, cover the hors d'oeuvres with a damp paper towel or plastic wrap. They can be made up to 1 hour ahead and refrigerated if the filling requires it. To keep tea sandwiches fresh on a buffet, stack them on top of one another. Canapés, on the other hand, must be arranged in a single layer.

....

gravlax with cucumber slaw on black bread

MAKES 3 DOZEN

Gravlax tastes best sliced paper thin: The long, thin, flexible blade of a salmon-slicing knife (see Equipment Sources, page 650) makes slicing easy; chilling the gravlax before cutting also helps.

2 tablespoons plus ½ teaspoon kosher salt

¼ cup plus ¾ teaspoon sugar

¼ teaspoon ground juniper berries

1 pound salmon fillet, tail end, skin on

1 tablespoon vodka

1 cup roughly chopped fresh dill

½ seedless cucumber

3 radishes, finely grated

½ teaspoon black or white sesame seeds

1 teaspoon freshly grated ginger

2½ tablespoons rice-wine vinegar

36 1½-inch squares black bread

1. Combine 2 tablespoons salt, ¼ cup sugar, and the juniper; sprinkle on the salmon flesh. Drizzle with the vodka; arrange the dill on top. Wrap with plastic wrap; place in a shallow nonreactive dish. Place a board on top, and weight it with about 10 pounds of cans. Refrigerate for 2 days.

2. On the medium holes of a box grater, grate the cucumber in long strokes. Place in a colander; press to extract the liquid. Transfer to a bowl; add the remaining sugar and salt, radishes, sesame seeds, ginger, and vinegar; toss.

3. Slice the salmon as thinly as possible, about ⅛ inch thick, on an angle; place a small piece on each bread slice. Top with ½ teaspoon of the slaw. Serve.

FIT TO EAT RECIPE PER PIECE: 39 CALORIES, 1 G FAT, 7 MG CHOLESTEROL, 4 G CARBOHYDRATE, 90 MG SODIUM, 3 G PROTEIN, 0 G DIETARY FIBER

caramelized onion and mascarpone tea sandwiches

MAKES 8

Cream cheese can be substituted for the mascarpone cheese.

- 2 teaspoons unsalted butter
- 2 small Vidalia or other sweet onions, finely chopped
- 4 slices raisin bread
- ¼ cup mascarpone cheese

1. Heat the butter in a medium skillet over low heat. Add the onions, and cook, stirring often, until they are brown and caramelized, 15 minutes. Remove from the heat, and let cool.

2. Generously spread the bread with the mascarpone. Spread the onions over 2 of the slices; cover with the remaining slices.

3. Chill until firm, trim the crusts, and cut each sandwich into 4 rectangles. Serve.

tomato, basil, and ricotta tea sandwiches

MAKES 8

Look for small, round tomatoes; the bread will be cut into circles about the same size.

- 8 slices thin white sandwich bread
- ½ cup ricotta cheese
  Kosher salt and freshly ground black pepper
- 2 tomatoes, cut into ¼-inch slices
- 8 basil leaves

Using a round cookie cutter about 2½ inches in diameter, cut 8 circles from the bread. In a small bowl, season the ricotta with salt and pepper. Spoon 1 tablespoon of the seasoned ricotta on each round. Place tomato slices over 4 of the rounds, top with the basil leaves, and cover with the remaining rounds. Cut the sandwiches in half. Serve.

marinated bocconcini

MAKES ABOUT 4 DOZEN

Bocconcini are "little mouthfuls" of fresh mozzarella cheese, often found where good-quality cheese is sold.

- 1 pound bocconcini
- 2 garlic cloves, minced
- 3 tablespoons coarsely chopped fresh flat-leaf parsley
- 1 teaspoon crushed red-pepper flakes
- 3 tablespoons extra-virgin olive oil
  Kosher salt

Combine all the ingredients in a large bowl, and season with salt. Let marinate at least 1 hour. Serve at room temperature.

warm goat cheese with walnuts and toast

SERVES 4

The walnuts and toast can be made ahead, leaving only 5 minutes of preparation time.

- 1 baguette, sliced on the diagonal into ½-inch-thick pieces
- 1 6-ounce log fresh goat cheese
- ½ teaspoon extra-virgin olive oil
- 1 cup walnut halves, toasted (see page 644)

1. Preheat the oven to 375°F. Toast the bread slices on a baking sheet until golden brown, 5 to 7 minutes per side.

2. Preheat the broiler. Place the goat cheese on a baking sheet, brush the top with the olive oil, and place as close to the heat as possible. Broil until the top of the cheese is flecked with brown and slightly bubbly, about 2 minutes. Arrange the cheese, walnuts, and toast on a dish, and serve immediately.

fresh goat cheese wrapped in grape leaves

MAKES 1 LOG; SERVES 4

Wrapping soft, fresh goat cheese in grape leaves allows it to be placed directly on the grill. Serve with slices of toasted country bread and fresh fruits such as pears or figs. If fresh grape leaves are unavailable, use vine leaves packed in jars; rinse first to remove the brine.

- 2 large, unsprayed fresh grape leaves
- 1 6-ounce log fresh goat cheese
  Extra-virgin olive oil, for brushing

1. Place one leaf, vein-side up, on a work surface. Place the goat cheese on the leaf, and wrap the leaf around the cheese, pressing it in slightly. Top with another leaf, vein-side down. Wrap the leaf around the cheese, enclosing it fully. Tie with kitchen twine, and set aside, or refrigerate until ready to grill.

2. Heat a grill or a grill pan to medium hot. Brush the leaf-wrapped cheese with olive oil. Toast on the edge of the grill until warmed; turn and grill the other side. The cheese should be slightly melted.

3. To serve, place the cheese on a platter, and remove the kitchen twine.

pears and camembert

SERVES 8

Make sure the cheese is cold so it can be easily sliced; the glaze will warm it when poured on top.

- 1 8-ounce wheel Camembert or Brie cheese, chilled
- 1 tablespoon unsalted butter
- 1 large Bosc pear, peeled and cut into ¼-inch dice
- 2 tablespoons brandy
- 1 teaspoon chopped fresh rosemary, plus more for garnish
- 2 tablespoons balsamic vinegar
- 1 tablespoon honey
- 8 walnut halves

1. Slice the cheese wheel in half crosswise; set aside. In a medium skillet over medium heat, melt the butter. Add the diced pear, and cook until tender, about 3 minutes. Stir in the brandy, and cook 1 minute more. Add the rosemary, and stir to combine. Remove from the heat, and spread over the bottom half of the reserved sliced cheese wheel, reserving 2 tablespoons of the mixture. Transfer the cheese to a serving plate.

2. Return the skillet to the stove, and heat the balsamic vinegar and honey until simmering. Simmer the mixture until slightly thickened, about 3 minutes. Set aside to cool, about 5 minutes. Pour half the glaze over the cheese and pear mixture; top with the remaining half of the cheese wheel and the reserved pears. Drizzle with the remaining glaze, and garnish with the walnut halves and rosemary. Serve immediately.

croccante di parmigiano

MAKES 2 TO 2½ DOZEN

These cheese crisps can be served plain or filled with mixed greens.

- 1 pound Parmigiano-Reggiano cheese, grated on the large holes of a box grater
- 1 tablespoon plus 1 teaspoon all-purpose flour

1. Heat a nonstick 12-inch skillet over medium-low heat. Combine the cheese and the flour in a medium bowl. Place three or four small overturned glasses next to your work area.

2. When the skillet is hot, sprinkle 3 tablespoons of the cheese mixture into a thin round, about 4 inches wide; repeat, making 3 more rounds. Cook until the cheese is golden brown on the bottom, 1½ to 2 minutes.

3. Carefully, using tongs and a flexible spatula, loosen the edges of the rounds, lift up, and turn over. Let the rounds cook about 10 seconds more; remove from the pan, and place on an overturned glass. Repeat with the remaining cheese mixture. Let cool until firm, about 1 minute. Transfer to a wire rack to fully cool; serve within 1 hour.

yogurt cheese with honey, mint, and sun-dried tomatoes

SERVES 8

Yogurt cheese is a good low-fat spread to have on hand; it will keep for several days.

- 1 quart low-fat plain yogurt
- 8 sun-dried tomatoes (not packed in oil)
- 2 tablespoons honey
- 1 large piece of lemon zest, cut into very thin strips
- 1 teaspoon fresh lemon juice
- 8 kalamata olives, pitted and coarsely chopped
- 1 teaspoon chopped fresh flat-leaf parsley
- 2 tablespoons thinly sliced fresh mint leaves
- 1 large sourdough baguette, cut into sixteen ½-inch slices

1. Line a colander or fine strainer with an 18-inch piece of doubled cheesecloth, and place over a large bowl. Pour the yogurt into the colander, and let sit for 15 minutes. Pour off the liquid. Tie the ends of the cheesecloth to a wooden spoon, and suspend over a tall pot. Cover and refrigerate overnight. Unwrap the yogurt, and carefully invert in the center of a large serving platter. Let warm to room temperature.

2. Place the sun-dried tomatoes in a small bowl, and pour 1 cup boiling water over them. Let stand for 20 minutes; drain and coarsely chop the tomatoes. Set aside.

3. In a small saucepan, combine the honey, lemon zest, and lemon juice, and bring to a simmer. Remove from the heat; let stand for 5 minutes for the flavors to infuse.

4. Mix together the olives, tomatoes, chopped parsley, and mint, and arrange around the yogurt cheese. Pour the honey mixture over the top, and serve with the sourdough slices on the side.

FIT TO EAT RECIPE PER SERVING: 194 CALORIES, 2 G TOTAL FAT, 10% CALORIES FROM FAT, 4 MG CHOLESTEROL, 36 G CARBOHYDRATE, 442 MG SODIUM, 8 G PROTEIN, TRACE OF DIETARY FIBER

grilled figs with goat cheese and prosciutto

SERVES 6

Make fragrant skewers using the longest, sturdiest rosemary sprigs you can find. Serve with crusty bread.

- 8 ounces fresh soft goat cheese
- 2 teaspoons finely chopped fresh rosemary
  Kosher salt and freshly ground black pepper
- 24 fresh figs, stemmed mixed varieties
- 4 ounces thinly sliced prosciutto
- 6 long woody sprigs fresh rosemary
  Extra-virgin olive oil, for brushing and drizzling

1. Combine the goat cheese, rosemary, and a pinch of salt and pepper in a small mixing bowl, and stir.

2. Make a small slit in the bottom or side of each fig. Fill a pastry bag fitted with a small plain tip with the cheese mixture. Pipe the cheese into each fig through the slit. Fill the figs with just enough cheese so they expand slightly.

3. Tear or cut the prosciutto slices into long strips. Wrap a strip of prosciutto around each fig, and skewer 4 figs on each rosemary sprig. Brush the figs with olive oil, and season with salt and pepper.

4. Preheat a grill or a grill pan to medium hot. Place the figs on the hot grill, rotating the skewers until the figs are very hot and the cheese starts to ooze, about 6 minutes. Remove from the grill; serve immediately with a drizzle of olive oil.

fingerling potatoes with goat cheese fondue

SERVES 12 TO 14

If fingerlings are unavailable, you can substitute other small potatoes, such as red bliss.

- 2 pounds (30 to 40) fingerling potatoes
  Kosher salt
- 8 ounces soft goat cheese, room temperature
- 1 cup nonfat buttermilk

½ teaspoon coarsely ground black pepper

1 bunch snipped chives

3 tablespoons finely chopped fresh thyme leaves

3 tablespoons finely chopped fresh tarragon leaves

3 tablespoons finely chopped fresh flat-leaf parsley

1. Place the fingerling potatoes in a large saucepan with enough cold salted water to cover generously. Place over high heat, and bring to a boil. Reduce to a simmer, and cook until the potatoes are tender when pierced with the tip of a knife, about 15 minutes. Remove from the heat, and drain in a colander. Transfer the potatoes to a platter; set aside.

2. Place the goat cheese and buttermilk in the top of a double boiler or in a heat-proof bowl set over a pan of simmering water. Warm the mixture, stirring until it is very smooth, about 7 minutes. Remove from the heat, and stir in the pepper, chives, thyme, tarragon, and parsley. Place in the bowl of a small fondue pot or in a warm serving bowl; serve immediately with the fingerling potatoes.

radishes with flavored salts and butter

SERVES 4

Softened butter soothes the peppery bite of fresh radishes. Serve the flavored salts, the softened butter, and the whole radishes in separate dishes, and allow guests to dip as they like.

3 tablespoons whole fennel seeds, toasted (see page 644)

2 tablespoons whole cumin seeds, toasted (see page 644)

2 cups kosher salt

2 teaspoons ground paprika

1½ teaspoons cayenne pepper

24 medium radishes, trimmed

8 tablespoons (1 stick) unsalted butter, room temperature

1. In a spice grinder; grind fennel seeds until they are no longer coarse. Repeat with cumin seeds.

2. In a small mixing bowl, stir the ground fennel seeds into ½ cup salt; transfer to a small serving bowl. Wipe out the mixing bowl, then mix the ground cumin seeds into ½ cup salt; transfer to another small serving bowl. Wipe out the mixing bowl, then stir the paprika and cayenne pepper into ½ cup salt; transfer to a third serving bowl.

3. Arrange the radishes on a serving platter. Pour the remaining salt into another serving bowl. Transfer the softened butter to a slightly larger bowl. Serve.

. . . .

CRUDITÉS

The key to appealing crudités is simple: Buy impeccable seasonal produce and lots of it. The best crudité platters have only a few carefully chosen vegetables in generous quantities. Below is a good basic list of vegetables and quantities to serve 12 people. If you cannot find one of the vegetables, simply make up for the quantity with another. Serve these vegetables with one or two dips on the side, or a dish of best-quality extra-virgin olive oil seasoned with chopped fresh herbs and kosher salt.

1 pound bunch (24 spears) thin asparagus

1 bunch (about 8) carrots

½ pint (about 12) cherry tomatoes

1 medium daikon

1 small jícama

1 cucumber or 3 Kirby cucumbers

2 bunches scallions

4 ounces haricots verts

1 yellow squash

1 zucchini

. . . .

gougères

MAKES ABOUT 50

Gougères are pâte à choux puffs with cheese added to the batter.

- 8 tablespoons (1 stick) unsalted butter, cut in small pieces, plus more for baking sheet
- 1 cup all-purpose flour
- ¾ teaspoon kosher salt
- ¾ teaspoon freshly ground black pepper
- 1 teaspoon dried thyme
  Pinch of cayenne pepper
- 1 cup milk
- 5 large eggs, room temperature
- ½ cup grated Parmesan cheese
- ½ cup grated Gruyère cheese

1. Preheat the oven to 400°F. Butter a baking sheet, and set aside. Sift together the flour, salt, pepper, thyme, and cayenne.

2. In a large heavy saucepan over high heat, combine the milk and butter, in pieces. Remove from the heat, add the flour mixture, and stir rapidly with a wooden spoon. Return the pan to the heat, and cook, stirring constantly, until the mixture comes together and pulls away from the sides of the saucepan as you stir, about 5 minutes. Remove the saucepan from the heat, and let cool for 5 minutes.

3. Add 4 eggs, one at a time, beating vigorously until they are completely incorporated and the pastry is smooth. Add the cheeses; stir well.

4. Pipe batter from a pastry bag fitted with a large star, or plain, tip into puffs onto the prepared baking sheet. In a small bowl, combine the remaining egg and 1 teaspoon water to make an egg wash. Brush the tops of the puffs sparingly with the egg wash.

5. Bake until lightly golden and puffed, about 20 minutes. Serve hot.

cherry tomatoes with mayonnaise and sunflower seeds

SERVES 8

Cherry tomatoes come in a variety of shapes, sizes, and colors. Use a combination of ripe ones for the best flavor. Serve the cherry tomatoes, fresh mayonnaise, and roasted sunflower seeds in separate dishes.

- 1 large egg
- 2 tablespoons fresh lemon juice
- ½ teaspoon kosher salt
- ½ teaspoon Dijon mustard
- 1 cup canola oil
- 2 pints assorted cherry tomatoes
- ½ cup roasted sunflower seeds

Place the egg, lemon juice, salt, and mustard in the bowl of a food processor; pulse until well combined. With the machine running, add the oil in a slow, steady stream. The mixture will become thick and creamy. To serve, dip the tomatoes in the mayonnaise, then in the sunflower seeds. The mayonnaise will keep, in an airtight container in the refrigerator, for up to 3 days.

NOTE *Raw eggs should not be used in food prepared for pregnant women, babies, young children, the elderly, or anyone whose health is compromised.*

hush puppies

MAKES ABOUT 3 DOZEN

- 4 cups peanut oil
- 1½ cups all-purpose flour
- ¾ cup yellow cornmeal
- 2 teaspoons baking powder
- 1½ teaspoons baking soda
- 1 teaspoon kosher salt
- ⅛ teaspoon cayenne pepper
- 1 jalapeño pepper, seeds and ribs removed, minced
- 2 large eggs
- 1 cup buttermilk

1. Heat the peanut oil in a 2½-quart saucepan over medium heat until a deep-frying thermometer registers 375°F.

2. Meanwhile, whisk together the flour, cornmeal, baking powder, baking soda, salt, and cayenne in a medium bowl. Mix in the jalapeño.

3. In another bowl, whisk together the eggs and buttermilk. Add to the flour mixture; stir to combine. The mixture will be slightly lumpy.

4. Drop heaping teaspoons of the batter into the hot oil without crowding. Fry until golden brown, turning once or twice, 2 to 3 minutes. Use a slotted spoon to transfer hush puppies to paper towels to drain. Serve immediately.

nyons olives with toasted rosemary

MAKES ABOUT 2 CUPS; SERVES 8 TO 10

- 10 *small sprigs fresh rosemary*
- 1 *teaspoon extra-virgin olive oil*
- ¼ *teaspoon freshly ground black pepper*
- 2 *cups Nyons olives*

Preheat the oven to 400°F Place rosemary sprigs on a nonstick baking sheet. Brush the sprigs with oil, season with pepper, and bake for 5 minutes, or until the sprigs are slightly brown. Remove from the oven, and toss with the olives. Serve.

cerignola olives with hot pepper garlic oil

MAKES ABOUT 2 CUPS; SERVES 8 TO 10

Any large green olive is good with this spicy oil.

- ¼ *cup extra-virgin olive oil*
- 6 *whole dried red chile peppers*
- 2 *large garlic cloves, sliced*
- 2 *cups Cerignola olives*

Heat the oil in a skillet over medium heat. Add the peppers and garlic; heat until the garlic is golden brown. Toss with the olives, and serve.

oil-cured olives baked with white wine and garlic

MAKES ABOUT 2 CUPS; SERVES 8 TO 10

- 1 *tablespoon extra-virgin olive oil*
- 5 *garlic cloves*
- 2 *cups oil-cured olives*
- ⅔ *cup dry white wine*
- 2 *teaspoons fresh oregano leaves*

1. Preheat the oven to 350°F. In an ovenproof skillet over medium heat, heat the oil and garlic just until fragrant. Remove from the heat, and let cool slightly. Stir in the olives and wine.

2. Place the pan in the oven, and bake until the olives are plump and the liquid is absorbed, about 15 minutes. Remove from the oven, and toss with the oregano leaves. Serve.

....

OLIVES

The flavor of olives is intensified when they are warmed. Serve them in ramekins with crusty pieces of bread for scooping.

....

simple white crackers

MAKES 1½ DOZEN

These crackers are a crisp, buttery homemade version of saltines. Discard any scraps since this dough can't be rolled out again.

- 1 *cup all-purpose flour, plus more for dusting*
- ½ *teaspoon table salt*
- 1 *teaspoon sugar*
- 1 *tablespoon unsalted butter, cut in pieces*
- ⅓ *cup plus 1 tablespoon milk*
  Kosher salt, for sprinkling

1. Preheat the oven to 325°F. In the bowl of a food processor, pulse the flour, salt, and sugar. Add the butter, and pulse until the mixture resembles coarse meal. With the machine running, gradually add the milk; process until dough comes together.

2. Transfer the dough to a lightly floured surface. Roll into a 10 x 12-inch sheet, ¹⁄₁₆ inch thick. Sprinkle with kosher salt; roll to gently press the salt into the dough.

3. Cut the dough into 2½-inch squares; carefully transfer to an ungreased baking sheet. Liberally pierce with a fork. Bake until just beginning to brown at the edges and firm to the touch, 20 to 25 minutes. Transfer to a wire rack to cool. Store in an airtight plastic container at room temperature.

whole-grain buttermilk cumin crackers

MAKES 5 DOZEN

1¼ cups whole-wheat flour, plus more for dusting

½ cup toasted wheat germ

¼ cup sunflower seeds

1 teaspoon ground cumin seed

½ teaspoon baking powder

½ teaspoon baking soda

½ teaspoon table salt

3 tablespoons unsalted butter, cut in pieces

½ cup nonfat buttermilk

Kosher salt, for sprinkling

1. Preheat the oven to 350°F with two racks centered. In the bowl of a food processor, pulse the flour, wheat germ, sunflower seeds, cumin, baking powder, baking soda, and table salt. Add the butter pieces, and process until the mixture resembles coarse meal. With the machine running, gradually add the buttermilk; process until the dough comes together and is moist.

2. Transfer the dough to a lightly floured surface, and allow to rest for 5 minutes. Roll until ¼ to ⅛ inch thick. Sprinkle with the kosher salt; roll gently to press the salt into the dough.

3. Cut the dough into 1½-inch squares, or other desired shape, and transfer the squares to two ungreased baking sheets. Pierce each cracker liberally with a fork. Bake until hard, about 15 minutes. Transfer to a wire rack to cool. Store in an airtight plastic container at room temperature.

cheddar pecan flowers

MAKES 16

½ cup all-purpose flour, plus more for dusting

¾ cup finely ground pecans, toasted (see page 644)

½ teaspoon table salt

¼ teaspoon freshly ground black pepper

¼ teaspoon cayenne pepper

2 tablespoons chilled unsalted butter, cut in pieces

4 ounces sharp Cheddar cheese, grated

Kosher salt, for sprinkling

1. Preheat the oven to 350°F. In the bowl of a food processor, pulse the flour, pecans, table salt, black pepper, and cayenne. Add the butter; pulse until the mixture resembles coarse meal. Add the cheese; pulse until the pieces are no longer visible. With the machine running, gradually add 2 tablespoons cold water; process until the dough comes together.

2. Transfer to a lightly floured surface; divide the dough into two equal parts. Roll out each to a ¼-inch thickness. Sprinkle with the kosher salt; roll to gently press the salt into the dough.

3. Cut the dough into 2½-inch flower shapes, or other desired shape using a cookie cutter no larger than 2½ inches; transfer to an ungreased baking sheet. Bake until the centers are firm to the touch, about 15 minutes. Cool on a wire rack. Store in an airtight plastic container at room temperature.

cheese coins with jalapeño jelly

MAKES ABOUT 6 DOZEN

1 cup all-purpose flour, plus more for rolling

1 teaspoon salt

1 teaspoon ground paprika

½ teaspoon cayenne pepper

1 cup (2 sticks) chilled unsalted butter, cut into small pieces

1 cup freshly grated sharp white Cheddar cheese

⅓ cup jalapeño jelly

1. Combine flour, salt, and spices in a food processor fitted with the metal blade; pulse to combine. Add the butter; pulse until mixture resembles coarse meal. Add the cheese; process until dough starts to hold together.

2. Turn out the dough onto a lightly floured surface; knead a few times. Divide into 4 equal pieces, and roll into logs, each about 6 inches long and 1¼ inches wide. Wrap in plastic; refrigerate until firm, at least 1 hour or up to 3 days. Dough can be stored in the freezer at this point up to 1 month.

3. Preheat oven to 350°F. Cut dough into ⅓-inch-thick slices; place 2 inches apart on a parchment-lined baking sheet. Bake until lightly browned, about 20 minutes. Remove from oven; let cool on baking sheet 1 minute, then transfer to a wire rack to cool completely.

4. When ready to serve, spoon a small amount of jelly onto the center of each coin.

mixed herb swatches
MAKES ABOUT 2 DOZEN

The dough in this recipe is very fragile. Let it rest for a minute or two before transferring to the baking sheet. These crackers take only about 15 minutes to make.

- *1 cup all-purpose flour, plus more for dusting*
- *½ teaspoon table salt*
- *¼ teaspoon freshly ground black pepper*
- *2 tablespoons snipped chives*
- *1 tablespoon fresh thyme*
- *1 tablespoon fresh oregano, coarsely chopped*
- *4 tablespoons chilled unsalted butter, cut in pieces*
- *¼ cup sour cream*
  Kosher salt, for sprinkling

1. Preheat the oven to 325°F. In the bowl of a food processor, pulse the flour, table salt, pepper, chives, thyme, and oregano. Add the butter; pulse until the mixture resembles coarse meal. With the machine running, add the sour cream; process until the dough comes together.

2. Transfer the dough to a lightly floured surface; divide into two equal parts. Roll out into 10 x 12-inch sheets, about ⅛ inch thick. Sprinkle with kosher salt; roll to gently press the salt into the dough.

3. Using a crimping wheel or fluted square cookie cutter, cut the dough into 2½-inch swatches (squares); transfer to an ungreased baking sheet. Pierce the swatches liberally with a fork. Bake until the swatches are just golden and feel firm to the touch, 10 to 15 minutes. Transfer to a wire rack to cool. Store in an airtight plastic container at room temperature.

caraway onion cards
MAKES 2 DOZEN

- *1 cup all-purpose flour*
- *1 cup rye flour*
- *½ teaspoon table salt*
- *¼ teaspoon freshly ground black pepper*
- *½ teaspoon sugar*
- *¼ cup caraway seeds, toasted (see page 644)*
- *6 tablespoons unsalted butter, cut in pieces*
- *1 cup minced onion*
- *1 large egg white*
  Kosher salt, for sprinkling

1. Preheat the oven to 350°F. In the bowl of a food processor, pulse the flours, table salt, pepper, sugar, and 2 tablespoons caraway seeds. Add the butter; pulse until the mixture resembles coarse meal. Add the onion; pulse until well combined, about 30 seconds. With the machine running, gradually add between 1 and 2 tablespoons cold water, until the dough comes together and is stiff.

2. Transfer the dough to a lightly floured surface; divide into two equal parts. Roll out as thinly as possible. Cut into 2 x 3½-inch rectangles.

3. Brush the egg white over the dough; sprinkle with the remaining 2 tablespoons caraway seeds and the kosher salt; roll to gently press the seeds and salt into the dough. Pierce the crackers liberally with a fork.

4. Bake on an ungreased baking sheet until firm to the touch, 20 to 25 minutes. Transfer to a wire rack to cool. Store in an airtight plastic container at room temperature.

potato chips with malt vinegar

SERVES 4

Oven-roasted golden potato chips make a fine substitute for the deep-fried kind.

- 4 medium (about 2½ pounds) Yukon gold potatoes, scrubbed
- 2 tablespoons olive oil
- 1 teaspoon kosher salt
- ½ teaspoon freshly ground black pepper
  Malt vinegar, for drizzling

1. Preheat the oven to 425°F with two racks centered. Place two baking sheets in the oven, and let heat for about 10 minutes.

2. Slice the potatoes into ¼-inch-thick rounds. Toss the potatoes with the olive oil, salt, and pepper.

3. Remove the baking sheets from the oven, and arrange potato slices on the sheets in a single layer. Bake until the potatoes are golden on the bottom side, about 30 minutes. Turn the potatoes over, and bake until golden brown all over, about 15 minutes more. Remove from the oven, drizzle with the vinegar, and serve immediately.

waffle chips

SERVES 6

- 6 Russet, Yukon gold, or Purple Peruvian potatoes, scrubbed
  Canola oil, for frying
  Kosher salt

1. Slice the potatoes ⅛ inch thick on the ripple edge of a mandoline or vegetable slicer, turning a quarter turn after each slice to create a perforated-waffle effect. (You may have to discard the first few slices.) Soak slices in cold water for 1 hour to extract some starch.

2. Fill a large, heavy skillet halfway with oil, and heat until a deep-frying thermometer registers 365°F. Drain potatoes, and dry thoroughly with paper towels. Fry potato slices in small batches until golden brown. Using a slotted spoon, transfer chips to paper towels; salt lightly. Serve immediately.

roasted pumpkin seeds

MAKES 2 CUPS

- 2 tablespoons dried rosemary
- 2 cups fresh pumpkin seeds
- 2 tablespoons olive oil
  Kosher salt

Preheat the oven to 350°F. Grind the rosemary in a spice grinder until fine. In a large bowl, combine the ground rosemary with the pumpkin seeds and oil, and season with salt. Spread the seeds on a baking sheet. Bake until crisp and brown, 10 to 12 minutes.

spiced nuts

MAKES 2½ CUPS; SERVES 6 TO 8

The egg white has been properly beaten when no clear liquid remains at the bottom of the bowl.

- 1 large egg white
- ¼ cup sugar
- 1 teaspoon kosher salt
- ½ teaspoon chili powder
- ¼ teaspoon ground allspice
- ½ teaspoon ground cumin
- 1¾ teaspoons cayenne pepper
- 2½ cups pecan halves or assorted nuts, such as cashews, walnuts, or almonds

1. Preheat the oven to 300°F Beat the egg white until soft and foamy. In a large bowl, combine the sugar, salt, chili powder, allspice, cumin, and cayenne; whisk into the egg white. Stir in the pecans until well coated; spread the mixture in a single layer onto an ungreased baking pan.

2. Bake the pecans for 15 minutes, and remove from the oven. Using a metal spatula, toss, stir, and separate the nuts. Reduce oven to 250°F, and return the nuts to bake until medium brown, about 10 minutes. Remove from the oven; toss, and stir again. Transfer the baking pan to a wire rack to cool. Break up any nuts that stick together; store in an airtight container for up to 2 weeks.

soups
AND
stews

....

summer borscht

SERVES 6

The soup will keep 2 days in the refrigerator or in the freezer for up to 3 months.

- 1½ pounds beets, scrubbed, stalks trimmed to ½ inch
- 1 tablespoon olive oil
- 1 small onion, finely chopped
- 1 garlic clove, minced
- 2 medium carrots
- 1 leek, white and pale-green parts, coarsely chopped, well washed (see page 646)
- ½ teaspoon kosher salt, plus more for seasoning
- ½ teaspoon freshly ground black pepper, plus more for seasoning
- ¼ cup fresh dill, loosely packed
- ¼ cup dry white wine
- 1¾ cups Homemade Chicken Stock (page 624), or low-sodium store-bought chicken broth, skimmed of fat
- ½ small cucumber, peeled and seeded
- ¼ cup plus 2 tablespoons crème fraîche or sour cream
- 2 tablespoons red-wine vinegar, optional

1. Fill a medium saucepan with water, add beets, and bring to a boil. Reduce heat to a simmer, and cook until beets are easily pierced with the tip of a knife, about 45 minutes. Drain the beets, reserving the cooking liquid, and let stand until cool enough to handle. Rub off the skins and discard.

2. Heat the olive oil in a stockpot over medium heat. Add onion and garlic, and cook until translucent, about 5 minutes.

3. Coarsely chop 1½ carrots; add to stockpot. Add leek, ½ teaspoon salt, and ½ teaspoon pepper. Coarsely chop half the dill; add to stockpot. Cook until carrots are almost tender, about 10 minutes.

4. Prepare an ice-water bath, and set aside. Cut the beets into 1-inch chunks, and add to the stockpot.

Add the wine, 2 cups of the reserved cooking liquid, and the chicken stock. Let simmer until the broth is flavorful, about 10 minutes. Season with salt and pepper. Remove the stockpot from the heat, and transfer the hot soup to a large bowl. Set the bowl in the ice-water bath to cool; skim off any fat.

5. Using the small holes of a box grater, grate the remaining ½ carrot and the cucumber. Serve the soup with a dollop of crème fraîche, garnished with the grated carrot and cucumber, and the remaining dill. Add a splash of red-wine vinegar, if desired.

cucumber soup

SERVES 6

This soup tastes best the day it is made.

- 5½ pounds (16 to 18) Kirby or other seedless cucumbers
- 1 tablespoon plus 1 teaspoon kosher salt
- 1 cup plain yogurt
- 2 tablespoons freshly chopped dill
  Freshly ground black pepper

1. Set aside 2 cucumbers for garnish. Peel the remaining cucumbers. Slice in half lengthwise. Scrape out any small seeds, and discard.

2. Sprinkle the cucumbers with 2 teaspoons salt. Let drain in a colander, about 30 minutes. Discard the juices; rinse the cucumbers in very cold water.

3. Cut the cucumbers into chunks. Working in batches if necessary, place the cucumbers in a blender with the remaining 2 teaspoons of salt, and process until the cucumbers are smooth. Set 1½ cups of the purée in the refrigerator. Press the remainder of the purée through a very fine sieve, pushing down on the solids with a rubber spatula. Discard the solids, and place the clear green cucumber water in the refrigerator to chill.

4. Cut the reserved cucumbers into quarters, lengthwise, and dice. Spoon the cucumber purée into serving bowls. Pour the cucumber water around the purée in each bowl. Top each with a dollop of yogurt. Garnish with the dill and diced cucumber, and season with pepper. Serve chilled.

summer corn chowder

SERVES 4

Small white new potatoes can be substituted for the fingerlings in this recipe. The soup will keep for 2 days in the refrigerator or may be frozen up to 1 week.

- 4   ounces bacon, cut into ¼-inch dice
- 1   small onion, peeled, cut into ¼-inch dice
- 2   celery stalks, strings removed, cut into ½-inch dice
- 8   sprigs fresh thyme
     Kosher salt and freshly ground black pepper
- 3   cups Homemade Chicken Stock (page 624), or low-sodium store-bought chicken broth, skimmed of fat
- 3   ears fresh yellow corn, kernels shaved from the cob (about 2½ cups)
- 5   ounces small fingerling potatoes, cut into ½-inch-thick slices
- 1   fresh poblano pepper, seeds and ribs removed, cut into ½-inch dice
- 1½ cups half-and-half

1. Place the bacon in small stockpot over medium-high heat. Cook, stirring occasionally, until it is deep golden brown and all the fat has been rendered, about 6 minutes. Remove the bacon with a slotted spoon, transfer to paper towel, and set aside. Discard all but 2 tablespoons of the bacon fat.

2. Add the onion, celery, thyme, and salt and pepper to taste; cook over medium-low heat until translucent, about 8 minutes. Add the stock, cover, and bring to a boil. Reduce heat to medium; simmer with the lid ajar for 15 minutes.

3. Add the corn, potatoes, and poblano pepper; cook uncovered until the potatoes are tender, about 8 minutes. Remove and discard the thyme. Add the half-and-half, and simmer until the soup is hot. Season with salt and pepper, and garnish with the reserved crisp bacon pieces. Serve hot.

roasted eggplant and red pepper soup

SERVES 8

The eggplant gives this soup a velvety texture. The soup will keep for 2 days in the refrigerator; it can be frozen up to 1 month.

- 3   large eggplants
- ¼   cup olive oil
- 3   large red onions, finely chopped
- 4   garlic cloves, minced
- 2¼   teaspoons kosher salt, plus more for seasoning
- ¼   teaspoon freshly ground black pepper, plus more for seasoning
- 4   red or yellow roasted bell peppers (see page 645), 3½ chopped, ½ intact
- 2   quarts Homemade Chicken Stock (page 624), or 1 quart low-sodium store-bought chicken broth, mixed with 1 quart water
      Pinch of cayenne pepper
- 3   tablespoons snipped chives

1. Heat a grill to hot, or turn on the broiler. Cook eggplants until charred, turning so all sides cook evenly, 8 to 10 minutes. Remove from heat. Slice open cooled eggplants; scoop out the flesh, taking care to avoid the charred skin as much as possible. Discard the charred skin, and set the flesh aside.

2. Heat olive oil in a stockpot over medium heat. Add onions and garlic; cook until soft and translucent, about 12 minutes. Add 2¼ teaspoons salt, and ¼ teaspoon black pepper, chopped peppers, and reserved eggplant flesh; simmer 15 minutes.

3. Add the chicken stock and cayenne pepper; simmer 15 minutes. Transfer the soup to a large bowl; set aside to cool.

4. Fill the bowl of a food processor with cooled soup; pulse until puréed. Transfer purée to a large bowl. Repeat, working in batches, with remaining soup. Return it to the stockpot. Warm soup over medium heat; season with salt and pepper. To serve, dice reserved pepper half; garnish soup with diced pepper and snipped chives. Serve hot.

garlic soup with rustic gruyère croutons

SERVES 4

For true garlic lovers, the croutons may be spread with a head of roasted garlic before being topped with cheese and broiled. The soup will keep for 2 days in the refrigerator or frozen up to 1 week.

- 1 tablespoon unsalted butter
- 2 large carrots, finely chopped
- 2 celery stalks, strings removed, finely chopped
- 6 sprigs fresh flat-leaf parsley
- 1 teaspoon kosher salt, plus more for seasoning
- ¼ teaspoon freshly ground black pepper, plus more for seasoning
- 4 heads of garlic
- 1 head of roasted garlic (see page 646)
- 1½ quarts Homemade Chicken Stock (page 624), or low-sodium store-bought chicken broth, skimmed of fat
- 3 slices white sandwich bread, crust removed
- ½ cup heavy cream
- ¼ cup sweet sherry
  Rustic Gruyère Croutons (recipe follows)
  Freshly grated nutmeg, for garnish

1. Preheat the oven to 450°F. Melt the butter in a small stockpot over medium heat. Add the carrots, celery, parsley, 1 teaspoon salt, ¼ teaspoon pepper, and the peeled cloves from 1 of head of raw garlic. Squeeze out the soft cloves from the roasted garlic, and add them to the stockpot. Cook, stirring often, until the vegetables are soft, about 15 minutes. Add the chicken stock, cover, and bring to a boil. Reduce heat, and simmer uncovered until the stock is very flavorful, about 30 minutes. Strain the soup through a fine sieve, or a cheesecloth-lined strainer, into a medium bowl, pressing down on the solids. Discard the solids; return the soup to the rinsed-out pot.

2. Slice the remaining 3 heads of garlic in half across the middle, removing any loose, papery skins; add to the stock. Simmer until the cloves are soft, about 20 minutes. Remove the garlic halves from the stock, remove the individual cloves (the cloves will easily push out from heads after being cooked), and discard the heads. Blend the stock, the soft garlic cloves, and the white bread in a food processor until smooth. Return the soup to the pot; simmer. Add the cream and sherry, and season with salt and pepper.

3. Place a crouton in each of four soup bowls; ladle soup over them. Sprinkle with the nutmeg. Serve hot.

rustic gruyère croutons

MAKES 4 LARGE CROUTONS

Thin shavings of a strong cheese like Gruyère add plenty of flavor. Emmental and Beaufort are also good choices.

- ½ small loaf whole-grain bread, broken into 4 rough pieces
- 2 ounces Gruyère cheese, shaved into 4 paper-thin slices
  Kosher salt and freshly ground black pepper

1. Preheat the broiler. On a baking sheet, toast the bread until it is golden brown on each side, 1 to 3 minutes per side.

2. Top each piece of bread with a slice of Gruyère; return to broiler until the cheese bubbles, 1 to 3 minutes. Season with salt and pepper; serve hot.

french onion soup

SERVES 6

Cooking onions for a long time over very low heat mellows their flavor. Avoid the temptation to stir too often, or the onions won't caramelize. Homemade Beef Stock (page 624) is best for this soup. Ungarnished soup keeps for 2 days in the refrigerator; it may be frozen up to 3 months.

- 4 tablespoons unsalted butter
- 2 pounds yellow onions, sliced into ¼-inch half circles
- 1 teaspoon sugar
- 1 tablespoon all-purpose flour
- ½ cup dry sherry
- 1½ quarts Beef Stock (page 624)
- 2 teaspoons chopped fresh thyme leaves, or ¾ teaspoon dried

  Kosher salt and freshly ground black pepper

- 1 small baguette, sliced crosswise into ½-inch pieces
- 8 ounces Gruyère cheese, grated on the large holes of a box grater (about 3 cups)

1. Melt the butter in a large Dutch oven, or in a heavy pot on medium-low heat. Add the onions, and spread out in as thin a layer as possible. Sprinkle with the sugar; cook, stirring just as needed to keep from sticking, until the onions are soft, golden brown, and beginning to caramelize, about 1 hour.

2. Sprinkle flour over onions; stir to coat. Add sherry, beef stock, and thyme, and bring to a simmer. Cook, partly covered, for about 30 minutes, to let flavors combine. Season with salt and pepper.

3. Preheat the broiler. Lightly toast the bread under the broiler; set aside. Ladle the hot soup into six ovenproof bowls. Arrange the bowls on a baking pan. Place 1 or 2 slices of toasted bread over each bowl of soup. Sprinkle ½ cup grated cheese over the bread in each bowl, and place under the broiler until the cheese is melted and turning brown around the edges. Serve hot.

sweet-pea soup with crushed mint ice

SERVES 10

This soup will be slightly thick at first but will thin as the mint ice melts. The ice may be made up to 2 days ahead; the soup tastes best if eaten within a day.

- 1 large bunch fresh mint, stems removed
- 2 tablespoons unsalted butter
- 1 medium (8 ounces) white onion, roughly chopped
- 1 teaspoon kosher salt
- ½ teaspoon freshly ground black pepper
- 1½ quarts Vegetable Stock (page 626), or low-sodium store-bought vegetable broth, plus more for thinning
- 2½ pounds sweet peas, shelled, or 4 10-ounce boxes frozen peas

1. Cover and bring 3 cups water to a boil. Remove from heat, add mint, reserving a few sprigs for garnish, and let steep for about 2 hours, until liquid is very flavorful and slightly green. Strain, discarding mint; transfer to 2 ice-cube trays, or an 8-inch square baking pan. Freeze until solid.

2. Meanwhile, melt the butter in a medium saucepan over medium-low heat. Add the chopped onion, salt, and pepper; cook, stirring often, until the onions are soft and translucent, about 8 minutes.

3. Add the stock, cover, and bring to a boil. Reduce heat; simmer, uncovered, 1 hour, until liquid is reduced by about half. Prepare an ice-water bath; set aside. Add peas; cook about 4 minutes, until they are just tender. Remove from heat; transfer to the ice bath. Stir until cold.

4. Working in batches, transfer soup to a blender; process until smooth. Adjust consistency with more stock. Chill until ready to serve.

5. Transfer mint ice cubes from freezer to a blender (if using an 8-inch square baking pan, cut ice into chunks first). Process mint ice cubes until crushed.

6. Place the chilled soup in bowls topped with a spoonful of crushed mint ice; garnish with mint sprigs. Serve chilled.

potato leek soup

SERVES 8 TO 10

- 2 dried bay leaves
- 6 sprigs fresh rosemary, or 2 teaspoons dried and crushed rosemary
- 4 sprigs fresh flat-leaf parsley
- 1 teaspoon whole black peppercorns
- 3 tablespoons olive oil
- 4 tablespoons unsalted butter
- 4 celery stalks, strings removed, cut in ¼-inch dice
- 6 leeks, white parts, thinly sliced and well washed (see page 646)
- 4 shallots, minced
- 6 garlic cloves, minced
- 2½ pounds Yukon gold potatoes, peeled, cut into 1-inch pieces
- 2 quarts Homemade Chicken Stock (page 624), or low-sodium store-bought chicken broth, skimmed of fat
- 1 cup milk
- ½ cup heavy cream
  Kosher salt and freshly ground black pepper

1. Tie the bay leaves, rosemary, parsley, and peppercorns in a piece of cheesecloth to make a bouquet garni. Set aside.

2. Heat the olive oil and butter in a medium stockpot. Add the celery, leeks, shallots, and garlic; cook on low heat until very soft, about 45 minutes, stirring only occasionally. Do not brown. Add the potatoes, chicken stock, and reserved bouquet garni. Cover, and bring to a boil; reduce to a gentle simmer. Cook, uncovered, until the potatoes are very tender, about 40 minutes. Remove the bouquet garni, and discard.

3. Working in batches, pass only half of the soup through a food mill fitted with a medium disk, into a large saucepan. Add the remaining chunky soup. Place the saucepan on medium-low heat to warm the soup. Slowly stir in milk and cream, and season with salt and pepper. Serve hot.

roasted apple, onion, and potato soup

SERVES 6

Roasting the apples brings out their sweetness and adds a smoky flavor to this soup.

- 1 tablespoon whole fennel seeds, toasted (see page 644)
- 1 pound (2 medium) white onions, quartered
- 3 large (1¾ pounds) Yukon gold potatoes, peeled and quartered
- 3 tart apples, such as Fuji or Granny Smith
- 1 tablespoon plus 1 teaspoon olive oil
- 1½ teaspoons ground cumin
- ½ teaspoon kosher salt, plus more for seasoning
- ¼ teaspoon freshly ground black pepper
- 3½ to 4 cups Homemade Chicken Stock (page 624), or low-sodium store-bought chicken broth, skimmed of fat
- 3 sprigs fresh tarragon

1. Transfer the seeds to a spice mill, and grind to a fine powder. Reserve 1½ teaspoons of the ground fennel. (Any remaining ground fennel may be saved in an airtight container for later use.)

2. Preheat the oven to 450°F. Arrange onions and potatoes in a large roasting pan. Core 2 apples (skin on); add to pan. Drizzle with 1 tablespoon olive oil; sprinkle with the cumin, reserved ground fennel, ½ teaspoon salt, and ¼ teaspoon pepper. Roast 25 minutes. Remove apples from pan; let cool. Using a spatula, turn the vegetables over, and continue to roast until the onions are tender when pierced with the tip of a knife, 25 to 40 minutes.

3. Remove 2 potato quarters and 2 onion quarters; cut into bite-size chunks, and reserve. Transfer remaining onions and potatoes to the bowl of a food processor. Add ½ cup stock to the pan; place over medium-high heat. Scrape up any brown bits with a wooden spoon; add warm liquid to a food processor. Add 1½ cups stock to the processor. Purée until smooth. Transfer purée to a stockpot. Remove peel from cooked apples, and discard. Add the apple flesh to the food processor. Add 1½ cups of the stock, and purée until smooth. Transfer to the stockpot, stir, and warm over medium heat. (If the soup is too thick, add the remaining ½ cup of stock, and warm.) Season with salt and pepper.

4. Meanwhile, peel and core the remaining apple; cut into ½-inch chunks. Heat the remaining teaspoon of oil in a skillet over medium-high heat. Add the apples, and cook, until the chunks are crisp and golden brown, about 10 minutes.

5. To serve, add the apple, potato, and onion chunks; warm over medium heat. Season with salt and pepper. Sprinkle with tarragon sprigs. Serve hot.

FIT TO EAT RECIPE PER SERVING: 173 CALORIES, 1 G FAT, 1 MG CHOLESTEROL, 37 G CARBOHYDRATE, 538 MG SODIUM, 6 G PROTEIN, 5 G DIETARY FIBER

yellow pepper soup

SERVES 4

2 tablespoons extra-virgin olive oil, plus more for drizzling

4 medium leeks, white and pale-green parts, thinly sliced, well washed (see page 646)

6 yellow bell peppers (2 pounds), seeds and ribs removed, cut into chunks

6 large sprigs fresh tarragon, plus more leaves for garnish

2¾ cups Homemade Chicken Stock (page 624), or low-sodium store-bought chicken broth, skimmed of fat

Kosher salt and freshly ground black pepper

1 large slice Italian bread, cut into ½ x 3-inch pieces, toasted

1. In a small stockpot, heat the oil over low heat. Add the leeks, and cook until wilted, about 10 minutes. Add the peppers, tarragon, and chicken stock, and season with salt and pepper. Raise heat to high; cover and bring to a boil. Reduce heat, and simmer with the lid ajar, until the peppers are very tender, about 20 minutes.

2. Remove the pot from the heat, and discard the tarragon sprigs. Transfer the soup to the bowl of a food processor, and purée. Strain the purée through a fine sieve, or a cheesecloth-lined strainer, into a bowl. Season with salt and pepper. Divide the soup among four bowls, and place 2 of the toast pieces in each. Garnish with the tarragon leaves, and drizzle with olive oil, if desired. Serve hot.

butternut squash soup

SERVES 6

2 butternut squash

2 medium leeks, white and pale-green parts, cut into ½-inch-thick slices, well washed (see page 646)

Grated zest of 1 orange

¼ teaspoon ground cinnamon

¼ teaspoon ground nutmeg

1½ quarts Homemade Chicken Stock (page 624), or low-sodium store-bought chicken broth, skimmed of fat

1½ teaspoons kosher salt

¼ teaspoon freshly ground black pepper

1 Cut the squash in half lengthwise; remove the seeds and discard, or save for toasting (see page 644). Peel and cut the flesh into ½-inch dice.

2. In a large saucepan over medium-low heat, cook the leeks in 2 tablespoons water until they soften, about 10 minutes. Add the squash, orange zest, cinnamon, and nutmeg; cook for 2 minutes. Add 5 cups of the chicken stock, the salt, and pepper; stir to combine, and cook until the squash is tender when pierced with the tip of a knife, about 25 minutes.

3. Working in batches, transfer the mixture to the bowl of a food processor, and purée. Return the soup to the pot; reheat, and add more stock to thin to desired consistency, if necessary. Serve hot.

FIT TO EAT RECIPE PER SERVING: 89 CALORIES, 1 G TOTAL FAT, 2 MG CHOLESTEROL, 15 G CARBOHYDRATE, 761 MG SODIUM, 6 G PROTEIN, 2 G DIETARY FIBER

creamy tomato soup

MAKES 3 QUARTS

This tomato soup is also delicious without any
half-and-half—or with twice as much. Add 2 cups
of cooked white rice to it to make another classic:
tomato-rice soup. The soup will keep for up to 2
days in the refrigerator; it can be frozen for up to
3 months without the half-and-half.

- 2 tablespoons unsalted butter
- 1 medium onion, finely chopped
- 3 garlic cloves, minced
- 3 26½-ounce boxes vacuum-packed crushed
  tomatoes, or 10 cups canned crushed
  tomatoes
- 5¼ cups Homemade Chicken Stock (page
  624), or low-sodium store-bought chicken
  broth, skimmed of fat
- 3 sprigs fresh oregano, plus more for
  garnish
- ½ cup half-and-half
  Kosher salt and freshly ground
  black pepper

1. Melt the butter in a medium saucepan over
medium-low heat. Add the onion and garlic, and
cook, stirring, until translucent, about 8 minutes.

2. Add the tomatoes, stock, and oregano; cover, and
bring to a boil. Reduce heat, and simmer gently, uncovered, until thickened, about 45 minutes. Remove
the oregano sprigs.

3. Slowly add the half-and-half, stirring constantly.
Season with salt and pepper. Garnish with oregano.
Serve hot.

summer squash soup
with basil pistou

SERVES 4

Pistou, a French version of pesto, is a mixture of
basil, garlic, and olive oil. Prepare the pistou just
before serving.

- 1 tablespoon unsalted butter
- 1 medium leek, white and pale-green parts,
  thinly sliced, well washed (see page 646)
- 1 garlic clove, minced
  Kosher salt and freshly ground
  black pepper
- 2¼ pounds yellow summer squash, trimmed
  and cut into half-moons
- 2 cups Homemade Chicken Stock (page
  624), or low-sodium store-bought chicken
  broth, skimmed of fat
- 2 cups loosely packed fresh basil leaves,
  plus more for garnish
- ⅓ cup extra-virgin olive oil

1. Melt the butter in a medium stockpot over
medium-high heat. Add the leek and half the garlic. Season well with salt and pepper; cook, stirring
until soft and tender, about 5 minutes.

2. Add the squash, and cook, stirring, about 5 minutes. Add the chicken stock, cover, and bring to a
boil. Reduce heat to a simmer, and cook with the lid
ajar until tender, about 20 minutes. Remove the
soup from the heat; let cool slightly.

3. Fill the bowl of a food processor with the basil
and the remaining garlic. With the machine running, drizzle the olive oil through the feed tube;
process until smooth. Season with salt and pepper.
Transfer the basil pistou to a bowl; place a piece of
plastic wrap over the surface, and set aside.

4. Place the slightly cooled soup in the cleaned bowl
of the food processor, and process until the soup
is still slightly chunky.

5. Return the soup to the stockpot; cook, uncovered,
over medium-high heat to reduce the liquid and
thicken just slightly, about 5 minutes. Season with
salt and pepper. Ladle into soup bowls, and garnish
with the basil pistou and a basil leaf. Serve hot.

pappa al pomodoro

SERVES 4

This recipe for the classic Florentine bread soup should be reserved for tomatoes at the height of the season.

- 4 pounds (6 to 8 large) tomatoes
- 2 tablespoons extra-virgin olive oil, plus more for drizzling
- 2 garlic cloves, minced
- ¾ cup thinly sliced leeks, white parts, well washed (see page 646)
- 2½ cups cubed peasant bread, crusts removed
- ½ teaspoon kosher salt
- ¼ teaspoon freshly ground black pepper
- 20 leaves fresh basil leaves, torn into pieces

1. Cover and bring a large pot of water to a boil. Prepare an ice-water bath. Using a paring knife, score the nonstem end of each tomato with a shallow "x." Blanch the tomatoes in the boiling water for 30 seconds. With a slotted spoon, transfer tomatoes to the ice-water bath. Slip off the skins with a knife. Cut the tomatoes in half crosswise; seed by squeezing over a strainer set in a bowl to collect the juice. Cut the tomatoes into chunks; set the tomatoes and juice aside. Discard the solids in the strainer.

2. In a small, nonreactive stockpot, heat 2 tablespoons olive oil over medium-low heat. Add the garlic and leeks; cook, stirring occasionally, until translucent, about 8 minutes. Raise heat to medium high, and add the tomatoes and juice. Simmer, stirring occasionally, until the tomatoes are disintegrating and very juicy, about 20 minutes.

3. Add the bread; cook, stirring and breaking up the bread with a wooden spoon until the liquid is absorbed, about 5 minutes. Stir in the salt and pepper. Remove from heat; let stand to come to room temperature. Just before serving, stir in torn basil. Drizzle each serving with extra-virgin olive oil, if desired. Serve warm or at room temperature.

spring-greens soup

SERVES 12

- 3 tablespoons unsalted butter
- 4 cups (about 1 pound) finely chopped shallots
- 4 cups (about 1½ pounds) chopped leeks, white and pale-green parts, well washed (see page 646)
- 4 cups (about 1¾ pounds) chopped sweet onions, such as Vidalia
- 4 cups (10 ounces) chopped scallions, white and light-green parts
- 3 quarts Homemade Chicken Stock (page 624), or low-sodium store-bought chicken broth, skimmed of fat
- 10 cups chopped (2 pounds) Boston or other soft lettuce, plus 1 leaf, julienned, for garnish
- ¼ cup plus 2 tablespoons snipped chives
- ½ cup packed fresh dill sprigs, plus more for garnish
- 1½ cups (about 2½ bunches) packed fresh tarragon leaves, plus more for garnish
- 1 cup (1 large bunch) packed fresh flat-leaf parsley leaves

  Kosher salt and freshly ground black pepper

1. Melt butter in a stockpot set over medium-low heat. Add shallots, leeks, onions, and scallions. Cover; cook, stirring occasionally, until softened, about 20 minutes. Add 4 cups stock, and stir well.

2. Add lettuce; cook, covered, until wilted, about 10 minutes. Add chives, dill, tarragon, and parsley; cook, covered, until aromatic, about 10 minutes.

3. Fill a blender halfway with the mixture; blend until well combined but some texture remains, being careful not to purée completely. Transfer the soup to a large bowl; blend the remaining mixture. Rinse out the stockpot.

4. Return the soup to the cleaned stockpot, and set over medium heat. Stir in the remaining 8 cups of stock; season with salt and pepper. Cook, uncovered, until heated throughout. Before serving, garnish with dill, tarragon, and the julienned lettuce. Serve hot.

provençal vegetable soup

SERVES 6

- ¾ cup dried navy beans
- 1 teaspoon olive oil
- 4 (1½ pounds) leeks, white and pale-green parts, well washed (see page 646)
- 1 medium garlic clove, thinly sliced
- 2 tablespoons coarsely chopped fresh flat-leaf parsley
- ½ teaspoon finely chopped fresh rosemary
- ½ teaspoon finely chopped thyme leaves
- 2 large carrots, cut into ½-inch dice
- 2 medium all-purpose potatoes, peeled, cut into ½-inch dice
- ¼ teaspoon freshly ground black pepper
- 2 quarts Homemade Chicken Stock (page 624), or low-sodium store-bought chicken broth, skimmed of fat
- 1 teaspoon kosher salt
- 8 ounces fresh spinach, washed, stemmed, and sliced into ¼-inch strips
- ¼ cup fresh chervil, for garnish
  Rustic Gruyère Croutons (page 104), optional

1. Pick over the dried beans, discarding any stones or broken beans, and rinse. Place in a saucepan; cover with cold water by 2 inches. Bring to a strong boil over high heat. Cover, and remove from heat. Let stand 1 hour. Drain; set aside.

2. In a heavy-bottomed stockpot, heat olive oil over medium-low heat. Add leeks and garlic; cook until translucent, stirring occasionally, about 8 minutes. Add parsley, rosemary, thyme, carrots, potatoes, and pepper. Cover; cook until vegetables are soft, stirring occasionally, about 15 minutes.

3. Add beans and stock. Cover, bring to a boil, and reduce heat to low; cook until beans are tender, about 40 minutes. About 10 minutes before beans are done, add salt. Add spinach; cook 1 to 2 minutes more. Divide soup among bowls; serve hot with chervil and croutons, if using.

FIT TO EAT RECIPE PER SERVING: 338 CALORIES, 4 G FAT, 5 MG CHOLESTEROL, 66 G CARBOHYDRATE, 609 MG SODIUM, 15 G PROTEIN, 11 G DIETARY FIBER

vegetable barley soup

SERVES 10

- ½ ounce dried porcini mushrooms
- 2 tablespoons unsalted butter
- 2 small onions, cut into ¼-inch dice
- 1 teaspoon fresh thyme leaves
- 2 teaspoons kosher salt, plus more for seasoning
- 1 teaspoon freshly ground black pepper
- 1 cup barley
- 1 cup Madeira wine
- 1 28-ounce can whole peeled tomatoes, drained and liquid reserved, tomatoes seeded, cored, and cut into ½-inch pieces
- 2 quarts Vegetable Stock (page 626), or low-sodium store-bought vegetable broth
- 2 large (1¼ pounds each) butternut squash, halved, seeded, flesh cut into ½-inch pieces
- ½ bunch (12 ounces) red or green Swiss chard, washed and drained

1. Place mushrooms in a bowl; cover with very hot water. Let stand until soft, about 20 minutes.

2. Meanwhile, melt butter in a large pot over medium heat. Add onions; cook, stirring often, until soft and translucent, about 8 minutes. Add thyme, 1 teaspoon salt, and ½ teaspoon pepper.

3. Stir in barley, and cook until it begins to brown and smell sweet, about 8 minutes.

4. Using a slotted spoon, remove porcinis from soaking liquid. Strain liquid through a fine sieve or cheesecloth-lined strainer into a bowl; set aside. Chop porcinis; add to barley mixture. Add ½ cup Madeira; raise heat to medium high. Cook until liquid is nearly evaporated. Reduce heat to medium; add reserved porcini liquid. Cook until liquid is almost completely reduced, about 8 minutes.

5. Add reserved tomato liquid to barley, along with the stock. Add squash pieces, 1 teaspoon salt, and ½ teaspoon pepper. Simmer until squash is tender, about 50 minutes, skimming foam occasionally. Add tomatoes for last 20 minutes of cooking time.

6. Chop chard stems into ½-inch pieces; add to barley. Chop leaves into ½-inch pieces; set aside.

7. Just before serving, stir the chopped Swiss chard leaves into the soup, and add the remaining ½ cup Madeira. Cook until the chard is just tender, about 2 minutes. Season with salt. Serve hot.

chilled minestrone
SERVES 6

Look for small, tender vegetables. Pattypan squash make beautiful bowls for this soup.

- 2 large beefsteak tomatoes
- ½ cup dried flageolets, rinsed and picked over
- 2 medium onions
- 1 head of garlic, cut in half crosswise, loose papery skins removed
- 1 handful fresh marjoram
- 1 dried bay leaf
- 1 tablespoon whole black peppercorns
- 1 teaspoon kosher salt, plus more to taste
- 6 large pattypan squashes, optional
- 2 tablespoons extra-virgin olive oil, plus more for drizzling
- 1 large garlic clove
- ½ large or 1 small bulb fennel, thinly sliced and chopped
- 3 thin carrots, sliced into ¼-inch-thick circles
- 1½ quarts Homemade Chicken Stock (page 624), or low-sodium store-bought chicken broth, skimmed of fat
- 1 medium Yukon gold potato, or any other floury potato, cut into ½-inch pieces
- 1 ear fresh corn, kernels shaved from the cob
- 1 to 2 young small zucchini, quartered, cut into ⅓-inch-thick quarter moons
- 4 ounces mixed fresh green beans, such as wax beans, string beans, and haricots verts, sliced into 1-inch pieces
- Freshly ground black pepper
- Juice of 1 lemon
- Basil Purée (recipe follows), optional

1. Cover and bring a pot of water to a boil. Prepare an ice-water bath. Using a paring knife, score non-stem end of each tomato with a shallow "x." Blanch for 30 seconds. Transfer tomatoes to ice bath. Slip off skins with a knife. Coarsely chop; set aside.

2. Place flageolets in a saucepan; cover with 2 inches of cold water. Halve 1 onion; add to pot. Add garlic. Reserve 2 tablespoons marjoram leaves. Tie remaining marjoram, bay leaf, and peppercorns in a piece of cheesecloth to make a bouquet garni; add to pot. Set over high heat; cover, and bring to a boil, reduce heat, and simmer, uncovered, until beans are tender, about 45 minutes. Stir in the salt 10 minutes before beans finish cooking. Remove from heat; cool in liquid. Drain beans; reserve 1 cup liquid. Discard onion, garlic, and bouquet garni.

3. For squash bowls, trace a circle 2 inches around outside of core of each squash. Cut on the diagonal to remove core in a cone-shaped piece. Scoop out flesh with a melon baller and discard; cover squash with plastic wrap, and chill until needed.

4. Heat oil in a stockpot over medium heat. Coarsely chop remaining onion; add to stockpot with garlic clove. Cook until translucent, about 8 minutes. Add reserved marjoram, fennel, and carrots; cook, stirring, until just soft, about 10 minutes. Add stock and the reserved cup of bean liquid. Add potato and tomatoes; simmer 10 minutes. Add flageolets and corn; simmer until the potato is tender and liquid is stewy, about 5 minutes. Prepare an ice-water bath. Raise heat to high. Stir in zucchini and green beans. Cook 2 minutes; remove from heat. Transfer to a bowl; place bowl in ice bath; stir occasionally until cold. Remove from ice bath; season with salt, pepper, and lemon juice. Ladle into bowls; add a spoonful of basil purée, or a drizzle of oil, to each. Serve chilled.

basil purée
MAKES ⅔ CUP

- 1 large bunch fresh basil leaves
- ½ cup extra-virgin olive oil
- ½ teaspoon kosher salt

Process ingredients in a blender until smooth; transfer to a glass jar. It is best used the same day.

chicken noodle soup

SERVES 8 TO 10

Chicken noodle soup tastes best when it's homemade. This recipe calls for soft egg noodles, but your favorite noodles will work fine. Use the shredded chicken from the Homemade Chicken Stock recipe (page 624) in this soup. The soup will keep 2 days in the refrigerator; it can be frozen up to 3 months.

- 3 quarts Homemade Chicken Stock (page 624), chilled
- 3 carrots, cut into ⅛-inch-thick rounds
  Kosher salt
- 8 ounces medium egg noodles
  Cooked shredded chicken meat, from Homemade Chicken Stock
  Freshly ground black pepper
- ¼ cup chopped fresh dill, or 1 tablespoon dried dill
- ¼ cup chopped fresh flat-leaf parsley

1. Remove the chilled chicken stock from the refrigerator. Use a spoon to remove the layer of fat that has formed and discard. Transfer the stock to a large stockpot; bring just to a simmer. Add the carrots; simmer until tender, about 6 minutes.

2. Meanwhile, bring a large saucepan of salted water to a boil. Cook the noodles just until tender, about 6 minutes. Drain; add the noodles to the stockpot, along with the shredded chicken meat. Season with salt and pepper. Heat until hot. When ready to serve, stir in the dill and parsley. Serve hot.

chicken soup north african style

SERVES 8

- 3 medium carrots
- 2 whole chicken breasts, split, bone in, skin removed
- 1 leek, white and pale-green parts, quartered lengthwise, well washed (see page 646)
- 1 celery stalk, strings removed, cut into 1-inch lengths
- 3 sprigs fresh flat-leaf parsley
- 2 sprigs fresh thyme
- 2 dried bay leaves
- 1½ teaspoons kosher salt
- ¼ teaspoon freshly ground black pepper
- 3 whole canned tomatoes, drained, seeded, and quartered
- 1 teaspoon ground cumin
- ½ teaspoon ground ginger
- 1 cup diced butternut squash
- 1 cup quick-cooking couscous
- 1 jalapeño pepper, seeds and ribs removed, minced
- ⅓ cup finely chopped fresh cilantro leaves, plus sprigs for garnish
- 2 small zucchini, seeded, cut into ½-inch dice
- ½ cup cooked or canned chickpeas, drained
- 2 limes, cut into wedges

1. Halve 1 carrot; place in a stockpot. Add chicken, 2 quarts water, leek, celery, parsley, thyme, bay leaves, and 1 teaspoon salt. Cover; bring to a boil. Reduce heat to low; simmer, uncovered, 1 hour; skim off any foam. Remove chicken. Strain the stock through a fine sieve or cheesecloth-lined strainer into a bowl. Discard solids, reserving meat. Slice chicken into ½-inch-thick strips, and set aside.

2. Rinse pot; add stock. Set over medium-low heat; add pepper. Dice remaining carrots. Add carrots, tomatoes, cumin, ginger, and squash; simmer over medium heat until tender, about 25 minutes.

3. Meanwhile, bring 1 cup water to a boil in a saucepan. Add couscous and remaining salt. Cover; remove from heat. Let stand 5 minutes. Fluff. Stir in the jalapeño and cilantro.

4. Add zucchini and chickpeas; cook until tender, 5 minutes. Add chicken; simmer 5 minutes. Season with salt and pepper. Place couscous in bowls; add soup; add cilantro sprigs and lime wedges.

FIT TO EAT RECIPE PER SERVING: 197 CALORIES, 2 G FAT, 25 MG CHOLESTEROL, 33 G CARBOHYDRATE, 470 MG SODIUM, 14 G PROTEIN, 6 G DIETARY FIBER

chicken and root vegetable soup with cornmeal spaetzle

SERVES 8

 2 *tablespoons fresh lemon juice*

 7 *sprigs fresh tarragon*

 ¼ *cup plus 1 tablespoon olive oil*

 1 *teaspoon kosher salt*

 ¼ *teaspoon freshly ground black pepper*

 1 *whole chicken breast (about 1 pound), boned, skin on*

 3 *carrots, cut in ¼ x 2-inch lengths*

 ½ *medium (about 8 ounces) celery root, cut in ¼ x 2-inch lengths*

 ½ *medium turnip, cut in ¼ x 2-inch lengths*

 1 *medium parsnip, cut in ¼ x 2-inch lengths*

 2 *leeks, white and light-green parts, cut in ¼ x 2-inch lengths, well washed (see page 646)*

 2 *quarts Homemade Chicken Stock (page 624), or low-sodium store-bought chicken broth, skimmed of fat*

   Cornmeal Spaetzle (recipe follows)

 3 *cups watercress leaves (about 2 bunches)*

1. In a small, shallow nonmetal dish combine lemon juice, 2 sprigs tarragon, 2 tablespoons olive oil, ½ teaspoon salt, and ⅛ teaspoon pepper. Place chicken in marinade, turning several times to coat. Cover and place in refrigerator for 1 hour.

2. Preheat oven to 400°F. Remove the leaves from the remaining sprigs of tarragon, and set aside. In a medium skillet with an ovenproof handle, heat 1 tablespoon olive oil over medium-high heat. Add chicken breast, skin-side down, and cook until golden brown, about 4 minutes. Turn and cook until golden brown, about 2 minutes. Discard the fat that has accumulated, place the skillet in the oven, and

roast until chicken is cooked through, about 10 minutes. Remove from oven, and set aside to cool.

3. In a 6-quart stockpot, heat remaining 2 tablespoons olive oil over medium heat. Add carrots, celery root, turnip, parsnip, ½ teaspoon salt, and ⅛ teaspoon pepper, and cook, stirring frequently, until wilted, about 5 minutes. Add leeks, and cook until just wilted, 3 to 4 minutes. Add the chicken stock, raise heat to medium high, and cook for 5 minutes. Add cooked spaetzle, and cook until heated through, about 2 minutes. Stir in the reserved tarragon leaves and watercress, adjust seasoning with salt and pepper if necessary, and remove from heat. Cut chicken breast in ¼-inch slices. Divide soup and chicken among eight bowls, and serve immediately.

cornmeal spaetzle

SERVES 8

There are a variety of ways to form spaetzle. Cutting the dough directly into boiling water results in large and irregularly shaped dumplings. Push the dough through a potato ricer, food mill, or colander for smaller spaetzle. Spaetzle may also be eaten hot with butter, salt, and pepper.

 1 *tablespoon plus 1 teaspoon kosher salt*

 1¼ *cups all-purpose flour*

 ½ *cup plus 1 tablespoon instant polenta*

 ¼ *teaspoon freshly ground black pepper*

 4 *large eggs*

 3 *tablespoons milk*

1. Fill a large pot with cold water, add 1 tablespoon salt, cover, and bring to a boil. Meanwhile, place flour, polenta, 1 teaspoon salt, and pepper in a large bowl. Mix with a wooden spoon. Whisk eggs and milk together in a small bowl, slowly add to dry ingredients, and mix until well combined. The dough will be wet and tacky.

2. Fill a potato ricer fitted with a ¼-inch-hole attachment with half the dough, and push it through into the boiling water. Repeat immediately with the rest of the dough, cooking all the spaetzle together. (Alternatively, dip a long, narrow wooden cutting board with a handle into the boiling water, then spread all dough out to a thickness of approximately ¼ inch on the board. Rest the board against the edge of the pot so it almost touches the water, and slice the dough into thin slivers using a sharp, wet knife. Allow the spaetzle to drop directly into the water. While cutting, dip board and knife frequently into the simmering water.)

3. Cook spaetzle until they float to the surface, reduce heat to medium high, and cook 6 to 8 minutes more, or until cooked through to the center. Remove the spaetzle with a slotted spoon, and drain in a colander.

matzo ball soup
SERVES 4 TO 6

Cooking matzo balls in chicken stock may make the soup a bit cloudy, but it is well worth it for the flavor the matzo balls will soak up from the rich broth. If you desire a clearer soup, strain the cooked matzo balls and vegetables, and heat them in the strained stock. Rendered chicken fat is available at butcher shops and in the meat department of some grocery stores.

- 3   *large eggs*
- 3   *tablespoons rendered chicken fat, or canola oil*
- 1½ *teaspoons kosher salt*
- ¾   *cup plus 2 tablespoons matzo meal*
- 2½ *quarts Homemade Chicken Stock (page 624), or low-sodium store-bought chicken broth, skimmed of fat*
- 3   *medium carrots, sliced into ½-inch-thick rounds*
- 2   *medium parsnips, sliced into ½-inch-thick rounds*
     Fresh dill, for garnish

1. In a medium bowl, whisk eggs and chicken fat until combined. Whisk in salt and ½ cup water. Add the matzo meal, and whisk until combined. Cover, and refrigerate until firm, about 2 hours.

2. Line a baking sheet with parchment paper. Bring the chicken stock to a boil in a large wide saucepan, and reduce heat to a simmer.

3. Slightly dampen your fingertips; form 2 heaping tablespoons of batter into a 1½-inch ball, being careful not to compress the mixture too much; place on the prepared sheet. Form remaining balls.

4 Using a large spoon, slide the matzo balls into the simmering stock. Once all the balls have been added, cover and cook for 10 minutes. Add the carrots and parsnips, cover, and continue cooking for about 20 minutes, until the vegetables are tender and the matzo balls are cooked through. To test if the matzo balls are done, remove a ball from the water, and slice in half. The color should be light throughout. If the center is darker, cook 5 to 10 minutes more. To serve, ladle broth, vegetables, and 1 or 2 matzo balls into each bowl. Garnish with the fresh dill, and serve hot.

turkey soup with little herbed dumplings
SERVES 4

To make turkey stock, substitute a 3-pound turkey breast and 2 pounds turkey wings for the chicken in the recipe for Homemade Chicken Stock (page 624).

for the dumplings

- 1   *large egg*
- 1   *teaspoon finely chopped celery leaves*
- ¾   *teaspoon finely chopped fresh tarragon*
- ¾   *teaspoon snipped chives*
- ¼   *teaspoon kosher salt*
     Freshly ground black pepper to taste
- ½   *cup plus 1 tablespoon all-purpose flour*

for the soup

- 1   *quart turkey stock*
- 1   *small parsnip, cut in matchsticks*
- ½   *carrot, cut in matchsticks*
- 4   *ounces cooked skinless turkey-breast meat, cut in thin strips*

1. To make the dumplings, beat the egg with celery leaves, herbs, salt, pepper, and ¼ cup water in a bowl. Add the flour, and stir to make a thick batter; if it isn't, add more flour or water accordingly. Cover; let sit for 1 hour.

2. To make the soup, bring the turkey stock to a simmer; add the parsnip and carrot. Cook the vegetables until tender, about 3 minutes, and remove with a slotted spoon. Set aside.

3. With a rubber spatula, push the dumpling batter through the holes of a slotted spoon into the simmering stock, about ½ cup at a time, until all the batter is used. The dumplings are done as soon as they come to the surface, about 4 minutes. When they are cooked, return the vegetables and add the turkey to the pot. Heat through; serve hot.

FIT TO EAT RECIPE PER SERVING: 170 CALORIES, 3 G TOTAL FAT, 14% CALORIES FROM FAT, 79 MG CHOLESTEROL, 17 G CARBOHYDRATE, 407 MG SODIUM, 17 G PROTEIN, TRACE OF DIETARY FIBER

spring pork stew
SERVES 6

- 1 cup white rice
- 2 teaspoons extra-virgin olive oil
- 1 pound lean pork roast or stew meat, trimmed of fat, cut into 1-inch cubes
- 1 cup Homemade Chicken Stock (page 624), or low-sodium store-bought chicken broth, skimmed of fat
- 2 garlic cloves, minced
- 1 medium onion, cut into ½-inch dice
- 2 celery stalks, strings removed, cut into ½-inch dice
- 2 medium carrots, cut into ½-inch dice
- 1 zucchini, cut in half lengthwise, cut into ½-inch half-moons
- 1 yellow squash, cut in half lengthwise, cut into ½-inch half-moons
- 1 yellow bell pepper, seeds and ribs removed, cut into ½ x 2-inch strips
- 1 red bell pepper, seeds and ribs removed, cut into ½ x 2-inch strips
- 1 28-ounce can plum tomatoes
- 2 teaspoons chopped fresh thyme
- 2 teaspoons chopped fresh flat-leaf parsley
- 1 teaspoon kosher salt
- ½ teaspoon freshly ground black pepper

1. Bring a saucepan of water to a boil. Stir in rice; simmer. Cook until tender, about 20 minutes. Drain; rinse with warm water. Set aside, covered.

2. Heat oil in a high-sided skillet on medium-high heat. Add pork; stir occasionally. Cook until brown on all sides, 3 to 4 minutes. Transfer to a plate; cover.

3. Place ½ cup stock, the garlic, onion, celery, and carrots in pan. Cook, stirring occasionally until they soften, about 3 minutes. Add zucchini, squash, and peppers. Toss; cook until soft, about 5 minutes.

4. Stir in remaining ½ cup stock and tomatoes with their juice, breaking tomatoes apart with a spoon. Stir in thyme and parsley. Return pork to pan, reduce heat to low, cover, and simmer until tender, about 20 minutes. Season with salt and pepper; serve warm over the reserved rice.

FIT TO EAT RECIPE PER SERVING: 315 CALORIES, 6 G FAT, 70 MG CHOLESTEROL, 39 G CARBOHYDRATE, 731 MG SODIUM, 27 G PROTEIN, 5 G DIETARY FIBER

savory fall stew
SERVES 4

To make peeling the onions easier, soak in warm water for 30 minutes to wrinkle the skins.

- 2 tablespoons olive oil
- 12 ounces hot Italian sausage, cut into small chunks
- 12 cipollini or pearl onions, peeled
- 1½ cups canned crushed tomatoes
- 3 cups Homemade Chicken Stock (page 624), or low-sodium store-bought chicken broth, skimmed of fat
- 1 handful of herbs, such as rosemary, thyme, or oregano
- 1 large (2½ pounds) butternut squash, peeled, seeded, cut into 1-inch chunks
- 3 carrots, cut into ½-inch pieces
- 3 parsnips, cut into 2-inch-long sticks
- 1 fennel bulb, halved, cored, cut into ¼-inch-thick slices
- 12 brussels sprouts, trimmed, cut in half
  Kosher salt and freshly ground black pepper

1. Heat the oil in a saucepan over medium heat. Cook sausage, stirring until it breaks into small pieces and is no longer pink, about 10 minutes. Remove sausage with a slotted spoon, and set aside.

2. Pour off all but 2 tablespoons of the rendered fat, and discard. Raise heat to medium high, and add the onions; cook, stirring, until golden, about 8 minutes. Add tomatoes, stock, and herbs; simmer over medium heat until the liquid starts to thicken, about 20 minutes. Add the sausage, squash, carrots, parsnips, and fennel; cover and simmer until the vegetables are tender, about 10 minutes. Add brussels sprouts; cook, covered, about 5 minutes more.

3. Uncover; cook, stirring occasionally, until the liquid thickens, 10 to 15 minutes more. Season with salt and pepper; serve hot.

pho (vietnamese beef and rice-noodle soup)

SERVES 6

In Vietnam, a bowl of this noodle soup—or one of its variations—is often served for breakfast. Use homemade beef stock if you can; canned versions are watery and salty.

for the soup

- 1 pound very lean sirloin of beef, trimmed of visible fat
- 4 ounces dry Chinese or Vietnamese rice noodles
- 3 cups Beef Stock (page 624)
- 3 tablespoons Asian fish sauce (nam pla)
- 1⅓ cups fresh bean sprouts

for optional accompaniments

- 1 small onion, thinly sliced
- 4 scallions, white and light-green parts, thinly sliced crosswise
- 2 small Thai chile peppers, or 1 small jalapeño, seeds and ribs removed, thinly sliced crosswise
- ⅓ cup fresh cilantro, or Thai basil leaves, coarsely chopped
   Hot red chile paste, optional

1. Wrap the beef in plastic wrap; freeze for about 1 hour. (Freezing the beef for a short time firms it up so thin slices are easy to cut. Don't freeze the beef overnight or it will be too frozen to cut.)

2. Meanwhile, fill a bowl with cold water, and add rice noodles. Soak until soft, about 30 minutes. Drain, and set aside.

3. Combine stock, 1½ cups water, and fish sauce in a large saucepan; set over medium-high heat.

4. Remove beef from freezer. Using a mandoline or a sharp knife, slice beef into ⅛-inch-thick strips.

5. Divide noodles among six bowls; top with meat. Raise heat; bring stock to a boil. Pour boiling stock over meat and noodles, pushing beef into the liquid so it cooks. Top with sprouts and other accompaniments; serve hot with chile paste, if using.

FIT TO EAT RECIPE PER SERVING: 208 CALORIES, 4 G FAT, 42 MG CHOLESTEROL, 22 G CARBOHYDRATE, 946 MG SODIUM, 19 G PROTEIN, 1 G DIETARY FIBER

mushroom beef barley soup

SERVES 8 TO 10

- 1 small bunch fresh dill
- 1 pound boneless beef chuck, cut into ½-inch pieces
   Kosher salt and freshly ground black pepper
- 3 tablespoons olive oil
- 1 medium onion, cut in ½-inch dice
- 1¼ cups hulled barley
- 1 12-ounce bottle dark beer
- 3 quarts Beef Stock (page 624)
- 3 carrots, cut in ¾-inch dice
- 8 ounces button mushrooms, wiped clean, quartered
- 1 tablespoon fresh thyme, roughly chopped
- 2 parsnips, cut in ½-inch dice

1. Place all but 7 sprigs dill into a piece of cheesecloth; tie with kitchen twine. Roughly chop the remaining sprigs; set both aside.

2. Sprinkle beef with salt and pepper. Heat 1½ tablespoons olive oil in a large stockpot over medium-high heat. Add the beef, and cook until browned on all sides, about 4 minutes. Remove beef and any liquid, and set aside.

3 Add remaining olive oil to stockpot, and place over medium-high heat. Add onion, barley, and salt and pepper to taste, and cook until onion is soft and barley is aromatic, about 8 minutes. Add beer, stirring with a wooden spoon to loosen any brown bits on the bottom of the pot; cook until liquid is reduced by half, about 10 minutes.

4 Add stock, reserved beef, and dill bundle; partially cover; bring to a boil. Reduce heat to medium low, and simmer for 30 minutes.

5 Add the carrots, mushrooms, and thyme, and simmer about 15 minutes. Add the parsnips; simmer about 20 minutes. Stir in the reserved chopped dill, and adjust the seasoning with salt and pepper, if necessary. Remove dill bundle, and serve hot.

kale, white bean, and sweet potato soup
SERVES 6

For a vegetarian version of this soup, use homemade or frozen vegetable broth.

- ½ cup dried white cannellini beans
- 2 sprigs fresh rosemary
- 1 small onion, cut into quarters
   Kosher salt
- ½ cup tubetti (small tube-shaped pasta)
- 1 tablespoon olive oil
- 2 small leeks, white and pale-green parts, thinly sliced, well washed (see page 646)
- 1 head of roasted garlic (see page 646)
- 1 sweet potato, peeled, cut into ½-inch cubes
- 1 bunch (12 ounces) kale
- 1½ quarts Homemade Chicken Stock (page 624), or low-sodium store-bought chicken broth, skimmed of fat
   Freshly ground black pepper

1. Pick over the dried beans, discarding any stones or broken beans, and rinse. Place in a large saucepan, cover with cold water by 2 inches, and bring to a strong boil over high heat. Cover and remove from the heat, and let stand 1 hour. Drain the beans, and set aside.

2. Tie 1 rosemary sprig in a small piece of cheesecloth. Place the beans, rosemary, onion, and 6 cups water in a large saucepan. Cover, and bring to a boil over medium-high heat. Reduce heat to a simmer, and cook, uncovered, until the beans are just tender, about 25 minutes. Drain the beans in a colander. Discard the onion and the rosemary; set the beans aside.

3. Cover, and bring a large saucepan of salted water to a boil over high heat. Add the tubetti, and cook until al dente, about 8 minutes. Transfer to a colander, drain, and set aside.

4. Place a 6-quart low-sided saucepan over medium heat. Add the olive oil; heat until the oil is hot, but not smoking. Add the leeks, the remaining sprig of rosemary, and the soft roasted garlic cloves, removed from their skins. Cook until the leeks become translucent, about 5 minutes. Add the sweet potato; cook, stirring, until the potato pieces just begin to soften, about 8 minutes.

5. Add the kale; cook until the kale begins to wilt, about 4 minutes. Add the chicken stock; cook until the potato pieces are tender, about 10 minutes. Add the reserved beans and pasta; season with salt and pepper. Cook until heated through, about 5 minutes. Divide among six soup bowls. Serve hot.

FIT TO EAT RECIPE PER SERVING: 472 CALORIES, 4 G FAT, 0 MG CHOLESTEROL, 93 G CARBOHYDRATE, 726 MG SODIUM, 17 G PROTEIN, 5 G DIETARY FIBER

red-lentil soup
with sage and bacon

SERVES 4

5 slices (4 ounces) bacon, cut
into ¼-inch dice

2 garlic cloves, minced

1 medium onion, finely chopped

4 medium carrots, cut into ¼-inch dice

6 fresh sage leaves, minced,
plus more for garnish

1½ cups dried red lentils

1 teaspoon ground cumin

5 cups Homemade Chicken Stock (page
624), or low-sodium store-bought chicken
broth, skimmed of fat

1. In a large saucepan over medium heat, cook the bacon until crisp, about 5 minutes. Transfer the bacon to a paper towel, and set aside. Discard all but 1 tablespoon of the rendered fat from the pan.

2. Add the garlic, onion, and carrots to the saucepan. Cook the vegetable mixture over medium heat until tender, about 5 minutes. Add the minced sage, and cook 1 minute more.

3. Add the lentils, cumin, and chicken stock; stir to combine. Simmer until the lentils are cooked and falling apart, about 25 minutes. To serve, divide the hot soup among four bowls, and garnish with the reserved bacon and additional sage. Serve hot.

. . . .

QUICK-SOAKING BEANS

If you don't have time for overnight soaking (8 hours), quick-soak your beans. Place beans in a pot, and cover with 2 inches of water. Bring to a boil, and immediately remove from heat. Cover, and let stand for an hour until the beans have plumped up. Drain, and use as directed.

. . . .

pasta e fagioli

SERVES 6

8 ounces (1¼ cups) dried great
Northern beans

1 tablespoon unsalted butter

2 celery stalks, strings removed, cut
into ¼-inch dice

1 medium onion, cut into ¼-inch dice

2 garlic cloves, minced

2 tablespoons finely chopped fresh
rosemary

3½ cups Homemade Chicken Stock
(page 624), or low-sodium store-bought
chicken broth, skimmed of fat

1 medium Yukon gold potato, peeled
(about 6 ounces)

2 whole canned tomatoes, seeded and
roughly chopped

⅛ teaspoon freshly ground black pepper

1 teaspoon kosher salt, plus more for water

4 ounces orecchiette pasta, or other
medium pasta

¼ cup packed fresh basil leaves

¼ cup packed fresh flat-leaf parsley leaves

5 large fresh sage leaves

¼ cup plus 2 tablespoons freshly grated
Parmesan cheese

1. Pick over the dried beans, discarding any stones or broken beans, and rinse. Place in a large saucepan, cover with cold water by 2 inches, and bring to a strong boil over high heat. Cover, remove from the heat, and let stand 1 hour. Drain the beans, and set aside.

2. Melt the butter in a small stockpot over medium-low heat. Add the celery, onion, and three-quarters of the garlic; cook until translucent, about 8 minutes. Add the beans, 1 tablespoon rosemary, the chicken stock, potato, tomatoes, pepper, and 3½ cups water. Raise heat to high, cover, and bring to a boil. Reduce heat to medium low; simmer, with lid ajar, until beans are tender, about 1¼ hours. Ten minutes before the soup is done, stir in the salt.

3. Meanwhile, cook the pasta in salted boiling water until slightly underdone, about 5 minutes; drain, and set aside. Pass the soup through a food mill fitted with a medium disk, holding back one-third of the whole beans. Return the soup and the beans to the stockpot, along with the pasta. Keep warm over low heat.

4. Chop the remaining garlic and 1 tablespoon rosemary, with the basil, parsley, and sage until finely minced. Stir into the soup, and divide the soup among six bowls. Sprinkle each bowl with 1 tablespoon Parmesan; serve hot.

FIT TO EAT RECIPE PER SERVING: 377 CALORIES, 7 G FAT, 24 MG CHOLESTEROL, 61 G CARBOHYDRATE, 697 MG SODIUM, 23 G PROTEIN, 7 G DIETARY FIBER

black-bean and tomato chili

SERVES 6

Serve this pungent chili, infused with raw and cooked garlic, over yellow rice. For guajillo chiles, see Food Sources, page 648.

1¾ cups dried black beans

3 large or 4 small dried guajillo chiles, toasted (see page 645)

1 tablespoon olive oil

2 medium onions, finely chopped

8 garlic cloves, minced

1 tablespoon plus 1 teaspoon ground cumin

1¾ cups Vegetable Stock (page 626), or low-sodium store-bought vegetable broth

2 pounds assorted tomatoes, seeded, cut into 1-inch chunks

½ cup fresh basil leaves, roughly chopped

1½ teaspoons kosher salt

¼ teaspoon freshly ground black pepper

2 tablespoons balsamic vinegar

1. Pick over the dried beans, discarding any stones or broken beans, and rinse. Place in a large saucepan, cover with cold water by 2 inches, and bring to a strong boil over high heat. Cover and remove from the heat, and let stand 1 hour. Drain the beans, and set aside.

2. Place the chiles in a small bowl, and cover with very hot water. Let stand until the chiles are soft, about 20 minutes. Cut the chiles in half, and remove the seeds and stems. Transfer the chile flesh, along with the soaking liquid, to the bowl of a food processor. Process until a purée forms.

3. Heat the oil in a medium saucepan over medium heat. Add the onions, three-quarters of the minced garlic, and the cumin. Cover, and cook until softened and slightly browned, about 15 minutes. Add the chile purée, and cook 2 minutes more. Add the vegetable stock and the black beans. Cover, and cook until the beans are soft, about 1½ hours. If the beans seem dry, add another ½ cup hot water.

4. In a large bowl, toss together the tomatoes, remaining garlic, basil, salt, pepper, and vinegar. Let sit 5 minutes. Stir half of the tomato mixture into the beans. Cover, and simmer 1 minute more.

5. Divide the chili among six soup bowls. Top with the remaining tomato mixture, and serve hot.

FIT TO EAT RECIPE PER SERVING: 280 CALORIES, 2 G FAT, 1 MG CHOLESTEROL, 52 G CARBOHYDRATE, 634 MG SODIUM, 18 G PROTEIN, 9 G DIETARY FIBER

lentil soup from granada

SERVES 6

1 teaspoon olive oil

1 large onion, cut into ½-inch dice

1 medium carrot, cut into ½-inch dice

1 garlic clove, coarsely chopped

1¾ quarts Homemade Chicken Stock (page 624), or low-sodium store-bought chicken broth, skimmed of fat

1½ cups dried French green lentils, picked over

1 tablespoon fresh mint, chopped, plus more for garnish

1 small dried red chile pepper, or ⅛ teaspoon crushed red-pepper flakes

1 teaspoon kosher salt

¼ teaspoon freshly ground black pepper

½ teaspoon sweet paprika

1 tablespoon fresh lemon juice

1 lemon, cut into wedges

1. Heat oil in a stockpot over medium-low heat. Add onion, carrot, and garlic. Cook, stirring occasionally, until onion is translucent, about 8 minutes.

2. Add the chicken stock, and stir in the lentils, chopped mint, chile pepper, salt, and pepper. Simmer until the lentils are tender, about 45 minutes.

3. Remove chile pepper, if used, and discard. Remove soup from the heat, stir in the paprika and lemon juice; season with salt and pepper. Serve hot, garnished with fresh mint and lemon wedges.

FIT TO EAT RECIPE PER SERVING: 215 CALORIES, 1 G FAT, 0 MG CHOLESTEROL, 33 G CARBOHYDRATE, 447 MG SODIUM, 14 G PROTEIN, 4 G DIETARY FIBER

white bean and sausage stew in pumpkin shells

SERVES 12

Individual sugar pumpkins filled with a hearty stew—rich with sausage, beans, and potatoes—make a dramatic and welcoming presentation. This soup can also be made when pumpkins are not in season; just serve in soup bowls. To make peeling pearl onions easier, soak them in hot water for 30 minutes to wrinkle the skins. This soup will keep 2 days in the refrigerator or up to 1 week in the freezer.

2 cups dried navy beans

12 small sugar pumpkins, about 2 pounds each

¼ cup olive oil

Kosher salt and freshly ground black pepper

2 dried bay leaves

2 sprigs fresh thyme, plus thyme leaves for garnish, optional

1 teaspoon whole black peppercorns

5 cups Homemade Chicken Stock (page 624), or low-sodium store-bought chicken broth, skimmed of fat

1 large onion, roughly chopped

3 tablespoons unsalted butter

2 large leeks, white and pale-green parts, thinly sliced crosswise, well washed (see page 646)

4 medium carrots, sliced in ¼-inch rounds

1 celery stalk, strings removed, diced

36 red or white pearl onions, peeled

12 ounces small red fingerling or new potatoes, halved lengthwise

1 pound turkey sausage, cut into ½-inch pieces

1 cup baby peas, fresh or frozen, defrosted

8 ounces white-button mushrooms, wiped clean, quartered

¼ cup all-purpose flour

1¼ cups milk

2 tablespoons fresh sage, coarsely chopped

1. Pick over the dried beans, discarding any stones or broken beans, and rinse. Place them in a large saucepan, cover with cold water by 2 inches, and bring to a strong boil over high heat. Cover and remove from the heat; let stand 1 hour. Drain the beans, and set aside.

2. Preheat the oven to 350°F. Line two baking sheets with parchment paper. Cut a lid into the top of each pumpkin. Remove the seeds, and reserve for toasting. Rub the inside of each pumpkin with the olive oil, and sprinkle lightly with salt and pepper. Place the pumpkins, right-side up, and the lids on the baking sheets, and bake for 30 minutes. Turn the pumpkins over, and continue to bake until tender but firm, about 30 minutes more. Set aside.

3. Tie the bay leaves, thyme, and peppercorns in a small piece of cheesecloth to make a bouquet garni. Set aside. Place the beans in a medium stockpot. Add the chicken stock, onion, and bouquet garni. Cover and bring to a boil, reduce heat, and simmer until the beans are tender, about 30 minutes. Drain the beans, reserving the cooking liquid. Discard the bouquet garni.

4. In a large stockpot, melt the butter over medium-high heat. Add the leeks, carrots, celery, pearl onions, and potatoes. Cook until softened, about 12 minutes. Add the sausage, and cook until browned, about 5 minutes. Stir in the peas and mushrooms.

Sprinkle in the flour, and cook 2 minutes. Reduce heat to medium, stir in the milk and reserved cooking liquid, and stir the stew often until it thickens, about 20 minutes. Stir in the beans and sage. Divide the stew among the pumpkins, and return the baking sheets to the oven; bake until the pumpkins are soft and the stew is heated through, about 15 minutes. Garnish with the thyme leaves, if using. Serve hot.

vietnamese fisherman's soup

SERVES 8

You can use any kind of seafood you like in this sweet-and-spicy soup. Look for many of these ingredients in the international section of grocery stores.

- 8 ounces boneless, skinless salmon, cut into bite-size pieces
- 4 ounces bay scallops
- 1 tablespoon canola oil
- 1 teaspoon hot red chile paste
- 1 large garlic clove, minced
- 5 cups Homemade Chicken Stock (page 624), or low-sodium store-bought chicken broth, skimmed of fat
- 2 medium (1 pound) tomatoes, cored and cut into ½-inch dice
- 2 cups diced fresh pineapple
- ½ medium onion, sliced lengthwise ¼ inch thick
- 2 tablespoons Asian fish sauce (nam pla)
- ¼ cup sugar
- ¼ teaspoon kosher salt
- ¼ cup fresh lime juice
- 3 scallions, white and light-green parts, cut diagonally ¼ inch thick
- 2 cups fresh bean sprouts
- 2 tablespoons chopped fresh Thai or regular basil leaves
- 2 tablespoons chopped fresh cilantro
- 2 tablespoons Fried Shallots (recipe follows), optional

1. Blanch the salmon in boiling water for 10 to 20 seconds. Remove with a slotted spoon, and drain in a colander. Blanch the scallops for 10 seconds; drain.

2. Heat the oil in a small stockpot over medium heat. Add the chile paste and garlic. Cook until fragrant, about 10 seconds. Add the chicken stock, cover, and bring to a boil. Reduce heat to medium; stir in the salmon and scallops, tomatoes, pineapple, onion, fish sauce, sugar, salt, and lime juice. Cook just until the seafood is cooked through, about 5 minutes. Remove from the heat, stir in the scallions, bean sprouts, basil, and cilantro. Divide among eight soup bowls, garnish with the shallots, if using, and serve hot.

fried shallots

MAKES ⅔ CUP

- 4 to 5 medium shallots, thinly sliced
- 1 cup canola oil

1. Spread the shallots on a paper-towel-lined baking sheet, and let dry for 15 to 20 minutes at room temperature.

2. Heat the oil in a small heavy skillet over medium-low heat until it's so hot that a shallot slice dropped in the oil bubbles and floats to the surface. Stir in all shallots; fry until golden, stirring often, about 5 minutes. Remove the fried shallots with a slotted spoon; drain on paper towels.

chilled corn soup
with radish and crab

Simmered corncobs make a rich stock. If white corn is not available, use more yellow corn. This soup will keep for 2 days in the refrigerator; do not freeze.

for the stock

- 2 tablespoons unsalted butter
- 1 large white onion, chopped medium
- 1 garlic clove, roughly chopped
- 1 teaspoon kosher salt
- 10 whole black peppercorns
- 4 ears fresh yellow corn, kernels shaved from the cob, cobs reserved
- 2 ears fresh white corn, kernels shaved from the cob, cobs reserved

for the soup

- ½ cup milk, plus more for thinning
- 8 ounces jumbo lump crabmeat
  - Juice of 1 lime
- ¼ teaspoon kosher salt, plus more for seasoning
- ¼ teaspoon freshly ground black pepper, plus more for seasoning
- 3 radishes
- 1 small bunch chives
  - Freshly grated nutmeg, for garnish, optional
  - Pinch of cayenne pepper, optional

1. Melt the butter in a large saucepan over medium-low heat. Stir in the onion, garlic, salt, and peppercorns. Cook until the onion is soft and translucent, about 8 minutes.

2. Add 8 cups water to the onion mixture, along with the reserved corncobs, cover, and bring the mixture to a boil. Reduce heat, and let simmer uncovered until the liquid is reduced by almost half and is milky and very flavorful, about 1 hour. Remove the corncobs, scraping as much liquid as possible off the cobs back into the pan. Discard the cobs. Transfer the corn stock to a large bowl, and cool to room temperature.

3. Meanwhile, cover and bring a medium pot of water to a boil. Add the reserved corn kernels, and blanch 1 minute. Remove from heat, strain, and run under cold water to stop the cooking.

4. Set aside ⅓ cup of the corn kernels for garnish. Process the remaining kernels and the cooled corn stock in the bowl of a food processor until smooth, working in batches if necessary. Transfer the mixture to a fine sieve set over a bowl. Press down hard on the solids, using a ladle or rubber spatula, to extract the liquid; discard the solids. Stir in the milk to thin the soup to desired consistency; transfer the liquid to the refrigerator. Chill.

5. Meanwhile, pick over the crabmeat, removing any shells or cartilage. Season with the lime juice, ¼ teaspoon salt, and ¼ teaspoon pepper. Grate the radishes using the small holes of a box grater, and set aside. Snip the chives into ¼-inch pieces with sharp kitchen scissors; set aside.

6. Season the chilled soup with salt and pepper. Ladle into soup bowls. Place ¼ cup of the crabmeat mixture in each bowl. Divide the remaining ⅓ cup of corn among the bowls, and garnish with the grated radish and snipped chives. If desired, sprinkle with the freshly grated nutmeg and cayenne, if using. Serve chilled.

bouillabaisse

Classic bouillabaisse calls for Mediterranean fish, many of which—John Dory, weever, and rascasse—are hard to find; halibut, red snapper, and monkfish are suitable. Avoid oily fish when making your selection. See page 644 for toasting seeds; for harissa, see Food Sources, page 648.

- 3 pounds fish heads and bones from nonoily fish, such as sole, flounder, snapper, or bass
- 8 sprigs fresh tarragon
- 8 sprigs fresh flat-leaf parsley
- 1 28-ounce can whole plum tomatoes
- 2 tablespoons olive oil
- 2 leeks, white and light-green parts, quartered lengthwise, sliced ¼ inch thick, well washed (see page 646)

4   small carrots, cut into ¼-inch dice

4   celery stalks, strings removed,
    cut into ¼-inch dice

2   small onions, cut into ¼-inch dice

4   garlic cloves, minced

1   teaspoon sweet paprika

8   sun-dried tomato halves
    (dry, not oil packed)

1   teaspoon crumbled saffron threads

½   teaspoon ground turmeric

2   teaspoons harissa, optional

½   teaspoon whole coriander seeds, toasted

½   teaspoon whole fennel seeds, toasted

½   teaspoon whole cumin seeds, toasted

    Zest from 3 oranges

3   live lobsters (1½ pounds each)

3   pounds mussels, scrubbed, debearded,
    and washed clean

    Kosher salt and freshly ground
    black pepper

8   small baking potatoes (2 pounds), peeled

4   pounds fish fillets, such as halibut, red
    snapper, and monkfish, cut into 1½-inch
    pieces

⅔   cup Rouille (recipe follows)

1   baguette, sliced into rounds and toasted

1. Remove the gills and any traces of blood from fish heads. Thoroughly wash the fish bones; cut them to fit inside a 12-quart stockpot. Set aside.

2. Tie tarragon and parsley sprigs in a small piece of cheesecloth to make a bouquet garni. Set aside.

3. Strain the tomatoes over a small bowl, reserving the liquid. Remove and discard the seeds; place the tomatoes in a bowl with the liquid. Set aside.

4. Heat the oil in a 12-quart stockpot over medium heat; add the sliced leeks, carrots, celery, onions, garlic, and paprika. Cook until the onions become translucent, about 8 minutes. Add the reserved whole tomatoes and their liquid, and the sun-dried tomatoes, saffron, turmeric, harissa (if using), and the toasted coriander, fennel, and cumin seeds. Stir to combine.

5. Raise heat to high, add the reserved fish heads and bones, and cook, stirring frequently, until the

bones are opaque, about 5 minutes. Add the orange zest and the bouquet garni. Add enough water to just cover the bones, about 1 gallon. Cover and bring to a boil; skim the foam from the surface. Reduce heat; simmer, uncovered, 30 minutes. Pour the stock through a sieve into a large bowl; discard the solids. Return the liquid to the rinsed-out pot.

6. Bring a large stockpot of water to a boil over high heat. Prepare an ice-water bath. Add lobsters; once water returns to a boil, cook about 10 minutes. Remove pan from the heat. Transfer lobsters to the ice-water bath to stop the cooking. Drain.

7. Place 1 cup of the reserved stock in a large saucepan. Add 1 cup water. Cover and bring to a boil; add the mussels. Cover; cook until the mussels open, about 5 minutes. Remove from the heat. Discard any mussels that do not open.

8. Meanwhile, place the stockpot with the stock over medium-high heat; cover, and bring to a boil. Reduce heat to a simmer. Season with salt and pepper. Add the potatoes; cook until tender when pierced with the tip of a knife, about 20 minutes. Add the fish fillets; cook until opaque, and cooked through, about 5 minutes more. Remove the tails and claws from the lobsters (discard the bodies or reserve for other use). Crack open the claws and tail; add with the mussels to the pot; cook just long enough to warm. Serve hot with the rouille and toasted bread rounds.

rouille
MAKES ABOUT ¾ CUP

4   garlic cloves

¼   teaspoon kosher salt

2   large egg yolks

¼   teaspoon crumbled saffron threads

¼   teaspoon cayenne pepper

½   cup extra-virgin olive oil

Place garlic, salt, yolks, saffron, and cayenne in the bowl of a food processor; process until combined. With the machine running, slowing drizzle the olive oil through the feed tube until a thick paste forms, about 5 minutes.

new england clam chowder

SERVES 6 TO 8

- 6 strips bacon, cut into 1-inch pieces
- 2 celery stalks, strings removed, cut into ¼-inch dice
- 1 cup very small pearl onions, peeled
- 3 tablespoons all-purpose flour
- 2 cups unsalted clam juice
- 4 small (about 1 pound) Yukon gold potatoes, peeled and cut into ½-inch dice
- 2 dried bay leaves
- ¼ teaspoon freshly ground black pepper
- 5 large sprigs fresh thyme
- 8 pounds quahog clams, shucked, liquid reserved, and chopped into ½-inch pieces (2 pounds shucked clams)
- 2 ears fresh yellow corn, kernels shaved from the cob
- 2½ cups milk
- 2 tablespoons unsalted butter
- 1 teaspoon kosher salt
- 1 tablespoon sherry, optional

1. In a stockpot, cook bacon until crisp. Drain on a paper towel; discard all but 2 tablespoons of the rendered fat. Add celery and onions; cook, stirring occasionally, until translucent, 8 minutes.

2. Sprinkle the flour over the onion mixture; cook, stirring with a wooden spoon, about 3 minutes. Add the clam juice, ½ cup water, the potatoes, bay leaves, and ⅛ teaspoon pepper; cover; bring to a boil. Pick the thyme leaves from stems; add both to the pot. Reduce heat to medium low; simmer until the potatoes are almost tender when pierced with the tip of a knife, about 12 minutes.

3. Add the clams and reserved liquid, cover, and cook 4 minutes over medium heat. Add the corn, cover, and cook about 5 minutes. Add the milk and butter; cook until the butter melts, 5 minutes. Remove the bay leaves and thyme stems; add ⅛ teaspoon pepper and 1 teaspoon salt.

4. Divide soup among bowls, drizzle with the sherry, and garnish with crumbled bacon. Serve.

shrimp and scallop stew

SERVES 4

The chopped Italian tomatoes that come in cartons have the best consistency for this recipe, but canned tomatoes may also be used. Serve this stew over plain white rice or Couscous Pilaf (page 206) made with Israeli couscous.

- 2 tablespoons olive oil
- 2 large leeks, white and light-green parts, cut into ½-inch dice, well washed (see page 646)
- 3 garlic cloves, minced
- ½ jalapeño pepper, seeds and ribs removed, finely chopped (about 1 teaspoon)
- 1 medium carrot, cut into ¼-inch dice
- ¾ teaspoon ground cumin
- ⅛ teaspoon cayenne pepper
- ¼ teaspoon ground cinnamon
- 1½ teaspoons kosher salt
- 1½ cups chopped tomatoes, with juice
- 1 cup dry white wine
- 12 ounces (about 24) medium shrimp, peeled and deveined, tails intact
- 12 ounces sea scallops or large bay scallops, muscle removed
- 3 tablespoons coarsely chopped fresh cilantro leaves

1. In a stockpot, heat the oil over medium heat. Add the leeks and garlic; cook, stirring, until translucent, about 8 minutes. Add the jalapeño, carrots, cumin, cayenne, cinnamon, and salt; reduce heat to medium low, and cook until the carrots are almost tender, about 5 minutes. Add the tomatoes, wine, and 1 cup of water. Bring to a boil, and reduce heat to medium; cook 5 minutes.

2. Stir in the shrimp and the scallops; cook until opaque and cooked through, 3 to 5 minutes. Remove from the heat; add the cilantro. Serve hot.

gazpacho with shrimp and mussels

SERVES 8 TO 10

Sweet shrimp and plump mussels may not be traditional gazpacho ingredients, but they turn this spicy tomato-based soup into a hearty meal. You can also chill the tomato purée in the freezer for about an hour before serving so that it becomes slightly slushy.

- 10 *beefsteak tomatoes (about 5 pounds)*
- 1 *small garlic clove*
- 2 *small fresh jalapeño peppers, seeds and ribs removed*
- *Juice of 4 limes*
- 1½ *teaspoons kosher salt*
- ¼ *teaspoon freshly ground black pepper*
- 1 *shallot, minced*
- 1 *cup dry white wine*
- 8 *ounces mussels, scrubbed, debearded, and washed clean*
- 8 *ounces medium shrimp, peeled and deveined*
- 8 *ounces yellow cherry tomatoes*
- 2 *Kirby cucumbers, peeled, seeded, finely chopped*
- 1 *small red onion, finely chopped*
- ½ *cup loosely packed fresh cilantro leaves, finely chopped*

1. Cover and bring a large pot of water to a boil. Prepare an ice-water bath. Using a paring knife, score the nonstem end of each tomato with a shallow "x." Blanch the tomatoes in boiling water for 30 seconds. With a slotted spoon, transfer the tomatoes to the ice-water bath. Peel and halve the tomatoes. Remove and discard most of the seeds, without wasting the pulp.

2. Place the tomatoes in a blender, and add the garlic and half of 1 jalapeño. Blend the mixture, working in batches if necessary, until smooth. Season the mixture with the lime juice, 1½ teaspoons salt, and ¼ teaspoon pepper. Transfer to the refrigerator, and chill.

3. Meanwhile, combine the shallot, white wine, and 2 cups water in a large skillet. Bring the mixture to a boil, and add the mussels. Cover the skillet, and let the mussels cook until the shells open, about 5 minutes. Using a slotted spoon, transfer the mussels from the skillet to a bowl. (Discard any that have not opened.) Allow the mussels to cool slightly, cover with plastic wrap, and refrigerate.

4. Return the skillet to the heat, and bring to a simmer. Add the shrimp, and poach until the shrimp are pink and cooked through, about 2 minutes. Transfer the shrimp from the poaching liquid to a bowl, let cool slightly, and refrigerate.

5. Dice the remaining 1½ jalapeños. Slice the yellow cherry tomatoes in half. Season the chilled soup with salt and pepper. Stir in the chopped jalapeños, cucumbers, red onion, and sliced cherry tomatoes. Ladle the soup into bowls. Divide the chilled seafood among bowls. Sprinkle each bowl with chopped cilantro, and serve chilled.

shrimp and fennel noodle soup

SERVES 4

Soba noodles are available in health-food stores and Asian markets. Linguine can be substituted.

- 3 tablespoons sherry or rice wine
- 1 tablespoon fresh lemon juice
- 2 tablespoons low-sodium soy sauce
- 1 large garlic clove, minced
- ½ fresh jalapeño pepper, seeds and ribs removed, minced
- ½ teaspoon freshly grated ginger
- 1 teaspoon homemade Chinese Five-Spice Powder (page 633) or prepared
- 16 medium shrimp (about 8 ounces), peeled and deveined
- 4 ounces dry soba noodles
- 2 teaspoons peanut oil
- 1 medium yellow onion
- 1 fennel bulb, halved, cored, and thinly sliced (about 1 pound)
- 5 cups Homemade Chicken Stock (page 624), or low-sodium store-bought chicken broth, skimmed of fat
- 1 cup thinly sliced Napa cabbage
- 1 red bell pepper, seeds and ribs removed, sliced into ¼-inch strips
- 2 tablespoons snipped chives

1. In a bowl, whisk sherry, lemon juice, soy sauce, garlic, jalapeño, ginger, and spices. Add shrimp; toss to coat. Cover with plastic; marinate at room temperature for 30 minutes or in the refrigerator for up to 4 hours. Cook noodles in a pot of boiling water, according to package directions. Drain, and set aside.

2. In a skillet, heat oil over medium-high heat. Add onion and fennel; stir-fry until just wilted, about 2 minutes. Add shrimp and marinade; stir-fry until shrimp are pink, 2 to 3 minutes. Add stock; bring to a boil. Reduce heat to low; simmer 1 to 2 minutes. Add cabbage, noodles, and pepper; cook until hot. Divide among bowls; garnish with chives. Serve.

FIT TO EAT RECIPE PER SERVING: 226 CALORIES, 5 G TOTAL FAT, 89 MG CHOLESTEROL, 25 G CARBOHYDRATE, 1126 MG SODIUM, 21 G PROTEIN, 3 G DIETARY FIBER

chilled bloody mary soup with crabmeat

SERVES 8 TO 10

A cold soup is always a refreshing first course on a hot day; this one doesn't require any time on the stove.

- 6 tomatoes
- 4 large red bell peppers, seeds and ribs removed
- 2 large green bell peppers, seeds and ribs removed
- 2 cucumbers, peeled and seeded
- 3 celery stalks, strings removed
- 1 small garlic clove
- 1 red onion
- 3 tablespoons extra-virgin olive oil
  Juice of 2 limes, or to taste
- ¼ cup Worcestershire sauce
  Hot red-pepper sauce, to taste
- 2 tablespoons freshly grated horseradish, or to taste, plus more for garnish
- ½ cup (4 ounces) vodka, optional
  Kosher salt and freshly ground black pepper
- 1 pound jumbo lump crabmeat, picked over for shells and cartilage

1. Cut the tomatoes, peppers, cucumbers, celery, garlic, and onion into large chunks. Working in batches, purée the vegetables in a blender or in the bowl of a food processor, adding some olive oil to each batch.

2. Strain the puréed vegetables through a fine sieve or a cheesecloth-lined strainer into a large bowl. (This will remove the skins and seeds.)

3. Stir in the lime juice, Worcestershire sauce, hot sauce, horseradish, and vodka, if using, and season with salt and pepper. Cover with plastic wrap, and chill at least 2 hours, or overnight. Before serving, taste and adjust seasoning. The amount of lime juice needed will depend on the acidity of the tomatoes.

4. Ladle the soup into bowls, and place about ¼ cup of crabmeat in the center of each bowl. Garnish with fresh horseradish, if desired. Serve chilled.

salads

....

mixed chicories with honey vinaigrette

SERVES 4

If you prefer the bitter flavor of the greens, adjust the sweetness of the vinaigrette by gradually adding the honey to taste.

- 1 tablespoon plus 1½ teaspoons fresh lemon juice
- 1½ teaspoons sherry vinegar
- 1 tablespoon honey
- ¼ cup plus 1½ teaspoons extra-virgin olive oil
- ½ teaspoon kosher salt, plus more for seasoning
- ¼ teaspoon freshly ground black pepper, plus more for seasoning
- 1 teaspoon anise seed
- 1 small (about 8 ounces) head escarole
- 1 head (about 6 ounces) radicchio
- 1 small (about 4 ounces) red onion, thinly sliced
- 1 medium (about 9 ounces) fennel bulb, trimmed and cut into ½-inch dice

1. Combine the lemon juice, vinegar, and honey in a small bowl. Whisk in the olive oil, ½ teaspoon salt, ¼ teaspoon pepper, and anise seed. Set aside.

2. Remove the tough outer leaves from the escarole and the radicchio, and discard. Slice escarole into ¼-inch strips. Tear radicchio into bite-size pieces. Combine escarole, radicchio, red onion, and fennel in a serving bowl; add vinaigrette; toss well. Season with salt and pepper, and serve.

frisée, orange, and toasted hazelnut salad

SERVES 4

Let the nuts cool completely before chopping them.

- 2 tablespoons fresh orange juice
- 1 tablespoon white balsamic or white-wine vinegar
- ¼ teaspoon grated orange zest
- ⅛ teaspoon ground cardamom
- ⅛ teaspoon ground ginger
- ½ teaspoon whole mustard seeds
  Kosher salt and freshly ground black pepper to taste
- 3 tablespoons extra-virgin olive oil
- 2 seedless oranges, peel and pith removed
- 1 medium head frisée
- ¼ cup toasted hazelnuts (see page 644), roughly chopped

1. In a medium bowl, whisk together the orange juice, vinegar, zest, cardamom, ginger, mustard seeds, salt, and pepper. Slowly whisk in the olive oil until combined, and set aside.

2. Slice the oranges thinly, crosswise, and arrange on four salad plates; set aside. Place the frisée in a large bowl, and toss with the dressing. Divide the frisée among the plates, and sprinkle with the chopped hazelnuts. Serve immediately.

REMOVING THE PEEL AND PITH FROM CITRUS

To remove the peel and pith from citrus fruit, first slice off the stem and flower end. Place the fruit on a work surface, cut-side down, and use a sharp knife to cut away the white and peel in a single curved motion, from end to end.

bacon, lettuce, and tomato salad

SERVES 6

Use a variety of greens in this easy-to-assemble salad inspired by the classic sandwich. Prepare the dressing as the bacon cooks.

- 12 strips (about 8 ounces) ¼-inch thick-cut bacon
- 1½ bunches lettuce, such as romaine, Bibb, or green oakleaf
- ½ cup Avocado Dressing (page 163)
- 1 pound tomatoes, preferably red and yellow
- ½ pint cherry tomatoes
  Kosher salt and freshly ground black pepper

1. Preheat the oven to 425°F. Arrange the bacon strips on a wire rack over a baking pan. Place the pan in the oven until the bacon is golden brown and crisp, about 20 minutes. Remove from the oven, being careful of the bacon fat that has collected under the rack, and set aside.

2. Arrange the lettuce in the bottom of a salad bowl; drizzle with half the avocado dressing. Cut the tomatoes into ¼-inch-thick slices; cut the cherry tomatoes, depending on size, in half. Arrange the tomato slices over the lettuce; scatter the cherry tomatoes over the tomato slices.

3. Arrange the whole bacon strips over the tomatoes. Drizzle with the remaining avocado dressing, season with salt and pepper, and serve immediately.

. . . .

FROSTY SALAD PLATES

Icy-cool plates bring out the crispness—preserving the chill of the refrigerator right to the table. Place plates, stacked, in the fridge for at least an hour. Don't use the freezer, which could crack ceramics.

. . . .

endive and warm pear salad

SERVES 4

Sautéed pears wilt the greens ever so slightly in this satisfying winter salad.

- 2 Bartlett pears, ripe but firm
- 1 tablespoon plus 2 teaspoons extra-virgin olive oil
- 1 teaspoon honey
- ½ teaspoon dry mustard
- ½ teaspoon kosher salt, plus more for seasoning
- ⅛ teaspoon freshly ground black pepper, plus more for seasoning
- ½ medium red onion, thinly sliced into rings
- 2 heads Belgian endive, sliced crosswise into 1-inch pieces
- 1 bunch watercress, tough stems removed
- 4 ounces Stilton, Roquefort, or Maytag blue cheese, crumbled
- 1½ teaspoons red-wine vinegar
- 1 teaspoon Worcestershire sauce

1. Cut pears lengthwise into quarters. Peel, core, and cut each quarter into approximately 1-inch chunks; place in a bowl. Add 2 teaspoons olive oil, honey, dry mustard, salt, and pepper, and toss well.

2. Place a medium skillet over medium-high heat. Add the pears and onions; cook, shaking the skillet a few times, until the pears are golden brown and the onions are slightly wilted, about 3 minutes.

3. Transfer the pears, onions, and any juices to a bowl. Add the endive, watercress, cheese, the remaining tablespoon olive oil, the vinegar, and Worcestershire sauce, and toss together gently. Season with salt and pepper, and serve warm.

herb salad

SERVES 4

1½ cups lightly packed mixed fresh
    herb leaves, such as mint,
    flat-leaf parsley, basil, chervil,
    tarragon, and snipped chives

1 tablespoon plus 1 teaspoon extra-virgin
   olive oil

1 teaspoon red-wine vinegar
   Kosher salt and freshly ground
   black pepper

Combine the herbs, oil, and vinegar in a medium
bowl; toss to combine, and season with salt and pepper. Serve immediately.

spinach, egg, and bacon salad

SERVES 8

12 ounces slab bacon, cut into ¼-inch cubes

1 garlic clove, minced

1 small shallot, minced
   Juice of ½ lemon

1½ tablespoons sherry vinegar

¼ cup extra-virgin olive oil

1 tablespoon chopped fresh flat-leaf
   parsley

1 teaspoon kosher salt, plus more to taste

¼ teaspoon freshly ground black pepper,
   plus more to taste

2 pounds baby or flat-leaf spinach, washed

4 large hard-boiled eggs (see page 571),
   chopped

1. Cook the bacon in a heavy skillet over medium-high heat until golden brown and crisp, 6 to 8 minutes. Transfer the bacon to a plate lined with a double thickness of paper towels. Reserve 1 teaspoon of the bacon fat, and discard the rest.

2. Meanwhile, combine the garlic, shallot, lemon juice, and sherry vinegar in a small bowl. Whisk in the olive oil; add the parsley and the salt and pepper.

3. In a large bowl, toss together the spinach, cooked bacon, reserved warm bacon fat, the vinaigrette, and the chopped eggs. Season with salt and pepper, if necessary, and serve immediately.

winter salad

SERVES 4

Blood oranges are available at many grocery stores from late fall to spring. Their ruby-red juice and bright-orange wedges make an exquisite presentation.

2 blood oranges, peel and pith removed

1 small head (about 6 ounces) chicory,
   torn into small pieces

2 heads Belgian endive, sliced
   into ¼-inch-thick slivers

½ small red onion, thinly sliced

¼ cup oil-cured black olives, pitted and
   coarsely chopped

2 teaspoons extra-virgin olive oil

¼ teaspoon kosher salt

⅛ teaspoon freshly ground black pepper

1. Working over a bowl to catch the juices, use a paring knife to carefully slice between the sections and membranes of each orange; remove the segments whole. Place each segment in a separate large bowl as completed. Squeeze any remaining juice from the membranes into the bowl with the reserved juice, and set aside.

2. Add the chicory, endive, onion, and olives to the bowl with orange sections. Drizzle with olive oil; sprinkle with the salt and pepper. Pour reserved orange juice over salad, toss well, and serve.

GREEN SALAD ADD-INS

*Spiced Nuts (page 100) and
pomegranate seeds*

Pear slices with crumbled blue cheese

Toasted pecans and jícama

Sliced red onion and oranges

Black olives, asparagus, and feta cheese

Edible flowers such as calendula, Johnny-jump-ups, and nasturtiums

classic caesar salad

SERVES 4 TO 6

If you prefer not to use the raw yolk in this recipe, substitute 1 tablespoon prepared mayonnaise. To make a version of the dressing that you can store, simply mince the garlic and anchovies, and place with the salt, pepper, lemon juice, Worcestershire, mustard, egg, and olive oil in a jar. Screw the lid on the jar tightly, and shake to combine. Shake the jar before each use. Store, refrigerated, up to 2 days. The croutons are best made no more than half an hour before assembling the salad.

for the croutons

- 2 tablespoons unsalted butter, melted
- 2 tablespoons extra-virgin olive oil
- 1 8- to 10-ounce loaf rustic Italian bread, crusts removed, cut into ¾-inch cubes
- 2 teaspoons kosher salt
- ¾ teaspoon ground cayenne pepper
- ½ teaspoon freshly ground black pepper

for the salad

- 2 garlic cloves
- 4 anchovy fillets
- 1 teaspoon kosher salt
- 1 teaspoon freshly ground black pepper
- 1 tablespoon fresh lemon juice
- 1 teaspoon Worcestershire sauce
- ½ teaspoon Dijon mustard
- 1 large egg yolk
- ⅓ cup extra-virgin olive oil
- 2 10-ounce heads romaine lettuce, outer leaves discarded, inner leaves washed and dried
- 1 cup freshly grated Parmesan or Romano cheese, or 2½ ounces shaved with a vegetable peeler

1. Preheat the oven to 450°F. Combine the butter and olive oil in a large bowl. Add the bread, and toss until coated. Sprinkle with the salt, cayenne pepper, and black pepper; toss until evenly coated. Spread the bread in a single layer on a 12 x 17-inch baking pan. Bake until the croutons are golden, about 10 minutes. Set aside until needed.

2. Place the garlic, anchovy fillets, and salt in a wooden salad bowl. Using two dinner forks, mash the garlic and anchovies into a paste. Using one fork, whisk in the pepper, lemon juice, Worcestershire, mustard, and egg yolk. Whisk in the olive oil.

3. Chop the romaine leaves into 1- to 1½-inch pieces. Add the croutons, romaine, and cheese to the bowl, and toss well. Serve immediately.

NOTE *Raw eggs should not be used in food prepared for pregnant women, babies, young children, or anyone whose health is compromised.*

crunchy summer salad with oven-dried cherries

SERVES 6

- 1 golden or red beet, trimmed and scrubbed, skin on
- 1 small bulb fennel, trimmed
- 3 yellow cherries, stemmed and pitted
- 1 tablespoon sherry vinegar
- 1½ tablespoons crème fraîche
- ½ teaspoon Dijon mustard
- 1 teaspoon kosher salt
- ⅛ teaspoon freshly ground black pepper
- 2 tablespoons extra-virgin olive oil
- ¼ cup pine nuts, toasted (see page 644)
- 2 heads Belgian endive, cut in matchsticks lengthwise
- 2 small ears fresh corn, kernels shaved from the cob
- 1 small yellow bell pepper, seeds and ribs removed, cut into ¼-inch dice
- 5 cups (4 ounces) mâche or other baby-lettuce leaves
- ¾ cup Oven-Dried Cherries (page 619)

1. Using a mandoline, slice the beet and the fennel into very thin slices. In the bowl of a food processor or blender, purée the yellow cherries, vinegar, crème fraîche, mustard, salt, and black pepper. Transfer the purée to a medium bowl. Whisk in the olive oil, and set the dressing aside.

2. In a large serving dish, combine toasted pine nuts, endive, corn, pepper, mâche, and oven-dried cherries. Drizzle dressing over salad; toss. Serve.

escarole and roasted vegetable salad

SERVES 6

1   bunch beets, stalks removed, peeled and cut into ½-inch-thick wedges

6   small red potatoes, cut into ½-inch-thick wedges

2   cups cauliflower florets (from 1 small head)

1   small red onion, cut into ¼-inch-thick rounds

2   carrots, cut into ¼-inch rounds

1   yellow or red bell pepper, seeds and ribs removed, cut into ½-inch dice

1   tablespoon extra-virgin olive oil

½   teaspoon kosher salt

¼   teaspoon freshly ground black pepper

1   head escarole, roughly chopped

¼   cup red-wine vinegar

½   cup apple cider

1. Preheat the oven to 425°F. In a large roasting pan, combine the beets, potatoes, cauliflower, onion, carrots, bell pepper, olive oil, salt, and black pepper; stir to combine. Roast until the vegetables are tender and golden brown, stirring occasionally, about 50 minutes. Transfer the vegetables to a large bowl. Add the escarole; toss.

2. Place the pan over high heat; add the vinegar. Using a wooden spoon, scrape up any brown bits on the bottom. Add the cider; cook until the liquid has reduced by two-thirds. Add the cider mixture to the roasted vegetables. Toss, and serve.

FIT TO EAT RECIPE PER SERVING: 188 CALORIES, 3 G FAT, 0 MG CHOLESTEROL, 39 G CARBOHYDRATE, 262 MG SODIUM, 5 G PROTEIN, 6 G DIETARY FIBER

shaved beet salad

SERVES 6

8   ounces beets, such as Chioggia, Golden Globe, or Little Ball, trimmed and scrubbed

1   tablespoon balsamic vinegar

3   tablespoons extra-virgin olive oil
    Kosher salt and freshly ground black pepper

2   bunches arugula (about 10 ounces), stems removed

Using a mandoline or a sharp knife, slice beets as thinly as possible into nearly translucent rounds. Transfer beets to a bowl; drizzle with vinegar and oil; season with salt and pepper. Toss to combine. Divide arugula among serving plates; spoon beets over arugula. Drizzle greens with any dressing that has collected in the bowl. Serve.

chunky avocado salad

SERVES 12

6   avocados, peeled and pitted (page 647)

2   navel oranges, peel and pith removed

3   Kirby or small cucumbers, peeled, seeded, and cut into ½-inch dice

6   ounces cherry or pear tomatoes, halved

¼   cup coarsely chopped fresh cilantro leaves, plus more for garnish

7   red pearl onions, peeled, cut into rounds

½   cup Guava Vinaigrette (page 163) or other fruity vinaigrette

1. Using a soupspoon, scoop out the avocado flesh in one piece; reserve the shell. Cut the flesh into ½-inch dice; set aside. Repeat with the other avocados. Working over a bowl to catch the juices, use a paring knife to carefully slice between the sections and membranes of each orange; remove the segments whole. Place each segment in the bowl.

2. Add the cucumbers, three-quarters of the tomatoes, the cilantro, onions, and vinaigrette to the oranges; toss. Add the avocado; gently toss. Divide the salad among the avocado shells. Garnish with the cilantro and remaining tomatoes. Serve.

raw artichoke salad

SERVES 4

Baby artichokes are used in this recipe because they have no choke and are entirely edible. This salad tastes best if served right after it is made.

- 12 anchovy fillets
- 1 large garlic clove
- 1 large egg
- ½ cup extra-virgin olive oil
- ½ cup fresh lemon juice (3 lemons)
  Freshly ground black pepper
- 1 small head frisée
- 10 baby artichokes

1. Use a mortar and pestle or a food processor to combine anchovies and garlic into a paste. Add egg, and combine. Drizzle in oil, a few drops at a time at first, whisking until emulsified. Whisk in 2 tablespoons lemon juice. Season with pepper.

2. Coarsely chop or tear the frisée; set aside. Make a small bowl of acidulated water with the remaining lemon juice and water. Trim the artichokes; leave stems on, and remove the tough outer leaves, leaving only the pale-green edible ones. Pare the base and stem; cut off the top of the artichokes; place in the lemon water.

3. Thinly slice the artichokes lengthwise on a mandoline, or by hand; immediately place in the lemon water. When ready to combine, drain well; mix with the frisée. Toss with the dressing, and season with pepper. Serve.

NOTE *Raw eggs should not be used in food prepared for pregnant women, babies, young children, or anyone whose health is compromised.*

beet, endive, and orange salad

SERVES 6

- 1½ tablespoons canola oil, plus more for brushing
- 6 large beets (about 2 pounds), trimmed and scrubbed
- 6 navel oranges, peel and pith removed
- 1 tablespoon red-wine vinegar
- ½ teaspoon kosher salt
- ½ teaspoon freshly ground black pepper
- 1 cup fresh flat-leaf parsley, coarsely chopped
- 3 heads Bibb lettuce (8 ounces), or 1 head Boston lettuce, cut into ½-inch strips
- 2 heads Belgian endive (8 ounces), cut into ½-inch pieces
- 4 ounces ricotta salata, or feta cheese, crumbled

1. Preheat the oven to 425°F. Brush an 8 x 8-inch baking pan with oil, and add the beets; cover with aluminum foil. Transfer pan to the oven; roast until tender when pierced with the tip of a knife, about 1 hour, depending on beets' size. Allow beets to cool, remove skins, and cut into ¾-inch chunks, reserving half a peeled beet for the vinaigrette.

2. Working over a bowl, use a paring knife to slice between sections and membranes of each orange; remove segments whole. Place each segment in the bowl as completed. Squeeze any remaining juice from the membranes before discarding. Drain the segments, and set aside, reserving ¼ cup of juice.

3. Place the reserved half beet, the reserved orange juice, the vinegar, salt, and pepper in a blender; purée until smooth. With the machine running, add the 1½ tablespoons canola oil, and process until combined. Stir in 2 tablespoons parsley.

4. Place lettuce, endive, beets, oranges, and remaining parsley in a bowl. Add vinaigrette; toss. Garnish with ricotta salata; serve.

FIT TO EAT RECIPE PER SERVING: 157 CALORIES, 6 G FAT, 8 MG CHOLESTEROL, 32 G CARBOHYDRATE, 321 MG SODIUM, 11 G PROTEIN, 3 G DIETARY FIBER

arugula with roasted beets and grilled baby leeks

SERVES 8 TO 10

If available, use a mixture of beets, such as ruby, ivory, golden, and Chioggia.

- 2 pounds (16 small) beets, trimmed and scrubbed
- ¼ cup extra-virgin olive oil
- 1½ teaspoons kosher salt
- ⅜ teaspoon freshly ground black pepper
- 1 teaspoon grated orange zest
- 2 teaspoons fresh orange juice
- 1 teaspoon grated lemon zest
- 1 teaspoon fresh lemon juice
- 2 tablespoons red-wine vinegar
- 1 tablespoon sherry vinegar
- ½ small shallot, minced
- 1 tablespoon walnut oil
- 16 baby leeks (2 to 3 ounces each) or scallions, white and pale-green parts, well washed (see page 646)
- 1 pound arugula, stems removed

1. Preheat the oven to 425°F. Cut the larger beets (more than 2 ounces) in half. Toss with 1 tablespoon olive oil, ½ teaspoon salt, and ⅛ teaspoon pepper. Enclose the beets in a packet of aluminum foil, and roast until they are easily pierced with the tip of a knife, about 1 hour. When cool enough to handle, peel the beets, and slice into ¼-inch rounds. Set aside in a bowl.

2. Meanwhile, prepare the vinaigrette. In a medium bowl, combine the orange zest and juice, lemon zest and juice, both vinegars, the shallot, ¾ teaspoon salt, and ⅛ teaspoon pepper. Gradually whisk in 2 tablespoons olive oil and the walnut oil. Add half the vinaigrette to the roasted beets; toss to coat, and set aside.

3. Cover and bring a large pot of salted water to a boil. Heat a grill pan or the broiler to medium hot. Add the leeks to the boiling water, and cook for 5 minutes. Drain and transfer to a small bowl. Let the leeks cool slightly, then add 1 tablespoon olive oil, ¼ teaspoon salt, and ⅛ teaspoon pepper. Cook the leeks on the grill for several minutes or under the broiler for 3 minutes on each side. Toss the grilled leeks with the remaining half of the vinaigrette.

4. Place the arugula on a large serving platter. Arrange the beets and leeks, with the vinaigrette, over the arugula; serve immediately.

shaved fennel salad

SERVES 4

Pecorino is a dry, aged sheep's-milk cheese. Its sharp taste makes it a perfect addition to raw salads and vegetables.

- 2 medium fennel bulbs (about 2 pounds total), trimmed
- 2 tablespoons extra-virgin olive oil
  Juice of 1 lemon
- 1½ ounces pecorino cheese
  Kosher salt and freshly ground black pepper

1. Using a mandoline, thinly shave the fennel. Toss in a medium bowl with the olive oil and lemon juice.

2. Using a vegetable peeler, shave the pecorino over the fennel. Season with salt and pepper, and toss gently. Serve.

warm mushroom salad with pistou vinaigrette

SERVES 4

Classic pistou is a mixture of crushed basil, garlic, and olive oil, but it's good with almost any other herb, such as parsley, thyme, or oregano.

- 1 pound mixed mushrooms, such as shiitake and oyster, wiped clean, trimmed, cut into 1½-inch pieces
- ¼ cup dry white wine
- ¼ cup olive oil
  Kosher salt and freshly ground black pepper
- 2 small garlic cloves
- ¼ cup grated pecorino cheese, plus shavings for garnish
- 1¼ cups loosely packed fresh herbs, such as basil, parsley, thyme, or oregano, coarsely chopped
- 6 ounces mixed lettuce greens
- 1 tablespoon sherry vinegar

1. Preheat the oven to 350°F. Arrange the mushrooms on a piece of aluminum foil; sprinkle with the wine, 3 tablespoons oil, and salt and pepper to taste. Slice 1 garlic clove; scatter over the mushrooms. Fold the foil to create a loose package. Bake until the mushrooms are tender when pierced with the tip of a knife, 15 to 20 minutes. Transfer to a large bowl.

2. Finely chop the remaining garlic clove; add to the bowl along with the pecorino and chopped herbs. Toss, and season with salt and pepper.

3. Place the greens in a bowl; season with the remaining tablespoon of oil, the salt, pepper, and vinegar. Arrange the greens on serving plates, and top with the warm mushroom mixture. Garnish with the shavings of pecorino. Serve.

crudite salad à la grecque

SERVES 8

This salad is best prepared several hours in advance and served at room temperature.

- 4 shallots, minced
- 1½ cups extra-virgin olive oil
- 1 tablespoon dried oregano
- 1 large (2½ pounds) head cauliflower
- 1 large (1½ pounds) head broccoli
- 24 white mushrooms, wiped clean, stemmed
- 6 celery stalks, strings removed
- 6 carrots
- 24 small (about 10 ounces) radishes
  Kosher salt and freshly ground black pepper
- 1 cup fresh lemon juice (6 lemons)

1. Combine the shallots, olive oil, and dried oregano in a small saucepan, and place over medium-low heat. Let cook until the shallots are translucent and very soft, about 20 minutes. If the oil starts to sputter or brown, reduce heat.

2. Meanwhile, cut the vegetables, and set each aside in its own bowl: Cut the cauliflower and broccoli into bite-size florets. Cut the mushroom stems in half. Slice each celery stalk and carrot into 3-inch-long pieces, and slice each piece into long, thin matchsticks. Slice the larger radishes in half, keeping the smaller ones whole.

3. Season each bowl of vegetables with salt and pepper. Add the lemon juice to the shallots and warm oil; stir to combine. Pour just less than ⅛ of the mixture over each bowl of vegetables, keeping in mind that the mushrooms will absorb the dressing and require a little more than the other vegetables. Toss each bowl of vegetables; let stand for between 1 and 4 hours. Arrange the vegetables on a serving platter, and serve.

winter crudité salad

SERVES 4

Choose celeriac, also known as celery root, that is heavy for its size.

½ teaspoon Dijon mustard
1½ teaspoons sherry vinegar
1½ tablespoons extra-virgin olive oil
  Kosher salt and freshly ground black pepper
1 medium (about 12 ounces) celeriac
4 carrots, cut into 2½-inch matchsticks
8 red radishes, thinly sliced

1. In a bowl, combine mustard and vinegar. Whisk in oil until creamy. Season with salt and pepper.

2. Peel celeriac with a sharp knife. Cut root in half crosswise; slice each half as thinly as possible. Keep slices in a bowl of cold water until needed. Drain and pat dry when ready to toss with vinaigrette.

3. Place the vegetables in separate bowls; season with salt and pepper and toss. Add 1½ teaspoons dressing to each bowl, and toss again. Arrange vegetables in piles on salad plates. Serve.

flageolet and frisée salad

SERVES 4

Dried flageolets, small French pale-green to white kidney beans, are available in most grocery stores. Use navy beans if you can't find them.

⅔ cup dried flageolet beans
3 tablespoons extra-virgin olive oil
15 anchovy fillets
3 tablespoons fresh lemon juice
1 large garlic clove, minced
¼ teaspoon freshly ground black pepper
1 tablespoon fresh flat-leaf parsley, roughly chopped
1 small head frisée, roughly chopped

1. Pick over the dried beans, discarding any stones or broken beans, and rinse. Place in a large saucepan, cover with cold water by 2 inches, and bring to a boil over high heat. Cover and remove from the heat, and let stand 1 hour. Drain the beans, and place them in a medium saucepan with 1 quart fresh water. Cover and bring to a boil, reduce to a simmer, and cook the beans, uncovered, until tender, 50 minutes to 1 hour. Rinse the beans under cold water; drain, and set aside.

2. Place the olive oil, anchovy fillets, lemon juice, garlic, and pepper in the bowl of a food processor. Pulse until the fillets are finely chopped, about 5 seconds. Place the parsley, frisée, beans, and the anchovy dressing in a medium bowl, and toss to combine. Serve immediately.

endive spears with lobster, avocado, and grapefruit

SERVES 10 TO 12

Shaped perfectly for fillings and sturdy enough to be picked up, endive spears are an excellent base for hors d'oeuvres. These are especially nice to serve at a bridal- or baby-shower luncheon. Crab or shrimp may be substituted for lobster.

1 pink grapefruit, peel and pith removed
1 avocado, peeled and pitted (see page 647)
  Juice of 1 lemon
3 ounces cooked lobster meat
4 heads Belgian endive (about 8 ounces total)
  Kosher salt and freshly ground black pepper
3 sprigs fresh tarragon

1. Working over a bowl to catch the juices, use a paring knife to slice between the sections and membranes of each grapefruit; remove the segments whole. Place each segment in the bowl. Cut each segment in half crosswise. Set aside.

2. Cut avocado into ⅛-inch-thick slices; cut the slices into 1-inch lengths. Toss in a large bowl with the lemon juice, and set aside.

3. Cut the lobster into bite-size pieces; set aside.

4. Trim the bottom from each endive; separate the spears. Place a grapefruit section on top of each endive spear. Top each with a piece of avocado, then a piece of lobster. Season with salt and pepper; garnish with the tarragon. Repeat with the remaining ingredients. Serve immediately.

avocado and lobster cocktail with herb mayonnaise

SERVES 4

The lobster can be cooked ahead of time, but the avocado should be prepared just before serving to prevent it from turning brown.

- 2 live lobsters (1½ pounds each)
- 1 large egg yolk
- 1 tablespoon fresh lemon juice
- ½ teaspoon Dijon mustard
- ¾ cup canola oil
- ¾ cup loosely packed picked herbs, such as flat-leaf parsley, dill, chervil, and tarragon, finely chopped

   Kosher salt and freshly ground black pepper
- 2 avocados, peeled and pitted (see page 647)
- ¼ ounce (2 teaspoons) golden caviar, optional

1. Prepare an ice-water bath. Cover and bring a large pot of water to a boil. Add the lobsters, cover, and let the water return to a boil. Cook the lobsters, covered, about 10 minutes. Remove the lobsters from the water, and submerge in the ice-water bath. Transfer the lobsters to a colander, drain, and keep refrigerated.

2. In a small bowl, whisk together the egg yolk, lemon juice, and mustard. Slowly add the canola oil in a steady stream, whisking, until all the oil is incorporated and the mayonnaise is thick and creamy. Add the herbs to the mayonnaise, and season with salt and pepper. Cover with plastic wrap; refrigerate until needed.

3. Using lobster crackers and scissors, carefully remove the lobster meat from the tail, claws, and knuckles. Cut the lobster meat into bite-size pieces; arrange in four serving dishes.

4. Using a standard-size melon baller, scoop out the avocado flesh, and scatter over the lobster. Serve each cocktail with the herb mayonnaise and ½ teaspoon of golden caviar, if using.

NOTE *Raw eggs should not be used in food prepared for pregnant women, babies, young children, the elderly, or anyone whose health is compromised.*

grapefruit and avocado salad with spicy lime vinaigrette

SERVES 10 TO 12

- 4 avocados, peeled and pitted (see page 647)
- ½ cup fresh lime juice (about 3 limes)
- 4 ruby-red grapefruit, peel and pith removed
- 1 tablespoon honey
- ½ cup extra-virgin olive oil
- ½ teaspoon crushed red-pepper flakes

   Kosher salt and freshly ground black pepper
- 3 heads (about 2 pounds) red-leaf lettuce

1. Cut the avocados into 1-inch pieces; toss in a bowl with ¼ cup of the lime juice.

2. Slice the grapefruit flesh crosswise into ¼-inch-thick rounds; place in a separate bowl.

3. Make the vinaigrette: Combine the remaining ¼ cup lime juice and the honey in a small bowl. Gradually whisk in the olive oil and red-pepper flakes; season with salt and pepper.

4. Place the lettuce in a serving bowl. Season with salt and pepper; drizzle with a quarter of the vinaigrette. Toss well.

5. Drizzle the avocado pieces with three-quarters of the remaining vinaigrette. Season with salt and pepper; toss well. Scatter the avocado and grapefruit slices over the greens; drizzle the salad with the remaining vinaigrette. Serve.

winter squash salad
with goat cheese "truffles"

SERVES 8 TO 10

Use another peppery green, such as mustard greens, if dandelions are not in season.

- 2 11-ounce logs fresh goat cheese
- 1 cup dark-green olives, pitted, finely chopped
- 1 cup kalamata olives, pitted, finely chopped
- 1 bunch fresh flat-leaf parsley, leaves removed and finely chopped

  Kosher salt
- 2 medium (about 4 pounds) butternut squash, peeled, seeded, and cut into ¾-inch dice
- 2 tablespoons balsamic vinegar
- 2 scallions, white and pale-green parts, thinly sliced on a diagonal
- 1½ teaspoons whole black or brown mustard seeds

  Freshly ground black pepper
- ¼ cup plus 2 tablespoons extra-virgin olive oil
- 1 pound dandelion or other bitter greens, long stems removed

1. Cut each goat-cheese log into 13 equal pieces, and roll into 1¼-inch balls.

2. Place the green olives in one bowl and the kalamata olives in another. Roll half of the goat-cheese balls in the green olives, pressing firmly to coat well. Roll the remaining balls in the kalamata olives, pressing firmly to coat well.

3. Spread the parsley out on a clean work surface, and roll all the balls in the parsley. Transfer the cheese truffles to a plate, and cover loosely with plastic wrap. Refrigerate the truffles until ready to serve.

4. In a medium stockpot, cover and bring 3 quarts salted water to a boil. Add the squash, and cook until tender when pierced with the tip of a knife, about 8 minutes. Drain the squash in a colander, and set aside.

5. In a medium bowl, combine the balsamic vinegar, scallions, and mustard seeds. Season with salt and pepper. Slowly whisk in the olive oil. Set the dressing aside.

6. When ready to serve, transfer the squash to a large bowl, and season with salt and pepper. Add half of the dressing; toss to combine. Arrange the greens on a serving platter, and arrange the squash salad over the top; the heat of the squash will wilt some of the greens. Drizzle the remaining dressing over the entire salad. Garnish with the chilled goat-cheese truffles. Serve.

watermelon salad with
red onion and black olives

SERVES 6

When the season calls for watermelon but the occasion requires something more formal than a simple slice, combine chunks of the ripest watermelon you can find with tangy onions and oil-cured olives.

- 1 8- to 10-pound yellow or red watermelon
- ½ red onion, sliced very thinly into rounds
- ¼ cup oil-cured black olives, pitted
- ½ cup loosely packed fresh cilantro leaves
- 1 tablespoon extra-virgin olive oil
- 2 teaspoons sherry vinegar
- ½ teaspoon kosher salt
- ⅛ teaspoon freshly ground black pepper

Cut watermelon flesh into 1½-inch chunks; remove seeds. Toss flesh with onion, olives, and cilantro. Drizzle with olive oil and vinegar, and sprinkle with salt and pepper.

warm plum salad with prosciutto and arugula

SERVES 4

Spoon the warm plums over the greens just before serving.

- 1 pound (about 8) small red plums
- ½ teaspoon kosher salt
- ½ teaspoon freshly ground black pepper
- 1 tablespoon fresh thyme leaves
- 2 tablespoons extra-virgin olive oil
- ½ cup dry white wine
- 2 tablespoons balsamic vinegar
- 1 small bunch arugula, stems removed
- 8 ounces thinly sliced prosciutto

1. Slice the plums in half, and remove the pits. Transfer the plum halves to a mixing bowl. Add the salt, pepper, and thyme.

2. Heat the olive oil in a large skillet over medium heat. Add the plum halves, cut-sides down, and cook, shaking the skillet often, until the plums release their juices but still hold together, about 5 minutes. Add the wine and vinegar; cook until the juice slightly thickens, about 2 minutes more.

3. Arrange the arugula in a mound on a serving platter. Drape the prosciutto over the arugula. Spoon the plums and sauce on top, and serve.

broccoli rabe, carrot, and radicchio salad

SERVES 4

Bittersweet best describes the combination of vegetables in this colorful salad—the peppery bite of broccoli rabe and radicchio is sweetened by carrots and honey.

- Kosher salt
- 1½ pounds broccoli rabe, tough stems removed, cut into 4-inch lengths
- 1 teaspoon fresh lemon juice
- 1 teaspoon sherry vinegar
- ½ teaspoon honey
- 1 teaspoon low-sodium soy sauce
- 1 tablespoon extra-virgin olive oil
- ⅛ teaspoon freshly ground black pepper
- 4 small carrots, sliced into thin strips using a vegetable peeler
- ¼ head of radicchio, thinly sliced crosswise to make about 1¼ cups

1. Prepare an ice-water bath. Cover and bring 3½ quarts salted water to a boil in a large pot. Add the broccoli rabe, and cook just until tender, about 1½ minutes. Drain and place in the ice-water bath. Drain again, and place on paper towels to absorb the remaining water.

2. In a small bowl, whisk together the lemon juice, vinegar, honey, soy sauce, and olive oil. Season with salt and pepper.

3. Combine the broccoli rabe, carrots, and radicchio in a medium bowl. Add the vinaigrette, toss well, and serve.

carrot, mint, and golden raisin salad

SERVES 4

- 1 pound large carrots
- 3 tablespoons golden raisins
- ⅔ cup fresh mint leaves, cut into ¼-inch strips
- 2 teaspoons fresh lemon juice
- 1 tablespoon extra-virgin olive oil
  Kosher salt and freshly ground black pepper

Grate the carrots on the large holes of a box grater, or with a food processor using the grater blade. In a medium bowl, combine the grated carrots with the golden raisins, mint, lemon juice, and olive oil. Season with salt and pepper, and toss to combine well. Serve.

cucumber mint salad

SERVES 4

If you cannot find seedless cucumbers, Kirbys can be used instead.

- 1 large seedless cucumber
- 2 tablespoons coarsely chopped fresh mint leaves
- 1 medium shallot, minced
- 2 teaspoons champagne or white-wine vinegar
- 1 tablespoon extra-virgin olive oil
  Kosher salt and freshly ground black pepper

Use a vegetable peeler to remove alternating strips of cucumber peel, creating white and green stripes. Halve the cucumber lengthwise, and scrape out the seeds, if necessary. Cut each half into ⅛-inch-thick slices, and place in a bowl. Add the mint, shallot, vinegar, and olive oil, and season with salt and pepper. Toss to combine, and serve.

cucumber, peanut, and coconut salad

SERVES 8

Deputy Creative Director Ayesha Patel grew up eating this salad in her native India; the ingredients are staples in an Indian kitchen. Let the salad sit at room temperature for 30 minutes to allow the flavors to develop. For black mustard seeds, see Food Sources, page 648.

- 1½ cups dry-roasted peanuts
- 1 unwaxed, seedless cucumber, unpeeled, cut into ¼-inch pieces
  Kosher salt
- 1 small coconut, cracked open, shell removed, liquid discarded
- 3 tablespoons canola oil
- 1½ tablespoons black mustard seeds
- ¼ cup fresh lime juice
- ½ cup chopped fresh cilantro

1. Toast the peanuts in a dry, heavy skillet over medium-high heat until slightly charred, about 5 minutes, turning them to keep from burning. Transfer the nuts to a cutting board; when cool enough to handle, roughly chop them.

2. Combine the cucumber and the nuts in a medium bowl. Sprinkle with salt to taste; set aside.

3. Use a vegetable peeler to remove the thin brown skin from each piece of coconut. Grate the coconut flesh on the medium holes of a box grater to yield about 1 cup. Combine with the cucumber mixture.

4. Heat the oil in a very small skillet over medium-high heat until very hot. Add the mustard seeds; let fry until they pop, about 5 seconds. Immediately pour all of the oil and the seeds over the cucumber mixture. Toss. Add the lime juice and cilantro; season with salt, and serve immediately.

jícama and jerusalem artichoke salad
SERVES 6 TO 8

6 radishes, trimmed

3 medium (about 8 ounces) Jerusalem artichokes

8 spring onions or scallions, washed, cut into ¼-inch pieces

1 medium (about 1½ pounds) jícama, peeled, cut into 2-inch matchsticks

½ bunch fresh watercress, stems removed

18 to 24 garlic-mustard green leaves or arugula, cut crosswise into thin strips

1 green bell pepper, seeds and ribs removed, cut into ¼-inch dice

1 red bell pepper, seeds and ribs removed, cut into ¼-inch dice

1½ tablespoons red-wine vinegar

¼ teaspoon kosher salt

Freshly ground black pepper

1 teaspoon chopped fresh thyme, or ½ teaspoon dried

¼ cup extra-virgin olive oil

1. If radishes are 1 ounce each or larger, cut them into eighths; quarter the smaller ones. Place in a bowl. Scrub the Jerusalem artichokes well. Use a small knife to trim off any bad spots, but do not peel. Slice the Jerusalem artichokes in half lengthwise, then crosswise into thin pieces. Add to the radishes; add the spring onions, jícama, watercress, mustard greens, and bell peppers. Toss to combine.

2. In a small bowl, combine the vinegar, salt, pepper to taste, and thyme. Gradually whisk in olive oil. Pour vinaigrette over salad; toss well. Let stand at room temperature for about 1 hour before serving.

....

FLAVORFUL OIL

Combine a half cup (2½ ounces) Moroccan or kalamata olives in 1 cup of extra-virgin olive oil. Let steep for at least a day, and use as olive oil in salads or marinades.

....

chunky radish salad
SERVES 4

16 medium (12 ounces) radishes, trimmed

1 medium cucumber, peeled if waxed

8 ounces feta cheese

8 ounces yellow cherry tomatoes

2 tablespoons roughly chopped fresh dill

2 tablespoons red-wine vinegar

¾ teaspoon kosher salt

¼ teaspoon freshly ground black pepper

⅓ cup extra-virgin olive oil

¾ cup fresh basil leaves

1. Cut the radishes, cucumber, and feta into 1-inch pieces. Transfer all the pieces to a medium bowl. Halve the cherry tomatoes. Add the tomato halves and dill to the radish mixture. Toss to combine.

2. In a small bowl, combine the vinegar, salt, and pepper. Whisk in the olive oil. Drizzle the vinaigrette over the radish mixture, and toss well. Tear basil into medium pieces, add, and toss. Serve.

tomatoes with anchovy dressing
SERVES 4

In this summer side dish, wedges of tomatoes are tossed in an anchovy dressing. Anchovies are very salty; season the tomatoes sparingly.

2 tablespoons extra-virgin olive oil

1 medium garlic clove, minced

5 anchovy fillets, coarsely chopped

4 medium tomatoes (red, yellow, or a mixture), cut into eighths

Kosher salt and freshly ground black pepper

2 tablespoons roughly chopped fresh flat-leaf parsley

1. Heat olive oil and garlic in a small skillet over low heat. Stir in anchovies; cook about 1 minute.

2. Place the tomato wedges in a serving dish, and season with salt and pepper.

3. Pour the warm dressing over the tomatoes, add the parsley, and toss to coat. Serve immediately.

minted peach and tomato salad

SERVES 8 TO 10

- 3 tablespoons extra-virgin olive oil
- 1 tablespoon balsamic vinegar
- 1 tablespoon fresh lemon juice
- ¾ teaspoon kosher salt
- ½ teaspoon freshly ground black pepper
- 4 large (about 1½ pounds) peaches
- 3 large (about 2 pounds) red tomatoes
- 3 large (about 2 pounds) yellow tomatoes
- 1½ cups (about 10 ounces) cherry tomatoes
- 2 small inner celery stalks, strings removed, cut into ¼-inch pieces
- ¼ cup fresh mint leaves, plus sprigs for garnish

1. Whisk together the olive oil, vinegar, lemon juice, ½ teaspoon salt, and ¼ teaspoon pepper in a small bowl; set the vinaigrette aside.

2. Halve and pit the peaches. Cut the halves into quarters. Remove the cores from the stem ends of large tomatoes; slice into ½-inch rounds.

3. Arrange the peaches, tomato slices, cherry tomatoes, and celery on a serving plate. Sprinkle with the remaining ¼ teaspoon salt and ¼ teaspoon pepper. Coarsely chop the mint leaves; add to the vinaigrette. Pour the vinaigrette over the salad, and garnish with the mint sprigs. Serve.

chopped-tomato salads

SERVES 8

A simple chopped-tomato salad becomes a perfect summer entertaining side dish when spooned into a measuring cup and unmolded onto a salad plate. Use red, yellow, and green tomatoes to make these brightly colored individual salads. If you can't find shiso leaves, use large basil leaves. Reserve the tomato water to use in sauces or vinaigrettes.

- 4 pounds tomatoes
- 1 teaspoon kosher salt, plus more for seasoning
- ¼ cup extra-virgin olive oil, plus more for molding salads
- 1 garlic clove, minced
- 1 large shallot, minced
- 2½ tablespoons fresh marjoram or oregano leaves, roughly chopped
  Freshly ground black pepper
- 8 shiso or nasturtium leaves, for garnish

1. Cover and bring a large pot of water to a boil. Prepare an ice-water bath. Using a paring knife, score the nonstem end of each tomato with a shallow "x". Blanch the tomatoes in the boiling water for 30 seconds. With a slotted spoon, transfer the tomatoes to the ice-water bath. Drain the tomatoes in a colander. Peel the tomatoes; remove and discard the cores. Slice the tomatoes in half, and, using a melon baller, remove and discard all the seeds. Cut the tomato flesh into ¼-inch dice, and transfer to a medium bowl. Sprinkle the tomatoes with 1 teaspoon salt, and let them stand about 25 minutes.

2. Place the tomatoes in a sieve over a small bowl, and gently press down on the flesh, extracting as much of the liquid as possible. If your tomatoes are particularly juicy, let them stand 15 minutes more. Reserve the liquid for another use. Return the tomato flesh to the bowl, and add the olive oil, garlic, shallot, and marjoram. Season with salt and pepper; mix.

3. Generously brush a ½-cup dry measuring cup

with olive oil. Fill with the tomato mixture, and press down with the back of a spoon, extracting any excess liquid; pour off the liquid. Line a salad plate with a shiso leaf. Run a small knife between the tomato mixture and the measuring cup, and invert the cup on the shiso leaf. Gently tap the bottom, and unmold the salad. Repeat with the remaining tomato mixture and shiso leaves, and serve.

tomato and corn salad

SERVES 6

This colorful salad is great for a summer party; make it early in the day so the flavors develop.

Kosher salt

- 2 *ears fresh corn, kernels shaved from the cob*
- 1 *roasted yellow bell pepper (see page 645), cut into ½-inch dice*
- 4 *plum tomatoes, peeled, seeded, and cut into ½-inch dice*
- ¼ *cup minced red onion*
- 1 *jalapeño pepper, seeds and ribs removed, minced*
- 3 *tablespoons finely chopped fresh cilantro*
- 3 *tablespoons finely chopped fresh flat-leaf parsley*
- 1 *tablespoon fresh lime juice*
- 1 *tablespoon fresh lemon juice*
- 3 *tablespoons Homemade Chicken Stock (page 624), or low-sodium store-bought chicken broth, skimmed of fat*
- ¼ *teaspoon freshly ground black pepper*

1. Cover and bring a small saucepan of salted water to a boil. Add the corn; cook until tender, about 2 minutes. Drain and set aside.

2. In a large bowl, combine the corn and the remaining ingredients. Toss to combine. The salad may be stored, covered with plastic wrap in the refrigerator, for up to 8 hours. Bring to room temperature before serving.

FIT TO EAT RECIPE PER HALF-CUP SERVING: 53 CALORIES, 1 G TOTAL FAT, 0 MG CHOLESTEROL, 12 G CARBOHYDRATE, 374 MG SODIUM, 2 G PROTEIN, 2 G DIETARY FIBER

butter bean and sugar snap pea salad

SERVES 12

Butter beans resemble lima beans, which can also be used; pea shoots are available in the spring at green markets or farm stands.

Kosher salt

- 1 *pound butter beans, shelled*
- 1 *pound sugar snap peas, trimmed*
- 3 *tablespoons walnut oil, or more to taste*
- 12 *medium leeks, quartered lengthwise, well washed (see page 646)*

  Freshly ground black pepper
- ½ *cup fresh chervil or flat-leaf parsley leaves*
- ½ *ounce pea shoots, optional*
- 3 *cups (1 to 2 ounces) baby sorrel, spinach, or dandelion leaves*

1. Cover and bring a large pot of salted water to a boil; prepare an ice-water bath. Blanch butter beans just until tender, 5 to 15 minutes. Transfer to the ice bath, and cool. Drain in a colander.

2. Blanch the snap peas in the boiling water just until bright green and crunchy, about 1 minute. Transfer the peas to the ice-water bath, and cool. Drain in a colander. Peel the skins from the butter beans, and set beans aside.

3. Heat 2 tablespoons walnut oil in large skillet over medium heat. Add the leeks, and cook, stirring occasionally, until bright green and soft, about 12 minutes. Add ½ cup water, and stir well. Cover, and cook until the leeks are soft, about 5 minutes. Season with salt and pepper. Add the reserved beans and snap peas, and toss over low heat until hot throughout. Season with salt and pepper.

4. Transfer the mixture to a large serving bowl. Add the chervil, pea shoots, if using, and the sorrel; toss. Drizzle with the remaining tablespoon of walnut oil, or to taste, and serve.

white bean and tomato salad

SERVES 12 TO 14

- 1½ pounds dried French navy or great Northern beans
- 2 teaspoons kosher salt
- 1 small fennel bulb
- ½ cup plus 2 tablespoons extra-virgin olive oil
- 3 medium leeks, white and pale-green parts, well washed (see page 646), cut crosswise into ⅛-inch-thick slices
- 1 small red onion, coarsely chopped
- 2 cucumbers, peeled, seeded, and diced
- 1 bunch chives, snipped
- 1 bunch fresh oregano, coarsely chopped
- ½ bunch fresh flat-leaf parsley, leaves only
- ½ cup fresh lemon juice (3 lemons)
- 1 teaspoon freshly ground black pepper
- 5 medium (1¾ pounds) tomatoes, each cut into 8 wedges

1. Pick over the dried beans, discarding any stones or broken beans, and rinse. Place in a large saucepan, cover with cold water by 2 inches, and bring to a strong boil over high heat. Cover and remove from the heat, and let stand 1 hour. Drain the beans, and place them with 2½ quarts of fresh water in a medium stockpot; set over high heat. Bring to a boil, then reduce to a simmer. Cook until beans are tender, about 1 hour. When beans are almost done, add 1 teaspoon salt. Drain in a colander. Transfer to a large bowl; set aside.

2. Cut the fennel bulb in half lengthwise, and remove core. Cut into 1-inch wedges, and cut crosswise into ⅛-inch-thick slices, including stalks.

3. Heat a skillet over medium-high heat; add 2 tablespoons olive oil. Add leeks and fennel; cook until tender, about 5 minutes. Remove from heat; add to reserved beans. Add red onion, cucumbers, chives, oregano, and parsley; toss to combine. Add the remaining ½ cup olive oil, the lemon juice, the remaining teaspoon salt, and the pepper; toss to combine. Arrange tomato wedges along edge of a platter. Spoon the bean mixture in the center; serve.

sugar snap peas with mint dressing

SERVES 4

To trim a sugar snap pea, snap off the stem end, pull away the string, and discard; then pinch off the small fiber from the pointed end.

- Kosher salt
- 1 pound sugar snap peas, trimmed
- 3 tablespoons finely chopped shallots
- 3 tablespoons rice-wine vinegar
- 1 teaspoon honey
- 1 teaspoon Dijon mustard
- ¼ cup plus 2 tablespoons extra-virgin olive oil
- 1½ cups fresh mint leaves, roughly chopped
- Freshly ground black pepper

1. Cover and bring a medium saucepan of salted water to a boil; prepare an ice-water bath. Add the peas to the boiling water, and cook until bright green and crunchy, about 1 minute. Using a slotted spoon, transfer the peas to the ice-water bath until cold. Drain the peas in a colander, and transfer to a serving dish.

2. Combine the shallots, vinegar, honey, mustard, olive oil, and mint in a jar with a lid. Season with salt and pepper. Cover, and shake vigorously until well combined. Let the dressing stand 10 minutes to let the flavors combine. Pour the dressing over the peas. Toss, and serve.

chickpea and cucumber salad with fresh mint

SERVES 4

- 2 cucumbers (about 1½ pounds)
- 1¾ cups canned chickpeas, drained and rinsed (from one 15-ounce can)
- ½ cup roughly chopped fresh mint leaves
- 2 medium carrots, grated
- ½ cup currants
- 1½ teaspoons whole fennel seeds
- 3 tablespoons minced shallots

¼ cup fresh lemon juice

1½ tablespoons extra-virgin olive oil

Kosher salt and freshly ground black pepper

1. Peel the cucumbers if they are waxed, and cut in half lengthwise. Scoop out the seeds with a spoon, and discard them. Cut the cucumbers into ¼-inch dice. Place in a medium bowl.

2. Add the chickpeas, mint, carrots, currants, fennel seeds, shallots, lemon juice, and olive oil, and toss well to combine. Season with salt and pepper. Serve at room temperature.

chickpea salad with green mango
SERVES 8

Green mangos are about the size of a large lemon, tart, and very firm. They should not be confused with underripe mangos. If you can't find them, omit them from the recipe, and add a little more lime juice.

1½ tablespoons whole cumin seeds, toasted (see page 644)

2 15-ounce cans chickpeas, drained and rinsed

6 large radishes, cut into 1-inch matchsticks

2 green mangos, peeled and pitted (see page 647), grated on the large holes of a box grater

2 teaspoons kosher salt

6 scallions, white and green parts, cut into 1-inch matchsticks

Zest and juice of 2 limes

1 cup fresh mint leaves, torn into pieces

1 tablespoon dried pomegranate seeds, optional (see Food Sources, page 648)

1. Process the toasted cumin seeds in a spice grinder until finely ground.

2. In a large bowl, combine the chickpeas, radishes, mangos, ground cumin, salt, scallions, lime zest and juice, and half the mint. Sprinkle the remaining mint and the pomegranate seeds, if using, over the salad; serve.

CRISPING CUCUMBERS

To make freshly cut cucumber slices extra crisp for salads, arrange them in a colander placed inside a bowl. Sprinkle with salt, cover with ice cubes, and refrigerate for an hour. Pat dry, and refrigerate until using.

five-bean salad
SERVES 6

Our version of the summer picnic classic features a combination of dried, fresh-shelled, and string beans. Assemble it several hours before you plan to serve it to let the flavors meld.

½ cup dried cannellini or gigande beans

1 tablespoon whole black peppercorns

1 head of garlic, cut in half, loose skin removed

1 teaspoon kosher salt, plus more for cooking water and seasoning

12 ounces fresh cranberry beans, shelled

8 ounces fresh green beans, trimmed

8 ounces fresh yellow beans, trimmed

12 ounces fresh fava beans, shelled

½ cup finely chopped flat-leaf parsley

3 scallions, white and light-green parts, thinly sliced

3 tablespoons extra-virgin olive oil

3 tablespoons fresh lemon juice

Freshly ground black pepper

1. Pick over the dried beans, discarding any broken beans or stones, and rinse. Place in a saucepan, cover with cold water by 2 inches, and bring to a boil over high heat. Cover and remove from the heat, and let stand 1 hour. Drain the beans, and set aside.

2. Tie the peppercorns in a small piece of cheesecloth. Set the bundle aside.

3. Return the cannellini beans to the saucepan; fill with cold water. Cover and bring to a boil. Add the garlic and the peppercorn bundle. Reduce heat, and simmer, uncovered, until the beans are tender, about 1 hour. Add 1 teaspoon salt approximately 50 minutes into the cooking time. Remove the beans from the heat; let cool in the cooking liquid.

4. Place the cranberry beans in a medium saucepan, and cover with cold water by ½ inch. Bring to a boil. Reduce heat, and simmer the beans until tender, 15 to 20 minutes. Remove from the heat; let cool in the cooking liquid.

5. Cover and bring a large saucepan of salted water to a boil. Prepare an ice-water bath. Blanch the green and yellow beans in the boiling water until crisp but tender, about 4 minutes. Leave the water boiling; using a slotted spoon, transfer the beans to the ice-water bath to stop the cooking. Transfer the beans to a colander. Then place them in a large bowl. Set aside.

6. Repeat step 5, blanching the fava beans until crisp but tender, 2 to 3 minutes. Peel and discard tough skins; add the fava beans to the bowl.

7. Drain the cannellini beans, discarding the peppercorn bundle and the garlic; add to the bowl. Drain cranberry beans; add to the bowl. Add the parsley, scallions, olive oil, and lemon juice. Toss to combine. Season with salt and pepper, and serve.

green beans with ricotta salata
SERVES 4

Ricotta salata is an aged and salted ricotta cheese. Unlike fresh ricotta, it can be sliced or crumbled.

- ¼ teaspoon kosher salt, plus more for cooking water
- 1 pound string beans, trimmed
- 2 ounces ricotta salata or mild feta, crumbled
- 20 small fresh basil leaves
- ½ teaspoon Dijon mustard
- 1 tablespoon red-wine vinegar
- 3 tablespoons extra-virgin olive oil
- ⅛ teaspoon freshly ground black pepper

1. Cover and bring a large pot of salted water to a boil. Prepare an ice-water bath. Add the beans, and cook just until bright green and tender, about 3 minutes. Drain, and immediately transfer the beans to the ice-water bath. Drain, pat dry, and place in a large bowl along with the ricotta salata and basil.

2. In a small bowl, whisk together the mustard, vinegar, olive oil, ¼ teaspoon salt, and the pepper.

3. Pour vinaigrette over bean mixture; toss. Serve.

summer black-eyed-pea salad
SERVES 4

Be careful not overcook the okra; it should be slightly crisp.

- 4 vine-ripened tomatoes
- 4 ears fresh corn
- 4 cups Traditional Black-Eyed Peas (page 333) with cooking liquid
- 8 sprigs fresh oregano or marjoram
- 1 teaspoon kosher salt, plus more for seasoning
- ½ teaspoon freshly ground black pepper, plus more for seasoning
- ¼ cup plus 2 tablespoons extra-virgin olive oil
- 1 pound fresh okra, trimmed
- ¼ cup red-wine or sherry vinegar

1. Cover and bring a large pot of water to a boil. Prepare an ice-water bath. Using a paring knife, score the nonstem end of each tomato with a shallow "x". Blanch tomatoes for 30 seconds. With a slotted spoon, transfer to the ice bath. When cool enough to handle, gently peel. Set tomatoes aside.

2. Place corn in same boiling water; cook until just tender, about 3 minutes. When cool enough to handle, stand 1 ear on a cutting board. Shave corn with a sharp knife; set aside. Repeat with remaining ears.

3. Discard water in the pot; refill to ¾-inch level with the pea cooking liquid or water. Add 5 sprigs oregano, 1 teaspoon salt, ½ teaspoon pepper, and 1 tablespoon olive oil. Arrange tomatoes and okra in the water; cover, and bring to just below the boiling point over medium-high heat. Keep covered; reduce heat so the liquid just simmers. Cook until the okra is just tender, 4 to 8 minutes; gently stir after 2 minutes so all of the okra is wet with the liquid. Do not overcook the okra. Using a slotted spoon, transfer the okra and tomatoes to a large serving platter. Discard the liquid.

4. In a small bowl, whisk vinegar and remaining 5 tablespoons olive oil; season with salt and pepper. Finely chop remaining oregano; whisk it into the vinaigrette. Arrange the corn and peas on the platter. Drizzle with the vinaigrette. Let sit at room temperature about 20 minutes; serve.

jícama and orange salad

SERVES 8

- 3 navel oranges
- 1 tablespoon sherry vinegar
- ½ teaspoon kosher salt
- ⅛ teaspoon freshly ground black pepper
- 1½ tablespoons extra-virgin olive oil
- 1 medium (about 1 pound) jícama, peeled, cut in 2-inch matchsticks
- 1 small red onion, sliced into thin half-moons

1. Slice 1 orange in half, and squeeze the juice from 1 half into a bowl. Add the sherry vinegar, salt, and pepper; slowly whisk in the oil.

2. Cut away the peel and pith of remaining 2½ oranges. Slice the oranges into ½-inch rounds, and use your hands to pull the slices apart into bite-size pieces. Set aside in a large bowl.

3. Add the jícama and onions to the orange pieces. Pour the vinaigrette over; toss to combine. Serve.

three-cabbage slaw with peanuts

SERVES 12 TO 15

The dressing on this salad is rather piquant; for a mellower flavor, make it a day ahead.

- ¾ cup plain yogurt
- ¾ cup Homemade Mayonnaise (page 632) or prepared
- 1 tablespoon dark sesame oil
- ¼ cup apple-cider vinegar
- ½ red onion, coarsely chopped
- 1 teaspoon celery seed
- ½ teaspoon cayenne pepper
- ½ teaspoon freshly ground black pepper
- 1 teaspoon kosher salt
- 1 tablespoon sugar
- 1 head savoy cabbage
- ½ head green cabbage
- ½ head red cabbage
- 6 large carrots
- 2 tablespoons unsalted butter
- 1 cup shelled peanuts

1. In a blender or in the bowl of a food processor, combine the yogurt, mayonnaise, sesame oil, vinegar, and onion. Purée until smooth. Add the celery seed, both peppers, the salt, and sugar, and blend for a few seconds to combine.

2. Remove the large outer leaves from the cabbages, and reserve to line the serving bowl. Shred cabbages with a large knife; set aside. Grate carrots, or cut into matchsticks on a mandoline. Set aside.

3. Melt the butter in a small skillet, and add peanuts. Toast, shaking the pan frequently, until brown. Do not burn. Let cool.

4. In a large bowl, combine the shredded cabbages and the grated carrots. Add the dressing; mix well. Crush the peanuts slightly with the side of a knife and, just before serving, add three-quarters of them to the slaw.

5. Line a serving bowl with the reserved cabbage leaves, and fill with the coleslaw. Garnish with the remaining peanuts, and serve immediately.

endive slaw

SERVES 4

1½ tablespoons champagne or
    white-wine vinegar

3   tablespoons extra-virgin olive oil
    Kosher salt and freshly ground
    black pepper

4   heads Belgian endive (about 12 ounces)

1   red bell pepper, seeds and ribs removed

20 fresh tarragon leaves

⅓   cup fresh pomegranate seeds
    (from ½ pomegranate)

1. In a small bowl, whisk vinegar and oil until smooth. Season with salt and pepper. Set aside.

2. Cut the endive lengthwise into ⅛- to ¼-inch-wide pieces. Transfer to a medium bowl. Cut the red pepper lengthwise into ⅛-inch-wide pieces. Transfer to the bowl with the endive. Just before serving, toss with the reserved vinaigrette. Top with the tarragon and pomegranate seeds.

asparagus, celeriac, and jícama slaw

SERVES 4

Avoid overcooking the asparagus; it will become mushy. Cooking time will vary depending on how thin the asparagus spears are.

    Kosher salt

1   pound thin asparagus, tough
    ends removed

1   lemon

1½ tablespoons Homemade Mayonnaise
    (page 632) or prepared

2   teaspoons heavy cream
    Freshly ground black pepper

¼   small (about 8 ounces) celeriac, peeled,
    cut into matchsticks

¼   small (about 8 ounces) jícama, peeled,
    cut into matchsticks

2   large radishes, cut into matchsticks

½   bunch chives, snipped into 2-inch lengths

1   tablespoon fresh thyme leaves,
    plus sprigs for garnish

1. Cover and bring a large saucepan of salted water to a boil; prepare an ice-water bath. Cook the asparagus in the boiling water just until bright green, about 30 seconds. Immediately transfer to the ice-water bath. Drain, and slice the spears in half lengthwise.

2. Grate 1 teaspoon of zest from the lemon, and transfer to a bowl. Squeeze 2 teaspoons of juice from the lemon, and add to the bowl. Add the mayonnaise, heavy cream, and 2 teaspoons water; season with salt and pepper. Whisk until combined; set the dressing aside.

3. Toss asparagus, celeriac, jícama, and radishes in a serving bowl. Add dressing, chives, and thyme; toss. Garnish with thyme sprigs. Serve.

summer slaw with poppy-seed dressing

SERVES 4

Raw fennel tastes best if sliced thinly. The poppy-seed dressing is delicious tossed with almost any raw, sliced vegetables like bell peppers, jícama, carrots, and tomatoes.

3   tablespoons crème fraîche or sour cream

1   1½-inch piece fresh ginger, peeled
    and grated

2½ tablespoons fresh orange juice

1   teaspoon poppy seeds
    Kosher salt and freshly ground
    black pepper

1   small (about 8 ounces) fennel bulb,
    thinly sliced crosswise

4   ounces green beans, trimmed,
    cut in long strips

2   small carrots, cut in matchsticks

1. In a small bowl, whisk together the crème fraîche, ginger, orange juice, and half the poppy seeds. Season with salt and pepper. Refrigerate until needed.

2. Combine the fennel, green beans, and carrots in a medium bowl, and toss with the dressing immediately before serving. Garnish with remaining poppy seeds. Serve.

jícama slaw

SERVES 4

- 1 tablespoon plus 1 teaspoon fresh lime juice
  Pinch of cayenne pepper
- 1 tablespoon chopped fresh cilantro leaves
- 1 small jalapeño pepper, seeds and ribs removed, minced
- ½ teaspoon kosher salt
- 1 large jícama, peeled, cut in matchsticks (5 cups)

In a medium bowl, combine the lime juice, cayenne, cilantro, jalapeño, and salt. Add the jícama, and toss well to combine. Serve.

zucchini slaw

SERVES 6

For crisp, colorful slaw, pick small, firm zucchini—the flesh is tender and the skin is delicate.

- 5 small zucchini
- 3 carrots
- 1 yellow bell pepper, seeds and ribs removed
- 4 large radishes
- 1 celery stalk, strings removed
- 3 ears fresh corn, kernels shaved from cob
- ¾ cup Homemade Mayonnaise (page 632) or prepared
- ½ cup plus 2 tablespoons cider vinegar
- ¾ teaspoon celery seed
- 1½ tablespoons sugar
- ¾ teaspoon kosher salt
- ½ teaspoon freshly ground black pepper
  Zucchini blossoms, for garnish, optional

1. Using the largest holes on a box grater, grate the zucchini and carrots, and transfer to a large bowl. Cut the yellow pepper and radishes into 1-inch matchsticks, and add to the bowl. Slice the celery as thinly as possible on a diagonal, and add to the bowl; add the corn. Toss to combine.

2. In a bowl, whisk together the mayonnaise, vinegar, celery seed, sugar, salt, and pepper. Pour over the salad; toss to combine. Garnish with the zucchini blossoms, if desired, and serve.

all-american potato salad

SERVES 10 TO 12

Cooking potatoes in their skins prevents them from absorbing too much water and losing flavor; it also maintains their shape. The cooking time will vary according to the size of the potatoes. They are done when a paring knife easily glides into the center of the potato. The potatoes must be peeled while they are steaming hot to better absorb the vinegar. (For cornichons, see Food Sources, page 648.)

- 4 pounds (about 8) russet potatoes
- 1 tablespoon plus 2 teaspoons kosher salt
- 3 tablespoons cider vinegar
- 3 large hard-boiled eggs (see page 571), 2 roughly chopped, 1 sliced into ¼-inch-thick rounds, for garnish
- 1 cup Homemade Mayonnaise (page 632) or prepared
- ½ teaspoon whole celery seeds
- 1 teaspoon dry mustard
- ½ teaspoon freshly ground black pepper
- 3 celery stalks, strings removed, cut into ¼-inch dice
- 1 red bell pepper, seeds and ribs removed, cut into ¼-inch dice
- 1 medium onion, finely diced
- 10 cornichons, cut into ¼-inch dice
- 3 scallions, white and pale-green parts, thinly sliced
- 2 tablespoons chopped fresh flat-leaf parsley
- 1 teaspoon paprika

1. Place the potatoes in a large pot with enough water to cover by several inches. Bring to a boil over high heat, add 1 tablespoon salt, and reduce to a simmer. Cook until the potatoes are tender when pierced with the tip of a knife, about 25 minutes. Drain into a colander. Using gloves or a kitchen towel to protect your hands, peel the potatoes, and cut into 1-inch dice while still hot. Drizzle with the vinegar; set aside.

2. Combine the chopped eggs, mayonnaise, celery seeds, mustard, 2 teaspoons salt, and the black pepper in a large bowl, and whisk to combine. Add the reserved potatoes to the mayonnaise mixture. Add the celery, red pepper, onion, cornichons, scallions, and chopped parsley. Stir to combine. Chill for 30 minutes before serving. Garnish with paprika and hard-boiled egg rounds.

curried potato salad
SERVES 10 TO 12

Homemade potato salads will keep 2 to 3 days in an airtight container in the refrigerator.

- 3 pounds baby white potatoes, scrubbed
- 1 tablespoon plus 1 teaspoon kosher salt
- 2 tablespoons white-wine vinegar
- 1 cup Homemade Mayonnaise (page 632) or prepared
- 3 tablespoons Curry Powder (page 633) or prepared
- 5 large hard-boiled eggs (see page 571), cut in quarters lengthwise
- 1 medium onion, thinly sliced into slivers
- ¼ cup fresh cilantro, finely chopped

1. Place the potatoes in a large pot with enough water to cover by several inches. Cover and bring to a boil over high heat; add 1 tablespoon salt, and reduce to a simmer. Cook until the potatoes are tender when pierced with the tip of a knife, 15 to 20 minutes. Drain into a colander. Using a kitchen towel to protect your hands, cut the potatoes into wedges while they are still hot. Drizzle with the vinegar, and set aside to cool.

2. Place the mayonnaise, curry powder, and the remaining teaspoon of salt in a large bowl; whisk to combine. Add the potatoes to the mayonnaise mixture. Add the eggs, onion, and cilantro. Stir to combine. Chill until ready to serve.

potato salad with crème fraîche dressing
SERVES 12

Cornichons (see Food Sources, page 648), tart pickles made from tiny gherkin cucumbers, flavor this updated version of an old-fashioned favorite. The dressing can be made up to 2 days ahead and stored, refrigerated in an airtight container. Homemade Mayonnaise (page 632) can be used in place of the crème fraîche.

- 4 pounds total (12 to 15 of each) small white and red potatoes, scrubbed
- 2 teaspoons kosher salt, plus more for seasoning
- ½ cup dry vermouth
- ¼ cup white-wine vinegar
- 1 tablespoon sugar
- 1½ cups crème fraîche or sour cream
- 1 teaspoon whole celery seeds
  Freshly ground black pepper
- 6 ounces (about ¾ cup) cornichons, drained, thinly sliced crosswise
- 2 bunches scallions, white and green parts, cut into ¼-inch slices on a diagonal
- ½ cup loosely packed fresh flat-leaf parsley, coarsely chopped

1. Place the potatoes in a large stockpot; fill with enough cold water to cover by 3 inches. Add 2 teaspoons salt; bring to a boil. Reduce heat, and let simmer until the potatoes are just tender when pierced with the tip of a knife, 35 to 40 minutes.

2. Remove from the heat, drain, and sprinkle with the vermouth. Let stand until cool.

3. In a medium bowl, whisk together the vinegar, sugar, crème fraîche, and celery seeds. Season with salt and pepper.

4. Cut the potatoes into bite-size pieces, and transfer to a serving bowl. Pour the dressing over the potatoes. Add the cornichons, scallions, and parsley; toss to combine. Season with salt and pepper, and serve at room temperature.

grilled mediterranean potato salad

SERVES 6 TO 8

- 2 pounds medium red-skinned potatoes, sliced ¼ inch thick
- ¼ cup plus 2 tablespoons extra-virgin olive oil
- 1 teaspoon kosher salt
- 4 anchovy fillets
- ¼ cup red-wine vinegar
- ¼ teaspoon freshly ground black pepper
- 2 roasted red bell peppers (see page 645), cut into ¼-inch-thick strips
- ¼ cup capers, drained
- 1 cup black olives, pitted
- ½ cup fresh flat-leaf parsley leaves

1. Heat a grill or a grill pan to medium hot, or pre-heat oven to 400°F. In a bowl, combine potatoes, 2 tablespoons oil, and ½ teaspoon salt. Grill potatoes until tender when pierced with the tip of a knife and brown on both sides. Alternatively, roast on a baking sheet until browned, about 40 minutes, turning halfway through cooking time.

2. Finely chop the anchovy fillets, and place in a medium bowl. Add the vinegar, the remaining ½ teaspoon salt, and the pepper; whisk to combine. Slowly whisk in the remaining ¼ cup olive oil.

3. Combine potatoes, roasted peppers, capers, olives, parsley, and vinaigrette in a serving bowl, and toss. Serve warm or at room temperature.

....

POTATO SALAD ADD-INS

Cut blanched asparagus

Chopped fresh dill

Sugar snap peas

Hard-boiled eggs

Diced celery or fennel

Chopped red onion

Capers

....

german potato salad

SERVES 8 TO 10

Small regular Yukon gold or Idaho potatoes can be substituted for the baby ones; adjust the cooking time accordingly.

- 4 pounds baby Yukon gold potatoes, peeled
- 1 tablespoon plus 2 teaspoons kosher salt
- ½ cup cider vinegar
- 1 tablespoon sugar
- 1 pound bacon, cut into ½-inch pieces
- 2 small white onions, finely chopped (about 1 cup)
- 2 cups Beef Stock (page 624) or low-sodium beef broth, skimmed of fat
- ½ cup chopped fresh flat-leaf parsley

1. Place the potatoes in a large pot with enough water to cover by several inches. Cover and bring to a boil over high heat; add 1 tablespoon of the salt, and reduce to a gentle boil. Cook until the potatoes are tender when pierced with the tip of a knife, about 10 minutes.

2. While the potatoes cook, combine the vinegar, sugar, and the remaining 2 teaspoons of salt in a small saucepan, and place over medium heat until the sugar is dissolved.

3. Drain the potatoes in a colander. Using a kitchen towel to protect your hands, slice the hot potatoes into ⅛-inch-thick rounds and place in a large bowl. Drizzle with the hot vinegar mixture, gently stirring until all the potatoes are coated. Set aside.

4. Cook the bacon in a large skillet over medium-low heat, stirring frequently, until browned and crispy. Using a slotted spoon, transfer the bacon to a paper-towel-lined plate. Drain the excess fat from the skillet, and discard, leaving a thin coating on the bottom. Add the onions; cook until translucent but not browned, about 8 minutes.

5. Add the beef stock; bring to a boil over high heat. Reduce to a simmer, and cook until reduced by half, about 20 minutes. Pour over the reserved warm potato mixture, and sprinkle with the reserved bacon and chopped parsley. Gently stir to combine, and serve immediately.

new potatoes with gremolata

SERVES 8 TO 10

Buy the smallest new potatoes available for this salad. Gremolata is traditionally made from equal parts minced fresh parsley, garlic, and lemon peel; here we've substituted shallots for the garlic for a more mellow flavor.

- 3 lemons
- 3 large shallots, minced
- ½ cup finely chopped fresh flat-leaf parsley
- ½ cup medium-chopped fresh dill
- 1 tablespoon plus 1 teaspoon kosher salt
- ¼ cup plus 1 tablespoon extra-virgin olive oil
- 4 pounds white and red new potatoes, scrubbed
- ⅛ teaspoon freshly ground black pepper
- 1 large hard-boiled egg (see page 571)

1. To make the gremolata, zest the lemons to yield 2 tablespoons. Juice the lemons; reserve the juice. Cover and bring a small pan of water to a boil, add the zest, and blanch for 30 seconds. Drain, run under cool water, and drain again. Transfer the zest to a cutting board; finely chop. Add the shallots, parsley, dill, and ½ teaspoon salt to the cutting board. Drizzle 1½ teaspoons oil over the ingredients. Use a large knife to chop the ingredients until very fine but still retaining some texture. (A food processor may be used, but pulse only.) Transfer the mixture to a medium bowl. Stir in 3 tablespoons oil and 1 tablespoon lemon juice, until the mixture is slightly thickened. Set the gremolata aside.

2. Put the potatoes in a large saucepan, and cover with cold water by 1 inch. Add 1 tablespoon salt, and bring to a boil. Reduce the heat to medium; simmer until the potatoes are tender when pierced with the tip of a knife, 15 to 25 minutes. Drain. Let stand until cool enough to handle; cut the potatoes in half or quarters. While still warm, season with salt and pep-

per and 1½ tablespoons oil. Add the gremolata, and toss to combine. The warm potatoes will absorb the flavors of the gremolata. Set aside.

3. Peel the hard-boiled egg, and cut in half. Dice finely. Set aside. Transfer the potato mixture to a serving bowl. Sprinkle with the diced hard-boiled egg, and serve.

warm potato and watercress salad

SERVES 4

- 12 small (about 1 pound 6 ounces) red potatoes, scrubbed
- 3 tablespoons olive oil
- 1 teaspoon kosher salt
- ½ teaspoon freshly ground black pepper
- 2 teaspoons fresh lemon juice
- 1 teaspoon sherry-wine vinegar
- 1 bunch (about 6 ounces) watercress, tough stems removed
  Grated zest of ½ lemon

1. Preheat the oven to 375°F. Arrange the potatoes in a roasting pan, and add 1 tablespoon olive oil, ½ teaspoon salt, and ¼ teaspoon pepper; toss the potatoes to coat. Roast until the potatoes are tender when pierced with the tip of a knife, about 40 minutes. Remove from the oven, and let stand just until cool enough to handle.

2. Meanwhile, whisk together the lemon juice, vinegar, the remaining 2 tablespoons olive oil, ½ teaspoon salt, and ¼ teaspoon pepper in a medium bowl; set aside.

3. Break the warm potatoes in half, and transfer to a serving bowl. Add the vinaigrette, and toss to coat. Add the watercress and lemon zest, toss, and serve immediately.

potatoes and green beans with mint pesto

SERVES 8

The pesto (step 3) can be made up to 2 days in advance: Transfer to a bowl, and pour a very thin layer of olive oil on top; cover, and refrigerate.

- 1½ pounds fingerling or other small potatoes, scrubbed
- 1 tablespoon plus ¾ teaspoon kosher salt
- 1 pound green beans, cut into 2-inch lengths
- ½ cup packed fresh basil leaves
- 1 cup packed fresh mint leaves
- ½ cup spinach leaves, washed, stems removed
- 1 tablespoon pine nuts, toasted (page 644)
- 1 small garlic clove
- ¼ cup plus 1 tablespoon extra-virgin olive oil
- 3 tablespoons grated Parmesan cheese
- 1 tablespoon unsalted butter, room temperature
- 6 scallions, white parts only, thinly sliced

1. Place the potatoes in a medium saucepan, and cover with cold water by 1 inch. Add 1 tablespoon salt, and place over high heat. Bring to a boil, and reduce heat to medium. Cook until the potatoes are tender when pierced with the tip of a knife, 10 to 20 minutes. Using a slotted spoon, transfer them to a colander. Slice them in half lengthwise. Transfer to a large mixing bowl.

2. Prepare an ice-water bath. Raise the heat to high, and add the beans to the boiling water. Cook until bright green and al dente, about 3 minutes. Transfer them to the ice-water bath. Drain them in a colander and transfer to the bowl with the potatoes.

3. Place the basil, mint, spinach, pine nuts, garlic, and ¾ teaspoon salt in the bowl of a food processor. With the machine running, slowly add the olive oil. Process until a purée forms. Add the Parmesan cheese and the butter; process until puréed.

4. Pour the pesto over the warm potatoes and beans, and toss to combine. Transfer the vegetables to a serving dish, and sprinkle the scallions over the top. Serve warm.

sweet potato salad

SERVES 4 TO 6

Any leafy green, such as spinach, green-leaf lettuce, or Boston lettuce, works well in this recipe.

- 2 large, or 3 small, sweet potatoes, peeled, cut into 1-inch dice
- 2 tablespoons extra-virgin olive oil
- 3 tablespoons fresh lime juice
- 1 tablespoon ketchup
- 1½ teaspoons sugar
- 1 large garlic clove, minced
- 1 tablespoon Dijon mustard
- 3 dashes hot red-pepper sauce
- 2 dashes Worcestershire sauce
  Kosher salt and freshly ground black pepper
- 1 red bell pepper, seeds and ribs removed, cut into ¼-inch dice
- 1 green bell pepper, seeds and ribs removed, cut into ¼-inch dice
- 1 small red onion, cut into ¼-inch dice
- 3 tablespoons whole cumin seeds, toasted (see page 644)
- ¼ cup roughly chopped fresh cilantro
- 2 cups loosely packed mixed greens, roughly chopped

1. Cover and bring a medium pot of water to a boil. Add the sweet potatoes, and cook until they can be easily pierced with a fork but still offer some resistance, 8 to 10 minutes. Drain, and rinse with cold water. Chill in the refrigerator, about 1½ hours.

2. In a medium bowl, whisk together the olive oil, lime juice, ketchup, sugar, garlic, mustard, red-pepper sauce, and Worcestershire sauce, and season with salt and pepper; set aside.

3. In a large bowl, combine the sweet potatoes, red and green peppers, onion, cumin, cilantro, greens, and the dressing. Season with salt and pepper, and serve at room temperature or chilled.

asparagus panzanella

SERVES 6

Kosher salt

1 *pound medium asparagus, tough ends removed*

1 *seedless cucumber, peeled, cut into ½-inch wedges*

8 *cherry tomatoes, cut in half*

2 *small red or yellow tomatoes, cut into 8 wedges*

1 *medium red onion, cut into ¼-inch-thick wedges*

¾ *cup kalamata olives, pitted*

¼ *cup capers, drained*

6 *½-inch-thick slices country-style bread, crusts on, torn into 1-inch chunks*

2 *tablespoons red-wine vinegar*

2 *tablespoons extra-virgin olive oil*

Freshly ground black pepper

1. Cover and bring a medium saucepan of salted water to a boil; prepare an ice-water bath. Cook the asparagus in the boiling water until bright green and just tender, about 3 minutes. Transfer immediately to the ice-water bath. Drain; place on a clean kitchen towel.

2. In a large bowl, combine the asparagus, cucumber, tomatoes, red onion, olives, capers, and bread; toss to combine.

3. In a small bowl, whisk together the red-wine vinegar and olive oil; season with salt and pepper. Pour the vinaigrette over the asparagus mixture, and toss until well coated. Let sit until the bread absorbs the juices, and serve.

fatoush

SERVES 6

Fatoush is a Middle Eastern salad of bell peppers, chopped cucumbers, and tomatoes with crisp pita toasts. Zahtar and Moroccan Preserved Lemons (page 617) can be ordered by mail (see Food Sources, page 648).

1 *red bell pepper, seeds and ribs removed, cut into 1-inch pieces*

1 *large cucumber, cut into 1-inch pieces*

2 *bunches arugula leaves*

1½ *pounds tomatoes, cut into 1-inch pieces*

4 *scallions, white and green parts, cut into ½-inch pieces*

3 *tablespoons fresh lemon juice*

½ *teaspoon kosher salt*

¼ *teaspoon freshly ground black pepper*

½ *teaspoon zahtar*

1 *tablespoon olive-cured olive oil or extra-virgin olive oil*

6 *ounces whole-wheat pita bread, toasted, cut into 1½-inch pieces*

2 *wedges Moroccan Preserved Lemons (page 617), rinsed and finely chopped, for garnish, optional*

¼ *ounce low-salt feta cheese, for garnish, optional*

1. Combine the red pepper, cucumber, arugula, tomatoes, and scallions in a large bowl. In a small bowl, combine the lemon juice, salt, black pepper, and zahtar. Use a fork to whisk in the olive oil. Drizzle over the vegetables, and toss to combine.

2. Just before serving, toss in the toasted pita. Garnish with the preserved lemons and crumbled feta, if using. Serve.

FIT TO EAT RECIPE PER SERVING: 126 CALORIES, 2 G FAT, 1 MG CHOLESTEROL, 27 G CARBOHYDRATE, 401 MG SODIUM, 5 G PROTEIN, 4 G DIETARY FIBER

dig-deep layered summer salad

SERVES 8 TO 10

Layer the ingredients in a large glass trifle bowl instead of tossing them. Pearl barley can be substituted for wheat berries, which are found at health-food stores. The salad must be made a day in advance.

- 2 cups hard wheat berries
- ¼ cup plus 2 tablespoons fresh lemon juice
- ¼ cup white-wine vinegar
- 1 tablespoon plus 1 teaspoon Dijon mustard
- 1½ teaspoons kosher salt
- ¼ teaspoon freshly ground black pepper
- 1 tablespoon sugar
- ½ teaspoon celery seed
- 1 cup extra-virgin olive oil
- ¾ head celery, strings removed, sliced thinly on a diagonal (about 2¼ cups)
- 1½ cups dried cherries
- 10 ounces Maytag or other good blue cheese, crumbled (2⅓ cups)
- 1 small head green cabbage, thinly shredded (about 5 cups)
- 5 large carrots, grated (about 5 cups)

1. Place the wheat berries in a small stockpot, and add 2 quarts water. Cover, and bring to a boil. Reduce the heat to low, and simmer the berries until tender, about 40 minutes. Drain in a colander, and transfer to a large glass serving bowl.

2. In a medium bowl, whisk together the lemon juice, vinegar, mustard, salt, pepper, sugar, and celery seed. In a slow, steady stream, whisk in the olive oil until completely combined. Drizzle 2 tablespoons of the dressing over the wheat berries.

3. Arrange the celery slices over the wheat berries, and drizzle with 2 tablespoons of the dressing. Cover the celery with the cherries, and drizzle with 2 tablespoons of the dressing.

4. Crumble half the blue cheese over the cherries, and drizzle with 2 tablespoons of the dressing.

5. In a medium bowl, toss together the shredded cabbage and 3 tablespoons of the dressing; layer the cabbage over the blue cheese. Layer the carrots over the cabbage, and drizzle with 2 tablespoons of the dressing. Crumble the remaining blue cheese over the carrots, and drizzle with the remaining dressing. Cover the salad with plastic wrap, and transfer to the refrigerator for 24 hours to allow the flavors to develop. Remove the salad from the refrigerator, and serve at room temperature.

....

BLUE CHEESE

Combine a pungent blue cheese with hearty greens just before serving so the cheese doesn't overpower the salad. Try Roquefort and frisée with shaved fennel and dried apricots, and toss with Shallot Vinaigrette (page 163).

....

chickpea, asparagus, and herbed orzo salad with feta dressing

SERVES 6

- 18 yellow and red cherry tomatoes, cut in half lengthwise
- 3 tablespoons extra-virgin olive oil, plus more for drizzling

  Kosher salt
- ¼ teaspoon freshly ground black pepper, plus more for seasoning
- 2 cups uncooked orzo
- 2½ pounds asparagus, tough ends removed
- 2½ cups canned chickpeas, drained and rinsed (from two 15-ounce cans)
- 14 chives, cut into 1¼-inch lengths
- ¼ cup plus 2 tablespoons fresh lemon juice
- 2 ounces feta cheese
- 2 lemons, cut into wedges

1. Preheat the oven to 250°F with a rack in the center. Place tomatoes on a parchment-lined baking sheet, cut-side up. Drizzle lightly with oil, and sprinkle with salt and pepper. Cook until they start to dry out and edges have shriveled, about 1 hour.

2. Cover a large pot of salted water, and bring to a boil. Cook the orzo until al dente. Drain; place under cool running water to stop the cooking. Set aside in a strainer.

3. Cover a large pot of water, and bring to a boil. Prepare an ice-water bath. Blanch the asparagus until tender, about 3 minutes. Transfer immediately to the ice-water bath to cool. Strain; set aside.

4. Combine the chickpeas and half the chives in a large bowl. Set aside.

5. In a blender, blend the lemon juice, ¼ teaspoon pepper, feta, and 3 tablespoons oil until creamy. Add the orzo to the chickpeas. Pour on the dressing; toss to combine with the remaining chives. Season with salt and pepper. To serve, arrange the orzo salad and asparagus on a platter, and scatter the tomatoes over the salad. Place the lemon wedges around the platter for seasoning. Serve.

FIT TO EAT RECIPE PER SERVING: 430 CALORIES, 12 G FAT, 8 MG CHOLESTEROL, 66 G CARBOHYDRATE, 406 MG SODIUM, 17 G PROTEIN, 7 G DIETARY FIBER

chicken salad

SERVES 6

This healthy salad is blended with yogurt and mustard instead of the traditional mayonnaise.

- 1   tablespoon olive oil
- 1   pound boneless, skinless chicken breasts
     Kosher salt and freshly ground black pepper
- ¾   cup plain nonfat yogurt
- 1   tablespoon Dijon mustard
- 2   tablespoons snipped chives
- 1   tablespoon chopped fresh tarragon
- 1   Granny Smith apple
     Juice of ½ lemon
- 1   small fennel bulb, trimmed, finely diced
- 2   stalks celery, strings removed, finely diced
- 2   cups red seedless grapes, cut in half
- 6   slices pumpernickel bread, optional
- 1   bunch watercress, tough stems removed

1. Heat oil in a large skillet over medium-high heat. Season chicken with salt and pepper; place in the hot skillet. Reduce heat to medium. Cook until chicken is cooked through, about 6 minutes per side. Remove chicken from pan; set aside.

2. In a bowl, combine the yogurt, mustard, chives, and tarragon, and season with salt and pepper. Core the apple, and cut into ¼-inch dice. Place in a medium bowl with the lemon juice, and toss to combine. Add the fennel, celery, and grapes. Cut the reserved chicken into ½-inch pieces. Add to the salad with the yogurt dressing; stir to combine. Serve on the pumpernickel bread, open-faced, if desired, and the watercress.

FIT TO EAT RECIPE PER SERVING: 238 CALORIES, 4 G FAT, 59 MG CHOLESTEROL, 24 G CARBOHYDRATE, 681 MG SODIUM, 27 G PROTEIN, 3 G FIBER

warm chicken, mushroom, and spinach salad

SERVES 4

- 1   tablespoon olive oil
- 1   cup loosely packed fresh flat-leaf parsley leaves, coarsely chopped
- 2   whole boneless chicken breasts, skin on, split
     Kosher salt and freshly ground black pepper
- 1   small onion, roughly chopped
- 10 white mushrooms, wiped clean, trimmed, cut into ¾-inch pieces
- 1   cup dry white wine
- 2   tablespoons balsamic vinegar
- 1   tablespoon unsalted butter
- 4   handfuls (8 to 10 ounces) fresh baby or flat-leaf spinach, stems removed

1. Preheat the oven to 400°F. Heat the olive oil in a large skillet over medium heat. Press 1 tablespoon parsley onto the skin side of each breast. Season both sides with salt and pepper. Place the breasts, skin-side down, in the skillet; cook until golden, about 8 minutes per side.

2. Remove the chicken from the skillet; transfer to a roasting pan. Transfer the pan to the oven until the chicken cooks through, 15 to 20 minutes.

3. Meanwhile, return skillet to stove. Add the onion; cook, stirring, until just golden, about 2 minutes. Add mushrooms; cook until soft, about 5 minutes. Add wine; use a wooden spoon to loosen any browned bits from the bottom of the pan. Cook until the wine is almost evaporated, about 5 minutes. Add vinegar; cook 1 minute more. Stir in remaining parsley; season with salt and pepper. Remove from heat; stir in the butter.

4. Remove the chicken from the oven. Place the spinach on the plates. Slice each breast into sixths; arrange over the spinach. Spoon the mushroom mixture over the chicken, drizzling the juices over the spinach, and serve.

chicken and spring-vegetable salad
SERVES 6

Buttermilk is an excellent—and low-fat—substitute for mayonnaise and other high-fat ingredients. Mixed with plain nonfat yogurt, it produces a remarkably creamy dressing. This salad can be made through step 2 up to 8 hours ahead; the vegetables should be prepared and tossed in no more than an hour ahead.

5¼ cups Homemade Chicken Stock (page 624), or low-sodium store-bought chicken broth, skimmed of fat

3 dried bay leaves

1 teaspoon whole black peppercorns

½ small onion

2 whole boneless, skinless chicken breasts

¼ cup nonfat buttermilk

3 tablespoons plain nonfat yogurt

Zest and juice of 1 lemon

¼ teaspoon kosher salt, plus more for cooking water

¼ teaspoon freshly ground black pepper

8 ounces snow peas, strings removed, cut diagonally into ¾-inch pieces

1 pound fresh peas, shelled (1 cup)

1 bunch asparagus (about 1 pound), tough ends removed, cut into 1-inch lengths

1 14-ounce can artichoke hearts, drained and quartered

¼ cup fresh mint leaves, roughly chopped

1 head Boston lettuce

1. Place the stock, bay leaves, peppercorns, and onion in a large saucepan, cover, and bring to a boil over high heat. Reduce heat to a simmer, and add the chicken breasts. Cook the chicken until cooked through, about 10 minutes. Transfer the chicken and stock to a bowl to cool.

2. Combine the buttermilk, yogurt, lemon zest, lemon juice, and salt and pepper in a large bowl. Remove the chicken from the stock mixture, setting aside the liquid for soup-making. Cut the chicken into ¾-inch chunks, and add to the buttermilk mixture. Stir to combine.

3. Cover and bring a large pot of salted water to a boil. Prepare an ice-water bath. Cook the snow peas, uncovered, until bright green and tender, about 1 minute. Remove with a slotted spoon, and transfer to the ice-water bath. Add fresh peas to boiling water; cook until bright green and tender, about 1 minute. Remove with a slotted spoon; transfer to the ice bath with the snow peas. Add asparagus to boiling water, and cook until bright green and tender, about 2 minutes. Remove with a slotted spoon, and transfer to the ice-water bath.

4. When vegetables are cool, drain, and transfer to paper towels to dry. Add to chicken mixture; toss to combine. Add artichoke hearts and mint. Arrange lettuce leaves among six plates; divide the chicken salad evenly among the plates. Serve.

FIT TO EAT RECIPE PER SERVING: 190 CALORIES, 2 G FAT, 49 MG CHOLESTEROL, 15 G CARBOHYDRATE, 828 MG SODIUM, 25 G PROTEIN, 5 G DIETARY FIBER

louisiana crab salad
with lemon vinaigrette

SERVES 6

When Patrick Dunne, the owner of Lucullus, an antiques shop in the French Quarter in New Orleans, entertains, he may serve this simple, elegant salad created by restaurateur and friend Hubert Sandot. Keep the crabmeat on ice as you pick it over.

- 1½ tablespoons fresh lemon juice
- 1½ teaspoons rice-wine vinegar
- ¼ cup extra-virgin olive oil
- 2 tablespoons finely chopped fresh basil leaves
- ¼ cup finely chopped fresh flat-leaf parsley
- ½ tablespoon kosher salt
- 1½ tablespoons freshly ground pink and black peppercorns
- 2 pounds jumbo lump crabmeat, shells and cartilage removed
- ½ bunch chives, for garnish

1. In a medium bowl, whisk together the lemon juice, vinegar, oil, basil, parsley, salt, and ground peppercorns until well combined. Set vinaigrette aside at room temperature for 1½ hours for the flavors to combine.

2. In a large bowl, toss together the crabmeat and the vinaigrette, being careful not to break up the crabmeat. Let salad stand at room temperature for 15 minutes. Garnish with chives; serve.

crab salad with noodles
and spicy carrot sauce

SERVES 6

If you can't find chile oil, make your own by mixing canola oil and cayenne pepper to taste.

- 1 5-ounce cucumber
- 8 ounces carrots, finely chopped
- 1 tablespoon freshly grated ginger
- ½ teaspoon ground cardamom
- ¾ teaspoon kosher salt, plus more for cooking water
- 1 teaspoon fresh lemon juice
- 1 teaspoon chile oil
- 1 tablespoon rice-wine vinegar
- 2 ounces thin rice noodles
- 1 cup fresh jumbo lump crabmeat, shells and cartilage removed
- 1 mango, peeled, pit removed (see page 647), cut into ¼-inch dice
- 2 ounces mesclun, watercress, or other mixed greens

1. Seed the cucumber, and cut lengthwise into very thin strips; set aside.

2. Place the carrots, ginger, cardamom, ¼ teaspoon salt, and 1 cup water in a saucepan. Cover and simmer until tender, 15 minutes.

3. Purée the carrot mixture in the bowl of a food processor; strain through a fine sieve or cheesecloth-lined strainer, extracting as much liquid as possible by pressing on the solids with the back of a spoon. Add the lemon juice, chile oil, vinegar, and ½ teaspoon salt to the carrot sauce; refrigerate. (This can be made a day in advance.)

4. Cover and bring a large pot of salted water to a boil. Cook the noodles in the boiling water until tender, about 5 minutes. Rinse in cold water.

5. Toss together the noodles, crab, mango, cucumber, and half the carrot sauce. Divide the greens and crab mixture among serving plates, pour the remaining sauce over, and serve.

FIT TO EAT RECIPE PER SERVING: 136 CALORIES, 1 G TOTAL FAT, 16 MG CHOLESTEROL, 24 G CARBOHYDRATE, 776 MG SODIUM, 8 G PROTEIN, 2 G DIETARY FIBER

mediterranean tuna salad

SERVES 6

Bound with oil and vinegar and studded with roasted red peppers and kalamata olives, this tuna salad needs little more accompaniment than a glass of cold, crisp white wine.

- 6 red new potatoes, cut into ½-inch-thick wedges
- 2 tablespoons plus 1 teaspoon extra-virgin olive oil
- ½ teaspoon kosher salt, plus more for cooking water
- 1 pound haricots verts, trimmed
- 1½ cups loosely packed fresh basil leaves
- 2½ tablespoons white-wine vinegar
- ½ teaspoon freshly ground black pepper
- 1 bunch fresh spinach leaves, chopped (5 cups)
- 12 cherry tomatoes, halved
- 2 celery stalks, strings removed, cut into ¼-inch-thick slices
- 1 cucumber, halved lengthwise, seeded and cut into ¼-inch-thick slices
- 2 scallions, white and pale-green parts, thinly sliced
- 1 roasted red pepper (see page 645), cut in 1-inch pieces
- 2 6-ounce cans water-packed solid white tuna, drained
- 6 kalamata olives, pitted and chopped

1. Preheat the oven to 450°F. Place the potatoes in a roasting pan, and drizzle with 1 teaspoon oil. Toss, then roast until browned, about 30 minutes.

2. Cover and bring a pot of salted water to a boil. Prepare an ice-water bath. Add the haricots verts to the boiling water, and cook until bright green and just tender, about 2 minutes. Drain; transfer the haricots verts to the ice-water bath until cool. Drain again, and set aside.

3. Place the basil, vinegar, ½ teaspoon salt, the pepper, and 2 tablespoons warm water in a blender, and purée until smooth. With the machine running, add 2 tablespoons olive oil, and purée until combined.

4. In a large bowl, combine the spinach, tomatoes, celery, cucumber, scallions, roasted potatoes, roasted pepper, reserved basil purée, and tuna; toss. Divide the haricots verts among six plates; top with the tuna salad. Garnish with the chopped kalamata olives, and serve.

FIT TO EAT RECIPE PER SERVING: 255 CALORIES, 8 G FAT, 23 MG CHOLESTEROL, 29 G CARBOHYDRATE, 519 MG SODIUM, 20 G PROTEIN, 6 G DIETARY FIBER

papaya, jícama, and avocado salad

SERVES 4

Martha loves this salad as a main course for a light lunch.

- ¼ cup fresh lime juice
- 2 tablespoons extra-virgin olive oil
- 1 teaspoon kosher salt, plus more for seasoning
- ⅛ teaspoon freshly ground black pepper, plus more for seasoning
- 1 small avocado, peeled and pitted (see page 647)
- 1 papaya (about 1½ pounds), peeled, seeded, and cut into ½-inch dice
- 1 medium (about 1 pound) jícama, peeled, cut into ½-inch dice
- ¼ cup fresh cilantro leaves, coarsely chopped

1. In a small bowl, whisk together the lime juice, olive oil, 1 teaspoon salt, and the pepper; set aside.

2. Cut the avocado into ½-inch cubes. In a medium bowl, combine the papaya, jícama, and avocado. Add the lime vinaigrette, and toss well to combine. Add the cilantro, season with salt and pepper, and toss to combine. Serve.

healthy chopped salad

SERVES 6

Chopping the ingredients allows you to scoop a little bit of each into every forkful.

- ¾ teaspoon kosher salt, plus more for cooking water
- 8 ounces haricots verts, trimmed
- 3 tablespoons balsamic vinegar
- ½ teaspoon freshly ground black pepper
- 2 tablespoons extra-virgin olive oil
- 2½ ounces mesclun, or any small lettuce
- 2 6-ounce cans water-packed solid white tuna, drained
- 2 red, yellow, or orange bell peppers, seeds and ribs removed, cut into ½-inch dice
- 1 small head radicchio, cut into ¼-inch strips
- 1 head Belgian endive, cut into 1-inch pieces
- 1 pound yellow or red tomatoes, cut into ½-inch dice
- 5 white-button mushrooms, wiped clean, quartered, stems intact

1. Cover and bring a large pot of salted water to a boil. Prepare an ice-water bath. Cook the haricots verts in the boiling water until bright green and just tender, 1 to 3 minutes. Transfer the beans immediately to the ice-water bath to stop the cooking. Drain; cut into 1-inch lengths; set aside.

2. Combine the vinegar, black pepper, and ¾ teaspoon salt in a small bowl. Whisk in the oil until combined. Toss the vinaigrette with the mesclun, tuna, peppers, radicchio, endive, tomatoes, and mushrooms, or arrange the salad in rows on a platter, and drizzle with the vinaigrette. Serve.

FIT TO EAT RECIPE PER SERVING: 173 CALORIES, 6 G FAT, 23 MG CHOLESTEROL, 12 G CARBOHYDRATE, 510 MG SODIUM, 18 G PROTEIN, 4 G DIETARY FIBER

summer shrimp salad

SERVES 6

- 1½ pounds (about 18) jumbo shrimp, peeled and deveined
- 2 tablespoons olive oil, plus more for brushing
- ¾ teaspoon kosher salt
- ½ teaspoon freshly ground black pepper
- 2 limes
- 2 tablespoons roughly chopped fresh cilantro, or flat-leaf parsley, plus sprigs for garnish
- 2 mangos, peeled, pit removed (see page 647), cut into ½-inch dice
- 2 cucumbers, seeded, cut into ½-inch dice
- ½ small red onion, finely diced
- 1 small (about ¾ pound) jícama, peeled and cut into ½-inch dice

1. Preheat the oven to 400°F. Place the shrimp on a sheet brushed with olive oil. Sprinkle the shrimp with ¼ teaspoon salt and ¼ teaspoon pepper. Transfer to the oven, and roast until opaque and cooked through, about 8 minutes.

2. Zest the limes; squeeze them to yield ¼ cup of juice. In a small bowl, combine the lime juice, zest, 2 tablespoons olive oil, cilantro, and the remaining ½ teaspoon salt and ¼ teaspoon pepper. In a medium bowl, combine 2 tablespoons of the lime dressing with the shrimp; toss to coat. In a large bowl combine the mangos, cucumbers, red onion, jícama, and the remaining lime dressing; toss to coat. Divide the salad and the shrimp among six bowls. Garnish with the remaining cilantro sprigs, and serve.

FIT TO EAT RECIPE PER SERVING: 225 CALORIES, 7 G FAT, 172 MG CHOLESTEROL, 17 G CARBOHYDRATE, 439 MG SODIUM, 24 G PROTEIN, 1 G DIETARY FIBER

creamy vinaigrette

MAKES ABOUT 1/4 CUP

2 teaspoons raspberry vinegar or
   red-wine vinegar
   Kosher salt and freshly ground black
   pepper
1 tablespoon plus 1½ teaspoons sour cream
2 tablespoons extra-virgin olive oil

In a medium bowl, whisk together the vinegar, salt and pepper, and sour cream. Slowly whisk in the oil until combined.

pink peppercorn vinaigrette

MAKES ABOUT 3/4 CUP

Pink peppercorns (see Food Sources, page 648) are not actually true peppercorns but the berries from the Baies rose plant.

1 teaspoon Dijon mustard
2 tablespoons white-wine vinegar
2 tablespoons whole pink peppercorns
½ cup extra-virgin olive oil
   Kosher salt and freshly ground
   black pepper

Place the mustard, vinegar, and peppercorns in a medium bowl; whisk. Slowly whisk in the oil until combined. Season with salt and pepper.

STORING VINAIGRETTES

Most vinaigrettes can keep for at least a week in a jar in the refrigerator.

Those with fresh herbs should be used within a day or two of making them. Bring to room temperature before serving.

---

herb vinaigrette

MAKES ABOUT 1/2 CUP

½ small shallot, peeled and finely chopped
1 garlic clove, smashed and minced
1 tablespoon red-wine vinegar
2 teaspoons sherry vinegar
1 tablespoon balsamic vinegar
½ teaspoon kosher salt
⅛ teaspoon freshly ground black pepper
3 tablespoons extra-virgin olive oil
1 tablespoon plus 1 teaspoon minced
   fresh herbs, such as thyme, chives, basil,
   and tarragon

In a bowl, whisk together the shallot, garlic, vinegars, salt, and pepper. Slowly whisk in the oil until combined. Add the herbs, and whisk to combine.

pumpkin vinaigrette

MAKES ABOUT 2 CUPS

Pumpkin seeds, also called pepitas, are available at health-food stores and Mexican markets. This vinaigrette is delicious poured over grilled sweet white or red onion rounds.

½ cup extra-virgin olive oil
1 cup pumpkin seeds
   Kosher salt
¼ cup fresh lemon juice
   Freshly ground black pepper

1. Heat 2 tablespoons olive oil in a medium skillet over medium-low heat. Add the pumpkin seeds, and cook, stirring occasionally, until golden, about 15 minutes, being careful that the seeds don't jump from the skillet as they pop. Set the skillet aside to cool.

2. Place half of the cooked pumpkin seeds in the bowl of a food processor; add a pinch of salt, and pulse until finely ground. With the machine running, slowly add the remaining ¼ cup plus 2 tablespoons olive oil. Add the lemon juice, and season with salt and pepper.

lemon-parsley vinaigrette

MAKES 1 CUP

Use this dressing the day you make it.

- 1   bunch fresh flat-leaf parsley, stems and leaves separated
- ¼   cup fresh lemon juice
- ½   cup extra-virgin olive oil
      Kosher salt and freshly ground black pepper

1. Line a small bowl with a double layer of dampened cheesecloth. In the bowl of a food processor, combine the parsley stems, one-quarter of the leaves, and the lemon juice. Process 5 minutes, scraping down the sides of the bowl as needed with a rubber spatula. Transfer the purée to the cheesecloth-lined bowl. Squeeze out as much liquid as possible; discard any solids.

2. Coarsely chop the remaining parsley leaves; transfer to a medium bowl. Add the reserved parsley juice to the bowl, and slowly whisk in the olive oil until combined. Season with salt and pepper.

blood-orange vinaigrette

MAKES 1 CUP

Fresh-squeezed juice from any orange can be used.

- ¾   cup fresh blood-orange juice (4 blood oranges)
- 1   tablespoon Dijon mustard
- 1   tablespoon plus 1 teaspoon white-wine vinegar
- ¾   teaspoon crushed red-pepper flakes
- 1   tablespoon whole yellow mustard seeds
      Kosher salt
- 3   tablespoons extra-virgin olive oil

In a medium bowl, whisk together the orange juice, mustard, vinegar, pepper flakes, seeds, and salt. Slowly whisk in the olive oil until combined.

yellow-tomato vinaigrette

MAKES 1 CUP

- 2   medium yellow tomatoes, quartered
- 2½ tablespoons white balsamic or white-wine vinegar
- 1   teaspoon kosher salt
- ⅛   teaspoon freshly ground black pepper
- ¼   cup extra-virgin olive oil
- 1   teaspoon fresh tarragon leaves, coarsely chopped

1. Place the tomatoes in the bowl of a food processor. Pulse until puréed, yielding ½ cup. Set a strainer over a medium bowl, and pass the purée through the strainer, pressing on the solids with a rubber spatula. Set aside the juice, and discard any solids.

2. Whisk in the balsamic vinegar, salt, and pepper. Slowly whisk in the olive oil until combined. Add the tarragon leaves 15 minutes before serving.

black-olive vinaigrette

MAKES 1 CUP

Black-olive paste is available at specialty food stores and Italian markets. To make your own, pit oil-cured olives, and chop into a fine paste.

- ¼   cup plus 1 tablespoon black-olive paste
- 1   teaspoon Dijon mustard
      Freshly ground black pepper
- ¼   cup red-wine vinegar
- ¼   cup plus 3 tablespoons extra-virgin olive oil

In a medium bowl, whisk together the black-olive paste, mustard, pepper, and vinegar until well combined. Slowly whisk in the oil until combined.

guava vinaigrette

MAKES ½ CUP

Canned or bottled guava nectar can be found in Latin American markets and in the international sections of large grocery stores.

- ¼ cup guava nectar
- 1 tablespoon fresh lime juice
- ½ teaspoon Dijon mustard
  Kosher salt and freshly ground black pepper
- ¼ cup extra-virgin olive oil

In a medium bowl, whisk together the guava nectar, lime juice, and mustard. Season with salt and pepper. Slowly whisk in the olive oil. The vinaigrette may be made up to 1 day ahead and refrigerated in an airtight container.

orange vinaigrette

MAKES ½ CUP

- 3 tablespoons Orange-Juice Reduction (recipe follows)
- 2 tablespoons white-wine vinegar
  Kosher salt and freshly ground black pepper
- 2 tablespoons extra-virgin olive oil

In a bowl, whisk together the orange-juice reduction and vinegar. Season with salt and pepper. Slowly whisk in the olive oil until combined. Store in an airtight container, refrigerated, up to 5 days.

orange-juice reduction

MAKES ½ CUP

- 3 cups fresh orange juice (about 9 oranges)

Place the juice in a small nonreactive saucepan over medium-high heat. Gently boil until the liquid has reduced to ½ cup and is syrupy, about 1 hour. Store the reduction in an airtight container, refrigerated, up to 5 days.

shallot vinaigrette

MAKES ABOUT ½ CUP

- 1 shallot, minced
- 1 teaspoon Dijon mustard
- 2 tablespoons sherry vinegar
- 1 tablespoon chopped fresh flat-leaf parsley
- ½ teaspoon kosher salt
- ¼ teaspoon freshly ground black pepper
- ¼ cup walnut oil

Place the shallots, mustard, vinegar, parsley, salt, and pepper in a medium bowl, and whisk to combine. Still whisking, slowly add the walnut oil.

avocado dressing

MAKES 1 CUP

This dressing should not be made too far ahead—avocado flesh turns brown when exposed to air. Drizzle this over grilled chicken or fish.

- 1 avocado
- ¼ cup loosely packed fresh basil leaves
- 1 small garlic clove
  Juice of 2 limes
- 3 tablespoons red-wine vinegar
- ½ cup extra-virgin olive oil
  Kosher salt and freshly ground black pepper

1. Slice the avocado in half lengthwise. Remove and discard the pit and peel, and place the flesh in the bowl of a food processor. Add the basil, garlic, lime juice, and vinegar; process until combined.

2. With the machine running, slowly add the olive oil through the feed tube, and process until the dressing is smooth. It should have a thick but pourable consistency; give an extra squeeze or two on the limes to adjust the consistency. Season with salt and pepper, and use promptly.

creamy lemon-buttermilk vinaigrette

MAKES ¾ CUP

- 2 lemons
- ¼ cup plus 2 tablespoons nonfat buttermilk
- 3 tablespoons nonfat yogurt
- 1 medium shallot, minced
   Kosher salt and freshly ground black pepper

Using the smallest holes of a box grater, remove the zest from 1 lemon; set aside. Squeeze the juice from both lemons, yielding ¼ cup. In a small bowl, whisk together the buttermilk, yogurt, lemon zest and juice, and shallot; season with salt and pepper. Store in an airtight container, refrigerated, up to 3 days.

creamy tomato dressing

MAKES ABOUT 1 CUP

- 3 small (12 ounces) tomatoes, quartered
- ¼ cup low-fat cottage cheese
- 3 tablespoons fresh lemon juice
- 1 teaspoon extra-virgin olive oil
- 2 tablespoons chopped fresh marjoram
- 1 teaspoon kosher salt
- ⅛ teaspoon freshly ground black pepper

1. Process the tomatoes in a food processor until smooth. Pass all the liquid through a fine strainer into a bowl; discard the seeds and skin.

2. Using a rubber spatula, press the cottage cheese through a strainer into the tomatoes. Add the remaining ingredients; whisk to combine. Refrigerate until ready to use.

FIT TO EAT RECIPE PER TABLESPOON: 7 CALORIES, 0 G FAT, 0 MG CHOLESTEROL, 1 G CARBOHYDRATE, 100 MG SODIUM, 0 G PROTEIN, 0 G DIETARY FIBER

creamy lemon-herb dressing

MAKES 1 CUP

This salad dressing is a delicious nonfat alternative to mayonnaise-based dressings.

- 2 teaspoons grated lemon zest
- 1 tablespoon fresh lemon juice
- 2 tablespoons snipped chives
- 1 tablespoon chopped fresh basil
- 2 tablespoons chopped fresh dill
- 1 tablespoon chopped fresh tarragon
- 8 ounces silken tofu
- 1 tablespoon Dijon mustard
- 1 tablespoon white-wine vinegar
   Kosher salt and freshly ground black pepper

Place all the ingredients in the bowl of a food processor. Process until smooth and creamy. Season with salt and pepper.

FIT TO EAT RECIPE PER TABLESPOON: 11 CALORIES, 0 G FAT, 0 MG CHOLESTEROL, 1 G CARBOHYDRATE, 88 MG SODIUM, 1 G PROTEIN, 0 G DIETARY FIBER

sandwiches

AND

savory pies

....

caesar salad sandwiches

MAKES 6

Choose a rectangular rustic loaf with a crisp crust and a soft interior for this portable salad.

- 1 pint cherry tomatoes, halved
- ½ cup plus 3 tablespoons extra-virgin olive oil
- 1 tablespoon balsamic vinegar
  Kosher salt and freshly ground black pepper
- 1 garlic clove, pressed or smashed to a paste
  Juice of 2 lemons
- 3 anchovy fillets, chopped
- ½ teaspoon Dijon mustard
- 1 12- to 16-ounce loaf rustic bread
- 1 head (about 1¼ pounds) romaine lettuce, limp outer leaves discarded, inner leaves separated and left whole
- 2 ounces Parmigiano-Reggiano cheese, shaved as thinly as possible

1. Preheat oven to 250°F. Line a baking sheet with parchment paper. Place the tomatoes in a mixing bowl with 3 tablespoons olive oil and the vinegar, sprinkle with salt and pepper, and toss to coat. Spread tomatoes, cut-side up, on the sheet; bake until wrinkled and starting to dry but still juicy, about 1 hour. Remove from the oven, and set aside to cool. Raise oven temperature to 375°F.

2. In a small jar with a lid, combine the garlic, lemon juice, anchovies, ½ cup olive oil, salt and pepper to taste, and mustard. Tighten the lid, and shake well; set aside.

3. Slice the loaf of bread lengthwise, leaving a hinge on one side, and remove most of the crumb so there is more crust than bread (use the crumb to make bread crumbs; see page 647). Place the bread shell in the oven, and toast until golden, about 6 minutes.

4. Drizzle a small amount of the dressing over the bread; toss the remaining dressing with the romaine, about half of the cheese, and pepper to taste. Arrange the romaine on the bottom half of the bread, sprinkle the tomatoes and the remaining cheese over the romaine, and close the sandwich. Slice crosswise into 6 sandwiches; serve.

inside-out tomato "sandwich" with warm vinaigrette

MAKES 4

More a salad than a sandwich, this version of the sublime summer treat must be eaten with a knife and fork. A slice of bread is sandwiched between thickly sliced, very ripe tomatoes.

- 2 large (about 1½ pounds) beefsteak tomatoes
- 4 ½-inch-thick slices sourdough bread
- 2 teaspoons finely chopped fresh flat-leaf parsley
- 1 teaspoon finely chopped fresh basil
- 1 teaspoon snipped chives
- ½ teaspoon finely chopped fresh mint
- ½ teaspoon finely chopped fresh tarragon
- ¼ teaspoon finely chopped fresh sage
- 1 tablespoon red-wine vinegar
- ¼ teaspoon kosher salt, plus more to taste
- ⅛ teaspoon freshly ground black pepper, plus more to taste
- 3 tablespoons extra-virgin olive oil

1. Use a small sharp paring knife to cut out the stem end of each tomato. Slice the tomatoes crosswise into ½-inch-thick rounds, and set aside.

2. Cut each piece of bread into a square as wide as the diameter of the tomato slices; set bread aside.

3. Heat a grill pan or the broiler to medium hot. Toast bread until golden, about 2 minutes per side.

4. Place 1 tomato slice on a plate. Cover with 1 piece of bread, and place 1 more tomato slice on top. Repeat, making three more sandwiches with the remaining tomato and bread slices.

5. In a small heat-resistant bowl, combine the parsley, basil, chives, mint, tarragon, sage, vinegar, ¼ teaspoon salt, and ⅛ teaspoon pepper. Heat the olive oil in a small saucepan over medium heat until very hot but not smoking, about 1 minute. Remove from the heat, and pour oil over the herb mixture.

6. Spoon warm herb-and-oil mixture evenly over each sandwich. Season with salt and pepper. Let sandwiches stand for 5 minutes before serving.

pan bagnat

MAKES 4

This salad, made portable by sandwiching it between sliced rolls brushed with olive oil, is composed of tuna, olives, hard-boiled eggs, and fresh vegetables, and drizzled with a vinaigrette.

- 4   *ounces young string beans or haricots verts*
- ½   *red onion, thinly sliced*
- ½   *fennel bulb, thinly sliced*
- 1   *pint cherry tomatoes, quartered*
- ½   *red bell pepper, seeds and ribs removed, cut into strips*
- ½   *cup black oil-cured or Niçoise olives, pitted and halved*
- 2   *tablespoons capers, drained*
- 2   *6½-ounce cans solid tuna, drained*
- 1   *bunch watercress, stems removed*
     Watercress Vinaigrette (recipe follows)
     Kosher salt and freshly ground black pepper
- 4   *large crusty rolls*
- 2   *hard-boiled eggs (see page 571), sliced*

In a bowl, combine beans, onion, fennel, tomatoes, bell pepper, olives, capers, tuna, and watercress with ¾ cup vinaigrette. Season with salt and pepper. Slice open rolls; scoop out some of the top halves. Brush remaining vinaigrette on insides of rolls. Pile salad mixture on the bottom pieces, and top with the egg slices. Cover with the tops of the rolls. Serve immediately.

watercress vinaigrette

MAKES 1 CUP

- 1   *garlic clove*
- 1   *cup watercress leaves and some stems, loosely packed*
- 2   *thin slices fennel bulb*
     Juice of 3 lemons
- 1   *teaspoon kosher salt*
- ½   *teaspoon freshly ground black pepper*
- 1   *cup extra-virgin olive oil*

1. Combine the garlic, watercress, fennel, lemon juice, salt, and pepper in a blender until smooth. With the motor running, slowly add the oil.

2. Blend until the oil is completely incorporated. Store, covered, for up to 3 days in the refrigerator. Shake well before using.

mediterranean melt

MAKES 4

- 3   *lemons*
- 8   *baby artichokes*
- ½   *cup oil-cured black olives, pitted and coarsely chopped*
- ¼   *cup olive oil*
- 1   *small garlic clove, minced*
     Kosher salt and freshly ground black pepper
- 1   *cup loosely packed fresh flat-leaf parsley, roughly chopped*
- 4   *plum tomatoes, sliced ¾ inch thick*
- 4   *rustic-style rolls*
- 8   *ounces Taleggio or fontina cheese, sliced ¼ inch thick*

1. Slice 2 lemons in half; squeeze the juice into a bowl of cold water. Add lemon halves to bowl.

2. Trim the tips and outer leaves from the artichokes; thinly slice, lengthwise; submerge in the lemon water. Combine the olives with 1 tablespoon oil in a small bowl.

3. Heat 1½ tablespoons oil in a skillet over medium heat; add the garlic. Cook until fragrant, about 30 seconds. Pat the artichoke slices dry; add to the skillet. Cook until golden, about 5 minutes. Squeeze the juice of the remaining lemon over the artichokes; season with a generous pinch of salt and pepper. Add ½ cup chopped parsley; toss. Transfer to a small bowl; cover with aluminum foil.

4. Return the skillet to the heat; add the remaining 1½ tablespoons of oil. Arrange the tomatoes in the skillet. Sprinkle with remaining ½ cup parsley, and season with salt and pepper. Cook until the tomatoes are golden around edges, about 5 minutes. Turn; cook 1 to 2 minutes.

5. Preheat the broiler to medium high. Slice the rolls; scoop out the bottom, creating a cavity for the filling; spread with the olive mixture. Mound artichokes over the olives; arrange several tomatoes over the artichokes. Arrange the cheese over the tomatoes. Place the sandwiches and the tops of the rolls, crumb-side up, on a baking sheet; broil until the cheese is melted and the bread is golden, about 2 minutes. Close the sandwiches. Serve hot.

classic burgers

MAKES 4

Ask your butcher to custom-grind the meat: The fresher the grinding, the better the burger. To achieve a crunchy exterior and juicy interior, handle the meat as little as possible. Resist the temptation to press down on the hamburger with the back of a spatula; it squeezes out the juices and results in a dry burger.

- 2 *pounds ground beef, preferably chuck*
- 2 *teaspoons kosher salt*
- ¼ *teaspoon freshly ground black pepper*
- 4 *Homemade Hamburger Buns (recipe follows) or prepared*
- 8 *Bibb lettuce leaves*
- 2 *medium tomatoes, thickly sliced*
  Homemade Spicy Ketchup (opposite), optional

Preheat a grill or a grill pan to medium high. Season the meat with salt and pepper; mix very lightly. Shape into 4 patties, and place them on the hot grill. Cook 4 to 6 minutes per side for rare, and 9 to 11 minutes for well done. Serve on warm or toasted buns, topped with lettuce, tomato, and ketchup.

homemade hamburger buns

MAKES 12

- 1½ *cups warm water (110°F)*
- ⅔ *cup instant nonfat dry milk*
- ⅓ *cup unsalted melted butter, cooled*
- 3 *tablespoons sugar*
- 2 *¼-ounce packages active dry yeast (1 tablespoon plus 1 teaspoon)*
- 1 *large egg*
- 2 *large egg yolks*
- 5 *cups all-purpose flour, plus more for dusting*
- 1½ *teaspoons kosher salt*
  Canola oil, for bowl
- 2 *tablespoons milk*
- 1 *tablespoon seeds, such as sesame, poppy, fennel, or cumin, optional*

1. Place the warm water, dry milk, butter, and sugar in a large mixing bowl, and stir to combine. Sprinkle the yeast over the mixture, whisk, and let stand until yeast is foamy, about 10 minutes.

2. Add egg, 1 egg yolk, 2 cups flour, and salt; whisk until smooth. Add 2½ cups flour; stir with a wooden spoon. When mixture becomes too thick to stir, use your hands. Add up to another ½ cup flour until dough is tacky when pinched but not sticky. Turn out onto a lightly floured work surface; knead for 1 minute. Let stand 10 minutes.

3. Knead dough again until smooth and elastic, about 5 minutes. Place in a lightly oiled bowl; cover with plastic wrap. Leave in a warm place until doubled in size, about 45 minutes. Punch down dough; divide in half. Cut each half into sixths; form flattened balls. Arrange buns 3 inches apart on parchment-lined baking sheets. Cover; let stand until doubled in size, 45 minutes.

4. Preheat the oven to 400°F. Whisk remaining egg yolk and milk; brush egg wash lightly over buns. Top buns with the seeds, if using. Bake until golden and hollow sounding when tapped, 13 to 15 minutes. Cool on a wire rack. Buns can be frozen in resealable plastic bags up to 2 months.

WHAT TO PUT ON YOUR BURGER

Cheddar, Swiss, mozzarella, blue cheese, or Gorgonzola cheese

Mushrooms sautéed with Marsala wine

Chopped chipotles in adobo sauce

Asian chili paste

Grilled eggplant

Pickled jalapeño peppers

A slice of pickled-green tomato

Hummus

Good-quality prepared salsa

Good-quality prepared mango chutney

homemade spicy ketchup
MAKES ABOUT 1½ CUPS

1 *28-ounce can plum tomatoes*

1½ *teaspoons olive oil*

1 *small onion, finely chopped*

½ *jalapeño pepper, seeds and ribs removed, minced*

1 *medium garlic clove, minced*

3 *tablespoons packed dark-brown sugar*

4 *whole cloves*

¼ *teaspoon ground mace*

½ *teaspoon whole cardamom seeds*

½ *teaspoon whole black peppercorns*

2 *whole star anise*

1 *large dried bay leaf*

1 *small cinnamon stick*

1 *tablespoon dry mustard*

1½ *tablespoons cider vinegar*

¼ *teaspoon cayenne pepper*

1½ *teaspoons fresh lime juice*

½ *teaspoon kosher salt*

1. Pass tomatoes and their juice through a food mill fitted with a large disk or a strainer into a bowl. Discard solids; set tomatoes aside.

2. Heat the olive oil in a large heavy saucepan over medium-low heat. Add the onion, jalapeño pepper, and garlic, and cook until translucent, about 10 min-

3. Cut a double thickness of cheesecloth into a 7-inch square. Place the cloves, mace, cardamom, peppercorns, star anise, bay leaf, and cinnamon stick in the center. Fold the sides of the cheesecloth around the spices, roll up, and tie with kitchen string. Add the bouquet garni and the mustard to the tomato mixture, and cook over medium-low heat until the mixture is reduced by two-thirds, about 25 minutes.

4. Stir in the vinegar, cayenne, lime juice, and salt. Reduce heat to low, and cook for 10 minutes. Keep refrigerated up to 2 weeks.

turkey burgers
MAKES 4

If the turkey is custom-ground for these burgers, ask the butcher for a mix of light and dark meat.

1½ *pounds ground turkey*

¼ *red bell pepper, seeds and ribs removed, finely chopped*

¼ *yellow bell pepper, seeds and ribs removed, finely chopped*

1 *medium shallot, minced*

2 *scallions, minced*

1 *teaspoon hot red-pepper sauce*

2 *teaspoons Worcestershire sauce*

2 *teaspoons fresh thyme leaves or 1 teaspoon dried*

1 *teaspoon kosher salt*

¼ *teaspoon freshly ground black pepper*

4 *Homemade Hamburger Buns (opposite) or prepared*

½ *bunch watercress (about 1 cup)*

1. Preheat a grill or a grill pan to medium high. Combine turkey, peppers, shallot, scallions, pepper sauce, Worcestershire, thyme, salt, and pepper in a large bowl; mix very lightly to combine.

2. Form 4 patties, and place them on the hot grill; cook through, about 7 minutes per side.

3. Serve on buns, toasted if desired, topped with watercress.

open-face turkey sandwiches with mushroom gravy

MAKES 4 SANDWICHES

This sandwich can be made with the recipe for Roast Turkey Breast and Gravy (page 272), or with your own turkey and gravy leftovers.

- 1 tablespoon unsalted butter
- 1 shallot, minced
- 1 teaspoon fresh thyme leaves
- 1 pound mixed domestic and wild mushrooms, such as shiitake, oyster, or cremini, wiped clean and quartered
  Kosher salt and freshly ground black pepper
- ½ cup Madeira wine
- 1½ cups turkey gravy
- 4 thick slices white sandwich bread
- 3 pounds roast turkey breast
- ½ small bunch watercress

1. Preheat the oven to 400°F. Melt the butter in a large skillet over medium heat. Add the shallot and thyme; cook until translucent, about 2 minutes. Add the mushrooms; cook until they release their liquid and are soft, about 5 minutes. Season with a generous pinch of salt and pepper. Add the Madeira, raise heat to high, and cook until the liquid is cooked away, about 5 minutes. Add the gravy; cook until thick enough to coat the back of a spoon.

2. Meanwhile, toast the bread until golden but still soft, about 2 minutes. Slice the turkey into ¼-inch-thick slices; submerge in the gravy. Cook until the turkey is hot, about 1 minute.

3. Place toast on serving plates, spoon 1 or 2 tablespoons of gravy over toast, and scatter watercress on top. Arrange turkey over toast, and spoon the mushrooms and gravy over the meat. Serve hot.

savory pea pie

MAKES ONE 9-INCH PIE; SERVES 8 TO 10

A perfect main-course savory pie, this recipe combines black-eyed peas with other favorite Southwest flavors. Look for raw chorizo, a highly seasoned pork sausage, at specialty meat markets and Latin grocery stores. Hot Italian sausage may be substituted for the chorizo.

- 3 tablespoons olive oil
- 12 large white-button mushrooms, wiped clean, sliced into ¼-inch pieces
  Kosher salt and freshly ground black pepper
- 1 medium onion, thinly sliced
- 8 ounces raw chorizo sausage, casing removed, crumbled
- 1 jalapeño pepper or fresh red-chile pepper, seeds and ribs removed, finely diced
- 1 bunch (12 ounces) fresh spinach, washed, stems removed
- 3 cups Traditional Black-Eyed Peas (page 333)
- 6 ounces Monterey Jack cheese, grated on the large holes of a box grater
- 2 tablespoons chopped fresh cilantro
- 2 large eggs
- ½ cup heavy cream
- ½ teaspoon cayenne pepper
  All-purpose flour, for dusting
  Martha's Perfect Pâte Brisée (page 634)

1. Preheat the oven to 375°F with a rack in the center. In a large, heavy skillet, warm 2 tablespoons olive oil over medium heat. Add the mushrooms, and cook until softened and moisture is released, about 10 minutes. Season with salt and pepper. Transfer the mushrooms to a colander placed over a bowl to cool.

2. Add the remaining tablespoon of oil to the skillet with the onion. Cook until the onions are very soft, about 10 minutes. Add the sausage, and cook, stirring as needed, until very soft and meat is cooked through, 5 to 10 minutes; onions will begin to caramelize. Add the jalapeño, and cook to soften, about 4 minutes. Season with salt and pepper. Transfer to a colander to cool slightly.

3. In the bowl of a food processor, working in batches if necessary, place the spinach, half the black-eyed peas, the cheese, cilantro, 1 egg, the cream, and cayenne pepper. Process until well combined but the mixture still has some texture. Season with salt and pepper.

4. On a lightly floured surface, roll out half the dough to a 12-inch circle. Transfer the dough to a 9-inch pie plate, allowing the excess dough to hang over the edge. Layer the filling in the following order: sausage mixture, mushrooms, and spinach mixture. Top with an even layer of the remaining black-eyed peas.

5. Roll out the remaining dough to a 9-inch circle; transfer to the top of the pie. Fold the excess dough of the bottom crust over the edge of the top crust. Use a fork to seal the edges. Using kitchen scissors, cut a 2-inch cross in the center of the dough. Fold back each of the four corners.

6. Whisk together the remaining egg with 1 teaspoon water for an egg wash. Brush the top of the dough with the wash. Bake the pie on a baking sheet to catch any drips, until the dough is golden brown, rotating the pie halfway through for even baking, 45 to 60 minutes. Let the pie rest at least 15 minutes; serve hot.

cherry tomato "pie" with gruyère crust

MAKES ONE 10-INCH PIE; SERVES 8

Gruyère cheese and cherry tomatoes provide a savory version of that summer classic, the double-crusted fruit pie. Resist the temptation to eat this pie straight from the oven. Wait until it has reached room temperature; the juice from the tomatoes will have had time to collect. Serve it as a light lunch or as a side dish.

- 2¾ cups plus 2 tablespoons all-purpose flour
- 2½ teaspoons kosher salt
- 2½ teaspoons sugar
- 1¼ cups grated Gruyère cheese
- 1 cup (2 sticks) plus 1 tablespoon cold unsalted butter, cut into pieces
- 1 large onion, diced
- 3 garlic cloves, minced
- 2 pounds assorted cherry tomatoes
- ½ cup chopped fresh basil leaves
  Pinch of freshly ground black pepper
- 1 large egg

1. In the bowl of a food processor, combine 2½ cups flour, 1 teaspoon salt, 1 teaspoon sugar, and 1 cup grated cheese. Add 1 cup butter pieces; process until mixture resembles coarse meal, 8 to 10 seconds. With machine running, gradually pour ¼ cup of ice water through the feed tube. Pulse until dough holds together without becoming wet or sticky; do not process more than 30 seconds. To test, squeeze a small amount of the mixture together: If it is crumbly, add more ice water, 1 tablespoon at a time.

2. Divide dough into two equal balls. Flatten each into a disk; wrap in plastic wrap. Chill 1 hour.

3. Melt remaining tablespoon butter in a large skillet over medium heat. Add onion and garlic. Cook, stirring occasionally, until translucent and softened, about 8 minutes. Transfer to a bowl to cool slightly.

4. Place tomatoes in a large bowl. Toss with remaining ¼ cup plus 2 tablespoons flour, 1½ teaspoons salt, and 1½ teaspoons sugar, and the basil and pepper; when the onion mixture is cooled, add to tomato mixture; toss to combine. Transfer the mixture to a deep 9- or 10-inch pie plate. Set aside.

5. Preheat the oven to 375°F. Roll out half the dough into a circle 1 inch larger than the pie plate. (The remaining dough may be frozen up to 2 months for later use.) Transfer rolled dough to top of plate; tuck in edges to seal. Make 3 to 4 small slits in the top crust; form a decorative edge.

6. In a small bowl, mix the egg with 1 teaspoon water for an egg wash. Brush the egg wash over the crust; sprinkle the crust with the remaining ¼ cup of grated cheese. Place the pie plate on a baking sheet to catch drips; bake until the crust is golden and the insides are bubbling, about 50 minutes. Bring to room temperature, and serve.

oven-dried tomato tartlets

MAKES SIX INDIVIDUAL 4-INCH TARTLETS

Inspired by tarte tatin, the classic French apple dessert, these savory individual tartlets can be made with puff pastry or Martha's Perfect Pâte Brisée (page 634). Use 4-inch tartlet pans with nonremovable bottoms to prevent the juice from running out of the molds (see Equipment Sources, page 650).

- 2 ounces fontina or Gruyère cheese
- 1 17¼-ounce package frozen
  puff pastry, thawed
  All-purpose flour, for dusting
- 2 tablespoons extra-virgin olive oil
- 2 tablespoons roughly chopped
  fresh herbs, such as thyme, oregano,
  or marjoram
- 5 dozen dried-cherry tomato or
  32 dried plum-tomato halves (see
  Oven-Dried Tomatoes, page 618)
  Kosher salt and freshly ground
  black pepper
- 1 large egg

1. Preheat the oven to 400°F. Line a baking sheet with parchment paper. Have ready six 4-inch tartlet pans with nonremovable bottoms. Using the large holes of a box grater, grate the cheese into a large bowl. Set aside.

2. Place 1 sheet of puff pastry on a lightly floured surface. Without rolling out the dough, cut out four 4-inch circles. Transfer the circles to the prepared baking sheet. From the second sheet of puff pastry, cut out two more 4-inch circles; transfer these to the baking sheet. Cover the dough with plastic wrap, and transfer the baking sheet to the refrigerator.

3. Arrange the tartlet pans on a clean work surface. Drizzle 1 teaspoon olive oil into the bottom of each pan. Sprinkle half the chopped herbs in an even layer over the oil. Arrange the dried tomatoes on top of the herbs, evenly covering the pan bottoms. Sprinkle with the reserved grated cheese and the remaining herbs. Season with salt and pepper.

4. In a small bowl, whisk together the egg and 1 teaspoon water to make a wash. Remove the chilled dough from the refrigerator. Place the pastry rounds over the tomato filling in the pans. Brush rounds with the egg wash. Transfer tartlet pans to the freezer, and chill 15 minutes.

5. Remove tartlet pans from freezer, and transfer to the baking sheet. Bake until pastry is golden brown, about 20 minutes. Transfer baking sheet to a wire rack until pans are cool enough to handle.

6. Using your fingers, gently unstick crusts from rims as needed. Turn out each tartlet onto a serving plate, tapping to loosen any tomatoes. Serve tartlets warm or at room temperature.

potato and root vegetable tarts

MAKES FOUR INDIVIDUAL 4-INCH TARTS

Thinly sliced potatoes create a delicious crust in these hearty tarts. One large 8- to 9-inch tart may also be made in a tart pan with a removable bottom (the cooking time will be slightly longer).

- 3 large Yukon gold potatoes
- 1 small onion, cut into 1½-inch pieces
- 1 medium parsnip, cut into 1½-inch pieces
- 1 small turnip, cut into 1½-inch pieces
   Kosher salt and freshly ground black pepper
- ½ teaspoon dried thyme
- ¾ cup Homemade Chicken Stock (page 624), or low-sodium store-bought chicken broth, skimmed of fat
- ¼ cup Madeira wine
   Extra-virgin olive oil
- 4 sprigs fresh thyme

1. Preheat the oven to 425°F. Peel 2 potatoes; cut into 2-inch pieces; combine with onions, parsnips, and turnips in a roasting pan. Season with salt, pepper, and thyme; toss well. Add stock. Roast until vegetables are tender and liquid evaporates, about 45 minutes. Remove from oven, add Madeira, and scrape up any brown bits with a wooden spoon.

2. Pass the vegetables and liquid through a food mill with a fine or medium disk. Season with salt.

3. With a mandoline or sharp knife, slice remaining potato lengthwise paper-thin to yield at least 24 slices. Brush four 4-inch tart pans lightly with olive oil. Arrange 6 slices in each pan in an overlapping pinwheel pattern so the potatoes touch in center of tin; overhang edge by about 1 inch.

4. Place a baking sheet in the oven to heat. Spoon about ¼ cup of the vegetable purée into the center of each pan. Place a sprig of thyme on top, and fold the potato slices inward. Brush lightly with more olive oil. Transfer pans to the heated baking sheet, and bake until puffed and golden brown, about 20 minutes. Brush with more oil, and serve.

FIT TO EAT RECIPE PER SERVING: 215 CALORIES, 2 G TOTAL FAT, 0 MG CHOLESTEROL, 43 G CARBOHYDRATE, 481 MG SODIUM, 5 G PROTEIN, 4 G DIETARY FIBER

spanakopita

MAKES ONE 11 X 15-INCH PIE; SERVES 8 TO 10

Spanakopita is a traditional Greek spinach pie with a flaky phyllo crust. Many people use Cream of Wheat in this savory pie as it helps to bind the other ingredients together.

- 4 tablespoons unsalted butter
- ¼ cup olive oil
- 1 1-pound package frozen phyllo pastry
- 4 bunches (3¼ pounds) fresh spinach, washed, stems removed, coarsely chopped
- 1½ cups finely chopped scallions, white and pale-green parts (4 large bunches)
- 1 cup finely chopped fresh flat-leaf parsley (2 large bunches)
- 6 large eggs, beaten
- 8 ounces small-curd cottage cheese
- 1 pound feta cheese, crumbled
- 2 tablespoons chopped fresh dill
- ¼ cup uncooked Cream of Wheat

1. Preheat the oven to 350°F. with a rack in the center. Melt butter and oil in a small saucepan over medium heat. Brush an 11 x 15 x 2-inch baking pan with the butter-oil mixture. Layer 7 sheets of phyllo in the pan, brushing each with the butter mixture. In a large bowl, thoroughly combine the spinach, scallions, parsley, eggs, cottage cheese, feta, dill, and Cream of Wheat.

2. Spread about 2 cups spinach filling over the phyllo in the pan. Cover with 2 more sheets of phyllo, brushing each with the butter mixture. Repeat layering 2 cups filling and 2 sheets of the phyllo, brushing each with the butter mixture, until all filling has been used, about 4 more layers.

3. Top with 7 more sheets of the phyllo, brushing each with the butter mixture. Press gently around the edges so the layers adhere to one another. Prick the surface all over with a toothpick.

4. Bake 15 minutes, reduce heat to 300°F, and continue baking until the pastry is golden, about 1 hour. Let stand 1 hour before serving.

spinach ricotta tart

MAKES ONE 8½-INCH TART; SERVES 6

This crustless tart must be made in a springform pan for easy serving. Cooked frozen spinach can be substituted for fresh; the texture of the tart will be slightly rougher though no less flavorful. Whatever spinach you use, thoroughly dry it to prevent the tart from becoming watery.

- 1 15-ounce container part-skim ricotta
  Olive oil, for brushing
- 1 bunch (12 ounces) fresh spinach, washed, stems removed
- 1½ cups loosely packed fresh basil leaves
- 1 teaspoon kosher salt
- ¼ teaspoon freshly ground black pepper
- ¼ teaspoon ground nutmeg
- 2 large eggs
- 1 large egg white

1. Wrap the ricotta tightly in fine cheesecloth; place in a colander over a bowl. Place a heavy bowl or cans on top, and let drain, refrigerated, for 3 hours or overnight.

2. Preheat the oven to 350°F. Brush an 8½-inch springform pan with olive oil. Place the drained ricotta, spinach, basil, salt, pepper, and nutmeg in the bowl of a food processor. Blend until smooth; scrape sides as needed, about 1 minute. Add the eggs and egg white; blend about 5 seconds. Pour the mixture into the prepared pan; bake until set and just brown around the edges, 40 to 45 minutes. Transfer to a wire rack to cool, about 5 minutes; run a paring knife around edges before unmolding. Cut into wedges; serve warm or at room temperature.

FIT TO EAT RECIPE PER SERVING: 139 CALORIES, 7 G FAT, 6 MG CHOLESTEROL, 93 G CARBOHYDRATE, 517 MG SODIUM, 12 G PROTEIN, 1 G DIETARY FIBER

sorrel and onion tart

MAKES TWO 7 X 11-INCH TARTS;
EACH SERVES 6 TO 8

Sorrel is a tender, slightly sour green. It is available in most large grocery stores and gourmet shops in the spring. If you can't find it, use spinach. Serve this for brunch or a lunch buffet.

- 4 tablespoons unsalted butter
- 5 Vidalia onions, thinly sliced
- 2 bunches (about 1½ pounds) fresh sorrel or spinach, washed
  Kosher salt and freshly ground black pepper
  All-purpose flour, for dusting
- 2 8-ounce sheets frozen puff pastry
- 2 large egg yolks
- ¼ cup heavy cream

1. Melt the butter in a heavy, deep saucepan over medium-low heat. Add the onions. Cook, stirring frequently, until the onions are soft and translucent, about 15 minutes.

2. Strip and discard tough center ribs from sorrel leaves. Cover and bring a large stockpot of salted water to a boil. Add sorrel, and cook just until the leaves wilt, 1 to 2 minutes. Drain in a colander, let cool, and squeeze out any excess liquid.

3. Add the sorrel to the onions; cook over low heat until the mixture breaks down and is almost soupy, about 20 minutes. Season with salt and pepper. Remove from the heat, and let cool.

4. Preheat the oven to 400°F with two racks. Line two baking sheets with parchment paper. On a lightly floured surface, roll 1 sheet of puff pastry into a 7 x 11-inch rectangle, about ⅛ inch thick. Transfer the dough to one of the baking sheets, and chill in the refrigerator 30 minutes. Repeat the process with the second sheet of puff pastry.

5. Remove both sheets of puff pastry from the refrigerator. Using a sharp knife, score a ½-inch border around the perimeter of each sheet, creating a picture-frame look. Using a fork, prick the entire surface within the scored edges on each sheet. In a small bowl, combine 1 egg yolk and 2 tablespoons of the heavy cream to make a wash; carefully brush the egg wash onto the borders.

6. Transfer both the sheets of dough to the oven, and bake until the pastry has puffed up and is golden brown, about 15 minutes. Remove the pastry from the oven.

7. Add remaining egg yolk and remaining 2 tablespoons of cream to the sorrel mixture, and stir to combine. Divide filling in half, and spread one half over each puff pastry. Return the tarts to the oven, and bake until filling is hot throughout, about 20 minutes. Remove the tarts from the oven, and transfer to a wire rack to cool, about 10 minutes. Cut the tarts into 2-inch squares, and serve warm.

vidalia onion tarte tatin

MAKES ONE 10-INCH TART; SERVES 10

- 1 tablespoon unsalted butter
- 2 teaspoons sugar
- 9 to 11 small (about 2½ pounds) Vidalia or other sweet onions
- 1 leek, white part only, halved lengthwise, well washed (see page 646)
- 1 tablespoon fresh thyme or 1 teaspoon dried, plus more for garnish

  Kosher salt and freshly ground black pepper
- 1½ cups Homemade Chicken Stock (page 624), or low-sodium store-bought chicken broth, skimmed of fat, or water
- 1 teaspoon balsamic vinegar

  All-purpose flour, for dusting

  Herbed Pastry Dough (page 636)

1. Melt butter in a 10-inch ovenproof nonstick skillet; sprinkle with sugar; remove from heat.

2. Cut 6 onions in half crosswise; fit them snugly into pan, cut-sides down. Cut leek into lengths the same height as onion halves, and fit them into spaces near the center of the pan. Sprinkle with half the thyme leaves; season with salt and pepper.

3. Slice remaining onions ¼ inch thick; place over onion halves. Sprinkle with remaining thyme and salt and pepper. Cook over medium-high heat for 5 minutes. Reduce heat to medium; cook 5 minutes, until onions are golden brown on cut side. Shake pan gently and rotate on burner for even browning.

4. Pour stock and vinegar over onions, bring to a simmer, cover, and cook over low heat for 25 minutes, or until onions are tender. Uncover, raise heat, and cook until liquid is syrupy and almost completely reduced. Remove from heat; cool slightly.

5. Preheat the oven to 375°F. On a lightly floured surface, roll out pastry ⅜ inch thick and just larger than the pan. Wrap the dough around the rolling pin; unroll over the pan, tucking in the excess.

6. Bake 30 to 35 minutes, until pastry is golden brown and juices are bubbling. Cool in pan 10 minutes; invert onto a serving plate. Serve warm, garnished with fresh thyme.

zwiebelkuchen
(savory bacon-and-onion tart)

MAKES ONE 10 X 16-INCH TART;
SERVES 8 TO 10

This German tart has a slightly sweet base, with a savory topping made from eggs, sour cream, onions, bacon, caraway seeds, and salt.

¾ cup milk

5 tablespoons unsalted butter, room temperature, plus more for bowl

¼ cup sugar

Kosher salt

Grated zest of ½ lemon

3 large egg yolks

1 ¼-ounce package (2 teaspoons) active dry yeast

3 cups plus 1½ teaspoons all-purpose flour, plus more for dusting

3 slices bacon, cut into ½-inch dice

3 large onions, finely chopped

⅓ cup plus 2 tablespoons sour cream

1 large egg

1 teaspoon caraway seeds

1. Place the milk and 4 tablespoons butter in a small saucepan, and heat until the butter has melted. Remove the pan from the heat, and let the mixture cool until tepid.

2. Place the milk mixture in the bowl of an electric mixer fitted with the paddle attachment. On low speed, add the sugar, salt to taste, the lemon zest, egg yolks, and yeast. Gradually add 3 cups flour, creating a dough that is soft but not sticky.

3. Turn the dough out onto a lightly floured surface, and knead until it is smooth and elastic and springs back when you poke it with your finger, about 5 minutes. Place the dough in a large buttered bowl, and cover tightly with buttered plastic wrap. Let rise in a warm place until the dough has doubled in size, about 1 hour.

4. Preheat the oven to 400°F. Line a 12 x 17-inch baking sheet with parchment paper. Punch the dough down, and roll out to a ¼-inch thickness. Place on the baking sheet, and cover with buttered plastic wrap; let rise until the dough doesn't spring back when you poke it with a finger, about 20 minutes.

5. Melt the remaining tablespoon of butter in a large skillet over medium heat. Add the bacon, and cook until golden and crisp and most of the fat has been rendered, about 6 minutes. Add the onions, and cook, stirring occasionally, until translucent, 8 minutes. Reduce heat to low. Sprinkle 1½ teaspoons flour over the onions, and stir in. In a small bowl, whisk together the sour cream and the egg, and stir into the onion mixture. Cook, stirring, until the mixture thickens, about 1 minute. Remove the skillet from the heat, and season with salt.

6. Spread the mixture on top of the dough, and let rise 15 minutes more. Sprinkle the top with caraway seeds. Bake until the edges are crisp and brown, about 30 minutes. Transfer to a wire rack to cool, and serve. The tart will keep, wrapped and unrefrigerated, up to 3 days.

pizza 101

MAKES TWO 12- TO 14-INCH PIZZAS

Since you are setting your oven to 500°F to bake the pizza properly, make sure that the oven is clean to avoid unwanted smoke.

Pizza Dough (page 178)
All-purpose flour, for dusting
Coarse-grain yellow cornmeal, for dusting
Pizza Sauce (page 178)

1 *pound fresh mozzarella cheese, thinly sliced*

1. Preheat the oven to 500°F for at least 10 minutes with the oven rack in the lower third of the oven. If using a pizza stone, place it in the lower third of the oven, and preheat the oven to 500°F for at least 30 minutes.

2. Place the pizza dough on a clean surface. Using a sharp knife, divide the dough in half, and knead each half four or five turns into a ball. Set aside one of the dough balls, and cover with plastic wrap. On a lightly floured surface, place the dough; pat into a flattened circle, cover lightly with plastic wrap, and let rest 5 minutes. Remove the plastic wrap and, using your fingers, flatten and push the dough evenly out from the center until it measures about 7 to 8 inches in diameter. Do not press the dough all the way to the edges. Leave a slightly raised border, about ½ inch wide, around entire circumference of pizza dough.

3. Dust a baking sheet or wooden pizza peel with cornmeal; set aside. Pick up the dough, and center it on top of your fists. Hold your fists about 1 to 2 inches apart. Rotate and stretch the dough, opening your fists until they are 6 to 8 inches apart and the dough is several inches larger. Then place your fists under the inside of the outer edge, and continue to stretch it a little at a time until it reaches about 12 inches in diameter. The dough will drape down over your forearms. At this stage, it is important to keep your fists along the inside of the outer edge and watch that the dough does not get too thin or tear in the center. At the same time, make sure to maintain the slightly raised border on the edges. The dough is surprisingly resilient and will not tear if this step is done carefully and slowly.

4. Set the pizza dough on top of the baking sheet or peel. Pour 9 tablespoons of the pizza sauce onto the dough. Using the back of a tablespoon, evenly spread the sauce, leaving the ½-inch border of dough uncovered. Arrange half of the mozzarella slices on top of the sauce.

5. If using a pan, transfer it directly onto the oven rack. If using a peel, slide the pizza off the wooden paddle directly onto the heated stone using a slight jerking motion to loosen the pizza from the paddle. Slightly tilt the peel, and place the front tip of it on the backside of the stone. Slide the pizza off the peel, centering it on the stone. Bake until the crust is golden brown and crisp on the edges and the bottom, 10 to 12 minutes, using tongs to turn the pizza halfway through baking. Using tongs, lift the edge of the pizza, and slide the peel under it to remove it from the oven. Using a pizza wheel or serrated knife, slice the pizza into eight pieces, and serve immediately. While first pizza is baking, shape and assemble a second pizza using remaining dough, sauce, and cheese.

PIZZA BITES

Cut any pizza into bite-size pieces for instant hors d'oeuvres. One 12-inch pizza makes enough hors d'oeuvres for 8 to 10 people.

pizza dough

MAKES ENOUGH FOR
TWO 12- TO 14-INCH PIZZAS

1   cup warm water (110°F.)

¼   teaspoon sugar

1   ¼-ounce package active dry yeast
    (2 teaspoons)

2¾ to 3¼ cups all-purpose flour

1   teaspoon kosher salt

1½ tablespoons olive oil, plus more for bowl

1. Pour the warm water into a small bowl. Add the sugar, and sprinkle in the yeast. Using a fork, stir the mixture until the yeast is dissolved and water has turned tan. Let yeast stand until foamy, about 10 minutes. In a food processor, combine 2¾ cups flour and the salt, and pulse 3 to 4 times. Add the yeast mixture and the olive oil. Pulse until the dough comes together, adding more flour as needed until dough is smooth, not tacky, when squeezed. Transfer to a clean surface; knead four or five turns into a ball.

2. Place the dough in a lightly oiled bowl, smooth-side up. Cover tightly with plastic wrap. Let the dough rise in a warm place until doubled in size, about 40 minutes. Remove the plastic wrap, and place your fist in the center of the dough to punch it down. Fold the dough back onto itself four or five times. Turn the dough over, folded-side down, cover with the plastic wrap, and let rise again in a warm place until the dough has doubled in size, about 30 minutes. Use as directed in the recipe, or see Make-Ahead Pizza Dough box (page 180).

WHAT TO PUT ON YOUR PIZZA

*Sautéed wild mushrooms and
fresh mozzarella*

*Crumbled spicy Italian sausage
and sliced green olives*

*Fresh chopped tomatoes, buffalo
mozzarella, and basil leaves*

Prosciutto and Parmigiano-Reggiano cheese

*Clams, chopped garlic, and
extra-virgin olive oil*

Grilled eggplant and zucchini

*Robiola cheese and truffle oil
(drizzled on after pizza is baked)*

Sliced potatoes, bacon, and sage

*Feta cheese, tomatoes, kalamata olives,
and fresh oregano*

pizza sauce

MAKES ENOUGH FOR
TWO 12- TO 14-INCH PIZZAS

This classic pizza sauce may be refrigerated for up to 2 days or frozen for up to 2 months.

2   tablespoons olive oil

1   28-ounce can whole Italian peeled plum
    tomatoes

¾   teaspoon dried oregano

1½ teaspoons kosher salt

⅛   teaspoon freshly ground black pepper

1. Pour the olive oil into a large skillet, and place over medium heat. Using your hands, squeeze the tomatoes in the can to crush them. Add to the warm olive oil, along with the remaining ingredients. Cook over medium-low heat, breaking up tomatoes with a wooden spoon, until the sauce is thick, 40 to 50 minutes.

2. Pass sauce through a food mill fitted with a medium disk, discard the seeds, and let cool.

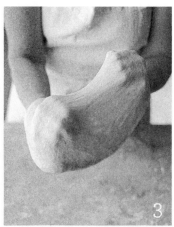

MAKING A PIZZA DOUGH

1. Allow the dough to rise until doubled in bulk, a visual rule of thumb indicating that the dough is ready. Punch back the dough and let it rise again. Pushing down the dough releases the gasses and redistributes the sugars and starches that yeast lives on.

2. Work on a lightly floured surface to keep the dough from sticking, but make sure not to be too liberal with the flour; too much can make the dough tough. Press out from the center until the dough is about 8 inches in diameter, leaving about a ½-inch raised border all around.

3. Lift the pizza, shifting your fists away from the center of the dough toward but not touching the border, so that it drapes over your fists (careful; it will tear if stretched too thin). Pull the dough out into a circle of about 12 inches in diameter; at the same time, make sure to maintain the border. If this seems too daunting, don't worry; a rolling pin can be used to roll out the dough instead.

4. Use a pizza peel to transfer the pizza to the oven and a preheated pizza stone. Using a slight jerking motion, slide the pizza back and forth on the paddle to loosen it. Slightly tilt the peel, place the front tip onto the back of the stone, and slide the pizza off, centering it on the stone. The more quickly you do this, the better; the pizza should cooperate without trouble. When the pizza is finished baking, use the peel to remove it from the oven.

caramelized onion, goat cheese, and turkey sausage pizza

MAKES TWO 12-INCH PIZZAS

This pizza has been a favorite at Sara Foster's Chapel Hill Market. A slice of the pizza and a green salad make a perfect lunch.

- ¼ cup olive oil, plus more for baking sheets
- 2 tablespoons unsalted butter
- 8 medium (3 pounds) red onions, sliced into ¼-inch rounds
- 10 garlic cloves
- 2 tablespoons balsamic vinegar
- 2 teaspoons sugar
- 1 teaspoon kosher salt
- ¼ teaspoon freshly ground black pepper
- 8 ounces turkey sausage
    Pizza Dough (page 178)
- 5 ounces goat cheese
- 2 teaspoons chopped fresh herbs, such as rosemary, parsley, and thyme

1. Heat 2 tablespoons oil and the butter in a large skillet over medium-low heat. Add the onions and garlic cloves, and cook until they begin to soften, stirring often, about 20 minutes. Add the vinegar, sugar, salt, and pepper, and cook until golden brown, stirring often, about 50 minutes. Set aside.

2. Heat 1 tablespoon olive oil in a large skillet on medium-high heat. Add the sausage, and cook until browned on all sides, about 10 minutes. Transfer the sausage to a cutting board, and slice into ¼- to ½-inch rounds. Set aside.

3. Preheat the oven to 400°F with two racks. Brush two baking sheets with olive oil, and set aside. Divide the pizza dough in half. Cover one of the pieces with plastic wrap, and set aside. Place the remaining half on a lightly floured surface. Roll the dough out to a 12-inch circle. Transfer to one of the baking sheets; repeat with the remaining dough. Brush the tops of the pizza dough rounds with the re-

maining tablespoon of olive oil. Top each pizza with a layer of the onion mixture, the sausage, and the goat cheese. Bake until the dough is golden brown and crisp, about 15 minutes. Transfer to a wire rack to cool slightly. Sprinkle the pizzas with the chopped fresh herbs; serve hot.

....

MAKE-AHEAD PIZZA DOUGH

Pizza dough can be made in advance and refrigerated for up to 12 hours or frozen for up to 3 weeks.

To make the dough in advance, follow the Pizza Dough recipe (page 178) through step 2, tightly cover with plastic wrap, and refrigerate. When ready to use, remove the plastic wrap, punch the dough down with your fists, and let it sit at room temperature until soft and pliable, about 30 minutes.

To freeze the dough, punch it down after the first rise in step 2. Fold it back onto itself 4 or 5 times as instructed. Divide the dough, and roll it out to the desired-size rounds. Stack the rounds, separated by parchment paper, then double wrap the stack tightly in plastic wrap, and freeze. To use, unwrap the frozen dough, and thaw slightly until the rounds are easily separated. Place each round in a lightly oiled bowl, and thaw at room temperature for 3 to 3½ hours, until each is completely thawed and the dough has doubled in size. Proceed as in step 2 of the Pizza 101 recipe (page 177).

....

ricotta pizza

MAKES THREE 6 X 12-INCH PIZZAS;
SERVES 6

1   tablespoon olive oil

2   teaspoons minced garlic

7   large (12 ounces) shallots, sliced into rings

4   anchovy fillets, chopped

1   14-ounce can artichoke hearts, drained
    and cut lengthwise into ¼-inch-thick slices

2   teaspoons chopped fresh thyme leaves

1   roasted red bell pepper (see page 645),
    cut into ¾-inch pieces

1   cup part-skim ricotta

¼   cup finely chopped fresh flat-leaf parsley
    Pizza Dough (page 178)
    All-purpose flour, for dusting
    Yellow cornmeal, for dusting

3   tablespoons grated Parmesan cheese

1. Place a pizza stone, if using, in the oven on the lowest shelf; preheat to 400°F. Heat the oil in a large skillet over medium-low heat. Add the garlic and shallots; cover. Cook until translucent, about 4 minutes. Add the anchovy fillets; cook about 2 minutes. Add the artichokes; cook until heated through, about 3 minutes. Stir in the thyme and the red pepper; remove from heat. Set aside. In a separate bowl, combine the ricotta and parsley.

2. Divide dough into three pieces. Cover two pieces with plastic wrap, and place the third piece on a lightly floured surface. Roll the dough out to an approximately 6 x 12-inch rectangle. Dust a baking sheet or wooden pizza peel with cornmeal, and place the dough on top. Arrange one-third of the artichoke mixture over the dough; using one-third of the ricotta mixture, drop teaspoonfuls onto the dough. Sprinkle with 1 tablespoon Parmesan. If using a baking sheet, transfer directly to the oven. Alternatively, transfer pizza from the peel to the pizza stone (see pages 178–79); bake until the dough is golden brown and crisp, about 10 minutes. Transfer to a wire rack to cool. Repeat with the remaining dough and toppings; serve hot.

FIT TO EAT RECIPE PER SERVING: 297 CALORIES, 5 G FAT, 15 MG CHOLESTEROL, 49 G CARBOHYDRATE, 624 MG SODIUM, 14 G PROTEIN, 4 G DIETARY FIBER

fig pizzas

MAKES 4 INDIVIDUAL 6-INCH PIZZAS

8   ounces pancetta or bacon,
    cut into small cubes

2   medium onions, thinly sliced

2   teaspoons sugar
    Freshly ground black pepper
    Pizza Dough (page 178)
    All-purpose flour, for dusting
    Cornmeal, for dusting

12 ripe figs, sliced lengthwise ¼ inch thick

½   cup kalamata olives, pitted and
    coarsely chopped

½   cup fresh ricotta cheese

1. Place a pizza stone, if using, in the oven on the lowest shelf; preheat the oven to 400°F. Cook pancetta in a skillet over medium-low heat until golden brown and crisp and most of the fat is rendered, about 15 minutes. Transfer pancetta to paper towels to drain. Pour off all but 3 tablespoons of fat.

2. Add the onions to the skillet, sprinkle with sugar, and season with pepper; raise heat to medium high. Cook the onions, stirring occasionally, until golden brown and slightly caramelized, about 15 minutes. Remove from the heat, and set aside.

3. Divide the pizza dough into quarters. On a lightly floured surface, roll out each portion to make a 6- to 7-inch rough circle about ¼ inch thick. Dust two baking sheets or a pizza peel with cornmeal; set aside. Arrange the pizza dough on the peel or sheets. Prick each circle of dough several times with a fork, leaving a ¾-inch border.

4. Divide cooked onions among pizzas; spread over dough, leaving a ¾-inch border between onions and the edge of the dough. Arrange sliced figs over onions, sprinkle with cooked pancetta and olives; dot the pizzas with the ricotta cheese.

5. Slide the pizzas onto the stone or onto the rack if using baking sheets, and bake until the pizza dough is crisp and golden and the topping is hot and bubbly, about 20 minutes. Serve hot.

escarole pizza

MAKES TWO 12-INCH PIZZAS

On this Mediterranean-inspired pizza, heady Gruyère cheese rounds out the slightly bitter escarole and the sweet sliced almonds.

Yellow cornmeal, for dusting
All-purpose flour, for dusting
Pizza Dough (page 178)
2 tablespoons currants
2 tablespoons golden raisins
1 tablespoon olive oil
1 small red onion, cut into thin wedges
1 head escarole, roughly chopped
1 tablespoon balsamic vinegar
1 cup coarsely grated Gruyère cheese
Freshly grated nutmeg, for sprinkling
2 tablespoons finely grated Parmesan cheese
2 tablespoons sliced almonds

1. Place a pizza stone, if using, in the oven on the lowest shelf; preheat oven to 400°F. Dust a baking sheet or wooden peel with cornmeal; set aside. On a lightly floured surface, roll out one half of the dough into a 12-inch circle. Transfer dough to the baking sheet or peel; cover with plastic wrap. Roll out the second piece of dough, and transfer to a baking sheet dusted with cornmeal. Cover with plastic wrap.

2. Place the currants and raisins in a small bowl. Cover with ¼ cup warm water; set aside. Heat the oil in a wide 6-quart saucepan over medium-high heat. When hot, add the onion; cook until translucent, about 2 minutes. Add the escarole and vinegar; cook until the escarole has wilted, about 2 minutes. Drain the currants and raisins, discarding the liquid, and add to the escarole mixture. Remove from the heat; set aside.

3. Remove the plastic wrap from the dough on the baking sheet or peel. Sprinkle half of the Gruyère over the dough, leaving a 1-inch border. Sprinkle nutmeg over the cheese, and cover with half of the escarole mixture. Top with 1 tablespoon of the Parmesan and 1 tablespoon of the sliced almonds.

4. Transfer the pizza to the stone in the oven, or onto the rack if using baking sheets; cook until crust is golden and crisp, 15 to 20 minutes. Transfer to a wire rack to cool slightly. Repeat with second piece of dough. Cut each pizza into wedges; serve hot.

FIT TO EAT RECIPE PER SERVING: 250 CALORIES, 10 G FAT, 13 MG CHOLESTEROL, 32 G CARBOHYDRATE, 212 MG SODIUM, 9 G PROTEIN, 4 G DIETARY FIBER

....

GRILLED PIZZA

Grilled pizza is infused with the unmistakable smoky flavor only a grill can provide. To grill, transfer the rolled-out pizza dough to a preheated grill brushed with olive oil, and cook until the bottom is golden brown and the top starts to bubble, 3 to 5 minutes. Quickly turn the crust over, and cook about 2 minutes more to ensure that the crust cooks through. Turn the crust over again. Scatter the toppings on top of the crust. Cover the grill, and let cook until the toppings are hot and bubbly, 6 to 8 minutes.

....

pasta, rice,
AND
grains

....

fresh pasta

MAKES 1 POUND

This pasta can be used for any recipe that calls for ribbon or filled pasta. Fresh pasta must be dried for several hours, until no moisture remains, before it is stored. This recipe can easily be halved; work in smaller quantities until you are comfortable with the technique. Rolling pasta by hand is undeniably a challenge. The dough must be rolled and stretched rapidly before it dries out, and rare is the novice who produces a flawless sheet on the first try … or the second, third, or fourth. No matter. Perfectly good pasta can be cut from less-than-perfect sheets. For pasta machines, see Equipment Sources, page 650.

  2   *cups all-purpose flour, plus more for work surface*

  4   *large eggs*

1. To make the dough by hand, mound the flour in the center of a work surface, and make a well in the middle. Crack the eggs into the well.

2. Beat the eggs with a fork until smooth, then begin to work the flour into the eggs with the fork.

3. Use a bench scraper to work in the rest of the flour, a bit at a time.

4. Once all the flour has been incorporated, start working the dough with your hands to form a rounded mass for kneading. Be sure your work surface is clean of all loose bits of dough; lightly dust with flour. Knead the dough about 10 minutes, or until smooth and elastic.

5. Cover the dough with an inverted bowl or plastic wrap, and allow to rest 1½ hours at room temperature, or refrigerate overnight.

6. Roll out the dough. (If rolling by hand, see note,

below). To roll using a pasta machine: Divide the dough into four pieces. Quickly knead and flatten a portion of the dough into a disk shape somewhat narrower than the machine opening; very lightly dust the dough with flour. Feed the dough through at the machine's widest setting. (If the pasta pulls or tears when passing through, simply sprinkle a little more flour over the dough before it's fed. When finished, remove the excess flour with a dry brush.) As the pasta sheet emerges, gently support it with your palm, and guide it onto the work surface. Fold the sheet lengthwise into thirds. Repeat the sequence twice with the same setting to smooth the dough and increase its elasticity. Thin the dough by passing it through ever finer settings, one pass on each setting from the widest to the narrowest (machine settings differ; some have as many as ten, others only six). Roll the remaining three portions of dough as soon as the first is finished. (For filled pasta, it's best to roll and cut a single portion at a time, otherwise the dough will dry out.) If your pasta machine comes with cutting rollers (most are equipped to make capellini, linguine, or fettuccine pasta), cut the sheets in the desired width. Alternatively, cut the sheets by hand (see below).

....

WORKING BY HAND

Lightly flour a clean work surface. Vigorously roll the dough into a very thin circle; apply even pressure. As the dough stretches, roll constantly. Do not bear down too hard or it will tear. Roll for several minutes, until the dough is as thin as possible, almost translucent. If it shrinks back as you roll, cover with a towel, and let rest 10 minutes.

To cut the sheets, lightly fold the sheets one at a time into thirds. Cut crosswise with a sharp knife to desired thickness.

....

pasta with roasted chestnuts and hazelnuts

SERVES 4

Kosher salt

¼ *cup extra-virgin olive oil*

1 *tablespoon unsalted butter*

2 *medium shallots, minced*

8 *fresh large chestnuts, peeled (see page 645), cut into quarters, or 8 vacuum-packed chestnuts (see Food Sources, page 648)*

¼ *cup dry white wine*

1 *cup Homemade Chicken Stock (page 624), or low-sodium store-bought chicken broth, skimmed of fat*

¼ *cup heavy cream*

16 *4-inch-square sheets fresh pasta (about 8 ounces) or pappardelle*

½ *cup blanched hazelnuts, toasted (see page 644), coarsely chopped*

1 *tablespoon fresh thyme leaves*

3 *tablespoons fresh flat-leaf parsley, coarsely chopped*

Freshly ground black pepper

¼ *cup pine nuts, toasted (see page 644)*

1. Cover and bring large pot of salted water to a boil. Add 2 tablespoons oil. In a skillet, heat remaining oil and the butter over low heat. Add shallots and chestnuts; cook until shallots are translucent, about 7 minutes. Add wine, stock, and cream; raise heat to high; cook until liquid is reduced by one-third, about 5 minutes. Cut pasta sheets in half with a fluted pastry wheel; place in boiling water. Cook until al dente, 2 to 3 minutes. Drain in a colander.

2. Reduce cream mixture's heat to medium low; stir in hazelnuts, thyme, and 2 tablespoons parsley. Season with salt and pepper; cook 2 minutes. Add pasta; toss. Remove from heat. Divide pasta among plates; drizzle sauce over top. Garnish with pine nuts and remaining parsley. Serve.

In Italy, fresh pasta, made with the soft white flour milled from the wheat of the Po Valley, is used for everyday cooking only in the northern region of Emilia-Romagna. Elsewhere, fresh pasta is often reserved for special occasions.

Making fresh pasta by hand is appealing for the pure sensual pleasure of it—kneading the dough into a plump, silky ball, then rolling it out into sheets of pale gold can be very satisfying. Handmade pasta doesn't necessarily require special skill—the dough is very forgiving. It does, however, require time and space. Before you crack a single egg, be sure to clear enough tabletops and chair backs for draping the dough after rolling and cutting; cover chairs with clean dishcloths, and lightly dust the flat surfaces with semolina flour. Like bread dough, pasta dough must be thoroughly worked to release and develop the flour's gluten, which gives the dough the elasticity necessary to produce a pasta both chewy and tender. When kneading and cutting by hand isn't an option, a food processor and hand-cranked roller can do the job.

spaghetti and tomato sauce 101

SERVES 2 TO 4

This is our simplest—and best—version of the classic spaghetti and red sauce. Two types of tomatoes can be used with our basic method: sweet, ripe cherry tomatoes or canned Italian plum tomatoes.

- ¼ teaspoon kosher salt, plus more for water
- 1½ pounds cherry tomatoes or vine-ripened tomatoes, or one 28-ounce can Italian plum tomatoes
- 8 ounces thin spaghetti
- ¼ cup extra-virgin olive oil
- 4 garlic cloves, cut into ⅛-inch-thick slices
- ¼ teaspoon crushed red-pepper flakes
- ¼ cup loosely packed fresh basil or fresh flat-leaf parsley leaves, torn

  Freshly grated Parmigiano-Reggiano cheese, optional

1. Cover and bring 3 quarts of salted water to a boil in a large stockpot.

2. If using cherry tomatoes, wash and stem. If using vine-ripened tomatoes, prepare an ice-water bath, and bring a large pot of water to a boil. Using a paring knife, score the nonstem end of each tomato with a shallow "x". Blanch the tomatoes in the boiling water for 30 seconds. With a slotted spoon, transfer the tomatoes to the ice-water bath (keep the water simmering on the stove). Using a chef's knife, cut the outer flesh away from the seedy cores of each tomato. Cut the flesh into ¼-inch-thick strips; set aside. Press the cores of the tomatoes through a sieve, and discard the seeds. If using canned tomatoes, strain, and pass through a food mill fitted with a fine disk.

3. Drop the spaghetti into the boiling water; stir to keep the pasta from sticking together. Cook until al dente, about 11 minutes.

4. Meanwhile, place a 12-inch skillet over medium heat; add the oil. Add the garlic, and cook, stirring occasionally, until the garlic is lightly golden, about 30 seconds. Add the red-pepper flakes and ¼ teaspoon salt. Cook until the garlic is medium golden, about 1 minute.

5. Increase heat to high. Tilting the pan at an angle, add the tomato strips and pulp from sieve. Cook, swirling pan occasionally, until the tomatoes begin to break down, the cherry tomatoes begin to burst, or the canned tomatoes begin to thicken, 5 to 6 min-utes. If using cherry tomatoes, mash a few with a spoon. If cherry tomatoes start to get too dry, add a little water from the pasta stockpot.

6. Drain the pasta in a colander, reserving 1 cup of the cooking liquid in case the sauce gets too dry. Add the pasta to the sauce in the skillet; cook until the sauce begins to cling to the pasta, 3 to 4 min-utes. Stir in the basil; cook 30 seconds more. Divide among serving bowls, and sprinkle with the cheese, if using.

SPAGHETTI AND TOMATO SAUCE TIPS

1. Add pasta to the water one handful at a time (or about a fourth of a 1-pound package at a time). It's important to stir the pasta frequently as it begins to boil to keep the strands from sticking together; stir only occasionally after that. Begin cooking the pasta right before the sauce. (Try to time it so that the sauce is done a little bit before the pasta, so the pasta can go directly into it to finish cooking.)

2. Tilt the pan away from you to avoid spattering as you pour the tomatoes and juices into the hot pan of garlic. Swirling occasionally, cook until tomatoes break down and become saucelike, about five minutes. Drain the pasta while the tomatoes continue to cook, reserving 1 cup of cooking water. Do not rinse the pasta; the starch that remains on the surface will help the sauce cling.

3. Rather than pouring the sauce over the pasta off the heat, slide the drained pasta into the pan with the sauce, gently tossing with tongs to coat. This way, the pasta gets a chance to absorb some of the sauce and become saturated with its rich flavors. If the sauce seems too dry, add some of the reserved pasta water.

spaghetti with veal bolognese sauce

SERVES 6

1 ¼-ounce package dried porcini mushrooms

1 large garlic clove

1 small (about 5 ounces) onion, cut into quarters

2 small carrots, cut into chunks

1 large celery stalk, strings removed, cut into chunks

1 tablespoon extra-virgin olive oil

1 pound veal shoulder, trimmed of all fat and cut into ¼-inch dice

½ cup dry red wine

¼ cup Tomato Sauce (recipe follows) or prepared

3½ cups Homemade Chicken Stock (page 624), or low-sodium store-bought chicken broth, skimmed of fat

¾ teaspoon kosher salt, plus more for water

⅛ teaspoon freshly ground black pepper

⅛ teaspoon ground nutmeg

1 pound spaghetti

¼ cup plus 2 tablespoons freshly grated Parmesan cheese (about 1 ounce), for garnish, optional

1. Place the porcini mushrooms in a small bowl, and cover with very hot water. Let stand until the porcini are soft, about 20 minutes. Lift mushrooms from liquid, and chop medium fine; set aside. Strain the liquid through cheesecloth; set liquid aside.

2. Place the garlic in the bowl of a food processor; process until finely chopped. Add the onion; process until finely chopped. Transfer the onions and garlic to a small bowl. Process the carrots in the food processor until coarsely chopped, about 15 pulses. Add the celery; process until the carrots and celery are finely chopped; set aside.

3. Heat the oil in a straight-sided skillet over medium-low heat. Add the vegetables, cover, and cook until translucent, about 8 minutes.

4. Add the veal, and raise heat to high; cook until the veal turns opaque, about 5 minutes. Add the wine; cook until evaporated. Stir in the tomato sauce, mushrooms, stock, reserved mushroom liquid, ¾ teaspoon salt, pepper, and nutmeg; bring to a boil. Reduce heat to medium low; simmer until the meat is tender and most of the liquid has been absorbed, about 2 hours.

5. Cover a large pot of salted water, and bring to a boil. Drop the pasta into the boiling water; stir to keep the pasta from sticking together. Cook until al dente. Drain and transfer to a large serving dish. Pour the sauce over the pasta; toss. Sprinkle with the Parmesan, if using. Serve hot.

FIT TO EAT RECIPE PER SERVING: 486 CALORIES, 9 G FAT, 76 MG CHOLESTEROL, 63 G CARBOHYDRATE, 613 MG SODIUM, 32 G PROTEIN, 4 G DIETARY FIBER

tomato sauce

MAKES 1 CUP

This classic tomato sauce may be refrigerated up to 1 week in an airtight container, or frozen up to 6 months. To serve, warm over low heat.

1½ tablespoons extra-virgin olive oil

2 garlic cloves

10 plum tomatoes (about 1½ pounds), cored, cut into eighths

Kosher salt and freshly ground black pepper

Heat oil in a medium skillet over medium heat. Add garlic; cook until golden, about 15 minutes. Add tomatoes; season with salt and pepper. Simmer until thickened, about 35 minutes. Remove from heat. Remove garlic; pass the sauce through a food mill fitted with a fine disk. The sauce may be used immediately, or stored as indicated above.

spaghetti with garlic three ways

SERVES 4

Garlic is toasted, roasted, and sautéed in this delicious dish.

- 1 head roasted garlic (see page 646), plus 8 raw cloves
  Kosher salt
- 1 pound spaghetti
- 2 tablespoons extra-virgin olive oil
- ¾ cup dry white wine
- 1 cup loosely packed fresh flat-leaf parsley leaves, roughly chopped
- 1 teaspoon crushed red-pepper flakes
  Freshly ground black pepper
  Freshly grated Parmesan cheese, for garnish

1. Squeeze the soft garlic out from each roasted clove into a small bowl. Set aside.

2. Cover and bring a large pot of salted water to a boil. Drop pasta into boiling water; stir to keep pasta from sticking together. Cook until al dente.

3. Meanwhile, thinly slice 5 cloves of the raw garlic. Finely chop the remaining 3 cloves. Heat the oil in a large skillet over medium heat. Add the sliced garlic; toast until golden and crisp, about 30 seconds. Remove the garlic with a slotted spoon; set aside. Add the chopped garlic; cook until translucent, about 1½ minutes. Add the reserved roasted garlic and the wine; let simmer about 3 minutes.

4. Drain the pasta, reserving a few tablespoons of the cooking liquid, and transfer the pasta to the skillet. Add the parsley, red-pepper flakes, and salt and pepper to taste, and toss. Add some of the reserved cooking liquid if the pasta seems too dry. Serve sprinkled with the toasted garlic slivers. Grate Parmesan over each serving. Serve.

perciatelli with garlic, walnuts, and tomatoes

SERVES 4

Perciatelli, also called bucatini, is hollow pasta slightly thicker than spaghetti. Use linguine or spaghetti if perciatelli is unavailable.

  Kosher salt
- 1 pound perciatelli pasta
- ¼ cup extra-virgin olive oil
- 3 large garlic cloves, peeled
- ¾ cup finely chopped fresh flat-leaf parsley
- 4 whole canned tomatoes, drained, seeded, and sliced ⅛ inch thick
- 2 tablespoons dry bread crumbs (see page 647), toasted
- 2 tablespoons finely chopped walnuts
  Pinch of crushed red-pepper flakes
- ¼ cup freshly grated pecorino cheese, plus 1 ounce shaved, for garnish, optional
  Freshly ground black pepper

1. Cover a large pot of salted water; bring to a boil. Drop pasta into boiling water; stir to keep pasta from sticking together. Cook until al dente; drain, reserving a few tablespoons of cooking liquid.

2. Meanwhile, in a large deep skillet, heat 3 tablespoons olive oil over medium-low heat. Add the garlic, and cook, turning, until browned, about 8 minutes. Add the cooked pasta, parsley, tomatoes, bread crumbs, walnuts, red-pepper flakes, grated pecorino, and the remaining tablespoon of olive oil, and season with salt and pepper; cook, tossing to combine, 1 to 2 minutes. Add some of the reserved cooking liquid if the pasta seems too dry.

3. Divide pasta among four plates; serve immediately, garnished with shaved pecorino, if using.

garden linguine with ricotta
SERVES 4

If fresh fava beans are not available, blanch thin asparagus instead, and cut into 1-inch-long pieces.

- 1 tablespoon kosher salt, plus more for water and seasoning
- 1 pound fresh fava beans, shelled
- 1 pound fresh or frozen peas, defrosted
- 1 pound linguine
- 1 cup ricotta cheese
- ½ cup freshly grated Parmesan cheese (from 1½ ounces)
- ¼ cup coarsely chopped mint leaves, plus more leaves for garnish
- ¼ teaspoon freshly ground black pepper, plus more for seasoning
- 2 tablespoons extra-virgin olive oil

1. Cover a large pot of salted water, and bring to a boil. Prepare an ice-water bath. Place the beans in a sieve, and lower into the boiling water. Let the water return to a boil, about 1 minute; blanch 1 minute more. Transfer the beans to the ice bath. Transfer to a colander; drain. Peel and discard the tough skins; set the beans aside.

2. Using the same boiling water and sieve, blanch the peas until just tender and bright green, about 3 minutes. Remove the sieve from the water; transfer the peas to the ice bath. Transfer the peas to the colander, drain, and set aside.

3. Discard the blanching water; fill the pot with fresh water. Add 1 tablespoon salt, cover, and bring to a boil. Drop the pasta into the water; stir to keep it from sticking together. Cook until al dente; drain, reserving 1 cup of the cooking water.

4. Meanwhile, combine ricotta, Parmesan, chopped mint, and ¼ teaspoon pepper in a bowl. Just before pasta finishes cooking, add reserved cup of cooking water to cheese mixture; stir to combine.

5. Drain the pasta in a colander, and transfer to a serving bowl. Add the olive oil; toss. Add the ricotta mixture, reserved fava beans, and reserved peas; toss to combine. Season with salt and pepper, sprinkle with the mint leaves, and serve.

pappardelle with osso buco sauce
SERVES 6

The sauce can be made a day ahead and reheated; the meat will be even more tender.

- 1 whole veal shank (about 1½ pounds osso buco), cut into 3 pieces
- 1 tablespoon extra-virgin olive oil
- 1 medium onion, diced
- 4 medium carrots, diced
- 3 celery stalks, strings removed, diced
- 1 red bell pepper, seeds and ribs removed, diced
- ½ cup dry white wine
- 1½ quarts Homemade Chicken Stock (page 624), or low-sodium store-bought chicken broth, skimmed of fat
- ½ ounce dried porcini mushrooms, broken into small pieces
- 1 cup canned chopped tomatoes
- ¼ teaspoon crushed red-pepper flakes
  Kosher salt
- 1 pound dried pappardelle or tagliatelle
- 1 tablespoon finely chopped fresh rosemary

1. Preheat the oven to 400°F. Trim the silver skin from the veal. Heat the oil in a Dutch oven, or shallow stockpot, over medium heat until very hot. Add the veal; cook until browned, turning as needed, about 5 minutes. Add the onion, carrots, celery, and red pepper; stir to combine. Reduce heat to medium low, and cook until the vegetables are softened, about 6 minutes. Increase heat to high, and add the wine; cook until almost all the wine has evaporated, about 5 minutes.

2. Add the stock, mushrooms, and tomatoes; bring to a boil. Cover the Dutch oven; transfer to oven. Cook 1 hour; uncover, and cook until the veal is falling off the bone and the sauce is quite thick, about 1 hour 10 minutes more. Using a wooden spoon, break the veal into smaller pieces, and remove and discard bones. Stir in red-pepper flakes.

3. Meanwhile, cover and bring a large stockpot of salted water to a boil. Drop the pasta into the boiling water; stir to keep the pasta from sticking together. Cook until al dente; drain and transfer to serving bowls, and top with the sauce. Garnish with the chopped rosemary, and serve hot.

FIT TO EAT RECIPE PER SERVING: 463 CALORIES, 8 G FAT, 69 MG CHOLESTEROL, 65 G CARBOHYDRATE, 215 MG SODIUM, 30 G PROTEIN, 13 G DIETARY FIBER

linguine with spicy clam sauce
SERVES 4

Littleneck clams can be substituted for the Manila clams.

- *1 tablespoon extra-virgin olive oil*
- *1 small garlic clove, thinly sliced*
- *½ teaspoon kosher salt, plus more for water*
- *¼ teaspoon freshly ground black pepper, plus more for seasoning*
- *1 pound linguine*
- *1 cup unsalted clam juice*
- *1 cup dry white wine*
- *2½ pounds Manila clams, scrubbed*
- *2 tablespoons capers, drained*
- *½ teaspoon crushed red-pepper flakes*
- *2 tablespoons unsalted butter*
- *½ cup loosely packed fresh flat-leaf parsley, coarsely chopped*

1. Heat the oil in a deep skillet over medium heat. Add garlic; cook until just golden, 1 to 2 minutes. Add ½ teaspoon salt and ¼ teaspoon pepper.

2. Cover a large pot of salted water, and bring to a boil. Drop pasta into boiling water; stir to keep pasta from sticking. Cook until al dente; drain, reserving a few tablespoons of the cooking liquid.

3. Meanwhile, add clam juice and wine to skillet; cook until liquid is reduced by a third, about 5 minutes. Add clams, capers, and red-pepper flakes; cover and cook until clams open, 10 to 12 minutes; discard unopened clams. Whisk in butter and parsley. Add pasta, and toss to combine, adding some of the reserved cooking liquid if pasta seems too dry. Season with salt and pepper. Serve hot.

fettuccine with mint, peas, ham, and cream
SERVES 4 TO 6

The mint enhances all the flavors and adds its own wonderfully fresh taste. Any variety of ham can be used instead of the Parma (see Food Sources, page 648).

- *2 tablespoons extra-virgin olive oil*
- *2 leeks, white parts only, very thinly sliced, well washed (see page 646)*
- *2 garlic cloves, minced*
- *1 cup Homemade Chicken Stock (page 624), or low-sodium store-bought chicken broth, skimmed of fat*
- *1 cup heavy cream*
- *3 ounces cooked Parma ham, cut into ⅛-inch-thick matchsticks*
- *1 cup frozen peas, defrosted*
- *Kosher salt and freshly ground black pepper*
- *1 pound fresh or dried fettuccine*
- *1 cup small fresh mint leaves, or chopped large leaves*

1. Heat the olive oil in large skillet over medium-low heat. Add the leeks and garlic, and cook until softened, about 3 minutes. Raise the heat to medium high. Add the chicken stock, cream, ham, and peas, and season with salt and pepper. Let the sauce cook until it is reduced by half, stirring frequently until it has thickened, about 6 minutes.

2. Cover a large pot of salted water, and bring to a boil. Drop the pasta into the boiling water; stir to keep the pasta from sticking together. Cook until al dente (about 4 minutes for fresh); drain, reserving a few tablespoons of the cooking liquid, and return the pasta to the pot. Add the sauce to the fettuccine, and toss to combine, adding cooking liquid if the pasta seems too dry. Transfer to a serving dish, sprinkle with the mint, and serve hot.

tagliatelle with asparagus and prosciutto

SERVES 4 TO 6

> 1   pound Fresh Pasta dough (page 184, made through step 6) or good-quality packaged pasta
>
>   All-purpose flour, plus more for dusting
>
> 1   pound asparagus, tough ends removed
>
> 1   tablespoon kosher salt
>
> 1   teaspoon olive oil
>
> 4   ounces prosciutto (or ham), cut into pieces
>
> 2   tablespoons thinly sliced fresh sage leaves
>
> 2½ cups heavy cream
>
> ¼   teaspoon ground nutmeg
>
>   Freshly ground black pepper
>
> 2   ounces freshly grated Parmesan cheese

1. Roll dough through remaining settings on machine (widest to narrowest), using as little additional flour as possible, until very thin. Place dough on a lightly floured surface; cut in half. Dry dough 5 to 10 minutes before cutting (this keeps pasta from clumping). To cut, lightly fold sheets one at a time into thirds. Cut crosswise with a sharp knife to desired thickness. Drape cut pasta over a chair back covered with a towel, on a rack, or spread on towels on a table to dry (dry completely if storing). Repeat with remaining pasta dough.

2. Prepare an ice-water bath. Cover and bring a pot of water to a boil. Cook asparagus just until tender when pierced with the tip of a knife, about 5 minutes. Transfer asparagus to ice bath. When cool, drain and cut into 2-inch lengths; set aside.

3. Cover and return water to a boil. Add salt; cook pasta until al dente, about 1 minute. Drain; set aside.

4. Heat a skillet over medium heat; add oil. Add prosciutto; cook until browned, about 3 minutes. Add sage and cream; cook until cream is slightly reduced and thickened, about 8 minutes. Add asparagus and pasta; warm about 3 minutes. Serve hot with nutmeg, pepper, and grated cheese.

orecchiette with raw tomato sauce

SERVES 8

The sauce would also be good over grilled meat or fish.

> 1   head of roasted garlic (see page 646)
>
> 10 large (about 2 pounds) plum tomatoes, coarsely chopped
>
> ¼   red onion, minced (2 tablespoons)
>
> ½   cup coarsely chopped fresh basil leaves, plus more for garnish
>
> ½   teaspoon crushed red-pepper flakes
>
> 4   oil-cured black olives, pitted and coarsely chopped
>
> 1   tablespoon capers, drained
>
> 1   teaspoon kosher salt, plus more for water
>
> ¼   teaspoon freshly ground black pepper
>
> 1   pound orecchiette pasta
>
> 1   ounce goat cheese, crumbled, optional

1. In a large nonreactive bowl, combine the roasted garlic, tomatoes, onion, basil, red-pepper flakes, olives, capers, 1 teaspoon salt, and pepper, and mix to combine. Cover with plastic wrap, and let stand at room temperature, stirring occasionally, for at least 2 hours and up to 6 hours.

2. Cover a large pot of salted water, and bring to a boil. Drop the pasta into the boiling water; stir to keep the pasta from sticking together. Cook until al dente; drain and combine with the tomato sauce. Add the goat cheese, if using, and toss to combine. Transfer to a large serving dish, garnish with more chopped basil, and serve immediately.

FIT TO EAT RECIPE PER SERVING: 255 CALORIES, 2 G TOTAL FAT, 2 MG CHOLESTEROL, 50 G CARBOHYDRATE, 359 MG SODIUM, 9 G PROTEIN, 3 G DIETARY FIBER

fusilli with shell beans and sausage

SERVES 6

2 dried bay leaves

½ teaspoon whole black peppercorns

1½ pounds fresh shell beans, such as cranberry, shelled (3 cups shelled)

1 large onion, halved

1½ teaspoons kosher salt, plus more for water

1 tablespoon olive oil

2 pounds sweet Italian sausage, casings removed

2 leeks, white and pale-green parts, sliced into ¼-inch-thick rounds, well washed (see page 646)

2 garlic cloves, minced

1 tablespoon fresh thyme leaves

1 pound fusilli pasta

¼ cup roughly chopped fresh flat-leaf parsley

Freshly ground black pepper

Freshly grated Parmesan cheese, optional

1. Tie the bay leaves and peppercorns in a piece of cheesecloth to make a bouquet garni, and place in a medium saucepan; add the beans, onion, and 1½ teaspoons salt. Cover with cold water, cover, and bring to a boil over medium-high heat. Reduce heat to low, and simmer until the beans are just tender, 15 to 20 minutes. Remove from the heat, and let the beans stand in the liquid until cool. Drain, reserving the liquid. Set aside. Discard the bouquet garni and the onion.

2. Cover and bring a large pot of salted water to a boil for the pasta. Pour the olive oil into a large skillet, and place over medium-high heat. Add the sausage, and cook, stirring with a wooden spoon to break up the large pieces, until well browned, 8 to 10 minutes. Add the leeks, garlic, and thyme; cook, stirring frequently, until softened, about 4 minutes. Reduce heat to low; add beans and 1 cup of the reserved cooking liquid. Bring to a simmer.

3. Drop the pasta into the boiling water; stir to keep the pasta from sticking together. Cook until al dente, about 9 minutes. Meanwhile, cover the skillet with the sausage mixture, and keep at a low simmer. Drain the pasta, reserving a few tablespoons of the cooking liquid. Transfer the pasta to the sausage mixture. Add the parsley, season with salt and pepper, and toss to combine, adding some of the reserved pasta water if the mixture is dry. Serve hot, topped with grated Parmesan, if desired.

gemelli with asparagus, mozzarella, and bacon

SERVES 6

12 ounces thickly sliced bacon

Kosher salt

1 pound gemelli or other tubular pasta, such as penne

1¼ pounds medium asparagus, tough ends removed, cut on a diagonal into 1-inch pieces

⅛ teaspoon crushed red-pepper flakes

2 tablespoons fresh marjoram or oregano leaves

12 ounces fresh buffalo or plain mozzarella cheese, cut into ½-inch cubes

Freshly ground black pepper

1. Cook the bacon in a skillet over medium heat until it is crisp and all the fat has been rendered, about 10 minutes. Remove the bacon from the pan, and drain on paper towels. Crumble the cooked bacon, and set aside. Remove skillet from heat.

2. Cover a large pot of salted water, and bring to a boil. Drop the pasta into the boiling water; stir to keep the pasta from sticking together. Cook until al dente; drain, reserving a few tablespoons of the cooking liquid.

3. Meanwhile, discard all but ¼ cup of the rendered bacon fat, and return the skillet to medium heat. Add the asparagus and the red-pepper flakes to the skillet. Cook until the asparagus is lightly browned. Add the pasta to the skillet with the crumbled bacon, and the marjoram; season with salt. Toss together until combined and heated through. Remove the skillet from the heat.

4. Add mozzarella; toss to combine, adding some of the cooking liquid if the pasta seems too dry. Divide the pasta among six plates. Garnish each serving with black pepper, and serve immediately.

cavatelli with beets and swiss chard

SERVES 6

Because this dish tastes good at room temperature, it is perfect for entertaining a crowd. Heat the goat cheese under a broiler immediately before serving.

- 6 slices good-quality white bread
- 2 tablespoons plus 1 teaspoon chopped fresh rosemary, plus 1 sprig
- ½ cup extra-virgin olive oil, plus more to taste
- 1 8-ounce log chilled fresh goat cheese, cut into eight ½-inch-thick rounds
- 2 pounds small beets, trimmed
- 1 tablespoon plus ½ teaspoon kosher salt, plus more for water and seasoning
- ½ teaspoon freshly ground black pepper, plus more for seasoning
- 1 pound red Swiss chard
- 1 pound cavatelli or orecchiette
- 8 garlic cloves, thinly sliced

1. Remove the crusts from the bread, and pulse the bread in the bowl of a food processor into soft, small crumbs. Line a baking sheet with parchment paper. Combine the bread crumbs and 2 tablespoons chopped rosemary in a small bowl. Pour 3 tablespoons olive oil onto a plate or into a shallow bowl. Coat each round of goat cheese with the olive oil, and dredge in the bread-crumb mixture. Arrange the cheese on the prepared baking sheet; cover with plastic wrap. Chill until firm, at least 1 hour or overnight.

2. Preheat the oven to 425°F. Line a baking sheet with aluminum foil. Cut the beets in half, and toss with 2 tablespoons oil, 1 teaspoon salt, and ¼ teaspoon pepper. Arrange the beets in one layer on the aluminum foil, cut-side down, and place the rosemary sprig on top of the beets. Cover the beets with another piece of aluminum foil, and seal the edges all around, creating a rectangular packet. Bake on the lowest shelf of the oven until the beets are tender when pierced with the tip of a knife, about 30 minutes. Let stand until cool enough to handle. Peel beets. Cut larger ones in half; set aside.

3. Strip the chard leaves from the stems. Discard the stems or reserve for later use. Rinse and drain the leaves in a colander. Do not dry them. Place the chard in a large pot over medium heat, and sprinkle with 2 teaspoons salt. Cover the pot, and cook over medium heat, opening the lid only to stir, until just wilted. Remove from the heat, return to the colander, and rinse with cold running water to stop the cooking. Using your hands, gently squeeze any excess water from the chard, and coarsely chop; you should have about 2 cups. Set the chard aside, but leave the pot on the stove.

4. Cover a large pot of salted water, and bring to a boil. Drop the pasta into the boiling water; stir to keep the pasta from sticking together. Cook until al dente; drain, reserving a few tablespoons of the cooking liquid.

5. Heat about 3 tablespoons olive oil in the chard pot over medium heat. Add the garlic, and cook slowly until the garlic is just toasted, stirring often. Add the chard, the remaining 1 teaspoon rosemary, ½ teaspoon salt, and ¼ teaspoon pepper, and cook until the chard is hot, about 3 minutes. Add the pasta, toss, and cook just until hot. Season with salt, pepper, and more olive oil; transfer the pasta to a serving platter. Arrange beets over the pasta.

6. Bake the cheese in the oven until soft to the touch, heated through, and golden brown, about 7 minutes. Remove from oven, arrange hot cheese around the platter of pasta, and serve.

tuna and farfalle puttanesca
SERVES 6

3 tablespoons extra-virgin olive oil

3 medium garlic cloves, minced

2 medium red onions, cut lengthwise into ¼-inch-thick slices

Kosher salt

1 pound farfalle

10 whole canned plum tomatoes, seeded, sliced ¼ inch thick lengthwise, plus 1 cup juice

3 tablespoons capers, drained

1 tablespoon finely chopped fresh rosemary

½ cup kalamata olives, pitted, cut into quarters

Freshly ground black pepper

2 6-ounce cans oil-packed Italian-style light tuna, drained

2 tablespoons roughly chopped fresh flat-leaf parsley

1. Warm the oil in large skillet over medium heat. Add the garlic and onions; cook until the onions are translucent, about 8 minutes.

2. Cover a large pot of salted water, and bring to a boil. Drop the pasta into the boiling water, and stir to keep the pasta from sticking together. Cook until al dente.

3. Meanwhile, add the tomatoes, juice, capers, rosemary, and olives to the onions; season with salt and pepper. Raise the heat to medium high, and cook until the tomatoes are heated through, about 4 minutes. Drain the pasta, and transfer to a large serving bowl. Add the sauce, tuna, and parsley; toss gently to combine. Serve hot.

caramelized garlic and shallot pasta
SERVES 6

Caramelizing the garlic tends to mellow and sweeten its flavor, so you can use more than you might expect.

2 tablespoons unsalted butter

1½ pounds (about 15 medium) shallots, sliced crosswise into ¼-inch rings

1 cup peeled garlic cloves (about 3 heads), large cloves halved lengthwise

2 teaspoons sugar

1½ teaspoons kosher salt, plus more for water

¼ teaspoon freshly ground black pepper

2 cups Homemade Chicken Stock (page 624), or low-sodium store-bought chicken broth, skimmed of fat

1 pound farfalle, rigatoni, or cavatelli

Fresh basil leaves, for garnish

Parmigiano-Reggiano cheese, for garnish

1. Heat the butter in a large skillet over medium-low heat. Add the shallots and garlic cloves, stirring to coat. Sprinkle with the sugar, 1 teaspoon salt, and the pepper, and stir to combine. Cook until very soft and golden, about 1 hour, adding water 2 tablespoons at a time if the pan seems dry.

2. Using a slotted spoon, transfer the garlic and shallots to a bowl, and set aside. Add the chicken stock, and bring to a boil, using a wooden spoon to scrape up any browned bits from the pan. Cook, stirring occasionally, until the mixture is reduced by one-quarter, about 5 minutes. Remove from the heat, return the garlic and shallots to the pan, and keep warm while cooking the pasta.

3. Cover a large pot of salted water, and bring to a boil. Drop the pasta into the boiling water; stir to keep pasta from sticking. Cook until al dente; drain and return to saucepan. Stir in ½ teaspoon salt, reserved garlic and shallots, and sauce. Cut basil leaves into thin strips. Divide pasta and sauce among six serving bowls; garnish with the basil and shaved Parmigiano-Reggiano. Serve hot.

FIT TO EAT RECIPE PER SERVING: 389 CALORIES, 7 G FAT, 14 MG CHOLESTEROL, 69 G CARBOHYDRATE, 694 MG SODIUM, 15 G PROTEIN, 2 G DIETARY FIBER

sicilian rigatoni

SERVES 4

Pasta served with cauliflower, saffron, and raisins is a familiar dish in Sicily.

- ½ cup golden raisins
- 3 tablespoons extra-virgin olive oil
- 4 garlic cloves, minced
- ½ teaspoon crushed red-pepper flakes
- 7 anchovy fillets, minced
- 3 tablespoons capers, drained
- 2 pinches crushed saffron threads
- 1 cup Homemade Chicken Stock (page 624), or low-sodium store-bought chicken broth, or dry white wine
- 1 medium head cauliflower, trimmed to 1-inch pieces
  Kosher salt and freshly ground black pepper
- 1 pound rigatoni
- 10 fresh basil leaves, for garnish
- ½ cup pine nuts, lightly toasted (see page 644)

1. Cover the raisins with warm water in a bowl, and let sit for 10 minutes to plump; drain.

2. Heat the oil in a medium skillet over medium-low heat. Add the garlic, and cook until the garlic begins to brown, 2 to 4 minutes. Add the pepper flakes, anchovies, capers, saffron, and stock. Stir; cook until combined, about 3 minutes. Stir in the cauliflower and raisins; season with salt and pepper. Cook, covered, until the cauliflower is tender, about 10 minutes. Uncover; let liquid reduce slightly over high heat, 1 to 2 minutes.

3. Meanwhile, cover a large pot of salted water, and bring to a boil. Drop the pasta into the boiling water; stir to keep the pasta from sticking together. Cook until al dente; drain, reserving a few tablespoons of the cooking liquid. Toss the pasta into the warm cauliflower mixture. Just before serving, tear the basil leaves and toss into the pasta along with the pine nuts. Add some of the cooking liquid if the pasta seems too dry. Serve hot.

macaroni and cheese 101

SERVES 12

This is quite possibly the most popular recipe we have ever created. Baked macaroni and cheese is a wonderful combination of comforting textures—al dente pasta, a velvety cream sauce made with two types of cheese, and crunchy, buttery bread crumbs. For the maximum crust, bake macaroni in a broad, shallow casserole dish. You can easily divide this recipe in half; if you do, use a 1½-quart casserole.

- 8 tablespoons (1 stick) unsalted butter, plus more for casserole
- 6 slices good white bread, crusts removed, torn into ¼- to ½-inch pieces
- 5½ cups milk
- ½ cup all-purpose flour
- 2 teaspoons kosher salt, plus more for water
- ¼ teaspoon ground nutmeg
- ¼ teaspoon freshly ground black pepper
- ¼ teaspoon cayenne pepper
- 4½ cups (about 18 ounces) grated sharp white Cheddar cheese
- 2 cups (about 8 ounces) grated Gruyère or 1¼ cups (about 5 ounces) grated Pecorino Romano cheese
- 1 pound elbow macaroni

1. Preheat the oven to 375°F. Butter a 3-quart casserole dish; set aside. Place the bread in a medium bowl. In a small saucepan over medium heat, melt 2 tablespoons butter. Pour the melted butter into the bowl with the bread, and toss. Set the bread crumbs aside.

2. Warm the milk in a medium saucepan set over medium heat. Melt the remaining 6 tablespoons butter in a high-sided skillet over medium heat. When the butter bubbles, add the flour. Cook, stirring, 1 minute.

3. While whisking, slowly pour in the hot milk a little at a time to keep mixture smooth. Continue cooking, whisking constantly, until the mixture bubbles and becomes thick, 8 to 12 minutes.

4. Remove the pan from the heat. Stir in salt, nutmeg, black pepper, cayenne pepper, 3 cups Cheddar cheese, and 1½ cups Gruyère (or 1 cup Pecorino Romano); set the cheese sauce aside.

5. Cover a large pot of salted water, and bring to a boil. Cook the macaroni until the outside of pasta is cooked and the inside is underdone, 2 to 3 minutes. Transfer the macaroni to a colander, rinse under cold running water, and drain well. Stir the macaroni into the reserved cheese sauce.

6. Pour the mixture into the prepared dish. Sprinkle the remaining 1½ cups Cheddar cheese, ½ cup Gruyère (or ¼ cup Pecorino Romano), and the bread crumbs over the top. Bake until golden brown, about 30 minutes. Transfer the dish to a wire rack for 5 minutes; serve.

MACARONI AND CHEESE ADD-INS

To add broccoli to your macaroni and cheese, blanch the florets from one bunch for 5 seconds; plunge into an ice bath. Drain, stir into cheese sauce with pasta, and bake. Other add-ins we like: cubed baked ham, shredded prosciutto, and sautéed chorizo or other sausage.

macaroni and four cheeses

SERVES 10 TO 12

Goat cheese, scallions, and Parmesan cheese update the classic recipe. Be sure to choose sharp, full-flavored cheeses to give this dish the most impact.

- 8 tablespoons (1 stick) plus 1 tablespoon unsalted butter, plus more for casserole
- 5 cups milk
- ½ cup plus 1 tablespoon all-purpose flour
- 1 teaspoon kosher salt, plus more for water
- ¼ teaspoon freshly ground black pepper
- ¼ teaspoon cayenne pepper
- 2 cups grated sharp yellow Cheddar cheese (from 8 ounces)
- 2 cups grated sharp white Cheddar cheese (from 8 ounces)
- 1 cup freshly grated Parmesan cheese (from 3 ounces)
- 20 scallions, white and pale-green parts, thinly sliced
- 5 ounces fresh goat cheese
- 4 cups elbow macaroni

1. Preheat the oven to 375°F. Lightly butter a 2-quart casserole. Set aside.

2. Warm the milk in a medium saucepan over medium-low heat. Melt the butter in a large saucepan over medium heat. Gradually whisk in the flour, and cook for 2 minutes, or until the mixture is thick and smooth. Whisking constantly, gradually add the milk. Cook over medium-low heat 8 to 10 minutes, whisking occasionally. Remove white sauce from heat; add the salt, pepper, and cayenne.

3. In a bowl, combine ¼ cup each of the yellow and white Cheddar cheeses and ¼ cup Parmesan; set aside. Set aside 1 tablespoon scallions. Add the remaining 1¾ cups of both Cheddar cheeses and ¾ cup Parmesan to the warm white sauce. Stir well. Stir in the remaining scallions and the goat cheese in 1-inch pieces; fold gently to combine. Set the sauce aside.

4. Cover a large pot of salted water, and bring to a boil. Cook the macaroni until the outside is cooked and the inside is underdone, 2 to 3 minutes. Transfer the macaroni to a colander, rinse under cold running water, and drain well. Stir the macaroni into the reserved cheese sauce.

5. Pour the mixture into the prepared casserole; top with the reserved scallions and cheeses. Bake until golden brown and bubbling, about 30 minutes. Serve hot.

penne with tomatoes, pancetta, and sage

SERVES 4

- ¼ cup extra-virgin olive oil
- 4 ounces pancetta, cut into ¼-inch cubes
- 1 onion, cut into ½-inch dice
- 2 small garlic cloves, minced
- ½ teaspoon kosher salt, plus more for water
- ¼ teaspoon freshly ground black pepper
- 2 28-ounce cans plum tomatoes, drained, juice reserved, seeded and cut into ½-inch pieces
- 4 carrots, cut into ½-inch pieces
- 1 28-ounce can white kidney or cannellini beans, drained and rinsed
- 2 tablespoons coarsely chopped fresh sage leaves, plus 8 whole leaves
- 1 pound penne
  Shaved Parmesan cheese, for garnish

1. Heat 1 tablespoon oil in a large heavy saucepan over medium heat. Add the pancetta; cook, stirring often, until golden brown, about 10 minutes. Add the onion, garlic, ½ teaspoon salt, and ¼ teaspoon pepper. Cook, stirring often, until the onions are golden, about 10 minutes.

2. Add the reserved tomato juice and the carrots to the pan. Cook until the carrots are tender, about 10 minutes. Reduce heat to medium low; add the tomatoes, beans, and chopped sage. Simmer until heated through, about 5 minutes.

3. Cover a large pot of salted water, and bring to a boil. Drop the pasta into the boiling water; stir to keep the pasta from sticking together. Cook until al dente; drain, reserving a few tablespoons of the cooking liquid. Meanwhile, heat the remaining 3 tablespoons oil in a small skillet over medium heat. Fry the sage leaves until they begin to curl. Using a slotted spoon, transfer the leaves to paper towels to drain. Drain the pasta, and transfer to a serving bowl. Top with the sauce; toss to combine. Serve sprinkled with sage leaves and Parmesan.

summer penne with lobster
SERVES 4

After removing the lobsters' tails and claw meat, use their empty shells to flavor the broth.

- 1 onion, quartered
- 1 carrot, cut into 1-inch pieces
- 3 dried bay leaves
- 1 garlic clove, smashed
- 1 1-inch piece fresh ginger, sliced
    Zest of 1 orange
- 1 tablespoon whole black peppercorns
- 2 live lobsters (1¼ pounds each)
    Kosher salt
- 8 ounces penne or garganelli
- 4 small (about 1 pound) zucchini
- 1 tablespoon extra-virgin olive oil
- 1 Vidalia onion, cut in ⅛-inch wedges
- 2 tablespoons minced garlic
- 4 ears corn, kernels shaved from the cob
- 2 bunches arugula, stems trimmed, chopped
- 2 tablespoons fresh marjoram or
    oregano leaves

1. Prepare an ice-water bath. In a large stockpot, combine the onion, carrot, bay leaves, garlic, ginger, zest, and peppercorns with 2 quarts water; cover, and bring to a boil. Add the lobsters, cover, and return the water to a boil, then cook 8 minutes. Remove the lobsters, reserving the liquid; transfer the lobsters to the ice bath.

2. When the lobsters are cool enough to handle, break the tails and claws from the body; crack open to remove the meat. Set the meat aside. Add the bodies and empty shells to the reserved liquid; cover, and return to a boil. Reduce heat; simmer 30 minutes with the lid ajar. Drain through a fine sieve; discard solids. Return the liquid to the pot; cook over medium-high heat until reduced to 1 cup, about 45 minutes. Cut the lobster-tail and claw meat into bite-size pieces; set aside.

3. Cover a large pot of salted water, and bring to a boil. Drop the pasta into the boiling water; stir to keep the pasta from sticking together. Cook until al dente; drain, reserving a few tablespoons of the cooking liquid.

4. Cut the zucchini lengthwise into quarters and crosswise into ½-inch pieces. Heat the oil in a low-sided 6-quart saucepan over medium-high heat until very hot. Add the onion and garlic; reduce heat to medium low. Cook until the onions are translucent, about 8 minutes. Add the zucchini; cook until tender, about 7 minutes. Add the corn, reserved lobster meat, cooked pasta, reserved lobster liquid, arugula, and marjoram; stir to combine. Add some of the reserved pasta cooking liquid if the pasta seems too dry. Serve hot.

FIT TO EAT RECIPE PER SERVING: 490 CALORIES, 6 G FAT, 89 MG CHOLESTEROL, 81 G CARBOHYDRATE, 142 MG SODIUM, 34 G PROTEIN, 8 G DIETARY FIBER

green orzo

SERVES 4

Arugula purée gives this orzo its emerald hue.

- 1 teaspoon kosher salt, plus more for water
- 2 bunches (about 1 pound) arugula
- 1¼ cups orzo
- 1 garlic clove
- 3 tablespoons extra-virgin olive oil
- ¼ teaspoon freshly ground black pepper, plus more for seasoning

1. Bring a large pot of salted water to a boil. Prepare an ice-water bath. Blanch the arugula until bright green in color, 5 to 10 seconds. Using a slotted spoon, transfer the arugula to the ice-water bath to stop the cooking. Keep the water boiling. Drain, and squeeze out any excess water from the arugula.

2. Cook the orzo in the boiling water until al dente. Drain and transfer to a serving bowl; set aside.

3. Meanwhile, place the arugula and garlic in the bowl of a food processor. Using the feed tube, slowly add the olive oil while pulsing the machine on and off. Add 1 teaspoon salt and ¼ teaspoon pepper; process until puréed.

4. Add the arugula purée to the orzo; toss to combine. Season with salt and pepper. Serve.

cheese tortelloni

MAKES ABOUT 3 DOZEN

Serve this tender pasta hot, drizzled with extra-virgin olive oil, unsalted butter, coarse salt, and freshly ground black pepper. For pasta machines, see Equipment Sources, page 650.

- 2 cups whole-milk ricotta cheese

for the pasta dough
- 3 large eggs
- 1½ cups all-purpose flour, plus more for dusting

for the filling
- 2 teaspoons olive oil
- 2 shallots, minced (about ¼ cup)
- 1 6-ounce log aged goat cheese, rind removed, grated on small holes of a box grater
  Grated zest of 1 lemon
- ½ teaspoon chopped fresh tarragon
- 2 tablespoons chopped fresh flat-leaf parsley
- 2 teaspoons kosher salt, plus more for water
- ½ teaspoon freshly ground black pepper
  Semolina or cornmeal, for dusting

1. Wrap the ricotta in a large piece of cheesecloth. Place the wrapped ricotta in a sieve set in the sink, and weigh down with a heavy skillet to help press out the moisture. Let drain 30 minutes.

2. Meanwhile, in the bowl of a food processor, combine the eggs and flour; process until the dough comes together. Run the processor for 5 minutes to start kneading the dough. Transfer the dough to a work surface, and knead 4 to 5 minutes. The dough should be soft and smooth and should not stick to your fingers when you pinch it. Cover the dough with plastic wrap, and let stand 30 minutes.

3. Heat a small skillet over medium heat. Add the olive oil and shallots; cook until translucent, about

3 minutes. Transfer to a large mixing bowl; add the drained ricotta, goat cheese, lemon zest, tarragon, parsley, salt, and pepper. Mix until well combined.

4. Divide the dough into 3 pieces. Using a pasta machine, roll out the dough until very thin (see Fresh Pasta, step 6, page 184). Place the pasta sheet on a lightly floured surface; use a pastry wheel to cut the sheet into 4-inch squares. Place a heaping tablespoon of the filling in center of each square. Brush the edges lightly with water. Fold into a triangle; seal, eliminating any air inside. Pull the two corners on folded side together; attach with a little water. Brush off excess flour with a dry brush.

5. Place the tortelloni on a tray generously dusted with the semolina; chill, covered tightly with plastic wrap, until ready to cook.

6. Cover a large pot of salted water, and bring to a boil. Add the tortelloni in batches of 12. Cook until al dente, about 5 minutes. Serve hot.

ravioli with peas and chervil

MAKES 4 TO 4½ DOZEN

With filled pastas, it is best to roll out only one sheet of dough at a time.

- 2 *teaspoons extra-virgin olive oil*
- 2 *shallots, minced*
- 2 *cups fresh peas, or 10 ounces frozen, defrosted*
- ⅓ *cup ricotta cheese*
- 2 *tablespoons fresh chervil, plus more for garnish*

  Kosher salt and freshly ground pepper
- ½ *recipe Fresh Pasta dough (page 184, made through step 5) or 8-ounces good-quality prepared pasta*

  All-purpose flour, for dusting
- ½ *cup semolina or cornmeal, for dusting*
- 4 *tablespoons unsalted butter*
- 3 *ounces freshly grated Parmesan cheese*

MAKING FILLED PASTA

To make ravioli (above left), divide a single leaf of thinned dough lengthwise. Place fillings in rows, evenly spaced. Layer with a second sheet, press down around the filling with your fingers, and cut into squares, sealing with a little water.

To make tortellini (above, center and right), follow directions for making ravioli, forming rounds instead of squares, then fill and fold, pinching ends to seal.

Holding the folded dough with the straight side facing you, wrap around your finger to form a small loop; pinch edge to seal.

1. Heat a skillet over medium heat; add the oil. Add the shallots; cook until translucent, about 6 minutes. Add the peas; cook until soft, about 8 minutes. Remove from heat; stir in the ricotta and chervil; season with salt and pepper. Mash with a fork.

2. Divide the dough into 2 pieces. Using a pasta machine, roll one piece of dough through widest opening, brushing very lightly with flour. Fold the dough into thirds; pass through machine again, folded-side up. Repeat the process three more times, or until dough is smooth.

3. Roll the dough through the remaining settings on the machine (widest to narrowest), using as little additional flour as possible, until very thin. Place the sheet on a lightly floured surface; cut in half lengthwise. Cover half with plastic wrap. With the remaining half, place teaspoons of the filling 1 inch apart in two rows. Moisten the pasta around each mound of filling, using a pastry brush dipped in water. Top with the remaining half sheet of pasta; press around the filling to seal. Use a pastry wheel to cut into squares. Brush with a dry brush to eliminate excess flour. Place the ravioli on a tray dusted with the semolina. Repeat with the remaining dough and filling. Chill until ready to cook.

4. Cover a large pot of salted water, and bring to a boil. Cook ravioli until tender, but al dente, about 2 minutes. Divide ravioli among serving plates.

5. Meanwhile, place the butter in a small skillet over medium heat; cook until lightly browned, about 6 minutes. Pour over the ravioli; top with the shaved Parmesan and chervil, and season with salt and pepper. Serve hot.

manicotti

SERVES 6

Look for "no-boil" boxes of manicotti. They require soaking, rather than precooking, which saves time. After soaking them, gently pat dry; the sauce will adhere better to the pasta.

1½ ounces (15 halves) sun-dried tomatoes
  6 sheets no-boil manicotti
  1 16-ounce container nonfat ricotta
  2 tablespoons plus 1 teaspoon roughly chopped fresh flat-leaf parsley
  ¼ cup roughly chopped fresh basil leaves
  1 large egg yolk
  ⅛ teaspoon ground nutmeg
  1 teaspoon kosher salt
  ¼ teaspoon freshly ground black pepper
    Extra-virgin olive oil, for brushing
1½ cups Tomato Sauce (page 188)
  3 tablespoons grated Parmesan cheese

1. Preheat the oven to 450°F. Place tomatoes in a bowl; cover with very hot water. Let stand until soft, about 20 minutes. Dry with paper towel, and cut into ¼-inch dice; set aside in a medium bowl.

2. Fill an ovenproof baking dish with very hot water; place the manicotti sheets, one at a time, in the water. Let stand 10 minutes, until softened.

3. To the tomatoes, add ricotta, 2 tablespoons parsley, basil, egg yolk, nutmeg, salt, and pepper; mix well. On a clean work surface, place one sheet of manicotti lengthwise. Spoon ⅓ cup of the ricotta mixture along the front edge; roll to form a cylinder. Repeat with all the manicotti. Brush a 9 x 13-inch ovenproof baking dish with olive oil; spoon about ¼ cup tomato sauce on the bottom.

4. Transfer manicotti to the dish in a single layer; cover with remaining tomato sauce and Parmesan. Cover with foil; bake 10 minutes. Remove foil; bake until top is browned and sauce is bubbling, 15 minutes. Garnish with parsley. Serve hot.

FIT TO EAT RECIPE PER MANICOTTI: 240 CALORIES, 3 G FAT, 65 MG CHOLESTEROL, 38 G CARBOHYDRATE, 840 MG SODIUM, 20 G PROTEIN, 4 G DIETARY FIBER

potato gnocchi

SERVES 6

Use a potato ricer (see Equipment Sources, page 650) to blend the potatoes into a delicate, soft purée. Gnocchi can be frozen, uncooked, up to 6 weeks.

- *4 large (about 2 pounds) Idaho potatoes, scrubbed*
- *1 tablespoon plus 2½ teaspoons kosher salt*
- *2 cups plus 2 tablespoons all-purpose flour, plus more for dusting*
- *2 large eggs*
- *⅛ teaspoon freshly ground black pepper*

1. Place unpeeled potatoes in a saucepan; cover by 2 inches with cold water. Add 1 tablespoon salt; cover. Bring to a boil. Reduce heat to medium high; cook, uncovered, until tender, about 40 minutes.

2. Drain potatoes; peel while hot, holding with a clean kitchen towel. Pass potatoes through a potato ricer or a food mill fitted with the finest disk onto a lightly floured work surface. Make a well in the center, and sprinkle the flour evenly over the potatoes. Break the eggs into the well, and add 2½ teaspoons salt and the pepper. Using a fork, lightly beat the eggs, and incorporate the flour-potato mixture to form a dough. Knead lightly on the work surface until the dough is soft and smooth.

3. Lightly dust work surface with flour. Divide dough into 4 balls; shape each ball into a rope ¾ inch in diameter. Cut each rope into 1-inch pieces. Shape the gnocchi: Hold a dinner fork in one hand, and use your index finger to hold a cut edge of a piece of gnocchi against the curved back of the tines of the fork. Press into the center of the gnocchi with your index finger to make a deep indentation. While you are pressing the piece against the tines, flip it away over the tip of the fork, allowing the gnocchi to drop to the work surface. If gnocchi becomes sticky, dip fork and your finger into flour. The finished gnocchi will have ridges on one side and a depression on the other. At this point, the gnocchi can be refrigerated on a lightly floured baking sheet, covered with plastic wrap, for several hours before cooking.

4. Cover a large pot of salted water, and bring to a boil. To cook gnocchi, drop half of them into boiling water; cook until they float, 2 to 3 minutes. Remove with a slotted spoon; place in a colander to drain. Repeat process with the other half of the gnocchi. Use as directed in the following recipes.

potato gnocchi with wild mushroom sauce

SERVES 6

For white truffle oil, see Food Sources, page 648.

- *1 pound assorted wild mushrooms, such as shiitake, cremini, hedgehog, or oyster, wiped clean*
- *2 tablespoons unsalted butter*
- *2 large shallots, minced*
- *2 sprigs fresh thyme*
- *¼ cup Homemade Chicken Stock (page 624), or low-sodium store-bought chicken broth, skimmed of fat*
- *1½ cups heavy cream*
- *1 teaspoon kosher salt*
- *⅛ teaspoon freshly ground black pepper*
- *Potato Gnocchi (recipe, left)*
- *1 tablespoon white truffle oil, optional*
- *½ cup freshly grated Parmesan cheese (from 1½ ounces)*
- *1 tablespoon fresh marjoram or oregano leaves*

1. Cover and bring a large pot of water to a boil. Remove the stems from the shiitake mushrooms, and trim stems of the others. Cut all the mushrooms into ¼-inch slices, and set aside.

2. In a large skillet, melt the butter over medium-low heat. Add the shallots, and cook until translucent, about 8 minutes. Raise heat to medium high, add the mushrooms and thyme sprigs, and cook until mushrooms begin to brown on the edges, about 4 minutes. Remove the thyme, add the chicken stock, and reduce to 1 tablespoon, about 30 seconds. Add the cream, salt, and pepper; cook until the cream thickens slightly, 2 to 3 minutes.

3. Drop the precooked gnocchi into the pot of boiling water, and cook until heated through, about 3 minutes. Lift the gnocchi out of the water with a slotted spoon, and transfer to the mushroom sauce, stirring until evenly coated. Cook for 1 to 2 minutes. Divide among six plates, drizzle with the truffle oil, if using, and garnish with the grated Parmesan and marjoram leaves. Serve hot.

gnocchi with brown butter and sage

SERVES 4

Leftover mashed potatoes can be used to make gnocchi, as it is here. You may also use this classic sauce with the Potato Gnocchi on page 203.

2½ cups cold leftover mashed potatoes
 1 large egg yolk
 1 teaspoon finely grated lemon zest
 3 tablespoons extra-virgin olive oil
1¼ cups all-purpose flour, plus more for dusting
 1 teaspoon kosher salt, plus more for water
 3 tablespoons unsalted butter
    Pinch of freshly ground black pepper
 8 fresh sage leaves, thinly sliced
 ¼ cup freshly grated Parmesan cheese

1. In a medium bowl, combine the potatoes, egg yolk, lemon zest, olive oil, flour, and ¾ teaspoon salt. Using a wooden spoon, stir until incorporated. Divide the dough into quarters. Line a baking sheet with parchment paper.

2. Form gnocchi as in step 3 for Potato Gnocchi (page 203).

3. Cover a large pot of salted water, and bring to a boil. Have ready a colander set over a bowl. Add one-fourth of the gnocchi, and cook until they float to the top, 2 to 3 minutes. Using a slotted spoon, transfer the cooked gnocchi to the colander. Cook the remaining gnocchi.

4. Place a large skillet over medium-high heat. Add the butter. When the butter begins to brown, about 2 minutes, add the pepper and ¼ teaspoon salt. Increase heat to high. Add the gnocchi and sage. Cook, stirring occasionally, until the sage has wilted and the gnocchi have heated through, about 2 minutes. Serve immediately, sprinkled with Parmesan.

ricotta dumplings

SERVES 4

The ricotta for the dumpling filling must drain overnight, so plan ahead.

 1 pound fresh ricotta cheese
1¼ teaspoons kosher salt, plus more for water
 6 tablespoons unsalted butter
 1 large egg
 ½ cup freshly grated Parmesan cheese (from 1½ ounces), plus 1 ounce freshly shaved, for garnish
 ¾ cup plus 1 tablespoon all-purpose flour
    Pinch of freshly grated nutmeg
 ¼ teaspoon freshly ground black pepper
 8 fresh sage leaves

1. Drain the ricotta by placing it in a 15-inch-square double thickness of cheesecloth. Gather up the corners, and tie into a knot. Slide the handle of a wooden spoon through the knot, and suspend the ricotta over a deep bowl, so that the ricotta ball is not touching the bottom of the bowl. (Alternatively, place ricotta in a sieve lined with cheesecloth and allow it to drain over a bowl.) Cover with plastic wrap, and place in refrigerator overnight.

2. Cover a large pot of salted water, and bring to a boil. Melt 2 tablespoons butter, and set aside. Remove the ricotta from the cheesecloth, and place in the bowl of an electric mixer fitted with the paddle attachment or in a large mixing bowl. Add the egg, Parmesan, melted butter, flour, nutmeg, 1 teaspoon salt, and ⅛ teaspoon pepper, and mix well on medium speed or with a wooden spoon until well combined. Dip 2 large soup spoons in warm water, then scoop out a generous spoonful of the mixture.

Shape the mixture into an oval by scraping the dough from spoon to spoon. Set the dumpling aside on a plate, and repeat with the remaining dough. You should have 12 to 14 dumplings; they will not be completely uniform in shape.

3. Reduce heat under the boiling water to medium high, and drop the dumplings into the water one at a time. Cook at a gentle boil for 7 minutes. Remove the dumplings with a slotted spoon, and divide among four plates.

4. Meanwhile, place the remaining butter and sage in a small skillet over medium-low heat. Cook until the butter is melted, being careful not to brown the butter, and the sage leaves are crisp. Add 3 tablespoons water and cook, stirring with a wooden spoon, until emulsified. Season with ¼ teaspoon salt and the remaining ⅛ teaspoon of pepper. Pour the melted butter and sage over the dumplings, garnish with the shaved Parmesan, and serve.

semolina dumplings with braised broccoli rabe

SERVES 6

Semolina (see Food Sources, page 648) is a fine pale-yellow powder ground from hard durum wheat.

- 1 *quart milk*
- ½ *teaspoon ground nutmeg*
- ½ *teaspoon kosher salt, plus more for water and seasoning*
- 1 *cup semolina*
- 2 *large egg yolks*
- 1 *tablespoon unsalted butter*
- ½ *cup freshly grated Parmesan cheese (from 1½ ounces), plus more for garnish*
- 1 *bunch (about 1¼ pounds) broccoli rabe*
- 2 *tablespoons extra-virgin olive oil, plus more for baking sheet*
- 2 *garlic cloves, thinly sliced*
- ¼ *cup Homemade Chicken Stock (page 624), or low-sodium store-bought chicken broth, skimmed of fat*

  Freshly ground black pepper

1. Bring the milk, nutmeg, and ½ teaspoon salt to a boil in a medium saucepan. Using a whisk, stir vigorously while sprinkling in semolina. After all the semolina has been added, continue whisking until mixture is very thick, 30 to 45 seconds.

2. Remove from the heat. Beat in the egg yolks with a wooden spoon, stirring quickly and vigorously. Add the butter and cheese; stir until incorporated.

3. Spread the dough on a baking pan to a thickness of ½ inch. Let cool completely, and chill until firm, about 1 hour.

4. Trim the large, thick stems from the broccoli rabe (but not the thinner ones), and wash well. Cover and bring a large pot of salted water to a boil, add the broccoli rabe, and blanch briefly until bright green, about 1 minute. Drain and refresh with cold water to stop the cooking. Set aside.

5. Preheat the oven to 425°F. Using a 3-inch round cookie cutter or a drinking glass, cut the semolina dough into crescent shapes by cutting a row of overlapping circles. Transfer the dumplings to an oiled baking sheet, placing them 1 inch apart. Bake until golden brown, about 20 minutes.

6. Meanwhile, heat the olive oil in a large skillet over medium heat, and add the garlic. Cook, stirring, until light golden brown. Add the broccoli rabe, and cook for 1 to 2 minutes. Add the stock, raise heat to high, and cook until only a little bit of liquid remains, about 5 minutes. Season with salt and pepper. Arrange 3 dumplings on each plate, and top with the broccoli rabe. Garnish with grated Parmesan, if desired. Serve hot.

spaetzle with butter and parsley

SERVES 4

You will need a potato ricer with ¼-inch-diameter holes (see Equipment Sources, page 650), or a colander.

- 3½ cups all-purpose flour
- 2 teaspoons kosher salt, plus more for water
- ½ teaspoon freshly ground black pepper
- ¼ teaspoon ground nutmeg
- ⅔ cup milk
- 9 large eggs
- ¼ cup plus 1 tablespoon extra-virgin olive oil
- 3 tablespoons unsalted butter, cut into small pieces
- ¼ cup loosely packed fresh flat-leaf parsley, coarsely chopped

1. Whisk together the flour, 2 teaspoons salt, pepper, and nutmeg in a large bowl. In another bowl, whisk the milk, eggs, and olive oil to combine. Whisk the egg mixture into the flour mixture until smooth.

2. Cover a large pot of salted water, and bring to a boil. Fill a potato ricer fitted with a ¼-inch-hole attachment with the batter, and push the batter through the holes into the boiling water, or use a colander, pushing the batter through the holes with a rubber spatula. Cook the spaetzle briefly until it floats, about 30 seconds. Drain in a colander. Toss with the butter and parsley. Serve hot.

couscous pilaf

SERVES 4

- 1⅔ cups Israeli couscous or one 10-ounce box medium-grain couscous
- 1¼ teaspoons kosher salt
- ¼ teaspoon freshly ground black pepper
- 1 tablespoon olive oil
- 1 tablespoon unsalted butter
- 1 small onion, cut into ¼-inch dice
- ¾ teaspoon ground cumin
  Pinch of cayenne pepper
- 2 tablespoons coarsely chopped fresh flat-leaf parsley

1. If using Israeli couscous, bring 2½ cups water to a boil in a medium saucepan (for regular couscous, reduce amount of water to 2¼ cups). Stir the couscous, salt, and pepper into the boiling water. Cover and simmer over low heat until tender and the water is absorbed, about 10 minutes.

2. Meanwhile, in a large saucepan, heat the olive oil and butter over medium-low heat. Add the onions, and cook until lightly browned, about 8 minutes. Stir in the cumin and cayenne pepper, and cook 1 minute more. Add the parsley, and serve.

cold vietnamese shrimp-and-noodle salad

SERVES 4

This salad features thin Banh Pho (see Food Sources, page 648), a thin, flat rice noodle similar in shape to linguine.

- ¼ cup peanut oil
- 2 teaspoons toasted sesame oil
- 2 tablespoons dark soy sauce
- 1 tablespoon mirin
- 3 tablespoons sugar
  Kosher salt
- 2 tablespoons fresh lime juice
- 1 pound (about 16) jumbo shrimp, peeled, deveined, tails intact
- 1 1-pound bag thin Banh Pho rice noodles
- 5 cups mixed baby greens (from 8 ounces)
- 2 cups mixed fresh herb leaves, such as mint, basil, cilantro, chervil, and scallions or garlic chives

1. In a small bowl, whisk together the oils, soy sauce, mirin, sugar, a pinch of salt, and the lime juice. Put the shrimp and ½ cup of dressing in a resealable plastic bag, and marinate in the refrigerator for 2 hours.

2. Cover a large pot of salted water, and bring to a boil. Add the noodles, and cook until al dente, about 8 minutes. Drain in a colander; rinse with cold water. Divide the noodles among plates.

3. Heat a grill or a grill pan until very hot; grill shrimp until cooked through, 2 minutes per side.

4. In a large bowl, toss the greens and 1 cup of the herbs and 2 tablespoons of the dressing. Place a handful of the dressed greens and herbs on top of each serving of noodles, and top each plate with 4 grilled shrimp. Drizzle with the remaining dressing, and garnish with the remaining cup of herbs.

pad thai
SERVES 4

This popular Thai dish combines chewy noodles and crunchy vegetables. Dried flat rice noodles, or sen lek, and dried shrimp can be found in some grocery stores or in Asian markets (see Food Sources, page 648).

- 8 ounces dried flat rice noodles, ⅛ inch thick
- ¼ cup packed light-brown sugar
- 3 tablespoons white vinegar
- 3 tablespoons Asian fish sauce (nam pla)
- 1 tablespoon tamarind paste mixed with 1 tablespoon water, or 2 tablespoons molasses
- ¼ teaspoon coarsely ground dried red chile pepper, or to taste
- 1 tablespoon dried shrimp, minced
  Kosher salt
- 4 ounces string beans, thinly sliced lengthwise
- 4 ounces sugar snap peas, cut in half
- 2 tablespoons canola oil
- 2 shallots, minced
- 2 large garlic cloves, minced
- 12 medium shrimp, peeled, deveined
- 1 cup fresh bean sprouts
- 3 scallions, green parts only, very thinly sliced on the diagonal
- 1 tablespoon roasted peanuts, coarsely chopped, for garnish
- 1 lime, quartered lengthwise, for garnish
  Fresh cilantro sprigs, for garnish

1. Soak the noodles in a large bowl of warm water for 20 minutes, or until softened; drain well. Meanwhile, combine ¼ cup water, the sugar, vinegar, fish sauce, tamarind mixture, and dried chiles in a small saucepan. Simmer, stirring, for 5 minutes. Remove from heat; add the dried shrimp. Set aside.

2. Cover and bring a medium saucepan of salted water to a boil. Add the string beans, and cook for 1½ minutes. Add the sugar snap peas, and continue cooking for 30 seconds. Drain and set aside.

3. Heat oil in a large nonstick skillet or wok over medium heat. Add the shallots and garlic, and stir-fry for 2 minutes. Stir in the sugar mixture, and reduce heat to the lowest possible setting.

4. In another large nonstick skillet, cook the shrimp over medium-high heat, 3 minutes per side. Meanwhile, add the noodles, a quarter of the bean sprouts, and half the scallions to the hot shallot mixture. Raise heat to high, and boil, stirring, for 2 minutes. Add the shrimp, string beans, and sugar snap peas, and stir for 1 minute more. Turn out noodles onto a platter, sprinkle with peanuts and remaining scallions; arrange lime quarters, cilantro, and bean sprouts beside them. Serve.

FIT TO EAT RECIPE PER SERVING: 420 CALORIES, 10 G TOTAL FAT, 21% CALORIES FROM FAT, 22 MG CHOLESTEROL, 71 G CARBOHYDRATE, 2,143 MG SODIUM, 15 G PROTEIN, 2 G DIETARY FIBER

rice noodles with cilantro pesto
SERVES 4

If using fettuccine, you will need to cook it slightly longer, until al dente.

- 2 cups (about 1 bunch) fresh cilantro leaves
- 1 tablespoon fresh lime juice
- ¼ cup plus 1 tablespoon extra-virgin olive oil
- 1 tablespoon plus 1 teaspoon unsalted butter, room temperature
- 2 teaspoons kosher salt, plus more for water
  Freshly ground black pepper
- 3 tablespoons pine nuts
- 8 ounces wide rice noodles or fresh or dried fettuccine

1. Combine cilantro, lime juice, olive oil, 1 tablespoon butter, 2 teaspoons salt, and pepper to taste in the bowl of a food processor; purée. Transfer the cilantro pesto to a small bowl, and set aside.

2. Melt remaining teaspoon of butter in a skillet over medium-high heat. Add pine nuts; cook, tossing until golden brown, about 1 minute. Sprinkle with salt; drain on a paper towel and set aside.

3. Cover and bring a large saucepan of generously salted water to a boil. Cook noodles until al dente, about 2 minutes. Drain. Transfer to a large bowl. Add pesto, toss, and garnish with pine nuts.

vietnamese chicken noodle salad

SERVES 6

2   tablespoons peanut butter

3   tablespoons rice-wine vinegar

1   tablespoon low-sodium soy sauce

1   tablespoon honey

2   tablespoons fresh lime juice, plus 6 lime wedges for garnish

1   teaspoon minced garlic

1   teaspoon freshly grated ginger

1   tablespoon peanut oil

2   tablespoons finely chopped fresh mint leaves, plus sprigs for garnish

1   quart Homemade Chicken Stock (page 624), or low-sodium store-bought chicken broth, skimmed of fat

1½ pounds boneless, skinless chicken breast

1   pound rice vermicelli or capellini pasta

1   cucumber, seeded, cut into 3-inch-long matchsticks

1   red bell pepper, seeds and ribs removed, cut into 3-inch-long matchsticks

2   carrots, cut into 3-inch-long matchsticks

½   small red onion, thinly sliced

1. Place peanut butter, 1 tablespoon rice-wine vinegar, soy sauce, honey, 1 tablespoon lime juice, garlic, and ginger in the bowl of a food processor or in a blender. Process until smooth and creamy. Set the peanut sauce aside until ready to use.

2. Whisk together the remaining 2 tablespoons rice-wine vinegar, the remaining tablespoon of lime juice, the peanut oil, and mint in a small bowl, and set the vinaigrette aside.

3. Place the chicken stock in a large saucepan; cover and bring to a boil. Add the chicken, and simmer about 15 minutes, until chicken is completely cooked. Remove chicken from pan, and set aside to cool, reserving stock. Shred chicken into bite-size pieces, and toss with reserved peanut sauce.

4. Add 3 cups water to the stock, cover, and return to a boil. Add the vermicelli, and cook, uncovered, until al dente, about 4 minutes. Drain, and toss with the reserved vinaigrette.

5. Divide noodles, cucumber, red pepper, carrots, red onion, and chicken among six bowls, and garnish with the mint sprigs and lime wedges. Serve.

FIT TO EAT RECIPE PER SERVING: 539 CALORIES, 9 G FAT, 88 MG CHOLESTEROL, 73 G CARBOHYDRATE, 483 MG SODIUM, 39 G PROTEIN, 2 G FIBER

cellophane noodle salad

SERVES 8

Seedless cucumbers often have small seeds; remove them for this recipe. Do not rinse the noodles after cooking; it will make them stick.

1   8.8-ounce bag cellophane noodles

3   celery stalks, strings removed, thinly sliced on a diagonal

4   carrots, thinly sliced on a diagonal

1   tablespoon plus 1 teaspoon kosher salt

2   tablespoons plus 2 teaspoons rice-wine vinegar

1   teaspoon Szechuan hot-bean paste

1   seedless cucumber (1 pound), skin on, seeds removed, cut in matchsticks

2   teaspoons toasted sesame oil, or more to taste

1. Soak the noodles in a large bowl of cool water for 1 hour. Cut into 5-inch lengths with kitchen shears. Cover and bring a large pot of water to a boil. Cook the noodles in the boiling water until they change from opaque to clear, 2 to 3 minutes. Drain in a colander. Transfer to a bowl.

2. Add the celery, carrots, and salt. Toss with tongs for 2 to 3 minutes. Add the vinegar and bean paste; toss. When cool, toss in the cucumber and oil. Serve at room temperature.

chilled somen noodles with dipping sauce and garnishes

SERVES 4

Somen noodles are often served cold, making them ideal summer food for a crowd. Double the ingredients to make enough for 8 people. For somen noodles, see Food Sources, page 648.

Kosher salt

4 *ounces shiitake mushrooms, wiped clean, stems removed*

8 *ounces asparagus*

4 *ounces sugar snap peas*

3 *tablespoons sesame seeds, toasted (see page 644)*

2 *teaspoons toasted sesame oil*

3 *tablespoons soy sauce*

⅔ *cup loosely packed fresh cilantro leaves, roughly chopped*

3 *tablespoons rice-wine vinegar*

1 *8.8-ounce bag somen noodles*

1½ *ounces enoki mushrooms, ends trimmed*

3 *scallions, greens cut thinly on a diagonal, whites cut into matchsticks*

1 *ounce fresh shiso or mint leaves*

6 *ounces silken tofu, cut into 1-inch cubes*

1 *2-inch piece fresh ginger, peeled, cut into matchsticks*

1. Cover a large pot of salted water, and bring to a boil. Prepare an ice-water bath. Blanch the shiitakes in the boiling water for 20 seconds. Using a slotted spoon, transfer to the ice bath, drain, and transfer to a small bowl when cool. Repeat this process with the asparagus and sugar snap peas, blanching the asparagus for 1 minute and the sugar snap peas for 1½ to 2 minutes, until they are bright green but still crunchy.

2. With the back of a knife or a rolling pin, or in a spice grinder, crush the sesame seeds until almost powdery. Combine in a small bowl with the sesame oil, soy sauce, cilantro, and rice-wine vinegar. In a small bowl, toss the shiitake mushrooms with 2 teaspoons of the sesame-oil mixture, and divide the remaining mixture among four dipping bowls.

3. Cover a large pot of salted water, and bring to a boil. Add the noodles, and cook until al dente, about 5 minutes. Drain noodles; rinse with cold water to stop the cooking. Divide among serving bowls; put a small handful of ice cubes into each bowl to keep the noodles chilled. Arrange the remaining ingredients in various serving dishes so guests can help themselves. Serve.

cold soba in dashi with shredded vegetables

SERVES 4

Arrange all of the vegetables in tiny piles on top of the noodles for a beautiful presentation. For Japanese turning slicers, see Equipment Sources, page 650.

Kosher salt

1 *7½-ounce package green or plain soba noodles*

1 *medium carrot*

1 *6-ounce daikon radish, peeled*

1 *medium beet, peeled*

1 *4-ounce Japanese cucumber, peeled and cut in matchsticks*

½ *ounce snow-pea or radish shoots*

2 *Napa cabbage leaves, cut in matchsticks*

Dashi, chilled (page 628)

Freshly grated ginger, for garnish

1. Bring a large pot of salted water to a boil. Add the noodles, and cook until al dente, about 5 minutes. Drain in a colander, and rinse with cold water to stop the cooking.

2. Using a vegetable peeler, shave carrot into long strips. Use a Japanese turning slicer to cut daikon radish, and the beet into curls, or cut into fine matchsticks with a chef's knife or mandoline.

3. Divide the noodles among four bowls. Divide the cut carrot, radish, beet, Japanese cucumber, snow-pea shoots, and cabbage leaves among the bowls. Pour the chilled dashi into each bowl with a little grated ginger, and serve immediately.

sesame noodles

SERVES 4

Unhulled sesame seeds (light brown in color), available at Asian markets, will make the sauce creamy; the stark white (hulled) variety will not produce the same results. The neutral flavor of udon allows the flavor of the other ingredients to come through.

- 1 *pound udon noodles*
- 3 *tablespoons toasted sesame oil*
- ½ *cup unhulled sesame seeds, toasted (see page 644)*
- ¼ *cup soy sauce*
- ¼ *cup plus 2 tablespoons mirin*
- 2 *teaspoons rice-wine vinegar*
- 1 *teaspoon black sesame seeds, optional*
- 2 *scallions, white and light-green parts only, thinly sliced*

1. Cover and bring a stockpot of water to a boil. Stir in the noodles, and cook, according to package instructions, until al dente. Drain. Transfer the noodles to a serving bowl, and toss with 1 tablespoon sesame oil. Set aside.

2. Place the toasted sesame seeds, soy sauce, mirin, the remaining 2 tablespoons of sesame oil, and the rice-wine vinegar in a blender; process until smooth and creamy. Pour the dressing over the reserved noodles, and toss to combine. Sprinkle with the black sesame seeds, if using, and scallions. Serve immediately, or it may be made up to 8 hours ahead and refrigerated. Let the noodles sit at room temperature for 15 to 20 minutes, to remove the chill, before serving.

israeli couscous with mint and lemon

SERVES 4

- 1 *tablespoon olive oil*
- 1 *shallot, minced*
- 1 *cup Israeli couscous*
- 1½ *cups Homemade Chicken Stock (page 624), or low-sodium store-bought chicken broth, skimmed of fat*
- 1 *tablespoon lemon zest*
- 2 *tablespoons fresh lemon juice*
- 2 *teaspoons chopped fresh mint*
  Kosher salt and freshly ground black pepper

1. Heat the olive oil in a medium saucepan over medium-low heat. Add the shallot; cook until translucent but not browned, about 5 minutes. Add the couscous; stir to coat with the oil. Add the stock, cover, reduce heat to low, and cook, stirring occasionally, until the couscous is soft and all the liquid has been absorbed, about 15 minutes.

2. Remove the couscous from the heat; stir in the lemon zest and juice and mint. Season with salt and pepper, and serve.

whole wheat couscous salad

SERVES 6

- 2 *beets, trimmed and scrubbed*
- 2 *tablespoons olive oil*
- ½ *cup finely chopped onion*
- ¾ *teaspoon ground cumin*
- 1½ *cups whole-wheat couscous*
- ¾ *teaspoon kosher salt*
- ⅛ *teaspoon freshly ground black pepper*
- 3 *tablespoons fresh lemon juice*
- 1 *cucumber (8 ounces), cut into ½-inch dice*
- ½ *cup chopped fresh mint*
- ½ *cup chopped fresh flat-leaf parsley*
- 1 *bunch watercress (3 ounces), leaves only*
- 4 *wedges Moroccan Preserved Lemon (page 617), rinsed and thinly sliced, optional*

1. Preheat the oven to 425°F. Wrap the beets in aluminum foil, and bake until tender when pierced with the tip of a knife, 30 to 60 minutes, depending on the size of the beets. Unwrap, let cool enough to handle, and rub off the beet skins. Cut the beets into ½-inch pieces, and set aside.

2. Heat 1 tablespoon oil in a large skillet over medium heat. Add the onion and cumin, and cook, stirring, until translucent, about 8 minutes. Add the couscous, 1½ cups boiling water, salt, and pepper; stir. Turn off the heat, cover, and let sit 10 minutes, until all the water has been absorbed. Fluff with a fork. Transfer to a large serving bowl, add the lemon juice, cucumber, mint, parsley, watercress, and preserved lemons, if using, and toss to combine. Serve.

FIT TO EAT RECIPE PER SERVING: 259 CALORIES, 3 G FAT, 0 MG CHOLESTEROL, 64 G CARBOHYDRATE, 852 MG SODIUM, 8 G PROTEIN, 6 G DIETARY FIBER

garden vegetable couscous
SERVES 4

You can use any variety of bell pepper or cherry tomato in this recipe.

- 1 cup couscous
- ½ small orange bell pepper, seeds and ribs removed, cut into 1-inch matchsticks
- 4 small scallions, white and green parts, thinly sliced
- 12 small yellow cherry tomatoes, halved
- 2 tablespoons extra-virgin olive oil
- 1 tablespoon fresh lemon juice
  Kosher salt and freshly ground black pepper
  Grated lemon zest, for garnish, optional

1. Place the couscous in a medium heat-proof bowl. Pour 1 cup boiling water over the couscous. Cover and let sit until slightly cooled, about 10 minutes. Fluff with a fork.

2. In a large serving bowl, combine the couscous, peppers, scallions, and tomatoes.

3. In a small bowl, whisk the olive oil and lemon juice together. Season with salt and pepper. Drizzle over the vegetables and couscous, and toss. Garnish with lemon zest, if using, and serve.

coconut rice
SERVES 4 TO 6

Mild and creamy coconut milk mellows this spice-infused side dish.

- 6 cardamom pods or ¼ teaspoon ground cardamom
- 1 tablespoon unsalted butter
- ½ large yellow onion, finely chopped
- 1¼ cups basmati or jasmine rice
- 1 cinnamon stick
- ¾ cup unsweetened coconut milk
- 1 teaspoon kosher salt
- 1 teaspoon sugar
  Fresh coconut, shelled but unpeeled, shaved, for garnish, optional

1. Remove the seeds from cardamom pods, if using, and discard the pods. Grind the seeds to a powder in a spice grinder or a mortar.

2. In a medium saucepan with a tight-fitting lid, melt the butter over medium-low heat. Add the onion and cardamom, and cook, stirring frequently, until translucent, about 6 minutes.

3. Add rice; stir until the grains are well coated with the butter, about 1 minute. Add the cinnamon stick, coconut milk, 1¾ cups water, the salt, and the sugar. Stir well to combine. Bring to a boil, and immediately reduce heat to low. Cook, covered, for 25 minutes. Remove from heat, and let stand, covered, for 10 minutes. Use a fork to fluff the rice. Serve hot, garnished with coconut, if using.

fluffy brazilian white rice

SERVES 10

Rice is as important as beans in Brazilian cooking; it is always fried first in oil.

- 2 cups long-grain white rice
- ¼ cup canola oil
- 3¼ cups boiling water
- 1 tablespoon kosher salt

Rinse the rice in a sieve under cool running water. In a large, heavy pot with a tight-fitting lid, heat the oil over low heat. Add the rice, and cook, stirring constantly, for 10 minutes. Raise heat to high, add 2½ cups of the boiling water and the salt, stir, and bring to a boil. Reduce heat to low, and cover. Continue cooking until most of the water evaporates, about 10 minutes more. Add the remaining ¾ cup of boiling water without stirring, reduce heat to very low, and cover the pot. Cook for 20 minutes. Remove from heat; let stand, covered, for 10 minutes. Use a fork to fluff the rice. Serve.

lemon basmati rice

SERVES 8

Cardamom pods are the dried fruit of a perennial herb that belongs to the ginger family. Look for green cardamom pods (see Food Sources, page 648); when bleached they are sold as white pods. Brown and black cardamom pods may also be used; their flavor is coarser; most often they are used to flavor meat and vegetable dishes.

- 2 cups basmati rice
  Grated zest of 2 lemons
- 8 whole cardamom pods, lightly cracked open
- 2 teaspoons kosher salt
- 2 3-inch cinnamon sticks, halved crosswise

1. Rinse the rice in a sieve under cool running water. Transfer to a medium saucepan with 3½ cups water. Add the zest of 1 lemon, the cardamom, salt, and cinnamon. Cover; bring to a boil. Reduce heat to low. Cook, covered, until the water evaporates, 10 to 15 minutes.

2. Remove from the heat, and let stand, covered, for 10 minutes. Use a fork to fluff the rice, and transfer to a serving platter. Remove the cardamom pods and cinnamon sticks, if desired, and sprinkle with the remaining lemon zest. Serve.

cinnamon basmati rice with golden raisins

SERVES 4

Basmati rice has a sweet, nutty flavor; in Hindi, the word "basmati" means "queen of fragrance."

- 1 tablespoon unsalted butter
- 1 medium yellow onion, cut into ¼-inch dice
- ¼ teaspoon ground cloves
- 1 teaspoon ground cinnamon
- 1 cup basmati rice
- 1 dried bay leaf
- 1 cinnamon stick
- ⅔ cup golden raisins
- 1 teaspoon kosher salt, plus more for seasoning
- ¼ teaspoon freshly ground black pepper, plus more for seasoning

1. Melt butter in a medium high-sided saucepan set over medium heat. Add onion, cloves, and cinnamon; cook until onion becomes translucent and the mixture is very fragrant, about 8 minutes.

2. Place the rice in a sieve, and rinse under cold running water. Add rice to the saucepan, and stir until the grains are coated with the butter mixture.

3. Add the bay leaf, cinnamon stick, raisins, 1 teaspoon salt, and ¼ teaspoon pepper to saucepan. Stir in 2 cups water. Raise heat, and bring to a boil. Cover, and reduce heat to low. Cook until all the water has been absorbed and the rice has cooked, 10 to 15 minutes.

4. Remove from the heat, and let stand, covered, for 10 minutes. Use a fork to fluff the rice. Season with salt and pepper. Serve.

dirty rice

SERVES 10 TO 12

This classic Cajun rice is named for the color the rice becomes when it is tossed with the chicken livers.

- 1½ cups long-grain white rice
- 2½ teaspoons kosher salt
- 1 tablespoon unsalted butter
- 3 tablespoons canola oil
- 1 medium red onion, finely chopped
- 2 garlic cloves, minced
- 8 ounces chicken livers, cleaned and finely chopped
- 2 scallions, white and green parts, cut into ⅛-inch rounds
- 2 celery stalks, including leafy greens, strings removed, finely chopped
- ½ medium green bell pepper, seeds and ribs removed, finely chopped (about ¼ cup)
- 1 small red bell pepper, seeds and ribs removed, finely chopped (about ½ cup)
- 2 tablespoons chopped fresh flat-leaf parsley
- 2 tablespoons chopped fresh oregano, or 2 teaspoons dried
- 1 jalapeño pepper, seeds and ribs removed, minced
- ½ teaspoon freshly ground black pepper

1. Cover and bring 3 cups water to a boil in a medium saucepan. Stir in the rice, 1 teaspoon salt, and the butter. Cover, reduce heat to low; cook until water is absorbed, 15 to 17 minutes. Remove from the heat, and let stand, covered, for 10 minutes. Use a fork to fluff the rice.

2. Heat the oil in a cast-iron skillet over medium-high heat. Add the onions and garlic; reduce heat to medium. Cook, stirring occasionally, until brown, about 10 minutes. Add the chicken livers; cook, stirring, 5 minutes. Add the rice and all the remaining ingredients. Cook, tossing and stirring, until hot, about 3 minutes.

red bean and rice salad

SERVES 8 TO 10

Basmati and popcorn rice (see Food Sources, page 648) are both long-grain varieties of aromatic rice with a subtle, nutty flavor.

- ¼ cup dried red kidney beans
- 1 dried bay leaf
- 2½ teaspoons kosher salt
- 2 cups long-grain white rice, preferably basmati or popcorn rice
- 1 cucumber, peeled, seeded, cut into ¼-inch dice
- 2 celery stalks, strings removed, cut into ¼-inch dice
- 4 scallions, white and green parts, thinly sliced crosswise
  Spicy Vinaigrette (recipe follows)

1. Pick over the dried beans, discarding any stones or broken beans, and rinse. Place in a saucepan, cover with cold water by 2 inches, and bring to a strong boil over high heat. Cover and remove from the heat, and let stand 1 hour. Drain the beans, and place in a large saucepan. Add the bay leaf and water to cover by 2 inches. Cover and bring to a boil. Reduce heat, and cook at a steady simmer for 1 to 1½ hours (times will vary depending on the age of the beans). Toward the end of the cooking time, add 1½ teaspoons salt. Let the beans cool in the liquid; drain when at room temperature, and discard the bay leaf.

2. Place the rice in a 2-quart saucepan with a tight-fitting lid. Add 3½ cups water and 1 teaspoon salt. Cover and bring to a boil over high heat. Reduce heat to low, cover, and cook for 20 minutes. Remove from the heat, and let stand, covered, for 10 minutes. Use a fork to fluff the rice, and transfer to a bowl.

3. Add the cucumber, celery, scallions, and beans to the rice. Toss with the vinaigrette. The salad tastes best served at room temperature within 2 hours. It also may be refrigerated up to 6 hours; return to room temperature before serving.

spicy vinaigrette

MAKES 1 CUP

- 3 tablespoons fresh thyme leaves, or 1 tablespoon dried
- ¾ cup extra-virgin olive oil
- ¼ cup red-wine vinegar
- 2 tablespoons fresh lemon juice
- ⅛ teaspoon cayenne pepper
- ¾ teaspoon freshly ground black pepper
- ½ teaspoon kosher salt
- 1 garlic clove, slightly crushed

Chop the thyme leaves to release the flavor. In a small bowl, combine the thyme, oil, vinegar, lemon juice, cayenne and black peppers, the salt, and garlic. Whisk well. The vinaigrette may be made up to 1 day ahead.

wild rice salad

SERVES 8 TO 10

This is perfect for a buffet; the flavors develop when the salad sits at room temperature.

- 1½ teaspoons kosher salt
- 3 cups wild rice
- 4 blood oranges or navel oranges, peel and pith removed
- 3 tablespoons red-wine vinegar
- 3 tablespoons sherry vinegar
- 1 teaspoon freshly ground black pepper, plus more for seasoning
- ½ cup extra-virgin olive oil
- 6 scallions, white and green parts, cut into ⅛-inch rounds
- 1 cup dried cranberries
- 1 bunch fresh flat-leaf parsley, leaves finely chopped (½ cup)

1. Cover and bring a large saucepan three-quarters full of salted water and the rice to a boil over medium-high heat. Cook the rice just until tender, about 40 minutes. Drain in a colander.

2. Meanwhile, working over a bowl to catch the juices, carefully slice between the sections and membranes of an orange; remove the segments whole. Place each segment in the bowl as completed. Repeat the process with the other oranges.

3. Combine vinegars, 1½ teaspoons salt, and the pepper in a separate bowl. Slowly whisk in oil.

4. In a large serving bowl, combine the rice, scallions, dried cranberries, parsley, and the orange sections and their juice. Drizzle on the vinaigrette, gently toss, and season with salt and pepper. Serve.

summer corn and rice pilaf

SERVES 4

- 2 tablespoons unsalted butter
- 1 cup basmati or long-grain white rice
- 4 ears corn, kernels shaved from cobs
- 4 large shallots, cut into ¼-inch slices
  Pinch of sugar
  Kosher salt and freshly ground black pepper
- ¼ cup loosely packed fresh mint leaves, coarsely chopped

1. Melt 1 tablespoon butter in a small saucepan set over medium heat. Add the rice, and stir until it is well coated with the butter. Add 2 cups water, raise heat to high, and bring to a boil. Reduce heat to medium low, cover, and simmer until all of the water is absorbed and the rice is tender, 15 to 18 minutes. Remove from the heat, and let stand, covered, for 10 minutes. Use a fork to fluff the rice.

2. Meanwhile, in a large skillet over medium heat, melt the remaining tablespoon of butter. Add the corn, shallots, and sugar, and season with salt and pepper. Cook, stirring occasionally to prevent burning, until the corn and shallots are soft and tender, about 5 minutes. Remove from heat.

3. Combine the rice and corn mixture in a medium bowl. Add the mint, and toss to combine. Season with salt and pepper. Serve.

rice pilaf with herbes de provence, toasted almonds, and dried pears

SERVES 6

This aromatic pilaf combines wild and long-grain white rice. Dried pears are available in grocery and health-food stores.

- 1 cup wild rice
- 1 tablespoon unsalted butter
- 1 small onion, finely chopped
- 2 teaspoons Herbes de Provence (recipe follows) or prepared
- 2 celery stalks, strings removed, finely chopped
  Kosher salt and freshly ground black pepper
- 1 cup long-grain white rice
- ½ cup whole almonds, toasted (see page 644), coarsely chopped
- 8 dried pears, finely chopped
- 1 cup loosely packed fresh flat-leaf parsley, finely chopped

1. Fill a medium saucepan with water, and cover and bring to a boil. Add the wild rice, and reduce heat. Let simmer until the rice is tender but not split, about 45 minutes. Drain, and set aside.

2. Meanwhile, melt the butter in a medium saucepan with a tight-fitting lid over medium heat. Add the onion; cook until translucent, about 6 minutes. Stir in the herbes de Provence and the celery. Season the mixture with salt and pepper and cook a few minutes more. Stir in the white rice, and cook, stirring, until it just starts to turn translucent, 3 to 4 minutes. Add 1½ cups cold water, raise heat to high, and bring to a boil. Reduce heat to low, cover, and simmer about 20 minutes.

3. Remove from the heat, and let stand, covered, for 10 minutes. Transfer the rice pilaf to a bowl. Add the chopped almonds, reserved wild rice, dried pears, and chopped parsley. Toss to combine. Serve.

herbes de provence

MAKES ABOUT ⅓ CUP

This herb blend is composed of dried herbs commonly found in southern France, where it originated. It is often packaged in decorative clay crocks, or it can be found in the spice section of large grocery stores.

- 1 tablespoon dried lavender
- 1 tablespoon dried summer savory
- 1 tablespoon dried marjoram
- 1 tablespoon dried rosemary
- 1 tablespoon dried thyme
- 1 tablespoon whole fennel seeds

Combine all the ingredients in an airtight container, and store in a cool, dark place for up to 4 months.

mint jasmine rice

SERVES 4

Delicately fragrant jasmine rice is an excellent accompaniment to grilled lamb or chicken.

- 1 cup jasmine rice
- 1 tablespoon extra-virgin olive oil
- 1 small onion, finely chopped (about ½ cup)
- ¼ cup coarsely chopped fresh mint
  Grated zest of 1 lemon
- ¼ cup coarsely chopped fresh flat-leaf parsley
- 1 teaspoon kosher salt
- 2 teaspoons fresh lemon juice

1. Cover and bring a medium saucepan three-quarters full of water to a boil. Stir in the rice, and return the water to a boil. Reduce heat to a simmer, and cook until the rice is tender, about 20 minutes. Drain the rice into a strainer, and rinse with cold water until cool.

2. Heat 1 teaspoon olive oil in a small skillet over medium heat. Add onion; cook until translucent, about 6 minutes. Transfer rice and onion mixture to a medium bowl, and toss with the mint, lemon zest, parsley, salt, lemon juice, and the remaining 2 teaspoons of olive oil. Serve at room temperature.

parmesan risotto 101

SERVES 4

Encourage your family or guests to eat as Italians do, flattening out the outermost part of the mound to cool it slightly, and slowly eating your way into the center so every bite will be the right temperature. For Carnaroli rice, see Food Sources, page 648.

1½ to 2 quarts Homemade Chicken Stock (page 624), or low-sodium store-bought chicken broth, skimmed of fat

3 tablespoons extra-virgin olive oil

2 shallots, minced

1 cup Arborio or Carnaroli rice

½ cup dry white wine

4 to 6 tablespoons unsalted butter

½ cup freshly grated Parmigiano-Reggiano cheese (from 1½ ounces), plus more for garnish

¼ cup chopped fresh flat-leaf parsley

Kosher salt and freshly ground black pepper

1. Heat the stock in a medium saucepan over medium heat; keep at a low simmer. Heat the olive oil in a heavy-bottomed saucepan over medium heat. Add the shallots, and cook, stirring, until translucent, about 4 minutes. Add the rice, and cook, stirring, until the rice begins to make a clicking sound like glass beads, 3 to 4 minutes.

2. Add the wine to the rice mixture. Cook, stirring, until the rice absorbs the wine.

3. Using a ladle, add ¾ cup hot stock to the rice. Using a wooden spoon, stir the rice constantly, at a moderate speed. When the rice mixture is just thick enough to leave a clear wake behind the spoon, add another ¾ cup of the hot stock.

4. Add hot stock ¾ cup at a time, stirring constantly, until rice is mostly translucent but still opaque in the center. The rice should be al dente but not crunchy. Watch the rice carefully and add smaller amounts of liquid to make sure it does not over-

cook. The final mixture should be thick enough that the rice is suspended in liquid that is the consistency of heavy cream, a total of 20 to 25 minutes. It will thicken slightly when removed from heat.

5. Remove from heat. Stir in butter, cheese, and parsley; season with salt and pepper. Divide mixture among four shallow bowls, mounding risotto in the center, and grate or shave additional cheese over the risotto. Serve.

wild mushroom risotto

SERVES 4

For a subtler mushroom flavor, omit the dried mushrooms, and add two more ounces of fresh mushrooms. For wild mushrooms and Carnaroli rice, see Food Sources, page 648.

1½ to 2 quarts Homemade Chicken Stock (page 624), or Veal Stock (page 626), or low-sodium store-bought chicken broth, skimmed of fat

4 ounces dried wild mushrooms, such as porcini

9 ounces assorted fresh wild mushrooms, wiped clean

¼ cup plus 3 tablespoons extra-virgin olive oil

5 shallots, minced (about ½ cup)

1 cup Arborio or Carnaroli rice

½ cup dry white wine

4 to 6 tablespoons unsalted butter

½ cup freshly grated Parmesan cheese (from 1½ ounces), plus more for garnish

Kosher salt and freshly ground black pepper

1. Heat the stock in a medium saucepan over medium heat. Add the dried mushrooms; cook until tender, about 5 minutes. Remove with a slotted spoon; finely chop. Keep the stock at a simmer over low heat.

2. Remove the stems from the fresh mushrooms; finely chop. Slice the caps ¼ inch thick. Heat 1 tablespoon oil in a saucepan over medium heat. Add the mushroom caps; cook, stirring occasionally, until golden and soft, about 3 minutes. Transfer to a bowl. Add the remaining ¼ cup plus 2 tablespoons of oil, the mushroom stems, and the shallots to the pan. Cook, stirring, until translucent. Add the rice; cook, stirring, until the rice begins to sound like glass beads, 3 to 4 minutes.

3. Add wine. Cook, stirring, until wine is absorbed by rice. Using a ladle, add ¾ cup hot stock to the rice. Using a wooden spoon, stir rice constantly at a moderate speed. When the rice has absorbed most, but not all, of the liquid and mixture is just thick enough to leave a clear wake behind the spoon when stirring, add another ¾ cup stock.

4. Continue adding the stock in this manner, stirring constantly, until the rice is mostly translucent but still opaque in the center. Continue cooking until the rice is al dente but not crunchy. As the rice nears doneness, watch carefully; add smaller amounts of hot stock. The mixture should be thick enough that grains are suspended in liquid that is the consistency of heavy cream (a total of 20 to 25 minutes). The risotto will thicken slightly when removed from the heat.

5. Add the dried mushrooms and the mushroom caps, and stir until warmed through. Remove from heat. Stir in the butter and cheese; season with salt and pepper. Divide among four bowls; grate the cheese over the risotto. Serve immediately.

butternut squash risotto
SERVES 4 TO 6

5 to 6 cups Homemade Chicken Stock (page 624), or low-sodium store-bought chicken broth, skimmed of fat

1 pound butternut squash, peeled and cut into ¾-inch dice (about 2 cups)

2 teaspoons extra-virgin olive oil

4 ounces pancetta, cut into ½-inch dice

1 medium onion, finely chopped

1 garlic clove, minced

1½ cups Arborio rice

½ cup dry white wine

Kosher salt and freshly ground black pepper

2 tablespoons roughly chopped fresh tarragon or flat-leaf parsley

2 tablespoons Roasted Pumpkin Seeds (page 100), for garnish, optional

1. In a saucepan, combine stock and squash; bring to a boil over medium-high heat. Reduce heat to low; let simmer (squash will not cook completely).

2. Meanwhile, warm the oil in a medium saucepan over medium-low heat. Add the pancetta; cook, stirring, until the fat is rendered and the pancetta is crisp, about 10 minutes. Using a slotted spoon, set the pancetta on a paper towel to drain; set aside.

3. Add the onion and garlic to the rendered fat; cook, stirring, until translucent, 8 minutes. Add the rice, raise heat to high, and continue stirring until the edges of the rice are translucent, 3 to 4 minutes. Add the wine; cook, stirring, until the wine is absorbed, about 2 minutes. Reduce heat to medium high; season with salt and pepper. Add about 1 cup of the hot stock and squash. Cook, stirring, until nearly all the stock is absorbed. Continue adding stock and squash, about ¾ cup at a time. Cook, stirring, allowing each addition to be nearly absorbed before adding the next, until rice is creamy but a little firm in the center, 20 to 25 minutes. Stir in the tarragon and reserved pancetta; garnish with the pumpkin seeds, if using. Serve.

....

RISOTTO

While little could be better than classic Parmesan risotto, other ingredients and flavorings are perfectly suited to this versatile grain. Among our favorites:

Crumbled saffron

Asparagus and lemon zest

Fresh and dried porcini mushrooms

Shellfish and peas

Fresh zucchini flowers

Fresh corn kernels

Spicy Italian sausage

Butternut squash and sage

Spring peas, mint, and lemon zest

Beets, beet greens, and pancetta

White truffle oil

....

lemon mint risotto

SERVES 6

The flavors of this risotto are bright and clean. Substitute 1 cup of frozen peas if asparagus is unavailable.

- 3 yellow bell peppers, seeds and ribs removed, cut into 1-inch dice
- 5 cups Homemade Chicken Stock (page 624), or low-sodium store-bought chicken broth, skimmed of fat
- 1 teaspoon kosher salt, plus more for water
- 8 ounces thin asparagus, tough ends removed, cut diagonally into 1½-inch lengths
- 6 sprigs fresh mint, plus 2 tablespoons finely chopped leaves
- 6 sprigs fresh flat-leaf parsley, plus 2 tablespoons finely chopped leaves
- 1 sprig fresh rosemary
- 1 tablespoon extra-virgin olive oil
- 8 ounces shallots, minced
- 1 medium fennel bulb, trimmed, diced to yield 1 cup
- 3 medium garlic cloves, minced
- 1¼ cups Arborio rice
- ½ teaspoon ground coriander
- ½ cup dry white wine
- Grated zest of 2 lemons
- ⅛ teaspoon freshly ground black pepper
- ¼ cup freshly grated Parmesan cheese
- 2 teaspoons lemon juice

1. In a small saucepan, combine the peppers, ¼ cup plus 2 tablespoons water, and ¼ cup chicken stock; cover and cook over medium-low heat, stirring frequently, until the peppers are very soft, 25 to 30 minutes. Remove from the heat, and let cool. In the bowl of a food processor, purée the peppers with the liquid until smooth. Strain through a coarse sieve into a small bowl. Set aside.

2. Prepare an ice-water bath. Cover and bring a medium saucepan of salted water to a boil, and add the asparagus. Cook until bright green and still slightly crunchy, 1 to 2 minutes. Remove the asparagus with a slotted spoon, and transfer to the ice bath to stop the cooking. Drain and set aside.

3. In a medium saucepan, combine the remaining 4¾ cups of chicken stock with the sprigs of mint, parsley, and rosemary; cover and bring to a boil. Reduce the heat to low, and keep the stock at a bare simmer.

4. Meanwhile, heat the olive oil in a heavy 4-quart saucepan over medium heat. Add the shallots, fennel, and garlic, and cook, stirring frequently with a wooden spoon, until very soft but not browned, about 6 minutes. Stir in the rice and coriander, and cook, stirring constantly, until the edges of the rice are translucent, about 3 minutes. Add the wine and lemon zest, and cook, stirring constantly, until nearly all the wine is absorbed, about 30 seconds.

5. Remove the herb sprigs from the stock with tongs or a slotted spoon, and discard. Add the salt and pepper and about ¾ cup of the simmering stock to the rice, and cook over medium-high heat, stirring constantly, until nearly all the stock is absorbed. Continue adding the stock, about ¾ cup at a time, stirring constantly and allowing each addition to be nearly absorbed before adding the next, until the rice is creamy-looking and each grain is tender but still firm in the center, 20 to 25 minutes.

6. Remove pan from heat; stir in the pepper purée, asparagus, cheese, 1 tablespoon of the chopped mint, the chopped parsley, and lemon juice. Season with salt and pepper, if necessary. Divide the risotto among six plates, and sprinkle with the remaining mint. Serve immediately.

FIT TO EAT RECIPE PER SERVING: 269 CALORIES, 6 G TOTAL FAT, 19% CALORIES FROM FAT, 7 MG CHOLESTEROL, 43 G CARBOHYDRATE, 633 MG SODIUM, 11 G PROTEIN, 5 G DIETARY FIBER

saffron and shellfish risotto

SERVES 4

Most Italians believe shellfish should not be paired with cheese; instead of cheese, we have added a little more butter.

1½ to 2 quarts Fish Stock (page 628) or Vegetable Stock (page 626), or frozen vegetable broth, thawed

12 littleneck clams, scrubbed

12 ounces medium shrimp, peeled and deveined, cut into thirds, shells reserved

3 tablespoons extra-virgin olive oil

4 shallots, minced

Pinch of crumbled saffron threads

1 cup Arborio rice

½ cup dry white wine

6 to 8 tablespoons unsalted butter

¼ cup chopped fresh flat-leaf parsley

Kosher salt and freshly ground black pepper

1. Heat the stock in a saucepan over high heat. Add the clams; cover. Cook until the clams are opened, 5 to 10 minutes. Using a slotted spoon, transfer the clams to a bowl. Discard the unopened clams. Remove the clams from the shells, and discard the shells. Chop the clam meat; set aside. Add shrimp shells to the stock. Cover; simmer 15 minutes. Pour the stock through a fine sieve or cheesecloth-lined strainer, discarding the solids and sand left in the pan. Return the stock to the cleaned saucepan on the stove; keep at simmer over medium heat.

2. Heat the oil in heavy-bottomed saucepan over medium heat. Add the shallots and saffron; cook, stirring, until translucent, about 6 minutes. Add the rice; cook, stirring, until the rice begins to sound like glass beads, 3 to 4 minutes.

3. Add wine. Cook, stirring, until wine is absorbed. Using a ladle, add ¾ cup hot stock to rice. Using a wooden spoon, stir rice constantly at a medium speed. When rice has absorbed most but not all of the liquid, and the mixture is just thick enough to leave a clear wake behind the spoon when stirring, add another ¾ cup of hot stock.

4. Continue adding the stock in this manner, stirring constantly, until the rice is mostly translucent but still opaque and slightly crunchy in the center. Add the shrimp; continue stirring and adding the hot stock until the rice is still al dente but not crunchy, and the shrimp is cooked through, about 3 minutes. As the rice nears doneness, watch carefully, and add smaller amounts of the hot stock. The mixture should be thick enough that grains of rice are suspended in liquid that is the consistency of heavy cream (a total of 20 to 25 minutes). It will thicken slightly when removed from heat.

5. Remove from heat. Stir in the chopped clams, butter (or a little more if the risotto seems dry), and the parsley; season with salt and pepper. Divide among four bowls. Serve immediately.

risotto balls

Leftover risotto is used to make these wonderful bite-size hors d'oeuvres.

Leftover risotto, chilled

Fontina cheese, cut into ½-inch cubes

Dry bread crumbs (see page 647), for coating

Olive oil, for frying

1. With moistened hands, form 2 tablespoons of risotto into a 1½-inch ball. Make a well in the center with your thumb, and fill it with a cube of cheese. Form a ball around the cheese, packing risotto firmly. Repeat with remaining risotto.

2. Place bread crumbs in a small bowl; roll the balls in the bread crumbs to lightly coat. Set aside.

3. In a medium skillet, heat ¾-inch olive oil over medium-high heat, until it registers 350°F. on a deep-frying thermometer. Carefully place the balls in the oil, 4 at a time. Fry until golden brown on one side, 2 to 2½ minutes. With a slotted spoon, turn the balls over and fry until deep golden brown, about 2 minutes more. Remove from the oil with the slotted spoon, and drain on paper towels. Repeat with the remaining risotto balls. Serve hot.

torta di riso

SERVES 10 TO 15

This "torta"—or cake—must be chilled overnight before serving, so plan ahead.

- 6 tablespoons unsalted butter, plus more for pan
- ½ cup dry bread crumbs (see page 647)
- 2½ quarts Homemade Chicken Stock (page 624), or low-sodium store-bought chicken broth, skimmed of fat
- 1 medium onion, finely chopped
- 2 garlic cloves, minced
- 1 cup finely chopped mixed fresh herbs, such as thyme, rosemary, basil, parsley, and oregano
- 3 cups Arborio rice
- 1 cup dry white wine
- ½ cup freshly grated Parmesan cheese (from 1½ ounces), plus more for garnish
  Kosher salt and freshly ground black pepper

1. Butter an 8-inch springform pan, and coat with the bread crumbs, shaking out the excess. Set aside. In a large saucepan, heat the stock to boiling, then lower to a simmer.

2. In a large, heavy saucepan over low heat, melt 3 tablespoons butter. Add onion, garlic, and ⅔ cup herbs, and cook until translucent, about 8 minutes. Raise heat to medium, and add the rice. Stir well to coat the grains; cook about 3 minutes.

3. Add wine; simmer, stirring constantly, until mostly evaporated. Add ¾ cup hot stock and simmer, stirring constantly, until mostly absorbed, about 3 minutes. Add the remaining stock ¾ cup at a time, stirring constantly. Always wait until one ladleful is nearly absorbed before adding the next.

4. Continue in this manner until the rice is al dente but not crunchy in the center, a total of 20 to 25 minutes. Add the remaining ⅓ cup of the herbs about halfway through the cooking time.

5. Stir in the remaining 3 tablespoons of butter, the Parmesan, and salt and pepper to taste. Pour into the prepared pan, and cool completely. Refrigerate overnight covered with plastic wrap.

6. Preheat the oven to 400°F. Bake the torta for about 30 minutes, or until heated through (test by inserting a knife into the center for 15 seconds and checking its temperature).

7. Unmold the torta carefully onto a serving plate, sprinkle grated Parmesan over the top, slice into wedges, and serve warm.

baked sage and saffron risotto

SERVES 4

When risotto is baked rather than cooked on the stove, it does not require constant stirring.

- 2 tablespoons extra-virgin olive oil
- 3 shallots, minced
- 1 cup Arborio rice
- ⅛ teaspoon crumbled saffron threads
- ½ cup dry white wine
- 2 cups Homemade Chicken Stock (page 624), or low-sodium store-bought chicken broth, skimmed of fat
- 6 fresh sage leaves, coarsely chopped (about 1 tablespoon), plus more for garnish
- 1 teaspoon kosher salt
- ⅛ teaspoon freshly ground black pepper
- 1 tablespoon unsalted butter, cut into small pieces

1. Preheat the oven to 450°F. In a medium ovenproof saucepan, heat the oil over medium heat. Add the shallots; cook, stirring until the shallots are translucent, about 4 minutes. Add the rice, and stir until the grains are shiny and well coated with the oil, about 2 minutes more. Add the saffron and wine, and continue cooking and stirring until the liquid is absorbed, 3 to 5 minutes.

2. Add the stock, sage, salt, and pepper. Cover the saucepan; transfer to the oven. Bake until stock is absorbed and rice is tender, about 25 minutes.

3. Uncover saucepan. Dot rice with the butter, arrange sage over rice, and bake until butter is melted, about 5 minutes more. Serve immediately.

tomato, cucumber, and barley salad

SERVES 12

Inspired by the classic Middle Eastern bulgur dish, this salad is every bit as refreshing.

- ¾ cup barley
- 2 teaspoons kosher salt
- 3 large (about 2 pounds) tomatoes, seeded, cut into ¾-inch dice
- 1½ cucumbers (about 1 pound), peeled, seeded, cut into ½-inch dice
- 2 celery stalks, strings removed, finely chopped
- 2 scallions, white part only, thinly sliced crosswise
- ½ cup finely chopped fresh flat-leaf parsley
- 1 cup finely chopped fresh mint
- ⅛ teaspoon cayenne pepper
- 3 tablespoons fresh lime juice
- 1 tablespoon plus 1 teaspoon extra-virgin olive oil
- ¼ teaspoon freshly ground black pepper

1. Cover and bring 5 cups water to a boil in a saucepan. Stir in barley and 1 teaspoon salt. Reduce heat to medium; cook until tender, about 35 minutes. Drain; rinse with cool water. Set aside.

2. Combine diced tomatoes and cucumbers in a large bowl. Add barley, celery, scallions, parsley, mint, and cayenne. Toss to combine; set aside.

3. In a small bowl, whisk together lime juice, olive oil, remaining teaspoon salt, and the pepper; add to barley mixture. Toss to combine. Serve immediately, or refrigerate, covered, for up to 8 hours.

FIT TO EAT RECIPE PER ½-CUP SERVING: 78 CALORIES, 2 G TOTAL FAT, 0 MG CHOLESTEROL, 14 G CARBOHYDRATE, 371 MG SODIUM, 2 G PROTEIN, 2 G DIETARY FIBER

tangy tabbouleh salad

SERVES 8

Tabbouleh is traditionally made with tomatoes, onions, parsley, and mint; this version was created with a mixture of our favorite vegetables.

- 1 cup bulgur wheat
- 12 ounces asparagus, tough ends removed, cut into 1¼-inch-long pieces
- 2 ears fresh corn, kernels shaved from the cob, or 1 cup frozen corn, defrosted
- 1 small fennel bulb, cut into matchsticks (about 1 cup)
- 3 scallions, white and green parts, thinly sliced diagonally
- ¼ cup roughly chopped fresh cilantro leaves
- 2 tablespoons fresh lime juice
- 2 tablespoons nonfat sour cream
- 1 tablespoon extra-virgin olive oil
- ¾ teaspoon kosher salt
- ⅛ teaspoon freshly ground black pepper

1. In a bowl, cover bulgur with 3 cups boiling water. Let stand 45 minutes. Drain well; return to the bowl. Meanwhile, cover and bring a large pot of water to a boil. Prepare an ice-water bath. Cook the asparagus in the boiling water until bright green and crisp, about 3 minutes. Using a slotted spoon, transfer to the ice-water bath to cool; drain and pat dry. In the same boiling water, cook the corn kernels for 3 minutes; drain and let cool.

2. Add the asparagus, corn, fennel, scallions, and cilantro to the bulgur; toss to combine.

3. In a bowl, whisk together the lime juice, sour cream, oil, salt, and pepper. Pour the vinaigrette over the salad; toss. Serve at room temperature, or refrigerate.

FIT TO EAT RECIPE PER SERVING: 114 CALORIES, 3 G FAT, 0 MG CHOLESTEROL, 21 G CARBOHYDRATE, 208 MG SODIUM, 5 G PROTEIN, 6 G DIETARY FIBER

polenta triangles

MAKES 8

Chicken stock gives the polenta a richer flavor. If you use store-bought chicken broth, you may not need to add salt.

- 1¼ cups Homemade Chicken Stock (page 624), or low-sodium store-bought chicken broth, skimmed of fat, or water
- 1¼ cups milk
- 2 teaspoons chopped fresh rosemary or thyme, optional
- 1 cup coarse yellow cornmeal
  Kosher salt
- 5 tablespoons unsalted butter, cut in tablespoons

1. Cover and bring the stock, milk, and herbs, if using, to a boil in a small, deep saucepan over medium heat. Lower heat, and slowly sprinkle in the cornmeal, stirring constantly. Cook, stirring constantly, for 20 minutes over low heat. If the polenta becomes too thick, add up to 1 more cup of boiling liquid. The polenta should resemble a thick porridge. Season with salt; stir in 4 tablespoons butter.

2. Pour the polenta into a 9 x 13 x ½-inch baking pan, and smooth out. Cover with plastic wrap, and refrigerate until firm, or overnight.

3. Cut the polenta into 8 triangles. Heat the remaining tablespoon of butter in a large nonstick skillet over medium heat. Cook the polenta triangles until brown on both sides. Serve immediately.

roasted barley pilaf

SERVES 4

Pan-roasting the barley gives it a rich, nutty flavor.

- 1 tablespoon olive oil
- 1 cup pearl barley, rinsed
- 2 shallots, minced
- 4 ounces white or wild mushrooms, wiped clean, sliced
- 2 cups Homemade Chicken Stock (page 624), or low-sodium store-bought chicken broth, skimmed of fat, or water
- ¼ teaspoon kosher salt, plus more for seasoning
  Freshly ground black pepper

1. Heat the oil in a heavy, medium saucepan over medium heat. Add the barley, and cook, stirring frequently, for 10 minutes. The barley should start to brown and give off an aroma.

2. Add shallots, and cook for 2 minutes. Add mushrooms, and cook until wilted, 2 to 3 minutes. Add stock and salt. Bring to a boil; then reduce heat to a bare simmer. Cover and cook for 45 minutes, or until the liquid is absorbed. Stir well, season with salt and pepper, if needed; serve.

herbed quinoa

SERVES 4

Parsley juice gives this quinoa a beautiful color.

- 1 cup quinoa, rinsed and drained
- 1½ cups Homemade Chicken Stock (page 624), or low-sodium store-bought chicken broth, skimmed of fat
- 1 large bunch fresh flat-leaf parsley
- 1 bunch chives, snipped into ¼-inch lengths
- 1 tablespoon unsalted butter
  Kosher salt and freshly ground black pepper

1. Place the quinoa and the stock in a medium saucepan. Cover and bring to a boil over medium-high heat. Reduce heat; simmer until all the stock has been absorbed, about 20 minutes. Transfer the quinoa to a large bowl; set aside in a warm place.

2. Meanwhile, pick ½ cup parsley leaves from the stems, chop the leaves coarsely, and set aside. Place the remaining parsley leaves, parsley stems, and ¼ cup water in the bowl of a food processor; process until puréed. Transfer the purée to a double layer of cheesecloth placed over a small bowl. Squeeze all the liquid from the purée, discard the solids, and set the parsley juice aside.

3. Add the snipped chives, butter, reserved parsley juice, and chopped parsley to the cooked quinoa, and mix until combined. Season with salt and pepper, and serve.

meat

....

beef tenderloin with shallots and red wine glaze

SERVES 4

To give the meat more flavor, tie several rosemary sprigs to the top of the tenderloin with kitchen twine before roasting.

2¼ *pounds beef tenderloin, trimmed and tied*

8 *sprigs fresh rosemary*

16 *shallots, peeled and trimmed*

2 *tablespoons olive oil*

Kosher salt and freshly ground black pepper

½ *cup dry red wine*

½ *cup Homemade Chicken Stock (page 624), or store-bought low-sodium chicken broth, skimmed of fat, or water*

1. Let the tenderloin come to room temperature, about 45 minutes. Preheat the oven to 425°F with a rack in the center. Arrange 7 rosemary sprigs in a medium roasting pan; place tenderloin on top. Arrange shallots around tenderloin. Rub meat and shallots with the oil; season with salt and pepper.

2. Roast 25 minutes. Turn the shallots for even browning; if the roast is dry, baste with more olive oil or pan juices. Cook 10 to 15 minutes more, until the shallots are golden; transfer to a small bowl; reserve. Meat should register about 125°F (for rare) with an instant-read thermometer; timing will vary with the thickness of the meat. Transfer beef to a medium platter. Let sit at least 10 minutes at room temperature before carving.

3. Meanwhile, chop the remaining sprig of rosemary into small pieces. Place the roasting pan over high heat. Add the wine and the stock. Cook, scraping the bottom of the pan to collect any cooked-on bits, until the liquid has reduced by half, about 6 minutes. Pass through a strainer; discard solids. Serve the beef with the gravy and reserved shallots.

beef tenderloin with cipollini onions agrodolce

SERVES 12

"Agrodolce" means "sweet and sour" in Italian and refers to the sweet and tangy glaze that coats the cipollini onions (flat, yellow Italian onions). Pearl onions may be substituted.

3 *pounds cipollini onions, peeled*

6 *tablespoons unsalted butter*

¼ *cup sugar*

2 *teaspoons kosher salt*

¾ *teaspoon freshly ground black pepper*

¼ *cup red-wine vinegar*

1 *tablespoon fresh thyme leaves, plus sprigs for garnish*

1 *whole beef tenderloin (4½ pounds), trimmed, cut into 2 pieces and tied with kitchen twine*

1 *tablespoon olive oil*

1. Place the onions, butter, sugar, ½ teaspoon salt, and ¼ teaspoon pepper in single layer in a large straight-sided skillet; add 1 inch of water. Cover and bring the water to a boil. Reduce heat to medium, and simmer, covered, 1 hour; the onions should be very soft. Uncover; add the vinegar. Cook, turning occasionally, until the liquid evaporates and the onions caramelize, about 1 hour. Stir in the thyme leaves. Set aside.

2. Preheat the oven to 400°F. Sprinkle the meat with the remaining 1½ teaspoons salt and ½ teaspoon pepper. Place an ovenproof skillet over high heat. Add the olive oil; heat until almost smoking. Place the beef in the pan; sear until well browned on all sides. Transfer to the oven; roast until an instant-read thermometer inserted in the thickest part registers 140°F (for medium rare), about 35 minutes. Allow to rest at least 10 minutes before slicing. The beef may be served warm or at room temperature. Slice just before serving. Place on a platter with the reserved cipollini onions; garnish with thyme sprigs. Serve.

brisket of beef

SERVES 10 TO 12

- 1 28-ounce can plum tomatoes with juice
- 1 brisket (about 5½ pounds), top flap removed and fat trimmed

   Kosher salt

- ¼ teaspoon freshly ground black pepper, plus more for seasoning
- 3 tablespoons olive oil
- 3 large (about 2½ pounds) onions, thinly sliced
- 2 garlic cloves
- 2 cups dry red wine
- 5 medium carrots, cut into 2-inch pieces
- 2 celery stalks, strings removed, cut into 2-inch pieces

1. Preheat the oven to 325°F. Pass the tomatoes and juices through a food mill fitted with a medium disk into a medium bowl. Set aside. Trim any remaining excess fat from the brisket. Season both sides of the brisket well with the salt and pepper.

2. Heat 2 tablespoons olive oil in a heavy ovenproof casserole over medium-high heat. Add the brisket, and brown very well, about 5 minutes per side. Transfer to a plate, and set aside.

3. Reduce heat to medium low, add the remaining tablespoon olive oil, the onions, and garlic, and cook, stirring frequently, until quite brown and very soft, about 25 minutes. Add the red wine, raise heat to high, and bring to a boil. Cook about 2 minutes, scraping up the brown bits on the bottom of the pot. Add the carrots, celery, and reserved tomatoes with juice, and stir well to combine.

4. Return brisket to pot, spooning some of the liquid and vegetables over it. Cover; transfer to the oven. Cook until beef is very tender, about 3 hours, carefully turning meat after 1½ hours.

5. Let cool slightly, and remove the brisket, being careful not to shred it. Transfer the sauce and the vegetables from the pot to the bowl of a food processor, and process until very smooth. Season with salt and pepper if necessary. If preparing the day before, return the brisket to the pot, pour the sauce over it, and refrigerate. If serving right away, return sauce to pot. Slice meat against the grain into ¼-inch-thick slices; place in the sauce. Warm over medium-low heat for about 5 minutes.

6. If refrigerated overnight, remove brisket from refrigerator; slice against the grain. Add sliced meat to sauce; reheat over medium-low heat until warmed through, about 30 minutes.

prime rib roast 101
with yorkshire pudding
SERVES 6 TO 8

for the pudding

2   cups all-purpose flour
1   teaspoon kosher salt
6   large eggs
2½ cups milk

for the roast

1   3-rib prime-rib roast, first cut, trimmed
    and tied, room temperature
2   tablespoons kosher salt
1   tablespoon freshly ground black pepper
3   short ribs, tied
1½ cups dry red wine

1. Sift together the flour and salt. Place in a large bowl; make a well, and place the eggs in the center. Slowly whisk the eggs into the flour mixture until a paste forms. Gradually whisk in the milk. Cover with plastic wrap; chill in the refrigerator at least 4 hours or overnight (it must be cold).

2. Preheat the oven to 450°F with a rack on the lowest level. Rub the roast all over with the salt and pepper. Transfer to a heavy 13 x 16-inch metal roasting pan. Arrange the meat, fat-side up. Place the short ribs in the pan.

3. Cook 20 minutes. Reduce the heat to 325°F, and continue cooking until an instant-read thermometer inserted in the thick end of the roast (not touching a bone) reaches 115°F, about 1 hour 25 minutes. If it is not done, return to the oven; check the temperature at 10-minute intervals.

4. Transfer the roast to a platter; set aside in a warm place. Let the roast rest for at least 30 minutes before carving to allow the meat juices to redistribute themselves back through the roast. (As the roast rests, the temperature will increase by about 10°F, to 125°F, rare.) Do not tent, or the crust will get soggy. Raise the oven to 425°F.

5. Pour the fat and drippings into a fat separator or a glass measuring cup; set aside.

6. Place the roasting pan over medium-high heat. Pour the red wine into the pan; scrape the bottom with a wooden spoon, loosening any cooked-on bits to deglaze pan. Cook until reduced by half, about 6 minutes. Place a fine sieve in a medium heat-proof bowl. Strain the sauce into the bowl. Do not clean the pan. Using the wooden spoon, press down on the solids to extract the juices. Discard the solids. Cover the bowl with aluminum foil, and set it over a saucepan with 1 inch of barely simmering water to keep warm.

7. Pour ¼ cup of the reserved pan drippings into the roasting pan. Place the pan with the drippings into the oven until very hot, about 5 minutes. Remove the batter from the refrigerator, and shake or whisk well; quickly and carefully pour the batter into the hot pan. Cook until the Yorkshire Pudding is crisp and golden, about 25 minutes. Cut each person a large wedge of warm pudding with the crispy edge, which will help it hold its shape. Transfer the reserved red-wine sauce into a gravy boat, and serve with the prime rib.

....

TIPS FOR PREPARING
PRIME RIB ROAST

● *Have the butcher tie the roast to keep the outer layer from pulling away from the rib eye. The roast will cook and carve more evenly. Tie short ribs for easy handling.*

● *Bring roast to room temperature about 2 hours before cooking so it cooks evenly.*

● *To season the roast, place the short ribs and roast, fat-side up, in a heavy metal pan (not nonstick). Beef roasted on the bone is more flavorful. Rub the meat all over, evenly, with salt and pepper. An even layer applied to the fat will make the roast more beautiful.*

....

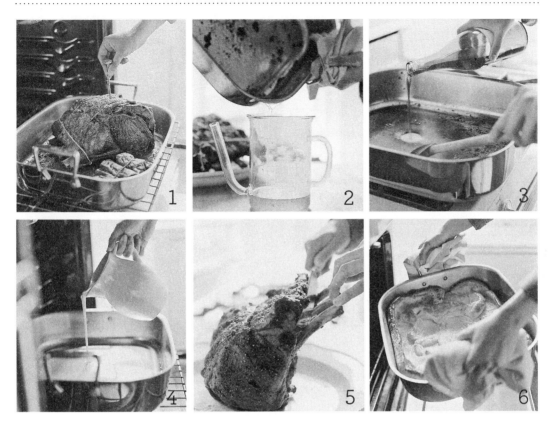

MAKING PRIME RIB WITH YORKSHIRE PUDDING

1. Use a heavy stainless-steel or other metal pan (nonstick pans yield fewer of the tasty cooked-on bits). Starting with a higher temperature helps initiate browning; reducing the heat ensures the roast cooks evenly throughout. Use an instant-read thermometer to determine the internal temperature: insert the probe into the thick end between two ribs, making sure it's not near a bone (bones may cause an improper reading).

2. Place roast on a platter and keep it near the stove to keep warm. Do not cover the roast, or the crisp exterior will get soggy. (If you like, save the short ribs to use in flavoring stock.) Pour all the drippings from the pan into a fat separator. If you don't have

one, use a liquid measuring cup; once the fat has risen to the top, pour or spoon it off.

3. Place the pan over medium-high heat, and add liquid, such as red wine. With a wooden spoon, scrape off the bits that are stuck to the pan. As you cook and reduce the liquids, adjust the seasoning with salt and pepper. These drippings are the essential ingredient in making the best-tasting Yorkshire pudding.

4. There is no need to use multiple pans. The reaction between the hot pan and the very cold batter is what makes the pudding puff.

5. Ready the roast for presentation by first removing the twine. Place the bones perpendicular

to a serving platter, and grip with one hand. With the other hand, slide the sharpened knife straight down between the meat and bones, separating the two as you cut down. Continue until the bones are completely separated. Transfer to the platter where it can easily be sliced.

6. Make sure the pudding is well browned. Undercooked pudding will collapse sooner (and have a raw taste). Serve each person a large wedge of pudding with the crispy edge, which will hold the shape nicely.

steak au poivre

SERVES 2

The creamy sauce mellows the peppercorns on the steak in this quick and luscious version of the classic. This recipe can be doubled.

- 2 tablespoons whole black peppercorns
- 1 tablespoon whole white peppercorns
- 1 tablespoon dried green peppercorns
- 2 boneless shell steaks (about 12 ounces each)
- 4 tablespoons unsalted butter
- 1 tablespoon canola oil
- 1 large shallot, minced
- ½ cup cognac
- 1 cup Beef Stock (page 624), or frozen, thawed
- 1 tablespoon green peppercorns in brine, drained and coarsely chopped
- ½ cup heavy cream
  Kosher salt

1. Place the peppercorns in a heavy resealable plastic bag; crush with the smooth side of a meat tenderizer or the bottom of a heavy skillet. (Or pulse in a spice grinder until coarsely ground; don't overprocess.) Pat the steaks dry; coat both sides with the peppercorn mixture. Heat 2 tablespoons butter and the oil in a large skillet over medium-high heat until very hot but not smoking. Add steaks to pan; cook until seared on both sides, 4 to 5 minutes on each side for medium rare. Transfer to a platter; cover with aluminum foil.

2. Drain all the fat from the skillet; melt the remaining 2 tablespoons butter over medium heat. Add the shallot, and cook until it begins to soften but not brown, about 2 minutes. Add the cognac; boil, scraping up browned bits from pan. Add the stock, green peppercorns, and the liquid that has collected around the steaks; boil until reduced slightly, about 2 minutes. Stir in the cream, and boil until sauce thickens, about 3 minutes. Season with salt. Pour the hot sauce over the steaks. Serve.

boeuf bourguignon with golden mashed potato crust

SERVES 10 TO 12

The key to this classic beef stew is in searing the meat: If the cubes of meat are too crowded in the pan, they will not form that delectable crust.

- 1 pound pearl onions, peeled
- 5 pounds stewing beef, cut into 1-inch cubes
- ½ cup all-purpose flour
- 1 tablespoon plus 1 teaspoon kosher salt, plus more for cooking water
- 1½ teaspoons freshly ground black pepper
- ½ cup canola oil
- 1 750-ml bottle red Burgundy wine
- 8 ounces pancetta or thick bacon, cut into ¼-inch cubes
- 2 onions, cut into ⅛-inch-thick rounds
- 5 (about 1 pound) carrots, cut into ¼-inch-thick rounds
- 3 (about 1 pound) parsnips, cut into ¼-inch-thick rounds
- 1 dried bay leaf
- 3 sprigs fresh thyme
- 5 sprigs fresh flat-leaf parsley
- 10 whole black peppercorns
- 4 pounds (8 to 10) Yukon gold potatoes, peeled, cut into ¼-inch-thick rounds
- 1½ cups heavy cream
- 12 tablespoons (1½ sticks) unsalted butter
- ½ teaspoon freshly grated nutmeg
- 1½ pounds button mushrooms, wiped clean, cut in quarters
- 10 to 12 small sprigs fresh oregano, for garnish

1. Cover and bring a medium saucepan of water to a boil. Cook the onions in the boiling water for 30 seconds to loosen the skins. Drain; let cool. Carefully peel the onions, leaving the root and stem ends intact. Set aside.

2. Place the beef in large bowl. In small bowl, whisk together the flour, 2 teaspoons salt, and 1 teaspoon pepper. Sprinkle the flour mixture over the beef; toss to coat the beef evenly.

3. Heat a 12-inch heavy-bottomed skillet over medium heat. Add 1 tablespoon canola oil; swirl to coat the bottom of the skillet. Heat the oil to just below the smoking point; test by placing one piece of the beef in the hot pan. It should sizzle the moment it touches the pan. If the beef spits, sputters, and smokes, the pan is too hot; remove it from the heat to cool. If the beef does not sizzle, the pan is not hot enough; wait a minute or two more. Brown the beef in manageable batches, about eight cubes at a time. Arrange an eighth of the meat in the skillet so the cubes do not touch. Cook until a dark crust has formed and the beef easily releases from the pan when lifted with tongs, about 3 minutes. Brown all sides of each piece in this manner.

4. Transfer the first batch of the browned beef to a large Dutch oven or large heat-proof skillet. Return the skillet to the heat. Deglaze the skillet: Pour in an eighth of the wine (about 3 ounces); use a wooden spoon to loosen the bits that have cooked onto the skillet. Pour the wine and deglazed juices into the Dutch oven. Return the skillet to the heat. Quickly wipe out with a paper towel. Add another tablespoon of the canola oil. Repeat the process of cooking the beef cubes with 1 tablespoon oil at a time and deglazing the skillet with the wine.

5. When the last batch of beef is browned and the skillet is deglazed, return the skillet to medium-low heat. Add the pancetta; cook, stirring occasionally, until golden brown, about 10 minutes. With a slotted spoon, transfer the pancetta to the Dutch oven. Pour half the oil from the skillet into a small bowl; set aside. In the oil that remains in the skillet, cook half the sliced onions, carrots, and parsnips, stirring often, until onions are transparent and carrots and parsnips have softened, about 8 minutes. With a slotted spoon, transfer to Dutch oven. Cook remaining half of the vegetables in the reserved oil from the skillet; transfer to Dutch oven.

6. Tie the bay leaf, thyme, parsley, and peppercorns in a small piece of cheesecloth to make a bouquet garni; add to the Dutch oven. Pour enough water into the Dutch oven to barely cover the meat, about 2 quarts. Cover and bring to a boil; reduce heat, and gently simmer, partly covered, until the beef is tender, about 2½ hours.

7. Meanwhile, place the potatoes in a medium saucepan, cover with salted water, and bring to a boil over high heat. Reduce heat; simmer, uncovered, until tender when pierced with the tip of a knife. Warm the cream in a small pan over medium heat. Drain the potatoes; when cool enough to handle, press through a potato ricer, or a food mill fitted with a fine disk, into a medium bowl. Stir with a wooden spoon until smooth, 1 to 2 minutes. Cut 8 tablespoons butter into chunks; add to the potatoes, and whisk to incorporate. Drizzle in the hot cream, whisking constantly. Whisk in 2 teaspoons salt, ½ teaspoon pepper, and the nutmeg. Set aside.

8. In a large skillet over medium-high heat, melt 2 tablespoons butter; add the reserved pearl onions, and cook until golden, about 10 minutes. Remove from the heat; add to the Dutch oven. Return the skillet to the heat; melt the remaining 2 tablespoons butter. Add the mushrooms; cook just until the mushrooms release their liquid, about 4 minutes. Transfer to the Dutch oven. Continue to simmer the stew until the beef is very tender and the pearl onions are soft, about 30 minutes more. Remove the bouquet garni; discard.

9. Preheat the oven to 475°F. For individual servings, spoon the stew into ovenproof ramekins about 5 inches wide and 3 inches tall (or for 1 large serving, spoon into a large ovenproof serving bowl). Top each with a large spoonful, about 1 cup, of the reserved mashed potatoes. Garnish each with an oregano sprig. Place the ramekins on a baking sheet; bake until the crust is golden, about 15 minutes. Serve hot.

short ribs ragu with pappardelle
SERVES 4

Have your butcher cut flanken-style short ribs for this dish. These ribs are cut across the rib bones instead of between the rib bones and make a rich and intensely flavored stew. They must be cooked in liquid over a long period of time to achieve the "falling off the bone" texture.

- 2 tablespoons canola oil
- 3½ to 4 pounds short ribs, each about 2 inches long, cut flanken style (across the bone)
- 1 tablespoon kosher salt, plus more for pasta water
- 1 teaspoon freshly ground black pepper
- 1 dried bay leaf
- 1 sprig fresh rosemary
- 5 sprigs fresh thyme
- 2 sprigs fresh flat-leaf parsley
- 4 small carrots, cut into ¼-inch pieces
- 2 celery stalks, strings removed, cut into ¼-inch pieces
- 1 medium onion, cut into ¼-inch pieces
- 2 medium shallots, cut into ¼-inch pieces
- 2 teaspoons all-purpose flour
- 2 teaspoons tomato paste
- ½ cup ruby port
- 2 cups red wine, such as Cabernet
- ½ head of garlic
- 3½ cups Veal Stock (page 626), Beef Stock (page 624), or frozen, thawed
- 1 pound pappardelle or other long, flat pasta

1. Preheat the oven to 275°F. Place a 5-quart oven-proof casserole or Dutch oven over medium heat. Add the oil, and heat until it is very hot but not yet smoking. Sprinkle the short ribs generously with salt and pepper. Working in batches if necessary to keep the short ribs from touching at all during this crucial browning step, add the short ribs to the hot oil (they should sizzle the moment they hit the pan). Cook the ribs until well browned, 10 to 15 minutes. Reduce heat to medium low if necessary to keep

the ribs from overbrowning; do not rush this step. Remove the ribs from the casserole, and transfer to a large bowl. Set aside.

2. Meanwhile, tie the bay leaf, rosemary, thyme, and parsley in a small piece of cheesecloth to make a bouquet garni. Set aside.

3. Add the carrots, celery, onion, and shallots to the oil in the casserole, and cook over medium heat, stirring occasionally, until the vegetables are soft and golden, about 10 minutes.

4. Add the flour and tomato paste to the casserole, and stir to combine. Add the ruby port; stir with a wooden spoon until all the browned bits have been scraped from the pan and the bottom of casserole is clean. Add the red wine; simmer until the liquid is reduced by a third, about 10 minutes. Add the garlic, veal stock, and the reserved bouquet garni.

5. Return the browned ribs to the casserole. Bring the liquid to a simmer over medium-high heat. Cover the casserole, and place it in the oven. Cook until the ribs are very tender, about 3½ hours.

6. Remove cooked ribs from casserole. Set casserole on top of the stove over medium heat, and simmer to thicken the sauce just slightly. As soon as short ribs are cool enough to handle, remove the meat from the bones, and shred into small pieces. (If you like, you can leave the meat on the bone for serving, too.) Discard any fat not rendered during cooking; discard the bouquet garni. Return shredded meat to casserole; simmer to reduce sauce by about half, until sauce is of desired consistency, about 10 minutes.

7. Meanwhile, fill a large pot with salted water. Set over high heat, and bring to a boil. Add the pasta; cook until the pasta is al dente, following the package instructions. Drain the pasta, and serve hot with the short-rib ragu.

grilled flank-steak tostada

SERVES 8

Corn and flour tortillas are available in the refrigerated section of your grocery store.

- 3 Vidalia or other sweet onions
- 1 jalapeño pepper, seeds and ribs removed, minced
- 1 large garlic clove
- 2 cups fresh cilantro leaves (from 1 large bunch)
- 1 tablespoon olive oil
- ¾ teaspoon kosher salt
- 1¼ pounds flank steak, trimmed of excess fat
- 4 small zucchini, cut lengthwise into ½-inch wedges
- 8 8-inch corn or flour tortillas
- 2 heads romaine lettuce, stacked and sliced across into ⅛-inch-wide strips
- 6 tomatoes, cut into ¼-inch-thick rounds
- 4 radishes, sliced into paper-thin rounds
- 4 limes, halved

1. Halve an onion crosswise, and place one half in the bowl of a food processor. Add the jalapeño, garlic, 1 cup cilantro, the olive oil, and ½ teaspoon salt; purée about 1 minute. Cut the remaining onions into ¼-inch-thick rounds.

2. Preheat the oven to 400°F. In a large nonreactive bowl, coat the flank steak, onion slices, and the zucchini with the cilantro purée. Cover; marinate at least 30 minutes.

3. Place the tortillas on baking sheets, 2 at a time, and place in the oven until dry and golden brown, 10 to 12 minutes. If baking two trays at a time, rotate halfway through baking. Repeat with the remaining tortillas.

4. Heat a grill or a grill pan to medium high. Place the steak on the grill; cook about 10 minutes. Turn and cook until medium rare, about 10 minutes more. Remove from the heat; set aside. Place the zucchini and onions on the grill. Cook until tender and browned, 8 to 12 minutes; turn as needed.

5. Thinly slice the beef against the grain of the meat. Toss the lettuce with ½ cup cilantro. Layer each tortilla with the tomatoes, lettuce, zucchini, beef,

onions, and radishes. Garnish with the remaining ½ cup cilantro; squeeze half a lime over each tostada, and season with a pinch of salt. Serve.

FIT TO EAT RECIPE PER SERVING: 329 CALORIES, 11 G FAT, 36 MG CHOLESTEROL, 40 G CARBOHYDRATE, 425 MG SODIUM, 22 G PROTEIN, 6 G DIETARY FIBER

steak with chimichurri sauce

SERVES 6; MAKES 1 CUP SAUCE

Chimichurri, a thick herb condiment from Argentina, is the ketchup of South America. This garlicky sauce is tamed by parsley, oregano, and olive oil.

- ⅓ cup finely chopped garlic (from ½ head)
- ½ cup finely chopped fresh flat-leaf parsley
- 2 teaspoons dried oregano
- 1 tablespoon paprika
- 1 teaspoon ground cumin
- 1 tablespoon extra-virgin olive oil
- 2 tablespoons balsamic vinegar
- 1 teaspoon hot red-pepper sauce
- 1 teaspoon kosher salt
- ¼ teaspoon freshly ground black pepper
- 1¼ pounds flank steak, trimmed of excess fat

1. Combine the garlic, parsley, oregano, paprika, cumin, olive oil, vinegar, hot sauce, salt, and pepper in a nonreactive container with a tight-fitting lid. Add ½ cup water, and shake well until mixed thoroughly. Refrigerate until ready to serve; the sauce will keep up to 1 week in the refrigerator.

2. When ready to serve, heat a grill or a grill pan to medium high. Place the steak on the grill; cook until well browned, about 10 minutes. Turn and cook until medium rare, about 10 minutes more.

3. Remove from the heat; set the steak aside for 10 minutes before cutting for juices to collect. Serve the steak with the chimichurri sauce on the side.

FIT TO EAT RECIPE PER SERVING: 245 CALORIES, 12 G FAT, 63 MG CHOLESTEROL, 3 G CARBOHYDRATE, 440 MG SODIUM, 25 G PROTEIN, 0 G DIETARY FIBER

sirloin and vegetable kebabs

SERVES 4

If using wooden skewers, soak in water about 20 minutes before using.

- 2 teaspoons ground coriander
- 2 teaspoons ground anise seed
- 2 garlic cloves, minced
- 1 tablespoon paprika
- ¼ teaspoon cayenne pepper
- ½ cup olive oil
  Kosher salt
- 1½ pounds boneless sirloin steak, fat and gristle trimmed, cut into 1¼-inch cubes
- 20 small (10 ounces) white-button mushrooms, wiped clean
- 12 red pearl onions, peeled and cut in half lengthwise
  Freshly ground black pepper

1. Heat a grill or a grill pan until hot. Combine the coriander, anise seed, garlic, paprika, cayenne pepper, and ¼ cup olive oil in a medium bowl. Season the marinade with salt, and stir until combined. Add the sirloin cubes, and stir to coat.

2. In a medium bowl, combine the mushrooms, onions, and remaining ¼ cup olive oil. Season with salt and pepper; toss to coat.

3. Divide the steak among 4 wooden skewers; thread, leaving ½ inch between each cube, so the meat will cook more evenly. Divide the vegetables among 4 other skewers; thread.

4. Grill the sirloin kebabs until well browned and medium rare, and grill the vegetable kebabs until tender and slightly charred, turning as needed, 5 to 7 minutes for both. Serve the meat and vegetables on the skewers.

grilled rib-eye steak and quail

SERVES 12 TO 14

Quail are now farm-raised in many parts of the South and sold by most butchers. These delicate birds should be grilled over low heat, and brushed with oil periodically to keep them from drying out.

- 12 quail
- ¼ cup plus 3 tablespoons olive oil, plus more for brushing
- ½ cup loosely packed fresh thyme leaves (from 2 bunches)
- ½ teaspoon freshly ground black pepper
- 12 boneless 1-inch-thick rib-eye steaks
  Kosher salt

1. Rinse the quail under cold water; pat dry. Arrange in a large, shallow baking pan. Add ¼ cup oil, ¼ cup thyme, and ¼ teaspoon pepper to the pan; coat the quail thoroughly. Cover and refrigerate for up to 24 hours.

2. Arrange the steaks in a large, shallow baking pan. Add the remaining 3 tablespoons oil, ¼ cup thyme, and ¼ teaspoon pepper to the pan; coat the steaks thoroughly. Cover and refrigerate, up to 24 hours.

3. Return the meat to room temperature. Heat a grill or a grill pan to medium high. Season the steaks and quail with salt. Grill the steak until seared outside and cooked to desired doneness inside, 10 to 12 minutes per side for medium rare. Grill the quails, breast-side first, until golden brown and cooked through, 10 to 12 minutes per side. Serve.

beef tacos with pico de gallo

MAKES 14

Masa harina (see Food Sources, page 648) is prepared ground cornmeal available in large grocery stores. Packaged corn tortillas may be used; warm in a cast-iron skillet before folding.

- 2 cups masa harina
- 2 teaspoons kosher salt
- ¼ teaspoon baking powder
- 1 cup plus 3 tablespoons warm water (110°F)
  All-purpose flour, for dusting
- 1 tablespoon canola oil
- 1 small onion, cut into ¼-inch dice
- 1 pound ground beef
- 2 large tomatoes, cut into ½-inch dice
- 1 tablespoon ground cumin
- ½ tablespoon dried oregano
- ¼ teaspoon freshly ground black pepper
- 1 cup shredded green cabbage (from ¼ head)
  Pico de Gallo (page 606)

1. Combine masa harina, 1 teaspoon salt, and the baking powder. Add the warm water, and quickly knead together by hand to form a smooth dough.

2. On a lightly floured surface, pinch off a 1½-inch ball of dough; roll into a 4-inch disk. Repeat with the remaining dough.

3. Heat a heavy skillet, preferably cast iron, to medium high. Cook the small corn tortillas, 1 or 2 at a time, until just puffed and slightly golden, 2 to 3 minutes; turn and cook 1 to 2 minutes more. Remove from the heat; fold in half to create a shell. Repeat with the remaining dough.

4. Heat oil in a skillet over medium-high heat. Add onions; cook until soft, about 6 minutes. Add beef; cook, stirring, until well browned, about 7 minutes. Drain excess fat. Stir in tomatoes, cumin, oregano, and remaining salt; season with pepper. Simmer until mixture is saucy, about 5 minutes.

5. Fill each shell with about 1 tablespoon shredded cabbage and 1 tablespoon beef. Spoon pico de gallo over the beef, or serve it on the side.

meatballs

SERVES 4

Serve these meatballs with spaghetti, or sandwich them in a hero roll, and top with Tomato Sauce (page 188) or Pizza Sauce (page 178) and melted cheese. They can be made up to a month ahead and frozen, uncooked, in an airtight container.

- 2 slices good-quality white bread, crusts removed, cut in small pieces
- ¼ cup milk
- 8 ounces ground veal
- 8 ounces ground pork
- ½ medium onion, finely chopped
- 3 small garlic cloves, minced
  Grated zest of ½ lemon
- 8 sprigs fresh flat-leaf parsley, chopped
- ¾ teaspoon kosher salt
- ¼ teaspoon freshly ground black pepper
- 1 large egg, lightly beaten
- 1 tablespoon olive oil

1. Place the bread in a bowl; pour the milk over it. In another bowl, mix the veal and pork. Add the onion, garlic, zest, parsley, salt, and pepper, and mix. Mash the bread mixture to form a paste; add to the meat mixture. Mix, and add the egg. Combine well. Cover with plastic wrap; chill 1 hour.

2. Preheat the oven to 350°F. Form the mixture into 12 to 16 1½-inch balls. Heat ½ tablespoon oil in a skillet over medium heat. Brown half the meatballs, a few minutes on each side. Transfer to a pan large enough to hold all the meatballs. Repeat with the remaining oil and meatballs. Transfer to the oven to finish cooking, about 20 minutes. Serve warm.

meat loaf 101

SERVES 6

- 3 slices white bread
- 1 large carrot, cut into ¼-inch-thick rounds
- 1 celery stalk, strings removed, cut into ½-inch pieces
- ½ medium yellow onion, roughly chopped
- 2 garlic cloves, smashed
- ½ cup fresh flat-leaf parsley leaves, loosely packed
- ½ cup plus 3 tablespoons ketchup
- 4½ teaspoons dry mustard
- 8 ounces ground pork
- 8 ounces ground veal
- 8 ounces ground round
- 2 large eggs, beaten
- 2 teaspoons kosher salt
- 1 teaspoon freshly ground black pepper
- 1 teaspoon hot red-pepper sauce, or to taste
- ½ teaspoon chopped rosemary, plus more for sprinkling
- 2 tablespoons packed dark-brown sugar
- 1 tablespoon olive oil
- 1 small red onion, cut into ¼-inch-thick rings

1. Preheat the oven to 400°F. Remove crusts from bread; place slices in the bowl of a food processor. Process until fine crumbs form, about 10 seconds. Transfer to a mixing bowl. (Do not use dried bread crumbs; they will make meat loaf rubbery.)

2. Place carrot, celery, yellow onion, garlic, and parsley in the bowl of the food processor. Process until vegetables are minced, about 30 seconds, scraping down the sides of the bowl once or twice. Transfer vegetables to bowl with bread crumbs.

3. Add ½ cup ketchup, 2 teaspoons dry mustard, the pork, veal, beef, eggs, salt, pepper, hot sauce, and rosemary. Using your hands, knead the ingredients just until thoroughly combined, about 1 minute. Do

MAKING MEAT LOAF

1. Mix together all the ingredients for the meat loaf (except the glaze) in a bowl with your hands, kneading until thoroughly combined, about 1 minute. Do not overwork, or the loaf will be heavy and dense. The mixture should be wet but hold together.

2. Cut a 5 × 11-inch piece of parchment paper and place it over the wire rack in the baking pan. Using your hands, form the meat mixture into an elongated loaf covering the parchment. The paper will keep the meat-loaf from falling through the wire rack.

3. Using a pastry brush, generously brush the glaze over the top of the loaf. Once the onions have cooled, scatter them over the glaze, covering the length of the loaf.

not overknead; doing so will result in a heavy and dense loaf. The texture should be wet, but tight enough to hold a free-form shape.

4. Set a wire baking rack in a 12 x 17-inch baking pan. Cut a 5 x 11-inch piece of parchment paper, and place over the center of the rack to prevent the meat loaf from falling through. Using your hands, form an elongated loaf covering the parchment.

5. Place the remaining 3 tablespoons ketchup, the remaining 2½ teaspoons mustard, and the brown sugar in a bowl. Mix until smooth. Using a pastry brush, generously brush the glaze over the loaf. Place the oil in a medium saucepan set over high heat. When the oil is smoking, add the red onion. Cook, stirring occasionally, until the onion is soft and golden in places. Add 3 tablespoons water, and cook, stirring, until most of the water has evaporated. Transfer the onion to a bowl to cool slightly, then sprinkle the onion over the meat loaf.

6. Bake 30 minutes, then sprinkle rosemary needles on top. Continue baking until an instant-read thermometer inserted into the center of the loaf registers 160°F, about 25 minutes more. Let the meat loaf cool on the rack, 15 minutes. Serve.

· ·

MEAT LOAF TIPS

● *Use a combination of meat for perfect meat loaf: beef for flavor, veal for tenderness and easy slicing, pork for juiciness.*

● *Don't use fillers like cracker crumbs or corn flakes. Fresh bread crumbs (see page 647) and eggs are all you need to lighten the texture and bind the ingredients.*

● *For a moist loaf, use raw fresh vegetables rather than cooked ones, which lose moisture and flavor through cooking.*

● *Ketchup is essential to flavoring the meat loaf; there is simply no substitute.*

● *Cooking the meat loaf in a free-form loaf as opposed to in a pan maximizes the amount of flavorful, roasted crust.*

· ·

shepherd's pie with rutabaga topping

SERVES 8 TO 10

This dish tastes best if the stew is made a day ahead of time; remove and discard any solidified fat before topping with the vegetable purée.

- 1 *celery stalk*
- 1 *sprig fresh rosemary, plus 1 tablespoon chopped fresh rosemary*
- 1 *sprig fresh thyme*
- 2 *dried bay leaves*
- 1 *garlic clove*
- 1½ *teaspoons unsalted butter, plus more for topping*
- 2 *pounds boneless beef or lamb for stew*
- 2 *medium onions, chopped*
- 2 *tablespoons all-purpose flour*
- 2 *cups dry red wine*
- 1 *cup Beef Stock (page 624), or frozen, thawed*
- 4 *carrots, cut into 3-inch lengths*
  Kosher salt and freshly ground black pepper
- 3 *(about 3 pounds) rutabagas*
- 4 *(about 2 pounds) russet or Yukon gold potatoes*
- ½ *cup hot milk, or as needed*

1. Tie the celery, rosemary sprig, thyme, bay leaves, and garlic in a small piece of cheesecloth to make a bouquet garni; set aside. Heat a wide, heavy-bottomed pan over medium heat until hot. Melt the butter, and brown the meat in two batches, taking care not to crowd the pieces or they will steam and not brown. Add the onions; cook until slightly softened, about 8 minutes. Sprinkle the flour over the meat, and cook until well browned, about 8 minutes, stirring often.

2. Add the wine, and bring to a boil, scraping the bottom of the pan to loosen brown bits. Add the stock and bouquet garni, bring to a boil, cover, and cook on low heat until the meat is tender, about 1½ hours. Remove the lid after 1 hour; add the carrots, and cook, uncovered, for the last 30 minutes. Season with salt and pepper.

3. Meanwhile, peel the rutabagas and potatoes, and cut into chunks. Place in separate saucepans, and cover with cold salted water. Bring to a boil, and simmer until tender, 30 to 40 minutes for the rutabagas and 25 minutes for the potatoes. Drain; return to the saucepans to dry out any moisture from the vegetables for a few minutes.

4. Put the rutabagas and the potatoes through a food mill fitted with a fine disk, or ricer, or mash by hand. Add the butter to taste, and enough hot milk to make a creamy purée. Season with salt and pepper; stir in the chopped rosemary.

5. Preheat the oven to 350°F. Remove bouquet garni; transfer stew into a deep 2-quart baking dish. Top with purée; dot lightly with butter. Bake 1 hour, or until top is brown and crusty. Serve hot.

LAMB

grilled butterflied leg of lamb
SERVES 8

When your butcher is butterflying the lamb, ask him to remove the silver skin and to trim the fat. For toasting seeds, see page 644.

- 3 tablespoons whole coriander seeds, toasted
- 3 tablespoons whole dill seeds, toasted
- 3 tablespoons whole fennel seeds, toasted
- 12 large garlic cloves, minced
- 3 tablespoons finely chopped fresh rosemary
- 3 tablespoons finely chopped fresh sage
- 3 tablespoons finely chopped fresh mint leaves
- ½ cup plus 2 tablespoons olive oil
- 1 7- to 9-pound leg of lamb, boned, butterflied, and cut into 4 sections
  Kosher salt and freshly ground black pepper

1. Have ready a dish large enough to accommodate the lamb in a single layer. Place the coriander, dill, and fennel seeds in a spice grinder, and finely grind.

2. In a medium bowl, combine the ground spice mixture, garlic, rosemary, sage, mint, and olive oil. Spread the mixture on both sides of each lamb section. Place the lamb in the dish, and transfer to the refrigerator. Marinate, covered with plastic wrap, at least 3 hours or overnight.

3. Heat a grill or a grill pan until medium hot. Season lamb with salt and pepper, and transfer to the grill. Cook until medium rare, 6 to 8 minutes per side.

4. Transfer the lamb to a cutting board. Let the meat stand 5 minutes. Slice thinly, and serve.

roast rack of lamb and mint
SERVES 4

Ask your butcher to trim off as much of the fat as possible from the lamb. This will help to keep the rub crisp. Fresh mint has a livelier flavor, aroma, and color than dried. To store fresh mint, gently roll the washed leaves in a paper towel, and seal in a plastic bag; it will keep in the refrigerator for several days.

- 1 medium shallot, coarsely chopped
- 4 garlic cloves
- 2 teaspoons Dijon mustard
- ¼ cup olive oil
- 1½ cups fresh mint leaves (no stems)
  Kosher salt and freshly ground black pepper
- 1 half-rack (8 bones, about 2 pounds trimmed) rib lamb chops

1. Preheat the oven to 425°F. In the bowl of a food processor, combine the shallot, garlic, mustard, 3 tablespoons olive oil, and the mint, and season with salt and pepper. Pulse until a medium-textured paste forms, about 30 seconds; set aside.

2. Heat a cast-iron skillet, large enough to accommodate the half-rack of ribs, over medium-high heat. Add the remaining tablespoon olive oil. Season the lamb with salt and pepper, and place in the skillet, fat-side down. Sear meat on both sides until well browned, 4 to 5 minutes. Remove skillet from the heat, and transfer lamb to a clean surface.

3. Spread the reserved mint paste on the meaty side of the lamb, and place in a shallow baking pan. Roast until the lamb is medium rare, or an instant-read thermometer inserted in the thickest part registers 130°F, about 20 minutes. Remove from the oven, and place the lamb on a cutting board; let rest for 10 minutes before slicing. Slice between the bones, and serve.

lamb and sweet-potato pie
SERVES 6

The sweet prunes and the spices give this dish a Moroccan flavor. It takes time to prepare, but the results are worth it.

- 2 teaspoons ground cinnamon
- 1 tablespoon plus 1 teaspoon ground cumin
- 1 tablespoon ground coriander
- 2 tablespoons freshly grated ginger
- 1 tablespoon all-purpose flour
- 1½ teaspoons kosher salt, plus more for seasoning
- ¼ teaspoon freshly ground black pepper, plus more for seasoning
- 2 pounds lean leg of lamb, cut into 1-inch cubes
- 3 tablespoons olive oil
- 4 tablespoons unsalted butter, plus more for casserole
- 2 large onions, thinly sliced
- 1 tablespoon sugar
- 3 large garlic cloves, minced
- 3 cups Beef Stock (page 624), or frozen, thawed
- 1 28-ounce can whole Italian plum tomatoes
- 2 whole star anise
- 2 cinnamon sticks, about 3 inches long
- 2 medium carrots, cut into ½-inch rounds
- 2 pounds sweet potatoes, peeled and cubed
- 12 ounces fresh spinach, washed, stems removed, optional
- ½ cup dried cherries
- ½ cup dried pitted prunes, cut in half
   Freshly grated nutmeg, for sprinkling

1. In a mixing bowl, combine cinnamon, 2 teaspoons cumin, 1 teaspoon coriander, 1 tablespoon ginger, flour, ½ teaspoon salt, and ¼ teaspoon pepper. Toss lamb pieces with spice mixture to coat.

2. In a Dutch oven or a large saucepan, heat 2 tablespoons olive oil over medium-high heat. Add the lamb in two to three batches, in a single layer, and sear until dark brown on all sides, about 6 minutes per batch. Add the remaining tablespoon olive oil during the searing if the pan becomes dry. Remove the lamb pieces, and set aside.

3. Reduce heat to medium; add 1 tablespoon butter. Add the onions and sugar; cook 10 minutes, stirring frequently, scraping up brown bits on the bottom of the pan while stirring the onions.

4. Reduce heat to medium low, add the minced garlic, and cook until brown and well caramelized, about 15 minutes.

5. Stir in the stock, tomatoes, star anise, cinnamon sticks, carrots, the remaining 2 teaspoons cumin, 2 teaspoons coriander, 1 tablespoon ginger, 1 teaspoon salt, and the reserved lamb. Bring to a boil, reduce heat to medium, and simmer, stirring occasionally, uncovered, for about 1 hour, until the lamb is tender and the sauce is thick.

6. Preheat the oven to 325°F. Meanwhile, place the sweet potatoes in a large saucepan; cover with cold water. Cover and bring to a boil, reduce heat to medium, and simmer, uncovered, for 15 minutes, until very tender when pierced with a fork. Drain the potatoes; return to saucepan. Dry potatoes over medium-low heat, for 1 minute. Pass potatoes through a food mill fitted with a medium disk into a medium bowl. Stir in the remaining 3 tablespoons butter; season with salt and pepper. Set aside, loosely covered with plastic wrap.

7. If using spinach, place in a large skillet over medium-high heat. Season with salt and pepper, cover, and cook until wilted, about 1½ minutes. Drain and set aside.

8. Remove the star anise and cinnamon sticks from the stew. Stir in the cherries and prunes. Transfer the mixture to a deep 2-quart buttered casserole, and place a layer of spinach, if using, over the stew. Spoon the sweet-potato mixture onto the stew. Transfer to a baking sheet, and bake for 30 minutes. Sprinkle with freshly grated nutmeg, and serve hot.

lamb tagine with prunes
SERVES 4

Flat breads, such as lavash, are traditionally used to eat this highly spiced Moroccan stew. Harissa sauce can be found in the international section of many grocery stores.

- 3 *pounds lamb shanks, cut into 1-inch pieces*
- 3 *medium onions, 1 grated, 2 thickly sliced*
- 1 *tablespoon Ras El Hanout (recipe follows), plus more to taste*
  Kosher salt and freshly ground black pepper
- 1 *tablespoon plus 1 teaspoon unsalted butter*
  Large pinch of saffron threads
- 1 *cinnamon stick*
- 1 *teaspoon olive oil*
- 2 *teaspoons sugar*
- ½ *cup canned crushed tomatoes*
- 1 *cup canned chickpeas, drained*
- 3 *cups pumpkin or butternut squash chunks, from 1 large squash*
- ¾ *cup pitted prunes, halved*
  Harissa sauce, optional

1. Coat lamb with grated onions and ras el hanout; season with salt and pepper. Marinate in the refrigerator, covered with plastic wrap, for 30 minutes or up to 2 hours. Melt 1 tablespoon butter in a wide, heavy-bottomed pan. Add meat, and brown lightly on all sides. Add the saffron, 3 cups water, and the cinnamon stick; bring to a boil. Reduce heat to a simmer, and cook, covered, for 1½ hours.

2. Let cool slightly, and remove the shanks. Pull the meat from the bones, keeping the pieces as large as possible; discard the fat, gristle, and bones. Season with salt and pepper. Skim the fat from the liquid, or refrigerate overnight and remove the fat. Refrigerate the meat.

3. In a skillet, heat 1 teaspoon butter and the oil. Add sliced onions; sprinkle with sugar, and season with salt and pepper. Cook over medium-high heat for 15 minutes, tossing or stirring only when brown. Reduce heat to low; cook until the onions are very soft and brown, about 20 minutes more.

4. Add the tomatoes and cooking liquid from the lamb, and bring to a boil. Add the meat, chickpeas, and pumpkin, and simmer, covered, for 15 minutes. Remove the lid, stir in the prunes, and simmer until thick, 15 to 20 minutes more. Season with salt, pepper, and ras el hanout. Serve immediately with harissa sauce on the side, if using.

ras el hanout
MAKES ¼ CUP

For galangal and long pepper, see Food Sources, page 648.

- 1 *teaspoon whole or ground allspice*
- 1 *teaspoon whole cardamom seeds*
- 1 *cinnamon stick*
- 1 *teaspoon whole coriander seeds*
- 1 *teaspoon whole cumin seeds*
- 1 *teaspoon ground mace*
- ½ *teaspoon cayenne pepper*
- ½ *teaspoon whole cloves*
- 1 *teaspoon ground ginger*
- 1 *teaspoon whole black peppercorns*
- 1 *1-inch piece galangal, optional*
- 1 *piece long pepper, optional*
- 1 *teaspoon grains of paradise, optional*

1. Place allspice, cardamom seeds, cinnamon, and coriander and cumin seeds in a small skillet over medium heat, and dry-roast, shaking the pan often, until they give off an aroma, about 5 minutes.

2. Combine all the ingredients in a mortar or a spice grinder, and grind to a powder. Store in an airtight container in a cool, dark place.

red-chile lamb chops

SERVES 8 TO 10

It is important to use "hot" paprika (see Food Sources, page 648) in this recipe, to create the spicy red-chile coating for the lamb chops. Paprika, finely ground dried red-pepper pods, can vary in intensity from mild to pungent; most supermarkets only carry the mild variety. The lamb must marinate overnight or up to 3 days before grilling.

- 3 roasted red bell peppers (see page 645)
- 2 tablespoons whole cumin seeds, toasted (see page 644)
- 2 tablespoons whole coriander seeds, toasted (see page 644)
- ¼ cup freshly ground dried ancho or other dried chiles
- ¼ cup hot paprika
- 1 teaspoon cayenne pepper
- 2 teaspoons dried oregano
- 2 to 3 garlic cloves, minced
- ½ cup olive oil
- 3 tablespoons red-wine vinegar
- 1 teaspoon kosher salt, plus more for seasoning
- 16 1-inch-thick lamb shoulder chops

1. Transfer the roasted peppers to the bowl of a food processor; process until smooth, and set aside. Grind the toasted cumin and coriander seeds in a spice grinder until powdered, and set aside.

2. In a medium bowl, combine the puréed peppers, ground cumin and coriander, the ground chiles, the paprika, cayenne, oregano, garlic, oil, vinegar, and salt. Mix well.

3. Salt the chops. Place in a nonreactive bowl. Add the spice mixture to the lamb, and toss to coat the chops. Cover with plastic wrap; refrigerate overnight or up to 3 days.

4. Heat a grill or a grill pan to medium-hot. Grill the chops, turning frequently, for 20 to 30 minutes, until they are juicy but cooked through. Serve hot.

mixed grill of baby lamb chops, spring onions, and white eggplant

SERVES 12

- 2½ pounds white or any purple eggplant
- 12 rib lamb chops
- 2 bunches spring onions
- ½ cup olive oil
  Kosher salt and freshly ground black pepper
- 2 tablespoons fresh rosemary, chopped
- 2 tablespoons fresh thyme leaves
  Romesco Sauce (recipe follows)

1. Heat a grill or grill pan until very hot. Slice any large eggplants in half or in quarters lengthwise.

2. Brush the eggplants, the lamb chops, and the spring onions with the olive oil. Sprinkle with salt, pepper, rosemary, and thyme; grill until lamb is tender and eggplant and spring onions are slightly charred and cooked through. (If cooking on an outdoor grill, make sure to cook the lamb over an even heat.) Serve with sauce on the side.

romesco sauce

MAKES 2 1/3 CUPS

- ½ dried ancho chile, seeds and stem removed, broken into pieces
- ½ cup boiling water
- 3 tablespoons extra-virgin olive oil
- ½ fresh serrano chile, seeds and ribs removed
- 3 garlic cloves, cut in half lengthwise
- 2 tablespoons (¾ ounce) blanched almonds
- 2 tablespoons (½ ounce) blanched hazelnuts
- 10 plum tomatoes, cut in half lengthwise
  Kosher salt and freshly ground black pepper
- 1 roasted red pepper (see page 645), chopped
- 1¾ loafs (about 1½ pounds) rustic white bread, crusts removed and torn into pieces
- 1 tablespoon sherry-wine vinegar
- ½ cup chopped fresh cilantro

1. Place the ancho chile in a small heat-proof bowl. Pour the boiling water over the chile; let soften 20 minutes.

2. Meanwhile, heat 1 tablespoon olive oil in a medium skillet over medium heat. Add the serrano chile, garlic, and nuts, and cook until the ingredients become deep golden, about 5 minutes. Using a slotted spoon, transfer the ingredients to a small bowl, leaving the oil in the skillet.

3. Raise heat to high. In two or three batches, place tomato halves cut-side down in skillet at least ¾-inch apart; sprinkle with salt and pepper. When edges of tomatoes begin to turn brown, turn them cut-side up, cover, and continue to cook 1½ minutes more. Seed and peel the tomatoes into a strainer placed over a bowl, reserving liquid. Cut tomatoes into ½-inch chunks, and set aside.

4. In the bowl of a food processor, place the serrano-chile mixture, roasted red pepper, and the softened ancho chile with its soaking liquid. Pulse until finely ground. Add the bread, and pulse 10 times, until the bread is in small pieces. Add the tomatoes and their liquid, sherry vinegar, remaining olive oil, and cilantro; pulse until just combined. Season with salt and pepper.

lamb medallions with black-olive wine sauce

SERVES 4

Marinating the lamb for several hours or overnight will intensify the flavor. Black-olive paste, also known as tapenade, is available in grocery and specialty food stores.

- ¼ cup plus 1 tablespoon olive oil
- 2 medium garlic cloves, minced
- 1 tablespoon finely chopped fresh rosemary
- ½ loin of lamb (about 2 pounds), boned and trimmed of fat

  Kosher salt and freshly ground black pepper
- ½ cup dry red or white wine
- ¾ cup Homemade Chicken Stock (page 624), or low-sodium store-bought chicken broth, skimmed of fat
- 2 teaspoons black-olive paste
- 2 tablespoons unsalted butter

1. Pour the olive oil into a shallow dish, and distribute half the garlic and one-third of the rosemary in the oil. Slice the lamb across into 8 rounds, lightly pound each into a ¼-inch-thick medallion, and place in the oil. Sprinkle the lamb with one-third of the chopped rosemary, the remaining half of the garlic, and salt and pepper to taste; set aside for 20 minutes at room temperature.

2. Pour 2 tablespoons of the oil-garlic marinade into a large skillet; place over medium-high heat. Add the medallions; cook until browned on the outside, medium rare inside, about 1 minute per side. Transfer to a platter, cover with aluminum foil to keep warm, and pour off the fat from the skillet.

3. Add the wine and the stock; cook, stirring constantly to loosen any cooked-on browned bits. Add the remaining third of the rosemary and the olive paste, and cook until the liquid has reduced by two-thirds. Swirl in the butter until the sauce has thickened slightly, about 1 minute. Arrange the medallions on a serving platter, pour the sauce over the lamb, and serve immediately.

eggplant and lamb al forno

SERVES 4

- 1 teaspoon kosher salt, plus more for seasoning
- 2 medium (about 1½ pounds total) eggplants, ends trimmed and cut into six ¼-inch-thick rounds
- 1 tablespoon olive oil
- 1 medium onion, cut into ¼-inch dice
- ¾ teaspoon freshly ground black pepper
- 1 teaspoon dried oregano
- 1 teaspoon ground cinnamon
- 1 teaspoon ground cumin
- ¼ teaspoon cayenne pepper
- 1¼ pounds ground lamb
- 1 28-ounce-can whole, peeled plum tomatoes, drained
- 2 teaspoons coarsely chopped fresh flat-leaf parsley
- 1 tablespoon dry bread crumbs (see page 647)

1. Preheat the oven to 375°F. Salt eggplants well; arrange in colanders. Place weighted bowls on top; drain for 30 minutes. Rinse and pat dry with paper towels. Meanwhile, heat the oil in a large skillet over medium heat. Add the onion, 1 teaspoon salt, and ¾ teaspoon black pepper; cook until translucent, about 10 minutes. Add the oregano, cinnamon, cumin, and cayenne; cook 2 minutes more. Add lamb; cook until it browns, about 5 minutes. Drain fat from the pan. Break up the tomatoes, and add to pan. Cook over medium heat, stirring often, until the sauce starts to thicken, about 8 minutes.

2. Place 4 eggplant slices in an 8-inch square baking pan, and top with a third of the meat sauce. Repeat twice, making four 3-layer stacks. Combine 1 teaspoon parsley and the bread crumbs in a small bowl; sprinkle over the top.

3. Cover with aluminum foil; bake for 1 hour. Remove foil; bake for 10 to 15 minutes more. Sprinkle with remaining parsley, and serve.

PORK

baked country ham

SERVES 3 TO 5 DOZEN

Salli LaGrone, Martha's good friend in Franklin, Tennessee, prefers to serve her country ham without a glaze, so there's just the pure, smoked-ham flavor. She finds it easiest to prepare the night before serving. The ham should be cut into very, very thin slivers; it is quite salty and is best eaten in small quantities. Once baked, the country-cured ham (see Food Sources, page 648) may be frozen. It keeps very well wrapped in the freezer, and slivers can be removed from the frozen ham as you need them. A ham-slicing knife can help make the job easier (see Equipment Sources, page 650).

- 1 16-pound country-cured ham
   Cornmeal Biscuits (page 554) or Herbed Cheddar Biscuits (page 555)

1. Soak the ham in a very large kettle or pot, or fill your sink with water, and soak it there. Soak the ham 4 to 8 hours to lose some of the saltiness; change the water 2 or 3 times if possible. Rinse well, and scrape off any mold or green rind.

2. Wrap ham well in aluminum foil. Place on a baking sheet. At 7 p.m. the night before you plan to serve it, preheat the oven to 500°F. Place the wrapped ham in a large roasting pan filled with 1 inch of water; bake for 30 minutes. Turn off oven, but do not open the door. At 10 p.m. turn the oven back on to 500°F. Bake the ham for 15 minutes more. Turn off the oven, but do not open the door. Leave the ham in the closed oven overnight.

3. Remove ham from oven, then remove the foil. Using a very sharp knife, trim the rind and all the fat from the ham. Serve warm or at room temperature; cut with a ham-slicing knife into very thin slivers. Serve slivers of ham tucked into split biscuits.

fresh ham 101
with green-herb paste
SERVES 12 TO 20

For fewer than 12 people, buy just the shank end of a fresh ham. You might need to order this from your butcher a few days ahead. Prepare as described below; check for doneness with an instant-read thermometer after 3 to 4 hours. The herb paste (step 1) can be made a day ahead and refrigerated.

for the green-herb paste

- 3 *heads of garlic*
- 2 *bunches fresh rosemary, yielding 1 cup needles*
- 2 *bunches fresh oregano, yielding 1 cup leaves*
  Kosher salt and freshly ground black pepper
- ¾ *cup extra-virgin olive oil*

for the ham

- 4 *large onions, unpeeled, cut into ½-inch rounds*
- 16 *sprigs fresh rosemary, plus more for platter*
- 3 *dozen fresh bay leaves or dried*
- 1 *18- to 22-pound whole fresh ham, skin on*
- 5 *garlic cloves, cut into slivers*
  Kosher salt and freshly ground black pepper
- 3¾ *cups dry white wine*
  Spring greens and herbs, for garnish, optional

1. Preheat the oven to 325°F. with a rack on the lowest level. In the bowl of a food processor, combine garlic, rosemary, oregano, 1 tablespoon salt, and 2 teaspoons pepper; pulse to combine. With machine running, add oil through feed tube; process until just combined.

2. Arrange the onion rounds in the bottom of a 14 x 18-inch roasting pan. Place 8 rosemary sprigs and 2 dozen bay leaves on top of the onions; this onion-herb bed will keep the ham from burning and will make an aromatic gravy.

3. Score the skin and fat: Using a sharp slicing knife, cut large diamonds, spaced about 2½ inches apart, through both the skin and the fat. Using a paring knife, make a slit in the meat at each diamond-intersection; insert a sliver or two of garlic and a tuft of rosemary into each.

4. Transfer ham to pan. Rub ½ cup green-herb paste into the cut areas, over the skin, and over the exposed end piece. Sprinkle liberally with salt and pepper.

5. Tie the ham crosswise in 2 or 3 places with kitchen twine. Make a bay wreath around the shank bone: Tie a piece of twine around the bone; tuck the remaining bay leaves under the twine. Let the ham sit at room temperature until no longer cold to the touch, about 30 minutes; if it goes into the oven too cold, it won't cook through. Cook ham 1 hour.

6. Slide out the pan on the rack. Slowly pour ¾ cup wine over ham; rub more paste into the cut areas as they expand and release juices. Bake 3½ to 5 hours more, basting with wine every hour and rubbing in more paste as needed, until an instant-read thermometer registers between 145°F and 155°F when it is inserted into two different sections of the center; be careful not to insert the thermometer next to the bone, or the reading will be incorrect. Cooking times will vary with the size of the ham, the weight of the pan, and the heat of the oven, so an instant-read thermometer is essential. While roasting, reverse the orientation of the pan for even browning, and tent the ham with foil if the outside is cooking too quickly.

7. Remove the ham from the oven, and let rest; the internal temperature will rise 5°F to 10°F more. When cool enough to handle, transfer the ham to a platter garnished with the spring greens and herbs, if using. Remove the twine.

8. For easiest slicing, let ham rest 1 hour. Discard onions and rosemary; pour remaining liquid in pan into a fat separator. Place pan over high heat. Add ½ cup water; once the liquid bubbles, scrape the bottom with a wooden spoon to loosen cooked-on bits. Reduce slightly, about 5 minutes. Remove fat from reserved liquid, and add liquid to pan. Heat through; strain. Serve with ham.

HOW TO MAKE FRESH HAM

1. You will need a large roasting pan; we used a 14 × 18-inch one. If you can cook a 20-pound turkey in the pan, the ham will fit; just make sure the pan fits in your oven. Arrange the onion rounds in the pan, then scatter the rosemary sprigs and bay leaves on top. This onion-herb bed will keep the ham from burning and will make an aromatic gravy.

2. Scoring the ham allows the fat to render and the seasonings to penetrate deeper into the meat; it also makes a pretty presentation, especially when fresh rosemary sprouts out of each diamond. Use a slicing knife to score the ham while it is still cold, being sure to cut all the way through the skin and the fat. Don't be alarmed by the amount of fat under the skin; it melts, shrinks, and crisps during cooking, making the meat more tender. Cut a slit at each intersection with a paring knife; this will make it easier to insert the garlic and rosemary.

3. Keep the ham scored side up in the pan, then rub all over with the garlicky herb paste, using your fingers to work the paste into all the scored parts and to cover the entire exposed surface of the ham. Besides giving it more flavor, slathering the ham with herbs helps keep the ham moist during cooking.

4. Tying the ham will help preserve its shape and keep the scored sections from gaping too much during cooking (which would deplete the meat of moisture). Bay leaves are tucked under the twine to give the ham even more flavor; wine is poured over during cooking to help infuse the meat with the flavor of the aromatics. To ensure that the meat has been properly cooked, use a meat thermometer.

glazed ham 101

SERVES 16

This is the traditional American ham, served across the country for holidays and gatherings. A ham this size can serve 16 people for dinner and up to 50 for hors d'oeuvres. Using both light- and dark-brown sugar keeps the glaze from getting too dark while the ham cooks. Fresh bay leaves are soft and flexible and can be used as an attractive garnish.

- 1 14- to 18-pound whole smoked ham, bone in and rind on
- 1 cup apple cider
- ¼ cup yellow mustard seeds, toasted (see page 644)
- 1 tablespoon whole fennel seeds, toasted (see page 644)
- 2 teaspoons ground cinnamon
- 1 tablespoon ground ginger
- ¾ cup Dijon mustard
- 1 cup plus 2 tablespoons packed light-brown sugar
- ¾ cup packed dark-brown sugar
- 3 tablespoons light corn syrup
- 2 tablespoons unsulfured molasses
- 2 to 3 tablespoons whole cloves
- 4 fresh bay leaves, optional

1. Rinse the ham with cool water, and dry with paper towels. Let the ham stand for 2 hours at room temperature. Preheat the oven to 350°F with a rack on the lowest level. Line a roasting pan with heavy-duty aluminum foil. Place a roasting rack in the pan. Transfer the ham, with the thicker rind on top, to the rack. Pour the apple cider over the ham. Cook for 2 hours, or until an instant-read thermometer inserted in the thickest part of the ham registers 140°F.

2. Place the toasted mustard and fennel seeds in a spice grinder or mortar and pestle, grind to a rough powder, and transfer to a medium bowl. Add the cinnamon, ginger, mustard, 2 tablespoons light-brown sugar, 2 tablespoons dark-brown sugar, the corn syrup, and the molasses. Combine well; set aside.

3. Remove the ham from the oven, and let it cool for about 30 minutes. Using kitchen shears or a sharp knife, trim away the hard rind from the ham. Use a sharp knife to trim the fat to a layer of about ¼ inch all over the ham; it does not need to be perfectly even. The bottom of the ham will have less fat and more skin. Place ham bottom-side down. Score remaining fat on top of the ham into a pattern of 1- to 2-inch diamonds, cutting about ¼ to ½ inch through the fat and into the meat.

4. Insert a whole clove into the intersection of each diamond. Using a pastry brush or your fingers, rub the spice glaze all over the ham and deep into the cut diamonds. In a medium bowl, combine the remaining cup of light-brown sugar and ½ cup plus 2 tablespoons dark-brown sugar. Using your fingers, gently pack the sugar mixture all over scored fat. If using bay leaves, secure them with toothpick halves around the shank bone. Cover the toothpicks by inserting the cloves on top of them.

5. Return the ham to the oven, and cook for 20 minutes. The sugar will begin to crystallize, but there will be some hard spots of sugar; gently baste these areas with the remaining glaze. Cook 40 minutes more, basting with the remaining glaze after 20 minutes; do not baste with any pan juices (the melted fat from the ham will make the glazed ham less attractive). The ham should be dark brown and crusty; cook 15 minutes more if necessary. Remove and let cool slightly. Transfer to a serving platter, and let stand 30 minutes before carving.

cider-braised pork loin and ribs
SERVES 4

This recipe may be made with just the pork loin for a slightly smaller yield.

- 1 pork loin and 1 rack of 8 ribs (about 5 pounds total)
- 2 tablespoons kosher salt, plus more for seasoning
- 2 teaspoons freshly ground black pepper, plus more for seasoning
- 2 tablespoons canola oil, plus more for frying
- 1 quart apple cider
- 1½ quarts Homemade Chicken Stock (page 624), or low-sodium store-bought chicken broth, skimmed of fat
- 2 tablespoons apple-cider vinegar
- 2 medium onions, cut in half
- 4 sprigs fresh thyme
- 2 sprigs fresh flat-leaf parsley
- 4 Granny Smith apples
- 2 teaspoons sugar
- 8 fresh sage leaves, optional

1. Preheat the oven to 250°F. Rub the rack of ribs with 1 tablespoon salt and 1 teaspoon pepper. Place a 7-quart ovenproof casserole or Dutch oven over medium heat. Add 1 tablespoon oil, and heat until the oil is hot but not smoking. Add the rack of ribs; brown, 8 to 10 minutes on each side, and remove. Pour out the excess fat from the casserole.

2. Add 2 cups apple cider, and stir with a wooden spoon until the bottom of the casserole is clean. Add the chicken stock, cider vinegar, onions, thyme, and parsley. Cut 2 apples in half; add to casserole. Return the ribs to the casserole. Bring to a simmer, transfer the casserole, covered, to the oven, and cook for 2 hours.

3. Heat remaining tablespoon of oil in a skillet. Season pork loin with 1 tablespoon salt and 1 teaspoon pepper. When oil is hot but not smoking, add pork. It should sizzle. Sear until golden brown on all sides, 10 to 15 minutes.

4. Transfer 2 cups of the cooking liquid from the casserole to a shallow bowl or fat separator, and let stand to cool. Add the loin to the casserole, return to the oven, and cook until an instant-read thermometer inserted into the loin registers 150°F., about 40 minutes more.

5. Skim the fat from the reserved cooking liquid. Strain the liquid; combine in a medium saucepan with the remaining 2 cups cider. Set over medium heat; simmer until reduced by a little more than half and amber in color; the liquid will have a slightly viscous consistency.

6. Place a large skillet over medium heat. Peel and core the remaining 2 apples, slice into eighths, and arrange in a single layer in the hot skillet. Sprinkle with the sugar, and season lightly with salt and pepper. Cook until the sugar melts, 2 to 3 minutes, and reduce heat. Continue cooking until the sugar starts to caramelize, about 8 minutes. Apples should soften and puff, and the seared side should start to brown. When the apple slices loosen naturally from the pan, turn and cook on the other side for about 5 minutes. Add the apple-cider sauce to the skillet; cook just to heat the sauce and dissolve any sugars that have cooked onto the pan.

7. If using sage leaves, heat about ½ inch of canola oil in a small heavy skillet over medium heat to just below smoking point. Add the sage leaves, and fry until crisp. With a slotted spoon, transfer to a piece of paper towel.

8. Slice the loin ¼ inch thick, and cut the rack into individual ribs. Serve with the apples and the sauce. Garnish with fried sage leaves.

mustard-rubbed pork
with blackberry-mustard sauce

SERVES 6

You will have spice mixture leftover; sprinkle it on Baked Oven Frites (page 363) just before baking, and serve with the pork. For toasting seeds, see page 644. Brown mustard seeds (see Food Sources, page 648) are smaller and spicier than yellow mustard seeds.

- 3 tablespoons whole brown or yellow mustard seeds, toasted
- 1 teaspoon whole fennel seeds, toasted
- 2 teaspoons whole coriander seeds, toasted
- 1 teaspoon whole cumin seeds, toasted
- 1 teaspoon whole black peppercorns, toasted
- 2 teaspoons dried thyme
- 1 tablespoon dry mustard
- 1 teaspoon ground ginger
- 1½ teaspoons kosher salt
- 1 teaspoon sugar
- 1¼ pounds pork tenderloin
- 2 tablespoons Dijon mustard
- 2 tablespoons dry white wine
- 2 cups Homemade Chicken Stock (page 624), or low-sodium store-bought chicken broth, skimmed of fat
- 1 tablespoon all-purpose flour
- ½ pint (about 5 ounces) blackberries
- 2 teaspoons chopped fresh thyme, for garnish

1. Place seeds and peppercorns in a spice grinder; pulse until finely chopped but not powdery. Transfer to a small bowl; stir in thyme, dry mustard, ginger, 1 teaspoon salt, and sugar. Set aside.

2. Preheat the oven to 425°F with a rack in the upper third. Meanwhile, rub the pork with 1 tablespoon Dijon mustard. Sprinkle with the remaining ½ teaspoon salt and 2 tablespoons of the spice mixture; pat with your hands to make it stick, and place the

pork in a roasting pan. Cook until the pork is 150°F on an instant-read thermometer, about 25 minutes. Transfer the pork to a cutting board and cover loosely with aluminum foil to keep warm. Don't clean the pan.

3. Place roasting pan on stove over medium-high heat. Stir in wine; scrape pan to loosen any browned bits on the bottom. Stir in stock; cook, stirring occasionally, until reduced by half, 5 to 7 minutes. Whisk flour with ¼ cup water in a bowl; whisk into simmering stock. Whisk in remaining mustard; cook until mixture thickens, 2 to 3 minutes more. Stir in berries; cook until they soften, about 2 minutes. Slice pork; transfer to a serving platter. Serve with the blackberry-mustard sauce and thyme.

barbecued pork ribs
with maple rub

SERVES 12 TO 16

Granulated maple sugar (see Food Sources, page 648), available at specialty food stores, adds a distinctive taste, but light-brown sugar can be substituted.

- 2 pounds maple sugar
- ¼ cup kosher salt
- 2 tablespoons paprika
- ¼ cup freshly ground black pepper
- 2 tablespoons fresh thyme leaves
- 4 garlic cloves, minced
  Grated zest of 2 lemons
- 4 racks pork spareribs (3 pounds each)
- ¼ cup olive oil

1. Combine the sugar, salt, paprika, pepper, thyme, garlic, and zest; spread on a sheet pan; let stand at room temperature overnight so the sugar will be hard and dry. Grind in the bowl of a food processor to a fine powder.

2. Brush the ribs with oil, and lightly coat with the sugar mixture.

3. Heat a grill or a grill pan to medium hot; grill the ribs, fat-side-down first, until the meat is just coming off the bone, 20 to 30 minutes per side. Cool slightly. Slice into individual ribs, and serve.

braised pork chops
with cabbage

SERVES 4

- 4 10-ounce pork chops (1 inch thick)

  Kosher salt and freshly ground black pepper

- 2 tablespoons extra-virgin olive oil

- ½ small (about 1 pound) head red cabbage, thinly sliced

- 1 teaspoon caraway seeds

- 1 teaspoon dried thyme

- ¾ cup apple cider

- ½ cup Homemade Chicken Stock (page 624), or low-sodium store-bought chicken broth, skimmed of fat

- 1 large leek, white and pale-green parts, cut into matchsticks, well washed (see page 646)

1. Season the pork chops with salt and pepper. Heat the oil in a large, straight-sided skillet over high heat. Add the pork chops; cook until brown, about 3 minutes on each side. Transfer to a plate; set aside.

2. Add the cabbage, caraway seeds, thyme, cider, and stock to the skillet, and season with salt and pepper; bring to a boil. Cover, reduce heat to medium, and simmer, stirring occasionally, 12 minutes.

3. Add the leeks to the cabbage, replace the cover, and cook 5 minutes. Add the reserved pork chops in a single layer. Cover, and cook until the pork chops are tender or when an instant-read thermometer registers 145°F when inserted into the thickest part of the chop, about 8 minutes. Remove from the heat, and serve immediately.

roasted pork tenderloins
with bacon and herbs

SERVES 10 TO 12

Pork tenderloins can be prepared in advance and cooked shortly before serving. Tying two tenderloins together ensures even cooking.

- 6 8-ounce pork tenderloins, rinsed and patted dry, trimmed of excess fat

- 1 head of roasted garlic (see page 646)

- 6 sprigs fresh sage

- 6 sprigs fresh rosemary

- 6 sprigs fresh thyme

- 18 (about 12 ounces) bacon strips

  Kosher salt and freshly ground black pepper

- 1 tablespoon olive oil

- 1 tablespoon unsalted butter

1. Preheat the oven to 400°F. Arrange 3 tenderloins on a work surface, flat-side up. Spread the flat side of each tenderloin with one-third of the roasted garlic. Strip the leaves from the fresh sage, rosemary, and thyme; discard the stems. Place one-third of each herb on each tenderloin, scattering the leaves over the garlic. Place remaining tenderloins on top of the herb-coated tenderloins, with flat sides down, and matching the larger ends to the tapered ends. Wrap 6 strips of bacon around each pair of tenderloins; tie bacon in place with kitchen twine. Sprinkle with salt and pepper on all sides.

2. Place a large, heavy-bottomed skillet over high heat. Add the oil and the butter; once melted, arrange the tenderloins in the skillet in batches to keep them from touching. Sear until golden brown on all sides, rotating as needed, about 10 minutes per tenderloin. Transfer the seared tenderloins to a large roasting pan; place in the oven. Roast until an instant-read thermometer inserted into the thickest part of the meat registers 150°F., about 15 minutes. Transfer the tenderloins to a cutting board; let stand 10 minutes. Remove twine before carving.

choucroute garni

SERVES 10 TO 12

If some meats are hard to get, such as dry-salted bacon, substitute other more available meats, such as sausage. Quantity is more important than variety. White-veal sausages, smoked country sausages, and knackwurst sausages are available from specialty butchers. Though the goose fat will yield the best flavor, lard or shortening can be used in its place. For sausages, goose fat, and juniper berries, see Food Sources, page 648.

- 5 to 6 pounds drained sauerkraut
- 25 whole black peppercorns
- 1½ teaspoons whole coriander seeds
- 5 whole cloves
- 15 whole juniper berries
- 6 sprigs fresh flat-leaf parsley
- 4 sprigs fresh thyme
- 2 dried bay leaves
- ½ cup goose fat
- 4 medium onions, sliced ⅛ inch thick
- 1½ cups Riesling or other dry white wine
- 2 cups Homemade Chicken Stock (page 624), or low-sodium store-bought chicken broth, skimmed of fat
- 1 slab (1½ pounds) dry-salted bacon, rinsed and dried
- 1 slab (1½ pounds) smoked bacon
- 2 (about 1½ pounds) dry-salted pig's knuckles
- 1 pound smoked pork butt
- 3 carrots
- ¼ cup finely minced garlic
- 2 teaspoons kosher salt
- 8 small red potatoes, peeled
- 4 white veal sausages (weisswurst or bockwurst; about 4 ounces each)
- 4 smoked country sausages (bauerwurst; about 4 ounces each)
- 4 knackwurst sausages (about 4 ounces each)

1. Place the sauerkraut in a colander set in the sink; rinse with warm water, and drain.

2. Tie the peppercorns, coriander seeds, cloves, juniper berries, parsley, thyme, and bay leaves in a small piece of cheesecloth to make a bouquet garni.

3. Melt the goose fat in a very large Dutch oven or large high-sided skillet over medium heat. Add sliced onions; cook, stirring frequently, until they are translucent but not brown, about 8 minutes.

4. Add the wine, chicken stock, and 2 cups water to the Dutch oven; stir to combine. Add the dry-salted bacon, smoked bacon, pig's knuckles, pork butt, carrots, garlic, salt, and the bouquet garni. Arrange the washed and drained sauerkraut on top of the mixture. Add enough cold water to bring the liquid to 1 inch below the sauerkraut. Cover, raise heat to high, and bring the liquid to a boil. Reduce heat to low; cook at a strong simmer for 1½ hours.

5. Add the potatoes; simmer, covered, until the potatoes are just becoming tender, about 30 minutes more. Add the sausages; simmer, covered, until heated through, about 10 minutes more.

6. Remove bouquet garni; discard. To serve the choucroute garni on a platter, remove the meat, potatoes, and carrots. Drain the sauerkraut, and place in the middle of the serving platter. Slice the bacon and pork butt. Arrange the meat, potatoes, and carrots around the sauerkraut on the platter. Serve.

sausage with sautéed red onions and thyme

SERVES 4

Parsley-and-cheese sausage is available at butcher shops, but you can substitute any sausage you like.

- 1 tablespoon olive oil
- 1½ pounds parsley-and-cheese pork sausage
- 4 small (1¼ pounds) red onions, sliced into ¼-inch-thick rounds
- 2 tablespoons fresh thyme leaves

  Kosher salt and freshly ground black pepper

1. Preheat the oven to 350°F. Place a large skillet over medium-low heat. When hot, add olive oil and sausage, pricked every few inches with the point of a knife; cook until nicely browned, about 10 minutes. Turn the sausage over, prick with knife, and cook until browned, about 10 minutes.

2. Transfer the sausage to a baking pan, and place in the oven, leaving the rendered fat in the skillet. Add the onions to the skillet, and stir. Add ½ cup water, and stir, using a wooden spoon to loosen any browned bits from the bottom of the pan. Cover, and cook over medium heat, stirring occasionally, until the onions are very soft, 15 to 20 minutes, adding a second ½ cup water if the pan becomes dry. Remove the lid, and stir in the thyme. Season with salt and pepper. Remove the sausage from the oven, and serve with the onions.

VEAL

herbed veal chops

SERVES 4

Ask your butcher to remove the chine bone, cut the rib bone to a 5-inch length, and then french the rib bone; the butcher can also remove all the fat and pound the chops to a ¼-inch thickness.

- ¼ cup plus 2 tablespoons olive oil
- 3 tablespoons fresh lime juice
- 3 garlic cloves, smashed
- ¼ cup plus 2 tablespoons finely chopped fresh flat-leaf parsley
- 2 tablespoons finely chopped fresh rosemary
- 3 tablespoons coarsely chopped fresh marjoram
- 4 8-ounce rib veal chops

  Freshly ground black pepper

  Kosher salt

1. In a dish large enough to accommodate the 4 chops, combine the olive oil, lime juice, and garlic; sprinkle half of the parsley, rosemary, and marjoram on top. Season the chops with pepper, and place in marinade. Turn chops over several times to coat both sides well. Sprinkle the remaining herbs on top of the chops, and turn several times. Cover loosely with plastic wrap, and set aside at room temperature to marinate, 20 to 30 minutes.

2. Heat a grill or a grill pan until hot. Season the chops with salt, and place on the grill. Cook until the chops are medium rare, about 1½ minutes on each side. Remove from the heat, and transfer to a serving dish. Serve.

veal stew with shallots and wild mushrooms

SERVES 4

Serve this easy yet elegant stew with wide egg noodles.

- 1 tablespoon olive oil
- 1 pound lean veal shoulder, cut into 1½-inch cubes
- ½ teaspoon kosher salt
  Freshly ground black pepper
- 20 (about 1½ pounds) shallots
- 2 garlic cloves, minced
- 1 tablespoon all-purpose flour
- ½ cup dry white wine
- 1½ cups Homemade Chicken Stock (page 624), or low-sodium store-bought broth, skimmed of fat
- 8 fresh sage leaves, or 1 teaspoon dried
- 2 large sprigs fresh thyme, or ⅛ teaspoon dried
- 2 (about 8 ounces) Yukon gold potatoes, peeled, cut into ¾-inch pieces
- 4 ounces cremini or button mushrooms, wiped clean, thinly sliced
- 4 ounces oyster or shiitake mushrooms, wiped clean, stemmed and thinly sliced
- 2 tablespoons snipped chives

1. Heat the oil in a large saucepan or Dutch oven over medium-high heat. Season the veal with salt and pepper, and cook quickly, stirring to brown the pieces on all sides. Remove to a platter.

2. Reduce heat to medium, add the shallots and 3 tablespoons water, and cook until the water has evaporated, about 1 minute. Add the garlic and flour, and cook, stirring, for 1 minute more. Add the wine, and simmer for 2 minutes. Add the stock, the veal with any juices from the platter, the sage, and the thyme, and bring to a boil. Reduce heat so that the stew is barely simmering, cover, and cook for 30 minutes. Add the potatoes, cover, and cook for 25 minutes more, or until the meat and potatoes are tender when pierced with the tip of a knife.

3. Heat a large nonstick skillet over medium-high heat until it is very hot. Add mushrooms; cook, stirring, for about 3 minutes (if mushrooms stick to pan, add 1 tablespoon water). Add mushrooms to stew; stir briefly. Just before serving, remove thyme sprigs, and stir in the chives.

FIT TO EAT RECIPE PER SERVING: 336 CALORIES, 12 G FAT, 31% CALORIES FROM FAT, 130 MG CHOLESTEROL, 20 G CARBOHYDRATE, 474 MG SODIUM, 34 G PROTEIN, 2 G DIETARY FIBER

osso buco

SERVES 4

Ask your butcher for four veal shanks of similar size, each tied so the meat is secured to the bone. The initial searing of the meat is essential to the outcome of this dish. Don't let the pieces touch in the pan while you're browning them, or they may steam rather than sear. Dried porcini mushrooms are available in most grocery stores (see Food Sources, page 648).

- 3 tablespoons canola oil
- ¼ cup all-purpose flour
- 2 tablespoons kosher salt
- 2 teaspoons freshly ground black pepper
- 4 veal shanks, tied to secure meat to bone
- 1 cup dried porcini mushrooms (about ¾ ounce)
- 1 dried bay leaf
- 1 sprig fresh rosemary
- 2 sprigs fresh thyme
- 3 fresh sage leaves
- 3 sprigs fresh flat-leaf parsley
  Zest of half a lemon, cut into long strips, pith removed
- 10 whole black peppercorns
- 2 medium carrots, chopped into ¼-inch pieces
- 1 celery stalk, strings removed, chopped into ¼-inch pieces
- 1 medium onion, cut into ¼-inch pieces
- 2 canned plum tomatoes, crushed
- 1½ cups dry white wine
- 1¼ cups Veal Stock (page 626), Beef Stock (page 624), or frozen, thawed

1. Preheat the oven to 275°F with a rack centered. In a 7-quart ovenproof casserole or Dutch oven over medium heat, heat the canola oil until hot but not smoking. In a medium bowl, combine the flour, salt, and pepper. Coat each veal shank well with the seasoned flour; tap off the excess. Working in batches if necessary to keep the veal shanks from touching at all, add the shanks (they should sizzle the moment they hit the pan). Cook until well browned on all sides, 10 to 15 minutes; do not rush. Remove the veal shanks from the casserole; set aside.

2. Place the porcini mushrooms in a small bowl, and cover with very hot water. Let stand until the mushrooms are soft, about 20 minutes. Strain the mushrooms through a fine sieve, reserving ½ cup of the soaking liquid.

3. Tie the bay leaf, rosemary, thyme, sage, parsley, zest, and peppercorns in a small piece of cheesecloth to make a bouquet garni. Add the carrots, celery, and onion to the casserole; cook until softened and lightly browned, about 10 minutes. Add the tomatoes, wine, stock, mushrooms and soaking liquid, and bouquet garni.

4. Return the browned shanks to the casserole; stir gently to combine. Bring to a simmer, cover, and place in the oven; cook until the meat is very tender, about 2½ hours. Check occasionally to ensure a gentle simmer; adjust the heat as needed.

5. Transfer the shanks to a platter, and cover with aluminum foil to keep warm. Place the casserole over medium heat; simmer until the sauce is thickened, about 15 minutes. Return the shanks to the casserole just to heat and coat with sauce. Serve hot.

veal fricadelles with lingonberries

SERVES 12 AS PART OF A BUFFET

Look for preserved lingonberries in specialty stores, or serve with Cranberry Orange Relish.

- *1 large (about 8 ounces) Idaho potato*
- *2 to 3 tablespoons unsalted butter*
- *1 small red onion, coarsely chopped*
- *2 pounds ground veal*
- *1 tablespoon kosher salt*
-    *Freshly ground black pepper*
-    *Pinch of ground nutmeg*
-    *Pinch of ground allspice*
- *1 large egg*
- *3 tablespoons all-purpose flour*
- *¼ cup milk*
-    *Mashed Potatoes 101 (page 364) with 1 tablespoon chopped rosemary stirred in*
- *1 10-ounce jar lingonberries in sugar, or Cranberry Orange Relish (page 611)*

1. Scrub potato; place in a saucepan of cold water. Bring to a boil; reduce heat, and simmer until tender when pierced with the tip of a knife. Drain, let cool, then chill. Peel potato; shred on the largest holes of a box grater. Set aside. Meanwhile, melt 1 tablespoon butter in a skillet over medium-low heat. Add onion; cook until soft, about 12 minutes.

2. In the bowl of an electric mixer fitted with the paddle attachment, combine potato, onion, and veal; beat on low speed. Beat in salt; season with pepper, nutmeg, and allspice. Add egg, flour, and milk; beat until completely combined. Cover and chill for at least 1 hour or overnight.

3. Form ¼ cup of the mixture into an elongated egg shape, and place on a parchment-paper-lined baking sheet. Repeat until the mixture is used up (there will be about 25 meatballs).

4. Heat 1 tablespoon butter in a nonstick skillet over medium heat. Cook meatballs in batches, adding butter as necessary, until browned on all sides, 12 to 15 minutes. Serve with potatoes and lingonberries.

GAME

loin of venison with red currant bordelaise

SERVES 8 TO 10

For venison, see Food Sources, page 648. Ask for a boneless saddle, which will yield two 2-pound loins. Many butchers and specialty food stores sell good-quality frozen veal stock.

- 1 tablespoon whole juniper berries
- 1 tablespoon whole black peppercorns
- 1 tablespoon whole allspice
- 1 4-pound boneless saddle of venison (2 loins)
- 4 shallots, minced
- 1 750-ml bottle dry red wine
- 2 cups Veal Stock (page 626), or frozen, thawed
- 3 tablespoons red-currant jelly
  Kosher salt and freshly ground black pepper
- 2 teaspoons canola oil

1. Combine the juniper berries, peppercorns, and allspice in a spice grinder, and grind to a powder. Rub the mixture into the venison loins, and refrigerate, covered with plastic wrap, for 2 hours.

2. Combine the shallots and red wine in a medium saucepan. Bring to a boil; simmer until reduced by three-quarters, about 45 minutes. Add the stock, and bring to a boil again. Simmer until reduced by half, about 30 minutes. The sauce should be thick enough to coat the back of a spoon. Stir in the jelly, and season with salt and pepper; set the sauce aside.

3. Preheat the oven to 400°F. Heat the oil in a large, heavy skillet over medium heat. Add the venison loins, and brown quickly on all sides. Transfer to a roasting pan; place in the oven for 6 to 8 minutes per pound for rare to medium rare.

4. Remove the venison from the pan, and sprinkle lightly with salt. Let sit for 10 minutes. Slice on an angle, and serve with the prepared sauce.

grilled game sausage and pears over cabbage

SERVES 8 TO 10

For venison sausage, see Food Sources, page 648. Kielbasa and chicken sausages can be substituted.

- Kosher salt
- 1 large head cabbage, cut into 8 or 10 wedges
- 1½ pounds venison sausage
- 1½ pounds pheasant sausage
- 5 Bartlett pears, cut in half lengthwise
  Quince Barbecue Sauce (recipe follows)

Heat a grill or a grill pan until medium hot. Fill a stockpot with salted water; cover; bring to a boil. Add cabbage. Reduce heat to medium; cook until tender, about 25 minutes. Drain. Place sausage and pears on grill. Cook, turning as needed, until lightly charred on all sides. Brush barbecue sauce on sausages and pears. Serve with cabbage.

quince barbecue sauce

MAKES 1½ QUARTS

Firm Bartlett pears can be substituted for quince.

- 2 tablespoons olive oil
- 4 garlic cloves
- 1 cup Tomato Sauce (page 188) or prepared
- 8 (5 to 6 pounds total) quince, peeled, cored, and cut into 1-inch chunks
- 1 cup packed light-brown sugar
- 1 cup red-wine vinegar
- 1 jalapeño pepper, minced
- ⅛ teaspoon ground cinnamon
- 1 teaspoon kosher salt
  Juice of 1 lemon
- 3 ounces grappa or brandy, optional

Heat oil in a large skillet over medium heat. Add garlic; cook until golden, about 3 minutes. Add sauce; simmer. Add remaining ingredients. Cook, stirring occasionally, until sauce thickens and quince are soft, 50 to 60 minutes. Sauce will keep, refrigerated in an airtight container, up to 5 days.

poultry

....

CHICKEN

roast chicken 101

SERVES 4

A golden-brown chicken, its skin crisp and its meat juicy, makes a meal that is equally appropriate for a casual gathering or a small dinner party.

- 1 *6-pound roasting chicken*
- 2 *tablespoons unsalted butter*
- *Kosher salt and freshly ground black pepper*
- 2 *medium onions, sliced crosswise ½ inch thick*
- 1 *lemon*
- 3 *large garlic cloves*
- 4 *sprigs fresh thyme*
- 1 *cup Homemade Chicken Stock (page 624), or low-sodium store-bought chicken broth, skimmed of fat, wine, or water*

1. Let the chicken and 1 tablespoon butter stand at room temperature for 30 minutes. Preheat the oven to 425°F. Remove and discard the plastic pop-up timer from the chicken if there is one. Remove the giblets and excess fat from the chicken cavity. Rinse the chicken inside and out under cold running water. Dry it thoroughly with paper towels. Tuck the wing tips under the body. Sprinkle the cavity liberally with salt and pepper, and set aside.

2. Place the onion slices in two rows down the center of a heavy-duty roasting pan, touching.

3. Press down on the lemon with your palm, and roll it back and forth several times (this softens the lemon and allows the juice to flow more freely). Pierce the entire surface of the lemon with a fork. Using the side of a large knife, gently press on the garlic cloves to open slightly. Place garlic cloves, thyme sprigs, and lemon in the chicken cavity. Place the chicken in the pan, on the onion slices. Cut about 18 inches of kitchen twine, bring the chicken legs forward, cross them, and tie together.

4. Spread the softened butter over the entire surface of the chicken, and sprinkle liberally with salt and pepper. Place in the oven, and roast until the skin is deep golden brown and crisp and the juices run clear when pierced, about 1½ hours. Insert an instant-read thermometer into the breast, then the thigh. The breast temperature should read 180°F and the thigh 190°F.

5. Remove the chicken from the oven, and transfer to a cutting board with a well. Let the chicken stand 10 to 15 minutes so the juices settle.

6. Meanwhile, pour the pan drippings into a shallow bowl or fat separator, and leave the onions in the pan. Leave any brown baked-on bits in the bottom of the roasting pan, and remove and discard any blackened bits. Using a large spoon or a fat separator, skim off and discard as much fat as possible from the pan drippings.

7. Pour the remaining drippings and the juices that have collected under the resting chicken back into the roasting pan. Place on the stove over medium-high heat to cook, about 1 minute. Add the chicken stock, raise heat to high, and, using a wooden spoon, stir to loosen the browned bits from the bottom of the pan; combine with the stock until the liquid is reduced by half, about 6 minutes. Strain the gravy into a small bowl, pressing on the onions to extract any liquid. Discard the onions, and stir in the remaining tablespoon of cold butter until melted and incorporated. Untie the chicken legs, and remove and discard the garlic, thyme, and lemon. Carve, and serve the gravy on the side.

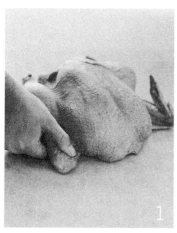

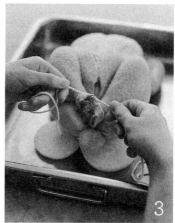

ROASTING CHICKEN

1. Tucking the tips under the bird will prevent them from cooking too fast and possibly burning before the rest of the bird has finished cooking.

2. A bed of onions in the roasting pan will flavor the chicken as well as the gravy; it also provides a rack for the bird, allowing the juices to drain off and preventing the skin from sticking to the bottom of the pan. An aromatic stuffing will also impart flavor during cooking.

3. Placing the chicken breast side up ensures the most even cooking; tying the legs together helps keep the stuffing inside and preserves the shape of the bird for a pretty presentation.

4. A delicious gravy is made in the roasting pan with reserved pan drippings and tasty cooked-on bits.

roast chicken
with potatoes and garlic
SERVES 6

Roast the whole chicken breasts with the skin on
and bone in to yield maximum flavor and juiciness, but remove the skin before eating if you're
counting calories—it's the most fattening part of
the chicken.

- 3 1½-pound whole chicken breasts,
     bone in and skin on
- 2 tablespoons olive oil, plus more
     for brushing
- 3 pounds mixed small potatoes,
     such as red new potatoes, Yukon golds,
     and fingerlings
- 1 head of garlic
- 1½ teaspoons kosher salt
- ½ teaspoon freshly ground black pepper
     Fresh rosemary sprigs, for garnish

1. Let the chicken breasts stand at room temperature for 15 minutes. Preheat the oven to 400°F with
two racks centered. Lightly brush two 14 x 12-inch
roasting pans with oil. The potatoes may be peeled
or not, as desired. If the potatoes are larger than
1½ inches in diameter, cut them into 1½- to 2-inch
chunks.

2. Separate the garlic head into cloves. Divide the
potatoes and garlic cloves between the roasting
pans. Drizzle the potatoes and garlic in each pan
with 1 tablespoon olive oil. Lightly toss the potatoes and garlic until they are covered with the oil.
Place 1 whole chicken breast, skin-side up, in one
pan. Place the remaining 2 whole breasts in the
other pan, skin-sides up. Sprinkle the ingredients
in each pan with ¾ teaspoon of salt and ¼ teaspoon
pepper. Roast for 30 minutes. Rotate the pans in the
oven, and use a spatula to turn the potatoes for even
browning. Continue to cook until the chicken skin
is crisp and an instant-read thermometer inserted
into the breast meat reads 180°F, 20 to 25 minutes.
(Don't touch any bones with the thermometer; it
will give a false reading.)

3. To serve, divide the potatoes evenly among six
plates with a few cloves of roasted garlic for each
person. Use a sharp knife to remove each half of the
breast meat from the bone. Remove the skin from
each serving before eating. Garnish with rosemary
sprigs. Serve.

FIT TO EAT RECIPE PER SERVING: 365 CALORIES, 7 G FAT,
91 MG CHOLESTEROL, 34 G CARBOHYDRATE, 626 MG
SODIUM, 38 G PROTEIN, 3 G DIETARY FIBER

roast poussin
with prunes and thyme
SERVES 6

Poussin, which are very small young chickens,
can be purchased from your butcher, but it may
be necessary to order them in advance. Cornish
game hens can also be used.

- 3 1¼-pound poussin
     Kosher salt and freshly ground
     black pepper
- 3 small onions, quartered
- 9 prunes, pitted
- 1 bunch fresh thyme
- 3 celery stalks
- 3 tablespoons unsalted butter,
     room temperature
- ¼ cup brandy
- 1 cup Homemade Chicken Stock
     (page 624), or low-sodium store-bought
     chicken broth, skimmed of fat

1. Preheat the oven to 425°F. Remove the neck from
the inside of the poussin cavity, and set aside. Rinse
the inside and outside of the poussin, and pat dry.

2. Season each of the poussin cavities with salt and
pepper. Fill each of the cavities with 2 onion quarters, 3 prunes, and ⅓ bunch of thyme. Tie the legs
of the poussin together with kitchen twine, and set
aside. Scatter the bottom of a large roasting pan
with the remaining onion quarters and the celery.

3. Rub the poussin with 2 tablespoons softened butter; season with salt and pepper. Arrange the
poussin in the roasting pan. Transfer to the oven.
Roast the poussin until golden brown and the thigh
juices run clear when pierced with a fork, about 55
minutes. Transfer to a serving platter.

4. Add the brandy and chicken stock to the pan over high heat; stir with a wooden spoon to loosen any browned bits from the bottom of the pan. Strain the gravy through a fine sieve or a cheesecloth-lined strainer, and discard the solids. Season the gravy with salt and pepper. Stir in the remaining tablespoon of butter. Use the gravy to glaze the poussin, or serve on the side.

fried chicken 101

SERVES 8

Cook dark meat, which takes a bit longer, separately from white meat to ensure doneness. Small chickens called fryers, about 3 pounds, are tender and best for frying. Use kosher salt for this recipe; if you measure with table salt it will be too salty. We conducted a test in the kitchen to see just how much oil the chicken absorbs during the frying process. We were amazed at the results: Every 16 pieces of fried chicken absorbed only 2¾ tablespoons of oil.

  6 *cups buttermilk*
  ¼ *cup plus 1 tablespoon kosher salt*
  ⅓ *cup hot red-pepper sauce, optional*
  2 *2- to 3-pound chickens, each cut into 8 pieces for frying*
  3 *cups all-purpose flour*
  1 *tablespoon freshly ground black pepper*
1½ *teaspoons cayenne pepper*
  2 *tablespoons baking powder*
  2 *pounds pure vegetable shortening*
  ¼ *cup plus 2 tablespoons bacon drippings, optional*

1. Combine the buttermilk, 1 tablespoon salt, and the red-pepper sauce, if using, in a large airtight container. Add the chicken pieces, turning to coat in the liquid. Cover, and refrigerate at least 2 hours or overnight.

2. Combine the flour, the remaining ¼ cup salt, the black and cayenne peppers, and the baking powder in a large brown paper bag. Shake vigorously.

3. One at a time, place the chicken pieces in the bag, and shake to coat. Place the coated pieces on a clean plate or tray. Heat the vegetable shortening (and bacon drippings, if using) in two 10-inch cast-iron skillets over medium-low heat. (One large cast-iron skillet may be used; it will just take longer to fry all the chicken.) Using a frying thermometer to measure the temperature, bring the shortening to 375°F; it should be at a medium, not a rolling, boil. Use tongs to place the thighs and drumsticks in the skillets. Fry until the coating is dark golden on the bottom, 10 to 14 minutes; then, using tongs, turn the chicken over. Cook until the coating is dark golden, another 10 to 14 minutes. An instant-read thermometer inserted into a thigh should register 190°F. Drain on brown paper bags or several layered paper towels. Using a slotted spoon, remove any bits of crisp coating left in the skillets, and discard. Place the breasts and wings in the skillets. Cook 10 to 14 minutes on each side. Drain on brown paper bags. Serve warm.

....

MAKING FRIED CHICKEN

● *Use baking powder in the batter; it causes the batter to puff up in the hot oil, giving it extra crunchiness.*

● *Marinate chicken overnight in buttermilk to give it a rich, slightly tangy flavor.*

● *Fry the chicken in shortening with a bit of bacon fat to produce chicken that is crispy, juicy, and light, with just a hint of the bacon's smokiness.*

● *Use a cast-iron skillet. It allows the chicken to brown evenly without burning because it keeps the fat hot and at an even temperature.*

....

silky braised chicken with wild mushrooms and pearl onions

SERVES 4

Splurge on the wild mushrooms. You do not need many, and they add a fantastic flavor to this dish.

- 1   6-pound chicken, cut into 8 pieces, skin on
      Kosher salt and freshly ground black pepper
- 2   medium onions, cut into ⅛-inch-thick slices
- 2   garlic cloves, slightly crushed
- 40 sprigs fresh thyme (3 to 4 bunches)
- 2   dried bay leaves
- 2   sprigs fresh rosemary
- 2   cups Riesling or other medium-dry white wine
- 1½ cups Homemade Chicken Stock (page 624), or low-sodium store-bought chicken broth, skimmed of fat
- 1   tablespoon plus 1 teaspoon grainy mustard
- 3   tablespoons unsalted butter
- 5   ounces (about 1 cup) red pearl onions, peeled and halved
- 8   ounces fresh wild mushrooms, such as chanterelle, wiped clean, cut into 1-inch pieces
- ¼   cup Madeira wine
- 10 strips best-quality bacon

1. Preheat the oven to 300°F. Sprinkle the chicken pieces with salt and pepper. Spread a third of the onion slices and all the garlic in the bottom of a 7-quart ovenproof casserole or Dutch oven. Scatter 5 sprigs thyme, 1 bay leaf, and 1 rosemary sprig over the onion layer. Arrange half the chicken pieces on top of the herb layer. Repeat with another third of the onion slices, the same amounts of each of the herbs as before, and the remaining chicken pieces; finish with a layer of all the remaining onion slices. Pour the Riesling and chicken stock over the onions and chicken. Cover the casserole, and place in the oven to cook until the chicken is tender, about 1 hour 15 minutes.

2. Remove the chicken pieces from the casserole, and let sit until cool enough to handle. Remove the skin from the chicken; cut each breast piece in half. Spread each chicken piece with ½ teaspoon of the mustard, season with salt and pepper, and top with the sprigs of thyme. Set aside. With a ladle, remove about 1 cup of the chicken cooking liquid from the casserole, straining it into a shallow bowl or fat separator; set aside to separate.

3. Melt the butter in a large skillet over medium heat. Add the pearl onions, and season with salt and pepper. Cook, shaking the skillet often, until the onions start to soften and turn golden brown, 3 to 4 minutes. Add the mushrooms, and season with salt and pepper. Cook, shaking the skillet often, until the mushrooms soften and release their juices, about 5 minutes. Cook until the juices have evaporated, about 2 minutes. Add 2 tablespoons Madeira to skillet, and cook until evaporated, about 1 minute. Transfer the mixture to a bowl, and set aside.

4. Return the skillet to medium heat. Arrange 5 bacon strips in a single layer in the skillet. Cook until the bacon renders most of its fat and is golden brown. Place a piece of the chicken on each piece of bacon, and, using tongs, wrap the chicken in the bacon. Breasts may need 2 pieces of bacon. Do not worry if the chicken unwraps; it can be easily rewrapped before serving. Remove the chicken from the skillet, place on a platter, and cover with aluminum foil to keep warm. Drain the fat from the skillet. Repeat with the remaining bacon and chicken.

5. Add the reserved cooked mushrooms and the onions and all the chicken to the skillet. Add the remaining 2 tablespoons of Madeira and the reserved chicken cooking liquid, skimmed of fat. Cook until the chicken and vegetables are hot. Serve.

chicken stuffed
with savory duxelles

SERVES 4

A duxelles is a thick paste of mushrooms, shallots, and herbs.

- 2 tablespoons olive oil
- 1 garlic clove, minced
- 1 shallot, minced
- 1 pound white-button mushrooms, wiped clean, finely chopped

   Kosher salt and freshly ground black pepper

- ¼ cup dry white wine
- ¼ cup finely chopped fresh flat-leaf parsley
- 2 whole boneless chicken breasts, split

1. Preheat the oven to 400°F. In a large skillet over medium heat, heat 1 tablespoon oil. Add the garlic and shallot; cook, stirring, until fragrant, about 1 minute. Add the mushrooms; cook, stirring, until the mushrooms release their juices, about 4 minutes. Season with salt and pepper. Add the white wine, and continue cooking until the liquid has evaporated, about 10 minutes. Remove from the heat, and stir in the parsley.

2. Pull the skin back from one chicken breast, keeping the skin attached at one end. Season with salt and pepper. Mound ⅓ cup of the mushroom filling on the breast; pull the skin back over the filling. Tuck the ends under the breast, forming a ball. Secure with toothpicks. Repeat with the remaining chicken and filling.

3. Place the stuffed breasts in a roasting pan, keeping them close together but not touching. Drizzle the remaining tablespoon of olive oil over the top. Transfer to the oven; roast until the skin is golden brown and the chicken has cooked through, about 35 minutes. Remove from the oven, and serve.

grilled chicken with
spicy barbecue sauce

MAKES 3 CUPS SAUCE;
SERVES 8

Use this rich, smoky sauce for marinating and basting meat or chicken before grilling. It is very spicy, so don't eat it by itself. For dried chile peppers, see Food Sources, page 648.

- 6 dried mora peppers
- 4 dried cascabel peppers
- 3 dried pequín peppers
- 3 pounds tomatoes, cored and quartered
- 2 teaspoons kosher salt
- ½ teaspoon freshly ground black pepper
- 2 teaspoons ground ginger
- 1 teaspoon ground allspice
- ½ cup packed dark-brown sugar
- ¼ cup cider vinegar
- ¼ cup unsulfured molasses
- 8 chicken-breast halves, bone in and skin on

1. Toast the dried peppers in a skillet on medium-high heat; using tongs, turn so they brown evenly. Remove when just browned (peppers can burn quickly, so watch closely). Transfer the peppers to a medium bowl. Cover with hot water, and soak until they are softened, about 30 minutes. When the peppers are cool enough to handle, pat dry, break apart, and remove the stems and seeds. Chop the peppers and set aside. Strain and reserve the liquid for making stews and soups.

2. Place the tomatoes and peppers in a medium saucepan, and simmer with 3 tablespoons water over low heat until the mixture is very liquidy, 20 to 30 minutes. Pass the mixture through a food mill fitted with a medium disk to remove the seeds and skins.

3. Return the tomato liquid to the saucepan. Add the salt, pepper, ginger, allspice, sugar, vinegar, and molasses. Bring to a boil over high heat, reduce to a simmer, and cook, uncovered, stirring occasionally, until reduced by half, 50 to 60 minutes. Transfer to a bowl to cool to room temperature. The sauce will keep in an airtight container in the refrigerator for up to 1 month.

4. Place the chicken in a large nonreactive pan. Measure out 2 cups of the sauce; return the remaining sauce to the refrigerator to use another time. Rub ¼ cup of the barbecue sauce over each breast. Heat a grill or a grill pan to medium hot (the chicken can also be cooked under the broiler in a baking pan). Cook over even heat, turning as needed to keep from scorching, 6 to 8 minutes per side. (If the chicken breasts are thick, finish cooking them all the way through by moving them to the coolest part of the grill and covering them with aluminum foil, or by putting them in a 350°F oven for 15 to 20 minutes, until the juices run clear.) Serve.

grilled chicken with cilantro mint rub
SERVES 8

Don't overcook the chicken, or the rub will darken; serve with extra Cilantro-Mint Sauce on the side.

> Cilantro-Mint Sauce (recipe follows), made without the water
> 3 tablespoons canola oil
> 8 boneless, skinless chicken-breast halves, each half cut into thirds
> Kosher salt and freshly ground black pepper

1. In a medium bowl, combine the cilantro-mint sauce and the oil. Place chicken in a nonreactive dish. Spread sauce over each piece of chicken.

2. Heat a grill or a grill pan to medium hot. Season chicken with salt and pepper. Cook until meat is cooked through, about 4 minutes per side.

cilantro-mint sauce
MAKES 1 CUP

This sauce tastes best when eaten within 3 or 4 hours of being made. Make a double batch if you are making it for the Grilled Chicken with Cilantro-Mint Rub, so you will have enough to serve on the side.

> 2 cups packed fresh flat-leaf parsley
> 2 cups packed fresh cilantro leaves
> 1 cup fresh mint leaves
> 3 small garlic cloves, minced
> 1 small jalapeño pepper, seeds and ribs removed, roughly chopped
> ¼ cup plus 2 tablespoons fresh lemon juice
> 1½ teaspoons kosher salt
> ½ teaspoon ground cumin

Combine parsley, cilantro, mint, garlic, jalapeño, lemon juice, salt, and cumin in the bowl of a food processor with ¼ cup water. Blend until well combined; mixture should still have some texture. Serve.

chicken paillard
with prosciutto and figs
SERVES 8

"Paillard" refers to thin, pounded chicken breasts; chicken prepared this way cooks very quickly.

- ¼ cup plus 2 tablespoons dry white wine
- 3 tablespoons finely chopped fresh rosemary, plus 8 sprigs
- 1 teaspoon crushed red-pepper flakes
- 2 tablespoons fresh lemon juice
- 1 teaspoon kosher salt
- ¼ teaspoon freshly ground black pepper
- ¼ cup olive oil
- 8 boneless, skinless chicken-breast halves, pounded ¼ inch thick
- 1 lemon, sliced into ⅛-inch rounds
- 16 fresh figs, preferably Black Mission
- 1 1-pound loaf country bread, cut into 1½-inch-thick slices
- 8 to 10 thin slices prosciutto di Parma Balsamic Fig Sauce (recipe follows)

1. Combine the wine, chopped rosemary, pepper flakes, lemon juice, salt, pepper, and oil in a large, shallow nonreactive dish.

2. Add the chicken breasts, lemon slices, and 3 rosemary sprigs to the dish with the marinade. Cover with plastic wrap; refrigerate 3 hours or up to overnight, turning the chicken occasionally.

3. Heat a grill or a grill pan to medium hot. Grill the chicken until the juices run clear, 3 to 5 minutes per side; set aside.

4. Grill the whole figs on the coolest part of the grill until soft and warm, 3 to 6 minutes. Grill the bread until browned on both sides.

5. Wrap the prosciutto loosely around each chicken breast. Arrange on a platter. Garnish with the remaining rosemary sprigs, and serve with the fig sauce, grilled figs, and bread.

balsamic fig sauce
MAKES 1 CUP

- 1 pound fresh figs, preferably Black Mission, chopped into ¾-inch pieces
- ⅓ cup red wine
- 1 tablespoon balsamic vinegar
  Pinch of kosher salt
- ⅛ teaspoon freshly ground black pepper
- ½ teaspoon sugar
- 1 sprig fresh thyme

1. Combine figs, red wine, vinegar, pinch of salt, the pepper, sugar, and thyme with ½ cup water in a small saucepan. Cover; bring to a boil over high heat. Reduce to a simmer; cook, partially covered, until the fruit has broken down, 20 to 30 minutes.

2. Let cool slightly; remove the thyme sprig. Press the mixture through a large-holed sieve with a rubber spatula. Discard the solids. Serve. The sauce may be made up to 6 hours ahead of time; keep refrigerated, in an airtight container, and return to room temperature before using.

GRILLING CHICKEN BREASTS

If your grill is hot enough and sufficiently well seasoned, you don't need any oil to prevent chicken from sticking. If your grill is brand-new, you may need to brush it with oil before the first few times you use it to help it develop its seasoned, nonstick coating.

grilled orange sesame chicken and vegetables

SERVES 6

The cooking time depends on the grill's heat.

- 3 navel oranges
- Juice of 1 lemon
- 1 tablespoon white-wine vinegar
- ¼ teaspoon freshly ground black pepper
- 2 teaspoons Dijon mustard
- 2 tablespoons toasted-sesame oil
- 6 boneless, skinless chicken-breast halves, cut in half
- 2 pounds asparagus, tough ends removed
- 6 small (2 pounds) zucchini, cut on a diagonal, ¼ inch thick
- 1 teaspoon extra-virgin olive oil
- Kosher salt
- 2 teaspoons sesame seeds, toasted (see page 644)

1. Cut 1 orange into wedges (peel intact); set aside. Remove the zest of 1 orange and the juice of 2 oranges; place in a nonreactive bowl. Add the lemon juice, vinegar, pepper, and mustard; whisk. Slowly whisk in the sesame oil; set aside.

2. Place the chicken between two sheets of plastic wrap; pound with a meat tenderizer to ½ inch thick. Place the chicken in a nonreactive bowl; pour half the reserved vinaigrette over the chicken. Coat thoroughly, cover with plastic wrap, and refrigerate 1 to 2 hours.

3. Heat a grill or grill pan until very hot. Brush the asparagus and zucchini with olive oil; season with salt. Grill the vegetables and the reserved orange wedges until tender when pierced with the tip of a knife. Remove the chicken from the marinade; season with salt; discard the marinade. Grill until the chicken is browned and cooked through, about 6 minutes per side. Arrange the chicken and vegetables on a platter; sprinkle with the sesame seeds. Serve with the remaining reserved vinaigrette.

FIT TO EAT RECIPE PER SERVING: 325 CALORIES, 11 G FAT, 117 MG CHOLESTEROL, 10 G CARBOHYDRATE, 653 MG SODIUM, 47 G PROTEIN, 2 G DIETARY FIBER

chicken tonnato

SERVES 4

"Tonno" is Italian for tuna, and the name of this dish refers to the primary ingredient in the sauce. The tuna is blended with capers, olive oil, and lemon juice to make a rich, flavorful sauce that is traditionally served with veal cutlets. The sauce can also be served chilled over room-temperature chicken.

- 1 tablespoon olive oil
- 4 boneless chicken-breast halves
- Kosher salt and freshly ground black pepper
- 1 small carrot, finely chopped
- 1 celery stalk, strings removed, finely chopped
- 1 small onion, finely chopped
- 1 medium garlic clove, minced
- 1 cup dry white wine
- 3 fresh sage leaves
- 1 sprig fresh rosemary
- 1½ teaspoons capers, drained
- 1 6-ounce can light tuna packed in oil, drained
- ½ cup Homemade Mayonnaise (page 632) or prepared
- 1 tablespoon fresh lemon juice
- 4 cups arugula leaves (1 large bunch)

1. Preheat the oven to 425°F. Heat the oil in an ovenproof skillet over high heat. Season the chicken with salt and pepper. Place in the skillet, skin-side down, and cook until brown, 3 to 4 minutes. Turn over; cook 1 minute. Remove the chicken; add the carrot, celery, onion, and garlic. Reduce heat to medium low; cook about 6 minutes.

2. Add the wine, and bring to boil. Stir in the sage, rosemary, capers, and tuna; add the chicken. Transfer the skillet to the oven, and roast until the chicken is cooked through, about 15 minutes. Remove the chicken; transfer to a cutting board.

3. Discard herbs. Let tuna mixture cool; purée in the bowl of a food processor until smooth. Add the mayonnaise and lemon juice. Slice the chicken; arrange over the arugula. Top with the sauce. Serve.

spring chicken ragout

SERVES 4

2 whole chicken breasts, bone in, split and skinned

Kosher salt and freshly ground black pepper

2 teaspoons olive oil

1¾ cups Homemade Chicken Stock (page 624), or low-sodium store-bought chicken broth, skimmed of fat

4 canned plum tomatoes, seeded and quartered

12 baby carrots, trimmed

8 ounces asparagus, tough ends removed, cut into 1½-inch pieces

1 leek (about 6 ounces), white and pale-green parts, cut into ¼-inch rounds, well washed (see page 646)

1 cup shelled peas, preferably fresh

Fresh flat-leaf parsley, for garnish, optional

1. Season the chicken breasts with salt and pepper. Heat the olive oil in a large skillet, add chicken, and cook over medium-high heat until golden brown on both sides, about 4 minutes per side.

2. Add the stock and tomatoes, bring to a boil, and cover. Cook on medium-low heat for about 20 minutes; remove the chicken, and set aside.

3. Add the carrots to the skillet, and cook, covered, until almost tender, about 5 minutes. Add the asparagus, leek, and peas, and cook until all the vegetables are tender, about 5 minutes more.

4. Meanwhile, pull the chicken from the bone, and shred into large bite-size pieces. Return the chicken to the skillet, and cook until heated through, about 2 minutes. Garnish with sprigs of parsley, if using, and serve.

chicken cacciatore

SERVES 6

This sauce is prepared hunter-style—with mushrooms, tomatoes, and onions—thus the name "cacciatore," the Italian word for hunter.

3 tablespoons olive oil

6 boneless, skinless chicken-breast halves

Kosher salt and freshly ground black pepper

4 ounces small white-button mushrooms, wiped clean, sliced ¼ inch thick

1 small onion, sliced lengthwise ¼ inch thick

2 celery stalks, strings removed, sliced crosswise ¼ inch thick

2 small carrots, sliced ⅛ inch thick

1 large garlic clove, minced

¼ cup dry white wine

2 cups chopped canned tomatoes

½ yellow bell pepper, seeds and ribs removed, sliced lengthwise ¼ inch thick

1½ teaspoons finely chopped fresh rosemary

¼ cup Homemade Chicken Stock (page 624), or low-sodium store-bought chicken broth, skimmed of fat

1. Heat 1 tablespoon oil in a medium skillet over high heat. Season the chicken with salt and pepper. Cook in the skillet until browned on both sides, about 6 minutes. Transfer to a plate.

2. Wipe out the skillet, and heat 1 tablespoon olive oil. Add the mushrooms, and cook until browned, about 5 minutes; set aside. Reduce heat to low.

3. Heat the remaining tablespoon of oil in the skillet, and add the onion, celery, carrots, and garlic; cook, stirring, until onion slices are translucent, 8 minutes. Add wine; raise heat to high. Cook until the wine is almost evaporated, about 30 seconds.

4. Add tomatoes, yellow pepper, rosemary, and stock; season with salt and pepper. Stir to combine. Add chicken and mushrooms; bring to a boil. Reduce heat to medium low, cover, and simmer until chicken is tender, about 30 minutes. Serve.

FIT TO EAT RECIPE PER SERVING: 187 CALORIES, 3 G FAT, 73 MG CHOLESTEROL, 9 G CARBOHYDRATE, 601 MG SODIUM, 29 G PROTEIN, 3 G DIETARY FIBER

poule au pot

SERVES 6

The recipe name is French for "chicken in a pot."

- 1 lemon, halved
- 1 tablespoon olive oil
- 6 shallots, sliced ¼ inch thick
- 2 teaspoons sugar
- Flavorful Chicken Stock (recipe follows), skimmed, plus chicken breasts from recipe
- 1 small leek, well washed (see page 646)
- 12 small carrots
- 8 ounces haricots verts
- 1 large celeriac
- Kosher salt
- ½ teaspoon freshly ground black pepper
- 1½ teaspoons fresh thyme leaves

1. Fill a large bowl with 1 quart of cold water. Squeeze the juice from the lemon into the water; add the lemon halves, and set aside.

2. Heat the oil in a medium skillet over medium heat. Add the shallots; cover, and cook, stirring, over medium-low heat until brown, about 15 minutes, adding 1 to 2 tablespoons water if the pan gets dry. Add the sugar, stir, cover, and cook 2 to 4 minutes more to caramelize the shallots.

3. Add the stock, using a wooden spoon to stir and loosen any browned bits from the bottom of the pan. Cover, and bring to a simmer.

4. Meanwhile, cut 6 half-inch-wide strips from the leek; reserve remaining leek for another use. Wash the strips; set aside. Cut carrots in 5-inch lengths; set aside. Cover and bring a large pot of water to a boil. Prepare an ice-water bath. Blanch haricots verts in the boiling water, just until bright green, 1 to 2 minutes. Using a slotted spoon, transfer to the ice bath to stop the cooking; drain. In the same boiling water, blanch the leek strips for 10 seconds; transfer to the ice-water bath; drain. Set aside. Peel and cut celeriac into ½-inch-thick wedges; transfer to the lemon water. Slice the reserved chicken diagonally into ½-inch-thick pieces; set aside.

5. Add carrots, celeriac, salt to taste, pepper, and thyme to simmering stock. Cook until carrots can

be pierced with a knife, 10 to 15 minutes. Meanwhile, divide the haricots verts into 6 bundles. Tie each with a leek strip. Add the haricots verts and the sliced chicken to the stock; cook until warm, 3 to 5 minutes. Serve hot in individual bowls.

FIT TO EAT RECIPE PER SERVING: 187 CALORIES, 3 G FAT, 73 MG CHOLESTEROL, 9 G CARBOHYDRATE, 601 MG SODIUM, 29 G PROTEIN, 3 G DIETARY FIBER

flavorful chicken stock

MAKES 6 TO 7 CUPS

- 6 skinless chicken-breast halves (about 3½ pounds total), bone in, trimmed of all fat
- 3 medium onions, unpeeled, quartered
- 4 carrots, scrubbed, cut into 1-inch chunks
- 3 celery stalks, cut into 1-inch chunks
- 3 garlic cloves, unpeeled
- 2 dried bay leaves
- 4 sprigs fresh thyme
- 1½ teaspoons whole black peppercorns

1. Place the chicken, onions, carrots, celery, and garlic in a stockpot. Add 3 quarts of cold water, cover, and bring to a boil. Reduce heat to medium low, skim the foam that rises to the surface, and add the bay leaves, thyme, and peppercorns. Simmer until the chicken is cooked through, 25 to 35 minutes. Transfer the breasts to a cutting board, and remove the breast meat from the bone in two pieces, keeping each half breast intact, and return the bones to the stock. Reserve the breast meat for Poule au Pot (recipe, left). Simmer the stock until flavorful, 30 to 40 minutes more.

2. Strain the stock through a fine sieve or a cheesecloth-lined strainer into a narrow container (a narrow container makes a thicker layer of fat, which is easier to collect). Discard the solids. Cool the stock to room temperature. Chill the stock in the refrigerator, and when cold, remove the layer of fat from the top. The stock may be made 1 day ahead, and kept refrigerated in an airtight container, or kept frozen up to 4 months.

FIT TO EAT RECIPE WHOLE RECIPE: 176 CALORIES, 7 G FAT, 13 MG CHOLESTEROL, 0 G CARBOHYDRATE, 410 MG SODIUM, 26 G PROTEIN, 0 G DIETARY FIBER

spicy stir-fried chicken and vegetables

SERVES 6

For dried wood ear mushrooms, see Food Sources, page 648.

- 1 ounce dried wood ear mushrooms or dried shiitake mushrooms
- 1 tablespoon cornstarch
- 1 large egg white
- 1 tablespoon rice-wine vinegar
- ½ teaspoon kosher salt
- 4 boneless, skinless chicken-breast halves, cut into strips
- ½ head broccoli, cut into florets
- 3 medium carrots, thinly sliced
- 2 tablespoons canola oil
- 1½ teaspoons freshly grated ginger
- 1 garlic clove, minced
- 2 scallions, white and green parts, sliced into thin rings
- ½ teaspoon crushed red-pepper flakes
- 1 medium onion, cut into ¾-inch pieces
- 1 medium red bell pepper, seeds and ribs removed, cut into ¾-inch pieces
- 1 1-pound cabbage, shredded
- ½ small jalapeño pepper, seeds and ribs removed, minced
- 2 tablespoons soy sauce
- 1 tablespoon balsamic vinegar
- ½ teaspoon dark sesame oil
  Kosher salt and freshly ground black pepper

1. Place the mushrooms in a small bowl, and cover with very hot water. Let stand until the mushrooms are soft, about 20 minutes; drain in a colander.

2. Dissolve cornstarch in 1½ tablespoons water. In a large bowl, combine cornstarch mixture, egg white, vinegar, and salt; whisk to combine. Add the chicken, cover, and refrigerate 30 minutes.

3. Cover and bring a large stockpot of water to a boil. Blanch broccoli in the boiling water for 1 minute; remove from water, and rinse under cold running water to stop cooking. Add carrots to the boiling water, and cook 2 minutes. Drain; rinse under cold running water to stop the cooking.

4. Heat a large wok over medium-high heat. Add canola oil, ginger, garlic, scallions, and red-pepper flakes. Stir-fry 30 seconds. Add onion and bell pepper; cook 1 minute more. Add carrots; cook 2 minutes more. Stir in broccoli, cabbage, jalapeño, and mushrooms; cook until cabbage starts to wilt, about 4 minutes. Remove chicken from marinade; add to wok. Cook until chicken is cooked through, about 5 minutes. Stir in soy sauce, vinegar, and sesame oil, and season to taste with salt and pepper. Serve immediately.

FIT TO EAT RECIPE PER SERVING: 208 CALORIES, 7 G FAT, 31 MG CHOLESTEROL, 23 G CARBOHYDRATE, 695 MG SODIUM, 17 G PROTEIN, 6 G DIETARY FIBER

tortilla casserole

SERVES 6

This casserole is baked in a springform pan and served in wedges. For a more traditional presentation, bake it in a casserole dish, and scoop out the servings.

- 2 boneless, skinless chicken-breast halves
- ¼ cup yellow cornmeal
- ½ teaspoon chili powder
- ¼ teaspoon kosher salt
- 2 tablespoons olive oil, plus more for brushing
- 1 small onion, finely diced
- 2 garlic cloves, minced
- 1½ pounds tomatillos, husks removed, cut into eighths
- 2 small jalapeño peppers, seeds and ribs removed, minced
- 4 8-inch whole-wheat or white corn tortillas
- 1 14½-ounce can diced tomatoes with chiles
- 1 ounce queso blanco or feta cheese

1. Preheat the oven to 400°F. Cut chicken into ½-inch cubes. Combine cornmeal, chili powder, and salt; sprinkle over the chicken. Toss to coat, and place in a colander; shake off any excess cornmeal.

2. Heat 1 tablespoon oil in a large skillet over medium-high heat; add the chicken. Cook, stirring occasionally, until browned on all sides and cooked through, about 6 minutes. Remove the chicken from the pan, and set aside. Wipe the pan with a paper towel; add the remaining tablespoon of olive oil, and place over low heat. Add the onion and garlic; cook until translucent, about 8 minutes. Add the tomatillos, jalapeño peppers, and ½ cup water; cover. Cook until the tomatillos are tender, about 20 minutes. Remove the lid; increase heat to medium high. Cook until most of the liquid has evaporated, about 8 minutes. Stir in the chicken.

3. Place 1 tortilla in the bottom of an 8-inch spring-form pan brushed with olive oil. Place half the chicken mixture over the tortilla, and spread to coat evenly. Place a second tortilla on top, cover with half the tomatoes, and top with a third tortilla. Cover with the remaining chicken mixture and the last tortilla. Spread the remaining tomatoes over the top; sprinkle with cheese.

4. Bake until golden brown, 25 to 30 minutes. Transfer from the oven to a cooling rack for about 15 minutes. Release the springform; remove the sides. Cut into 6 wedges using a serrated knife. Serve hot.

FIT TO EAT RECIPE PER SERVING: 230 CALORIES, 4 G FAT, 41 MG CHOLESTEROL, 28 G CARBOHYDRATE, 435 MG SODIUM, 19 G PROTEIN, 3 G DIETARY FIBER

chicken with grainy mustard sauce
SERVES 4

4	skinless chicken-breast halves, bone in
2	carrots, scrubbed
2	small onions, cut in half
2	celery stalks, cut into 3-inch pieces
1	dried bay leaf
10	sprigs fresh flat-leaf parsley
1	cup dry white wine
1	tablespoon whole black peppercorns
¾	cup dried apricots
2	cups fresh pineapple in 1-inch cubes
	Kosher salt and freshly ground black pepper
½	teaspoon chopped fresh tarragon
1	teaspoon grainy mustard
4	ounces baby lettuce, such as mâche

1. Place the chicken, carrots, onions, celery, bay leaf, parsley, wine, and peppercorns in a stockpot. Add cold water to cover (about 3 quarts); cover and bring to a boil. Reduce heat. Poach, adjusting the heat to maintain a bare simmer and skimming foam off the top, until chicken is cooked, 20 to 25 minutes.

2. Remove chicken from stock; use a sharp knife to remove the meat from the bones. Place in a dish; add enough stock to just cover. Return bones to the remaining stock; simmer until very flavorful, about 1 hour. Pass the stock through fine sieve or a cheesecloth-lined strainer; discard the solids.

3. In a clean saucepan, return stock to a boil. Reduce heat; bring stock to a simmer. Add apricots and pineapple; poach until tender, about 10 minutes. Remove fruit with a slotted spoon; season with salt, pepper, and ¼ teaspoon tarragon.

4. Raise heat to high; cook the stock until reduced to ⅓ cup, about 45 minutes. Reduce heat to low; whisk in the mustard; season with salt, pepper, and remaining ¼ teaspoon tarragon. Divide the lettuce among plates. Slice chicken; place on greens. Pour sauce over chicken; serve with fruit mixture.

FIT TO EAT RECIPE PER SERVING: 318 CALORIES, 3 G FAT, 53 MG CHOLESTEROL, 21 G CARBOHYDRATE, 377 MG SODIUM, 32 G PROTEIN, 4 G DIETARY FIBER

chicken potpie

SERVES 6

This savory pie should be generously seasoned since the flavors mellow as it cooks.

- 1 4-pound chicken
- 1 quart Homemade Chicken Stock (page 624), or low-sodium store-bought chicken broth, skimmed of fat
- 1 large yellow onion, cut in half
- 2 dried bay leaves
- ½ teaspoon whole black peppercorns
- 1 small bunch fresh thyme
- 1 celery stalk, cut into thirds
- 1¼ cups plus 1 tablespoon all-purpose flour
- 2¼ teaspoons kosher salt
- 8 tablespoons (1 stick) plus 7 tablespoons chilled unsalted butter
- 2 large egg yolks
- 9 ounces red potatoes, scrubbed and cut into ½-inch pieces
- 12 pearl onions, peeled and cut lengthwise if large
- 1 medium leek, white and pale-green parts, sliced into ¼-inch-thick rounds, well washed (see page 646)
- 2 medium carrots, sliced into ¼-inch-thick rounds
- 6 ounces white-button mushrooms, wiped clean, quartered if large
- 1 cup milk
- 2 tablespoons chopped fresh flat-leaf parsley
  Zest of 1 lemon
- ½ teaspoon freshly ground black pepper
- 1 tablespoon heavy cream

1. Combine the chicken, chicken stock, yellow onion, bay leaves, peppercorns, 3 thyme sprigs, and celery in a stockpot, and add enough water just to cover the chicken. Cover and bring the stock to a boil, reduce heat, and simmer, uncovered, for 1 hour.

2. Pick enough thyme leaves to make 3 tablespoons. Combine 1 cup flour, ¼ teaspoon salt, and 1 tablespoon thyme leaves in the bowl of a food processor, and set the remaining 2 tablespoons of thyme aside. Add 10 tablespoons of the chilled butter, cut into small pieces, and pulse until mixture resembles coarse meal. While the food processor is running, add 3 tablespoons of ice water and 1 egg yolk, and process until the dough holds together. Turn the dough out onto plastic wrap, flatten into a circle, and wrap well; refrigerate at least 1 hour.

3. Drain the chicken, and reserve the stock. Remove the skin from the chicken, and remove all the chicken from the carcass. Shred the chicken meat into bite-size strips, and set aside. Strain the stock, discarding the solids, and set aside 2 cups of the stock. Reserve the remaining stock for another use.

4. Preheat the oven to 375°F. Melt the remaining 5 tablespoons butter in a large skillet over medium-high heat. Add red potatoes and pearl onions; cook, stirring occasionally, about 5 minutes, until potatoes begin to turn golden. Add leek, carrots, and mushrooms; cook 5 minutes more. Add remaining ¼ cup plus 1 tablespoon flour, and cook, stirring, for 1 minute. Stir in the reserved chicken stock and the milk, and bring to a simmer. Cook until thick and bubbly, stirring constantly, 2 to 3 minutes. Add the reserved chicken pieces, parsley, the remaining 2 tablespoons of thyme, the lemon zest, remaining 2 teaspoons salt, and the pepper; transfer to an ovenproof casserole. Set aside.

5. Roll out the dough until it is ¼ inch thick, and transfer to a baking sheet. Place in the refrigerator, and allow the dough to chill 15 minutes. In a small bowl, whisk together the remaining yolk and heavy cream to make an egg wash. Working quickly, place the dough over the top of the chicken mixture, and tuck the extra dough around the edges. Cut slits on the top to allow the steam to escape. Brush with the egg wash, and place on a baking sheet. Bake until crust is golden, 35 to 40 minutes. Serve hot.

arroz con pollo

SERVES 6

Serve this with Cuban Black Beans (page 334).

- 1½ cups long-grain rice
- 1½ cups canned tomatoes, with juice
- ½ cup finely chopped red onion
- 2 garlic cloves, minced
- 1 tablespoon plus 2 teaspoons dried oregano
- 2 teaspoons ground cumin
- 2 teaspoons chili powder
- 1½ teaspoons kosher salt
- ¾ teaspoon freshly ground black pepper
- 6 skinless chicken-breast halves, bone in, each half cut into 3 pieces
- 3 tablespoons canola oil
- 1 small jalapeño pepper, seeds and ribs removed, minced
- 2½ cups Homemade Chicken Stock (page 624), or low-sodium store-bought chicken broth, skimmed of fat
- 1 cup frozen baby peas, thawed
- 10 cherry tomatoes, cut in half
    Fresh cilantro, for garnish, optional

1. Preheat the oven to 375°F. Place the rice in a medium bowl, and cover with 2 inches of hot water. Let the rice soak 10 minutes. Transfer to a colander; drain. Rinse with cold water; set aside.

2. Place the canned tomatoes, onion, and garlic in a blender. On high speed, blend the mixture until puréed, about 30 seconds. Set aside. In a small bowl, combine 1 tablespoon plus 1 teaspoon oregano with the cumin, chili powder, 1 teaspoon salt, and ½ teaspoon pepper. Rub each piece of chicken with the mixture, and set aside.

3. Heat 2 tablespoons oil in a large Dutch oven or a large, deep ovenproof skillet. Cook the chicken in two batches over medium-high heat until browned on each side, about 2 minutes per side. Add 1 tablespoon oil to the pot before browning second batch. Transfer all the chicken to a bowl, and set aside. Add the reserved rice to the pot, and cook over medium-low heat, stirring, until the rice be-

comes slightly golden, about 2 minutes. Add the jalapeño, and cook 1 minute more. Add the tomato purée, and cook, stirring, until the liquid has been absorbed, 2 to 3 minutes. Add remaining 1 teaspoon dried oregano, ½ teaspoon salt, and ¼ teaspoon pepper. Add stock, peas, cherry tomatoes, and chicken; bring to a simmer over high heat.

4. Cover, and transfer the pot to the oven. Bake until the chicken is cooked through and the liquid has been absorbed, 25 to 35 minutes. Garnish with the cilantro, and serve warm.

FIT TO EAT RECIPE PER SERVING: 551 CALORIES, 12 G FAT, 143 MG CHOLESTEROL, 43 G CARBOHYDRATE, 910 MG SODIUM, 59 G PROTEIN, 3 G DIETARY FIBER

chicken saltimbocca

SERVES 4

- 4 boneless, skinless chicken-breast halves
- 4 ounces fontina cheese, thinly sliced
- 6 ounces prosciutto, thinly sliced
- 16 large fresh sage leaves
- 1 teaspoon kosher salt
- ¼ teaspoon freshly ground black pepper
- 3 tablespoons unsalted butter
- 1 cup Madeira wine

1. Slice the tenderloin (the small flap of meat) from chicken; set aside. Cut each breast on the bias into 3 medallions. Place tenderloins and medallions between two layers of plastic wrap, and pound to ¹⁄₁₆ inch thick. Layer a slice of fontina, half a slice of prosciutto, and a sage leaf on each; secure by piercing the layers with a toothpick. Sprinkle underside of each with salt and pepper.

2. Melt 1 tablespoon butter in a skillet over high heat. Cook half the pieces, chicken-side down, until golden, 2 to 3 minutes. Turn and cook 1 minute more. Remove the chicken from the pan, and keep warm. Repeat with 1 tablespoon butter and the remaining chicken. Remove and keep warm.

3. Pour the Madeira into the skillet, and let reduce slightly, about 1 minute. Add the remaining tablespoon of butter, and cook, swirling the pan, until the sauce thickens, about 30 seconds. Pour the sauce over chicken, remove toothpicks, and serve.

TURKEY

perfect roast turkey 101

SERVES 12 TO 14

If your roasting pan only fits sideways in the oven, turn the pan every hour so the turkey cooks and browns evenly. The cheesecloth is dipped in butter and wine to keep the breast meat moist and the skin from burning. Unlike frozen turkeys, fresh birds release a lot of juice as they cook. Watch your roasting pan for overflow, and scoop out liquid from the pan as the turkey cooks.

- 1 20- to 21-pound fresh whole turkey, neck and giblets (heart, gizzard, and liver) removed from cavity and reserved
- 1½ cups (3 sticks) unsalted butter, melted, plus 4 tablespoons unsalted butter, room temperature
- 1 750-ml bottle dry white wine
- 2 teaspoons kosher salt, plus more for seasoning
- 2 teaspoons freshly ground black pepper, plus more for seasoning
- 1 cup dry red or white wine, or water, for gravy, optional
  Homemade Turkey Stock (recipe follows)

1. Rinse the turkey inside and out with cool water, and dry with paper towels. Let stand for 1 to 2 hours at room temperature.

2. Preheat the oven to 450°F. with a rack on lowest level. Combine melted butter and wine in a bowl. Fold a large piece of cheesecloth into quarters, and cut it into a 17-inch, 4-layer square. Immerse the cheesecloth in the butter and wine; let soak.

3. Place the turkey, breast-side up, on a roasting rack in a heavy metal roasting pan. If the turkey comes with a pop-up timer, remove it; an instant-read thermometer is a much more accurate indication of doneness. Fold the wing tips under the turkey. Sprinkle ½ teaspoon salt and ½ teaspoon pepper inside the turkey. If stuffing the turkey, do so now. Tie the legs together loosely with kitchen twine (a

bow will be easy to untie later). Fold the neck flap under, and secure with toothpicks. Rub the turkey with the softened butter, and sprinkle with 1½ teaspoons salt and 1½ teaspoons pepper.

4. Lift the cheesecloth out of the liquid, and squeeze it slightly, leaving it very damp. Spread it evenly over the breast and about halfway down the sides of the turkey; it can cover some of the leg area. Place the turkey, legs first, in the oven. Cook for 30 minutes. Using a pastry brush, baste the cheesecloth and exposed parts of the turkey with the butter and wine. Reduce oven temperature to 350°F., and continue to cook for 2½ hours more, basting every 30 minutes and watching the pan juices; if the pan gets too full, spoon out the juices, reserving them for the gravy.

5. Carefully remove and discard cheesecloth. Turn roasting pan so the breast is facing the back of the oven. Baste turkey with pan juices. If there are not enough juices, continue to use the butter and wine. The skin gets fragile as it browns, so baste carefully. Cook 1 hour more, basting after 30 minutes.

6. Insert an instant-read thermometer into the thickest part of the thigh. Do not poke into a bone. The temperature should reach 180°F. (the stuffing should be between 140°F. and 160°F.) and the turkey should be golden brown. The breast does not need to be checked for temperature. If the legs are not yet fully cooked, baste the turkey, return to the oven, and cook 20 to 30 minutes more.

7. When fully cooked, remove from the oven, and let rest for about 30 minutes. Transfer to a carving board. Make the gravy: Pour all the pan juices into a glass measuring cup. Let stand until the fat rises to the surface, about 10 minutes, then skim it off. Meanwhile, place the roasting pan over medium-high heat. Add 1 cup red or white wine to the pan. Using a wooden spoon, scrape the pan until the liquid boils and all the browned bits are loosened from the pan. Add the turkey stock to the pan. Stir well and return to a boil. Cook until the liquid has reduced by half, about 10 minutes. Add the defatted pan juices, and cook over medium-high heat 10 minutes more. You will have about 2½ cups of gravy. Season to taste with salt and pepper, strain into a warm gravy boat, and serve with turkey.

homemade turkey stock

MAKES ABOUT 1 QUART

The giblets are the secret to a fine stock and gravy. It can be prepared while the turkey roasts or a day in advance.

  Giblets (heart, gizzard, and liver) and neck reserved from turkey
4 tablespoons unsalted butter
1 onion, cut into ¼-inch dice
1 celery stalk with leaves, strings removed, stalk cut into ¼-inch dice, leaves roughly chopped
1 small leek, white and pale-green parts, cut into ¼-inch dice, well washed (see page 646)
  Kosher salt and freshly ground black pepper
1 dried bay leaf

1. Trim fat or membrane from the giblets. If the liver has the gallbladder attached, trim it off carefully, removing part of the liver if necessary. Do not pierce the sac; the liquid it contains is very bitter. Rinse the giblets and neck, and pat dry.

2. In a medium saucepan, melt 3 tablespoons butter over medium heat. Add the onion, celery and leaves, and leek. Cook, stirring occasionally, until the onion is translucent, about 8 minutes. Season with salt and pepper; cook 5 minutes more. Add 7 cups cold water, the bay leaf, gizzard, heart, and neck. Cover and bring to a boil, then reduce to a simmer. Cook 45 minutes, or until the gizzard is tender when pierced with the tip of a knife.

3. Chop the liver finely. Melt the remaining tablespoon butter in a skillet over medium-low heat. Add liver; cook, stirring constantly, 4 to 6 minutes, until liver no longer releases any blood. Set aside.

4. Simmer the stock until reduced to 2½ cups, about 45 minutes. Increase the heat, and cook 10 to 15 minutes more if necessary.

5. Strain the stock. Chop gizzard and heart very fine; add to the strained stock along with the chopped liver. Pick the meat off the neck, and add to stock. Set aside until needed to make the gravy.

STUFFING A TURKEY

Fill the large cavity and neck cavity loosely with as much stuffing as they hold comfortably. Do not pack tightly, or the stuffing will not cook through (this is particularly dangerous if the stuffing has raw eggs in it). If all the stuffing does not fit, transfer the extra to a buttered baking dish, and bake for 45 minutes in a 375°F. oven. Among our favorite add-ins for stuffing are:

VEGETABLES *They not only add texture and flavor to your stuffing; they also add moisture. Celery and onions are a good place to start, because they have strong flavors that are very compatible, but you may also want to add garlic, carrots, or whatever else looks abundant and delicious in the grocery store. For extra crunch, add the vegetables raw to the stuffing, and let them cook in the bird.*

OYSTERS *The tradition of adding oysters to stuffing dates back to the 19th century, when oysters were cheap and plentiful. While they are more expensive these days, they are worth the splurge and add incomparable flavor and texture to stuffings.*

EGG YOLKS *To add richness to your stuffing, add 2 to 3 egg yolks to it before cooking.*

CARVING A TURKEY

You will need a platter, kitchen scissors, and a 10-inch slicing knife (do not use a serrated blade; it will tear the flesh). Let the bird rest in the pan at room temperature for 20 to 30 minutes after removing it from the oven. Transfer to a carving board. Use your hand to hold the turkey steady while you slice; a carving fork will tear the flesh.

1. With the kitchen scissors, cut through the trussing, and remove all the string.

2. Remove drumsticks. Place the knife against the thigh; cut to expose the leg's second joint. Apply pressure at the joint with the knife, twist, and cut to sever drumstick. Repeat with other drumstick.

3. Slice neck cavity with an oval incision so you can remove stuffing with the skin on top intact. Use a long-handled spoon to scoop out stuffing; transfer it to a bowl.

4. Slice the thigh meat from the bone. The dark meat should be tender from resting in the juices. Repeat on the other side.

5. Place the knife horizontally at the bottom curve of the breast; slice in toward the rib cage to create a "guide cut." Slice again down along the rib cage at the top. This allows the sliced breast to fall away. Cut vertically through the breast meat to create medallion slices (make sure to preserve some skin on each medallion). Repeat on the other side of the breast.

6. Insert knife at first wing joint and twist to sever wing. Repeat with other wing.

Arrange medallions around rim of a platter. Place thigh meat in center; lay drumsticks crossed at one end. Top the platter with wings facing each other, skin-side up.

deep-fried turkey

SERVES 10 TO 12

Martha discovered this most amazing way to cook a turkey during a visit to Auldbrass Plantation in Yemassee, South Carolina. Making this turkey requires effort, but the crisp skin and moist meat that result are well worth it. The 10-gallon "frying" pot is available at large housewares stores. This turkey must be cooked outdoors.

- 1   *12- to 15-pound fresh turkey*
- 25   *medium whole dried bay leaves*
- 1   *tablespoon plus ¼ teaspoon dried thyme*
- 1   *tablespoon plus ¼ teaspoon dried oregano*
- 1½   *teaspoons whole black peppercorns*
- 3   *tablespoons Konriko brand, or other hot, Creole seasoning*
- 2   *teaspoons garlic powder*
- 4   *gallons peanut oil*

1. Rinse turkey inside and out with cool running water; pat dry with paper towels. Finely grind bay leaves in a spice grinder; transfer to a small bowl. Finely grind thyme, oregano, and peppercorns separately; add to bay leaves. Mix in Creole seasoning and garlic powder. Rub one-third of the spice mixture on the inside of turkey, one-third under the skin of the breasts, and one-third on the outside of the turkey; place in a roasting pan. Cover; marinate in the refrigerator overnight or up to 24 hours.

2. Bring the turkey to room temperature, about 1 hour. Using a wooden skewer, thread the neck flap securely to the bottom of the turkey. Fold the wing tips under. Using a steel or aluminum wire, tie the legs and pope's nose together securely; form a handle with the wire. This will enable you to hold the turkey while submerging it in the hot oil.

3. Heat oil in a 10-gallon pot with a liner basket over high heat until the temperature registers 360°F. Holding turkey by wire handle, carefully immerse in the hot oil. Maintain temperature at 360°F. while frying. Fry until golden brown, about 45 minutes, or 3 minutes per pound. Carefully lift turkey from oil; transfer to a wire rack over a roasting pan. Drain 15 minutes. Serve.

roast turkey breast and gravy

SERVES 8; MAKES 1½ CUPS GRAVY

Fresh turkey breast is easy to find frozen in your grocery store, or ask your butcher. Reserve the other half of the turkey breast for Open-Face Turkey Sandwiches (*page 170*).

- 1 6-pound turkey breast, room temperature
- 1 teaspoon kosher salt
- ¼ teaspoon freshly ground black pepper
- 3 large onions, sliced in half
- 3 carrots, sliced in half lengthwise
- 3 celery stalks
- 3 tablespoons all-purpose flour
- ¼ cup Madeira wine
- 2 cups Homemade Turkey Stock (page 270), or low-sodium store-bought chicken broth, skimmed of fat

1. Preheat the oven to 425°F. Rinse the turkey breast with cool water; pat dry with paper towels. Rub the breast with the salt and pepper.

2. Scatter a roasting pan with the onions, carrots, and celery; place the turkey over the vegetables. Roast until the breast is cooked through and an instant-read thermometer inserted into the thickest part registers 170°F, about 1½ hours.

3. Cut the breast in half; transfer half to a cutting board, tent with foil to keep warm, and set aside.

4. Place the roasting pan over two medium-high heat burners on the stove. Sprinkle the cooked vegetables and drippings with the flour, and cook, stirring constantly, until the flour forms a golden-brown film over the bottom of the roasting pan and the vegetables are completely coated with the film and the turkey drippings, 2 to 3 minutes. Do not let the pan get too hot, or the drippings will burn.

5. Pour the Madeira slowly into the pan, and cook, scraping up the film from the pan with a wooden spoon until a thin paste forms, about 1 minute.

Slowly add the stock, stirring, until the paste thins to a thick liquid. Continue adding the stock, stirring, until the gravy is the desired consistency. Season with salt, pepper, and a splash more Madeira, if desired. Strain the gravy through a fine sieve or cheesecloth-lined strainer, pressing down on the solids with a rubber spatula to extract the juices and flavor. Discard the solids; transfer the gravy to a heat-proof bowl set over a pan of simmering water until ready to serve with the roast turkey.

turkey picadillo

SERVES 12

- ¼ cup olive oil
- 2 medium onions, finely diced
- 6 garlic cloves, minced
- 2 red bell peppers, seeds and ribs removed, finely diced
- 2 green bell peppers, seeds and ribs removed, finely diced
- 4 pounds ground turkey
- 2½ teaspoons ground cumin
- 1 tablespoon ground oregano
- 2 teaspoons dried tarragon
- 1 teaspoon ground coriander
- 5 dried bay leaves
  Kosher salt and freshly ground black pepper
- 2 cups dry white wine
- 2 cups tomato purée
- ½ cup Homemade Chicken Stock (page 624), or low-sodium store-bought chicken broth, skimmed of fat
- ¾ cup raisins
- 1 cup pimiento-stuffed green olives, thinly sliced crosswise
  Cuban Black Beans (page 334)
- 12 Fried Eggs (page 571), optional

1. Heat oil in a wide, shallow stockpot over medium heat. Add onions and garlic; cook, without browning, 4 minutes. Add bell peppers; cook until onions are soft and translucent, about 8 minutes.

2. Raise heat to high; add turkey, cumin, oregano, tarragon, coriander, and bay leaves. Season with salt and pepper. Break the meat up into small pieces; cook until opaque, about 7 minutes. Add wine; cook until most of the liquid has been absorbed, about 15 minutes. Reduce heat to medium low. Add the tomato purée and chicken stock; stir to combine. Simmer until most of the liquid has been absorbed, about 20 minutes. Stir in the raisins and olives; cook 2 minutes. Serve with black beans; top with fried eggs, if using.

turkey and green chile burritos
SERVES 4

Look for poblano peppers with smooth skins and no dark spots.

- 3 roasted poblano peppers (see page 645)
- 1 medium onion, coarsely chopped
- 1 garlic clove, minced
- 1 tablespoon olive oil
- ½ fresh boneless turkey breast (about 1½ pounds), cut into 1-inch cubes
    Kosher salt and freshly ground black pepper
- 8 small red potatoes, unpeeled, cut into 1-inch cubes
- 1¾ cups Homemade Chicken Stock (page 624), or low-sodium store-bought chicken broth, skimmed of fat
- 4 12-inch flour tortillas
- 4 ounces Monterey Jack cheese, grated

1. Cut roasted peppers into strips, and set aside.

2. Preheat the oven to 350°F. Cook the onion and the garlic in the olive oil in a deep skillet over medium-low heat until translucent, about 5 minutes. Add the turkey, raise heat to medium, and cook until the meat is golden brown, about 5 minutes. Season with salt and pepper; add the potatoes and the stock. Reduce heat to medium low, cover, and simmer until the potatoes and turkey are cooked, about 10 minutes. Uncover; raise heat to medium; cook to reduce liquid, about 8 minutes. Add the reserved poblano peppers.

3. Place a quarter of the mixture on a tortilla, midway between the center and the edge nearest you.

Sprinkle with a quarter of the cheese. Fold the right and left sides of tortilla over the filling and roll up the tortilla away from you. Repeat with the other tortillas, place in a baking dish, cover with foil, and bake until heated through, about 15 minutes.

....
GAME BIRDS
....

grilled duck breasts with cherry-plum sauce
SERVES 4

Whole Szechuan peppercorns (see Food Sources, page 648) are a mildly hot spice with a distinctive flavor and fragrance. Make this dish in early summer, when cherries and plums are in season.

- ½ cup Sour-Cherry Preserves (page 615) or prepared
- 1 tablespoon whole Szechuan peppercorns
- 2 whole boneless duck breasts (about 1 pound each)
    Kosher salt and freshly ground black pepper
- 4 tablespoons unsalted butter
- 6 ounces red cherries, stemmed, pitted, and halved
- 4 red plums, pitted, cut into eighths
- 1 tablespoon plus 2 teaspoons sugar
- 1 teaspoon finely chopped fresh thyme
- 1 cup ruby port
- 2 tablespoons red-wine vinegar

1. Preheat the oven to 500°F. Place the sour-cherry preserves in the bowl of a food processor, and purée. Transfer to a small bowl; set aside. Place the peppercorns on a clean cutting board. Using the side of a heavy knife, press down on the peppercorns until they are coarsely crushed, and set aside.

2. Cut both the duck breasts in half, and trim away any excess fat, leaving the skin attached to the breasts. Season both sides of the duck breasts with salt and pepper. Spread 1 tablespoon of the puréed preserves on the flesh side of each breast; sprinkle with half of the crushed peppercorns.

3. Place the duck breasts, flesh-side down, in a medium ovenproof skillet. Spread 1 tablespoon of the puréed preserves on the skin side of each breast; sprinkle with the remaining crushed peppercorns. Place the skillet in the oven; roast until medium rare, 10 to 12 minutes. Remove from the oven; set aside in a warm place.

4. Melt the butter in large skillet over medium-high heat. Add the cherries, plums, sugar, and thyme. Season with salt and pepper. Cook until the sugar dissolves, 1 to 2 minutes. Add the port. Strike a match, and carefully ignite the port; cook until the flame dies out. Add the vinegar, and cook until the juices thicken, 10 to 15 minutes. Remove from the heat. Transfer the duck to a serving dish, and pour the fruit sauce over top. Serve hot.

braised duck with sparkling cider and wild mushrooms

SERVES 2

Use nonalcoholic sparkling cider to give this dish a sweet-tart flavor. Ask your butcher to quarter the duck for you.

- 1 *5-pound duck, quartered*
- 2 *shallots, minced*
- 1 *tablespoon fresh rosemary, finely chopped, or a large pinch dried*
- 6 *sprigs fresh thyme or a large pinch dried*
- 1 *pound turnips, cut into 1½- to 2-inch pieces*
- 1 *teaspoon sugar*
- 2 *cups sparkling cider*
- 1 *cup Brown Game Stock (recipe follows), Homemade Chicken Stock (page 624), or low-sodium store-bought chicken broth, skimmed of fat*
- *Kosher salt and freshly ground black pepper*
- 1 *tablespoon olive oil*
- 8 *ounces assorted wild mushrooms, wiped clean and trimmed*
- ½ *teaspoon cider vinegar*

1. Cut the wing tips from the duck below the first joint. Trim the flesh from the wing bone and discard. Remove the excess skin and fat from the duck. Save the bones for the stock.

2. Prick the skin all over with a fork. In a large, deep, heavy skillet, cook the duck over medium heat, skin-side down, until most of the fat is rendered and the skin is golden brown, about 15 minutes. Drain and discard the fat from the pan periodically. Turn and cook 5 minutes more. Transfer the duck to a plate. Drain the remaining fat from the pan.

3. Add the shallots to the skillet, and cook over low heat for 2 minutes, scraping up the brown bits. Add the rosemary, 4 sprigs thyme, and turnips. Cook 2 minutes more. Add the sugar, cider, and stock; season with salt and pepper. Bring to a boil. Return the duck to the pan, reduce heat, cover, and simmer for 10 minutes. Remove the breasts, and continue cooking the legs until tender, about 25 minutes more.

4. Remove the legs and turnips. Strain the stock; discard the solids. Skim and discard the fat. Pour the sauce into a clean skillet.

5. In a medium pan, heat the oil over high heat. Add the mushrooms; cook until soft, about 5 minutes. Season with salt and pepper.

6. Add the mushrooms, turnips, and legs to the sauce. Add the vinegar and the remaining thyme. Bring to a boil, and cook over medium heat until the sauce is thick enough to coat the back of a spoon, 5 to 10 minutes, turning the legs once or twice. Add breasts to heat through, and serve hot.

brown game stock

MAKES ABOUT 1 QUART

For the clearest stock, simmer the liquid over very low heat, and don't stir it.

- 2 pounds game-bird or poultry bones
- 3 carrots, coarsely chopped
- 3 celery stalks, coarsely chopped
- 1 onion, quartered, with skin on
- 1 tablespoon tomato paste
- 2 garlic cloves, peeled
- 2 dried bay leaves
  Fresh flat-leaf parsley stems
- 1 sprig fresh rosemary or a large pinch of dried
- 4 sprigs fresh thyme or a large pinch of dried
- 1 tablespoon whole black peppercorns

1. Preheat the oven to 400°F. Rinse and pat the bones dry. Place in a roasting pan, and roast for 20 minutes, or until they begin to brown.

2. Add the carrots, celery, onion, and tomato paste to the roasting pan, and continue roasting, stirring occasionally, for 30 minutes more, or until brown and caramelized. (These two steps are what will give this game stock its rich color and flavor.)

3. Transfer the bones and vegetables to a large stockpot. Skim off and discard the fat from the pan; add 1 cup water. Cook over medium heat, scraping up any browned bits with a wooden spoon. Transfer to the stockpot. Add 2 quarts plus 3 cups water, the garlic, bay leaves, parsley stems, rosemary, thyme, and peppercorns.

4. Cover and bring the stock to a boil and simmer over very low heat for about 5 hours, skimming often to remove any foam from the top of the stock.

5. Remove the pot from the heat, and let cool slightly. Strain the stock carefully through a fine sieve or a cheesecloth-lined strainer. Cool completely. The stock may be frozen up to 4 months.

cornish hens with kasha pilaf

SERVES 4

- 4 tablespoons butter
- 1 medium onion, cut into ¼-inch dice
- 8 ounces white mushrooms, wiped clean, stemmed, quartered
- ½ cup whole kasha
- 2½ cups Homemade Chicken Stock (page 624), or low-sodium store-bought chicken broth, skimmed of fat
  Kosher salt and freshly ground black pepper
  All-purpose flour, for dredging
- 2 2-pound Cornish hens, split, with backbones reserved
- ¼ cup dry white wine
- 8 ounces orecchiette pasta
- ⅓ cup loosely packed fresh flat-leaf parsley, finely chopped

1. Preheat the oven to 425°F; place a roasting pan in it. Melt 2 tablespoons butter in a skillet over medium heat. Add onion, cook about 10 minutes. Add mushrooms; cook until tender. Add kasha and 2 cups stock. Cook until kasha is tender and the liquid has been absorbed, about 20 minutes. Season with salt and pepper, and set aside.

2. Flour the hens, shaking off any excess flour, and set aside on a plate. Melt 1½ tablespoons butter in a cast-iron skillet over medium-high heat. Cook the hens, skin-side down, with the backbones, until golden brown, 6 to 8 minutes. Turn and cook 3 to 5 minutes more. Transfer to the roasting pan; roast until the skin is dark brown and the juices run clear when pierced with a fork, about 20 minutes.

3. Discard the grease from the skillet. Over high heat, add the wine to the skillet, and use a wooden spoon to loosen any browned bits from the bottom of the pan. Reduce heat, add the remaining ½ cup of stock, and cook until reduced by a third, 5 minutes. Stir in the remaining ½ tablespoon of butter.

4. Cover and bring a large pot of salted water to a boil. Drop the orecchiette into the boiling water; stir to keep the pasta from sticking together. Cook until al dente; drain. Stir the pasta and parsley into the kasha. Season with salt and pepper, and heat through. Serve the hens over the kasha pilaf, and spoon the sauce over the hens.

roast goose with dressing 101

SERVES 6

A holiday roast goose served with apricot stuffing makes a beautiful presentation. Unlike a roast chicken or turkey, roast goose requires no basting as it cooks; its high fat content keeps the goose moist and tender. Unless you have a special source for fresh geese, most are only available frozen.

- 1 12-pound frozen goose, giblets reserved
  Kosher salt and freshly ground black pepper
- 3 medium carrots, scrubbed and cut in half
- 3 celery stalks, cut in half
- 1 head of garlic, cut in half crosswise
- 1 bunch fresh thyme
- 1 bunch fresh sage
- 1 medium onion, cut in half
- 8 sprigs fresh flat-leaf parsley
- 1 dried bay leaf
- 1 teaspoon whole black peppercorns
- ½ cup dry white wine
- 1 tablespoon unsalted butter

1. If the goose is frozen, place it in the refrigerator overnight to thaw. Remove the goose from the refrigerator, and let it stand at room temperature for 30 minutes. Preheat the oven to 400°F. Rinse the goose inside and out with cool water, and pat it dry with paper towels. Trim as much of the excess fat as possible from the opening of the cavity. Remove the first and second joints of the wings, and set them aside for use in making the stock.

2. With the point of a sharp knife, prick the entire surface of the goose skin, being careful not to cut into the flesh. Fold the neck flap under the body of the goose, and pin the flap down with a wooden toothpick. Generously sprinkle the cavity with salt and pepper, and insert 2 carrot halves, 2 celery-stalk

halves, the garlic, thyme, and sage. Using a piece of kitchen twine, tie the legs together. Generously sprinkle the outside of the goose with salt and pepper, and place it, breast-side up, on a wire rack set in a large roasting pan.

3. Roast the goose in the oven until it turns golden brown, about 1 hour. With a baster, remove as much fat as possible from the roasting pan every 30 minutes. Reduce heat to 325°F, and roast until the goose is very well browned all over and an instant-read thermometer inserted into a breast, without touching a bone, registers 180°F, about 1 hour after reducing the temperature.

4. Meanwhile, prepare the goose stock, which will be used when making the gravy and the dressing. Trim and discard any excess fat from the wing tips, neck, and giblets, and place them in a small stockpot. Add 4 carrot halves, 4 celery-stalk halves, both onion halves, the parsley, bay leaf, peppercorns, and enough water to cover the bones and vegetables by 1 inch (about 2½ quarts water). Place the stockpot over high heat, and bring to a boil. Reduce heat to medium low, and simmer the stock, skimming the foam as it rises, for 2 hours. Strain the stock through a fine sieve or cheesecloth-lined strainer. Remove and discard the fat floating on the surface of the stock, and set the stockpot aside.

5. Remove the goose from the oven, and transfer it to a cutting board that has a well. Let the goose stand 15 to 20 minutes.

6. Meanwhile, prepare the gravy. Pour off all the fat from the roasting pan, and place the pan on the stove over high heat. Pour in the wine, and cook, stirring with a wooden spoon to loosen any browned bits from the bottom of the pan, until the cooking liquid is reduced by three-quarters. Add 2 cups of the goose stock, and cook, stirring until the liquid is again reduced by three-quarters. Season with salt and pepper. Stir in the butter, and cook until slightly thickened. Pass the gravy through a fine sieve or cheesecloth-lined strainer into a gravy boat, and serve with the goose.

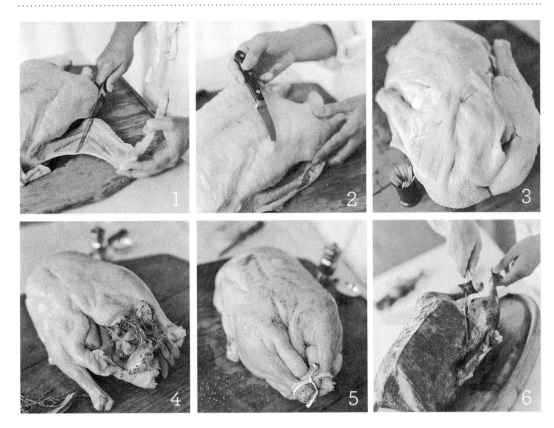

ROASTING A GOOSE

1. A 12-pound goose ought to provide enough meat to serve six people. The wings contain little meat, so first and second joints should be removed before cooking (otherwise, they will burn). Save the wings to make the goose stock, which will be used to make the gravy.

2. Because geese have so much fat, it helps to trim away as much of it as possible before cooking. You should be able to remove between a third and a half pound from the cavity alone. Even so, plenty will remain to keep the meat moist. A 12-pound goose yields about 2 cups of fat during roasting, as compared with virtually none from a turkey of similar size.

3. If not properly secured, the flap of neck skin may dangle and burn during roasting. To prevent this, turn the goose breast side down, fold the flap over the body, and secure it with toothpicks or skewers.

4. Because of the amount of fat that drips as the bird roasts, any dressing is best cooked separately. Instead, stuff the cavity with a head of garlic, some celery and carrots, and a bundle of fresh thyme and sage to impart aroma and flavor to the bird.

5. Rather than trussing the bird, all that's required is to tie the legs together with kitchen twine. This will keep the legs from splaying as the goose cooks,

thereby ensuring that the bird retains its form for serving at the table.

6. To carve the goose, first gently pull one leg away from the body, and cut through the joint. Remove the other leg the same way, and set them aside. Find the breast bone, and cut down along one side between the breast bone and the meat until you reach the wing joint. Holding the meat with the fork, gradually cut the meat away from the breast bone and rib cage.

roast-goose dressing

SERVES 6

A goose is always served with dressing because it releases so much fat while roasting—stuffing would be too greasy. Prepare the dressing in an ovenproof casserole; the dressing may be made up to 1 day ahead and refrigerated, uncooked and covered with plastic wrap, in the casserole. Cooked chestnuts are available in jars from specialty food stores (12 nuts weigh about 3 ounces).

2½ cups plus 2 tablespoons homemade goose stock (see step 4 of Roast Goose recipe, page 276), Homemade Chicken Stock (page 624), or low-sodium store-bought chicken broth, skimmed of fat

1 cup wild rice

4½ tablespoons unsalted butter

4 ounces shiitake, cremini, or white-button mushrooms, wiped clean, stemmed, quartered

1 medium onion, cut into ¼-inch dice

2 garlic cloves, minced

1 celery stalk, strings removed, cut into ¼-inch dice

Kosher salt and freshly ground black pepper

½ cup white rice

1 Granny Smith apple, peeled cored, cut into ¼-inch dice

⅔ cup dried apricots (3 ounces), quartered

12 canned or vacuum-packed cooked chestnuts, cut in half

½ cup slivered almonds, toasted (see page 644)

2 teaspoons finely chopped fresh rosemary

1 tablespoon finely chopped fresh sage

2 tablespoons finely chopped fresh thyme

2 tablespoons finely chopped fresh flat-leaf parsley

1. In a small saucepan over medium-low heat, bring 1½ cups stock to a simmer. Add the wild rice, cover, reduce heat to low, and cook until all the liquid is absorbed, 45 to 60 minutes. Meanwhile, in a medium skillet over high heat, melt 1 tablespoon butter. Add mushrooms; cook until browned, about 3 minutes. Remove skillet from heat; set aside.

2. Preheat the oven to 375°F. Melt 2 tablespoons butter in a medium saucepan over medium heat. Add the onion, garlic, celery, salt, and pepper, and cook, stirring occasionally, until the onions begin to brown, about 15 minutes. Stir in the white rice, and cook for 2 minutes. Add ¾ cup stock, and bring to a simmer. Cover, reduce heat to low, and cook until the liquid is absorbed, about 20 minutes.

3. Butter a 1½-quart ovenproof casserole with ½ tablespoon butter, and set aside. In a medium bowl, combine the white- and wild-rice mixtures, the apple, apricots, chestnuts, almonds, the remaining ¼ cup plus 2 tablespoons of the stock, the rosemary, sage, thyme, parsley, and salt and pepper; transfer to the prepared casserole. Dot the dressing with the remaining tablespoon of butter, and cook until hot, about 20 minutes. Remove from the oven, and serve immediately with the roast goose.

citrus marinated quail

SERVES 4

These small birds have delicately flavored white meat. The perfect size for a first course, the quail also make an elegant lunch.

- 4 5-ounce quail
- 1 teaspoon dark sesame oil
- 1 teaspoon canola oil
   Zest and juice of 1 orange
   Juice of 1 lime
- 2 tablespoons honey
- 2 tablespoons soy sauce
- 1 garlic clove, smashed
- ½ teaspoon freshly ground black pepper
- 1 1-inch piece of fresh ginger, peeled, finely chopped
   Kosher salt
- 4 ounces soba noodles or spaghetti
- 2 tablespoons sesame seeds, toasted (see page 644)
- 3 cups loosely packed pea shoots or watercress leaves

1. Butterfly the quail by placing it on a cutting board, breast side up, inserting a knife into the cavity, and cutting down through the backbone. Cut off and discard the wing tips.

2. In a medium nonreactive bowl, mix together the sesame and canola oils, the orange zest and juice, the lime juice, honey, soy sauce, garlic, black pepper, and ginger until combined. Add the quail, and cover with plastic wrap. Refrigerate for several hours, turning several times.

3. Heat a grill or a grill pan to medium hot. Remove the quail from the marinade, and place on the hot grill, skin-side down. Cook until brown, 5 to 7 minutes, basting occasionally with the marinade. Turn quail, baste, and cook for 5 minutes more.

4. Meanwhile, cover large pot of salted water, bring to a boil, and add the noodles. Cook until al dente, about 3 minutes. Drain in a colander, and set aside.

5. Pour the remaining marinade into a saucepan. Bring to a strong boil over high heat. Boil until slightly thickened, 2 to 3 minutes. Strain and place in a clean saucepan. Add the noodles; simmer until heated through. Stir in the sesame seeds. Divide the noodles and pea shoots among four plates. Place a quail on top, and serve hot.

spice-rubbed hens

SERVES 4

The spice mixture forms a crisp crust on the hens when cooked, creating a juicy and flavorful interior. The mixture may also be used on chicken.

- 4 poussin (baby chickens) or Cornish game hens
- ¼ cup sweet paprika
- ¼ cup hot paprika
- ¼ cup cumin seeds, toasted (see page 644)
- 1½ teaspoons kosher salt

1. Preheat the oven to 400°F. Rinse the birds and pat dry. Mix the spices with the salt and rub the birds inside and out. Transfer to a roasting pan. Cook for 15 minutes, reduce heat to 350°F.

2. Cook until the juices run clear, about 45 minutes. Baste every 10 minutes or so. (Don't baste for the last 10 minutes to allow the skin to crisp.) Let the hens rest for 10 minutes before serving.

FOR ASIAN-RUBBED HENS *Substitute 1 cup Chinese Five-Spice Powder (page 633) for the paprika mix.*

FOR CURRY HENS *Rub hens with 2 teaspoons honey and substitute 1 cup Curry Powder (page 633) for the paprika mix.*

fish
AND
shellfish

·······················

braised flounder
with chinese cabbage

SERVES 6

Look for high-quality frozen fish stock at specialty food stores. It will keep in the freezer up to 3 months.

 1 1½-inch piece fresh ginger, peeled

 3 cups Fish Stock (page 628), or frozen fish stock, thawed

 1 large leek, white and pale-green parts, cut into ¼-inch-thick slices, well washed (see page 646)

 3 whole star anise

 3 tablespoons dry sherry

1½ tablespoons low-sodium soy sauce

 1 teaspoon canola oil

 2 shallots, minced

 3 garlic cloves, minced

12 ounces white-button mushrooms, wiped clean, cut into ¼-inch-thick pieces

    Freshly ground black pepper

10 canned water chestnuts, cut crosswise into ¼-inch-thick slices

 1 head Napa cabbage, cut crosswise into ½-inch-thick slices

 6 scallions, white and green parts, thinly sliced on a diagonal, plus more for garnish

 6 5-ounce flounder fillets

    Kosher salt

1. Thinly slice half the ginger; cut the remaining half into 1½-inch-long matchsticks, and reserve. Place the sliced ginger, the stock, leek, star anise, sherry, and soy sauce in a small saucepan. Cover; bring to a boil. Reduce heat; simmer 15 minutes. Strain stock through a fine sieve or cheesecloth-lined strainer; discard solids and reserve stock.

2. In a straight-sided skillet, heat oil over medium-low heat. Add shallots and garlic; cook until translucent, about 5 minutes. Add mushrooms; season with pepper. Raise heat to medium high; cook until golden brown, about 7 minutes. Add chestnuts; cook 2 minutes. Transfer mixture to a bowl.

3. Place the cabbage and the sliced scallions in the skillet. Season the fillets with salt and pepper. Roll up the fillets; place on the cabbage. Add the reserved fish stock and the cooked vegetables. Cover and bring to a boil. Reduce heat; simmer until the fish has cooked through, about 15 minutes. Garnish with the ginger matchsticks and the scallions.

FIT TO EAT RECIPE PER SERVING: 215 CALORIES, 3 G FAT, 69 MG CHOLESTEROL, 11 G CARBOHYDRATE, 430 MG SODIUM, 32 G PROTEIN, 2 G DIETARY FIBER

panfried trout with lemon

SERVES 8

 8 medium (9 to 10 ounces each) brook trout, scaled, gutted, and cleaned (gills removed)

 2 teaspoons kosher salt, plus more for seasoning

 ¼ teaspoon freshly ground black pepper, plus more for seasoning

 ½ cup all-purpose flour

 4 lemons, cut into ¼-inch rounds

1½ tablespoons unsalted butter

1½ tablespoons olive oil

1½ tablespoons sesame oil, optional

1. Rinse the trout and pat dry. Combine salt, pepper, and flour on a plate. Season the insides of the fish with salt and pepper. Insert 3 slices of lemon inside each; dredge in flour, and shake off excess.

2. Heat ½ tablespoon butter, ½ tablespoon olive oil, and ½ tablespoon sesame oil, if using, in an 11-inch skillet over medium-high heat. Add 3 trout, and arrange 4 or 5 lemon slices around the fish. Cook until golden brown, 5 to 6 minutes. If the lemon slices begin to burn, put them on top of the fish. Turn the fish, and cook until it has a golden crust and is flaky and moist, 5 to 6 minutes more.

3. Remove fish from skillet, and keep warm on a plate covered with aluminum foil. Repeat twice with remaining trout, butter, oils, and lemon slices. Serve fish with cooked lemon slices.

grilled lemon-rosemary trout

SERVES 4

Using fish-grilling baskets (see Equipment Sources, page 650) prevents the skin of the fish from sticking to the grill and makes grilling and turning whole fish easy. The lemon slices inside the trout flavor the fish and prevent it from drying out.

- 2 tablespoons olive oil, plus more for brushing
- 2 large lemons
- 1 tablespoon capers, drained
- ½ teaspoon kosher salt, plus more for seasoning
- ¼ teaspoon freshly ground black pepper, plus more for seasoning
- 2 1-pound whole trout, scaled and gutted (gills and fins removed)
- 2 sprigs fresh rosemary
- 1 fennel bulb

1. Brush a grill or grilling basket with olive oil. Heat grill until very hot. Slice half of 1 lemon as thinly as possible. Squeeze the other half to yield 2 tablespoons juice. Place lemon juice, capers, 1 tablespoon oil, ½ teaspoon salt, and ¼ teaspoon pepper in a small bowl; whisk to combine. Set aside. Stuff each trout with half the lemon slices and a rosemary sprig. Season with salt and pepper.

2. Cut the fennel into wedges and the remaining lemon into ¼-inch-thick slices. Brush trout, fennel, and lemon slices with the remaining tablespoon of oil. Place fennel and lemons on the grill; cook until golden brown, about 1½ minutes per side for lemons and 3 minutes per side for fennel. Remove from grill; arrange on a serving platter.

3. Place trout in grilling basket, if using; transfer to grill; cook several minutes, until browned and cooked through (times will vary depending on the heat of the grill and the distance of the fish from the heat). The fish should feel firm; the skin should pull away from the flesh. Transfer to the serving platter. Spoon sauce over fish, fennel, and lemons.

When ready to serve, cut along the back, and lift fillet away from bones, then pull up to remove skeleton and head from bottom fillet. Serve.

FIT TO EAT RECIPE PER SERVING: 215 CALORIES, 3 G FAT, 69 MG CHOLESTEROL, 11 G CARBOHYDRATE, 430 MG SODIUM, 32 G PROTEIN, 2 G DIETARY FIBER

sole grenobloise

SERVES 4

The delicate flavor of sole is complemented by briny capers and lemon in this classic French preparation.

- 1½ cups milk
- 1 cup all-purpose flour
- ¼ cup olive oil
- 4 5-ounce lemon- or gray-sole fillets
  Kosher salt and freshly ground black pepper
- 5 tablespoons unsalted butter
- ¼ cup capers, drained
  Juice of 1 lemon
  Fresh flat-leaf parsley, for garnish

1. Pour the milk into a shallow bowl. Put the flour on a dinner plate or other flat dish. In a medium skillet set over medium-high heat, heat 2 tablespoons oil until hot. Place 2 fillets in the milk. Remove one; dredge both sides in the flour. Tap off excess flour, and transfer the fish to the oil. Repeat with the second fillet. Season each with salt and pepper. Cook the fish until browned on both sides, about 2 minutes per side. Transfer to a serving plate. Repeat with the remaining oil and fish.

2. Wipe the pan clean with folded paper towels; return to medium heat. Add the butter; cook until melted and starting to brown, about 1½ minutes. Stir in the capers; cook until the butter is golden brown, 1 to 2 minutes. Remove from the heat. Squeeze the lemon juice over the fish. Top with the hot butter and capers. Garnish with the parsley. Serve immediately.

roasted sea bass

SERVES 4

Bring the fish to the table whole, with the warm sauce poured over it, and cut it using a fish server for a dramatic presentation.

- 1 2½-pound sea bass, scaled, gutted, and cleaned (gills removed)
- ½ cup plus 2 tablespoons extra-virgin olive oil, plus more for brushing
  - Kosher salt and freshly ground black pepper
- 2 small fresh red chile peppers
- 20 sprigs fresh thyme
- 1 lime, thinly sliced crosswise
- 1 large beefsteak tomato, sliced ¼ inch thick
- 1 large onion, sliced crosswise ⅛ inch thick
- ¼ cup plus 2 tablespoons sweet white wine, such as a sweet Riesling
- 1 tablespoon fresh lime juice

1. Preheat the broiler. Score the sea bass at 1-inch intervals. Brush the inside cavity of the fish with olive oil, and season with salt and pepper on both sides. Place the chile peppers and 10 thyme sprigs inside the cavity. Brush both sides of the fish with olive oil, and season with salt and pepper.

2. In a 10 x 18-inch roasting pan, or one large enough to hold the fish, arrange the lime, tomato, and onion slices so they form a bed for the fish, and season with salt and pepper. Place the fish on top, and pour 6 tablespoons olive oil over it.

3. Transfer roasting pan to broiler, and cook the fish for 10 minutes, until the skin is slightly crisp on top. Remove the pan from the oven, and reduce heat to 400°F. Add the wine to the roasting pan, and return the fish to the oven to roast until it is opaque and cooked through, about 35 minutes.

4. Remove the pan from the oven, and transfer the fish to a large serving platter.

5. Pick 1 teaspoon thyme leaves from the remaining sprigs. Place the vegetables from the roasting pan into a sieve, and strain the juices into a bowl, pressing out any additional juices from the vegetables to create a sauce. Stir the thyme leaves and

the remaining olive oil into this sauce; season with salt and pepper, and add lime juice to taste. Gently reheat the sauce in a small saucepan over low heat; do not to let it boil. Fillet the fish. Pour the sauce over the fillets, and serve.

striped bass with ginger-lime sauce

SERVES 8

- 3 medium garlic cloves
- 3 Thai bird chiles or 2 serrano peppers
- 1 1½-inch piece fresh ginger, peeled
- ½ teaspoon ground-chile paste, or to taste
- 2 tablespoons Asian fish sauce (nam pla)
- 1 tablespoon fresh lime juice
- 2 tablespoons sugar
- 4 8-ounce boneless striped-bass fillets, skin on
- 2 tablespoons canola oil
- 2 scallions, white and green parts, cut in matchsticks
- ½ medium carrot, cut in matchsticks
- 5 sprigs fresh cilantro

1. Smash 1 garlic clove. Halve 1 chile lengthwise. Grate 1-inch piece of ginger. Mix these with the chile paste on a cutting board. Mince together to form a paste, and transfer to a bowl. Stir in the fish sauce, lime juice, sugar, and 2 tablespoons water. Thinly slice remaining chiles diagonally; cut remaining ginger into matchsticks; add to the bowl. Thinly slice remaining garlic, and set aside.

2. Cut the fillets in half crosswise. In a large non-stick skillet, heat the oil over high heat. Add the fillets, skin-side down, and scatter the sliced garlic over the fish. Cook just until golden brown, and very crisp on the outside, 2 to 3 minutes per side. Transfer to a platter. Pour the sauce over the fish, and sprinkle with the scallions, carrots, and cilantro. Serve hot.

striped bass en papillote
SERVES 2

Cooking "en papillote," or in paper, locks in the steam created as the fish cooks, keeping it super moist. Aluminum foil will produce the same results in less time; bake for 12 to 15 minutes.

- 1 teaspoon extra-virgin olive oil, plus more for drizzling
- 4 large garlic cloves
- 2 tablespoons unsalted butter, melted
- 2 6- to 8-ounce striped-bass fillets, skin removed
    Kosher salt and freshly ground black pepper
- 2 shallots, thinly sliced
- 2 plum tomatoes, sliced
    Grated zest of 1 orange
    Several sprigs of fresh thyme or ½ teaspoon dried
- ¼ cup oil-cured olives, pitted
- 2 tablespoons dry white wine or fresh orange juice

1. Preheat the oven to 375°F. Heat the oil in a small skillet, and cook the garlic until well browned on all sides. Set aside.

2. Fold two large pieces of parchment paper in half, and cut half a heart shape, 3 inches larger than the fillets, out of each. Brush the insides with melted butter. Place a fillet on the parchment, about 2 inches away from the crease on each sheet.

3. Season the fillets with salt and pepper, and divide the garlic, shallots, tomatoes, zest, thyme, olives, and white wine between the fillets. Drizzle with olive oil.

4. Starting at top of heart shape, fold over and make long pleats around edges of parchment to make an airtight seal. Finish by twisting the end.

5. Place the packets on a baking sheet, and bake until they are browned and puffed, 15 to 20 minutes. Serve immediately in the parchment, or remove and transfer to a plate.

roast cod with leeks, plum tomatoes, and wilted spinach
SERVES 6

If your fillets have skin on one side, begin cooking the fish skin-side down. If using cod steaks, remove the dark skin from around the edges before serving.

- 2 tablespoons olive oil, plus more for brushing
- 2 tablespoons freshly grated ginger with juices
- 2 tablespoons low-sodium soy sauce
- ¼ cup plus 1 tablespoon fresh lime juice
    Freshly ground black pepper
- 2 pounds leeks, white and pale-green parts, cut in ¾-inch rings, well washed (see page 646)
- 2 pounds plum tomatoes, quartered into wedges
- 6 5- to 6-ounce codfish fillets or steaks, skin on, 1 to 1¼ inches at thickest point
    Kosher salt
- 1 pound fresh spinach, washed, stems removed

1. Preheat the oven to 425°F. with two racks centered. Brush two 12 x 14-inch roasting pans with olive oil. In a bowl, combine ginger, soy sauce, lime juice, olive oil, and pepper to taste. Set aside.

2. Arrange the leeks and tomatoes in one pan and the cod in the second pan. Brush liberally with the ginger marinade. Season the fillets with salt and pepper. Cook vegetables 15 minutes. Turn the vegetables with a spatula for even browning, and begin to cook the cod. Continue to cook until the cod is opaque throughout, 10 to 14 minutes more. Transfer the cod to a serving plate, and keep warm. Add the spinach to the pan, and cook just long enough to wilt, about 5 minutes. To serve, arrange the spinach on each plate; add 1 cod fillet. Divide the tomato mixture evenly among the plates. Serve hot.

FIT TO EAT RECIPE PER SERVING: 297 CALORIES, 7 G FAT, 78 MG CHOLESTEROL, 24 G CARBOHYDRATE, 385 MG SODIUM, 37 G PROTEIN, 5 G DIETARY FIBER

codfish cakes

SERVES 4

Using a food processor is an easy way to make the batter for these fish cakes, but you can also mix it together by hand.

- 3 tablespoons olive oil
- 1 large onion, finely chopped (about 1½ cups)
- 1½ teaspoons kosher salt
- ¼ teaspoon freshly ground black pepper
- 1¼ pounds codfish or scrod fillets, bones removed
- 2 tablespoons finely chopped fresh tarragon leaves
- 1 large egg, lightly beaten
- 3 dashes hot red-pepper sauce, or to taste
- ⅓ cup dry bread crumbs (see page 647)
  Horseradish Tartar Sauce (recipe follows)

1. Preheat the oven to 200°F. Heat 1 tablespoon olive oil in a medium skillet over medium heat. Add the onion, ½ teaspoon salt, and ⅛ teaspoon pepper. Cook, stirring occasionally, until the onions are translucent, about 10 minutes. Set aside.

2. Cut the fish into large chunks; pulse in the bowl of a food processor to coarsely chop. Transfer to a medium bowl. Add the reserved onion, tarragon, egg, and hot sauce, and combine well. Add the remaining teaspoon salt and ⅛ teaspoon pepper. Form eight 3-inch patties, and dredge them in the bread crumbs, shaking off the excess.

3. Heat 1 tablespoon oil in a large skillet over medium-low heat. Cook 4 patties until browned, about 5 minutes per side. Transfer to a baking sheet, cover with aluminum foil, and keep warm in the oven. Wipe out the skillet, and return to heat; add the remaining tablespoon of olive oil. Cook the remaining patties; serve with the tartar sauce.

horseradish tartar sauce

SERVES 4

Adjust the amount of horseradish to taste.

- 1 celery stalk, strings removed, finely chopped
- 2 tablespoons finely chopped cornichons or sour pickles
- 1 tablespoon Fresh Horseradish (page 632) or prepared
- 2 tablespoons coarsely chopped fresh flat-leaf parsley
- ½ teaspoon dry mustard
- ¼ cup plus 2 tablespoons Homemade Mayonnaise (page 631) or prepared
- 1 teaspoon fresh lemon juice
  Kosher salt and freshly ground black pepper

In a bowl, combine celery, cornichons, horseradish, parsley, mustard, mayonnaise, and lemon juice. Season with salt and pepper. Tartar sauce will keep, refrigerated in an airtight container, up to 4 days.

braised cod with plum tomatoes

SERVES 4

A cod steak has a row of bones running down its center; to remove them, cut around them with a sharp knife, dividing the fish into two pieces.

- 4 7-ounce codfish steaks, skin and bones removed
- 1 teaspoon dried oregano leaves
- 2 teaspoons kosher salt
- ½ teaspoon freshly ground black pepper
- ⅛ teaspoon cayenne pepper
- 4 plum tomatoes, cut into ½-inch-thick slices
- 1½ teaspoons olive oil
- ½ teaspoon minced garlic
  Fresh flat-leaf parsley, for garnish, optional

1. Sprinkle both sides of the cod steaks with oregano, ½ teaspoon salt, ¼ teaspoon black pepper, and cayenne pepper. Sprinkle tomato slices with 1½ teaspoons salt and ¼ teaspoon black pepper.

2. Heat the olive oil in a large skillet over high heat. When hot, add the cod and tomato slices. Cook until the cod steaks are golden on the bottom, about 4½ minutes. Using a metal spatula, turn the cod steaks and the tomatoes. Add 1 cup of water and the garlic, and bring the liquid to a simmer.

3. Simmer until cod begins to feel firm and it starts to flake, about 4 minutes. Divide the cod, tomatoes, and broth among four shallow soup bowls. Garnish with the parsley, and serve.

halibut with lemon sauce

SERVES 4

Preserved lemons are a staple in the Middle Eastern pantry, used to infuse all manner of dishes with a briny, mellow lemon flavor. Make your own (page 617), or look for them in specialty food stores (see Food Sources, page 648). They will keep, refrigerated, indefinitely.

1   Moroccan Preserved Lemon (page 617) or prepared
    Grated zest of 3 lemons
2   tablespoons sugar
1   tablespoon kosher salt
⅓   cup plus 1 tablespoon fresh lemon juice
3   tablespoons chopped fresh dill
4   8-ounce fillets halibut or other firm white fish
1   tablespoon olive oil
3   tablespoons butter, cut into thirds

1. Cut preserved lemon rind into ¼-inch-thick strips. Set aside. In a bowl, combine the lemon zest, sugar, salt, 1 tablespoon lemon juice, and the dill. Place the fillets in a shallow, nonreactive container. Cover with the lemon-dill marinade, cover with plastic wrap, and refrigerate 3 hours.

2. Remove the fish from the container, and set the marinade aside. Heat the olive oil in a large skillet over medium heat. Cook the fillets until golden and cooked through, about 5 minutes per side. Remove from the heat, and transfer the fillets to a platter. Cover with aluminum foil to keep warm.

3. Raise heat to high, and add the reserved marinade. When it bubbles and browns, add the remaining ⅓ cup lemon juice. Cook 1 minute. Reduce heat to low. Add the butter, swirling the pan to melt it. Remove the pan from the heat, and strain sauce into a small pan. Warm the preserved lemon with the sauce in the pan. Pour the sauce over the fillets, and serve hot.

halibut with puttanesca sauce

SERVES 4

1   28-ounce can plum tomatoes
3   tablespoons olive oil
2   garlic cloves, minced (about 1 teaspoon)
1   large onion, thinly sliced
⅓   cup oil-cured black olives, halved and pitted
2   tablespoons capers, drained
4   anchovy fillets, minced
1   teaspoon finely chopped fresh rosemary
4   6- to 8-ounce halibut steaks
    Kosher salt and freshly ground black pepper
⅓   cup chopped fresh flat-leaf parsley

1. Drain the tomatoes, reserving ½ cup of the liquid. Seed and coarsely chop them. Heat 1½ tablespoons olive oil in a large skillet over medium-low heat. Add the garlic, and cook until aromatic, 1 to 2 minutes. Add the onion, and cook until transparent, about 8 minutes. Raise heat to medium high; add the tomatoes, reserved liquid, olives, capers, anchovies, and rosemary, and cook, stirring often, to let the flavors combine and the liquid reduce slightly, 2 to 3 minutes. Remove from the heat, and set aside.

2. Heat the remaining 1½ tablespoons oil in a large nonstick skillet over medium-high heat. Season both sides of the halibut steaks with salt and pepper. Cook the steaks until golden brown, 4 to 5 minutes on each side.

3. Reheat the sauce until it simmers. Stir in parsley. Serve halibut with a little sauce on each steak.

salt-roasted red snapper

SERVES 2 TO 4

Whole red snapper is roasted in coarse salt infused with lemon and fresh herbs. The salt forms a hard crust as it bakes, sealing in moisture and flavor. The crust is cracked open and discarded. You can use any whole medium-size fish, such as sea bass.

- 1   2- to 3-pound whole red snapper, scaled, gutted, and cleaned (gills removed)
- 3   pounds kosher salt
- 4   large egg whites
- 2   lemons, sliced into ¼-inch-thick rounds
- ½   bunch fresh flat-leaf parsley
- ½   bunch fresh thyme, stems removed
- 4   dried bay leaves

1. Preheat the oven to 450°F with a rack in the center. Rinse the fish thoroughly inside and out until no traces of blood remain. Pat the fish dry with paper towels.

2. In a large bowl, stir together the salt and egg whites until thoroughly combined. Place a ½-inch layer of salt mixture in the bottom of a 13 x 9 x 2-inch baking pan. Place the lemon rounds, parsley, thyme, and bay leaves on top of the salt, arranging the ingredients so they form the shape of the fish and reserving some of each ingredient. Fill the fish cavity with the reserved lemons and herbs, and place the fish on top of the mixture.

3. Pour the remaining salt over the fish, completely covering the body; the tail can stick out of the pan. Using your fingers, pat down the salt, completely sealing the fish.

4. Bake fish until cooked through, allowing 15 minutes per pound. Insert a carving fork or metal skewer through the salt crust and into fish, then place it on your chin under your lower lip for 15 seconds; if the metal feels very warm, the fish is done. Remove pan from oven; let sit 5 minutes.

5. Gently break away the salt crust. Transfer the fish to a cutting board. Using a paring knife and your fingers, peel away the skin. Separate, and serve.

red snapper with roasted red pepper and onion sauce

SERVES 4

Sliced red and white pearl onions form overlapping layers on the snapper. Depending on the thickness of your fillets, the cooking time may vary slightly.

- 1   roasted red bell pepper (see page 645), cut in half
- 1   medium yellow onion, cut into ¼-inch-thick rounds
- 1½   teaspoons kosher salt
- ½   teaspoon freshly ground black pepper
- 2   teaspoons balsamic vinegar
- 4   8-ounce red-snapper fillets
- 8   ounces red and white pearl onions, thinly sliced
- ¼   teaspoon ground cumin
    Olive oil, for brushing

1. Preheat the oven to 400°F. Place the roasted pepper and the onion on a large piece of aluminum foil, and fold the foil into a package. Place the package in the oven, and cook until the onion is very soft and golden, about 1 hour.

2. Transfer the contents of the package to the bowl of a food processor. Add ¾ teaspoon salt, ¼ teaspoon black pepper, and the vinegar. Pulse until smooth, about 2½ minutes. Set the sauce aside.

3. Preheat the broiler. Place the snapper fillets on a 12 x 17-inch baking sheet. Layer the red and white pearl onions in a scale-like pattern over the fillets. Sprinkle the remaining ¾ teaspoon salt, ¼ teaspoon pepper, and the cumin over the onions, and brush lightly with olive oil.

4. Broil until the fillets are cooked through and the onions are slightly brown, about 10 minutes. If the onions start to brown too rapidly, cover the baking sheet with a piece of aluminum foil.

5. Transfer the snapper to individual serving plates. Drizzle the reserved sauce over the fillets, and serve.

FIT TO EAT RECIPE PER SERVING: 270 CALORIES, 3 G FAT, 83 MG CHOLESTEROL, 10 G CARBOHYDRATE, 946 MG SODIUM, 48 G PROTEIN, 2 G DIETARY FIBER

pecan-crusted catfish with wilted greens and tomato chutney

SERVES 8

Restaurant chefs use this technique for dredging fish: Use one hand for flouring and coating the fish with nuts, the other for dipping it in the egg.

- 4 cups pecans
- ½ cup all-purpose flour
  Kosher salt and freshly ground black pepper
  Cayenne pepper to taste
- 1 large egg
- 3 tablespoons milk
- 8 4-ounce catfish or red-snapper fillets
- 2 bunches (about 1½ pounds) mustard greens or kale
  Juice of 1 lemon
  Tomato Chutney (recipe follows)

1. Preheat the oven to 450°F. Place the pecans in the bowl of a food processor, and pulse until some pecans are almost a powder and others remain in large pieces. Spread on a plate, and set aside.

2. Mix the flour with salt, pepper, and cayenne to taste. Spread out on a plate. Whisk together the egg and milk in a shallow bowl.

3. Rinse the fish and pat dry. Coat with the flour mixture, shaking off the excess. Dip in the egg mixture, letting the excess drip off. Press each fillet firmly in the pecans on the plate, coating the fish completely.

4. Arrange the fillets on a baking sheet, being careful not to overlap. Cook for 15 minutes.

5. While the fish is cooking, wash the greens, allowing a little moisture to cling to the leaves. Tear into medium-size pieces, and place in a large pot. Season with salt, cover, and cook over medium heat, stirring occasionally until the greens are wilted and bright green, about 4 minutes. Season with the lemon juice and pepper.

6. Place a serving of greens on each of eight plates, and lay a fish fillet on top. Spoon a few tablespoons of chutney on each fillet, and serve immediately.

tomato chutney

MAKES 1 CUP

This simple sweet-and-sour condiment tastes delicious with fish or chicken. The chutney may be refrigerated, in an airtight container, for up to 1 week.

- 4 tomatoes
- 4 shallots, cut into ⅛-inch-thick slices
- ¼ cup sugar
- ¼ cup balsamic vinegar
- 3 drops hot red-pepper sauce, or to taste

1. Cover a large pot of water, and bring to a boil. Prepare an ice-water bath. Using a paring knife, score the nonstem end of each tomato with a shallow "x". Blanch the tomatoes in the boiling water for 30 seconds. With a slotted spoon, transfer the tomatoes to the ice-water bath. Peel them, and cut off flesh in large pieces. Discard the cores. Cut the tomatoes into long strips about ¼ inch wide. Place in a colander over a bowl, and allow to drain.

2. Place the shallots in a shallow skillet with 1 cup water and the sugar. Cook over medium heat, swirling pan occasionally, until the liquid is reduced to a thick, clear syrup, 15 to 20 minutes.

3. Add vinegar, tomatoes, and hot sauce; cook for 5 minutes, gently stirring. The chutney should be thick, but the tomatoes shouldn't break down very much. Let cool. Serve cold or at room temperature.

whole poached salmon 101

SERVES 10 TO 12

A magnificent salmon can be poached, glazed, and prepared for the table in a couple of hours, then kept in the refrigerator overnight. The equipment is basic; a fish poacher is helpful, but you can make do with a large, deep roasting pan with a cooling rack placed in the bottom. The other materials are likely to be found around the kitchen: cheesecloth, kitchen twine, and a good knife. If the salmon is too long to fit in your poacher, you may cut off the head and tail, although Martha thinks the presentation is more beautiful with the entire fish intact. A 6-pound salmon will feed about 8 people.

1   *8-pound whole salmon, scaled, gutted,*
    and cleaned (gills removed)
    Court Bouillon (page 627)

6   *large egg whites*

2   *tablespoons plus ¾ teaspoon unflavored*
    gelatin
    Fennel fronds, for garnish

1   *ounce each golden and salmon caviar,*
    for garnish, optional

1   *lemon, 1 orange, and 2 or 3 kumquats*
    if available, all sliced into ¼-inch-thick
    rounds for garnish

1. Rinse the fish under cold running water, washing away any blood around the gills, which would cloud the stock. Pat fish dry inside and out with paper towels; place on a clean work surface. Trim fins from back and belly, and near the gills with kitchen scissors. If the fish is too long to fit in the poacher, remove the head and tail with a sharp knife; cut off the tail right below the tail fins.

2. Cut a double thickness of cheesecloth 17 inches wide and 8 inches longer than the salmon. Place the cheesecloth on a clean work surface. Lay the fish lengthwise on the cloth, and wrap the cloth around the fish. Tie the ends of the cheesecloth with kitchen twine.

3. Place the rack in the bottom of the poacher, and fill with the cooled court bouillon. Using the ends of the cloth as handles, lower the salmon into the poacher, adding water if necessary to cover the fish.

Cover, and set the poacher over two burners. Bring the liquid to a simmer; reduce heat to very low. Cook at a bare simmer for 25 minutes (the water should not be boiling).

4. Slide a wooden spoon through each handle of the poaching rack; lift out the rack, and prop the spoons on the edges of the poacher so the fish is elevated. Raise one of the spoons to lift the side of the rack that supports the head end, and expose the widest part of the fish's back. Insert an instant-read thermometer near where the fin was. The fish is fully cooked when the temperature registers 135°F. (For a larger salmon this may take up to an hour.) If it is not done, return the fish to the liquid, and continue poaching, checking the temperature every 10 minutes.

5. Drain the poacher, reserving the court bouillon. When the salmon is cool enough to handle, about 15 minutes, transfer to a clean work surface; let cool completely, about 45 minutes.

6. To make the aspic glaze, pour court bouillon through a fine sieve. Place 6 cups bouillon in a stockpot. In a separate bowl, whisk the egg whites until frothy, then whisk into bouillon. Whisk the mixture over medium heat until it comes to a simmer, about 10 minutes. The egg whites will draw all the cloudy particles from the stock and begin to coagulate on top. Stop whisking; simmer over the lowest heat, until the foam has risen to the surface and the broth is clear, about 15 minutes.

7. Using a slotted spoon, carefully lift out the foam. Soak a 12-inch square piece of cheesecloth in ice water. Squeeze out any excess water, and line the sieve with the cold cheesecloth. Pour the broth through the sieve. Repeat, using fresh cheesecloth each time, until all the foam has been removed from the stock. Place ⅓ cup cold water in a small bowl, and evenly sprinkle the gelatin over the top. Let sit until softened, about 10 minutes. Add gelatin mixture to clarified stock, and bring to a simmer over medium heat, whisking constantly, until all the gelatin has dissolved; do not boil. Remove from heat. Prepare an ice-water bath, and set aside.

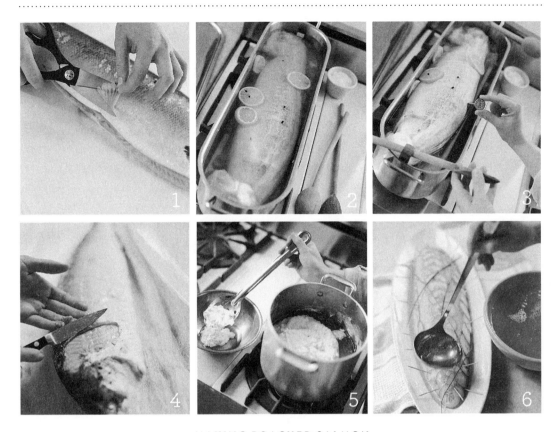

MAKING POACHED SALMON

1. A whole salmon will require a bit of trimming before cooking; if you prefer, ask the fishmonger to do this. Once it's trimmed, wrap the fish in several layers of cheesecloth, and tie the loose ends for easy handling.

2. Small fish (two to four pounds) can go straight into hot court bouillon, but most salmon needs to be started in cool liquid and heated very slowly so the outside doesn't cook before the inside. Court bouillon imparts subtle flavor to the fish as it cooks; lemon slices and white wine act as a counterpart to the richness of the fish, and their acidity helps the fish retain its shape by causing the proteins to contract.

3. Use wooden spoons to lift out and prop up the fish, then insert an instant-read thermometer into the widest part of the back, to determine the internal temperature.

4. Once the poached fish has cooled, peel off the skin (it comes off very easily) and then gently scrape off the brown fat. Leave the fish on the cheesecloth as you work, as the cloth will help you in flipping and moving the fish to the platter. Trim the side that was on the rack first so that the prettier side faces up on the serving platter.

5. Making aspic requires some patience (and a bit of science). First, the court bouillon is clarified by simmering with beaten egg whites, which draw all the cloudy particles out of the stock into a coagulated foam. Then the clarified stock is mixed with gelatin, simmered some more, and set in an ice bath. Don't worry; just when you've given up, it will gel. Arrange the garnishes on the fish before setting the aspic in the ice bath.

6. Ladle the thickened aspic over the fish. One coating will be enough to give the fish a gloss, but the ambitious cook may want to chill the fish and glaze it a second or third time. If the aspic becomes too solid for glazing, warm it slightly over a double boiler until it liquefies, then use it immediately.

8. Unwrap the fish, leaving the cheesecloth in place underneath. If the head and tail are still attached and are in good shape, you may want to leave them on for decoration. If not, remove the tail with kitchen scissors. The head will pull off easily. Turn the fish over, so that the side that was on the rack faces up. Peel the skin off using a paring knife and your fingers. Using cheesecloth to support the fish, flip it onto a serving platter, skin-side up. Remove skin from top of fish. Using the back of a paring knife, gently scrape off any brown fat.

9. Arrange the garnishes on top of the fish; temporarily secure with toothpicks. Pour the aspic into a large bowl set over the ice-water bath. Stir the aspic until it begins to thicken, 5 to 10 minutes. Remove the aspic from the ice-water bath, and ladle a coating over the salmon. Refrigerate the salmon 20 minutes. Repeat the glazing process, if desired. If the aspic becomes too thick to ladle, warm in a double boiler until liquid again. Remove the toothpicks. Keep the salmon in the refrigerator, uncovered, up to 24 hours. (The aspic coating keeps the fish from drying out.)

10. When ready to serve, clean away any aspic collected around the bottom of the fish; cut with a fish server. Start at the wide end of the fish; slide the server under or between the garnishes, rather than cutting through them. Cut down to the bone, working the server gently between the flakes. Lift a section of the fish with the garnishes on top, and transfer to a dinner plate. Continue cutting and serving as needed.

cedar-planked salmon

SERVES 8 TO 10

A Native American method of cooking fish, planking originally entailed securing a fish to a piece of driftwood and propping it vertically in the sand downwind from a fire. Here, it is suspended horizontally above the embers between two stacks of bricks. As it cooks, the fish takes on the flavors from both smoke and wood. Use the planking method if cooking fish for a crowd.

YOU WILL NEED nails, braided picture wire, one untreated cedar or oak plank (1 inch thick, 10 inches wide, and 4 feet long), and 13 to 15 bricks

- *1 tablespoon kosher salt*
- *1 teaspoon freshly ground black pepper*
- *1 teaspoon dry mustard*
- *3 tablespoons olive oil*
- *20 large sprigs fresh dill*
- *1 4-pound whole side of salmon, scaled, gutted, and cleaned (gills removed)*
  Roasted Pepper Relish (recipe follows)

1. Place a nail on the long, thin edge of the plank, 3 inches from the end. Hammer it halfway into the plank. Continue hammering nails along the plank at 2-inch intervals. Repeat on the opposite edge, with the first nail 4 inches from the end.

2. Combine the salt, pepper, and dry mustard in a small bowl, and set aside.

3. Brush one side of the plank with 1 tablespoon olive oil, and arrange 10 dill sprigs on it. Place salmon, skin-side down, over dill. Brush salmon with the remaining 2 tablespoons olive oil, and rub the mustard mixture over the entire surface. Arrange the remaining dill sprigs over the salmon.

4. Wrap one end of the braided picture wire around the head of the first hammered nail. Pull wire across top of salmon to the first nail on the opposite side; wrap wire around the nail head, keeping wire taut. Continue lacing until the wire has been fastened to all nails and salmon is secure.

5. Stack the bricks (long sides facing each other) in two columns 3 feet apart—one column should be six bricks and the other five. Build a medium-hot wood fire between them.

6. Center the plank, fish-side down, over the fire with the salmon's tail closest to the six-brick stack. Cook over the fire until the flesh is firm and flaky, 30 to 35 minutes (time will vary depending on the heat of the fire and the thickness of the fish). Spritz fish and plank with water if they smolder. If the fish begins to burn before the flesh is cooked through, add another brick to each stack. If the fire is too cool, remove a brick from each stack.

7. When cooked, remove the fish from the fire, and unwrap the wire. Discard the dill, and cut the fish on the plank. Serve with the roasted-pepper relish.

roasted pepper relish
MAKES ABOUT 1 CUP

If you can't find fresh poblano peppers, use a yellow bell pepper and more jalapeño pepper.

- 3 roasted red bell peppers (see page 645), cut into ½-inch pieces
- 2 roasted fresh poblano peppers (see page 645), cut into ½-inch pieces
- 1 small jalapeño pepper, seeds and ribs removed, minced
- 1 tablespoon extra-virgin olive oil
- 1 teaspoon balsamic vinegar
- ½ teaspoon kosher salt
  Pinch of freshly ground black pepper
- ¼ cup loosely packed fresh basil leaves, coarsely chopped

Combine the roasted peppers, jalapeño, olive oil, vinegar, salt, and pepper in a small bowl, and toss. Add the basil, toss again, and serve.

salmon roasted on chardonnay twigs
SERVES 10 TO 12

Cooking times will vary with the size of your salmon. Roasting the fish on aromatic Chardonnay twigs (or dried fennel branches; see Food Sources, page 648) prevents sticking—vegetables alone will do the same thing.

- 1 8-pound whole salmon, scaled, gutted, and cleaned (gills removed)
  Olive oil
  Kosher salt and freshly ground black pepper
- 2 lemons, thinly sliced
- 1 to 2 bunches fresh rosemary
- 5 large carrots
- 4 celery stalks, cut in half
- 2 onions, quartered lengthwise
  Chardonnay twigs, optional
- ¼ cup dry white wine

1. Preheat oven to 500°F. Rinse salmon inside and out, making sure there are no traces of blood in the cavity or gills. Rub the cavity with oil, salt, and pepper. Arrange lemon slices in the cavity, layer with rosemary, and top with more lemon slices.

2. Using a trussing needle and kitchen twine, sew up the cavity. (Use toothpicks or small metal skewers if you don't have a needle.) Rub surface of salmon with more oil, and sprinkle with more salt and pepper. Toss the vegetables with oil to coat.

3. Transfer vegetables to a large, shallow roasting pan. Arrange twigs on top. Place fish on twigs. You may have to place fish on a diagonal to fit. Don't worry if the head or tail hangs over the pan.

4. Place the pan in the oven with the fish head toward the back. Roast for 15 minutes, then reduce oven to 425°F. Add wine, and roast for 1 hour more or until done. To check for doneness, insert a knife into the thickest part of the fish to see if flesh is opaque. (An instant-read thermometer should read 130°F when inserted.)

5. Serve fish whole, hot or at room temperature, with roasted vegetables. Peel back skin (or eat, if desired), and lift salmon off bones. Remove large central bone, and continue to serve bottom half.

horseradish-crusted salmon

SERVES 6

- 5 slices white bread, crusts removed
- 1½ teaspoons kosher salt
- ½ teaspoon freshly ground black pepper
- 1 small shallot, minced
- 2 tablespoons chopped fresh dill
- ½ cup freshly grated horseradish (grated on small holes of box grater)
- 2 tablespoons olive oil, plus more for pan
- 6 6-ounce salmon fillets, skin removed

1. Preheat the oven to 450°F. Position a rack 8 to 12 inches from the heat. Place the bread in the bowl of a food processor, and pulse until coarsely chopped (¼- to ⅛-inch pieces). Add 1 teaspoon salt, ¼ teaspoon pepper, the shallot, dill, horseradish, and 2 tablespoons olive oil. Pulse just until combined, and set aside.

2. Rub the bottom and sides of a 12 x 17-inch pan with olive oil. Place the salmon in the pan, spacing the fillets 2 inches apart. Sprinkle with remaining salt and pepper. Pat the mixture onto each fillet. Bake until cooked through, 5 to 6 minutes. Raise oven heat to broil, and cook until the tops are golden, 1 to 2 minutes. Serve hot.

dill-marinated salmon with pickled cucumbers

SERVES 4

- 2 cucumbers, peeled
- 3 tablespoons rice-wine or red-wine vinegar
- ½ cup chopped fresh dill
- 1 teaspoon sugar
- 1 teaspoon kosher salt
- 4 5-ounce salmon fillets, skin removed
- ¼ teaspoon freshly ground black pepper

1. Heat a grill or a grill pan until very hot. Slice cucumbers into very thin rounds. Transfer to a bowl with vinegar, 3 tablespoons dill, the sugar, and ¾ teaspoon salt. Toss to combine; set aside.

2. Place the salmon on a tray, sprinkle with the remaining salt and pepper, and coat with the remaining dill. Transfer to the hot grill, and cook until nicely browned, 4 to 6 minutes. Turn over, and continue grilling until just cooked through, 4 to 6 minutes. Salmon will appear flaky when done. Place pickled cucumbers on a platter, top with salmon fillets, and serve.

FIT TO EAT RECIPE PER SERVING: 291 CALORIES, 29 G PROTEIN, 15 G FAT, 94 MG CHOLESTEROL, 8 G CARBOHYDRATE, 863 MG SODIUM, 1 G DIETARY FIBER

grilled swordfish steaks with olive pesto

SERVES 8

- 8 6-ounce swordfish steaks (about 1 inch thick), cut into 8 pieces
  Kosher salt and freshly ground black pepper
- ½ cup plus 1 tablespoon extra-virgin olive oil, plus more for brushing
- ¼ cup pitted oil-cured olives
- 1 small garlic clove
- 1½ cups loosely packed arugula leaves (from 1 bunch)
- ¼ cup fresh flat-leaf parsley leaves
- ¼ teaspoon dried oregano

1. Arrange swordfish steaks in a shallow baking dish, season well with salt and pepper, and coat with 3 tablespoons olive oil. Marinate at room temperature up to 30 minutes, until ready to grill (or longer in the refrigerator, covered with plastic wrap; return to room temperature before grilling).

2. Heat a grill or a grill pan until very hot. Meanwhile, to make the pesto, combine the olives, garlic, arugula, parsley, oregano, and salt to taste in the bowl of a food processor. Pulsing the machine, slowly add the remaining ¼ cup plus 2 tablespoons olive oil. Add 1½ tablespoons hot water, pulsing until coarsely puréed. Set aside.

3. Place the fish on the grill. Cook for about 5 minutes on one side, and turn. Grill until nearly cooked through, about 5 minutes. Transfer to a shallow serving dish. Spoon the pesto over the hot fish, turning the fish to coat well. Serve hot.

swordfish kebabs

SERVES 6

Soak the wooden skewers in water for at least 20 minutes before cooking to prevent charring.

- 1 garlic clove, minced
- 1½ teaspoons ground cumin
- 1½ teaspoons chili powder
- ½ cup white-wine vinegar
- ¼ cup unsulfured molasses
- ½ cup fresh orange juice
- ½ cup fresh lime juice (about 4 limes)
- 3 large lemons
- 18 dried bay leaves
- 2¼ pounds swordfish, skin removed, cut into 2-inch cubes
- 12 cherry tomatoes
  Kosher salt and freshly ground black pepper

1. Combine the garlic, cumin, chili powder, vinegar, molasses, and orange and lime juices in a small saucepan. Bring to a boil over high heat. Boil for 2 minutes, remove from the heat, and set aside. Halve lemons crosswise; cut each half into 4 wedges.

2. On each of six long metal or wooden skewers, arrange 4 lemon wedges, 3 bay leaves, 3 pieces of fish, and 2 tomatoes. Kebabs can be prepared up to this point and refrigerated for up to 6 hours.

3. Heat a grill or a grill pan until medium hot. Season the kebabs with salt and pepper, and spoon the glaze over them. Grill until the fish is opaque to the center and lightly charred, 3 to 4 minutes per side. Brush with the glaze several times while cooking. Remove the skewers, and serve.

FIT TO EAT RECIPE PER SERVING: 284 CALORIES, 7 G TOTAL FAT, 66 MG CHOLESTEROL, 23 G CARBOHYDRATE, 696 MG SODIUM, 35 G PROTEIN, 0 G DIETARY FIBER

grilled tuna with balsamic glaze

SERVES 6

- ¼ cup plus 2 tablespoons dry white wine
- 1 cup plus 2 tablespoons balsamic vinegar
- 2 tablespoons sugar
- 1 teaspoon freshly ground black pepper
- 1½ pounds ripe fresh tomatoes, cut into ½-inch dice
- 2 teaspoons olive oil
- 2 teaspoons kosher salt
- 12 ounces haricots verts or green beans
- 1 teaspoon fresh lemon juice
- 6 6-ounce fresh tuna steaks (1 inch thick)
- ¼ cup loosely packed fresh basil leaves, very thinly sliced

1. Combine the wine, vinegar, sugar, and ¼ teaspoon pepper in a small saucepan over medium-high heat. Simmer until slightly thickened and syrupy, about 30 minutes. Remove from the heat, and set aside.

2. Combine the tomatoes, 1 teaspoon olive oil, ½ teaspoon salt, and ¼ teaspoon pepper in a medium bowl. Toss and set aside.

3. Heat a grill or a grill pan until medium hot. Combine the haricots verts, lemon juice, the remaining teaspoon olive oil, ½ teaspoon salt, and ¼ teaspoon pepper in a bowl, and toss well. Arrange the beans on the hot grill, and cook, turning, until just limp and lightly charred, 2 to 4 minutes. Transfer to a serving platter.

4. Sprinkle the remaining teaspoon salt and ¼ teaspoon pepper on all sides of the tuna steaks. Brush the wine-and-vinegar mixture on the tops and sides of the steaks, and place, glazed-side down, on the grill. Grill, brushing with more glaze, until lightly charred, about 3 minutes per side for rare, 6 to 7 for well done. Transfer to the serving platter with the beans. Add the basil to the tomatoes, toss, and spoon over the tuna. Serve immediately.

FIT TO EAT RECIPE PER SERVING: 279 CALORIES, 4 G TOTAL FAT, 74 MG CHOLESTEROL, 20 G CARBOHYDRATE, 787 MG SODIUM, 41 G PROTEIN, 2 G DIETARY FIBER

seared tuna steaks
with caper butter

SERVES 4

The tuna can also be grilled on a very hot grill or grill pan. Place it on the grill directly from the refrigerator; this will ensure that the outside will sear and the inside will remain rare.

- 4 8-ounce tuna steaks (about ¾ inch thick)
- 1 tablespoon extra-virgin olive oil
   Kosher salt and freshly ground black pepper
- 4 tablespoons unsalted butter, room temperature
- 2 tablespoons capers, drained
- 1 tablespoon finely diced red or yellow bell pepper
- 1 large bunch arugula

1. Rub the tuna with the olive oil, and season with salt and plenty of pepper. Set aside to marinate for at least 20 minutes at room temperature (if longer than 30 minutes, transfer, covered with plastic wrap, to the refrigerator; return to room temperature before cooking).

2. In a small bowl, combine the butter, capers, and diced peppers until well blended. Turn the butter mixture onto a square of parchment paper or wax paper, and roll into a log about ½ inch in diameter. Refrigerate until firm, about 30 minutes.

3. Heat a cast-iron skillet slowly over low heat until very hot (a few drops of water splashed in the pan should evaporate almost immediately). Arrange the tuna in the skillet, and cook for about 5 minutes on each side. It should be well browned and crisp on the outside and rare to medium on the inside.

4. Arrange the arugula on plates or a platter. Place the tuna on top with a slice of caper butter on each steak. Serve immediately.

poached monkfish
with red onion, oranges, and
kalamata olives

SERVES 6

for the quick court bouillon

- 1 onion, cut into 8 wedges
- 1 celery stalk, cut into 4 pieces
- 1 carrot, cut into 4 pieces
- 3 sprigs fresh flat-leaf parsley
- 2 dried bay leaves
- 1 teaspoon whole black peppercorns
   Zest of 1 orange
- ½ cup dry white wine

for the monkfish

- 2 oranges, peel and pith removed
- 2 1-pound monkfish fillets, skin and black membranes removed
- 2 ounces pitted kalamata olives (about ½ cup), cut into quarters lengthwise
- 1 medium red onion, cut into ½-inch-wide slivers

1. Place the onion, celery, carrot, parsley, bay leaves, peppercorns, zest, and wine in a wide shallow saucepan with 1 quart plus 2 cups water. Cover and bring to a boil; reduce to a simmer. Cook 20 minutes to allow the flavors to blend.

2. Meanwhile, working over a bowl to catch the juices, use a paring knife to carefully slice between the sections and membranes of each orange; remove the segments whole. Place each segment in the bowl as completed; set aside.

3. Strain the court bouillon; discard the solids. Return liquid to pan, and bring to a boil; reduce to just simmering. Place the fish in the stock (it will be partly submerged). Top with the oranges, olives, and red onion. Cover, and cook until the fish is just cooked through, about 10 minutes.

4. Transfer the fish with a spatula or slotted spoon to a serving platter. Garnish with the orange segments, olives, and onion. Serve immediately.

FIT TO EAT RECIPE PER SERVING: 142 CALORIES, 4 G FAT, 24 MG CHOLESTEROL, 8 G CARBOHYDRATE, 175 MG SODIUM, 15 G PROTEIN, 2 G DIETARY FIBER

boiled maine lobster

SERVES 12

Each summer, many lobsters' tough shells are replaced by thin ones. These lobsters, called "shedders," are a delight to eat—it takes no effort to get at the tail and claw meat. Keep a pair of crackers on hand, just in case. If seawater isn't available, prepare Court Bouillon, a flavorful stock used to poach seafood. As a rule, a 1½-pound lobster is cooked 10 minutes after the water returns to a boil; for each pound thereafter, cook an additional 3 to 4 minutes.

> Court Bouillon (page 627)
>
> 12 live lobsters (about 1½ pounds each), "shedders" if available
>
> 1 pound (4 sticks) unsalted butter, melted, or Clarified Butter (page 633)
>
> 6 lemons, halved

1. Place the court bouillon in a large stockpot. Cover and bring to a boil over high heat. Depending on the size of the stockpot, quickly add 4 to 6 lobsters to the boiling court bouillon, making sure the liquid covers all the lobsters. Cover and allow the court bouillon to return to a boil again. Only then start timing the cooking. Cook the lobsters about 10 minutes. Using tongs, remove the lobsters; transfer to a platter. Repeat with remaining lobsters, working in batches if necessary.

2. Using kitchen scissors, trim the tip of each lobster claw; allow the liquid to drain, and discard. Serve the lobsters with the melted butter and lemons on the side.

lobster on the grill

SERVES 4

If you're not squeamish, the lobsters can also be prepared for grilling by inserting the point of a sharp knife through the cross mark on their backs. Lobsters should not be alive when they are grilled or sautéed.

> Kosher salt
>
> 4 live lobsters, 1 to 2 pounds each
>
> 1 cup (2 sticks) melted butter, optional
>
> 4 lemon wedges, halved

1. Cover a large stockpot of salted water, and bring to a boil over high heat. Heat a grill to medium hot. Plunge the lobsters headfirst into the boiling water, and cook for 1 minute. Using tongs, remove the lobsters from the water, and drain.

2. Transfer lobsters to the grill. Cook 10 minutes, turning occasionally to avoid burning the shells.

3. Crack a claw to see if it is fully cooked (the meat should be opaque). If not, detach the claws and return to the grill for a few minutes more. Using kitchen scissors, split the lobsters lengthwise by cutting along the underside of the tail, leaving the back of the shell intact. Scrape out the red coral, if any, and green tomalley, and combine with the melted butter for a dipping sauce, if desired. Keep the lobsters warm on a platter covered with aluminum foil until serving. Garnish with lemon wedges, and serve with melted butter on the side.

. . . .

LOBSTER TIP

After steaming or boiling, cut the tip off each lobster claw and hold the lobster up by the tail to let the water drain out.

. . . .

lobster newburg

SERVES 6

Newburg is a traditional New England dish of shellfish in a rich butter sauce flavored with sherry. The lobsters and stock (the first four steps) may be made a day ahead. This recipe is written for individual servings; to make a larger, single version, cook one Newburg in a soufflé dish. The cooking time will increase by 15 to 20 minutes.

- 1 teaspoon kosher salt, plus more for cooking water
- 3 live lobsters, 1¼ pounds each
- 4 tablespoons unsalted butter
- 1 medium onion, coarsely chopped
- 2 celery stalks, strings removed, coarsely chopped
- 2 medium leeks, white and pale-green parts, well washed (see page 646)
- 4 medium carrots
- 8 sprigs fresh tarragon
- 2 tablespoons all-purpose flour
- ¼ cup dry sherry
- 2 teaspoons tomato paste
- ½ cup heavy cream
- ⅛ teaspoon freshly ground black pepper
- 1 large egg yolk

1. Cover and bring a large stockpot of salted water to a boil over high heat. Prepare an ice-water bath. Add lobsters to the stockpot, making sure each one is completely submerged (work in batches if necessary). Cover and let water return to a boil; cook lobsters about 8 minutes. Using tongs, transfer the lobsters to the ice bath to cool. Drain the lobsters in a colander.

2. Carefully remove the lobster meat from the tails, claws, and legs, and remove any cartilage from the claw meat. Cut the meat into bite-size pieces. Transfer the meat to a bowl, cover with plastic wrap, and refrigerate until ready to use. Discard the lobster bodies, but reserve the shells from the tails, claws, and legs for making stock.

3. Melt 2 tablespoons butter in a large saucepan over medium heat. Add the onion and celery to the pan. Coarsely chop 1 leek and 2 carrots; add to the pan. Add reserved lobster shells, 4 sprigs tarragon, and enough water to cover the shells by 3 inches.

4. Cover and bring the liquid to a boil, reduce heat, and simmer with the lid ajar, skimming surface often, until stock is flavorful, about 1½ hours.

5. Prepare an ice-water bath. Strain the stock through a fine sieve, pushing down on the solids to extract the liquid. Transfer the stock to a clean saucepan, and discard the solids. Continue cooking the stock until the liquid has reduced to 2 cups. Remove from the heat, and transfer to the ice bath to chill. Transfer the chilled stock to an airtight container, and refrigerate until ready to use.

6. Split the remaining leek in half lengthwise. Cut the leek and the remaining 2 carrots into ½-inch pieces, and set aside.

7. Melt the remaining 2 tablespoons butter in a medium saucepan over medium-low heat. Sprinkle the flour into the saucepan, and cook, stirring constantly, so the mixture foams and forms a paste but does not turn brown, about 2 minutes.

8. Carefully add the sherry, stirring constantly to loosen any flour that has cooked onto the bottom of the saucepan, being careful that no lumps form. Add the tomato paste and 2 cups of the reserved lobster stock. Add the chopped leek and carrots to the saucepan, and cook until just tender, about 4 minutes. Stir in the cream, and bring to a boil. Reduce heat, and simmer until the sauce just starts to thicken, about 6 minutes. Add 1 teaspoon salt and the pepper. Pick the tarragon from the remaining 4 sprigs, chop, and add.

9. In a medium bowl, whisk the egg yolk. Whisk in a ladleful of the hot sauce to combine. Return the mixture to the saucepan over low heat; whisk to combine. Remove from the heat.

10. Preheat the oven to 350°F. Bring a large kettle of water to a boil; set six 6-ounce ramekins in a roasting pan. Add the reserved lobster meat to the sauce, and stir to combine. Divide the Newburg among the ramekins. Transfer the roasting pan to oven, and fill with 1 inch of boiling water. Cook until the Newburg bubbles, about 25 minutes. Remove the roasting pan from the oven, and carefully transfer the ramekins to serving plates. Serve.

seafood pot au feu

SERVES 6

- ¾ teaspoon kosher salt, plus more for cooking water
- 2 live lobsters, 1 pound each
- 2 small leeks, white and pale-green parts, well washed (see page 646)
- 3 medium carrots
- 1 celery stalk
- 1 medium fennel bulb
- 2 medium garlic cloves, peeled
- 1 tablespoon unsalted butter
- 1 medium onion, cut into ¼-inch dice
- 1 teaspoon whole fennel seeds, toasted (see page 644)
- 8 sprigs fresh thyme
- 4 sprigs fresh tarragon
- 1 cup dry white wine
- 1 dried bay leaf
- 4 whole canned tomatoes, roughly chopped, with juice
- 10 sprigs fresh flat-leaf parsley
- ⅛ teaspoon freshly ground black pepper
- 12 sea scallops (¾ pound), muscle removed
- 1 pound halibut or other firm white fish, cut into 1½-inch cubes
- 1 small bunch watercress, stems removed
- 2 tablespoons Sauternes or other sweet wine, optional

1. Cover a large stockpot of salted water, and bring to a boil over high heat. Add the lobsters, making sure that each lobster is completely submerged in the water. Cover, and let the water return to a boil. Cook 3 minutes; using tongs, transfer the lobsters from the water, and set aside to cool. Hold the lobsters with a towel, and twist off the tails and claws. Remove the meat from the tails and claws; refrigerate. (The lobster meat will be just undercooked.) Reserve the lobster shells and bodies.

2. Cut 1 leek, 1 carrot, celery, half the fennel, and 1 clove garlic into ¼-inch dice.

3. Heat 1 teaspoon butter in a large saucepan over medium heat. Add the chopped leek, carrot, celery, fennel, garlic, onion, fennel seeds, 6 sprigs thyme, and tarragon; cook, stirring occasionally, until the vegetables are soft and aromatic, about 5 minutes. Add the lobster shells and the bodies; cook, stirring occasionally, about 3 minutes.

4. Add the wine, bay leaf, tomatoes, parsley, and 8 cups water. Raise heat to high; cover and bring to a boil. Reduce heat to medium low; simmer until the liquid is very flavorful, about 1 hour.

5. Meanwhile, halve the remaining leek; cut into ¼-inch-thick slices. Cut the remaining 2 carrots into ⅛-inch-thick matchsticks. Cut the remaining fennel into ¼-inch dice. Smash the remaining garlic clove. Set the vegetables aside.

6. Remove the stock from the heat; strain through a fine sieve or cheesecloth-lined strainer, pressing on the solids to extract the liquid. Discard solids.

7. Melt the remaining 2 teaspoons butter in a large shallow saucepan over medium heat. Add the sliced leeks, carrots, fennel, garlic, remaining 2 sprigs thyme, ¾ teaspoon salt, and pepper; cook until tender, about 8 minutes. Add the stock; raise heat, and bring to a boil. Reduce heat to medium low; simmer for 20 minutes. Meanwhile, slice the lobster-tail meat into medallions, but leave the claw meat whole; set aside. Add the scallops and halibut to the stock; adjust heat to maintain a bare simmer, and poach for about 1 minute. Add lobster meat, adjust heat again, and poach until the fish is opaque and the lobster is cooked through, 3 to 4 minutes. Discard garlic clove and thyme sprigs. Stir in watercress and Sauternes, if using. Serve.

FIT TO EAT RECIPE PER SERVING: 236 CALORIES, 5 G FAT, 86 MG CHOLESTEROL, 5 G CARBOHYDRATE, 417 MG SODIUM, 34 G PROTEIN, 1 G DIETARY FIBER

soft-shell crabs with arugula

SERVES 4

1   cup yellow cornmeal

1   teaspoon kosher salt

¼   teaspoon freshly ground black pepper

2   large egg whites

8   soft-shell crabs (about 2½ pounds total)

¼   cup plus 2 tablespoons olive oil

1   bunch (about 6 ounces) arugula, washed
    and tough stems removed

    Red Pepper and Lemon Confit
    (recipe follows)

1. Combine the cornmeal, salt, and pepper in a shallow bowl or plate.

2. Whisk egg whites in a small bowl just until frothy. Dip crabs into the egg whites to coat. Dredge in the cornmeal, shake off excess, and set aside.

3. Preheat the oven to 300°F. Heat 1½ tablespoons olive oil in a large nonstick skillet over medium-high heat; arrange 4 crabs on their bellies in the pan. Cook until golden and crisp, about 5 minutes. Transfer the crabs to a plate, and add 1½ tablespoons olive oil to the pan. Return the crabs to pan, on their backs, and cook until crisp, about 5 minutes more. Remove the crabs from the pan, and keep warm on a baking sheet in the oven. Repeat with the remaining olive oil and crabs.

4. Divide the arugula among four plates. Arrange 2 crabs over each plate of arugula, spoon the confit over or around the crabs, and serve.

red pepper and lemon confit

SERVES 4

1½   tablespoons olive oil

5   shallots (about 5 ounces), sliced into ¼-inch rounds

4   red bell peppers (about 1¾ pounds), seeds and ribs removed, cut into long, thin strips

1   cup dry white wine

½   teaspoon kosher salt

⅛   teaspoon freshly ground black pepper

1   lemon

1. Heat the oil in a large skillet over medium-low heat. Add the shallots, and cook until they begin to brown, about 15 minutes. Add the bell peppers, wine, salt, and pepper. Cover and cook until the wine is almost absorbed, about 20 minutes, stirring occasionally. Uncover and reduce heat to low. Cook, stirring occasionally, until the peppers are tender, about 15 minutes.

2. Meanwhile, remove the zest from the lemon in long thin strips, and set aside. Cut the white pith away from the lemon. Working over a bowl to catch the juices, slice between the sections and membranes of the lemon; remove the segments whole. Place each segment in the bowl as completed. Cut the segments in half, and add to the peppers along with the zest. Toss to combine, and serve.

crab boil

SERVES 4 TO 6

Serve with wooden mallets (see Equipment Sources, page 650) and lots of napkins. There are many brands of crab boil; look locally, or see Food Sources, page 648.

8   lemons, halved

2   pounds onions, cut in quarters

1   cup kosher salt

4   bags crab boil

2   tablespoons cayenne pepper

3   heads of garlic, cut crosswise

6   dried bay leaves

¼   cup whole black peppercorns

18   live crabs

10   pounds live crayfish (also called crawfish, crawdads, and freshwater crab or lobster)

1. Fill a large stockpot with water. Squeeze the lemon into it, and add the rinds. Add the onions, salt, crab boil, cayenne, garlic, bay leaves, and peppercorns. Cover and bring to a boil over high heat. Boil for 10 minutes. Add crabs, cover, and return to a boil. Add crayfish, cover, and return to a boil.

2. Remove the pot from the heat, and let the seafood stand in the water for 10 minutes. Drain, discarding the seasonings. Serve on a large tray.

maquechoux oysters

SERVES 8

This spicy fried oyster dish hails from Parlange, a beautiful eighteenth-century home outside Baton Rouge, Louisiana. Maquechoux is a traditional Cajun dish, and refers to the piquant topping of red and jalapeño peppers with corn.

3½ dozen fresh oysters, in the shells

1 tablespoon olive oil

1 large onion, finely diced

4 ears fresh corn, kernels shaved from the cob

½ teaspoon kosher salt

Pinch of cayenne pepper

1 large red bell pepper, seeds and ribs removed, cut into ¼-inch dice

2 jalapeño peppers, seeds and ribs removed, minced

Canola oil, for frying

2 cups yellow cornmeal

Red Pepper Mayonnaise (recipe follows)

1. Scrub the oysters well with a brush under running water. Discard any that are open or have broken shells. Shuck the oysters, saving all the liquid and bottom halves of shells. Scrub the shells inside and out, and set aside. Refrigerate the oysters in the reserved liquid, covered, until ready to use.

2. Heat the olive oil in a medium skillet over medium-low heat. Add the onion, and cook, covered, until translucent, about 8 minutes.

3. Add the corn, and cook, stirring, for about 5 minutes, or until the corn is softened. Add the salt, cayenne, red pepper, and jalapeños, and cook for 2 minutes. Set aside.

4. Drain the oysters, reserving the liquid. Measure the liquid, and add enough water to make 1 cup. Pour into the skillet. Raise the heat to medium, and cook about 10 minutes, or until the liquid is mostly reduced. Set aside.

5. In a large skillet, heat 1 inch of canola oil until it registers 375°F on a deep-frying thermometer.

Dredge the oysters in the cornmeal, coating them completely. Fry the oysters in the hot oil in batches (don't let them overlap). Drain the fried oysters on paper towels.

6. Arrange 4 or 5 oyster shells on each plate. Spoon about 1 teaspoon of the mayonnaise into each shell, and top with a fried oyster and some of the corn mixture. Serve immediately.

red pepper mayonnaise

MAKES 1 CUP

1 large roasted red bell pepper (see page 645)

1 large egg yolk

1 teaspoon kosher salt

¼ teaspoon cayenne pepper

1 large garlic clove

Juice of 1 lemon

¾ cup extra-virgin olive oil

1. Place the roasted pepper in a blender or a food processor with the egg yolk, salt, cayenne pepper, garlic, and lemon juice. Blend until smooth.

2. With the machine running, add the oil a few drops at a time. As the mixture starts to thicken, pour in the remaining oil in a slow, steady stream, and mix until incorporated. The mayonnaise will keep, in an airtight container in the refrigerator, for up to 3 days.

NOTE *Raw eggs should not be used in food prepared for pregnant women, babies, young children, the elderly, or anyone whose health is compromised.*

steamed shrimp

SERVES 8 AS PART OF A BUFFET OR
3 TO 4 AS A MAIN COURSE

- 1 tablespoon rice wine
- 2 tablespoons soy sauce
- ½ teaspoon sugar
- 1 pound (about 24) large shrimp, heads and shells left on
- 1 tablespoon thinly sliced scallion greens

1. In a small bowl, whisk together the rice wine, soy sauce, and sugar; set aside.

2. Divide the shrimp between the two compartments of a bamboo steamer; cover. Set the steamer over a wok filled with 5 to 6 cups water; place the wok over medium heat, and steam until the shrimp are opaque and cooked through, about 8 minutes. (Alternatively, steam the shrimp, working in batches if needed, in a steamer basket placed over 1 inch of water.) Transfer the shrimp to a serving plate, pour the sauce over, and garnish with the scallion greens. Serve immediately.

shrimp sautéed with bacon and herbs

SERVES 4

- 1½ pounds (about 36) large shrimp, peeled and deveined, tails intact
- 1 large garlic clove, sliced thinly
- 1½ teaspoons finely chopped fresh rosemary
- 1½ teaspoons fresh thyme leaves
- 1½ tablespoons olive oil
- 4 ounces bacon, cut into 1½-inch dice
  Kosher salt and freshly ground black pepper
- 2 teaspoons fresh lemon juice
- ½ cup Homemade Chicken Stock (page 624), or store-bought low-sodium chicken broth, skimmed of fat
- 1½ tablespoons unsalted butter

1. In a medium bowl, toss together the shrimp, garlic, rosemary, thyme, and oil. Set aside to marinate at room temperature for 30 minutes.

2. Arrange the bacon in a large skillet, and cook over medium-high heat, stirring occasionally, until almost all the fat is rendered, about 8 minutes. Pour off and discard all but 2 tablespoons of the bacon fat. Add the shrimp, marinade ingredients, and salt and pepper to taste; cook over medium-high heat, until the shrimp are opaque and cooked through, about 2½ minutes per side.

3. Remove the shrimp and bacon, and transfer to a serving dish. Add the lemon juice and stock to the skillet; cook, stirring up the cooked-on brown bits. Cook until the liquid is reduced by half, about 2 minutes. Swirl in the butter; cook, swirling the skillet until the butter has melted. Pour the sauce over the shrimp, and serve hot.

firecracker prawns

SERVES 8

- 4 large shallots
- 1 pound (about 24) large shrimp
- 3 tablespoons cornstarch
- ½ teaspoon paprika
- 1½ teaspoons kosher salt
- ½ teaspoon freshly ground black pepper
- 3 tablespoons canola oil
- 1 teaspoon minced garlic
- 1 teaspoon sugar
- 1 teaspoon Asian fish sauce (nam pla)
- ½ red or yellow bell pepper, seeds and ribs removed, thinly sliced
- 2 scallions, white and light-green parts, sliced diagonally ½ inch wide
- 1 fresh serrano chile pepper or ½ jalapeño pepper, seeds and ribs removed, thinly sliced
- ½ teaspoon whole black peppercorns
- ½ teaspoon whole white peppercorns
- 3 sprigs fresh cilantro, for garnish

1. Thinly slice 2 of the shallots; set aside. Finely chop the remaining 2 shallots. Using kitchen shears, cut through the shrimp shells along the back. Leaving the shells on, use a small sharp knife to devein the shrimp.

2. Carefully lift one side of the shrimp shells; tuck about ½ teaspoon chopped shallot onto the shrimp. Gently press the shells back in place.

3. Combine the cornstarch, paprika, salt, and pepper. Add the shrimp, and toss to coat.

4. In a large nonstick skillet, heat the oil over medium-high heat. Add the shrimp, and cook just until opaque, about 2 minutes on each side. Scatter the garlic and reserved sliced shallots over the shrimp, and cook, shaking the pan often, about 1 minute. Add the sugar, fish sauce, 3 tablespoons water, bell pepper, scallions, serrano pepper, and black and white peppercorns. Toss to combine. Cook, shaking the pan often, 1 minute. Serve immediately, garnished with the cilantro.

jumbo shrimp with cilantro stuffing

SERVES 4

- 2 *lemons*
- 2 *cups loosely packed fresh cilantro leaves, finely chopped, plus more for garnish*
- 1 *garlic clove, minced*
- 1 *large shallot, minced*
- ¼ *cup plus 4 teaspoons olive oil*
- 1 *teaspoon kosher salt*
- ½ *teaspoon freshly ground black pepper*
- 1¼ *pounds (about 16) jumbo shrimp*
- ¼ *cup dry white wine*

1. Squeeze the juice from 1 lemon into a small bowl. Add the cilantro, garlic, shallot, ¼ cup olive oil, and the salt and pepper. Combine, and set aside.

2. Using a paring knife, split each shrimp down the back, cutting just enough to expose the vein; remove the vein, leaving the shell and tail intact.

3. Using your fingers, fill the spaces between the shells and flesh with the cilantro mixture.

4. Cut the second lemon into 8 wedges. Heat 2 teaspoons olive oil in a large skillet over medium-high heat. Arrange 8 shrimp and 4 lemon wedges in the skillet; cook until the shrimp is opaque and cooked through, about 4 minutes per side. Remove from the pan, and set aside. Repeat with the remaining

shrimp and lemon, adding the remaining 2 teaspoons olive oil. Pour the white wine into the empty skillet. Using a wooden spoon, scrape up any cooked-on bits; cook over medium-high heat until reduced by half, about 1 minute. Pour the sauce over the shrimp, and garnish with the cilantro.

curried shrimp skewers with rice salad

SERVES 4

- 1 *cup basmati rice*
- 2 *lemons*
- ⅓ *cup chopped fresh mint leaves*
- ⅓ *cup chopped fresh cilantro leaves*
- ⅓ *cup chopped fresh flat-leaf parsley*
- 1½ *tablespoons olive oil*
- ¾ *teaspoon kosher salt*
- ¼ *teaspoon freshly ground black pepper*
- 1 *pound (about 24) large shrimp, peeled and deveined, tails intact*
- 2 *teaspoons Curry Powder (page 633) or prepared*

1. Place rice and 1¾ cups water in a small saucepan, cover, and bring to a boil. Reduce heat to low. Simmer, covered, until all the water is absorbed, 20 minutes. Let sit 5 minutes, fluff, and let cool.

2. Grate zest from 1 lemon into a bowl; squeeze lemons to yield ¼ cup plus 2 tablespoons juice. Add juice to bowl. Add rice, mint, cilantro, parsley, 1 tablespoon oil, salt, and pepper; toss to combine.

3. Heat a grill or a grill pan until very hot. Place the shrimp in a medium bowl. Add the remaining ½ tablespoon olive oil and curry powder. Toss until shrimp are well coated. Thread shrimp onto skewers; place on hot grill. Cook until cooked through, about 2½ minutes per side; serve over the rice.

FIT TO EAT RECIPE PER SERVING: 371 CALORIES, 27 G PROTEIN, 8 G FAT, 172 MG CHOLESTEROL, 47 G CARBOHYDRATE, 574 MG SODIUM, 0 G DIETARY FIBER

steamers with asian broth and cilantro butter

SERVES 6 TO 8

Though categorized as soft-shell clams, the shells of steamers are hard to the touch; their shells are simply softer than quahog shells. Steamers can be easily identified by the necklike protrusion from the shell.

- 1 cup unsalted clam juice
- 1 cup loosely packed fresh Thai basil or basil leaves
- 1 2-inch piece lemongrass, coarsely chopped
- 3 limes, cut into wedges, plus 3 tablespoons fresh juice
- 1 tablespoon Asian fish sauce (nam pla)
- 1 teaspoon kosher salt
- 1 cup loosely packed fresh cilantro leaves
- ¾ cup (1½ sticks) unsalted butter
- 8 pounds steamer clams, scrubbed, or littlenecks or cherrystones

1. Combine 2 cups water, the clam juice, basil, lemongrass, lime juice, fish sauce, and the salt in a large stockpot. Cover and bring to a boil over high heat, reduce heat, and simmer until flavorful, about 30 minutes.

2. Meanwhile, combine the cilantro and the butter in a food processor; mix until cilantro is chopped in tiny flecks. Set aside in a small saucepan.

3. Pass the liquid in the stockpot through a fine sieve or cheesecloth-lined strainer. Return the liquid to the stockpot, and set over medium-high heat. Add the clams to the liquid, or use a bamboo steamer, if desired; cover the pan. Cook until the clams open, 10 to 12 minutes; discard any unopened ones. Melt the cilantro butter.

4. Serve the clams with the lime wedges, broth for rinsing off the sand, and the melted cilantro butter for dipping.

seafood paella

SERVES 6

Brands of clam juice vary in sodium content; choose one that contains 60 milligrams per ounce or less.

- 3 cups Homemade Chicken Stock (page 624) or low-sodium store-bought chicken broth, skimmed of fat
- 2 cups low-sodium clam juice
  Pinch of saffron threads
- 1 cup sugar snap peas, stems trimmed, strings removed, cut in half on the bias
- 2 tablespoons olive oil
- 2 links fresh chicken sausage, cut into ½-inch rounds
- 12 medium shrimp, peeled and deveined
- 12 squid (about 1 pound), cleaned and cut into 1-inch rings
- 1 medium onion, finely diced
- 2 tablespoons minced garlic
- 1 red bell pepper, seeds and ribs removed, cut into 1-inch-long matchsticks
- 1 yellow bell pepper, seeds and ribs removed, cut into 1-inch-long matchsticks
- 1 pound uncooked paella rice
- 1 pound cockles (baby clams) and mussels, scrubbed, debearded, and washed clean
- ¼ teaspoon paprika
- ¼ teaspoon freshly ground black pepper
- 6 plum tomatoes, seeded and cut into ¼-inch dice
- ¼ cup coarsely chopped fresh flat-leaf parsley

1. Place the stock, clam juice, and saffron in a medium saucepan over medium-high heat. Cover and bring to a boil; reduce heat, and simmer 15 minutes. Remove from the heat; set aside.

2. Prepare an ice-water bath. Bring a medium saucepan of water to a boil, and blanch the sugar snap peas until bright green and just tender, about 1 minute. Using a slotted spoon, transfer the peas to the ice bath; let cool. Drain, and set aside.

3. Heat the olive oil in a paella pan (or a 6-quart Dutch oven that measures about 11 inches in diameter and 5 inches in height) over medium-high heat. Add the sausage, and cook until well browned, turning, about 5 minutes.

4. Add the shrimp, and cook 1½ minutes. Add the squid, and cook until opaque, about 1½ minutes more. Transfer the seafood and the sausage to a plate, and set aside.

5. Add the onion, garlic, and bell peppers to the pan; cook until the onions are translucent, about 5 minutes. Add the uncooked rice; cook until translucent, 1 to 2 minutes more. Add 4 cups of the reserved stock mixture; cover and bring to a boil. Reduce heat to medium low, and cover. Cook until most of the liquid has been absorbed and the rice is just tender, about 10 minutes.

6. Meanwhile, place the remaining cup of stock, the cockles, and mussels in a medium skillet over medium-high heat. Cover, and bring to a boil. Cook until all the shells have opened, about 5 minutes; discard any that remain closed.

7. Add the paprika, black pepper, tomatoes, shrimp, squid, and sausage to the rice mixture, and combine. Add the cockles, mussels, and cooking liquid to the mixture, being careful to leave behind any gritty residue in the skillet. Stir in the parsley; garnish with the peas. Serve immediately.

FIT TO EAT RECIPE PER SERVING: 585 CALORIES, 11 G FAT, 258 MG CHOLESTEROL, 77 G CARBOHYDRATE, 904 MG SODIUM, 44 G PROTEIN, 4 G DIETARY FIBER

clam pan roast
with sausage and fennel
SERVES 6

1 *garlic clove, minced*

8 *ounces sweet Italian sausage, casings removed*

4 *ounces kielbasa, cut into ½-inch cubes*

12 *small red new potatoes, cut in half*

3 *small (about 3 pounds total) fennel bulbs, cut into ¼-inch-thick slices*

1 *small leek, white and pale-green parts, cut into ¼-inch rounds, well washed (see page 646)*

¼ *cup Pernod or other anise liqueur*

1½ *cups unsalted clam juice*

½ *teaspoon kosher salt*

½ *teaspoon freshly ground black pepper*

2½ *pounds littleneck clams, scrubbed*

2 *large tomatoes, cut into 8 wedges each*

¼ *cup coarsely chopped fresh tarragon leaves*

1. In a Dutch oven or deep skillet over medium heat, cook the garlic and the sausage, breaking up the meat, about 5 minutes; using a slotted spoon, transfer to a bowl. Drain off and discard all but 1 tablespoon of the rendered fat; cook the kielbasa until crisp, about 8 minutes. Add to the bowl.

2. Arrange the potatoes in the pan, cut-side down; cook over medium heat until golden brown, about 7 minutes. Turn; cook about 5 minutes more, until just tender. Scatter the fennel among the potatoes. Cook about 10 minutes more, stirring often.

3. Add the leek, Pernod, clam juice, salt, and the pepper; cook until the vegetables are tender, about 5 minutes. Return the sausages to the pan; mix to combine. Add the clams, cover, and cook about 5 minutes. Add the tomatoes; cook, covered, until the clams open, about 7 minutes; discard the unopened clams. Stir in the tarragon, and serve.

baked clams with
pine nuts and basil

MAKES 6

- ⅓ cup pine nuts, toasted (see page 644)
- 2 pounds quahog clams, shucked, liquid and shells reserved, coarsely chopped
- 5 pounds cherrystone clams, shucked, liquid reserved, coarsely chopped
- 1 garlic clove, minced
- 1 tablespoon unsalted butter, room temperature, cut into very small pieces, plus 1 tablespoon melted butter
- 1 cup loosely packed fresh basil leaves, coarsely chopped
- 1 tablespoon fresh lemon juice, plus 1 lemon, sliced into wedges
- 1 tablespoon dry vermouth
- ½ teaspoon kosher salt
- ¼ teaspoon freshly ground black pepper
- ¼ cup dry bread crumbs (see page 647)

1. Preheat the oven to 400°F. Finely chop the pine nuts, and set aside.

2. Wash and dry 6 of the quahog shells; set aside.

3. Combine the clams, pine nuts, garlic, 1 tablespoon softened butter, the basil, lemon juice, vermouth, salt, and the pepper; add 1 to 2 tablespoons of the clam liquid. In a separate bowl, mix the bread crumbs with the melted butter.

4. Divide the clam mixture among the reserved shells on a baking sheet; sprinkle with the bread crumbs, and bake until golden brown, about 15 minutes. Serve hot with the lemon wedges.

orange-flavored scallops

SERVES 6

To stir-fry properly, constantly toss, turn, and stir ingredients with tongs or a long-handled spoon.

- 1 pound sea scallops, muscle removed
- ¾ cup fresh orange juice (about 3 oranges)
- 1 tablespoon freshly grated ginger, plus 3 tablespoons fresh ginger cut in matchsticks
- 2 tablespoons rice-wine vinegar
- 1 orange
- 1 tablespoon canola oil
- 2 garlic cloves, thinly sliced
- 2 small leeks, white and pale-green parts, cut into 3-inch-long matchsticks, well washed (see page 646)
- 6 medium carrots, cut into 3-inch-long matchsticks
  Kosher salt
- 1¾ cups Homemade Chicken Stock (page 624) or low-sodium store-bought chicken broth, skimmed of fat
- 2 tablespoons fresh cilantro leaves

1. In a medium bowl, combine scallops, orange juice, grated ginger, and vinegar, and set aside.

2. Use a vegetable peeler to remove long strips of zest from the orange. Do not remove the white pith. Cover and bring a small saucepan of water to a boil. Add the orange zest, and blanch 2 minutes. Remove from the heat, drain, and place under cold running water to stop the cooking. Cut the zest into matchsticks. Set aside.

3. Set a large straight-sided skillet over high heat until very hot. Add the oil, and swirl to cover the bottom. Remove the scallops from the marinade; pat dry. Set aside the marinade. Cook the scallops, stirring constantly, 2 minutes. Add the matchstick ginger and the garlic; cook until the scallops have cooked through, about 2 minutes. Using a slotted spoon, transfer the scallops to a covered bowl.

4. Add the leeks, carrots, and reserved orange zest. Season with salt. Cook 1 minute. Add the stock and the marinade; cover. Cook until the carrots are tender, about 10 minutes. Remove the lid; cook to reduce the liquid by half, about 5 minutes. Return the scallops to the pan; cook 1 minute. Garnish with the cilantro. Serve hot.

FIT TO EAT RECIPE PER SERVING: 164 CALORIES, 4 G FAT, 25 MG CHOLESTEROL, 16 G CARBOHYDRATE, 218 MG SODIUM, 15 G PROTEIN, 3 G DIETARY FIBER

seared scallops niçoise

SERVES 6

Slice very large scallops in half crosswise before sprinkling with the peppercorn mixture.

1½   teaspoons whole pink peppercorns
1½   teaspoons whole dried green peppercorns
1½   teaspoons whole white peppercorns
1½   teaspoons whole black peppercorns
2½   tablespoons red-wine vinegar
 2   teaspoons Dijon mustard
 ¼   cup plus 3 tablespoons olive oil
     Kosher salt and freshly ground
     black pepper
1½   pounds haricots verts, trimmed
1½   pounds fresh fava beans, shelled (about 2
     cups shelled)
 1   pound sea scallops, muscle removed
 ½   cup niçoise olives (about 3 ounces)
 1   small red onion, thinly sliced lengthwise
24   small red or orange tomatoes, halved
 3   large hard-boiled eggs (page 571),
     cut into 8 wedges
     Fresh tarragon, for garnish
     Lemon wedges, optional

1. In a spice grinder, coarsely grind each type of peppercorn separately. Transfer to a small bowl, and toss to combine. Set aside.

2. In another small bowl, mix together the vinegar and mustard; add ¼ cup plus 2 tablespoons oil in a slow, steady stream, whisking continuously. Season to taste with salt and pepper, and set the dressing aside.

3. Prepare an ice-water bath; set aside. Cover a large pot of salted water, and bring to a boil. Add the haricots verts, and cook until bright green and just tender, about 1 minute. Using a slotted spoon, lift the beans from the water, and transfer to the ice-water bath until cool. Remove the beans from the ice bath with a slotted spoon, and transfer to a clean kitchen towel. Pat the beans dry, and transfer them to a large bowl. Set aside.

4. Return the water to a boil. Add the fava beans, and cook until just tender, 2 to 3 minutes. Drain and transfer to the ice-water bath. Drain in a colander. Remove and discard the inner skins from the fava beans, and add the fava beans to the haricots verts.

5. Sprinkle the scallops with salt and the reserved peppercorn mixture. Heat a heavy iron skillet until very hot over medium-high heat. Add 1½ teaspoons olive oil. Add half the scallops, and cook until well browned, 2 to 3 minutes per side. Transfer to a plate, and set aside.

6. Add the remaining 1½ teaspoons olive oil to the skillet. Repeat with the remaining scallops, and transfer to the plate.

7. Add the olives, onion, tomatoes, and reserved dressing to the beans, and toss to combine.

8. Arrange the bean-and-tomato salad on six plates. Top with the eggs and scallops; garnish with the tarragon. Serve with lemon wedges, if desired.

sautéed scallops
over spaghetti squash

SERVES 4

2 *1-pound spaghetti squash, cut in half lengthwise and seeded*

2 *tablespoons olive oil, plus more for pan*

4 *leeks, white and pale-green parts, thinly sliced lengthwise, well washed (page 646)*

2 *medium shallots, thinly sliced lengthwise*

¼ *cup all-purpose flour*

10 *large sea scallops, muscle removed, sliced in half*

   Kosher salt and freshly ground black pepper

¾ *cup dry white wine or water*

2 *tablespoons unsalted butter, chilled, cut into small pieces*

1 *bunch snipped chives*

1. Preheat the oven to 375°F. Place the squash, cut-sides down, on an oiled baking pan. Cook until the squash is easily pierced with a knife tip, about 45 minutes. Using a fork, separate the flesh into strands, and transfer to a bowl; cover.

2. Heat 1 tablespoon oil in a saucepan over medium heat. Cook the leeks and the shallots, stirring, until crisp, about 10 minutes. Transfer to a plate.

3. Place the flour in a small bowl; dredge the scallops. Return the pan to the heat; add the remaining tablespoon of oil. Shake off any excess flour, and cook half of the scallops until golden, about 3 minutes per side. Season with salt and pepper. Cook the remaining scallops.

4. Increase heat to medium high; add the wine. Using a wooden spoon, scrape up any brown bits on the bottom of the pan. Cook until the liquid has reduced by half. Slowly whisk in the butter until the sauce begins to thicken, about 2 minutes; season with salt and pepper.

5. Divide the squash and the leek mixture among four dinner plates; top with scallops. Drizzle with the sauce, and garnish with the chives. Serve hot.

meatless main dishes

·······················

chunky vegetable potpie

SERVES 6

½   medium (about 8 ounces) butternut squash, peeled and cut into ¾-inch cubes

1   small head celeriac, cut into ½-inch cubes

2   medium carrots, cut into thick matchsticks

½   cup yellow cauliflower florets

½   cup green cauliflower florets

8   ounces brussels sprouts, cleaned and trimmed, sliced lengthwise if large

1   medium beet, trimmed and scrubbed, cut into ¼-inch pieces

1   small turnip or 2 parsnips, cut into thick 1-inch-long matchsticks

¼   cup olive oil

     Kosher salt and freshly ground black pepper

3   garlic cloves, minced

2   medium shallots, minced

½   cup dry white wine

1½   cups Vegetable Stock (page 626), or low-sodium store-bought vegetable broth

1   cup plus 2 tablespoons all-purpose flour

2   teaspoons baking powder

2   tablespoons plus 2 teaspoons chopped fresh tarragon

3   tablespoons unsalted butter

½   cup milk

2   tablespoons freshly grated Parmesan cheese

1   medium zucchini, cut into thick 1-inch-long matchsticks

1. Preheat the oven to 425°F. Place squash, celeriac, carrots, yellow and green cauliflower, brussels sprouts, beet, and turnip in a roasting pan. Toss with 2 tablespoons olive oil; season with salt and pepper. Roast for 35 to 40 minutes, stirring twice during the cooking. Remove; reduce oven to 375°F.

2. Heat remaining olive oil in a medium skillet over medium heat. Add the garlic and shallots; cook until soft, about 5 minutes. Raise heat to high, and add the wine. Let the wine reduce by half, about 2 minutes. Add the vegetable stock, and simmer over medium-high heat for 5 minutes. Set aside.

3. Combine 1 cup flour, the baking powder, 2 teaspoons tarragon, and a sprinkling of salt in the bowl of a food processor. Pulse in butter until mixture resembles coarse meal. Add the milk and Parmesan, process until combined, and set aside.

4. Transfer vegetables to a large bowl. Add zucchini and the remaining 2 tablespoons flour and 2 tablespoons tarragon; toss to combine. Stir in stock mixture; season with salt and pepper. Transfer to a shallow, ovenproof glass pie dish; bake for 15 minutes. Remove from the oven, and drop heaping tablespoons of the biscuit dough over the vegetables, leaving some vegetables exposed. Place the pie dish on a baking sheet, and bake until the biscuits are golden, about 25 minutes. Serve hot.

curry chickpea potpie

SERVES 6

4   tablespoons unsalted butter

1   cup millet

2   cups boiling water

2   large eggs

¾   teaspoon kosher salt, plus more for seasoning

2   tablespoons chopped fresh flat-leaf parsley

8   ounces broccoli, cut into bite-size pieces

1   medium onion, chopped

2   cups (from ½ head) shredded green cabbage

2   garlic cloves, minced

1   tablespoon freshly grated ginger

1   tablespoon Curry Powder (page 633) or prepared

2   large carrots, cut into ½-inch dice

8   ounces small white potatoes, quartered

⅓   cup dried red lentils

½   cup canned chickpeas, drained

     Freshly ground black pepper

1. Melt 1 tablespoon butter in a skillet over medium-high heat. Add millet; cook until golden brown, about 3 minutes, stirring frequently. Add another tablespoon butter and the boiling water; return to a boil. Reduce heat to low; simmer, covered, 25 minutes. Transfer to a bowl to cool slightly; tent with foil. When cool, stir in eggs, ¾ teaspoon salt, and parsley.

2. Prepare an ice-water bath. Bring a large pot of salted water to a boil. Add the broccoli, and blanch for 20 seconds, until bright green. Transfer to the ice-water bath to cool. Drain, and set aside.

3. Preheat the oven to 350°F. Melt 1 tablespoon butter in a saucepan over medium-high heat. Add onion; cook, stirring occasionally, to soften, 5 minutes. Add cabbage; cook, stirring occasionally, 3 minutes. Add garlic, ginger, and curry powder; cook 2 minutes. Pour in 2 cups water; using a wooden spoon, scrape up any brown bits on the bottom of the pan. Add carrots, potatoes, lentils, and chickpeas; bring to a boil. Reduce heat to medium low; simmer, covered, for 20 minutes. Stir in reserved broccoli; season with salt and pepper.

4. Place the stew in a 1½-quart ovenproof casserole; cover with millet mixture. Dot with the remaining butter; place on a baking sheet. Bake 30 minutes, until golden brown and crisp. Serve hot.

scallion ravioli in fresh tomato sauce

SERVES 4

- 1   *pound firm tofu*
- ¾   *teaspoon kosher salt, plus more for seasoning*
- ¼   *teaspoon freshly ground black pepper plus more for seasoning*
- ⅓   *cup thinly sliced scallions*
- 1   *large egg white*
- 24   *2½-inch round gyoza wrappers*
- 6   *plum tomatoes*
- 1   *tablespoon olive oil*
- ¾   *teaspoon minced garlic*
      Pinch of cayenne pepper
- 1   *tablespoon balsamic vinegar*
- 1½ *tablespoons freshly grated Parmesan cheese*

1. Place the tofu, ¾ teaspoon salt, and ¼ teaspoon black pepper in the bowl of a food processor. Process until the texture resembles that of ricotta cheese, about 40 seconds. Add the scallions, and process until incorporated, 10 seconds more.

2. In a small bowl, whisk together the egg white and 1 teaspoon water to make an egg wash; set aside.

3. Lay 6 gyoza wrappers on a clean work surface. Place a tablespoon of the tofu mixture in the center of each wrapper. Lightly brush the edges of the wrappers with the egg wash. Fold ravioli in half, and press the edges together to seal. Cover the sealed ravioli with plastic wrap, to keep it from drying out, and repeat with remaining filling and wrappers.

4. Cut the tomatoes lengthwise into quarters. Set a strainer over a small bowl. Hold a tomato quarter over the strainer, and scoop out the seeds and juice; set the flesh aside. Repeat with the remaining tomatoes. Using a rubber spatula, press all the tomato juice through the strainer. Discard the seeds and pulp; reserve the juice. Dice the reserved tomato flesh into ¼-inch pieces.

5. Heat the oil in a medium nonstick skillet over medium heat. Add the garlic, cover, and let cook until translucent, stirring occasionally, about 3 minutes. Add the diced tomatoes, reserved tomato juice, and the cayenne pepper. Season with salt and black pepper; cook 1 minute. Add the balsamic vinegar, and cook for 30 seconds more. Cover, and remove from the heat.

6. Cover a stockpot of salted water, and bring to a boil. Add the ravioli, and simmer until tender, about 4 minutes. Use a slotted spoon to transfer the ravioli to a colander, and drain. Over medium heat, quickly reheat the tomato sauce, about 30 seconds. Pour ¼ cup of the tomato sauce onto each of four plates. Place 6 ravioli on each plate. Sprinkle with the grated Parmesan; serve.

FIT TO EAT RECIPE PER SERVING: 265 CALORIES, 8 G FAT, 5 MG CHOLESTEROL, 31 G CARBOHYDRATE, 559 MG SODIUM, 19 G PROTEIN, 4 G DIETARY FIBER

couscous-stuffed eggplant

SERVES 6

This can be made 4 to 6 hours in advance; reheat before serving.

- 4 small eggplants
- 3 tablespoons olive oil
- 1 medium onion, finely chopped
- 1 yellow or red bell pepper, seeds and ribs removed, cut into ¼-inch dice
- 1 teaspoon kosher salt
- ½ teaspoon freshly ground black pepper
- ¾ cup uncooked couscous
- 1 cup boiling water
- Grated zest of 2 lemons
- ¼ cup low-fat ricotta cheese
- ¼ cup roughly chopped fresh flat-leaf parsley leaves, plus more for garnish
- ½ head of roasted garlic (see page 646)
- 8 ounces red and yellow cherry tomatoes, cut into eighths

1. Cut 3 eggplants in half lengthwise, and place the 6 halves, cut-sides up, on a cutting board. Using a paring knife, cut around the perimeters, leaving a ⅓-inch-wide border and being careful not to cut through the skin. Cutting down through the flesh, slice lengthwise into ¼-inch-wide strips. Using a small spoon, scoop out the strips, keeping the skin intact. Cut strips into ¼-inch dice. Set both the diced eggplant and the shells aside. Cut the remaining eggplant, skin on, into ¼-inch dice. Set aside.

2. Heat 2 tablespoons olive oil in a large skillet over medium heat. Add the onion, and cook, stirring occasionally, until soft and slightly browned, about 8 minutes. Add all the diced eggplant, the bell pepper, ½ teaspoon salt, and ¼ teaspoon black pepper. Cover; cook, stirring occasionally, until browned, about 6 minutes. If the mixture starts to become dry, add the additional tablespoon of oil. Set aside.

3. Preheat the oven to 400°F. Place the couscous in a medium heat-proof bowl. Pour 1 cup boiling water over the couscous. Cover and let sit until slightly cooled, about 10 minutes. Fluff with a fork. Add the lemon zest, ricotta, parsley, and the remaining ½ teaspoon salt and ¼ teaspoon pepper. Add the reserved eggplant mixture, the roasted garlic, and the cherry tomatoes. Stir to combine.

4. Fill each eggplant shell with couscous mixture; arrange on a baking sheet. Cover with aluminum foil. Bake until warm throughout and the shell has softened, about 20 minutes. Remove foil; cook until tops are toasted and brown, about 20 minutes. Remove from oven. Garnish with parsley; serve hot.

FIT TO EAT RECIPE PER SERVING: 222 CALORIES, 8 G FAT, 3 MG CHOLESTEROL, 35 G CARBOHYDRATE, 379 MG SODIUM, 6 G PROTEIN, 5 G DIETARY FIBER

wild mushroom and spinach lasagna

SERVES 10 TO 12

The meaty texture of wild mushrooms will satisfy even the most serious of meat eaters. Frozen spinach can be substituted for fresh, and fresh plain lasagna sheets can be substituted for the spinach sheets.

- 1 cup (2 sticks) unsalted butter
- 3 garlic cloves, finely sliced
- 5 pounds fresh spinach, washed, stems removed
- 1 pound ricotta cheese
- 2 tablespoons kosher salt
- 1¾ teaspoons freshly ground black pepper
- 3 pounds wild mushrooms (such as chanterelle, oyster, and shiitake), wiped clean, trimmed, cut into 1-inch pieces
- ¾ cup Madeira wine
- ½ cup chopped fresh flat-leaf parsley
- 1 quart plus ½ cup milk
- ½ cup all-purpose flour
- ½ teaspoon ground nutmeg
- 1 cup (3 ounces) grated Pecorino Romano cheese
- 1 1-pound package fresh spinach lasagna sheets

1. Melt 1 tablespoon butter in large pan over medium heat. Add half the garlic; cook until light golden, about 2 minutes. Add half the spinach leaves, cover, and cook, stirring occasionally, until wilted, about 5 minutes. Drain the spinach in a colander. Repeat with another tablespoon of the butter and the remaining garlic and spinach. When the spinach is cool enough to handle, squeeze to extract all the liquid. Roughly chop the spinach; place in a medium bowl. Add the ricotta, 2 teaspoons salt, and 1 teaspoon pepper; mix well.

2. Melt 2 tablespoons butter in a large skillet over medium heat. Add one third of the mushrooms; season with 1 teaspoon salt and ¼ teaspoon pepper. Cook until the mushrooms are softened and browned, about 10 minutes. Pour ¼ cup Madeira into the hot skillet with the mushrooms, and use a wooden spoon to loosen any browned bits cooked onto the skillet. Cook the mushrooms until the liquid has almost evaporated. Transfer mushrooms to a medium bowl. Repeat with another 2 tablespoons butter, another third of the mushrooms, and ¼ cup Madeira. (Reserve remaining mushrooms and Madeira for the topping.) Stir in two-thirds of the chopped parsley with the mushrooms.

3. In a medium saucepan over medium heat, heat 1 quart milk. Melt 1 stick butter in a medium saucepan over medium heat. When the butter bubbles, sprinkle in the flour; cook, whisking constantly, 1 minute. Slowly add the warmed milk; cook, whisking constantly, until the mixture bubbles and becomes thick. Remove the pan from the heat. Stir in 2 teaspoons salt, ¼ teaspoon pepper, the nutmeg, and ½ cup grated cheese.

4. Preheat the oven to 350°F. Set aside ½ cup of the sauce. Assemble the lasagna: Spread ½ cup of the sauce in the bottom of a 9 x 13-inch roasting pan. Place a layer of lasagna sheets in the pan, trimming to fit; spread 1 cup of the spinach mixture, 1 cup of the mushroom mixture, and ½ cup of the sauce on top of the lasagna sheets. Repeat the layers several times. For the last layer, place lasagna sheets on top; spread ½ cup of the sauce over the sheets. Sprinkle with the remaining ½ cup grated cheese. Bake until the top is golden brown, 1 to 1¼ hours. Let stand 20 minutes before serving.

5. Just before serving, melt the remaining 2 tablespoons butter in the skillet over medium heat. Add the remaining third of the uncooked mushrooms; season with 1 teaspoon salt and ¼ teaspoon pepper. Cook until golden and tender, about 10 minutes. Add the remaining ¼ cup Madeira, and stir with a wooden spoon to loosen any cooked-on bits from the bottom of the pan. Stir in the remaining fresh parsley.

6. In a small saucepan, combine the reserved ½ cup of sauce with the remaining ½ cup of milk. Over medium heat, whisk until warm and smooth. Spoon the cooked mushrooms over each serving, or serve on the side. Serve the lasagna hot with the sauce.

spinach and cheese soufflé
MAKES ONE 1-QUART SOUFFLE; SERVES 4

You can make a plain cheese soufflé by omitting the chopped spinach, or make an all-green soufflé by doubling the amount of spinach and not dividing the base. Frozen spinach can be used if necessary, but the color and flavor won't be as vibrant.

- 3 tablespoons unsalted butter, room temperature, plus more for dish
  Finely grated Parmesan cheese, for dish
- 8 ounces fresh spinach, washed, stems removed
  Kosher salt
- 2 shallots, minced
- ¼ cup all-purpose flour
- 1 cup milk
  Pinch of freshly grated nutmeg
  Freshly ground black pepper
  Pinch of cayenne pepper
- 1 cup grated cheese (choose a dry, strong cheese such as Gruyère or aged goat cheese)
- 4 large egg yolks
- 6 large egg whites
  Pinch of cream of tartar

1. Preheat the oven to 400°F. Butter a 1-quart soufflé dish well, dust with Parmesan, and tap out the excess cheese. Cut out a parchment-paper collar to extend 3 inches above the rim of the dish. Tie the collar around the dish with kitchen twine, then, using a pastry brush, butter the inside of the paper. Transfer the dish to the freezer to chill.

2. Place the spinach with the water that clings to the leaves in a large saucepan over medium-high heat. Sprinkle with salt, and cover. Cook until the spinach starts to wilt, about 1 minute. Stir, cover, and cook 1 minute more, or until spinach is completely wilted. Drain spinach in a colander; refresh with cold water. Squeeze to remove as much moisture as possible. Chop finely by hand or in the bowl of a food processor. Set aside ¼ cup chopped spinach; set aside remainder for another use.

3. Heat 3 tablespoons butter in a medium saucepan over medium-low heat. Add shallots; cook until translucent, about 6 minutes. Add flour; cook 2 to 3 minutes. Add milk, nutmeg, salt and pepper to taste, and cayenne; stir until smooth. Cover and bring to a boil; lower heat, and simmer 5 minutes, stirring constantly. Add cheese; stir until melted. Season with salt and pepper—the base should be overseasoned, because the egg whites will dilute the flavor. Stir in egg yolks, one at a time. Transfer to a large bowl; cover with plastic wrap, pressing it onto the surface to prevent a skin from forming. Keep warm.

4. For a two-tone soufflé, divide base in half; place each half in a bowl. Stir ¼ cup chopped spinach into one bowl. In a large bowl, beat whites and cream of tartar until stiff peaks form. Mix a little egg white into each bowl to lighten mixtures, then divide the remaining whites between bowls. Fold in gently and quickly, then pour in both the batters side by side up to the rim of the dish. Bake for 15 minutes at 400°F., then reduce heat to 375°F.; bake until puffed and golden, about 15 minutes more. Carefully remove collar; serve immediately.

stuffed swiss chard rolls
SERVES 6

Swiss chard makes a sturdy yet tender wrapping for the mixed-mushroom filling.

- *1 pound cremini mushrooms, wiped clean*
- *1 pound shiitake mushrooms, wiped clean*
- *1 cup quinoa*
- *5 cups Vegetable Stock (page 626), or low-sodium store-bought vegetable broth*
- *½ teaspoon kosher salt, plus more for cooking water*
- *2 bunches red Swiss chard*
- *1 tablespoon unsalted butter*
- *2 tablespoons olive oil, plus more for brushing*
- *2 shallots, minced*
- *2 large carrots, cut into ⅛-inch dice*
- *¼ teaspoon freshly ground black pepper*
- *2 tablespoons fresh marjoram or oregano leaves*
- *2 tablespoons Marsala wine or sherry*

1. Preheat the oven to 350°F. Prepare an ice-water bath. Remove and discard the stems from all the mushrooms. Cut the cremini caps into quarters and the shiitake caps into ¼-inch slices; set aside.

2. Place the quinoa and 2¼ cups stock in a saucepan. Cover and bring to a boil over medium-high heat. Reduce heat; simmer until all the stock has been absorbed, about 20 minutes. Transfer the quinoa to a large bowl; set aside in a warm place.

3. Bring a large stockpot of lightly salted water to a boil. Place the chard in the boiling water, and blanch until tender and bright green, about 2 minutes. Using a slotted spoon, transfer the chard to the ice-water bath; let cool. Transfer the chard to paper towels, and pat dry. Carefully remove the stem from each leaf. Reserve the leaves, being careful not to tear them. Chop the stems into ¼-inch pieces.

4. Heat the butter and olive oil in a large skillet over medium-high heat. Add the shallots and carrots; cook until the shallots are translucent, about 5 minutes. Add the mushroom caps, chard stems, ½ teaspoon salt, and the pepper; cook until tender, stirring occasionally, about 8 minutes.

5. Remove 1½ cups of the mushroom mixture from the pan; add to the reserved quinoa. Set the remaining mushroom mixture aside. Coarsely chop 1 tablespoon marjoram; stir into the quinoa.

6. Divide the chard leaves into 6 portions. Form one portion into a 6 x 10-inch rectangle, overlapping the leaves so there are no gaps. Place ½ cup of the quinoa mixture at one short end. Starting at this end, roll, enclosing the sides. Brush the outside lightly with olive oil; place in a baking pan. Repeat, making five more rolls.

7. Transfer the pan to the oven, and cook the rolls until they are heated through, 5 to 10 minutes.

8. Meanwhile, place the remaining mushroom mixture over medium-high heat. Add the Marsala; cook, stirring, until most of the liquid has been absorbed. Add the remaining 2¾ cups stock; cook until slightly thickened, about 6 minutes. Stir in the remaining tablespoon marjoram.

9. Cut each chard roll in half; place in the center of a plate. Spoon the mushroom mixture around the chard, and serve immediately.

FIT TO EAT RECIPE PER SERVING: 197 CALORIES, 8 G FAT, 6 MG CHOLESTEROL, 24 G CARBOHYDRATE, 781 MG SODIUM, 7 G PROTEIN, 6 G DIETARY FIBER

cambodian-style tofu salad
SERVES 6

- 1 pound firm tofu, cut into 1-inch cubes
- 1 1-inch piece fresh ginger, peeled and coarsely chopped
- 3 large garlic cloves, coarsely chopped
- 1 jalapeño pepper, seeds and ribs removed, minced
- 1 tablespoon sugar
- 2 teaspoons Asian fish sauce (nam pla)
- ½ cup fresh lime juice
- 2 tablespoons rice-wine vinegar
  Kosher salt
- 1 pound green beans
- 3 medium carrots, cut into 2-inch matchsticks
- 7 scallions, white and pale-green parts, cut into 2-inch slivers
- 3 long (about 11 ounces) red Italian frying peppers or 2 red bell peppers, seeds and ribs removed, thinly sliced
- 1 head (8 ounces) Boston lettuce, shredded
- 1 cup fresh mint leaves
- ¼ cup roasted unsalted peanuts, coarsely chopped

1. Place the tofu between two layers of paper towel on a dish. Place a baking sheet over the tofu, and set a heavy book on top of the baking sheet to weight the tofu so it releases excess water; let stand about 30 minutes.

2. Combine the ginger, garlic, jalapeño, sugar, fish sauce, lime juice, and vinegar in a small saucepan. Cover and bring to a boil over medium-high heat, remove from the heat, and set aside.

3. Cover a large saucepan of salted water, and bring to a boil. Prepare an ice-water bath. Add the beans to the boiling water; cook until they are just tender and bright green, 3 to 4 minutes. With a slotted spoon, transfer them to the ice-water bath. When chilled, drain and pat dry.

4. Distribute the beans, carrots, scallions, red peppers, lettuce, and mint evenly among six plates.

5. Meanwhile, heat a large nonstick skillet over medium heat. Add the tofu, and cook until golden brown and slightly crisp, about 3 minutes per side. Add the ginger mixture, toss to coat the tofu, and cook about 1 minute more. Spoon the tofu and the sauce over the vegetables, sprinkle with the peanuts, and serve.

FIT TO EAT RECIPE PER SERVING: 196 CALORIES, 8 G FAT, 0 MG CHOLESTEROL, 21 G CARBOHYDRATE, 623 MG SODIUM, 13 G PROTEIN, 3 G DIETARY FIBER

tostada salad

SERVES 6

Cotija cheese is pungent and salty, much like feta. It is delicious crumbled into soups, over pasta, and onto pizza. Baking the tortillas until crisp, instead of frying them, cuts down significantly on fat and calories.

- 12   *corn tortillas*
- ¼   *teaspoon cayenne pepper, plus more for sprinkling*
- 5   *cups (3 15½-ounce cans) canned black beans, drained, liquid reserved, beans rinsed*
- ¾   *teaspoon ground cumin*
- 1½   *teaspoons dried oregano*
- ¾   *teaspoon kosher salt, plus more for seasoning*
- ¼   *teaspoon freshly ground black pepper, plus more for seasoning*
- 1½   *tablespoons sherry or red-wine vinegar*
- 5   *ounces romaine lettuce, cut across into ¼-inch strips*
- 3   *tomatoes, chopped into ½-inch dice*
- 2   *ounces Cotija or feta cheese, crumbled*
- 2   *scallions, white and green parts, halved lengthwise and cut into 1-inch lengths*
- 2   *radishes, trimmed and cut into thin slices*
- ¼   *cup chopped fresh cilantro leaves*
- 1   *jalapeño pepper, seeds and ribs removed, minced*

1. Preheat the oven to 375°F with a rack in the center. Place 6 tortillas on a baking sheet. Bake until just toasted, about 5 minutes per side. Set aside. Quarter the remaining 6 tortillas; place on baking sheet. Sprinkle with cayenne. Bake until just toasted, about 4 minutes per side. Set aside.

2. Heat the beans in a medium saucepan until hot. Place half in a medium bowl. Add 3 to 4 tablespoons of the reserved bean liquid, ¼ teaspoon cayenne, the cumin and oregano, ¾ teaspoon salt, ¼ teaspoon pepper, and the vinegar. Toss; set aside. Place the remaining beans in a medium bowl. Add 3 to 4 tablespoons of the bean liquid; mash until smooth.

3. Place 1 crisp whole tortilla on each plate. Spread each with the mashed black beans. Arrange the whole beans, lettuce, and half the tomatoes in layers on top of the tortilla. Sprinkle on the cheese and half the scallions, radishes, cilantro, and jalapeño. Combine the remaining half of the tomatoes, scallions, cilantro, and jalapeño in a small bowl to make a salsa. Season with salt and pepper. Drizzle the salsa over the tostadas, and serve with the crisp corn tortilla chips.

FIT TO EAT RECIPE PER SERVING: 352 CALORIES, 4 G FAT, 8 MG CHOLESTEROL, 63 G CARBOHYDRATE, 311 MG SODIUM, 18 G PROTEIN, 14 G DIETARY FIBER

roasted mushrooms with asparagus and parmesan

SERVES 6

- 1 tablespoon olive oil, plus more for brushing
- 2 pounds portobello mushrooms, wiped clean, stems removed and reserved
- 12 ounces shiitake mushrooms, wiped clean, stems removed and reserved
- 1½ cups dry white wine
- 1 ounce dried porcini mushrooms
- 8 sprigs fresh thyme
- 2 medium Yukon gold potatoes, peeled
- 12 medium shallots
- 6 garlic cloves
- 1 teaspoon kosher salt
- ¼ teaspoon freshly ground black pepper
- 1 pound thin asparagus, ends trimmed
- 1 tablespoon chopped fresh flat-leaf parsley

  Shaved Parmesan cheese, optional

1. Preheat the oven to 450°F. Brush two roasting pans with olive oil. Roughly chop the reserved stems of the portobello and shiitake mushrooms; transfer the stems to one pan. Arrange the mushroom caps in the second pan. Transfer both pans to the oven, and roast until the juices have been released, about 15 minutes. Remove the pan with mushroom caps from the oven, and set aside. Remove the pan with the stems, add the wine, and cook, stirring, over high heat 2 to 3 minutes; set aside.

2. Place the dried porcinis in a saucepan. Pour the stems and liquid from the roasting pan into the saucepan. Add 4 cups water and 4 sprigs thyme. Cover; simmer 45 minutes. Strain through a fine sieve or a cheesecloth-lined strainer. Press down on the solids with a spatula to rid the mushrooms of any excess liquid. Set aside. Discard the solids.

3. Cut the portobello caps in half; reserve. Slice the potatoes into 4 x 1-inch strips; set aside in a bowl of cold water.

4. Heat the olive oil in a large skillet over medium heat. Add the shallots and garlic; cover, and cook, turning until brown, about 5 minutes. Add the reserved broth, the remaining 4 sprigs thyme, 1 teaspoon salt, the pepper, the reserved caps, and the collected juices. Drain the potatoes; add to the broth. Simmer, covered, until the potatoes and shallots are soft, about 15 minutes, stirring once.

5. Cover a large pot of water, and bring to a boil. Prepare an ice-water bath. Blanch the asparagus in the boiling water just until bright green, 1 to 2 minutes. With a slotted spoon, transfer the asparagus to the ice-water bath. Drain. Add the asparagus to the broth; cook until heated through, about 3 minutes. Garnish with the parsley and shaved Parmesan, if using. Serve hot.

FIT TO EAT RECIPE PER SERVING: 223 CALORIES, 3 G FAT, 5 MG CHOLESTEROL, 39 G CARBOHYDRATE, 446 MG SODIUM, 12 G PROTEIN, 5 G DIETARY FIBER

roasted fall-vegetable salad

SERVES 4 TO 6

Serve this salad with a side dish of brown rice.

- 2 large (1¾ pounds) beets, scrubbed
- 3 large carrots
- 2 large portobello mushrooms, wiped clean
- 2 large leeks, white and green parts, cut into bite-size pieces, well washed (see page 646)
- 1 large butternut squash, peeled, seeded, cut into 1-inch pieces
- 3 shallots, halved
- 3 tablespoons extra-virgin olive oil
- 2 sprigs fresh rosemary
- 2 sprigs fresh thyme
- 1½ teaspoons kosher salt
- ½ teaspoon freshly ground black pepper
- 1 large bunch (1½ pounds) kale or mustard greens, cleaned, stems removed
- 2 tablespoons walnut oil
- 3 tablespoons red-wine vinegar

1. Preheat the oven to 450°F with two racks in it. Trim the beet stems to 1 inch. Place the beets on a sheet of aluminum foil; fold to make a packet. Cook until the tip of a knife slips easily into the beets; timing will vary with size, 35 to 75 minutes. When cool, peel; cut into ½-inch pieces. Reserve.

2. Meanwhile, cut carrots and portobellos into bite-size pieces. Transfer to a roasting pan; add leeks, squash, and shallots. Toss with 2 tablespoons olive oil. Add rosemary and thyme. Sprinkle with 1 teaspoon salt and ¼ teaspoon pepper. Bake, uncovered, until vegetables are tender, about 20 minutes.

3. Just before serving, heat the remaining tablespoon of oil in a medium skillet over medium heat until hot but not smoking. Add the kale in batches, sprinkle with 1 tablespoon water, cover, and cook until wilted, about 2 minutes. Set aside.

4. In a bowl, combine walnut oil, vinegar, and the remaining ½ teaspoon salt and ¼ teaspoon pepper.

5. Arrange the vegetables in rows on a serving platter. Drizzle with the vinaigrette, and serve.

FIT TO EAT RECIPE PER SERVING: 287 CALORIES, 10 G FAT, 0 MG CHOLESTEROL, 48 G CARBOHYDRATE, 811 MG SODIUM, 7 G PROTEIN, 9 G DIETARY FIBER

avocado enchiladas

SERVES 12 TO 14

Dried ancho chiles (see Food Sources, page 648) are available at specialty-food stores and many supermarkets.

- 2 dried ancho chiles
- 1 quart plus 1 tablespoon canola oil
- ½ medium onion, cut into ¼-inch dice
- 2 garlic cloves, minced
- 2 tablespoons packed light-brown sugar
- ¼ cup plus 1 tablespoon ground cumin
- 2 tablespoons dried oregano
- 2 cups dry white wine
- 1 28-ounce can crushed plum tomatoes
- 2 cups Vegetable Stock (page 626), or low-sodium store-bought vegetable broth
- 8 avocados, peeled and pitted (see page 647), roughly chopped
- 1 cup loosely packed fresh cilantro leaves, roughly chopped
- ¼ cup fresh lime juice
- ¾ teaspoon kosher salt
- ¼ teaspoon freshly ground black pepper
- 25 corn tortillas
- 1½ pounds Monterey Jack cheese, grated

1. Place the chiles in a saucepan; add water to cover. Bring to a boil over medium-high heat. Reduce heat; simmer 5 to 10 minutes. Cool slightly, remove the stems, and purée the chiles and the liquid in the bowl of a food processor. Set aside.

2. Heat 1 tablespoon oil in a deep skillet over medium heat. Add onion, garlic, sugar, cumin, and oregano; cook until onion is soft, about 5 minutes. Add wine, purée, tomatoes, and stock; simmer 20 minutes more, until the consistency of stew.

3. In a medium bowl, toss the avocados with the cilantro, lime juice, salt, and pepper. Set aside.

4. Preheat the oven to 400°F. Heat the remaining quart of oil in a wide, heavy saucepan over medium heat until very hot but not smoking, about 8 minutes. Using tongs, fry 6 tortillas, one at a time, for 2 to 3 seconds. Drain on a paper towel.

5. Dip the fried tortillas in the chile sauce to lightly coat both sides. Spoon 2 tablespoons of the avocado filling onto each tortilla; roll up. Spread ½ cup of the chile sauce into a large, deep casserole. Arrange the rolled tortillas in the casserole so they fit snugly and cover the bottom of casserole; pour 1 cup of the sauce over the tortillas; sprinkle with half of the cheese. Make a second layer using the remaining ingredients. Top with the remaining sauce and cheese.

6. Bake the enchiladas until heated through, about 15 minutes. Serve immediately.

spaghetti squash with cherry tomatoes and ricotta

SERVES 4

Juicy cherry tomatoes cooked with garlic and onion form a "sauce" for spaghetti squash garnished with herbed ricotta. The squash is cut in half and baked with sprigs of fresh herbs, then pulled away from its skin in long strands that resemble spaghetti.

15 ounces part-skim ricotta

1 tablespoon olive oil, plus more for brushing

4 garlic cloves, thinly sliced, plus ¼ teaspoon minced

¼ teaspoon crushed red-pepper flakes

¼ cup chopped fresh basil

¼ cup chopped fresh oregano

1 large (about 5 pounds) spaghetti squash

1 large onion, finely diced (2 cups)

2 pints cherry tomatoes, halved

½ cup dry white wine

½ teaspoon kosher salt

1. Wrap the ricotta tightly in a piece of fine cheesecloth; place in a colander over a bowl. Place a heavy bowl or cans on top, and let drain, refrigerated, for 3 hours or overnight.

2. Preheat the oven to 350°F. Brush a baking pan with olive oil, and place the sliced garlic on the pan. Bake 15 minutes; stir every 3 minutes. Remove pieces as they turn golden; set aside. Place the drained ricotta, red-pepper flakes, 3 tablespoons basil, and 3 tablespoons oregano in a bowl; combine. Cover with plastic wrap; set aside. Halve the squash lengthwise; remove the seeds. Place the squash, cut-sides down, on a lightly oiled baking pan. Bake until skin yields to pressure and flesh is soft, about 1 hour.

3. Heat a large skillet over medium-high heat. Add the olive oil, minced garlic, and onion to the pan; cover. Cook until translucent, about 8 minutes. Remove the lid; add the tomatoes, wine, and salt. Cook uncovered until the tomatoes are juicy, about 5 minutes. Stir in the remaining basil and oregano. Remove the herbs from the squash; discard. Pull the strands from the squash with a fork; transfer the squash strands to a serving bowl. Top with the tomato mixture, ricotta, and garlic slices; serve hot.

FIT TO EAT RECIPE PER SERVING: 195 CALORIES, 8 G FAT, 22 MG CHOLESTEROL, 19 G CARBOHYDRATE, 272 MG SODIUM, 10 G PROTEIN, 3 G DIETARY FIBER

vegetable egg donburi

SERVES 4

This is the vegetarian version of a Japanese dish in which either meat, fish, or eggs are served over rice. Japanese or sushi rice is available in grocery stores in the international-foods section (see Food Sources, page 648).

- 1½ cups Japanese or sushi rice
-   2 large whole eggs
-   4 large egg whites
      Pinch of freshly ground black pepper
-   1 tablespoon olive oil
-   6 shiitake mushrooms, wiped clean, thinly sliced
- 10 snow peas, stems trimmed, strings removed
-   1 medium carrot, cut into matchsticks
-   3 scallions, white parts cut into thin rounds and green parts cut into 1½-inch lengths
- 1½ cups Vegetable Stock (page 626), or low-sodium store-bought vegetable broth
- 1½ teaspoons freshly grated ginger
-   2 tablespoons low-sodium soy sauce
-   1 ounce radish sprouts or other sprouts

1. Place the rice and 2 cups water in a medium saucepan, and set over high heat; bring the water to a boil. Cover the saucepan, and reduce heat to a bare simmer. Cook the rice until the water has been absorbed, about 20 minutes. Remove the saucepan from the heat, and set the rice aside, covered, until ready to serve.

2. In a medium bowl, lightly whisk the eggs, egg whites, and pepper. Set the egg mixture aside.

3. Heat the oil in a medium nonstick skillet over medium-high heat. Add the mushrooms; cook until browned, 2 to 3 minutes.

4. Add the snow peas, carrot, and scallions to the skillet. Cook until the snow peas turn bright green, about 1 minute.

5. Add the vegetable stock, ginger, and soy sauce to the skillet. Cook until the liquid has been reduced by half, about 6 minutes. Gently pour in the reserved egg mixture without stirring. Cover skillet, and cook until eggs have just set, about 5 minutes.

6. Divide the rice among four soup plates or soup bowls. Divide the omelet into 4 servings; spoon the omelet and any remaining broth over the rice. Garnish with the radish sprouts. Serve.

FIT TO EAT RECIPE PER SERVING: 385 CALORIES, 3 G FAT, 107 MG CHOLESTEROL, 76 G CARBOHYDRATE, 401 MG SODIUM, 15 G PROTEIN, 2 G DIETARY FIBER

tea tofu

SERVES 8

Use firm tofu for this unusual dish. Serve over rice.

-   1 pound firm tofu
-   2 tablespoons soy sauce
-   1 tablespoon sugar
-   1 teaspoon dark Chinese sesame oil
- ¼ cup plus 1 tablespoon loose-leaf green tea
-   1 large egg, lightly beaten
- ½ cup canola oil
-   1 tablespoon thinly sliced scallion greens

1. Cut the tofu into 1 x ¾-inch pieces, and blot on a paper towel to dry. In a small bowl, whisk together the soy sauce, sugar, and sesame oil; set aside.

2. Rub tea between fingers to carefully crush it; do not crush to a powder. Place on a plate.

3. Dip the tofu pieces in the egg, and roll in the tea leaves. Brush off the excess leaves.

4. Heat the oil in a skillet over medium-high heat. Fry the tofu pieces, turning, until golden brown on all sides, about 8 minutes. Transfer the tofu to a paper towel to absorb any excess oil.

5. Transfer the tofu to a serving dish or bowl, drizzle with the soy-sauce mixture, garnish with the scallions, and serve immediately.

wild mushroom ragu with polenta

SERVES 6

For lump-free polenta, hold a fistful of cornmeal over the boiling stock and let it trickle out through a small opening in your fist. With your other hand, briskly whisk continuously until all the grain is absorbed.

- 2 *ounces assorted dried wild mushrooms, such as shiitake, morel, oyster, and porcini*
- 2 *tablespoons olive oil*
- 4 *tablespoons unsalted butter*
- 8 *ounces white-button mushrooms, wiped clean, sliced ¼ inch thick*
- 1 *medium onion, finely chopped*
- 3 *garlic cloves, minced*
- 2 *celery stalks, strings removed, finely chopped*
- ½ *teaspoon dried savory*
- 1 *teaspoon dried thyme*
- 1 *teaspoon dried marjoram or oregano*
- 1 *teaspoon kosher salt, plus more for seasoning*

  Freshly ground black pepper
- 1 *cup chopped tomatoes (from 1 large tomato)*
- ½ *cup Marsala wine or sherry*
- 7 *cups Vegetable Stock (page 626) or low-sodium store-bought vegetable broth*
- 1⅓ *cups quick-cooking polenta*

1. Place the dried mushrooms in a small bowl, and cover with very hot water. Let stand until the mushrooms are soft, about 20 minutes. Lift the mushrooms from the water, and gently squeeze the liquid back into the bowl. Cut the larger mushrooms in half, and strain the liquid through a fine sieve or cheesecloth-lined strainer; set aside.

2. In a large high-sided skillet, combine the olive oil and 2 tablespoons butter, and place the skillet over medium-high heat. Add the button mushrooms, and cook, stirring frequently, until the mushrooms are golden, about 10 minutes. Add the onions, garlic, celery, savory, thyme, and marjoram, and season with salt and pepper. Reduce the heat to medium low, and cook until the onions are translucent and softened, about 10 minutes.

3. Add the dried mushrooms, reserved mushroom liquid, tomatoes, Marsala, and 2 cups vegetable stock; cover, and bring to a boil. Reduce heat to medium, and simmer the ragu with the cover ajar until the liquid has thickened slightly and is reduced by two-thirds, about 35 minutes.

4. Meanwhile, in a medium saucepan, combine the remaining 5 cups vegetable stock, 2 tablespoons butter, and 1 teaspoon salt; cover and bring to a boil. While whisking rapidly, add the polenta in a thin, steady stream. Reduce the heat to low, and cook the polenta, stirring occasionally, 3 to 4 minutes. Divide the polenta among six plates, and cover each serving with the mushroom ragu; serve.

parsnip pierogies
with pickled red cabbage slaw
and sautéed apples

MAKES 2 DOZEN

Making these pierogies with her mother is one of Martha's favorite childhood memories. They can be assembled ahead of time; refrigerate them on a lightly floured baking sheet, with waxed paper between the layers. This dough is lighter than traditional pierogi dough; it contains no potatoes, butter, or cornstarch.

for the pickled red cabbage slaw

¼   cup red-wine vinegar
1½ tablespoons sugar
1   teaspoon whole caraway seeds, crushed
¼   small red cabbage, finely shredded
    Kosher salt and freshly ground black pepper

for the pierogi dough

1   large egg
½   cup milk
1½ tablespoons sour cream
2¼ cups all-purpose flour, plus more for dusting

for the pierogi filling

1½ pounds parsnips
    Kosher salt
2   shallots
1   teaspoon unsalted butter
    Freshly grated nutmeg
    Freshly ground black pepper
2   teaspoons Fresh Horseradish (page 632) or prepared
4   ounces farmer cheese or goat cheese

for the sautéed apples

2   teaspoons unsalted butter
2   apples, peeled if desired, cored, and thinly sliced
1   tablespoon sugar

1. To make the red cabbage slaw: Whisk together the vinegar, sugar, and caraway seeds in a medium bowl. Toss in the cabbage. Season with salt and pepper. Let marinate for at least 1 hour, or overnight.

2. To make the pierogi dough: Whisk together the egg, milk, sour cream, and ½ cup water. Stir in the flour a little at a time, until the dough comes together. Turn out onto a lightly floured surface, and knead until smooth and elastic, up to 10 minutes. Incorporate more flour if the dough is too sticky. Cover the dough with plastic wrap, and let rest for 1 hour.

3. To make the filling: Place the parsnips in a medium saucepan, and cover with cold salted water. Cover pan, bring to a boil, and simmer until tender when pierced with the tip of a knife, 20 to 25 minutes. Drain and put through a food mill fitted with the fine disc to purée.

4. In a small skillet, cook the shallots in butter until soft, 1 to 2 minutes. Stir into the purée, and season with nutmeg, salt, and pepper. Remove from the heat, and let cool slightly; mix in the horseradish and cheese.

5. On a lightly floured surface, roll out the dough to ⅛ inch thick. Cut out circles using a 3¾-inch-round cutter. Set the circles aside on a lightly floured baking sheet. Place a rounded tablespoon of the filling on each circle. Lightly wet the edges, fold over, and seal by pinching. Cover with plastic wrap to keep from drying out.

6. To make the sautéed apples: Heat a medium skillet over medium-high heat. Melt the butter, add the apple slices, and toss to coat. Add the sugar, and toss again to coat evenly. Cook until brown, about 5 minutes.

7. When ready to serve, cover and bring a large pot of salted water to a boil. Add the pierogies, and boil for 5 minutes after they float to the surface; drain. The pierogies can be eaten right away or browned in a small amount of butter. Serve warm with the red-cabbage slaw and sautéed apples.

side dishes

panfried artichokes, jewish style

SERVES 4

These panfried artichokes were inspired by the deep-fried version that originated in the Jewish neighborhoods of Rome. After they are browned in the pan, the leaves are fanned out like a flower and returned to the pan to crisp.

- 8 baby artichokes (about 1 pound total)
- 2 lemons, halved
- ½ cup extra-virgin olive oil
- 4 garlic cloves
  Kosher salt and freshly ground black pepper
  Parmesan cheese, for shaving

1. Pare the artichoke bases flat, and remove the tough outer leaves, leaving the pale-green edible ones. Trim the tops off. Rub the cut surfaces with a lemon half. Work quickly to prevent the artichokes from turning brown; do not soak in water.

2. Heat 3 tablespoons oil and the garlic in a skillet over medium-high heat. Brown the artichokes, cooking on all sides 2 to 3 minutes. If the garlic gets too brown, discard. Stand the artichokes on the bottoms; cook 1 to 2 minutes, or until tender.

3. Leave the pan with the oil on the stove; transfer the artichokes to a paper towel to drain upside down until slightly cool. Spread the leaves like a flower (scrape out the choke with a melon baller).

4. Season the artichokes with salt and pepper; add 3 tablespoons oil to the pan on the stove; when hot, add enough artichokes to fit comfortably without overlapping, bases facing up. Cook over medium-high heat, pressing the leaves down, until brown and crisp, 3 to 5 minutes. Keep warm while cooking the second batch. Blot well on paper towel. Season lightly with salt, and serve hot with shaved Parmesan and the remaining lemon halves.

steamed artichokes

SERVES 6

- 6 large artichokes
- 4 lemons, halved
  Kosher salt
- 1 teaspoon whole black peppercorns
  Large sprig fresh thyme
- 2 cloves garlic
- 2 tablespoons olive oil
  Lemon Mayonnaise (recipe follows)

1. Trim artichokes (see page, opposite). Squeeze the juice of ½ lemon onto the heart; squeeze the other ½ lemon into a bowl of ice water, and add lemon halves and the artichoke while preparing the rest.

2. Fill a large pot with 2 inches of water. Juice the remaining 3 lemon halves; add the juice and the lemon halves to the pot with salt, the peppercorns, thyme, garlic, and olive oil; bring to a simmer. Add artichokes, stem-end up; cover pot. Steam until tender, 25 to 30 minutes. The leaves should pull off easily; the heart should feel tender when pierced with the tip of a knife. Drain well; serve at room temperature or chilled with lemon mayonnaise.

lemon mayonnaise

MAKES 1 CUP

- 1 large egg, room temperature
  Kosher salt
- ¼ cup canola oil
- ½ cup extra-virgin olive oil
  Juice of ½ lemon, plus more to taste

Combine egg and a pinch of salt in the bowl of a food processor; blend until foamy. With machine running, add the canola and olive oils, a few drops at a time, then in a slow steady stream. Add the lemon juice; blend briefly. Season with salt and more lemon juice. Refrigerate, in an airtight container, until needed, or up to 2 days.

NOTE Raw eggs should not be used in food prepared for pregnant women, babies, young children, or anyone whose health is compromised.

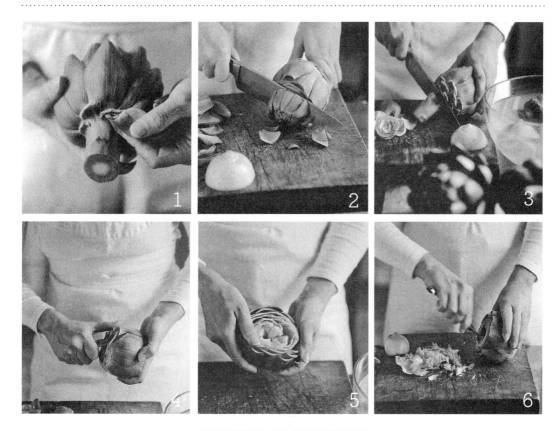

CLEANING AN ARTICHOKE

Although there are variations on this method, this is a basic way to prepare an artichoke for steaming, either plain or stuffed. Before getting started, you will need to cut a lemon in half; squeeze one half into a bowl of cool water (this is called acidulated water, which keeps artichokes from discoloring) and keep the other half for rubbing on the cut parts.

1. Snap off the tough outer leaves (or bracts), and discard. Rub the exposed surfaces of the artichoke with a halved lemon.

2. Using a large knife, cut off about the top third of the artichoke. If any tips remain below the cut, snip off the thorny points with scissors.

3. Trim the stem so the artichoke will sit upright, and rub well with lemon.

4. Use a stainless-steel paring knife (or a curved "bird's beak" knife, perfect for this task) to neatly trim the stem and base.

5. Spread the leaves open to expose the choke.

6. Using a melon baller, scoop out the prickly hairs, or the choke. Keep scraping until you no longer see any fuzz. Squeeze lemon juice directly on the heart, and place artichoke in a bowl of acidulated water while preparing the rest.

stuffed artichokes

SERVES 5

- 5   large globe artichokes
- 2   lemons, halved
- 2   tablespoons extra-virgin olive oil
- 4   large (2½ pounds) onions, sliced lengthwise into ¼-inch wedges
- 3   garlic cloves, minced
- 2½ cups fresh bread crumbs (see page 647)
- ½   cup niçoise olives, pitted and coarsely chopped
- ½   cup chopped fresh flat-leaf parsley
- 6   anchovy fillets, minced to a paste
- 1   tablespoon fresh thyme leaves
     Kosher salt and freshly ground black pepper
- 1   cup Homemade Chicken Stock (page 624), or low-sodium store-bought chicken broth, skimmed of fat
- 2   tablespoons freshly grated Parmesan cheese

1. Trim artichokes (see page 325). Squeeze juice of ½ lemon onto heart; squeeze another ½ lemon into a bowl of ice water, and add the lemon halves and the artichoke while preparing the rest.

2. In a large skillet, heat oil over medium heat. Cook onions and garlic until tender and lightly caramelized, 45 minutes to 1 hour; let cool. Coarsely chop two-thirds of onion. Place in a bowl; add bread crumbs, olives, parsley, anchovies, and thyme. Season with salt and pepper; mix well.

3. Preheat the oven to 375°F. Drain the artichokes upside down on a paper towel; gently open leaves. Fill the centers with the mixture; place small amounts in the crevices of the leaves. Place a piece of kitchen twine around the outside of the artichokes; tie snugly.

4. Scatter remaining onions on the bottom of large Dutch oven or deep skillet. Fit in artichokes; add stock. Sprinkle each artichoke with the Parmesan. Cover; transfer to the oven, and bake 30 minutes. Uncover; bake until golden and crusty on top and the hearts are tender when pierced with the tip of a knife, about 10 minutes. Serve.

baby artichokes with warm vinaigrette

SERVES 4

- 2¼ teaspoons kosher salt
- ¼   cup plus 1 teaspoon extra-virgin olive oil
- 1   lemon
- 8   baby artichokes
- 1   medium shallot, minced (3 tablespoons)
- ¼   cup grainy mustard
- ¼   teaspoon freshly ground black pepper
- 3   tablespoons red-wine vinegar.

1. Fill a stockpot with water; add 2 teaspoons salt and 1 tablespoon olive oil. Halve lemon; squeeze juice into water. Add squeezed halves. Remove tough outer artichoke leaves, and pare down stems using a vegetable peeler. Add artichokes to lemon water, cover, and bring to a boil. Reduce to a simmer; cook until leaves are easily removed and heart is tender when pierced with the tip of a knife, 15 to 20 minutes. Drain in a colander; set aside.

2. Place 1 teaspoon olive oil in a skillet over medium-low heat; add minced shallot. Cook until translucent, about 2 minutes. Remove from heat; add mustard, remaining ¼ teaspoon salt, the pepper, and vinegar. Slowly whisk in remaining 3 tablespoons olive oil. Serve the reserved artichokes with the warm vinaigrette on the side for dipping.

BABY ARTICHOKES

Unlike large artichokes, of which only the heart is completely edible, baby artichokes, once they are trimmed of their spiky leaves and fibrous stem, can be eaten whole. If you are unable to find baby artichokes (which are at their peak in the fall), frozen artichoke hearts make an acceptable substitute—most frozen artichokes are actually baby artichokes that have been trimmed and halved.

artichokes à la barigoule
SERVES 4

"Barigoule" traditionally refers to large artichokes filled with a flavorful paste. These are not stuffed but incorporate the flavors of Provence.

- 24 baby artichokes
- 2 lemons, halved
- 3 ounces pancetta or bacon, cubed (½ cup)
- 1 tablespoon olive oil
- 5 medium shallots, cut into ¼-inch slices
- 2 garlic cloves
- 5 medium carrots, cut into ¼-inch slices
- 2 sprigs fresh thyme
- 2 dried bay leaves
-    Kosher salt and freshly ground black pepper
- ½ cup dry white wine
- 1 to 1½ cups Homemade Chicken Stock (page 624), or low-sodium store-bought chicken broth, skimmed of fat, or more as needed
- ½ cup chopped fresh flat-leaf parsley
-    Balsamic vinegar, for drizzling

1. Pare artichoke bases flat. Remove tough outer leaves, leaving pale-green edible ones. Trim tops. Rub cut surfaces with a lemon half. Work quickly to keep artichokes from turning brown.

2. In a Dutch oven or deep skillet, cook pancetta in oil over medium heat until brown and crisp and the fat is rendered, about 10 minutes. Remove pancetta with a slotted spoon; reserve. Add shallots and garlic; cook 5 minutes, stirring and picking up the brown bits from the bottom, until golden.

3. Add carrots, thyme, bay leaves, salt, and pepper; cook until just tender, about 4 minutes. Add wine and stock; stir until boiling. Place artichokes on vegetables. Cover; simmer on medium-low heat until tender, stirring occasionally, 20 to 30 minutes. If liquid has evaporated, add ½ cup stock. Raise heat, reduce liquid to thicken slightly; season with salt and pepper. Stir in parsley and pancetta.

4. Place artichokes on a platter with the vegetables and sauce. Drizzle with balsamic vinegar; serve.

artichoke bottoms au gratin
SERVES 8

The artichoke bottoms and the béchamel sauce can be prepared the day before you need them, then assembled and baked just before serving.

- 8 medium artichokes
- 2 lemons, halved
- 1 sprig fresh thyme
- 1 teaspoon whole black peppercorns
- 1 dried bay leaf
-    Béchamel Sauce (page 629)
- 1 tablespoon unsalted butter
-    Kosher salt and freshly ground black pepper
- 4 slices prosciutto, cut in half crosswise

1. Snap off most of the tough outer leaves from the artichokes. Trim 1½ inches from the top. In a large pot, place the artichokes, 1½ lemons, the thyme, peppercorns, and bay leaf. Fill the pot with enough water to cover by ½ inch. Cover with a smaller-size lid to keep the artichokes submerged. Bring to a boil; reduce heat to a simmer, and cook over medium heat until the hearts are tender when pierced with the tip of a knife, about 30 minutes.

2. Preheat the oven to 350°F. When the artichokes are tender, drain, remove the remaining leaves, and discard all but the smallest, most tender ones. Set those aside. Remove the choke completely with a melon baller or spoon, and rub the artichoke bottoms with the remaining lemon half. In a glass pie pan or gratin dish, scatter the leaves, and mix in half of the béchamel. Lightly butter the artichoke bottoms, season with salt and pepper, and place on top of the béchamel. Place a folded piece of prosciutto in each bottom; fill with a rounded mound of béchamel.

3. Bake until golden, 20 to 25 minutes. Rub the tops with the remaining butter, and bake for 5 minutes more. Serve 1 bottom per person along with some of the leaves.

grilled asparagus

SERVES 4

- 2 pounds jumbo asparagus, tough ends removed
- 1½ tablespoons extra-virgin olive oil
  Kosher salt and freshly ground black pepper
- 4 ounces pea shoots, for garnish, optional
  Caramelized-Shallot Vinaigrette (recipe follows)

Heat a grill or a grill pan until medium hot. Place the asparagus in a bowl. Drizzle the oil over the asparagus; season with salt and pepper. Grill, turning every few minutes, until tender, about 12 minutes. Garnish with the pea shoots, if using; serve with the vinaigrette.

caramelized-shallot vinaigrette

MAKES ½ CUP

- ½ tablespoon unsalted butter
- 3 shallots, minced
- 2 teaspoons sugar
  Kosher salt and freshly ground black pepper
- 1 teaspoon Dijon mustard
- 2 tablespoons red-wine vinegar
- ¼ cup extra-virgin olive oil

1. Melt the butter in a medium skillet over medium heat. Add the shallots and sugar; season with salt and pepper. Cook, stirring, until the shallots are caramelized and tender but still retain some crunch, about 8 minutes; set aside.

2. In a bowl, combine mustard and vinegar; season with salt and pepper. Slowly whisk in oil until combined; stir in shallots. Drizzle over grilled asparagus. Vinaigrette is best used the same day.

oven-roasted asparagus and leeks

SERVES 4

If thick asparagus is unavailable, use thin spears, and adjust the cooking time; thin asparagus will cook faster.

- 20 thick (about 1 pound) asparagus spears, tough ends removed
- 6 medium leeks, white and pale-green parts, halved lengthwise, well washed (see page 646)
- 1 tablespoon extra-virgin olive oil
- ½ teaspoon kosher salt
  Freshly ground black pepper
  Balsamic vinegar, for drizzling

1. Preheat the oven to 400°F. In a large bowl, combine the asparagus and leeks. Drizzle the olive oil over the vegetables, and toss to coat. Add the salt, and season with pepper; toss to combine.

2. Place the vegetables in a heavy roasting pan, and transfer to the oven. Roast until the vegetables start to turn brown and are tender when pierced with the tip of a knife, turning once, about 25 minutes. Remove the pan from the oven, and set on a heat-proof surface until the vegetables are cool enough to eat. When ready to serve, drizzle with the vinegar.

sautéed white asparagus and endive in orange sauce

SERVES 4

- 1 navel orange
- 1 pound medium white asparagus, tough ends removed
- 2 tablespoons unsalted butter
- 2 heads Belgian endive, quartered lengthwise
- ½ cup plus 2 tablespoons fresh orange juice
- ¾ teaspoon kosher salt
- 1 tablespoon dry white wine
- 2 tablespoons Grand Marnier

1. Using a citrus zester, remove the orange zest in very thin strips from half of the orange, and set aside. Using a sharp knife, remove and discard the peel and pith from the orange; cut the orange cross-wise into ¼-inch-thick rounds; cut the rounds into quarters, and set aside.

2. Using a vegetable peeler, remove the outer layer of the asparagus. Melt 1 tablespoon butter in a large skillet over medium-high heat. Add the asparagus and endive; cook until the endive is golden brown, about 4 minutes.

3. Add ¼ cup plus 1 tablespoon orange juice and ¾ teaspoon salt; bring the liquid to a simmer, cover, and cook until just tender, about 8 minutes. Transfer the asparagus and endive to a serving platter; set aside in a warm place.

4. Add the wine, the remaining ¼ cup plus 1 tablespoon of orange juice, and the Grand Marnier to the pan. Swirl the liquid, deglazing the pan. Remove from the heat; swirl in the remaining tablespoon of butter. Drizzle the sauce over the asparagus and endive; garnish with the reserved orange pieces and zest. Serve immediately.

- -

ASPARAGUS: THICK OR THIN?

Some people think the thinner the asparagus spear, the better. This is most likely based on the belief that slender spears are younger. But in fact, the fat spears are already fat when they poke up from the ground, and the thin spears don't get thicker as they age. Indeed, fat stalks tend to be more succulent. But no matter the size, the keys to delicious asparagus are freshness and proper preparation. Since asparagus is highly perishable, the journey from field to cooking pot should be as brief as possible. It's best to buy asparagus that has been grown locally and to buy it in season (in the United States, fresh local asparagus is available roughly from March through June). When choosing asparagus, look for compact tips and firm, smooth stems free of yellowing. If you must store asparagus before cooking, treat it like a bunch of flowers, placing the trimmed stalks in a glass with an inch or two of water.

- -

sesame asparagus and tofu
SERVES 4

This recipe calls for extra-firm tofu, but the firm variety will also work: Wrap a piece in paper towels, place between two plates, and place a can on top. Refrigerate for 30 minutes while the paper towels absorb the excess liquid.

- 3 *tablespoons low-sodium soy sauce*
- 1½ *teaspoons Dijon mustard*
- 1 *teaspoon toasted sesame oil*
- 1 *teaspoon white-wine vinegar*
- 2 *teaspoons snipped chives*
- 12 *asparagus, tough ends removed*
- 1 *tablespoon plus 1 teaspoon sesame seeds*
- 8 *ounces extra-firm tofu, cut into ½ x ½ x 2½-inch batons*
- 2 *tablespoons canola oil*

1. In a medium bowl, whisk together 1 tablespoon soy sauce, the mustard, sesame oil, vinegar, and chives. Set aside. Cover a large stockpot of water, and bring to a boil. Prepare an ice-water bath. Blanch the asparagus just until tender, 1 to 2 minutes. With a slotted spoon, transfer to the ice-water bath. Set aside.

2. Pour the sesame seeds onto a small plate. Place the remaining 2 tablespoons of soy sauce and the tofu in a medium bowl. Turn the tofu in the soy sauce to coat; let sit 30 seconds. Remove a baton; dip one side in the sesame seeds. Transfer to a clean plate. Repeat with the remaining batons.

3. Heat the canola oil in a large skillet over medium-high heat. Arrange the tofu, with the sesame seeds down, in the pan. Cook until golden brown on the bottoms, about 5 minutes. Brown the remaining sides, about 2 minutes per side; remove from the skillet.

4. In a bowl, toss the asparagus in the vinaigrette. Divide the asparagus and tofu among four plates, and drizzle with any remaining vinaigrette. Serve.

FIT TO EAT RECIPE PER SERVING: 99 CALORIES, 6 G FAT, 0 MG CHOLESTEROL, 4 G CARBOHYDRATE, 167 MG SODIUM, 8 G PROTEIN, 1 G DIETARY FIBER

camembert-asparagus bread pudding

SERVES 8

Pungent Camembert cheese, mushrooms, onions, and bread are layered with asparagus to produce the ultimate side dish.

- 1½ tablespoons unsalted butter, plus more for dish
- 1½ pounds medium asparagus, tough ends removed
- 1½ teaspoons kosher salt, plus more for cooking water
- 1½ tablespoons olive oil
- 8 ounces small white-button or wild mushrooms
- 1 small Vidalia or Spanish onion, cut into ¼-inch-thick wedges
- ½ loaf (10 ounces) country-style white bread, crusts on, cut into ¾ x 1½ x 1½-inch pieces
- 2 teaspoons chopped fresh rosemary
- 4 ounces ripe Camembert cheese, cut into ½-inch cubes
- 1½ cups milk
- 1½ cups heavy cream
- 5 large eggs, room temperature
- ¼ teaspoon freshly ground black pepper

1. Preheat the oven to 350°F. Generously butter a 2½-quart casserole dish, and set dish aside. Using a vegetable peeler, carefully peel the outer layer from the bottom 2 inches of the asparagus spears.

2. Fill a large, straight-sided skillet with salted water, cover, and bring to a boil; prepare an ice-water bath. Add the asparagus, and cook until bright green, about 1 minute. Transfer the asparagus to the ice-water bath, and let cool. Drain, transfer to a clean kitchen towel, and pat dry. Set asparagus aside.

3. Melt ½ tablespoon of the butter with ½ tablespoon of the olive oil in a medium skillet over medium heat. Add the mushrooms, and cook, stirring once or twice, until the mushrooms turn golden brown, about 5 minutes. Transfer mushrooms to a plate; set aside.

4. Melt the remaining tablespoon of butter with the remaining tablespoon of oil in the skillet; add the onion. Cook until the onion is soft and translucent, about 8 minutes. Remove the pan from the heat, and set aside.

5. Randomly arrange half of the bread pieces on the bottom of the prepared casserole dish. Sprinkle half of the rosemary over the top. Place half of the asparagus, onions, mushrooms, and cheese on top. Make a second layer with the remaining bread, rosemary, asparagus, onions, mushrooms, and cheese.

6. To make the custard, combine the milk and cream in a medium saucepan, and set over medium-high heat; cook until the mixture is hot. Meanwhile, in a medium bowl, whisk together the eggs, 1½ teaspoons of salt, and the pepper until combined. Slowly drizzle the hot milk mixture into the eggs, whisking constantly.

7. Pour the custard over the pudding. Press down on the pudding, completely soaking the top layer of bread, and place a plate on top. Weigh down the plate with a can or other heavy object. Let the pudding stand 20 minutes. Remove plate.

8. Bake until the custard has set and the top is golden, about 45 minutes. Transfer the dish to a wire rack to cool, about 5 minutes. Serve hot.

stir-fried fava beans

SERVES 8 AS AN APPETIZER

These warm, spiced beans make unusual hors d'oeuvres as well as a simple side dish.

- Kosher salt
- 1 pound fresh or frozen shelled fava beans
- 1 tablespoon canola oil
- 1 teaspoon Asian fish sauce (nam pla)
- 2 tablespoons thinly sliced scallion greens

1. Cover and bring a large pot of salted water to a boil. Prepare an ice-water bath. Add beans to boiling water, return to a boil, reduce heat to low, and simmer until beans are tender but still firm, 10 minutes. Transfer to the ice-water bath to stop the cooking. Drain. (If beans have outer skins, use your fingers to pop each bean out. Discard the skins.)

2. Heat the oil in a wok or a large skillet over medium-high heat, and add the fava beans, salt to taste, and the fish sauce; stir-fry for about 2 minutes. Add the scallions, and stir-fry until the beans are tender, about 1 minute. Serve immediately.

fava bean fritters

MAKES 1 DOZEN

Fava beans are available fresh only in the spring; use frozen favas during the other seasons. Serve these fritters with thick-sliced tomatoes or a mixed-green salad for a perfect springtime lunch.

 3 *pounds fresh fava beans, shelled
    (about 4 cups shelled)*
 ¼ *cup finely grated pecorino cheese*
 ¼ *cup finely chopped fresh flat-leaf parsley*
 ¼ *cup dry bread crumbs (see page 647)*
 2 *large eggs, lightly beaten*
 2 *tablespoons heavy cream*
    *Kosher salt and freshly ground
    black pepper*
 2 *tablespoons olive oil*

1. Prepare an ice-water bath; set aside. Cover and bring a large pot of water to a boil. Add the fava beans, and cook, uncovered, 2 to 3 minutes. Drain the beans, and transfer to the ice-water bath. Remove from the ice bath, and peel and discard the inner skins from the beans.

2. Place the beans in the bowl of a food processor, and pulse until coarsely chopped. Transfer the beans to a medium bowl, add the cheese, parsley, bread crumbs, eggs, and cream, and season with salt and pepper. Mix until well combined. Shape the mixture into 2-inch patties.

3. In a medium skillet, heat 1 tablespoon olive oil over medium heat. Add 6 patties, and cook until golden brown, about 2 minutes per side. Repeat with remaining oil and patties. Serve warm.

haricots verts with hazelnuts

SERVES 8 TO 10

 1 *teaspoon kosher salt, plus more
    for cooking water*
 1½ *pounds haricots verts or green beans,
    trimmed*
 3½ *tablespoons unsalted butter*
 5 *large shallots*
 ¼ *teaspoon freshly ground black pepper*
 ⅓ *cup hazelnuts, preferably blanched,
    toasted (see page 644)*

1. Preheat the oven to 375°F. Cover and bring a large pot of salted water to a boil. Prepare an ice-water bath. Add the haricots verts; cook until just tender, 3 to 4 minutes. Transfer the beans to the ice-water bath. Drain and set aside. (This can be done up to 6 hours in advance.)

2. In a medium skillet, melt 1½ tablespoons of the butter over medium-high heat. Add the shallots, ½ teaspoon salt, and ⅛ teaspoon pepper, and cook, turning, until the shallots start to brown on all sides, about 3 minutes. Cover, reduce heat to low, and cook, turning frequently, until the shallots are well browned, about 10 minutes. Let cool slightly, then cut into slivers. Crush the toasted hazelnuts roughly with the flat side of a knife.

3. In a large skillet, heat the remaining 2 tablespoons butter over medium-high heat. Add the haricots verts and the remaining ½ teaspoon salt and ⅛ teaspoon pepper; cook, stirring, until heated through, about 3 minutes. Add the shallots and hazelnuts; cook 1 minute more. Transfer to a serving dish, and serve immediately.

mixed beans with crisp rosemary and sage leaves

SERVES 6

When using beans that are different sizes, blanch each type separately to ensure even cooking.

Kosher salt

1½ pounds mixed yellow and green beans, such as string beans, haricots verts, and Romano beans, trimmed

2 tablespoons extra-virgin olive oil

⅓ cup fresh sage leaves

⅓ cup fresh rosemary needles

Freshly ground black pepper

1. Cover and bring a large pot of salted water to a boil. Add beans; simmer until the color has brightened and beans are just tender, 30 seconds to 2 minutes, depending on their size. Drain in a colander; pat dry with a clean towel. Transfer to a bowl.

2. Heat the oil in a large skillet over medium-high heat. Add the sage and rosemary; cook, stirring to keep the sage leaves separated until crisp, 2 to 3 minutes. Remove from heat; pour over the beans. Season with salt and pepper, toss to combine; serve.

sesame green beans

SERVES 6

¼ cup plus 2 tablespoons Homemade Chicken Stock (page 624), or low-sodium store-bought chicken broth, skimmed of fat

2 tablespoons low-sodium soy sauce

2 tablespoons dry sherry

2 teaspoons toasted sesame oil

1½ pounds green beans, trimmed

3 large garlic cloves, thinly sliced

1 tablespoon freshly grated ginger

2 teaspoons unhulled sesame seeds, optional

1. Combine the stock, soy sauce, and sherry in a small bowl, and set aside.

2. Set a wok or a large skillet over high heat for 1 minute. Add the oil; swirl to cover the bottom and sides. Add the beans; cook, stirring and tossing, 5 minutes. Add the garlic, ginger, and the reserved stock mixture. Stir to combine; cook 1 minute. Cover; cook until the beans are bright green and crunchy, about 2 minutes. Remove the cover; cook until no liquid remains. Sprinkle with the sesame seeds, if using; serve immediately.

FIT TO EAT RECIPE PER SERVING: 68 CALORIES, 2 G FAT, 0 MG CHOLESTEROL, 9 G CARBOHYDRATE, 222 MG SODIUM, 3 G PROTEIN, 3 G DIETARY FIBER

west texas baked beans

SERVES ABOUT 14

6 cups (2½ pounds) dried pinto beans

1 pound sliced bacon

2 onions, cut into ¼-inch dice

1 tablespoon plus 1 teaspoon chili powder

4 garlic cloves, minced

1¼ cups packed light-brown sugar

2 12-ounce bottles dark beer

Kosher salt and freshly ground black pepper

1. Pick over the dried beans, discarding any stones or broken beans, and rinse. Place in a large saucepan, cover with cold water by 2 inches, and bring to a strong boil over high heat. Cover and remove from the heat, and let stand 1 hour. Drain the beans, and set aside.

2. In heavy skillet, cook the bacon over medium heat until crisp. Remove the bacon, and set aside.

3. Pour off all but 3 tablespoons of the rendered bacon fat. Add onions, chili powder, and garlic; cook, stirring, until onions are soft, about 5 minutes.

4. Place the beans in a large stockpot or Dutch oven. Cover with water by 2 inches. Crumble bacon into small pieces; add to beans with the onion mixture, sugar, and beer. Cover and bring to a boil over high heat. Reduce heat to medium, and cook, covered, stirring occasionally, until the beans are soft and liquid is almost absorbed, about 2½ hours. Season with salt and pepper. Serve hot.

traditional black-eyed peas

SERVES 6 TO 8

Fresh black-eyed peas cook much more quickly than dried ones; check for tenderness after 20 minutes. We found that dried black-eyes don't need presoaking, which saves a lot of time.

- 1 pound fresh shelled black-eyed peas or one 1-pound package (2½ cups) dried black-eyed peas
- 5 whole black peppercorns
- 1 dried bay leaf
- 1 medium onion, quartered
- 1 jalapeño pepper, halved
- 1 ham hock or 8 ounces slab bacon
- 1 small bunch fresh flat-leaf parsley
- 4 garlic cloves
  Kosher salt and freshly ground black pepper

1. Place either the fresh or dried black-eyed peas in a colander, and rinse them under cool running water. Transfer to a medium stockpot. Cover with about 2 inches of water. Add the peppercorns, bay leaf, onion, jalapeño pepper, ham hock, parsley (including stems), and garlic. Cover, and bring just below the boiling point over medium-high heat. Uncover, reduce heat to a simmer, and cook just until the peas are tender when bitten, about 20 minutes for fresh and 45 minutes for the dried peas (though the cooking time will vary with the age of dried peas). Do not stir the peas while cooking because they can break down. Season with salt and pepper during the last 10 minutes of cooking.

2. The peas will keep in their cooking liquid for about 3 hours at room temperature. Then they may be stored in an airtight container in the refrigerator for 1 to 2 days. Serve the black-eyed peas hot, along with their cooking liquid, in individual bowls. If desired, the meat from the ham hock may be shredded and served with the peas, along with the garlic and jalapeño peppers from the pot.

texas caviar

MAKES 3 PINTS

These three variations on Texas caviar—highly seasoned, pickled black-eyed peas—can be used as side dishes or condiments. Try all three in separate 1-pint jars; or use a 3-pint jar and make just one, and triple the spice mixture of your choice.

- 6 cups Traditional Black-Eyed Peas (recipe, left)
- 4 sprigs fresh oregano
- 2 teaspoons whole cumin seeds
- 2 small fresh serrano chile peppers or other hot chile peppers
- 1 small Hungarian wax pepper, cut into ¼-inch rounds
- 2 teaspoons whole mustard seeds
- 2 small dried red-chile peppers
- 2 teaspoons crushed red-pepper flakes
- 2 teaspoons whole fennel seeds
- 2¼ cups white or cider vinegar
- 2 tablespoons kosher salt

1. In a 1-pint canning jar, using 2 cups of the black-eyed peas, alternate layers of the peas with oregano, cumin seeds, and serrano chiles. In a second jar, layer 2 cups of peas with the wax peppers and mustard seeds. In a third jar, layer the remaining 2 cups of peas with the dried chile peppers, red-pepper flakes, and fennel seeds. Set aside.

2. In a saucepan, combine the vinegar and salt. Heat until the mixture just comes to a boil. Pour ¾ cup of the vinegar mixture over each jar of peas to cover all layers. Seal the jars. When the mixture cools to room temperature, refrigerate at least 1 week and up to 1 month.

cuban black beans

SERVES 12

If you cannot find black-bean purée, make it by processing canned black beans in the bowl of a food processor until smooth.

- ¼ cup plus 1 tablespoon olive oil
- 2 medium onions, finely diced
- 4 garlic cloves, minced
- 2 green bell peppers, seeds and ribs removed, finely diced
- 4 15½-ounce cans black beans, with juice
- 1½ cups canned black-bean purée
- 5 dried bay leaves
- 2 teaspoons ground cumin
- 2 teaspoons dried oregano
  Kosher salt and freshly ground black pepper
- 1 tablespoon white vinegar
- 3 tablespoons chopped fresh cilantro, plus more for garnish
- 2 tablespoons finely diced red bell pepper, for garnish, optional

1. Heat the olive oil in a medium stockpot set over medium-low heat. Add the onions, garlic, and green bell peppers; cook until the onions are soft but still translucent, about 25 minutes.

2. Add the black beans, black-bean purée, bay leaves, cumin, and oregano. Season with salt and pepper; stir.

3. Cook the mixture until thickened, about 10 minutes. Stir in the vinegar and cilantro. Garnish with the cilantro and red pepper, if using. Serve.

boiled beets with sautéed beet greens

SERVES 6

Beet greens are just as delicious as the beets themselves.

- 3 pounds medium beets, scrubbed, with greens
  Kosher salt
- 1 tablespoon olive oil, plus more for drizzling
- 1 garlic clove, thinly sliced
  Freshly ground black pepper

1. Place the beets in a large saucepan of salted water, cover, and bring to a boil. Cook the beets, uncovered, until the beets are tender when pierced with the tip of a knife, about 45 minutes. Drain, let cool, and rub off the skins.

2. Heat the olive oil in a large skillet over medium heat. Add the garlic, and cook just until golden, about 3 minutes. Add the beet greens, and season with salt and pepper. Cook, tossing the greens until wilted. Remove the skillet from the heat. Arrange the whole boiled beets over warm greens. Drizzle with olive oil, and serve.

roasted beets and shallots

SERVES 6 TO 8

Beets in bunches are much fresher than loose ones.

- 7 medium beets, trimmed and scrubbed
- 10 large shallots, unpeeled, cut in half
- 2 tablespoons olive oil
- 1½ teaspoons kosher salt
- ½ teaspoon freshly ground black pepper
- 1½ tablespoons sherry vinegar

1. Preheat the oven to 400°F. Place beets and shallots in a large bowl. Drizzle with 1 tablespoon olive oil; season with 1 teaspoon salt and ¼ teaspoon pepper. Toss well; transfer to a large roasting pan.

2. Cover the pan with aluminum foil, and transfer to the oven. Bake until the beets are tender when pierced with the tip of a knife, about 1 hour.

3. Remove the pan, and let stand until cool enough to handle. Peel the beets and shallots, and cut the beets into 1-inch pieces. Combine in a serving bowl. Add the sherry vinegar, the remaining tablespoon of olive oil, ½ teaspoon salt, and ¼ teaspoon pepper, and toss well to combine. Serve.

lentils with scallions and peppers
SERVES 4

Ordinary brown lentils can be substituted for French green lentils; they will require about 8 minutes less cooking time.

- 1 cup dried French green lentils or brown lentils
- 1 very large shallot (1½ ounces)
- 1 large garlic clove
- 1 dried bay leaf
- 3 cups Homemade Chicken Stock (page 624), or low-sodium store-bought chicken broth, skimmed of fat
- 3 tablespoons olive oil
- 4 scallions, white and green parts, sliced crosswise ¼ inch thick
- ½ yellow bell pepper, seeds and ribs removed, cut into ¼-inch dice
- 1 teaspoon balsamic vinegar
  Kosher salt and freshly ground black pepper

1. In a small saucepan, combine the lentils, shallot, garlic, bay leaf, and chicken stock; cover and bring to a boil. Reduce heat to low, and simmer, uncovered, until the lentils are tender, about 40 minutes. Drain, and discard the seasonings.

2. In a large skillet, heat the oil over medium-high heat. Add the scallions and yellow pepper, and cook just to slightly soften the vegetables, about 5 minutes. Add the lentils and vinegar, and season with salt and pepper; cook, tossing until well heated, about 5 minutes. Transfer to a serving dish, and serve immediately.

sautéed broccoli rabe
SERVES 4

Broccoli rabe is a bitter green with long, thick stalks and broccoli-like buds at the tips.

- 2 tablespoons olive oil
- 2 garlic cloves, sliced ⅛ inch thick
- 1 bunch (about 1 pound) broccoli rabe, trimmed
  Kosher salt and freshly ground black pepper
- ¼ cup Homemade Chicken Stock (page 624), or low-sodium store-bought chicken broth, skimmed of fat

In a large skillet over medium heat, heat the olive oil. Add the garlic, and cook until golden brown, about 3 minutes. Add the broccoli rabe, and season with salt and pepper. Add the chicken stock, and cook, covered but stirring often, until the broccoli rabe is softened, about 10 minutes. Serve hot.

brussels sprouts with vinegar-glazed red onions
SERVES 4

The sweetness of the onions is a nice contrast to the assertive flavor of brussels sprouts. Garnish with toasted hazelnuts (see page 644), if desired.

- Kosher salt
- 10 ounces brussels sprouts, trimmed
- 1 tablespoon unsalted butter
- 1 tablespoon olive oil
  Freshly ground black pepper
- 1 small red onion, thinly sliced lengthwise
- 2 tablespoons balsamic vinegar

1. Cover and bring a medium pot of salted water to a boil. Prepare an ice-water bath. Add the brussels sprouts and cook, uncovered, until tender but still bright green, about 4 minutes. Remove from heat, drain, and plunge sprouts into ice-water bath to stop the cooking. Drain well, and cut in half.

2. Heat ½ tablespoon butter and ½ tablespoon olive oil in a large heavy skillet over medium-high heat. Add the brussels sprouts, and cook, tossing occasionally, until they are brown and crisp on the edges, about 3 minutes. Season with salt and pepper and transfer to a large bowl. Cover with aluminum foil to keep warm.

3. Add the remaining butter and oil to the same pan over medium-low heat. Add the onion, and cook, tossing occasionally, until wilted and transparent, 3 to 4 minutes. Add the vinegar (stand back to avoid the fumes), and stir to loosen any brown bits on the bottom of the pan. Cook until the vinegar is reduced and the onions are glazed, about 30 seconds.

4. Add the onions to the brussels sprouts, and toss well. Serve immediately.

creamy red and green cabbage

SERVES 6

1   small head red cabbage
1   small head green cabbage
    Kosher salt
4   tablespoons unsalted butter
1   shallot, minced
1½ teaspoons celery seeds
1   cup heavy cream
    Freshly ground black pepper

1. Trim both the red and green cabbages, discarding the tough outer leaves and cores. Slice into ¼-inch-thick slices. Cover and bring a large stockpot of salted water to a boil. Cook the red cabbage for 1 minute. Using a slotted spoon, transfer the cabbage to a colander, and drain. Repeat with the green cabbage. Pat the cabbage dry, and set aside.

2. Melt the butter in a large skillet over medium heat. Add the shallot and celery seeds; cook until fragrant, about 2 minutes. Add the cream; bring to a boil. Reduce heat; simmer until the cream has slightly thickened, about 5 minutes. Add the cabbage to the skillet, and season with salt and pepper. Cook the cabbage until heated through, 3 to 5 minutes. Serve hot.

brussels sprouts purée

SERVES 6 TO 8

1   pound (about 4 cups) brussels sprouts, trimmed
1¼   teaspoons kosher salt, plus more for cooking water
½   cup heavy cream
2   tablespoons unsalted butter
¼   teaspoon freshly ground black pepper
¼   teaspoon ground nutmeg

1. With a knife, cut a shallow "x" into the base of each brussels sprout. Separate about 25 large outer green leaves; set aside.

2. Prepare an ice-water bath, and set aside. Cover and bring a large pot of salted water to a boil. Cook the brussels sprouts, uncovered, until just tender but still bright green, 6 to 8 minutes. With a slotted spoon, transfer the sprouts to the ice-water bath to stop the cooking.

3. Blanch reserved leaves in the boiling water, until bright green, 1 to 2 minutes. Strain; transfer to the ice-water bath. Drain; reserve. Transfer sprouts to the bowl of a food processor.

4. Heat the cream and butter in saucepan over low heat until the butter has melted. Add 1¼ teaspoons salt, the pepper, and the nutmeg; add to the brussels sprouts. Process until completely combined. Transfer to a serving bowl. Arrange the reserved leaves around the edge of the bowl. Serve.

sweet and sour red cabbage

SERVES 4

This side dish can be made ahead and reheated before serving.

1 small (about 2 pounds) head red cabbage
2 tablespoons canola oil
¼ cup plus 3 tablespoons red-wine vinegar
3 tablespoons honey
1 teaspoon ground cinnamon
 Pinch of ground allspice
 Kosher salt and freshly ground black pepper
1 Granny Smith apple

1. Cut the cabbage in half lengthwise, remove the core, and slice as thinly as possible.

2. Heat the oil in a large saucepan over medium-low heat. Add the cabbage, and cook, stirring, until wilted, about 10 minutes. Add the vinegar, honey, cinnamon, and allspice. Season well with salt and pepper. Add 3 tablespoons water, and continue cooking the cabbage until almost soft, 1 to 1½ hours. (Add more water, if needed, while the cabbage is cooking.)

3. Cut apple in half lengthwise, remove core, and slice into very thin wedges. Add to cabbage, and continue cooking until cabbage is soft and almost dry, about 20 minutes more. Serve immediately.

buttered carrots with parsley

SERVES 4

7 medium carrots
 Kosher salt
2 tablespoons unsalted butter
2 tablespoons roughly chopped fresh flat-leaf parsley
 Freshly ground black pepper

1. Cut the carrots into 3 x ½ x ⅛-inch batons. Cover and bring a large saucepan of salted water to a boil. Cook the carrots until they start to soften but are still firm, about 2½ minutes. Transfer to a colander; rinse under cold water; set aside.

2. In a large skillet over medium heat, melt the butter. Add the blanched carrots, and toss in the butter to coat. Cook the carrots until tender, 5 to 7 minutes. Stir in the parsley, and season with salt and pepper. Serve.

carrot and parsnip purée

SERVES 4

 Kosher salt
6 medium (about 1 pound) carrots, cut in 2-inch pieces
2 large garlic cloves
4 sprigs fresh thyme, plus 1 tablespoon leaves, plus more for garnish, optional
3 medium parsnips, cut in 2-inch pieces
2 tablespoons unsalted butter
1 tablespoon heavy cream
 Freshly ground black pepper

1. Cover and bring a medium saucepan with 6 cups cold salted water to a boil. Place the carrots, garlic, and 4 sprigs of thyme in the water, reduce heat, and simmer for about 5 minutes. Add the parsnips, and continue cooking until both the carrots and parsnips are tender when pierced with the tip of a knife, about 15 minutes.

2. Remove from the heat, drain, and discard the thyme sprigs. Transfer the carrots, parsnips, and garlic to the bowl of a food processor. Add the butter, cream, and 1 tablespoon thyme leaves, and process until completely smooth. Season with salt and pepper. Serve immediately, garnished with fresh thyme, if using. This purée can be made ahead of time and warmed in a saucepan over low heat before serving.

cauliflower gratin with endive

SERVES 8

Sardinian pasta, also known as fregola or friulli (see Food Sources, page 648), is a flour-based, nutty-flavored pasta; it absorbs the juices in the gratin beautifully. Small pasta such as tubettini may be used instead; boil it for 3 minutes, and rinse under cool water before using in recipe.

- 4 tablespoons unsalted butter, plus more for the dish
- 2 heads Belgian endive, cut lengthwise into sixths
- 1 cup large-style Freula Sarda, Sardinian pasta, or 1 cup parboiled tubettini pasta
- 2 pounds cauliflower florets (from 2 large heads)
- ¼ cup all-purpose flour
- 3 cups hot milk
  Kosher salt and freshly ground black pepper
- ⅛ teaspoon cayenne pepper
- 2 tablespoons minced fresh marjoram or oregano
- 10 ounces Gruyère cheese, grated on the small holes of a box grater
- ¼ cup fresh bread crumbs (see page 647)
- 2 ounces Parmesan cheese, grated on the large holes of a box grater to yield ¼ cup

1. Preheat the oven to 400°F with a rack in the lower third. Lightly butter a deep 1½-quart heat-proof dish. Arrange the endive in the bottom of the dish. Spread the pasta evenly over the endive. Arrange the cauliflower florets in the dish; the florets will mound up out of the dish generously.

2. Melt 4 tablespoons butter in a medium saucepan over medium heat; when bubbling, stir in flour with a wooden spoon. Reduce heat to medium low; stir for 2 minutes to cook the flour. Whisk in the hot milk, whisking constantly until the mixture thickens, about 4 minutes. Remove from the heat, and whisk in salt and pepper to taste, cayenne pepper, and marjoram. When well blended, whisk in the Gruyère until smooth. Pour the mixture over the cauliflower. Wipe any spills from the sides of dish. Sprinkle with the bread crumbs. Transfer the gratin dish to a baking sheet.

3. Bake 30 minutes. Remove from the oven, and sprinkle with the Parmesan. Reduce temperature to 350°F, and continue baking until the tip of a knife pierces the larger cauliflower pieces, about 40 minutes. (Cover the gratin with aluminum foil if the top darkens before the cauliflower is cooked through.) Remove from the oven, and place on a cooling rack to rest for 10 minutes before serving. Serve hot.

miniature cauliflower with tuscan ragoût

SERVES 6 TO 8

Tender and delicate miniature cauliflower is available in the fall. Serve this ragoût as a side dish or over rice, or cut the cooked cauliflower into smaller pieces, and use the ragoût as an omelet or frittata filling.

- 2 tablespoons olive oil
- 1 medium onion, chopped into ½-inch pieces
- 8 garlic cloves, 4 minced, 4 whole
- 5 anchovy fillets, minced
- 8 large cremini or white-button mushrooms, wiped clean, quartered
- 2 28-ounce cans (7 cups) whole Italian tomatoes
- 1 tablespoon finely chopped fresh rosemary
- 4 ounces (½ cup) niçoise olives, pitted
- 3 tablespoons capers, drained
- 2 dried bay leaves
- 8 heads baby cauliflower, trimmed, leaves on, or 1½ pounds cauliflower, cored, cut into 3½-inch pieces

1. Preheat the oven to 350°F. Heat the oil in a 3-quart ovenproof casserole or pan over medium heat. Add onion; cook, stirring occasionally, until translucent, about 8 minutes. Add garlic and minced anchovy fillets; cook until garlic is softened, about 3 minutes. Add mushrooms; cook until their liquid is released and evaporates, about 5 minutes.

2. Stir in the tomatoes, rosemary, olives, capers, and bay leaves. Cook over medium-high heat, stirring occasionally, until all the flavors combine, about 10 minutes. Transfer half of the mixture to the bowl of a food processor, and process until it is slightly chunky; return to the pan. Use a large spoon to break up the larger pieces of tomato.

3. Arrange the cauliflower over the sauce in the pan. Cover, and cook until the cauliflower is tender, about 30 minutes. (If mixture is too soupy, continue to cook another 5 to 10 minutes, uncovered, to reduce the liquid.) Serve hot.

corn on the cob

SERVES 12

For the sweetest corn possible, keep fresh ears at room temperature; refrigeration causes the natural sugars to convert to starch, which toughens the kernels.

½ teaspoon sugar

12 ears fresh corn

   Kosher salt and freshly ground black pepper

   Herbed Butter (recipe follows)

Fill a large stockpot with cold water. Cover and bring to a boil over high heat. Add the sugar and the corn, and let simmer until just tender, 3 to 5 minutes. Remove from water with tongs. Serve hot, sprinkled with salt and pepper, with herbed butter.

herbed butter

MAKES ½ POUND

Molding butter into a long, flat rectangle makes it perfect for buttering corn on the cob. As a substitute for fresh herbs, try 1½ tablespoons lemon zest or ½ tablespoon freshly grated nutmeg.

1 cup (2 sticks) unsalted butter, room temperature

¼ cup fresh chopped herbs such as flat-leaf parsley, cilantro, and basil

¼ teaspoon kosher salt

⅛ teaspoon freshly ground black pepper

1. Combine butter and herbs in the bowl of an electric mixer fitted with the paddle attachment. Season with salt and pepper; mix until well combined.

2. Using a rubber spatula, turn the butter out onto the center of a 12-inch square piece of parchment paper. Shape the butter into an approximate 4 x 8-inch rectangle. Fold up the parchment, and cover with plastic wrap. Transfer to refrigerator until ready to use.

corn on the grill

SERVES 6

6 ears fresh white or yellow corn, husks on

   Unsalted butter

   Kosher salt and freshly ground black pepper

1. Heat a grill or a grill pan until medium hot. Pull the husks back from the corn, keeping husks attached. Remove as much silk from the corn as possible; replace the husks, covering the kernels. Using kitchen twine, secure the husks at tops. Place corn in a large bucket of cold water. Let soak 1 hour.

2. Transfer the corn to the grill. Cook until the husks are charred and the corn has steamed, about 15 minutes. Remove from the grill; discard the husks. Serve hot with the butter and sprinkled with salt and pepper.

COOKING CORN

Cooking times for corn may vary. To test if it is done, use tongs to remove an ear from the water, and pierce a kernel with the tine of a fork. If the kernel bursts easily, it is done. Refrigerate extra boiled corn in a resealable plastic bag in the refrigerator, and eat it cold as a snack the next day (it is so sweet and delicious that it needs no butter, only a sprinkling of salt).

individual corn puddings

SERVES 8

These puddings are best served piping hot; you may serve them at room temperature, but they will lose their puff.

- 5 tablespoons unsalted butter
- 2 tablespoons all-purpose flour
- 4 ears fresh corn, kernels shaved from the cob
- 2 large eggs, separated
- 1¾ cups milk
- 1 teaspoon kosher salt
- ¼ teaspoon freshly ground black pepper
- ⅛ teaspoon ground nutmeg
- Pinch of cayenne pepper

1. Preheat the oven to 325°F. Melt 1 tablespoon butter, and use to brush eight 6-ounce ramekins; set the ramekins aside. Melt the remaining 4 tablespoons of butter in a small saucepan, and whisk in the flour.

2. Whisk together the corn, egg yolks, milk, salt, black pepper, nutmeg, and cayenne pepper in a bowl. Add the melted-butter mixture, and whisk to combine.

3. In a small bowl, whisk the egg whites until soft peaks form. Fold into the corn mixture.

4. Bring a kettle filled with water to a boil. Pour the corn mixture into the buttered ramekins, making sure to distribute the corn and batter evenly. Don't overfill; leave ¾-inch spaces at the top to allow the puddings to rise. Place the ramekins in a shallow baking pan, and transfer to the oven. Fill the baking pan with enough boiling water to cover the ramekins halfway up. Bake until the puddings are puffed and golden, 50 to 55 minutes. Remove from the oven, and serve immediately. Serve the puddings on individual saucers since they are extremely hot right out of the oven.

corn boiled in milk

SERVES 8

Boiling corn in milk gives it a sweet flavor; adding sugar brings out even more sweetness.

- 2 quarts milk
- 1 tablespoon sugar
- 8 ears fresh corn
- Unsalted butter
- Kosher salt and freshly ground black pepper

In a large, heavy saucepan, cover and bring the milk, 2 quarts water, and the sugar to a rapid boil. Add the corn, and cook 3 to 5 minutes, or until desired doneness. Remove the corn from the liquid with tongs. Serve hot with butter and sprinkled with salt and pepper.

braised endive with orange

SERVES 4

This dish can be prepared ahead of time and rewarmed over low heat; add the orange slices just before serving.

- 2 cups Homemade Chicken Stock (page 624), or low-sodium store-bought chicken broth, skimmed of fat
- 1 cup fresh orange juice
- ¼ cup triple sec or other orange-flavored liqueur
- 1 teaspoon kosher salt
- ⅛ teaspoon freshly ground black pepper
- 4 heads (1¼ pounds) Belgian endive
- 1 orange, peel and pith removed, sliced into ¼-inch-thick rounds

1. Combine stock, orange juice, liqueur, salt, and pepper in a large, shallow, nonreactive saucepan. Cover, bring to a boil, and add the endive. Cover endive with a piece of cheesecloth to keep it submerged, reduce heat to medium low, and cover; simmer until tender, about 45 minutes.

2. Transfer the endive to a plate, and cover with the cheesecloth to keep warm. Continue simmering until syrupy and slightly thick, about 20 minutes.

3. Slice the heads of endive in half lengthwise; add to the syrup. Add the orange slices, and toss to coat. Toss again, and serve hot.

FIT TO EAT RECIPE PER SERVING: 118 CALORIES, 1 G TOTAL FAT, 1 MG CHOLESTEROL, 19 G CARBOHYDRATE, 666 MG SODIUM, 4 G PROTEIN, 5 G DIETARY FIBER

spoon bread with leeks and corn

SERVES 8

Any shape of dish can be used, but spoon bread will bake best in one that is slightly wider than it is high. The baking time will be slightly different, depending on the size of the pan.

Unsalted butter, for dish
3 large eggs, separated
2½ cups milk
½ teaspoon cayenne pepper
1 teaspoon kosher salt
1 cup yellow cornmeal, preferably stone-ground
2 teaspoons baking powder
2 ears fresh corn, kernels shaved from the cob (1 cup)
2 leeks, white and pale-green parts, halved lengthwise, sliced, well washed (see page 646)

1. Preheat the oven to 400°F. Butter a 2½-quart casserole. Lightly beat the egg yolks in a medium bowl; set aside.

2. In a saucepan over medium heat, cover and bring 2 cups milk, the cayenne, and salt to a boil. Sprinkle the cornmeal into the liquid, stirring constantly, and cook until thick and smooth, about 3 minutes. Stir in the remaining ½ cup milk, baking powder, and egg yolks.

3. In a mixing bowl, beat the egg whites until stiff. Stir 1 large spoonful of the whites into the cornmeal mixture to lighten it, then gently fold in the remaining whites.

4. Pour half of the batter into the prepared dish. Sprinkle on the corn and leeks. Cover with the remaining batter. Bake until set and golden brown, 35 to 40 minutes. Serve immediately.

eggplant ragoût

SERVES 6

2 teaspoons whole fennel seeds, toasted (see page 644)
2 tablespoons olive oil
1 white onion, cut into ½-inch dice
2 garlic cloves, minced
2 teaspoons chopped fresh thyme leaves, plus sprigs for garnish
¼ cup dry white wine
2 pounds mixed eggplant, cut into 1-inch dice
1 large zucchini, cut into 1½-inch-long matchsticks
5 medium plum tomatoes, quartered lengthwise
Kosher salt and freshly ground black pepper

1. Place the fennel seeds in a spice grinder, and process until finely ground. Set aside.

2. Heat the olive oil in a large skillet over low heat. Add onion; cook, stirring often, on low heat until caramelized and slightly golden, 15 to 25 minutes.

3. Add the garlic, ground fennel, and thyme. Stir well; cook about 1 minute. Increase heat to medium high. Add the white wine, and stir, using a wooden spoon to loosen any browned bits from the bottom of the skillet. Cook until the liquid has been reduced by half, 1 to 2 minutes.

4. Add the eggplant and zucchini. Cover, and cook until the vegetables have softened but still retain their shapes and colors, 8 to 12 minutes. Add the tomatoes and ¼ cup water. Cook on medium-high heat, covered, until tomatoes release their juices but still retain shape, about 5 minutes. Season with salt and pepper. Garnish with the thyme sprigs; serve.

FIT TO EAT RECIPE PER SERVING: 124 CALORIES, 5 G FAT, 0 MG CHOLESTEROL, 17 G CARBOHYDRATE, 364 MG SODIUM, 3 G PROTEIN, 3 G DIETARY FIBER

roasted eggplant and bell pepper terrine

SERVES 6

Make this terrine a day ahead, and bring it to room temperature before serving. Fromage blanc, a fresh cream cheese that has the consistency of yogurt, is available in the dairy section of many supermarkets.

- 2 tablespoons extra-virgin olive oil, plus more for brushing
- 2 medium (2 pounds total) eggplants, cut into ¼-inch-thick rounds
- 1 small shallot, minced
- 1 tablespoon balsamic vinegar
- ½ teaspoon kosher salt
- ⅛ teaspoon freshly ground black pepper
- 4 roasted red bell peppers (see page 645), cut into 1-inch-wide strips
- ¼ cup fromage blanc or low-fat ricotta cheese
- 2 cups loosely packed fresh basil leaves, plus more for garnish

1. Preheat the oven to 400°F. Brush two baking sheets with oil. Working in batches, arrange eggplant rounds on baking sheets in a single layer. Roast until tender, 20 to 25 minutes, turning rounds over after about 12 minutes to ensure even cooking. Using a spatula, transfer rounds to a wire rack to cool. Repeat with the remaining eggplant.

2. In a small bowl, combine shallot, vinegar, salt, and pepper. Whisk in the remaining 2 tablespoons of olive oil until smooth. Set vinaigrette aside.

3. Brush a 9 x 4½ x 2½-inch loaf pan with oil, and line the pan with plastic wrap. Arrange one-third of the eggplant rounds, slightly overlapping, to cover the bottom of the pan. Brush lightly with the reserved vinaigrette. Arrange half of the bell pepper strips, slightly overlapping, over the eggplant. Using an offset spatula, spread half of the fromage blanc over the bell peppers. Top with half of the basil. Brush with the vinaigrette.

4. Make another layer of eggplant, vinaigrette, bell pepper, fromage blanc, and basil; brush with the vinaigrette. Top with a third layer of the eggplant;

brush with the vinaigrette. Using your hands, press down firmly but gently on the terrine, compressing the layers.

5. Cover tightly with plastic wrap; marinate, refrigerated, 12 to 24 hours. To serve, unmold terrine onto a serving platter; garnish with basil. Serve.

FIT TO EAT RECIPE PER SERVING: 113 CALORIES, 6 G FAT, 3 MG CHOLESTEROL, 14 G CARBOHYDRATE, 195 MG SODIUM, 4 G PROTEIN, 2 G DIETARY FIBER

steamed eggplant with black bean sauce

SERVES 4

Japanese eggplant is the long, thin, light-purple variety. Fermented black-bean sauce is made from small black soybeans that have been preserved in salt.

- 4 medium Japanese eggplants, halved lengthwise
- 1 tablespoon canola oil
- 3 garlic cloves, smashed
- 1 2-inch knob of fresh ginger, cut into ¼- inch-thick slices
- 2 tablespoons fermented black-bean sauce
- 1 teaspoon sugar
- 1 tablespoon very thinly sliced scallions, white parts only

1. Divide the eggplant halves between two compartments of a bamboo steamer, and set over a wok filled with 5 cups water. Steam the eggplants over medium heat until they are tender, about 45 minutes. Set aside.

2. Pour out the water from the wok. Add the oil, garlic, and ginger, and cook over medium-high heat until they begin to turn brown, about 1 minute. Remove garlic and ginger from pan, and discard.

3. In a small bowl, mix together the black-bean sauce, sugar, and 1½ tablespoons water. Add the sauce and scallion to pan, and mix well.

4. Transfer the eggplants from the steamer to a serving plate. Pour the sauce over eggplants, and serve immediately.

braised fennel with chestnuts and shallots

SERVES 8 TO 10

Baby fennel is in season around Thanksgiving; cut the bulbs in half instead of in quarters, and reduce the cooking time as necessary. This is one of our favorite Thanksgiving side dishes.

- 8 ounces fresh, frozen, or vacuum-packed chestnuts, peeled
- 15 small shallots
- 4 tablespoons unsalted butter
- 6 fennel bulbs or 12 baby fennel bulbs (about 6 pounds total), trimmed, quartered lengthwise, fronds reserved for garnish
- 2 tablespoons sugar
- 2¼ cups Homemade Chicken Stock (page 624), or low-sodium store-bought chicken broth, skimmed of fat
- 1½ teaspoons kosher salt
- ¼ teaspoon freshly ground black pepper

1. If using frozen chestnuts, bring a medium saucepan of water to a boil. Add the chestnuts, and boil for 3 minutes. Drain and set aside.

2. Peel shallots, leaving root ends intact. In a large, wide saucepan, melt 1 tablespoon butter over medium-high heat. Add the shallots and chestnuts, and cook, stirring occasionally, until browned on all sides, about 5 minutes. Cover the skillet, reduce heat to low, and cook, shaking the pan occasionally, until slightly tender, about 5 minutes. Remove the shallots and chestnuts from the pan; set aside.

3. Add remaining 3 tablespoons butter; melt over medium-high heat. Add fennel and sugar; cook, turning, until browned on all sides, about 12 minutes. If sugar begins to burn, reduce heat.

4. Add shallots, chestnuts, stock, salt, and pepper; stir to combine, scraping up any crisp bits in the bottom of the pan. Cover and bring to a boil. Reduce heat to medium; cook, carefully turning vegetables occasionally, until they are tender, about 20 minutes. Uncover, raise heat to medium high, and cook until the liquid is reduced to a glaze, about 12 minutes. Transfer to a serving dish, garnish with reserved fennel fronds, and serve.

fennel and celeriac gratin

SERVES 10 TO 12

Celeriac, a brown, knobby vegetable, is also called celery root or knob celery.

- 1 large onion
- 1½ tablespoons unsalted butter
- 3 medium (1¼ pounds) celeriac, peeled
- 2 small (1¾ pounds) fennel bulbs
- 3 tablespoons fresh lemon juice
- ½ cup Homemade Chicken Stock (page 624), or low-sodium store-bought chicken broth, skimmed of fat

  Kosher salt and freshly ground black pepper
- 1½ tablespoons balsamic vinegar
- 1 teaspoon finely chopped fresh sage
- 2 teaspoons finely chopped fresh marjoram or oregano
- 2 tablespoons coarsely chopped fresh flat-leaf parsley
- ½ cup freshly grated Parmesan cheese (from 2 ounces)

1. Slice onion in half lengthwise, and then slice each half into ¼-inch-thick slices. Melt butter in a large straight-sided skillet over medium-low heat. Add onions to skillet, cover, and cook, stirring occasionally with a wooden spoon, until the onions are translucent, about 8 minutes.

2. Preheat the broiler. Slice the celeriac into 1-inch pieces, and then slice each piece as thinly as possible. Transfer the celeriac to a medium mixing bowl. Slice the fennel as thinly as possible, add to the celeriac, and toss with 2 tablespoons lemon juice. Stir the fennel-celeriac mixture into the onions along with the chicken stock and salt and pepper to taste. Cover the skillet, raise the heat to medium, and cook, stirring occasionally, until the vegetables are tender, about 10 minutes.

3. Remove the cover, and stir the balsamic vinegar, the remaining tablespoon of lemon juice, the sage, marjoram, and parsley into the vegetable mixture. Transfer the vegetables to an ovenproof gratin dish, and sprinkle the top of the mixture with the Parmesan. Place the dish under the broiler until the top of the mixture is golden brown. Remove the gratin from the oven, and serve immediately.

FIT TO EAT RECIPE PER SERVING: 59 CALORIES, 4 G FAT, 8 MG CHOLESTEROL, 5 G CARBOHYDRATE, 408 MG SODIUM, 3 G PROTEIN, 4 G DIETARY FIBER

grilled leeks vinaigrette

SERVES 4

If you like, set aside the dark-green ends of the leeks for making stock.

- Kosher salt
- 8 leeks, white and pale-green parts, sliced in half lengthwise, ½ inch from the root end (which stays intact), well washed (see page 646)
- 1 tablespoon Dijon mustard
- 2 tablespoons sherry vinegar
- 3 tablespoons extra-virgin olive oil
- Freshly ground black pepper

1. Prepare an ice-water bath; set aside. Cover and bring a large pot of salted water to a boil. Add the leeks, and cook until very tender, about 4 minutes. Transfer the leeks to the ice-water bath. Once the leeks are cold, drain them, pat them dry, and set them aside.

2. In a small bowl, combine mustard and vinegar. Slowly drizzle oil into the bowl, whisking to form a thick vinaigrette. Season with salt and pepper.

3. Heat a grill or a grill pan to medium hot. Lightly brush the leeks with some of the vinaigrette, and arrange them on the hot grill. Grill the leeks until they are hot and have grill marks, about 2 minutes per side. Remove the leeks from the grill, and toss with the remaining vinaigrette. Serve.

mess o' greens

SERVES 10 TO 12

- 2 tablespoons olive oil
- 5 medium leeks, white and pale-green parts, cut into ¼-inch rounds, well washed (see page 646)
- 2 garlic cloves
- 1 teaspoon crushed red-pepper flakes
- 1 smoked turkey wing (4 to 6 ounces), cut into 3-inch pieces
- 3 pounds greens, such as collard, mustard, turnip, and kale, washed, trimmed, and torn into pieces
- ¼ cup dry white wine
- ¾ teaspoon kosher salt
- ¼ teaspoon freshly ground black pepper

1. Heat the oil in a large stockpot or casserole over medium-high heat until hot, 2 to 3 minutes. Add the leeks and garlic; stir to coat. Cook, stirring, until the leeks are softened but not brown, about 3 minutes. Add the red-pepper flakes, smoked turkey wing, and greens; if necessary add the greens in a few batches.

2. Add the wine; cover. Steam the greens, turning occasionally, 8 to 10 minutes. Uncover, add the salt and pepper, and cook, tossing occasionally, 3 minutes more. Discard the turkey wing and garlic cloves, and serve hot.

portobello mushrooms stuffed with gratinéed potatoes

SERVES 6

This dish can be assembled several hours ahead through step 5. Reheat in a 350°F oven for 30 minutes before broiling.

- 3 large (about 1½ pounds) Yukon gold or Yellow Finn potatoes, scrubbed
- 1 teaspoon kosher salt, plus more for cooking water and seasoning
- ½ cup milk
- 8 medium roasted garlic cloves (see page 646)
- 3 tablespoons freshly grated Parmesan cheese
- 2 tablespoons unsalted butter
- ¼ teaspoon freshly ground black pepper, plus more for seasoning
- 6 portobello mushrooms, 4 inches in diameter, wiped clean, stems removed
- 3 tablespoons olive oil
- 1 tablespoon fresh thyme leaves

1. Place the potatoes in a large pot, and cover with 2 inches of cold salted water. Cover and bring the water to a boil, and reduce heat. Gently cook the potatoes until they are tender when pierced with the tip of a knife, 40 to 50 minutes. Remove from the heat, and drain. Peel and set aside.

2. While the potatoes are cooking, warm the milk in a small saucepan over medium-low heat until bubbles form around the edges.

3. Cover and bring a large pot of water to a simmer. Using a ricer or a food mill fitted with a fine disk, purée the potatoes into a large metal bowl, then place the bowl over the pot of simmering water. Add the roasted garlic, warm milk, Parmesan, butter, 1 teaspoon salt, and ¼ teaspoon pepper to the potatoes, and stir until smooth and creamy. Cover the bowl with aluminum foil, and keep warm over the barely simmering water until ready to use.

4. Place the mushroom caps in a large roasting pan, stem-side down, and drizzle with 1½ tablespoons olive oil. Season with salt and pepper. Turn and driz-

zle with the remaining 1½ tablespoons olive oil, and season with salt, pepper, and the thyme leaves. Place the pan in the oven, and bake the mushrooms until tender, about 15 minutes.

5. Remove the mushrooms from the oven, and preheat the broiler. Spoon about ½ cup of the potato purée onto each mushroom cap.

6. Place pan under broiler until potatoes are golden brown, about 2 minutes. Serve immediately.

wild mushroom ragoût

SERVES 4

- 2 tablespoons unsalted butter
- 1 tablespoon extra-virgin olive oil
- 2 garlic cloves, minced
- 1½ pounds wild mushrooms, such as chanterelle or shiitake, wiped clean, trimmed, cut into ½-inch pieces
- ¼ cup dry white wine
   Kosher salt and freshly ground black pepper
   Juice of ½ lemon
- 3 tablespoons roughly chopped fresh flat-leaf parsley

1. Melt the butter with the olive oil in a large skillet set over high heat. Add the garlic, and cook until fragrant but not brown, about 30 seconds.

2. Add mushrooms, and toss quickly in the butter mixture to coat. Add the wine. Continue cooking until the mushrooms release their juices, the pan is almost dry, and the mushrooms turn golden, about 8 minutes. Season well with salt and pepper. Add the lemon juice and parsley; toss. Serve hot.

fried okra

SERVES 10 TO 12

5   cups pure vegetable shortening
4   large eggs
2   tablespoons milk
2   cups all-purpose flour
2   cups cornmeal
1½ teaspoons kosher salt
½   teaspoon freshly ground black pepper
1   pound fresh okra, stems trimmed

1. Melt and heat the shortening in a 12-inch cast-iron skillet over medium heat until a deep-frying thermometer registers 375°F.

2. Meanwhile, whisk together the eggs and the milk in a bowl. Place the flour, cornmeal, salt, and pepper in another bowl; whisk to combine.

3. Place 8 pieces of the okra in the egg mixture to coat, then dredge in the flour mixture. Fry until golden brown, turning as necessary, 3 to 4 minutes. Drain on paper towels. Repeat coating and frying the remaining okra; serve warm.

baked stuffed onions

SERVES 8

8   medium yellow onions, unpeeled
1   cup fresh basil leaves, loosely packed
½   cup fresh flat-leaf parsley leaves, loosely packed
1   head of roasted garlic (see page 646)
2½ teaspoons kosher salt, plus more for water
¼   teaspoon freshly ground black pepper
3   medium (about 1 pound) Yukon gold potatoes, peeled, cut into ½-inch cubes
1   tablespoon olive oil, plus more as needed and for brushing
10 ounces assorted mushrooms, such as chanterelle, shiitake, or oyster, wiped clean, sliced into ¼-inch-thick pieces
¼   cup dry white wine

1. Preheat the oven to 450°F. Cut off the top quarter from each onion; wrap each onion in aluminum foil. Cook onions until soft, about 1½ hours.

2. Remove the onions from the oven, unwrap, and let cool 15 minutes. Peel, and discard the skins. Working from the center of each onion, pull out all but two outer layers, leaving a shell. Place the shells in a small baking dish. Measure 3 cups of onion flesh, and set the rest aside.

3. Place half of the onion flesh in the bowl of a food processor. Add the basil, parsley, roasted garlic, 1 teaspoon salt, and ⅛ teaspoon black pepper. Purée, and set aside.

4. Place the potatoes in a large saucepan and cover with 2 inches of salted water. Cover and bring to a boil. Cook the potatoes until tender when pierced with the tip of a knife, about 20 minutes; drain.

5. Pass the potatoes through a ricer set over a large bowl. Slowly whisk in the puréed onion mixture. Set the potato filling aside.

6. Heat the oil in a small skillet over medium heat. Add one variety of mushroom. Season with some of the remaining 1½ teaspoons salt and ⅛ teaspoon pepper. Cook, stirring occasionally, until tender and slightly golden. Transfer the mushrooms to a bowl. Repeat the cooking process with the remaining mushrooms, adding more oil as necessary. Roughly chop the remaining onion flesh; stir into the mushroom filling.

7. Stuff the onion shells with alternating spoonfuls of the potato and mushroom fillings. Brush the stuffed onions with olive oil. Add the wine to the baking dish. Bake the stuffed onions until they are soft and golden, about 30 minutes. Serve hot.

FIT TO EAT RECIPE PER SERVING: 99 CALORIES, 0 G FAT, 0 MG CHOLESTEROL, 0 G CARBOHYDRATE, 675 MG SODIUM, 3 G PROTEIN, 4 G DIETARY FIBER

pan-roasted balsamic onions

SERVES 8 TO 10

We mixed leeks with equal amounts of red and white pearl onions and cipollini, but you can use any combination of small, sweet onions.

- 10 ounces white pearl onions
- 10 ounces red pearl onions
- 10 ounces cipollini onions
- ¼ cup plus 1 tablespoon olive oil
- 1½ teaspoons kosher salt, plus more for seasoning
- ¼ teaspoon freshly ground black pepper, plus more for seasoning
- 2¼ pounds leeks, white and pale-green parts, cut in half lengthwise, well washed (see page 646)
- ¼ cup balsamic vinegar
- 1 cup Homemade Chicken Stock (page 624), or low-sodium store-bought chicken broth, skimmed of fat
- 2 tablespoons unsalted butter
- ½ teaspoon fresh thyme leaves

1. Preheat the oven to 450°F, cover, and bring a saucepan of water to a boil. Add onions; boil for 1 minute. Drain. Let stand until cool enough to handle, then carefully peel, leaving root and stem ends intact. Transfer to a bowl; add 2 tablespoons olive oil, 1 teaspoon salt, and the pepper; toss.

2. In a large bowl, combine leeks, 1 tablespoon olive oil, and ½ teaspoon salt; toss to combine.

3. Heat a large skillet over medium-high heat; add 1 tablespoon olive oil and the leeks. Cook the leeks until slightly tender and lightly browned, about 5 minutes. Remove the leeks from the skillet, and set aside.

4. Add remaining tablespoon of oil and onions to the skillet, and cook, turning occasionally, until browned all over, about 8 minutes.

5. Reduce heat to medium low; add vinegar and stock. Cover skillet; cook until onions are tender, about 30 minutes, adding leeks after 10 to 15 minutes. Uncover and add butter; increase heat to high, and cook, shaking pan occasionally, until liquid reduces and coats onions, about 4 minutes. Transfer to a serving dish; garnish with thyme leaves. Season with salt and pepper; serve.

fire-roasted vidalia onion halves

SERVES 8

Pair these roasted onions with grilled salmon.

- 8 Vidalia or other sweet onions, cut in half crosswise
-    Extra-virgin olive oil
-    Balsamic vinegar
-    Kosher salt and freshly ground black pepper
- 2 bacon strips, cut into 16 pieces

1. Place each onion half, cut-side up, on a 10-inch square of aluminum foil. Drizzle with olive oil and vinegar. Sprinkle with salt and pepper. Turn the onions cut-side down; pat a piece of bacon onto the side of each one. Fold the foil into neat packets.

2. Heat a grill or a grill pan to medium hot. Place the foil packets on grill; cook 20 to 30 minutes (if the grill becomes too hot, move the onions to a cooler part), until tender and slightly charred. Let the onions cool in packets for 15 minutes.

3. Remove the foil, reserving the juices; discard the bacon. Serve the onions warm or at room temperature, drizzling the reserved juices over the tops.

glazed pearl onions

SERVES 6 TO 8

1½ pounds (about 6 cups) pearl onions,
    roots trimmed
1 tablespoon olive oil
2 cups dry white wine
2 tablespoons unsalted butter
   Kosher salt and freshly ground
   black pepper

1. Cover and bring a large saucepan of water to a boil. Cook the onions in the boiling water for 2 minutes. Drain; let cool. Carefully peel the onions, leaving the root and stem ends intact.

2. Heat oil in a medium skillet over high heat. Add onions, and cook, stirring occasionally until dark brown, about 5 minutes. Add wine; cover and bring to a boil. Reduce heat to medium low; simmer with the lid ajar, until liquid is almost completely reduced and onions are very tender, about 25 minutes. Add butter, and stir until incorporated. Season with salt and pepper. Serve immediately.

caramelized roasted parsnips

SERVES 10 TO 12

8 tablespoons (1 stick) unsalted butter,
   melted
2 tablespoons granulated sugar
2 teaspoons packed light-brown sugar
3 pounds parsnips, cut into ¼ x 3-inch
   julienne
1 teaspoon garlic powder
   Kosher salt and freshly ground
   black pepper
1 tablespoon snipped chives

1. Preheat the oven to 350°F. Place melted butter and granulated and brown sugars in a large roasting pan; whisk until incorporated. Add the parsnips; toss. Sprinkle with the garlic powder, and season with salt and pepper; toss. Cover with aluminum foil; bake 20 minutes.

2. Remove foil; stir. Roast parsnips, uncovered, until lightly browned and easily pierced with the tip of a knife, about 20 minutes. Stir; season with salt and pepper. Sprinkle with chives, and serve.

peperonata

SERVES 8

The juice content of peppers varies. If peppers seem too juicy toward the end of cooking time, remove the lid sooner to cook off more liquid.

3 tablespoons olive oil
6 garlic cloves
2 large red onions, cut into ½-inch rings
6 red, yellow, or green bell peppers, seeds
   and ribs removed, cut into ¾-inch-thick
   strips
   Kosher salt and freshly ground
   black pepper
1 sprig fresh rosemary, coarsely chopped
2 tablespoons balsamic vinegar
½ cup kalamata olives, pitted and cut in half
10 fresh basil leaves

1. Heat the oil in a skillet over medium heat. Add the whole garlic cloves; gently cook over low heat until golden, about 10 minutes. Add the onions; cook over medium-low heat, turning often, until they soften, about 5 minutes.

2. Add the bell peppers, salt and pepper to taste, and rosemary to the skillet; stir to coat with the oil, and cook, covered, over low heat, stirring occasionally, until the peppers are soft and the juices are released, about 35 minutes. Stir in the vinegar and olives. Cook 5 minutes. Just before serving, roughly tear the basil leaves, reserving two for garnish. Stir in the torn basil. Serve warm or at room temperature, garnished with reserved basil.

pumpkin gratin

SERVES 8

Cheese pumpkins have light-brown or tan skins and orange flesh. If you cannot find this variety, substitute a variety of squash, such as butternut.

- 1 garlic clove, cut in half
- 1 tablespoon unsalted butter, plus more for pan
- ½ cup dried bread crumbs (see page 647)
  Kosher salt and freshly ground black pepper
- 2 teaspoons chopped fresh flat-leaf parsley
- 5 pounds cheese pumpkin, peeled, seeded, cut into 2-inch-long matchsticks
- 2 tablespoons fresh thyme leaves
- 3 tablespoons snipped chives
- 1½ cups heavy cream
- ⅛ teaspoon ground nutmeg

1. Preheat the oven to 375°F. Rub a 2½-quart gratin dish with the garlic clove, and generously spread with butter. Set aside.

2. Melt 1 tablespoon butter in a small skillet over medium heat. Add the bread crumbs. Season with salt and pepper, and stir until the crumbs have separated, 2 to 3 minutes. Transfer to a medium bowl, and stir in the parsley. Set aside.

3. Place the pumpkin in the prepared dish. Combine with the thyme and chives. Season with salt and pepper.

4. In a small saucepan, combine the cream and nutmeg. Bring to a boil. Reduce heat to medium; simmer 5 minutes to reduce slightly. Pour the cream over the pumpkin mixture.

5. Bake the gratin for 20 minutes. Remove from the oven; stir gently. Return to oven, and bake until the cream has thickened and is bubbling, about 10 minutes. Remove from the oven.

6. Preheat broiler. Sprinkle gratin with reserved bread-crumb mixture; broil until top is deep golden brown, about 2 minutes. Serve immediately.

grilled radicchio and fontina

SERVES 4

- 1 10-ounce head radicchio
- 2 tablespoons balsamic vinegar
  Kosher salt and freshly ground black pepper
- 2 teaspoons chopped fresh oregano
- ¼ cup extra-virgin olive oil
- ¾ cup (3 ounces) finely grated fontina cheese
  Lemon wedges, for serving

1. Keeping the base intact, quarter the radicchio so that the head opens out into 4 wedges. Combine the vinegar, salt, pepper, and 1½ teaspoons oregano. Whisk in the oil. Brush half the vinaigrette over and into the cut radicchio.

2. Heat a grill pan until medium hot. Place the radicchio, cut-side down, on the pan. Cover the radicchio with a metal bowl. Cook until the leaves start to soften, 2 to 4 minutes. Turn the radicchio over. Tuck some of the grated cheese into the leaves, separating the layers a little; sprinkle some more cheese over the surface, leaving a little left over for garnish. Cover, and cook on the grill on low heat until the outer leaves are soft and cheese has melted, 3 to 5 minutes. Transfer to a serving platter, drizzle with the remaining half of the vinaigrette, ½ tablespoon oregano, and the cheese. Serve hot with lemon wedges.

spinach sautéed with indian spices

SERVES 4

Spinach releases a lot of water when cooked, so dry the leaves well to keep the water from accumulating.

- 3 tablespoons unsalted butter
- 4 large shallots, thinly sliced lengthwise
- 2 large garlic cloves, thinly sliced
- 1 1-inch piece fresh ginger, cut in matchsticks
- 2 teaspoons ground cumin
- 2 teaspoons ground turmeric
- 2 pounds fresh spinach, washed
- 2 teaspoons whole yellow mustard seeds

  Kosher salt and freshly ground black pepper

1. In a high, straight-sided skillet, melt butter over medium-high heat. Add shallots and garlic, and cook until shallots are lightly browned, 6 minutes.

2. Stir in the ginger, cumin, and turmeric, and cook for 30 seconds. Add the spinach and mustard seeds; season with salt and pepper; cook, tossing, until the spinach is just wilted, 1 to 2 minutes. Remove from the skillet, and serve immediately.

twice-baked butternut squash

SERVES 6

- 6 butternut squash (about 9 pounds total)

  Kosher salt and freshly ground black pepper
- ½ cup plus 1 tablespoon nonfat sour cream
- 2 teaspoons paprika
- 6 chives, snipped into ⅛-inch pieces
- 3 tablespoons fresh bread crumbs (see page 647), lightly toasted

1. Preheat the oven to 450°F with the rack in the center. Halve the squash lengthwise, and remove the seeds and fibers. Season the squash with salt and pepper. Fill a roasting pan with ¼ inch of water. Place the squash, cut-sides up, in the pan. Cover with aluminum foil, and bake until the squash is

tender when pierced with the tip of a knife, 35 to 45 minutes. Remove from the oven, transfer the squash to a cool surface, and let cool enough to handle. Reduce oven temperature to 425°F.

2. Use a spoon to scoop the baked flesh out of each half into a large bowl, leaving a ¼-inch border around 6 of the halves so they will keep their shape (discard the other halves). To the bowl, add the sour cream, paprika, and chives, and season with salt and pepper. Mix with a handheld electric mixer or potato masher until smooth and well combined. Fill the 6 squash halves with the mixture. Sprinkle the tops with the toasted bread crumbs. Bake until golden brown and warm throughout, 20 to 30 minutes. Serve hot.

FIT TO EAT RECIPE PER SERVING: 292 CALORIES, 3 G FAT, 2 MG CHOLESTEROL, 67 G CARBOHYDRATE, 637 MG SODIUM, 13 G PROTEIN, 13 G DIETARY FIBER

spaghetti squash with herbs

SERVES 10 TO 12

- 1 7-pound spaghetti squash, cut in half lengthwise and seeded
- 6 tablespoons unsalted butter, cut into tablespoons
- 3 tablespoons finely chopped fresh thyme, chives, or flat-leaf parsley

  Kosher salt and freshly ground black pepper

1. Preheat the oven to 350°F. Place the squash halves, cut-side down, in a large roasting pan. Add 1 cup water; cover with aluminum foil. Bake until translucent and the flesh pulls away from the skin, about 50 minutes. Let cool 5 minutes.

2. Using a fork, scrape the flesh; it will separate into spaghetti-like strands. Discard the skins. In a large bowl, toss together the squash, butter, and herbs. Season with salt and pepper. Serve hot.

baked stuffed spaghetti squash

SERVES 4

- 2 medium spaghetti squash
- 16 plum tomatoes
- 2 teaspoons minced garlic
- 2 tablespoons olive oil
- 4 ounces basil leaves, plus sprigs for garnish
- 1 teaspoon kosher salt
- ¼ teaspoon freshly ground black pepper
- ¼ cup plus 2 tablespoons grated Parmesan cheese (from 1 ounce)

1. Place both whole spaghetti squash in a large stockpot, and cover with 2 inches of water. Cover and bring the water to a boil. Reduce heat to a simmer, and cook the squash until it is slightly tender when you press it with your fingers, 20 to 30 minutes. Drain. Using a serrated knife, cut the squash in half crosswise. Stand the halves on end, with cut-sides up, and set aside to cool 15 minutes.

2. Preheat the oven to 450°F. Remove seeds from squash halves; discard. Using a fork, scrape the flesh; it will separate into spaghetti-like strands. Transfer the strands to a mixing bowl, and transfer squash shells to a baking pan; set both aside.

3. Chop 12 tomatoes into ½-inch pieces; add to squash. Slice remaining 4 tomatoes into ¼-inch-thick rounds; set aside.

4. Place the garlic, olive oil, basil leaves, salt, and pepper in the bowl of a food processor. Process until basil is very finely chopped, about 2 minutes.

5. Transfer the basil mixture to the mixing bowl with the squash strands and the tomato pieces; toss with the vegetables to combine. Divide the mixture among the reserved squash shells, and top each shell with several tomato slices. Sprinkle 1½ tablespoons of the Parmesan cheese over each shell.

6. Transfer pan to the oven; bake the stuffed squash until the cheese is golden and a metal skewer inserted down into the stuffing comes out hot when held there for 15 seconds, about 30 minutes. Garnish with the basil sprigs. Serve hot.

FIT TO EAT RECIPE PER SERVING: 209 CALORIES, 11 G FAT, 6 MG CHOLESTEROL, 26 G CARBOHYDRATE, 703 MG SODIUM, 7 G PROTEIN, 5 G DIETARY FIBER

braised squash with moroccan spices

SERVES 6

- 1 2½-pound winter squash such as kabocha
- ½ cup golden raisins
- 1 tablespoon olive oil
- 4 shallots, quartered
- 4 whole cardamom pods
- ¾ teaspoon ground cumin
- 2 teaspoons dried savory or oregano
- ½ cup dried apricots
- ½ cup pitted prunes
- ½ cup Homemade Chicken Stock (page 624), or low-sodium store-bought chicken broth, skimmed of fat
- ¼ cup fresh orange juice

  Kosher salt and freshly ground black pepper
- 2 teaspoons grated lemon zest
- 1 tablespoon fresh lemon juice
- 1 teaspoon almond slices, lightly toasted (see page 644)
- 2 teaspoons chopped fresh mint leaves

1. Halve squash lengthwise. Remove seeds and fibers; peel. Cut in 1-inch pieces to yield 4 cups. Soak raisins in a bowl with warm water.

2. Preheat oven to 375°F. Heat oil in a medium oven-proof skillet over medium heat. Add shallots, and cook until they begin to brown, about 10 minutes. Add cardamom, cumin, savory, and squash, and stir well. Cover; cook over medium-low heat until squash begins to color, 5 to 10 minutes.

3. Add apricots, prunes, drained raisins, stock, and orange juice. Season with salt and pepper. Cover and bring to a boil. Transfer to oven; cook until liquid has been absorbed and squash is tender, 20 to 30 minutes. Be sure the liquid does not evaporate so quickly that the squash burns. Transfer to a serving dish; add half the lemon zest and the lemon juice. Stir to combine. To serve, sprinkle with almonds, mint, and remaining zest. Serve hot.

FIT TO EAT RECIPE PER SERVING: 186 CALORIES, 1 G FAT, 0 MG CHOLESTEROL, 46 G CARBOHYDRATE, 30 MG SODIUM, 5 G PROTEIN, 4 G DIETARY FIBER

creamed swiss chard

SERVES 4

Swiss chard, a member of the beet family, has dark-green, bumpy leaves, and white or pink stalks.

- 2 tablespoons unsalted butter
- 2 medium shallots, minced
- 1 tablespoon all-purpose flour
- 1 cup milk
- ½ teaspoon ground nutmeg
- 1 teaspoon kosher salt
- ¼ teaspoon freshly ground black pepper
- 1 large bunch (about 1 pound 10 ounces) green Swiss chard, washed, ribs removed, leaves roughly chopped

1. In a large skillet, melt the butter over medium heat. Add the shallots, and cook until translucent, about 6 minutes. Add the flour, and cook, stirring constantly, for 1 minute. Add the milk, nutmeg, salt, and pepper; raise heat to high and cook, stirring constantly, until the mixture is reduced by half, about 2 minutes.

2. Add the chard, and cook until it is tender and coated with the thickened milk mixture, about 5 minutes. Serve immediately.

slow-roasted tomatoes

SERVES 6

Serve these tomatoes over grilled or toasted rustic bread; spread any of the oil remaining in the skillet over the bread before grilling.

- 2 pints red and yellow cherry tomatoes
- 3 sprigs fresh basil
- 6 garlic cloves
- ½ cup extra-virgin olive oil
  Kosher salt and freshly ground black pepper

1. Preheat the oven to 300°F. Arrange the tomatoes, basil, and garlic in a large cast-iron skillet. Pour the olive oil over the tomatoes; toss to coat.

2. Transfer skillet to oven. Roast until tomatoes are soft, melted, and the skins start to pop, about 40 minutes. Remove from oven, and season with salt and pepper. Serve warm or at room temperature.

grilled tomatoes with yogurt

SERVES 4

Thick, creamy Greek or Middle Eastern yogurt, available at specialty food stores, is especially good with these tomatoes, but plain full-fat yogurt will also work.

- 4 red tomatoes
- 1 teaspoon dried oregano
- 1 teaspoon dried thyme
- 1 teaspoon fresh lemon juice
- 1 teaspoon extra-virgin olive oil
  Kosher salt and freshly ground black pepper
- 1 cup plain yogurt, preferably Greek or Middle Eastern

1. Cut ½ inch off the top of the tomatoes. Sprinkle the cut surfaces of the tomatoes with the oregano, thyme, lemon juice, oil, salt, and pepper.

2. Heat a grill or grill pan until hot. Grill tomatoes cut-side down until slightly charred, 3 to 5 minutes. Turn and grill until soft and warm, 3 to 5 minutes . Transfer to a dish; serve immediately with the yogurt on the side.

cherry tomato kebabs

SERVES 6

If you're using wooden skewers, soak them in water for at least 1 hour before using.

- 36 (about 12 ounces) cherry or pear tomatoes
- 1 tablespoon extra-virgin olive oil
  Kosher salt and freshly ground black pepper

1. Place tomatoes in a bowl. Drizzle oil over tomatoes; season with salt and pepper. Toss to combine.

2. Thread 6 tomatoes, spaced at least ½ inch apart, on each of six wooden or metal skewers.

3. Heat a grill or a grill pan until medium hot. Arrange the skewers on the grill. Grill until the tomatoes have grill marks and start to soften, 2 to 4 minutes. Turn the skewers over, and grill the other side, 1 to 2 minutes more. Remove the skewers from the grill, sprinkle with salt, and serve.

baked plum tomatoes with herbed rice stuffing

SERVES 4

Serve these as an antipasto or as a side dish.

- 8 large plum tomatoes
- 1 teaspoon kosher salt, plus more for seasoning
- 1½ tablespoons finely chopped fresh basil
- 1 tablespoon finely chopped fresh tarragon, plus more, coarsely chopped, for garnish
- 2 tablespoons minced shallots
- ¼ teaspoon freshly ground black pepper
- ¼ cup plus 1 tablespoon Arborio rice
- 2 teaspoons freshly grated Parmesan cheese
- 1 teaspoon extra-virgin olive oil
- ¼ cup dry white wine

1. Preheat the oven to 375°F. Using a sharp knife, cut a very thin slice from the bottom of the tomatoes to enable them to stand upright. Cut ⅛ inch from the stem end of each tomato; discard the ends. Use a spoon or a melon baller to scrape the flesh, seeds, and juice from 6 of the tomatoes into a medium bowl. Repeat with the remaining 2 tomatoes, but scrape the flesh, seeds, and juice into a separate bowl.

2. Sprinkle salt in each tomato; stand them in a small baking dish.

3. To the reserved pulp of the 6 tomatoes, add 1 teaspoon salt, the basil, finely chopped tarragon, shallots, pepper, and Arborio rice; mix to combine.

4. Fill the tomatoes with the rice mixture, gently tapping the bottom of each tomato to distribute the filling evenly. Sprinkle the Parmesan over the tops, and drizzle with olive oil.

5. Add the wine to the reserved pulp of the 2 tomatoes, mix to combine, and pour into the bottom of the dish.

6. Bake until the tops are golden brown and the rice is tender, 45 minutes to 1 hour. Remove from the oven, and garnish with the coarsely chopped tarragon. Serve immediately.

FIT TO EAT RECIPE PER STUFFED TOMATO: 60 CALORIES, 1 G TOTAL FAT, 1 MG CHOLESTEROL, 11 G CARBOHYDRATE, 285 MG SODIUM, 2 G PROTEIN, 1 G DIETARY FIBER

gratin of yellow tomatoes, potatoes, and caramelized onions

SERVES 6

This gratin has a lovely golden color when yellow tomatoes are used.

- 2 teaspoons olive oil, plus more for brushing
- 3 large (2 pounds) Vidalia or other sweet onions, thinly sliced
- 2 teaspoons kosher salt
- ½ teaspoon freshly ground black pepper
- ½ cup Homemade Chicken Stock (page 624), or low-sodium store-bought chicken broth, skimmed of fat

  Pinch of crushed saffron threads
- 3 medium (1½ pounds) Yukon gold potatoes, sliced paper thin
- 3 garlic cloves, minced
- 1 tablespoon finely chopped fresh oregano, or 1 teaspoon dried
- 1 tablespoon finely chopped fresh thyme, or 1 teaspoon dried
- 3 yellow tomatoes, sliced into ½-inch-thick rounds
- 1 tablespoon freshly grated Parmesan cheese

1. Heat the olive oil in a large skillet over medium-low heat. Add the onions, ½ teaspoon salt, and ⅛ teaspoon pepper; cook until soft and caramelized, stirring occasionally, about 30 minutes. Remove from the heat, and set aside.

2. Preheat the oven to 350°F. Meanwhile, in a small saucepan, heat the stock and saffron over low heat until the stock turns yellow and is infused with saffron, about 3 minutes. Remove from the heat, and set aside.

3. Combine potatoes, garlic, oregano, and thyme in a large bowl, and add the saffron-infused stock. Gently toss with a rubber spatula to combine well.

4. Brush an ovenproof dish with oil, and arrange half the potato mixture evenly in the dish. Sprinkle with ½ teaspoon salt and ⅛ teaspoon pepper, and spread the caramelized onions over the potatoes. Arrange the tomato slices on top of the onions, and season with ½ teaspoon salt and ⅛ teaspoon pepper. Layer the remaining half of the potatoes over the tomatoes, and sprinkle with the remaining ½ teaspoon salt and ⅛ teaspoon pepper. If any stock remains in the bowl, pour it over the gratin.

5. Cover gratin with aluminum foil; bake 1 hour. Remove foil, baste with the juices from the pan, sprinkle with the Parmesan, and bake, uncovered, until the top is golden brown and crisp, about 25 minutes more. Let stand about 15 minutes before serving. This dish can be made up to 4 hours in advance and served at room temperature or reheated in a 300°F oven for 15 minutes.

FIT TO EAT RECIPE PER SERVING: 159 CALORIES, 3 G TOTAL FAT, 1 MG CHOLESTEROL, 31 G CARBOHYDRATE, 766 MG SODIUM, 5 G PROTEIN, 5 G DIETARY FIBER

tomatoes gratinée

SERVES 4

- 4 small (4 to 6 ounces) yellow tomatoes
- 4 small (4 to 6 ounces) red tomatoes

  Kosher salt and freshly ground black pepper
- 1 tablespoon extra-virgin olive oil
- 2 ounces Gruyère cheese, grated on the large holes of a box grater
- 1 garlic clove, minced
- 1 small Idaho potato
- ¼ teaspoon ground nutmeg

1. Preheat the oven to 400°F. Slice and discard stem and top of each tomato; arrange tomatoes in a baking dish. Season with salt and pepper, and drizzle with olive oil.

2. Combine grated cheese and garlic in a small bowl. Peel the potato; grate on the large holes of the box grater. Squeeze out moisture; toss with cheese mixture. Add nutmeg, and stir to combine. Sprinkle evenly over tomatoes. Bake until tomatoes are soft and crust is golden and crisp, 20 to 25 minutes. Remove from oven, and serve hot.

sautéed zucchini and yellow squash with mint

SERVES 4 TO 6

Don't crowd the vegetables in the pan; they will steam rather than brown. If your skillet is not large enough, cook them in two batches.

- 3   tablespoons olive oil
- 1   medium garlic clove, minced
- 1   small onion, thinly sliced
- 2   medium (about 12 ounces) zucchini, cut into ½-inch pieces
- 2   medium (about 12 ounces) yellow squash, cut into ½-inch pieces
- ⅛   teaspoon crushed red-pepper flakes
- 1   tablespoon fresh lemon juice
      Kosher salt and freshly ground black pepper
- ⅓   cup fresh mint leaves, cut into ¼-inch-thick strips

1. Heat 1½ tablespoons olive oil in a large skillet over medium-low heat. Add the garlic and onion, and cook until translucent but still crunchy, about 2 minutes.

2. Raise heat to medium high. Add the remaining 1½ tablespoons of olive oil, the zucchini, yellow squash, and red-pepper flakes. Cook, stirring occasionally, until the vegetables are tender and golden brown, 5 to 10 minutes. Remove from the heat, stir in the lemon juice, and season with salt and pepper. Transfer to a serving dish, sprinkle the mint on top, and serve hot.

zucchini fritters

SERVES 4

- 2   medium (about 1 pound) zucchini
- 1   teaspoon kosher salt
- 1   tablespoon grated lemon zest
- 10 sprigs fresh flat-leaf parsley, stems removed and leaves finely chopped, plus more for garnish
- 1   medium garlic clove, minced
- ¼   teaspoon freshly ground black pepper
- 2   large eggs, lightly beaten
- ½   cup all-purpose flour
- ¼   cup olive oil
- 1   lemon, cut into 8 wedges, optional

1. Using the large holes of a box grater, grate the zucchini into a medium bowl. Add the salt, lemon zest, parsley, garlic, pepper, and eggs. Mix well to combine. Slowly add the flour, stirring so no lumps form.

2. Heat 2 tablespoons olive oil in a large skillet over medium-high heat until the oil sizzles when you drop a small amount of the zucchini mixture into the pan. Carefully drop about 2 tablespoons of the zucchini mixture into the pan; repeat, spacing the fritters 2 inches apart.

3. Cook the fritters until golden, 2 to 3 minutes. Reduce heat to medium. Turn the fritters, and continue cooking until golden, 2 to 3 minutes more. Transfer the fritters to a plate; set aside in a warm place. Cook the remaining zucchini mixture, adding more oil to the pan if necessary. Garnish with the parsley sprigs and lemon wedges, if using; serve.

sautéed spring vegetables

SERVES 4

This dish makes a pretty bed for cooked fish or a colorful accompaniment to grilled meat.

- ½ teaspoon kosher salt, plus more for cooking water
- 6 ounces carrots, cut diagonally into 1-inch-long pieces
- 6 ounces wax or green beans, trimmed, cut diagonally into 1-inch-long pieces
- 6 ounces white or green asparagus, tough ends removed, cut diagonally into 1-inch-long pieces
- 6 ounces sugar snap peas, trimmed, strings removed, cut diagonally into 1-inch-long pieces
- 2 tablespoons olive oil
- ½ small red onion, cut into ¼-inch dice
- 6 ounces yellow or orange cherry tomatoes, cut in half
- ⅛ teaspoon freshly ground black pepper
- ½ cup fresh basil leaves, torn in half

1. Cover and bring a large pot of salted water to a boil. Prepare an ice-water bath. Add the carrots; cook 2 minutes. Add the beans, asparagus, and sugar snap peas; cook until tender but still crisp, about 2 minutes. Drain and transfer the vegetables to the ice-water bath to cool. Drain again.

2. Heat the oil in a large skillet over low heat. Add the onion; cook, stirring occasionally, until translucent, about 8 minutes. Add blanched vegetables, tomatoes, ½ teaspoon salt, and the pepper. Raise heat to medium high; cook, stirring occasionally, until all the vegetables are tender, about 5 minutes. Remove from the heat, stir in the basil, and toss to combine. Serve warm.

vegetables steamed in parchment

SERVES 4

This recipe calls for baby vegetables; larger vegetables can be halved or quartered and cooked the same way.

- 16 white or red pearl onions
- 4 baby orange or red beets, cut into ¼-inch-thick slices
- 8 sugar snap peas
- 8 medium asparagus spears, tough ends removed, cut diagonally into 1½-inch-long pieces
- 8 baby carrots, scrubbed
- 4 baby artichokes, trimmed and quartered
- 4 small ripe tomatoes, cored and quartered
- 10 green beans, trimmed and cut into 1½-inch lengths
- 2 garlic cloves, minced
- 2 tablespoons olive oil
- 1 teaspoon kosher salt
- ⅛ teaspoon freshly ground black pepper
- 3 tablespoons dry white wine
- 8 sprigs fresh thyme
- 4 sprigs fresh rosemary

1. Preheat the oven to 400°F. Cut four 16-inch-square sheets of parchment paper; set aside. Place the pearl onions in a heat-proof bowl; cover with boiling water. Let stand 5 minutes, and peel.

2. In a large bowl, toss all the ingredients. Divide mixture into four batches, distributing vegetables and herbs evenly. Transfer one batch to the center of a parchment square. Gather the four corners of the square, forming a bundle; tie tightly with kitchen twine. Repeat with the remaining batches.

3. Transfer bundles to a baking sheet, arranging them close together but not touching. Bake until tender, about 20 minutes. Remove from the oven.

4. Transfer bundles to plates. Cut off tops; discard. Spread bundles open. Discard herb sprigs and tomato skins, if desired. Serve hot.

FIT TO EAT RECIPE PER SERVING: 178 CALORIES, 8 G FAT, 0 MG CHOLESTEROL, 25 G CARBOHYDRATE, 613 MG SODIUM, 5 G PROTEIN, 7 G DIETARY FIBER

roasted fall vegetables

SERVES 6

- 3 tablespoons olive oil
- 1 medium onion, cut into 1½-inch wedges
- 1 medium red onion, cut into 1½-inch wedges
- 1 rutabaga, cut into 1-inch pieces
- 4 small turnips, cut in half
- 3 medium carrots, cut in half lengthwise
- 1 pound butternut or acorn squash, cut into 2-inch pieces
- 12 ounces brussels sprouts, trimmed
- 1 teaspoon kosher salt
- ½ teaspoon freshly ground black pepper
- 1 tablespoon chopped fresh rosemary
- 2 teaspoons chopped fresh thyme

1. Preheat the oven to 450°F with two racks centered. Brush two 12 x 14-inch roasting pans with 1 tablespoon olive oil. Arrange the onions, rutabaga, turnips, carrots, squash, and brussels sprouts evenly in the pans. Drizzle the vegetables with 1 tablespoon olive oil, and toss lightly to coat the vegetables. Sprinkle each pan with ½ teaspoon salt and ¼ teaspoon pepper. Sprinkle the rosemary and thyme evenly over each pan.

2. Roast for 25 minutes; turn the vegetables with a spatula for even browning. Continue to cook the vegetables until they are tender when pierced with the tip of a knife, 15 to 25 minutes more. The brussels sprouts may cook faster than the other vegetables; if so, transfer to a serving platter, and keep warm until the remaining vegetables are tender. Serve hot.

FIT TO EAT RECIPE PER SERVING: 162 CALORIES, 5 G FAT, 0 MG CHOLESTEROL, 28 G CARBOHYDRATE, 405 MG SODIUM, 5 G PROTEIN, 7 G DIETARY FIBER

summer vegetable gratin

SERVES 4

Once the leeks have been sliced, handle them carefully so they don't fall apart.

- 3 tablespoons extra-virgin olive oil, plus more for brushing
- 2 large leeks, white and pale-green parts, cut into ¼-inch-thick diagonal rounds, well washed (see page 646)
- 1 medium zucchini, sliced on a diagonal, ¼ inch thick
- 1 medium yellow squash, sliced on a diagonal, ¼ inch thick

  Kosher salt and freshly ground black pepper
- 2 tablespoons dry bread crumbs (see page 647)
- 2 tablespoons freshly grated Parmesan cheese
- 1 medium garlic clove, minced
- 2 teaspoons fresh thyme leaves

1. Preheat the oven to 425°F. Brush a 9-inch ovenproof glass pie plate or gratin dish with oil. In a medium bowl, gently toss the leeks, zucchini, yellow squash, and 2 tablespoons olive oil, and season with salt and pepper. Arrange vegetable slices in the bottom of pie plate, slightly overlapping them.

2. In a small bowl, combine the bread crumbs, Parmesan, garlic, and thyme, and season with salt and pepper. Mix in the remaining tablespoon of oil until the mixture is crumbly. Sprinkle the crumb mixture over the vegetables, and bake until the bread crumbs are golden brown and the vegetables are tender, about 25 minutes. Serve hot.

potatoes in salt crust

SERVES 6

Small red potatoes are embedded in coarse salt, baked, and unmolded in one piece for a dramatic presentation. The salt absorbs the moisture from the potatoes as they cook, giving them soft, velvety flesh and crackled, salt-tinged skin.

- 2 garlic cloves, cut in half
  Extra-virgin olive oil
- 2 tablespoons fresh rosemary leaves
- 3 pounds (30 to 40) Yellow Finn, new, or fingerling potatoes, scrubbed
- 1½ pounds kosher salt
- ¼ cup all-purpose flour
- 1 cup sour cream

1. Preheat the oven to 450°F. Rub the garlic over the bottom and sides of a 12-inch round gratin dish or a cast-iron skillet. Brush a thin layer of olive oil over the pan. Sprinkle the rosemary over the bottom of the pan, and place the potatoes in a snug layer over the rosemary.

2. In a large bowl, whisk together the salt and flour. Slowly stir in ½ cup water until thoroughly combined. Pour the salt mixture over the potatoes in an even layer, making sure to fill in any gaps between the potatoes.

3. Roast the potatoes 1 hour 15 minutes. Remove the pan from the oven, and let the potatoes cool 5 minutes. Invert the pan onto a serving platter or into a large bowl. The potatoes will be embedded in the salt. Drizzle the potatoes with olive oil, pull them out of the salt, and serve hot with sour cream.

twice-baked potatoes

SERVES 6

- 6 Idaho potatoes, scrubbed
- 1 tablespoon olive oil
- 4 small garlic cloves, minced
- 8 medium shallots, minced
- ¼ cup plus 2 tablespoons nonfat ricotta cheese
- ¼ cup plus 2 tablespoons skim milk
- 1½ teaspoons kosher salt
- ¼ teaspoon freshly ground black pepper
- 4 medium tomatoes, seeded, cut into ¼-inch dice
- 1 tablespoon roughly chopped fresh marjoram, basil, or oregano

1. Preheat the oven to 400°F. Prick each potato several times with a fork or paring knife. Bake the potatoes on a baking sheet until tender, about 1 hour. Make about a 4-inch-long cut lengthwise along the top of each. Using a spoon or melon baller, remove the flesh of each potato; transfer flesh to a medium bowl. Reserve the skins. Pass the potatoes through a ricer or a food mill fitted with a fine disc into a medium bowl.

2. Heat the oil in a nonstick skillet over medium-low heat. Add the garlic and shallots; cook, stirring frequently, about 6 minutes. Stir half the garlic and shallots into the riced potatoes. Set the remaining half aside in the skillet.

3. In the bowl of a food processor, purée the ricotta until smooth; mix into the riced potatoes along with the milk, 1 teaspoon salt, and ⅛ teaspoon pepper. Fill the potato skins with the cheese-and-potato mixture until brimming over the edges. Transfer to a baking sheet; place in the oven until potatoes are heated through, about 15 minutes.

4. Return the remaining garlic and shallots to medium heat. Add the tomatoes and remaining ½ teaspoon salt and ⅛ teaspoon pepper; cook, tossing, until tomatoes are warm, about 3 minutes. Stir in ½ tablespoon marjoram; cook 1 minute. Spoon 3 tablespoons tomato mixture over each potato; garnish with the remaining marjoram. Serve hot.

FIT TO EAT RECIPE PER SERVING: 313 CALORIES, 4 G FAT, 3 MG CHOLESTEROL, 62 G CARBOHYDRATE, 844 MG SODIUM, 11 G PROTEIN, 5 G DIETARY FIBER

baked potatoes with roasted garlic

SERVES 4

Baking potatoes in aluminum foil makes them soggy; any time saved using this "steaming" technique is not worth the limp and flavorless skin that results. Roast a few extra heads of garlic to spread on bread or add to sauces; it will keep for up to 3 days in the refrigerator.

- 4 Idaho potatoes, scrubbed
- 4 heads of roasted garlic (see page 646)
    Kosher salt and freshly ground black pepper
    Extra-virgin olive oil

1. Preheat the oven to 400°F. Prick each potato several times with a fork or paring knife, and place on a baking sheet. Transfer the sheet to the oven, and bake until the potatoes are tender when pierced with the tip of a knife, about 1 hour.

2. Serve each potato with a head of garlic; squeeze roasted garlic from the skin, and mix into the baked potato with salt, pepper, and olive oil to taste.

BAKED POTATO TOPPINGS

Butter, Dijon mustard, salt, and freshly ground black pepper

Crumbled bacon and scallions

Crème fraîche, dill, and golden caviar

Crumbled goat cheese and roasted red peppers

Spicy chili and scallions

Mascarpone cheese and chives

Poached egg and a drizzle of truffle oil

provençal potatoes

SERVES 2

Cooking in parchment eliminates the need for cooking oil. The potatoes can also be cooked in a small roasting pan, if desired; toss in 1 tablespoon oil, and cover with aluminum foil.

- 6 small red potatoes, skin on, quartered
- 6 (about 4 ounces) cipollini or pearl onions, peeled and quartered
- 10 medium garlic cloves
- 2 plum tomatoes
- 4 kalamata or niçoise olives, pitted and halved
- 1 teaspoon olive oil
- ½ teaspoon kosher salt
- ¼ teaspoon freshly ground black pepper
- 2 sprigs fresh rosemary
- 2 sprigs fresh thyme

1. Preheat the oven to 400°F. Place the potatoes, onions, garlic, tomatoes, and olives in a medium bowl. Add the olive oil, salt, and pepper, and toss to coat the vegetables.

2. Fold a 24-inch length of parchment paper in half, cut into a half-heart shape, and open. Place the vegetable mixture on the parchment, 2 to 3 inches from the crease, and scatter the rosemary and thyme sprigs on top. Fold the other half of parchment over the ingredients. Make small overlapping folds to seal the edges, starting at the top of the heart.

3. Two inches from the end, twist the parchment twice, gently but firmly, to seal the packet. Place the packet on a baking sheet; bake until potatoes are tender, about 30 minutes. Remove from the oven, and open the packet. Use your fingers to crumble the herbs, discarding the stems. (Don't worry about burning your fingers; the sprigs will have dried during cooking and the leaves will come off the stems easily.) Carefully pull off the skin of the tomatoes. Using a fork, break up the tomatoes; stir into the potatoes. Serve immediately.

FIT TO EAT RECIPE PER SERVING: 243 CALORIES, 6 G TOTAL FAT, 0 MG CHOLESTEROL, 46 G CARBOHYDRATE, 714 MG SODIUM, 5 G PROTEIN, 5 G DIETARY FIBER

sweet potatoes
with caramelized apples
SERVES 8 TO 10

This dish can be assembled up to a day in advance and refrigerated; allow it to come to room temperature before baking.

- 6 (about 4 pounds) sweet potatoes
- 1 teaspoon kosher salt
- 3 Granny Smith apples, peeled and cored
- 1 tablespoon fresh lemon juice
- 8 tablespoons (1 stick) plus 1 tablespoon unsalted butter, plus more for casserole
- ¼ cup plus 2 tablespoons packed dark-brown sugar
- ¼ cup plus 2 tablespoons heavy cream
- ¼ cup Calvados or brandy
- ¼ cup fresh orange juice

1. Preheat the oven to 425°F. Prick each potato several times with a fork or a paring knife. Bake the potatoes until tender when pierced with the tip of a knife, 40 to 45 minutes. When cool enough to handle, peel and place the flesh in a medium bowl; add the salt, and mash with a fork.

2. Meanwhile, slice the apples into ⅛-inch-thick wedges, and place in a medium bowl. Add the lemon juice, and toss to combine.

3. In a medium skillet, melt 3 tablespoons butter over medium-high heat. Add 2 tablespoons brown sugar, and cook, stirring, until the sugar dissolves. Cook the apple slices in the butter and sugar in three or four batches, until golden and caramelized, about 1 minute on each side. As they finish cooking, transfer to a plate, and set aside.

4. In a medium skillet, melt 3 tablespoons butter over high heat. Add 2 tablespoons brown sugar, and cook until the sugar dissolves. Stir in ¼ cup cream and the Calvados, and cook until slightly thickened, about 1 minute. Remove from the heat, and add to the sweet potatoes, mixing well to combine. Transfer the potato mixture to a buttered 3-quart ovenproof casserole. Arrange the apple slices over the potatoes; set aside.

5. In a medium skillet, melt the remaining 3 tablespoons butter over medium heat. Add the remaining 2 tablespoons brown sugar, and cook until dissolved. Add the remaining 2 tablespoons cream, and cook, stirring, for 30 seconds. Stir in the orange juice, and cook for 1 to 2 minutes, until thickened and dark brown. Pour over the apples, and cover with aluminum foil.

6. Bake until heated through, about 30 minutes. Remove from oven and serve, or let stand at room temperature up to 30 minutes before serving.

lemon roasted potatoes
SERVES 8

- 4 pounds (8 medium) Idaho potatoes, peeled and quartered
- ½ cup extra-virgin olive oil
- ½ cup fresh lemon juice (about 4 lemons)
- 1 tablespoon dried oregano, plus more for garnish
- 1 tablespoon kosher salt
- ¼ teaspoon freshly ground black pepper

1. Preheat the oven to 500°F. Place the potatoes in a 10 x 15-inch baking dish. Add 1 cup water and the olive oil, lemon juice, oregano, salt, and pepper. Toss the potatoes until well coated.

2. Bake, uncovered, until tender when pierced with the tip of a knife and brown on the edges, about 40 minutes. Turn the potatoes halfway through for even browning; add more water if all the liquid has been absorbed. Garnish with oregano. Serve hot.

cuban-style roasted sweet potatoes

SERVES 4

Seasoned with garlic, lime juice, and parsley, these potatoes are delicious with any simple grilled meat.

3   large (about 3 pounds) sweet potatoes, peeled and quartered

¼   cup extra-virgin olive oil

    Kosher salt and freshly ground black pepper

1   large garlic clove, minced

1   tablespoon fresh lime juice

1½ tablespoons roughly chopped fresh flat-leaf parsley

1. Preheat the oven to 400°F. Line a roasting pan with parchment paper, and set aside. Place the sweet potatoes in a medium bowl, toss with 2 tablespoons olive oil, and season with salt and pepper. Transfer the potatoes to the roasting pan, and roast until they can be pierced easily with the tip of a knife but still offer some resistance, about 30 minutes. Cool on a wire rack, about 15 minutes.

2. Transfer the potatoes to a large bowl. Toss with the garlic, lime juice, chopped parsley, and the remaining 2 tablespoons olive oil; season with salt and pepper. Serve warm or at room temperature.

balsamic roasted sweet potatoes and butternut squash

SERVES 10 TO 12

4   large sweet potatoes, peeled, cut into ¾ x 3-inch wedges

2   medium butternut squash, peeled, seeded, and cut into ¾ x 3-inch wedges

¼   cup olive oil, plus more for drizzling

3   tablespoons balsamic vinegar, plus more for drizzling

2   tablespoons unsalted butter, melted

1   tablespoon chopped fresh rosemary

1   teaspoon kosher salt

½   teaspoon freshly ground black pepper

1   small bunch arugula, stems removed

1. Preheat the oven to 400°F. In a large bowl, toss together the potatoes, squash, olive oil, vinegar, butter, rosemary, salt, and pepper.

2. Arrange the vegetables in a single layer in two 9 x 13-inch baking pans. Transfer the pans to the oven, and roast the vegetables until golden and tender, about 45 minutes, rotating the pans between the racks halfway through roasting.

3. Remove the pans from the oven, and allow the vegetables to cool slightly. Toss the vegetables with the arugula. Drizzle with additional olive oil and balsamic vinegar, and serve immediately.

roots anna

SERVES 8 TO 10

We add rutabaga to pommes Anna, a French dish traditionally made only with potatoes.

1½	pounds Yukon gold or Idaho potatoes
1	large (about 2 pounds) rutabaga
6	tablespoons unsalted butter
1½	teaspoons kosher salt
⅜	teaspoon freshly ground black pepper
1½	teaspoons fresh thyme leaves
3	large roasted garlic cloves (see page 646)

1. Preheat the oven to 425°F. Peel the potatoes, and slice them as thinly as possible; place them in a bowl, and put a damp paper towel on top to keep them from turning brown. Peel the rutabaga, cut in half, slice as thinly as possible, and cover with a damp paper towel.

2. In a 10-inch nonstick ovenproof skillet, melt 2 tablespoons butter, swirling the pan to coat the bottom and sides. Remove from the heat; starting at the sides of the pan, arrange about half of the rutabaga slices in overlapping concentric circles, covering the bottom of the pan; press to compress. Sprinkle the rutabaga with ½ teaspoon salt, ⅛ teaspoon pepper, ½ teaspoon thyme, and a third of the roasted garlic; dot with 1 tablespoon butter.

3. Arrange the potato slices in tight concentric circles over the rutabaga, and press down. Season with ½ teaspoon salt, ⅛ teaspoon pepper, ½ teaspoon thyme, and half of the remaining garlic; dot with 1 tablespoon butter. Arrange the remaining rutabaga on top, and season again with ½ teaspoon salt, ⅛ teaspoon pepper, and the remaining garlic; dot with 1 tablespoon butter.

4. Spread the remaining tablespoon of butter over a large piece of aluminum foil. Cover the skillet tightly with the foil, buttered side down. Place a cast-iron skillet on top of the foil to weigh it down, and transfer to the oven. Bake until the vegetables are tender when pierced with the tip of a knife, 50 to 60 minutes.

5. Let stand on a wire rack for 15 minutes. Remove foil, and invert pan carefully onto a serving dish. Garnish with the remaining ½ teaspoon thyme; serve warm. This can be made a few hours ahead of time and reheated: Cover loosely with foil, and place in a 350°F. oven until hot, about 20 minutes.

potato torta with olives

SERVES 4 TO 6

2	large Spanish onions
3	tablespoons olive oil
2	tablespoons fresh rosemary
	Kosher salt and freshly ground black pepper
½	cup oil-cured black olives, pitted and torn into pieces
6	medium (about 2½ pounds) Yukon gold or Yellow Finn potatoes, peeled
4	ounces fontina cheese, cubed

1. Cut the onions into ½-inch-thick slices. Heat 1 tablespoon oil in a large skillet over medium heat. Add the onions, and cook, stirring frequently, until golden brown and soft, about 20 minutes.

2. Reduce heat to low; add the rosemary and salt and pepper to taste. Cook about 5 minutes, stirring often. Add the olives; set aside.

3. Preheat the oven to 400°F. Cut 3 potatoes into ¼-inch-thick slices. In an 8-inch cast-iron skillet, heat 1 tablespoon oil over medium heat. Arrange the potato slices in overlapping circles in the pan. Season lightly with salt and pepper. Spread the onion mixture over the potatoes. Cook for 10 minutes.

4. Dot the onions with the cheese. Slice remaining potatoes, and arrange a second layer in overlapping circles atop the onion mixture. Season lightly with salt and pepper, and brush with the remaining oil. Transfer to the oven, and cook until a toothpick goes through the torta easily, about 25 minutes.

5. Let the torta cool about 3 minutes in the pan. Carefully run a small, sharp knife around the edge, then invert torta onto a plate. Serve hot.

potato, sweet potato, and onion latkes

MAKES 2 DOZEN 2-INCH LATKES

1   large Idaho or Yukon gold potato, peeled
1   large sweet potato, peeled
¼   large white onion
1   large egg, room temperature
2   tablespoons all-purpose flour
1   teaspoon kosher salt
¼   teaspoon freshly ground black pepper
¼   cup canola oil

1. Grate the potatoes and onion using the largest holes of a box grater. Combine in a bowl; add the egg, flour, salt, and pepper, and stir well to combine.

2. Place the oil in a large skillet over medium-high heat until the oil is very hot but not smoking. Line a plate with a paper towel, and set aside.

3. Spoon about 1 tablespoon of the potato mixture into the hot oil. Repeat with the remaining potato mixture, working in batches if necessary. Cook the latkes until golden brown, about 4 minutes per side. Transfer the latkes to the paper-towel-lined plate. Serve hot.

FOR POTATO, CARROT, AND PARSNIP LATKES *Use 2 Yukon gold potatoes, 1 medium carrot, and 1 small parsnip (omit sweet potato and onion).*

FOR POTATO, ONION, AND HORSERADISH LATKES *Use 2 Yukon gold potatoes, ¼ large white onion, and 2 tablespoons Fresh Horseradish (page 632) or prepared horseradish (liquid pressed out).*

ultimate french fries

SERVES 6

The secret to perfect French fries is to fry them twice—once to cook, and again to color them.

3   pounds Idaho or large Yukon gold potatoes, scrubbed
2   quarts canola or peanut oil
    Kosher salt

1. Cut the potatoes (with the skin on or off) into uniform fries by hand or with a mandoline.

2. Rinse the fries in warm water, drain, and dry. In an electric deep-fryer or a large stockpot, heat the oil until a deep-frying thermometer registers 325°F.

3. Using a slotted spoon or frying basket, carefully lower about 2 cups of the fries at a time into the oil. Fry for 4 to 5 minutes, until they begin to color. Remove the fries from the oil, and drain on paper towels. Let cool at least 10 minutes. The fries can be prepared to this point several hours ahead of time and kept at room temperature.

4. Raise the oil temperature to 365°F. Lower the fries, 2 cups at a time, into the oil for 1 to 2 minutes, until deep golden brown. Drain on paper towels; sprinkle with the salt. Serve immediately.

baked oven frites

SERVES 4

4   medium baking potatoes, scrubbed
2   tablespoons extra-virgin olive oil
1½ teaspoons kosher salt
¼   teaspoon freshly ground black pepper

1. Preheat the oven to 400°F. Place a heavy-duty baking sheet in the oven. Cut potatoes lengthwise into uniform batons. Place in a medium bowl. Toss with the olive oil, salt, and pepper.

2. When the baking sheet is hot, about 15 minutes, carefully remove from oven. Place potatoes on the baking sheet in a single layer. Return baking sheet to the oven, and cook until the potatoes are golden on the bottom, about 30 minutes. Turn the potatoes over, and continue cooking until golden all over, about 15 minutes more. Serve immediately.

mashed potatoes 101

SERVES 4 TO 6

For stiffer mashed potatoes, use only ¾ cup milk or cream; for richer mashed potatoes, add another 2 tablespoons butter.

- 2 *pounds russet, Yukon gold, or long white potatoes*
- 1 *tablespoon kosher salt, plus more for seasoning*
- 1 *cup milk or cream*
- 4 *tablespoons unsalted butter*
- ¼ *teaspoon freshly ground black pepper*
- ¼ *teaspoon ground nutmeg*

1. Peel and cut the potatoes into 1½-inch-thick slices. Place in a medium saucepan, and cover with cold water by 2 inches; add 1 tablespoon of salt. Bring to a simmer. If using a potato ricer, fill another saucepan or the bottom of a double boiler with water; place over low heat. Cook the potatoes until the tip of a knife slips in and out easily. Drain the potatoes in a colander. Place the milk in a small saucepan set over medium-high heat.

2. If using a potato ricer, place a heat-proof bowl or the top of a double boiler over the pan of simmering water. Press the hot, drained potatoes through the ricer into the bowl. (If using an electric mixer, proceed to step 4.)

3. Stir the potatoes with a wooden spoon until smooth, about 1 minute. Using a whisk, incorporate the butter. Drizzle in the hot milk, whisking continuously. Add the pepper, nutmeg, and salt to taste; whisk to combine. Serve immediately.

4. For the electric-mixer method, transfer the hot, drained potatoes to the bowl of an electric mixer fitted with the paddle attachment. Mix on medium-low speed until most lumps have disappeared, about 1 minute. Add the butter; mix until blended. On low speed, add the hot milk in a slow stream, then add the pepper, nutmeg, and salt to taste. Mix to combine. Do not overmix; do not increase speed. Serve immediately.

MAKING MASHED POTATOES

1. A potato ricer produces the fluffiest mashed potatoes. To use, place a heat-proof bowl over a pan of simmering water. After the potatoes have been drained but are still hot, press them through the ricer into the bowl.

2. Use a handheld whisk (rather than a wooden spoon) to incorporate the butter, milk, and seasonings; this is the best way to avoid overmixing and to achieve a smooth, creamy texture.

mashed potatoes
and fava beans

SERVES 6

Fava beans are sold fresh in springtime, with the shells on. Frozen lima beans can be substituted.

  1 *pound fava beans with shells on*
     (about 1½ cups shelled beans)
     Mashed Potatoes 101 (recipe opposite)

1. Split bean pods lengthwise with your fingers, and remove the beans. Cover a small saucepan of water, bring to a boil, and add the beans. Cook until the beans are very tender, about 3 minutes; drain.

2. Peel one end of each bean; squeeze gently to pop the bean from the skin. Discard the skins. Roughly mash half the beans, and stir into the mashed potatoes. Garnish with the remaining whole fava beans, and serve immediately.

caramelized onion
and fennel mashed potatoes

SERVES 6

  1 *tablespoon olive oil*
  1 *Vidalia or other sweet onion, coarsely chopped*
  1 *fennel bulb, core removed, coarsely chopped*
  2 *teaspoons sugar*
  1 *teaspoon kosher salt*
  ¼ *teaspoon freshly ground black pepper*
  1 *8-ounce container sour cream*
  1 *cup milk*
     Mashed Potatoes 101 (recipe opposite)

1. Heat the oil in a large skillet over medium heat. Add the onion, fennel, sugar, salt, and pepper, and cook until the onions are tender and caramelized, about 15 minutes. If the pan begins to brown before the fennel and onion are cooked, add water, ¼ cup at a time, and continue cooking.

2. Transfer the fennel mixture to the bowl of a food processor, add the sour cream, and purée until the mixture is smooth. Place the milk in a small saucepan, and bring to a boil. Whisk the milk and sour-cream mixture into the mashed potatoes until smooth and fully incorporated. Serve hot.

. . . .

PERFECT MASHED POTATOES

- *Simmer potatoes; roasting results in unevenly cooked potatoes.*

- *Russet potatoes make fluffy, grainy mashed potatoes; Yukon gold and long white potatoes make super-creamy mashed potatoes; new potatoes make more dense mashed potatoes.*

- *Use a potato ricer (see Equipment Sources, page 650) for the smoothest, creamiest mashed potatoes; an electric mixer fitted with the paddle attachment produces nicely mashed potatoes, too, but be careful not to overmix (or the texture will be grainy).*

- *Never use a hand-held mixer with a whisk attachment or a food processor to mash potatoes—the potatoes will turn to paste within seconds.*

- *Avoid undercooked, cold, microwaved, or potatoes puréed in a food processor; they require extra mashing to smooth out the lumps. The vigorous mashing breaks down the walls of the potatoes' starch granules and turns the potatoes into glue.*

- *Serve mashed potatoes immediately whenever possible; if you must make ahead, mash up to 40 minutes before serving time, reserve a third of the hot milk, place potatoes in a heat-proof bowl set over a pan of barely simmering water, and pour the reserved milk over the top of the potatoes. Stir the milk into the potatoes just before serving.*

MASHED POTATO MIX-INS

SAFFRON MASHED POTATOES *While heating the milk for mashed potatoes, add a pinch of saffron; let steep for 5 minutes before adding mixture to potatoes.*

ROASTED-GARLIC MASHED POTATOES *Stir smashed roasted garlic cloves (see page 646) into warm mashed potatoes.*

HERBED MASHED POTATOES *Add fresh chopped herbs such as flat-leaf parsley, dill, chives, mint, or basil directly to mashed potatoes. Or, for bright-green potatoes, substitute an herb-infused olive oil for the butter—purée the herbs and olive oil in the bowl of a food processor until they are finely minced and the olive oil is bright green.*

MASHED POTATOES AND ROOT VEGETABLES *Substitute 6 ounces cooked carrots, sweet potatoes, celery root, or turnips for 6 ounces potatoes. Sweet potatoes and carrots make rose-colored potatoes.*

---

tzimmes
SERVES 10

Tzimmes, a stew made from a combination of sweet potatoes and dried fruit, is a traditional dish served on Rosh Hashanah.

 4 *medium (about 2 pounds) sweet potatoes*

 9 *medium (about 1 pound) carrots, cut into 2-inch pieces*

 6 *ounces pitted prunes, cut into bite-size pieces (about 1 cup)*

 5 *ounces dried apricots (about 1 cup)*

 2 *tablespoons fresh lemon juice*
    Grated zest of 1 orange

 ⅓ *cup fresh orange juice*

 ¼ *cup honey*

 1 *teaspoon ground cinnamon*

 ¼ *teaspoon kosher salt*

1. Preheat the oven to 350°F. Cover a large saucepan of water, bring to a boil, then reduce heat to medium; add the sweet potatoes in their skins, and cook for 20 minutes, adding the carrots after 10 minutes. Drain in a colander; set aside until cool enough to handle.

2. Peel the sweet potatoes, and cut into 1-inch chunks. Place in a large bowl along with the carrots, prunes, apricots, lemon juice, orange zest, orange juice, honey, cinnamon, and salt. Mix well, and transfer to a 2-quart baking dish.

3. Cover with aluminum foil, and bake for 30 minutes, basting with the pan juices after 15 minutes. Remove from the oven, and serve immediately.

classic stuffing
MAKES 12 CUPS

Stale bread gives this stuffing texture. If you like a moist, soft stuffing, use a sturdy, chewy loaf.

 12 *tablespoons (1½ sticks) unsalted butter*

  4 *onions (2 pounds), cut into ¼-inch dice*

 16 *celery stalks, strings removed, cut into ¼-inch dice*

 10 *large fresh sage leaves, chopped, or 2 teaspoons crushed dried sage*

 1½ *quarts Homemade Chicken Stock (page 624), or low-sodium store-bought chicken broth, skimmed of fat*

  2 *loaves stale white bread (about 36 slices), crusts on, cut into 1-inch cubes*

  2 *teaspoons kosher salt*

  1 *tablespoon plus 1 teaspoon freshly ground black pepper*

  3 *cups coarsely chopped fresh flat-leaf parsley leaves (about 2 bunches)*

  2 *cups pecans, toasted (see page 644), chopped, optional*

  2 *cups dried cherries, optional*

1. Melt the butter in a large skillet. Add the onions and celery, and cook over medium heat until the onions are translucent, about 8 minutes. Add the sage, stir to combine, and cook 3 minutes. Add ½ cup stock, and stir well. Cook for about 5 minutes, until the liquid has reduced by half.

2. Transfer the onion mixture to a large mixing bowl. Add the bread, salt, pepper, parsley, pecans, and cherries, if using, and the remaining 1 quart plus 1½ cups stock; mix to combine. Use to stuff the turkey immediately.

roasted garlic, sage, and sausage stuffing

SERVES 10

Corn bread makes an excellent base for stuffing because as it cooks, it never looses its toothsome texture. The recipe calls for half of the Skillet Corn Bread; serve the remainder to your guests.

- 3 heads of roasted garlic (see page 646)
- 9 tablespoons unsalted butter, plus more for pan
- ½ recipe Skillet Corn Bread (page 562), crumbled (about 5 cups)
- 3 cups cooked long-grain white rice, cold
- 3 medium carrots, cut into ¼-inch dice
- 1 large onion, cut into ¼-inch dice
- 3 large celery stalks, strings removed, cut into ¼-inch dice
- 1 green bell pepper, seeds and ribs removed, cut into ¼-inch dice
- 1½ pounds sweet fennel sausage, casings removed
- 2 tablespoons poultry seasoning
- 2 tablespoons finely chopped fresh sage
  Kosher salt and freshly ground black pepper
- 1 quart Homemade Chicken Stock (page 624), or low-sodium store-bought chicken broth, skimmed of fat

1. Preheat the oven to 375°F. Squeeze the soft garlic out from each clove. Set aside. Butter a 9 x 13-inch baking dish; set aside.

2. In a large bowl, combine the corn bread and rice, and set aside. In a large skillet, melt 5 tablespoons butter over medium-high heat. Add the carrots, and cook until they begin to soften, about 2 minutes.

Add the onion and celery, and cook until the onion is translucent, 8 minutes. Add the green pepper, and cook 1 minute. Add the vegetables to the corn-bread mixture.

3. In the same skillet, cook sausage over medium heat, stirring frequently with a wooden spoon to break up any large pieces, until browned and cooked through, about 8 minutes. Remove the sausage with a slotted spoon; mix with the corn-bread mixture, along with the poultry seasoning, sage, and salt and pepper to taste. Discard the rendered fat from the skillet. Add the stock to the corn-bread mixture, 1 cup at a time, until the stuffing is well moistened; you may not need all of the stock.

4. Add the soft roasted garlic to the corn-bread mixture, and mix lightly to keep the cloves whole. Season with salt and pepper. Transfer to the prepared baking dish. Melt the remaining 4 tablespoons butter; drizzle over the top of stuffing. Bake until the top is golden and the stuffing is heated through, 45 to 60 minutes. To reheat, bring to room temperature, cover with aluminum foil, and bake at 350°F. for 20 minutes. Remove the cover; bake until heated through, about 10 minutes more. Serve hot.

. . . .

STUFFING VS. DRESSING

These terms refer to the same dish: bread or corn-bread crumbs or cubes (and sometimes rice or potatoes) that are highly seasoned with aromatic vegetables (such as onions and celery), fresh herbs, spices, and often dried fruits, nuts, seafood, or mushrooms. The difference lies in how they are cooked: Stuffings are baked inside the cavity of poultry, meats, or even vegetables, while dressings are baked separately in their own dish.

. . . .

chestnut stuffing

MAKES 6 CUPS

Fresh bread crumbs (see page 647) improve the flavor of any stuffing; try making them instead of using dry store-bought ones. Chestnuts add a wonderful earthy flavor and texture.

- 12 *slices white bread, crusts removed*
- 2 *tablespoons unsalted butter*
- 1 *small onion, cut into ¼-inch dice*
- 1 *celery stalk, cut into ¼-inch dice*
- 5 *chicken livers*
- 10 *chestnuts, blanched and peeled if fresh, roughly chopped (see page 645)*
- ½ *teaspoon coarsely chopped fresh rosemary*
- ¼ *cup heavy cream*
- 2 *tablespoons cognac*
- 1 *bunch watercress, large stems removed, finely chopped*

   Kosher salt and freshly ground black pepper

- ⅓ *cup Homemade Chicken Stock (page 624), or low-sodium store-bought chicken broth, skimmed of fat (see note)*

1. Preheat the oven to 350°F. Using 12 slices white bread, make the bread crumbs (see page 647).

2. Heat butter in a medium skillet over medium heat. When hot, add onion and celery. Cook, stirring occasionally, until onion is softened, about 3 minutes. Push to one side of pan; add the chicken livers. Brown the chicken livers on both sides, about 5 minutes. Remove the pan from the heat.

3. Remove the livers from the pan, and chop into ⅛- to ¼-inch pieces. Toss in a large bowl with the onion, celery, bread crumbs, chestnuts, rosemary, cream, cognac, and watercress; season with salt and pepper. Use to stuff the turkey immediately.

NOTE *If baking stuffing outside the turkey, preheat the oven to 400°F. Add ⅓ cup of the chicken stock, and place in a 9 x 13-inch buttered baking pan. Bake until crusty and golden, 30 to 45 minutes.*

fruit desserts

oven-roasted apples with cider sabayon

SERVES 4

Crisp apples are best for this dish. They keep their shape and won't soften into a sauce while cooking. Sabayon is a light custard sauce.

- 4 Mutsu or any firm, crisp apples, such as Golden Delicious or Granny Smith, peeled, cored, cut in half lengthwise
- ⅓ cup plus 1 tablespoon sugar
- ¼ cup maple syrup
   Zest of 1 orange, cut into matchsticks
   Zest of 1 lemon, cut into matchsticks
- 3 tablespoons fresh lemon juice
- 2 dried bay leaves
- ½ vanilla bean, split lengthwise and scraped
- ¼ teaspoon ground cinnamon
- ¼ teaspoon ground mace
   Pinch of ground nutmeg
- 1 whole star anise
- 4 tablespoons unsalted butter
   Apple-Cider Sabayon (recipe follows)

1. Preheat the oven to 250°F. Place the apples, 1 tablespoon sugar, the maple syrup, orange zest, lemon zest, lemon juice, bay leaves, vanilla bean and seed scrapings, the cinnamon, mace, nutmeg, and star anise in a medium mixing bowl. Toss the mixture well.

2. Melt the remaining sugar in a 12-inch cast-iron skillet over medium-high heat until the sugar has caramelized, about 4 minutes. If the sugar starts to brown unevenly, stir occasionally with a wooden spoon. Add the butter, and cook until melted.

3. Reduce the heat to medium. Carefully place the apple halves, cut-side down, into the skillet, and pour the rest of the ingredients from the mixing bowl over the apples. Cook until the apples begin

to caramelize and the sauce starts to thicken slightly, about 5 minutes. Transfer the skillet to the oven, and bake for 40 minutes. Remove the skillet from the oven, and, using a spatula or tongs, carefully turn the apples over. Bake until the apples are very tender, about 20 minutes more. Serve warm with the sabayon.

apple-cider sabayon

MAKES 3 CUPS

For best results, when setting the sabayon over simmering water in step 2, choose a bowl that fits snugly inside the pot to prevent moisture from dripping into the sabayon.

- ¼ cup sugar
- 4 large egg yolks
- ½ cup sparkling apple cider
- 2 tablespoons Calvados or regular brandy
- ¼ cup heavy cream

1. Fill a large saucepan with 2 inches of water, cover, and bring to a simmer over medium-high heat. Prepare an ice-water bath; set aside. Combine the sugar and egg yolks in the bowl of an electric mixer fitted with the paddle attachment, and beat until the mixture is pale and has a thick consistency, 2 to 3 minutes. Scrape down the sides of the bowl with a rubber spatula once while beating. Add the cider and Calvados, and beat for 2 minutes more.

2. Transfer the yolk mixture to a large metal bowl, and set it over the pan of simmering water (the bottom of the bowl must not be touching the water). Whisk constantly until the sabayon thickens and is fluffy and slightly stiff, about 6 minutes. The sabayon should begin to look satiny and start sticking to the bowl slightly. The air bubbles will become very fine instead of large and loose.

3. Transfer the bowl into the ice-water bath. Continue whisking the sabayon until chilled, about 3 minutes. In a large bowl, whip the cream until soft peaks form, and fold into the chilled sabayon. The sabayon will keep, covered with plastic wrap in the refrigerator, for up to 24 hours.

cider-glazed baked apples

SERVES 6

Baking time for this recipe will vary depending on the type and firmness of the apples used.

- 6 Rome or other firm red apples, cored to within ½ inch of base
- Juice and zest of 1 lemon, zest minced
- 1 vanilla bean
- 1 teaspoon ground cinnamon
- 1½ teaspoons packed dark-brown sugar
- 2 cups cider, or more as needed

1. Preheat the oven to 425°F. with a rack in the center. Using a vegetable peeler, remove ½ inch of skin around the top of each apple; reserve the peelings. Brush the lemon juice inside and around the top of each apple to prevent browning. Arrange the apples in a 9 x 12¾ x 2½-inch roasting pan. Divide zest evenly among the apple cavities. Cut the vanilla bean crosswise into six even pieces. Split one piece lengthwise; scrape out the seeds, and place the seeds and the bean into an apple. Repeat with remaining apples. Divide the cinnamon and brown sugar evenly among the apples. Pour the cider into the pan, and arrange the reserved peelings around the apples.

2. Bake 20 minutes. Using a slotted spoon, remove the peelings, and set aside. Baste the apples, and continue cooking 15 to 20 minutes more. Insert the tip of a knife into base of one apple; if soft, transfer the apples to a platter; proceed to step 3. Baste the apples again. If the cider has almost evaporated, add enough fresh cider to cover the bottom of the pan. Continue to cook apples until they are soft when pierced with the tip of a knife, 10 to 20 minutes more. Transfer to a serving platter.

3. Place the pan with the remaining cider over high heat on the stove. Cook until the liquid is reduced to a syrupy glaze, 4 to 6 minutes. Garnish each apple with the glaze and the reserved peelings, and serve warm.

FIT TO EAT RECIPE PER SERVING: 126 CALORIES, 1 G FAT, 0 MG CHOLESTEROL, 33 G CARBOHYDRATE, 4 MG SODIUM, 0 G PROTEIN, 2 G DIETARY FIBER

baked meringue apples

SERVES 6

The meringue may be piped into a dramatic topping using a star-shaped pastry tip. You will get the best results if you use one of the apples listed here. Microwaving cooks the shells quickly and preserves their color.

- Juice of 1 lemon
- 10 medium Cortland, Jonathan, or Granny Smith apples, cored to within ½ inch of base
- ¼ cup plus 1 tablespoon sugar for sprinkling
- 2 tablespoons unsalted butter
- 2 tablespoons brandy or cognac
- ½ recipe Swiss Meringue (page 643)
- Caramel Sauce (page 406)

1. Brush the lemon juice inside and around the top of each apple to prevent browning. Sprinkle each apple with ½ teaspoon sugar. Place 3 apples on a microwave-safe plate, and loosely cover with plastic wrap. Microwave on high power until the apples are translucent and cooked through but not caving in, about 4 minutes. Remove from the microwave, and repeat with 3 more apples (time will vary from oven to oven, so turn and check them periodically). They will bubble up with juices when almost done.

2. Preheat the oven to 450°F. Peel, core, and slice the remaining 4 apples into ¼-inch-thick wedges. Melt the butter in a large saucepan over high heat. Add the apples, and toss to coat. Cook for 1 minute, and sprinkle ¼ cup sugar over the apples. Cook, tossing often, until the apples are brown and translucent. Standing back, carefully add the brandy (adding the alcohol may cause mixture to ignite briefly), and toss again; cook until the alcohol evaporates.

3. Transfer the apples to a baking sheet, and fill with the apple wedges. Set aside in a warm place.

4. Fill a pastry bag fitted with an Ateco #5 star or any other large star tip with meringue, and pipe out the meringue onto each apple in decorative swirls. Bake until the meringue just starts to brown, 1 to 2 minutes. Serve warm with the caramel sauce.

vacherin with
red raspberry sauce
SERVES 10

This French dessert is composed of layers of meringue, cream, and berries, and is so called because of its resemblance to the famous cheese of the same name. We used fraises des bois, raspberries, and fresh red currants, but you may use whatever fruit is in season.

- 6 large egg whites, room temperature
- 1½ cups granulated sugar
- 2 teaspoons pure vanilla extract
- 1½ cups heavy cream
- 2 tablespoons confectioners' sugar, plus more for dusting
- 1½ pints mixed berries, such as red and white fraises des bois, red and golden raspberries, and fresh red currants
  Red Raspberry Sauce (recipe follows)

1. Preheat the oven to 200°F. with two racks centered. Trace a 9-inch circle on each of 2 pieces of parchment paper. Turn over, and use each piece to line a baking sheet. Set aside.

2. Place the egg whites in the bowl of an electric mixer fitted with the whisk attachment. Beat on high speed until soft peaks form, about 2 minutes. Add ¼ cup granulated sugar; beat to combine. Gradually add the remaining 1¼ cups granulated sugar, 1 tablespoon at a time, until the whites are very stiff and glossy. Add 1 teaspoon vanilla; beat just until combined.

3. Divide the batter among the traced circles, and use an offset spatula or rubber spatula to spread evenly to the edges of the circles.

4. Transfer the baking sheets to the oven, and bake about 3½ hours, switching the upper and lower sheets every 30 minutes. When fully cooked, the meringues should be white and dried and crisp on the outside, yet soft and somewhat chewy inside; test by tapping the center lightly with a fork. (If the meringues start to color, reduce heat to 175°F.) Remove from the oven, and let cool completely on the baking sheets.

5. Combine the cream, the remaining vanilla, and 2 tablespoons confectioners' sugar in a large bowl; whip until soft peaks form.

6. Place one meringue on a serving plate, and spread three-quarters of the whipped cream over it. Scatter half of the berries over, and place the second meringue on top. Spoon the remaining cream onto the center of the meringue, and heap the remaining berries on top. Dust the top with confectioners' sugar. Slice the vacherin with a thin sharp knife, and serve immediately with the red raspberry sauce on the side.

red raspberry sauce
MAKES ABOUT ¾ CUP

- 1 pint raspberries
- ¼ cup sugar
- 2 tablespoons fresh lemon juice
  Pinch of kosher salt

Combine the raspberries, sugar, lemon juice, and salt in a small nonreactive saucepan over low heat. Cook until the berries release their juice and just start to break down, about 5 minutes. Use a rubber spatula to press the berries through a fine sieve; discard the solids. Let cool, and refrigerate until ready to use. May be made 1 day ahead.

rhubarb-raspberry pavlova
SERVES 8

Poached rhubarb and fresh raspberries seemingly float on a cloud of sweet, crisp meringue in this special dessert. Spread in swirls over the bottom of an overturned mixing bowl, the meringue is left overnight in a barely warm oven to dry out. Whipped cream flavored with vanilla is spooned into the snow-white shell, then topped with fruit poached in kirsch. Resist the urge to slice this dessert neatly; instead tap it all over with a pie server, and it will crack into pieces. Prepare steps 1 through 6 a day ahead, and store the poached rhubarb, refrigerated, in an airtight container.

2 large egg whites

1¼ cups granulated sugar

Pinch of cream of tartar

½ teaspoon pure vanilla extract

1 tablespoon kirsch, optional

1 pound (10 stalks) rhubarb, trimmed and cut into ½-inch chunks

2 cups heavy cream

1 vanilla bean, split lengthwise and scraped

½ pint raspberries

Confectioners' sugar, for dusting

1. Preheat the oven to 200°F. Invert a 9-inch metal bowl on a work surface. Cut an 18-inch-square sheet of aluminum foil, and place over the bowl, shiny side out. Using the plastic handle of a rubber spatula, smooth the foil against the bowl, eliminating any creases; set the bowl aside. Fill a medium saucepan one-quarter full with water. Set the saucepan over medium heat, and bring the water to a simmer.

2. Combine the egg whites, ½ cup sugar, and the cream of tartar in the bowl of an electric mixer. Holding the bowl over the simmering water, whisk constantly until the sugar has dissolved and the whites are warm to the touch, 3 to 4 minutes.

3. Attach the bowl to the mixer fitted with the whisk attachment. Start beating on low speed; gradually increase to high until stiff, glossy peaks form, about 10 minutes. Add vanilla; mix to combine.

4. Spoon meringue over the foil on the inverted bowl. Using an offset spatula or a large spoon, gently spread meringue to make a shell that is ½ inch to 1 inch thick and 2 inches deep. Without going over rim of bowl, make decorative swirls around the rim. Coat what will be the base of the shell evenly so it is flat; avoid making thin spots.

5. Transfer bowl, still inverted, to a baking sheet. Bake in the oven 25 minutes. Watch carefully; if shell begins to brown, open oven door for about 10 minutes. Lower temperature to 175°F. Bake 2 hours more at 175°F. Turn off heat; leave bowl in oven 12 hours or overnight to dry completely.

6. Prepare an ice-water bath; set aside. Combine 1 cup water, the remaining sugar, and kirsch, if using, in small saucepan; cover and bring to a boil. Add the rhubarb chunks. Reduce heat to medium low; simmer until the rhubarb is tender, about 6 minutes. Remove from the heat. Transfer the rhubarb to an empty bowl set over the ice-water bath; let cool completely. Chill until ready to use.

7. To assemble the dessert: Prepare an ice-water bath; set aside. Drain the rhubarb through a strainer set over a bowl, reserving both the syrup and the rhubarb. Transfer the syrup to a small saucepan over medium heat; reduce by half or until the syrup coats the back of a wooden spoon, about 5 minutes. Transfer the syrup to a bowl set over the ice-water bath; let cool completely.

8. Pour the heavy cream into the bowl of an electric mixer fitted with the whisk attachment. Add the vanilla-bean scrapings, reserving the pod for another use. Beat on high speed until stiff peaks form.

9. Unwrap the aluminum-foil edges from the bowl, and slide the bowl out of the meringue shell. Turn the shell right-side up. Gently pull the foil away from the meringue, starting at the rim and working toward the bottom, until the shell is free.

10. Place the meringue shell on a rimmed cake stand or plate. Spoon the whipped cream into the shell. (If the shell breaks, press it back together.) Spoon the rhubarb chunks over the whipped cream, and garnish with the raspberries. Serve the remaining rhubarb syrup on the side. Dust with confectioners' sugar. Using a pie server or spoon, break into wedges and serve immediately.

figs in meringue

SERVES 4

2   large egg whites

1   cup confectioners' sugar

3   large figs, stemmed, cut in quarters,
     lengthwise

1. Preheat the oven to 250°F with a rack in the center. In the bowl of an electric mixer fitted with the whisk attachment, beat the egg whites on medium speed until soft peaks form, about 7 minutes. Reduce the speed to low, and slowly add the confectioners' sugar. Once the sugar is fully incorporated, increase the speed to high; you may need to scrape down the bowl a few times. Whisk until the whites are firm but not dry, about 10 minutes more.

2. Line a baking sheet with parchment paper. Divide the meringue into 4 equal dollops on the parchment, and place 3 fig quarters in the center of each dollop. Using a small offset spatula, smooth the meringue around the bottom of the figs, sealing the bottom of each fig in the meringue.

3. Transfer the baking sheet to the oven, and bake until the meringues are firm, about 1 hour. Remove the baking pan from the oven, and, using a spatula, transfer the meringues to a serving platter. Serve immediately.

crêpes with caramelized apples and whipped crème fraîche

SERVES 6

Fresh-made crêpes may be wrapped in aluminum foil and kept warm in the oven for 2 hours. You may make them 1 day in advance; stack the completely cooled crêpes directly on top of each other, wrap the stack in plastic wrap, and refrigerate until the following day. To freeze crêpes for up to 2 weeks, double-wrap them in plastic wrap. Remove plastic wrap and warm refrigerated crêpes for about 20 minutes in a 250°F oven before serving. To reheat frozen crêpes, remove the plastic, wrap in foil, and place in a 250°F oven for 30 minutes, or until warm throughout.

6   Mutsu, Granny Smith, or other
     crisp apples, peeled, quartered, cored,
     cut into 1-inch cubes

     Grated zest and juice of 1 lemon

½   teaspoon ground cinnamon

½   teaspoon ground ginger

½   cup all-purpose flour

     Pinch of kosher salt

2   large eggs

1   large egg yolk

1¼ cups milk

1½ teaspoons pure vanilla extract

6   tablespoons unsalted butter

¼   cup plus 2 tablespoons granulated sugar

3   tablespoons Calvados or regular brandy

1   cup crème fraîche

3   tablespoons confectioners' sugar,
     plus more for dusting

1. Place the apples in a medium bowl. Add the lemon zest and juice, cinnamon, and ginger; toss to coat well. Set aside.

2. Sift together the flour and salt into a medium mixing bowl. Whisk in the eggs, egg yolk, and 1 tablespoon milk to form a smooth batter with a paste-like consistency. Add the remaining milk and 1 teaspoon vanilla, and mix well so there are no lumps. Melt 4 tablespoons butter in a well-seasoned or nonstick skillet, and stir into the batter. (Leave a film of butter in the skillet for cooking the crêpes later.) Let the batter rest at room temperature for about 30 minutes.

3. Preheat the oven to 200°F. Heat the skillet over medium-low heat until warm. Stir the batter, and carefully ladle about ¼ cup batter into the skillet. Lift the skillet, and rotate so that the batter spreads out and thinly coats the bottom and edges of the skillet. Return the skillet to the heat, and cook until the edges of the crêpe are golden brown, lacy, and start to pull away from the skillet, about 2 minutes. Using a knife or an offset spatula, carefully turn the crêpe over, and cook the other side until just golden, 30 to 40 seconds. Slide the crêpe out of the skillet, and place on a heat-proof plate. Cook the remaining crêpe batter, stirring the batter still in the bowl as you work and stacking the finished crêpes on top of one another.

4. Loosely wrap aluminum foil over the plate of crêpes, and place in the oven to keep warm.

5. Melt the remaining 2 tablespoons of butter in a 12-inch cast-iron skillet over medium heat. Add the sugar to skillet, and cook, stirring occasionally, until the sugar turns to an amber caramel, about 5 minutes. Remove the skillet from the heat if the caramel starts to get too dark. Add the apples and spices, and cook, turning the apples over until soft and completely caramelized. Pour the Calvados into a measuring cup, then pour into the skillet, and ignite with a match. Carefully cook until the flames die down, about 2 minutes, shaking the skillet to toss the apples in the syrup. Remove the apples from the heat; let cool slightly.

6. Meanwhile, combine the crème fraîche, the remaining ½ teaspoon of vanilla, and the confectioners' sugar in the bowl of an electric mixer fitted with the whisk attachment. Beat until light and fluffy and almost doubled in volume.

7. Remove the crêpes from the oven, and arrange on six serving plates. Spoon ½ cup caramelized apples over each crêpe, dust lightly with confectioners' sugar, and spoon a generous amount of the crème-fraîche mixture over the apples. Fold the crêpes over the apples, and serve immediately.

baked stuffed apricots
SERVES 4

Amaretti cookies (see Food Sources, page 648) sold in vacuum-packed bags in the grocery store vary in size; crush enough to yield 1 cup. Plain biscotti may be substituted for the cookies.

- 4 ripe apricots, halved lengthwise, pitted
- 8 (3 to 4 ounces) amaretti cookies
- 1 tablespoon unsalted butter, room temperature
- 1 tablespoon brandy
- 1 large egg yolk
   Whipped cream, for serving, optional

1. Preheat the oven to 375°F. Place apricot halves in a baking dish, cut-side up. Place cookies on a clean surface. Using a rolling pin, crush cookies into fine crumbs; transfer to a small bowl. Add the butter, brandy, and egg yolk, and mix to combine.

2. Place about 1 tablespoon of the cookie mixture into cavity of each apricot half. Bake until apricots are tender, 25 to 35 minutes, depending on ripeness and size. Serve warm with a dollop of the whipped cream on the side, if using.

oven-dried apricot compote
SERVES 4

- 20 oven-dried apricot halves (see Oven-Dried Fruit, page 618)
- 1 375-ml bottle late-harvest Riesling or other dessert wine
- 3 whole cinnamon sticks
- 1 teaspoon whole pink peppercorns, plus more for garnish
- 1 tablespoon crystallized ginger pieces
- 12 small fresh mint leaves

1. Cut 4 apricot halves into bite-size pieces; transfer to a saucepan. Add Riesling, cinnamon sticks, peppercorns, and ginger. Cover and bring to a boil over medium-high heat. Reduce heat to a simmer; cook, stirring occasionally, 15 minutes for the flavors to combine and the liquid to reduce.

2. Strain the liquid through a fine sieve or cheesecloth-lined strainer into a glass measuring cup, yielding about ¾ cup. Reserve the ginger; discard the other solids.

3. Divide remaining apricots among four dessert bowls. Pour the syrup over the fruit; garnish with the reserved ginger, peppercorns, and mint leaves, and serve.

blueberry and gooseberry fools

SERVES 3

Fools can be made with any soft fruit; the amount of sugar will vary with the tartness of the fruit. Very soft fruits like strawberries, raspberries, and blackberries can be used without cooking; just mash them with the back of a spoon and combine with only ½ cup of sugar.

- 4 *tablespoons unsalted butter*
- 1 *pound 2 ounces (3½ cups) gooseberries or blueberries (3¾ cups), stems removed*
- 1 *cup sugar for gooseberries, ½ cup for blueberries*
- ¾ *cup heavy cream*

1. Melt the butter in a large skillet on medium heat, and add the berries and sugar. Cover, reduce heat to low, and cook gently, stirring occasionally, until the sugar has dissolved and the berries have softened, about 5 minutes. Remove the pan from the heat, and lightly squash the fruit with the back of a wooden spoon. Don't mash to a purée; some texture should remain. Cool completely in the refrigerator before proceeding.

2. In a large bowl, whip the cream to soft but not stiff peaks. Gently fold the cream into the cooled fruit mixture, leaving the mixture marbled. Serve immediately in individual bowls.

....

PITTING CHERRIES

With a simple paper clip, pitting cherries is a cinch: Unfold a paper clip at its center and, depending on the size of the cherry, insert the large or small end through the top (where the stem was), loosen the pit, and pull out. To leave the stems intact, simply remove the pit from the bottom.

....

cherries in moscato

SERVES 6

Moscato d'Asti is a sparkling Italian dessert wine; any other sparkling wine may be substituted.

- 3 *tablespoons sugar*
- 1 *lemon wedge*
- 1 *pound fresh red cherries, pitted*
- 1 *750-ml bottle chilled Moscato d'Asti*

1. Pour the sugar into a shallow dish. Run the lemon wedge around the rim of a champagne flute. Invert the flute, and dip into the sugar, coating the entire rim. Set the flute aside, and repeat with five more flutes.

2. Place the cherries in a medium bowl. Using the back of a wooden spoon, slightly crush the cherries. Divide the cherries evenly among the flutes, and fill with the chilled Moscato. Serve immediately.

spiced poached figs

SERVES 4

The figs should not be overly ripe because they may fall apart when poaching. The cooking time will vary with the ripeness and the size of figs.

- 2 *cups sweet white wine, such as Sauternes*
- ¾ *cup granulated sugar*
- 2 *2-inch strips lemon zest*
- 8 *whole black peppercorns*
- 1 *2-inch cinnamon stick*
- 2 *dried bay leaves*
- 2 *sprigs fresh thyme*
- 2 *¼-inch-thick slices fresh ginger*
- 2 *whole star anise*
- 3 *green cardamom pods*
- 8 *large fresh green or purple figs, stemmed*
- ½ *cup mascarpone cheese*
- 1½ *tablespoons confectioners' sugar, sifted*
- ½ *vanilla bean, split lengthwise and scraped*

1. Combine wine, sugar, lemon zest, peppercorns, cinnamon stick, bay leaves, thyme, ginger, star anise, and cardamom pods in a small, deep saucepan. Place mixture over medium-high heat, and bring to a boil. Reduce heat to low, and simmer for 10 minutes. Cover the saucepan, and continue to simmer the mixture for 20 minutes more.

2. Add the whole figs to the syrup, return to a simmer, cover, and poach gently until the figs are soft but not mushy, 10 to 15 minutes. Transfer the figs and syrup to a bowl, and let stand to cool, until no more steam rises. When cool, cover the bowl with plastic wrap, and refrigerate overnight.

3. Combine mascarpone, confectioners' sugar, and vanilla bean and seed scrapings in a mixing bowl. Stir with a spoon or rubber spatula until combined.

4. Remove figs from the refrigerator; let stand until the fruit comes to room temperature. Transfer to another bowl; strain the syrup (discard solids).

5. Place two figs, sliced in half, in the center of each plate. Spoon some of the poaching liquid onto the plate to cover, and place a dollop of the vanilla mascarpone next to the figs. Serve.

roasted peaches
SERVES 4

- 2 tablespoons unsalted butter
- ½ cup packed light-brown sugar
- ½ teaspoon pure vanilla extract
- 1 tablespoon orange-flavored liqueur, such as Grand Marnier
- 4 medium peaches, halved lengthwise, pitted

Preheat the oven to 375°F. Place the butter, sugar, and 3 tablespoons water in a 9 x 13-inch glass baking dish. Place in the oven until the sugar is dissolved, about 6 minutes. Remove from the oven; whisk in the vanilla and liqueur. Place the peaches in the dish, cut-side down; bake until tender, about 15 minutes. Cool in the pan on a wire rack. Slip off the peach skins. Serve.

peaches in sauternes
SERVES 12

The peaches must marinate in Sauternes overnight so that they fully absorb the flavor of the sweet wine.

- 4 cups sugar
- 1 large strip lemon zest
- 1 vanilla bean, split lengthwise and scraped
- 2 cups Sauternes or other sweet dessert wine
- 12 ripe (about 5 pounds) peaches

1. Add sugar, lemon zest, vanilla bean and seed scrapings to 3 cups cold water in a medium saucepan. Cook over medium-high heat, covered, until the sugar is completely dissolved, about 10 minutes. Uncover and cook for 2 minutes more. Remove from the heat, and let stand about 10 minutes. Stir in the Sauternes, and set aside.

2. Prepare an ice-water bath; set aside. Bring a large pot of water to a boil. Using a paring knife, score the nonstem end of each peach with a shallow "x". Blanch the peaches in the boiling water for 30 seconds. With a slotted spoon, transfer the peaches to the ice-water bath to cool.

3. Peel the peaches, place in a canning jar or serving bowl, and pour the warm Sauternes syrup over. Drape cheesecloth over the peaches to keep them submerged; set aside until cool. Leave the cheesecloth in place, cover with plastic wrap, and refrigerate overnight, turning occasionally to keep the peaches from browning. Store in refrigerator for up to 2 days. Serve slightly chilled.

baked pears with cream

SERVES 8

Though technically a custard, this bakes like a crustless tart—the filling is firm enough to cut into wedges.

- 1 lemon, scrubbed and quartered
- 4 pears, such as Comice or Anjou, peeled and cored
- 2½ cups milk
- ¾ cup sugar
- 3 large eggs
- 3 large egg yolks
- 1 tablespoon pear or regular brandy

1. Preheat the oven to 275°F. Fill a large bowl with cold water, and squeeze the juice from the lemon quarters directly into the water; add the rinds. Slice the pears ⅜ inch thick; add to the lemon water.

2. In a medium saucepan, bring the milk to a boil. Meanwhile, whisk the sugar, eggs, egg yolks, and brandy in a large bowl until the batter leaves a ribbonlike trail on the surface for 3 seconds when you raise the whisk. Slowly add the hot milk to the egg mixture, whisking constantly, until the milk has been incorporated.

3. Bring a large kettle full of water to a boil. Using a slotted spoon, lift the pears from the water, and pat dry with paper towels. In a 10-inch-round pie plate, arrange the pears in a circular pattern. Pour the milk-and-egg mixture over the pears.

4. Place the pie plate in a shallow baking pan, and transfer to the oven. Fill the pan with enough boiling water to cover the pie plate halfway up, and bake until the custard has set and is just brown, about 1½ hours. Cool slightly on a wire rack before serving.

CORING PEARS

Use a melon baller to quickly and neatly core pears. Halve them lengthwise, then scoop out the core with the melon baller.

sautéed pear parfaits

SERVES 4

Buy pears that are ripe but still firm so they don't get too soft while cooking. For amber crystal sugar, see Food Sources, page 648.

- 2 tablespoons unsalted butter
- 3 tablespoons granulated sugar
- 3 large Anjou or Bartlett pears, peeled, cored, quartered, and cut into ¼-inch-thick slices
- 3 sprigs fresh rosemary
- 8 ounces sour cream or crème fraîche
- 1 teaspoon amber crystal sugar, for garnish, optional

1. Melt butter and granulated sugar in a large skillet over medium-high heat. Cook, stirring frequently until the sugar begins to caramelize, about 2 minutes. Add the pears and rosemary; raise heat to high; cook, stirring occasionally, until pears are browned and caramelized all over, about 5 minutes. (If pears begin to burn, reduce heat to medium.) Remove the pears, and spread out on a plate to cool.

2. Return the skillet to high heat, stir ¼ cup water into the browned sugar and butter. Cook, stirring and swirling the pan, until reduced to a thick syrup.

3. Arrange a layer of pears in four glasses. Spoon sour cream over each. Repeat with remaining pears and sour cream. Drizzle with syrup, sprinkle with crystal sugar, if using, and serve.

pears poached in red wine with black pepper and vanilla

SERVES 6

The pears will keep up to 2 days in the refrigerator if left in the poaching liquid and covered.

- 1 750-ml bottle dry red wine
- 1½ cups sugar
- 2 tablespoons whole black peppercorns
- 1 vanilla bean, split lengthwise and scraped
- 6 firm but ripe Bosc pears

1. Combine wine, sugar, peppercorns, and vanilla bean and seeds in a large saucepan. Add 4 cups water; bring to a boil over medium-high heat, and stir until the sugar dissolves. Remove from heat. Carefully peel the pears, leaving the stem intact.

2. Place the pears in the cooking liquid, cover, and bring to a boil. Reduce heat to low, and weigh down the pears with a saucer or small pot lid to keep them submerged. Simmer until tender when pierced with the tip of a knife, about 30 minutes. Using a slotted spoon, transfer the pears to a medium bowl to cool.

3. Bring the cooking liquid to a boil. Simmer until reduced by half, about 30 minutes. Pour over pears. Transfer the pears and syrup, covered, to the refrigerator to chill until cold and deep red in color, at least 6 hours or overnight. Serve the pears with the reduced syrup, hot or cold.

QUICK FRUIT DESSERTS

Navel oranges, peel and pith removed, with Caramel Sauce (page 406)

Melons with chilled Beaumes de Venise or other sweet dessert wine

Blueberries and fresh cream

Strawberries and raspberries with kirsch and fresh mint

Grapefruit sections drizzled with Ginger Syrup (page 595) or Tarragon Syrup (page 595)

Plums with fresh ricotta cheese and honey

Broiled apricots with whipped cream and amaretto

Peaches with crème fraîche and cinnamon-sugar

Fresh figs with goat cheese and honey

Frozen seedless grapes

grilled summer fruit

SERVES 4

4   *tablespoons unsalted butter, melted*

¼   *cup packed dark-brown sugar*

4   *ripe yellow or white peaches, halved and pitted*

4   *ripe red plums, halved and pitted*

4   *miniature ripe bananas, cut in half lengthwise*

1. Heat a grill or a grill pan to medium hot, or preheat the broiler. In a bowl, combine melted butter and brown sugar. Add all the fruit; toss.

2. Fold the edges of a piece of heavy-duty aluminum foil to form a shallow baking pan, and place on the grill. Arrange the fruit, cut-sides down, on the foil. Cook the fruit until browned and caramelized around the edges, rearranging occasionally to prevent burning. Turn the fruit over, and repeat; serve warm.

roasted plums with crème fraîche

SERVES 4

Italian plums, sometimes called prune plums, can be found at farmer's markets during the summer. They are smaller, denser, and less juicy than North American plums, and ideal for roasting.

16   *(about 2 pounds) Italian plums or other variety, halved and pitted*

3   *tablespoons packed light-brown sugar*

1   *cup crème fraîche*

1. Preheat the oven to 425°F. In a medium bowl, toss the plum halves with 2 tablespoons brown sugar; place in an ovenproof skillet.

2. Transfer skillet to oven; roast plums until they are soft and the juice is bubbling, 15 to 20 minutes. Remove from the oven, and let cool slightly.

3. Just before serving, place the crème fraîche in a small clean mixing bowl, and whip with a whisk until soft peaks form like whipped cream. Spoon the plums into four serving bowls. Top the plums with a dollop of whipped crème fraîche. Sprinkle the remaining brown sugar on top, and serve.

sautéed plums with citrus dumplings

SERVES 8

When you uncover the casserole in step 4, don't let condensation run off into the dumplings.

- 1 lemon
- 7 large (2 pounds) plums, halved and pitted
- ¼ cup plus 3 tablespoons sugar
- 3 tablespoons kirsch or Triple Sec
- 1 cup all-purpose flour
- 2¼ teaspoons baking powder
- ½ teaspoon baking soda
- ¼ teaspoon kosher salt
- 1 tablespoon grated lime zest
- 2 tablespoons heavy cream
- ½ cup buttermilk

  Homemade Vanilla Ice Cream (page 390) or prepared, optional

1. Grate the zest and squeeze the juice from the lemon; set both aside. Quarter each plum half lengthwise, and place in a round 12 x 2-inch casserole or skillet. Sprinkle the plums with ¼ cup sugar, and drizzle with the lemon juice, kirsch, and 3 tablespoons water.

2. Place over high heat, cover, and bring to a boil. Reduce heat to medium low, and simmer until the plums begin to break down, about 15 minutes, depending on ripeness.

3. Meanwhile, sift together the flour, remaining sugar, baking powder, baking soda, and salt. Whisk in the lemon and lime zests. Stir in the cream and buttermilk until just combined.

4. Drop batter by the heaping tablespoon over the plums; there should be enough to make 8 dumplings. Cover the casserole (with a lid or foil), reduce heat to low, and simmer until the dumplings are doubled in size and cooked through, about 20 minutes. Remove from the heat, uncover, and transfer to a wire rack to cool for 10 minutes. Serve warm with ice cream, if using.

FIT TO EAT RECIPE PER SERVING: 181 CALORIES, 2 G FAT, 6 MG CHOLESTEROL, 40 G CARBOHYDRATE, 300 MG SODIUM, 3 G PROTEIN, 2 G DIETARY FIBER

caramel fondue with fresh fruit and toasted pound cake

SERVES 10 TO 12

- 2 cups sugar
- 1 cup heavy cream
- 1 vanilla bean, split lengthwise and scraped

  Brown-Sugar Pound Cake (page 470) or Vanilla Tea Cake (page 468) or prepared
- 2 pints strawberries, hulled
- 2 mangos, peeled, pit removed (see page 647), cut into 1½-inch-long wedges
- 2 Asian pears, cut into 1½-inch wedges

1. In a heavy saucepan, combine the sugar and ¼ cup water. Bring the mixture to a boil over medium-high heat, brushing down the sides of the pan with a pastry brush dipped in water to prevent the sugar from crystallizing. Don't stir. Reduce heat to low; simmer until the caramel is dark amber, 10 to 12 minutes. At arm's length, quickly add the cream and the vanilla seed scrapings (reserving the pod for another use), and stir.

2. Preheat the oven to 350°F. Cut the pound cake into 1 x 2-inch rectangles; place on an ungreased baking sheet. Toast until golden all over.

3. Serve cake pieces and fruit on skewers. Place a heat-proof serving dish over a warming candle, and pour the warm caramel into the dish. Serve.

compote of poached fruit and yogurt

SERVES 8

The yogurt in this dish is drained overnight, which gives it a dense consistency. The fruit may also be poached the day before serving and chilled in its poaching liquid.

- 2 pounds nonfat plain yogurt
- 4 firm ripe pears, such as Bosc or Anjou
    Juice of 1 lemon
- 8 dried Calimyrna figs
- 8 dried whole apricots
- ¼ cup dried cherries or cranberries
- 1 750-ml bottle Riesling wine
- 2 whole cinnamon sticks
- 4 whole star anise
- 1 vanilla bean, split lengthwise and scraped

1. Line a sieve with a double thickness of cheesecloth, and place over a deep bowl or a stockpot. Place the yogurt in the cheesecloth, and wrap securely. Return wrapped yogurt to sieve, and allow to drain overnight in the refrigerator; the whey will run out into the bowl; discard.

2. Peel the pears, cut in half lengthwise, and pour the lemon juice over them. Place the pears cut-side down in a large saucepan. Add the dried figs, apricots, cherries, wine, cinnamon, star anise, and the vanilla bean and seed scrapings. Cover and bring to a simmer over medium heat. Cook over low heat for 10 minutes, until the pears are soft when pierced with the tip of a knife but still hold their shape. Uncover and allow the fruit to cool in the liquid.

3. Remove core from pears using a melon baller. Arrange a pear half, the dried fruit, and the yogurt in each of the compote dishes. Strain the remaining poaching liquid, and discard the solids. Drizzle the compotes with the poaching liquid, and serve.

FIT TO EAT RECIPE PER SERVING: 241 CALORIES, 1 G FAT, 2 MG CHOLESTEROL, 38 G CARBOHYDRATE, 95 MG SODIUM, 8 G PROTEIN, 4 G DIETARY FIBER

apple-rhubarb brown betty

SERVES 4

This classic dessert has been baked in American kitchens for over a century. Rhubarb reaches its peak between April and June; hothouse rhubarb is available from late winter to early summer.

- 12 ounces (2 to 3 stalks) rhubarb, trimmed
- 1 6-ounce loaf brioche or other soft bread, crusts removed
- 8 tablespoons (1 stick) unsalted butter, melted, plus 1 tablespoon for topping and more for dish
- 1 Granny Smith apple, peeled, cored, and sliced into ¼-inch-thick wedges
- ½ cup plus 2 tablespoons packed dark-brown sugar
- ¼ teaspoon ground cinnamon
    Pinch of ground nutmeg
    Zest and juice of ½ lemon
    Homemade Vanilla Ice Cream (page 390) or prepared

1. Preheat the oven to 375°F with a rack in the center. Cut the rhubarb into ¼-inch-thick cubes, yielding about 3 cups. Tear the brioche into ½-inch pieces, yielding 3 to 3½ cups.

2. Butter a shallow 1-quart baking dish. In a medium bowl, combine the melted butter and the brioche; cover the bottom of the baking dish with 1 to 1½ cups brioche. In another bowl, combine the rhubarb, apple, brown sugar, cinnamon, nutmeg, and lemon zest and juice. Let sit until the juices begin to run, about 5 minutes. Spread half of the rhubarb mixture over the brioche. Cover with 1 cup brioche. Add the remaining rhubarb mixture and juices; cover with the remaining brioche. Dot with 1 tablespoon of the butter. Spoon ¼ cup plus 2 tablespoons warm water over the top.

3. Cover with aluminum foil, and bake until the rhubarb is tender, 25 to 35 minutes. Raise heat to 400°F; uncover, and bake until the rhubarb is soft, the top is crusty, and the juices begin to bubble at the edges of the baking dish, 10 to 15 minutes more. Serve warm with vanilla ice cream.

individual pear-blueberry brown betties

SERVES 8

This could also be made in one large dish and served hot, straight from the dish.

- 2 tablespoons plus 1 teaspoon unsalted butter, melted, plus more for ramekins
- 2 tablespoons granulated sugar
- 10 ounces good-quality white bread, crusts removed
- 4 medium Bartlett pears, peeled
- ¼ cup packed light-brown sugar
- 1 tablespoon cornstarch
- 1 teaspoon grated fresh ginger
- ¼ cup pear or regular brandy
- ¼ cup plus 1 tablespoon pear nectar or apple cider
- ¾ cup blueberries, picked over
- 8 ounces plain nonfat yogurt

1. Preheat the oven to 325°F. Butter eight 4-ounce ramekins or custard cups; coat each with ¾ teaspoon granulated sugar. Cut the bread into ¼-inch cubes; place on a baking sheet, and toast until golden brown, about 15 minutes. Let cool. Raise heat to 400°F.

2. Slice the pears in half lengthwise; core. Cut each half crosswise into ¼-inch-thick slices; place in a bowl. Add 3 tablespoons brown sugar, the cornstarch, ginger, brandy, and ¼ cup pear nectar; toss to combine.

3. Place the bread cubes in a bowl; add the melted butter and half the liquid from the pear mixture; toss to combine. Place 1 heaping tablespoon of the bread in each ramekin to cover the bottom. Distribute half the pears among the ramekins. Distribute the blueberries evenly among ramekins; cover with the remaining pears. Divide the remaining bread over the pears; drizzle with the remaining pear liquid.

4. Cover each ramekin with aluminum foil; press down on the tops, and place on a baking sheet.

Place a baking pan on top of the ramekins, and fill with dried beans to weight it down. Bake until the puddings are golden, about 50 minutes. Remove the pan and the weight, and transfer the ramekins to a wire rack to cool for about 20 minutes. Remove the foil. Unmold onto serving plates.

5. Meanwhile, whisk the yogurt with the remaining brown sugar and pear nectar. Serve the yogurt sauce on the side of the warm betties.

FIT TO EAT RECIPE PER SERVING: 207 CALORIES, 4 G FAT, 10 MG CHOLESTEROL, 40 G CARBOHYDRATE, 140 MG SODIUM, 4 G PROTEIN, 2 G DIETARY FIBER

winter fruit crisp

SERVES 8 TO 10

The cooking time for the figs will vary depending on how moist they are. Dried figs are available near the raisins in the grocery store.

- 1 teaspoon whole black peppercorns
- 3 cups dried Calimyrna or other dried figs, stemmed
- ¼ cup honey
- ¼ cup sugar
- 2 cinnamon sticks
- 2 cups dry red wine
- ¾ cup dried cherries
- 4 large Granny Smith apples
- 4 Bartlett pears, ripe but firm
- 2 tablespoons fresh lemon juice
- 4 cups Crisp Topping (recipe follows)
  Crème fraîche, whipped cream, or ice cream, for serving

1. Tie the peppercorns in a small piece of cheesecloth; set aside. Cut the figs in half lengthwise if small or in quarters if large. Place them in a small saucepan along with the honey, sugar, peppercorn bundle, cinnamon sticks, and wine. Stir well, cover, and bring to a boil. Reduce heat to low, and simmer, uncovered, for about 30 minutes, stirring gently occasionally, until the figs are soft and the liquid is reduced to about ¼ inch. Remove the cinnamon sticks and peppercorn bundle, and discard. Add the cherries. The recipe can be prepared up to this point 4 to 6 hours ahead of time.

2. Preheat the oven to 375°F. Peel and core the apples, and cut each into 16 wedges. Peel and core the pears, and cut into 1-inch chunks. Sprinkle both with the lemon juice to prevent discoloration.

3. In a large bowl, combine the fig mixture with the apples and pears, and mix well. Turn into a 3½-quart oval gratin dish, and sprinkle the crisp topping evenly over the top. Bake for 30 minutes. Reduce heat to 350°F, and bake for 15 minutes more, or until the topping is brown and the juices are bubbling (if the top is getting too brown, cover it loosely with aluminum foil). Transfer to a wire rack to cool slightly. Serve warm with crème fraîche, whipped cream, or ice cream.

crisp topping

MAKES 2 QUARTS

Martha's friend Susie Tompkins introduced her to this delicious topping from the Downtown Bakery & Creamery in Healdsburg, California. This makes enough for two large crisps—freeze the extra in an airtight plastic bag up to 2 months. The almonds may be blanched or unblanched.

- ½ cup almonds, toasted (see page 644)
- 2¼ cups all-purpose flour
- ¾ cup packed light-brown sugar
- ⅓ cup granulated sugar
- ½ teaspoon ground cinnamon
- ½ teaspoon kosher salt
- 1 cup (2 sticks) chilled unsalted butter, cut into small pieces

Finely grind the almonds in the bowl of a food processor; transfer to the bowl of an electric mixer fitted with the paddle attachment. Add the flour, both sugars, cinnamon, and salt, and mix just until combined. Add butter; mix on low speed until pea-size clumps form, about 4 to 5 minutes. Sprinkle the topping over the crisp.

mango and raspberry crisp

SERVES 4

The recipe for this topping can be doubled or tripled. Store up to 1 week in the refrigerator or 1 month in the freezer; if frozen, thaw before using.

for the filling

- 3 mangos, peeled, pit removed (see page 647)
- 2 tablespoons fresh lemon juice
- 3 tablespoons sugar
- 1 tablespoon all-purpose flour
- ½ pint raspberries

for the crisp topping

- ⅔ cup finely ground blanched hazelnuts (from 2 ounces)
- ⅛ teaspoon kosher salt
- ¾ cup all-purpose flour
- ⅓ cup sugar
- 6 tablespoons unsalted butter, room temperature

1. Preheat the oven to 350°F. Slice the mangos into ¾-inch pieces; transfer to a medium bowl. Stir in the lemon juice, 3 tablespoons sugar, and 1 tablespoon flour, and set aside.

2. In a medium bowl, whisk together the hazelnuts, salt, and the remaining flour and sugar until combined. Using a pastry cutter or two knives, cut the butter into the flour mixture until it is crumbly. Continue working in the butter until completely incorporated and there are no dry crumbs. Squeeze the mixture together to create pea-size clumps.

3. Add the raspberries to the reserved mangos, and divide mixture among four small baking dishes. Place one-quarter of the nut-and-flour mixture on top of each baking dish, allowing some of the fruit to show through. Bake until the top is golden brown and the fruit juices are thick and bubbling, 35 to 40 minutes. Transfer to a wire rack to cool slightly. Serve warm.

blackberry and blueberry cobbler

SERVES 8

Cobblers often have a thick, biscuit-dough topping. In this deep-dish version, the berries are enclosed in classic pâte brisée.

- 1½ pints blueberries
- 2 pints blackberries
- ½ cup sugar, or to taste
- 2 tablespoons all-purpose flour, plus more for dusting
- 2 tablespoons fresh lemon juice
  Dash of ground cinnamon
- ½ finished recipe (1 disk) Martha's Perfect Pâte Brisée (page 634)
- 1 large egg yolk
- 1 tablespoon heavy cream

1. Preheat the oven to 400°F. Place the berries in a large bowl. Add the sugar, flour, lemon juice, and cinnamon. Toss to combine, and set aside.

2. On a lightly floured surface, roll out the dough to ⅛-inch-thick circle, about 18 inches in diameter. With a dry pastry brush, brush off the excess flour; roll the dough around the rolling pin, and lift it over an 8½ x 2½-inch round gratin dish or deep-dish pie plate. Line the pan with the dough, pressing it into the bottom, allowing excess to hang over the edge.

3. Spoon the berry mixture into the prepared dish, and fold the pastry in over the fruit. Trim away the excess pastry, leaving an opening of about 3 inches in the center. Place the cobbler in the refrigerator, and chill until the dough is firm, about 30 minutes.

4. In a small bowl, combine the egg yolk and cream to make an egg wash. Brush the pastry with the egg wash, and transfer the cobbler to the oven. Bake until the crust is golden brown, about 30 minutes. Reduce the heat to 350°F., and continue baking until the juices start to bubble up over the crust, about 35 minutes more. Transfer to a wire rack to cool slightly, and serve warm.

pear-and-golden-raisin clafouti

SERVES 4

Clafouti is a shallow puddinglike dessert made with fruit, almost like a dense pancake. Early recipes called for unpitted black cherries because the pit was thought to add flavor to the batter. Using a blender to mix the batter will make the clafouti light and airy. The batter may also be combined in an electric mixer.

- Unsalted butter, for dish
- 2 medium Bosc pears, peeled, cored, cut crosswise into ¼-inch slices
- 2 large eggs
- 1¾ cups heavy cream
- ¼ cup all-purpose flour
- ¼ cup granulated sugar
- ⅛ teaspoon ground nutmeg
  Pinch of kosher salt
- ¼ cup golden raisins
- 1½ tablespoons packed light-brown sugar, plus more for garnish

1. Preheat the oven to 400°F. Generously butter a 12-inch-round gratin dish; set aside. Arrange the pear slices in the bottom of the prepared gratin dish. Set aside.

2. In a blender, combine the eggs, 1 cup cream, the flour, granulated sugar, nutmeg, and salt, and process until a batter is formed. Pour the batter around the pears, and sprinkle the top with raisins.

3. Bake until the top begins to set, about 12 minutes. Sprinkle with the light-brown sugar; continue to bake until the clafouti is set and golden brown on top, about 8 minutes. In a large bowl, whip the remaining ¾ cup cream until soft peaks form. Remove the clafouti from the oven; serve immediately with the whipped cream and sprinkled with more brown sugar.

dried fruit compote

SERVES 4 TO 6

Mascarpone, a slightly sweet cream cheese, is available at specialty stores and Italian markets.

3½ tablespoons granulated sugar
 4 chamomile tea bags
 4 dried peach halves
 4 dried pear slices
12 dried apricots
12 dried pitted prunes
12 dried apple slices
⅓ cup dried cherries
 4 ounces mascarpone cheese, room temperature
 1 teaspoon orange-flavored liqueur, such as Grand Marnier
1½ teaspoons confectioners' sugar

1. Cover and bring 3½ cups water and the granulated sugar to a boil. Add tea bags, remove from the heat, and let steep, covered, for 15 minutes.

2. Remove the tea bags, and bring back to a boil. Add the peaches and pears, reduce heat to medium, and simmer for about 4 minutes. Add the apricots, prunes, and apples, and simmer for 2 to 3 minutes. Add the cherries, and simmer for 1 minute more. Remove from the heat, and set aside.

3. In a bowl, mix together the mascarpone, orange liqueur, and confectioners' sugar. To serve, divide the fruit among bowls, pour some of the poaching liquid over, and top with the mascarpone.

lemon terrine

SERVES 8 TO 10

You will need one 4-cup porcelain or other non-reactive terrine mold to make this terrine.

for the lemon gelatin

1¾ cups fresh lemon juice (10 to 12 lemons)
 3 tablespoons unflavored gelatin
 1 cup sugar
 8 to 10 fresh mint leaves

for the lemon confit

 3 lemons, scrubbed, sliced into ¼-inch-thick rounds
1¼ cups sugar

for the mint syrup

 1 cup sugar
 1 cup fresh mint leaves

1. Make the lemon gelatin. Place 1 cup lemon juice in a bowl. Sprinkle the gelatin evenly over the juice, and let stand to soften, 5 minutes.

2. Bring the sugar and 3½ cups water to a boil over high heat, stirring to dissolve the sugar. Pour the syrup over the gelatin mixture; whisk to dissolve the gelatin. Add the remaining ¾ cup lemon juice.

3. Pour ⅓ cup gelatin mixture into a 4-cup porcelain or other nonreactive terrine mold. Press the mint leaves into the gelatin. Cover; refrigerate just until set, 45 to 50 minutes. Add the remaining gelatin mixture. Cover; refrigerate until firm, 4 hours.

4. Make the confit. Preheat the oven to 300°F. Place lemons in a single layer in a heat-proof glass dish. Combine sugar and 1 cup water in a saucepan; bring to a boil; stir to dissolve sugar. Pour over lemons. Bake until lemons are translucent, about 45 minutes. Let cool.

5. Make the mint syrup. Bring the sugar and ¼ cup water to a boil over high heat, stirring to dissolve the sugar. Let cool to room temperature. Refrigerate to chill. Bring a small saucepan of water to a boil. Prepare an ice-water bath; set aside. Blanch the mint in the boiling water for 30 seconds, strain, and plunge into ice-water bath. Drain; squeeze in a kitchen towel to dry. Purée the syrup and mint in a blender. Strain the syrup, and refrigerate for 1 hour before serving.

6. To serve: Unmold the terrine by dipping it briefly into hot water and carefully running the tip of a knife around the edge; invert onto a serving platter. Serve with the lemon confit and mint syrup.

champagne gelatin with peaches and plums

SERVES 8

You will need one 4- or 5-cup gelatin mold or Bundt pan.

- 3 cups rosé champagne
- 3½ cups sugar
- 6 chamomile tea bags (or ⅓ cup loose tea)
- 6 (2¼ pounds) peaches
- 1 tablespoon plus 1½ teaspoons unflavored gelatin
- 2 medium plums

1. Bring the champagne, 2 cups sugar, the tea, and 6 cups water to a boil; reduce heat, and simmer 10 minutes. Add the peaches; simmer gently for 5 to 20 minutes, depending on the ripeness of the peaches (the tip of a knife should insert easily into each peach). Let the peaches cool in the liquid, 3 hours. Peel the peaches; slice 2 into 8 sections each. Set aside the remaining peaches. Strain the liquid. Transfer 2 cups of the liquid to the refrigerator to chill. Sprinkle the gelatin over the cold liquid; let stand to soften, 5 minutes.

2. Bring 2 cups of the room-temperature liquid to a boil. Add to the gelatin mixture; whisk to dissolve the gelatin, about 5 minutes. Pour 3 tablespoons of the mixture into the mold to coat the bottom. Cover; refrigerate 30 minutes, until just set.

3. Combine the remaining sugar and poaching liquid in a skillet; bring to a boil, stirring to dissolve the sugar. Reduce heat; let the syrup simmer. Halve the plums, and remove the pits. Add the plums, cut-side down, and poach until the skin loosens, 5 to 10 minutes. Remove from the syrup; let cool. Remove the skins. Slice each into 4 wedges. Transfer to the refrigerator to chill.

4. Arrange the plums over the gelatin in the mold. Add ¾ cup gelatin mixture. Cover with plastic wrap; refrigerate 45 minutes, or until set. Add the remaining gelatin; arrange peach slices on top. Cover with plastic; chill until set, 6 hours.

5. To unmold, dip the mold briefly into hot water, and run the tip of a knife around the edge. Invert onto a serving platter. Cut the reserved peaches in half, discard the pits, and serve with the gelatin.

honeydew gelatin

SERVES 6

- 2 large (8½ pounds total) honeydew melons, rinds and seeds removed, cut in medium pieces
- 3 tablespoons plus 2¼ teaspoons unflavored gelatin
- ¾ cup sugar, or less if the fruit is very ripe
- 1 tablespoon fresh lemon juice

1. Purée the melon in the bowl of a food processor in two batches.

2. Let purée drain through a cheesecloth-lined strainer over a large bowl for 1 hour; do not press on solids or the liquid may become cloudy. Discard the solids; strain the juice through a cheesecloth-lined strainer into a bowl (use 2 bowls and strainers if necessary). You should have 5 cups of juice.

3. Pour 1 cup melon juice into a bowl. Sprinkle the gelatin evenly over the juice; let stand to soften, about 5 minutes.

4. Bring the sugar and ¼ cup water to a boil over medium-high heat, stirring to dissolve the sugar. Pour the syrup over the gelatin mixture; whisk to dissolve the gelatin. Add the remaining melon juice and lemon juice; stir to combine.

5. Pour into a 9 x 13-inch glass pan, cover, and refrigerate until set, about 2 hours. When ready to serve, cut the gelatin into 1-inch cubes, and serve in tall glasses.

grape gelatin

SERVES 6

½ cup Concord grape juice

3½ cups white grape juice

1 tablespoon plus 1½ teaspoons unflavored gelatin

¼ cup sugar

1. Combine the grape juices. Pour 1 cup juice into another bowl; sprinkle the gelatin evenly over it. Let stand to soften, 5 minutes.

2. Bring the sugar and 1 cup juice to a boil over medium-high heat, stirring to dissolve. Add to the gelatin mixture; whisk to dissolve the gelatin.

3. Stir the remaining juice into the gelatin mixture. Pour into a 9 x 13-inch glass pan, cover, and refrigerate to set, 2 hours.

4. When ready to serve, cut the gelatin into 1-inch cubes, and serve in tall glasses.

. . . .

WORKING WITH GELATIN

The texture of gelatin is directly related to its temperature, and it can go from liquid to solid and back again as the temperature changes. So if the day is hot and you plan to leave a dish out of the refrigerator for a while, you may want to increase the amount of gelatin in a recipe. Setting times and textures are affected by sugar and acid concentrations as well. Molds that have fresh fruit in them as well as large molds require extra chilling time to set. All of our recipes are designed to produce a pleasantly melting texture, but gelling can vary with the temperature and the sugar content of the fruit. It's best to prepare these recipes the day or night before you want to serve them, but no earlier.

. . . .

berry gelatins

MAKES 8 HALF-CUP SERVINGS

Any small summer berry may be used to make these light, colorful gelatins. They may be unmolded or eaten from their molds.

1 cup sugar

2 tablespoons well-strained strawberry purée, from ½ cup (4 ounces) ripe strawberries (blackberries, loganberries, olallieberries, or other berries can be substituted)

¼ cup fresh lemon juice

2 tablespoons unflavored gelatin

¾ cup (6 ounces) small strawberries or fraises des bois, for layering, plus more for garnish

1. Place sugar and 2 cups of water in a medium saucepan. Bring to a boil, reduce to a simmer, and cook, stirring occasionally, until sugar is dissolved, about 2 minutes. Remove pan from heat, stir in purée and lemon juice, and set aside to cool for 10 minutes. Strain mixture through a mesh sieve into a bowl, and set aside.

2. Place 6 tablespoons water in a small shallow heatproof bowl; sprinkle gelatin evenly over water. Let sit 5 minutes to soften. Place bowl over a pan of barely simmering water. Stir until dissolved and foamy. Stir some of the berry mixture into gelatin to reduce temperature. Stir gelatin back into berry mixture; strain into a large measuring cup or bowl to remove any undissolved gelatin.

3. To make layered jellies, fill each mold half full with the mixture; add a few berries; refrigerate until jelly begins to set, about 30 minutes. Fill remaining half of molds; add a few more berries.

4. Chill until completely set, 2 hours or overnight. Unmold when ready to serve, or eat from cups; garnish with more berries.

frozen desserts

....

homemade vanilla ice cream

MAKES 1½ QUARTS

- 2 vanilla beans, split lengthwise and scraped
- 2 cups milk
- 6 large egg yolks
- ¾ cup plus 2 tablespoons sugar
- 2 cups very cold heavy cream
- 1 teaspoon pure vanilla extract

1. Place vanilla beans and seed scrapings in a saucepan with the milk. Bring to a gentle boil; cover. Remove from heat. Let steep for 30 minutes.

2. Combine egg yolks and sugar in the bowl of an electric mixer fitted with the whisk attachment. Beat at medium-high speed until thick and pale, about 4 minutes. Alternatively, whisk in a bowl.

3. Return milk to medium-high heat, and bring just to a simmer. Using a ladle or measuring cup, slowly pour about ½ cup hot milk into the egg-yolk mixture, whisking constantly on low speed until blended. Keep adding milk, about ½ cup at a time, until all of it is added. Whisk until combined.

4. Pour mixture back into saucepan; cook over low heat, stirring constantly with a wooden spoon, until mixture is thick enough to coat back of a spoon, 3 to 5 minutes. Custard should retain a line drawn across back of spoon with your finger.

5. Prepare an ice-water bath. Remove the pan from the heat, and immediately stir in the cold cream to stop the mixture from cooking. Pour the custard through a fine sieve into a medium bowl set in the ice-water bath to chill, and stir occasionally until cooled. Stir the vanilla into the cooled custard. Cover the bowl, and transfer to the refrigerator until chilled, at least 30 minutes or overnight.

6. Freeze in an ice-cream maker according to the manufacturer's instructions. Transfer the soft ice cream to a plastic container, and freeze at least 4 hours. Store in the freezer for up to 1 week.

mango ice cream

MAKES 1 QUART

Dried mango (see Food Sources, page 648) can be found in most health- or specialty food stores.

- ½ cup (2 ounces) dried mango
- ½ cup dark rum
- 1½ large, very ripe mangos, peeled, pit removed (see page 647), cut in large chunks
- 1¼ cups heavy cream
- ¼ cup milk
- 2 large egg yolks
- ¼ cup plus 2 tablespoons sugar

1. In a bowl, combine dried mango and rum; set aside to soak, turning occasionally, 2 hours. Drain in a colander set over a bowl. Reserve rum for another use. Dice mango into ¼-inch pieces. Set aside.

2. In the bowl of a food processor, purée the fresh mango until smooth. Set aside.

3. Prepare an ice-water bath; set aside. In a medium saucepan, bring 1 cup cream and the milk to a simmer over medium-high heat.

4. In the bowl of an electric mixer fitted with the whisk attachment, combine the egg yolks and sugar, and beat on medium-high speed until very thick and pale yellow, about 5 minutes.

5. Add half the hot cream to the egg-yolk mixture, and whisk until blended. Stir the egg-yolk mixture back into the saucepan with the remaining hot cream; cook over low heat, stirring constantly, until the mixture is thick enough to coat the back of a spoon. Remove from the heat.

6. In a clean mixer bowl, beat the remaining ¼ cup cream until soft peaks form. Add the whipped cream, rum-soaked mango, and mango purée to the hot cream mixture. Mix to combine. Freeze in an ice-cream maker according to the manufacturer's instructions. Store in a plastic container in the freezer for up to 1 week.

peach ice cream

MAKES 1 ½ QUARTS

Enjoy this summertime treat straight from the bowl, or put a scoop between two spicy cookies in Ginger Crisp Ice Cream Sandwiches (page 409).

- 5 *large (about 2 pounds) ripe peaches*
- 1 *tablespoon plus 1 teaspoon fresh lemon juice*
- 1¾ *cups sugar*
- 2 *tablespoons peach schnapps*
- 2¼ *cups milk*
- 2⅔ *cups heavy cream*
- 8 *large egg yolks*
  Pinch of kosher salt
- 1 *teaspoon pure vanilla extract*

1. Cover and bring a large pot of water to a boil. Prepare an ice-water bath. Using a paring knife, score the nonstem end of each peach with a shallow "x". Blanch the peaches in the boiling water for 30 seconds. With a slotted spoon, transfer the peaches to the ice-water bath. Drain the peaches, and reserve the ice-water bath.

2. Peel and pit peaches, reserving skin and pits. Slice each peach into 10 wedges; place in a nonreactive saucepan; stir in the lemon juice and 2 tablespoons sugar. Cook over medium-high heat, stirring occasionally, until peaches are tender and liquid has thickened slightly, 10 to 15 minutes. Remove saucepan from heat and let cool.

3. Stir the peach schnapps into the peach mixture. Transfer to the bowl of a food processor, and pulse to a chunky purée, 10 to 15 pulses; set aside.

4. In a medium saucepan, bring the milk, cream, peach skins, and pits to a simmer over medium heat. Reduce heat to medium low; simmer 5 minutes. Cover and remove from the heat. Allow to steep for 15 minutes. Strain the mixture, and reserve the milk; discard the solids.

5. In the bowl of an electric mixer fitted with the whisk attachment, combine the egg yolks, remaining sugar, salt, and vanilla, and beat on medium-high speed until very thick and pale yellow, about

5 minutes. Return the milk to a medium saucepan, and bring to a simmer over medium-low heat.

6. Add half the hot milk to the egg-yolk mixture, and whisk until blended. Stir the egg-yolk mixture back into the saucepan with the remaining milk, and cook over low heat, stirring constantly with a wooden spoon, until the mixture is thick enough to coat the back of a spoon. Remove from the heat.

7. Pass the mixture through a fine sieve or cheesecloth-lined strainer into a bowl set in the ice-water bath. When chilled, stir in the peach purée. Freeze the mixture in an ice-cream maker according to the manufacturer's instructions, in two batches if necessary. Store in a plastic container in the freezer for up to 1 week.

. . . .

ICE-CREAM-MAKING TIPS

- *Make sure that the custard mixture is cold before putting it in the machine.*

- *In order to give the ice cream an opportunity to aerate in the machine, do not fill the ice-cream maker more than three-quarters full.*

- *Vanilla and other extracts lose their flavor if added while the custard is hot; add when the custard base is cool.*

- *Not only does the flavor of ice cream fade over time, but it has a tendency to absorb the odors of food around it; seal it tightly and eat within a week.*

- *Storing ice cream in a shallow container makes it easier to form scoops for a cone or sundae.*

. . . .

pear ice cream

MAKES 1 QUART

- 2 cups milk
- 1 cinnamon stick
- 6 Bartlett or Anjou pears, peeled, cored, roughly chopped
- 6 large egg yolks
- ½ cup sugar
- 2 cups heavy cream
- 2 tablespoons brandy, optional

1. In a medium saucepan, bring the milk and cinnamon stick to a simmer over medium-high heat. Cover and remove from the heat. Allow to steep for 30 minutes. Remove the cinnamon stick, and discard. Set the milk aside.

2. In a large saucepan, cook the pears over medium-high heat until they make a thick sauce, about 45 minutes. Let cool a bit, then purée in the bowl of a food processor or in a blender. Set aside.

3. Prepare an ice-water bath; set aside. In the bowl of an electric mixer fitted with the whisk attachment, combine the egg yolks and sugar, and beat on medium-high speed until very thick and pale yellow, about 5 minutes. Meanwhile, return the milk to a simmer over medium-low heat.

4. Add half the hot milk to the egg-yolk mixture, and whisk until blended. Stir the egg-yolk mixture back into the saucepan with the remaining milk, and cook over low heat, stirring constantly, until the mixture is thick enough to coat the back of a spoon.

5. Remove from the heat, and immediately stir in the cream. Pass the mixture through a fine sieve or a cheesecloth-lined strainer into a medium mixing bowl set in the ice-water bath. Stir in pear purée and brandy, if using, and let chill. Freeze in an ice-cream maker according to the manufacturer's instructions. Store in a plastic container in the freezer for up to 1 week.

rich lemon ice cream

MAKES 1 QUART

- 2 large eggs
- 4 large egg yolks
- 1¼ cups sugar
- ¾ cup fresh lemon juice (about 5 lemons)
- 1 tablespoon grated lemon zest
- 1¼ cups heavy cream
- 1 cup milk

1. Prepare an ice-water bath. In a medium saucepan set over medium heat, whisk together the eggs, egg yolks, sugar, lemon juice, and zest.

2. Using a wooden spoon, stir constantly until the mixture coats the back of the spoon, 7 to 8 minutes. Remove from the heat; stir in the cream and milk. Pour the mixture through a fine sieve or cheesecloth-lined strainer into a clean bowl set over the ice-water bath to chill.

3. Transfer the chilled mixture to an ice-cream maker, and freeze according to the manufacturer's instructions. Store in a plastic container in the freezer for up to 1 week.

burnt-sugar ice cream

MAKES 1 QUART

- 1 cup plus 3 tablespoons sugar
- 2 cups milk
- 2 cups heavy cream
- 6 large egg yolks

1. Place 1 cup sugar in a medium saucepan, and cook over high heat until the sugar is half melted and beginning to turn golden brown. Reduce heat to medium high. Using a wooden spoon, stir continuously until all the sugar is melted, clear, and golden, about 2 minutes. Clip a candy thermometer onto the saucepan. Brush down sides of pan with a pastry brush dipped in cold water to prevent crystallizing. When the sugar becomes dark and golden and the temperature reaches 350°F, remove from the heat, and continue stirring until the temperature registers 372°F. Using a wooden spoon, immediately stir in the milk and cream; return to the heat, stirring constantly until all the sugar is dissolved, about 6 minutes.

2. Prepare an ice-water bath; set aside. In a medium bowl, whisk together the egg yolks and the remaining 3 tablespoons sugar. Add half the milk mixture to the egg yolks; whisk until blended. Stir back into the remaining milk mixture, and place over medium heat. Cook, stirring constantly, until thick enough to coat the back of a wooden spoon, about 5 minutes. Pass the mixture through a fine sieve or cheesecloth-lined strainer into a medium bowl set in the ice-water bath. Let chill, stirring occasionally. Freeze in an ice-cream maker according to the manufacturer's instructions. Store in a plastic container in the freezer for up to 1 week.

HAZELNUT-BRITTLE CARAMEL ICE CREAM VARIATION
Fold 1 cup finely chopped Hazelnut Brittle (page 539) into the 1 quart of Burnt-Sugar Ice Cream; transfer to a plastic container and freeze overnight.

chunky ginger ice cream
MAKES 1 QUART

- 1 cup milk
- 3 cups heavy cream
- 1 cup sugar
- 1 tablespoon freshly grated ginger
  Pinch of kosher salt
- 6 large egg yolks
- ⅓ cup finely chopped candied ginger, plus more cut in strips for garnish
- 1 teaspoon pure vanilla extract
- ½ teaspoon fresh lemon juice

1. In a medium saucepan, bring the milk, 1 cup cream, ½ cup sugar, fresh ginger, and salt to a simmer over medium heat. Cover, remove from the heat, and allow to steep for 30 minutes.

2. Prepare an ice-water bath; set aside. In the bowl of an electric mixer fitted with the whisk attachment, combine the egg yolks and remaining ½ cup sugar, and beat on medium-high speed until very thick and pale yellow, about 5 minutes. Meanwhile,

return the milk to the heat, and bring to a simmer over medium-low heat.

3. Add half the hot milk mixture to the egg-yolk mixture; whisk to blend. Stir into the milk in the pan; cook over medium-low heat, stirring with a wooden spoon, until the mixture is thick enough to coat the back of a spoon.

4. Remove from the heat, and immediately pour in the remaining 2 cups cream. Pass the mixture through a fine sieve or cheesecloth-lined strainer into a bowl set in the ice-water bath. Let chill. Stir in the candied ginger, vanilla, and lemon juice. Freeze in an ice cream-maker according to the manufacturer's instructions. Store in a plastic container in the freezer for up to 1 week. Serve topped with candied ginger strips.

vanilla waffle cones
MAKES 6

You will need a pizzelle iron (see Equipment Sources, page 650), to make these cones. They are ideal for serving any of your favorite homemade or store-bought ice creams or other frozen desserts.

- 2 large egg whites
  Pinch of kosher salt
- ¾ cup confectioners' sugar
- ¼ teaspoon pure vanilla extract
- ½ cup all-purpose flour
- 4 tablespoons unsalted butter, melted and cooled
- 1 tablespoon canola oil

1. In the bowl of an electric mixer, beat the egg whites until soft peaks form. Add the salt and 1 tablespoon sugar and beat until stiff peaks form. Using a rubber spatula, gently fold in the vanilla and the remaining sugar. Fold in the flour and the cooled butter until incorporated.

2. Heat a pizzelle iron over medium heat, and brush lightly with the oil. Place a heaping tablespoon of the batter on the iron a third of the way in from the hinge. Close the iron, and press tightly together.

Scrape away the excess batter with a knife. Cook one side for 45 seconds, then flip the iron, and cook another 45 seconds, or until golden. Adjust heat as necessary. Open the iron, and remove the waffle with a fork or a thin spatula. Quickly roll the hot waffle into a cone shape. Repeat the process with the remaining batter. Let the cones cool; store in an airtight container.

CHOCOLATE-CONE VARIATION *Reduce the flour to ¼ cup and add with ¼ cup cocoa powder, sifted, to the butter in step 1.*

ricotta gelato

MAKES 1 QUART

The ricotta must be drained overnight.

- 2 cups fresh ricotta
- 2 cups milk
- ¼ teaspoon freshly ground nutmeg
- 5 large egg yolks
- 1 cup sugar
- 1 cup heavy cream

1. Place ricotta in a cheesecloth-lined sieve over a bowl. Drain overnight in refrigerator.

2. Bring the milk and nutmeg to a simmer in a medium saucepan. Meanwhile, combine the egg yolks and sugar in the bowl of an electric mixer fitted with the paddle attachment. Beat the mixture on medium-high speed until very thick and pale yellow, about 5 minutes.

3. Prepare an ice-water bath. Whisking constantly, add half of the milk to egg-yolk mixture. Stir into remaining milk, and cook over low heat, stirring constantly with a wooden spoon, until mixture is thick enough to coat the back of the spoon.

4. Remove from heat; immediately stir in cream. Pass mixture through a strainer into a medium bowl set over the ice bath to chill. Whisk in drained ricotta until blended; freeze in an ice-cream maker according to manufacturer's instructions. Freeze in a plastic container up to 1 week.

espresso gelato

MAKES 1 QUART

If an espresso-roast coffee bean is too strong for your taste, substitute a Viennese, French, or any dark-roast bean.

- ⅓ cup espresso beans
- 2 cups milk
- 5 large egg yolks
- ¾ cup sugar
- 1 cup heavy cream
- 1 tablespoon plus 2 teaspoons instant espresso

1. Place the espresso beans on a cutting board, and gently crush them using a heavy saucepan or a hammer (be careful not to pulverize the beans). In a medium saucepan, bring the milk and the espresso beans to a simmer over medium-high heat. Cover and remove from the heat. Allow to steep for 30 minutes. Strain the mixture, and reserve the milk; discard the solids.

2. Prepare an ice-water bath; set aside. In the bowl of an electric mixer fitted with the whisk attachment, combine the egg yolks and sugar, and beat on medium-high speed until very thick and pale yellow, about 5 minutes. Meanwhile, return the milk to the medium saucepan, and bring to a simmer over medium-low heat.

3. Add half the hot milk to the egg-yolk mixture, and whisk until blended. Stir the egg-yolk mixture back into saucepan with remaining milk, and cook over low heat, stirring constantly, until mixture is thick enough to coat the back of a wooden spoon.

4. Remove from the heat, and immediately stir in the cream. Pass the mixture through a fine sieve or a cheesecloth-lined strainer into a medium mixing bowl set in the ice-water bath. Stir in the instant espresso, and let chill. Freeze in an ice-cream maker according to the manufacturer's instructions. Store in a plastic container in the freezer up to 1 week.

low-fat ricotta gelato

MAKES 1½ QUARTS

Famously rich and high in calories, gelato can also be enjoyed in a low-fat form with nonfat milk and low-fat ricotta. Lactose-reduced milk, available at most supermarkets, tastes creamier than regular nonfat milk, which can be substituted.

15 ounces part-skim ricotta
2½ cups lactose-reduced nonfat milk
½ cup sugar
1 cinnamon stick
1 1 x 2-inch strip lemon zest
2 tablespoons light corn syrup
¼ teaspoon pure vanilla extract
    Finely ground espresso, for garnish, optional

1. Purée the ricotta in the bowl of a food processor until smooth, about 2 minutes. Transfer to a medium saucepan; add the milk, sugar, and cinnamon stick, and bring just to a simmer over medium-high heat. Remove from the heat, add the zest, cover, and allow to steep for 30 minutes.

2. Prepare an ice-water bath; set aside. Add the corn syrup and vanilla to the ricotta mixture; whisk to combine. Pass the mixture through a fine sieve or cheesecloth-lined strainer into a medium bowl set in the ice-water bath; let chill. Freeze in an ice-cream maker according to the manufacturer's instructions. If necessary, do this in 2 batches, refrigerating the remainder while freezing the first batch. Divide the gelato among twelve 4-ounce ramekins; cover with plastic wrap. Freeze until set, at least 4 hours.

3. To serve, unmold the gelato by dipping the ramekins three-quarters of the way into a bowl of hot water for about 10 seconds. Insert a table knife halfway into the center of the gelato, and twist to loosen. Invert onto a plate, sprinkle with the ground espresso, if using, and serve immediately.

FIT TO EAT RECIPE PER HALF-CUP SERVING: 105 CALORIES, 4 G TOTAL FAT, 14 MG CHOLESTEROL, 13 G CARBOHYDRATE, 68 MG SODIUM, 5 G PROTEIN, 0 G DIETARY FIBER

blood orange gelato

MAKES 1 QUART

2 cups milk
    Zest of 1 blood orange
1 cup blood orange juice (about 5 blood oranges)
5 large egg yolks
¾ cup sugar
1 cup heavy cream

1. In a medium saucepan, heat milk and orange zest. Bring to a gentle boil, cover, and remove from heat. Steep for 30 minutes.

2. In a small saucepan, cook juice over medium-low heat until reduced by three-quarters, 30 to 40 minutes. Allow syrup to cool completely.

3. Combine egg yolks and sugar in the bowl of an electric mixer fitted with a whisk attachment. Beat at medium-high speed until very thick and pale yellow, about 5 minutes. Meanwhile, return the milk and orange zest mixture to a simmer.

4. Prepare an ice-water bath. Whisking constantly, add half the milk to egg-yolk mixture. Stir into remaining milk and cook over low heat, stirring constantly with a wooden spoon, until mixture is thick enough to coat the back of the spoon.

5. Remove from heat and immediately stir in cream. Pass mixture through a fine sieve into a medium bowl set over the ice bath to chill. Stir in orange syrup, then freeze in an ice-cream maker according to manufacturer's instructions. Freeze in a plastic container up to 1 week.

pistachio gelato

MAKES 1 QUART

- 2 cups shelled pistachios (8 ounces)
- 3 cups milk
- 5 large egg yolks
- ⅔ cup sugar
- 1 cup heavy cream

1. Preheat oven to 350°F. Cover and bring a saucepan of water to a boil. Add pistachios and cook for 30 seconds. Remove from heat and drain. When pistachios are cool enough to handle, remove outer skins and discard. Spread nuts out on a baking pan and toast in oven until aromatic, about 5 minutes. Let cool completely; grind coarsely.

2. In a medium saucepan, heat milk and pistachios. Bring to a gentle boil, cover, and remove from heat. Steep for 2 hours at room temperature. Pass through a strainer lined with cheesecloth, pressing hard on solids, and reserve milk; discard solids.

3. Combine egg yolks and sugar in the bowl of an electric mixer fitted with the whisk attachment. Beat at medium-high speed until very thick and pale yellow, about 5 minutes. Meanwhile, return milk to a simmer.

4. Prepare an ice-water bath. Whisking constantly, add half the milk to egg-yolk mixture. Stir into remaining milk and cook over low heat, stirring constantly with a wooden spoon, until mixture is thick enough to coat the back of the spoon.

5. Remove from heat and immediately stir in cream. Pass mixture through a fine sieve into a medium bowl set over the ice bath to chill. Freeze in an ice-cream maker according to manufacturer's instructions. Freeze in a plastic container up to 1 week.

HAZELNUT VARIATION *Substitute hazelnuts for the pistachios. Toast for 8 to 10 minutes and peel. Stir in 1 tablespoon hazelnut liqueur before freezing in ice-cream maker.*

coconut gelato

MAKES 1 QUART

- 1 fresh coconut (about 12 ounces)
- 3 cups whole milk
- 5 large egg yolks
- ½ cup sugar
- ½ cup heavy cream
- ½ cup cream of coconut, such as Coco Lopez
- ½ cup sweetened coconut flakes

1. Puncture the eyes of the coconut with a nail, and drain the milk into a small saucepan. Crack open the coconut with a hammer. Remove the outer shell, and peel off the dark-brown skin with a vegetable peeler; discard. Grate the coconut flesh. Prepare an ice-water bath; set aside.

2. Heat the coconut milk over low heat until reduced to syrup consistency, about 20 minutes. In a medium saucepan, bring the whole milk and grated coconut to a simmer. Cover and remove from the heat. Allow to steep for 30 minutes. Strain the mixture and reserve the milk; discard the solids.

3. In the bowl of an electric mixer fitted with the whisk attachment, combine the egg yolks and sugar, and beat on medium-high speed until very thick and pale yellow, about 5 minutes. Meanwhile, return the milk to the medium saucepan, and bring to a simmer over medium-low heat.

4. Add half the hot milk to the egg-yolk mixture, and whisk until blended. Stir egg-yolk mixture back into saucepan with remaining milk, and cook over low heat, stirring constantly, until the mixture is thick enough to coat the back of a spoon.

5. Remove from the heat, and immediately stir in the cream. Pass the mixture through a fine sieve or a cheesecloth-lined strainer into a medium mixing bowl set in the ice-water bath. Stir in the reduced coconut milk and cream of coconut, and let chill. Freeze in an ice-cream maker according to the manufacturer's instructions. Add the sweetened coconut flakes, and mix in the machine until combined, about 30 seconds. Store in a plastic container in the freezer for up to 1 week.

mint chocolate chip gelato

MAKES 1 QUART

Homemade mint gelato is not bright green like the packaged varieties, which use food coloring.

2½ cups milk
14 sprigs fresh mint
5 large egg yolks
⅔ cup sugar
1 cup heavy cream
¼ teaspoon peppermint extract
4 ounces semisweet chocolate, chopped

1. In a medium saucepan, bring the milk and 12 sprigs mint to a simmer over medium-high heat. Cover and remove from the heat. Allow to steep for 30 minutes. Strain the mixture, and reserve the milk; discard the solids.

2. Prepare an ice-water bath; set aside. In the bowl of an electric mixer fitted with the whisk attachment, combine the egg yolks and sugar, and beat on medium-high speed until very thick and pale yellow, about 5 minutes. Meanwhile, return the milk to a medium saucepan, and bring to a simmer over medium-low heat.

3. Whisk half the hot milk into the egg-yolk mixture until blended. Stir the egg-yolk mixture back into the saucepan with the remaining milk, and cook over low heat, stirring constantly, until the mixture is thick enough to coat the back of a wooden spoon.

4. Remove from the heat, and immediately stir in the cream. Pass the mixture through a fine sieve or a cheesecloth-lined strainer into a medium mixing bowl set in the ice-water bath. Stir in the peppermint extract, and let chill. Freeze in an ice-cream maker according to the manufacturer's instructions. Finely chop the remaining 2 mint sprigs, and add with the chopped chocolate to the gelato in the ice-cream maker. Mix until combined, about 30 seconds. Store in a plastic container in the freezer for up to 1 week.

chocolate sorbet

MAKES 1 QUART

Cocoa powder and just a bit of chocolate make this sorbet rich enough to satisfy any chocolate lover. To make Mexican chocolate sorbet, add 1½ teaspoons ground cinnamon and 1½ teaspoons ground anise seeds to the water in step 1.

¾ cup packed dark-brown sugar
½ cup granulated sugar
⅔ cup unsweetened cocoa powder
1 ounce bittersweet chocolate, finely chopped
1½ teaspoons pure vanilla extract
1 teaspoon instant espresso powder

1. Combine 2½ cups water, the brown sugar, granulated sugar, and cocoa in a saucepan. Bring to a boil over medium-high heat and cook, whisking occasionally, until the sugar dissolves, about 5 minutes. Reduce heat to low; boil gently for 3 minutes.

2. Prepare an ice-water bath; set aside. Remove the syrup from heat and add the chocolate, vanilla, and espresso powder; whisk until the chocolate is melted and well incorporated. Pour the mixture into a bowl set over the ice-water bath, and stir occasionally until well chilled. Transfer to an ice-cream maker, and freeze according to the manufacturer's instructions. Store in a plastic container in the freezer for up to 1 week.

FIT TO EAT RECIPE PER HALF-CUP SERVING: 165 CALORIES, 3 G TOTAL FAT, 0 MG CHOLESTEROL, 38 G CARBOHYDRATE, 18 MG SODIUM, 2 G PROTEIN, 0 G DIETARY FIBER

plum sorbet

MAKES 1 QUART

For a colorful dessert, make 3 quarts, each with a different type of plum (such as purple, red, and green plums). Serve scoops of each color in every bowl.

2¼ pounds (about 9) Kelsey, Freedom, or Santa Rosa plums, pitted, cut in 1½-inch pieces

¾ cup sugar

¼ teaspoon kosher salt

2 teaspoons cognac

1 teaspoon balsamic vinegar

1. Combine the plums, ¾ cup water, the sugar, and the salt in a 5-quart nonreactive saucepan. Cook over medium heat until the plums break down, about 30 minutes. Stir occasionally to prevent the plums from scorching. Remove from the heat, and cool slightly.

2. Prepare an ice-water bath; set aside. Purée the mixture in the bowl of a food processor, and strain the mixture through a fine sieve or cheesecloth-lined strainer into a medium bowl set over the ice-water bath to chill. Stir in the cognac and vinegar.

3. Freeze the mixture in an ice-cream maker according to the manufacturer's instructions. Store in a plastic container in the freezer for up to 1 week.

. . . .

MAKING SORBET WITHOUT AN ICE-CREAM MAKER

If an ice-cream maker is unavailable, place the mixture in an 11 x 6 x 2¾-inch plastic container (this size container works best) in the freezer for 1 hour. After 1 hour, stir with a fork to break up the ice. Continue to freeze, stirring every 30 minutes, until the sorbet has set and is completely frozen, about 4 hours. This will make an icier sorbet (similar to granita) than those made in ice-cream makers.

. . . .

watermelon sorbet

MAKES 1 QUART

1 cup sugar

1 tablespoon white crème de menthe or Campari, optional

3 cups ripe watermelon flesh, seeds removed

1. Prepare an ice-water bath; set aside. Place the sugar and ¾ cup water in a small saucepan. Cover and bring to a boil over medium heat, stirring occasionally. When the sugar has dissolved, remove the pan from the heat, and stir in the crème de menthe, if using. Transfer the syrup to a bowl set in the ice-water bath to chill.

2. Place the watermelon in the bowl of a food processor; process until liquefied, about 2 minutes. Add the purée to chilled syrup; stir to combine.

3. Freeze the sorbet in an ice-cream maker according to the manufacturer's instructions. Store in a plastic container in the freezer for up to 1 week. ˋ

black-currant sorbet

MAKES 1 QUART

Crème de cassis is a black-currant-flavored liqueur sold in most liquor stores. To mail-order frozen black-current purée, see Food Sources, page 648.

1 pound frozen black-currant purée, or 1¼ pounds fresh black currants

1¼ cups plus 2 tablespoons Simple Syrup for Sorbet (recipe follows)

3 tablespoons crème de cassis

1. If using black-currant purée, proceed to step 2. If using fresh black currants, place the fruit in a medium saucepan with ½ cup water, and bring to a boil. Remove the pan from the heat, and pass the fruit through a fine sieve or cheesecloth-lined strainer set over a medium bowl; discard the seeds, and set aside to cool.

2. In a large bowl, stir together the currant purée, simple syrup, and crème de cassis. Freeze in an ice-cream maker according to the manufacturer's instructions. Store in a plastic container in the freezer for up to 1 week.

simple syrup for sorbet

MAKES 6 CUPS

4 cups sugar

Prepare an ice-water bath. In a large saucepan, combine the sugar and 4 cups water; bring to a boil over medium-high heat. Cook, stirring occasionally, until the sugar has completely dissolved, about 10 minutes. Transfer the syrup to a bowl set over the ice-water bath. Let stand, stirring occasionally, until chilled. The syrup will keep, in an airtight container in the refrigerator, up to 2 months.

lemon sorbet

MAKES 1 QUART

1 cup sugar
¾ cup light corn syrup
1 cup fresh lemon juice (about 6 lemons)

1. Prepare an ice-water bath. In a medium saucepan, combine the sugar, corn syrup, and 2½ cups water; cover and bring to a boil over medium-high heat. Cook, stirring occasionally, until the sugar completely dissolves, about 2 minutes.

2. Remove the pan from the heat; stir in the lemon juice. Pour the mixture into a medium bowl set over the ice-water bath. Freeze the mixture in an ice-cream maker, according to the manufacturer's directions. Store in a plastic container in the freezer for up to 1 week.

buttermilk sorbet

MAKES 1½ QUARTS

1¾ cups sugar
2 cups buttermilk
1½ teaspoons pure vanilla extract

1. Combine the sugar and 2 cups water in a medium saucepan. Stir over medium heat until the sugar dissolves completely, about 10 minutes. Increase heat, and bring just to a boil. Let cool.

2. In a large bowl, combine the sugar syrup with the buttermilk and vanilla. Transfer the mixture to an ice-cream maker, and freeze according to the manufacturer's instructions. Transfer the sorbet to an airtight container, and place in freezer for at least 1 hour before serving. Store in a plastic container in the freezer for up to 1 week.

cantaloupe sorbet

MAKES 1 QUART

1 2-pound, very ripe cantaloupe, rind and seeds removed
1¼ cups plus 2 tablespoons Simple Syrup for Sorbet (recipe at left)
⅓ cup fresh lime juice (3 limes)

1. Cut the cantaloupe into large chunks; transfer to the bowl of a food processor, and purée. Transfer to a medium saucepan over medium-high heat, and simmer, stirring occasionally, until reduced by one-quarter, about 6 minutes. Remove from the heat; set aside to cool.

2. In a large bowl, stir together the cooled cantaloupe purée, simple syrup, and lime juice until well combined. Freeze in an ice-cream maker according to the manufacturer's instructions. Store in a plastic container in the freezer for up to 1 week.

winter sorbet

SERVES 6

A small frozen pear creates an individual serving cup for each person.

¾ cup plus 2 tablespoons sugar
9 Comice or other green-skinned pears
½ cup fresh lemon juice
½ cup frozen or fresh cranberries

1. Prepare an ice-water bath; set aside. Combine the sugar with 1¾ cups water in a medium saucepan. Stir well, and cook over medium-high heat, stirring occasionally, until the sugar has dissolved, about 8 minutes. Transfer the syrup to a heat-proof bowl set over the ice-water bath to chill, or place in the refrigerator, about 30 minutes.

2. Meanwhile, peel and core 3 pears. Chop into ¼-inch dice, and transfer to a medium saucepan. Toss the pears with 2 tablespoons lemon juice. Add the cranberries. Cover, and cook over medium heat until the juices are released, 6 to 8 minutes. Reduce the heat to medium low, and cook, covered, until the pears are very soft, 12 to 18 minutes. Transfer the mixture to the bowl of a food processor, and process until smooth. (At this stage, the purée may be passed through a fine sieve or cheesecloth-lined strainer to get a smoother texture.) Transfer the purée to a metal bowl; let chill over the ice-water bath or in the refrigerator, about 30 minutes.

3. Combine purée with syrup and ¼ cup lemon juice. Transfer mixture to an ice-cream maker; freeze according to manufacturer's instructions.

4. Meanwhile, make the serving shells. Cut the top inch from the 6 remaining pears, and reserve the tops. Using a melon baller, scoop out as much flesh from the pears as possible, leaving the skin intact. Brush the insides of the pears with the remaining 2 tablespoons lemon juice. Place the pears and their tops in a large plastic container, and cover; transfer to the freezer for at least 2 hours. The shells may be prepared 2 to 3 days ahead. To serve, fill frozen shells with the sorbet; garnish with pear tops. Serve immediately. If not using right away, sorbet may be stored in a plastic container, frozen, for up to 1 week.

FIT TO EAT RECIPE PER SERVING: 171 CALORIES, 0 G FAT, 0 MG CHOLESTEROL, 44 G CARBOHYDRATE, 1 MG SODIUM, 0 G PROTEIN, 2 G DIETARY FIBER

cranberry buttermilk sorbet

MAKES 1 QUART

- 1½ cups sugar
- 2 cups fresh cranberries, or frozen, defrosted
- 1½ cups buttermilk
- 1 tablespoon pure vanilla extract

1. Bring sugar and 1½ cups water to a boil in a saucepan. Reduce heat to medium; cook, stirring with a wooden spoon, until sugar dissolves, about 10 minutes. Meanwhile, place cranberries in the bowl of a food processor; process to a smooth purée, about 2 minutes, scraping down sides of bowl several times with a rubber spatula. Add cranberries to hot syrup; stir. Cook 10 minutes more.

2. Prepare an ice-water bath. Pour cranberry syrup through a fine sieve into a bowl set in the ice-water bath to chill. Stir in the buttermilk and vanilla; transfer to an ice-cream maker, and freeze according to manufacturer's instructions. Store in a plastic container in the freezer for up to 1 week.

lime frozen yogurt

MAKES 1 ½ QUARTS

- 1 quart plain low-fat yogurt
- ¾ cup fresh lime juice (about 5 large limes)
- ¾ cup sugar
- ¼ cup light corn syrup
- 1 teaspoon grated lime zest
- 1 teaspoon pure vanilla extract

1. Place yogurt in a fine sieve or cheesecloth-lined strainer set over a medium bowl; chill for about 1 hour, until about 1 to 1⅓ cups liquid has drained from the yogurt. Discard liquid; set yogurt aside.

2. In a bowl, combine lime juice, sugar, corn syrup, lime zest, and vanilla; whisk until sugar dissolves, about 2 minutes. Add strained yogurt; whisk to combine. Transfer to an ice-cream maker; freeze according to manufacturer's instructions. If necessary, work in two batches, keeping remainder refrigerated while freezing the first batch. Store in a plastic container in the freezer for up to 1 week.

FIT TO EAT RECIPE PER HALF-CUP SERVING: 132 CALORIES, 1 G TOTAL FAT, 5 MG CHOLESTEROL, 26 G CARBOHYDRATE, 69 MG SODIUM, 4 G PROTEIN, 0 G DIETARY FIBER

bartlett pear and
black pepper frozen yogurt

MAKES 1¼ QUARTS

Peppercorns give a spicy edge to this unusual and delicious frozen yogurt.

2½ cups whole-milk plain yogurt

6 ripe (about 2½ pounds) Bartlett pears

1 cup sugar

3 tablespoons fresh lemon juice

1 vanilla bean, split lengthwise
   and scraped

½ teaspoon whole black peppercorns

1 dried bay leaf

1. Place the yogurt in a fine sieve or cheesecloth-lined strainer over a bowl. Refrigerate for about 1 hour, until about ½ cup liquid has drained from the yogurt. Discard the liquid; set yogurt aside.

2. Meanwhile, peel, core, and chop the pears into ½-inch pieces. Combine the pears, sugar, lemon juice, vanilla bean and seed scrapings, the peppercorns, and bay leaf in a medium saucepan, and simmer over medium-low heat until the syrup thickens and the pears are very soft, about 25 minutes. Discard the vanilla bean and bay leaf.

3. Prepare an ice-water bath; set aside. Transfer the pear mixture to the bowl of a food processor, and purée until smooth, about 2 minutes. Pass the purée through a fine sieve or cheesecloth-lined strainer into a bowl over the ice-water bath, discarding the solids. Let stand until chilled.

4. Remove the purée from the ice-water bath; whisk the yogurt into the pear mixture. Transfer to an ice-cream maker, and freeze according to the manufacturer's instructions. If necessary, do this in two batches, keeping the remainder refrigerated while freezing the first batch. Store in a plastic container in the freezer for up to 1 week.

FIT TO EAT RECIPE PER HALF-CUP SERVING: 185 CALORIES, 2 G TOTAL FAT, 8 MG CHOLESTEROL, 41 G CARBOHYDRATE, 30 MG SODIUM, 3 G PROTEIN, 4 G DIETARY FIBER

almond-crusted frozen
yogurt snowballs

SERVES 4

1 pint vanilla frozen yogurt

½ cup almonds, toasted (see page 644),
   cooled

2 tablespoons sugar

½ teaspoon ground cinnamon
   Honey

1. Line a square cake pan with parchment paper. Using a 1¾-inch ice-cream scoop, make 4 balls of frozen yogurt, place on the parchment, and transfer pan to freezer to harden for at least 30 minutes.

2. Place the almonds in the bowl of a food processor. Add the sugar and cinnamon, and pulse until finely chopped. Roll the yogurt balls in the nut mixture, and drizzle with honey. Serve immediately.

apricot almond ice milk

MAKES 1¾ QUARTS

1¼ pounds (about 9 medium) fresh ripe
    apricots, pitted, quartered

¾ cup sugar

1¾ cups milk

1¼ cups low-fat buttermilk

2 tablespoons almond liqueur,
   such as Amaretto

¼ teaspoon pure almond extract

1. In a medium bowl, combine the apricots and sugar; stir to combine. Let stand until the juices are released and the sugar dissolves, 30 to 60 minutes.

2. Transfer to the bowl of a food processor; purée until smooth, about 1 minute. Pass through a coarse sieve into a bowl, discarding solids. Add milk, buttermilk, almond liqueur, and almond extract; whisk to combine. Freeze in an ice-cream maker according to manufacturer's instructions, in two batches, if necessary. Keep the remainder refrigerated while freezing the first batch. Store in a plastic container in the freezer for up to 1 week.

FIT TO EAT RECIPE PER HALF-CUP SERVING: 93 CALORIES, 1 G TOTAL FAT, 5 MG CHOLESTEROL, 18 G CARBOHYDRATE, 38 MG SODIUM, 2 G PROTEIN, 1 G DIETARY FIBER

crème fraîche ice

MAKES 1 QUART

Serve this tart, icy dessert with fresh peaches and Peach-Vanilla Syrup (recipe follows).

- 1 cup sugar
- 1½ cups crème fraîche
- 1½ cups nonfat buttermilk

1. Prepare an ice-water bath; set aside. Combine sugar and 1 cup water in a saucepan; bring to a boil over medium-high heat. Reduce heat to low; simmer until sugar dissolves, about 5 minutes.

2. Pour the syrup into a bowl set over the ice-water bath to chill, about 10 minutes. In a medium bowl, combine the syrup, crème fraîche, and buttermilk; stir until smooth. Freeze in an ice-cream maker according to the manufacturer's directions. Store in a plastic container in the freezer for up to 1 week.

peach-vanilla syrup

MAKES 2 CUPS

- 2 cups sugar
- 2 peaches, preferably white, pitted, each cut into sixths
- 1 vanilla bean, split lengthwise and scraped
- ½ cup Sauternes wine or other rich dessert wine

1. Prepare an ice-water bath. Place the sugar in a small saucepan with 2 cups water; bring to a boil over medium-high heat. Add peaches, vanilla bean and seed scrapings, and Sauternes; simmer until the syrup is pink and flavorful, 40 to 45 minutes.

2. Set the pan over the ice-water bath to chill, about 15 minutes. Pour through a fine sieve or cheesecloth-lined strainer into a bowl, pressing on the peaches to obtain the fullest flavor. Serve.

sour-cherry granita

MAKES 1 QUART

- 2 pounds fresh or frozen sour cherries, defrosted and pitted
- 1 teaspoon balsamic vinegar
- 3 tablespoons sugar

1. Set a colander over a bowl, and drain the cherries, reserving all the liquid.

2. Place cherries in the bowl of a food processor or in a blender; purée. Pass purée through a fine sieve or cheesecloth-lined strainer set over a medium bowl. Using the back of a spoon, press cherries to extract the juice. If any solids remain, pass the juice through the sieve again. Discard the pulp left in the sieve. Add the reserved liquid from step 1 and the vinegar to the strained juice.

3. In a medium saucepan, combine the sugar with ⅔ cup water; cook over medium-high heat until the sugar has dissolved, about 4 minutes. Remove the pan from the heat, and let stand until cool.

4. Add cooled syrup to juice mixture; stir until combined. Pour new mixture into a shallow metal pan large enough to hold the liquid; place in the freezer until ice crystals begin to form around the edges, about 1 hour. Using a fork, stir the ice crystals into the center; return to the freezer. Stir the ice crystals once an hour until all the liquid has frozen and has a grainy consistency, about 5 hours. Serve, or store in the freezer, covered, up to 2 days.

poached grapefruit with grapefruit granita

SERVES 6

3 *pink grapefruit, peel and pith removed*

3 *cups fresh pink-grapefruit juice*

1 *cup sugar*

2 *tablespoons Campari liqueur*

¼ *cup fresh mint leaves, chopped*

1. Working over a bowl to catch the juices, use a paring knife to carefully slice between the sections and membranes of each grapefruit; remove the segments whole. Place each segment in the bowl as completed. Repeat the process with the other grapefruit. Set aside.

2. Prepare an ice-water bath; set aside. In a small stockpot, bring the juice, sugar, and 3 cups water to a boil; stir and remove from the heat. Add the grapefruit sections; let stand 5 minutes. Using a slotted spoon, remove the grapefruit; cover and refrigerate. Add the Campari to the liquid, and pour into a metal bowl set over the ice bath to cool.

3. Pour the mixture into a shallow metal pan large enough to hold the liquid; place in the freezer until ice crystals begin to form around the edges, about 1 hour. Using a fork, stir the ice crystals into the center; return to the freezer. Stir the ice crystals once an hour until all the liquid has frozen and has a grainy consistency, about 5 hours. Serve the granita with reserved grapefruit and fresh mint, or store in the freezer, covered, up to 2 days.

FIT TO EAT RECIPE PER SERVING: 227 CALORIES, TRACE FAT, 0 MG CHOLESTEROL, 56 G CARBOHYDRATE, 2 MG SODIUM, 1 G PROTEIN, 2 G DIETARY FIBER

....

GRANITA

Granita is an Italian water ice that is grainier than sorbets and is generally flavored with strong fruits or coffee. It is not made in an ice-cream maker; rather, the base is poured into a shallow pan and then transferred to the freezer, where it is stirred frequently with a fork to create the icy crystals for which it is prized.

....

caramelized banana split

SERVES 4

Adding ice cream to the caramel sauce makes it extra rich and especially silky.

¾ *cup sugar*

4 *tablespoons unsalted butter*

4 *bananas, cut into 2-inch pieces*

1 *pint plus ½ cup vanilla ice cream*

¼ *cup shaved semisweet or milk chocolate*

1. Heat sugar in a heavy skillet over medium-high heat. Bring mixture to a boil, brushing down sides of pan with a pastry brush dipped in water to prevent crystallizing. Don't stir. Reduce heat to low; simmer until golden brown, 6 to 8 minutes.

2. With the mixture on low, stir in the butter. Add the bananas, carefully roll in the caramel, and cook, turning the bananas occasionally until just soft, 3 to 5 minutes. Remove the bananas from the caramel, and transfer to four serving dishes. Add ½ cup vanilla ice cream to the caramel sauce, and stir until smooth and creamy. Scoop remaining ice cream over bananas; pour caramel over ice cream, and sprinkle with chocolate shavings. Serve immediately.

rocky road sundae

SERVES 4

8 *scoops (about 1 pint) chocolate ice cream*

4 *scoops (about ½ pint) coffee ice cream*

1 *cup Hard Chocolate Sauce (page 405)*

¾ *cup Marshmallow Sauce (page 406)*

½ *cup hazelnuts, toasted (see page 644)*

2½ *ounces milk chocolate, cut into chunks*

Place 2 scoops chocolate ice cream and 1 scoop coffee ice cream in each of four bowls. Top with the chocolate and marshmallow sauces. Sprinkle with hazelnuts and chocolate; serve.

very berry sundae

SERVES 4

¾ *pint strawberry ice cream*

¾ *pint raspberry or strawberry sorbet*

½ *cup Red Raspberry Sauce (page 406)*

½ *cup Marshmallow Sauce (page 406)*

½ *pint raspberries*

1. Line two small baking pans with parchment paper. Using a miniature ice-cream scoop, place small scoops of ice cream on the prepared pans; transfer to the freezer. Repeat process with sorbet. Let the scoops freeze for 30 minutes.

2. Arrange the scoops of ice cream and sorbet among four dishes; top with the raspberry sauce, marshmallow sauce, and raspberries. Serve.

mint parfait

SERVES 4

To make this parfait, we cut our ice cream into cubes. This is easiest if you cut the pint container in quarters from top to bottom. You can cut each quarter into two or three pieces. The best tool for making chocolate curls is a swiveling vegetable peeler; use a large block of best-quality soft chocolate to make shaving the curls easy.

Chocolate curls, from one 6- to- 8-ounce block milk chocolate

1 *pint mint-chip ice cream*

½ *recipe Chocolate Brownies, cut into 12 pieces (page 518)*

½ *cup Hot Fudge Sauce (page 405)*

4 *sprigs mint, for garnish, optional*

Make the chocolate curls for garnish: Use a vegetable peeler to shave the chocolate from the block; set aside. Cut the ice cream into 1½-inch chunks; stack in four glasses, alternating with the brownie pieces. Drizzle with the chocolate syrup. Garnish with the curls and mint sprigs, if using; serve.

mandarin fruit sundae

SERVES 4

Other fruits and sorbets can be substituted for those listed here.

2 *navel oranges, peel and pith removed*

½ *fresh pineapple, peeled and cored*

1 *small mango, peeled, pit removed (see page 647)*

1 *red or yellow papaya, peeled and seeded*

3 *tablespoons coconut-flavored or regular rum*

1 *tablespoon sugar*

½ *recipe Lemon Sorbet (page 399) or 1 pint prepared*

¼ *cup shredded sweetened coconut, toasted (see page 647)*

1. Working over a bowl to catch the juices, use a paring knife to carefully slice between the sections and membranes of each orange; remove the segments whole. Place each segment in the bowl as completed. Set aside.

2. Slice the pineapple, mango, and papaya into ⅛-inch-thick slices and then into bite-size pieces. Combine the pineapple, mango, papaya, rum, and sugar in the bowl with the oranges; toss to combine. Let the fruit stand at room temperature for 15 minutes.

3. Divide the fruit and liquid among four serving dishes. Add 2 small scoops of sorbet to each dish, and garnish with the toasted coconut. Serve.

neapolitan sundae

SERVES 4

This sundae is a play on the Neapolitan tradition of serving chocolate, vanilla, and strawberry ice cream together. Instead of being scooped out of their containers, the different ice creams are cut into disks and piled on top of one another in alternating colors. The disks may be stacked ahead of time and returned to the freezer to make ahead for a party. Use single-pint containers of ice cream for this recipe. The ice cream is easiest to slice if you leave it in its container. Cut the bottom end slightly thicker to compensate for the container rim.

- 1 cup heavy cream
- 1 pint chocolate ice cream
- 1 pint vanilla ice cream
- 1 pint strawberry ice cream
- 1 cup Hot Fudge Sauce (recipe follows)
- 4 strawberries, hulled, cut into thirds crosswise

In a medium bowl, whip the heavy cream until soft peaks form. Using a serrated knife, cut each pint of ice cream crosswise into four disks. Place a chocolate disk on each of four plates. Top each with a vanilla and strawberry disk. Pour the hot fudge over each stack, and add a dollop of whipped cream. Garnish with strawberries and serve.

. . . .

QUICK/EASY ICE CREAM DESSERT

Cool and delicious, ice cream is a natural choice for a summertime dessert—it's perfect for a party. And if you gently ease it from its cardboard containers, you will have an attractive, casual presentation. Remove a pint from the freezer, and let it sit for 1 minute. Carefully slide a spatula or thin knife between ice cream and the container, all the way around. Hold a serving dish facedown on top of the container, then invert both, and lift, removing container. Top your frosty tower with fresh berries, mint leaves, or other seasonal garnishes.

. . . .

ice cream toppings

Make a scoop of vanilla (or other flavors) ice cream more interesting with these rich, tasty sauces.

hot fudge sauce

MAKES ABOUT 2 CUPS

This sauce stays gooey on ice cream; it may be made ahead of time and warmed before serving.

- 1 cup heavy cream
- ⅓ cup light corn syrup
- 12 ounces dark bittersweet chocolate, finely chopped

Combine the heavy cream and corn syrup in a saucepan. Stir to combine, cover, and bring to a boil over medium-high heat. Remove from the heat, and add the chocolate. Whisk until the chocolate is melted. Serve.

hard chocolate sauce

MAKES 1 ¾ CUPS

This sauce hardens into a shell on the ice cream.

- 12 ounces bittersweet chocolate, finely chopped
- 8 tablespoons (1 stick) unsalted butter

Combine the chocolate and butter in the top of a double boiler or in a heat-proof bowl set over a saucepan of simmering water. Heat, stirring occasionally, until well combined, and serve. The sauce will keep, in an airtight container in the refrigerator, for up to 1 week. Rewarm before serving.

strawberry sauce

MAKES 1 1/2 CUPS

½ cup sugar

1 pint strawberries, hulled

Place the sugar and ¼ cup water in a small saucepan; stir, cover, and bring to a boil. Simmer until the sugar is completely dissolved. Allow the syrup to cool completely. Place half the berries in a blender; add the syrup. Purée until smooth; pass through a fine sieve or cheesecloth-lined strainer. Chop the remaining berries; stir into the strawberry purée. Serve. The sauce will keep, in an airtight container in the refrigerator, for up to 3 days.

caramel sauce

MAKES 2 1/2 CUPS

2 cups sugar

1½ cups heavy cream

2 tablespoons unsalted butter

1 teaspoon fresh lemon juice

Place the sugar and ½ cup water in a saucepan; stir. Bring the mixture to a boil over medium-high heat, brushing down the sides of the pan with a pastry brush dipped in water to prevent crystallizing. Don't stir. Reduce heat to low; simmer until the caramel is a rich amber color, about 10 minutes. Gradually add the cream while stirring with a wooden spoon. Add the butter and lemon juice; combine. Serve warm. The sauce will keep, in an airtight container in the refrigerator, for up to 1 week. Rewarm before serving.

marshmallow sauce

MAKES 2 CUPS

This sauce is best used right away; it has the fluffy texture of just-whipped marshmallows.

¾ cup light corn syrup

½ cup sugar

2 large egg whites, room temperature

1. Combine the corn syrup and sugar in a small saucepan with ¼ cup water. Bring the mixture to a boil over medium-high heat, and clip a candy thermometer onto the saucepan; brush down the sides of the pan with a pastry brush dipped in water to prevent crystallizing. Don't stir.

2. Meanwhile, in the bowl of an electric mixer fitted with the whisk attachment, beat the egg whites until medium peaks form. When the syrup reaches 240°F (soft-ball stage), about 7 minutes, remove from the heat. With the mixer running at medium speed, very slowly pour the syrup down the side of the bowl of egg whites in a steady stream, beating until the syrup is fully incorporated and the sauce is shiny and fluffy. Serve.

MORE IDEAS

In addition to the toppings listed in this chapter, sundaes can be topped with just about anything. Crumble thin pretzels onto chocolate ice cream, or sprinkle crushed mint candy over vanilla ice cream for an instant version of that classic childhood favorite, peppermint stick. Fresh berries, crushed toffee, or bite-size pieces of your favorite cookies will also make any sundae more memorable. And don't forget to pile on the whipped cream.

poached tropical fruit sauce

SERVES 4

This sauce is particularly good with passsion-fruit sorbet.

- 2 cups fresh pineapple juice
- ¼ cup sugar
- 2 teaspoons cracked black peppercorns
- ½ pineapple, peeled and cored, thinly sliced
- 2 mangos, peeled, pit removed (see page 647), thinly sliced
- 3 kiwis, peeled, each cut into 8 wedges

1. Combine the pineapple juice, sugar, 1 cup water, and the peppercorns in a small saucepan. Set over high heat, cover, and bring to a boil. Reduce heat to a simmer, and cook until flavorful, about 30 minutes. Remove from the heat, and pass the liquid through a fine sieve or cheesecloth-lined strainer set over a heat-proof bowl. Discard the solids.

2. Prepare an ice-water bath. Add the pineapple, mango, and kiwi to the poaching liquid, and let stand 15 minutes. Set the bowl in the ice bath; chill, stirring occasionally. Serve the chilled fruit with the remaining poaching liquid.

wet walnuts

MAKES 1 CUP

This old-fashioned sundae topping is usually sold in jars in the supermarket, but it is easy to make and so much more flavorful when made with fresh, toasted walnuts.

- 1 cup walnut pieces, toasted (see page 644)
- ¼ cup pure maple syrup
- ¼ cup light corn syrup

Combine toasted walnuts, maple syrup, and corn syrup in bowl; stir until nuts are coated. Serve.

strawberries and red wine

SERVES 4

Try serving this over Homemade Vanilla Ice Cream (page 390).

- 2 pints strawberries, hulled
- ¼ cup sugar
- ⅓ cup dry red wine
- 1 3-inch cinnamon stick
- ⅛ teaspoon freshly ground black pepper
- 4 sprigs fresh mint, for garnish

1. If strawberries are small, cut in half; if large, cut in quarters. Combine sugar, red wine, and cinnamon stick in a skillet; cook over medium-high heat until the sugar dissolves, about 3 minutes.

2. Add the strawberries and pepper; cook until the berries soften slightly, 4 to 5 minutes. Remove from the heat, discard the cinnamon stick, and divide the berries and sauce among four serving dishes; top with a sprig of mint. Serve immediately.

rum-raisin sauce

SERVES 4

- ½ cup packed dark-brown sugar
- ½ cup light corn syrup
- 1 tablespoon unsalted butter
- ¼ cup dark rum
- ¼ cup golden raisins
- ¼ cup dark raisins

1. In a saucepan, combine brown sugar and corn syrup. Set over medium-low heat. Stir until well combined and sugar has melted, about 5 minutes.

2. Remove from the heat, and add the butter, rum, and raisins, stirring until the butter has completely melted. Allow to cool slightly before serving.

coconut bonbons

MAKES 12

These frozen bonbons offer a rich contrast between the creamy coconut ice cream and the crisp, dark chocolate shell. Melt any excess chocolate that drips onto the baking pan, strain it, and reserve for a future use. Plain chocolate cookies are available in any grocery store.

- 12 chocolate wafer cookies
- ½ cup shredded coconut
- 2 pints coconut sorbet
- 12 whole almonds
- 26 ounces semisweet or bittersweet chocolate, chopped
- 1 tablespoon pure vegetable shortening

1. Set a wire rack over a baking pan. Arrange the wafers, top-sides down, on the rack, spaced evenly apart. Place 2 teaspoons shredded coconut in the center of each wafer. Using a 2-inch ice-cream scoop, scoop a ball of coconut sorbet onto each wafer. Place an almond on top of each scoop of sorbet. Transfer the pan to the freezer for 20 minutes.

2. In the top of a double boiler or in a heat-proof bowl set over a pan of barely simmering water, combine the chocolate and shortening. Stir until melted. Remove the bowl from the heat. Let cool slightly.

3. Remove the baking pan from the freezer. Generously ladle the melted chocolate over the bonbons, covering them entirely. Return the baking pan to the freezer for 30 minutes more or overnight to harden. Serve frozen.

cappuccino semifreddo

SERVES 6

Semifreddo, which in Italian means "half cold," refers to any dessert that is partially frozen, whether it is ice cream, cake, custard, or whipped cream. To find torrone, an Italian nougat and nut candy, see Food Sources, page 648.

- 1½ cups heavy cream
- 2 large eggs, separated
- ¼ cup plus 2 tablespoons sugar
- 2 tablespoons cognac
- 2 tablespoons instant espresso powder
- ¼ cup dry Marsala wine
- 2 ounces torrone, or almonds, chopped to equal ½ cup, optional

1. In the bowl of an electric mixer fitted with the whisk attachment, beat 1 cup cream until stiff peaks form. Transfer to the refrigerator until ready to use.

2. Prepare an ice-water bath. Combine the egg yolks and 2 tablespoons sugar in the top of a double boiler or in a heat-proof bowl set over a medium saucepan of barely simmering water. Whisk until pale yellow. Whisk in the cognac and espresso powder. Gradually whisk in the Marsala. Whisk vigorously until the mixture becomes thick and glossy, 2 to 3 minutes. Remove from the heat; whisk the mixture over the ice bath until cool. Set aside. Keep saucepan of water simmering.

3. In the detached bowl of the mixer, whisk together the egg whites and the remaining ¼ cup sugar. Place over the saucepan of barely simmering water; continue whisking until the sugar dissolves and the mixture is warm to the touch, 3 minutes. Return the bowl to the mixer fitted with the whisk attachment, and beat the mixture on medium speed until stiff and glossy.

4. Fold one-third of the whipped egg whites into the egg-yolk mixture to lighten it. Repeat with the remaining egg whites, one-third at a time. Gently fold in the chilled whipped cream. Spoon the mixture into cappuccino mugs, cover with plastic wrap, and freeze until frozen, about 1½ hours.

5. In a large bowl, whisk the remaining ½ cup cream until soft peaks form. Spoon over the frozen semi-freddo. Garnish with the chopped torrone, if using, and serve immediately.

melon-sherbet pops

MAKES 8

Freeze the sherbet in popsicle molds, available at grocery and housewares stores, or paper cups; use a stick or spoon in the center for a handle.

2½ pounds melon (such as 1 cantaloupe, ½ honeydew melon, or ¼ watermelon), rind and seeds removed, cut into large chunks

 ⅔ cup sugar

1¼ cups heavy cream

 1 tablespoon muscat wine or sweet white wine

1. In the bowl of a food processor, purée the melon until smooth. Pour 1¾ cups of the purée into a bowl; reserve the rest for another use.

2. Prepare an ice-water bath; set aside. In a small saucepan over medium-low heat, combine the sugar and 1 cup cream just until the sugar dissolves. Stir into the melon purée.

3. Stir the remaining cream and wine into the melon mixture. Place the bowl in the ice-water bath to chill. Freeze in an ice-cream maker according to the manufacturer's instructions.

4. Fill eight 4-ounce (½ cup) popsicle molds with the frozen melon sherbet, insert the handle or a wooden stick into the base of each mold, and freeze until hard, about 3 hours, or up to 4 days. Remove from freezer, let stand 2 to 3 minutes to soften, and remove from the mold. Serve immediately.

ginger crisp ice cream sandwiches

MAKES 12 SANDWICHES

These are best eaten within 2 days of being made; soften them in the refrigerator for 10 to 15 minutes before serving. Use your favorite flavor ice cream for these sandwiches; peach ice cream is particularly good.

 5 tablespoons unsalted butter, room temperature

 1 cup sugar

 ½ teaspoon pure vanilla extract

 4 large egg whites, room temperature

 1 cup sifted all-purpose flour
    Pinch of kosher salt

 2 teaspoons ground ginger

 1 tablespoon minced crystallized ginger
    Peach Ice Cream (page 390)

1. Preheat the oven to 375°F with two racks centered. Trace twelve 3½-inch circles on each of two 12 x 16-inch pieces of parchment paper with a pencil. Place each pencil-side down, on a baking sheet.

2. In the bowl of an electric mixer fitted with the paddle attachment, beat the butter and sugar on medium-high speed until pale yellow, about 4 minutes. Add the vanilla and egg whites; beat until combined, scraping down the sides of the bowl with a rubber spatula. Add the flour, salt, ground ginger, and crystallized ginger; beat on low speed until just incorporated.

3. Spoon a heaping tablespoonful of the batter onto each circle, and spread the batter to the edges with the back of the spoon. Bake until the cookies are golden brown on the edges, about 12 minutes, rotating the sheets between oven racks twice while baking to ensure even baking, if necessary. Transfer to a wire rack to cool.

4. When cool, spoon about ½ cup of partially frozen ice cream onto the bottom side of 1 cookie. Cover with another cookie; press down gently. Wrap in wax paper or plastic wrap, and freeze. Repeat process to make 11 more sandwiches. Freeze for at least 2 hours before serving.

lime cream pops

MAKES 16 POPS OR 1 QUART OF SORBET

These are half sorbet, half frozen yogurt; for sorbet alone, follow steps 1 and 2 only. Freeze the pops in popsicle molds, available at grocery and housewares stores, or paper cups; use a stick or spoon in the center for a handle.

> 2 cups sugar
> 1½ cups fresh lime juice
> 1 tablespoon grated lime zest
> Lime Frozen Yogurt (page 400)

1. Combine the sugar and 2 cups water in a medium saucepan, and bring to a boil. Reduce heat to low; simmer until the sugar dissolves, about 5 minutes.

2. Prepare an ice-water bath; set aside. Pour the sugar syrup into a bowl set in the ice bath; set aside until chilled. Remove the bowl from the ice bath, and stir in the lime juice and zest. Transfer to an ice-cream maker and freeze according to the manufacturer's instructions.

3. Spoon ¼ cup frozen lime sorbet into each of 16 4-ounce (½ cup) popsicle molds or paper cups. Place molds in the freezer to set for about ½ hour.

4. Remove the molds from the freezer. Spoon ¼ cup frozen yogurt on top of the sorbet. (If the frozen yogurt has hardened in the freezer, allow it to soften until it is spoonable.) Insert wooden sticks three-quarters of the way into the molds, and place in the freezer until the entire pop is fully set, at least 4 hours. Freeze the remaining frozen yogurt in an airtight container for up to 5 days.

FIT TO EAT RECIPE PER POP: 109 CALORIES, TRACE FAT, TRACE CHOLESTEROL, 28 G CARBOHYDRATE, 4 MG SODIUM, TRACE PROTEIN, 0 G DIETARY FIBER

blackberry frozen yogurt pops

MAKES 12 POPS OR
1½ QUARTS OF FROZEN YOGURT

This is an excellent way to use berries that have softened and are slightly past their prime. Freeze the pops in popsicle molds, available at grocery and housewares stores, or paper cups; use a stick or spoon in the center for a handle.

> 2 cups plain low-fat yogurt
> 1 pint (about 12 ounces) fresh blackberries
> 1 cup sugar
> 1 cup half-and-half
> 1 cup whole milk
> ½ teaspoon pure vanilla extract

1. Place the yogurt in a fine sieve or cheesecloth-lined strainer over a bowl. Refrigerate for about 1 hour, until about ½ cup liquid has drained from the yogurt. Discard the liquid; set yogurt aside.

2. Meanwhile, in a medium saucepan, combine blackberries and sugar. Simmer over medium-low heat, stirring occasionally, until the syrup is thick and the berries are very soft, about 15 minutes.

3. Prepare an ice-water bath. Transfer the berries and syrup to the bowl of a food processor, and purée until smooth, about 1 minute. Pass through a coarse strainer into a bowl set over the ice-water bath until chilled.

4. Remove from the ice-water bath; add the yogurt, half-and-half, milk, and vanilla. Whisk to combine. Transfer to an ice-cream maker, and freeze according to the manufacturer's instructions. If necessary, do this in 2 batches, keeping the remainder refrigerated while freezing the first batch.

5. Spoon ½ cup of the frozen yogurt into each of twelve 4-ounce (½ cup) popsicle molds or paper cups. Insert a wooden stick three-quarters of the way into each, and freeze until fully set, at least 4 hours. Freeze the remaining frozen yogurt in an airtight container for up to 3 days.

FIT TO EAT RECIPE PER POP: 143 CALORIES, 4 G TOTAL FAT, 13 MG CHOLESTEROL, 25 G CARBOHYDRATE, 45 MG SODIUM, 3 G PROTEIN, 1 G DIETARY FIBER

semifreddo al caffe

MAKES ONE LOAF CAKE; SERVES 12 TO 16

This coffee-and-chocolate-flavored dessert can be prepared up to 4 days ahead of time.

    6   large egg yolks
    ½   cup sugar
    ⅓   cup coffee-flavored liqueur
    2   tablespoons instant espresso mixed
        with 2 teaspoons hot water
    2   cups heavy cream
        Chocolate Sheet Cake (recipe follows)
        Coffee Syrup (page 412)
        Warm Chocolate Sauce (page 412)
        Cocoa powder, for dusting

1. Place the egg yolks in the bowl of an electric mixer fitted with the paddle attachment, and beat until they turn pale. Gradually add the sugar; beat until fluffy. Slowly add the liqueur, and beat again until fluffy.

2. Place the bowl (if mixer bowl is not heat-proof, transfer to a heat-proof bowl) over a pan of barely simmering water. Do not let water touch the bottom of the bowl.

3. Whisk constantly until fluffy, thick, and hot, 8 to 10 minutes. Add espresso mixture. Remove bowl from heat and return to the electric mixer; beat on medium speed until cool, about 10 minutes.

4. Whip cream in a chilled bowl until it holds soft peaks. Add a quarter of it to the egg-espresso mixture, and whisk thoroughly. Fold in remainder of whipped cream. Keep semifreddo mixture cold in the refrigerator or over a bowl of ice water.

5. Cut a 4 x 10-inch strip of Chocolate Sheet Cake. Fit into bottom of a 5½ x 10½ x 3-inch loaf pan, and soak well with a third of the Coffee Syrup. Spoon a third of the semifreddo mixture over cake.

6. Cut remaining cake into two 5½ x 10-inch strips. Continue layering as in step 5, ending with semifreddo mixture. Cover with plastic wrap and freeze overnight. When ready to serve, thaw in refrigerator until slightly softened, 10 to 20 minutes.

7. Using an ice-cream scoop, place 1 to 2 scoops of semifreddo on each plate. Pour warm Chocolate Sauce over top; dust with cocoa, if desired. Serve.

chocolate sheet cake

MAKES ONE 10 X 15-INCH CAKE

This is a moist, all-purpose sponge cake.

        Unsalted butter, for the pan
    ½   cup all-purpose flour
    ½   cup unsweetened cocoa powder
        Pinch of kosher salt
    ½   teaspoon baking powder
    4   large eggs, separated
    1   cup sugar
    3   tablespoons boiling water
    1   teaspoon pure vanilla extract

1. Preheat the oven to 350°F. Butter and flour, or line with parchment, a 10¼ x 15¼ x ¾-inch jelly-roll pan.

2. Sift together the flour, cocoa, salt, and baking powder. Set aside.

3. In the bowl of an electric mixer fitted with the whisk attachment, beat together the egg yolks and sugar until fluffy, on medium-low speed. Beat in boiling water and vanilla.

4. Fold in dry ingredients in three additions.

5. In a separate bowl, beat the egg whites until stiff but not dry, and whisk a quarter of them into the batter. Fold in the remainder of the whites, and spread the batter evenly in the prepared pan. Bake until the cake springs back when gently pressed, about 15 minutes. Cool in the pan.

coffee syrup

MAKES ABOUT ½ CUP

½ cup sugar

2 tablespoons coffee-flavored liqueur

Combine the sugar and ¼ cup water in a small saucepan. Bring to a boil, and stir until the sugar is dissolved. Remove from heat. Stir in liqueur; let cool completely before using.

warm chocolate sauce

MAKES ABOUT 1 CUP

6 ounces bittersweet chocolate, finely chopped

¾ cup plus 1 tablespoon heavy cream

Place the chocolate in a small bowl. In a small saucepan, scald the cream. Pour over chocolate; let stand 5 minutes. Stir until smooth. Set over a pan of warm water to keep warm until ready to use.

frozen tiramisù

SERVES 12

This frozen version of the popular Italian dessert includes sponge cake soaked with an espresso-Kahlúa syrup, espresso and coffee ice creams, and a fine dusting of ground espresso. Serve right from the pan.

1 cup sugar

1½ cups strong, freshly brewed espresso

⅓ cup Kahlúa liqueur, optional
   Vanilla Sponge Cake (recipe follows)

¼ cup finely ground espresso

2 pints espresso or coffee ice cream

2 pints coffee ice cream
   Chocolate Curls (recipe opposite)

1. Place sugar and ⅔ cup water in a saucepan. Bring to a boil over medium heat, stirring occasionally, until sugar dissolves. Remove from heat; stir in espresso and Kahlúa. Let the syrup cool.

2. Using a long serrated knife, cut the sponge cake in half horizontally, making two layers. Place one layer in the bottom of a 9 x 2-inch baking pan. Using a pastry brush, brush the layer with ¾ cup of the cooled syrup. Sift 2 tablespoons ground espresso over the cake layer.

3. Place the espresso ice cream in the bowl of an electric mixer fitted with the paddle attachment. Beat on low speed until spreadable. Spread the ice cream over the cake; top with a second layer of sponge cake. Brush with the remaining syrup. Transfer the cake to the freezer for 20 minutes.

4. Remove the cake from the freezer; sift the remaining 2 tablespoons of ground espresso evenly over the cake. Place the coffee ice cream in the mixer bowl. Beat on low speed until spreadable. Spread the ice cream over the cake, forming large swirls. Return to the freezer; freeze until completely hardened. To serve, garnish with the chocolate curls.

vanilla sponge cake

MAKES ONE 9-INCH SQUARE CAKE

This cake is also used for the Watermelon Bombe (page 415). Make a half batch of this recipe; divide the batter between two 6-inch-round layer-cake pans, and bake 35 minutes. Use one layer for the bombe, and freeze the second layer for future use.

1 tablespoon unsalted butter, for pan

½ cup all-purpose flour, plus more for pan

½ cup cornstarch

4 large eggs, separated

1 teaspoon pure vanilla extract

¾ cup sugar
   Pinch of kosher salt

1. Preheat the oven to 350° F with a rack in the center. Butter a 9 x 2-inch square baking pan. Line the pan with parchment paper. Butter and flour the paper, tapping out the excess flour; set aside. In a small bowl, sift together the flour and cornstarch; set aside.

2. In the bowl of an electric mixer fitted with the whisk attachment, beat egg yolks, vanilla, and ½ cup sugar on high speed until thick and pale, about 5 minutes. Transfer mixture to a large bowl. Wash and dry bowl and whisk attachment.

3. Combine egg whites and salt in mixer bowl; beat on medium until the whites hold soft peaks, about 1½ minutes. With the mixer running, slowly add the remaining ¼ cup of sugar. Continue beating until stiff and glossy, about 1 minute.

4. Stir about one-third of the egg-white mixture into the egg-yolk mixture to lighten it. Fold in the remaining egg-white mixture into the egg-yolk mixture. In three additions, fold the reserved flour mixture into this new mixture. Transfer the batter to the pan, and smooth the top with an offset spatula. Bake until a cake tester inserted into middle comes out clean, 30 to 40 minutes. Transfer the pan to a wire rack to cool; turn out the cake, and wrap it in plastic wrap until ready to use. May be made up to 1 day ahead.

chocolate curls
MAKES ENOUGH TO DECORATE
A 9-INCH CAKE

8 ounces semisweet or bittersweet chocolate, chopped into ½-inch pieces

1 teaspoon pure vegetable shortening

1. In the top of a double boiler or in a heat-proof bowl set over a pan of simmering water, melt the chocolate and shortening, stirring occasionally, with a rubber spatula, until smooth.

2. Divide the chocolate between two 12 x 17-inch baking pans; spread evenly with an offset spatula. Chill until your finger makes a mark but not a hole when touching the chocolate.

3. Remove the pans from the refrigerator. Hold a sturdy metal pancake spatula at a 45° angle to the pan; scrape away from you, forming curls. If the chocolate is too brittle, quickly wave the pan over the top of a warm stove. If too soft, briefly return to the refrigerator to harden. Refrigerate the curls in an airtight container up to 2 weeks.

kulfi cake
SERVES 8

Kulfi is a traditional type of Indian ice-cream dessert, made by reducing milk that has been flavored with sugar, cardamom, and nuts. It is shaped in conical containers (see Equipment Sources, page 650, for molds) and frozen. Freezing this cake in stages makes the beautiful colored layers. Only the first layer of the mixture is strained; this makes the finished surface smooth. Serve with wedges of fresh mango on the side.

2 cups unsweetened coconut milk

8 whole cardamom pods

½ cup whole, shelled green pistachio nuts or whole blanched almonds

1½ cups sweetened condensed milk

½ cup blanched almond slivers

¾ cup heavy cream

1 small mango, peeled, pit removed (see page 647), cut into large pieces

2 tablespoons light corn syrup

1. In a small saucepan over medium heat, warm the coconut milk and cardamom pods until the milk just reaches a boil. Remove from the heat, cover, and set aside to steep for 30 minutes.

2. Preheat the oven to 350°F. Place the pistachios on a baking sheet; toast until aromatic, about 8 minutes. While warm, transfer the nuts to a clean kitchen towel; rub to remove the brown skins. Set the nuts aside. (If using whole blanched almonds, simply toast, see page 644, and set aside.)

3. Place the condensed milk, pistachio nuts, and almond slivers in the bowl of a food processor. Process until well blended and the nuts are finely chopped. Strain the coconut milk into the nut mixture. Pulse until just combined. Transfer the mixture to a large bowl.

4. In the bowl of an electric mixer fitted with the whisk attachment, whip the heavy cream until soft peaks form. Gently whisk the cream into the coconut mixture.

5. Strain 1 cup of the mixture through a fine sieve into the bottom of a 5-cup oval pudding mold or any 5-cup mold. Transfer mold to freezer; let chill until firm, 1 hour to 1¼ hours. (Poke the mixture lightly with your finger to test for firmness.) Pour 1½ cups of the remaining coconut mixture (not strained) over the frozen mixture, return to freezer, and chill until firm, about 1½ hours.

6. In the bowl of a food processor, purée the mango; it should yield about ½ cup. Combine the purée and the corn syrup in a bowl. Pour the mango mixture over the frozen mixture; freeze until firm, 30 to 40 minutes. Stir well; pour the remaining coconut mixture (not strained) over the frozen mango layer until the mold is full. Cover with plastic wrap; freeze overnight.

7. To unmold the cake, remove the plastic wrap; place the mold, metal-side up, on a serving platter. Wet a kitchen towel with very hot water; wring out. Place the towel over the mold, and press into the mold, being careful to press the warm towel into any curves or flutes of the mold. Repeat this step as needed, until kulfi slips out onto the platter. Return cake to freezer on the platter until firm again, at least 30 minutes. The cake may be made up to this point 1 day ahead. To serve, chill about 20 minutes, until soft enough to cut with a serrated or slicing knife. Serve.

black-and-white peanut bar
SERVES 8

This cake is an homage to the Nutty Buddy ice-cream cone. Crisp cookie wafers are layered with vanilla and chocolate ice cream. The parchment collar crafted in step 7 allows you to pour a generous amount of chocolate on top of the cake, finishing it with a handful of roasted peanuts. You can also make this cake without the collar; just let the melted chocolate drip down the sides.

- 1 quart chocolate ice cream
- 64 Nabisco's Biscos Sugar Wafers "Creme Filling" (about 1 box)
- 1 quart best-quality vanilla ice cream
- 6 ounces semisweet chocolate, chopped
- 2 teaspoons pure vegetable shortening
- ⅓ cup unsalted roasted peanuts, roughly chopped

1. Cut a 5 x 24-inch rectangle out of parchment paper, and set aside. Cut a 4 x 7½-inch rectangle out of cardboard.

2. Using a spoon, spread 1 tablespoon chocolate ice cream across the cardboard. Arrange 16 sugar wafers over the cardboard; we laid 10 wafers side by side over the lower half of the cardboard; then we made two rows of three wafers, laid end to end, over the top half of the cardboard. You should have a flat, single layer of wafers. This will become the bottom of the cake.

3. Microwave both the chocolate and the vanilla ice creams until softened, about 20 seconds. Transfer the chocolate ice cream to a medium mixing bowl, and transfer the vanilla ice cream to another one. Stir both ice creams with a rubber spatula until smooth; place the vanilla ice cream in the freezer.

4. Using a small offset spatula, spread 2 cups of the chocolate ice cream as evenly as possible over the wafer layer. Arrange 16 more sugar wafers, as described in step 2, on top of the ice cream. Transfer the cake and the bowl of chocolate ice cream to the freezer for 15 minutes.

5. Remove the cake and the bowl of vanilla ice cream from the freezer. Stir the ice cream with a rubber spatula to resoften it, and spread 2 cups of the vanilla ice cream as evenly as possible over the wafers. Arrange 16 more sugar wafers, as described in step 2, on top of the ice cream. Transfer the cake and the bowl of vanilla ice cream to the freezer for 15 minutes more.

6. Repeat the layering process, making one more chocolate and one more vanilla layer, with only one wafer layer in between; chill the cake after making each new layer. End with the layer of vanilla ice cream on the top. Transfer the cake to the freezer and chill until completely hard, at least 1 hour.

7. Using a long serrated knife, trim ¼ inch from all sides of the cake, making them even. Wrap the parchment paper around the sides of the cake, extending ½ inch above the top layer; secure the seam with a small dollop of ice cream. Return the cake to the freezer.

8. In the top of a double boiler or in a heat-proof bowl set over a pan of simmering water, melt the chocolate and shortening, stirring occasionally, with a rubber spatula, until smooth. Remove the bowl from the heat; let the chocolate stand until cool but still liquid.

9. Remove the cake from the freezer, and pour the melted chocolate over the top. Using a spatula, quickly spread the chocolate so it meets all four edges of the paper collar and does not go down the sides. Sprinkle the chopped peanuts over the chocolate. Return the cake to the freezer, and chill until it has completely hardened.

10. When ready to serve, place the cake on a serving plate, and remove the paper collar. Serve. May be made up to 2 days ahead.

ICE-CREAM-CAKE TECHNIQUES

● *To achieve the right consistency for spreading ice cream without melting it, it is vital to "temper" it by beating it in a mixer, or softening it and beating it by hand, to remove as much air as possible. (Use premium ice creams for these cakes, since they have less air than other brands and will not lose as much volume.) Beating the chilled ice cream also loosens up any ice crystals and makes it creamier and easier to spread without breaking the cookie or cake bases.*

● *Do not rush the freezing process. The freezer is the "oven" for ice-cream cakes; just as baking times are followed for baked cakes, freezing times should be adhered to for ice-cream cakes.*

watermelon bombe

SERVES 12

Slices of this bombe not only resemble sweet wedges of watermelon but are just as refreshing. A pistachio ice-cream "rind" is lined with vanilla ice cream and filled with watermelon sorbet that is studded with chocolate wafer bits for the seeds. For the mold, choose a deep metal (3-quart) mixing bowl with a nice dome shape. The bombe may be made up to 2 days ahead.

- *1   quart pistachio ice cream*
- *1   pint best-quality vanilla ice cream*
- *1   quart watermelon sorbet or other red or pink sorbet*
- *4   Nabisco Famous Chocolate Wafers, broken into ¼-inch pieces*
- *1   6-inch-round layer Vanilla Sponge Cake (page 412)*

1. Line a 3-quart metal mixing bowl with plastic wrap, and leave the edges overhanging by a few inches. Place the lined bowl in the freezer for 10 minutes; this will be the mold. Chill the bowl of an electric mixer in the freezer as well.

2. Place the pistachio ice cream in the chilled mixer bowl. Using the paddle attachment, beat on low speed until the ice cream is spreadable, about 30 seconds. Remove the chilled mold from the freezer. Using a rubber spatula, coat the inside of the mold with all the pistachio ice cream, making a ½-inch-thick layer. Return the mold and the empty mixer bowl to the freezer for 30 minutes.

3. Place the vanilla ice cream in the chilled mixer bowl. Beat on low speed until spreadable, about 30 seconds. Remove the mold from the freezer. Using the rubber spatula, coat the pistachio layer with the vanilla ice cream, making a ¼-inch-thick layer. Return the mold and the empty mixer bowl to the freezer for 30 minutes.

4. Place the sorbet in the chilled mixer bowl. Beat on low speed until the sorbet has softened, about 1 minute. Fold in the wafer pieces (these will represent the seeds). Remove the mold from the freezer. Pack the sorbet into the center, making an even layer ⅓ inch below the ice cream. Cover the sorbet portion with the sponge cake; trim the cake if necessary. Return the mold to the freezer until completely hardened.

5. To serve, place a serving plate upside-down on top of the mold. Holding the plate against the mold, invert both. Place a hot wet kitchen towel over the mold. Remove the metal bowl. Immediately before serving, remove the plastic wrap.

rainbow sorbet cake

MAKES ONE 7-INCH LAYER CAKE; SERVES 10

Brightly colored fruit sorbets are layered between delicate, snowy disks of meringue to create a lofty frozen cake.

- 1½ cups sugar
- 6 large egg whites
- ⅔ pint mango sorbet
- ⅔ pint grapefruit sorbet or other pink sorbet
- ⅔ pint raspberry sorbet
- ⅔ pint green apple sorbet or other green sorbet

1. Preheat the oven to 185°F. Cut a 7-inch circle from a 10-inch square of ¼-inch-thick cardboard or Foamcore. Set the circle aside to use for bottom of the cake, and reserve the cut-out square as a template. Cut three 12 x 17-inch rectangles out of parchment paper, and set the rectangles aside.

2. Fill a medium saucepan with 2 inches of water, and bring to a simmer. Place the sugar and egg whites in the bowl of an electric mixer. Hold the bowl over the simmering water, and whisk until warm to the touch and the sugar has dissolved, about 3 minutes.

3. Attach the bowl to the mixer fitted with the whisk attachment; beat egg whites on medium until stiff and glossy, about 4 minutes. Do not overbeat.

4. Place the template over one end of a piece of parchment. Scoop 1 cup of the egg-white mixture into the center. Using an offset spatula, spread the mixture into an even layer. Remove the template. Make another disc on the other end of the parchment. Create 3 more discs on the remaining 2 pieces of parchment for a total of five. Slide onto 12 x 17-inch baking sheets.

5. Transfer meringue discs to oven, and bake 1½ hours, making sure they don't brown. Turn off the heat, and let the discs dry completely in the oven, 6 hours to overnight. The cake can be prepared up to this point and the meringues stored in an airtight container up to 5 days ahead.

6. Place 1 meringue disc on the reserved 7-inch cake round. Using a large spoon, make an even layer of scoops of the mango sorbet on top of the disc (the layer should not be smooth; rough scoops are fine). Top with a second meringue disc. Continue layering, using remaining grapefruit, raspberry, and green-apple sorbets and meringue discs. Top with a disc. Transfer cake to the freezer, and freeze until hardened. Using a serrated knife, cut in wedges and serve. May be assembled up to 4 hours before serving and kept in the freezer.

baked alaska

SERVES 6 TO 8

You will need one 8-inch cake pan and one pastry bag fitted with an Ateco #5 star tip.

Unsalted butter, room temperature, for pan

¼ *cup plus 2 tablespoons sugar*

3 *large egg yolks*

1 *teaspoon pure vanilla extract*

3 *ounces bittersweet chocolate, melted and cooled*

3 *large egg whites, room temperature*

Pinch of kosher salt

1½ *pints pistachio or other flavor ice cream, slightly softened*

1½ *pints cherry ice cream or any berry sorbet, slightly softened*

Swiss Meringue (page 643)

1. Preheat the oven to 350°F with a rack in the center. Line an 8-inch cake pan with parchment paper, and coat with butter; set aside.

2. Combine 3 tablespoons sugar and the yolks in the bowl of an electric mixer fitted with the whisk attachment, and beat on medium speed until pale yellow and thick, about 15 minutes. Add the vanilla, and fold in the melted chocolate just to combine.

3. Clean the whisk attachment. Combine the egg whites and a pinch of salt in a clean mixer bowl, and whisk on medium speed until frothy. Add 3 tablespoons sugar; beat until stiff peaks form. Fold the egg whites into the chocolate mixture.

4. Carefully pour the batter into prepared cake pan. Bake until a cake tester inserted in the center comes out clean and the top is dull, about 20 minutes. Transfer to a wire rack to cool completely. Remove cake from the pan, and remove parchment paper.

5. Butter a 5-cup-capacity metal bowl; line with plastic wrap. Pack the base of the bowl with the pistachio ice cream; layer the cherry ice cream over the pistachio. Pack firmly, cover the surface with plastic wrap, and place in the freezer. Freeze until the ice cream is very hard, at least 2 hours or up to 24 hours in advance.

6. Transfer the cake to a baking sheet. Remove the ice cream from the freezer, and invert the bowl over the cake. Keep the ice cream covered with plastic wrap, and return to the freezer.

7. Preheat the oven to 500°F with a rack in the center. Fill a pastry bag fitted with an Ateco #5 star tip with the meringue; pipe onto the ice cream in a decorative fashion, or spoon the meringue over the ice cream, and smooth or swirl with a rubber spatula. If the ice cream starts to soften, return to the freezer for 15 minutes.

8. Transfer to the oven, and bake until the meringue just starts to brown in spots, 1 to 2 minutes, watching constantly. Remove from the oven, and serve immediately.

brownie ice-cream bars

MAKES 12

These homemade ice-cream bars are of course fresher than store-bought. Beating the ice cream with a paddle makes it softer and easier to spread. It is best to bake brownies a day in advance so they have time to set completely. Make space in your freezer before you begin to accommodate the ice-cream bars and the baking sheet.

14 tablespoons (1¾ sticks) unsalted butter

46 ounces semisweet chocolate, cut into 1-inch pieces

3 large eggs

½ teaspoon kosher salt

1 cup granulated sugar

½ cup packed light-brown sugar

1 teaspoon pure vanilla extract

¾ cup all-purpose flour

2 quarts Homemade Vanilla Ice Cream (page 390) or prepared

1. Preheat the oven to 350°F. Line a 10 x 13-inch pan with parchment paper. In the top of a double boiler or in a heat-proof bowl set over a pan of simmering water, combine 12 tablespoons of the butter and 6 ounces of the chocolate. Stir occasionally until the chocolate is melted and smooth.

2. Whisk the eggs together in a large bowl; add the salt, both sugars, and the vanilla, and stir to combine. Stir in the butter-and-chocolate mixture, then fold in the flour. Pour the batter into the prepared pan, spread evenly, and place in the oven to bake until the top is shiny, about 20 minutes. Do not overbake; a cake tester should not come out clean. Transfer to a wire rack to cool completely. Store in an airtight container overnight.

3. The next day, loosen the corners of the brownie. Lift it from the pan, keeping the brownie intact. Invert onto a cutting board, and peel off the parchment. Trim about ¼ inch from each edge, and discard or snack on.

4. Place a fresh piece of parchment in the baking pan, allowing the excess to stick out over the edges of the pan. Return the brownie to the pan, top-side up, and set aside.

5. Meanwhile, working quickly, scoop half of the ice cream into the bowl of an electric mixer fitted with the paddle attachment. Beat the ice cream until soft and smooth but not melted. Using a rubber spatula, transfer the ice cream to the brownie pan, and spread, creating an even layer. Place the pan in the freezer to chill. Repeat with the remaining 2 pints of ice cream, adding a second layer to the brownie, and return the pan to freezer. Let chill until very hard, at least 1 hour (overnight produces the best result).

6. In the top of a double boiler or in a heat-proof bowl set over a pan of simmering water, combine the remaining chocolate and 2 tablespoons butter. Stir until melted and smooth.

7. Remove the pan from the freezer. Place a cooling rack over a baking sheet, and set aside. Using the edges of the parchment paper, lift the brownie and the ice cream out of the pan, and transfer to a cutting board. Working quickly and using a sharp knife dipped in hot water, trim the outside edges to even them, wasting as little of the ice cream and brownie as possible. Use the hot knife to cut the brownie into twelve 2¼ x 4¼-inch rectangles, and transfer each rectangle to the cooling rack.

8. Remove the bowl of chocolate from the saucepan, wiping the bottom until dry. Fill a ½-cup ladle with the melted chocolate; carefully ladle the chocolate over each bar, working from front to back. Cover as much of the ice cream as you can. Work quickly; do not worry if some of the ice cream shows. Return the rack and baking sheet to the freezer. Let stand until the chocolate hardens, about 30 minutes. Serve the bars frozen, or store in freezer in an airtight container up to 1 week.

custards

AND

puddings

. . . .

double hot chocolate pudding

SERVES 4 TO 6

The taste of the chocolate will come through very clearly in this pudding, so buy only the best. A pinch of cayenne gives it a slight bite. The pudding may be served lukewarm or refrigerated (with plastic wrap over the surface) for up to 1 day and served chilled.

- ¼ cup cornstarch
- ¼ cup plus 2 tablespoons sugar
- 3 tablespoons Dutch-process cocoa powder
- ¼ teaspoon ground cinnamon
- 1 tablespoon espresso powder, optional
  Pinch of kosher salt
  Pinch of cayenne pepper, optional
- 1¼ cups heavy cream
- 1¼ cups milk
- 7 ounces bittersweet chocolate, finely chopped
- 1½ tablespoons unsalted butter, cut into small pieces

1. In a medium saucepan, whisk together the cornstarch, sugar, cocoa, cinnamon, espresso powder, salt, and cayenne, if using. In a measuring cup, combine the cream with the milk. Whisk 1 cup cream mixture into the dry ingredients until the cornstarch is dissolved. Whisk in the remaining cream mixture; place saucepan over medium-high heat.

2. Cook, whisking constantly, until the mixture comes to a boil and thickens, about 5 minutes. Add the chocolate; cook, whisking, 1 minute more. Remove from the heat; whisk in the butter until melted. Transfer to a bowl; place plastic wrap directly on the surface of the pudding to prevent a skin from forming. Let stand until lukewarm, about 45 minutes. Transfer the pudding to serving bowls or goblets.

steamed chocolate sponge pudding

SERVES 4 TO 6

Serve this pudding warm from the bowl, or allow it to cool slightly, and invert onto a plate.

- 2 tablespoons unsalted butter, plus more for bowl
- ½ cup sugar
  Pinch of kosher salt
- 2 tablespoons all-purpose flour
- 1 teaspoon unsweetened cocoa powder
- 2½ ounces bittersweet chocolate, chopped
- ¾ cup milk
- 2 large eggs, separated
- 1 teaspoon pure vanilla extract
- ½ cup coarsely chopped hazelnuts, toasted (see page 644), for garnish

1. Preheat the oven to 325°F. Butter a 5-cup pudding bowl, and set aside.

2. Whisk ¼ cup plus 1 tablespoon sugar with the salt, flour, and cocoa in a large bowl. Set aside.

3. Combine the chocolate and 2 tablespoons butter in the top of a double boiler or in a heat-proof bowl set over a pan of simmering water. Stir until melted and smooth.

4. Meanwhile, bring the milk just to a simmer in a small saucepan over medium heat. Whisk the hot milk into the melted chocolate mixture. Beat the egg yolks. Stir a little of the hot chocolate mixture into the yolks; whisk the yolks back into the chocolate mixture. Add the vanilla; stir until well combined. Stir into the flour mixture.

5. Bring a kettle filled with water to a boil. In a large bowl, beat the egg whites with the remaining sugar until stiff peaks form. Stir one-third of the beaten egg whites into the batter to lighten it; gently fold in the remaining egg whites.

6. Pour the batter into the pudding bowl. Tap the mold sharply down on the counter to distribute the batter evenly. Place the mold on a wire rack or a folded kitchen towel in a deep roasting pan. Pour the boiling water into the pan halfway up the sides of the bowl. Bake until the pudding is set and a toothpick inserted in the center of the pudding comes out clean, 40 to 50 minutes. Add boiling water to pan if needed to maintain the water level.

7. Let cool slightly in the bowl, and invert onto a plate. Garnish with hazelnuts. Serve warm.

warm brownie cups

MAKES 5

This puddinglike dessert is baked in individual custard cups or ramekins.

  4   ounces semisweet chocolate
  8   tablespoons (1 stick) unsalted butter
  ½   cup all-purpose flour
  ½   teaspoon baking powder
      Pinch of salt
  ½   cup cocoa powder
  4   large eggs, at room temperature
  1   teaspoon pure vanilla extract
  1   cup granulated sugar
      Confectioners' sugar, for dusting

1. Preheat the oven to 350°F. Place a baking pan half full of water on a lower rack in the oven.

2. Bring a saucepan of water to a simmer. Place the chocolate and butter in a heat-proof bowl. Place over water and stir with a rubber spatula until almost melted. Remove bowl from heat and let cool, stirring occasionally.

3. Sift together twice all the dry ingredients except the sugars. Set aside.

4. In an electric mixer fitted with the whisk attachment, beat the eggs and vanilla until foamy and light. Add the granulated sugar and beat until fluffy. Stir in the chocolate-butter mixture. Fold in the dry ingredients. Pour into five 8-ounce custard cups, filling each nearly to the rim. Place in the prepared baking pan; water should come halfway up sides of cups.

5. Bake for 30 minutes or until brownies have risen to just above the rim and tops are cracked. They should be firm. Let cool for 5 minutes, then serve dusted with confectioners' sugar.

chocolate pots de crème

MAKES 6

You will need six 3-ounce pot-de-crème molds or ovenproof ramekins to make these custards. Each spoonful of pot de crème is dense and intensely flavorful, unlike pudding, which has a less assertive flavor and a more satiny texture.

  ¼   cup Dutch-process cocoa powder, sifted
  ½   cup plus 1 tablespoon skim milk
  ¼   cup evaporated milk
  2   large eggs
  1   large egg white
  ¾   cup granulated sugar
      Pinch of kosher salt
      Confectioners' sugar, for sprinkling

1. Preheat the oven to 325°F with a rack in the center. Line a shallow baking pan with a kitchen towel; set aside. Place cocoa in a bowl. In another bowl, combine milks. Slowly whisk about 3 tablespoons of the milk mixture into the cocoa until it forms a thick paste. Whisk in the remaining milk mixture until thoroughly combined; set aside.

2. Bring a kettle filled with water to a boil. In a large bowl, combine the eggs, egg white, granulated sugar, and salt, and whisk together until thoroughly combined. Whisk in the cocoa-milk mixture until completely combined. Divide the mixture among six 3-ounce pot-de-crème molds or ovenproof ramekins, and place in the prepared baking pan. Transfer the pan to the oven, and fill the baking pan halfway with the boiling water.

3. Bake until the puddings are set and leave no residue on your finger when lightly touched, about 25 minutes. Remove pan from oven, then remove puddings from water bath. Transfer puddings to a wire rack, and let cool 20 to 30 minutes. When ready to serve, dust the puddings with confectioners' sugar. Serve warm.

FIT TO EAT RECIPE PER SERVING: 64 CALORIES, 3 G FAT, 72 MG CHOLESTEROL, 4 G CARBOHYDRATE, 134 MG SODIUM, 5 G PROTEIN, 0 G DIETARY FIBER

caramel pots de crème

MAKES 6

The name of this delicate dessert comes from the small lidded porcelain pots in which the desserts are traditionally baked; be careful not to overcook them, as doing so would ruin the velvety texture. The cover is not used while the crème is baking, but for an elegant presentation. You may also use small white ceramic soufflé ramekins or oven-proof custard cups.

¾ cup sugar

1½ cups heavy cream

1 cup milk

1 vanilla bean, split lengthwise and scraped

5 large egg yolks

¼ teaspoon kosher salt

1. Preheat the oven to 300°F with a rack in the center. Place six 4-ounce ramekins or pot-de-crème molds in a 13 x 9 x 2-inch roasting pan; set aside.

2. Place ½ cup sugar in a medium saucepan set over medium heat. Cook, without stirring, until the sugar has caramelized and is golden brown, about 3 minutes, brushing down the sides of the pan with a pastry brush dipped in water to prevent crystallizing. Swirl the pan, dissolving the unmelted sugar; reduce heat to low.

3. Slowly whisk in 1 cup cream and the milk. Scrape the vanilla seeds into the pan, and add the pod. Increase heat to medium high, cover, and bring to a boil; remove the pan from the heat.

4. In a bowl, whisk together the remaining sugar, the egg yolks, and salt; continue whisking until pale yellow in color. Slowly add the hot cream mixture to the egg mixture, whisking constantly. Pour this new mixture through a fine sieve set over a large liquid measuring cup; discard vanilla pod.

5. Bring a kettle filled with water to a boil. Using a tablespoon or a small ladle, skim the surface to remove any visible air bubbles. Pour approximately ½ cup of the liquid into each ramekin. Transfer the

pan to the oven. Fill the roasting pan with the boiling water to within 1 inch of the ramekin tops. Cover pan with aluminum foil, and poke small holes in two opposite corners for vents.

6. Bake until the custard is set and is no longer liquid when lightly touched in the center, about 35 minutes. Remove the foil; transfer the ramekins to a wire rack to cool completely. Cover with plastic wrap; refrigerate until chilled. When ready to serve, place remaining ½ cup cream in a mixing bowl. Whip cream until soft peaks form. Add a dollop of whipped cream to each serving.

vanilla bean custard

MAKES 4 INDIVIDUAL CUSTARDS

1¼ cups heavy cream

1¼ cups milk

1 whole vanilla bean, split lengthwise and scraped

6 large egg yolks

½ cup sugar

1. Preheat the oven to 300°F with a rack in the lower third. Choose a small roasting pan large enough to hold four 6-ounce custard cups, and fill it with enough water to go halfway up the sides of the cups. Place the pan without the cups in the oven. Meanwhile, in a medium saucepan, combine the cream, milk, and the vanilla-bean scrapings, reserving the pod for another use; cover and bring to a boil.

2. Whisk together the yolks and the sugar in a medium bowl until light and fluffy. Slowly whisk in the hot milk until completely combined, then pour into the custard cups, and place them in the pan of hot water. Bake until the custard has set and is no longer liquid when lightly touched in the center, 30 to 40 minutes. Remove the pan from the oven, remove the custard cups from the water, and place on a wire rack to cool. Serve warm, at room temperature, or chilled. The custard with keep, refrigerated, wrapped in plastic wrap, up to 4 days.

coffee custard

MAKES 4 INDIVIDUAL CUSTARDS

Serve this dessert warm or chilled.

> *Unsalted butter, melted, for custard cups*
>
> 1 *cup heavy cream*
>
> ½ *cup whole milk*
>
> 2 *tablespoons instant espresso powder*
>
> 3 *large egg yolks*
>
> 1 *large egg*
>
> ¼ *cup sugar*
>
> 1 *teaspoon pure vanilla extract*
>
> *Pinch of kosher salt*
>
> *Chocolate Curls (page 413)*

1. Preheat the oven to 300°F with a rack in the lower third. Place a roasting pan three-quarters full of hot water in the oven. Brush four 6-ounce custard cups with melted butter, and set aside.

2. Combine the cream, milk, and espresso powder in a small saucepan over medium heat. Bring almost to a simmer, then remove from the heat.

3. Whisk together the egg yolks, egg, sugar, vanilla, and salt in a medium bowl. Add a little of the hot milk mixture to the egg mixture, and whisk well. Add the remaining milk mixture, and whisk again to combine well. Strain the mixture through a fine sieve into a large bowl.

4. Pour the mixture into the custard cups, and place in the water bath in the oven, making sure that the water comes three-quarters of the way up the sides of the cups. Bake until the custard is set and is no longer liquid when lightly touched in the center, about 35 minutes.

5. Remove the custard cups from the water bath, and transfer to a wire rack to cool for about 20 minutes. Loosen the custards with a knife, and invert onto serving dishes; sprinkle with the chocolate. Alternatively, refrigerate the custards and turn out when ready to serve.

buttermilk panna cotta with strawberries

MAKES 6 INDIVIDUAL PUDDINGS

Panna cotta, Italian for "cooked cream," is a silky custardlike pudding that is set with gelatin. Like other gelatins, it is served cold.

> 1½ *teaspoons unflavored gelatin*
>
> 2 *cups buttermilk*
>
> ⅔ *cup heavy cream*
>
> ¾ *cup sugar*
>
> 1 *pint strawberries, hulled and quartered*

1. In the top of a double boiler or in a heat-proof bowl (not set over heat), sprinkle the gelatin evenly over 1 cup buttermilk; let soften, about 5 minutes.

2. Meanwhile, bring the cream and ½ cup sugar to a boil in a medium saucepan. Whisk into gelatin mixture; place the double boiler over a pan of simmering water; whisk until the gelatin dissolves, 5 minutes. Stir in remaining buttermilk. Pass mixture through a fine sieve or cheesecloth-lined strainer. Divide mixture among six 4-ounce ramekins or small bowls; transfer to a baking sheet. Cover with plastic wrap; refrigerate until set, 4 hours.

3. Sprinkle the strawberries with the remaining sugar; let stand about 1 hour at room temperature.

4. Unmold by dipping the ramekins briefly into hot water and running the tip of a knife around the edges; invert onto plates, and serve with the strawberries and their juice.

café gelatin

SERVES 6

This layered dessert features three flavors of gelatin; use tall, slender glasses to properly showcase each one.

for the espresso-panna-cotta layer

1½ cups heavy cream
3 tablespoons sugar
1 tablespoon finely ground espresso
1 teaspoon unflavored gelatin

for the espresso-gelatin layer

1¼ cups chilled strong brewed espresso
1¼ teaspoons unflavored gelatin
3 tablespoons sugar

for the vanilla-panna-cotta layer

1½ cups heavy cream
3 tablespoons sugar
¼ vanilla bean, split lengthwise
    and scraped
1 teaspoon unflavored gelatin

1. For the espresso panna cotta: Heat ¾ cup cream, the sugar, and ground espresso over medium-low heat, stirring to dissolve. Bring just to a boil; remove from heat. Cover; steep 5 minutes.

2. Meanwhile, pour the remaining cream into the top of a double boiler or a heat-proof bowl (not over heat). Sprinkle the gelatin evenly over; let stand to soften, 5 minutes. Add the warm espresso mixture; place double boiler over simmering water; whisk until gelatin is dissolved, 3 to 5 minutes. Strain mixture through a cheesecloth-lined strainer.

3. Pour ¼ cup espresso panna cotta into each of six tall 8-ounce glasses. Cover with plastic wrap; refrigerate until set, about 1 hour.

4. For the espresso gelatin: Place ½ cup chilled brewed espresso in a bowl. Sprinkle the gelatin over; let stand to soften, about 5 minutes.

5. Bring the sugar and the remaining espresso just to a boil; add to the espresso-gelatin mixture; whisk to dissolve. Cool to room temperature. Add 2 ta-

blespoons of the espresso gelatin to each glass. Cover; refrigerate to set, 40 minutes. Refrigerate the remaining espresso gelatin in a small baking dish, covered, to set.

6. For the vanilla panna cotta: Combine ¾ cup cream and the sugar in a saucepan; add vanilla bean and seed scrapings, and bring just to a boil. Remove from the heat; cover and steep 5 minutes.

7. Meanwhile, in the top of a double boiler or in a heat-proof bowl (not over heat), sprinkle the gelatin evenly over the remaining ¾ cup of cream; let stand to soften, 5 minutes.

8. Pour the hot cream over the gelatin mixture; set over simmering water; whisk until the gelatin dissolves, 5 minutes. Pour through a cheesecloth-lined strainer; cool to room temperature. Pour ¼ cup vanilla panna cotta into each glass. Cover; refrigerate 1½ hours to set.

9. Using a small spoon, scoop up the remaining espresso gelatin into small amounts, and transfer them into glasses on top of the vanilla layer; divide evenly among the glasses creating a loose, jumbled final layer for the dessert. Serve.

citrus sponge pudding with rhubarb sauce

MAKES 4 INDIVIDUAL PUDDINGS

2 tablespoons unsalted butter, room
    temperature, plus more for ramekins
¾ cup sugar, plus more for ramekins
    Pinch of kosher salt
1 teaspoon grated lemon zest
1 teaspoon grated lime zest
2 large egg yolks
3 tablespoons all-purpose flour
1½ tablespoons fresh lemon juice
1½ tablespoons fresh lime juice
¾ cup plus 1 tablespoon milk
3 large egg whites
1½ cups fresh or frozen rhubarb, trimmed,
    cut into ½-inch dice

1. Preheat the oven to 325°F with a rack in the center. Butter four 6-ounce glass custard cups; coat with the sugar, tapping out the excess. Line a baking pan with a kitchen towel, and set aside.

2. In the bowl of an electric mixer fitted with the paddle attachment, combine 2 tablespoons butter, ½ cup plus 1 tablespoon sugar, and the salt; mix on medium speed until crumbly. Mix in the zests and yolks until combined. Mix in the flour until combined, then the juices and milk.

3. Bring a kettle filled with water to a boil. In a large bowl, beat the egg whites until stiff peaks form. Gently fold the whites into the egg-yolk mixture. Ladle into the custard cups; place in the prepared baking pan. Transfer the pan to the oven, and fill the pan halfway with the boiling water. Bake until the puddings have set (the tops may crack), about 25 minutes. Transfer the puddings to a wire rack to cool for 30 minutes. Chill or let stand at room temperature.

4. Meanwhile, combine the rhubarb, remaining sugar, and 1 tablespoon water in a small skillet; cook over medium-high heat until tender when pierced with the tip of a knife, about 4 minutes. Let cool. To unmold, run a knife carefully around the edge of each pudding; invert puddings onto serving plates, and serve chilled or at room temperature with the rhubarb sauce.

coconut-rum flan

MAKES ONE 9-INCH FLAN; SERVES 12

This flan is best when refrigerated overnight right in the pie plate and served the next day.

1½ cups sugar
     Pinch of kosher salt
  5 large egg yolks
  3 large eggs
1¾ cups canned coconut milk
  1 cup milk
  3 tablespoons dark rum

1. Preheat the oven to 325°F with a rack in the center. Bring a kettle filled with water to a boil. Have ready a 9-inch-round glass pie plate. Place a clean kitchen towel in the bottom of a shallow baking pan large enough to hold the pie plate. Transfer the baking pan to the oven, and fill the baking pan with enough boiling water to come halfway up the sides of the dish.

2. Place ¾ cup sugar in a heavy-bottomed medium skillet. Place over medium-high heat; cook until the sugar begins to melt, swirling the pan and brushing down the sides of the pan with a pastry brush dipped in water to prevent crystallization. Cook until the sugar is melted and medium-dark brown, about 5 minutes. Remove from the heat; pour the caramelized sugar into the pie dish. Swirl the dish until the caramel evenly coats the bottom; let cool.

3. In a large bowl, whisk together the remaining sugar, the salt, egg yolks, and eggs until combined. Whisk in the coconut milk, milk, and rum until combined. Pour into the pie dish; transfer the dish to the hot-water bath in the oven. Bake until the flan is just set and is no longer liquid when lightly touched in the center, 40 to 50 minutes. Transfer the pie dish to a wire rack until cool.

4. When ready to serve, run a knife between the flan and the pie dish. Place a serving dish on top of the flan and invert it. Garnish with any remaining syrup. Slice and serve.

whim-whams

MAKES 4 INDIVIDUAL DESSERTS

This centuries-old British dessert is reminiscent of trifle with layers of brandy-soaked cookies, custard, and berries. For amaretti cookies, see Food Sources, page 648.

- 6 ounces mixed berries, such as blackberries, raspberries, loganberries, and strawberries, hulled, plus more for garnish
- ¼ cup plus 2 tablespoons sugar
- ¼ cup plus 2 tablespoons brandy
- ¼ cup (2 ounces) Muscat or sweet white wine
- 1 cup heavy cream
- 12 to 16 amaretti cookies
  Soft Custard (recipe follows)

1. Combine 6 ounces of the berries, 3 tablespoons sugar, and 1 tablespoon brandy in a medium bowl. Stir gently to combine and dissolve the sugar. Set aside for about 1 hour at room temperature to release the berry juices.

2. Place the wine and 1 tablespoon brandy in the bowl of an electric mixer fitted with the whisk attachment. Stir in the remaining 3 tablespoons sugar until dissolved. Turn the mixer to low; slowly add the cream. Increase speed; whisk until the cream is thick enough to hold its shape. Place the bowl in the refrigerator while preparing the glasses.

3. Divide the cookies among four 8-ounce glasses, and spoon 1 tablespoon brandy into each glass. Cover with some of the fruit and a layer of soft custard. Repeat with another layer of fruit and custard, reserving any remaining berry juice. Top with the cream. Serve immediately, or set aside in refrigerator for 1 hour. Just before serving, garnish with more berries and juice of the reserved berries.

soft custard

MAKES 1 ⅓ CUPS

- 1 vanilla bean, split lengthwise and scraped
- ½ cup heavy cream
- 1 cup milk
- 8 large egg yolks
- ⅓ cup sugar

1. Heat the vanilla bean and seed scrapings, the cream, and milk in the top of a double boiler or in a heat-proof bowl set over simmering water, stirring occasionally, until almost boiling. Discard the vanilla pod.

2. Prepare an ice-water bath. In a medium bowl, whisk together the egg yolks and sugar. Pour a little of the hot milk into the eggs, whisking constantly. Pour the remaining hot milk back into the eggs, still whisking constantly. Transfer the egg mixture back to the double boiler, and cook, whisking constantly, until the mixture thickens, about 3 minutes. Be sure not to let the mixture boil, because it will curdle.

3. Remove the pan from the heat, and pour the custard through a fine-mesh sieve into a clean bowl set in the ice-water bath. Stir the mixture as it cools to stop the cooking. When cool, transfer to an airtight container, and store in the refrigerator until ready to use, up to 2 days.

blancmange

SERVES 6

The secrets to a delicious blancmange are to warm the almonds to develop more flavor, let the almond-milk mixture steep overnight, and use as little gelatin as possible. Use the leftover almonds to make Blancmange Macaroons (recipe follows).

- 4 cups (1½ pounds) whole blanched almonds
- 1 cup sugar
- 4 to 5 cups milk

2   cinnamon sticks

½   cup heavy cream

1½ tablespoons unflavored gelatin

   Fresh berries, for serving, optional

1. Preheat the oven to 200°F. Place the almonds on a baking pan, and let warm in the oven for 10 minutes. (Do not let almonds color, or the blancmange will not be white.) Allow the almonds to cool slightly, and transfer to the bowl of a food processor. Purée the almonds and the sugar until very fine and clumps start to form, about 2 minutes. Transfer to a medium saucepan, and add 1 quart milk, the cinnamon sticks, and 1½ cups water. Warm on medium heat until hot but not bubbling. Turn off the heat, and allow to steep, covered, overnight, or up to 24 hours in the refrigerator. (The longer the mixture steeps, the more flavor it will have.)

2. Fill a 4- to 4½-cup mold with ice water, and set aside. Rinse a large piece of heavy-duty cheesecloth (if thin, use a double layer) in hot water, and wring as dry as possible. Place a sieve over a bowl, line the sieve with the cheesecloth, and pour in the almond mixture. Let the almond milk drip through for 30 minutes, then carefully gather up the ends of the cheesecloth, and wring as much of the liquid out as possible. The milk mixture should be smooth; if any pieces of almond pass through, strain the mixture through a very fine sieve. Discard the cinnamon sticks. Reserve the remaining almond mixture to make the macaroons, if using. Pour the almond milk into a measuring cup (there should be at least 3 cups of almond milk), and add enough of the remaining milk to make 1 quart of liquid. Transfer the mixture to a bowl.

3. Pour 1 cup almond milk into a wide heat-proof bowl. Add cream, then sprinkle gelatin evenly over mixture. Let stand for 5 minutes to soften. Place bowl over a shallow pan of simmering water over low heat. Stir gently until the mixture is smooth and creamy, indicating gelatin has dissolved, about 3 minutes. Remove the bowl from the heat. Stir half the remaining almond milk into the gelatin mixture to reduce the temperature, then stir the gelatin mixture into the remaining almond milk. Pour the ice water out of mold, but do not dry out the mold—this makes the blancmange easier to unmold later. Pour the almond milk into the mold through a sieve to catch any bits of congealed gelatin. Chill until firm, about 6 hours or overnight.

4. To unmold, carefully run a small knife around edge of the mold to break the seal; use your fingers to gently pull the pudding away from edges. Invert a serving platter on top; quickly turn over. Jiggle to loosen; remove the mold. Serve chilled with berries, if using.

blancmange macaroons
MAKES 6 DOZEN

1¼ cups all-purpose flour

  1   cup sugar, plus more for sprinkling

½   teaspoon kosher salt

¾   teaspoon baking soda

   Almond-sugar mixture from Blancmange (recipe, above); use 4 cups total

  3   large eggs

  1   teaspoon pure vanilla extract

50 to 60 (2 to 3 ounces) whole blanched almonds

1. Preheat the oven to 375°F. In a bowl, whisk together the flour, sugar, salt, and baking soda.

2. In another bowl, combine the almond mixture with 2 eggs and the vanilla.

3. Stir flour mixture into almond mixture. Drop by rounded tablespoons, 1 inch apart, onto a parchment-paper-lined baking sheet. Press an almond into the top of each cookie.

4. Lightly beat remaining egg in a small bowl with 1 teaspoon water; brush over cookies. Sprinkle with sugar. Bake until cookies are light golden and firm, 20 to 25 minutes. Cool on rack; serve.

floating island

SERVES 6

Floating island, or *île flottante* in French, is a light, airy dessert consisting of a large baked meringue served in a pool of custard sauce. Caramel sauce, which is traditionally drizzled over the meringue, is replaced in this recipe with a show-stopping crown of golden spun sugar. If you prefer to pool and drizzle each serving with caramel sauce, see page 406.

Unsalted butter, room temperature,
for mold and parchment

10 large egg whites

½ teaspoon cream of tartar

1 cup sugar

Strawberry-Lemon Sauce (recipe opposite)

Spun Sugar (recipe opposite), optional

1. Preheat the oven to 350°F. with a rack in the lower third. Generously butter an 8-cup charlotte or other mold. In the bowl of an electric mixer fitted with the whisk attachment, beat the egg whites on medium-low speed until frothy. Add the cream of tartar. Gradually beat in the sugar; beat until the meringue is stiff and shiny, about 10 minutes.

2. Using a large rubber spatula, lightly pack the meringue into the prepared mold. Smooth the top. Tap the mold on the counter several times to remove any air pockets. Lightly butter a sheet of parchment or aluminum foil; place it, buttered-side down, on top of the meringue in the mold.

3. Transfer the mold to a large roasting pan, and place in the oven. Pour in enough hot tap water to reach halfway up the sides of the mold. Bake until the meringue is puffed slightly over the top of the mold and is pulling away from the sides of the pan, 20 to 30 minutes. Transfer the mold to a wire rack, and remove the parchment paper. Allow to cool for 30 minutes. The floating island may be kept in the mold, refrigerated, for 1 day.

4. To serve, unmold the floating island directly onto a serving platter. Some of the liquid may have condensed in the pan as the floating island chilled; simply drain it off of the serving platter. Pat the platter dry, and spoon the sauce around the sides. Arrange the spun sugar, if using, over the floating island, and serve immediately.

MERINGUES

● *Eggs are easier to separate when they are cold, but the egg whites create more volume when they are beaten once they have reached room temperature.*

● *When beaten, egg whites will rapidly turn into a foam that is basically a stable mass of bubbles.*

● *If egg whites do not turn into foam as they are beaten, it may be due to a trace of egg yolk—the tiniest bit of which will decrease the volume of the foam by as much as two-thirds—or fat, which manifests itself in surprising ways. For example, it clings to the surface of plastic bowls, even when washed. This is why bakers use metal, glass, or especially copper bowls, which have a stabilizing effect on egg foams.*

● *Acid, usually a small amount of cream of tartar, stabilizes egg foams.*

● *If you don't beat whites long enough, the bubbles won't stiffen and the foam will lack volume. Overbeat the whites and the proteins bond too much, causing the egg whites to turn liquidy or curdle.*

● *To beat the foam just long enough, whip it with a whisk or an electric mixer. Begin on low speed. The clear liquid will turn white and smooth as you gradually increase the speed to medium high. Stop beating when the foam is stiff enough to stand up in peaks. You should be able to turn the bowl upside down without disturbing the egg foam. If the foam turns lumpy, you have beaten too long and must start again with new whites.*

strawberry-lemon sauce

MAKES 2½ CUPS

Frozen strawberries make a delicious sauce when fresh are out of season. Lemon juice brightens their flavor, no matter the season.

- ¼ cup sugar
- 1 20-ounce bag unsweetened frozen strawberries, defrosted
- 2 tablespoons fresh lemon juice

1. Combine the sugar with ½ cup water in a small saucepan. Place over medium heat, and warm, stirring occasionally, until the sugar has dissolved. Increase heat; bring just to a boil. Remove from the heat, and let the sugar syrup cool.

2. Place the defrosted berries in the bowl of a food processor. Process until smooth, about 2 minutes. Add the lemon juice and ¼ cup reserved room-temperature sugar syrup (reserve any extra syrup to use as a sweetener). Process to combine. Transfer the mixture to an airtight container, and refrigerate until serving with floating island. May be made 1 day ahead.

. . . .

SPUN SUGAR TIP

Snip the looped ends of a wire whisk to make the perfect tool for throwing spun sugar.

. . . .

spun sugar

MAKES ENOUGH FOR 1 FLOATING ISLAND

A tiny amount of beeswax can be added to the mixture to keep the spun sugar soft and malleable. Martha never uses beeswax, but you may find it makes working with the sugar easier. If the syrup gets too thick, reheat gently for about 1 minute over low heat; if it only makes dots when thrown, it is too hot.

- Canola oil
- ½ cup sugar
- ⅓ cup light corn syrup
- 1 teaspoon grated beeswax, optional

1. Lightly oil a wooden laundry rack or two wooden spoons, securely taped side by side to your work surface with the handles extending. Cover the floor generously with layers of newspaper to protect it from the sugar.

2. In a small saucepan, combine the sugar and the corn syrup. Bring the mixture to a boil, and clip a candy thermometer onto the pan. Boil the mixture until it turns a pale amber color and the candy thermometer reads 320°F., about 6 minutes. Remove from the heat, and let cool for 2 minutes. Stir in the beeswax, if using.

3. Cool the mixture, stirring occasionally, until it reaches 250°F. Stand on a step stool so you are about 2 feet above your work surface. Dip a cut whisk or 2 forks, held side by side, into the syrup; wave the sugar back and forth over the drying rack, allowing the strands to fall in long, thin threads. Let stand until cooled slightly and the strands have set. Wrap the strands around the floating island within 30 minutes.

eton mess

SERVES 8 TO 10

This is a traditional English dessert served at Eton, the prestigious boys' school in England. It is a favorite recipe of Martha's friend and former neighbor, Caroline Santandrea.

- 3 large egg whites, room temperature
  Pinch of kosher salt
- ¾ cup plus 3 tablespoons sugar
- 2¼ pounds strawberries, hulled and quartered, if large, plus 10 reserved whole, for serving
- 3 tablespoons kirsch
- 2¼ cups heavy cream

1. Preheat the oven to 200°F with two racks centered. Line two baking sheets with parchment paper; set aside. In the bowl of an electric mixer fitted with the whisk attachment, beat the egg whites on low speed until foamy, about 2 minutes. Increase speed to medium high, add the salt, and gradually add ½ cup sugar. Beat until soft peaks form, 2 to 4 minutes. Increase speed to high. Gradually add ¼ cup sugar, 1 tablespoon at a time, until stiff and glossy, 2 to 4 minutes more.

2. Spoon ¼ cup meringue onto the baking sheet; use an offset spatula or rubber spatula to spread out to make a circle roughly 3 inches in diameter and ¾ inch high, making 8 to 10 circles.

3. Transfer the sheets to the oven, and bake 30 minutes; switch the upper and lower sheets. Bake another 30 minutes; if meringues are still white, cook 15 minutes more. When beginning to brown, remove from the oven. The meringues should be white and dry to the touch. Turn off the heat, and leave the oven door open about 20 minutes. Return the meringues to the oven, with the door closed, about 1 hour, to dry completely. The meringues may be made 2 to 3 days ahead and kept in an airtight container at room temperature.

4. While the meringues are baking, place the strawberries in a large bowl; combine with the kirsch and 3 tablespoons sugar. Refrigerate until needed, at least 1 hour, tossing occasionally.

5. In a large bowl, whip the cream until stiff peaks form. Break the meringues into 3 or 4 pieces. Arrange a layer of meringues in the bottom of a glass serving bowl. Spoon a layer of the strawberries and juices over the meringues. Top with a layer of the whipped cream. Continue to layer until all the ingredients are used, reversing the last two layers so the cream follows the meringues and the strawberries are the final layer. Arrange the whole strawberries around edge. Serve immediately.

the best chocolate soufflé

SERVES 6

Be sure to use high-quality chocolate—look for 4-ounce bars in the candy or baking sections of the supermarket.

- Unsalted butter, room temperature, for dish and parchment paper
- ¼ cup plus 2 tablespoons granulated sugar, plus more for dish
- 4 ounces bittersweet chocolate, chopped
- 1 cup milk
- 3 large egg yolks
- ¼ cup all-purpose flour
- 5 large egg whites
  Pinch of cream of tartar
  Confectioners' sugar or cocoa for dusting, optional

1. Preheat the oven to 400°F with a rack in the lower third. Butter a 1-quart soufflé dish well, dust with sugar, and tap out the excess sugar. Cut out a parchment-paper collar to extend 3 inches above the rim of the dish. Tie the collar around the dish with kitchen twine; using a pastry brush, butter the inside of the paper. Transfer the dish to the freezer to chill.

2. In the top of a double boiler or in a heat-proof bowl set over a pan of simmering water, melt the chocolate. Stir with a rubber spatula until smooth; keep warm.

3. In a medium saucepan, bring the milk just to a simmer; remove from the heat.

4. Meanwhile, in the bowl of an electric mixer fitted with the whisk attachment, beat yolks and ¼ cup sugar until pale and fluffy, about 3 minutes. Beat in the flour until well combined. With mixer running, slowly add half the hot milk.

5. Add warm egg mixture back to saucepan with remaining hot milk. Bring to a boil over medium-low heat, stirring constantly. Simmer 2 to 3 minutes more; whisk in melted chocolate. Transfer to a large bowl, and cover with plastic wrap, pressing it onto the surface. Keep warm until ready to use.

6. In a large bowl, beat the egg whites and cream of tartar until soft peaks form. Gradually add the remaining sugar. Beat until stiff and glossy.

7. Spoon a third of the whites into the chocolate base to lighten it, and whisk thoroughly until smooth. Quickly fold in the remaining whites until combined. (Don't worry if some streaks remain.) Transfer the mixture to the prepared dish.

8. Bake for 15 minutes at 400°F, then reduce heat to 375°F and bake until the soufflé is puffed and golden, about 15 minutes more. Carefully remove the collar, and dust with confectioners' sugar or cocoa, if using, and serve immediately.

lime raspberry soufflés

MAKES 4 INDIVIDUAL SOUFFLÉS

Fresh fruit is best used only in small soufflés; the short baking time prevents the fruit from becoming too watery.

Unsalted butter for dishes

½ cup plus 2 tablespoons granulated sugar, plus more for dishes

3 bright-skinned limes, washed and dried

1½ cups milk

4 large egg yolks

¼ cup plus 2 tablespoons all-purpose flour

6 large egg whites

Pinch of cream of tartar

½ pint raspberries

Confectioners' sugar for dusting, optional

1. Preheat the oven to 400°F with a rack in the lower third. Butter four 6-ounce soufflé dishes well, coat with sugar, and tap out the excess. Transfer to the freezer to chill.

2. Grate the zest of 2 of the limes into a small bowl using the fine holes of a box grater. Pour some of the milk into the bowl to pick up the zest and lime oil. Pour the lime-scented milk into a medium saucepan, and add the remaining milk. Cover and bring the milk to a simmer, and immediately remove from the heat; let steep for 15 minutes. Strain, discarding the solids, and return the milk to the saucepan over medium heat.

3. In the bowl of an electric mixer fitted with the whisk attachment, beat the yolks and ½ cup sugar until pale and fluffy, about 3 minutes. Beat in the flour until well combined. With the mixer running, slowly add half the hot-milk mixture.

4. Return the warm egg mixture to the saucepan with the remaining hot milk. Bring to a boil over medium-low heat, stirring constantly. Simmer for 2 to 3 minutes more. Transfer to a large bowl; grate the zest of the remaining lime, and add to the mixture. Cover the surface with plastic wrap to prevent a skin from forming. Keep warm until ready to use.

5. In a large bowl, beat the egg whites and cream of tartar until soft peaks form. Gradually add the remaining sugar. Beat until stiff and glossy.

6. Spoon about a third of the whites into the lime base to lighten it, and whisk until smooth. Quickly fold the remaining whites into the mixture until combined. (Don't worry if some streaks remain.) Fill the prepared dishes to about ¼ inch from top. Place a few raspberries in each dish, pressing them gently into the batter. Run your thumb around the edge of the dishes to make a groove. Transfer the dishes to a baking sheet.

7. Bake for 10 minutes at 400°F, then reduce heat to 375°F; bake 10 minutes more. Dust with confectioners' sugar, if using, and serve immediately.

pear ginger soufflés
MAKES 4 INDIVIDUAL SOUFFLÉS

This soufflé has a fruit-purée base, which makes it very light and intensely flavored.

> Unsalted butter, room temperature, for dishes
> ¼ cup plus 1 tablespoon sugar, plus more for dishes
> 3 large, ripe pears, preferably Bartlett
> 1 lemon, halved
> 1 3-inch piece of fresh ginger, peeled and cut into smaller pieces
> 2 tablespoons cornstarch
> 3 large egg yolks
> 6 large egg whites
> Pinch of cream of tartar
> 2 tablespoons poire William (pear brandy), optional

1. Preheat the oven to 400°F with a rack in the lower third. Butter four 10-ounce soufflé dishes well, coat with the sugar, and tap out the excess. Transfer the dishes to the freezer to chill.

2. Peel, quarter, and core the pears. Cut into 1-inch pieces. Squeeze the lemon halves over the pears to prevent discoloration. Place the pears and 2 tablespoons sugar in a small saucepan, and cook, stirring frequently, over medium heat until a chunky sauce forms, about 10 minutes. Transfer to the bowl of a food processor, and purée. Return to the pan.

3. Using a clean garlic press, squeeze juice from ginger into purée. Discard pulp. Continue cooking purée over low heat until thick and a spoon drawn through it leaves a trail, about 15 minutes.

4. In a small bowl, dissolve the cornstarch in 2 tablespoons water. Stir into the purée, and bring to a boil, stirring constantly. Simmer a few minutes more. Transfer to a large bowl, and beat in the egg yolks. Cover surface with plastic wrap to prevent a skin from forming. Keep warm until ready to use.

5. In a large bowl, beat the egg whites and cream of tartar until soft peaks form. Gradually add the remaining sugar. Beat until stiff and glossy.

6. Spoon a third of the whites into the pear base to lighten it. Add the poire William, if using, and whisk until smooth. Quickly fold in the remaining whites until combined. (Don't worry if there are some streaks.) Fill the prepared dishes to about ¼ inch from the top. Run your thumb around the edge of the dishes to make a groove. Sprinkle with granulated sugar.

7. Bake 10 minutes at 400°F, then reduce heat to 375°F, and continue baking for 10 minutes more. Serve immediately.

little lemon soufflés
MAKES 8 INDIVIDUAL SOUFFLÉS

This recipe uses the lemon itself as a baking dish for each individual soufflé.

> 8 large lemons, preferably Meyer
> 3 large eggs, separated
> ½ cup granulated sugar
> 2 tablespoons all-purpose flour
> Confectioners' sugar, for dusting

1. Preheat the oven to 350°F with a rack in the lower third. Trim the stem end from a lemon so that the fruit sits level. Cut the top end one-third of the way down, making sure the cut is parallel with the bottom; reserve the top. Repeat with all the lemons.

2. Hold a lemon above a strainer set over a bowl, and scoop out the pulp. Squeeze and reserve the juice. Discard the pulp. Repeat with all the lemons.

3. In the bowl of an electric mixer fitted with the whisk attachment, combine the egg yolks, ¼ cup granulated sugar, ¼ cup reserved lemon juice, and the flour. Beat on medium speed until the mixture is pale yellow, about 3 minutes. Set a small saucepan filled one-quarter with water over medium heat, and bring to a simmer. Place the bowl over the simmering water, and whisk constantly until very thick, about 8 minutes. Remove the bowl from the heat, and return to the mixer. Beat on medium speed until cool, scraping down the sides several times with a rubber spatula, about 10 minutes. Transfer to a medium bowl, and set aside. Wash and dry the mixer bowl and attachment.

4. Combine the egg whites and the remaining granulated sugar in the mixer bowl. Set a small saucepan filled with water over medium heat, and bring to a simmer. Place the bowl over the simmering water, and whisk until the sugar has dissolved and the mixture is warm. Remove from the heat, and return to the mixer fitted with the whisk attachment; beat on low speed until frothy. Gradually increase the speed until the meringue is shiny and soft peaks form, 2 to 3 minutes; do not overbeat.

5. Whisk one-third of the meringue into the yolk mixture to lighten it, and whisk until smooth. Gently fold in the remaining meringue. Carefully fill the prepared lemon shells to just the rims. Transfer to a parchment-lined baking sheet.

6. Bake until the meringue is slightly golden and rises about 1 inch above the lemons, about 15 minutes. Remove the soufflés from the oven, and transfer them to serving plates. Dust with confectioners' sugar, and garnish with the reserved lemon tops. Serve immediately.

SOUFFLÉ TIPS

● *All the equipment that comes into contact with the egg whites (including your hands!) must be perfectly clean and dry—any grease or water will prevent the whites from reaching full volume. Use lemon juice or vinegar to clean the bowls and beaters, then rinse with cold water and dry.*

● *A copper bowl produces the most stable beaten egg whites. It also makes them hard to overbeat. A second choice is stainless steel, third is glass—never use plastic. Omit the cream of tartar if using a copper bowl.*

● *Use eggs that are at least 3 days old—the foam will be fluffier and more stable than that from fresh eggs.*

● *Keep in mind that it is better to underbeat the egg whites than to overbeat them.*

● *If you want to do most of the work in advance, prepare the base, press plastic wrap tightly against the surface, and refrigerate for up to 2 days. Rewarm in a double boiler—all that's left to do is to beat the egg whites, fold them in, and bake.*

● *Refrigerate or freeze the buttered dishes; this will help the soufflé to rise straight up.*

● *A parchment collar allows for a higher, more stable soufflé. Tie the string in a bow so you can remove it easily. Pour the batter to the very top of the dish if using a collar; if not, fill to within 1 inch of the top for large dishes. If not using a collar, make a groove in the batter by running your thumb around the edge of the dish; the soufflé will rise in a top-hat shape.*

● *Make sure the oven is fully heated before baking—preheat at least 15 minutes. An oven thermometer is helpful; precise temperature is important when baking soufflés. Place the oven rack in the lower third of the oven, and remove the others.*

● *A soufflé should be served straight from the oven, but you can keep it at its peak for up to 5 minutes by turning off the oven and leaving the door ajar. Avoid drafts.*

● *Use a fork and a spoon back-to-back to break open the top of the soufflé, then spoon out the servings.*

peach melba soufflé

SERVES 6

This should be made in a soufflé dish that is 8 inches in diameter and 4 inches high.

Unsalted butter, room temperature, for dish

½ *cup plus 3 tablespoons sugar, plus more for dish*

4 *ripe peaches (about 1¼ pounds), pitted and cut into chunks*

1 *tablespoon fresh lemon juice*

3 *tablespoons Cuarenta y Tres (a Spanish liqueur) or peach schnapps*

2 *tablespoons cornstarch*

5 *large egg whites, room temperature*

¼ *teaspoon cream of tartar*

1½ *pints raspberries (about 5 cups)*

1. Preheat the oven to 350°F with a rack in the lower third. Butter a 1½-quart soufflé dish; coat with sugar, and tap out excess. Transfer to the freezer to chill.

2. In a nonreactive saucepan, combine the peaches, ¼ cup plus 1 tablespoon sugar, the lemon juice, and ¼ cup water. Cover and bring to a boil over high heat. Reduce heat to medium, and cook until the peaches are broken down and reach a saucelike consistency, about 20 minutes. Purée in the bowl of a food processor, and return to the saucepan.

3. Prepare an ice-water bath; set aside. In a small bowl, stir together the Cuarenta y Tres and cornstarch until dissolved. Place the peach purée over medium heat; whisk in the cornstarch mixture until the mixture comes to a boil, 3 to 4 minutes; continue whisking for about 30 seconds. Transfer the mixture to a large bowl set over the ice-water bath to cool; stir frequently for 5 to 10 minutes so that the cornstarch continues to thicken the mixture before the egg whites are added.

4. In a large bowl, beat egg whites and cream of tartar until soft peaks form. Gradually add 3 tablespoons sugar. Beat the mixture until stiff and glossy.

5. Gently fold about a quarter of the beaten egg whites into the chilled peach purée to lighten it; whisk until smooth. Fold in the remaining egg whites and ¾ cup raspberries; gently spoon the mixture into the prepared soufflé dish.

6. Bake until the soufflé is firm and has risen 1 to 2 inches over the top rim of the dish and is a deep golden brown, 40 to 50 minutes.

7. While the soufflé is baking, make the sauce: In a small saucepan, combine the remaining raspberries and the remaining sugar; place over medium-high heat. Simmer until the berries release their juices and are somewhat broken down, about 5 minutes. Pass through a fine strainer two times, discarding the seeds, and let cool for 5 minutes. Remove the soufflé from the oven, and serve with the warm raspberry sauce.

autumn parfait

MAKES 6

¾ *cup Arborio rice*

2¼ *cups milk*

¾ *cup sugar*

2 *lemons*

1 *vanilla bean, split lengthwise and scraped*

3 *large egg yolks*

¾ *cup heavy cream*

¼ *teaspoon pure almond extract*

9 *small (1¾ pounds) figs*

2 *tablespoons unsalted butter*

½ *cup tawny port*

1 *cup whole almonds*

2 *tablespoons honey*

1. Combine the rice and 1¼ cups water in a small saucepan. Bring to a boil, stirring occasionally. Reduce to a simmer. Continue cooking, stirring gently, 4 minutes more. Transfer to a sieve, drain, and discard the liquid.

2. Place the parboiled rice in a medium saucepan. Add 1¾ cups milk and ¼ cup sugar. Place over high heat, and bring to a boil. Reduce heat to a simmer, and cook, stirring occasionally with a wooden spoon, until the rice is soft and the liquid has evaporated, about 15 minutes. Spread out cooked rice on a baking pan and cool; cover with plastic wrap.

3. Using a vegetable peeler, remove the zest from 1 lemon, being careful not to remove the bitter white pith. Place the lemon zest, the remaining milk, and ¼ cup sugar in a small heavy-bottomed saucepan. Add the vanilla bean and seed scrapings, and stir to combine; bring the mixture to a boil over medium-high heat. Remove from the heat, and cover. Let stand 15 minutes.

4. Prepare an ice-water bath, and set aside. In a medium bowl, combine 2 tablespoons sugar and the egg yolks; whisk until pale yellow. Set the egg-yolk mixture aside.

5. Uncover infused milk mixture; return to a boil over medium-high heat. Slowly add boiling milk mixture to egg-yolk mixture, whisking constantly.

6. Return the mixture to the saucepan, and set over medium-high heat. Cook, stirring constantly with a wooden spoon, until the mixture is thick enough to coat the back of the spoon, about 2 minutes. Remove the pan from the heat immediately, and pour the vanilla sauce through a fine sieve set over a medium bowl. Discard the solids, and place the bowl in the ice-water bath to chill. Cover, and refrigerate until ready to use.

7. Place the heavy cream and almond extract in a medium bowl. Whisk until soft peaks form. Whisk one-quarter of the whipped cream into the vanilla sauce. Using a rubber spatula, gently fold in the remaining cream.

8. Place the cooked rice in a medium bowl. Stir in half of the vanilla cream, loosening the grains. Gently fold in the remaining vanilla cream; cover, and refrigerate.

9. Squeeze 2 tablespoons of juice from the peeled lemon into a small bowl; set aside. Wash, dry, and quarter the figs. Melt 1 tablespoon butter in a large skillet over medium-high heat. Add half of the figs, and sprinkle with 1 tablespoon sugar. Cook, shaking the skillet occasionally, until the sugar has melted and starts to caramelize. Add 1 tablespoon lemon juice and ¼ cup port; return the skillet to the heat. Carefully ignite the alcohol, and gently swirl the pan, loosening the cooked sugar and figs. Let the flame burn out, and cook until the liquid has reduced by half. Transfer the figs and syrup to a small bowl, and repeat the cooking process with the remaining figs, sugar, lemon juice, and port.

10. Preheat the oven to 375°F, and line a baking pan with parchment paper; set aside. In a small bowl, combine the almonds and the honey. Transfer to the baking pan, and toast until aromatic, about 12 minutes. Transfer the pan to a wire rack to cool. Roughly chop the nuts; set aside.

11. When ready to assemble, use a zester to remove the zest from the remaining lemon. Place three fig quarters in the bottom of a wide-mouthed wine glass. Top with ⅓ cup rice pudding and 1½ tablespoons chopped almonds. Make a second layer with ¼ cup pudding and another 1½ tablespoons almonds. Drizzle with the port syrup; garnish with zest. Repeat layering in five more glasses; serve.

....

RICE PUDDINGS

Choosing the rice for your pudding is important; different varieties of rice yield different textures. Using Arborio rice will yield a creamier, thicker pudding with grains of rice that are slightly al dente (the same quality that this rice gives to risotto). Basmati, jasmine, or other long-grain white rices yield soft and tender grains and a lighter pudding that can be enhanced with delicate flavors like rosewater or citrus zests.

....

tapioca with sautéed nectarines

Use the quick-cooking variety of tapioca, which looks like tiny grains and can be found in grocery stores. "Pearl" tapioca takes much longer to cook and often requires overnight soaking. The pudding may seem loose while it is hot, but it will continue to firm up as it cools; make sure not to overcook the tapioca, or the pudding will have the consistency of glue.

- 3 tablespoons quick-cooking tapioca
- ¼ cup sugar
- ¼ cup honey
- ¼ teaspoon kosher salt
- 2 large eggs
- 2 cups milk
- 2 large (about 10 ounces total) nectarines, each sliced into 10 wedges
- ¼ teaspoon ground ginger
- 4 sprigs fresh mint, optional

1. Prepare an ice-water bath; set aside. Combine the tapioca, sugar, 2 tablespoons honey, the salt, eggs, and milk in a medium saucepan, and whisk to combine. Let stand, without stirring, for about 5 minutes. Cook over medium heat, stirring, until the mixture comes to a full boil.

2. Transfer to a medium bowl set over the ice-water bath. Let stand until cool, stirring occasionally, about 15 minutes. When cool, the pudding can be refrigerated for up to 1 day before serving.

3. Just before serving, heat the remaining honey in a medium skillet over medium heat. Add the nectarine wedges, and sprinkle with the ground ginger. Cook until the fruit is just tender, about 3 minutes. Divide the pudding among four dishes, and spoon the warm nectarines over the top. Top each with a sprig of mint, if using. Serve.

creamy orange rice pudding

If you want to make this dish ahead of time, simmer the rice for 15 minutes. When ready to serve, return to a simmer, and cook for 5 to 10 minutes more before adding the cream. If too much of the milk has been absorbed to bring back to a simmer, add a little more.

- 1 orange
- 1¼ cups Arborio rice
- 1 quart milk
  Zest of 1 lemon
- ½ vanilla bean, split lengthwise and scraped
  Kosher salt
- ½ cup sugar
- ½ cup heavy cream

1. Remove the zest from the orange using the smallest holes on a box grater, and set aside. Cut the ends off the orange, and remove the peel, pith, and outer membranes, following the curve of the fruit with a paring knife. Working over a bowl to catch the juices, use the paring knife to carefully slice between the sections and membranes of the orange; remove the segments whole. Place each segment in the bowl as completed. Squeeze juice from the membranes over the sections before discarding them.

2. Place the Arborio rice, milk, the reserved orange zest, lemon zest, vanilla bean and seed scrapings, salt, and sugar in a medium saucepan, and bring to a simmer over medium-low heat. Cook, stirring occasionally, until the rice is tender and most but not all of the liquid has been absorbed, 20 to 25 minutes. Stir in the heavy cream. Remove the vanilla bean, and serve the pudding in small bowls garnished with the reserved orange sections. Serve hot.

individual summer puddings

MAKES 6

Layers of bread are saturated with berry juice in this classic English dessert. Use firm, good-quality unsliced white sandwich bread.

- 1 pint strawberries, hulled and sliced ¼ inch thick
- ¾ cup granulated sugar
- 1 pint blueberries, picked over
- 1½ pints raspberries
- ½ pint blackberries
- 2 tablespoons fresh lemon juice
  Pinch of kosher salt
- 1 large loaf fresh white bread, cut in 18 slices
- 1 cup heavy cream
- 1 teaspoon pure vanilla extract
- 1 tablespoon confectioners' sugar

1. Combine the strawberries and sugar in a large straight-sided skillet over medium heat. Cook until the berries release their juices and the sugar dissolves, about 5 minutes. Add the blueberries, raspberries, and blackberries, and cook until they release their juices but still hold their shape, about 5 minutes; the mixture will look like a thick soup. Remove from the heat, and transfer to a mixing bowl to cool. Stir in the lemon juice and salt.

2. Line six ½-cup ramekins with plastic wrap. Cut 1 circle from each slice of bread to the same size as the ramekin's diameter.

3. Spoon 2 tablespoons of the berry mixture into each ramekin. Dip 6 circles of the bread into the bowl of berries one at a time, saturating them, and place one in each ramekin. Cover with 2 tablespoons more of the berry mixture. Continue until you have 3 layers of bread and berries, ending with the bread. If there is not enough juice to saturate all the bread, press the remaining berries through a coarse sieve to yield more juice. When complete, the bread and berries should be brimming over the tops of the ramekins.

4. Arrange the ramekins in a shallow baking pan, cover with the plastic wrap, and place a cutting board or another baking pan on top large enough to cover them all. Weight the board with heavy cans (about 5 pounds), and refrigerate overnight.

5. To serve, combine the cream, vanilla, and confectioners' sugar in a large bowl; whip until stiff but soft peaks form, about 3 minutes. Invert the puddings, removing the ramekins and plastic wrap, onto serving plates. Serve the puddings with a dollop of whipped cream.

chocolate bread pudding

SERVES 8 TO 10

A 9 x 13-inch glass baking dish may be used in place of a gratin dish. If you use white bread, trim the crusts.

- 2 cups heavy cream
- 2 cups milk
- 1 vanilla bean, split lengthwise and scraped
- 3 cinnamon sticks, optional
- 1 1-pound loaf brioche or good-quality white bread
- 12 ounces bittersweet chocolate, roughly chopped
- 8 large egg yolks
- ¾ cup sugar
- 1 8-ounce container crème fraîche or heavy cream

1. Preheat the oven to 325°F. Place cream, milk, vanilla bean and seed scrapings, and cinnamon sticks, if using, in a medium saucepan; bring to a boil. Remove from heat, cover with plastic wrap, and let sit for 30 minutes to infuse the flavors.

2. Cut the brioche into ¼-inch-thick slices. Cut the slices into quarters, setting aside the rounded top pieces. Fill a 9 x 12-inch gratin dish or a deep oval roasting dish with the quartered pieces.

3. Return the milk mixture to a boil, remove from heat, and discard the vanilla pod and cinnamon sticks. Add the chocolate, and whisk until smooth. Combine the egg yolks and sugar in a large bowl, and whisk to combine. Pour the hot chocolate mixture very slowly into the egg-yolk mixture, whisking constantly, until fully combined.

4. Bring a kettle filled with water to a boil. Slowly pour half the chocolate custard over the bread, making sure all the bread is soaked through. Arrange the reserved bread on top in a decorative pattern, and press firmly so the bottom layer of bread absorbs the chocolate mixture. Spoon the remaining custard over the bread until completely covered and all cracks are filled. Place a piece of plastic wrap over the dish; press down to soak the bread thoroughly. Remove the plastic wrap; wipe the edges of the dish with a damp towel; allow to sit for 30 minutes. Place the gratin dish in a roasting pan; transfer the pan to the oven. Fill the roasting pan with boiling water halfway up the sides of the gratin dish. Bake until set, about 35 minutes. Transfer the gratin dish to a wire rack to cool for 15 minutes.

5. Whisk crème fraîche until soft peaks form. Serve pudding warm, garnished with crème fraîche.

caramel-apple bread puddings
MAKES 6 INDIVIDUAL PUDDINGS

Brioche gives a rich flavor to this pudding while producing a lighter texture than white bread.

- 2 *Granny Smith apples, unpeeled and cut into matchsticks*
- *Juice of 1 lemon*
- 1 *tablespoon unsalted butter, room temperature*
- 1 *day-old, 8-ounce loaf brioche or white bread, crusts trimmed*
- 1¼ *cups heavy cream*
- 3 *large eggs*
- ½ *cup sugar*
- ½ *teaspoon kosher salt*
- 2 *teaspoons pure vanilla extract*
- ¼ *teaspoon ground nutmeg*
- *Caramel Bourbon Vanilla Sauce (page 642)*

1. Preheat the oven to 325°F with a rack in the center. Place apples in a bowl; toss with lemon juice; set aside. Butter six 8-ounce ramekins or custard cups; place in a roasting pan. Cut brioche into 8 slices, quarter each slice, and set aside.

2. In a bowl, whisk together cream, eggs, sugar, salt, vanilla, and nutmeg. Add brioche; toss to coat.

3. Bring a kettle filled with water to a boil. Place 1 tablespoon caramel sauce in each ramekin. Add ⅓ cup apple mixture, then ⅓ cup bread mixture. Add a second layer of sauce, apple, and bread.

4. Transfer roasting pan to oven; fill pan with boiling water to within ½ inch of ramekin tops. Cover pan with aluminum foil. Cook for 20 minutes. Remove foil; cook until the puddings are set, about 20 minutes more. Transfer ramekins to a wire rack to cool 5 minutes. Using a towel, invert ramekins onto a serving platter. Serve warm with the remaining caramel sauce on the side.

banana bread puddings

MAKES 4 INDIVIDUAL PUDDINGS

- 2 tablespoons unsalted butter, plus more for ramekins
- 1¼ cups heavy cream
- 3 large eggs
- ¾ cup packed dark-brown sugar
- ½ teaspoon kosher salt
- 2 teaspoons pure vanilla extract
- 2 tablespoons dark rum
- 3 small (about 1 pound) bananas, sliced into ¼-inch-thick rounds
- 8 ounces peasant bread (about ½ loaf), crusts removed, torn into 32 small pieces

1. Preheat the oven to 325°F with a rack in the center. Place a baking pan filled with ½ inch of water in the oven. Butter four 6-ounce ramekins; set aside. Whisk together the cream, eggs, ½ cup sugar, salt, vanilla, and rum; set aside.

2. Cut the butter into 8 pieces. Place 1 piece of butter and ½ teaspoon sugar in each ramekin. Place an eighth of the banana slices in an even layer over the butter and sugar. Cover the banana with 4 pieces of bread; sprinkle each with ½ teaspoon sugar. Pour about half the cream mixture among the ramekins to soak the bread. Divide the remaining banana slices among the ramekins, sprinkle each with ½ teaspoon sugar, and top with the remaining bread; pour the remaining cream mixture over. Press to soak bread. Place 1 piece of butter in each; sprinkle with the remaining sugar.

3. Cover each ramekin loosely with aluminum foil; bake in the hot-water bath 30 minutes. Uncover; bake 30 minutes more. Transfer ramekins to cool on a wire rack for about 10 minutes before serving.

apple charlotte

SERVES 8

You will need one charlotte mold (see Equipment Sources, page 650) or one round, flat-bottomed 2-quart casserole. The applesauce filling can be made several days ahead of time.

- 11 tablespoons unsalted butter, room temperature
- 6 pounds tart apples such as McIntosh or Gravenstein, peeled, cored, and thinly sliced
- 2 tablespoons fresh lemon juice
- 1 vanilla bean, split lengthwise and scraped
- ¾ cup sugar
- 3 tablespoons brandy or Calvados, optional
- 1 loaf thin-sliced white bread or brioche
  Whipped cream, for serving, optional

1. Melt 4 tablespoons butter in large saucepan over medium-low heat. Add the apples, lemon juice, vanilla bean and seed scrapings, the sugar, and brandy, if using. Cook until the apples break down and become a chunky applesauce, about 20 minutes. Continue cooking over low heat until the mixture is stiff enough to hold its shape when you press a spoon into it, 10 to 15 minutes more. Remove and discard the vanilla bean. Let the sauce cool, and refrigerate until cold.

2. Preheat the oven to 400°F. Trim the crusts from the bread, and discard. Place 4 slices of bread together in a square, and place a 7-inch charlotte mold on top. Trace shape of mold onto bread with a knife tip; cut it to fit in bottom of mold. Butter the bread on both sides, and fit it into the mold.

3. Reserve at least 4 slices of bread for top; cut remaining slices in half lengthwise. They should be the same height as the mold. Butter rectangles on both sides; fit them against the walls of mold, overlapping like shingles. Fill with apple mixture. Cut reserved bread to fit top of mold; butter, and fit into place. Chill for 15 minutes.

4. Bake until bread is golden brown, 30 to 40 minutes. Let cool in pan at least 30 minutes. Unmold and serve warm with whipped cream, if using.

sussex pond pudding

SERVES 6

As it steams, the lemon softens and forms a tart marmalade-like pool, hence the pond reference in the name of this most famous of English puddings. Do not use a Meyer lemon for this recipe.

- 2 cups all-purpose flour, plus more for dusting
- 1 tablespoon baking powder
- ¾ teaspoon kosher salt
- 12 tablespoons (1½ sticks) chilled unsalted butter, cut into pieces
- ¾ cup packed light-brown sugar
- 1 large lemon, washed

1. Put a clean dish towel in the bottom of a large stockpot; fill halfway with water. Cover and bring to a boil over medium heat; simmer until ready to use.

2. Place flour, baking powder, and salt in the bowl of a food processor; pulse to combine. Add 8 tablespoons butter; pulse until mixture resembles coarse meal, about 10 seconds. With machine running, add ½ cup ice water, and process until the dough just holds together. Wrap the dough in plastic wrap, and refrigerate for at least 1 hour.

3. Remove two-thirds of the dough (leave the remaining dough in the refrigerator). On a lightly floured surface, roll out to ⅛-inch thickness; line a 1-quart pudding bowl or soufflé dish with dough.

4. On a lightly floured surface, roll out the remaining dough. Layer the lined pudding bowl with half the light-brown sugar and 2 tablespoons butter. Prick the lemon all over with the point of a paring knife. Place the lemon in the center of the bowl, sprinkle with the remaining sugar and butter, and cover with the remaining dough. Trim the edges.

5. Place a 10-inch circle of parchment paper over the bowl. Secure with a large rubber band. Place in the stockpot with the towel and simmering water, adding more water if it does not come halfway up the sides of the bowl. Cover; steam for 5 hours, making sure the water remains at a bare simmer. Add more water if the level drops. Carefully remove the pudding bowl from the pot, and invert onto a serving platter; serve immediately.

pies
AND
tarts

....

deepest-dish apple pie

MAKES ONE 8-INCH SINGLE-CRUST PIE;
SERVES 6 TO 8

This pie couldn't be simpler to make: Mound seasoned apple pieces in an ovenproof bowl, and drape the crust over it. Deep-dish pie plates are considered to be deeper than 1½ inches.

- 1 cup sugar
- ½ teaspoon ground cinnamon
- 1 teaspoon ground cardamom
- 6 tablespoons unsalted butter
- 15 (about 8 pounds) Granny Smith apples, peeled, cored, cut into eighths
- ¾ teaspoon pure vanilla extract
- ¼ cup plus 2 tablespoons Calvados or regular brandy
- ½ cup plus 2 tablespoons heavy cream
  All-purpose flour, for dusting
- 1 disk Martha's Perfect Pâte Brisée (page 634)
- 1 large egg yolk

1. Combine the sugar, cinnamon, and cardamom in a small mixing bowl; set aside.

2. In a large skillet, melt 2 tablespoons butter over medium-high heat. Add ⅓ the apples, ⅓ the sugar mixture, and ¼ teaspoon vanilla. Cook until the apples are golden brown, about 4 minutes. Remove from the heat, measure 2 tablespoons Calvados into a measuring cup, and add to the skillet; return to the heat, and cook 3 minutes (the Calvados may ignite; proceed with caution until the alcohol burns off, about 30 seconds). Add 3 tablespoons cream; cook, stirring, until thick, 2 to 3 minutes. Transfer to a large bowl. Repeat the step in two batches with the remaining apples.

3. On a lightly floured surface, roll out the pâte brisée to ⅛ inch thick. Measure the diameter of the ovenproof bowl (we used a bowl 8 inches wide and 6 inches deep); roll dough out to extend over the sides by 3 inches all the way around. In the center of the dough, cut a ¼-inch round hole with a paring knife or a small biscuit cutter.

4. Place apple mixture in the ovenproof bowl; drape the rolled-out pastry on top, positioning the hole in the center. Allow edge of pastry to overhang sides of bowl. Trim the edges to create a scalloped, or zigzag, edge, if desired; decorate the top with the excess dough, cut into decorative shapes, using cold water to seal it.

5. Whisk together the egg yolk and the remaining tablespoon of cream to make an egg wash; brush the wash evenly over the pie. Chill for 30 minutes.

6. Preheat the oven to 400°F. Bake until the top becomes golden brown, then loosely drape a piece of aluminum foil over the top to prevent further browning, and continue to bake until the pie bubbles, about 1 hour. Let stand about 45 minutes before serving. Serve warm or at room temperature.

classic greenmarket apple pie

MAKES ONE 9-INCH DOUBLE-CRUST PIE;
SERVES 8 TO 10

Inspired by the huge variety of apples available at the Union Square farmer's market in New York City, this pie is one of Martha's favorites. The best apple pies feature a mix of apple varieties. Look for Macoun, Granny Smith, Cortland, Jonagold, and Empire.

- 3 tablespoons all-purpose flour, plus more for dusting
  Martha's Perfect Pâte Brisée (page 634)
- 1 large egg yolk
- 1 tablespoon heavy cream
- 3 pounds assorted apples such as Macoun or Granny Smith, peeled, cored, and cut into ¼-inch-thick slices
- 2 tablespoons fresh lemon juice
- ¼ cup sugar, plus more for sprinkling
- 1 teaspoon ground cinnamon
- ¼ teaspoon ground nutmeg
- ⅛ teaspoon kosher salt
- 1 tablespoon unsalted butter, cut into small pieces

1. On a lightly floured surface, roll out one disk of the pâte brisée to a ⅛-inch-thick circle, about 13 inches in diameter. With a dry pastry brush, brush off the excess flour; roll the dough around the rolling pin, and lift it over a 9-inch pie plate. Line the pie plate with the dough, pressing it into the corners. Trim the dough so that it hangs over the pie by about ¼ inch. Transfer the pie plate to the refrigerator, and chill 30 minutes.

2. Preheat the oven to 425°F. Whisk together the egg yolk and cream to make an egg wash; set aside.

3. In a large bowl, toss together the apples, lemon juice, sugar, flour, cinnamon, nutmeg, and salt; arrange in the chilled crust. Dot with butter.

4. Roll out the remaining disk of pâte brisée as in step 1. Brush the rim of the bottom crust with the egg wash. Place the second piece of dough on top, and trim so that 1 inch overhangs all the way around. Tuck the dough under, and crimp the edges with a fork or your fingers. Transfer the pie to the refrigerator, and chill until firm, about 15 minutes.

5. Remove the pie from the refrigerator, brush with the egg wash, and sprinkle generously with sugar. Cut 4 vents in the top, allowing the steam to escape.

6. Bake until the crust begins to turn light brown, about 25 minutes. Reduce temperature to 350°F, and bake until golden brown and the juices are bubbling, 25 to 30 minutes. Let stand 30 minutes before serving. Serve warm or at room temperature.

EXTRA-CRISP PIECRUST

What better way to show off a juicy pie filling than with an extra-crisp crust? Before baking, just brush water onto the crust, and sprinkle it with sugar. This simple trick will give your crust a beautiful golden color and a delightful texture.

mrs. dunlinson's plate cakes

MAKES ONE 9-INCH DOUBLE-CRUST PIE;
SERVES 6 TO 8

Design Director James Dunlinson grew up eating these very juicy double-crust fruit pies in his native England. This is his mother Julia's recipe.

- 2 pounds Granny Smith apples, peeled, cored, and cut into 1½-inch chunks
- Juice of 1 lemon
- 1 pound raspberries
- 1 teaspoon unsalted butter, for plate
- Martha's Perfect Pâte Brisée (page 634)
- All-purpose flour, for dusting
- ½ cup sugar, plus 1 tablespoon for sprinkling
- 1 large egg

1. Preheat the oven to 375°F with a rack in the center. In a bowl, toss apples and lemon juice. Gently fold in raspberries. Set aside. Coat an 8- or 9-inch ovenproof plate with the butter. Set aside.

2. Roll half the pâte brisée on a lightly floured surface to a circle 1 inch larger than the plate, about ⅛ inch thick. Transfer to plate. Mound fruit in center of plate; sprinkle with ½ cup sugar. Brush edge with water to seal the crust.

3. Roll out remaining pastry, a few inches larger than plate; place on top of fruit. Trim off any excess, then turn edges under to seal. Flute edges; make 2 or 3 slits in the top for steam to escape. Combine egg and 1 teaspoon water in a bowl to make an egg wash; brush evenly over the cake, and sprinkle with remaining sugar. Place plate on a baking pan to catch drips. Bake until crust is golden and fruit is bubbling, 40 to 50 minutes. Transfer to a wire rack to cool about 10 minutes before serving.

NOTE *For gooseberry or currant plate cakes, replace the fruit in step 1 above with 1½ cups sugar tossed with 2 pounds (5 cups) of gooseberries (brown stems removed) or black currants. Pile sugared fruit onto the plate with the rolled-out bottom crust. Sprinkle with ½ cup sugar. Brush the pastry edge with water to seal crust. Continue with step 3 in the recipe above.*

apple-butter hand pies

MAKES 14

These hand pies are easy to transport, making them perfect for picnics and hostess gifts.

Cream Cheese Dough (page 636)

All-purpose flour, for dusting

2 cups Apple Butter (recipe follows) or prepared

¼ cup sugar

¼ teaspoon ground cinnamon

1. Divide the refrigerated dough in half. On a lightly floured work surface, roll out one half of the dough to a ⅛-inch thickness. Using a 4½-inch-round cookie cutter, cut 7 circles out of the rolled dough. Transfer the circles to a parchment-lined baking sheet, and place in the refrigerator to chill for about 30 minutes. Repeat the rolling, cutting, and chilling process with the remaining half of the dough.

2. Remove the chilled dough from the refrigerator, and let stand at room temperature until just pliable, about 3 minutes. Spoon about 2 tablespoons of the apple butter onto one half of each circle of dough. Using your fingers or the back of a spoon, spread the apple butter into the half circle to within ½ inch of the edge. Do not spread the butter too thinly. Quickly brush a little cold water around the edges of the entire circle, and fold it in half so the other side comes down over the apple butter, creating a semicircle. Seal the hand pie, and make a decorative edge by pressing the edges of the dough together with the back of a fork. Repeat with the remaining rounds. Return the hand pies to the parchment-lined baking sheet, and chill for 30 minutes more in the refrigerator.

3. Preheat the oven to 375°F. Combine sugar and cinnamon in a small mixing bowl. Remove chilled hand pies from the refrigerator, and lightly brush with cold water. Sprinkle the cinnamon sugar generously over the pies. Bake until they are golden brown and just slightly cracked, about 20 minutes. Transfer the pies to a wire rack to cool slightly before serving. Serve warm or at room temperature.

apple butter

MAKES 2 CUPS

20 apples, such as empire or Golden Delicious (about 6½ pounds), peeled, cored, and quartered

1 cup apple cider

2 tablespoons Calvados

1 large cinnamon stick

1 teaspoon ground ginger

½ teaspoon ground cardamon

½ teaspoon ground nutmeg

¼ teaspoon ground mace

Small pinch of ground cloves

1 cup sugar

2 tablespoons fresh lemon juice

1. Combine all the ingredients in a large heavy-bottomed saucepan; place over medium-high heat, and cook, stirring often with a large wooden spoon to prevent scorching, until apples are broken down and saucy, about 1 hour. Mash any large pieces of apple with the wooden spoon.

2. Reduce heat to medium. Using a rubber spatula, transfer apple mixture to a small saucepan. Continue cooking, stirring occasionally, until apples are completely broken down and butter is thick and dark, about 2½ hours. Watch carefully for scorching as it thickens. Remove from heat, and let stand to cool. Store, refrigerated, in an airtight container for up to 1 month or frozen up to 6 months.

blueberry pie

MAKES ONE 9-INCH DOUBLE-CRUST PIE; SERVES 8 TO 10

To make an extra-wide lattice-top crust, roll out dough to ⅛ inch thick, and cut four 3-inch-wide strips. Chill the strips until firm. Weave the strips over the filling, and seal the lattice to the side of the bottom crust with a wash of egg and milk.

¼ cup all-purpose flour, plus more
  for dusting

  Martha's Perfect Pâte Brisée (page 634)

1 large egg

1 tablespoon milk

3 pints blueberries, picked over

2 tablespoons fresh lemon juice

½ cup sugar

¼ teaspoon ground cinnamon

2 tablespoons unsalted butter, cut
  into pieces

1. On a lightly floured surface, roll out half the dough to a ⅛-inch-thick circle, about 13 inches in diameter. With a dry pastry brush, brush off excess flour; roll the dough around the rolling pin; lift it over a 9-inch pie plate. Line pie plate with dough, pressing it into the corners. Trim dough so that it hangs over the pie plate by about ¼ inch. Turn the overhanging dough under, forming a rim, and crimp the edges of the pastry. Chill 30 minutes.

2. Preheat the oven to 425°F. Whisk together the egg and milk to make an egg wash, and set aside. Combine the blueberries, lemon juice, sugar, flour, and cinnamon in a large bowl, and turn onto the chilled bottom crust. Dot with the butter.

3. Roll out remaining dough to the same size and thickness. Brush rim of bottom crust with the egg wash, place the other piecrust on top, trim to ½ inch over the edge of the pan, and crimp the edges with a fork or your fingers. Transfer the pie to the refrigerator to chill until firm, about 15 minutes.

4. Brush evenly with the egg wash, and bake for 20 minutes. Reduce heat to 350°F, and bake until golden brown and the juices are bubbling, 30 to 40 minutes more. Let stand for 30 minutes before serving. Serve warm or at room temperature.

sour-cherry pie

MAKES ONE 9-INCH DOUBLE-CRUST PIE;
SERVES 8 TO 10

Sour cherries are usually too tart to eat raw, but they make excellent fillings for pie. Since they are only available for a few weeks at the end of June, freeze them for use throughout the summer.

¼ cup plus 2 tablespoons all-purpose flour,
  plus more for dusting

  Martha's Perfect Pâte Brisée (page 634)

1 large egg

1 tablespoon milk

7 cups fresh sour cherries, pitted

1 tablespoon fresh lemon juice

1 cup sugar

2 tablespoons unsalted butter, cut into
  small pieces

1. On a lightly floured surface, roll out half the dough to a ⅛-inch-thick circle, about 13 inches in diameter. With a dry pastry brush, brush off the excess flour; roll the dough around the rolling pin, and lift it over a 9-inch pie plate. Line the plate with the dough, pressing it into the corners. Trim the dough so that it hangs over the pie plate by about ¼ inch. Turn the overhanging dough under, forming a rim, and crimp the edges of the pastry.

2. Preheat the oven to 425°F. Whisk together the egg and milk, and set aside. Combine the cherries, lemon juice, sugar, and flour, and turn onto the chilled bottom crust. Dot with the butter. Roll out the remaining dough to the same size and thickness. Brush the rim of the bottom crust with the egg wash, place the other crust on top, trim, and crimp the edges with a fork or your fingers. Transfer to the refrigerator until firm, about 30 minutes.

3. Brush the crust evenly with the egg wash, and bake 20 minutes. Reduce heat to 350°F, and bake until the crust is golden and the juices are bubbling, 30 to 40 minutes more. Serve warm or at room temperature.

pear pie in cornmeal crust

MAKES ONE 9-INCH DOUBLE-CRUST PIE;
SERVES 8 TO 10

This recipe is as much a European tart as it is an American pie. Poach the pears the day before you make the pie.

  1 *750-ml bottle dry red wine*
  1 *cup sugar*
  4 *whole cloves*
  2 *to 3 cinnamon sticks*
 10 *ripe but firm Bartlett or Anjou pears, peeled and cut into 1-inch cubes*
  1 *tablespoon all-purpose flour, plus more for dusting*
     Cornmeal Pastry (recipe follows)
  1 *large egg beaten with 2 tablespoons heavy cream, for egg glaze*
  8 *ounces Gorgonzola cheese, sliced, optional*

1. Combine the wine, sugar, cloves, and cinnamon sticks in a large saucepan. Bring to a boil over medium heat. Reduce heat, and simmer until reduced by a third, about 10 minutes. Add the pears, and poach at a gentle simmer until tender, 15 to 30 minutes, depending on ripeness. Keep pears submerged with a pot lid slightly smaller than pan.

2. Transfer pears to a large bowl using a slotted spoon. Reduce liquid by half over high heat. Pour over pears, and let cool to room temperature; refrigerate, covered, overnight.

3. On a lightly floured surface, roll out half the pastry to a thickness of ⅛ inch and use to line a 9-inch pie plate. Chill until needed. Roll out remaining dough to a thickness of ⅛ inch and a diameter of 11 inches. Transfer to a parchment-lined baking sheet and cover; chill.

4. Preheat oven to 375°F. Sprinkle the tablespoon of flour over bottom of chilled crust. Remove spices from poaching liquid and discard. Remove pears with a slotted spoon and place in crust. (A little of the poaching liquid may end up in the pie.)

5. Let the top crust warm at room temperature for a few minutes before moving it. Brush edges of bottom crust lightly with ice water. Carefully cover pears with top crust; crimp edges, sealing well. Cut a few small vents near the center of the pie, and lightly brush the egg glaze over the crust. Bake until top is golden brown and juices start to bubble out, 50 to 60 minutes. Let cool for 1 hour. Serve with a slice of Gorgonzola, if desired.

cornmeal pastry

MAKES TWO 9-INCH CRUSTS

This pastry is more crumbly than pâte brisée; roll out dough between sheets of plastic wrap.

 1½ *cups all-purpose flour*
  ½ *cup yellow cornmeal*
  ½ *cup sugar*
  1 *teaspoon kosher salt*
  8 *tablespoons (1 stick) cold unsalted butter, cut into small pieces*
  2 *large egg yolks*
  3 *to 4 tablespoons ice water*

1. In a large bowl, mix together flour, cornmeal, sugar, and salt. Rub in the butter with your fingers, or a pastry cutter, until crumbly.

2. Mix together the egg yolks and ice water in a small bowl. Mix into dry ingredients, stirring with a fork. Knead lightly in the bowl until dough holds together; add more water if it seems dry. Divide dough in half, and press into two flat disks; wrap in plastic. Chill until firm, about 30 minutes.

....

PIE CARRIER

A freshly baked pie is always a welcome gift—even more so when it arrives wrapped inside an unusual container. A bamboo steamer is the ideal size to transport a pie and can hold two pies at once. After placing the lid on the steamer, secure it with a bow.

....

plum crumb pie

MAKES ONE 9-INCH SINGLE-CRUST PIE;
SERVES 8

Using a round tart ring makes rustic pies simple to prepare (see Equipment Sources, page 650). When making the pâte brisée for this pie, form a single large disk instead of two.

- ¼ cup plus 1 tablespoon all-purpose flour, plus more for dusting

   Martha's Perfect Pâte Brisée (page 634); form dough into 1 disk

- 6 black or red plums (2 pounds total), pitted, quartered

- ¼ cup sugar, plus more for sprinkling

- 1 teaspoon ground cinnamon

- 1 cup Crumb Topping (recipe follows)

1. Preheat the oven to 425°F. Prepare a 9 x 1¾-inch round tart ring set on a parchment-lined baking sheet. On a lightly floured surface, roll out the dough to a ⅛-inch-thick circle. Trim it into a 15-inch circle, and fit into the tart ring, leaving the excess dough overhanging.

2. Combine the plums, sugar, flour, and cinnamon in a large bowl; toss to coat.

3. Place the mixture in the shell. Fold the excess pastry over the plums, leaving the center open. Sprinkle the crumb topping over the exposed plums. Transfer the baking sheet to the refrigerator; chill until firm, about 20 minutes.

4. Bake until the crust begins to brown, about 20 minutes. Reduce heat to 375°F; bake until the crust has browned and the fruit is bubbling, about 1 hour. Let stand for 25 minutes before serving. Remove tart ring, and serve warm or at room temperature.

crumb topping

MAKES 3 CUPS

Use leftover topping for fruit crisps and cobblers.

- ¼ cup whole blanched almonds, toasted (see page 644)

- 3 tablespoons granulated sugar

- 1 cup plus 2 tablespoons all-purpose flour

- ¼ cup plus 2 tablespoons packed light-brown sugar

- ¼ teaspoon ground cinnamon

- ¼ teaspoon kosher salt

- 8 tablespoons (1 stick) chilled unsalted butter, cut into small pieces

1. Place the almonds and granulated sugar in the bowl of a food processor; process until finely ground. Transfer to the bowl of an electric mixer fitted with the paddle attachment.

2. Add the flour, light-brown sugar, cinnamon, and salt; mix on low speed until combined. Add the butter, and mix just until small clumps begin to form, about 1½ minutes. Store in an airtight container, refrigerated, up to 1 week, or frozen, up to 1 month.

EXTRA DOUGH

If you find yourself with extra dough, cut dough scraps into strips and practice your lattice-weaving technique: Braid, twist, or tie the dough in knots; scrunch each into a free-form fan. Sprinkle them with cinnamon and sugar and bake at 350°F. Alternatively, roll the dough into a small circle, pinch the sides into a cup, and spoon some jam into the center to make a miniature tart. Bake at 350°F for 10 minutes.

peach-raspberry pie

MAKES ONE 9-INCH DOUBLE-CRUST PIE;
SERVES 8

Raspberries make a better filling when mixed with another fruit; on their own, they are excessively juicy and result in a runny pie. This pie also tastes good topped with a sugary crust: Omit the egg wash, brush the pastry with cold water, and sprinkle with sugar.

- ¼ cup all-purpose flour, plus more for dusting
  Martha's Perfect Pâte Brisée (page 634)
- 1 large egg
- 1 tablespoon milk
- 4 pounds (about 8 large) peaches, cut into ¾-inch-thick pieces
- ½ pint raspberries
- ½ cup sugar
- 2 tablespoons unsalted butter, cut into pieces

1. On a lightly floured surface, roll out half the dough to a ⅛-inch-thick circle, about 13 inches in diameter. With a dry pastry brush, brush off excess flour; roll dough around rolling pin, and lift it over a 9-inch pie plate. Line pan with dough, pressing it into the corners. Trim the dough so that it hangs over the pie plate by about ¼ inch. Turn the overhanging dough under, forming a rim, and crimp the edges of the pastry. Transfer to the refrigerator to chill for about 30 minutes.

2. Preheat the oven to 425°F. In a small bowl, whisk egg and milk to make an egg wash, and set aside. Combine peaches, raspberries, sugar, and flour; turn onto chilled bottom crust. Dot with butter.

3. Roll out remaining dough to the same size and thickness. Add an extra tablespoon of flour if the peaches are very juicy. Brush rim of crust with the egg wash, place other crust on top, trim to ½ inch over the edge of the plate, and crimp the edges with a fork or your fingers. Chill pie until firm, about 30 minutes. Brush with egg wash; bake for 20 minutes. Reduce heat to 350°F, and bake until crust is golden and the juices are bubbling, 30 to 40 minutes more. Let stand for 15 minutes before serving. Serve warm or at room temperature.

lemon meringue pie

MAKES ONE 9-INCH SINGLE-CRUST PIE;
SERVES 8 TO 10

Make mini lemon meringue pies by cutting six 7-inch circles from the dough; bake in six 4½-inch pie plates.

for the crust

- All-purpose flour, for dusting
- ½ finished recipe (1 disk) Martha's Perfect Pâte Brisée (page 634)
- 1 large egg
- 2 tablespoons heavy cream

for the filling

- 1¼ cups sugar
- ¼ cup plus 2 tablespoons cornstarch
- ½ cup fresh lemon juice (3 lemons)
- 5 large egg yolks
  Kosher salt
- 2 tablespoons grated lemon zest
- 4 tablespoons unsalted butter, cut into pieces
  Swiss Meringue for Pies (page 642)

1. Preheat the oven to 400°F. On a lightly floured surface, roll out the dough to a ⅛-inch-thick circle, about 13 inches in diameter. With a dry pastry brush, brush off excess flour; roll dough around rolling pin; lift it over a 9-inch pie plate. Line pan with dough, pressing it into the corners. Trim dough so it hangs over pie plate by about ¼ inch. Turn the overhanging dough under, forming a rim, and crimp the edges of the pastry. Transfer to the refrigerator to chill for about 30 minutes.

2. In a small bowl, combine the egg and cream to make an egg wash. Prick bottom of dough shell with a fork, brush edges with egg wash, and line with parchment paper. Weight the paper down with pie weights or dried beans. Bake until edges begin to turn brown, 10 to 15 minutes. Remove the paper and the weights; continue baking until golden brown, 7 to 10 minutes more. Let cool.

3. To make filling, sift sugar and cornstarch in a bowl. Stir in 2 cups water until mixture is smooth.

4. In a nonreactive saucepan over medium heat, combine the lemon juice, egg yolks, and salt. Stir in the cornstarch mixture. Cook, stirring constantly, until the mixture comes to a boil. Lower heat until the mixture falls off spoon in thick clumps, 2 to 3 minutes. Remove from the heat; stir in the zest and the butter until smooth. Pour into a bowl, and let cool to room temperature, stirring occasionally so a skin doesn't form.

5. Pour the filling into the cooled pie shell, and refrigerate, covered with plastic wrap, until firm, about 1 hour.

6. Preheat the broiler. Spread the meringue over the pie so that it covers the filling and touches the crust all around. Broil just until golden brown on parts of the meringue, watching constantly. Serve at room temperature.

shaker citrus pie

MAKES ONE 9-INCH SINGLE-CRUST PIE;
SERVES 8

This Shaker-style pie uses the whole fruit, rind and all. To get the best flavor, choose lemons and oranges with very thin skin. The citrus zest must soak overnight.

- 2 *medium thin-skinned or juice oranges, washed*
- 1 *lemon, washed*
- 2 *cups sugar*
  All-purpose flour, for dusting
- 1 *disk Martha's Perfect Pâte Brisée (page 634)*
- 4 *large eggs*
- 1 *large egg yolk*
- 1 *tablespoon heavy cream*
  Cranberry Compote (recipe follows)

1. Cut the oranges and the lemon into paper-thin slices, and remove the seeds. Cut all but 4 slices of the lemon and 4 slices of the oranges into eighths. Place the rings and slices into a plastic container, add the sugar, mix gently, and refrigerate overnight.

2. On a lightly floured surface, roll out the dough to a ⅛-inch-thick circle, about 13 inches in diameter. With a dry pastry brush, brush off the excess flour; roll the dough around the rolling pin, and lift it over a 9-inch pie plate. Line pie plate with dough, pressing it into the corners. Trim the dough so that it hangs over the pie plate by about ¼ inch. Turn the overhanging dough under, forming a rim, and crimp the edges of the pastry. Transfer to the refrigerator to chill for about 30 minutes.

3. Preheat the oven to 400°F. Drain the oranges and lemons, reserving the fruit syrup at the bottom of the container; separate the whole slices from the cut pieces; set aside.

4. In the bowl of an electric mixer fitted with the paddle attachment, combine eggs and fruit syrup. Beat on medium high for 5 minutes, until pale yellow and fluffy. Remove the bowl from the mixer; stir in the orange and lemon eighths. Pour into the pie shell; top with the reserved whole fruit slices.

5. In a small bowl, combine the egg yolk and cream to make an egg wash. Using a pastry brush, gently brush the dough edges with the egg wash. Place the pie on a baking sheet; bake 15 minutes. Reduce heat to 350°F; continue to bake until the pie is set, 35 to 40 minutes more. Transfer to a wire rack to cool completely, 2 to 3 hours. Serve the pie at room temperature with the compote on the side.

cranberry compote

MAKES 1 CUP

This compote may be made up to 2 days in advance; return to room temperature or warm before serving.

- 2 cups fresh cranberries
  Grated zest of ½ orange
- 3 tablespoons fresh orange juice
- 1 cup sugar
- ¼ teaspoon ground cinnamon
- ½ teaspoon pure vanilla extract

Combine the cranberries, orange zest and juice, the sugar, cinnamon, and vanilla in a medium saucepan. Place over medium-high heat; cook, stirring occasionally, until the berries start to pop but are still whole, 7 to 10 minutes. Transfer to a bowl until cool.

lemon ice-box pie with coconut crust

MAKES TWO 9-INCH SINGLE-CRUST PIES;
EACH SERVES 8

- 2½ cups all-purpose flour, plus more for dusting
- 3 tablespoons sugar
- 1 cup (2 sticks) chilled unsalted butter, cut into small pieces
- 1 cup shredded sweetened coconut
- ¼ cup ice water
- 2 large egg yolks
- 2 cups heavy cream
- 4 large egg whites
- 1⅓ cups sugar
- 2 tablespoons grated lemon zest
- ½ cup fresh lemon juice (3 lemons)

1. Place flour and sugar in the bowl of a food processor. Add butter; pulse until mixture resembles coarse meal, about 10 seconds. Add ½ cup coconut, and pulse.

2. In a small bowl, beat together the ice water and the egg yolks. With the machine running, add the liquid to the flour mixture in a slow, steady stream, until the dough just holds together. (You may not need all the liquid.) Do not overprocess.

3. Turn the dough out onto a work surface. Divide into 2 equal pieces, and place on 2 separate sheets of plastic wrap. Flatten, and form two disks. Wrap, and refrigerate at least 1 hour or overnight.

4. In the bowl of an electric mixer fitted with the whisk attachment, beat the cream until stiff peaks form (do not overwhip the cream). Transfer to a bowl, and refrigerate. In a clean mixer bowl, whip the egg whites until soft peaks form. Add the sugar in a steady stream while beating. Continue to beat whites until stiff, 4 to 5 minutes. Whip in lemon zest and juice. Fold in whipped cream until just incorporated. Cover filling; chill at least 1 hour but no more than 2 hours or it might separate.

5. Preheat the oven to 400°F. On a lightly floured surface, roll out half the dough to a ⅛-inch-thick circle, about 13 inches in diameter. Using a dry pastry brush, brush off excess flour; roll dough around rolling pin, and lift it over a 9-inch pie plate. Line pie plate with dough, pressing it into the corners. Trim the dough so it hangs over the pie plate by about ¼ inch. Turn the overhanging dough under, forming a rim, and crimp the edges of the pastry. Transfer to the refrigerator to chill for about 30 minutes. Repeat with remaining dough.

6. Prick bottom of shell with a fork. Bake until golden, 18 to 25 minutes. Cool completely. While crusts cool, spread remaining ½ cup coconut on a baking sheet. Toast until golden, 5 to 7 minutes. Set aside to cool.

7. Spread the reserved cream filling in the cooled crusts, and refrigerate until ready to serve. Sprinkle with toasted coconut. Serve chilled.

NOTE *Raw eggs should not be used in food prepared for pregnant women, babies, young children, the elderly, or anyone whose health is compromised.*

eggnog cups

MAKES 8

These individual pies are made in cups, each draped with flaky pie crust and topped with the holiday flavors of eggnog. If you're not sure if your cups are ovenproof, use ordinary 6-ounce glass custard dishes instead.

- 7 large egg yolks
- ⅔ cup granulated sugar
- 2 tablespoons all-purpose flour, sifted, plus more for dusting
- 2 cups milk
- ½ vanilla bean, split lengthwise and scraped
- 1 teaspoon nutmeg, preferably fresh grated
  Martha's Perfect Pâte Brisée (page 634)
- 1 tablespoon, plus 1 cup heavy cream
- 2 tablespoons confectioners' sugar, sifted
- 1 tablespoon rum

1. Combine 6 egg yolks and sugar in electric mixer fitted with whisk attachment. Mix on high until thick and pale yellow, and ribbon forms when beaters are lifted, about 5 minutes. Add flour; mix until fully incorporated.

2. While mixing egg yolks, in a 2-quart stainless-steel saucepan, bring milk, vanilla, and nutmeg to a boil over medium-high heat. With mixer running, pour about one-quarter milk mixture into egg mixture. Slowly add egg-milk mixture to pan with remaining milk. Cook over medium heat, whisking constantly, until mixture thickens and bubbles in the center, about 5 minutes. Pass through a fine sieve into a medium bowl. Place plastic wrap directly on the surface of custard to prevent a skin from forming. Let cool, 30 to 45 minutes. When cool, chill until set, at least 2 hours.

3. On a lightly floured surface, roll out pâte brisée ⅛ inch thick. Cut into eight 6-inch squares. Place a square of dough in an ovenproof ceramic cup; let excess drape 1 to 1½ inches over edges. Repeat with remaining cups.

4. In a small bowl, mix remaining egg yolk and 1 tablespoon cream; brush over surface of dough, and refrigerate at least 1 hour.

5. Preheat the oven to 350°F. Transfer cups to a baking sheet, and gently prick bottom of dough inside cups 3 to 4 times with a fork. Bake 20 to 25 minutes, until crust is deep golden and inside of pastry shell is dry. Let cool completely on a wire rack.

6. Meanwhile, chill bowl and whisk attachment of an electric mixer. Whip remaining 1 cup cream on medium high. When cream starts to thicken, add confectioners' sugar; mix until soft peaks form. Add rum; continue to whip until soft peaks form.

7. Spoon ¼ cup chilled custard into each cooled pastry shell. Add a dollop of whipped cream; serve.

coconut cream pie

MAKES ONE 9-INCH SINGLE-CRUST PIE;
SERVES 8 TO 10

An American classic with an original topping; fluffy meringue replaces traditional whipped cream on this delicious pie.

- 1 large egg, lightly beaten
  All-purpose flour, for dusting
- 1 disk Martha's Perfect Pâte Brisée (page 634)
- ¼ cup cornstarch
- 1¼ cups plus 2 tablespoons sugar
- ¼ teaspoon kosher salt
- 2 cups milk
- ⅔ cup cream of coconut
- 3 large egg yolks
- 1 teaspoon pure vanilla extract
- 1 tablespoon unsalted butter
- 1¼ cups unsweetened coconut flakes
  Swiss Meringue for Pies (page 642)

1. In a small bowl, whisk together the egg with 2 teaspoons water to make an egg wash, and set aside. On a lightly floured surface, roll out the dough to a ⅛-inch-thick circle, about 13 inches in diameter. With a dry pastry brush, brush off the excess flour; roll the dough around the rolling pin, and lift it over a 9-inch pie plate. Line plate with the dough, pressing it into the corners. Trim the dough so that it hangs over the pie plate by about ¼ inch. Turn the overhanging dough under, forming a rim, and crimp the edges of the pastry. Lightly prick bottom of dough with a fork; brush rim with the beaten egg. Transfer the crust to the freezer for 30 minutes.

2. Preheat the oven to 375°F with a rack positioned in the lower third. Line the chilled crust with parchment paper. Weight the paper down with pie weights or dried beans. Bake until the edges begin to turn brown, 15 to 20 minutes. Remove the paper and the weights; continue baking until golden brown, 7 to 10 minutes more. Let cool. Carefully remove the weights and the paper from the crust. Continue baking until the crust is just golden, about 10 minutes more. Transfer the crust to a wire rack to cool completely.

3. Combine cornstarch, ½ cup sugar, the salt, milk, and cream of coconut in a large saucepan. Set over medium heat; cook, stirring constantly, until the mixture has thickened and some bubbles just start to appear around the edges, about 10 minutes.

4. In a medium bowl, whisk the egg yolks. Slowly whisk in the hot milk mixture. Return the mixture to the saucepan, and continue cooking over medium heat, stirring constantly, just until the bubbles begin to appear around the edges, about 10 minutes, making sure that the custard does not boil. The custard will be smooth and thick and will thicken more as it rests. Remove the saucepan from the heat.

5. Stir in the vanilla and the butter. Fold in 1 cup coconut flakes. Lay a piece of plastic wrap on the surface of the custard to keep it hot and to prevent a skin from forming. Place the lid on the saucepan.

6. Prepare the Swiss meringue. Preheat the broiler with a rack positioned in lower third of oven. Transfer the warm custard to the cooled crust. Using a large spatula, pile the meringue onto the center of the custard. Lightly spread the meringue over the custard; the meringue should cover the filling and touch the crust all around.

7. Broil just until parts of the meringue are golden brown, watching constantly.

8. Transfer the pie to a wire rack to cool for at least 2 hours. Sprinkle with the remaining ¼ cup coconut. Slice; serve. Refrigerate any leftover pie.

key lime pie

MAKES ONE 9-INCH SINGLE-CRUST PIE;
SERVES 8 TO 10

Key limes (see Food Sources, page 648) are also called Mexican limes and may be labeled as such. It is always best to use the juice of fresh fruit for pies, but bottled Key-lime or Persian-lime juice can be substituted.

1½   *cups graham-cracker crumbs,*
      about 10 cracker sheets

¾   *cup sugar*

6   *tablespoons unsalted butter, melted*
     and cooled, plus more for pie plate
     Pinch of kosher salt

1   *14-ounce can sweetened condensed milk*

4   *large eggs, separated*

¾   *cup fresh Key-lime juice*
     (about 20 Key limes)

¾   *cup heavy cream*

1. Preheat the oven to 375°F with a rack in the center. In a bowl, combine graham-cracker crumbs, 3 tablespoons sugar, butter, and salt. Press mixture into a buttered pie plate; bake until lightly browned, about 12 minutes. Cool completely on a wire rack. Reduce oven temperature to 325°F.

2. In a bowl, whisk together the condensed milk, yolks, and lime juice. Pour into the cooled crust.

3. Return pie to oven; bake until center is just set, about 15 minutes. Cool completely on a wire rack.

4. In the bowl of an electric mixer, whisk together the remaining sugar and egg whites. Place the bowl over a pot of simmering water, and stir until warm to the touch and the sugar is dissolved. Attach bowl to mixer fitted with the whisk attachment; mix on medium-high speed until stiff peaks form and meringue is glossy, about 5 minutes.

5. In a large bowl, beat cream until soft peaks form, being careful not to overmix. Gently whisk a third of the cream into the meringue to lighten it. Using a rubber spatula, fold in remaining cream.

6. Top pie with the meringue mixture; freeze just until the topping is firm enough to slice. Serve.

maple bourbon pecan pie

MAKES ONE 9-INCH SINGLE-CRUST PIE;
SERVES 8 TO 10

All-purpose flour, for dusting
1 disk Martha's Perfect Pâte Brisée (page 634)
1 cup sugar
4 tablespoons unsalted butter, melted
4 large eggs
1 cup plus 2 tablespoons dark corn syrup
½ cup pure maple syrup
2 tablespoons bourbon or dark rum
1 teaspoon pure vanilla extract
1½ cups pecan halves
2 large egg yolks
2 tablespoons heavy cream

1. On a lightly floured surface, roll out the dough to a ⅛-inch-thick circle, about 13 inches in diameter. With a dry pastry brush, brush off the excess flour; roll the dough around the rolling pin, and lift it over a 9-inch pie plate. Line the pan with the dough, pressing it into the corners. Trim the dough so it hangs over pie plate by about ¼ inch. Turn overhanging dough under, forming a rim, and crimp the edges. Using a paring knife, carefully cut out leaves from scraps of dough. Gently score leaves with veins. Place leaves on a baking sheet; chill leaves and pie crust for at least 30 minutes.

2. Preheat the oven to 400°F. In a bowl, whisk the sugar, butter, eggs, corn syrup, maple syrup, bourbon, and vanilla. Fold in half the pecan halves. Pour the filling into the chilled pie shell; arrange the remaining pecan halves on top of the pie.

3. Score outer rim of pie dough. Beat 1 egg yolk; brush beaten egg evenly over hatch marks. Adhere chilled leaves to dough in a decorative pattern. Chill pie for 30 minutes. Add 2 tablespoons heavy cream to remaining egg yolk to make an egg wash. Brush egg wash evenly over leaves; transfer pie to oven.

4. Bake 15 minutes; reduce heat to 350°F. Bake until a knife tip inserted into center comes out clean, about 1 hour 15 minutes. Serve.

chocolate pecan pie with chocolate crust

MAKES ONE 9-INCH SINGLE-CRUST PIE;
SERVES 8 TO 10

⅔ cup sugar
1 cup light corn syrup
4 ounces semisweet chocolate, chopped into ½-inch pieces
2 tablespoons unsalted butter
All-purpose flour, for dusting
Chocolate Crust (page 635)
3 large eggs
1 teaspoon pure vanilla extract
1½ cups pecan halves

1. Combine the sugar and corn syrup in a saucepan over medium-high heat; stir to partly dissolve the sugar. Bring to a boil, reduce the heat to low; simmer for 2 minutes, stirring occasionally. Cool for 45 minutes. Let thicken.

2. In the top of double boiler, or in a heat-proof bowl set over a pan of simmering water, combine 2 ounces chocolate and butter over medium-low heat; cook until melted, stirring occasionally. Cool.

3. Preheat the oven to 400°F. On a lightly floured surface, roll out the chocolate dough to a ⅛-inch-thick circle, about 13 inches in diameter. With a dry pastry brush, brush off the excess flour; roll the dough around the rolling pin, and lift it over a 9-inch pie plate. Line the plate with the dough, pressing it into the corners. Trim dough so it hangs over the plate by about ¼ inch. Turn overhanging dough under, forming a rim, and crimp the pastry edges. Chill for about 30 minutes.

4. In a large bowl, beat the eggs until foamy. Combine with the chocolate and corn-syrup mixtures. Stir in the vanilla and pecan halves; set aside.

5. Pour the filling into the chilled crust. Bake 20 minutes. Reduce heat to 350°F, and bake until the filling has set, about 20 minutes. Sprinkle with the remaining 2 ounces of chocolate, and bake 5 minutes more. Transfer to a wire rack to cool for 1¼ hours, and serve.

mary ellen's raisin pie

MAKES ONE 9-INCH DOUBLE-CRUST PIE; SERVES 8

1½ cups golden raisins

1½ cups dark raisins

1 cup sugar

¼ cup all-purpose flour, plus more for dusting

Zest of 1 lemon

2 tablespoons fresh lemon juice

1 teaspoon unsalted butter, for pie plate

Martha's Perfect Pâte Briseé (page 634)

1 large egg yolk

1 tablespoon heavy cream

1. Place raisins in a bowl, cover with boiling water, and soak for 15 minutes. Drain in a colander, discarding water; return raisins to bowl. Add sugar, flour, and lemon zest and juice. Mix thoroughly; set filling aside to thicken for 10 minutes.

2. Lightly butter a 9-inch pie plate; set aside. On a lightly floured work surface, roll out half the dough to ⅛ inch thick; drape over the pie plate. Trim the dough to fit to the plate's lip, with no overhang. Roll out remaining dough to a thickness of ⅛ inch. Measure a 9-inch circle across center; mark lightly without cutting through dough. With a round ¼-inch pastry tip or a straw, punch holes in dough; make 10 to 12 rows of holes. Work quickly so dough remains cold and is pierced easily.

3. Fill the prepared pie plate with raisin mixture. With a pastry brush, gently brush the rim of the dough with cool water; top with the perforated dough, making sure it is centered. With scissors, trim excess dough so that it creates an overhang of ½ inch. Tuck the dough overhang under itself to just sit on top of rim. Refrigerate for 30 minutes.

4. Preheat the oven to 425°F with a rack centered. Mix egg yolk and cream in a small bowl. Brush pie sparingly with egg-yolk mixture. Place pie on a baking sheet; transfer to oven. Bake 20 minutes, reduce temperature to 375°F, and bake until golden, 35 to 40 minutes more (if pie starts to brown, drape with a piece of aluminum foil). Transfer to wire rack; cool at least 30 minutes before serving.

fresh apricot almond tart

MAKES ONE 8 X 11-INCH TART; SERVES 12

This tart is fancy enough to serve for a special brunch or dinner party. It may be made up to 8 hours ahead.

for the crust

6 tablespoons unsalted butter, room temperature, plus 1 tablespoon, melted, for pan

3 ounces (about ¾ cup) whole blanched almonds

2 tablespoons plus ¼ teaspoon sugar

1 cup all-purpose flour

Pinch of kosher salt

¼ teaspoon pure almond extract

for the filling

½ cup plus 1 tablespoon granulated sugar

Pinch of kosher salt

¼ cup plus 2 tablespoons all-purpose flour

¼ cup plus 2 tablespoons blanched almond flour or very finely ground blanched almonds

½ teaspoon baking powder

2 large eggs, lightly beaten

1½ tablespoons unsalted butter, melted

¼ cup plus 2 tablespoons half-and-half

10 to 12 fresh apricots, halved and pitted

3 tablespoons blanched sliced almonds, toasted (see page 644)

Confectioners' sugar, for dusting

1. Preheat the oven to 350°F with a rack in the center. Brush an 8 x 11-inch tart pan with a removable bottom with melted butter. Set aside.

2. Place the almonds and 1 tablespoon sugar in the bowl of a food processor, and pulse until the almonds are finely ground. Add the butter, and process until combined. Pulse in the flour, the remaining 1 tablespoon plus ¼ teaspoon sugar, the salt, and the almond extract until combined. The dough will be crumbly.

3. Transfer the dough to the prepared pan. Using your fingers, pat out the dough evenly to make a thin crust along the bottom and up the sides of the pan. Chill the crust 30 minutes.

4. Bake the crust until golden, 20 to 25 minutes. Transfer to a wire rack to cool.

5. Make the filling: In a large bowl, combine ½ cup granulated sugar, the salt, all-purpose flour, almond flour, and baking powder; whisk together. Whisk in the eggs, melted butter, and the half-and-half until well combined. Pour the filling into the baked crust.

6. Arrange the apricot halves, cut-sides up, on top of the filling, packing the fruit closely together. Sprinkle the tops of the apricots with the remaining tablespoon of granulated sugar. Sprinkle the toasted almonds over the entire tart.

7. Bake the tart until the filling is puffed and golden brown, 60 to 70 minutes, rotating the pan for even browning after 30 minutes. Transfer the tart to a wire rack to cool. Unmold, and sprinkle with confectioners' sugar just before serving.

caramelized apple galette
MAKES ONE 7-INCH TART; SERVES 4

A galette is a round, flat pie or tart made from puff-pastry dough. This tart, which is caramelized on both the top and the bottom, bakes best in a cast-iron skillet. Use firm apples such as Mutsu, Golden Delicious, or Northern Spy.

All-purpose flour, for dusting

Quick Puff Pastry (page 637), or 1 sheet frozen puff pastry (from a 17¼-ounce package), thawed

1 firm baking apple, such as Northern Spy

¼ cup sugar

2 tablespoons unsalted butter

2 tablespoons Calvados or regular brandy

1. On a lightly floured surface, roll out an eighth of the puff pastry dough to about ⅛-inch thickness. Using a sharp paring knife, cut the dough into a circle about 7½ inches in diameter. Transfer to a parchment-lined baking sheet, and place in the refrigerator to chill, about 15 minutes.

2. Preheat the oven to 425°F. Place chilled dough in a cast-iron skillet that measures 6½ inches in diameter at bottom. Peel, core, and slice apple in half lengthwise. Using a mandoline or very sharp knife, slice apple halves widthwise into 25 ⅛-inch-thick slices. Arrange in a fanned pattern, overlapping apples, keeping them ½ inch in from edge of pastry dough; fill center with smaller or broken apple slices as you create fanned-out circle.

3. Sprinkle 2 tablespoons sugar over the apples, and dot with 1 tablespoon butter, cut into very small pieces. Place the skillet in the oven, and bake until the pastry has puffed up along the edges of the pan and is golden brown, about 30 minutes.

4. Remove skillet from oven. Using a spatula, remove tart from skillet; transfer to a plate; set aside. Add remaining tablespoon of butter to the skillet; place over medium heat. Add remaining 2 tablespoons of sugar; cook until sugar dissolves and forms a light caramel, about 5 minutes. Stir Calvados into caramel; cook out alcohol, about 3 minutes.

5. Return tart to skillet, apple-side down, and cook 4 to 5 minutes, until the caramel bubbles up over the tart and starts to look a little thick. Remove the skillet from the heat, and carefully invert the tart onto a plate large enough to catch the hot caramel as it drips out of the skillet. Serve warm.

caramelized lemon tart

MAKES ONE 12-INCH TART; SERVES 6 TO 8

    2 cups sugar, plus more for
       caramelizing top

    1 cup fresh lemon juice (6 lemons)

   12 large egg yolks

       Grated zest of 2 lemons

    1 cup (2 sticks) unsalted butter,
       cut into pieces

    1 12-inch Pâte Sucrée tart shell (page 635),
       baked and cooled

1. Place the sugar, lemon juice, and egg yolks in a large stainless-steel bowl, and whisk to combine.

2. Set the bowl over a pot of simmering water, and whisk until the mixture thickens, 15 to 20 minutes. Cook 5 minutes more.

3. Remove bowl from heat, and stir in the zest. Stir in the butter piece by piece until completely melted. Pour into the cooled 12-inch tart shell. Cover the surface of the lemon curd with plastic wrap to prevent a skin from forming; transfer to the refrigerator to chill until firm, at least 1 hour.

4. Preheat the broiler. Remove the outer ring from the tart pan, and place the tart on a large baking sheet. Place the outer ring (which was just removed) upside down on top to protect the pastry edges from burning.

5. Sift a thin layer of sugar evenly over the top, and place under the broiler. Watch carefully; remove the tart when the top is evenly golden brown and caramelized. Serve.

rustic cherry tart

MAKES ONE 9-INCH TART; SERVES 8 TO 10

    ½ cup blanched almond flour,
       plus more for dusting

    1 sheet frozen puff pastry, from a 17¼-ounce
       package, thawed

    5 tablespoons unsalted butter,
       room temperature

    ⅓ cup plus 4 teaspoons sugar

    1 large egg

    ½ teaspoon pure almond extract

    1 large egg yolk

    1 tablespoon heavy cream

    1 pound fresh red cherries, pitted

1. Preheat the oven to 425°F. Line a surface with parchment paper; sprinkle lightly with flour. Roll out puff pastry to an ⅛-inch thickness on the paper. Cut a 12-inch circle out of the dough. Roll up edges, making a 10-inch crust. Transfer parchment and crust to a baking sheet, and transfer to the refrigerator to chill, about 30 minutes.

2. Place the butter, ⅓ cup sugar, ½ cup almond flour, the egg, and almond extract in a bowl; mix until combined.

3. Remove crust from refrigerator; prick entire surface with a fork. In a small bowl, combine egg yolk and heavy cream to make an egg wash; brush the egg wash evenly over the surface and edges of the crust. Using an offset spatula, spread the almond mixture evenly in an ⅛-inch-thick layer in the bottom of the crust; chill 15 minutes more.

4. Remove the tart from the refrigerator, and spread the cherries in a single layer over the almond mixture. Bake 15 minutes.

5. Sprinkle the remaining 4 teaspoons of sugar over the tart, and continue baking until the edges turn deep-golden brown, 5 to 10 minutes. Transfer the tart to a wire rack to cool. Serve warm or at room temperature.

thin pear tart

MAKES ONE 8-INCH TART; SERVES 4

Pat this dough out on parchment paper—no special pans are needed.

- 2 ounces cream cheese
- 4 tablespoons unsalted butter, room temperature
- ½ cup all-purpose flour, plus more for dusting
- ½ cup plus 1½ tablespoons sugar
- ⅛ teaspoon kosher salt
- 2 tablespoons fresh lemon juice
- 2 tablespoons pear or regular brandy
- 1 Bosc or Red Bartlett pear
- ⅛ teaspoon ground cinnamon

1. Preheat the oven to 400°F with a rack in the center. Line a baking sheet with parchment paper. Combine cream cheese and butter in the bowl of a food processor. Add flour, ¼ cup sugar, and salt; process until combined. Turn the dough out onto the prepared baking sheet. With lightly floured fingers, pat the dough out into a flat 8-inch circle.

2. In a bowl, combine ¼ cup sugar with lemon juice and brandy. Halve pear lengthwise; core; leave skin on. Cut into ¼-inch-thick slices; transfer to lemon-juice mixture; coat well. Drain in a strainer. Arrange lengthwise around border, overlapping slightly; add remaining slices in center. Sprinkle with remaining 1½ tablespoons sugar. Dust with cinnamon. Bake until golden, 25 to 30 minutes. Serve warm or at room temperature.

. . . .

ALMOND FLOUR

Blanched almond flour is available at gourmet food markets and by mail (see Food Sources, page 648). If it is unavailable, you can make your own by grinding whole blanched almonds as finely as possible in a food processor. The flour will keep in your freezer for up to 6 months.

. . . .

grapefruit tarts with tarragon cream

MAKES TWO 5 X 10-INCH TARTS; EACH SERVES 4

Make this tart during the winter months, when grapefruit is especially luscious. Mint or rosemary can also be used in place of the tarragon to flavor the rich pastry cream. For leaf-shaped cookie cutters, see Equipment Sources, page 650.

- 2 large pink or ruby-red grapefruit, peel and pith removed
- 2 large white grapefruit, peel and pith removed
- 2 cups milk
- 1 vanilla bean, split lengthwise and scraped
- ½ cup plus 2 tablespoons granulated sugar
- 6 sprigs fresh tarragon
- ¼ cup plus 2 tablespoons cornstarch
- 3 large eggs
- ½ cup plus 1 tablespoon heavy cream
  All-purpose flour, for dusting
- 1 17¼-ounce package frozen puff pastry, thawed
  Superfine or granulated sugar, for sprinkling

1. Working over a bowl to catch the juices, use a paring knife to carefully slice between the sections and membranes of each grapefruit; remove the segments whole. Place each segment in the bowl as completed. Repeat the process with the remaining pink and white grapefruit. When finished, transfer the bowl to the refrigerator to chill.

2. Combine milk, vanilla bean and seed scrapings, ¼ cup sugar, and 2 sprigs of tarragon in a medium saucepan over high heat. Stir to combine, cover, and bring to a boil. Remove the pan from the heat. Allow to steep 20 minutes. Strain the mixture through a fine sieve or cheesecloth-lined strainer into a clean saucepan; discard the solids. Set aside.

3. Prepare an ice-water bath. In a bowl, whisk the cornstarch and the remaining ¼ cup plus 2 tablespoons sugar. Break 2 eggs into a bowl; whisk. Add the cornstarch mixture; whisk thoroughly.

4. Bring the infused milk to a boil again, and slowly pour over the egg mixture, whisking constantly. Return the milk-egg mixture to the saucepan, and set over medium heat. Bring to a boil, whisking constantly. Continue whisking until very thick, about 3 minutes.

5. Remove pan from heat, and transfer the mixture to a medium bowl. Place the bowl in the ice-water bath, and let sit, whisking occasionally, until room temperature. Cover the surface with plastic wrap to prevent a skin from forming, and transfer the pastry cream to the refrigerator to chill.

6. Preheat the oven to 350°F, and line a baking sheet with parchment paper; set aside. In a small bowl, whisk together remaining egg and 1 tablespoon heavy cream to make an egg wash; set aside.

7. On a lightly floured surface, roll out 1 sheet puff pastry just enough to smooth the creases. Cut a 5 x 10-inch rectangle, and place the rectangle on the baking sheet; chill. Using a paring knife or a leaf-shaped cookie cutter, cut 22 small leaves from the pastry scraps.

8. Remove the rectangle from the refrigerator. Brush the bottoms of the leaves with a dab of cold water; place them around the perimeter of the rectangle, arranging them in an overlapping pattern. Prick the inside of the rectangle with a fork. Brush the pastry evenly with the egg wash; return to the refrigerator to chill.

9. Repeat steps 7 and 8 with the remaining sheet of puff pastry.

10. Bake both pieces of pastry until puffed and golden brown, about 35 minutes. Transfer the shells to a wire rack to cool completely.

11. When ready to serve, lightly brush the remaining 4 tarragon sprigs with the remaining egg wash; sprinkle with superfine sugar. Dry on an unlined baking sheet, about 30 minutes.

12. In the bowl of an electric mixer fitted with the whisk attachment, beat remaining ½ cup cream until soft peaks form. Place the pastry cream in a bowl, and whisk to loosen; fold in the whipped cream. Spoon half of the lightened pastry cream onto each pastry shell, and smooth with an offset spatula. Top with alternating pink- and white-grapefruit segments; garnish with sugared tarragon sprigs. Slice each tart into four pieces; serve.

fig tart with cornmeal crust and cream cheese filling

MAKES ONE 14-INCH TART; SERVES 8 TO 10

If fresh figs are not available, use any fresh stone fruit or large berries. Form only one large disk of dough; do not divide the dough in half.

for the crust

>   Unsalted butter, for the pan
>   Cornmeal Pastry (page 446)

for the filling

>   4   ounces cream cheese, room temperature
>   ½   cup crème fraîche
>   1½ tablespoons confectioners' sugar
>   1   pint black or purple figs, stemmed and quartered

for the glaze

>   ¼   cup fig or red-currant jam
>   2   tablespoons red wine

1. Butter a 4½ x 14-inch rectangular fluted tart pan, and set aside. Roll out the chilled dough between two pieces of plastic wrap to about a ⅛-inch thickness. Discard the top plastic wrap, and gently invert the dough over the prepared tart pan. Discard the remaining piece of plastic wrap. Using your fingers, press the dough into the tin, and trim so the dough is flush to the edges. Repair any tears or cracks in the dough by pressing it together with your fingers. Transfer to the refrigerator to chill for about 30 minutes.

2. Preheat the oven to 350°F with a rack in the center. Prick the crust several times with a fork, and bake until the crust begins to color, 15 to 20 minutes. Transfer to a wire rack to cool completely. When cool, remove from the pan. Transfer to a serving platter.

3. Place the cream cheese in the bowl of an electric mixer fitted with the paddle attachment, and beat until smooth. Add the crème fraîche and confectioners' sugar, and beat until the mixture is smooth and fluffy, about 2 minutes. Transfer to the refrigerator to chill for 30 minutes. Spread the filling into the cooled crust, and arrange the figs on top, pressing them in slightly.

4. To make the glaze, combine the jam and wine in a small saucepan. Set over medium-high heat, and bring to a boil, stirring frequently. Reduce heat, and simmer until the mixture is thick and syrupy, about 2 minutes. Cool slightly, and brush the warm glaze over the figs with a pastry brush. Chill the tart in the refrigerator if not serving right away. Serve within several hours.

lemon-blueberry tart

MAKES ONE 8-INCH TART; SERVES 8

To make miniature unadorned lemon tartlets for bite-size desserts: Use 1- to 2-inch tartlet pans (see Food Sources, page 648) in place of the single 8-inch tart pan. Prepare pâte sucrée, line, and blind bake the tartlets in the same manner as below; the baking time will be shorter for the tiny tartlets. Watch carefully after 10 minutes when the tartlets are weighted and then about 5 minutes when they are not. Fill each with lemon curd, and return to oven to set curd, about 5 minutes. One recipe will make several dozen.

    All-purpose flour, for dusting
1 *disk Pâte Sucrée (page 635)*
    Lemon Curd for Tart Fillings (recipe follows)
1 *cup crème fraîche*
1 *tablespoon confectioners' sugar*
1 *cup blueberries, picked over*
3 *tablespoons apricot jam*

1. Preheat the oven to 375°F. On a lightly floured surface, roll out the dough to a ⅛-inch-thick circle, about 11 inches in diameter. With a dry pastry brush, brush off excess flour; roll dough around rolling pin, and lift it over an 8-inch tart pan. Line tart pan with the dough; using your fingers, gently press the dough into the pan. Trim any excess dough flush with edges of pan; chill 30 minutes.

2. Place the chilled tart pan on a baking sheet. Prick the crust all over with a fork. Line the crust with parchment paper. Weight the paper down with pie weights or dried beans. Bake until the edges begin to turn golden, 15 to 20 minutes. Carefully remove paper and weights; continue baking until golden brown, 10 minutes more. Remove from the oven, and spread the lemon curd into the tart shell. Return to the oven, and bake until the curd is set, about 10 minutes. Transfer to a cooling rack, and let cool to room temperature.

3. Place crème fraîche and confectioners' sugar in a medium bowl. Whisk until stiff peaks form, 2 to 3 minutes. Spoon into the center of cooled tart.

4. Place blueberries in a bowl. In a small saucepan, warm the apricot jam with 2 teaspoons water over medium heat, 3 to 4 minutes. Using a fine sieve, strain jam directly over blueberries. Toss blueberries until coated with jam mixture. Pile glazed blueberries on top of crème fraîche. Serve.

lemon curd for tart fillings

MAKES 1¼ CUPS

This lemon curd is a looser version of the curd used to fill layer cakes; it is held in by the sides of the tart.

- 4 large egg yolks, lightly beaten
- 1 large egg, lightly beaten
- 1 cup sugar
- ½ cup fresh lemon juice (3 lemons)
- 8 tablespoons (1 stick) unsalted butter, cut into pieces
- 1 tablespoon grated lemon zest

1. Strain the egg yolks and the egg through a fine sieve into a heavy-bottomed medium saucepan. Add the sugar and lemon juice; whisk to combine.

2. Cook over low heat, stirring constantly with a wooden spoon until the mixture thickens and coats the back of the spoon, 10 to 12 minutes. Remove from the heat; transfer to a heat-proof bowl. Stir in the butter, one piece at a time, until fully incorporated. Stir in the lemon zest. If not using immediately, cover the surface of the lemon curd with plastic wrap to keep a skin from forming. Transfer to the refrigerator to chill until firm, about 1 hour, before using. The curd may be refrigerated in an airtight container for up to 3 days.

apricot-and-berry tart with cornmeal crust

MAKES ONE 8-INCH TART; SERVES 4 TO 6

This delectable crust is pressed right into the pan—there's no rolling.

- 6 apricots, pitted and cut into eighths
- ¾ cup assorted berries, such as raspberries, blueberries, and blackberries
- ½ cup sugar
- ¾ cup all-purpose flour
- ½ cup yellow cornmeal
- ¼ teaspoon kosher salt
- 7 tablespoons unsalted butter, cut into small pieces
- 1 large egg yolk
- ½ teaspoon pure vanilla extract
  Whipped cream, for serving, optional

1. Preheat the oven to 400°F, and have ready an ungreased 8-inch tart pan with a removable bottom. In a medium bowl, toss together the apricots, berries, and ¼ cup sugar. Set aside.

2. In the bowl of a food processor, combine the flour, cornmeal, 3 tablespoons sugar, the salt, butter, egg yolk, and vanilla; pulse until dough begins to come together. Press dough into tart pan; set pan on a baking sheet. Bake until golden and slightly puffy, about 15 minutes. Remove from oven.Using a spatula, gently flatten the bottom of the crust.

3. Reduce heat to 350°F. Arrange the fruit in the tart pan. Bake 30 minutes; sprinkle with the remaining tablespoon of sugar. Bake until the apricots are juicy and tender, about 15 minutes more. Transfer to a wire rack to cool. Remove the tart from the frame; serve warm or at room temperature with whipped cream, if desired.

mango tart

MAKES ONE 9-INCH TART; SERVES 8

Assemble this tart no more than 2 hours before serving.

All-purpose flour, for dusting
1 *disk Pâte Sucrée (page 635) or Martha's Perfect Pâte Brisée (page 634)*
1½ *cups Lime Curd (page 641)*
2 *mangos, peeled and pit removed (see page 647), cut in ⅛-inch thick wedges*
¼ *cup apricot jam*

1. Preheat the oven to 400°F. On a lightly floured surface, roll out the dough to ⅛-inch-thick circle, about 12 inches in diameter. With a dry pastry brush, brush off the excess flour; roll the dough around the rolling pin, and lift it over a 9-inch tart pan. Line the pan with the dough; using your fingers, gently press the dough into the pan. Trim any excess dough flush with the edges of the pan. Prick the surface of the dough with a fork. Transfer to the refrigerator to chill for 30 minutes.

2. Line the chilled crust with parchment paper. Weight the paper down with pie weights or dried beans. Bake until the edges begin to turn brown, 15 to 20 minutes. Carefully remove the paper and the weights; reduce heat to 350°F. Return to the oven, and continue baking until golden brown, about 10 minutes more. Transfer to a wire rack to cool.

3. When the tart shell is completely cool, fill with the lime curd, using a small offset spatula to smooth the top. Arrange the mango wedges in a spiraling design on top of the lime curd.

4. Place the apricot jam and 1 tablespoon water in a saucepan over medium heat until warm and thin. Pass mixture through a fine-mesh sieve. Using a pastry brush, coat mangos with the warm jam. Refrigerate until ready to serve. Serve chilled.

summer fruit tart

MAKES ONE 12-INCH TART; SERVES 10

This recipe makes one large rustic tart; we used a paella pan, but a 12-inch pizza pan works, too. You can also use a parchment-lined baking sheet.

4 *cups plus 3 tablespoons all-purpose flour, plus more for dusting*
1 *teaspoon kosher salt*
½ *cup plus 2 teaspoons sugar, plus more for sprinkling*
1½ *cups (3 sticks) chilled unsalted butter, cut into ⅛-inch pieces*
1 *cup ice water*
6 *plums or peaches, pitted, sliced into ½-inch pieces*
4 *to 5 pints fresh berries*
Milk, for brushing dough

1. In the bowl of an electric mixer fitted with the paddle attachment, combine 4 cups flour, salt, and 2 teaspoons sugar. Add half the butter. Mix on low speed to combine, then on medium speed until mixture resembles coarse meal, about 3 minutes. Add remaining butter and ice water; mix 20 seconds. Dough will be chunky. Transfer to a piece of plastic wrap. Press into an inch-thick flattened rectangle; wrap in plastic wrap. Chill at least 1 hour.

2. Preheat oven to 375°F with a rack in center. Toss plums with 3 tablespoons flour and ½ cup sugar.

3. On a lightly floured surface, roll out dough to a ⅛-inch thickness, about 4 inches larger than pan (see headnote). With a dry pastry brush, brush off excess flour; roll dough around rolling pin, and lift it over the pan. Drape dough in pan, leaving excess dough hanging over the edge of the pan. Chill for 30 minutes. Toss berries with plums. Pile the fruit into the pan; fold the overhanging dough toward the center. Brush the dough with the milk; sprinkle with sugar. Bake until the fruit is bubbling and the crust is brown, 30 to 40 minutes. Serve.

shortbread fruit tart

MAKES ONE 9 X 11-INCH RECTANGULAR OR
10-INCH ROUND TART; SERVES 6

1½ cups all-purpose flour

⅓ cup sugar plus 1 teaspoon, plus
   more to taste

1 teaspoon baking powder

8 tablespoons (1 stick) chilled unsalted
   butter, cut into small pieces

1 large egg yolk

1 tablespoon heavy cream

3½ cups mixed summer fruit, such as plums,
   berries, currants, and apricots

2 tablespoons cognac, optional

1. Preheat the oven to 375°F with a rack in the center. Place the flour, 1 teaspoon sugar, and the baking powder in the bowl of a food processor, and pulse to combine. Add the butter, the egg yolk, and the heavy cream; process mixture until a crumbly dough forms.

2. Transfer the crumbs into a 9 x 11-inch or 10-inch round tart pan with a removable bottom. Distribute the crumbs evenly over the bottom and sides; press down with your fingers. Transfer to the refrigerator to chill for 30 minutes.

3. Remove the crust from the refrigerator, and prick the entire surface with a fork. Bake just until the crust starts to turn golden, 20 to 25 minutes. Transfer the crust to a wire rack to cool.

4. Remove any pits or seeds from fruit; cut larger fruit into wedges, leaving smaller fruit whole.

5. Place the fruit in a large bowl, and toss with the remaining ⅓ cup sugar and cognac, if using; add more sugar, depending on the sweetness of the fruit. Arrange the fruit in a single layer over the crust.

6. Bake tart until the crust is golden and the fruit is hot and bubbly, 30 to 35 minutes. Transfer the tart to a wire rack to cool slightly before serving.

shortbread with dried plum petals

MAKES ONE 14-INCH TART; SERVES 5 TO 6

Use shortbread as a base for any fruit topping. It may be made up to 2 days in advance and kept at room temperature wrapped in plastic.

8 tablespoons (1 stick) unsalted butter,
   plus 1 tablespoon, melted, for pan

¾ cup granulated sugar

1¼ cups all-purpose flour

½ teaspoon kosher salt

½ teaspoon pure vanilla extract
   Dried Plum Petals (recipe follows)

½ cup heavy cream

2 tablespoons confectioners' sugar,
   plus more for dusting

1. Preheat the oven to 275°F with a rack in the center. Brush melted butter over a 4½ x 14-inch fluted tart pan with a removable bottom; set aside.

2. In the bowl of an electric mixer fitted with the paddle attachment, cream 8 tablespoons butter and ¼ cup granulated sugar on medium-high speed until light and fluffy, about 2 minutes. Add the flour, salt, and vanilla; mix, beginning on low speed and increasing to medium, until the flour is incorporated. Using your fingers, gently press the dough evenly into the pan. Using a fork, score the dough evenly into five even pieces.

3. Bake until the edges start to take on color but the center remains pale, 45 to 55 minutes. Transfer to a wire rack to cool; unmold.

4. Place ½ cup granulated sugar in a saucepan. Add ½ cup water; bring to a boil; cook, stirring until the sugar has completely dissolved. Reduce heat to a high simmer. Cut 6 dried plum petals into smaller pieces; add. Reduce the liquid to a thick pink syrup, 10 to 20 minutes. Strain the syrup through a sieve into a medium bowl; discard the solids. Set aside.

5. In the bowl of an electric mixer fitted with the whisk attachment, beat the heavy cream and 2 tablespoons confectioners' sugar until soft peaks form, about 3 minutes.

6. To serve, top the shortbread with whipped cream, the remaining plum petals, and the syrup. Dust with confectioners' sugar. Serve.

dried plum petals

MAKES 30 PETALS

Oven drying the plums concentrates their flavors, making them tart, juicy, and sweeter all at the same time. Petals may be made up to a day ahead and kept refrigerated in an airtight container, or frozen for up to 2 months.

- 10 *plums*
- 1 *to 2 tablespoons sugar*

1. Preheat the oven to 225°F with a rack in the center. Line a baking pan with parchment paper. Slice about ⅛ inch off both ends of the plums; discard the pits. Cut each remaining piece in half, making two wedges. Arrange the plum pieces on pan, spaced ½ to 1 inch apart. Sprinkle with sugar.

2. Transfer to the oven. Dry the plums until the thinner pieces begin to curl inward and the color has deepened, 1 to 2 hours. Dry the wedges up to 30 minutes more, if necessary. Transfer to a wire rack to cool completely.

mini jam tarts

MAKES SIXTEEN 2- TO 3-INCH TARTLETS

Use whatever jam you like as the filling for these little tarts; a combination of flavors and colors always makes a pretty presentation.

- 1¾ *cups all-purpose flour, plus more for dusting*
- 2 *tablespoons sugar*
- ¼ *teaspoon kosher salt*
- ¾ *teaspoon ground cinnamon*
- 12 *tablespoons (1½ sticks) unsalted butter, cut into small pieces*
- 2 *large egg yolks*
- 2 *tablespoons ice water*
- 1 *cup homemade or prepared jam, in assorted flavors*
- 1 *tablespoon heavy cream*

1. Preheat the oven to 350°F with a rack in the center. In a food processor, combine the flour, sugar, salt, and cinnamon; process for 10 seconds. Add the butter, and process until mixture resembles coarse meal, 15 to 20 seconds.

2. Combine 1 egg yolk with the ice water, and add to the flour mixture. Process until the dough comes together, about 7 seconds. Transfer the dough to a piece of plastic wrap. Press into a flattened rectangle, wrap in plastic, and chill at least 1 hour.

3. On a lightly floured surface, roll out dough to just thinner than ¼ inch. Using a round or square cookie cutter, cut out the shapes, and press into 2- to 3-inch round tartlet pans or a small muffin-top pan. Shape the crust as desired, fill each tart with 1½ to 2 teaspoons of jam, and decorate the tops with cutouts of the remaining dough. Arrange the filled tart pans on a baking pan, and refrigerate for 15 minutes or several hours.

4. Combine the remaining egg yolk with the cream to make an egg wash; lightly brush the exposed dough with the egg wash. Bake until golden brown, 20 to 25 minutes. Transfer the tarts from the pans to a wire rack to cool. Serve.

plum-frangipane tart

MAKES ONE 4 X 13-INCH TART; SERVES 8

All-purpose flour, for dusting

1 *disk Martha's Perfect Pâte Brisée (page 634)*

Frangipane (recipe follows), room temperature

9 *Italian purple plums or 3 large black or red plums (1 pound total), halved and pitted*

1. Preheat the oven to 375°F. On a lightly floured surface, roll out dough into a ⅛-inch-thick 8 x 16-inch rectangle. With a dry pastry brush, brush off excess flour; roll dough around rolling pin, and lift it over the pan. Line pan with dough; using your fingers, gently press dough into pan. Trim any excess dough flush with edges of pan. Spread frangipane on bottom of shell; chill for 30 minutes.

2. Gently press plums, cut-sides up or down, into chilled frangipane. Place tart on a baking sheet. Bake until frangipane is brown and crust is golden, about 45 minutes. Transfer to a wire rack to cool. Serve.

frangipane

MAKES 1¾ CUPS

8 *tablespoons (1 stick) unsalted butter, room temperature*

½ *cup sugar*

1 *large egg*

4½ *ounces (1 cup) finely ground blanched almonds*

1 *tablespoon dark rum*

1 *teaspoon pure almond extract*

1 *tablespoon all-purpose flour*

In the bowl of an electric mixer fitted with the paddle attachment, cream butter and sugar on medium-low speed until light and fluffy, about 2 minutes. Add egg, almonds, rum, almond extract, and flour; beat until smooth, about 2 minutes. Frangipane will keep, refrigerated, up to 4 days.

rich chocolate tart

MAKES ONE 4 X 14-INCH TART; SERVES 8

Decorate the top of this tart by making a stencil out of cardboard, gently placing it on top of the tart, and dusting it with cocoa and confectioners' sugar. For tart pans and pre-made stencils, see Equipment Sources, page 650.

All-purpose flour, for dusting
Chocolate Dough (recipe follows)

¾ *cup heavy cream*

¼ *cup milk*

2 *tablespoons granulated sugar*

7 *ounces semisweet chocolate, chopped*

2 *large eggs, lightly beaten*

1 *teaspoon pure vanilla extract*

¼ *cup cocoa powder*

¼ *cup confectioners' sugar*

1. Preheat the oven to 375°F. On a lightly floured piece of parchment paper, roll dough into a 6 x 16-inch rectangle, ⅛ inch thick. With a dry pastry brush, brush off excess flour; roll dough around rolling pin; lift it over a 4 x 14-inch tart pan. Line pan with dough; using your fingers, gently press dough into pan. Trim any excess dough flush with edges of pan. Chill for 30 minutes.

2. Prick bottom of crust in several places with a fork. Line chilled crust with parchment paper. Weight paper down with pie weights or dried beans. Bake until edges begin to harden, 15 to 20 minutes. Transfer to a wire rack to cool completely.

3. In a pan over medium-high heat, cook cream, milk, and sugar, stirring to dissolve sugar, until just the boiling point. Place chocolate in a metal bowl. Pour cream mixture over chocolate; whisk gently. Add eggs; whisk gently. Add vanilla; whisk gently.

4. Pour filling into crust. Bake until filling is set, 30 to 35 minutes. Let cool in the pan on a wire rack.

5. Using a small sifter, sift 2 tablespoons cocoa over the tarts. Combine the remaining 2 tablespoons cocoa with the confectioners' sugar. If using, place the stencils over the tart. Sift the sugar mixture over the tart and remove the stencils. Serve.

chocolate dough

MAKES ONE 4 X 14-INCH CRUST

This makes a very soft dough; it is best rolled directly on plastic wrap or parchment paper for easier handling. The dough may be refrigerated for up to 2 days or frozen for up to 1 month.

- 1 cup all-purpose flour
- 2 tablespoons cocoa powder
- ¼ cup plus 3 tablespoons confectioners' sugar
- 8 tablespoons (1 stick) chilled unsalted butter, cut into small pieces
- 1 large egg yolk, lightly beaten
- 1 to 2 tablespoons ice water

1. Place the flour, cocoa powder, and confectioners' sugar in the bowl of a food processor; pulse to combine. Add the butter; pulse until the mixture resembles coarse meal.

2. With the motor running, add the egg yolk, then 1 to 2 tablespoons ice water; process just until dough begins to come together.

3. Shape dough into a disk; wrap in plastic and chill at least 1 hour or overnight.

chocolate macadamia-nut tart

MAKES ONE 11-INCH TART; SERVES 8 TO 10

This tart is best baked several hours in advance and left at room temperature until served.

- ½ cup all-purpose flour, plus more for dusting
- 1 disk Pâte Sucrée (page 635)
- 2 large eggs
- 1 cup sugar
- ½ tablespoon bourbon
- ¼ teaspoon kosher salt
- 12 tablespoons (1½ sticks) unsalted butter, melted and cooled
- 6 ounces semisweet chocolate, chopped
- 2½ cups (10½ ounces) unsalted whole macadamia nuts

1. Preheat the oven to 400°F with a rack centered. On a lightly floured surface, roll out the dough to ⅛-inch-thick circle, about 14 inches in diameter. With a dry pastry brush, brush off the excess flour; roll the dough around the rolling pin, and lift it over an 11-inch tart pan. Line the pan with the dough; using your fingers, gently press the dough into the pan. Trim any excess dough flush with the edges of the pan. Transfer to the refrigerator to chill for 30 minutes.

2. In a large bowl, whisk eggs, sugar, and bourbon until combined. Whisk in flour and salt. Whisk in the butter. Stir in the chocolate. Pour the mixture into the chilled tart shell. Cover the top with the nuts, pressing them halfway down into the filling.

3. Bake for 10 minutes. Reduce heat to 350°F., and continue baking until the crust and nuts are golden, about 35 minutes more. If the tart gets too brown, place a piece of aluminum foil over the top for the remainder of the cooking time. Transfer to a wire rack to cool completely. Serve.

date and pine-nut tart

MAKES ONE 4 1/4 X 13 1/2-INCH TART;
SERVES 8

½ cup all-purpose flour, plus more
for dusting

1 disk Martha's Perfect Pâte Brisée
(page 634)

½ cup pitted dates, finely chopped

4 tablespoons unsalted butter,
room temperature

½ cup sugar

2 large eggs, lightly beaten

½ cup honey

1 teaspoon pure vanilla extract

Grated zest of 1 lemon

½ teaspoon ground cinnamon

1 cup pine nuts, toasted (see page 644)

1. Preheat the oven to 350°F with a rack in the center. On a lightly floured surface, roll the pâte brisée into an 8 x 18-inch rectangle. With a dry pastry brush, brush off the excess flour; roll the dough around the rolling pin, and lift it over the tart pan. Line the pan with the dough; using your fingers, gently press the dough into the pan. Trim any excess dough flush with the edges of the pan. Transfer to the refrigerator to chill for 30 minutes.

2. In a small bowl, toss and separate the chopped dates with 2 tablespoons flour; set aside.

3. In the bowl of an electric mixer fitted with the paddle attachment, cream the butter and sugar. Add eggs, honey, vanilla, and lemon zest. Stir in the remaining ¼ cup plus 2 tablespoons of flour, the cinnamon, and the floured-dusted dates. Pour the batter into the chilled shell; sprinkle with the toasted pine nuts. Bake until the filling has browned and set, about 35 minutes. Transfer to a wire rack to cool. Serve.

cakes

. . . .

vanilla tea cake

MAKES ONE 10-INCH LOAF; SERVES 10

YOU WILL NEED one 10 x 5 x 3-inch loaf pan.

Serve this dense, buttery cake with fresh mixed berries on the side.

- 1 cup (2 sticks) unsalted butter, room temperature, plus more for pan
- 2 cups cake flour (not self-rising), plus more for pan
- ½ teaspoon kosher salt
- 1 teaspoon baking powder
- 1½ cups sugar
- 5 large eggs
- 2 teaspoons pure vanilla extract

1. Preheat the oven to 325°F with a rack in the center. Butter a 10 x 5 x 3-inch loaf pan. Line with parchment paper, and butter and flour the paper, tapping out the excess flour. Place a baking sheet on the oven rack to heat. Sift together the flour, salt, and baking powder; set aside.

2. In the bowl of an electric mixer fitted with the paddle attachment, cream butter on medium speed until light and fluffy, 3 to 4 minutes. Gradually add sugar; beat until creamy. Beat in the eggs one at a time. Add the vanilla; beat until creamy.

3. With the mixer on lowest speed, gradually add the flour mixture. Mix just until incorporated.

4. Scrape the batter into the prepared pan; tap on the countertop to settle. Place the pan on the baking sheet in the oven. Bake until the cake is golden on top and a cake tester inserted into the center comes out clean, 1 hour to 1 hour 15 minutes.

5. Transfer the pan to a wire rack to cool for 1 hour. Slide knife around the edge of the cake to loosen. Invert the pan to remove the cake, remove the parchment paper, then place cake upright on the rack. When completely cool, wrap tightly in plastic, and let stand 24 hours for the best flavor.

apple-rosemary tea bread

MAKES THREE 5½-INCH LOAVES; SERVES 10 PER LOAF

YOU WILL NEED three 5½ x 2½ x 2-inch loaf pans.

Drizzle warm clover honey on this fragrant bread.

- 4 tablespoons plus 1 teaspoon unsalted butter, plus more for pans
- 1½ cups all-purpose flour, plus more for pans
- ¾ cup plus 1 tablespoon milk
- ½ cup raisins, coarsely chopped
- 2 apples, peeled, cored, and diced
- ½ cup plus 1 tablespoon sugar
- 1 teaspoon chopped fresh rosemary
- 2 teaspoons baking powder
- ¼ teaspoon kosher salt
- 1 large egg

1. Preheat the oven to 350°F with two racks centered. Butter three 5½ x 2½ x 2-inch loaf pans. Line with parchment paper; butter and flour the paper, tapping out the excess flour. Set aside.

2. In a saucepan, heat milk over medium-high heat; bring just to a boil. Remove from heat; add raisins. Stir in 4 tablespoons butter, and let cool.

3. In a skillet over medium heat, melt the remaining teaspoon butter. Add apples; cook with 1 tablespoon sugar until apples are glazed and soft, about 3 minutes. Add rosemary; stir to combine.

4. Combine flour, the remaining ½ cup sugar, baking powder, and salt. Whisk egg into the cooled milk-raisin mixture.

5. Add the diced apples to the dry ingredients, but don't combine. Pour the wet mixture over the dry, and mix with a few quick strokes, until dry ingredients are just moistened. Do not overmix.

6. Fill prepared pans three-quarters full. Bake until a cake tester inserted in the middle comes out clean, rotating pans during baking, 20 to 30 minutes. Transfer to a wire rack to cool slightly. Turn cakes out of pans; remove parchment. Serve.

lemon–poppy seed snacking cake

YOU WILL NEED one 9 x 13-inch cake pan.

- 1 cup (2 sticks) unsalted butter, room temperature, plus more for pan and parchment
- 3 cups cake flour (not self-rising), plus more for pan
- 1¾ teaspoons baking powder
- ¼ teaspoon baking soda
- ½ teaspoon kosher salt
- 2 cups plus 2 tablespoons granulated sugar
- 4 large eggs
-    Grated zest of 3 lemons
- 1 cup nonfat buttermilk
- ½ cup plus 2 tablespoons plus 1 teaspoon fresh lemon juice
- 1 cup confectioners' sugar
- 1 teaspoon poppy seeds
- 2 tablespoons Candied Lemon Peel (page 643), for garnish

1. Preheat the oven to 350°F with a rack in the center. Butter a 9 x 13-inch cake pan; line with parchment paper. Butter and flour parchment, tapping out excess flour. Set aside. Sift together flour, baking powder, baking soda, and salt; set aside.

2. In the bowl of a mixer fitted with the paddle attachment, cream butter. Gradually add 2 cups granulated sugar; beat 1 to 2 minutes. Add eggs, one at a time, until blended. Add zest; combine.

3. Beginning and ending with the dry ingredients, alternately add the flour mixture and the buttermilk to the egg mixture. Beat until combined.

4. Spread the batter evenly in the cake pan. Bake until golden brown and a cake tester inserted in the center comes out clean, about 35 minutes. Transfer to a wire rack; let cool completely.

5. In a saucepan, combine ½ cup lemon juice and remaining granulated sugar. Cook, stirring, over medium heat until sugar is dissolved, about 2 minutes. Set syrup aside to cool. Poke holes 1 inch apart from each other in cake with a toothpick. Brush entire surface with syrup, letting it run into holes.

6. Whisk confectioners' sugar and remaining lemon juice until smooth. Spread over cake. Sprinkle with poppy seeds. Garnish with candied peel. Cut in squares; serve. The cake will keep at room temperature, covered with plastic wrap, up to 3 days.

gingerbread snacking cake

YOU WILL NEED one 9 x 13-inch cake pan.

- 8 tablespoons (1 stick) unsalted butter, room temperature, plus more for pan
- 2½ cups all-purpose flour, plus more for pan
- 1 cup boiling water
- 2 teaspoons baking soda
- 1 tablespoon ground ginger
- 1½ teaspoons ground cinnamon
- ½ teaspoon ground cloves
- ½ teaspoon ground nutmeg
- ½ teaspoon kosher salt
- 2 teaspoons baking powder
- ⅔ cup packed dark-brown sugar
- 1 cup unsulfured molasses
- 2 large eggs, room temperature, lightly beaten
-    Confectioners' sugar, for dusting

1. Preheat the oven to 350°F with a rack in the center. Butter and flour a 9 x 13-inch cake pan, tapping out excess; set aside. In a bowl, combine the boiling water and baking soda; set aside. In a bowl, sift together the flour, ginger, cinnamon, cloves, nutmeg, salt, and baking powder; set aside.

2. In the bowl of an electric mixer fitted with the paddle attachment, cream butter on medium until light. Beat in brown sugar until fluffy, 3 minutes. On low, beat in molasses, baking-soda mixture, and flour mixture. Beat in eggs, one at a time.

3. Pour batter into pan; bake until a toothpick inserted in center comes out clean, 30 to 40 minutes. Cool on a wire rack. Dust with confectioners' sugar before serving. Gingerbread will keep at room temperature, covered with plastic wrap, several days.

blueberry upside-down cake

MAKES ONE 5½-INCH CAKE; SERVES 4

YOU WILL NEED one 1-quart, 5½-inch-diameter soufflé dish.

The milk must be at room temperature to keep the butter from curdling, which prevents the cake from achieving a fluffy texture.

- 4 tablespoons unsalted butter, melted, plus more for dish
- ⅓ cup plus 3 tablespoons packed light-brown sugar
- 1½ cups blueberries
- ¾ cup cake flour (not self-rising)
- 1 teaspoon baking powder
- ¼ teaspoon kosher salt
- 1 large egg
- ¼ cup milk, room temperature

1. Preheat the oven to 350°F with a rack in the center. Butter a 1-quart, 5½-inch-diameter soufflé dish. Pour 2 tablespoons melted butter into the bottom of the soufflé dish. Sprinkle 3 tablespoons brown sugar over the melted butter. Scatter 1 cup blueberries over the sugar. Set aside.

2. In a medium bowl, whisk together the flour, baking powder, and salt. In another medium bowl, whisk together the remaining 2 tablespoons of melted butter, the remaining ⅓ cup brown sugar, and the egg. Whisk the milk into the egg mixture. Add flour mixture; whisk until batter is smooth.

3. Pour half the batter into the soufflé dish. Sprinkle the remaining ½ cup of blueberries over the batter. Spread the remaining batter over the blueberries. Bake until a cake tester inserted in the middle of the cake comes out clean, about 45 minutes. Immediately unmold the cake, inverting it onto a serving dish. Serve warm.

brown-sugar pound cake

MAKES ONE 9-INCH LOAF; SERVES 8

YOU WILL NEED one 9 x 4½ x 2¾-inch loaf pan.

- 1 cup (2 sticks) unsalted butter, room temperature, plus more for pan
- 1½ cups plus 2 tablespoons all-purpose flour, plus more for pan
- 1 cup packed light-brown sugar
- ½ teaspoon pure vanilla extract
- ½ teaspoon pure almond extract
- 4 large eggs, room temperature, lightly beaten
- 1½ teaspoons baking powder
- ½ teaspoon kosher salt

1. Preheat the oven to 375°F with a rack in the center. Butter a 9 x 4½ x 2¾-inch loaf pan; line with parchment paper, and butter and flour the paper; tap out the excess flour. Set aside.

2. In the bowl of an electric mixer fitted with the paddle attachment, cream butter and brown sugar on medium speed until light and fluffy, 2 to 4 minutes. Add vanilla and almond extracts; mix until combined. Drizzle in beaten eggs, a little at a time, mixing to incorporate after each addition.

3. In a medium bowl, whisk together the flour, baking powder, and salt.

4. Gradually add the flour mixture to the butter mixture, and mix, on low speed, just until the flour is incorporated. Using a spatula, spread the batter evenly into the prepared pan.

5. Bake until richly browned on top and a cake tester inserted into the center comes out clean, 35 to 45 minutes. Transfer to a wire rack to cool completely, about 1 hour. Run a knife around inside of pan, and turn out cake and remove the parchment. Wrap in plastic wrap, and store at room temperature up to 2 days.

honey cake with honey cream-cheese frosting

MAKES ONE 8-INCH CAKE; SERVES 8

YOU WILL NEED one 8 x 2-inch baking pan.

This recipe makes a dense, moist cake much like poundcake. It can be made several days in advance; store, covered, at room temperature. Frost the cake just before serving. Experiment with different types of honey for different flavors; the stronger the flavor, the more it will come through in the cake.

- 1 cup (2 sticks) unsalted butter, room temperature, plus more for pan
- 2 cups sifted all-purpose flour, plus more for pan
- ¼ teaspoon kosher salt
- ¼ teaspoon ground nutmeg
- 5 large eggs, room temperature
- 1½ teaspoons pure vanilla extract
- ¾ cup sugar
- ½ cup honey
  Honey Cream-Cheese Frosting (page 492)

1. Preheat the oven to 325°F with a rack in the center. Butter an 8 x 8 x 2-inch baking pan. Line with parchment paper; butter and flour the paper, tapping out the excess flour. Set aside. In a medium bowl, whisk together the flour, salt, and nutmeg, and set aside. In a small bowl, whisk together the eggs and vanilla, and set aside.

2. In the bowl of an electric mixer fitted with the paddle attachment, cream the butter on medium high until light and fluffy, scraping down sides of bowl as necessary, about 3 minutes. Add sugar and honey; beat the mixture until light and fluffy, about 3 minutes.

3. Add the egg mixture a few tablespoons at a time, beating well for 2 to 3 minutes after each addition. Raise speed to high, and beat, scraping down the sides of the bowl as necessary, until very thick and light in color, 4 to 5 minutes.

4. Add the flour mixture in 3 batches, beating just to combine after each addition. Pour the batter into the prepared pan.

5. Bake until a cake tester inserted in the center comes out clean, 40 to 50 minutes. Transfer to a wire rack for 5 minutes. Turn the cake out of the pan, and place on the wire rack, top-side up, to cool completely. Remove the parchment paper.

6. Transfer the cake to a serving platter. Using an offset spatula, spread the frosting evenly over the top of the cake. Serve.

lemon chiffon cake

MAKES ONE 7-INCH CAKE; SERVES 6

YOU WILL NEED one 7-inch tube pan, also known as an angel-food cake pan (see Equipment Sources, page 650).

- ¾ cup cake flour (not self-rising)
- ¼ teaspoon baking soda
- ¼ teaspoon kosher salt
- ¾ cup plus 1 tablespoon granulated sugar
- 3 large eggs, separated
- ¼ cup canola oil
- 2 tablespoons grated lemon zest
- 1 tablespoon fresh lemon juice
- ½ teaspoon pure vanilla extract
- ¼ teaspoon cream of tartar
  Confectioners' sugar, for dusting

1. Preheat the oven to 325°F, with a rack in the lower third. In a medium bowl, sift together the flour, baking soda, salt, and ¾ cup granulated sugar; set aside.

2. In a large bowl, whisk together egg yolks, oil, ⅓ cup water, lemon zest and juice, and the vanilla. Stir in the reserved dry ingredients until smooth.

3. In the bowl of an electric mixer fitted with the whisk attachment, beat the egg whites on medium speed until foamy. Add the cream of tartar; beat on high speed until soft peaks form, about 1 minute. Gradually add the remaining tablespoon of granulated sugar; beat on high speed until stiff peaks form, about 2 minutes more.

4. Gradually fold the egg-white mixture into the batter; start by stirring in one-third to lighten it, then fold in the remaining two-thirds. Pour the batter into an ungreased 7-inch tube pan. Using an offset spatula, smooth the top. Bake until a cake tester inserted in the center comes out clean and the cake is golden, about 45 minutes.

5. Remove the cake from the oven; invert the pan over a glass soda or other bottle for 2 hours to cool (the cake must cool upside down). Turn the cake right-side up. Run a table knife all the way down between the cake and the pan; invert again, and remove the cake. Dust the cake with confectioners' sugar before serving.

almond torte with peach sauce

MAKES ONE 8½-INCH TORTE; SERVES 8

YOU WILL NEED one 8½-inch springform pan.

Unsalted butter, for pan

¾ cup all-purpose flour, plus more for pan

1½ cups whole blanched almonds

1½ cups granulated sugar

1 tablespoon Grand Marnier or other
   orange-flavored liqueur

1 teaspoon pure vanilla extract

1 tablespoon finely grated orange zest

8 large egg whites, room temperature

½ teaspoon kosher salt

4 ounces dried peach halves or
   dried apricots, chopped (about ¾ cup)

3 tablespoons fresh lemon juice
   Confectioners' sugar, optional

1. Preheat the oven to 350°F with a rack in the center. Butter an 8½-inch springform pan; line with parchment paper, and butter and flour the parchment; tap out the excess flour.

2. Combine the almonds and 1¼ cups sugar in the bowl of a food processor. Process until the almonds are finely ground, about 1 minute. Add 1 teaspoon Grand Marnier, the vanilla, and the zest, and pulse until blended, 1 to 2 minutes.

3. In the bowl of an electric mixer, combine the egg whites and salt, and beat until the whites are stiff but not dry. Gradually fold the almond mixture into the whites.

4. Sift the flour over the egg-white mixture; fold together. Pour the batter into the pan, and smooth the top. Bake until a cake tester inserted in the center comes out clean, 40 to 45 minutes. Transfer to a wire rack to cool completely.

5. Meanwhile, combine the peaches with 1½ cups of hot water and the remaining ¼ cup sugar. Soak until the peaches are soft, about 30 minutes. Transfer the peaches and liquid to the food processor; add the lemon juice and the remaining 2 teaspoons Grand Marnier. Blend until smooth; strain through a fine sieve into a small bowl. Cover and refrigerate until well chilled.

6. Remove the torte from the pan, and remove the parchment. Dust with confectioners' sugar, if using. Cut into 10 wedges; serve with sauce on the side.

FIT TO EAT RECIPE PER SERVING: 275 CALORIES, 9 G TOTAL FAT, 30% CALORIES FROM FAT, 0 MG CHOLESTEROL, 44 G CARBOHYDRATE, 154 MG SODIUM, 7 G PROTEIN, 2 G DIETARY FIBER

angel food swirl cake

MAKES ONE 10-INCH CAKE; SERVES 10

YOU WILL NEED one round or heart-shaped 10-inch tube pan with legs or a removable bottom (see Equipment Sources, page 650).

Raspberry purée is layered in the batter and then swirled by drawing a knife through the mix. This technique creates a unique design in every slice.

1¼ cups sifted cake flour (not self-rising)

1½ cups sugar, preferably superfine
   Pinch of kosher salt

½ pint raspberries

1¾ cups egg whites (about 12 large eggs)

1 teaspoon cream of tartar

1½ teaspoons pure vanilla extract

1. Preheat the oven to 350°F with a rack in the lower third. Cut parchment to fit the bottom of the tube pan. Fit the paper into the pan. Do not grease pan.

2. Sift the flour, ½ cup sugar, and the salt together. Sift again into a bowl. Using a fork, mash ½ cup whole raspberries; strain to yield about ¼ cup mashed raspberries.

3. In the bowl of an electric mixer fitted with the whisk attachment, beat the egg whites on medium-low speed until foamy. Beat in the cream of tartar and vanilla. Raise speed to medium high; beat until the whites are nearly stiff. Reduce speed to medium low; beat in the remaining cup of sugar, 2 tablespoons at a time. Beat until the peaks are almost stiff but not at all dry. Transfer the egg whites to a large bowl.

4. Sift the flour mixture over the egg whites; fold in gently with large rubber spatula. Gently transfer one-third of the batter to the tube pan. Spoon 2 tablespoons of the mashed berries over the egg whites, keeping away from the edges. Spoon another third of the batter into the pan; repeat with the remaining mashed berries. Top with the remaining batter. Run a knife through the mixture, touching the bottom of the pan to eliminate any air pockets. Leave the top very textured with peaks in the meringue; do not smooth.

5. Bake until the top of the cake is lightly golden and the cake springs back when pressed lightly, 35 to 45 minutes. (If top darkens too quickly, tent with aluminum foil.)

6. Invert the pan onto its legs or hang it over the neck of a bottle or funnel; let the cake stand, in the pan, until completely cool, about 1 hour. Run a knife around the edges of the cake to loosen the sides. Unmold cake, and remove parchment paper. Serve with remaining whole raspberries.

1-2-3-4 lemon cake

MAKES ONE 8-INCH 4-LAYER CAKE;
SERVES 8 TO 10

YOU WILL NEED two 8 x 2-inch cake pans.

The name of this old-fashioned cake comes from its simple formula: 1 cup butter, 2 cups sugar, 3 cups flour, and 4 eggs.

- 1 cup (2 sticks) unsalted butter, room temperature, plus more for pans
- 3 cups sifted all-purpose flour, plus more for pans
- 1 tablespoon baking powder
- 1 teaspoon baking soda
- ½ teaspoon kosher salt
- 2 cups granulated sugar
- 4 large eggs, lightly beaten
- 1¼ cups buttermilk
- 1½ teaspoons pure vanilla extract
  Grated zest of 2 lemons
  Large-Quantity Lemon Curd Filling (page 640)
  Vanilla Whipped Cream (page 495)
- 12 ounces assorted fresh berries
  Confectioners' sugar, for dusting

1. Preheat the oven to 350°F with two racks centered. Butter two 8 x 2-inch cake pans, and line with parchment paper. Dust the bottoms and sides with flour, and tap out any excess. In a large bowl, sift together the flour, baking powder, baking soda, and salt; set aside.

2. In the bowl of an electric mixer fitted with the paddle attachment, cream butter on low speed to soften, increase speed to medium, and beat until light in color and fluffy. Keep beating while gradually adding the granulated sugar; beat until fluffy, about 3 minutes. Gradually drizzle in beaten eggs, beating between each addition until the batter is no longer slick, scraping down the sides twice.

3. With the mixer on low speed, alternate adding the flour mixture and the buttermilk, a little of each at a time, starting and ending with the flour. Beat in the vanilla and the lemon zest. Divide evenly between the two pans. Bake until a cake tester inserted into the center of each comes out clean, rotating the pans for even baking, if needed, 45 to 55 minutes. Transfer the pans to a wire rack to cool for 10 minutes. Remove the cakes from the pans, and return to the rack to cool, top-sides up.

4. To assemble the cake, remove the parchment paper from the bottom of each cake. Use a long serrated knife to cut each cake layer in half horizontally, creating four layers. Reserve the prettiest dome top to use for the top of the cake. Place the other top, dome-side down, on a serving platter to make the first layer. Spread with 1 cup lemon curd to within a ½ inch from the edge. Place the second cake layer over the first, and spread with 1 cup curd, covering with the third layer, and spreading with another cup of the lemon curd. One hour before serving, transfer the platter with the cake to the refrigerator to firm up the lemon curd (if the kitchen is warm and the curd gets runny, refrigerate the layers as they are completed).

5. Just before serving, place the reserved domed layer on top of the cake. Spoon on the sweetened whipped cream. Sprinkle with the mixed berries and a dusting of confectioners' sugar. Serve.

old-fashioned yellow cake with mocha buttercream frosting

MAKES ONE 8-INCH 2-LAYER CAKE;
SERVES 8 TO 10

YOU WILL NEED TWO 8 X 2-INCH CAKE PANS.

- 1 cup (2 sticks) unsalted butter, cut into 1-inch pieces, plus more for pan
- 3 cups sifted cake flour (not self-rising), plus more for pan
- 1 tablespoon baking powder
- ½ teaspoon kosher salt
- 2 cups superfine sugar
- 1½ teaspoons pure vanilla extract
- 4 large eggs, lightly beaten
- 1 cup milk
  Mocha Buttercream Frosting (page 494)

1. Preheat the oven to 350°F with two racks centered. Butter two 8 x 2-inch cake pans; line with parchment paper. Dust bottoms and sides with flour, tapping out excess; set aside. Sift together flour, baking powder, and salt three times. Set aside.

2. In the bowl of an electric mixer fitted with the paddle attachment, cream the butter on low speed to soften, increase speed to medium, and beat until light in color and fluffy. Keep beating while gradually adding the sugar; beat until fluffy, about 3 minutes. Beat in the vanilla.

3. Gradually drizzle in beaten eggs, beating between additions until the batter is no longer slick, scraping down the sides twice. With mixer on low, alternate adding flour mixture with the milk; starting and ending with the flour. Mix until just incorporated after each addition. Scrape sides of the bowl, and mix 10 seconds longer.

4. Divide evenly between the pans. Bake until a cake tester inserted into the center of each comes out clean, about 45 minutes. Transfer the pans to a wire rack to cool for 10 minutes. Remove the cakes from the pans, remove parchment, and return to the rack to cool, top-sides up.

5. To assemble, place one layer on serving platter; spread with the buttercream; top with a second layer and frost cake thinly. Chill until firm, at least 30 minutes; frost again for a smooth final layer.

lemon meringue cake

MAKES ONE 7-INCH 3-LAYER CAKE; SERVES 8

YOU WILL NEED one 7-inch tube pan, also known as an angel-food cake pan (see Food Sources, page 648).

Lemon-chiffon cake and tart lemon curd are clad in a cloud of meringue. The recipe can be doubled; use a standard 10-inch tube pan, and increase the baking time to 60 to 65 minutes. It's best to make the cake at least 4 hours before icing it with the meringue.

- 1 cup plus 2 tablespoons sifted cake flour (not self-rising)
- 1½ teaspoons baking powder
- ¼ teaspoon kosher salt
- 3 large eggs, separated, room temperature
- ¾ cup superfine sugar
- ¼ cup canola oil
- 1 teaspoon grated orange zest
- 1 teaspoon grated lemon zest
- ¼ cup fresh orange juice
- 2 tablespoons fresh lemon juice
  Pinch of cream of tartar
  Lemon Curd (page 640)
  Swiss Meringue (page 643)

1. Preheat the oven to 325°F with a rack in the lower third. In a large bowl, sift the flour, baking powder, and salt. Sift again. Set aside.

2. Place the egg yolks in the bowl of an electric mixer fitted with the whisk attachment. Beat on medium high until pale and foamy, 3 to 5 minutes. Gradually add ½ cup sugar, beating until very pale and fluffy, 5 to 7 minutes.

3. Add the oil in a steady stream. Add the orange and lemon zests; beat for 1 minute. Reduce speed to low, and add the flour mixture alternately with the orange and lemon juices, the flour in 4 parts and the liquid in 3 parts, beginning and ending with the flour. Set aside.

4. In a clean mixer bowl fitted with whisk attachment, beat egg whites on low speed until foamy. Add cream of tartar, and increase speed to medium

high. Beat until soft peaks form. Gradually add remaining ¼ cup sugar, and beat until the whites are glossy and stiff peaks form, 1½ minutes.

5. Stir a quarter of the whites into the flour-yolk mixture to lighten it. Fold in the remaining whites carefully, trying not to deflate the batter. Gently pour into an ungreased 7-inch tube pan. Bake until the cake is golden brown and a cake tester inserted into the center comes out clean, about 40 minutes.

6. Remove the cake from oven, and invert immediately onto a wire rack. Cool completely in the pan. Run a knife around the sides to loosen, and remove the outer part of the pan. Loosen the cake from the inner tube; run a knife along the bottom of the pan and around the tube to loosen. Lift cake off. Turn cake upside down onto a cake round (see Note) slightly smaller than cake. Using a long, serrated knife, horizontally slice cake into 3 layers.

7. Spread half the curd on the bottom layer. Stack a second layer over the curd; spread remaining curd on middle layer; cover with the top layer. Refrigerate overnight, or at least 4 hours. Brush off any excess crumbs with a dry pastry brush.

8. Preheat the oven to 400°F. Prepare the meringue, and spread all over the cake, swirling with an offset spatula, as desired, for design. Set the cake, still on the cake round, on an oiled baking sheet, and place in the oven. Bake, watching carefully, until the meringue is brown around the edges and beginning to brown elsewhere. Transfer to a serving plate, and serve immediately. For clean cutting, slice using a knife dipped in hot water and wiped dry.

NOTE *A cake round is useful for moving layers when assembling cakes. Use the bottom of a springform pan, or make one out of corrugated cardboard wrapped in foil.*

MAKING LAYER CAKES

- *Bring ingredients to room temperature before using them in cakes.*

- *Do not substitute self-rising cake flour for cake flour. The self-rising variety has baking powder and salt added to it. Cake flour produces a finer crumb than all-purpose flour, but if you cannot find cake flour, follow this conversion: Remove 2 tablespoons of all-purpose flour for every 1 cup of cake flour called for. For example, 2 cups cake flour equals 1¾ cups all-purpose flour (1 cup equals 16 tablespoons).*

- *If a recipe calls for a quantity of sifted cake flour, sift it first, and then measure.*

- *Use the exact pan size called for. Place the cake pan on a preheated baking sheet as it is slid into the oven. For easy removal from the pan and uniform layers, line the pan bottom and sides with parchment paper.*

- *Don't crowd the cake pans. They should not touch each other or the sides of the oven, or hot air will not circulate and bake layers evenly.*

- *Cake layers must be cool before splitting and icing. For best results, bake them a day ahead, wrap layers in plastic, and keep at room temperature.*

- *Use wooden skewers to support the layers as you stack and fill them.*

- *A rotating cake stand (see Equipment Sources, page 650) and an offset spatula make icing easy.*

boston cream pie

MAKES ONE 9-INCH 2-LAYER CAKE;
SERVES 8 TO 10

YOU WILL NEED one 9 x 2-inch cake pan.

This American classic, first made by a chef at a Boston hotel in the 1850s, isn't a pie at all. Though it is a cake made from two sponge layers, it was probably first baked in pie pans, which were more common in 19th-century New England. This version is baked in one 9-inch cake pan and split horizontally into two layers; an 8-inch pan is too small for the batter.

for the hot-milk sponge cake

Unsalted butter, for cake pan

1 cup sifted cake flour (not self-rising), plus more for pan

¼ teaspoon kosher salt

4 large eggs

1 cup sugar

¼ cup plus 2 tablespoons milk

1 vanilla bean, split lengthwise and scraped

for the custard-cream filling

6 large egg yolks

¾ cup sugar

¼ cup plus 2½ tablespoons cornstarch

⅛ teaspoon kosher salt

3 cups milk

2 teaspoons pure vanilla extract

for the shiny chocolate glaze

4 ounces best-quality semisweet chocolate, coarsely chopped

½ cup heavy cream

1. Make the hot-milk sponge cake. Preheat the oven to 350°F with a rack in the center. Place a baking sheet on the rack below to catch any spills. Butter one 9 x 2-inch cake pan, and line with parchment paper. Dust the bottoms and sides with flour, and tap out the excess. Set aside.

2. Sift together the cake flour and the salt. Sift again, twice; set aside. In the bowl of an electric mixer fitted with the whisk attachment, beat the eggs and sugar until well combined. Place the bowl over a pan of simmering water; whisk until the mixture is warm, about 110°F, and the sugar is dissolved, about 5 minutes. Remove from the heat; return the bowl to the mixer. Beat the egg mixture on high until thickened and pale, about 6 minutes.

3. In a small saucepan, combine the milk and vanilla bean and seed scrapings. Place over medium heat until hot, being careful not to boil. Remove and discard the vanilla bean. With egg mixture beating, pour hot milk into egg mixture in a slow, steady stream. Transfer to a large bowl, and fold in flour mixture. Pour batter into the prepared pan.

4. Bake until the cake is golden brown and springs back when gently pressed with a finger, about 30 minutes. Transfer the pan to a wire rack to cool for 15 minutes. Remove from pan; cool completely. Remove parchment paper.

5. Make the custard-cream filling. While the cake is baking, make the filling. Prepare an ice-water bath. In a large bowl, whisk the egg yolks; set aside. In a medium saucepan, combine the sugar, cornstarch, and salt. Gradually stir in the milk. Cook over medium heat, stirring constantly with a wooden spoon, until the mixture thickens and begins to bubble, about 5 minutes. (It is essential that the mixture comes to a boil.) Remove from the heat.

6. Whisking constantly, slowly pour the hot milk mixture into the egg yolks. Return the mixture to the saucepan. Cook over medium heat, stirring constantly with the wooden spoon, until the mixture begins to bubble, about 3 minutes. (It is essential that the mixture bubbles again.) Remove from the heat; stir in the vanilla.

7. Transfer the filling to a medium bowl. Place the bowl in the ice-water bath. Stir from time to time until the mixture cools; it thickens as it cools. Once completely cool the filling is very thick; it must be covered with plastic wrap, pressing the wrap against the filling to prevent a skin from forming; the filling may be refrigerated overnight at this stage, or it is ready to use.

8. Use a long serrated knife to cut the cake layer in half horizontally, creating two layers; spread the bottom half with chilled filling, to within only ½ inch of the edge so filling does not ooze out. Transfer bottom layer to the refrigerator to set, about 30 minutes. Wrap remaining half of the cake with plastic wrap; set aside.

9. In the top of a double boiler or in a medium heatproof bowl set over a pan of simmering water, combine chocolate and heavy cream. Stir occasionally until the chocolate melts, about 12 minutes. Remove from heat; set aside to cool for 10 minutes.

10. To assemble, remove cake from the refrigerator; top with reserved layer. Transfer cake to a serving platter; pour the warm chocolate glaze over top. Allow to set 20 minutes before serving.

banana cake

MAKES ONE 8-INCH 4-LAYER CAKE;
SERVES 8 TO 10

YOU WILL NEED two 8 x 2-inch cake pans.

A fancy version of the classic snack cake, this layer cake is swathed in shiny cream-cheese frosting and filled with a layer of chocolate and sautéed bananas. Make the frosting first so it can chill while the cake is being prepared.

- 8 tablespoons (1 stick) unsalted butter, room temperature, plus more for pans
- 2½ cups sifted cake flour (not self-rising), plus more for pans
- ½ teaspoon baking powder
- ¾ teaspoon baking soda
- ½ teaspoon kosher salt
- 2 tablespoons pure vegetable shortening
- 1½ cups superfine sugar
- 3 large eggs, lightly beaten
- 1 cup (about 3) puréed ripe bananas
- 1 teaspoon pure vanilla extract
- ¼ cup buttermilk
- ¼ cup confectioners' sugar, or more to taste
- 3 cups sour cream
  Chocolate Glaze and Curls (page 478)
  Sautéed Banana Filling (page 478)
  Shiny Cream-Cheese Frosting (page 492)

1. Preheat the oven to 350°F with two racks centered. Butter two 8 x 2-inch cake pans, and line with parchment paper. Butter the parchment. Dust the pans with flour, tap out any excess. In a large bowl, sift together the flour, baking powder, baking soda, and salt; set aside.

2. In the bowl of an electric mixer fitted with the paddle attachment, cream the butter and shortening on medium low until very soft, about 1 minute. Gradually add the sugar until the mixture is fluffy, about 3 minutes; scrape down the sides twice with a rubber spatula. Gradually drizzle in the beaten eggs on the lowest speed, beating after each addition until the batter is no longer slick, about 5 minutes; scrape down the bowl three times. In a medium bowl combine the puréed bananas with the vanilla and the buttermilk. On low speed, slowly add the flour mixture and the buttermilk mixture, alternating between them, a little of each at a time, starting and ending with the flour; scrape down the sides twice.

3. Divide the batter evenly between the two pans. Bake, rotating the pans after 25 to 30 minutes for even browning if needed, until a cake tester inserted into the center of each comes out clean, about 10 minutes more.

4. Transfer the pans to wire racks to cool for 10 minutes. Remove the cakes from the pans; return to cool completely on the racks, top-sides up.

5. Meanwhile, sift the confectioners' sugar over the sour cream in a medium bowl. Gently fold them together with a rubber spatula. Transfer to the refrigerator to chill, and reserve to use for the filling.

6. To assemble the cake, remove the parchment paper from the bottoms of the cakes. Use a long serrated knife to cut each cake layer in half horizontally, creating four layers. Set aside the prettiest dome for the final layer. Place another domed layer, dome-side down, on the serving platter. Spread the chocolate glaze on all three layers, not the reserved final. Set aside to let the chocolate dry slightly. Arrange one-third of the sautéed banana filling over the chocolate-covered cake layer. Fill in between the bananas with the sweetened sour cream. Stack a second layer over the first. Repeat the filling-and-stacking process with the remaining layer, top with the reserved domed layer. Let the cake chill, and set 1 hour before frosting. Frost with the cream-cheese frosting; top with chocolate curls. Serve.

chocolate glaze and curls
MAKES ENOUGH FOR ONE CAKE

Do not use a wooden spoon to stir the chocolate; wood can retain moisture, and any bit of water will cause the chocolate to seize or appear curdled. For bench scrapers, see Equipment Sources, page 650.

13 *ounces semisweet chocolate, finely chopped*

1. Place chocolate in the top of double boiler or in a heat-proof bowl set over a pan of simmering water. Stir with a rubber spatula until the chocolate is melted, about 3 minutes.

2. Pour ¼ cup of the melted chocolate onto a flat baking sheet. Repeat with a second baking sheet and ¼ cup of melted chocolate. Use an offset spatula to spread the chocolate as evenly as possible over each sheet. Transfer the baking sheets to the refrigerator to chill, about 20 minutes.

3. Transfer the baking sheets to a flat surface. Use a bench scraper to firmly scrape along the bottom of the sheet in the direction away from your body. Hold the bench scraper at a slight angle to the sheet; push to form curls. If the chocolate is too cold, it will splinter. Let the sheet sit 2 to 4 minutes at room temperature. Scraps of the chocolate may be melted and used again. Refrigerate the best curls for the cake.

4. Use the remaining ¾ cup of melted chocolate to spread on the three banana-cake layers.

sautéed banana filling
MAKES 4½ CUPS

3 *tablespoons unsalted butter*
¼ *cup packed light-brown sugar*
2½ *pounds ripe bananas, cut into ¾-inch slices*
¼ *cup bourbon*

1. Melt 1½ tablespoons butter in a large skillet over medium-high heat. Add 2 tablespoons sugar; stir until the sugar melts, 1 to 2 minutes.

2. Add half the banana slices; let sit, shaking the pan occasionally, until the bananas are lightly golden on the bottom, about 2 minutes. Turn the bananas over; cook 1 minute more. Remove from the heat; add 2 tablespoons bourbon. Cook 30 seconds to cook off the alcohol. Transfer in a single layer to a plate to cool. Repeat with the remaining ingredients. Cool completely before using.

fig trifle

SERVES 6

Just a few minutes of last-minute assembly are needed to serve this dessert; the cake and lemon curd can be made several days in advance.

- 1 pint (about 18) green or black figs, stemmed, quartered
- 1 pint mixed berries, such as red raspberries, golden raspberries, blackberries, and strawberries, large ones hulled and quartered
- ¼ cup sugar
- 1 tablespoon Grand Marnier or other orange-flavored liqueur
  Yellow Genoise Cake (recipe follows)
  Lightened Lemon-Curd Filling (page 480)
  Confectioners' sugar, for dusting

1. Combine the figs and berries in a small bowl. Sprinkle with the sugar and the liqueur. Let sit at room temperature, tossing gently once or twice, until the juices have released, about 30 minutes.

2. Preheat the oven to 425°F. Slice the cake into twelve 3-inch squares (you will have a few extra squares), and toast on a baking sheet in the oven until golden brown, 6 to 8 minutes. Remove from the oven.

3. Arrange half the toasted cake squares on six serving plates. Spoon lemon curd and fruit over the cake squares. Cover each with another slice of cake, dust with the confectioners' sugar, and serve.

yellow genoise cake

MAKES ONE 12 × 17-INCH SHEET; ENOUGH FOR 1 TRIFLE

YOU WILL NEED ONE 12 X 17-INCH JELLY-ROLL PAN.

Génoise, a tender, flavorful French sponge cake, differs from other sponge cakes in that butter is added to the batter. For jelly-roll pans, see Equipment Sources, page 650.

- 6 tablespoons unsalted butter, melted, plus more for pan
- 1⅓ cups all-purpose flour, plus more for pan
- 1 cup sugar
- 6 large eggs
- 1 teaspoon pure vanilla extract

1. Preheat the oven to 350°F with a rack in the center. Butter a 12 x 17-inch jelly-roll pan, line with parchment paper, butter and flour the paper, and set aside.

2. Set the bowl of an electric mixer over, but not touching, a pot of simmering water. Combine the sugar and eggs in the bowl, and whisk until mixture is warm to the touch, about 2 minutes.

3. Transfer the bowl to the electric mixer fitted with the whisk attachment, and beat on high speed until the mixture is very thick and pale, 6 to 8 minutes. With a rubber spatula, gently transfer the mixture to a large mixing bowl. Sift in the flour in three additions, folding gently after each. Combine the butter and the vanilla, and add in a steady stream as you fold in the third addition of flour. Fold gently, and pour out onto the prepared pan. Smooth the top with an offset spatula.

4. Bake until the cake is springy to the touch and golden brown, 18 to 20 minutes. Transfer the pan to a wire rack to cool completely. Wrap the cake in the pan tightly with plastic wrap, and refrigerate for up to 3 days or freeze up to 1 month. When ready to use, turn out cake onto a cutting board covered with a clean piece of parchment or wax paper, and carefully peel the paper off the cake.

lightened lemon-curd filling

MAKES 2¾ CUPS

Whipped cream is folded into lemon curd to create this lightened filling. The base for the lemon curd should be prepared at least a few hours in advance and chilled. It can be made up to several days before using; fold in the whipped cream on the day you need the filling.

- 6 large egg yolks
- 1 cup granulated sugar
- ½ cup fresh lemon juice
  Grated zest of 1 lemon
- ½ cup unsalted butter, cut into small pieces
- ⅔ cup heavy cream
- 1 tablespoon confectioners' sugar

1. Whisk together the egg yolks, sugar, and lemon juice in a small, heavy-bottomed saucepan. Cook over low heat, stirring constantly with a wooden spoon until the mixture coats the back of a spoon, 8 to 10 minutes.

2. Transfer to a small bowl. Stir in zest and butter, piece by piece. Let cool completely. Cover surface with plastic wrap to prevent a skin from forming, and transfer to the refrigerator for 2 to 3 days.

3. In a large metal bowl, whip together the cream and confectioners' sugar until stiff peaks form. Fold the mixture into the curd; chill in the refrigerator at least 20 minutes before using.

....

HOMEMADE CRÈME FRAÎCHE

To make crème fraîche at home, combine 1 cup whipping cream with 2 tablespoons buttermilk. Cover, and let stand at room temperature overnight or until thick.

....

ginger-pecan cake

MAKES ONE 8-INCH 3-LAYER CAKE;
SERVES 8 TO 10

YOU WILL NEED three 8 x 2-inch cake pans.

Use thin wooden skewers or toothpicks to support the layers if they begin to slip, and remove before serving.

- 1½ cups (3 sticks) unsalted butter, room temperature, plus more for pans
- 3 cups sifted all-purpose flour, plus more for pans
- 1½ tablespoons baking powder
- ¾ teaspoon kosher salt
- 1 tablespoon ground ginger
- 7 ounces pecan halves, toasted (see page 644), finely ground (1½ cups), plus 9 toasted pecan halves, for garnish
- 3 cups packed light-brown sugar
- 6 large eggs, lightly beaten
- 1 cup plus 2 tablespoons milk
- ¾ teaspoon freshly grated ginger
- 2 teaspoons pure vanilla extract
- 1 pint crème fraîche
- 2 teaspoons bourbon, optional
- 3 tablespoons confectioners' sugar, or more to taste
  Glossy Caramel Icing (page 495)
- ¼ ounce crystallized ginger, cut into thin strips

1. Preheat the oven to 350°F with two racks centered. Butter three 8 x 2-inch cake pans, and line with parchment paper. Dust the bottoms and sides with flour; tap out any excess. Sift the flour, baking powder, salt, and ground ginger into a medium bowl. Add the ground pecans, and whisk to combine; set aside.

2. In the bowl of an electric mixer fitted with the paddle attachment, cream butter on medium speed until fluffy. Gradually add the brown sugar until fluffy, about 4 minutes. Drizzle in the beaten eggs, a little at a time, beating each time until the batter is no longer slick, about 5 minutes; scrape down the sides twice with a rubber spatula.

3. On low speed, add the flour mixture to the sugar-butter mixture, alternating with the milk, a little of each at a time, starting and ending with the flour mixture; scrape down the bowl twice. Beat in the grated ginger and vanilla. Divide the batter evenly between the pans. Bake, rotating the pans, if necessary, for even browning, after 30 minutes. Continue baking until a cake tester inserted into center of cakes comes out clean, 5 to 10 minutes more.

4. Transfer the pans to wire racks to cool for 10 minutes. Turn out the cakes from the pans, and return to the wire racks to cool completely, top-sides up.

5. Meanwhile, in the clean bowl of the electric mixer fitted with the whisk attachment, beat the crème fraîche until soft peaks form. Add the bourbon and confectioners' sugar; beat until soft peaks return. Transfer to a medium bowl, cover, and refrigerate until firm, about 1 hour.

6. To assemble the cake, remove the parchment paper from the bottoms of the cakes. Set aside the prettiest layer; it will be used for the top of the cake. Place one layer on a serving platter, and spread with half the crème-fraîche filling; repeat with second layer. Top the cake with reserved third layer. Chill the cake while the icing is being prepared. Pour the icing onto the center point on the top of the cake, and let it flow down the sides. When the icing has set slightly, 5 to 10 minutes, arrange the pecan halves and crystallized ginger on the top. Serve.

carrot-ginger layer cake

MAKES ONE 8-INCH 2-LAYER CAKE;
SERVES 8 TO 10

YOU WILL NEED two 8 x 2-inch cake pans.

This tiered carrot cake is wrapped like a gift with candied carrots for ribbon. To make two 6-inch layer cakes: Use four 6 x 2-inch-round cake pans, and spread each layer with ½ cup of frosting.

Unsalted butter, for pans

3 cups all-purpose flour, plus more for pans

1 pound large carrots

3 large eggs, room temperature

⅓ cup nonfat buttermilk

1 teaspoon pure vanilla extract

2 cups sugar

1½ cups canola oil

1 tablespoon freshly grated ginger

2 teaspoons baking powder

1 teaspoon baking soda

1 teaspoon kosher salt

1 teaspoon ground cinnamon

1 cup pecan halves, toasted (see page 644), finely chopped

Orange Cream-Cheese Frosting (page 493)

Candied Carrot Strips (recipe follows), optional

1. Preheat the oven to 375°F with two racks centered. Butter two 8 x 2-inch cake pans, and line with parchment paper. Dust the bottoms and sides with flour, and tap out any excess. Set the pans aside.

2. Using the smallest holes (less than ¼ inch in diameter) of a box grater, grate the carrots, yielding 2½ cups. Place the carrots, eggs, buttermilk, vanilla, sugar, oil, and ginger in a large bowl; whisk until well combined.

3. In a bowl, whisk the flour, baking powder, baking soda, salt, and cinnamon. Using a rubber spatula, fold the flour mixture into the carrot mixture until combined. Fold in the toasted pecans.

4. Divide evenly between the pans. Bake until a cake tester inserted into the center of each comes out clean, rotating pans for even baking, if needed, about 1 hour. Transfer pans to a wire rack to cool for 10 minutes. Remove the cakes from the pans, and return to the rack to cool, top-sides up.

5. To assemble, remove the paper from the bottoms of the cakes. Use a long serrated knife to trim the tops of the cakes flat. Cut each cake layer in half horizontally, creating four layers. Place a layer on a cake stand or cardboard round, and spread ¾ cup of the frosting over the top. Place a second cake layer on top, and spread with another ¾ cup of frosting. Repeat with the third layer and another ¾ cup of frosting. Place the last cake layer on the top, and spread the remaining frosting over the sides and top of the assembled cake. Transfer to the refrigerator, and chill 3 to 4 hours.

6. If using the candied carrot strips, set a wire rack over a baking pan. Using your fingers, lift one candied carrot strip from the sugar syrup, holding it over the container. With the thumb and forefinger of your other hand, gently squeeze carrot strip and slide your fingers along its length, removing excess syrup; lay the carrot strip on the wire rack. Repeat with the remaining carrot strips.

7. Gently place the tapered end of a drained carrot strip in the center of the cake, and gently press it down the side; place a second strip next to it. Continue applying strips around entire cake. Form 2 or 3 strips into a decorative bow, and place on top. Cut the cake, and serve.

candied carrot strips
DECORATES TWO 6-INCH CAKES
OR ONE 8-INCH CAKE

Use a mandoline to slice the carrots whisper thin.

12 large carrots
7 cups sugar

1. Using a mandoline, slice carrots lengthwise into thin strips, no more than ⅛ inch thick; set aside.

2. In a small stockpot, combine 4 cups sugar and 2 cups water. Place over high heat, and bring to a boil, brushing the sides of the saucepan with cold water to prevent the sugar from crystallizing. Add the carrots; reduce the heat to medium. Simmer until the carrots are translucent, about 25 minutes.

3. In another small stockpot, combine the remaining 3 cups sugar with 1 cup water. Place over high heat, and bring to a boil, brushing the sides of the saucepan with cold water to prevent the sugar from

crystallizing. When the sugar has completely dissolved, remove from the heat. Use a slotted spoon to transfer the candied carrots from the syrup in which they boiled to this new sugar syrup. Let stand until completely cooled; discard the old syrup. Transfer the carrot strips and the new sugar syrup to an airtight container, and store, refrigerated, for up to 3 days.

coconut layer cake
MAKES ONE 6-INCH 6-LAYER CAKE; SERVES 8

YOU WILL NEED three 6 x 2-inch cake pans.

This teetering creation of tender sour-cream cake, coconut filling, and piles of Seven-Minute Frosting is the last word on coconut. Sweetened angel-flake coconut is available in grocery stores. You can bake the batter in two 8 x 2-inch cake pans, but the layers will be slightly thinner (place a baking sheet on the bottom rack in the oven to catch any spills).

12 tablespoons (1½ sticks) unsalted butter, room temperature, plus more for pans
2 cups sifted cake flour (not self-rising), plus more for pans
½ teaspoon baking powder
½ teaspoon baking soda
¼ teaspoon kosher salt
1 cup superfine sugar
1 teaspoon pure vanilla extract
4 large egg yolks, lightly beaten
⅔ cup sour cream
11 ounces (about 3¾ cups) sweetened angel-flake coconut
Coconut-Cream Filling (recipe follows)
Seven-Minute Frosting (page 492)

1. Preheat the oven to 350°F with two racks centered. Butter three 6 x 2-inch cake pans, and line with parchment paper. Dust the bottom and the sides with flour; tap out any excess. In a large bowl, sift together the flour, baking powder, baking soda, and salt; set aside.

2. In the bowl of an electric mixer fitted with the paddle attachment, cream the butter on low speed to soften, increase speed to medium, and beat until light in color and fluffy, 1 to 2 minutes. Keep beating while gradually adding the sugar, until the mixture is fluffy, about 3 minutes. Beat in the vanilla. Gradually drizzle in the beaten eggs, beating between each addition until the batter is no longer slick, scraping down the sides twice. Beat until the mixture is fluffy again, about 3 minutes more.

3. With the mixer on low speed, alternate adding the flour mixture and the sour cream, a little of each at a time, starting and ending with the flour. Divide evenly among the three pans. Bake until a cake tester inserted into the center of each comes out clean, rotating the pans for even baking, if needed, 30 to 40 minutes. Transfer the pans to a wire rack to cool for 10 minutes. Remove the cakes from the pans, and return to the rack to cool, top-sides up.

4. To assemble, remove the parchment paper from the bottoms of the cakes. Use a long serrated knife to cut each cake layer in half horizontally, creating six layers. Set aside the prettiest dome; it will be used for the final layer. Place another domed layer, dome-side down, on the serving platter. Sprinkle 2 to 3 tablespoons of the flaked coconut over the cake. Spread ½ cup of the coconut-cream filling over the coconut flakes. Repeat the sprinkling and spreading process on the remaining layers until all but the reserved domed layer are used. Top the cake with the reserved domed layer. Transfer the cake to the refrigerator to firm for 1 hour. Remove from the refrigerator, and frost the outside of the cake with the just-made frosting. Sprinkle the remaining coconut flakes all over the cake while the frosting is soft; do not refrigerate.

coconut-cream filling

MAKES 1 QUART

- 6 large egg yolks
- ¾ cup sugar
- ¼ cup plus 2 tablespoons cornstarch
- ⅛ teaspoon kosher salt
- 3 cups milk
- 4 ounces (1½ cups) sweetened angel-flake coconut
- 1½ teaspoons pure vanilla extract
  Unsalted butter, for plastic wrap

1. Place egg yolks in a large bowl; whisk to combine; set bowl aside. Combine the sugar, cornstarch, and salt in a saucepan. Gradually add milk, whisking constantly. Cook, stirring, over medium heat until mixture thickens and just begins to bubble, 10 to 12 minutes. Remove from the heat.

2. Whisk ½ cup of the hot milk mixture into the reserved yolks to warm them. Slowly pour the warmed yolks back into the saucepan, stirring constantly. Cook, while continuing to stir, over medium heat until the mixture just begins to bubble, about 2 minutes. Remove from the heat. Stir in the coconut and vanilla.

3. Transfer the filling to a medium mixing bowl. Lightly butter a piece of plastic wrap, and place it directly on top of the filling to prevent a skin from forming; set aside to cool slightly, about 10 minutes. Transfer the filling to the refrigerator until firm and chilled, at least 1 hour. The filling may be made 1 day ahead.

maple layer cake

MAKES ONE 9-INCH 2-LAYER CAKE;
SERVES 10 TO 12

YOU WILL NEED two 9 x 2-inch round cake pans.

- 8 tablespoons (1 stick) unsalted butter, room temperature, plus more for pans
- 2¾ cups all-purpose flour, sifted, plus more for pans
- 2 cups pure maple syrup, preferably grade-A dark amber
- 3 large eggs, lightly beaten
- 1 tablespoon baking powder
- ¼ teaspoon kosher salt
- 1 teaspoon ground ginger
- 1 cup milk
- 1 teaspoon pure vanilla extract
- 1½ cups (6 ounces) walnuts, chopped medium fine
  Maple-Buttercream Frosting (page 493)

1. Preheat the oven to 350°F with one rack centered. Butter two 9 x 2-inch round cake pans, and line with parchment paper. Butter the parchment. Dust the inside of the pans with flour, tapping out the excess; set aside.

2. In the bowl of an electric mixer fitted with the paddle attachment, cream the butter on low speed to soften, increase speed to medium, and beat until light in color and fluffy, 1 to 2 minutes. Keep beating while gradually adding the maple syrup, beat until fluffy, about 2 minutes, scraping down the sides of the bowl once or twice with a rubber spatula. Gradually drizzle the beaten eggs into the bowl on medium-low speed, beating after each addition until the batter is no longer slick but is smooth and fluffy, about 5 minutes. Stop to scrape down the bowl once or twice so the batter will combine well.

3. In a large bowl, sift together the flour, baking powder, salt, and ginger. With the mixer on low speed, alternate adding the flour mixture and the milk to the butter mixture, a little of each at a time, starting and ending with the flour. Beat in vanilla. Stir in ¾ cup walnuts. Divide evenly between the two pans. Bake until a cake tester inserted into the center of each comes out clean, rotating the pans for even baking, if needed, about 40 minutes. Transfer the pans to a wire rack to cool for 10 minutes. Remove the cakes from the pans, and return to the rack to cool, top-sides up.

4. To assemble the cakes, remove the papers from the bottom of the cakes. Using a serrated knife, trim the tops of the cakes flat. Place one layer, top-side up, on a cardboard round or serving platter. Spread 1½ cups of the maple-buttercream frosting evenly over the top. Place the second cake layer on top, and spread the remaining 2½ cups of frosting around the sides and over the top. Using your hands, gently press the remaining ¾ cup of walnuts onto the sides of the cake. Serve.

old-fashioned berry shortcake

MAKES ONE 9-INCH 4-LAYER CAKE;
SERVES 10 TO 12

YOU WILL NEED two 9 x 2-inch round cake pans.

This cake is best when assembled 6 to 8 hours ahead; arrange the top layer of fruit just before serving.

Unsalted butter, for pans
1   *cup all-purpose flour*
⅔   *cup cornstarch*
6   *large eggs, room temperature*
4   *large egg yolks, room temperature*
1   *cup granulated sugar*
¼   *teaspoon kosher salt*
2   *teaspoons pure vanilla extract*
¾   *cup canola oil*
1   *quart heavy cream*
½   *cup confectioners' sugar*
1   *vanilla bean, split lengthwise and scraped*
1   *pint small strawberries, hulled*
½   *pint blackberries*
½   *pint raspberries*
½   *pint blueberries*
    Fresh mint leaves, for garnish

1. Preheat the oven to 350°F with a rack in the center. Butter two 9 x 2-inch round cake pans; set aside. In a large bowl, sift together the flour and cornstarch; set aside.

2. In the bowl of an electric mixer fitted with the whisk attachment, combine the eggs, egg yolks, granulated sugar, salt, and 1 teaspoon vanilla. Beat on high speed until the mixture is thick and holds a ribbon-like trail on the surface when you raise the whisk, about 5 minutes.

3. Place the reserved flour mixture on a large piece of parchment paper. Holding the paper like a funnel, gradually add the flour mixture to the egg mixture. With machine running on low speed, mix until just combined. In a steady stream, immediately add the oil; mix until just combined. Remove the bowl from the mixer; detach the whisk. Using the whisk, fold mixture several times.

4. Divide the batter between the pans. Bake the cakes, rotating the pans halfway through baking time, until the centers spring back when you touch them with your finger, about 30 minutes.

5. Immediately turn the cakes out onto a wire rack to cool completely.

6. Combine the cream, confectioners' sugar, and the remaining teaspoon of vanilla in the clean mixer bowl. Add the vanilla seed scrapings, and reserve the pod for another use. Starting on low speed and increasing to medium high, beat until stiff peaks form, about 2 minutes.

7. Using a serrated knife, slice each cake in half horizontally; place one layer on a serving plate. Spread one-quarter of the whipped cream over the layer; arrange strawberries on top. Repeat the process with remaining layers, cream, and berries. Refrigerate until serving; garnish with mint. Serve.

warm chocolate cakes

MAKES SIX 3-INCH CAKES; SERVES 6

YOU WILL NEED six 3-inch metal baking rings (see Equipment Sources, page 650).

Tender and cakey on the outside, gooey on the inside, these decadent little cakes provide the perfect combination of both textures in every forkful.

14	ounces best-quality bittersweet chocolate, finely chopped
¼	cup plus 2 tablespoons heavy cream
6	tablespoons unsalted butter, plus more for rings
	All-purpose flour, for rings
5	large eggs, separated
½	cup plus 2 tablespoons granulated sugar
½	teaspoon pure vanilla extract
¾	cup ground almonds
	Confectioners' sugar, for dusting, optional

1. Place 2 ounces chocolate in a medium heat-proof bowl. Pour the cream into a small saucepan, and heat until bubbles appear around the edge. Pour the hot cream over the chocolate, let stand several minutes, and whisk until smooth. Pour the chocolate ganache into 6 squares of a plastic ice-cube tray. Freeze until solid.

2. Butter and flour six 3-inch metal baking rings, and place on a parchment-lined baking sheet, tapping out the excess flour; set aside.

3. Melt butter and remaining 12 ounces chopped chocolate in a heat-proof bowl over a pan of simmering water. Stir until smooth. Let cool slightly.

4. Meanwhile, in the bowl of an electric mixer fitted with the whisk attachment, combine the egg yolks, ¼ cup plus 2 tablespoons sugar, and the vanilla. Beat until thick and pale yellow, about 5 minutes. Add the chocolate-butter mixture, and thoroughly combine. Fold in the ground almonds.

5. In a clean mixer bowl fitted with the whisk attachment, beat the egg whites on low speed until frothy, 2 to 3 minutes, then on medium low until the whites are foamy and begin to thicken, just before soft peaks form. Gradually add the remaining ¼ cup of sugar, and beat until stiff peaks form. Stir one-third of the egg whites into the egg-yolk-chocolate mixture to lighten it. Fold the remaining egg whites into the mixture.

6. Spoon about 3 tablespoons of the batter into each ring. Remove the frozen ganache cubes from the freezer. (You may need to dip the bottom of the ice tray in hot water to get them out.) Place a cube in the center of each ring. Spoon the remaining batter into the rings, being careful to keep the ganache cubes in the center, and cover them completely. Freeze the filled molds until solid, about 1 hour.

7. Preheat the oven to 375°F with a rack in the center. Take the baking sheet from the freezer. Wrap any cakes to be saved and replace in the freezer; leave the rest on the sheet. Bake until the batter has set, 20 to 25 minutes. Transfer the sheet to a wire rack to cool for 5 to 10 minutes. To unmold, cover one hand with a clean dish towel, and pick a cake up on a spatula with the other. Invert the cake into your hand, pull off the ring, then invert again onto a serving plate. Dust with confectioners' sugar, if using. Serve hot.

luscious chocolate cake

MAKES ONE 9-INCH 3-LAYER CAKE;
SERVES 8 TO 10

YOU WILL NEED three 9 x 2-inch cake pans.

If you want to use 8-inch cake pans for this (you will have batter left over), fill them halfway, and place them on a baking sheet before sliding in the oven.

- 1 cup (2 sticks) plus 2 tablespoons unsalted butter, room temperature, plus more for pans and parchment
- ½ cup plus 1 tablespoon best-quality cocoa powder, plus more for pans
- ¼ cup plus 2 tablespoons boiling water
- ¾ cup milk
- 2¼ cups sifted cake flour (not self-rising)
- ¾ teaspoon baking soda
- ½ teaspoon kosher salt
- 1¾ cups sugar
- 2 teaspoons pure vanilla extract
- 3 large eggs, lightly beaten
  Whipped Ganache (page 494)
  Ganache Glaze (page 495)

1. Preheat the oven to 350°F with two racks centered. Butter three 9 x 2-inch cake pans, and line with parchment paper; butter and dust the bottoms and sides of the pans with cocoa; tap out the excess. Sift the cocoa into a medium bowl; stir in the boiling water until smooth; gradually whisk in the milk. Set aside to cool.

2. Sift the flour, baking soda, and salt into a bowl. Set aside. In the bowl of an electric mixer fitted with the paddle attachment, cream the butter on low until light and fluffy, about 3 minutes. Gradually beat in the sugar, scraping down sides twice. Beat in the vanilla.

3. Add the eggs, a third at a time, beating after each addition. With the mixer on low speed, alternate adding the flour mixture and the reserved cocoa mixture a little at a time, starting and ending with the flour mixture. Divide batter evenly among pans; spread with an offset spatula until level.

4. Bake, rotating pans if necessary, until a cake tester inserted into the center of each cake comes out clean, 20 to 25 minutes. Transfer the pans to a wire rack to cool, about 15 minutes. Remove the cakes from the pans, remove the paper, and return to the rack to cool, top-side up.

5. With a long serrated knife, trim the top of each cake layer until level. Transfer one layer to a cardboard cake round. Spread about 1¼ cups of the whipped ganache on the cake; top with a second layer. Repeat. Spread the remaining whipped ganache evenly over the top and sides of the cake to seal in the crumbs and form a smooth surface. Chill until the crumb coat is firm, about 30 minutes.

6. Place the cake (still on the cardboard cake round) on a wire rack set in a baking pan. Pour enough ganache glaze over the cake to fully coat, shaking the pan gently to help spread the ganache if necessary. Let sit for 15 to 20 minutes. The ganache in the baking pan may be strained through a fine sieve and added back into the glaze. Pour the remaining glaze over cake; allow excess to drip off sides. If top is not smooth, gently shake pan, or run an offset spatula quickly over the surface. Allow to set at least 30 minutes before serving.

moist devil's food cake

MAKES ONE 8-INCH 3-LAYER CAKE;
SERVES 8 TO 10

YOU WILL NEED three 8 x 2-inch cake pans.

Dutch-process cocoa powder mixed with boiling water gives this cake a rich color and strong chocolate flavor. Edible flowers, such as pansies, make a dramatic decoration for this cake.

- 1½ cups (3 sticks) unsalted butter, plus more for pans
- ¾ cup Dutch-process cocoa powder, plus more for pans
- ½ cup boiling water
- 2¼ cups sugar
- 1 tablespoon pure vanilla extract
- 4 large eggs, lightly beaten
- 3 cups sifted cake flour (not self-rising)
- 1 teaspoon baking soda

½ teaspoon kosher salt

1 cup milk

Mrs. Milman's Chocolate Frosting
(page 491)

1. Preheat the oven to 350°F with two racks centered. Butter three 8 x 2-inch cake pans, and line with parchment paper. Dust the bottoms and sides with cocoa; tap out the excess. Sift the ¾ cup cocoa into a medium bowl; whisk in the boiling water. Set aside and let cool.

2. In the bowl of an electric mixer fitted with the paddle attachment, cream the butter on low speed to soften, increase speed to medium, and beat until light in color and fluffy. Keep beating while gradually adding the sugar; beat until fluffy, about 3 minutes. Beat in the vanilla.

3. Gradually drizzle in the beaten eggs, beating between each addition until the batter is no longer slick, scraping down the sides twice.

4. Sift the flour, baking soda, and salt together in a large bowl. Whisk the milk into the cooled cocoa mixture. With the mixer on low speed, alternate adding the flour mixture and the cocoa mixture, a little of each at a time, starting and ending with the flour. Divide evenly among the three pans. Bake until a cake tester inserted into the center of each comes out clean, rotating the pans for even baking, if needed, about 45 minutes. Transfer the pans to a wire rack to cool for 10 minutes. Remove the cakes from the pans, and return to the rack to cool, topsides up.

5. To assemble the cake, remove the papers from the bottoms of the cakes. Save the prettiest layer for the top. Place one layer on a serving platter; spread with 1½ cups of the chocolate frosting, and repeat with the second layer; top with the third. Cover the outside of the cake with the remaining 3 cups of frosting. Serve.

chocolate cupcakes

MAKES 2 DOZEN STANDARD CUPCAKES

Large dark-chocolate curls crown these popular cupcakes.

2 cups cake flour (not self-rising)

1 cup plus 2 tablespoons cocoa powder

1 teaspoon baking powder

½ teaspoon kosher salt

1½ cups (3 sticks) unsalted butter, room temperature

2 cups sugar

5 large eggs

2 teaspoons pure vanilla extract

1 cup nonfat buttermilk

24 ounces semisweet chocolate morsels

2 cups heavy cream

½ teaspoon light corn syrup

1. Preheat the oven to 350°F with two racks centered. Line standard muffin tins with paper baking cups; set aside. In a bowl, sift together the flour, 1 cup cocoa powder, the baking powder, and salt.

2. In the bowl of an electric mixer fitted with the paddle attachment, cream the butter and sugar on medium speed until light and fluffy, about 3 minutes. With the mixer running, add the eggs and vanilla; beat until combined. Scrape down the sides of the bowl with a rubber spatula.

3. With the mixer on low speed, add 1 cup of the flour mixture; mix until combined. Add ½ cup buttermilk; combine. Alternate adding the remaining flour mixture and the buttermilk, ending with the flour. Scrape down the sides of the bowl with a rubber spatula.

4. Fill each baking cup in the prepared muffin tins with ⅓ cup of the batter. Bake until a cake tester inserted into the middle of a cupcake comes out clean, 25 to 30 minutes. Transfer the tins to a wire rack to cool completely.

5. In the top of a double boiler or in a heat-proof bowl set over a pan of simmering water, melt 12 ounces of the chocolate. Stir with a rubber spatula until smooth. Set aside.

6. To make the frosting, place the remaining 12 ounces of chocolate and the cream in a heavy medium saucepan. Cook over low heat, stirring constantly with a rubber spatula, until combined and thickened, 25 to 35 minutes. Increase heat to medium low; cook, stirring, about 10 minutes more. Remove from heat; stir in the corn syrup.

7. Combine 1 cup of the frosting with the melted chocolate; transfer the mixture to a shallow pie plate. Refrigerate until hardened.

8. Meanwhile, prepare an ice-water bath. Transfer the remaining frosting to a medium metal bowl, and set over the ice-water bath. Stir constantly, incorporating the chilled chocolate on the bottom of the bowl, until the frosting reaches the desired spreading consistency.

9. Using a small offset spatula, spread the frosting on the cupcakes.

10. Remove the hardened chocolate from the refrigerator; let stand 5 minutes. Using a teaspoon, gently scrape the surface of the chocolate to create loose curls. Using more pressure will create thicker curls. Transfer the curls to a plate as you work; if the curls get too soft, chill briefly. Sift the remaining 2 tablespoons of cocoa over the plate of curls. Arrange several curls over each cupcake, and serve.

three-cheese cake

MAKES ONE 8-INCH CAKE; SERVES 8

YOU WILL NEED one 8-inch springform pan.

- 8 *navel oranges, peel and pith removed*
- 6 *tablespoons unsalted butter, plus more for pan*
- 9 *whole graham crackers*
- ¾ *cup plus 2 tablespoons sugar*
- ¾ *cup hazelnuts, toasted (see page 644)*
- 5 *ounces cream cheese, room temperature*
- 6 *ounces mild and creamy goat cheese, room temperature*
- 1 *teaspoon grated orange zest*
- 1 *tablespoon plus 1 teaspoon all-purpose flour*
- ½ *teaspoon kosher salt*

- 1 *tablespoon plus 1 teaspoon Frangelico, optional*
- 4 *large eggs, separated*
- 5 *ounces mascarpone cheese*
- 1 *tablespoon plus 1 teaspoon fresh orange juice*
- 1 *tablespoon lavender-flavored or regular honey*
- ½ *teaspoon dried lavender, optional*
  Lavender blossoms, for garnish, optional

1. Working over a bowl to catch juices, use a paring knife to carefully slice between sections and membranes of an orange; remove segments whole. Place each segment in the bowl as completed. Repeat process with other oranges; set aside.

2. Preheat the oven to 350°F with a rack in the center. Butter an 8-inch springform pan. In a small saucepan over low heat, melt the butter; set aside.

3. In the bowl of a food processor, pulse the graham crackers into fine crumbs, yielding about 1 cup crumbs. Place in a medium bowl; add ¼ cup sugar, and set aside. Place ½ cup toasted hazelnuts in the food processor; pulse until fine but not powdery. Add to the graham-cracker-crumb mixture. Using a fork, add the melted butter; stir to combine. Put the crumb mixture in the bottom of the pan, and press evenly around the bottom and halfway up the sides, about 1½ inches.

4. Bake the crust until golden brown, about 10 minutes. Transfer to a wire rack to cool.

5. Reduce heat to 325°F. Place the cream cheese and goat cheese in the bowl of an electric mixer fitted with the paddle attachment, and beat on medium-high speed until light and fluffy, 2 to 3 minutes. Reduce speed to low. Add ½ cup sugar, the orange zest, flour, salt, and Frangelico, if using; mix until combined. Add the egg yolks one at a time, mixing after each addition. Add the mascarpone cheese and the orange juice; mix just until the batter is combined and smooth. Transfer the batter to a large mixing bowl, and set aside. Clean the mixer bowl.

6. Place the egg whites in the clean mixer bowl. Using the whisk attachment, beat on medium speed until frothy. Increase speed to medium high, and gradually add the remaining 2 tablespoons sugar, 1 teaspoon at a time. Continue beating the whites until stiff but not dry.

7. Using a hand whisk, mix one-third of the whipped egg whites into the batter to lighten it. Using a rubber spatula, gently fold in the remaining whites. Pour the batter into the cooled crust.

8. Bake the cheesecake until the top is golden brown and the center has barely set, about 1 hour; the top should be cracked and will sink upon cooling, forming a "bowl." Transfer the cheesecake to a wire rack to cool completely. Cover with plastic wrap, and transfer to the refrigerator to chill several hours or overnight. To unmold, wrap a hot towel around the sides of the pan to help release the cake, and run a thin knife around the inside of the pan. Carefully remove the outside of the pan, and slide cake onto a serving plate.

9. Combine the orange segments, honey, and dried lavender, if using, in a medium bowl. Coarsely chop the remaining ¼ cup of toasted hazelnuts, and add to the bowl. Spoon the topping into the bowl on top of the cheesecake. Garnish with the lavender blossoms, if desired. Serve.

no-bake chocolate-crust cheesecake

MAKES ONE 6-INCH CAKE; SERVES 4

YOU WILL NEED one 6-inch springform pan.

The crunchy chocolate crust on this cool, creamy cheesecake is made from crushed chocolate wafers. The cheesecake may be made a day ahead and kept, covered, in the refrigerator.

- 7 ounces chocolate wafer cookies
- ⅓ cup plus 3 tablespoons sugar
- 6 to 8 tablespoons unsalted butter, melted
- 1 8-ounce package cream cheese
- 2 tablespoons fresh lemon juice
- ¼ cup heavy cream
- 1 pint raspberries

1. Place the cookies in the bowl of a food processor; process until finely ground. Combine the cookies and 3 tablespoons sugar in a bowl. Add 6 table-

spoons butter, and mix well until the crumb mixture holds together. If needed, add the remaining 2 tablespoons melted butter. Transfer the cookie mixture to a 6-inch springform pan, and pat out evenly to make the crust, lining the sides of the pan only about three-quarters of the way up. Transfer to the freezer while proceeding.

2. Combine the cream cheese, lemon juice, and the remaining sugar in the bowl of an electric mixer fitted with the paddle attachment, and beat until combined. Lightly whip the cream to soft peaks, and fold into the cream-cheese filling. Remove the crust from the freezer, and pour the filling evenly into the pan. Cover with plastic wrap, place in the freezer for 30 minutes, then transfer to the refrigerator for at least 30 minutes, until firm, or up to 24 hours.

3. To serve, pass half the raspberries through a fine strainer to purée. Serve slices of the cake with the whole raspberries and the purée.

lemon cheesecake in a glass with blueberry sauce

SERVES 4

The flavors of classic blueberry cheesecake are served parfait-style.

- ½ teaspoon whole coriander seeds
- ½ teaspoon whole fennel seeds
- ½ cup low-fat milk
- 1 teaspoon grated lemon zest
- 1 large egg yolk, room temperature
- ½ cup plus 1 teaspoon sugar
- 2¼ teaspoons unflavored gelatin
- 2 pinches of kosher salt
- 15 ounces part-skim ricotta cheese
- ¼ cup fresh lemon juice
- ½ teaspoon pure vanilla extract
- 1½ cups fresh blueberries, or frozen, thawed and drained
  Pinch of ground cinnamon
- ½ teaspoon cornstarch
- 1 tablespoon plus 1 teaspoon graham-cracker crumbs

1. Crush coriander and fennel seeds by placing them under a heavy pot and pressing down. In a saucepan, combine milk, lemon zest, crushed coriander, and fennel; bring mixture to a boil. Remove pan from heat. Cover; let steep 15 minutes.

2. Strain the milk mixture through a sieve into a heat-proof bowl, and place the bowl over a saucepan of simmering water. Add the egg yolk, and whisk until very light, about 5 minutes. Add ½ cup sugar, the gelatin, and a pinch of salt, and continue to cook, whisking constantly, until the mixture thickens and the whisk leaves tracks in the custard, about 5 minutes. Remove from the heat; set aside to cool to room temperature.

3. Place ricotta in the bowl of a food processor; blend until smooth, about 1 minute. Add lemon juice and vanilla; process until combined. Fold ricotta into cooled gelatin mixture. Place in four glasses; chill, covered, until set, at least 2 hours.

4. Combine berries, 1 teaspoon water, remaining sugar, and a pinch of salt and cinnamon in a nonreactive saucepan. Cook over medium heat, stirring frequently, until berries are soft, about 3 minutes.

5. Blend 2 teaspoons water and the cornstarch in a small bowl. Bring the blueberries to a boil; stir in the cornstarch. Cook, stirring constantly, until slightly thickened, about 1 minute. Remove from the heat, and cool completely. Divide among the glasses, and sprinkle with the graham-cracker crumbs. Serve chilled or at room temperature.

FIT TO EAT RECIPE PER SERVING: 331 CALORIES, 11 G TOTAL FAT, 29% CALORIES FROM FAT, 87 MG CHOLESTEROL, 45 G CARBOHYDRATE, 176 MG SODIUM, 16 G PROTEIN, 1 G DIETARY FIBER

blood orange cheesecake
MAKES ONE 7-INCH CAKE; SERVES 6

YOU WILL NEED one 7-inch springform pan.

Decorated with a single candied orange slice in the center and glistening ruby-red glaze, this cake is fit for the most festive occasions. Ricotta cheese makes it lighter and less rich than a traditional cheesecake.

- 2 cups fresh ricotta cheese
- ¾ cup graham-cracker crumbs (6 or 7 crackers)
- ¾ cup sugar
- 4 tablespoons unsalted butter, melted
- 3 tablespoons fresh lemon juice
- 2¼ teaspoons unflavored gelatin
- 4 large egg yolks
- ½ cup plus 2 tablespoons milk
  Pinch of kosher salt
  Grated zest of ½ orange
- 1 teaspoon pure vanilla extract
- ½ cup heavy cream
- 4 ounces cream cheese, room temperature
- 1 Candied Blood Orange Slice (recipe follows)
  Blood Orange Glaze (recipe follows)

1. Line a sieve with cheesecloth, and leave the ricotta to drain over a large bowl in the refrigerator for several hours or overnight.

2. Preheat the oven to 350°F with a rack in the center. Fit a parchment circle into the bottom of a 7-inch springform pan. Combine the graham-cracker crumbs and 2 tablespoons sugar in a small bowl. Stir in the melted butter with a fork until the crumbs are moistened. Press into the bottom of the pan to make a crust. Bake until golden, about 10 minutes. Transfer to a wire rack to cool.

3. Place the lemon juice in a small bowl, and sprinkle the gelatin evenly over the surface. Set aside for 10 minutes to soften.

4. In a small, heavy saucepan, beat the egg yolks until smooth. Whisk in the milk. Gradually whisk in the remaining sugar. Add the salt. Cook over low heat, stirring constantly, until the mixture coats the back of a spoon, about 7 minutes. Do not allow to boil. Transfer to a bowl and stir.

5. Stir in the softened gelatin, orange zest, and vanilla, mixing until the gelatin is completely dissolved. Set the custard aside.

6. In a large bowl, whisk the cream until soft peaks form. Set aside. Place the drained ricotta in the bowl of a food processor, and process until smooth. Add the cream cheese, and process again until smooth. With the machine running, add the warm custard, and process just long enough to combine. Transfer to a bowl, and fold in the reserved whipped cream. Pour the mixture into the prepared pan, cover with plastic wrap, and chill overnight.

7. Place a candied orange slice in the center of the cake. Pour the glaze over the top, tipping the cake pan to cover the top completely. Chill until the glaze is set, about 1 hour.

8. To unmold, wrap a hot towel around the sides of the pan to help release the cake, and run a thin knife around the inside of the pan. Carefully remove the outside of the pan. Slide onto a serving plate, and chill until ready to serve.

candied blood orange slices
MAKES 5 TO 6 SLICES

Candy all of the slices and then choose the perfect one to garnish the cheesecake. Cooled candied blood-orange slices may be kept in their poaching liquid up to 2 days in the refrigerator.

- 1 blood orange, scrubbed
- ¾ cup sugar
- 2 tablespoons light corn syrup

Cut the orange into ⅛-inch slices. In a small saucepan over medium heat, combine the sugar, 2 cups water, and the syrup. Bring to a boil, cover, and simmer until clear and no sugar crystals cling to the sides of the pan, about 3 minutes. Add the orange slices in one layer; simmer over the lowest heat until transparent, about 1 hour. Transfer to a wire rack set over a baking pan to cool.

blood orange glaze
MAKES ENOUGH FOR ONE 7-INCH CAKE

- ¾ teaspoon unflavored gelatin
- ¼ cup plus 3 tablespoons blood-orange juice
- 2 tablespoons sugar
- ¼ teaspoon cornstarch

In a small bowl, sprinkle the gelatin evenly over 2 tablespoons juice; let stand until soft, about 10 minutes. In a small saucepan, bring the sugar and ¼ cup of the juice to a boil. Combine the remaining juice and cornstarch in a small bowl. Stir until dissolved; whisk into the boiling orange juice. Remove from the heat. Stir in the softened gelatin. Cool to lukewarm, and pour over the cake.

FROSTINGS

mrs. milman's chocolate frosting
MAKES 6 CUPS, ENOUGH TO FROST AND FILL A 3-LAYER CAKE

Crafts Editorial Director Hannah Milman made this frosting with her mother as a child. Use Nestle's chocolate morsels; the frosting will not set with more expensive chocolate. Keep the chocolate mixture over the heat until it thickens, or it will not thicken enough in the ice bath; timing will vary depending on the saucepan used and the stovetop heat.

- 24 ounces semisweet chocolate morsels
- 1 quart heavy cream
- 1 teaspoon light corn syrup

1. Place chocolate and cream in a heavy saucepan. Cook over medium-low heat, stirring constantly with a rubber spatula, until combined and thickened, 25 to 35 minutes. Increase heat to medium; cook, stirring, about 10 minutes more.

2. Remove from heat; stir in corn syrup. Transfer to a metal bowl; chill. Stir every 15 to 20 minutes; stir until cool enough to spread, 2 to 3 hours.

seven-minute frosting

MAKES ENOUGH FOR ONE
2- OR 3-LAYER CAKE

This cake frosting is named for the length of time it must be beaten in the final stage. Have the cake prepared for the billowy covering; it must be spread on while the beaten eggs whites and sugar are still pliable; once frosted, the cake may sit out for several hours before being served. Do not refrigerate.

- ¾ cup plus 2 tablespoons sugar
- 1 tablespoon light corn syrup
- 3 large egg whites

1. In a small heavy saucepan, combine ¾ cup sugar, the corn syrup, and 2 tablespoons water. Heat over medium heat, stirring occasionally, until the sugar has dissolved. Rub a bit between your fingers to make sure there is no graininess. Raise heat to bring to a boil. Do not stir anymore. Boil, washing down sides of pan with a pastry brush dipped in cold water from time to time to prevent the sugar from crystallizing, until a candy thermometer registers 230°F, about 5 minutes. (Depending on the humidity, this can take anywhere from 4 to 10 minutes.)

2. Meanwhile, in the bowl of an electric mixer fitted with the whisk attachment, whisk the egg whites on medium speed until soft peaks form, about 2½ minutes. Gradually add the remaining 2 tablespoons of sugar. Remove the syrup from the heat when the temperature reaches 230°F (it will keep rising as pan is removed from heat). Pour the syrup in a steady stream down the side of the bowl (to avoid splattering) containing the egg-white mixture, with the mixer on medium-low speed.

3. Beat the frosting on medium speed until it is cool, 5 to 10 minutes. The frosting should be thick and shiny. Use immediately.

CRUMB COAT

The secret to a flawlessly frosted cake is in the crumb coat. Professional bakers always apply a thin, even layer of icing to the cool, filled layers of the cake to seal in crumbs. It also allows you to smooth out any imperfections or uneven areas in the layers. The cake is chilled for 30 minutes, creating a sturdy surface onto which the final layer of icing is applied. The best icings to use for a crumb coat are any buttercreams, Whipped Ganache (page 494), and Mrs. Milman's Chocolate Frosting (recipe page 491). Generally cream-cheese frostings are applied to denser cakes that form a crust when they bake and don't need crumb coating.

honey cream-cheese frosting

MAKES 1¼ CUPS, ENOUGH FOR
ONE SINGLE-LAYER CAKE

This frosting can be made in advance and refrigerated. Bring to room temperature before using.

- 1 8-ounce package cream cheese, room temperature
- ¼ cup honey

In the bowl of an electric mixer fitted with the paddle attachment, beat cream cheese on medium speed until light and fluffy, about 2 minutes. Add honey; beat until smooth, about 1 minute. Use immediately or refrigerate, covered, until needed.

shiny cream-cheese frosting

MAKES 3 CUPS, ENOUGH FOR
ONE 2- OR 3-LAYER CAKE

- 12 ounces cream cheese, room temperature
- 6 tablespoons unsalted butter, room temperature
- 3 cups confectioners' sugar

In an electric mixer fitted with the paddle attachment, beat cream cheese on medium-low speed until smooth, about 1 minute. Add butter, and cream for 2 minutes, until smooth. Add confectioners' sugar on low speed; mix until completely combined. Beat on medium speed until smooth and fluffy, about 1 minute. Transfer to an airtight container; place in the refrigerator until mixture is chilled and firm, 3 to 4 hours, or overnight.

orange cream-cheese frosting

MAKES ENOUGH FOR TWO 6-INCH CAKES

- 12 tablespoons (1½ sticks) unsalted butter, room temperature
- 3 8-ounce packages cream cheese, room temperature
- 3 cups confectioners' sugar
- 1 tablespoon freshly grated orange zest
- 2 tablespoons freshly grated ginger
  Kosher salt

Place butter in the bowl of an electric mixture fitted with the paddle attachment; beat on medium-high speed until fluffy, about 2 minutes. Add cream cheese; beat until well combined and fluffy, about 2 minutes more. Gradually beat in sugar on low speed; beat in zest, ginger, and a pinch of salt; beat 5 minutes. Use immediately, or refrigerate and rewhip before using.

swiss-meringue buttercream

MAKES 3 CUPS, ENOUGH FOR ONE 2- OR 3-LAYER CAKE OR ABOUT 2 DOZEN CUPCAKES

This buttercream holds its shape particularly well, making it good for decorating. If the buttercream becomes too soft while piping, stir it over an ice-water bath until it stiffens. It can be made ahead and kept in an airtight container in the refrigerator up to 2 days. However, you must rewhip the buttercream before spreading it; let it sit at room temperature for about 30 minutes to soften slightly, then transfer to an electric mixer fitted with the paddle attachment. Beat on medium-high speed until the buttercream is smooth and spreadable. It will go through a curdle-like stage; just keep beating. (You can also beat the buttercream vigorously with a rubber spatula if you don't have an electric mixer.)

- 1¼ cups sugar
- 5 large egg whites
  Pinch of cream of tartar
- 1 pound (4 sticks) chilled unsalted butter, cut into small pieces
- 1 teaspoon pure vanilla extract

1. In a small saucepan over medium heat, bring the sugar and ⅓ cup water to a boil. Clip a candy thermometer onto the saucepan. Boil the syrup, brushing down the sides of the pan with a pastry brush dipped in water to prevent crystallization, until the syrup registers 240°F, soft-ball stage.

2. In the bowl of an electric mixer fitted with the whisk attachment, beat the egg whites on low speed until foamy. Add the cream of tartar and beat on medium high until stiff but not dry peaks form.

3. With the mixer running, pour the sugar syrup, down the sides of the bowl (to prevent splattering) into the egg whites in a steady stream, and beat on high speed until the steam is no longer visible, about 3 minutes. Beat in butter, piece by piece. Add vanilla; beat until smooth and spreadable, 3 to 5 minutes. If it looks curdled at any point during the beating process, continue beating until smooth.

maple-buttercream frosting

MAKES 4 CUPS, ENOUGH TO COVER ONE 4-LAYER CAKE

This frosting can be stored, refrigerated, in an airtight container up to 2 days. Before using, bring to room temperature, and beat with a hand whisk or the whisk attachment of an electric mixer for several minutes to restore the fluffiness. This frosting was developed for Maple Layer Cake (page 483).

- 6 large egg yolks
- 2 cups pure maple syrup, preferably grade-A dark amber
- 1 pound (4 sticks) chilled unsalted butter, cut into small pieces

1. Place egg yolks in the bowl of an electric mixer fitted with the whisk attachment, and beat on high speed until light and fluffy, about 5 minutes.

2. Meanwhile, pour the maple syrup into a medium saucepan. Place the pan over medium-high heat, and bring to a boil. Clip a candy thermometer onto the saucepan, and cook the syrup until the thermometer registers 240°F (soft-ball stage), about 15 minutes.

3. Remove the saucepan from the heat. While the electric mixer is running, slowly pour the syrup in a slow, steady stream down the side of the mixing bowl into the egg-yolk mixture (it is essential that the syrup touches the side of the bowl as you pour it in so the sugar will be very evenly incorporated and not splatter onto the sides of the bowl) until the syrup has been completely incorporated, about 1½ minutes. Beat until the bottom of the bowl is just slightly warm to the touch, 5 to 6 minutes.

4. Add the chilled butter, one piece at a time, until all of the butter has been completely incorporated and the frosting is fluffy, about 4 minutes more. (If the frosting appears to curdle, keep beating, and it will smooth itself out.)

mocha buttercream frosting

MAKES ABOUT 3 CUPS, ENOUGH FOR
ONE 2- OR 3-LAYER CAKE

You can substitute different extracts for the espresso, vanilla, and chocolate to change the flavor of the buttercream.

- 4 *large egg whites*
- ¾ *cup superfine sugar*
- 1 *tablespoon plus 1 teaspoon instant espresso powder*
- 1 *tablespoon pure vanilla extract*
- 1½ *cups (3 sticks) unsalted butter, cut into small pieces*
- 1 *ounce semisweet chocolate, melted and cooled*

1. Place the egg whites in the bowl of an electric mixer fitted with the whisk attachment. Beat on low speed until frothy, 2 to 3 minutes, then on medium low until the whites are foamy and begin to thicken, just before soft peaks form.

2. Set the bowl over a saucepan of simmering water. Whisk in the sugar by hand, 1 tablespoon at a time. Continue beating for 2 to 3 minutes, or until the whites are warm and the sugar is dissolved.

3. Remove the bowl from the heat, and return it to the mixer. Beat on medium-high speed until the mixture forms a very thick meringue and is cool, about 6 minutes. Do not overbeat.

4. In a small bowl, combine the espresso powder and vanilla, and stir to combine; set aside. On medium speed, beat the butter one piece at a time into the meringue mixture. Beat in espresso-vanilla mixture and chocolate until combined.

whipped ganache

MAKES 1 QUART

Ganache will not whip properly unless it is cold.

- 1 *pound bittersweet chocolate, finely chopped*
- 2½ *cups heavy cream*

1. Place the chocolate in a large heat-proof bowl.

2. Bring cream just to a boil over medium-high heat; pour over chocolate. Allow to sit for 10 minutes; use a rubber spatula or a small whisk to gently stir the chocolate and cream until combined.

3. Transfer the ganache to the refrigerator to chill; stir every 5 minutes until the mixture is cool to the touch, about 30 minutes (watching carefully and stirring so that it remains a uniform temperature). Remove the bowl from the refrigerator; whip the ganache with a wire whisk until it just barely begins to hold its shape and is slightly lighter in color. Do not overwhip, or the mixture will become grainy. The ganache will keep thickening after you stop whisking. Use immediately.

ganache glaze

MAKES 1 QUART

The longer the ganache sits undisturbed, the thicker it gets. Let it sit just long enough to remain easy to pour but not runny.

- 1 pound bittersweet chocolate, finely chopped
- 2½ cups heavy cream

1. Place the chocolate in a large heat-proof bowl.

2. Bring the cream just to a boil over medium-high heat; pour directly over the chopped chocolate. Allow to sit 10 minutes; use a rubber spatula to gently stir the chocolate and cream until combined. Allow to sit at room temperature until it is the consistency of corn syrup, about 15 minutes. Use immediately.

glossy caramel icing

MAKES 1½ CUPS, ENOUGH FOR ONE 2-LAYER CAKE

Be careful not to let the sugar get too hot while it melts; the hotter the caramel, the harder it gets as it cools, making the cake more difficult to slice.

- 1½ cups sugar
- ¾ cup heavy cream

1. Place sugar in a skillet over medium heat. Cook until it begins to melt and turns golden, 2 to 3 minutes. As sugar melts, stir with the back of a wooden spoon if needed, until amber and about 310°F on a candy thermometer, 3 to 4 minutes.

2. Slowly and carefully pour cream into skillet. Stir with the wooden spoon, reducing heat to medium low. Continue stirring; the hardened caramel will melt into the cream and become soft and liquid. Change to a whisk; continue stirring slowly to minimize bubbles, until completely smooth, 1 to 3 minutes. Remove from heat; let cool slightly, 3 to 4 minutes. Pour the icing directly onto the top of the chilled cake. If the caramel becomes too stiff to pour, warm over a double boiler or in a heat-proof bowl set over a pan of simmering water.

chocolate glaze for cupcakes

MAKES 1¾ CUPS, ENOUGH FOR 10 CUPCAKES OR 3 DOZEN MINI CUPCAKES

- 6 ounces best-quality bittersweet chocolate or semisweet chocolate, finely chopped
- 1 cup heavy cream

1. Place the chocolate in a medium heat-proof bowl. In a small saucepan, bring the cream just to a boil over medium-high heat. Immediately remove the cream from the heat, and pour it over the chocolate. Let the mixture stand 5 minutes, then stir until smooth. Let the glaze stand at room temperature for about another 10 minutes.

2. For the smoothest possible surface, carefully dip the cupcakes into the prepared chocolate glaze. Let the cupcakes drip, dipped-side down, for several seconds, and then turn right-side up. Allow the glaze to set, about 20 minutes, before serving.

vanilla whipped cream

MAKES 1¾ CUPS, ENOUGH FOR A DOZEN INDIVIDUAL SHORTCAKES, CRISPS, OR COBBLERS

Whisk the infused cream by hand for very soft peaks. Add up to another tablespoon confectioners' sugar for sweeter whipped cream.

- 1 cup heavy cream
- 1 vanilla bean, split lengthwise and scraped
- 1 tablespoon confectioners' sugar

1. Place the cream, vanilla bean, and seed scrapings in a saucepan over medium heat; bring just to a simmer; immediately remove from the heat. Cover and steep for 10 minutes. Discard the pod.

2. Prepare an ice-water bath. Pass cream through a fine sieve or a cheesecloth-lined strainer into a bowl set in the ice bath. Let stand, stirring occasionally, until cold. Add sugar; whisk by hand until soft peaks form, about 5 minutes.

pastries

·······················

roasted-strawberry napoleon

SERVES 4

Place an empty pan on top of the puff pastry while it bakes to ensure that it puffs evenly.

- 2 tablespoons light corn syrup
  All-purpose flour, for dusting
- 1 sheet frozen puff pastry (from a 17¼-ounce package), thawed
- 2 tablespoons unsalted butter, room temperature
- ½ vanilla bean, split lengthwise and scraped
- 14 medium (about 1 pint) strawberries, hulled
- 1 tablespoon granulated sugar
- 2 tablespoons Grand Marnier, optional
- 1 tablespoon fresh orange juice
- ½ cup heavy cream
- 1 tablespoon confectioners' sugar
  Orange Pastry Cream (recipe follows)
- 1 tablespoon finely chopped pistachios

1. Preheat the oven to 375°F. Line a baking pan with parchment paper, and set aside. Have ready another baking pan, unlined. In a small bowl, combine the corn syrup with 1 teaspoon warm water; set aside.

2. On a lightly floured surface, roll puff-pastry sheet into a 12-inch square; trim edges. Cut on the fold, making three 4 x 12-inch rectangles. Place on lined pan. Top with parchment. Place unlined pan on top of filled pan. Bake 8 minutes.

3. Remove top pan and top piece of parchment; return pastry to oven. Bake until pastry starts to puff and is light golden brown, about 8 minutes. Remove from oven; lightly brush with reserved corn-syrup mixture. Using a long metal spatula, gently flip. Brush again with the corn-syrup mixture. Bake until shiny and golden brown, about 8 minutes more. Using the spatula, transfer to a wire rack to cool completely. Store in an airtight container until ready to use.

4. Raise oven temperature to 450°F. Using a pastry brush, coat the bottom of a medium ovenproof skillet with 1 tablespoon butter; scrape the vanilla seeds into the butter. Place the strawberries, cut-sides down, in the pan. Sprinkle with the granulated sugar, and lay the vanilla pod on top. Roast until the strawberries start to "slump" and feel soft when squeezed, about 10 minutes. Using a slotted spoon, transfer all but two of the berries and the vanilla pod to a plate to cool. Reserve the juices in the pan.

5. Transfer the pan to the stove over high heat. If using the Grand Marnier, carefully add it to the pan, standing back while doing so. Carefully use a match to ignite the alcohol in the mixture; it will flame up only briefly and burn out in about 1 minute. Reduce heat to medium. Using a fork, mash the two remaining strawberries; add the orange juice. (If not using liqueur, add 2 tablespoons more orange juice.) Cook until thick and syrupy, 30 to 40 seconds; discard the vanilla pod. Remove from the heat. Swirl in the remaining butter, and set aside.

6. Combine the cream and confectioners' sugar in the bowl of an electric mixer fitted with the whisk attachment, and beat until stiff peaks form.

7. Without using a tip, close off the end of a pastry bag with a paper clip or clothespin; fill with the whipped cream. Repeat, filling a second pastry bag with the orange pastry cream. (Alternatively, use two resealable plastic bags, and cut off a corner on each; an offset spatula can also be used to spread both whipped and pastry creams.)

8. Pipe a tablespoon of the pastry cream in the middle of a serving plate. Center a rectangle of the puff pastry on top (this anchors the napoleon). Leaving a ½-inch border, pipe the orange pastry cream onto the puff pastry. Arrange the roasted strawberries on top of the pastry cream; scrape any remaining juices from the plate into the reserved sauce. Place a second rectangle of puff pastry on top of the strawberries. Leaving a ½-inch border, pipe the whipped cream onto the second rectangle of puff pastry. Sprinkle with the pistachios. Place a third rectangle of the puff pastry on top.

9. Using a serrated knife, slice the assembled napoleon into 4 pieces. Drizzle with the reserved sauce, and serve.

orange pastry cream

MAKES 1 CUP

- 1 cup milk
- 2 large strips orange zest
- ¼ cup sugar
- ½ vanilla bean, split lengthwise and scraped
- 2 tablespoons cornstarch
- 1 large egg
- 1 large egg yolk
- 2 tablespoons unsalted butter, cut into small pieces

1. In a small saucepan, combine the milk, orange zest, and 2 tablespoons sugar. Add the vanilla bean and seed scrapings. Bring the mixture to a boil over medium-high heat, stirring occasionally. Remove from the heat, and cover. Steep 10 minutes; discard the orange zest and vanilla pod.

2. Prepare an ice-water bath; set aside. In a small bowl, mix together the remaining sugar with the cornstarch. In a medium bowl, whisk together the egg and egg yolk; add the sugar mixture, and continue whisking until pale yellow.

3. Return the milk mixture to the heat. Bring to a boil, scraping the vanilla seeds from the sides of the pan.

4. Slowly ladle half the hot milk mixture into the egg-yolk mixture, whisking constantly. Transfer this mixture back to the saucepan over medium heat, whisking constantly and scraping the sides and edges of the pan. Once it comes to a boil, whisk vigorously until very thick, about 1½ minutes.

5. Remove the pan from the heat. Using a rubber spatula, scrape the pastry cream into a medium bowl; set over the ice-water bath. Whisk the butter, piece by piece, into the pastry cream while still warm. Let cool completely. Lay plastic wrap on the surface of the pastry cream to prevent a skin from forming; wrap tightly. Store the pastry cream, refrigerated, up to 1 day.

banana pillows

SERVES 4

Cut the dough along the folds of the puff pastry to prevent the pillows from rising unevenly.

- All-purpose flour, for dusting
- 1 sheet frozen puff pastry (from a 17¼-ounce package), thawed
- 8 tablespoons (1 stick) unsalted butter
- ⅓ cup packed light-brown sugar
- ¼ teaspoon pure vanilla extract
- Pinch of kosher salt
- 3 tablespoons heavy cream
- 4 (1½ pounds) bananas, sliced on a diagonal, ¼ inch thick
- Confectioners' sugar
- Chocolate shavings, for garnish

1. Preheat the oven to 400°F. On a lightly floured surface, roll the pastry to ⅛ inch thick; cut out four 5-inch squares. Place on a parchment-lined baking sheet; bake until golden, about 15 minutes. Remove from the oven; set aside to cool.

2. Place the butter, sugar, vanilla, and salt in a small skillet over medium heat. Cook, stirring frequently, until the butter and sugar are melted and combined, about 5 minutes. Stir in the cream until the mixture is smooth. Add the bananas; gently stir until coated. Remove from the heat.

3. Using a paring knife, remove and discard a 2-inch square from the top center of the reserved pastry pillows; keep the bottom intact. Fill with the banana mixture. Dust with the confectioners' sugar, and garnish with chocolate shavings. Serve.

chocolate turnovers

MAKES 9

All-purpose flour, for work surface
1 *sheet frozen puff pastry (from a 17¼-ounce package), thawed*
1 *large egg yolk*
2 *tablespoons heavy cream*
2¼ *ounces semisweet chocolate, cut into 9 pieces*

1. Preheat the oven to 400°F. On a lightly floured surface, roll out the puff pastry to form a 12-inch square. Trim the edges to make a perfect square.

2. Cut the puff pastry into nine 3½-inch squares, and transfer them to a parchment-lined baking sheet. Discard the excess, or save for another use.

3. In a small bowl, whisk together the egg yolk and heavy cream to make an egg wash. Neatly brush a little of the egg wash along 2 adjacent edges of each square. Place a piece of chocolate just below the center of each square, and fold down the unwashed edges to enclose the chocolate and form a triangle. Using your fingers, gently but firmly press the puff-pastry edges together to seal.

4. Place the baking sheet in the freezer until the pastry is chilled, about 20 minutes. Remove from the freezer, and brush the tops liberally with the remaining egg wash. Place in the oven, and bake until the triangles are puffed and golden brown, about 15 minutes. Transfer the sheet to a wire rack to cool slightly. Serve warm.

baklava

MAKES 4 DOZEN

Baklava is a popular Greek and Middle Eastern pastry made from layers of buttered phyllo dough filled with chopped nuts and soaked with a sugar or honey syrup. It is traditionally an Easter specialty, consisting of forty layers of phyllo to represent the forty days of Lent.

3 *cups very finely chopped walnuts, almonds, or a mix*
2 *teaspoons ground cinnamon*
¼ *teaspoon ground allspice*
½ *teaspoon ground cloves*
1 *pound frozen phyllo pastry, preferably extra-thin, thawed*
1¼ *cups (2½ sticks) unsalted butter, melted*
2 *cups sugar*

1. Preheat the oven to 350°F. Combine the nuts, cinnamon, allspice, and cloves in a bowl.

2. Unroll the phyllo; halve crosswise. Immediately cover with plastic wrap and then a damp towel. Keep covered while working.

3. Brush a 9 x 13 x 2-inch baking pan with melted butter. Lay 1 sheet phyllo in pan. Lightly brush with the melted butter; cover with another sheet of phyllo, and butter again. Layer the phyllo, and butter 5 more times each, ending with the phyllo.

4. Sprinkle phyllo with 2 tablespoons nut mixture. Lay 1 sheet phyllo over, brush with butter, and cover with a sheet of phyllo. Sprinkle with 2 tablespoons of the nut mixture; repeat layering with butter, phyllo, and nuts until the filling is used up, for a total of about 20 layers. Lay 1 sheet of phyllo over; brush with butter. Layer phyllo and butter 6 more times.

5. Using a sharp knife, score surface of pastry (¼ inch deep) diagonally into diamonds (about 2 inches long). Bake until golden brown, about 40 minutes. Transfer to a rack to cool 5 to 10 minutes.

6. Meanwhile, place the sugar and 1 cup water in a saucepan; bring to a boil over high heat. Reduce heat; simmer 3 to 4 minutes.

7. Pour the syrup over the surface of the baklava; let cool completely. To serve, use a sharp knife to cut into pieces along the scored lines.

....

WORKING WITH PHYLLO

Phyllo (Greek for "leaf") is a tissue-paper-thin pastry, made only of flour and water. Used in Greek and Middle Eastern savory and sweet recipes, phyllo (also spelled "filo") can be found frozen in supermarkets and fresh in Greek markets. (Packages labeled as strudel leaves may also be used.) Use fresh phyllo if you can find it. Frozen phyllo must be thawed in the refrigerator overnight before using. It should not be refrozen. If you are in a rush, frozen phyllo may be defrosted at room temperature in about an hour, but it may be more difficult to work with.

To work with the sheets, unfold and lay them flat on a work surface. Remove as many sheets as the recipe calls for plus one or two extra. Chill remaining sheets for another use. Cover the sheets with a damp kitchen towel so they do not dry out. (Because the dough is so thin, it dries out very easily and cannot be salvaged.) To form the pastry, brush the thin sheets one by one with melted butter or oil, as indicated in the recipe, before layering or folding them around the filling.

When working with phyllo, rips or tears are common; just mend the torn area by brushing it with the melted butter or oil and then patching it with another piece of phyllo. If the entire package of phyllo is torn or cracked in the same place throughout all of the layers, alternate the way you arrange the sheets on top of one another.

....

roasted plum strudels

SERVES 10

3½ pounds (10 to 12) large ripe but firm plums, halved, pits removed, halves cut into 1-inch pieces

  2 tablespoons fresh lemon juice

  ¼ cup sugar

  1 teaspoon ground cinnamon

  6 18¼ x 11½-inch sheets frozen phyllo pastry, thawed

  6 tablespoons unsalted butter, melted

  ⅓ cup shelled unsalted pistachios, finely chopped

1. Preheat the oven to 400°F. In a medium bowl, combine the plums, lemon juice, sugar, and cinnamon, and toss well.

2. Divide the plum mixture in half, and arrange in two 9 x 13-inch glass baking dishes. Roast, stirring occasionally with a wooden spoon, for 25 to 30 minutes. The plum juices will reduce to a glaze during roasting. Remove the plums from the oven, and cool completely. (The recipe can be prepared to this point 1 day ahead.)

3. Unroll the phyllo; cover the unused portion with a damp kitchen towel as you work to prevent it from drying out. Cover the work surface with parchment paper. Place a sheet of phyllo on the parchment paper. Brush evenly and lightly with the melted butter. Cover with another sheet of the pastry, and brush again with the butter. Sprinkle half the pistachios over this layer. Repeat the process with 2 more layers of phyllo and the remaining pistachios, then top with 2 more layers of the buttered phyllo.

4. With the long side of the pastry toward you, spoon the cooled plums along its length, 1 inch from the edge nearest you. Using the parchment to help you, gently roll up the pastry to encase the plums. Don't roll the pastry too tightly.

5. Brush the strudel lightly with the butter, and carefully lift it onto a large baking sheet. Bake until the pastry is golden brown and the fruit is bubbling, 35 to 45 minutes. Let cool on a pan for at least 20 minutes; use 2 spatulas to transfer to a serving platter. Serve warm or at room temperature.

galaktoboureko beggar's purses

MAKES 2 DOZEN

Galaktoboureko, like baklava, is a classic Greek dessert, hailing from Macedonia. "Gala" means milk in Greek, and "boureko" translates to stuffed, which aptly describes these crisp phyllo pastries filled with creamy milk custard. Phyllo comes in different thicknesses; if possible, use extra-thin. Traditional recipes call for Cream of Wheat as a thickener.

- 1 quart milk
- 8 tablespoons (1 stick) unsalted butter, room temperature, plus 12 tablespoons (1½ sticks) butter, melted
- ½ cup uncooked Cream of Wheat
- 4 large eggs, beaten
- 1½ cups sugar
- 1 teaspoon pure vanilla extract
- 12 ounces frozen phyllo pastry, thawed

1. Preheat the oven to 350°F. In a medium saucepan, bring the milk and the 8 tablespoons butter to a simmer over medium-high heat, and cook for 5 minutes. Slowly whisk in the Cream of Wheat. Lower heat to medium, and cook, stirring, 3 to 4 minutes. Slowly add the eggs; continue to cook, stirring with a wooden spoon, until the mixture begins to thicken, about 8 minutes. Add 1 cup sugar and the vanilla; stir, and cook 10 to 12 minutes, until the custard has a porridge-like consistency, about 10 minutes. Let cool.

2. Carefully unroll the phyllo. Immediately cover it with plastic wrap and then a damp towel. Keep covered as you work.

3. Place 1 sheet phyllo on a work surface. Lightly brush the phyllo with the melted butter, place another sheet on top, and brush with the butter; place a third sheet of phyllo on top and brush with the butter. Cut into 4 rectangles. Place 1 heaping tablespoon of the custard in the center of a rectangle. Gather and pinch the pastry around the custard, forming a purse shape with a ruffled top. Place in a muffin tin so it retains its shape while the others are formed. Repeat the process with remaining phyllo and custard, making a total of 24 purses.

4. Transfer the purses to a parchment-lined baking sheet; brush the sides of the purses with the melted butter. Bake until flaky and golden brown, 25 to 30 minutes. Transfer to a wire rack to cool slightly.

5. While the pastries are baking, place the remaining sugar and ¼ cup water in a small saucepan; bring to a boil over high heat. Reduce heat; simmer 3 to 4 minutes. Let cool. Drizzle the syrup over warm pastries. Serve.

profiteroles with whipped coconut cream and caramelized bananas

SERVES 12

Profiteroles are a classic dessert made with pâte à choux pastry, the same pastry used to make cream puffs. This recipe for pâte à choux is made with matzo cake meal (a finer grinding of regular matzo meal) to make it kosher for Passover. The unfilled profiteroles may be made up to 3 weeks ahead and kept in resealable plastic bags in the freezer, and the whipped coconut cream may be made up to 4 days ahead and kept in the refrigerator. Assemble profiteroles right before serving.

- 10 tablespoons butter
- ⅛ teaspoon kosher salt
- 2 tablespoons granulated sugar
- ¾ cup matzo cake meal
- ¼ cup potato starch
- 5 large eggs, room temperature
- 6 medium just-ripe bananas
- ¼ cup plus 2 tablespoons packed light-brown sugar
- ½ cup fresh orange juice, optional
  Whipped Coconut Cream (recipe follows)

1. Preheat the oven to 400°F. Place 1 cup water, 6 tablespoons butter, the salt, and granulated sugar in a medium saucepan. Bring to a boil over medium heat. Add the matzo meal and potato starch at the same time; stir vigorously with a wooden spoon. The mixture will become extremely stiff. Continue stirring for 4 minutes more.

2. Transfer to the bowl of an electric mixer fitted with the paddle attachment. On medium speed, add the eggs one at a time, fully incorporating each egg before adding the next. The mixture should be smooth and satiny but stiff enough to form a mound when dropped from a spoon.

3. Fit a pastry bag with a plain coupler. Line two baking sheets with parchment paper. Fill the pastry bag with profiterole batter. Pipe six 2½-inch mounds on each pan, spacing 3 inches apart.

4. Transfer to oven, and bake until profiteroles are puffed and golden, about 25 minutes. Transfer to a wire rack to cool.

5. Slice the bananas in half lengthwise; cut each half into thirds. Heat a large skillet over medium heat. Add 2 tablespoons butter and 1½ tablespoons brown sugar. When the butter has melted and is sizzling, add half the bananas; brown them, about 3 minutes per side. Transfer the bananas to a large shallow container to cool in a single layer. Melt another 2 tablespoons butter with 1½ tablespoons brown sugar in the skillet; brown the remaining bananas. Transfer to a plate.

6. To make the sauce, add the orange juice, the remaining brown sugar, and two pieces of the caramelized banana to the empty pan. Whisk the mixture over medium heat until thick and the banana dissolves, about 1 minute.

7. Slice the tops of the profiteroles, leaving a small hinge attached. Insert 2 or 3 pieces of the banana. Spoon 2 tablespoons of the coconut cream onto the banana. Serve immediately with sauce on the side.

whipped coconut cream
MAKES 1½ CUPS

When canned coconut milk is chilled in the refrigerator, the cream congeals at the top. Whipped with sugar, the cream makes a delicious nondairy topping.

- 3 cans chilled coconut milk
- 2 tablespoons superfine or granulated sugar

Place a large bowl and a wire whisk in the freezer for 10 minutes. Open the chilled coconut-milk cans, and skim the cream from tops. Make sure not to get the thin liquid from the bottom of the can, or the cream will not become stiff when whipped. Place the cream and sugar in a bowl; whisk until thick and stiff. Store, covered with plastic wrap, in the refrigerator until ready to use.

cookies

AND

candy

....

living large chocolate-chunk cookies

MAKES 13

Chill the dough for at least 2 hours or overnight; the extra butter in the dough causes the cookies to spread too thin unless the dough is very cold.

- 1 cup (2 sticks) unsalted butter, room temperature
- ¾ cup packed dark-brown sugar
- ½ cup granulated sugar
- 1 large egg
- 1 teaspoon pure vanilla extract
- 2 cups sifted all-purpose flour
- ½ teaspoon baking soda
- ½ teaspoon kosher salt
- 1 cup chocolate chunks or chopped bittersweet chocolate

1. In the bowl of an electric mixer fitted with the paddle attachment, cream butter and both sugars on medium-high speed until fluffy, about 3 minutes, scraping down sides of bowl once or twice during mixing. Add egg; mix on high speed to combine. Add vanilla; mix to combine. Scrape down sides of bowl. In a medium bowl, whisk together flour, baking soda, and salt. Add flour mixture; beat on low speed just until incorporated. Stir in chocolate. Refrigerate for at least 2 hours.

2. Preheat the oven to 400°F with two racks centered. Line three baking sheets with parchment paper. Roll ¼ cup dough into a ball. Place on a prepared baking sheet. Repeat, placing 4 on each of two baking sheets. Bake until just brown around the edges, rotating sheets between oven racks halfway through baking, 12 to 15 minutes. Meanwhile, prepare a third baking sheet. Transfer sheets to wire racks to cool, then transfer cookies to the racks to cool completely. Repeat with remaining dough. Store in an airtight container up to 1 week.

torie's chocolate-chunk toffee cookies

MAKES ABOUT 2½ DOZEN

Martha's friend Torie Hallock often makes these delicious cookies for her. Toffee bits can be found in the baking sections of grocery stores. If not, use the small pieces of Heath bars sold in bags.

- 1½ cups all-purpose flour
- 1 teaspoon baking soda
- 1 cup (2 sticks) unsalted butter, room temperature
- ¾ cup packed light-brown sugar
- ¾ cup granulated sugar
- 1 large egg
- 1 teaspoon pure vanilla extract
- 1½ cups old-fashioned rolled oats
- 1 cup dried cherries, optional
- 4½ ounces bittersweet chocolate, coarsely chopped
- 1 cup (about 7 ounces) toffee pieces, finely chopped

1. Preheat the oven to 350°F with two racks centered. Line two baking sheets with parchment paper (or use two nonstick baking sheets). In a large bowl, sift together the flour and baking soda.

2. In the bowl of an electric mixer fitted with the paddle attachment, cream the butter and sugars on medium high until light and fluffy, about 3 minutes, scraping down the sides of the bowl once or twice during mixing. Add the egg; mix on high speed to combine. Add the vanilla; mix to combine. Scrape down the sides of the bowl.

3. Working in additions, add the flour mixture to the egg mixture on low speed until well combined. Add the oats, cherries, chocolate, and toffee pieces; mix to combine.

4. Spoon dough by heaping tablespoons onto the baking sheets, spacing the cookies 2 inches apart.

5. Bake until golden brown, rotating sheets between oven racks halfway through baking for even browning, about 10 minutes. Transfer to a wire rack to cool. Store in an airtight container up to 1 week.

classic oatmeal cookies

MAKES 13 LARGE OR 3 DOZEN
MEDIUM COOKIES

- 1 cup (2 sticks) unsalted butter, room temperature
- 1 cup packed light-brown sugar
- 1 cup granulated sugar
- 2 large eggs, room temperature
- 1 teaspoon pure vanilla extract
- 3 cups old-fashioned rolled oats
- 1 cup plus 2 tablespoons all-purpose flour
- 1 teaspoon baking soda
- 1 teaspoon baking powder
- ½ cup wheat germ
- 12 ounces good-quality chocolate, chopped into chunks, or 1½ cups golden raisins, optional

1. Preheat the oven to 350°F with two racks centered. Line two baking sheets with parchment paper; set aside. In the bowl of an electric mixer fitted with the paddle attachment, cream the butter and both sugars on medium-high speed until light and fluffy, about 3 minutes, scraping down the sides of the bowl once or twice during mixing. Add the eggs; mix on high speed to combine. Add the vanilla; mix to combine. Scrape down the sides of the bowl.

2. Combine the rolled oats, flour, baking soda, baking powder, and wheat germ in a large bowl, and stir to combine. Add the dry mixture to the butter mixture, then mix on low speed just to combine, 10 to 15 seconds. Remove the bowl from mixer, and stir in your choice of chocolate chunks or golden raisins, if using.

3. Use a large (2½ ounce) or small (1¼ ounce) ice-cream scoop to form balls of the dough. Place the balls of dough about 4 inches apart on the baking sheets. Bake until golden and just set, rotating the sheets between the oven racks halfway through baking to ensure even browning, about 18 minutes for large cookies and 14 minutes for small cookies. Transfer the sheets to a wire rack to cool about 5 minutes before transferring the cookies to the rack. Store in an airtight container up to 1 week.

low-fat oatmeal cookies

MAKES ABOUT 4 DOZEN

- ¾ cup plus 2 tablespoons all-purpose flour
- ½ teaspoon baking powder
- ¾ cup old-fashioned rolled oats
- 3 tablespoons finely chopped golden raisins
- 3 tablespoons finely chopped dried cherries
- 2 tablespoons finely chopped crystallized ginger
- ¼ teaspoon kosher salt
- 4 tablespoons unsalted butter, room temperature
- ¼ cup packed dark-brown sugar
- 2 tablespoons granulated sugar
- 1 large egg yolk, room temperature
- ½ teaspoon pure vanilla extract

1. Preheat the oven to 400°F with two racks centered. Line two baking sheets with parchment paper, and set aside. In a medium bowl, combine the flour, baking powder, oats, raisins, cherries, crystallized ginger, and salt. Stir well.

2. In the bowl of an electric mixer fitted with the paddle attachment, cream the butter and both sugars on medium-high speed until light and fluffy, about 3 minutes, scraping down the sides of the bowl once or twice. Add the egg yolk, 1 teaspoon water, and the vanilla; mix on high speed to combine. Scrape down the sides of the bowl. Add the flour mixture, and beat on low speed just until combined.

3. Form the dough into ¾-inch balls, and place them 1 inch apart on the prepared baking sheets. Using a spatula, flatten the balls into ¼-inch-thick rounds. Bake until golden brown, rotating the sheets between the oven racks halfway through baking to ensure even browning, about 10 minutes. Transfer the sheets to a wire rack to cool for 3 minutes, then transfer the cookies to the rack, and let cool completely. Store in an airtight container for up to 1 week.

FIT TO EAT RECIPE PER COOKIE: 74 CALORIES, 2 G TOTAL FAT, 30% CALORIES FROM FAT, 14 MG CHOLESTEROL, 12 G CARBOHYDRATE, 54 MG SODIUM, 1 G PROTEIN, TRACE OF DIETARY FIBER

chewy ginger cookies

MAKES 2 DOZEN

- 2½ cups all-purpose flour
- 2¼ teaspoons baking soda
- ½ teaspoon kosher salt
- 1 tablespoon ground ginger
- ½ teaspoon ground allspice
- ½ teaspoon ground white pepper
- 1 cup (2 sticks) plus 2 tablespoons unsalted butter
- ½ cup packed light-brown sugar
- 1 cup granulated sugar
- 1 large egg
- ¼ cup plus 2 tablespoons unsulfured molasses

1. In a medium bowl, whisk together flour, baking soda, salt, ginger, allspice, and pepper; set aside.

2. In the bowl of an electric mixer fitted with the paddle attachment, cream the butter, brown sugar, and ½ cup granulated sugar until light and fluffy; about 5 minutes. Beat in the egg and molasses. Add the flour mixture; mix until combined. Form into a ball; wrap in plastic. Chill the dough at least 2 hours or overnight.

3. Preheat the oven to 350°F with two racks centered. Line two baking sheets with parchment paper and set aside. Pour the remaining granulated sugar into a bowl. Form the dough into 1-inch balls; roll each ball in the sugar. Place the coated balls on the prepared baking sheets, spaced 2 inches apart. Using the palm of your hand, flatten each ball slightly into a disk.

4. Bake the cookies until browned, rotating the sheets between the oven racks halfway through baking to ensure even browning, about 10 minutes. Transfer the cookies to a wire rack to cool completely. Store in an airtight container up to 1 week.

chocolate-gingerbread cookies

MAKES 2 DOZEN

- 7 ounces best-quality semisweet chocolate
- 1½ cups plus 1 tablespoon all-purpose flour
- 1¼ teaspoons ground ginger
- 1 teaspoon ground cinnamon
- ¼ teaspoon ground cloves
- ¼ teaspoon ground nutmeg
- 1 tablespoon cocoa powder
- 8 tablespoons (1 stick) unsalted butter
- 1 tablespoon freshly grated ginger
- ½ cup packed dark-brown sugar
- ¼ cup unsulfured molasses
- 1 teaspoon baking soda
- ¼ cup granulated sugar

1. Chop chocolate into ¼-inch chunks; set aside. In a medium bowl, sift together the flour, ground ginger, cinnamon, cloves, nutmeg, and cocoa.

2. In the bowl of an electric mixer fitted with the paddle attachment, cream the butter and grated ginger until whitened, about 4 minutes. Add the brown sugar; beat until combined. Add the molasses; beat until combined.

3. In a small bowl, dissolve the baking soda in 1½ teaspoons of very hot water. Beat half of the flour mixture into the butter mixture. Beat in the baking-soda mixture, then the remaining half of the flour mixture. Mix in the chocolate; turn out onto a piece of plastic wrap. Pat the dough out to about 1 inch thick; seal with the wrap; refrigerate until firm, 2 hours or overnight.

4. Preheat the oven to 325°F with two racks centered. Line two baking sheets with parchment paper. Roll the dough into 1½-inch balls; place, 2 inches apart, on the baking sheets. Refrigerate 20 minutes. Place the granulated sugar in a small bowl. Roll the cookie balls in the granulated sugar, and transfer them back to the sheets. Bake until the surfaces crack slightly, 10 to 15 minutes; let cool 5 minutes; transfer to a wire rack to cool completely. Store in an airtight container up to 1 week.

lemon-ginger drop cookies

MAKES 3 DOZEN

- 8 tablespoons (1 stick) unsalted butter
- ¾ cup plus 2 tablespoons sugar, plus more for sprinkling
- 1 large egg
- 1 tablespoon grated lemon zest
- 1⅓ cups all-purpose flour
- ½ teaspoon ground ginger
- ½ teaspoon baking soda
- ¼ teaspoon kosher salt
- ¼ cup finely chopped crystallized ginger

1. Preheat the oven to 350°F with two racks centered. Line two baking sheets with parchment; set aside. In the bowl of an electric mixer fitted with the paddle attachment, cream the butter and sugar on medium-high speed until light and fluffy, about 3 minutes, scraping down the sides of the bowl twice. Add the egg; mix on high speed to combine. Add the zest; mix to combine.

2. In a bowl, whisk together the flour, ground ginger, baking soda, salt, and crystallized ginger; add to the butter mixture; mix on medium-low speed to combine, about 20 seconds.

3. Using two spoons, drop about 2 teaspoons of the batter on the prepared baking sheet; repeat, spacing them 3 inches apart. Bake for 7 minutes. Sprinkle the cookies with sugar, rotate the sheets between the oven racks, and bake until just golden, about 7 minutes more. Slide the parchment with the cookies on it onto a wire rack; let cool 15 minutes. Store in an airtight container up to 1 week.

DROP COOKIES

For perfect, evenly shaped cookies every time, use a small ice-cream scoop to scoop chilled cookie dough onto baking sheets.

molasses drop cookies

MAKES 2 DOZEN

- 8 tablespoons (1 stick) unsalted butter
- ½ cup packed dark-brown sugar
- 1 large egg
- ¼ cup plus 2 tablespoons molasses
- 1¼ cups all-purpose flour
- ½ teaspoon baking soda
- ¼ teaspoon kosher salt
  Granulated sugar, for sprinkling

1. Preheat the oven to 350°F with two racks centered. Line two baking sheets with parchment; set aside. In the bowl of an electric mixer fitted with the paddle attachment, cream the butter and sugar on medium-high speed until light and fluffy, about 3 minutes, scraping down the sides of the bowl twice.

2. Add egg and molasses and mix on medium speed until combined, about 20 seconds, scraping down the sides of the bowl once.

3. In a medium bowl, whisk together the flour, baking soda, and salt; add to the butter mixture. Mix on low speed to combine, about 20 seconds.

4. Using two spoons, drop 2 teaspoons of the batter on the prepared baking sheet; repeat, spacing them 3 inches apart. Bake for 5 minutes. Sprinkle the tops of the cookies with granulated sugar, rotate the sheets between the oven shelves, and bake 8 minutes more. Rotate the sheets again, and bake until the cookies are just brown around the edges, about 6 minutes more. Slide the parchment with the cookies onto a wire rack; let cool for 15 minutes. Store in an airtight container up to 1 week.

almond crisps

MAKES 4 TO 5 DOZEN

1¾   cups unblanched almonds, finely ground
1½   cups sugar
 3   large egg whites
 1   teaspoon pure almond extract
 1   teaspoon pure vanilla extract
 ½   cup unblanched almond slices
     Nonstick cooking spray

1. Preheat oven to 375°F. Line a baking sheet with parchment; lightly coat with cooking spray. In the bowl of an electric mixer fitted with the paddle attachment, combine ground almonds, sugar, and egg whites. Beat on medium speed until thick, about 3 minutes. Beat in extracts.

2. Roll dough into 1-inch balls; place 2 inches apart on prepared baking sheet. Flatten each ball with dampened fingers; press 2 sliced almonds on top.

3. Bake until just brown on top, about 10 minutes. Transfer cookie sheet to a wire rack for 5 to 10 minutes. Remove cookies from baking sheet while still warm, and place on a wire rack to cool.

macaroons

MAKES 20

For chocolate-chunk macaroons, add ½ cup semisweet chocolate chunks (about 3 ounces).

 ¾   cup sugar
2½   cups unsweetened shredded coconut
 2   large egg whites
 1   teaspoon pure vanilla extract
     Pinch of kosher salt

1. Preheat the oven to 350°F with a rack in the center. Line a baking sheet with parchment paper; set aside. In a bowl, combine sugar, coconut, egg whites, vanilla, and salt. Use your hands to mix well, completely combining the ingredients.

2. Dampen your hands with cold water. Form 1½ tablespoons of the mixture into a loose haystack shape; place on baking sheet. Repeat with remaining mixture, placing macaroons about 1 inch apart.

3. Bake until golden brown, about 15 minutes. Transfer the baking sheet to a wire rack to cool. Store in an airtight container for up to 3 days.

chocolate macaroons

MAKES 2 DOZEN

 4   ounces semisweet chocolate, broken
     into small pieces
 ¼   cup unsweetened cocoa, sifted
 ¾   cup sugar
2½   cups unsweetened shredded coconut
 3   large egg whites
 1   teaspoon pure vanilla extract
     Pinch of kosher salt

1. Preheat the oven to 350°F with a rack in the center. Line a baking sheet with parchment paper.

2. In the top of a double boiler or in a heat-proof bowl set over a pan of simmering water, melt the chocolate. Stir with a rubber spatula until the chocolate is smooth, and set aside to cool.

3. In a bowl, combine cooled chocolate, cocoa, sugar, coconut, egg whites, vanilla, and salt. Completely combine ingredients with your hands.

4. Dampen your hands with cold water. Form 1½ tablespoons mixture into a loose haystack shape; place on the baking sheet. Repeat with remaining mixture, placing the macaroons about 1 inch apart.

5. Bake until golden brown, about 15 minutes. Transfer the baking sheet to a wire rack, and cool. Store in an airtight container for up to 3 days.

coconut pyramids

MAKES ABOUT 3½ DOZEN

One of our most popular cookies ever, these macaroons work best with unsweetened coconut (see Food Sources, page 648), but if you can't find it, use ½ cup sugar, 4 cups sweetened coconut, 3 large egg whites, ½ teaspoon almond extract, and ½ teaspoon vanilla extract in place of the amounts listed below.

- 1¾   cups sugar
- 5¼   cups unsweetened shredded coconut
- 7   large egg whites
    Pinch of kosher salt
- 2   tablespoons unsalted butter, melted
- 1   teaspoon pure almond extract
- 1   teaspoon pure vanilla extract
- 4   ounces semisweet chocolate
- ½   teaspoon pure vegetable shortening

1. Preheat the oven to 350°F with a rack in the center. Line a baking sheet with parchment paper; set aside. In a large bowl, using your hands, mix together the sugar, coconut, egg whites, and salt. Add the butter and extracts, and combine well. Refrigerate for at least 1 hour.

2. Moisten your palms with cold water. Roll 1 tablespoon of the coconut mixture in your palms, squeezing tightly together 2 or 3 times to form a compact ball. Place the ball on a clean surface and, using a spatula, flatten one side at a time to form a pyramid shape.

3. Place the pyramids on the prepared baking sheet about 1 inch apart, and bake until the edges are golden brown, about 15 minutes. Transfer the baking sheet to a wire rack to cool completely.

4. In the top of a double boiler or in a heat-proof bowl set over a pan of simmering water, melt the chocolate and shortening; stir occasionally with a rubber spatula until smooth. Dip top ½ inch of each pyramid in the melted chocolate. Transfer each dipped macaroon to a cooled baking sheet to allow chocolate to harden. Store in an airtight container up to 3 days.

fruit jumbles

MAKES 2½ DOZEN

The pecans may be replaced with other nuts or an additional cup of granola. Mini-muffin-cup liners are available in some grocery stores and party stores and also by mail (see Equipment Sources, page 650).

- 2   cups dried fruits, such as pineapple, apricots, cranberries, and golden raisins
- 1   cup unsalted pecans, toasted (see page 644), coarsely chopped
- 1½   cups Homemade Granola (page 581) or prepared
- ½   teaspoon kosher salt
- ⅔   cup light corn syrup
- 2   tablespoons unsalted butter
- 1   tablespoon fresh orange juice
- 1   teaspoon grated orange zest

1. Cut the dried fruit, except the raisins, into ¼-inch pieces. In a medium bowl, combine all of the dried fruit, the nuts, granola, and salt; set aside.

2. In a small saucepan, combine the corn syrup, butter, and orange juice. Set the pan over medium heat until the butter has melted, about 4 minutes. Remove from the heat, and stir in the orange zest.

3. Pour corn-syrup mixture over fruit mixture; stir well. Set aside until completely cool, about 1 hour.

4. Using a small 1¼-inch ice-cream scoop or a tablespoon, form the cooled mixture into 30 balls. Transfer the balls into paper mini-muffin cups or in a single layer in an airtight container, and refrigerate until cold, about 30 minutes. Store in an airtight container, refrigerated, up to 1 week.

· ·

COCONUT

Unsweetened coconut (see Food Sources, page 648), available in health-food stores and gourmet grocers, is essential for these macaroons. Don't use the thinly shredded, sweetened angel-flake kind—it's too sweet and results in gummy macaroons.

· ·

espresso biscuits

MAKES 16

1½ cups all-purpose flour

½ cup Dutch-process cocoa powder

1 tablespoon finely ground espresso beans

1 cup (2 sticks) unsalted butter, room temperature

¾ cup confectioners' sugar

1 teaspoon pure vanilla extract

1. Preheat the oven to 350°F with two racks centered. Line two baking sheets with parchment paper; set aside. Sift together the flour, cocoa, and espresso beans; set aside.

2. In the bowl of an electric mixer fitted with the paddle attachment, cream the butter, confectioners' sugar, and vanilla until light and fluffy, about 3 minutes. Gradually beat the flour mixture into the butter mixture on low speed, scraping down the sides of the bowl twice.

3. Roll 2½ tablespoons of the dough between the palms of your hand to form a ball. Transfer to the prepared baking sheet; repeat with the remaining batter, spacing the cookies 2 inches apart. Using a dinner fork, press the tines into the dough, and gently press into a biscuit shape. Bake just until firm to the touch, rotating the sheets between the oven racks halfway through to ensure even baking, 10 to 15 minutes. Transfer to a wire rack to cool. The biscuits will keep at room temperature in an airtight container up to 1 week.

vanilla tuiles

MAKES ABOUT 2 DOZEN

4 large egg whites

1 cup superfine sugar

1 cup all-purpose flour, sifted
   Pinch of salt

5 tablespoons unsalted butter, melted

3 tablespoons heavy cream

1 teaspoon pure almond, vanilla, orange, or lemon extract

1. Preheat the oven to 400°F with a rack in the center. Combine the egg whites and sugar in a large bowl. Using a wooden spoon beat until just combined and frothy, about 30 seconds. (Alternatively, combine the egg whites and sugar in the bowl of an electric mixer fitted with the paddle attachment; beat on medium speed until just combined and frothy, about 30 seconds.)

2. Beat in the flour and the salt. Add the butter, heavy cream, and extract; beat until combined. Spoon a heaping tablespoon of the batter onto a parchment-lined (or Silpat-lined) baking sheet. Using the back of a spoon, spread the batter into a very thin 6 x 3½-inch oval. Repeat, making 3 more ovals on the sheet.

3. Bake just until brown around the edges, about 5 minutes, but watch carefully for coloring. Meanwhile, prepare the second baking sheet. Working quickly, use a knife or an offset spatula to transfer a tuile to a work surface; drape the hot tuile over a small drinking glass to create a bowl, or over a rolling pin or dowel to create a wavy effect; place on wire rack to cool. Repeat with the remaining 3 cookies. If they get too stiff, return the baking sheet to the oven for 30 seconds. Repeat until all the batter is used. Store between layers of waxed paper in an airtight container for 2 to 3 days.

CHOCOLATE TUILE VARIATION *Use ¾ cup all-purpose flour and ¼ cup cocoa powder, sifted together, in place of the 1 cup flour for the vanilla tuiles. Process as in recipe above.*

Named for the curved French roofing tiles they resemble, tuiles (TWEELZ) are classic French wafer cookies gently molded into delicate and dramatic shapes, including cones and cups. As elegant and delicate as they are, it's easy to create these beautiful—and delicious—cookies that practically melt in your mouth. Traditionally tuiles are flavored with almond, but chocolate, vanilla, lemon, or orange flavorings are also popular.

Tuiles cook very quickly: Watch them closely as they bake. Bake only a few at a time so that they don't harden before you shape them. While they are still warm, drape the tuiles onto wooden dowels, overturned small bowls, and muffin tins. Tuiles may also be left flat. To make classic round or oval tuiles, a stencil may be cut from heavy plastic (such as a coffee-can lid), or form them freehand. To make Cigarettes Russes, use your fingers to roll the tuile around a chopstick or a thin wooden dowel, forming a cigarette shape. Once cooled on a wire rack, one end may be dipped into melted chocolate; these are delicious served with ice cream and sorbets.

For best results, bake tuiles on a dry day; they don't retain their shapes well in high humidity. Batter may be made a day ahead and refrigerated in an airtight container.

almond lace cookies

MAKES 2 ½ DOZEN

These cookies can be left flat or rolled into cones or cylinders. They can also be dipped in melted chocolate; allow them to set before serving.

- 4 tablespoons unsalted butter
- 2 tablespoons heavy cream
- 1 tablespoon orange liqueur
- ¾ cup whole unblanched almonds, ground medium fine
- 1 tablespoon all-purpose flour
- ½ cup sugar

1. Preheat oven to 375°F. Line a baking sheet with parchment. In a small saucepan over medium heat, combine butter, cream, and orange liqueur. When butter has melted, stir in remaining ingredients with a wooden spoon. Cook until gently bubbling, 2 to 3 minutes. Remove from heat and keep warm.

2. Place 5 half teaspoons of batter 1½ inches apart on prepared baking sheet (this is as many as you can mold while hot). Bake until lightly browned and crisp, 6 to 7 minutes.

3. Remove from oven. Working quickly, use an offset spatula, a small flat spatula, or fingers to lay each cookie over a cone-shaped object (we used a water-cooler cup), pressing edges together. Alternatively, roll cookies around the handle of a wooden spoon, pressing the edges together to form a cylinder. Continue baking and forming cookies until all the batter is used. Transfer cookies to a wire rack to cool. Store between layers of waxed paper in an airtight container for 2 to 3 days.

chewy orange almond cookies

MAKES 2 DOZEN

It's important to weigh nuts for accurate amounts, as volume can differ enormously. Extra cookies keep well; cover in plastic wrap and freeze.

- 4½ ounces sliced almonds (about 1¼ cups)
- ¾ cup granulated sugar
- ¼ cup all-purpose flour
  Finely grated zest of 2 oranges (about ¼ cup)
- 1 teaspoon anise seed, crushed
- 3 large egg whites, room temperature
- ¼ teaspoon kosher salt
- 2 tablespoons confectioners' sugar

1. Preheat the oven to 350°F. Line two baking sheets with parchment paper, and set aside.

2. In the bowl of a food processor, blend 3½ ounces of the almonds (about 1 cup) with ½ cup sugar until almonds are finely ground. Transfer the almond mixture to a medium bowl. Stir in flour, orange zest, and crushed anise seed.

3. Using an electric mixer fitted with the whisk attachment, whisk egg whites, salt, and remaining ¼ cup sugar to soft glossy peaks. Fold egg-white mixture into dry ingredients until just blended.

4. Spoon level tablespoons of the batter 2 inches apart on the prepared baking sheets. Using remaining almonds, arrange 3 sliced almonds on each cookie. Sift confectioners' sugar over the cookies. Bake until cookies are lightly browned along edges, about 12 minutes. Cool slightly before removing from sheets with a spatula.

meringue disks

MAKES 16

Try these with a cup of hot coffee or with softened ice cream sandwiched between two.

> *Unsalted butter, melted, for parchment*
> *All-purpose flour, for parchment*
> ¾ *cup plus 1½ tablespoons sugar*
> ½ *cup whole blanched almonds*
> 4 *large egg whites*
> ¼ *teaspoon cream of tartar*
> 1 *tablespoon plus 1 teaspoon cornstarch, sifted*
> ½ *teaspoon white vinegar*

1. Line two baking sheets with parchment paper. Trace eight 3¼-inch circles on each; turn over. Lightly brush the parchment with butter, and dust with flour. Tap off the excess. Set aside.

2. In a food processor, process ¼ cup plus 1½ tablespoons sugar and the almonds to a fine powder.

3. Preheat the oven to 225°F with two racks centered. In the bowl of an electric mixer fitted with the whisk attachment, beat the egg whites and cream of tartar on medium speed until foamy, about 5 minutes. Increase speed to medium high; slowly add the remaining sugar. Beat until glossy and firm, about 5 minutes. Reduce speed to low, sprinkle the cornstarch over, and mix 15 to 20 seconds. Add the vinegar; mix 15 to 20 seconds more.

4. Fold in the almond mixture with a rubber spatula. Evenly spread ¼ cup of the mixture onto each circle on the parchment.

5. Bake until the meringue is hard to the touch, but not browned, about 1 hour 15 minutes, rotating the pans between the shelves and reversing the positions halfway through. Transfer the meringues, on the parchment, to wire racks to cool completely. Peel off the parchment paper. Meringues may be made up to 2 days ahead and kept at room temperature in an airtight container.

brown sugar meringues

MAKES ABOUT 1 DOZEN

This twist on the classic meringue recipe calls for almonds and brown sugar, producing a golden-brown cookie that is crunchy on the outside and deliciously chewy inside. These should be dried overnight in the oven before serving.

> 6 *large egg whites*
> 1½ *cups packed light-brown sugar*
> ½ *teaspoon pure vanilla extract*
> 1 *cup whole almonds, toasted (see page 644)*

1. Preheat the oven to 200°F with two racks centered. Line two 12 x 17-inch baking sheets with parchment; set aside.

2. In the bowl of an electric mixer, combine the egg whites and sugar. Place the bowl over a pan of simmering water. Whisk until the sugar dissolves and the mixture is warm, about 3 minutes.

3. Transfer the bowl to the mixer fitted with the whisk attachment. Starting on low speed and gradually increasing to high, beat the mixture until stiff, glossy peaks form, about 5 minutes. Add the vanilla extract, and mix to combine. Fold in the almonds.

4. Place ⅓-cup ovals (or other shape) of meringue on a baking sheet. Repeat with the remaining meringue, about 6 per sheet. Bake until hard to the touch, about 1 hour. Turn off the heat; dry in the oven overnight. Store the meringues between layers of parchment paper in an airtight container in a cool, dry place up to 3 days.

chocolate-meringue cookies

MAKES 2½ DOZEN

¼ cup unsweetened cocoa powder, plus
2 teaspoons for dusting

Swiss Meringue (page 643)

1. Preheat the oven to 175°F Line a baking sheet with parchment paper.

2. Sift ¼ cup cocoa over the meringue, and fold so that streaks of cocoa remain.

3. Fill the pastry bag fitted with an Ateco #5 star tip or other decorative tip; pipe out the cookies onto a baking sheet. Sift the remaining cocoa over the cookies; bake until the cookies lift off the parchment easily, about 2 hours. Transfer the baking sheet to a wire rack to cool completely.

cherry-meringue bites

MAKES ABOUT 4 DOZEN

The meringue can be made several days in advance and stored in an airtight container at room temperature. Fill with crème fraîche and a cherry just before serving.

Swiss Meringue (page 643)

¾ cup crème fraîche or whipped heavy
cream

50 (about 1 pound) cherries, pitted
Confectioners' sugar, for dusting

1. Line two baking sheets with parchment paper. Using a 1-inch cookie cutter, draw 25 circles on each piece of parchment. Turn the paper over, and place on the sheets. Set aside.

2. Preheat the oven to 200°F with two racks centered. Fit a pastry bag with a Wilton #16 star tip or other small star tip, and fill the bag with the meringue. Cover one of the circles with an even layer of the meringue. Pipe around the circumference, making a 1-inch-high cup. Repeat the piping over the remaining circles. Transfer the baking sheets to the oven, and bake 20 minutes. Reduce the heat to 175°F, and bake until the meringue has dried but is still white, 35 to 40 minutes more. Transfer the sheets to a wire rack to cool.

3. Fit a pastry bag with a plain round tip, and fill the bag with the crème fraîche. Pipe about 1½ teaspoons crème fraîche into each of the meringue cups to almost fill, and top with a cherry. Dust the meringue bites with confectioners' sugar, and serve.

cranberry-lemon squares

MAKES ABOUT 16

6 tablespoons chilled unsalted butter, cut
into 12 pieces, plus more for pan

1½ cups dried cranberries

¼ cup confectioners' sugar, plus more
for dusting

1 cup all-purpose flour

2 large eggs

¾ cup granulated sugar

¼ cup plus 1½ teaspoons fresh lemon juice

1. Preheat the oven to 325°F. Butter an 8-inch square baking pan; set aside.

2. Combine the cranberries and 2 cups water in a medium saucepan; bring to a boil. Reduce heat to medium, and cook, stirring occasionally, until the water is absorbed, about 25 minutes. Transfer to the bowl of a food processor, and chop coarsely. Set aside in a bowl.

3. In the bowl of an electric mixer fitted with the paddle attachment, combine the confectioners' sugar and ¾ cup flour. Add the butter, beating on low speed until the mixture forms pea-size pieces. Press the batter into the baking pan; bake until golden, about 20 minutes.

4. Meanwhile, in the bowl of the electric mixer fitted with the whisk attachment, beat the eggs and granulated sugar until smooth. Add the lemon juice; beat to combine. Add the remaining ¼ cup of flour, and beat to combine; set aside.

5. Reduce heat to 300°F. Spread the cranberry mixture over the crust; pour the lemon mixture over the cranberries. Bake until set, about 40 minutes.

6. Transfer to a wire rack to cool for 30 to 40 minutes, then chill for about 4 hours. To serve, cut into squares, and dust with confectioners' sugar.

fruit crumb bars

MAKES ABOUT 5 DOZEN

- 2¼ cups all-purpose flour
- 1 teaspoon baking soda
- ¾ teaspoon kosher salt
- 1¼ teaspoons ground cinnamon
- 4 cups quick-cooking oats
- 1½ cups packed light-brown sugar
- 1½ cups (3 sticks) unsalted butter, cut into ½-inch pieces
  Apple Filling (recipe follows)

1. Preheat the oven to 375°F. In a large bowl, whisk together the flour, baking soda, salt, and cinnamon. Stir in the oats and brown sugar. Cut the butter into the mixture.

2. Line a 12 x 17-inch baking pan with parchment paper. Press 5 cups of the oat mixture into the bottom of the pan. Spread the filling over it. Top with remaining oat mixture. Bake until golden, about 40 minutes. Transfer to a wire rack to cool. Cut into about sixty 1¼ x 2½-inch pieces.

apple filling

MAKES 5 CUPS

- 4 tablespoons unsalted butter
- ¼ cup plus 2 tablespoons packed light-brown sugar
- 10 Granny Smith apples, cored, peeled, and cut into ½-inch pieces
- 1 tablespoon ground cinnamon
  Juice of ½ lemon

1. Heat 2 tablespoons butter and 3 tablespoons brown sugar in a large skillet over high heat. When the butter is melted and bubbling, add half the apples. Sprinkle with 1½ teaspoons cinnamon. Cook, stirring occasionally, until apples are soft, about 15 minutes. Transfer to a large bowl.

2. Heat remaining butter and sugar in the skillet. Add remaining apples and cinnamon. Cook according to step 1. Transfer to the bowl. Stir in lemon juice. Cool completely before using.

raisin bars

MAKES 2 DOZEN

- 2 cups raisins
- ½ cup pure maple syrup
- 1½ teaspoons grated orange zest
- ⅓ cup fresh orange juice
- 1 tablespoon all-purpose flour, plus more for dusting
  Classic Sugar Cookies (page 533), dough prepared through step 2
- 1 large egg yolk mixed with 1 tablespoon heavy cream, for egg wash

1. Combine raisins, syrup, zest and juice, and flour in a heavy saucepan. Bring to a boil over medium-low heat and cook until mixture thickens and raisins are plumped, about 5 minutes. Remove from heat and let cool slightly. Transfer to a food processor and pulse until almost puréed. Set side.

2. Cut disks of cookie dough in half; roll each half into a 9 x 6-inch rectangle, about ¼ inch thick. Cover lightly with plastic wrap and refrigerate for at least 30 minutes.

3. Place 1 dough rectangle on a lightly floured surface. Cut in half lengthwise. Lightly score one rectangle crosswise at 1½-inch intervals. Place 3 tablespoons raisin mixture on the unscored rectangle; spread evenly to ¼ inch from the edges. Using 2 large spatulas, lift the scored half and carefully place on top. Repeat this process three more times with the remaining dough for a total of 4 bars, placing each completed bar in the refrigerator until ready to bake.

4. Brush bars with egg wash. Bake until golden brown, about 20 minutes. Remove to a wire rack to cool. Use a sharp knife to cut the bars along the score marks into 6 pieces.

ORANGE MARMALADE COOKIE VARIATION Substitute ¾ cup orange marmalade for the raisin mixture.

shortbread wedges

MAKES 3 DOZEN

- 1 pound (4 sticks) unsalted butter, plus more for pans
- 1 cup packed light-brown sugar
- 5 cups all-purpose flour
- 1 teaspoon kosher salt
- 1 teaspoon pure vanilla extract

1. Preheat the oven to 275°F with a rack in the center. Butter three 8-inch springform pans. In the bowl of an electric mixer, cream the butter and sugar on medium high until light and creamy, about 2 minutes. Add the flour, salt, and vanilla, and mix, beginning on low speed and increasing to medium, until the flour is just combined.

2. Divide the dough evenly among the prepared pans. Using a spatula, spread the dough out to the edges, making sure the tops are smooth and level.

3. Lightly score the dough in each pan into 12 equal wedges. Prick a pattern into each wedge with the tines of a fork. Bake until shortbread is dry and barely golden, about 50 minutes. Transfer to a wire rack to cool. Using a sharp knife, follow the score marks to cut into neat wedges. Remove from pans. Shortbread may be stored in an airtight container at room temperature for up to 1 week.

pecan shortbread

MAKES 4 TO 6 BARS

- 8 tablespoons unsalted butter, room temperature, plus more for pan
- ¼ cup packed dark-brown sugar
- ¼ cup granulated sugar
- 1¼ cups all-purpose flour, sifted
- ½ cup finely ground pecans (2 ounces)
- ½ teaspoon kosher salt
- ½ teaspoon pure vanilla extract

1. Preheat the oven to 300°F with a rack in the center. Butter a 5 x 9-inch loaf pan. In the bowl of an electric mixer fitted with the paddle attachment, cream the butter and both sugars until light and fluffy, about 3 minutes. Add the flour, pecans, salt,

and vanilla; beat on low speed for 5 minutes. Transfer the dough to the prepared pan, and spread evenly. Score the dough into bars, and prick the surface decoratively with a fork.

2. Bake until the shortbread looks dry, about 1 hour. Transfer the pan to a wire rack to cool. Turn the shortbread out of the pan, and cut along the scored lines. The shortbread may be stored in an airtight container at room temperature for up to 1 week.

mocha shortbread wedges

MAKES 6 TO 8

This not-too-sweet shortbread can also be rolled out and cut, but baking it in a pan and cutting while it's warm is faster and easier.

- ½ cup plus 3 tablespoons all-purpose flour
- ½ cup unsweetened cocoa powder
  Pinch of kosher salt
- 1 tablespoon finely ground coffee beans, preferably espresso
- 8 tablespoons (1 stick) unsalted butter, room temperature
- ⅓ cup confectioners' sugar, plus more for sprinkling

1. Preheat the oven oven to 350°F. Sift together the flour, cocoa, and salt. Stir in coffee and set aside.

2. In the bowl of an electric mixer fitted with the paddle attachment, cream the butter until light and fluffy, about 3 minutes. Gradually add the sugar and beat well. Add the flour mixture and beat on low speed until combined.

3. Pat the dough into an ungreased 8-inch round pan. Bake until firm, 20 to 25 minutes. Transfer to a wire rack to cool for 5 minutes, then cut into wedges. Let cool completely. Sprinkle with confectioners' sugar before serving. The shortbread may be stored in an airtight container at room temperature for up to 1 week.

pecan squares

MAKES 32

Martha's Perfect Pâte Brisée (page 634)
All-purpose flour, for dusting
1 *pound (4 sticks) unsalted butter*
1 *cup honey*
2 *cups packed light-brown sugar*
½ *cup granulated sugar*
8 *cups chopped pecans (1 pound, 13 ounces)*
¾ *cup heavy cream*

1. Preheat the oven to 350°F with a rack in the center. Divide the pâte brisée in half; wrap one half in plastic wrap, and chill. On a lightly floured work surface, roll the other half of the pâte brisée into a 9 x 12-inch rectangle about ⅛ inch thick. Lay the rolled-out dough on one side of a 12 x 17-inch baking pan. Roll out remaining pâte brisée; lay it on the other side of pan, overlapping slightly. Press edges together to seal. Trim dough so it does not hang over the edges. Refrigerate until chilled, at least 30 minutes. Prick the dough all over with a fork; bake until golden, about 20 minutes (do not worry if small cracks form in the pastry crust).

2. In a saucepan over medium heat, combine butter, honey, brown sugar, and granulated sugar; bring to a boil. Let the mixture boil 7 minutes to dissolve the sugar and to bring the mixture to the correct temperature. Be careful not to let the mixture bubble over. Remove from the heat.

3. Stir in pecans and cream. Cool slightly; carefully pour over crust. Bake until filling is bubbling, about 20 minutes. Let cool completely in the pan on a wire rack. Cut into squares, and serve.

chocolate brownies

MAKES 1 DOZEN

The better the chocolate, the better the brownie.

1 *cup (2 sticks) unsalted butter, plus more for pan*
8 *ounces best-quality unsweetened chocolate, such as Callebaut or Valrhona*
5 *large eggs*
3½ *cups sugar*
2 *teaspoons instant espresso powder, optional*
1 *tablespoon pure vanilla extract*
1⅔ *cups sifted all-purpose flour*
½ *teaspoon kosher salt*
½ *cup semisweet chocolate chips*
1 *cup coarsely chopped walnuts, toasted (see page 644)*

1. Preheat the oven to 400°F with a rack in the center. Generously butter a 9 x 13-inch baking pan, and set aside. In the top of a double boiler or in a heatproof bowl set over a pan of simmering water, melt the chocolate and butter. Stir with a rubber spatula until smooth. Set aside.

2. In bowl of an electric mixer fitted with the paddle attachment, beat the eggs, sugar, and espresso, if using, at high speed for 10 minutes. Reduce speed to low, and add the melted-chocolate mixture and the vanilla; beat until combined. Slowly add the flour and salt; beat just until incorporated.

3. Remove the bowl from the mixer, and fold in the chocolate chips and toasted nuts. Pour the batter into the prepared pan. Bake until the edges are dry but the center is still soft, about 30 minutes. Remove the pan from the oven, and transfer to a wire rack to cool. Cut into 3-inch squares, and store in an airtight container at room temperature up to 2 days.

blondies

MARKS 1 DOZEN

12 tablespoons (1½ sticks) unsalted butter,
   plus more for pan

1½ cups all-purpose flour

 1 teaspoon baking powder

 1 teaspoon kosher salt

 1 cup packed light-brown sugar

 ⅔ cup granulated sugar

 2 large eggs

 1 teaspoon pure vanilla extract

 1 cup (6 ounces) butterscotch or semisweet
   chocolate chips

 ¾ cup pecans, coarsely chopped,
   toasted (see page 644)

1. Preheat the oven to 350°F with a rack in the center. Butter a 9-inch square cake pan, and set aside. In a medium bowl, whisk together the flour, baking powder, and salt; set aside.

2. In the bowl of an electric mixer fitted with the paddle attachment, cream the butter and both sugars until light and fluffy, about 3 minutes, scraping the sides occasionally. Add the eggs and vanilla; beat until well combined. Add the flour mixture; beat on low speed just until combined. Fold in the butterscotch chips and the toasted pecans.

3. Using an offset spatula, spread the batter into the pan. Bake until the surface is golden brown and a cake tester inserted into the center comes out barely clean, 45 to 55 minutes. Transfer to a wire rack to cool. Cut into squares. Store in an airtight container up to 3 days.

peanut butter no-bakes

MAKES ABOUT 3½ DOZEN

Creamy peanut butter works best in this recipe. If you prefer, the melted chocolate can be drizzled onto the cookies.

1½ cups old-fashioned rolled oats

 1 cup creamy peanut butter

1½ cups nonfat dry milk

 4 tablespoons unsalted butter

 2 tablespoons honey

 ½ cup (about 2 ounces) semisweet
   chocolate morsels, optional

1. Preheat the oven to 350°F. Spread oatmeal in an ungreased baking pan; toast until lightly browned, about 10 minutes, shaking once. Set aside to cool.

2. In a medium bowl, combine the peanut butter and the nonfat dry milk. Stir in the toasted oatmeal, and set aside.

3. In a small saucepan over medium heat, melt the butter. Stir in the honey. Pour the butter mixture over the peanut-butter mixture, and stir until well combined. Allow to cool slightly.

4. Shape into about 40 logs, each about 2½ inches long. Place the logs onto a wire rack or a parchment-lined baking sheet, and set aside.

5. In the top of a double boiler or in a heat-proof bowl set over a pan of simmering water, melt the chocolate morsels, if using. Stir occasionally until the chocolate is smooth, about 2 minutes. Remove from the heat, and transfer the melted chocolate to a pastry bag fitted with a #3 plain round tip, or a plastic freezer bag with a bottom corner snipped off. Pipe the chocolate onto the cookie logs. Serve immediately, or store in an airtight container, refrigerated, up to 1 week.

wheatmeal peanut-butter fingers

MAKES ABOUT 3 DOZEN

- 1   cup butter (2 sticks), room temperature
- ¾   cup confectioners' sugar
- 1   large egg
- 1¼ cups toasted wheat germ
- 1¼ cups whole-grain pastry flour
- ¼   teaspoon kosher salt
- ¼   cup cornstarch
- ¼   cup smooth peanut butter
- ¼   cup granulated sugar

1. Place butter and confectioners' sugar in the bowl of an electric mixer fitted with the paddle attachment. Beat until fluffy, about 3 minutes. Add the egg, and beat until fluffy.

2. In a medium bowl, whisk together the wheat germ, pastry flour, salt, and cornstarch. Add to the butter mixture, and beat on low speed until combined, about 1 minute.

3. Divide the dough into two equal parts, and place between 12-inch squares of parchment paper. Roll out each piece of the dough into a 7 x 10-inch rectangle, about ¼ inch thick.

4. Remove the top pieces of the parchment from the dough; spread the peanut butter over 1 rectangle. Invert the second rectangle on top of the first, folding any overhanging edges of the parchment; wrap the dough. Chill at least 1 hour.

5. Preheat the oven to 350°F with two racks centered. Line two baking sheets with parchment. Unwrap the dough. Generously sprinkle the top and bottom with the granulated sugar. Trim the edges, creating a clean rectangle. Cut into three dozen 3½ x ½-inch rectangles; place on the sheets, spaced 1½ inches apart.

6. Bake the cookies until barely golden, 20 to 25 minutes. Transfer to a wire rack to cool. Bake or freeze the remaining dough. Store in an airtight container up to 1 week.

hazelnut biscotti

MAKES ABOUT 2 DOZEN

Biscotti get their dry, crisp texture from a second baking. They are delicious dipped in coffee or dessert wine.

- 2½ cups all-purpose flour, plus more for dusting
- 1¼ cups sugar
- 1   teaspoon baking powder
- ½   teaspoon anise seeds
- 1   tablespoon orange zest
     Pinch of kosher salt
- 3   large eggs
- 2   large egg yolks
- 1   teaspoon pure vanilla extract
- ½   cup hazelnuts, toasted (see page 644)

1. Preheat the oven to 350°F with a rack in the center. Line one baking sheet with parchment paper. In the bowl of an electric mixer fitted with the paddle attachment, combine the flour, sugar, baking powder, anise seeds, zest, and salt.

2. Beat together the eggs, egg yolks, and vanilla. Add to the dry ingredients, and mix until a sticky dough is formed. Coarsely chop half of the hazelnuts. Work in the chopped and whole nuts.

3. Turn out the dough onto a well-floured board, and divide into 2 portions. With floured hands, roll into logs about 12 inches long, and transfer to the prepared sheet.

4. Bake until dough sets, about 30 minutes. Remove from oven; cool for 15 minutes. Reduce heat to 275°F. Slice the dough on a diagonal into ½-inch pieces; place, cut-side down, on the baking sheet. Bake 20 minutes. Turn over; bake 20 minutes more, until slightly dry. Transfer to a wire rack to cool. Biscotti will keep for several weeks in an airtight container at room temperature.

double-chocolate biscotti

MAKES 2 DOZEN

- 8 tablespoons (1 stick) unsalted butter
- 4 ounces bittersweet or semisweet chocolate, finely chopped
- ½ cup Dutch-process cocoa powder
- 1¾ cups all-purpose flour, plus more for dusting
- 1½ teaspoons baking powder
- ½ teaspoon kosher salt
- 1 cup sugar
- 2 large eggs
- 1 teaspoon pure vanilla extract
- 1 cup whole shelled pistachio nuts or blanched almonds, toasted (see page 644)
- 1 cup golden raisins

1. Preheat the oven to 350°F with one rack centered. Line a baking sheet with parchment paper, and set aside. In the top of a double boiler or in a heat-proof bowl set over a pan of simmering water, melt the butter and chocolate, stirring occasionally, until smooth.

2. Sift together the cocoa, flour, baking powder, and salt. In the bowl of an electric mixer fitted with the paddle attachment, cream the sugar and eggs on medium speed until lightened. Add the vanilla extract. On low speed, add the chocolate mixture, then the flour mixture. Stir in the nuts and raisins. The dough will be soft.

3. Turn the dough out onto a lightly floured surface. Form two 9 x 3½-inch logs, and transfer to the prepared baking sheet.

4. Bake until the dough sets, about 30 minutes. Remove from the oven, and cool for 15 minutes. Reduce heat to 275°F. Slice the dough on a diagonal into ½-inch pieces; place, cut-side down, on the baking sheet. Bake 20 minutes. Turn over; bake 20 minutes more, until slightly dry. Transfer to a wire rack to cool. Biscotti will keep for several weeks in an airtight container at room temperature.

pecan-cranberry biscotti

MAKES 2 DOZEN

- 1½ cups pecan halves, toasted (see page 644)
- 1 teaspoon baking powder
- 2½ cups all-purpose flour, plus more for dusting
- 1¼ cups sugar
- ⅛ teaspoon kosher salt
- 3 large eggs
- 2 large egg yolks
- 1 teaspoon pure vanilla extract
- 1 cup dried cranberries
- Finely grated zest of 1 lemon

1. Preheat the oven to 350°F with a rack in the center. Line a baking sheet with parchment paper, and set aside. Finely chop half the toasted pecans, leave the remaining ones in halves; set aside.

2. In the bowl of an electric mixer fitted with the paddle attachment, combine the baking powder, flour, sugar, and salt. In a separate bowl, beat the eggs, egg yolks, and vanilla. Add to the dry ingredients; mix on medium low until a sticky dough is formed. Stir in the pecans, cranberries, and zest.

3. Turn the dough out onto a lightly floured surface, and sprinkle with more flour; knead slightly. Shape into two 9 x 3½-inch logs. Transfer to the prepared baking sheet.

4. Bake until the dough sets, about 30 minutes. Remove from the oven, and cool for 15 minutes. Reduce heat to 275°F. Slice the dough on a diagonal into ½-inch pieces; place, cut-side down, on the baking sheet. Bake 20 minutes. Turn over; bake 20 minutes more, until slightly dry. Transfer to a wire rack to cool. Biscotti will keep for several weeks in an airtight container at room temperature.

s'mores squares

MAKES 9

S'mores taste best with homemade marsh-mallows (the first five steps below). They can be prepared up to 2 days ahead.

Canola oil, for brushing

3   *tablespoons unflavored gelatin*

3¼ *cups granulated sugar*

1¼ *cups light corn syrup*

¼   *teaspoon kosher salt*

2   *teaspoons pure vanilla extract*

1½ *cups confectioners' sugar*

7   *tablespoons unsalted butter, melted,
    plus 6 tablespoons, room temperature,
    plus more for pan*

14 *graham crackers, crushed to yield
    1½ cups crumbs*

12 *ounces semisweet chocolate, chopped
    into ½-inch pieces*

1. Brush a 9 x 13-inch baking dish with the oil. Cut a piece of parchment paper large enough to cover the bottom of the dish and to overhang the longer sides. Place the parchment in the dish, brush with oil, and set dish aside.

2. Pour ¾ cup cold water in the bowl of an electric mixer, and sprinkle the gelatin on top. Let stand 5 minutes to soften.

3. Place 3 cups granulated sugar, the corn syrup, salt, and ¾ cup water in a saucepan. Set the saucepan over high heat; bring to a boil. Clip on a candy thermometer, and cook until the mixture reaches 238°F (soft-ball stage), about 9 minutes.

4. Attach the mixer bowl to the mixer fitted with the whisk attachment. On low speed, drizzle the hot syrup down the sides of the bowl, beating it into the gelatin mixture. Gradually increasing speed to high, beat until the mixture is very stiff, white, and fluffy, about 12 minutes. Beat in the vanilla. Pour mixture into the prepared baking dish; smooth the surface with an offset spatula. Set the dish aside, uncovered, until the marshmallow becomes firm, at least 3 hours or overnight.

5. Place 1 cup confectioners' sugar in a fine strainer, and sift onto a work surface. Invert the large marsh-mallow onto the sugar-coated surface, and peel off the parchment paper. Lightly brush a sharp knife with oil, and cut the marshmallow into 2-inch squares. Sift the remaining ½ cup confectioners' sugar into a small bowl, and roll the marshmallows in the sugar to coat. Set aside.

6. Preheat the oven to 350°F with a rack in the center. Brush a 9-inch square baking pan with melted butter. In a large bowl, combine the graham-cracker crumbs, 7 tablespoons melted butter, and the remaining ¼ cup of granulated sugar. Using your hands, press the mixture firmly into the prepared pan. Bake until the crust has set, about 15 minutes. Transfer to a wire rack to cool.

7. In the top of a double boiler or in a heat-proof bowl set over a pan of simmering water, combine the chocolate with the remaining 6 tablespoons butter. Stir until chocolate and butter melt. Pour the chocolate mixture over the cooled graham-cracker crust. Using an offset spatula, spread chocolate mixture into an even layer. Transfer to the refrigerator, and chill until firm, about 30 minutes.

8. Preheat the broiler. Cut the chocolate crust into nine 3-inch squares. Top each square with a marsh-mallow, and place the assembled s'mores on a baking sheet. Place under the broiler just until the marshmallows turn golden brown, about 20 seconds, watching carefully. Serve immediately.

meringue porcupines with cream filling

MAKES 1 DOZEN

An oval of meringue is decorated with tiny spikes to resemble a porcupine. They may be eaten plain like a cookie or filled with preserves and almond cream and sandwiched together, as they are here.

Swiss Meringue (page 643)

½ *cup heavy cream*

2 *drops pure almond extract*

1 *cup plus 2 tablespoons best-quality peach or apricot preserves*

1. Preheat oven to 400°F with two racks centered. Line two baking sheets with parchment paper.

2. Scoop a spoonful of the meringue onto a large oval soup spoon, and use another soup spoon to form the meringue into shape of a small egg. Use the second spoon to push the meringue "oval" off the first spoon and onto the parchment. Spoon 12 ovals onto each prepared baking sheet. Using a small offset spatula, touch the meringue in several different spots, and pull out spikes of meringue, creating a porcupine effect.

3. Reduce oven to 200°F; bake until the meringues are crisp on the outside but have the consistency of marshmallow inside, about 1 hour. Reduce oven to 175°F if the meringue starts to brown. Remove from the oven, and gently press the bottom of each meringue so that it caves in and can be filled. Turn off heat, and return to oven to dry, about 20 minutes. Let meringues cool completely before filling.

4. Combine the cream and almond extract in the bowl of an electric mixer fitted with the whisk attachment, and beat on medium speed until stiff peaks form, about 2 minutes. Fill half the hollowed meringues with the cream, the remaining half with the preserves, and sandwich the halves together. Serve immediately.

MAKING MERINGUE PORCUPINES

1. This dessert starts with a quenelle, or oval-shaped mound: Fill a soup spoon generously with meringue; using a second spoon, pass the meringue from spoon to spoon until smooth. Use first spoon to gently scrape quenelle onto lined baking sheet.

2. Then spikes are formed: Use a small offset spatula to quickly pull up small spikes along the quenelle.

almond-meringue sandwiches

MAKES 2 DOZEN

- 5 large egg whites
- ¼ teaspoon cream of tartar
- 1 cup superfine sugar
- 1½ cups ground blanched almonds
- ½ cup heavy cream
- 6½ ounces semisweet chocolate, finely chopped

1. Preheat the oven to 200°F with two racks centered. Line two baking sheets with parchment paper.

2. Combine the egg whites and the cream of tartar in the bowl of an electric mixer fitted with the whisk attachment. Beat on medium speed until soft peaks form. Gradually add the sugar, 1 tablespoon at a time, beating until the whites are shiny and firm, about 3 minutes. Fold in the ground almonds.

3. Fill a pastry bag, fitted with an Ateco #864 star tip or other medium tip, with the meringue. Pipe out 2-inch round cookies onto the prepared baking sheets.

4. Bake until the meringues just start to color, about 15 minutes. Turn off the heat, and let the meringues cool for 4 hours or overnight in the oven. For a quicker method, reduce the heat after 15 minutes to 175°F, and cook for 1½ hours. Transfer the pans to wire racks to cool completely.

5. Meanwhile, bring the cream to a simmer in a small saucepan over medium-high heat. Place the chocolate in a medium heat-proof bowl, and pour the hot cream over the chocolate. Whisk until the chocolate is smooth and melted. Let cool completely. Fill a pastry bag with the chocolate filling, and pipe out onto the bottom side of half the cookies. Make sandwiches with the remaining cookies, and serve. Store in airtight containers at room temperature for 2 to 3 days.

linzer cookies

MAKES ABOUT 5 DOZEN

- 1 cup (2 sticks) unsalted butter
- ⅔ cup sugar
- 2 large eggs
- 1 teaspoon pure vanilla extract
- 2 cups all-purpose flour
- 1 teaspoon baking powder
- 1 teaspoon ground cinnamon
- ¼ teaspoon kosher salt
- 1 teaspoon grated lemon zest
- 1¼ cup hazelnuts, ground medium fine (from 4 ounces)
- ½ cup seedless raspberry or cherry jam

1. Preheat the oven to 350°F with a rack in the center. In the bowl of an electric mixer fitted with the paddle attachment, cream the butter and sugar at medium-high speed until light and fluffy, about 3 minutes. Add the eggs, and beat until smooth, about 3 minutes. Beat in the vanilla.

2. Combine the flour, baking powder, cinnamon, salt, and zest. Add to the butter mixture; beat on medium speed until combined, about 1 minute. Refrigerate for at least 30 minutes.

3. Roll the dough into ¾-inch balls, and roll in the ground hazelnuts. Place the balls on an ungreased baking sheet 1 inch apart. Bake until the cookies begin to set, about 8 minutes. Transfer to a wire rack. Working quickly, make a slight indentation in each cookie with your thumb. Return to the oven, and bake about 8 minutes more. Transfer the sheet to the wire rack to cool. When cool enough to handle, transfer the cookies to the rack.

4. Melt jam in a small saucepan over medium-low heat. Place ¼ to ½ teaspoon jam in each indentation. Cool cookies completely before serving.

chocolate thumbprints

MAKES 2 DOZEN

Named for the way the indentation in the center
is made—with your thumb—these popular cookies are filled with a pool of melted chocolate.

- 12 tablespoons (1½ sticks) unsalted butter
- ½ cup confectioners' sugar
- ¼ teaspoon kosher salt
- 1 teaspoon pure vanilla extract
- 1¼ cups all-purpose flour
- 4 ounces semisweet chocolate, chopped
- 1½ teaspoons corn syrup

1. Preheat the oven to 350°F with a rack in the center. In the bowl of an electric mixer fitted with the
paddle attachment, cream 8 tablespoons butter, the
sugar, salt, and vanilla on medium-high speed until
smooth, about 2 minutes. Beat in the flour, beginning on low speed and increasing to medium high.

2. Roll the dough by teaspoonfuls into balls, and
place 1 inch apart on an ungreased baking sheet.
Bake for 10 minutes, remove from the oven, and
press your thumb into the tops of the cookies to
make an indentation. Return to the oven, and bake
until light brown on the edges, 7 to 10 minutes
more. Transfer to a wire rack to cool.

3. Combine the chocolate, the remaining 4 tablespoons of butter, and the corn syrup in the top of a
double boiler or in a small heat-proof bowl set over
a pot of simmering water; stir occasionally with a
rubber spatula until melted and smooth. Allow to
cool slightly. When the cookies are cool, fill the
thumbprints with the chocolate mixture. The filling will harden as the cookies cool.

gingersnap-raspberry sandwiches

MAKES 2 DOZEN

- 8 tablespoons (1 stick) unsalted butter, room temperature
- ¼ cup pure vegetable shortening
- 2 cups sugar
- 2 cups all-purpose flour
- 2 teaspoons baking soda
- 1 teaspoon ground cinnamon
- 1 tablespoon ground ginger
- ¼ cup pure maple syrup
- 1 large egg, beaten
- 1 cup raspberry jam (with seeds)

1. Preheat the oven to 375°F with a rack in the center; line a baking sheet with parchment paper, and
set aside.

2. In the bowl of an electric mixer fitted with the
paddle attachment, cream butter, shortening, and 1
cup sugar on medium speed. In a bowl, sift together
flour, baking soda, cinnamon, and ginger.

3. Add the maple syrup to the butter mixture; beat
to combine. Beat in the egg until well combined.
Reduce mixer speed to low; slowly add the flour
mixture, a little at a time, until well blended.

4. Place the remaining cup of sugar in a bowl. Measure out 2 teaspoons of the dough; roll into a ball.
Roll the dough in the sugar; transfer to the prepared
sheet. Repeat, spacing the balls 3 inches apart. Bake
until golden, about 12 minutes. Transfer to a wire
rack to cool. Form and bake the remaining dough.
The cookies may be kept in an airtight container
at room temperature up to 1 week.

5. To make sandwiches, spread about 2 teaspoons
of the jam over half of the cooled cookies; place a
second cookie on top of each.

vienna tarts

MAKES 1 1/2 DOZEN

Martha's mother makes these fruit-filled triangles for the holidays. Prune lekvar is a rich fruit butter available in most grocery stores.

- 8 tablespoons (1 stick) unsalted butter
- 3 ounces cream cheese
- 1 cup sifted all-purpose flour, plus more for dusting
- 1/4 cup prune lekvar mixed with 1 teaspoon lemon zest
- 1 large egg yolk
- 2 tablespoons milk
  Confectioners' sugar, for sprinkling

1. In the bowl of an electric mixer fitted with the paddle attachment, cream the butter and cream cheese until light and fluffy, about 4 minutes. Add the flour, and beat until smooth. Wrap in plastic wrap, and refrigerate for 3 hours.

2. Preheat the oven to 400°F with a rack in the center. Line a baking sheet with parchment; set aside. On a lightly floured surface, roll out the dough to 1/8 inch thick, and cut into 3-inch squares. Place 1/4 teaspoon lekvar mixture in one corner of each square. Fold to make a triangle, press to seal, and roll up from the fold. Place on the prepared sheets, and shape into crescents.

3. In a small bowl, combine the egg yolk and milk to make an egg wash. Brush the crescents with the egg wash. Bake until golden, 12 to 15 minutes. Transfer to a wire rack to cool, and sprinkle with confectioners' sugar.

black and white dough

MAKES ENOUGH FOR 7 1/2 DOZEN BULL'S-EYE COOKIES OR 6 1/2 DOZEN STRIPED COOKIES

Bread flour has more protein than all-purpose flour and so absorbs more of the water in the butter to create a denser, crisper, and even more golden-brown cookie. All-purpose flour may be used, but the dough must be kept very cold.

- 2 pounds (8 sticks) unsalted butter, room temperature
- 1 teaspoon pure vanilla extract
- 3 cups confectioners' sugar
- 7 1/2 cups bread flour
- 1/3 cup Dutch-process cocoa powder

1. For white dough, place 1 pound butter, 1/2 teaspoon vanilla, 1 1/2 cups sugar, and 3 3/4 cups flour in the bowl of an electric mixer fitted with the paddle attachment. Mix on medium until well combined. Wrap in plastic; store, refrigerated, up to 2 weeks, or freeze up to 3 months.

2. For chocolate dough, combine remaining butter, vanilla, sugar, flour, and cocoa in a bowl. Mix on medium until combined. Wrap in plastic; store, refrigerated, up to 2 weeks, or freeze up to 3 months.

striped cookies

MAKES ABOUT 6 1/2 DOZEN

Black and White Dough (recipe above), room temperature

1. Divide black dough into 4 equal pieces. Place each piece between two pieces of parchment. Roll into 3 1/2 x 12-inch rectangles. Transfer to baking sheets; chill 30 minutes. Repeat with white dough.

2. Remove top parchment from rectangles. Using bottom piece for support, invert a white rectangle onto a black one; remove parchment. Repeat, for a total of 4 layers. Wrap in plastic. Make second brick with remaining 4 rectangles. Chill at least 1 hour.

3. Preheat the oven to 375°F with two racks centered. Line two baking sheets with parchment. Unwrap the bricks; trim evenly by 1/8 inch. Slice crosswise into 1/4-inch-thick rectangles; place on the sheets, spaced 2 inches apart.

4. Bake until barely golden, 10 to 12 minutes. Transfer the cookies to a wire rack to cool. Bake or freeze the remaining dough. Store in an airtight container at room temperature up to 1 week.

bull's-eye cookies

MAKES ABOUT 7½ DOZEN

You will need a kitchen scale for this recipe.

A slender log of chocolate dough is wrapped in a layer of white dough followed by a second layer of chocolate dough to create a perfect bull's-eye when the cookies are sliced.

Black and White Dough (recipe opposite), room temperature

1. Place 20 ounces of black dough between two pieces of parchment. Roll out to a 7 x 12-inch rectangle, about ⅓ inch thick. Repeat with 20 ounces of white dough. Chill rectangles at least 30 minutes.

2. Place 12 more ounces of the black dough between two 12 x 14-inch pieces of parchment. Roll out to a 4¾ x 12-inch rectangle. Repeat the process with 12 ounces of the white dough. Chill at least 15 minutes.

3. Place 6 ounces of the black dough on a work surface. Roll into a 12-inch-long log, about ¾ inch in diameter. Repeat with 6 ounces of the white dough. Wrap in parchment. Chill at least 15 minutes.

4. Remove the top piece of parchment from the smaller black rectangle. Unwrap the white log, and place lengthwise on the black rectangle. Using the bottom piece of parchment for support, wrap black dough around white log, pressing with your fingers to seal seam. Roll the log back and forth to smooth seam. The seam must be smoothed completely.

5. Repeat step 4 with the black log and the smaller rectangle of white dough.

6. Remove the top piece of parchment from the larger white rectangle. Place the white log wrapped in black dough lengthwise on the white rectangle. Using bottom piece of parchment for support, wrap white dough around log, pressing with your fingers to seal the seam. Roll the log back and forth to smooth the seam, making it as smooth as possible.

7. Repeat step 6 with black log wrapped in white dough and the larger rectangle of the black dough. Wrap both of the logs in parchment. Chill 1 hour.

8. Preheat the oven to 375°F with two racks centered. Line two baking sheets with parchment. Remove parchment from logs; slice crosswise into ¼-inch-thick rounds. Place on sheets, 2 inches apart.

9. Bake until barely golden, about 15 minutes. Transfer the cookies to a wire rack to cool. Bake or freeze the remaining dough. Store in an airtight container at room temperature up to 1 week.

ICEBOX COOKIES

For the busy holiday baker, icebox cookies are indispensable. Doughs prepared ahead of time (up to 3 months) and stored in the freezer can quickly be baked into an assortment of cookies that will appeal to everyone. Since one batch of dough can yield dozens of cookies, the dough itself or the baked cookies are ideal for holiday gift-giving. To give baked cookies as a gift, slice and bake a whole log, or cut a few slices from each for an assortment, and return the uncut dough to the freezer.

Several different doughs can be combined to form logs or bricks; when sliced, a cross-section can reveal a checkerboard, a spiral, or stripes. Or a single flavor of dough can be rolled in chopped nuts, candied fruit, cocoa powder, or sugar to create cookies with sparkly, crunchy, or chewy edges; don't defrost the dough before using.

chocolate black-pepper icebox cookies

MAKES ABOUT 4 DOZEN

Black pepper gives these chocolate cookies a subtle spicy flavor. Sanding sugar, which has larger crystals than granulated sugar, makes a distinctive decorative topping on the baked cookies; granulated sugar may also be used.

1½ cups all-purpose flour
¾ cup cocoa powder
¼ teaspoon kosher salt
¼ teaspoon freshly ground black pepper, plus more for sprinkling
1 tablespoon instant espresso powder
½ teaspoon ground cinnamon
12 tablespoons (1½ sticks) unsalted butter, room temperature
1 cup granulated sugar
1 large egg
1½ teaspoons pure vanilla extract
   Sanding sugar, for sprinkling

1. In a bowl, sift flour, cocoa powder, salt, pepper, espresso, and cinnamon; set mixture aside.

2. In the bowl of an electric mixer fitted with the paddle attachment, cream the butter and sugar until light and fluffy, about 3 minutes. Add the egg and vanilla; beat to combine. Add the reserved flour mixture, beating on low speed, until combined.

3. Have ready a large piece of parchment paper. Turn out the dough onto the parchment, and roll into a 2-inch-diameter log. Roll the log in the parchment. Transfer the log to the refrigerator, and chill the dough at least 1 hour or overnight.

4. Preheat the oven to 375°F with two racks centered. Line two baking sheets with parchment paper. Remove log from refrigerator; remove parchment. Pour sanding sugar onto a baking pan; roll log in sugar, gently pressing down to adhere sugar to dough. Transfer log to a cutting board; slice it

crosswise into ¼-inch-thick rounds. Place rounds on prepared baking sheets, spacing 1 inch apart. Sprinkle cookies with freshly ground pepper.

5. Bake the cookies until there is slight resistance when you lightly touch them in the centers, about 12 minutes. Transfer cookies to a wire rack to cool completely. Bake the remaining dough. Store the cookies in an airtight container at room temperature up to 2 days.

chewy coconut-chocolate pinwheels

MAKES ABOUT 3 DOZEN

9 tablespoons unsalted butter, room temperature
1 cup sugar
1 large egg
1 teaspoon pure vanilla extract
2 cups cake flour (not self-rising)
½ teaspoon baking soda
¼ teaspoon kosher salt
1½ cups shredded unsweetened coconut
6 ounces bittersweet chocolate, chopped
⅓ cup sweetened condensed milk

1. In the bowl of an electric mixer fitted with the paddle attachment, cream 8 tablespoons butter and the sugar until fluffy, about 3 minutes. Add the egg and vanilla, and beat until fluffy.

2. In a bowl, whisk the flour, baking soda, and salt. Add to the butter mixture, and beat on low speed until combined. Add the coconut, and beat until combined. Roll out the dough between two 12 x 17-inch pieces of parchment paper into a 10 x 15-inch rectangle, about ⅛ inch thick. Transfer to a baking sheet, and chill at least 1 hour.

3. Place the chocolate and the remaining butter in the top of a double boiler or in a heat-proof bowl set over a pan of simmering water. Stir occasionally until smooth, about 2 minutes, and remove from the heat. Stir in the condensed milk. Let sit until slightly thickened, about 5 minutes.

4. Remove the top piece of parchment from the dough. Using an offset spatula, spread the choco-

late mixture over the dough. Roll the dough into a log. Wrap the log in parchment, and chill overnight.

5. Preheat the oven to 350°F with two racks centered. Line two baking sheets with parchment paper. Unwrap the log, and slice it crosswise into ¼-inch-thick rounds. Place on the baking sheets, spaced 1½ inches apart. Bake until pale golden brown on edges, 8 to 12 minutes. Transfer the cookies to a wire rack to cool. Bake or freeze the remaining dough. Store the cookies in an airtight container at room temperature up to 1 week.

ginger cookies

MAKES ABOUT 6½ DOZEN

This cookie dough was inspired by one sold at the Downtown Bakery & Creamery in Healdsburg, California.

- 4¾ cups all-purpose flour
- 2 tablespoons baking soda
- ¾ teaspoon kosher salt
- ½ teaspoon baking powder
- 2 teaspoons ground cinnamon
- 1½ teaspoons ground ginger
- 1½ cups (3 sticks) unsalted butter, room temperature
- 1¾ cups sugar, plus 2 tablespoons for sprinkling
- 2 large eggs
- 1 teaspoon pure vanilla extract
- ½ cup molasses

1. Combine the flour, baking soda, salt, baking powder, cinnamon, and ginger in a large bowl; sift and set aside.

2. In the bowl of an electric mixer fitted with the paddle attachment, cream the butter and 1¾ cups sugar, starting on low speed and increasing to high, until mixture is fluffy, about 3 minutes, scraping the sides of the bowl down once using a rubber spatula. Add eggs one at a time and vanilla; beat on medium speed just until combined, scraping down the sides of the bowl after each addition.

3. Add the molasses, and mix on medium speed until just combined. Scrape the sides of the bowl, and add the dry ingredients. Mix, starting on low speed and increasing to medium high, until the ingredients are just combined, about 30 seconds.

4. Transfer the dough to a work surface. Roll the dough into four 1½-inch-diameter logs. Wrap in plastic wrap or parchment, and refrigerate until firm, at least 2 hours.

5. Preheat the oven to 350°F with two racks centered. Unwrap and slice the logs crosswise into ⅜-inch-thick rounds; place on ungreased baking sheets. Sprinkle with the remaining sugar. Bake until the cookies crack slightly on the surface, about 12 minutes. Bake or freeze the remaining dough. Remove from the oven, and let cool on the baking sheet for 2 minutes before transferring to a wire rack to cool completely. Store the cookies in an airtight container at room temperature up to 1 week.

lime meltaways

MAKES ABOUT 10 DOZEN

These citrus cookies are so tender that they literally melt in your mouth.

- 12 tablespoons (1½ sticks) unsalted butter, room temperature
- 1 cup confectioners' sugar
-    Grated zest of 2 limes
- 2 tablespoons fresh lime juice
- 1 tablespoon pure vanilla extract
- 1¾ cups plus 2 tablespoons all-purpose flour
- 2 tablespoons cornstarch
- ¼ teaspoon kosher salt

1. In the bowl of an electric mixer fitted with the whisk attachment, cream the butter and ⅓ cup sugar until fluffy. Add the lime zest and juice, and the vanilla; beat until fluffy.

2. In a medium bowl, whisk together the flour, cornstarch, and salt. Add to the butter mixture, and beat on low speed until combined.

3. Between two 8 x 12-inch pieces of parchment paper, roll the dough into two 1¼-inch-diameter logs. Chill at least 1 hour.

4. Preheat the oven to 350°F with two racks centered. Line two baking sheets with parchment. Place the remaining sugar in a resealable plastic bag. Remove the parchment from the logs; slice crosswise into ⅛-inch-thick rounds. Place the rounds on the sheets, spaced 1 inch apart.

5. Bake until barely golden, about 15 minutes. Transfer the cookies to a wire rack to cool slightly, about 10 minutes. While still warm, place the cookies in the sugar-filled bag; toss to coat. Bake or freeze the remaining dough. Store in an airtight container at room temperature up to 1 week.

french butter cookies

MAKES ABOUT 5 DOZEN

    1 cup (2 sticks) unsalted butter, room
       temperature
   ⅔ cup packed light-brown sugar
    1 large egg
    1 teaspoon pure vanilla extract
  2½ cups sifted all-purpose flour
    1 teaspoon kosher salt
   ½ cup granulated sugar

1. Combine the butter and light-brown sugar in the bowl of an electric mixer fitted with the paddle attachment, and cream on high speed until fluffy, 2 to 3 minutes. Add the egg and vanilla, and mix to combine. Add the flour and salt, and mix on low speed until the flour is incorporated.

2. Roll the dough into three 1½-inch-diameter logs. Wrap in plastic wrap, and refrigerate until firm, at least 1 hour or overnight.

3. Preheat the oven to 350°F with one rack in the center. Line a baking sheet with parchment paper. Roll the cookie logs in the granulated sugar, coating them evenly, and slice into ¼-inch rounds. Place the cookies on the baking sheet about 1 inch apart. Using a cake tester, toothpick, or small end of a piping tip, make 4 decorative holes in each cookie.

4. Bake until golden brown, 15 to 20 minutes. Remove from the oven, and transfer to a wire rack to cool completely. Cookies will keep at room temperature in an airtight container up to 1 week.

cornmeal-pecan biscuits

MAKES 2½ DOZEN

The dough for these biscuits must be chilled overnight, so plan accordingly.

    8 tablespoons (1 stick) unsalted butter
    1 cup granulated sugar
    1 large egg
    1 teaspoon pure vanilla extract
  1¼ cups all-purpose flour
   ½ cup yellow cornmeal
    1 teaspoon baking powder
   ¼ teaspoon kosher salt
   ½ cup whole pecans, toasted (see page 644)
    1 teaspoon ground cinnamon
    2 tablespoons packed dark-brown sugar
    1 large egg white

1. In the bowl of an electric mixer fitted with the paddle attachment, cream the butter and sugar on medium speed until light and fluffy, 3 minutes. Beat in the egg and vanilla.

2. In a medium bowl, whisk together the flour, cornmeal, baking powder, and salt. On low speed, add the flour mixture to the butter mixture. Mix until combined, about 30 seconds.

3. Transfer the dough to a work surface, and divide into 4 equal portions. Place one portion between two 12-inch-square pieces of parchment. Roll out the dough to a 3½ x 9-inch rectangle. Repeat with the remaining 3 portions of the dough. Transfer to baking sheets; chill at least 10 minutes.

4. In the bowl of food processor, process the toasted pecans, cinnamon, and brown sugar until the nuts have been finely chopped, about 15 seconds. Transfer the mixture to a medium bowl.

5. In a small bowl, combine the egg white with 1 tablespoon water to make an egg wash. Remove the top pieces of parchment paper from the dough. Brush one piece of the dough lightly with the egg wash, and sprinkle ¼ cup of the pecan mixture over the top. Brush the second rectangle lightly with the egg wash. Invert the second rectangle over the first, and remove the parchment on top. Repeat the layering and stacking process, leaving the top rectangle uncoated. Trim to a 3¼ x 8½-inch brick. Wrap, and chill in the refrigerator overnight.

6. Preheat the oven to 350°F with two racks centered. Line two baking sheets with parchment. Cut the brick into ¼-inch-thick rectangles; place on the baking sheets, spaced 2½ inches apart.

7. Bake the biscuits until light golden, 12 to 15 minutes. Transfer to a wire rack to cool. Bake or freeze the remaining dough. Store in an airtight container up to 1 week.

almond crescents
MAKES ABOUT 3½ DOZEN

Superfine sugar makes the texture of these cookies very crumbly, soft, and delicate.

- 2¼ cups all-purpose flour
- ⅛ teaspoon kosher salt
- ½ cup (3 ounces) blanched almonds
- ⅔ cup superfine sugar
- 14 tablespoons (1¾ sticks) chilled unsalted butter, cut into very small pieces
- 3 large egg yolks
- 1 teaspoon pure vanilla extract
- ¾ cup confectioners' sugar, for sifting

1. In a large bowl, sift together the flour and salt. In the bowl of a food processor, finely grind the almonds. Add the sugar and sifted flour and the salt to the processor. Pulse to combine. With the machine running, slowly add pieces of the butter through the feed tube. Add the yolks and vanilla. Process for 20 seconds. Divide the dough into 2 pieces. Roll each into a 1½-inch-thick log, wrap in plastic, and refrigerate for 3 hours.

2. Line two baking sheets with parchment paper. Cut the dough into ⅜-inch-thick pieces. Use your fingers to shape each piece into a 3-inch crescent; transfer to the prepared baking sheets about 1 inch apart. Refrigerate for 30 minutes.

3. Preheat the oven to 350°F with two racks centered. Bake, rotating the sheets between the oven racks halfway through baking to ensure even baking, about 15 minutes; the cookies should not brown. Transfer the parchment with the cookies to a wire rack; let cool 5 minutes. Sift the confectioners' sugar over the tops before serving.

pecan sandies
MAKES ABOUT 5 DOZEN

- 1 cup (2 sticks) unsalted butter
- ⅓ cup granulated sugar
- 1 teaspoon pure vanilla extract
- ⅔ cup pecans, finely ground
- 1⅔ cups all-purpose flour, plus more for dusting
- Pinch of kosher salt
- ¼ cup confectioners' sugar

1. Preheat the oven to 350°F with two racks centered. In the bowl of an electric mixer fitted with the paddle attachment, cream the butter and sugar on medium-high speed until light and fluffy, about 3 minutes. Beat in the vanilla.

2. In a medium bowl, combine the ground pecans, flour, and salt, and add to the butter mixture. Beat, beginning on low speed and increasing to medium, until combined, about 1 minute.

3. Lightly flour your palms, if necessary, and roll the dough into ¾-inch balls. Place on an ungreased baking sheet 1 inch apart. Bake until just brown on the edges, rotating the baking sheet halfway through baking to ensure even browning, 20 to 25 minutes. Remove the cookies from the baking sheet while still warm; sift the confectioners' sugar over the tops. Store in an airtight container at room temperature for up to 4 days.

gingerbread cookies

MAKES ABOUT 8 DOZEN 3-INCH COOKIES

This extra-stiff dough makes wonderful edible Christmas tree ornaments. It is sturdy enough to be used with giant cookie cutters (see Equipment Sources, page 650).

- 6 cups sifted all-purpose flour, plus more for dusting
- 1 teaspoon baking soda
- ½ teaspoon baking powder
- 1 cup (2 sticks) unsalted butter
- 1 cup packed dark-brown sugar
- 1 tablespoon plus 1 teaspoon ground ginger
- 1 tablespoon plus 1 teaspoon ground cinnamon
- 1½ teaspoons ground cloves
- 1 teaspoon finely ground black pepper
- 1½ teaspoons kosher salt
- 2 large eggs
- 1½ cups unsulfured molasses
  Royal Icing (recipe follows), optional

1. In a large bowl, sift together flour, baking soda, and baking powder. Set aside.

2. In an electric mixer fitted with the paddle attachment, cream the butter and sugar until fluffy. Mix in the spices and salt. Beat in the eggs and molasses. Add flour mixture; mix on low speed to thoroughly combine. Divide the dough in thirds and wrap in plastic. Chill for at least 1 hour.

3. Preheat the oven to 350°F. On a floured work surface, roll the dough to ⅛ inch thick. Cut into desired shapes, transfer to ungreased baking sheets, and chill until firm, 30 minutes. Bake until crisp but not darkened, 8 to 10 minutes. If making tree ornaments, immediately make a small hole for a hook or cord using a bamboo or metal skewer, then cool on wire racks. To decorate with Royal Icing, reinsert skewer to prevent icing from filling hole; make designs with the icing as desired.

royal icing

MAKES ABOUT 2½ CUPS

Substitute 5 tablespoons meringue powder (see Sources, page 648) and ⅓ cup water for raw eggs.

- 2 to 3 large egg whites
- 1 pound confectioners' sugar
  Juice of 1 lemon
- 2 to 3 drops food coloring, optional

In the bowl of an electric mixer fitted with the paddle attachment, combine egg whites and sugar on low speed. Stir in lemon juice until spreadable. Add food coloring, if using. Use immediately, or store in an airtight container 1 to 2 days; beat with a rubber spatula before using.

NOTE *Raw eggs should not be used in food prepared for pregnant women, babies, young children, the elderly, or anyone whose health is compromised.*

chocolate cookies

MAKES ABOUT 16 LARGE COOKIES

- 3 cups sifted all-purpose flour, plus more for dusting
- 1¼ cups unsweetened cocoa
- ¼ teaspoon kosher salt
- ½ teaspoon ground cinnamon
- 1½ cups (3 sticks) unsalted butter
- 2½ cups sifted confectioners' sugar
- 2 large eggs, lightly beaten
- 1 teaspoon pure vanilla extract

1. In a large bowl, sift together the flour, cocoa, salt, and cinnamon. Set aside.

2. In an electric mixer fitted with the paddle attachment, cream the butter and sugar on medium speed until fluffy. Beat in eggs and vanilla.

3. Add the flour mixture; mix on low speed until thoroughly combined. Divide the dough in half; wrap in plastic wrap. Chill at least 1 hour.

4. Preheat the oven to 350°F. On a floured surface, roll out dough until ⅛ inch thick. Cut into shapes. Transfer to ungreased baking sheets; chill until firm, about 30 minutes. Bake until crisp, 8 to 10 minutes. Cool on wire racks; decorate as desired.

classic sugar cookies

MAKES 7 DOZEN SMALL OR 2 DOZEN
LARGE COOKIES

This dough can be cut into shapes appropriate
for any occasion.

- 1 cup (2 sticks) unsalted butter
- ¾ cup sugar, plus 3 tablespoons for sprinkling
- 2 large egg yolks
- 1 teaspoon pure vanilla extract
- 1 tablespoon orange liqueur or cognac
- 2½ cups all-purpose flour, plus more for dusting
- 1½ teaspoons baking powder
  Pinch of salt
- 1 large egg yolk mixed with 1 tablespoon heavy cream, for egg wash

1. Preheat oven to 350°F. Line a baking sheet with parchment. In the bowl of an electric mixer fitted with the paddle attachment, beat butter and sugar on medium-high speed until smooth, about 2 minutes. Add yolks; beat until fluffy, 2 to 3 minutes. Beat in vanilla and liqueur. Add flour, baking powder, and salt; mix, beginning on low speed and increasing to medium, until flour is just incorporated.

2. Turn dough out onto a clean surface and divide evenly into 2 portions. Flatten each half to a 1-inch-thick disk, wrap in plastic, and refrigerate for at least 1 hour.

3. Lightly flour a clean surface. Roll dough to ¼ inch thick, and cut into desired shapes. Decorate as desired, brush with egg wash, or sprinkle with sugar. (Scraps can be combined and rolled one more time.) Bake until golden, 10 to 15 minutes. Remove cookies to a wire rack to cool.

grandma's sugar cookies

MAKES 22 DOZEN 1½-INCH COOKIES

The yield depends on the size cookie you make, and on whether you make sandwich cookies, as described in step 4. The recipe can be halved, or you can freeze part of the dough for up to three weeks.

- 1 cup (2 sticks) unsalted butter
- 2 cups sugar
- 2 large eggs
- 4⅔ cups all-purpose flour, plus more for work surface
- 1 teaspoon baking soda
- ¼ teaspoon salt
- ¼ cup buttermilk
- ½ cup pale-pink or white sanding sugar
  Petal dust in pink, orange, and violet
- 1 cup apricot or strawberry jam, slightly warmed (optional)

1. In the bowl of an electric mixer fitted with the paddle attachment, cream butter and sugar until fluffy, about 4 minutes. Add eggs, one at a time, beating well after each. Sift flour, baking soda, and salt into large bowl. On low speed, gradually add flour mixture to mixer bowl, alternating with buttermilk, until combined. Wrap dough in plastic; chill until firm, 1 hour or overnight.

2. To color with sanding sugar, if using: Place a few tablespoons in a small bowl. Mix in petal dust with a toothpick, a bit at a time, until desired shade is reached. Colored sanding sugar will last indefinitely.

3. Preheat the oven to 350°F, with racks in upper and lower thirds. Line two baking sheets with parchment paper. On a lightly floured surface, roll chilled dough to ⅛ inch thick. Cut out hearts using any 1- to 3½-inch heart cookie cutters. If desired, cut the centers out of some hearts. Transfer with a spatula to baking sheets. Chill for 30 minutes. Sprinkle with sanding sugar if using. Bake until just golden but not too brown, about 10 minutes. Transfer cookies to a rack. Continue with the rest of the dough; reroll scraps.

4. To make sandwich hearts, brush the bottom heart lightly with jam; cover with a second heart with the center cut out; the jam will adhere the hearts. Fill cut-out area with more jam.

5. Cookies will keep, in an airtight container, at room temperature for 1 week.

golden caramels

MAKES ABOUT 12½ DOZEN

Keep the pan still after caramel has been poured in, or it can separate and become greasy.

> *Canola oil, for pan and cutting board*
> 1   *quart heavy cream*
> 1   *cup sweetened condensed milk*
> 4   *cups light corn syrup*
> 4   *cups sugar*
> 1   *teaspoon kosher salt*
> 1   *cup (2 sticks) unsalted butter, cut into 16 pieces*
> 1   *tablespoon plus 1 teaspoon pure vanilla extract*

1. Lightly brush a 12 x 17-inch baking pan with canola oil. Set aside. In a 2-quart saucepan, combine the cream and milk; set aside.

2. In a heavy 6- to 8-quart saucepan, combine corn syrup, 1 cup water, sugar, and salt, and mix well. Clip a candy thermometer onto the saucepan. Bring to a boil over medium heat, stirring occasionally with a wooden spoon, 15 to 20 minutes. Brush down sides of pan with a pastry brush dipped in water to prevent crystallizing. Reduce heat to medium low; cook, without stirring, until temperature reaches 250°F (hard-ball stage), 45 to 60 minutes.

3. Meanwhile, cook cream mixture over low heat until just warm. Do not boil. When the sugar reaches 250°F, slowly stir in the butter and warm cream mixture, keeping the mixture boiling at all times. Stirring constantly with a wooden spoon, cook over medium heat until the thermometer reaches 244°F (firm-ball stage), 55 to 75 minutes more. Stir in the vanilla. Immediately pour into the prepared pan without scraping the pot. Let stand uncovered at room temperature for 24 hours.

4. To cut the caramels, lightly oil a large cutting board. Unmold the caramel from the pan onto it. Cut into 1 x 1¼-inch pieces. Wrap each in cellophane or waxed paper.

deep dark chocolate caramels

MAKES ABOUT 12½ DOZEN

The better the quality of chocolate used in these caramels, the more delicious they will be.

> *Canola oil, for pan and cutting board*
> 1   *quart heavy cream*
> 2½   *cups light corn syrup*
> 4½   *cups sugar*
> ½   *teaspoon kosher salt*
> 1   *pound, 2 ounces bittersweet chocolate, chopped in small pieces*
> 1   *cup (2 sticks) unsalted butter, cut into 16 pieces*

1. Lightly brush a 12 x 17-inch baking pan with canola oil. Set aside. In a heavy 4-quart saucepan, combine 2 cups cream, the corn syrup, sugar, and salt. Clip a candy thermometer onto the saucepan. Bring to a boil over medium heat, stirring occasionally with a wooden spoon, 15 to 20 minutes. Brush down the sides of the pan with a pastry brush dipped in water to prevent crystallizing.

2. Cook, stirring constantly, until the temperature reaches 220°F, 6 to 8 minutes; watch so the mixture doesn't boil over. Continue stirring, and add the chocolate and butter; keep the mixture boiling at all times, or it can separate. Slowly add the remaining 2 cups cream. Cook, still stirring, until the temperature reaches 240°F (soft-ball stage), about 60 minutes, keeping the mixture at a low boil.

3. Pour the mixture into the prepared pan without scraping the pot. Let stand uncovered at room temperature for 24 hours without moving.

4. To cut the caramels, lightly oil a large cutting board. Unmold the caramel from the pan onto the oiled surface. Cut into 1 x 1¼-inch pieces, or other shapes. Wrap each in cellophane or waxed paper.

pink peony popcorn balls

MAKES 1 DOZEN

- 2 tablespoons canola oil
- ¾ cups popping corn (enough to make 12 cups popped)
- ½ cup dried cranberries
- 1⅓ cups sugar
- ¼ cup plus 1 tablespoon light corn syrup
- ¼ teaspoon kosher salt
- ½ teaspoon white vinegar
- 1 or 2 drops red food coloring

1. Heat the oil in a large, heavy-bottomed stockpot over medium heat. When hot, add the popping corn. Cover, and let cook until the corn starts to pop, shaking the pot occasionally. When the popping noises become infrequent, remove the stockpot from the heat. Combine the popped popcorn and cranberries in a large mixing bowl, and set aside.

2. Combine the sugar, ¾ cup water, the corn syrup, salt, and vinegar in a small heavy saucepan. Clip a candy thermometer onto the side of the saucepan. Set the saucepan over high heat, and bring the mixture to a boil. Brush down the sides of the pan with a pastry brush dipped in water to prevent crystallizing. Cook until the mixture reaches 290°F, about 15 minutes. Add the food coloring, stirring, until the desired color is reached. Remove pan from the heat.

3. Pour the hot syrup over the reserved popcorn mixture; stir together with a wooden spoon until all the kernels have been well coated. Working quickly, use your hands to form a 2½-inch-diameter ball. Transfer the ball to parchment paper, and let cool completely. Repeat with the remaining popcorn mixture. Store the popcorn balls in an airtight container for up to 2 days.

coconut clusters

MAKES ABOUT 2 DOZEN

- Canola oil, for sheet
- 2 cups sugar
- 1½ cups unsweetened flaked coconut

1. Lightly oil a baking sheet; set aside. Combine sugar and ½ cup water in a saucepan. Bring mixture to a boil over medium-high heat, brushing down sides of pan with a pastry brush dipped in water to prevent crystallizing. Don't stir. Reduce heat to low; simmer until caramel is golden brown, about 11 minutes. Remove pan from heat.

2. Add the coconut, and gently fold it into the caramel, using a wooden spoon.

3. Working quickly and carefully, tilt pan slightly; using a fork, transfer 2 tablespoons of the coconut mixture to the baking sheet. Repeat, with the remaining coconut. Let the patties cool completely, and store in an airtight container for up to 2 days.

simple chocolate truffles

MAKES 3 DOZEN

- 1 pound bittersweet chocolate, finely chopped
- 1 cup heavy cream
- Best-quality cocoa powder

1. Place the chocolate in a large heat-proof bowl. Bring cream just to a boil over medium-high heat; pour directly over chopped chocolate. Allow to sit 10 minutes; use a rubber spatula to gently stir chocolate and cream until combined. Let sit at room temperature until thickened, about 15 minutes.

2. Pour the mixture into a shallow 8-inch square glass baking dish or pie plate. Cover with plastic wrap, and refrigerate until the mixture is very cold and set but still pliable, about 30 minutes.

3. Using a teaspoon, scoop out chocolate mixture into 1-inch nuggets; transfer to a parchment-lined baking sheet. Chill 10 minutes. Use your fingertips to mold truffles into round shapes. Roll in cocoa powder to coat; chill in an airtight container until ready to serve. Truffles can be stored in an airtight container in the refrigerator for up to 2 weeks.

chocolate armagnac truffles

MAKES 5 DOZEN

- 12 ounces best-quality semisweet chocolate
- ½ cup heavy cream
- 2 tablespoons Armagnac (brandy or orange liqueur may be substituted)
- ½ cup Dutch-process cocoa powder, sifted

1. Chop chocolate and place in a large heat-proof bowl. Bring cream to a boil in a small, heavy saucepan; pour over chocolate. Stir until chocolate is melted and smooth. Stir in liqueur. Refrigerate until firm, at least 3 hours or overnight.

2. Scoop up ½ teaspoon chilled chocolate; quickly roll into a ball. Continue until all the mixture is used. Place cocoa powder in a bowl; roll truffles in cocoa to coat. Chill until firm. Store in an airtight container in the refrigerator for up to 2 weeks.

....

FLAVORED TRUFFLES

Truffles can be flavored with both liquid and solid flavorings. The method you use depends on whether the flavoring is liquid or solid. The quantities below will flavor 1 pound of chocolate, regardless of how much cream is added.

LIQUID FLAVORINGS *After chocolate and cream are combined, while ganache is warm, stir in ¼ cup pure vanilla, other extracts, or liqueur, such as Grand Marnier or cognac.*

SOLID FLAVORINGS *Bring cream to a boil. Add one of the following: 1 sprig fresh rosemary, the zest of 2 oranges, 8 roughly ground cardamom pods, ¼ cup roughly ground espresso or coffee beans, or 1 vanilla bean, split lengthwise. Remove from heat; steep until flavor is infused, about 30 minutes. Strain, discarding solids, and boil cream again. Add to chopped chocolate.*

....

chocolate fudge

MAKES 2½ DOZEN SQUARES

- 2 tablespoons unsalted butter, plus more for pan
- 3 tablespoons best-quality cocoa powder
- 2 cups sugar
- ⅔ cup milk
- 3 ounces best-quality semisweet chocolate, finely chopped
- 2 tablespoons light corn syrup
- 1 cup walnut halves, cut into large pieces

1. Butter an 8 x 2-inch square pan. Sift cocoa powder and sugar into a medium bowl.

2. Prepare an ice-water bath. In a small saucepan, combine the milk and cocoa-powder mixture with a wooden spoon until a sandy, pastelike texture forms. Clip a candy thermometer onto the saucepan. Add the chocolate, butter, and corn syrup. Cook on low heat, stirring constantly, until the sugar has completely dissolved, 7 to 10 minutes, brushing down the sides of the pan with a pastry brush dipped in water to prevent crystallizing. Raise heat to medium. When the mixture reaches 236°F (just below the soft-ball stage), remove the pan from the heat, and place in the ice-water bath for 5 seconds. Transfer the pan to a heat-proof surface, and let sit until the thermometer registers 121°F, about 45 minutes.

3. Using a wooden spoon, stir the fudge briskly until it begins to lose its sheen, 2 to 3 minutes. Stir in the walnuts. Spread the fudge into the prepared pan with a wooden spoon. Using your fingers, smooth fudge. Cover with plastic wrap; chill 30 minutes. Cut into 1-inch squares. Store the fudge in an airtight container up to 1 week.

peanut butter and jelly fudge

MAKES ABOUT 16 PIECES

These sweet flower-shaped pieces of fudge have grape-jelly centers. Use a flower cookie cutter to make neat 1- to 1½-inch flowers. The fudge can also be cut with a knife into squares or diamonds.

- 2 tablespoons chilled unsalted butter, plus more for pan
- 3 tablespoons light corn syrup
- 1 cup granulated sugar
- ¾ cup packed light-brown sugar
- ¾ cup milk
-   Pinch of baking soda
- ½ teaspoon kosher salt
- ¼ cup plus 2 tablespoons creamy peanut butter
- 1 teaspoon pure vanilla extract
- 2 tablespoons red-currant or Concord grape jelly

1. Lightly butter an 8-inch square baking pan, and set aside. Combine the corn syrup, both sugars, milk, baking soda, and salt in a heavy medium saucepan. Clip a candy thermometer onto the saucepan. Bring the mixture to a boil over medium-high heat, stirring occasionally. Cook, brushing down the sides of the pan with a pastry brush dipped in water to prevent crystallizing, until the temperature registers 236°F (just below the soft-ball stage); don't overcook.

2. Immediately remove saucepan from heat, and add the chilled butter, then the peanut butter and vanilla, stirring until smooth. Pour the mixture into the prepared pan. Set aside in a cool, dry place, and let the fudge set.

3. Before the fudge cools completely, cut into desired shapes. Using a small melon baller, scoop out a small hole in the center of each fudge shape. Set the shapes aside to cool completely. Fill a resealable plastic bag with jelly; close, and cut off a corner. Neatly squeeze the jelly into the holes. Store the fudge in an airtight container up to 1 week.

PERFECT FUDGE EVERY TIME

When making fudge, follow the instructions to the letter, and make sure your candy thermometer works correctly. To test it, put it in a pan of boiling water; it should read exactly 212°F. Timing can vary greatly in candy making, depending on the weather and equipment, so follow your candy thermometer readings, using the times given in the recipes as guidelines. If fudge is overcooked, even a little, it will be dry and crumbly; it's always better to undercook it. To ensure success, remove fudge from heat just before it reaches the soft-ball stage (240°F).

caramel-molasses pecan logs

MAKES 6 LOGS OR 12 DOZEN PETITS FOURS

The logs should be refrigerated until serving. For petits-fours cups, see Equipment Sources, page 650.

- 2 cups sugar
- 1 cup light corn syrup
- 1 cup unsulfured molasses
- 1 cup (2 sticks) unsalted butter
- 1¾ cups heavy cream
- 3 cups (about 9 ounces) pecans, coarsely chopped
- 2 pounds best-quality bittersweet chocolate, finely chopped
- 1 tablespoon pure vegetable shortening

1. Line an 8-inch square baking pan with plastic wrap, leaving a 2-inch overhang. Set aside.

2. Combine the sugar, corn syrup, molasses, butter, and heavy cream in a large heavy-bottomed saucepan set over medium-high heat. Clip a candy thermometer onto the saucepan. Cook, stirring occasionally, until the mixture reaches 250°F, about 12 minutes. Pour the caramel into the prepared pan; freeze until cool and set, about 1 hour.

3. Invert the pan onto a cutting board, and pop out the caramel; remove plastic; and cut into six sticks.

4. Line a baking sheet with parchment paper. Place the chopped pecans on another piece of parchment. Roll each stick in the nuts, forming a log and coating completely. Place the logs on the baking sheet, and transfer to the refrigerator.

5. Place chocolate and shortening in the top of a double boiler or in a heat-proof bowl set over a pan of simmering water. Stir until melted; remove from the heat. Remove the logs from the refrigerator.

6. Using a pastry brush, coat each log with a layer of chocolate, and return to the baking sheet. Chill until set, about 15 minutes.

7. Meanwhile, pour remaining chocolate into a 4½ x 9-inch loaf pan. Roll logs in chocolate, one at a time, coating completely. Return logs to baking sheet; refrigerate until set, about 15 minutes more.

8. For petits fours, slice each log into 24 ⅓-inch-thick slices; place in petits-fours cups, and serve.

chocolate-covered almonds
MAKES ABOUT 2 POUNDS

1¼ cups granulated sugar
2½ cups (13 ounces) unblanched whole
    almonds, toasted (see page 644)
1   teaspoon ground cinnamon
1   pound best-quality semisweet
    chocolate, chopped
½   cup Dutch-process cocoa powder
½   cup confectioners' sugar

1. Line two baking pans with parchment paper, and set aside. In a medium saucepan, combine the granulated sugar, ¼ cup water, toasted almonds, and cinnamon. Cook, stirring constantly, until sugar becomes golden and granular and almonds are completely coated and separated. Pour nuts onto the prepared pans. Chill in the freezer, about 15 minutes.

2. Meanwhile, place the chocolate in the top of a double boiler or in a heat-proof bowl set over a pan of simmering water. Stir until melted. Transfer half the chilled almonds to a large bowl, and pour half the melted chocolate over the nuts. Stir until the nuts are thoroughly coated. Transfer the nuts onto the prepared baking pan. Using two forks, separate

the nuts so none stick together. Return the almonds to the refrigerator until the chocolate has set, about 20 minutes. Repeat with the remaining almonds.

3. Place the cocoa powder and confectioners' sugar into two separate bowls. Toss half the nuts in the cocoa and half in the sugar, and gently tap off any excess powder. Store separately in airtight containers, in a cool dry place, for up to 1 month.

pralines
MAKES ABOUT 1½ DOZEN

1   cup nonfat buttermilk
1   teaspoon baking soda
2   cups sugar
5   tablespoons unsalted butter
1   tablespoon bourbon
1   cup pecan halves

1. Line two baking pans with parchment paper; set aside. In a 4-quart saucepan, combine the buttermilk, baking soda, and sugar. Clip a candy thermometer onto the saucepan. Over medium-high heat, bring to a rolling boil, stirring constantly. Brush down the sides of the pan with a pastry brush dipped in water to prevent crystallizing.

2. Cook, stirring constantly, until mixture is 240°F (soft-ball stage), about 15 minutes. Remove from heat. Add butter and bourbon; stir with a wooden spoon until butter has melted. Stir in pecans; beat with the spoon for 30 seconds. Immediately spoon 1 tablespoon pecan mixture onto the prepared baking pan, forming a 2-inch patty. Repeat with remaining mixture. If mixture begins to harden, return to heat for 1 minute, scraping down sides and stirring. Let patties stand until set, about 1 hour. Wrap pralines individually in wax paper.

peanut brittle

MAKES 1½ POUNDS

Peanut brittle tends to draw moisture from the air; make it when the weather is sunny and dry.

  Canola oil, for pan and spatula
2½ *cups (12 ounces) dry-roasted salted peanuts*
 1 *cup sugar*
 1 *cup light corn syrup*
 1 *tablespoon unsalted butter*
 1 *tablespoon baking soda*

1. Brush a large baking pan with oil; set aside. Combine the peanuts, sugar, and corn syrup in a medium saucepan. Set over medium-high heat, and bring to a boil, stirring constantly.

2. Clip a candy thermometer onto the saucepan. Continue boiling, without stirring, until the temperature registers 295°F, about 6 minutes, brushing down the sides of the pan with a pastry brush dipped in water to prevent crystallizing. When the sugar begins to brown, stir the nuts gently to ensure even cooking. Remove the saucepan from the heat, and stir in the butter and baking soda; the mixture will begin to foam up, so mix quickly. Pour onto the prepared baking pan.

3. Using an oiled offset spatula, spread the brittle out as thinly as possible. Allow the brittle to cool completely, about 45 minutes, and break into bite-size pieces. Store the peanut brittle in an airtight container up to 2 weeks.

hazelnut brittle

MAKES ABOUT SIX 6 X 5-INCH RECTANGLES

You can also make this caramel brittle with other nuts, such as slivered almonds or pistachios.

  Canola oil, for pan and knife
 4 *cups sugar*
 ¼ *teaspoon apple-cider vinegar*
5½ *cups hazelnuts, toasted (see page 644)*

1. Oil a 12 x 17-inch baking pan; set aside. Combine the sugar, vinegar, and 1 cup water in a medium saucepan set over medium heat. Cook until amber in color, 20 to 22 minutes, brushing down the sides of the pan with a pastry brush dipped in water to prevent crystallizing. Stir in the hazelnuts.

2. Pour the hot mixture onto the prepared pan. Let set until firm but still soft enough to cut. Invert onto a cutting board, and unmold. Working quickly, use an oiled chef's knife to cut the sheet into six equal rectangles. Store the brittle in an airtight container up to 1 week.

french almond nougat

MAKES ABOUT 3½ DOZEN PIECES

A popular European confection, this snow-white chewy candy can be prepared plain or studded with nuts or dried fruit. The basis of this candy is a mixture of sugar syrup and egg whites known as mazetta. The candy can be stored, refrigerated, for up to 4 days.

for the mazetta

 2 *large egg whites, room temperature*
 ¾ *cup light corn syrup*
 ½ *cup sugar*

for the nougat

  Canola oil, for pan
1½ *cups light corn syrup*
1½ *cups sugar*
 4 *tablespoons unsalted butter, melted*
 1 *teaspoon pure vanilla extract*
 ¼ *teaspoon kosher salt*
3½ *cups unblanched, whole raw almonds*

1. Make the mazetta: In the bowl of an electric mixer fitted with the whisk attachment, beat the egg whites until stiff peaks form; set aside. In a 1-quart saucepan, combine the corn syrup, ¼ cup water, and the sugar. Clip a candy thermometer onto the saucepan. Bring to a boil over high heat, stirring with a wooden spoon, about 5 minutes. Brush down the sides of the pan with a pastry brush dipped in water to prevent crystallizing.

2. Cook over medium heat, stirring occasionally, until the temperature reaches 242°F (soft-ball stage), 15 to 20 minutes. Remove the sugar syrup from the heat. Beating constantly on medium speed, slowly pour the hot syrup into the egg whites. Continue beating until the syrup is incorporated, about 4 minutes. Use immediately, or cover and refrigerate until ready to use.

3. Make the nougat: Brush an 8-inch square baking pan with canola oil; set aside. Place the mazetta in a large bowl; set aside. In a 2-quart saucepan, combine the corn syrup and sugar. Clip a candy thermometer onto the saucepan. Bring to a boil over high heat, stirring constantly with a wooden spoon, 5 to 10 minutes. Brush down the sides of the pan with a pastry brush dipped in water to prevent crystallizing.

4. Over medium-high heat, cook the syrup until the temperature reaches 280°F (soft-crack stage), 12 to 15 minutes, without stirring. If the heat is too high it can boil over, so watch carefully. Remove from the heat; let stand for 2 minutes. Without scraping the pan, pour the syrup over the mazetta. Working quickly, stir with a wooden spoon until almost smooth. Stir in the butter, vanilla, and salt. Mix until the butter is incorporated. Stir in the nuts. Scrape into the prepared pan, and smooth the top; you may oil your hand with the canola oil and run it over the warm candy to smooth it. Let stand at room temperature, uncovered, until firm, 4 to 6 hours.

5. Lightly brush a cutting board with canola oil. Unmold the nougat from the pan onto the oiled surface. Cut the nougat into 3 x 1 x ¾-inch pieces or other desired shapes. Wrap each piece in waxed paper or cellophane.

pistachio-honey torrone

MAKES ONE 9 X 13-INCH SHEET

Torrone is an Italian nougat and nut candy. You can substitute almonds or hazelnuts for the pistachios, if desired. For edible wafer paper, see Food Sources, page 648.

> *Edible wafer paper, for 2 layers in pan*
> ⅓ *cup cornstarch*
> 3 *large egg whites*
> 1 *cup honey*
> 3 *cups granulated sugar*
> ½ *cup confectioners' sugar*
> 2 *cups shelled raw pistachio nuts*

1. Piece together the wafer paper, without overlapping, to fit the bottom of a 9 x 13-inch baking pan; set aside. Liberally sprinkle a surface with cornstarch. Pour egg whites into bowl of an electric mixer fitted with whisk attachment; set aside.

2. In a medium saucepan, combine the honey and granulated sugar. Place over medium heat; cook until the mixture just begins to simmer, about 4 minutes. Clip a candy thermometer onto the saucepan; continue to heat, stirring occasionally, brushing down the sides of the pan with a pastry brush dipped in water to prevent crystallizing.

3. Beat the whites until stiff peaks form; add the confectioners' sugar. When the thermometer registers 315°F, remove the honey mixture from the heat. The temperature will rise to 320°F. Stir until the temperature drops to 300°F, 1 to 2 minutes. With the mixer running, pour the honey mixture into the egg-white mixture (at this point, the whites will double in volume; let stand a few seconds; the volume will return to normal). Beat until the mixture thickens and begins to stick to the beaters; fold in the nuts.

4. Pour the mixture onto the cornstarch-covered surface; knead about 5 turns. Stretch and roll to fit the pan; place mixture in the wafer-lined pan. Cover with another layer of wafer paper; let cool on a wire rack until cool enough to touch. Leave in the pan and cut into slices while still warm; store in an airtight container, with parchment between the layers, up to 2 weeks.

toffee

MAKES ABOUT 6 DOZEN PIECES

The pans recommended below are the ideal fit for the toffee; if you use other pans, make sure they are perfectly flat, and pour the toffee to a thickness of an eighth of an inch.

> *Canola oil, for pan*
> 1 *pound (4 sticks) unsalted butter, each stick cut into 8 pieces*
> ¼ *cup light corn syrup*
> 2½ *cups sugar*
> 1 *pound best-quality bittersweet chocolate, chopped*
> 3 *cups pecans, very finely chopped, sieved to remove fine powder*

1. Brush two 15 x 10-inch baking pans (or two 12 x 17-inch baking pans) and one 8-inch square baking pan with oil. In a heavy 3-quart saucepan, combine butter, ½ cup water, corn syrup, and sugar; clip on a candy thermometer. Bring to a boil over high heat, stirring with a wooden spoon until thickened, about 2 minutes. Brush down sides of pan with a pastry brush dipped in water to prevent crystallizing. Reduce the heat to low; stop stirring. Let the mixture come to a boil.

2. Let boil, without stirring, until the temperature reaches 280°F (soft-crack stage). This will take from 35 minutes to 1 hour; it is essential that the mixture continues to boil. Remove from the heat. Without scraping the pot, pour into the prepared pans as evenly as possible, using a spatula if necessary. Let cool at room temperature for 1 hour.

3. When mixture has cooled 45 minutes, melt the chocolate in a double boiler or in a heat-proof bowl set over a pan of simmering water; stir until smooth. Pour chocolate over toffee; spread with a spatula if necessary. Let cool about 15 minutes. Sprinkle with the nuts, then press them into the chocolate.

4. Let stand at room temperature for 24 hours. Using a large knife, lightly score 1¾ x 2¾-inch rectangles over the chocolate. Cut along scored lines. Alternatively, the toffee may be broken into shards. Store in an airtight container for 3 to 4 weeks.

fruit jellies

MAKES 7 DOZEN

The jellies call for citric acid and various extracts and oils, available at baking-supply stores and by mail (see Food Sources, page 648).

> *Canola oil, for pans*
> *Fruit flavoring (recipes follow)*
> ¼ *cup plus 2 tablespoons unflavored gelatin*
> 4⅓ *cups granulated sugar*
> 1 *teaspoon citric acid*
> 1 *cup superfine or confectioners' sugar*

1. Lightly brush two 8-inch-square pans with oil. Prepare the flavoring.

2. In a 6-quart saucepan, sprinkle the gelatin evenly over 2 cups water; let gelatin soften for about 5 minutes. Add granulated sugar and citric acid. Heat slowly over low heat, stirring constantly with a wooden spoon, until sugar has dissolved, about 10 minutes. Brush down the sides of pan with a pastry brush dipped in water to prevent crystallizing.

3. Raise heat to high; bring to a boil. Reduce heat to medium low, and boil, without stirring, 15 minutes. If syrup starts to turn dark tan before the 15 minutes, it is ready. Remove from the heat.

4. Let stand for 5 minutes while bubbles dissipate; some white foam will remain. Whisk in the flavoring. Without scraping the pot, pour evenly into the prepared pans. Let stand, uncovered, for 24 hours. Unmold, cut into 1-inch squares or other desired shapes; roll in superfine or confectioners' sugar.

apricot jelly flavoring

4 ounces dried apricots

1 tablespoon apricot oil or
orange-flower water

1. Chop apricots medium fine, place in a saucepan, and add 1 cup water. Cover and bring to a boil; reduce heat to medium low, and cook, covered, for 10 to 20 minutes, until the water is absorbed.

2. Transfer apricots to the bowl of a food processor. Process to a fine purée. Transfer to a bowl, and add the apricot oil or the orange-flower water.

fig jelly flavoring

6 ounces (about 10) dried figs

1 cup dry red wine

½ teaspoon freshly ground black pepper

1 tablespoon pure vanilla extract

1. Chop figs medium fine. Place in a small saucepan, add the wine and pepper, and cover. Bring to a boil; reduce heat to medium low, and cook for 15 minutes, until most of the water is absorbed.

2. Transfer to the bowl of a food processor, and purée. Transfer purée to a bowl; stir in vanilla.

grape jelly flavoring

½ cup boysenberry or grape jelly

1 tablespoon anise extract or oil

Mix together the jelly and the anise extract or oil in a small bowl.

pineapple jelly flavoring

8 ounces dried pineapple

1 tablespoon lemon oil

1. Chop pineapple medium fine. Place in a saucepan with 1 cup water; cover. Bring to a boil. Cook over medium-low heat until most of the water has been absorbed, 15 minutes.

2. Transfer to the bowl of a food processor, and process until mixture is as smooth as possible. Transfer to a small bowl, and mix in the lemon oil.

cranberry jelly flavoring

2 cups fresh or frozen cranberries

1 tablespoon orange-flower water

1 cup dried cranberries

1. Place cranberries and 1 cup water in a saucepan; cover. Bring to a boil; reduce heat to medium low; cook until water is absorbed, 10 to 20 minutes.

2. Transfer to the bowl of a food processor. Process to a fine purée. Transfer to a bowl. Whisk in the orange-flower water and dried cranberries.

breads

....

ciabatta

MAKES 3 LOAVES

Named for its original slipper shape ("ciabatta" is Italian for "old shoe"), ciabatta makes excellent sandwich bread; slice it horizontally to make a sandwich, or cut the loaf into long slices and spread with butter.

- 1¼ cups plus 2 tablespoons warm water (110°F)
- 2½ ¼-ounce packages (1 tablespoon plus 2 teaspoons) active dry yeast
- 3 cups Sponge (page 546), pulled into small pieces
- 3¾ cups plus 2 tablespoons bread flour, plus more for dusting
- 2 tablespoons nonfat powdered milk
- 1 tablespoon kosher salt
  Olive oil, for bowl and plastic wrap

1. In the bowl of an electric mixer, whisk together 1 cup water and the yeast. Let stand until the yeast is foamy, about 10 minutes. Add the remaining ¼ cup plus 2 tablespoons of water and the sponge and, using the paddle attachment, mix on low speed until combined, about 2 minutes.

2. In a medium bowl, combine the flour, powdered milk, and salt; add to the yeast mixture, and mix on low speed for 1 minute. Switch to the dough-hook attachment, and mix on medium-low speed until the dough is smooth and sticks to fingers slightly when squeezed, about 8 minutes. (Or knead by hand, 15 to 20 minutes.)

3. Transfer the dough to a lightly floured surface, and knead 4 or 5 turns into a ball. Place the dough, smooth-side up, in a lightly oiled bowl, and cover with plastic wrap; let rise in a warm place until the dough has doubled in size and is slightly blistered and satiny, about 1 hour.

4. Punch the dough down, and fold over onto itself 4 or 5 times. Turn the folded side down in the bowl. Cover and let rise again in a warm place until doubled in size and satiny, about 50 minutes.

5. Turn the dough onto a floured surface, flour the top, and cut into 3 pieces.

6. Line 3 baking sheets with parchment paper; flour generously. Transfer a piece of the dough to each baking sheet. Gently pull each piece into a rough rectangle (about 7 x 11 inches). Cover the dough loosely with oiled plastic wrap; let it rise in a warm place until doubled in size and small air pockets appear, about 30 minutes.

7. Dimple the surface of the bread with your fingertips. Cover with plastic wrap, and let rise again for 30 minutes. Sprinkle with flour and dimple again; cover and let rise in a warm place for 30 minutes more. Thirty minutes before the rising is completed, place a baking stone, if using, in the lower third of the oven and a baking pan on the lowest shelf. Preheat the oven to 450°F In a large saucepan, bring 2 cups water almost to a boil.

8. Slide the loaves, along with the parchment, onto the baking stone. If not using a stone, cook on the parchment-lined baking sheets. Quickly pour the very hot water into the baking pan to create steam, and close the oven door. Bake until bread is golden brown and hollow sounding when tapped on the bottom, 20 to 25 minutes. Cool on a wire rack for at least 30 minutes before slicing.

FORMING A YEAST DOUGH LOAF

1. Turn out dough onto a floured work surface and knead into a smooth, elastic ball. Cover and let it rise. For a quick rise (about an hour), set the bowl in a warm spot in the kitchen, such as near a heated oven or on top of the clothes dryer. Refrigerate dough for a slower rise (if your schedule doesn't allow you to proceed after about an hour) and to allow the flavor more time to develop.

2. Punch down the dough three or four times and let rise again.

3. Turn out the dough onto a floured surface (it will be slightly sticky) and divide it into the number of loaves you plan to make.

4. Shape the dough; this one is rolled up lengthwise, then turned and rolled again to form a peasant loaf (see page 546).

5. Move the dough to an un-floured surface; using cupped hands, form the dough into a smooth ball and let it rise again.

6. Use a cornmeal-dusted pizza peel to slide the formed loaf onto the baking stone in the oven.

peasant bread

MAKES 2 LOAVES

If you like chewy bread, look for recipes that contain bread flour. It has more gluten, the protein that gives bread its structure, than breads baked with all-purpose flour. Rye flour is available at many supermarkets and health-food stores (see Food Sources, page 648); it gives this bread its slightly dark color.

2 cups plus 1 tablespoon warm water (110°F)

1¼ teaspoons active dry yeast

1 cup Sponge (recipe follows), pulled into small pieces

6 cups bread flour, plus more for dusting

½ cup white, light, or medium rye flour

1 tablespoon kosher salt

Olive oil, for bowl and plastic wrap

1. In the bowl of an electric mixer, whisk together ¼ cup water and the yeast. Let stand until the yeast is foamy, about 10 minutes.

2. Add ½ cup more warm water and the sponge. Using the paddle attachment, mix on low speed, about 2 minutes. Add the flours, salt, and the remaining 1¼ cups plus 1 tablespoon warm water; mix 1 minute more. Switch to the dough-hook attachment, and mix on medium-low speed, pulling the dough from the hook 2 or 3 times, until the dough is soft and sticks to the fingers when squeezed, about 8 minutes. (Or knead the dough by hand, 15 to 20 minutes.)

3. On a lightly floured surface, knead dough into a ball. Place smooth-side up in a lightly oiled bowl. Cover with plastic wrap; let the dough rise in a warm place until tripled in size, about 3 hours.

4. Turn the dough out onto floured surface. Flour the top, and cut in half. Roll up one piece of dough lengthwise, flatten slightly, and roll lengthwise again. On an unfloured surface, cup your hands around the sides of the dough, and move it in small, circular motions, until the top of the dough is rounded and the bottom is smooth. Flour a piece of parchment paper, and place the dough on it; cover loosely with oiled plastic wrap, then cover with a towel. Repeat the process with remaining dough. Let rise in a warm place until doubled in size, about 50 minutes. Thirty minutes before this final rise is completed, place a baking stone or heavy baking sheet in the oven and an empty baking pan on the lowest shelf. Preheat the oven to 450°F In a large saucepan, bring 2 cups water almost to a boil.

5. Sprinkle the dough with flour; dimple the surface with your fingertips. Let rise 10 minutes more. Using a baker's peel or baking sheet, slide the loaves and parchment onto the baking stone or baking sheet. Pour the hot water into the heated baking pan to create steam. Bake until dark golden brown and hollow sounding when tapped on the bottom, 25 to 30 minutes. Transfer to a wire rack to cool for at least 30 minutes before slicing.

sponge

MAKES ABOUT 3½ CUPS

The sponge can be put in a plastic or stainless-steel bowl, covered with plastic wrap, and refrigerated for up to 1 week. It can be frozen for up to 3 months, double wrapped in plastic wrap. Bring to room temperature before using.

1½ cups warm water (110°F)

½ teaspoon active dry yeast

3½ cups bread flour

Olive oil, for bowl

1. In the bowl of an electric mixer, combine ¼ cup warm water and the yeast. Let stand until the yeast is foamy, about 10 minutes. Add the remaining 1¼ cups of water and the flour; mix on low speed, 2 minutes. The dough will be wet.

2. Place the dough in a lightly oiled bowl. Cover with plastic wrap; let stand at room temperature for 24 hours. The sponge is ready to use.

*A sponge is made by combining a small
amount of yeast with flour and water. The
thick, batterlike mixture is covered and set
aside until it bubbles and becomes foamy.
Depending on the combination of ingredients, this may take up to 24 hours. The remaining ingredients are added, and the
bread is kneaded and baked. Breads baked
using a sponge are typically denser than
other breads. A sponge is important when
making sourdough or rye breads, both of
which derive their characteristic tang from
the fermentation of the sponge.*

multigrain bread

MAKES 2 LOAVES

For the most traditional approach, let the dough
for these dense round loaves rise in Brotformen,
ridged German bread-rising baskets (see Equipment Sources, page 650) that leave a distinctive
coiled imprint on the top crust. If the baskets are
not available, use any large ceramic or stainless-
steel bowl.

¼ cup plus 2 tablespoons whole dried
  wheat berries

2½ cups warm water (110°F)

1½ teaspoons active dry yeast

2 tablespoons honey

½ cup Sponge (recipe opposite), pulled
  into small pieces

4½ cups bread flour

¼ cup plus 2 tablespoons white, light, or
  medium rye flour, plus more for dusting

¾ cup whole-wheat bread flour

1 cup rye meal

¼ cup plus 2 tablespoons cracked wheat

½ cup millet

½ cup flax seeds

1 tablespoon plus 1 teaspoon kosher salt

½ cup raw, hulled sunflower seeds

  Olive oil, for bowl and plastic wrap

  Coarse cornmeal, for dusting

1. Bring a small saucepan of water to a boil. Add the
wheat berries, and gently boil for 20 minutes. Drain
and let cool. In the bowl of an electric mixer, whisk
together ¼ cup warm water, the yeast, and honey.
Let stand until the yeast is foamy, about 10 minutes.
Using the paddle attachment, mix the yeast mixture and the sponge on low speed until combined,
about 1 minute. Add the flours, rye meal, cracked
wheat, millet, flax, salt, and remaining 2¼ cups of
warm water; mix on low speed for 2 minutes. Switch
to the dough-hook attachment, and mix on
medium-low speed for 6 minutes. Add the sunflower seeds and the cooked wheat berries; mix for
1 minute. Pull the dough down from the hook, and
press dough into the seeds at the bottom of the
bowl. Continue to mix until the seeds are incorporated and the dough is wet and tacky, about 2 minutes. (Or knead by hand, 15 to 20 minutes.)

2. Transfer to a lightly floured surface, and knead
by hand, 4 or 5 turns, into a ball. Place the dough,
smooth-side up, in a lightly oiled bowl and cover
with plastic wrap. Let the dough rise in a warm place
until 1½ times its size, about 2½ hours.

3. Punch down the dough, and fold it over onto itself 4 or 5 times. Turn the folded side face down in
the bowl. Cover and let rise in a warm place until
doubled in size, 1 hour.

4. Liberally dust 2 braided Brotformen (or 2 ceramic
or stainless-steel bowls) with flour. Turn dough onto
a lightly floured surface; cut in half. Cover one piece
of dough loosely with oiled plastic wrap. On an un-
floured surface, knead remaining dough into a ball.
Cup your hands around it and move it on the work
surface in small, circular motions, until the top is
round and the bottom is smooth.

5. Place the shaped loaf, bottom up, in a Brotform
(or one of the bowls). Cover loosely with lightly
oiled plastic wrap and a towel. Repeat process with
the second piece of dough. Let the loaves rise in a
warm place until doubled in size, about 1 hour.
Thirty minutes before the final rise is completed,
place a baking stone, if using, in lower third of the
oven and an empty baking pan on the lowest shelf.
Preheat the oven to 450°F. In a large saucepan, bring
2 cups of water almost to a boil.

6. Transfer one loaf from a Brotform to a baker's peel or baking sheet sprinkled with coarse cornmeal. Using a razor blade or serrated knife, slash the top ¼ to ½ inch deep. Slide onto the stone. Repeat with the second loaf. If not using a stone, slash the tops and bake on a cornmeal-dusted baking sheet. Quickly pour hot water into the heated baking pan to create steam; close oven door. Bake until dark golden brown and hollow sounding when tapped on the bottom, 25 to 30 minutes. If the bread darkens too quickly, lower the temperature to 425°F after 15 minutes of the baking time. Let cool on a wire rack at least 30 minutes.

olive bread

MAKES 2 LOAVES

The type of olive used will affect the amount of moisture and salt in the dough.

- *1 cup oil-cured olives, pitted*
- *¼ cup warm water (110°F)*
- *1 ¼-ounce package (2 teaspoons) active dry yeast*
- *3 cups unbleached all-purpose flour, plus more for dusting*
- *4 to 5 cups bread flour*
- *1½ tablespoons kosher salt*
- *Vegetable oil, for bowl*
- *Coarse cornmeal, for dusting*

1. Coarsely chop half the olives. Set aside. Rinse a small bowl with hot water. Add the warm water, and sprinkle in the yeast. Let sit until foamy, about 10 minutes. Stir until smooth. Place the yeast in the bowl of an electric mixer fitted with the paddle attachment, with 3 cups of room-temperature water. Mix to combine.

2. Add both flours, 1 cup at a time, with mixer on low. After the first cup of bread flour, beat until smooth. Gradually add the rest of the flour, beating with each addition, until the dough feels tacky and just pulls away from the sides of the bowl.

3. Switch to the dough hook, and beat on low speed for 5 minutes, then on high for 2 minutes. Beat in the olives and salt. Turn dough out onto a lightly floured board.

4. Knead the dough until smooth and elastic, adding small amounts of flour as necessary; dough should remain somewhat sticky.

5. Shape into a ball, and place in an oiled bowl. Turn the dough until the outside is completely oiled. Cover with plastic wrap, and refrigerate to rise overnight until doubled. (A slow rise overnight will develop the most flavor, but the dough may also be set aside at room temperature to rise until doubled, generally several hours.)

6. Dust a heavy-gauge baking sheet with cornmeal. Turn out the dough onto a lightly floured surface, and divide in half. Shape each half into a flat rectangle. Roll tightly along the long side of one rectangle, then flatten the roll. Turn and roll the short way as tightly as possible. Repeat with other half. Shape each half into a smooth ball by tightly stretching dough surface, working from top down; tuck loose ends under to form a seam. Place loaves seam-side down on baking sheet. Cover with a clean kitchen towel; leave at cool room temperature for 1½ to 2 hours, or until doubled in bulk.

7. Preheat the oven to 450°F. Dust the loaves with flour, and dimple the tops with your fingers. Let stand 10 minutes.

8. Place the baking sheet in the bottom third of the oven, and immediately spray water around but not on the loaves. Repeat spraying 3 times in the first 10 minutes of baking. Bake until loaves sound hollow when tapped on the bottom, 35 to 50 minutes.

black bread

MAKES 2 LOAVES

This bread gets its color and flavor from molasses, coffee, and cocoa.

- 1 tablespoon instant coffee
- 2 cups plus 2 tablespoons warm water (110°F)
- ¼ cup molasses
- 2½ ¼-ounce packages (1 tablespoon plus 2 teaspoons) active dry yeast
- 2 tablespoons honey
- 4½ cups whole-wheat bread flour, plus more for dusting
- ½ cup plus 2 tablespoons bread flour
- 1 cup plus 3 tablespoons dark rye flour
- 2 tablespoons sifted cocoa powder
- 1 tablespoon plus 1 teaspoon kosher salt
- Olive oil, for bowl and plastic wrap
- Coarse cornmeal, for dusting
- 1 large egg white, lightly beaten

1. In a small bowl, dissolve the coffee in ¼ cup warm water, and set aside. In the detached bowl of an electric mixer, combine the remaining 1¾ cups plus 2 tablespoons of warm water and the molasses. Sprinkle the yeast on top, stir, and let stand until yeast is foamy, about 10 minutes.

2. Attach the bowl to the mixer fitted with the paddle attachment. Add the remaining ingredients, except the cornmeal and egg white, to the yeast mixture; mix on low speed for 1 minute. Switch to the dough hook, and mix on medium-low speed until dough is smooth and slightly tacky, 6 minutes. (Or knead by hand, 15 to 20 minutes.)

3. Transfer the dough to a lightly floured surface, and knead by hand, 4 or 5 turns, into a ball. Place the dough, smooth-side up, in a large lightly oiled bowl; cover with plastic wrap and let rise in a warm place until doubled in size, 1½ hours.

4. Turn the dough onto a lightly floured surface, and cut in half. Cover one piece of dough loosely with lightly oiled plastic wrap, and set aside. Press the other piece of dough into a 9-inch square. Fold one side of the dough into the middle, then fold the other side over it, like a letter. Turn the dough 90° and fold again, pinching the seam and sides closed. Place the seam side down on an unfloured surface, and roll the dough back and forth, shaping the loaf: It should be tapered to a point at both ends, thick and rounded in the middle, and 12 inches long. Repeat the shaping process with the remaining piece of dough. Dust a clean cloth with coarse cornmeal and place the loaves on top about 6 inches apart. Cover loosely with lightly oiled plastic wrap and then with a towel. Let the dough rise in a warm place for 45 minutes. Thirty minutes before this final rise is completed, place a baking stone, if using, in the lower third of the oven and an empty baking pan on the lowest shelf. Preheat the oven to 400°F. In a large saucepan, bring 2 cups water almost to a boil.

5. Transfer the loaves to a baker's peel or baking sheet that has been dusted with coarse cornmeal. Brush the top of the loaves with the egg white. Use a razor blade or serrated knife to make 4 diagonal cuts, ¼ to ½ inch deep, across each loaf. Slide each loaf onto the baking stone. If not using a stone, bake the loaves on a parchment-lined baking sheet that has been dusted with coarse cornmeal. Quickly pour the very hot water into the heated baking pan to create steam. Bake until dark brown and hollow sounding when tapped on the bottom, 30 to 40 minutes. Let cool on a wire rack for at least 30 minutes before slicing.

BREAD-MAKING TIPS

Making homemade bread is an art, and a great loaf takes time. To perfect this time-honored baking practice, all you need is patience and a few helpful hints:

• Buy an instant-read thermometer at your local housewares store. It will tell you the right temperature for the water (between 105°F and 115°F) and the correct heat for the rising dough (70°F to 75°F).

• Repeat the same recipe before moving on to a new bread. If you toy with the recipe one variable at a time, you will end up with a perfect loaf and a lot of learning.

• Let the dough rise in the refrigerator. If you have the luxury of time, allow the dough to slowly rise in the refrigerator overnight. The cool air slows down the fermentation, allowing flavor to develop.

• Use a spray bottle or plant mister filled with hot water to create steam. Spray the sides of the oven with hot water, and spray the bread a few times during the first 5 minutes of baking. If you are baking smaller loaves, spray them as you remove them from the oven to prevent their crusts from becoming too hard as they cool.

• Use proofing baskets, such as Brotformen (see Equipment Sources, page 650). These special baskets, usually lined with cloth, help the rising dough hold its shape. Dough that spreads too fast during the rising process will not rise properly in the oven. A basket is also preferable to a bowl, since the cloth continues to allow the dough to breathe.

rosemary flatbread

MAKES TWO 10- TO 12-INCH ROUND LOAVES

This flatbread can also be grilled. Fresh oregano, marjoram, or thyme can be substituted for the rosemary. To prevent the bread from getting soggy on the bottom, always cool on a wire rack.

¼ cup warm water (110°F)

1¼ teaspoons active dry yeast

½ cup milk, room temperature

1 tablespoon olive oil, plus more for bowl, pan, and drizzling

½ tablespoon kosher salt, plus more for sprinkling

2½ to 4 cups all-purpose flour, plus more for dusting

2 tablespoons chopped fresh rosemary

1. Pour the ¼ cup warm water in a large bowl. Sprinkle the yeast over the warm water, and let stand until foamy, about 10 minutes. Stir in the milk, ½ cup room-temperature water, oil, and salt. Add 1 cup flour; whisk until smooth. Add more flour, ½ cup at a time, and incorporate until the dough comes together and pulls away from the side of the bowl.

2. Turn the dough out onto a well-floured surface; knead until velvety and soft and no longer sticky, 6 to 8 minutes. Add more flour as needed.

3. Place the dough in a lightly oiled bowl, coating the dough with the oil. Cover tightly with plastic wrap, and let the dough rise in a warm place until doubled in size, about 1½ hours.

4. Preheat the oven to 400°F. If grilling, prepare a grill. Turn out the dough onto a lightly floured surface; divide into two pieces, shaping each into a ball. Place the balls on an oiled 12-inch-wide pan; with oiled fingers, press into 10- to 12-inch circles. Cover with plastic wrap, and allow to rise 30 minutes.

5. Dimple the dough by pressing with your fingertips; drizzle lightly with more olive oil, cover with moist towels, and let rise again for 10 minutes.

6. If grilling, lightly brush both sides of the dough with olive oil, and place directly on a hot grill; grill the flatbread until golden brown, about 2 minutes per side; remove from grill, and season with salt. To bake, sprinkle rosemary over the dough; sprinkle with salt. Bake 25 to 35 minutes, spraying with water a few times in the first 10 minutes to create a crisp surface. Bake until bottoms are golden. Transfer immediately to cooling racks.

....

YEAST

Yeast is the key ingredient to making airy loaves of fresh bread. Most recipes that call for yeast instruct you to "proof" it by combining it with warm water (110°F) and sugar to test its potency before baking. If the yeast is indeed "alive," the water and the sugar will cause the yeast to bubble up and turn foamy—yeast converts both sugars and starch into carbon dioxide, which causes the actual rising and the network of holes throughout the dough.

Bakers can buy commercial yeast, available in many forms. Cake yeast is also known as compressed fresh yeast. It is dry, crumbly, and white and comes in small 6-ounce squares. It is equivalent in potency to one ¼-ounce package of active dry yeast. Cake yeast is moist and extremely perishable, and must be used within a week or two of being made (or by the date indicated on the package). It may also be frozen; defrost it completely before using. Cake yeast is preferred by professional bakers because it is fresher.

Home bakers are better off using active dry yeast (fine, light-brown granules), which retains its potency for a long time. It is best stored in the freezer, where the yeast can remain for years, and is usually available in small ¼-ounce packages. Newer and a little less common is quick-rise yeast, which can cause bread to rise approximately twice as fast. It is available in larger, more porous pellets that are packaged in an airtight can.

....

curried parchment bread
MAKES 4 9½ × 11-INCH SHEETS

Whole spices ground just before using give these paper-thin free-form breads such depth of flavor that they are delicious—and addictive—plain.

1   tablespoon unsalted butter
1   tablespoon minced garlic
2   tablespoons freshly grated ginger (from a 1-inch piece)
1   medium onion, minced (about 1 cup)
⅛   teaspoon cayenne pepper
⅛   teaspoon ground cardamom
¼   teaspoon ground turmeric
¼   teaspoon ground coriander
½   teaspoon ground cumin
½   teaspoon Curry Powder (page 633) or prepared
1   teaspoon kosher salt
⅛   teaspoon freshly ground black pepper
½   cup all-purpose flour, plus more for dusting
1   tablespoon pure vegetable shortening

1. Preheat the oven to 325°F. Melt the butter in a small saucepan over medium heat. Add the garlic, ginger, and onion; cook until fragrant, about 3 minutes. Stir in the cayenne, cardamom, turmeric, coriander, cumin, curry, ½ teaspoon salt, and the pepper, and cook for 30 seconds. Remove from the heat, and allow to cool.

2 . In a food processor, pulse the flour with the remaining ½ teaspoon salt. Add the shortening, and pulse until mixture resembles coarse meal. With the machine running, gradually add 5 tablespoons spice mixture; process until dough comes together.

3. Transfer the dough to a lightly floured surface; divide into four equal parts. Roll out the dough as thinly as possible into a 9½ x 11-inch rectangle. If the dough is too wet, sprinkle with additional flour. Transfer to an ungreased baking sheet; repeat with a second piece of dough, and transfer to the sheet. Bake for 10 minutes. Turn, and bake an additional 5 minutes, until firm. Transfer the bread to a wire rack to cool. Store in an airtight container, at room temperature, for up to 1 week.

whole-wheat onion focaccia

MAKES TWELVE 4- TO 5-INCH LOAVES

You can freeze half of the dough in a resealable plastic bag after it has risen the first time; bring it to room temperature, let rise again, and bake.

- 1 tablespoon olive oil, plus more for bowl and brushing
- 5 medium yellow onions, cut into ¼-inch-thick rounds
- ½ cup warm water (110°F)
- 1 ¼-ounce package (2 teaspoons) active dry yeast
- 1½ teaspoons kosher salt
- 1¼ cups whole-wheat flour
- 3 cups all-purpose flour, plus more for kneading and dusting

  Yellow cornmeal, for dusting

- 12 red and yellow cherry tomatoes, quartered
- 2 teaspoons flaky or coarse sea salt
- ¼ teaspoon freshly ground black pepper
- 1 teaspoon whole fennel seeds

1. Heat the oil in a large skillet over medium-high heat. Add the onions; cover. Cook, stirring occasionally, until the onions are soft and slightly golden, about 25 minutes.

2. Transfer half of the onions to the bowl of a food processor; pulse until smooth, about 30 seconds. Set remaining onions aside.

3. Combine the warm water and yeast in a small bowl. Let sit until mixture becomes foamy, about 10 minutes.

4. Add the yeast mixture, salt, and whole-wheat flour to puréed onions, and pulse until smooth. Working in three batches, add the all-purpose flour, pulsing to incorporate after each addition; dough should be slightly sticky.

5. Transfer the dough to a lightly floured surface. Knead 10 times; place in a lightly oiled bowl; cover tightly with plastic wrap. Let the dough rise in a warm place until doubled in size, about 30 minutes; punch down. Let rise again until doubled in size, 30 to 40 minutes.

6. Preheat the oven to 400°F. Transfer the dough to a lightly floured surface. Using a sharp knife, cut the dough into 12 equal pieces. Form each piece into a ball. Sprinkle two 12 x 17-inch baking sheets with cornmeal, and place 6 balls of dough on each sheet. Cover tightly with plastic wrap; let rise in a warm place until puffed, 10 to 15 minutes.

7. Punch down each dough ball with your fingertips to create 4- to 5-inch rounds. Place 2 tablespoons of the reserved onions in center of each round. Place four tomato quarters on each round. Lightly brush the rounds with oil. Sprinkle with the salt, pepper, and fennel.

8. Bake until golden, about 30 minutes. Transfer to wire racks to cool. Serve warm.

FIT TO EAT RECIPE PER SERVING: 188 CALORIES, 1 G FAT, 1 MG CHOLESTEROL, 39 G CARBOHYDRATE, 464 MG SODIUM, 6 G PROTEIN, 4 G DIETARY FIBER

herb-scented flatbread

MAKES THREE 6-INCH ROUND LOAVES

Less chewy and a bit flatter than yeasted flatbread, this yeastless version is just as delicious and quicker to make. Use any combination of fresh herbs.

- 1 cup plus 3 tablespoons all-purpose flour, plus more for dusting
- ½ teaspoon baking powder
- ½ teaspoon kosher salt, plus more for sprinkling
- 1 teaspoon finely chopped fresh sage
- 1 teaspoon finely snipped chives
- 1 teaspoon finely chopped fresh flat-leaf parsley
- 2½ tablespoons pure vegetable shortening
- 3 tablespoons milk
- 1 tablespoon olive oil, for brushing

1. In the bowl of a food processor, combine flour, baking powder, salt, sage, chives, and parsley; process for 5 seconds. Add vegetable shortening; process until well combined, about 15 seconds. Add the milk and 2 tablespoons water, and process until the dough comes together, about 7 seconds.

2. Transfer the dough to a clean surface, and knead for about 1 minute, forming it into a ball. Cover with plastic wrap, and let stand for 30 minutes.

3. Heat a medium cast-iron skillet over medium-high heat until very hot. Meanwhile, cut the dough into 3 equal pieces; form each one into a ball. On a lightly floured surface, roll a piece of dough out into a very thin circle (it should be less than ¹⁄₁₆ inch thick and about 6½ inches in diameter). Using a fork, prick dough 7 or 8 times. Lightly brush one side of the dough with olive oil; sprinkle it with salt.

4. Preheat oven to 200°F. Transfer round of dough, oiled-side down, to the hot skillet, and reduce heat to medium; cook until surface is covered with gold speckles, 1 to 2 minutes on each side. If it begins to burn, lower the heat and continue to cook.

5. Remove bread from skillet; transfer to a baking sheet; place in oven to keep warm. Repeat with remaining dough. Cut the bread into wedges with a pizza wheel or sharp knife, and serve warm.

coca bread

MAKES TWO 8 × 17-INCH LOAVES

Slice this sweet Spanish yeast bread in long, thin rectangles, and drizzle it with your favorite honey.

- 2 ¼-ounce packages (1 tablespoon plus 1 teaspoon) active dry yeast
- ⅓ cup warm water (110°F)
- 1¼ cups sugar
- 5 to 6 cups all-purpose flour
- 1 teaspoon kosher salt
- 1 cup milk, room temperature
- 4 large eggs
- ½ cup (1 stick) unsalted butter, melted, plus more for bowl and pans
- ¼ cup honey, for drizzling

1. In a small bowl, combine yeast and warm water; let stand until foamy, about 10 minutes. In a bowl, combine 1 cup sugar, 4 cups flour, and salt. With a wooden spoon, stir in yeast mixture, milk, 3 eggs, and ½ cup melted butter until combined. Using your hands, work remaining flour into dough, ¼ cup at a time, until dough is no longer sticky.

2. On a lightly floured surface, knead the dough until it develops a smooth satiny texture and springs back when you poke it with your finger, about 5 minutes. Form the dough into a ball, and place in a lightly buttered bowl, rotating the dough in the bowl to coat with the butter. Cover with plastic wrap, and let rise in a warm place until doubled in size, about 1 hour.

3. Preheat the oven to 400°F. Generously grease two baking sheets with some of the melted butter. Turn the dough to a clean work surface, and cut in half. Place half of the dough on each prepared baking sheet, and press into two 8 x 17-inch rectangles. Allow the dough to proof for 15 minutes. In a small bowl, whisk the remaining egg with 1 tablespoon water, and brush onto the dough.

4. Generously sprinkle the dough with the remaining ¼ cup sugar, and drizzle with the honey. Bake until golden and crispy, about 18 minutes. Transfer the breads to wire racks to cool.

buttermilk kiss biscuits

MAKES 3 DOZEN

Because it contains yeast, this dough is a little sturdier and can be handled more vigorously than some others, making it easy to shape these light, airy biscuits. Fold the round biscuits in half to make them resemble kisses. If you don't have three baking sheets, after the first batch of biscuits is done, cool one of the baking sheets (place it under cold running water and dry thoroughly), line with parchment paper, and bake the remaining biscuits.

- 5 cups all-purpose flour, plus more for dusting
- 1 teaspoon baking soda
- 1 tablespoon baking powder
- 2 teaspoons kosher salt
- 2½ tablespoons sugar
- ¼ cup warm water (110°F)
- 2 ¼-ounce packages (1 tablespoon plus 1 teaspoon) active dry yeast
- 1 cup (2 sticks) unsalted butter, cut into small pieces
- 2 cups buttermilk
- 4 tablespoons unsalted butter, melted and cooled

1. Preheat the oven to 450°F with two racks. Line three baking sheets with parchment paper. Sift together the flour, baking soda, baking powder, salt, and sugar.

2. Place the warm water in a small bowl; sprinkle the yeast over, and let stand until foamy, about 10 minutes. Use a pastry cutter or 2 knives to cut the butter into the flour mixture until it resembles coarse meal. Stir in the yeast mixture and buttermilk. Turn onto a lightly floured surface, and knead until smooth, 2 to 3 minutes.

3. Roll the dough to a thickness of ¼ inch. Cut out the biscuits as close together as possible, using a floured 2½-inch-round biscuit or cookie cutter;

place 2 inches apart on the baking sheets. Knead the dough scraps lightly; continue cutting biscuits, using all the dough. Brush the edges with the melted butter, fold the rounds in half, and press the edges to seal. Brush the tops with butter. Place 2 of the baking sheets in the oven; leave the third at room temperature. Bake 6 minutes; rotate baking sheets between the oven racks and bake until lightly golden, about 5 minutes more. Bake the third sheet on a center rack until the biscuits are golden, about 10 minutes. Serve hot.

cornmeal biscuits

MAKES 8

Yellow cornmeal adds color and crunch to these leavened biscuits. Spread softened butter on the biscuits, and drizzle with honey. This recipe can be doubled.

- 1½ cups all-purpose flour, plus more for dusting
- ¼ cup plus 2 tablespoons yellow cornmeal
- 2 teaspoons baking powder
- ¾ teaspoon baking soda
- ¾ teaspoon kosher salt
- 1½ tablespoons sugar
- 6 tablespoons cold unsalted butter, cut into ½-inch pieces
- ¾ cup plus 1 tablespoon buttermilk

1. Preheat the oven to 400°F. In a medium bowl, whisk together the flour, cornmeal, baking powder, baking soda, salt, and sugar. Using a pastry cutter or 2 knives, cut the butter into the flour mixture. Using a fork, stir in ¾ cup buttermilk until the mixture holds together.

2. Line a baking sheet with parchment paper. On a lightly floured work surface, roll out the dough to a 1-inch thickness. Cut out 8 biscuits, as close together as possible, using a floured 2-inch-round biscuit or cookie cutter; discard the scraps of dough. Transfer the biscuits to the baking sheet. Brush the tops with the remaining buttermilk. Bake until golden and puffy, about 12 minutes. Serve hot.

herbed cheddar biscuits

MAKES 20

Martha's friend Sara Foster is famous for these savory biscuits, made by the dozens at her food market in Chapel Hill, North Carolina.

- 1 cup (2 sticks) cold unsalted butter, cut into small pieces, plus more for pan
- 7 cups all-purpose flour, plus more for dusting
- 1 tablespoon baking powder
- 1 tablespoon baking soda
- 1 tablespoon kosher salt
- ½ cup cold pure vegetable shortening
- ½ cup minced scallions
- ¼ cup minced fresh flat-leaf parsley
- 2 cups grated sharp Cheddar cheese
- 1½ cups buttermilk

1. Preheat the oven to 425°F. Lightly butter or parchment line a baking sheet. In a large bowl, whisk together the flour, baking powder, baking soda, and salt. Use a pastry cutter or 2 knives to cut the butter into the dry ingredients until the mixture resembles coarse meal. Cut in the shortening; mix in the scallions, parsley, and cheddar cheese.

2. Make a well in the center of the flour mixture, pour in the buttermilk, and stir with a fork just until dough comes together. Do not overmix. Turn dough onto a lightly floured surface, and knead gently 6 to 8 times.

3. On a clean work surface, pat the dough into a 1-inch-thick round. Cut out the biscuits, as close together as possible, using a floured 3-inch-round biscuit or cookie cutter. Do not twist the cutter. Gently pat together the scraps of dough, and cut out more biscuits.

4. Transfer the biscuits to the baking sheet, and bake until golden brown, 12 to 15 minutes, rotating baking sheet halfway through. Serve hot.

soda biscuits

MAKES 8

Soda biscuits are most often cut from the dough with a biscuit cutter, but shaping the dough into wedges directly on the baking sheet makes short work of this step. Make these when you are too rushed to use a biscuit cutter or want more rustic-looking biscuits.

- 1¾ cups all-purpose flour, sifted
- 1 teaspoon kosher salt
- 1½ tablespoons sugar
- 1½ teaspoons baking soda
- 2 teaspoons baking powder
- 5 tablespoons cold unsalted butter, cut into small pieces
- ¾ cup buttermilk

1. Preheat the oven to 425°F. Line a baking sheet with parchment paper. Combine the dry ingredients in the bowl of a food processor. Pulse once or twice to combine. Add the butter, and process until the dough resembles coarse meal. Add the buttermilk, and process a few seconds more, until the dough just comes together.

2. Turn out the dough onto the baking sheet, and pat into a 7-inch circle about 1 inch thick. Using a sharp knife, cut into the dough about ¼ inch to make 8 wedges; do not separate.

3. Bake the biscuits until golden brown on top and firm, about 20 minutes. Break apart into wedges, and serve hot.

. . . .

BREAD WARMER

Add a few clean unglazed terra-cotta tiles to the oven for the last 5 minutes of baking. Place the hot tiles in a towel-lined basket, add bread or rolls, cover, and serve.

. . . .

roasted garlic and sage parker house rolls

MAKES 2½ DOZEN

A roasted-garlic-and-sage filling gives these buttery rolls a savory flavor. To make classic Parker House rolls, omit the garlic and sage.

- 3 large leaves fresh sage, plus smaller leaves for garnish
- 1 head of roasted garlic (see page 646)
- 1¼ cups warm milk (110°F)
- 2 ¼-ounce packages (1 tablespoon plus 1 teaspoon) active dry yeast
- 10 tablespoons unsalted butter, plus more for bowl and pan
- 3 tablespoons sugar
- 1¼ teaspoons kosher salt
- 5½ cups all-purpose flour, plus more for dusting
- 3 large eggs, lightly beaten

1. Finely chop the large sage leaves, and combine them with the soft roasted garlic in a small bowl; set the filling aside.

2. Place ½ cup warm milk in a small bowl, and sprinkle the yeast evenly over the top. Let stand until foamy, about 10 minutes.

3. Pour the remaining ¾ cup milk into a medium saucepan, set over medium-high heat, and bring just to a boil. Cut 6 tablespoons butter into small

pieces. Remove the pan from the heat, and stir in the butter pieces, the sugar, and the salt. Stir until the butter has completely melted. Set the pan aside.

4. Place 4½ cups flour in the bowl of an electric mixer. Using your hand, make a well in the center of the flour. Place the yeast mixture, the butter mixture, and the eggs in the well. Attach the bowl to the mixer fitted with the dough-hook attachment, and, with the machine on low speed, blend just until it starts to come together, about 2 minutes.

5. Transfer the dough to a lightly floured surface. Knead until the dough becomes soft and smooth and is no longer sticky, 5 to 10 minutes, adding the remaining cup of flour as needed. Lightly butter a bowl and a 12 x 17-inch baking pan. Place the dough in the buttered bowl. Turn the dough to lightly coat with butter, and cover the dough with a clean kitchen towel. Let the dough rise in a warm place until doubled in size, about 1½ hours. Punch down the dough, and let rest 10 minutes.

6. Melt the remaining 4 tablespoons of butter. Divide the dough in half. Roll out one piece on a lightly floured surface, keeping the second piece covered, forming a 10 x 12-inch rectangle; trim the edges as needed. Cut each rectangle lengthwise into five 2-inch-wide strips. Cut each strip into three 4-inch-long rectangles. Working with one rectangle at a time, brush half of it with melted butter, and spread about ⅛ teaspoon of the garlic-sage filling in a thin layer over the melted butter. Fold the rec-

MAKING THE PARKER HOUSE ROLLS

Form the rolls one at a time: Brush melted butter over a piece of dough, spread garlic-sage purée over the butter, fold the dough, and put on the pan. Repeat with the remaining dough pieces, arranging them in a

slightly overlapping fashion, one row at a time. When you've filled the pan with one row, start another immediately adjacent to the first.

tangle in half, leaving a ½-inch overhang at the bottom. Transfer the roll to the prepared baking pan. Repeat forming and making rolls, arranging them on the baking pan so they overlap slightly. Roll out the remaining half of the covered dough, and form the remaining rolls. Cover the baking pan with a clean kitchen towel.

7. Preheat the oven to 375°. Let the rolls rise in a warm place until they have doubled in size, about 30 minutes. Brush the top of each roll with melted butter, and arrange 3 sage leaves on top. Bake the rolls until they become golden brown on the tops, 15 to 20 minutes. Serve.

potato rolls

MAKES ABOUT 2½ DOZEN

This easy and inexpensive potato dough lends itself to large-scale production, making these an excellent choice for big gatherings. Mixed in large batches, the dough can be rolled and cut quickly into triangles using a pizza cutter or knife.

- 2 *small russet potatoes, peeled and cut into 2-inch pieces*
- 2 *¼-ounce packages (1 tablespoon plus 1 teaspoon) active dry yeast*
- 2 *tablespoons plus a pinch of sugar*
- 1 *cup buttermilk, room temperature*
- 6 *tablespoons unsalted butter, melted and cooled, plus more for pans*
- 1 *tablespoon plus 1 teaspoon kosher salt*
- 5½ *to 6½ cups bread flour, plus more for dusting*

1. Line 3 baking sheets with parchment paper. Place the potatoes in a medium saucepan; cover with cold water. Bring to a boil; reduce to a simmer. Cook until tender when pierced with the tip of a knife, about 15 minutes. Drain, reserving ½ cup of the liquid. Mash the potatoes, and set aside.

2. Cool the reserved liquid to 105°F. In the bowl of an electric mixer, whisk together the reserved liquid, yeast, and pinch of sugar. Set aside until mixture is foamy, about 10 minutes.

3. Using an electric mixer fitted with the dough-hook attachment, mix the remaining sugar, the reserved mashed potatoes, the buttermilk, 4 tablespoons butter, and the salt on low speed until combined. Gradually add enough flour to make a slightly sticky dough. Mix the dough until smooth, about 2 minutes. Place the dough in a lightly buttered bowl; cover with buttered plastic wrap. Set aside to rise in a warm place until doubled in size, 1 to 1½ hours.

4. Preheat the oven to 375°F. Turn the dough out onto a lightly floured surface. Using a floured rolling pin, roll the dough out to ¾ inch thick. Cut the dough into 2-inch-wide strips. Cut the strips into triangles or squares; place at least 1¼ inches apart on the baking sheets. Brush the tops with the remaining butter; cover with buttered plastic wrap. Let rise until the dough does not spring back when pressed with a finger, about 15 minutes. Bake until golden, 18 to 20 minutes. Serve hot.

sopressata skillet rolls

MAKES 22

These are easy to make—strips of potato dough are rolled with fresh rosemary and chopped sausage and then baked in a skillet. Sopressata (see Food Sources, page 648) is short, wide salami made with ground pork, garlic, cracked black pepper, and other spices.

- ¼ *cup olive oil, for brushing*
- ½ *recipe Potato Rolls dough (recipe, at left), made through step 3*
  All-purpose flour, for dusting
- 1 *tablespoon finely chopped fresh rosemary*
- 8 *ounces sweet sopressata or salami, roughly chopped*

1. Preheat the oven to 350°F. Generously brush a large ovenproof cast-iron skillet with olive oil.

2. Turn dough out onto a lightly floured surface. Using a floured rolling pin, roll the dough into a 10 x 20-inch rectangle. Brush with olive oil; sprinkle with rosemary and sopressata. Halve lengthwise. Roll each strip lengthwise to form a long, narrow roll. Cut each roll into eleven 1¾-inch slices.

3. Place the slices, cut-side down, in the skillet. Brush the tops with the remaining olive oil. Cover with plastic wrap; let rise until the dough does not spring back when pressed with a finger, about 30 minutes. Bake until golden, about 35 minutes. Serve hot.

olive rolls

MAKES 1½ DOZEN

Olive paste comes in tubes and jars; it is available in supermarkets and specialty-food stores. Steam is essential for achieving the delicious crust on these rolls.

- 1¼ cups plus 1 tablespoon warm water (110°F)
- ¼ teaspoon active dry yeast
- ½ cup Sponge (page 546), pulled into small pieces
- ¼ cup plus 1 tablespoon olive oil, plus more for oiling
- 3¾ cups bread flour, plus more for dusting
- 2½ teaspoons kosher salt
- ¾ cup olive paste

1. Pour ¼ cup warm water into the bowl of an electric mixer. Sprinkle yeast over the top; let stand until yeast is foamy, about 10 minutes. Add sponge and 2 tablespoons olive oil. Using the paddle attachment, mix on low speed, about 2 minutes.

2. Add the flour, salt, and remaining cup of water; mix 1 minute more. Change to the dough-hook attachment, and mix on medium-low speed until the dough is soft and smooth, 6 minutes. (Or knead by hand, 15 to 20 minutes.)

3. Transfer the dough to a lightly floured surface, and knead by hand, 4 or 5 turns, into a ball. Place the dough, smooth-side up, in a large, lightly oiled bowl; cover with oiled plastic wrap. Let the dough rise in a warm place until doubled in size, about 2½ hours.

4. Brush two 9 x 5-inch loaf pans liberally with olive oil, and pour 1 tablespoon olive oil into each. Turn the dough out onto a lightly floured surface, and cut off a 2-ounce piece of dough. Using your fingertips, flatten the dough into a 4 x 5-inch rectangle. Spread with about 1 teaspoon olive paste, roll up tightly, and pinch the long edge to seal. Place the roll, seam-side down, in the prepared pan. Repeat this process until you have filled the bottom of the pan with the rolls fitting snugly; the pan should accommodate about nine. Repeat the process with remaining dough. Cover with lightly oiled plastic wrap, and let rise for 1 hour. Thirty minutes before the final rise is completed, place a baking stone, if using, in the lower third of the oven and a baking pan on the lowest shelf. Preheat the oven to 450°F. In a large saucepan, bring 2 cups water to a boil.

5. Using a razor blade or sharp knife, make a lengthwise slash on each roll, deep enough to expose the olive paste. Transfer the loaf pans to the hot baking stone; quickly pour the hot water into the baking pan to create steam, and close the oven door. Bake until dark golden brown, 30 to 40 minutes. Remove the pans from the oven, and turn rolls out onto a wire rack to cool. If the bottom and sides are not dark enough, return to the oven, and bake (out of the pans) until golden, about 10 minutes. Brush the tops with the remaining olive oil, and let cool on wire racks for at least 20 minutes before serving.

classic light rolls

MAKES 2 DOZEN

For really fluffy yeast dinner rolls like these classic light rolls, don't gather and reroll the scraps of dough, and be sure to give the dough generous rising time.

- ¼   cup warm water (110°F)
- ½   cup plus a pinch of sugar
- 1   ¼-ounce package (2 teaspoons) active dry yeast
- 1¼ cups milk
- ¾   cup (1½ sticks) unsalted butter, melted and cooled, plus more for the bowl
- 2½ teaspoons kosher salt
- 3   large eggs
- 4½ to 5 cups all-purpose flour, plus more for dusting
- 1   tablespoon poppy seeds

1. Line a baking sheet with parchment paper. In the bowl of an electric mixer, whisk together the warm water, a pinch of sugar, and the yeast. Set aside until the mixture is foamy, about 10 minutes.

2. Using the electric mixer fitted with the dough-hook attachment, mix together on low speed the milk, butter, the remaining sugar, the salt, and 2 eggs. Gradually add enough flour to form a sticky but manageable dough. Transfer the dough to a lightly buttered bowl; cover tightly with buttered plastic wrap. Let the dough rise in a warm place until doubled in size, about 2½ hours.

3. Turn the dough out onto a lightly floured surface. With a floured rolling pin, roll the dough out to a ¾-inch thickness. Cut out 24 rounds, as close together as possible, using a 2¼-inch-round biscuit or cookie cutter. Place the rounds ¼ inch apart on the baking sheet. Cover with buttered plastic wrap. Let rise until light and dough does not spring back when pressed with a finger, about 30 minutes.

4. Preheat the oven to 350°F. Whisk together the remaining egg and 1 tablespoon water. Brush the tops of the rounds with the egg wash. Sprinkle the rounds with the poppy seeds. Bake until the rolls are golden brown, 20 to 25 minutes. Transfer to a wire rack to cool for 5 minutes. Serve warm.

buttery crescents

MAKES ABOUT 3 DOZEN

Salted butter gives these rolls their light, flaky texture and just the right amount of seasoning.

- 1   cup (2 sticks) salted butter, cool but not cold
    Classic Light Rolls dough (recipe, left), made through step 2
    All-purpose flour, for dusting

1. Line two baking sheets with parchment paper. Place the butter in the bowl of an electric mixer fitted with the paddle attachment. Beat on low speed until the butter is spreadable. Turn the dough out onto a floured work surface. With a floured rolling pin, roll the dough into a rough 10 x 25-inch rectangle. Spread the dough with the butter. Fold both 10-inch edges of the dough into the middle, then fold in half to form a rectangle that is about 10 x 6 inches. Wrap the dough in plastic wrap; place on a baking sheet. Chill for 40 minutes.

2. On a lightly floured surface, roll the dough into a 10 x 25-inch rectangle. Fold into quarters as in step 1. Wrap in plastic wrap; return to the baking sheet. Chill 40 minutes more.

3. Roll the dough into a 15 x 25-inch rectangle. Using a pizza wheel or a sharp knife, trim the edges of the dough so they are straight. Discard the scraps. Cut the rectangle lengthwise into four equal strips. Cut each strip into elongated triangles, about 3 inches wide at the base. Starting at the base of the triangles, roll and shape into crescents. Transfer crescents to the prepared baking sheets, spacing them 1 inch apart. Cover with buttered plastic wrap. Let the dough rise in a cool place for 1 hour.

4. Preheat the oven to 350°F with two racks. Bake the crescents until golden and cooked through, about 20 minutes. Transfer to a wire rack to cool for 5 minutes before serving. Serve warm.

health rolls

MAKES 22

½ cup bulgur wheat

1 cup warm milk (110°F)

1 ¼-ounce package (2 teaspoons) active dry yeast

⅓ cup honey

2 large eggs, lightly beaten

½ cup quick-cooking oatmeal

1½ cups whole-wheat flour

1 teaspoon freshly ground black pepper

1 tablespoon kosher salt

2½ to 3½ cups all-purpose flour

2 tablespoons olive oil, plus more for pan

3 tablespoons mixed seeds, such as poppy, sesame, or fennel

1 tablespoon sea salt or kosher salt

1. Place the bulgur in a medium saucepan with 2 cups water. Bring to a boil, reduce to a simmer, and cook until the bulgur is tender and water is absorbed, 12 to 25 minutes. Let cool.

2. In the bowl of an electric mixer, whisk together the warm milk, yeast, and honey. Set aside until mixture is foamy, 10 minutes.

3. Using an electric mixer fitted with the dough-hook attachment, mix the milk mixture, eggs, oatmeal, whole-wheat flour, pepper, salt, and cooled bulgur on low speed. Slowly add enough all-purpose flour to make a soft, slightly sticky dough. Knead the dough on medium-low speed until it springs back when pressed with a finger, about 3 minutes. Place the dough in a lightly oiled bowl; cover with oiled plastic wrap. Let rise in a warm place until doubled in size, 1½ to 2 hours.

4. Generously brush two 8-inch round cake pans with olive oil. Measure the dough into 2-ounce portions. Roll each portion of dough into a ball. Place 11 balls of dough into each cake pan. Brush the tops generously with the 2 tablespoons olive oil. Cover with plastic wrap, and let rise until half again as large, 20 to 25 minutes.

5. Preheat the oven to 375°F. Sprinkle the tops of the rolls with the mixed seeds and flaky salt. Bake until dark golden brown on top, 20 to 25 minutes. Transfer to a rack to cool for about 12 minutes before unmolding. Serve warm.

rosemary shallot popovers

MAKES 6

To make popovers that really pop up and over, use a popover frame, available in kitchenware shops (see Equipment Sources, page 650); it enables the hot air to circulate around each popover. Traditionally, popover batter is refrigerated until very cold and poured into a very hot pan to rise properly; we created a batter that pops beautifully, even if it's not chilled ahead of time. This recipe can be doubled directly.

Canola oil, for the tins

2½ tablespoons plus 1 teaspoon unsalted butter

4 shallots, minced

1 tablespoon chopped fresh rosemary

1½ cups milk

1½ cups all-purpose flour

½ teaspoon kosher salt

4 large eggs

1. Preheat the oven to 450°F. Place a rack on the bottom level. Lightly oil the popover tins or a standard muffin tin and set aside.

2. Heat 1 teaspoon butter in a small skillet over low heat. Add shallots, and cook until soft and transparent, about 5 minutes. Add rosemary, and set aside.

3. Melt 1½ tablespoons butter. Combine with the milk, flour, and salt. Beat in the eggs one at a time. Add the shallot-rosemary mixture.

4. Heat the oiled tin for 5 minutes; remove from the oven. Divide the remaining tablespoon of butter among the tins, and heat until the butter sizzles. Divide the batter evenly among the cups.

5. Bake for 20 minutes, then reduce heat to 350°F without opening the oven. Bake 20 minutes more. When popovers are done, the sides should feel crisp and firm. Poke with a sharp knife to release steam, and serve immediately.

sunday best irish soda bread

MAKES ONE 3-INCH LOAF

    4   cups all-purpose flour
    ¼   cup sugar
    1   teaspoon kosher salt
    2   teaspoons baking powder
    2   tablespoons whole caraway seeds
    4   tablespoons cold unsalted butter
    2   cups golden or dark raisins
    1½ cups buttermilk
    1   large whole egg
    1   teaspoon baking soda
    1   large egg yolk
    1   tablespoon heavy cream

1. Preheat the oven to 350°F. Line a baking sheet with parchment paper; set aside. In a large bowl, whisk together the flour, sugar, salt, baking powder, and caraway seeds until well combined.

2. Using a pastry cutter or 2 knives, cut the butter into the flour mixture until it resembles coarse meal. Stir in the raisins until evenly distributed.

3. In a small bowl, whisk together the buttermilk, egg, and baking soda until well combined. Pour the buttermilk mixture into the flour-and-butter mixture all at once, and stir with a fork until all the liquid is absorbed and the mixture begins to hold together. Using your hands, press the dough into a round, dome-shaped loaf about 8 inches in diameter. Transfer it to the baking sheet.

4. In a small bowl, whisk together the egg yolk and cream. Using a pastry brush, brush the egg wash over the loaf. Using a razor blade or sharp knife, make an x-shaped slash about ½ inch deep into the top of the loaf. Bake, rotating halfway through, until it is deep golden brown and a cake tester comes out clean when inserted into the center, about 70 minutes. Transfer to a wire rack to cool.

fresh-ginger pain d'epice

SERVES 16

The flavors of this spice bread ("pain d'épice" in French) improves if it is wrapped and stored at room temperature for 2 or 3 days before eating.

        Canola oil, for the pan
    2¼ cups all-purpose flour (or 1¾ cup all-
        purpose flour and ½ cup whole-wheat
        flour), plus more for dusting
    ½   cup packed dark-brown sugar
    ¼   cup granulated sugar
    2   teaspoons baking powder
    ½   teaspoon baking soda
    1   tablespoon anise seeds
    ¼   teaspoon ground ginger
    ¼   teaspoon ground allspice
    ¼   teaspoon freshly ground black pepper
    ¾   teaspoon ground cinnamon
    ½   teaspoon kosher salt
    ½   teaspoon finely grated lemon zest
    ½   teaspoon finely grated orange zest
    ¾   cup plus 2 tablespoons honey
    3   tablespoons cognac
    1   tablespoon freshly grated ginger
    ½   cup chopped blanched almonds
    ⅓   cup finely diced dried pears
    ⅓   cup golden raisins

1. Preheat the oven to 350°F. Brush a 9 x 5-inch loaf pan with oil, and lightly flour it.

2. Combine the flour, sugars, baking powder and soda, spices, salt, and zests in a bowl.

3. Pour ¾ cup hot water over ¾ cup honey in the bowl of an electric mixer fitted with the paddle attachment; add the cognac and the fresh ginger. Mix on low speed for about 30 seconds.

4. Add the flour mixture; mix on low speed until smooth, about 1 minute. Add the almonds, pears, and raisins, and mix on low speed for about 30 seconds. Pour into the pan.

5. Bake until a cake tester inserted in the center comes out clean, about 1 hour 15 minutes. Cool on a wire rack, about 5 minutes.

6. Meanwhile, heat the remaining 2 tablespoons of honey in a small saucepan over low heat. Turn the loaf onto a wire rack, and use a pastry brush to coat the top and sides with the warm honey. Cool completely. Cut into ½-inch slices, and serve.

FIT TO EAT RECIPE PER SERVING: 208 CALORIES, 2 G TOTAL FAT, 9% CALORIES FROM FAT, 0 MG CHOLESTEROL, 45 G CARBOHYDRATE, 172 MG SODIUM, 3 G PROTEIN, 1 G DIETARY FIBER

skillet cornbread

SERVES 6 TO 8

¼ cup pure vegetable shortening
1 cup all-purpose flour
1 cup yellow cornmeal
1 tablespoon sugar
2 teaspoons kosher salt
2 teaspoons baking powder
1 cup milk
2 large eggs

1. Preheat the oven to 425°F with a rack in the center. Place the shortening in an 8-inch cast-iron skillet. Place the skillet in the oven.

2. In a medium bowl, whisk together the flour, cornmeal, sugar, salt, and baking powder. Set aside. In a small bowl, whisk together the milk and eggs until frothy. Pour the milk-egg mixture into the dry ingredients. Mix just until ingredients are incorporated. Do not overmix; the batter should be lumpy. Carefully pour the batter into the hot skillet. Cook until the top is golden brown and a skewer inserted in the center comes out clean, 25 to 30 minutes. Serve warm.

confetti cornbread

SERVES 8

This savory cornbread can also be made in a loaf pan or an iron skillet.

Canola oil, for cans
3 tablespoons unsalted butter
3 shallots, chopped into ¼-inch pieces
1 cup plus 2 tablespoons all-purpose flour
2¼ cups yellow cornmeal
2 teaspoons kosher salt
¾ teaspoon freshly ground black pepper
1½ tablespoons baking powder
¾ teaspoon baking soda
3 large eggs
2¼ cups buttermilk
8 ounces fresh hot or sweet red, yellow, and green peppers (about 2 small bell peppers and 1 hot pepper), seeds and ribs removed, cut into ⅛-inch dice to yield ¾ cup
¼ cup plus 2 tablespoons pure vegetable shortening

1. Preheat the oven to 375°F. Brush four clean 13¾-ounce cans with oil. Set aside. (If using a skillet, brush with oil.) Melt the butter in a skillet over medium heat. Add the shallots, and cook, stirring occasionally, over medium-low heat until soft, about 4 minutes; set aside.

2. Whisk together the flour, cornmeal, salt, pepper, baking powder, and baking soda in a large bowl. Make a well; add the eggs to the center. Whisk the eggs into the dry mixture. Add the buttermilk and mix to combine; the mixture will be thick.

3. Stir in the shallots and peppers. Melt the shortening in a pan over medium heat. Pour into the cornbread mixture. Stir well to combine. Spoon the batter evenly into prepared cans or skillet.

4. Bake until golden brown and pulling away from sides of the cans or skillet, 30 to 40 minutes; a cake tester inserted in the center should come out clean. Transfer to a cooling rack. When cool, gently run a knife around rim; unmold. If baked in cans, cut into 1-inch-thick slices. If made in the skillet, cut into wedges. Serve hot.

breakfast
AND
brunch

·······················

omelet 101

MAKES 1

1 tablespoon Clarified Butter (page 633)

3 large eggs

Kosher salt and freshly ground
black pepper

½ cup omelet filling (see box below)

1. Heat the clarified butter in a 10-inch nonstick skillet over medium-high heat. Place your hand above the skillet. When your palm feels warm, the skillet is ready.

2. Whisk together the eggs, and season with salt and freshly ground black pepper while the skillet is heating, not before. If they have to sit and wait for the skillet, the whisked eggs will deflate. You want to incorporate lots of air into the mixture so that your omelet is light and fluffy. Drop a little whisked egg into the skillet. If the egg sizzles and begins to fry, the pan is too hot (if so, remove skillet from heat briefly).

3. Working quickly, pour the whisked eggs into the skillet. Reduce heat to medium. If you want to serve several omelets at once, turn the oven to low heat, about 200°F, and place the serving plates in it.

4. Simultaneously whisk the eggs and shake the skillet vigorously back and forth over heat for less than a minute. Keep the eggs moving, incorporating some of the runny parts with the more-cooked parts until there are some curds swimming in the eggs. Stop whisking. The key to producing an omelet with a fluffy, very smooth surface is to stop whisking just before the egg sets.

5. Continue cooking, making sure eggs cover the entire surface of the skillet. Using a rubber spatula, spread the runny egg out to the edges of the skillet and over any holes that may have formed on the surface of the omelet.

6. With the handle of the skillet pointing directly toward you, sprinkle ½ cup filling over the left side of the eggs, leaving a small rim of egg around the edge. Run the rubber spatula along the right side of the omelet to loosen eggs from the skillet. Place the spatula under the right side of the eggs, mak-ing sure that the spatula is well underneath the eggs to offer maximum support, and lift the right side over the left in one fluid motion.

7. The folded omelet should look like a half moon. Lightly press down on the omelet with the spatula to seal the omelet together. Do not press hard; you do not want to flatten the curds. Check to make sure the handle of the skillet is still facing directly out toward you. Lift the skillet with one hand, and hold the plate with your other hand. Tilt the skillet, and let the curved edge of the omelet slide onto the plate. Quickly invert the skillet, folding the portion of the omelet that is left in the skillet over the curved edge already on the plate. Keeping the skillet at about stomach level with the handle facing you should help.

8. Traditionally, omelets are garnished with something that relates to the filling, but this does not need to be a hard-and-fast rule. A simple sprig of parsley is sufficient. A garnish that's been strategically placed can also help mask an imperfection.

OMELET FILLINGS

Smoked ham and tomatoes

Goat cheese, roasted red peppers, and fresh thyme

Cheddar cheese, tomatoes, and crumbled bacon

Cooked chorizo sausage and minced green chiles

Feta cheese, sautéed spinach, and cherry tomatoes

Parmesan cheese and diced grilled vegetables

Smoked salmon, shredded arugula, and cream cheese

Brie, prosciutto, and steamed asparagus

Monterey Jack cheese with prepared salsa

Fresh mozzarella, tomatoes, and basil

Gruyère cheese with sautéed red and yellow peppers

MAKING AN OMELET

1. The omelet pan needs to be hot but not scalding. Heat the clarified butter in a skillet over medium-high heat. Place your hand immediately above the skillet; when your palm feels warm, the skillet is ready.

2. While the pan is heating, whisk the eggs, salt, and pepper; don't do it before then, or the whisked eggs will deflate and your omelet won't be light and fluffy.

3. Quickly pour in the eggs; reduce heat to medium. Simultaneously, whisk the eggs and shake the pan vigorously back and forth over the heat for less than a minute. You want to keep the eggs moving, incorporating some of the runny parts with the

cooked parts until there are some curds swimming in the eggs. Stop whisking.

4. Continue cooking, being sure the eggs cover the entire surface of the pan; you can use a rubber spatula to push together any holes that may have formed. With the handle of the pan pointing directly out toward you, sprinkle the filling over the left side of the eggs, leaving a small border at the edge.

5. Run the rubber spatula along the right side of the omelet to loosen it from the pan. Place the spatula under the eggs, as far as you can go toward the middle of the omelet, then lift the right side over the left in one fluid motion. The folded omelet

should resemble a half moon. Lightly press down on the omelet with the spatula to seal the edges. Be careful not to press hard; you do not want to flatten the curds.

6. With the handle of the skillet still facing directly out toward you, lift up the skillet with one hand, and hold the serving plate with your other hand. Tilt the skillet, letting just the outer curved edge (about 1 inch) of the omelet slide onto the plate. Quickly invert the skillet, folding the portion of the omelet left in the skillet over the curved edge already on the plate.

cheese omelet

MAKES 1

The fresher the eggs, the better the omelet, so purchase organic eggs, available at most supermarkets, farmer's markets, and health-food stores, whenever possible. You may use regular unsalted butter in place of clarified, but you must watch carefully to make sure that it does not burn. Also, the omelet will brown faster with regular butter. It is important to heat the skillet before adding the butter; this will prevent the omelet from sticking.

- 1 tablespoon Clarified Butter (page 633)
- 3 large eggs
  Kosher salt and freshly ground black pepper
- 3 tablespoons finely grated Gruyère, Parmesan, or Fontina cheese

1. Heat the clarified butter in a 10-inch nonstick skillet over medium-high heat. Place your hand above the skillet. When your palm feels warm, the skillet is ready.

2. While the pan is heating, in a medium bowl whisk together the eggs, and season with salt and pepper; incorporate a lot of air into the eggs, so that the omelet will be light and fluffy.

3. Pour the eggs into the hot skillet. At the same time, briefly whisk the eggs, and shake the skillet vigorously back and forth over the heat, until the eggs begin to set. Stop whisking, and let cook until almost completely set, 1 to 1½ minutes.

4. With the handle of the skillet facing you, sprinkle the left half of the omelet with the grated cheese. Using a rubber spatula, carefully loosen the eggs from the edges of the skillet, and then fold the right half of the omelet over the filling, forming a half-moon shape. Lightly press down on the omelet with the spatula to seal it together.

5. Lift up the skillet with one hand and a serving plate with the other. Tilt the skillet, and let the curved edge of the omelet slip onto the plate. Quickly invert the skillet, folding the portion of the omelet that is left in the skillet over the curved edge already on the plate. Serve immediately.

spinach omelet with feta cheese and hot cherry-tomato sauce

MAKES 1

- 1 tablespoon Clarified Butter (page 633)
- 3 large eggs
  Kosher salt and freshly ground black pepper
- 1 cup loosely packed whole baby spinach leaves, stems removed
- ¼ cup crumbled feta cheese
- 2 teaspoons olive oil
- 1 small garlic clove, thinly sliced
- 1 tablespoon fresh oregano leaves
- 1 cup red and yellow cherry tomatoes
- ½ cup dry white wine or water

1. Heat a 10-inch nonstick skillet over medium heat; add the butter. When your palm placed over the skillet feels very warm, the skillet is ready.

2. While the pan is heating, in a medium bowl whisk together the eggs, and season with salt and pepper; incorporate a lot of air into the eggs, so that the omelet will be light and fluffy.

3. Wilt the spinach in the skillet, about 30 seconds. Pour in the eggs; cook, whisking constantly and shaking pan vigorously, until the eggs begin to set but are still quite loose. Stop whisking and cook until almost completely set, 1 to 1½ minutes.

4. With the handle of the skillet facing you, sprinkle the left half of the omelet with the feta. Using a rubber spatula, carefully loosen the eggs from the edges of the skillet, and then fold the right half of the omelet over the cheese, forming a half-moon shape. Lightly press down on the omelet with the spatula to seal it together. Fold the top half over the bottom half, and slide the omelet onto a plate. Keep warm.

5. Quickly return the skillet to the heat. Add the oil, garlic, and oregano, and cook until the garlic is golden, about 2 minutes. Add the tomatoes and the wine or water, raise heat to medium high, and simmer until the tomatoes burst and liquid is somewhat reduced, about 4 minutes. Ladle the sauce over the omelet, and serve immediately.

layered spring omelet

SERVES 6

This three-layer omelet is sliced and served in wedges, like a cake.

- 1 tablespoon olive oil
- 8 ripe tomatoes, seeded and diced into ½-inch dice
- ¾ teaspoon kosher salt, plus more for seasoning
- ½ teaspoon freshly ground black pepper, plus more for seasoning
- 21 large eggs
- ½ teaspoon ground nutmeg
- ½ teaspoon cayenne pepper
- 3 tablespoons unsalted butter
- ¾ cup grated Cheddar cheese
- ¾ cup grated Gruyère cheese
- ⅔ cup loosely packed fresh basil leaves, torn in half
- 8 ounces fresh spinach, leaves picked and torn in half
- 1 tablespoon chopped fresh thyme leaves or 1 teaspoon dried
- 1 small leek, white parts, well washed (see page 646), julienned, for garnish
- 2 tablespoons snipped chives, for garnish

1. Heat the olive oil in a medium saucepan over medium heat. Add the tomatoes, and simmer until almost all the liquid has evaporated, about 25 minutes. Season with salt and pepper. Transfer the tomatoes to a colander, and drain any excess liquid. Set aside.

2. Preheat the oven to 350°F. In a large bowl, combine the eggs, ¾ teaspoon salt, ½ teaspoon black pepper, the nutmeg, and cayenne pepper, and lightly beat the mixture with a fork.

3. Melt 1 tablespoon butter in a 10-inch ovenproof nonstick skillet over medium-high heat. Pour one-third of the egg mixture, about 1½ cups, into the skillet. Using a rubber spatula, stir the eggs until they just begin to set, about 1 minute. Sprinkle both cheeses over the top. Using a spatula, gently pull the sides of the omelet toward the center so any uncooked liquid runs underneath. Cook until the eggs have almost completely set, about 3 minutes.

4. Transfer the skillet to the oven, and bake until fluffy, about 4 minutes. Remove the skillet from the oven, and place a baking sheet on top of skillet; invert the skillet onto the baking sheet, releasing the omelet layer; hold both the baking sheet and skillet firmly so omelet doesn't slide. Set aside, and keep warm.

5. Carefully wipe out the hot skillet with a paper towel. Add 1 tablespoon butter, and melt over medium-high heat. Pour another third of the egg mixture into the skillet, and stir with the rubber spatula until the eggs just begin to set, about 1 minute. Add half the reserved cooked tomatoes and half the basil to the eggs. Using the spatula, gently pull sides of the omelet toward the center so any uncooked liquid runs underneath. When the eggs have almost completely set, spread the remaining tomatoes and basil over the top.

6. Transfer the skillet to the oven, and bake until fluffy, about 4 minutes. Remove from the oven, and place another baking sheet on top of the skillet; carefully invert the skillet to release second layer. Carefully slide on top of the first omelet layer, and set the two aside; keep warm.

7. Carefully wipe out the hot skillet with a paper towel. Add the remaining tablespoon butter, and melt over medium-high heat. Pour the remaining third of the egg mixture into the skillet, and stir with the rubber spatula until the eggs just begin to set, about 1 minute. Add half of the spinach and thyme, and incorporate into the eggs. Using the spatula, gently pull sides of the omelet toward the center so any uncooked liquid runs underneath. When the eggs have almost completely set, spread the remaining spinach and thyme on top.

8. Transfer the skillet to the oven, and bake until fluffy, about 4 minutes. Invert the third layer onto a baking sheet, and slide on top of the other second omelet layer.

9. Transfer the omelet to a serving platter; garnish with the leeks and chives. Serve immediately.

fresh tomato salsa and jack cheese omelet burrito

MAKES 1

- 1 tablespoon Clarified Butter (page 633)
- 3 large eggs

  Kosher salt and freshly ground black pepper
- ½ cup grated Monterey Jack cheese
- ½ cup Quick Tomato Salsa (recipe follows) or store-bought tomato salsa

  Several sprigs fresh cilantro
- 1 12-inch flour tortilla

  Avocado slices, optional

1. Heat the butter in a 10-inch nonstick skillet over medium heat. Whisk the eggs, and season with salt and pepper. Pour the eggs into the pan, and cook, whisking constantly and shaking pan vigorously until eggs begin to set but are still quite loose. Stop whisking; continue to cook until almost completely set, 1 to 1½ minutes, depending on the desired consistency. Sprinkle the cheese over the eggs, and spoon the salsa down the center of the eggs. Reduce heat to low, and let the cheese melt. Scatter the cilantro sprigs over the cheese.

2. Place the tortilla on a plate. Slide the omelet out of the pan, centering it over the tortilla. Roll up the tortilla, burrito-style, and serve with avocado slices, if using, on the side.

quick tomato salsa

MAKES 3 CUPS

- 1 pound tomatoes, seeded, cut into ¼-inch dice
- ½ cup finely diced red onion (from 1 small red onion)
- ⅓ cup finely chopped fresh cilantro
- 1 teaspoon minced garlic
- 1 large jalapeño pepper, seeds and ribs removed, minced
- 1 tablespoon extra-virgin olive oil

  Juice of 1 lime
- ⅛ teaspoon kosher salt
- ⅛ teaspoon freshly ground black pepper

Combine all the ingredients in a medium bowl, and let sit 30 minutes for the flavors to combine. The tomato salsa tastes best if it is not refrigerated, so use the salsa within 3 hours.

cherry tomato and ricotta omelets in toast cups

SERVES 6

The small toast cups can be made in advance and reheated before serving.

- 6 slices country white bread, cut into 5 x 3 x ¼-inch pieces
- 4 tablespoons unsalted butter, melted
- 12 large eggs

  Kosher salt and freshly ground black pepper
- 36 small (about 12 ounces) mixed red and orange tomatoes
- ⅔ cup ricotta cheese
- 2 ounces green and red oakleaf lettuces or other leaf lettuces

  Extra-virgin olive oil, for drizzling
- 2 tablespoons snipped chives, for garnish

1. Preheat the oven to 425°F. Brush both sides of each piece of bread with the melted butter. Set remaining butter, about 2 tablespoons, aside.

2. Gently press each piece of bread into a 3-inch cup of a muffin tin, allowing the bread to overlap cup slightly. Bake until the bread is golden, about 10 minutes. Remove tin from oven, and set aside.

3. Break the eggs into a large bowl. Add ½ cup cold water, and season with salt and pepper. Using a large balloon whisk, whisk the egg mixture until light and fluffy, about 12 minutes.

4. Heat the reserved butter in a 12-inch nonstick skillet set over medium heat. Add the tomatoes, and cook until just soft, about 3 minutes. Add the egg mixture, and cook until eggs begin to set, about 4 minutes. Using a spatula, lift up the edges of the omelet, letting the uncooked eggs flow to bottom of the pan. Continue cooking until the eggs have almost set. Add the ricotta cheese, and fold in to incorporate. Remove from the heat.

5. Place a handful of greens on each of six serving plates, and top with the toast cups. Cut the omelet into 6 wedges, divide evenly among the toast cups, and drizzle olive oil over the omelets and greens. Season with salt and pepper, and garnish with the chopped chives. Serve immediately.

chinese egg-white omelet with tomatoes

SERVES 8

Martha loves egg-white omelets. This recipe highlights the traditional Chinese method of cooking an omelet in a wok, a technique that Martha learned from her Chinese friend Lily, who is an excellent cook. You may use a 10-inch non-stick skillet if you don't have a wok; it will puff much less because the heat source is different. If there are no vine-ripened tomatoes available, use small cherry tomatoes.

2 tablespoons plus ½ teaspoon canola oil

2 large ripe red tomatoes, sliced into ¼-inch rounds

10 large egg whites

1 teaspoon kosher salt, plus more for seasoning

1. Heat a wok, without its stand, over high heat for 1 minute. Add ½ teaspoon oil, swirling to coat the sides of the wok. When hot, about 30 seconds, add the tomatoes. Quickly stir until they soften, 1 to 2 minutes. Set aside the tomatoes and their juices. Rinse the wok with hot water, and dry.

2. Whisk the egg whites in a medium bowl with 1 teaspoon salt until foamy, about 1 minute.

3. Return the wok to high heat for 1 minute, and add the remaining 2 tablespoons oil. When the oil is hot, about 1 minute, scoop up some of it using a large spoon; hold this oil over the wok while pouring the whites into the wok; immediately pour the hot oil onto the whites. Cook for 1½ minutes, without stirring. The egg whites will puff up. Add the tomatoes with their juices in a circular pattern. Continue to cook, without stirring, until the eggs are cooked through, adjusting heat as necessary, about 2 minutes. Season with salt. Slide the omelet out of the wok onto a serving plate, cut into wedges, and serve immediately.

martha's soft-boiled eggs

MAKES 4

Despite its name, the boiled egg shouldn't be boiled throughout the cooking process—a method that yields a rubbery result—but rather brought to a boil and then immediately removed from the heat. Serve with buttered toast.

4 large eggs
Kosher salt and freshly ground black pepper

Place the eggs in a saucepan large enough to accommodate them in a single layer. Fill the pan with cold water, covering the eggs by 1 inch. Set over medium-high heat, and bring to a boil. Remove from the heat, cover, and let stand 1½ to 2 minutes. Remove the eggs from the water. Serve immediately in egg cups—perfect for cracking and scooping the egg right from the shell. Season with salt and pepper as you eat.

poached eggs

MAKES 4

A flawless poached egg is compact, with glistening whites clinging to a barely set yolk. Use the freshest eggs you can find: The thick albumen will hold its shape better around a fresh yolk. To make classic eggs Benedict, slide the egg onto a toasted English-muffin half lined with a broiled piece of Canadian bacon or a slice of baked ham, and top with Hollandaise Sauce (page 629).

    1 tablespoon distilled white vinegar
    4 large eggs
      Kosher salt and freshly ground
      black pepper

1. Fill a large, wide saucepan with 1 inch of water. Cover and bring to a boil over high heat. Reduce heat to medium, so the water is just simmering (bubbles should be breaking the surface), and add the vinegar.

2. Break 1 egg at a time into a small heat-proof cup or ramekin, about the size of 1 egg. Partially immerse the cup into the simmering water, and quickly slide in the egg. Poach until the whites turn opaque and yolks are just set, 3 to 5 minutes. Using a slotted spoon, remove the eggs from the water in the same order that they were added, and set the spoon, with the egg inside, briefly on a clean kitchen towel to drain. Season with salt and pepper. Serve immediately.

MAKE-AHEAD POACHED EGGS

If you are planning on making poached eggs for a group of people, you can make them ahead of time to avoid a last-minute rush. This is how most poached eggs are prepared for brunch in restaurants. Poach the eggs until slightly underdone, then transfer to a bowl of ice water with a slotted spoon. Cool the eggs for up to 2 hours, and when ready to serve, slip them into gently simmering water until they are hot, about 1 minute.

coddled eggs

MAKES 4

Coddling is a gentle steaming method that yields a tender egg. The eggs are cooked individually in coddling cups—ceramic cups with screw-on lids, available in kitchen-supply stores. Four-ounce baby-food jars can be used as well. Garnish with chopped herbs, onion, or cooked bacon.

      Unsalted butter, for coddlers
    2 teaspoons heavy cream
    4 large eggs
      Kosher salt and freshly ground
      black pepper

1. Line the bottom of a saucepan with a kitchen towel. Fill the pan with enough water to come just below the rim of the coddlers. Place over medium-high heat, and bring to a boil.

2. Butter the inside of each coddler. Pour ½ teaspoon heavy cream in each. Crack 1 egg in each coddler, and season with salt and pepper. Screw on the lids tightly. Carefully place the egg coddlers into the boiling water.

3. Reduce heat to medium, and simmer for 4 minutes. Remove the entire pan with the coddlers from the heat, cover, and let stand for 6 to 7 minutes. Remove the coddlers from the water, unscrew the lids, and serve immediately.

shirred eggs

MAKES 2

Shirred eggs are baked in the oven in a shallow ovenproof dish (such as a gratin dish) that is just large enough to accommodate 2 eggs, enough for 1 serving. This technique sets the eggs quickly at a high heat; watch carefully to make sure they don't overcook.

Unsalted butter, for gratin dish

2 large eggs
Kosher salt and freshly ground black pepper

Preheat the oven to 500°F. Adjust the oven rack to the top third of the oven. Generously butter a 5-inch gratin dish. Break the eggs into the dish, and season with salt and pepper. Bake until the eggs are set, 4 to 5 minutes. Serve.

scrambled eggs

MAKES 4; SERVES 2

Our scrambled eggs are made without milk or water, seasoned with only salt and pepper, and cooked in butter. The key is to beat the eggs briskly, incorporating air into them to produce large fluffy curds.

4 large eggs
Kosher salt and freshly ground black pepper

2 teaspoons unsalted butter

1. Combine the eggs with salt and pepper to taste in a medium bowl, and whisk vigorously for 15 seconds. Melt the butter in a 7-inch nonstick skillet over medium-high heat.

2. When butter is melted and foamy, add the eggs. Reduce heat to medium. Using a rubber spatula or a flat wooden spoon, push eggs toward center while tilting skillet to distribute runny parts.

3. When eggs are almost set, scramble them some more, gently turning them over several times. Serve immediately.

fried eggs

MAKES 4

When a fresh egg is cracked into a skillet, the thickest part of the egg white clings to the yolk. To ensure that the whites set throughout, break these thick albumen sacs, and distribute the whites evenly. Fried eggs are more delicious made in the same skillet after the fried bacon comes out; leave the fat in so the eggs will sizzle and fry. To make just 2 eggs at a time, use a smaller skillet.

2 tablespoons unsalted butter

4 large eggs
Kosher salt and freshly ground black pepper

1. Melt the butter in a 10- to 12-inch nonstick skillet set over high heat. Crack the eggs into a bowl. When the butter is melted, carefully slide the eggs into the skillet, holding the bowl close to the pan to avoid breaking the yolks (or you may simply crack each egg into the hot skillet). Reduce heat to medium. Using the side of a spatula, gently poke the egg-white sacs surrounding the yolks, tilting and swirling the skillet to distribute the whites.

2. Cook eggs until whites are set, about 1 minute. Remove from the heat; let stand 1 minute. (For over-easy eggs, cook for 1 minute after breaking whites, then carefully turn the eggs. Cook for 30 seconds on the other side.) Season with salt and pepper, and serve immediately.

. . . .

PERFECT HARD-BOILED EGGS

This foolproof method will ensure that you have bright-yellow yolks with no darkened edges, which is a sign that the eggs have been overcooked: Place the eggs in a small saucepan, cover with cold water, and place over high heat. Bring to a boil; cook 1 minute. Remove from the heat, and cover. Let the eggs stand for 13 minutes. Drain, and place in cold water until cool. Peel.

. . . .

fried eggs with prosciutto and asparagus

SERVES 4

1 pound (about 16 spears) asparagus
  Kosher salt
4 ounces thinly sliced prosciutto
1 tablespoon unsalted butter, melted
  Fried Eggs (page 571)
2 tablespoons freshly grated
  Parmesan cheese
1 tablespoon coarsely chopped fresh
  flat-leaf parsley
  Freshly ground black pepper

1. Snap off and discard the tough ends of the asparagus. Bring a large pot of salted water to a boil. Cook the asparagus until just tender but still bright green, about 4 minutes. Transfer the asparagus to a colander, and place briefly under cool running water just to stop the cooking. Transfer the asparagus, using a slotted spoon or tongs, to a clean kitchen towel, and fold over. Set aside.

2. Place several slices of the prosciutto on each of four plates; arrange 4 spears of asparagus on each, and brush with the melted butter. Carefully place 1 fried egg on top of each plate, sprinkle with the Parmesan cheese and the parsley, season with salt and pepper, and serve immediately.

egg nest

MAKES 1

An egg white is beaten into a cloudlike nest with just a glimpse of the yolk peeking through in this baked dish. The exact cooking time will depend on the heat of your oven and the depth of your ramekins.

  Unsalted butter, for ramekin
2 tablespoons freshly grated Parmesan
  cheese
1 large egg
¼ teaspoon kosher salt, plus more
  for seasoning
1½ teaspoons finely chopped flat-leaf parsley
  Freshly ground black pepper

1. Preheat the oven to 375°F. Butter a 4-ounce ramekin, coat with 1 tablespoon grated Parmesan cheese, and set aside. Separate the egg, reserving the yolk, and whip the white until foamy. Add the ¼ teaspoon salt, and whip until firm but not dry; fold in the parsley. Fill the ramekin two-thirds full with egg white. Using the back of a tablespoon, make an indentation in the center of the white. Gently slide the yolk into the indentation. Spread the remaining white around the yolk, covering the sides and leaving the center showing. Season with salt and pepper; sprinkle the white with the remaining tablespoon of grated cheese.

2. Bake until the white is set and the cheese is slightly golden, about 6 minutes. Serve.

bacon and egg pie

SERVES 6

This is an ideal dish to serve for a brunch.

  Unsalted butter, for pie plate
8 ounces thickly sliced bacon
4 ounces small mushrooms, wiped clean,
  quartered
1 red, yellow, or orange bell pepper,
  seeds and ribs removed, diced
3 ounces soft goat cheese
½ cup freshly grated Parmesan cheese
1 tablespoon fresh thyme leaves
5 large eggs
1½ cups heavy cream
  Kosher salt and freshly ground
  black pepper

1. Preheat the oven to 325°F. Generously butter a 10-inch glass pie plate. Cook the bacon in a large skillet until very crisp. Remove; drain on paper towels. Pour off all but 2 tablespoons of the bacon fat from the skillet.

2. Return the skillet to medium-high heat; add the mushrooms. Cook until well browned, about 4 minutes. Remove from the skillet; spread the mushrooms in the prepared pie plate. Crumble the bacon; arrange over the mushrooms, along with the pepper, cheeses, and thyme.

3. Beat the eggs and cream in a large bowl, and season with salt and pepper. Pour the egg mixture over the bacon-vegetable mixture. Bake until the egg pie is set and deep golden brown, about 1 hour. Remove from the oven, and place on a wire rack for 10 minutes. Slice into wedges, and serve warm or at room temperature.

swiss chard and mushroom frittata
SERVES 8

This frittata features more egg whites than yolks, giving it an extra light and airy texture. Spinach may be substituted for the Swiss chard in this recipe.

- 2 tablespoons olive oil
- 8 ounces shiitake mushrooms, stems removed, quartered
- 8 ounces cremini or button mushrooms, wiped clean, stems trimmed, quartered
- 1 red onion, cut in half and thinly sliced lengthwise
- 8 ounces Swiss chard, stems trimmed, roughly chopped
- 1 tablespoon fresh thyme leaves, plus sprigs for garnish
- 1 teaspoon kosher salt
- ¼ teaspoon freshly ground black pepper
- 2 large whole eggs
- 8 large egg whites
- 2 tablespoons freshly grated Parmesan cheese

1. Preheat the oven to 400°F. Heat 1 tablespoon olive oil in a 12-inch ovenproof nonstick skillet over medium-high heat. Add the mushrooms and the onion, and cook until the mushrooms start to release their juices, stirring frequently. Reduce the heat to medium low, and cook until the mushrooms are soft and golden brown. Add the Swiss chard, thyme, ¼ teaspoon salt, and the pepper, and cook until the chard is wilted and all the liquid has evaporated. Transfer to a baking pan lined with paper towels, and set aside.

2. Combine the eggs, egg whites, and the remaining ¾ teaspoon salt in the bowl of an electric mixer fitted with the whisk attachment, and beat, on medium speed, until soft peaks form, 4 to 5 minutes. Heat the remaining tablespoon of oil in the skillet over medium-high heat. Add two-thirds of the egg mixture to the pan, layer with the reserved mushroom-chard mixture, and top with the remaining egg mixture. Sprinkle the top with the Parmesan, and transfer the pan to the oven. Cook until the eggs are set and the frittata is golden brown, about 15 minutes. Run a spatula around the edges of the pan to loosen frittata if necessary; transfer to a serving plate. Cut into wedges, garnish with thyme sprigs, and serve.

FIT TO EAT RECIPE PER SERVING: 67 CALORIES, 2 G FAT, 54 MG CHOLESTEROL, 6 G CARBOHYDRATE, 401 MG SODIUM, 7 G PROTEIN, 1 G DIETARY FIBER

green tomato and leek frittata
SERVES 6

- 1 teaspoon olive oil
- 1½ pounds leeks, white and pale-green parts, well washed (see page 646), sliced
- 2 medium (about 9 ounces) green tomatoes, cut into ½-inch dice
- 1½ teaspoons kosher salt
- ¼ teaspoon freshly ground black pepper
- 4 large whole eggs
- 2 tablespoons freshly grated Parmesan cheese
- ½ cup fresh basil leaves, torn into small pieces
- 2 large egg whites
- 1 teaspoon unsalted butter

1. Heat the oil in a 10-inch ovenproof nonstick skillet over medium-low heat. Add the leeks, and cook until golden, about 7 minutes. Add the tomatoes, ½ teaspoon salt, and ⅛ teaspoon pepper, and stir to combine. Raise heat to medium, and cook until the tomatoes are tender, about 5 minutes. Remove from the heat, and set aside to cool.

2. Preheat the broiler. Place the 4 eggs in a large bowl, and beat with a fork. Add the leek-tomato mixture, the remaining teaspoon of salt and ⅛ teaspoon of the pepper, the Parmesan cheese, and basil, and mix to combine.

3. In a separate bowl, whisk the egg whites until stiff but not dry. Using a rubber spatula, stir one-quarter of the whites into the egg mixture to lighten it. Gently fold in the remaining whites.

4. Heat the butter in a medium ovenproof nonstick skillet over medium heat. As soon as the butter begins to foam, but not brown, pour in the egg mixture. Reduce heat to low, cover the pan, and cook until the eggs start to set and thicken but the surface is still runny, about 6 minutes.

5. Remove the cover, and place the skillet under the broiler. Broil until the top of the frittata is set but not browned, about 4 minutes.

6. Run a spatula around and under the frittata to loosen. Transfer to a serving dish, cut into 6 wedges, and serve immediately, or let stand for up to 1 hour, and serve at room temperature.

FIT TO EAT RECIPE PER SERVING: 110 CALORIES, 6 G TOTAL FAT, 146 MG CHOLESTEROL, 8 G CARBOHYDRATE, 640 MG SODIUM, 7 G PROTEIN, 0 G DIETARY FIBER

··

FRITTATA

A frittata is an Italian omelet with the ingredients mixed into the eggs rather than sprinkled over them in a hot skillet, as in a French omelet. A frittata is firmer than an omelet because it's cooked very slowly over low heat (an omelet is cooked quickly over moderately high heat). The result is a soft, fluffy egg pie, delicious warm or at room temperature.

··

spanish onion and potato torta

SERVES 6 TO 8

Torta is both a Spanish and Italian word for cake. This savory cake is layered with potatoes and onions and served in a bread shell lined with crunchy greens.

- *7 tablespoons olive oil*
- *1 medium (about 12 ounces) Spanish onion, halved and sliced into ¼-inch-thick pieces*
- *3 medium (about 1 pound) Yukon gold or other floury potatoes sliced into ¼-inch-thick rounds*
- *8 large eggs*
  Kosher salt and freshly ground black pepper
- *1 12-inch-diameter round loaf rustic bread*
- *1 garlic clove*
- *1 small head frisée or other chicory lettuce*
- *2 teaspoons sherry-wine vinegar*

1. Preheat the oven to 325°F. Heat 1 tablespoon oil in a 10-inch ovenproof nonstick skillet over medium-high heat. Add onion; cook, stirring occasionally, until golden, about 8 minutes. Transfer to a small bowl.

2. Return the skillet to medium-high heat, and add 1 tablespoon oil. Add the potatoes, cover, and cook until soft, stirring, about 12 minutes. Transfer to the bowl with the onions, and toss to combine.

3. Whisk together the eggs, and season with salt and pepper. Transfer to the bowl with the onions and potatoes, and toss to combine.

4. Return the skillet to medium-high heat; add 1 tablespoon oil. Add the egg mixture; cook until the edges set and start to brown, about 1½ minutes. Cover and transfer to the oven; bake until set, about 10 minutes. Remove the cover, and broil until the top is golden.

5. Meanwhile, slice the bread in half crosswise, and reserve the top half for another use (for Fresh Bread Crumbs, see page 647). Remove some of the inside from bottom half, and discard the crumb (or save for bread crumbs). Toast the bread under the broiler until golden, about 4 minutes. Remove from the broiler, brush with 3 tablespoons oil, and rub with the garlic clove. Toss the frisée with the remaining tablespoon of oil and the vinegar, and season with salt and pepper. Scatter the greens into the bread, and slide the torta over the greens. Cut into wedges, and serve.

best buttermilk pancakes

MAKES NINE 6-INCH PANCAKES

If serving with bacon, reserve half a teaspoon of bacon drippings to grease the griddle. Batter can be poured onto the griddle in different shapes to appeal to young eaters.

- 2 cups all-purpose flour
- 2 teaspoons baking powder
- 1 teaspoon baking soda
- ½ teaspoon kosher salt
- 3 tablespoons sugar
- 2 large eggs, lightly beaten
- 3 cups buttermilk
- 4 tablespoons unsalted butter, melted, plus ½ teaspoon for griddle

1. Preheat an electric griddle to 375°F, or place a griddle pan or cast-iron skillet over medium-high heat. Whisk together the flour, baking powder, baking soda, salt, and sugar in a medium bowl. Add the eggs, buttermilk, and 4 tablespoons melted butter, and whisk to combine. The batter should have small to medium lumps.

2. Preheat the oven to 175°F. Test the griddle by sprinkling a few drops of water on it. If the water bounces and spatters, the griddle is hot enough. Using a pastry brush, brush the remaining ½ teaspoon butter onto the griddle. Wipe off the excess with a folded paper towel.

3. Using a 4-ounce ladle, about ½ cup, pour the batter in pools 2 inches apart. When the pancakes have bubbles on top and are slightly dry around the edges, about 2½ minutes, flip over. Cook until golden on bottom, about 1 minute.

4. Repeat with the remaining batter, keeping the finished pancakes on a heat-proof plate in the oven. Serve warm.

yeast-raised pancakes

MAKES TWELVE 4-INCH PANCAKES

- 1½ cups warm milk (110°F)
- 2 tablespoons sugar
- 1 ¼-ounce package (2 teaspoons) active dry yeast
- 1½ cups all-purpose flour
- ½ teaspoon kosher salt
- 4 tablespoons unsalted butter, melted, plus more for griddle
- 3 large egg yolks

1. In a large bowl, whisk together the warm milk, sugar, and yeast; let stand until foamy looking, about 5 minutes.

2. Whisk in the flour, salt, butter, and egg yolks until smooth. Cover tightly with plastic wrap; let rise in a warm place until doubled in size, about 1½ hours, or make the batter the night before, and let rise overnight in the refrigerator.

3. Preheat the oven to 175°F. Preheat an electric griddle to 375°F, or place a griddle pan or cast-iron skillet over medium-high heat. Test the griddle by sprinkling a few drops of water on it. If the water bounces and spatters, the griddle is hot enough. Using a pastry brush, brush a small amount of melted butter onto the griddle. Wipe off the excess with a folded paper towel.

4. Using a 2-ounce ladle, about ¼ cup, pour the batter in pools 2 inches apart. When the pancakes have bubbles on top and are slightly dry around the edges, about 3 minutes, flip over. Cook until golden on the bottom, about 1½ minutes. Repeat with the remaining batter; keep the finished pancakes on a heat-proof plate in the oven. Serve hot.

cornmeal pancakes

MAKES NINE 5-INCH PANCAKES

Pancakes can be easy to make at the last minute: Mix the dry ingredients ahead of time, then combine with liquid mixture just before cooking.

- ¾ cup all-purpose flour
- 2 tablespoons sugar
- ½ cup yellow cornmeal
- 1 tablespoon plus 1 teaspoon baking powder
- ¾ teaspoon kosher salt
- 1 cup milk
- 5 tablespoons unsalted butter
- 2 large eggs, beaten
  Canola oil, for griddle

1. Preheat an electric griddle to 375°F, or place a griddle pan or cast-iron skillet over medium-high heat. In a large bowl, whisk together the flour, sugar, cornmeal, baking powder, and salt.

2. Combine the milk and the butter in a small saucepan, and warm over low heat until the butter melts. Let cool to lukewarm, then beat in the eggs. Whisk the egg mixture into the dry ingredients. The batter should have small to medium lumps.

3. Preheat the oven to 175°F. Test the griddle by sprinkling a few drops of water on it. If the water bounces and spatters off griddle, the griddle is hot enough. Using a pastry brush, brush a small amount of canola oil onto the griddle. Wipe off the excess with a folded paper towel.

4. Using a 4-ounce ladle, about ½ cup, pour the batter in pools 2 inches apart. When the pancakes have bubbles on top and are slightly dry around the edges, about 2½ minutes, flip over. Cook until golden on the bottom, about 1 minute.

5. Repeat with the remaining batter, keeping the finished pancakes on a heat-proof plate in the oven. Serve hot.

dutch baby pancake

SERVES 4

A close relative of the popover and Yorkshire pudding, this large fluffy pancake rises and falls as it bakes so the center stays soft and eggy. The craterlike shape makes it perfect for filling with fresh or cooked fruit.

- 1½ tablespoons unsalted butter
- 1 Granny Smith apple, peeled, cored, and cut into ½-inch wedges
- ⅓ cup honey
- ¼ teaspoon ground cardamom
- 3 large eggs
- ¾ cup milk
- ¾ cup all-purpose flour
- ¼ teaspoon kosher salt
- 1 tablespoon confectioners' sugar

1. Preheat the oven to 400°F. Heat a well-seasoned 10-inch cast-iron skillet over high heat. Add the butter; when melted, add the apple wedges. Cook until softened and lightly golden, about 2 minutes. Stir in the honey and cardamom, and remove from the heat. Reserve.

2. Whisk together the eggs, milk, flour, and the salt in a medium bowl until smooth. Pour the batter over the apples. Bake until puffed and brown, about 20 minutes. Use a flat spatula to slide the pancake onto a serving platter. Serve immediately, cut into wedges, with confectioners' sugar sifted on top.

buttermilk waffles

SERVES 4 TO 6

Traditional buttermilk waffles can be transformed with different flavors. Fold 2 very ripe mashed bananas and ½ cup chopped nuts into the batter. Or sprinkle the batter with cinnamon sugar before closing the waffle iron for a sweet-and-spicy crust. The vanilla bean adds a delicious fragrance to these waffles.

- 2 cups all-purpose flour
- ¼ cup packed light-brown sugar
- 1 teaspoon baking soda
- 1½ teaspoons baking powder
- ½ teaspoon ground cinnamon
- ½ teaspoon kosher salt
- 3 large eggs, separated, room temperature
- 2 cups buttermilk, room temperature
- 8 tablespoons (1 stick) butter, melted, plus more for waffle iron
- 1 vanilla bean, split lengthwise and scraped

1. Preheat a waffle iron. In a large bowl, sift together the flour, sugar, baking soda, baking powder, cinnamon, and salt.

2. In a medium bowl, whisk together the egg yolks, buttermilk, butter, and vanilla-bean scrapings. Pour into the dry mixture, and whisk just until combined.

3. In a clean medium bowl, beat egg whites until stiff but not dry; fold the whites into the batter.

4. Preheat the oven to 200°F. Using a pastry brush, brush the waffle iron lightly with melted butter. Ladle about ⅓ cup of the batter onto each section of the waffle grid; spread the batter almost to the edges. Close the lid, and bake 3 to 5 minutes, until no steam emerges from the waffle iron.

5. Repeat with the remaining batter, keeping the finished waffles on a heat-proof plate in the oven. Serve hot.

oat and whole-wheat waffles with mango sauce and fresh fruit

SERVES 6

- ¾ cup old-fashioned rolled oats
- 1 cup plus 2 tablespoons whole-wheat flour
- 1 cup plus 2 tablespoons cake flour (not self-rising)
- 3 tablespoons instant nonfat dry milk
- ¼ cup sugar
- ¾ teaspoon kosher salt
- 1½ tablespoons baking powder
- 1½ teaspoons baking soda
- 1 large whole egg
- 2 large egg whites
- 2¼ cups buttermilk
- 3 tablespoons unsalted butter, melted, plus more for waffle iron
- Mango Sauce (recipe follows)
- 1½ pints assorted fresh fruit such as raspberries, blueberries, boysenberries, and peaches

1. Preheat a waffle iron. Place the oats in a food processor, and process until coarsely ground, about 30 seconds. Transfer to a medium bowl, and whisk in the whole-wheat flour, cake flour, dry milk, sugar, salt, baking powder, and baking soda.

2. In another medium bowl, whisk together the whole egg, egg whites, and buttermilk. Pour into the dry mixture, add the melted butter, and whisk until thoroughly combined.

3. Preheat the oven to 200°F. Using a pastry brush, brush the waffle iron lightly with melted butter. Ladle about ⅓ cup of the batter onto each section of the waffle grid; spread the batter almost to the edges. Close the lid, and bake 3 to 5 minutes, until no steam emerges from waffle iron.

4. Repeat with the remaining batter, keeping the finished waffles on a heat-proof plate in the oven. Cut the waffles into squares; serve hot, topped with mango sauce and fresh fruit.

FIT TO EAT RECIPE PER WAFFLE: 206 CALORIES, 4 G FAT, 27 MG CHOLESTEROL, 37 G CARBOHYDRATE, 342 MG SODIUM, 7 G PROTEIN, 3 G DIETARY FIBER

mango sauce
MAKES 1½ CUPS

If you can't find Meyer lemons, use regular ones.

- 1 mango, peeled, pit removed (see page 647)
- 2 tablespoons fresh Meyer lemon juice
- 1½ tablespoons sugar

Cut the mango into roughly 1-inch chunks, and transfer to a food processor with 5 tablespoons water, the lemon juice, and sugar. Process until the mixture is smooth, about 1 minute. Transfer to a small bowl and serve with hot waffles, or the sauce may be made up to 4 hours ahead and kept refrigerated, in an airtight container.

french toast
MAKES 4

- 3 large eggs
- 1 cup milk
- ¾ teaspoon kosher salt
- 1 tablespoon sugar
- ¼ teaspoon ground cinnamon
- 1 teaspoon pure vanilla extract
- 4 slices brioche, egg, or white bread, cut into ¾-inch slices
- 1 tablespoon butter, plus more if needed

1. In a large baking dish, combine the eggs, milk, ¼ teaspoon salt, sugar, ground cinnamon, and vanilla extract. Beat thoroughly with a wire whisk until well incorporated.

2. Soak four ¾-inch slices of brioche, egg, or white bread (see variations) in the egg mixture (in batches, if dish is too small), about 4 minutes, turning once to soak other side.

3. Meanwhile, in a large skillet set over medium heat, melt 1 tablespoon butter. Add the soaked bread and cook until golden brown on both sides, 2 to 3 minutes per side. If cooking in batches, add

an additional 1 tablespoon butter before adding the second batch. French toast can be kept in a 275°F oven on an ovenproof platter for up to 15 minutes.

BREAD VARIATIONS *Croissants cut in half lengthwise and French bread rounds also make wonderful French toast. The butter in the croissants will cause them to cook more quickly than the other breads, so watch them carefully. French bread rounds make a perfect child-size portion.*

FLAVOR VARIATIONS *Substitute ½ cup milk with an equal amount of orange juice for citrus flavor. Try ground cardamom or nutmeg, or add flavor to the soaking liquid with 1 tablespoon honey, 1 teaspoon grated orange zest, or 1 tablespoon of a flavored liqueur, such as amaretto.*

TOPPINGS *Melted butter, warm maple syrup, Chunky Fruit Syrup (below), Strawberry-Ginger Compote (below), honey, sautéed apples and cinnamon, confectioners' sugar, or brown sugar with a squeeze of lime juice.*

chunky fruit syrup
MAKES 3 CUPS

- 2 cups berries or diced fruit (pitted or cored), such as pears, peaches, or plums
- 1 cup maple syrup
- 1 vanilla bean, split lengthwise, optional

Combine fruit and syrup in a small bowl. If using berries, press with the back of a spoon until they just start to break apart. Add vanilla seeds and pod to mixture, if using. Store syrup in an airtight container in the refrigerator for up to 4 days. Before serving, syrup can be warmed in a saucepan over low heat.

strawberry-ginger compote
MAKES 1 CUP

- 1 pint strawberries, hulled and sliced lengthwise in thirds
- ¼ cup superfine sugar
- 2 teaspoons freshly grated ginger

In a medium bowl, gently toss the berries, sugar, and ginger. Let stand until juicy, about 1 hour. Serve.

unsoaked steel-cut oatmeal

SERVES 3

If you don't have time to soak the oats overnight, oatmeal can be made with unsoaked grains and cooked for a longer time. Resist the temptation to stir the oats too often while they cook; they will lose their chewy texture.

Pinch of kosher salt
1 *cup Irish, Scottish, or other steel-cut oats*

Cover and bring 4 cups water and the salt to a boil in a medium saucepan over high heat. Stir in the oats. Reduce to a simmer, and let cook, uncovered, stirring occasionally, until the oatmeal is tender but still retains some bite, about 30 minutes. Serve the oatmeal hot with the toppings of your choice.

toasted oatmeal

SERVES 4

Toasting dried oatmeal gives a smoky, nutty flavor to the cooked cereal.

1 *tablespoon unsalted butter*
1 *cup Irish, Scottish, or other steel-cut oats, or 2½ cups old-fashioned rolled oats*
Pinch of kosher salt

Melt the butter in a large heavy saucepan over medium heat. Add the oats, and toast, shaking the pan and turning the oats until browned and fragrant, about 4 minutes. Add 4 cups water and the salt, cover, and bring to a boil. Reduce to a simmer until most of the water has evaporated and the oatmeal is tender, about 30 minutes for the Irish oatmeal or 10 minutes for the old-fashioned rolled oats. Serve hot with the toppings of your choice.

hot cheddar grits

SERVES 4

Stone-ground grits (see Food Sources, page 648) have been a staple of the Southern kitchen for generations. They cook quickly and make a satisfying breakfast cereal.

1½ *teaspoons kosher salt*
1 *cup grits, stone ground if possible*
2 *tablespoons unsalted butter, plus more for serving*
1 *cup grated Cheddar cheese, plus more for serving*
Pinch of freshly ground black pepper
Pinch of cayenne pepper or hot-pepper sauce, optional

Cover and bring 4 cups water and the salt to a boil in a large saucepan over high heat. Slowly stir in the grits. Reduce heat to low, cover, and simmer, stirring occasionally until creamy, 4 to 6 minutes. Remove from heat, and stir in the butter, cheese, and pepper. Serve hot, garnished with extra butter, cheese, and cayenne pepper, if using.

breakfast polenta

SERVES 4

Quick-cooking polenta is now available in most grocery stores.

4 *cups milk, or more to taste*
1 *cup quick-cooking polenta*
4 *tablespoons unsalted butter*
½ *cup Infused Honey (page 580)*
4 *tablespoons mascarpone cheese (see Food Sources, page 648)*
4 *large fresh figs, cut into wedges*

Cover and bring the milk to a boil in a saucepan over high heat. Whisk in the polenta. Reduce heat to low, and whisk occasionally until creamy, about 2 minutes. Stir in butter and more milk, if desired. Serve hot with the honey, mascarpone, and figs.

five hot-cereal toppings

Hot cereal is a more complete breakfast when topped with something sweet, crunchy, or warm.

infused honey
MAKES 1 CUP

This flavorful honey can be made ahead and kept up to 10 days in an airtight container. It can also be used to sweeten hot tea or bread.

- 1 cup honey
- 4 whole star anise
- 4 cinnamon sticks

Warm the honey, star anise, and cinnamon sticks in a saucepan over medium-low heat for 5 to 10 minutes. Remove from heat, and let steep for at least 30 minutes or overnight. Serve over hot cereal.

vanilla cream
MAKES 2 CUPS

Remove and discard the vanilla bean before serving with oatmeal.

- 2 cups heavy cream
- 1 vanilla bean, split lengthwise and scraped

Heat the cream and the vanilla bean, with scrapings, in a saucepan over very low heat until the cream is just bubbling. Remove from heat, cover, and steep for about 20 minutes. Remove the vanilla bean, and serve warm over hot cereal.

maple syrup–glazed bananas
SERVES 4

- 3 tablespoons unsalted butter
- 3 ripe but firm bananas, cut into 1-inch-thick slices
- ½ cup plus 2 tablespoons pure maple syrup

Melt the butter in a large skillet over medium-high heat. Add the bananas, and cook, turning, until golden brown and caramelized, about 4 minutes. Add the maple syrup, and cook until thickened, 3 to 4 minutes. Serve warm over hot cereal.

crisp berry-nut topping
SERVES 4

The crisp topping can be made ahead and kept in an airtight container for up to 1 week.

- 2 tablespoons dried currants
- 2 tablespoons dried cranberries
- 2 tablespoons almond slivers
- 1 tablespoon plus 1 teaspoon sugar
- 2 tablespoons millet
- 1 egg white

Preheat the oven to 350°F. Line a 12 x 17-inch baking pan with parchment paper. In a small bowl, combine the currants, cranberries, almonds, sugar, and millet. In another small bowl, beat the egg white until soft peaks form. Add 1 tablespoon of the egg white to the dry mixture, and stir until coated. Discard any remaining egg white. Spread the mixture on the prepared baking sheet, and bake until the almonds are golden, about 10 minutes. Transfer to a wire rack to cool. Serve over hot cereal.

stewed fruit
MAKES 1 CUP

The stewed fruit may be rewarmed in a small saucepan over low heat.

- ¼ cup brandy or apple juice
- 1 vanilla bean, split lengthwise and scraped
- 8 pitted prunes
- 12 dried apricot halves
- ¼ cup golden raisins

Place all of the ingredients in a medium saucepan with 2 cups water. Cover and bring to a boil; reduce to a simmer. Cook the fruit, uncovered, until the liquid is reduced by about three-quarters. Serve warm over hot cereal.

homemade granola

SERVES 6

Rye flakes may be substituted for wheat in this recipe. Coconut flakes keep the granola moist, but add lots of fat; they are optional.

- 3 tablespoons canola oil, plus more for pans
- 4 cups old-fashioned rolled oats
- 1 cup wheat flakes
- 2 tablespoons toasted wheat germ
- ½ cup unsalted pumpkin seeds
- ¾ cup whole almonds, coarsely chopped
- 1 cup apple cider
- ⅓ cup pure maple syrup
- 1 teaspoon ground cinnamon
- ¼ teaspoon ground nutmeg
- 1 teaspoon kosher salt
- 1 teaspoon pure vanilla extract
- ½ cup dried cranberries
- ½ cup dried figs, quartered lengthwise
- ¼ cup unsweetened coconut flakes, toasted (see page 647), optional

1. Preheat the oven to 300°F. Lightly oil two baking pans. In a large bowl, combine the rolled oats, wheat flakes, wheat germ, pumpkin seeds, and almonds.

2. In a small saucepan, bring the cider to a boil; cook until the liquid has reduced to ½ cup, about 7 minutes. Stir in the canola oil, maple syrup, cinnamon, nutmeg, salt, and vanilla extract. Remove the pan from heat, pour the liquid over the oat mixture, and combine thoroughly.

3. Divide the mixture between the baking pans, and bake until golden brown, about 40 minutes, stirring every 15 minutes. Transfer the pans to wire racks to cool completely.

4. Transfer the mixture to a large bowl, and stir in the dried cranberries, figs, and toasted coconut. Store in an airtight container, at room temperature, for up to 2 weeks.

oat scones

MAKES 10

Freezing the dough for at least 2 hours before baking keeps the scones from spreading too much. Fresh sour cherries have a short season around June and July; defrosted, drained frozen sour cherries or dried cherries may be substituted. Sanding sugar creates a lustrous effect on the top of the scones, but regular sugar may be substituted.

- 1¼ cups whole-wheat flour
- 2 cups all-purpose flour
- ¾ cup granulated sugar
- ¾ teaspoon kosher salt
- 1 teaspoon baking soda
- 2½ teaspoons baking powder
- 2½ cups old-fashioned rolled oats
- 1 cup fresh, frozen, or dried sour cherries, roughly chopped
- 1 cup plus 4 tablespoons unsalted butter, chilled, cut into ½-inch pieces
- ⅔ cup buttermilk
- 1 tablespoon heavy cream
- 1 tablespoon sanding sugar, optional (see Food Sources, page 648)

1. Line a baking sheet with parchment paper. Combine both flours, the granulated sugar, salt, baking soda, baking powder, and oats with the cherries in the bowl of an electric mixer fitted with the paddle attachment. Add the butter, and mix on medium-low speed until the mixture resembles coarse meal. Add the buttermilk, and mix just until combined.

2. Turn out the mixture onto a clean work surface. With your hands, quickly pat the mixture into a 16 x 3½-inch rectangle that is 1½ inches thick. Score the rectangle into 10 triangles. Cover with plastic wrap, and transfer to the freezer for at least 2 hours (the dough can be frozen for up to 3 weeks).

3. Preheat the oven to 350°F. Remove the dough from the freezer, and cut into triangles with a sharp knife. Place the scones 2 inches apart on the baking sheet. Brush the scones with the heavy cream, and sprinkle with the sanding sugar. Bake until lightly golden, about 30 minutes.

skillet scones

MAKES 8

These skillet scones taste best when made in a cast-iron skillet.

- 2 cups all-purpose flour, plus more for dusting
- 2½ teaspoons baking powder
- 2 tablespoons sugar
- 1 teaspoon kosher salt
- 1¾ teaspoons cream of tartar
- 2 tablespoons instant nonfat dry milk
- 4 tablespoons unsalted butter, cut into small pieces
- 1 large egg, lightly beaten

1. Combine the flour, baking powder, sugar, salt, cream of tartar, and dry milk in a large bowl, and add the butter. Work the butter into the flour with your fingertips, fork, or pastry cutter until the mixture resembles coarse meal. Add 6 tablespoons water and the egg to the mixture, and, using a wooden spoon, mix just until combined.

2. On a lightly floured surface, pat the dough into an 8-inch circle, ½ inch thick. Cut into 8 wedges.

3. Heat an 11-inch cast-iron skillet over medium-low heat, and lightly dust with flour. Arrange the wedges in the skillet ¼ to ½ inch apart. Cook, uncovered, until golden and cooked through, about 10 minutes per side. Serve.

blueberry corn muffins

MAKES 6 LARGE MUFFINS

You will need six 2¾ x 2-inch pastry rings (see Equipment Sources, page 650), which give these muffins a unique shape. Jumbo or oversize muffin tins can also be used. Frozen blueberries may be used instead of fresh.

- 1 cup (2 sticks) plus 2 tablespoons unsalted butter, room temperature
- ¾ cup sugar, plus 2 tablespoons for sprinkling
- 3 tablespoons honey
- 2 large eggs
- 3 cups all-purpose flour
- 1 cup yellow cornmeal
- 1 tablespoon plus ½ teaspoon baking powder
- ½ cup milk
- 1 cup blueberries

1. Preheat the oven to 375°F with a rack in the center. Line a baking sheet with parchment paper; place six 2¾ x 2-inch pastry rings on it. Cut a sheet of parchment into six 10 x 3-inch strips; use them to line the rings (the paper will extend above the rims).

2. Place the softened butter, ¾ cup sugar, and the honey in the bowl of an electric mixer fitted with the paddle attachment. Beat on medium speed until fluffy, about 1 minute. Add the eggs; beat 1 minute more.

3. Whisk the flour, cornmeal, and baking powder together in medium bowl; add to the butter mixture in the mixer bowl. Beat until combined. Slowly pour in the milk, beating on low, just until combined. Fold in the blueberries. Divide the dough among the rings (do not pack too firmly; each will take about 1 cup). Brush the tops with cold water; sprinkle 1 teaspoon sugar over each.

4. Bake until the tops are browned and a cake tester inserted in the center of a muffin comes out clean, about 30 minutes. Let cool in the pans 5 minutes. Tie kitchen twine around the muffins to hold the parchment in place, if desired, or remove the parchment. Serve immediately.

bran and currant muffins

MAKES 9

If you make extra muffins, wrap each one in foil, and store them all in a resealable plastic bag in the freezer. Defrost at room temperature overnight or in the oven before breakfast.

- 3 *tablespoons canola oil, plus more for tins*
- 1 *cup unprocessed wheat bran*
- ½ *cup prune juice*
- ½ *cup plain nonfat yogurt*
- ½ *cup currants*
- 3 *tablespoons unsulfured molasses*
- 1 *large egg*
- ½ *teaspoon pure vanilla extract*
- 1 *cup all-purpose flour*
- 1 *teaspoon baking powder*
- ½ *teaspoon baking soda*
- ½ *teaspoon kosher salt*

1. Preheat the oven to 400°F. Lightly grease a standard muffin tin with oil, and set aside.

2. Combine the wheat bran, prune juice, yogurt, currants, molasses, 3 tablespoons canola oil, the egg, and vanilla in a large bowl. Let stand for 10 minutes.

3. In a separate bowl, whisk together the flour, baking powder, baking soda, and salt. Stir dry ingredients into the bran mixture just until the dry ingredients are moistened. Do not overmix.

4. Spoon the batter into the muffin cups, filling each about three-quarters full.

5. Bake for 20 minutes or until a toothpick inserted into a muffin comes out clean. Place the muffins on a wire rack to cool. Serve warm.

FIT TO EAT RECIPE PER SERVING: 187 CALORIES, 7 G TOTAL FAT, 32% CALORIES FROM FAT, 24 MG CHOLESTEROL, 26 G CARBOHYDRATE, 209 MG SODIUM, 7 G PROTEIN, 6 G DIETARY FIBER

crumb cake muffins

MAKES 12

These muffins are best eaten still warm from the oven. If you need to make them a day ahead, store them in an airtight container, and reheat in a 350°F oven for about 10 minutes. The batter can also be used to make coffee cake; bake it in an 8-inch springform pan for about 40 minutes.

for the crumb topping

- ½ *cup old-fashioned rolled oats*
- ¼ *cup packed light-brown sugar*
- 2 *tablespoons finely chopped crystallized ginger*
- 2 *tablespoons all-purpose flour*
- 2 *tablespoons unsalted butter, melted, plus more for tins*

for the cake

- 1½ *cups all-purpose flour*
- 2 *tablespoons sugar*
- 2 *teaspoons baking powder*
- 1 *teaspoon baking soda*
- ¼ *teaspoon ground cinnamon*
- ¼ *teaspoon ground ginger*
- ¼ *teaspoon kosher salt*
- ½ *cup buttermilk*
- ½ *cup unsweetened applesauce*
- ¼ *cup canola oil*
- 2 *large egg whites, lightly beaten*

1. In a medium bowl, combine the oats, brown sugar, crystallized ginger, flour, and 2 tablespoons melted butter, and stir until thoroughly combined. Set aside.

2. Preheat the oven to 350°F. Lightly grease a standard muffin tin with melted butter, and set aside. Combine the flour, sugar, baking powder, baking soda, cinnamon, ground ginger, and salt in a large mixing bowl, and stir to combine.

3. In a separate bowl, combine the buttermilk, applesauce, and canola oil. Stir the liquids into the flour mixture until well combined. Fold in the egg whites. Place 2 heaping tablespoons of batter into each muffin cup. Sprinkle with a generous tablespoon of reserved topping; press gently to adhere topping to cake.

4. Bake about 25 minutes or until a cake tester inserted into a muffin comes out clean. Cool in the pan for 15 minutes, and serve.

FIT TO EAT RECIPE PER MUFFIN: 168 CALORIES, 7 G FAT, 5 MG CHOLESTEROL, 24 G CARBOHYDRATE, 267 MG SODIUM, 3 G PROTEIN, 1 G DIETARY FIBER

cinnamon-pecan sticky buns
MAKES 12

The dough must be prepared a day in advance, but these mouthwatering buns are well worth the wait.

  2 ¼-ounce packages (1 tablespoon plus 1 teaspoon) active dry yeast
  1 cup plus 2 tablespoons warm milk (110°F)
  6 cups all-purpose flour
  ⅓ cup granulated sugar
  2 teaspoons kosher salt
  4 large eggs
  1 pound (4 sticks) unsalted butter, room temperature, cut in small pieces, plus more for tins
 3⅓ cups pecan halves
 2¼ cups light corn syrup
 1¼ cups packed dark-brown sugar
  ½ cup plus 3 tablespoons sour cream
  1 tablespoon ground cinnamon

1. Line a 13 x 18-inch baking pan with parchment paper, and set aside. In a small bowl, combine the yeast and the milk. Let stand until the yeast is creamy, about 10 minutes. In the bowl of an electric mixer fitted with the dough hook, combine the flour, granulated sugar, and salt. Add the yeast mixture and eggs, and mix on low speed until completely combined, about 3 minutes.

2. Raise the speed to high, and add the butter, several pieces at a time. When all the butter has been added, continue mixing the dough until it is smooth and shiny, 8 to 10 minutes. Transfer the dough to the baking pan, and use your hands to spread the dough out to fit the pan. Cover the pan with plastic wrap, and place in the refrigerator to chill overnight.

3. Preheat the oven to 350°F. Generously butter one 12-cup or two 6-cup, 7-ounce muffin tins. Chop 2 cups pecans, and break the remaining 1⅓ cups pecans in half lengthwise, keeping the two types separate. Pour 3 tablespoons corn syrup into each muffin cup, and add about 1 tablespoon brown sugar to each muffin cup. Add about 2 tablespoons halved pecans to each cup, and set the filled muffin tin aside.

4. Remove the dough from the refrigerator, and let stand at room temperature until slightly softened, about 15 minutes. Roll out the dough lengthwise, ¼ inch thick x 15 inches long x 20 inches wide. Using a spatula, spread the sour cream over the surface of the dough, leaving a ½-inch border. Dust the sour cream with the cinnamon, and sprinkle with ⅔ cup brown sugar. Cover the brown sugar with the chopped pecans, and roll the dough up lengthwise to form a roll 18 inches long x 3 inches in diameter.

5. Using a sharp knife, slice the dough into 1½-inch-thick slices, and place in the pan or pans, cut-side down, until every cup is filled. Cover the buns with parchment paper, and let rise in a warm place until they rise ½ inch above cups, 20 to 30 minutes. Transfer the sticky buns to the oven, placing a cookie sheet on the rack below to catch any drips. Rotate the pans between the shelves to ensure even baking, until the buns are dark golden brown, about 40 minutes.

6. Remove the pans from the oven, and immediately turn the buns out onto a parchment-paper-lined baking sheet. Replace any pecan halves that fall off the buns when turning them out. Place the cookie sheet on a wire rack to cool. Sticky buns are best eaten within 24 hours.

cinnamon raisin loaf

MAKES 2 LOAVES

This bread is good right out of the oven, or it may be wrapped in plastic and kept at room temperature for several days and toasted.

for the dough

- 2 cups plus 1½ teaspoons warm water (110°F)
- 1 ¼-ounce package (2 teaspoons) active dry yeast
- 5¾ cups bread flour
- 2 tablespoons nonfat powdered milk
- 1 tablespoon plus 1 teaspoon sugar
- 1 tablespoon kosher salt
- 3 tablespoons unsalted butter, melted and cooled, plus more for pans
- 2 cups raisins
  Canola oil, for bowl and plastic wrap

for the filling

- ¾ cup sugar
- 2 tablespoons plus 1 teaspoon ground cinnamon
  All-purpose flour, for dusting
- 1 large whole egg, beaten
- 4 tablespoons unsalted butter, melted and cooled
- 1 large egg white, beaten

for the topping

- 1 tablespoon sugar

1. In the bowl of an electric mixer fitted with the paddle attachment, combine ¼ cup warm water and the yeast. Let sit until the yeast is creamy, about 10 minutes. Add the flour, powdered milk, sugar, salt, 3 tablespoons melted butter, and the remaining warm water. Mix on low speed for 1 minute. Change to the dough-hook attachment, and mix on medium-low speed for 7 minutes. (Or knead by hand, 15 to 20 minutes.) Add the raisins, and mix on medium-low speed until the dough is firm but not dry, about 3 minutes.

2. Transfer the dough to a lightly floured surface, and knead by hand into a ball. Place the dough, smooth-side up, in a large, lightly oiled bowl. Cover with plastic wrap; let rise in a warm place until doubled in bulk, about 1½ hours.

3. Butter two 9 x 5-inch loaf pans generously, and set aside. In a small bowl, combine ¼ cup sugar and the cinnamon, and set aside. Transfer the dough to a lightly floured surface, and cut in half. Cover one piece of the dough loosely with lightly oiled plastic wrap.

4. Press the other piece of dough into a 10 x 12-inch rectangle. Brush with half the beaten egg, sprinkle with half the cinnamon sugar, and drizzle with half the melted butter. Rub the surface with the back of a spoon to blend the butter and cinnamon sugar. Starting at a short end, roll up the dough tightly, and pinch together along the crease. Roll the dough back and forth to make it cylindrical, and pinch the ends together. Transfer to a loaf pan, seam-side down, and cover loosely with lightly oiled plastic wrap. Repeat the process with the second piece of dough and the second loaf pan. Let the loaves rise in a warm place, 45 minutes to 1 hour. Thirty minutes before this final rise is completed, place a baking stone, if using, in the lower third of the oven. Preheat the oven to 425°F.

5. Brush the tops of the loaves with the egg white, and sprinkle each loaf with 1½ teaspoons sugar. Slide the loaves directly onto the baking stone, if using, or onto the rack. Bake 15 minutes; lower the oven to 400°F, and bake 15 minutes more. Remove from the oven; transfer to a wire rack to cool for at least 30 minutes before slicing.

crumpets

MAKES 10 LARGE OR 15 SMALL

You will need 4-inch flan rings (see Equipment Sources, page 650). For thinner crumpets that don't need to be split, use ⅛ cup of batter for each; bake for 16 minutes. Serve crumpets warm with lots of butter and jam.

1¼   cups milk

1   ¼-ounce package (2 teaspoons) active dry yeast

1   teaspoon sugar

3   cups all-purpose flour, sifted

1¼   teaspoons kosher salt

¾   teaspoon baking soda

Canola oil, for griddle

Unsalted butter, room temperature

1. Combine the milk and 1 cup water in a small saucepan; heat to 110°F. Transfer the mixture to a small bowl. Sprinkle the yeast and the sugar evenly over top. Let stand until foamy, about 10 minutes.

2. Sift flour and salt into the bowl of an electric mixer fitted with the paddle attachment. Mixing on low speed, slowly add some yeast mixture. Slowly increase speed to medium high as you add the remaining liquid, until all the flour is incorporated. Beat on medium high until smooth, 3 minutes.

3. Tightly cover the bowl with plastic wrap; let stand in a warm place until doubled in size and the dough is bubbly, 1 to 1½ hours. Return dough to the mixer. Dissolve the baking soda in 1 tablespoon hot water, and add to the dough; mix until well combined. Cover; set aside for 20 minutes.

4. Lightly oil a griddle or large cast-iron skillet; place over medium heat for 5 minutes. Generously butter the flan rings; place on the heated griddle. Reduce heat to medium low. Pour ½ cup of the batter into the rings; cook until bubbles rise to the surface and the top is dry, about 10 minutes. Remove the rings; turn the crumpets over. Cook until slightly golden, about 8 minutes. Transfer to a wire rack to cool. Repeat with the remaining batter. When ready to serve, preheat the broiler, and toast the crumpets whole or split open. Serve warm.

apple cheddar turnovers

MAKES 16

These are best eaten while still warm; you can form turnovers and freeze, well wrapped, for up to 3 weeks before baking.

2   large egg yolks, lightly beaten

Puff Pastry (page 637), or two 17¼-ounce packages puff pastry

All-purpose flour, for dusting

2   Granny Smith apples, peeled, cored, and cut into ½-inch chunks

4   ounces sharp Cheddar cheese, coarsely grated

1   tablespoon plus 1 teaspoon fresh thyme leaves

1. Preheat the oven to 425°F. Line two baking sheets with parchment paper. Whisk the egg yolks with 1 tablespoon water in a small bowl to make an egg wash; set aside.

2. Cut the puff pastry in half; wrap one half in plastic; chill. On a lightly floured surface, roll half the pastry 1/16 inch thick. Cut into eight 5-inch squares (if using store-bought pastry, cut 4 squares from each sheet).

3. Place 7 or 8 apple pieces and 1 tablespoon grated cheddar cheese in the center of each pastry square. Sprinkle with ¼ teaspoon thyme leaves. Brush the egg wash on the pastry edges. Fold up the edges of the pastry to create a small bundle; pinch the edges to seal. Place the turnovers on the baking sheet; chill 30 minutes. Repeat with the remaining pastry, apples, cheese, and thyme. The turnovers can be wrapped in plastic and frozen at this point.

4. Brush the turnovers with egg wash. Bake 15 minutes. Reduce heat to 375°F; cook until golden brown, about 30 minutes more. For store-bought pastry, bake according to manufacturer's instructions. Serve warm.

cake doughnuts

MAKES 20

It's important to use extra-large eggs for these. Look for nonmelting sugar in specialty-food stores (see Food Sources, page 648).

- 2   *quarts canola oil*
- 2   *cups all-purpose flour, plus more for dusting*
- ¼   *cup sour cream*
- 1¼ *cups cake flour (not self-rising)*
- ¾   *cup granulated sugar*
- 1½ *teaspoons baking powder*
- ½   *teaspoon baking soda*
- 1½ *teaspoons kosher salt*
- 1½ *teaspoons ground nutmeg*
- 1   *¼-ounce package (2 teaspoons) active dry yeast or 0.6 ounces cake yeast*
- ¾   *cup plus 2 tablespoons buttermilk*
- 1   *extra-large whole egg*
- 2   *extra-large egg yolks*
- 1   *teaspoon pure vanilla extract*
- 1¼ *cups nonmelting or confectioners' sugar*

1. Heat the oil in a low-sided 6-quart saucepan over medium-high heat until a deep-frying thermometer registers 375°F. Lightly dust a baking pan with flour; line a second with paper towels; set aside.

2. Meanwhile, place the sour cream in a heat-proof bowl or in the top of a double boiler, and set over a pan of simmering water. Heat until it is warm to the touch. Remove from the heat, and set aside.

3. In a large bowl, sift together the all-purpose flour, cake flour, granulated sugar, baking powder, baking soda, salt, and nutmeg. Make a large well, and place the yeast in the center. Pour the warm sour cream over the yeast, and let sit 1 minute.

4. Place the buttermilk, whole egg, egg yolks, and vanilla in a medium bowl, and whisk to combine. Pour the egg mixture over the sour cream. Using a wooden spoon, gradually draw the flour mixture into the egg mixture, stirring until smooth before drawing in more flour. The dough will be sticky.

5. Sift a heavy coat of flour onto a clean work surface. Turn out dough onto the floured surface. Sift another heavy layer of flour over dough. Using your hands, pat the dough until it is ½ inch thick. Using a 2¾-inch doughnut cutter, cut out the doughnuts as close together as possible, dipping the cutter in flour before each cut. Transfer the doughnuts to the floured pan, and let rest 10 minutes, but not more.

6. Carefully transfer 4 doughnuts to the hot oil. Cook until they are golden, about 2 minutes. Turn the doughnuts over, and continue cooking until evenly browned on both sides, about 2 minutes more. Using a slotted spoon, transfer the doughnuts to the paper-towel-lined pan. Repeat with the remaining doughnuts.

7. Gather the remaining dough scraps into a ball, and allow to rest 10 minutes. Pat the dough into a ½-inch-thick rectangle, cut into doughnuts, and fry, following the directions in step six. When cool enough to handle, sift the nonmelting sugar over the tops of the doughnuts. Serve immediately.

french doughnuts

MAKES 30

Made from the same egg-rich pâte à choux dough as cream puffs and éclairs, French doughnuts puff up when they fry, gaining an airy texture without any special leaveners. They are finished with a lemon-sugar glaze, poppy seeds, and candied lemon zest.

- 2   quarts canola oil, plus more for pans and parchment
- 2   cups all-purpose flour
- 2   cups milk
- 2   teaspoons kosher salt
- 2   teaspoons sugar
- 1   cup (2 sticks) unsalted butter, cut into small pieces
- 9   extra-large eggs
- 2½ teaspoons poppy seeds, plus more for sprinkling
     Lemon Glaze (recipe follows)
     Candied Lemon Peel (page 643)

1. Heat oil in a low-sided 6-quart saucepan over medium-high heat until a deep-frying thermometer registers 360°F. Cut thirty 4-inch squares out of parchment paper, and line two baking pans with paper towels. Set both aside.

2. Meanwhile, sift the flour into a medium bowl. In a medium saucepan, combine the milk, salt, sugar, and butter. Bring to a full boil over medium-high heat. Remove from the heat; add the sifted flour, all at once, stirring constantly until the flour has been incorporated. Return to the heat, and cook, stirring constantly, until the dough pulls away from sides, about 30 seconds. Remove from the heat.

3. Transfer the dough to bowl of an electric mixer fitted with the paddle attachment. Beat on low speed until the bowl is warm to the touch, 4 to 5 minutes. Add the eggs, one at a time, beating until each egg has been incorporated before adding the next. Stir in the poppy seeds.

4. Lightly brush a third baking pan with some of the oil, spread 5 squares of parchment on top, and oil the parchment paper. Fit a large pastry bag with a #4 star tip, and fill with the dough. In one continuous stroke, pipe a 2½-inch double-layer circle onto each square.

5. Carefully lifting the squares, gently slide 5 doughnuts into the hot oil. Cook until golden brown, about 2 minutes. Using a slotted spoon, turn over; continue cooking until evenly browned, about 2 minutes more. Transfer to the paper-towel-lined baking pans; let rest until cool enough to handle.

6. Repeat steps four and five with remaining parchment squares and dough. While warm, coat doughnuts with lemon glaze. Sprinkle with candied lemon zest and a pinch of poppy seeds. Transfer to a wire rack to allow the glaze to set. Serve.

MAKING FRENCH DOUGHNUTS

Piping dough from a pastry bag fitted with a star tip makes French doughnuts as decorative as they are delicious. Preparing them is easier if the dough is piped onto individual squares of parchment paper; formed doughnuts can slide right off the paper into the hot oil.

lemon glaze

MAKES 1½ CUPS

2½ cups confectioners' sugar

¾ cup heavy cream

1 tablespoon plus 2 teaspoons fresh
  lemon juice

Combine all the ingredients in a heat-proof bowl. Set over a pan of simmering water, and heat, stirring, just until warm. Use while still warm.

apple-cinnamon matzo brei

SERVES 4

Drizzle this matzo brei with honey for a wonderful breakfast treat. Since leavened bread is forbidden during the Jewish holiday of Passover, matzo brei is a nice alternative to sweet French toast.

5 tablespoons unsalted butter

2 Granny Smith apples, peeled, cut into
  ½-inch dice

5 tablespoons sugar

  Juice of ½ lemon

½ teaspoon ground cinnamon

½ cup golden or dark raisins

8 plain matzos

4 large eggs

  Pinch of kosher salt

¼ cup chopped pecans, toasted
  (see page 644)

1. In a medium skillet set over medium-high heat, melt 1 tablespoon butter. Add the apples, and cook until lightly browned, about 5 minutes. Sprinkle 3 tablespoons sugar over apples, and cook, stirring occasionally, until the sugar has dissolved and caramelized, about 8 minutes. Stir in the lemon juice, cinnamon, and raisins. Remove from the heat, and set aside.

2. Meanwhile, bring 3½ quarts of water to a boil in a large pan. Break the matzos into 3-inch pieces directly into a colander set in the sink, and pour the boiling water over them. Let the matzo stand until softened, about 3 minutes. Set aside.

3. In a medium bowl, whisk the eggs with the salt and the remaining 2 tablespoons sugar. Stir in the soaked matzo, and mix until well coated.

4. Melt the remaining 4 tablespoons butter in a large skillet set over medium-high heat. Add the matzo mixture, and cook, stirring frequently, until golden brown, about 10 minutes. Stir in two-thirds of the apple mixture, and cook until warm; transfer to a serving plate. Garnish with pecans and remaining apple mixture. Serve immediately.

hash browns

SERVES 6

These can be cooked in individual patties or in two large cakes cut into wedges.

4 Yukon gold or russet potatoes
  (2 pounds), peeled

1 large shallot

3 tablespoons fresh herbs, roughly
  chopped, such as flat-leaf parsley,
  thyme, and rosemary

  Kosher salt and freshly ground
  black pepper

¼ cup canola oil

1. Preheat the oven to 175°F. Prepare a baking sheet lined with paper towels. Grate the potatoes and shallot on the large holes of a box grater or with a food processor fitted with the grating blade. Transfer to a piece of cheesecloth or clean dishcloth; squeeze out as much of the liquid as possible. Place in a bowl, add the herbs, season with salt and pepper, and stir to combine.

2. Heat 2 tablespoons oil in a large nonstick skillet over medium-low heat. Drop ¼ cup of the mixture into the skillet; gently press to form a patty about 2½ inches in diameter. Repeat until there are 6 patties in the skillet. Cook until deep golden brown, about 8 minutes on each side. Remove from the skillet; transfer to the prepared baking sheet. Place in the oven to keep warm. Wipe out the pan; pour in the remaining 2 tablespoons oil. Repeat the process with the remaining potato mixture; serve warm.

celery root, potato, and leek home fries

SERVES 4

Celery root and leeks make home fries into a sophisticated side dish for breakfast and even lunch or dinner.

- 2 tablespoons olive oil
- 5 medium leeks (about 1½ pounds), white and pale-green parts, well washed (see page 646), cut into ¼-inch-thick rounds
- 2 medium Idaho potatoes (about 12 ounces), peeled and cut into matchsticks (1 inch long x ¼ inch wide)
- 1 celery root (about 1 pound), peeled and cut into matchsticks (1 inch long x ¼ inch wide)
- 1 tablespoon chopped fresh rosemary
- 2 teaspoons fresh thyme leaves
  Kosher salt and freshly ground black pepper

1. In a large nonstick skillet, heat the olive oil over medium-high heat. Add the leeks, potatoes, celery root, rosemary, and thyme, and cook, turning the vegetables frequently, until browned and crusty, about 15 minutes.

2. Reduce heat to medium, and continue to cook until the vegetables are tender, about 10 minutes. Season with salt and pepper, and serve immediately.

campfired potatoes

SERVES 8

- ¼ cup olive oil
- 1 large onion, cut into ½-inch dice
- 1¾ teaspoons kosher salt
- ¼ teaspoon freshly ground black pepper
- 3½ pounds (about 6) Yukon gold or Idaho potatoes, unpeeled, cut into ¾-inch dice

1. Heat the oil in a large cast-iron skillet over medium-low heat. Add the onion, ¾ teaspoon salt, and ⅛ teaspoon pepper. Cook, stirring, until the onion just starts to brown, about 10 minutes.

2. Add the potatoes, remaining 1 teaspoon salt, and ⅛ teaspoon pepper, and cook until golden brown on the bottom, about 10 minutes. Continue cooking, turning with a spatula, until the potatoes are golden brown all over and soft, about 40 minutes more. If the potatoes are too brown but not yet tender, cover with foil, reduce heat, and continue to cook until soft.

sweet-potato hash browns

SERVES 4

Chill the potatoes before cooking; it prevents them from falling apart in the skillet.

   Kosher salt
2 *large (2 pounds) sweet potatoes, cut into ¾-inch dice*
6 *tablespoons olive oil*
1 *medium onion, peeled and cut into ⅓-inch dice*
2 *tablespoons roughly chopped fresh flat-leaf parsley*
   Freshly ground black pepper

1. Bring a medium pot of salted water to boil over high heat. Add the sweet potatoes, and cook until they can be easily pierced with a fork but still offer some resistance, 3 to 4 minutes. Drain, and rinse under cold running water. Place in the refrigerator until completely chilled, about 1 hour.

2. Heat 2 tablespoons olive oil in a large skillet over medium heat. Add the onions, and cook, stirring occasionally, until onions are tender and golden brown, about 20 minutes. Transfer the onions to a small bowl, and set aside.

3. Pour the remaining olive oil into the skillet, and place over medium-high heat. Add the potatoes, and cook, stirring occasionally, until golden brown, about 8 minutes. Add the reserved onions, and cook 2 minutes. Toss in the parsley, and season with salt and pepper. Serve hot.

spring vegetable hash

SERVES 6 TO 8

The vegetables can be prepared the day before and refrigerated in separate plastic bags.

1¼ *pounds small red potatoes*
 4   *carrots*
 2   *teaspoons unsalted butter*
2½ *teaspoons olive oil*
 1   *large onion, chopped medium*
 3   *red bell peppers, cut into ½-inch cubes*
 1   *tablespoon fresh thyme leaves, or 1 teaspoon dried*
 1   *tablespoon chopped fresh rosemary, or 1 teaspoon dried and crumbled*
 8   *ounces asparagus*
 1   *cup Homemade Chicken Stock (page 624), or low-sodium store-bought chicken broth, or water*
     Kosher salt and freshly ground black pepper

1. Fill a medium saucepan with cold water, and add the potatoes. Bring to a boil, reduce heat, and simmer for 5 minutes. Add the carrots, and continue cooking for 10 minutes more, or until the vegetables are just tender when pierced with the tip of a knife. Remove from heat, drain, and set aside until cool enough to handle. Cut the potatoes and carrots into ½-inch cubes.

2. Heat the butter and oil in a large nonstick skillet over medium heat. Add the onion, and cook until transparent and golden at edges, about 10 minutes. Add the red peppers, and cook, stirring, another 10 minutes, or until soft. Add half the thyme and rosemary. Add the potatoes and carrots, and mix well. Cook over medium heat, stirring only occasionally, until a golden crust forms on the potatoes, about 15 minutes.

3. Cut off the asparagus tips, and cut the remaining tender parts into ½-inch lengths, discarding the woody ends. Add the tips and pieces, remaining thyme and rosemary, and stock to the skillet; cook 2 minutes more, until the stock reduces and thickens slightly and the asparagus is tender. Season with salt and pepper, and serve hot.

brown sugar–glazed bacon

SERVES 6

Cooking the bacon in the oven renders the fat very evenly and eliminates the need to turn the strips. For Martha's favorite bacon, look for the cob-smoked variety (see Food Sources, page 648).

- 1¼ pounds thickly sliced bacon
- ½ cup packed dark-brown sugar

Preheat the oven to 425°F. Line a baking pan with parchment paper. Arrange the bacon on the paper, and sprinkle the brown sugar liberally over the bacon. Transfer the pan to the oven, and bake for 10 minutes. Remove the pan from the oven, and carefully drain the fat into a container. Return the pan to the oven, and bake until the bacon is crisp, 6 to 7 minutes more. Transfer the bacon immediately to a wire rack to cool.

homemade pork sausage patties

SERVES 6

These homemade sausage patties can be made ahead of time and frozen until ready to use—up to 5 months. Defrost thoroughly before cooking.

- 1 pound coarsely ground pork shoulder
- 1½ teaspoons kosher salt
- ¼ teaspoon freshly ground black pepper
- ¼ teaspoon ground nutmeg
- ½ teaspoon ground cinnamon
- 1½ teaspoons packed dark-brown sugar
- 1 teaspoon olive oil

1. In a medium bowl, combine the ground pork, salt, pepper, nutmeg, cinnamon, and sugar.

2. Shape ¼ cup of the mixture into a flat 2½-inch oval patty. Repeat with the remaining mixture.

3. Heat the oil in a large skillet over medium-low heat. Place the patties in the skillet, and cook until golden brown, about 3 minutes per side. Remove from the skillet, and transfer to paper towels to drain. Place the sausages in a 175°F oven to keep warm until ready to serve.

chicken and apple sausage patties

MAKES 16 PATTIES

These savory patties can be made up to a day before cooking and serving. Have your butcher grind the chicken for you.

- 1 tablespoon plus 1 teaspoon olive oil
- 1 small onion, minced
- 2 Granny Smith apples, peeled, cored, cut into ¼-inch dice
- 1 pound ground chicken
- ⅓ cup fresh sage leaves, shredded
- ¾ teaspoon freshly ground black pepper
- ¾ teaspoon kosher salt
  Pinch of ground cinnamon

1. Heat 1 tablespoon oil in a small skillet over medium heat, and cook the onion until translucent and soft, about 3 minutes. Add the apples, and cook until soft, about 5 minutes. Remove from the heat, and allow to cool.

2. Combine the chicken with the onion-apple mixture and remaining ingredients, mixing thoroughly with your hands. Form the mixture into ½-inch round patties.

3. Preheat the oven to 350°F. Heat the remaining teaspoon of oil in a medium ovenproof skillet, and brown the sausage patties over medium-low heat, 2 minutes on each side; transfer the skillet to the oven, and bake until cooked through, about 10 minutes. Serve immediately.

drinks

....

lemonade or limeade

SERVES 8

This recipe makes a strong drink that will not get too watery when the ice melts. To make pink lemonade, add ½ cup of cranberry juice.

- 3 cups fresh lemon or lime juice (about 20 lemons or 25 limes)
- 2 cups superfine sugar
- 4 cups ice cubes
- 2 lemons or limes, thinly sliced, for garnish

In a large glass container or pitcher, combine the lemon or lime juice and the sugar, and stir until the sugar is dissolved. Add 4 cups cold water, and stir again until combined. Add the ice cubes, and fill with the lemon or lime slices. Serve cold.

orange pekoe lemonade

SERVES 6

- ¾ cup fresh lemon juice (4 to 5 lemons), plus wedges for garnish
- ½ cup honey
- 3 cups freshly brewed orange pekoe tea, chilled

In a small bowl, combine the lemon juice and honey; stir until the honey has completely dissolved. Transfer to a large pitcher. Add the tea and 1 cup cold water; stir. Fill the pitcher with ice; garnish with the lemon wedges. Serve cold.

cherry lemonade

SERVES 6 TO 8

Add sugar to make this drink as sweet as you like.

- 1¾ cups fresh lemon juice (10 to 12 lemons)
- 1 cup sugar
- 1 pound fresh cherries, pitted

In a gallon container, combine lemon juice and sugar until sugar is dissolved. Stir in 3 quarts cold water and the cherries until combined. Pour the lemonade into glasses filled with ice, and serve.

blueberry-mint lemonade

SERVES 6

- 1 pint blueberries, plus more for garnish
- ¾ cup plus 2 tablespoons fresh lemon juice (5 lemons), plus slices for garnish
- 1½ cups Mint Syrup (recipe follows)
  Mint sprigs, for garnish

1. Place the blueberries and lemon juice in the bowl of a food processor, and purée completely. Pass the purée through a fine sieve set over a bowl, and discard the pulp.

2. Transfer the juice to a large pitcher. Add the mint syrup and 2 cups cold water; stir to combine. Fill the pitcher with ice. Garnish with the blueberries, lemon slices, and mint sprigs. Serve cold.

mint syrup

MAKES 3 CUPS

- 1 cup sugar
- 2 bunches mint, cut into 2-inch lengths

In a small, tall saucepan, combine the sugar, mint, and 2¾ cups water; bring to a boil over medium-high heat. Cook until the sugar has completely dissolved, 1 minute. Remove from the heat; let stand 30 minutes. Pass through a fine sieve set over a bowl, and discard the mint. Store in an airtight container, refrigerated, up to 2 months.

tarragon limeade

SERVES 6

- 1½ cups fresh lime juice (about 15 limes), plus wedges for garnish
- 1½ cups Tarragon Syrup (recipe follows)
  Fresh tarragon sprigs, for garnish

In a large pitcher, stir together the lime juice, tarragon syrup, and 2 cups cold water. Fill pitcher with ice; garnish with lime wedges and tarragon sprigs. Serve cold.

tarragon syrup

MAKES ABOUT 3 CUPS

- 1¼ cups sugar
- 10 large sprigs fresh tarragon

In a saucepan, combine sugar, tarragon, and 2½ cups water; bring to a boil over medium-high heat. Cook until sugar has completely dissolved, about 1 minute. Remove from heat; let stand 30 minutes. Remove and discard tarragon sprigs. Store in an airtight container, refrigerated, up to 2 months.

watermelon-ginger limeade

SERVES 6

If using a food processor to juice the watermelon, remove the rind and seeds, and process flesh until liquid. Pass the purée through a fine strainer, and discard the pulp.

- 4 pounds red or yellow watermelon, rind and seeds removed, plus more wedges for garnish
- 1 cup fresh lime juice (10 limes), plus wedges for garnish
- 1 cup Ginger Syrup (recipe follows)

1. Place the watermelon flesh in a juice extractor, and process, extracting 3 cups of watermelon juice.

2. Transfer the juice to a large pitcher. Add the lime juice and ginger syrup to the pitcher, and stir to combine. Fill the pitcher with ice. Garnish with the watermelon and lime wedges. Serve cold.

ginger syrup

MAKES 4 CUPS

The strength of the syrup will depend on the amount of time the ginger steeps.

- 1¾ cups sugar
- 1 6-inch piece fresh ginger, peeled and thinly sliced lengthwise

In a medium saucepan, combine the sugar, ginger, and 3½ cups water; bring to a boil over medium-high heat. Cook until the sugar has completely dissolved, about 1 minute. Reduce heat to a simmer,

and cook 5 minutes more. Remove saucepan from heat, and let the syrup stand about 30 minutes. Remove and discard the ginger. Store syrup in an airtight container, refrigerated, up to 2 months.

kiwi-honeydew limeade

SERVES 6

This pale-green cooler is speckled with small black kiwi seeds and sweetened with ripe melon.

- 1 2-pound honeydew melon, rind and seeds removed
- 3 kiwis, peeled
- ¾ cup fresh lime juice (about 8 limes)
- 1 cup Simple Syrup (recipe follows)

1. Place the honeydew melon in a juice extractor; process, extracting 1¾ cups of juice. Place the kiwis in the bowl of a food processor; process, yielding 1½ cups of purée.

2. Transfer the melon juice and kiwi purée to a large pitcher. Add the lime juice, simple syrup, and 1½ cups cold water to the pitcher. Stir until combined. Pour over ice, and serve cold.

simple syrup

MAKES 6 CUPS

- 2¼ cups sugar

Prepare an ice-water bath. In a large saucepan, combine the sugar and 4¾ cups of water; bring to a boil over medium-high heat. Cook until the sugar has completely dissolved, about 10 minutes. Transfer the syrup to a bowl, and set the bowl over the ice bath. Let stand, stirring occasionally, until chilled. Store the syrup in an airtight container, refrigerated, up to 2 months.

orange boston cooler

SERVES 4

This frothy, ginger-spiked ice-cream cooler requires both a straw and a spoon to enjoy.

- 1 cup Ginger Syrup (page 595)
- 16 ounces cold club soda
- 4 scoops best-quality vanilla ice cream
- 8 scoops (about 1 pint) orange sherbet

1. Place the ginger syrup in a large pitcher; stir in the club soda.

2. Place 1 scoop vanilla ice cream in the bottom of each of four glasses. Top each with 2 scoops orange sherbet, and pour the ginger ale to fill glasses. Serve immediately.

tofu fruit smoothie

SERVES 2

Try different fruits in this shake; if you're using raspberries, purée them and strain the seeds before placing in the blender. Tofu is very high in protein, making this smoothie a perfect healthy breakfast.

- 6 ounces fruit, such as raspberries, blueberries, or mango
- 4 ounces silken tofu
- 2 tablespoons honey, or to taste
- 1 cup ice cubes

Place the fruit, tofu, 2 tablespoons honey (or to taste), and ice cubes in a blender. Blend on high speed until the texture is creamy and the ice has been finely ground. Serve immediately.

FIT TO EAT RECIPE PER SERVING: 141 CALORIES, 2 G FAT, 0 MG CHOLESTEROL, 29 G CARBOHYDRATE, 39 MG SODIUM, 6 G PROTEIN, 2 G DIETARY FIBER

MAKING FRESH FRUIT JUICES

An electric juicer makes fast work of fresh fruit juices, but it isn't absolutely necessary. Fresh fruit juices can be made by puréeing the fruit in the bowl of a food processor and passing the purée through a fine sieve to remove skin and fibers.

blueberry-strawberry layered smoothie

SERVES 2

Crushed ice makes this smoothie frothier when blended, but it may be omitted if you prefer.

- 6 ounces (about 6 large) strawberries, hulled and halved
- ½ cup blueberries (about 3 ounces)
- 1½ teaspoons fresh lemon juice
- 3 tablespoons sugar
- 1 cup nonfat plain yogurt
- ¼ cup whole milk
- 1 cup crushed ice

1. Place the strawberries, blueberries, lemon juice, and sugar in the bowl of a food processor, and purée. Pour the purée evenly into two glasses.

2. Combine the yogurt, milk, and ice in a blender, and blend until frothy. Pour the yogurt mixture over the fruit purée in each glass. Stir the smoothie several times to slightly incorporate the two layers, and serve immediately.

FIT TO EAT RECIPE PER SERVING: 201 CALORIES, 2 G FAT, 6 MG CHOLESTEROL, 40 G CARBOHYDRATE, 106 MG SODIUM, 8 G PROTEIN, 2 G DIETARY FIBER

mango lassi

SERVES 8

A lassi is a popular chilled yogurt drink served in India. Ripe mangos make all the difference in the flavor of this drink; they will also give the drink a more vibrant color.

- *3 pounds ripe mangos, peeled, pit removed (see page 647), cut into chunks*
- *1 cup plain whole-milk yogurt*
- *¼ cup plus 2 tablespoons fresh lime juice*
- *2 cups ice cubes*

1. Place the mango in a blender. Blend until puréed; the mixture should yield about 3½ cups. Add the yogurt and lime juice, and blend until combined.

2. Working in batches, if necessary, add 2 cups of ice; blend until combined. Serve cold.

pink grapefruit "margaritas"

SERVES 6

Colored sanding sugar (see Food Sources, page 648) is available at cake-decorating stores; it makes a beautiful garnish for these non-alcoholic drinks. Pomegranate syrup (see Food Sources, page 648) is a thick, condensed version of the juice.

- *2 tablespoons colored sanding sugar, optional*
- *1 lime*
- *2 tablespoons pomegranate syrup or grenadine*
- *1½ cups fresh pink-grapefruit juice*
- *2 cups crushed ice*

1. Place the sanding sugar on a shallow dish or plate, if using. Slice 6 thin rounds from the middle of the lime, and set aside. Rub the cut side of one end of the lime around the rims of six glasses; dip each glass in the sugar to coat the rim. Pour 1 teaspoon pomegranate syrup into the bottom of each glass.

2. Place the grapefruit juice and the ice in a blender. Process on high speed until the ice is crushed. Pour the frozen mixture over the pomegranate syrup in the glasses; garnish with the reserved lime rounds. Serve immediately.

malted milk shakes

SERVES 4

Malted-milk powder, such as Ovaltine, is available in most grocery stores.

- *1 cup milk*
- *¼ cup plus 2 tablespoons malted milk powder, plus more for garnish*
- *1 pint best-quality vanilla ice cream*
- *1 pint chocolate or strawberry ice cream*
- *Malted-milk balls, for garnish, optional*

1. Place ½ cup milk and 3 tablespoons malt powder in a blender, and process until the malt is dissolved. Add half the vanilla ice cream, and blend until smooth. With the machine running, add the remaining vanilla ice cream, 1 scoop at a time, until it is fully incorporated.

2. Pour half the shake into a glass measuring cup, and place in the freezer. Divide the remaining half between two glasses, and place the glasses in the freezer. Allow to chill for 10 minutes before proceeding to step 3.

3. Place the remaining ½ cup milk and 3 tablespoons malt powder in a clean blender; process until the malt is dissolved. Add half the chocolate or strawberry ice cream, and blend until smooth. With the machine running, add the remaining ice cream, 1 scoop at a time, until fully incorporated. Divide half the shake between two empty glasses, and top off the two partially filled glasses from the freezer with the remainder. Allow the half-filled glasses to freeze for 10 minutes. Stir the reserved vanilla shake before topping off the remaining glasses. Garnish with malted milk powder and malted milk balls, if using, and serve immediately.

chocolate milk shake

SERVES 2

Any flavor of ice cream can be substituted to make different milk shakes. If you find your milk shake is not blending properly and ice crystals begin to form, the ice cream is probably too cold. Try letting the milk shake stand for a few minutes to melt a bit, then blend again until smooth. Also, the ice cream should be placed in the blender by the scoop, not all at once.

1 pint chocolate ice cream, slightly softened
½ cup milk

In a blender, combine the ice cream and milk, and blend until the mixture is smooth, about 20 seconds. Pour into two tall glasses, and serve immediately.

ice cream sodas

SERVES 8

Old-fashioned seltzer in bottles is still available; check the Yellow Pages for beverage distributors.

Fruit Toppings for Sodas (recipe follows), or 4 peaches, pitted and halved
1½ quarts best-quality vanilla ice cream
1 pint heavy cream
1 to 2 bottles chilled old-fashioned seltzer
Fresh cherries and strawberries, for garnish

For each serving, place 1 to 2 tablespoons of fruit or a peach half in a large soda glass. Add 2 scoops ice cream and 3 to 4 tablespoons cream. Shake the seltzer bottle and squirt into glass. Garnish the soda with cherries or strawberries. Serve immediately.

fruit toppings for sodas

SERVES 8

strawberry compote
2 pounds fresh strawberries, hulled
3 tablespoons sugar, or to taste

rhubarb compote
2 pounds rhubarb, trimmed, cut into 1-inch pieces
¾ cup sugar, or to taste
½ cup heavy cream, or to taste

roasted peaches
2 tablespoons unsalted butter
¼ cup sugar
8 to 10 (about 4 pounds) ripe peaches

Strawberry compote: Combine the strawberries and sugar with 3 tablespoons water over medium-low heat. Cook, partially covered, until the berries release some juice but remain whole, 5 to 10 minutes. Let cool.

Rhubarb compote: Preheat the oven to 450°F. Place rhubarb and sugar in an ovenproof casserole; toss to coat. Cook until rhubarb is soft, 25 to 40 minutes. Let cool, then stir in cream.

Roasted peaches: Preheat the oven to 450°F. Melt the butter in a roasting pan over medium heat; sprinkle the sugar over it. Halve the peaches crosswise; discard the pits. Place them, cut-side down, in the pan. Roast 15 to 25 minutes, until the peaches are soft but still hold their shape. Reserve the juice to serve with the sodas. When the peaches cool, pull off the skins.

egg cream

SERVES 4

½ cup Chocolate Syrup (recipe follows)
1 cup milk
2 cups chilled club soda

Pour 2 tablespoons chocolate syrup into each of four 10-ounce glasses. Pour ¼ cup milk over the syrup. Add 4 ounces club soda to each glass, stirring vigorously. Serve immediately.

chocolate syrup

MAKES 1½ CUPS

Chocolate syrup is thinner than chocolate sauce and is generally used to make chocolate milk, milk shakes, and egg creams.

¾ cup sugar
¼ cup light corn syrup
4 ounces dark bittersweet chocolate, finely chopped
½ teaspoon pure vanilla extract

Combine the sugar, corn syrup, and ¼ cup hot water in a saucepan; cover and bring to a boil over medium-high heat. Reduce to a simmer; cook, uncovered, until the sugar dissolves, about 1 minute. Remove from the heat; add the chocolate, and stir until smooth. Stir in the vanilla and ¼ cup warm water. Serve. The sauce can be stored in an airtight container, refrigerated, up to 1 week. Rewarm before serving.

COCKTAILS

raspberry vodka martinis

SERVES 4

Framboise de Bourgogne, a raspberry liqueur, is available in most liquor stores.

20 ounces raspberry-flavored vodka, chilled
3 ounces Framboise de Bourgogne
⅓ cup fresh raspberries

Place four martini glasses in the freezer for at least 10 minutes. Fill a cocktail shaker with ice. Add the vodka and Framboise; shake or stir. Strain into the cold glasses; garnish with 2 or 3 raspberries. Serve.

blue parrot

SERVES 4

Legend has it that the flavorless liqueur curaçao originally got its blue color from crushed beetles; today food coloring is used.

1 lime wedge
    Kosher salt, for glasses
4 ounces tequila
2 ounces Cointreau
2 ounces blue curaçao
⅔ cup fresh lime juice
¼ cup superfine sugar
1½ cups crushed ice

Rub the rim of each glass with the lime wedge. Spread the salt out on a shallow plate, and dip the rims of the glasses in the salt to coat. Combine the tequila, Cointreau, curaçao, lime juice, sugar, and ice in a blender until smooth. Pour into the salt-rimmed glasses, and serve immediately.

BASIC BAR EQUIPMENT

When making party cocktails for a crowd, the following equipment is indispensable. Have everything set out before the guests arrive:

Ice bucket

Blender

Cocktail shakers

Glass pitchers

Jigger measures

Corkscrew

Bottle opener

Ice cracker

Sharp knife

Lemon zester

Cocktail napkins

Cocktail strainers

maestro's old-fashioned

SERVES 1

Martha's friend Salli LaGrone serves this traditional drink during the holidays.

1 cube of sugar
   Dash angostura bitters
   Ice cubes
2 ounces best-quality bourbon
   Orange zest
   Orange slice, for garnish

Put the sugar into an old-fashioned glass with the bitters and 2 drops cold water; stir a bit to dissolve the sugar. Add ice cubes to half fill the glass; add the bourbon. Stir. Twist the orange zest over the drink to release the oils, then drop in the zest. Garnish with the orange slice. Serve immediately.

ramos gin fizz

SERVES 1

This cocktail was created in New Orleans in the late 1800s by bar owner Henry Ramos, who added orange-flower water and cream to the traditional gin fizz. A dash is equal to an eighth of a teaspoon. Use superfine sugar in cocktails—it dissolves quickly. For orange-blossom water, see Food Sources, page 648.

1 ounce gin
3 dashes fresh lime juice
3 dashes fresh lemon juice
3 dashes orange-blossom water
2 teaspoons superfine sugar
1 large egg white
¼ cup light cream or half-and-half
2 ounces club soda
   Ground cinnamon, for garnish, optional

1. Combine the gin, lime juice, lemon juice, orange-blossom water, superfine sugar, egg white, and cream in a cocktail shaker. Shake over ice; pour into a glass.

2. Top the drink with club soda, and garnish with cinnamon, if using; serve immediately.

NOTE *Raw eggs should not be used in food prepared for pregnant women, babies, young children, the elderly, or anyone whose health is compromised.*

DRINK CONVERSION CHART

The ingredients in traditional beverage recipes are always written in ounces, but if you are making drinks in batches, it is easier to use standard kitchen measures:

½ ounce = 1 tablespoon

1 ounce = 2 tablespoons

2 ounces = ¼ cup

4 ounces = ½ cup

8 ounces = 1 cup

mint julep

SERVES 4

The debate continues over whether or not to crush the mint leaves—we tasted them both ways and found crushed leaves made a better drink.

- 2 tablespoons superfine sugar
- 2 tablespoons fresh lemon juice
- 24 fresh mint leaves, plus 4 sprigs for garnish
- 2 cups finely crushed ice
- 8 ounces bourbon

Combine the sugar, lemon juice, and mint leaves in a pitcher. Crush well with a wooden spoon. Add the ice and the bourbon, and mix well. Pour into tumblers, garnish with mint sprigs, and serve.

bloody mary

SERVES 4 TO 6

- 3 cups tomato juice
- 3 tablespoons Fresh Horseradish (page 633) or prepared to taste, plus more for garnish
- 4 ounces vodka
- 2 teaspoons Worcestershire sauce
  Juice of 1 lemon
- 1 teaspoon freshly ground black pepper, plus more for garnish
  Hot red-pepper sauce, to taste
  Celery stalks, for garnish
  Lemon wedges, for garnish

1. Combine the tomato juice, horseradish, vodka, Worcestershire, lemon juice, pepper, and the pepper sauce in a pitcher. Transfer to the refrigerator until very cold. The mixture may be made up to this point 8 hours ahead.

2. Stir well to combine. Pour into ice-filled glasses; garnish with the grated horseradish, pepper, celery, and lemon wedges. Serve.

frozen bloody mary

SERVES 4

A Bloody Mary made from puréed frozen cherry tomatoes combines the sweet, spicy taste of the traditional cocktail with the texture of a smoothie. The frozen tomatoes won't dilute the drinks the way ice cubes do. Freeze the tomatoes the night before you plan to make these drinks.

- 4 cups (1½ pounds) frozen cherry tomatoes, plus more for garnish
- 6 ounces chilled vodka
- ½ cup fresh lime juice (about 6 limes)
- 1 tablespoon Fresh Horseradish (page 633) or prepared to taste
- 1 teaspoon hot red-pepper sauce, or to taste
  Kosher salt and freshly ground black pepper
  Celery stalks, for garnish

Place the frozen tomatoes, vodka, lime juice, horseradish, pepper sauce, and salt and pepper to taste in a blender; purée until smooth but still very thick. Divide among chilled glasses; garnish with celery and cherry tomatoes. Serve immediately.

fresh tomato juice and aquavit cocktail

SERVES 8

Aquavit is traditionally served chilled in a shot glass. The Scandinavian liquor is distilled from grain or potatoes and is flavored with caraway seeds. Mixed with tomato juice and served over ice in larger glasses, it makes a particularly nice brunch cocktail.

- 6 large (about 5 pounds) red tomatoes
- 8 ounces chilled aquavit or vodka
  Kosher salt

Place tomatoes in the bowl of a food processor, working in batches if necessary. Purée until smooth. Pass through a sieve or a cheesecloth-lined strainer into a large bowl; refrigerate until well chilled, at least 1 hour. Add aquavit to tomato juice; stir. Ladle mixture into serving glasses filled with ice, sprinkle with salt, and serve.

mango-melon colada

SERVES 2

⅓ cantaloupe, rind and seeds removed,
    cut in chunks (about 2 cups)

1 mango, peeled, pit removed (see page
   647), cut in chunks (about 1½ cups)

3 tablespoons cream of coconut

2 tablespoons fresh lime juice

2 tablespoons superfine sugar

4 ounces light rum

2 cups crushed ice

Place the cantaloupe, mango, cream of coconut,
lime juice, sugar, rum, and ice in a blender. Purée
until smooth, about 20 seconds. Pour into 2 glasses;
serve immediately.

blood-orange
champagne cocktails

SERVES 10 TO 12

2¼ cups fresh or frozen blood-orange juice

2 750-ml bottles chilled champagne

Pour 3 tablespoons of juice in each champagne
flute. Fill the flutes with the chilled champagne, and
serve immediately.

guava champagne punch

SERVES 12

Guava nectar is sold in cans or as frozen concentrate in specialty grocery stores and large supermarkets.

2 quarts guava nectar, chilled

2 750-ml bottles chilled champagne
   or sparkling wine

3 guavas, cut into ⅛-inch-thick slices,
   for garnish, optional

Combine the guava nectar and champagne in a
punch bowl or large pitcher. Add the guava slices,
if using, and serve immediately over ice.

bellini

SERVES 4

The original bellini was created at Harry's Bar in
Venice. Look for white peaches at large super-
markets or farmer's markets during the summer.
If you cannot find white peaches, substitute
yellow-fleshed ones. For a nonalcoholic Peach
Fizz, substitute club soda for the sparkling wine.

5 white peaches

3 tablespoons fresh lemon juice

16 ounces chilled sparkling wine

1. Peel and pit the peaches, then purée in the bowl
of a food processor or in the jar of a blender. Refrigerate until chilled.

2. Combine 1 cup of the peach purée and the lemon
juice. Divide among four champagne flutes. Add
the sparkling wine, stir, and serve.

campari cooler

SERVES 1

5 ounces dry white wine

1 ounce Campari

2 ounces club soda

2 2-inch-long strips lime zest

Fill a large glass with ice. Add the wine, Campari,
and club soda. Run the lime twists around the rim
of the glass, and add the twists to the cocktail. Serve
immediately.

HOT DRINKS

the best hot chocolate

SERVES 4

For flavored hot chocolate, simmer the milk with 2 vanilla beans, split lengthwise and scraped, or 6 fresh mint sprigs or 3 dried chile peppers for 5 minutes to let the flavors infuse. Strain the milk before whisking in the chocolate.

- 1 *quart milk*
- 10 *ounces semisweet or milk chocolate, cut into small pieces*

Place the milk in a medium saucepan, and bring to a simmer over medium-low heat. Add the chocolate, and whisk until it is completely melted and the milk is frothy. Serve immediately.

mexican hot chocolate

SERVES 4

Mexican chocolate is a combination of chocolate, cinnamon, almonds, and sugar. It is available in Mexican markets and large supermarkets.

- 3 *ounces sweet Mexican chocolate, roughly chopped*
- 3 *cups milk*
- ½ *vanilla bean, split lengthwise and scraped, optional*
- 4 *cinnamon sticks, for stirrers, optional*

1. In a medium saucepan, combine the chocolate with 3 tablespoons water over medium heat. Using the back of a fork, mash the chocolate into the water, and stir until chocolate is melted and smooth and bubbles around the edges, about 2 minutes.

2. Add the milk and the vanilla bean and seed scrapings, if using, to the saucepan, and heat, stirring occasionally, until wisps of steam begin to rise from the surface of the milk. Remove from the heat, and discard the vanilla bean. For frothy hot chocolate, transfer it to a blender, and blend until foamy. Serve each cup of hot chocolate with a cinnamon-stick stirrer, if using. Serve hot.

sore-throat tea

SERVES 4

Echinacea-goldenseal extract is available at health-food stores.

- 1 *5-inch-long piece fresh ginger, roughly chopped*
  Grated zest of 1 lemon
- ¼ *cup chopped fresh mint leaves*
- 3 *tablespoons fresh lemon juice*
- 2 *tablespoons honey, or to taste*
- 1 *teaspoon echinacea-goldenseal extract*

1. Combine ginger, zest, mint, and 6 cups water in a saucepan. Cover, and bring to a boil. Reduce heat, and simmer, with the lid ajar, until the mixture has reduced to 5 cups, about 30 minutes.

2. Strain the mixture through a fine sieve set over a heat-proof bowl. Return the liquid to the saucepan, and discard the solids.

3. Add the lemon juice and honey to taste; simmer 2 minutes. Place ¼ teaspoon of echinacea into each of four teacups. Pour tea; serve hot.

RECYCLING TEA AND COFFEE

While your first instinct may be to toss out tea bags and coffee filters after they've fulfilled their duties, you might reconsider. Simply mix the used tea leaves and coffee grounds into the ground (before you do, be sure to remove the tags, strings, and staples from the tea bags). The nutrients from the tea and coffee will enrich the soil and give a boost to acid-loving plants like azaleas, rhododendrons, and blueberry shrubs.

HERBAL TEA BLENDS

For centuries, herbs were a primary source of medicine. Although pharmaceuticals have now taken over, herbal infusions are still a good source of relief from everyday ailments. Blend your own healing teas in time for flu season, when their soothing qualities will be as welcome as their more potent effects. Each blend makes 3 cups tea mixture. Use ¼ cup mixture to 4 cups boiling water; let steep in a teapot for 5 minutes before serving. See Food Sources, page 648, for dried herbs and spices.

LICORICE AND PEPPERMINT TEA

3 ounces dried licorice root, cut into ¼-inch pieces (cough suppressant)

½ ounce dried peppermint leaves (nausea)

GOLDENSEAL, THYME, SAGE, AND GINGER TEA

1 ounce each dried goldenseal (antibacterial) or echinacea, dried thyme leaves, and dried whole sage leaves (congestion)

1½ tablespoons ground ginger (nausea)

FENUGREEK, SLIPPERY ELM, CHAMOMILE, AND CINNAMON TEA

2½ ounces fenugreek, lightly toasted (nausea)

1½ ounces dried slippery elm (sore throat)

¾ ounce dried chamomile flowers (antispasmodic)

1 8-inch cinnamon stick, broken into ½-inch pieces (nausea)

cinnamon-thyme tea
SERVES 4

Thyme contains thymol, a natural antiseptic and antioxidant.

> 3 bunches fresh thyme (about 1½ ounces)
> 4 whole cinnamon sticks

Place the thyme and cinnamon in a medium saucepan. Add 8 cups water. Cover, and bring to a boil. Reduce heat, and simmer, with the lid slightly ajar, until the mixture has reduced to about 5 cups, 45 to 60 minutes. Strain; serve hot.

FIT TO EAT RECIPE PER SERVING: 4 CALORIES, 0 G FAT, 0 MG CHOLESTEROL, 1 G CARBOHYDRATE, 20 MG SODIUM, 0 G PROTEIN, 0 G DIETARY FIBER

hibiscus-flower tea
SERVES 4

Licorice root, a natural throat soother, can be found in most health-food stores.

> ¼ cup dried chamomile
> ¼ cup dried hibiscus flowers
> 4 to 5 large sprigs fresh rosemary
> 4 licorice-root sticks

Combine the chamomile, hibiscus, rosemary, and licorice root in a medium saucepan, and add 8 cups of water. Cover; bring to a boil. Reduce heat; simmer, with the lid slightly ajar, until the mixture has reduced to about 5 cups, 45 to 60 minutes. Strain, and serve hot.

FIT TO EAT RECIPE PER SERVING: 111 CALORIES, 3 G FAT, 0 MG CHOLESTEROL, 22 G CARBOHYDRATE, 69 MG SODIUM, 2 G PROTEIN, 6 G DIETARY FIBER

salsas, sauces, dips,

AND MORE

....

pico de gallo

MAKES 3 CUPS

- 2 medium tomatoes, cut into ½-inch dice
- 2 jalapeño peppers, seeds and ribs removed, minced
- 1 small red onion, cut into ¼-inch dice
- 2 scallions, white and green parts, finely chopped
- ¼ cup fresh lime juice
- ½ cup loosely packed fresh cilantro leaves, roughly chopped
- ½ teaspoon ground chili powder, preferably pasilla
- ½ teaspoon kosher salt
- ⅛ teaspoon freshly ground black pepper

Combine the ingredients in a mixing bowl; toss to combine. Serve. Pico de Gallo will keep, refrigerated in an airtight container, up to 2 days.

salsa verde

MAKES 1 QUART; SERVES 12 TO 16

"Salsa verde" means "green sauce." The tomatillos, jalapeños, and cilantro give this salsa its bright color. Blanching the tomatillos will take away any bitterness.

- 1 pound tomatillos, husks removed
- 1 cup loosely packed fresh cilantro leaves, roughly chopped
- 5 jalapeño peppers, seeds and ribs removed, minced
- 6 scallions, white and pale-green parts, chopped
- 2 garlic cloves, minced
- 2 tablespoons fresh lime juice
- ½ teaspoon kosher salt
- ⅛ teaspoon freshly ground black pepper

Cover and bring a large pot of water to a boil. Add tomatillos; cook just until soft, 3 to 5 minutes. Drain. Let cool; chop into ½-inch pieces; place in a bowl. Toss with the remaining ingredients. Cover with plastic wrap; transfer to the refrigerator for several hours before serving. Salsa will keep, refrigerated in an airtight container, for 2 to 3 days.

grilled peach salsa

SERVES 6

Serve the peach salsa over grilled chicken breasts, lamb chops, or flank steak. Grilled peach halves are also delicious as a side dish.

- 5 ripe peaches (about 2 pounds), halved, pits removed
- 1 tablespoon extra-virgin olive oil
- 2 small jalapeños
- ¼ cup tightly packed torn fresh cilantro leaves
- 2 tablespoons balsamic vinegar
  Kosher salt and freshly ground black pepper

1. Heat a grill or grill pan to medium-high heat. Brush the cut side of each peach with the olive oil, and place on the grill, cut-side down. Grill until peaches start to soften, about 10 minutes. Use tongs to turn the peaches over, and continue grilling until peaches start to fill up with their own bubbling juices, about 20 minutes. Remove from the grill, and let cool.

2. Place jalapeños on the grill, and cook until charred all over and soft, about 10 minutes. Remove from heat, and let cool slightly. Peel off all black skin. Remove stems and seeds, and slice the jalapeños lengthwise into ⅛-inch strips.

3. Remove skins from cooled peaches over a bowl to catch the juices. Slice peach halves into fifths, place in the bowl, and toss with jalapeño, cilantro, and balsamic vinegar. Season to taste with salt and pepper. Salsa is best eaten within 2 to 3 hours.

black bean and grilled corn salsa

MAKES 5 CUPS; SERVES ABOUT 15

- 1 roasted jalapeño pepper (see page 645), minced
- 1 roasted red bell pepper (see page 645), cut in ¼-inch pieces
- 4 ears fresh corn, husks removed
- ¼ cup fresh lime juice
- 1 15-ounce can black beans, drained and rinsed
- ½ cup loosely packed fresh flat-leaf parsley, coarsely chopped
- ¼ cup finely chopped red onion
- 1 small garlic clove, minced
- 1 tablespoon extra-virgin olive oil
- ¼ teaspoon cayenne pepper

  Kosher salt and freshly ground black pepper

1. Combine the roasted jalapeño and bell peppers in a large bowl, and set aside.

2. Heat a grill or a grill pan to medium hot. Place the ears of corn directly on the grill. Cook until brown and tender, turning often, about 10 minutes. Remove from the grill, and let cool slightly. Using a sharp knife, shave the kernels off the cob; add to the peppers.

3. Add the lime juice, black beans, parsley, red onion, garlic, olive oil, and cayenne to the corn and pepper mixture, and toss well. Season with salt and pepper, and serve.

FIT TO EAT RECIPE PER HALF-CUP SERVING: 146 CALORIES, 2 G TOTAL FAT, 0 MG CHOLESTEROL, 30 G CARBOHYDRATE, 155 MG SODIUM, 6 G PROTEIN, 3 G DIETARY FIBER

tropical fruit salsa

MAKES 5½ CUPS; SERVES ABOUT 15

Spoon this sauce over grilled fish or chicken, or scoop it up with tortilla chips. Make it just before serving or it will lose its texture; the papaya contains enzymes that break the salsa down.

- 1 pound sweet onions, such as Maui, Vidalia, or Texas 1015s, skins on
- 2 teaspoons extra-virgin olive oil
- 1 mango, peeled, pit removed (see page 647), cut into ¼-inch dice
- 1 papaya (about 1¼ pounds), peel and seeds removed, cut into ¼-inch dice
- ¼ pineapple, peeled, cored, cut into ¼-inch dice (about 1 cup)
- 3 plum tomatoes, cut into ¼-inch dice
- 1 jalapeño pepper, seeds and ribs removed, minced
- 2½ tablespoons fresh lemon juice
- 2 tablespoons fresh lime juice
- ¼ cup coarsely chopped fresh cilantro leaves
- ½ teaspoon kosher salt
- ⅛ teaspoon freshly ground black pepper

1. Preheat the oven to 400°F. Halve the onions crosswise, and brush the cut sides with the oil. Cook, cut-side down, in a roasting pan until caramelized, about 1 hour 20 minutes. Turn the onions over, and let cool. Peel the onions, and cut into ¼-inch dice.

2. Combine the onions in a medium bowl with the mango, papaya, pineapple, tomatoes, jalapeño, lemon and lime juices, cilantro, salt, and pepper. Toss well, and cover until ready to use.

green tomato chutney

MAKES 6 HALF-PINT JARS

For the most mint flavor, press on the mint bundle with the back of a spoon while stirring.

- 1   large bunch fresh mint, roughly chopped
- 4   pounds green tomatoes
- 2   yellow onions (1 pound), finely diced
- 1½ cups white vinegar
- 1½ cups sugar
- 1   teaspoon kosher salt
- 1   cup golden raisins

1. Cover and bring a large stockpot of water to a boil. Tie the mint in a piece of cheesecloth; set aside. Prepare an ice-water bath, and set aside.

2. Using a paring knife, remove the core and score the nonstem end of each tomato with a shallow "x". Blanch the tomatoes in the boiling water for 30 seconds. With a slotted spoon, transfer the tomatoes to the ice-water bath. Using a paring knife, peel off the skin, and discard. Repeat with the remaining tomatoes. Cut the tomatoes into ¾-inch chunks, and set aside.

3. Combine the onions, vinegar, mint bundle, sugar, salt, raisins, and 1 cup water in a low-sided, 6-quart saucepan. Cover and bring to a boil over medium-high heat.

4. Add the tomatoes, and reduce to a simmer. Cook, stirring frequently, until the tomatoes are tender, about 1 hour.

5. Increase heat to high, and continue cooking, stirring frequently, until almost all the liquid has been absorbed, about 5 minutes. Remove the pan from the heat, and discard the mint bundle.

6. Transfer chutney immediately to a large bowl set over the ice bath to chill; chutney can be stored, refrigerated in an airtight container, up to 4 weeks.

dried cherry, pearl onion, and pear chutney

MAKES 6 HALF-PINT JARS

- 1   pound red pearl onions
- 4   Bartlett pears, peeled, cored, cut into ¼-inch dice
     Juice of 2 lemons
- 2½ cups dried cherries
- 1½ cups red-wine vinegar
- 1   cup sugar
- 1   teaspoon kosher salt
- ¼   teaspoon ground cloves

1. Cover and bring a large saucepan of water to a boil. Cook onions in the boiling water for 2 minutes. Drain; let cool. Carefully peel onions; trim root ends. Cut in half lengthwise. Set aside. In a large bowl, toss the pears with lemon juice.

2. Place the cherries, pearl onions, half of the pears, the vinegar, sugar, salt, cloves, and 2 cups water in a low-sided, 6-quart saucepan. Set the saucepan over high heat, cover, and bring the liquid to a boil.

3. Reduce heat to medium low, and simmer, uncovered, until the fruit is tender, about 45 minutes.

4. Raise heat to high; cook until the liquid has been absorbed, about 10 minutes. Stir in the remaining pears, and reduce heat to low; cook just until the pears are heated through, about 5 minutes. Remove the pan from the heat.

5. Transfer chutney immediately to jars as directed in Safe Canning Procedures (page 622). Alternatively, prepare an ice-water bath; transfer chutney to a large bowl set over it to chill; chutney will keep, refrigerated in an airtight container, up to 4 weeks.

. . . .

CHUTNEYS

All of the chutneys on these pages may be kept in the refrigerator up to 1 month. To keep them longer, the chutneys must be preserved by following the Safe Canning Procedures, 622.

. . . .

mango and fresh pepper chutney

MAKES 2 QUARTS

- 8 mangos, peeled, pit removed (see page 647), cut in 1½-inch pieces
- 1 medium onion, halved, very thinly sliced
- 1 cup golden raisins
- ½ cup cider vinegar
- 1 cup packed light-brown sugar
- 3 to 4 fresh small red and green hot peppers, seeds and ribs removed, cut into ¼-inch pieces
- 1 roasted jalapeño or small poblano pepper (see page 645), cut in ⅛-inch strips
- Grated zest of 2 lemons
- Juice of 2 lemons
- 2 tablespoons freshly grated ginger
- ½ teaspoon ground cinnamon
- 1 teaspoon kosher salt
- ½ teaspoon freshly ground black pepper
- 1 cup blanched almonds, toasted (see page 644)

1. Place the mangos in a medium saucepan. Add the onion, raisins, vinegar, and sugar; stir. Place over medium-low heat; cook, stirring often, until the sugar has dissolved and the liquid has been released from the mangos, 8 to 10 minutes.

2. Add the hot peppers, roasted-pepper strips and their reserved liquid, the lemon zest and juice, the ginger, cinnamon, salt, and pepper. Reduce heat to low; continue cooking, stirring to avoid scorching, until the mixture has thickened, 35 to 50 minutes. Transfer to a medium bowl. Stir in the toasted almonds. Let cool to room temperature. The chutney will keep, refrigerated in an airtight container, for 4 weeks.

chunky fruit barbecue marinade and chutney

MAKES 1½ QUARTS; SERVES 8 TO 12

This recipe yields both a marinade and a chutney, which are both delicious with chicken, pork, or a lean cut of beef, such as flank steak.

- 16 small shallots (about 6 ounces), peeled, bottoms trimmed but intact
- 1¼ cups dry white wine
- 4 medium fresh apricots, pitted, cut into ½-inch wedges
- 2 large peaches, pitted, cut into ½-inch wedges
- 2 plum tomatoes, cut into ½-inch wedges
- 12 prunes, pitted, cut into quarters
- 2 medium garlic cloves, minced
- 2 tablespoons low-sodium soy sauce
- ½ cup packed dark-brown sugar
- ¼ teaspoon crushed red-pepper flakes

1. In a small saucepan, combine the shallots and wine; cover and bring to a boil over high heat. Reduce heat to medium low, and let simmer, uncovered, until the shallots are tender, 15 to 20 minutes.

2. Combine the apricots, peaches, tomatoes, prunes, garlic, soy sauce, sugar, and pepper flakes in a large saucepan, add the shallots and wine, and bring to a boil over high heat. Reduce heat to medium; cook until the fruits have broken down but are still somewhat chunky, 10 to 15 minutes. Let cool.

3. Transfer half of the sauce to the bowl of a food processor, and purée until smooth. Use this as a marinade (and to baste with while grilling; discard the marinade once the basting is complete). Serve the other half as a chutney.

FIT TO EAT RECIPE PER SERVING: 155 CALORIES, 0 G FAT, 0 MG CHOLESTEROL, 33 G CARBOHYDRATE, 163 MG SODIUM, 2 G PROTEIN, 2 G DIETARY FIBER

chunky raw tomato sauce

SERVES 6

Toss this sauce into hot pasta, spoon over grilled skirt steak, wrap in warm tortillas, or drizzle over grilled bread.

- 2 pounds tomatoes, assorted sizes
  Kosher salt
- 2 teaspoons white balsamic or white-wine vinegar
- 2 teaspoons grated orange zest
- 1½ tablespoons fresh orange juice
  Freshly ground black pepper
- 3 tablespoons extra-virgin olive oil
- 6 large green olives, pitted, roughly chopped
- 6 large black olives, pitted, roughly chopped
- 2 tablespoons capers, drained
- 1 garlic clove, smashed
- 1 tablespoon chopped fresh thyme leaves
- 2 tablespoons coarsely chopped fresh flat-leaf parsley
- 1 small fennel bulb, trimmed and cut into ½-inch dice
- 20 fresh basil leaves
- 3 ounces goat cheese

1. Cut the tomatoes into rough 1-inch pieces, and place in a large bowl. Season with salt. Toss to combine, and set aside.

2. In a medium bowl, combine the vinegar, orange zest, orange juice, and pepper to taste. Whisk in the olive oil until well combined.

3. Add the green and black olives, capers, garlic, thyme, parsley, and fennel to the vinegar mixture. Toss to combine. Pour this mixture over the tomatoes, and gently toss. Season with salt and pepper. The mixture may sit for the flavors to meld up to 2 hours at room temperature. Before serving, remove the garlic, and add the basil and goat cheese; toss to combine.

green herb sauce

SERVES 6

The combined flavors of lemon, vinegar, and anchovies give depth to the herbs. Spoon into warm tortillas, and roll up with skirt steak, grilled chicken, or shrimp. Drizzle over rice, squash, and grilled vegetables.

- 3 shallots, minced
- 1 teaspoon kosher salt
- ¼ teaspoon freshly ground black pepper
- 2 anchovy fillets, roughly chopped, optional
- 3 tablespoons walnut or canola oil
  Grated zest of 1 lemon
- 1 tablespoon fresh lemon juice
- 2 teaspoons tarragon vinegar or white-wine vinegar
- 2 cups mixed fresh herbs, such as mint, flat-leaf parsley, tarragon, and basil leaves, packed
- ¼ cup snipped chives

1. Place the shallots in a mortar. Add the salt, and, using the pestle, pound until a paste forms. (If a mortar is unavailable, place the shallots on a cutting board, and sprinkle the salt over the top. Using the side of a chef's knife, crush the shallots against the board. Continue crushing until a paste forms.) Add the pepper and the anchovies, if using. Work the mixture, with either pestle or knife, until a paste forms again. Transfer it to a medium bowl.

2. Using a small whisk or a fork, mix the oil, the lemon zest and juice, and the vinegar into the shallot paste.

3. Using a large chef's knife, chop the herbs until medium-fine. Add the herbs to the bowl with the shallot paste. Add the chives. Using a rubber spatula, gently combine ingredients. Serve the sauce the same day.

mark peel's pesto

MAKES ½ CUP

Mark Peel, chef/owner of Campanile in Los Angeles, makes this coarse-textured pesto using a mortar and pestle rather than a food processor. Basil leaves turn black if exposed to the air after they are cut, so pour extra-virgin olive oil over the surface of the sauce to preserve its brilliant color.

- 3 garlic cloves
- 3 tablespoons pine nuts, toasted (see page 644)
- ½ teaspoon kosher salt, plus more for seasoning
- ¼ cup plus 1 tablespoon extra-virgin olive oil
- 1 cup coarsely chopped fresh basil leaves
  Fresh lemon juice

Using a mortar and pestle, crush garlic and pine nuts with ½ teaspoon salt and 1 tablespoon oil until pulverized. Add basil; work until you have a rough paste. Whisk in remaining oil in a stream. Season with salt and lemon juice. Use immediately.

cranberry-orange relish

MAKES 2 CUPS

For a cranberry fig relish, substitute 8 ounces chopped dried figs for the crystallized ginger and orange zest.

- 3 cups fresh cranberries
- 1 cup sugar
  Zest and juice of 1 lemon
  Zest of 1 orange
- ¾ cup fresh orange juice
- ¼ cup crystallized ginger, finely chopped

In the bowl of a food processor, pulse 2 cups of the cranberries until chopped. In a saucepan over medium heat, combine sugar, lemon and orange zests, orange juice, and ginger. Bring to a simmer; cook for 10 minutes. Add the chopped cranberries; cook, stirring, until thickened, about 15 minutes. Remove from the heat. Stir in the remaining cranberries and lemon juice. Transfer to a medium bowl to cool, about 20 minutes. Cover; refrigerate.

sweet red pepper sauce

MAKES 1 CUP

- 1 teaspoon olive oil
- 1 large leek, white and light-green parts, halved lengthwise, cut in ¼-inch thick slices, well washed (see page 646)
- 1 red bell pepper, seeds and ribs removed, cut into chunks
- ¼ teaspoon kosher salt
- ⅛ teaspoon freshly ground black pepper
- 1 cup Homemade Chicken Stock (page 624), or low-sodium store-bought chicken broth, skimmed of fat

Heat the oil in a saucepan over medium heat. Add the leek, bell pepper, salt, and pepper; cook for 3 minutes. Add the stock; cover. Cook until the vegetables are tender, about 12 minutes. Transfer the vegetables to the bowl of a food processor; purée until smooth. Pass purée through a fine sieve back into saucepan. To serve, warm over low heat.

FIT TO EAT RECIPE PER TABLESPOON: 14 CALORIES, TRACE OF FAT, 0 MG CHOLESTEROL, 2 G CARBOHYDRATE, 53 MG SODIUM, 1 G PROTEIN, 1 G DIETARY FIBER

avocado mango sauce

SERVES 6

2 avocados, peeled and pitted (see page 647)

3 tablespoons fresh lime juice

1 ripe mango, peeled, pit removed (see page 647), cut into ¾-inch cubes

1 small seedless cucumber, cut into ½-inch dice

2 scallions, white and pale-green parts, cut into ¼-inch pieces

3 tablespoons coarsely chopped fresh cilantro leaves

1 small jalapeño pepper, seeds and ribs removed, cut into ⅛-inch dice

Kosher salt and freshly ground pepper

Cut avocados into ¾-inch cubes. In a bowl, toss gently with lime juice. Add mango, cucumber, scallions, cilantro, and jalapeño to the avocados. Toss very gently, being careful not to mash them. Season with salt and pepper. Serve within 1 hour, or store in an airtight container, refrigerated, for up to 3 hours.

carrot raita

SERVES 8

1½ pounds (about 5 large) carrots, cut into 1-inch matchsticks (5 cups), plus 1 small carrot, cut into long, thin strips

1 quart plain yogurt

3 tablespoons fresh lemon juice

3 tablespoons canola oil

2 teaspoons whole black or brown cumin seeds

1 tablespoon whole fennel seeds

Kosher salt

½ cup fresh mint leaves, torn into medium pieces, plus more leaves for garnish

Combine 5 cups carrots, yogurt, and lemon juice in a bowl. Heat oil in a very small skillet over medium-high heat until very hot. Add cumin and fennel seeds; let fry until they pop, about 5 seconds. Pour the oil and seeds over carrot mixture. Stir to combine. Season with salt; add the mint. Toss. Garnish with the mint leaves and carrot strips, and serve.

sweet-and-sour onion marinade and relish

MAKES 2½ CUPS; SERVES 6

As intensely sweet as it is sour, this marinade can stand up to richly flavored fish steaks or beef. Serve the relish on the side or as a spread on sandwiches.

1 pound sweet onions, such as Vidalia or Texas 1015s, sliced into thin rounds

2 medium garlic cloves, minced

1 teaspoon unsalted butter

2½ tablespoons balsamic vinegar

½ teaspoon kosher salt

Pinch of freshly ground black pepper

5 plum tomatoes

½ cup loosely packed fresh basil leaves

¼ cup Homemade Chicken Stock (page 624), or low-sodium store-bought chicken broth, skimmed of fat

1. In a large skillet, combine the onions, garlic, butter, vinegar, salt, and pepper with 1¾ cups water; cover and bring to a boil over high heat. Reduce heat to medium low; simmer until most of the liquid has evaporated, about 45 minutes. Continue to cook, stirring often, until the onions are caramelized, 15 minutes more.

2. Cut 3 tomatoes into thin wedges; add to the onions, and cook, stirring occasionally, until the tomatoes soften but retain their shape, 5 to 10 minutes. Set aside; this is the relish.

3. Quarter the remaining tomatoes; purée in the bowl of a food processor with the basil. Strain through a fine sieve; discard the solids. Return to the food processor; add the stock and half the relish; purée. This is the marinade; discard it after using. Serve the remaining half of the relish warm or at room temperature.

FIT TO EAT RECIPE PER SERVING: 54 CALORIES, 1 G FAT, 2 MG CHOLESTEROL, 11 G CARBOHYDRATE, 208 MG SODIUM, 2 G PROTEIN, 3 G DIETARY FIBER

west indian papaya sauce

MAKES 1½ CUPS

This recipe calls for the hottest of the hot fresh peppers, the habanero. Use with discretion, and eat it with something starchy to help neutralize the heat, like Skillet Cornbread (page 562). Use it sparingly with fish, chicken, and beef dishes.

- 1 papaya, peel and seeds removed, cut into small pieces
- 1 yellow or orange fresh habanero pepper, seeds and ribs removed, minced
- 1 small red onion, cut into ¼-inch dice to yield ¾ cup
- 2 garlic cloves, minced
- ½ teaspoon ground turmeric
- ½ teaspoon mustard powder
- 1 teaspoon ground cumin
- ¼ cup white-wine vinegar
- ½ teaspoon kosher salt
- ¼ teaspoon freshly ground black pepper

1. Process papaya and habanero in a blender just until smooth but retaining some texture. Add onion, garlic, turmeric, mustard powder, cumin, vinegar, salt, and pepper. Process until smooth.

2. Transfer the mixture to a saucepan. Bring to boil over high heat, reduce to simmer, and cook until thickened slightly, 10 to 15 minutes. Transfer to a bowl; cool to room temperature. Refrigerate in an airtight container for up to 3 weeks.

baked white bean purée

MAKES 3 CUPS; SERVES 6 TO 10

This dip uses basic pantry ingredients, making it perfect for a last-minute gathering. Serve with crostini and raw or steamed vegetables.

- 2 tablespoons plus 1 teaspoon extra-virgin olive oil
- 1 medium onion, finely chopped
- 1 tablespoon minced garlic
- 2 teaspoons finely chopped fresh rosemary
- 2 15½-ounce cans cannellini beans, drained, liquid reserved
- ½ teaspoon kosher salt
- ½ teaspoon freshly ground black pepper
- 1 tablespoon white-wine vinegar
- 1 tablespoon dry bread crumbs (see page 647)
- 1 tablespoon freshly grated Parmesan cheese

1. Preheat the oven to 350°F. Heat 1 tablespoon oil in a medium saucepan over medium heat. Add the onion and garlic, and cook until translucent, about 8 minutes. Add 1 teaspoon rosemary, the cannellini beans, and salt and pepper, and cook until very hot.

2. Transfer the bean mixture to the bowl of a food processor; add the vinegar, 1 tablespoon olive oil, and 3 tablespoons of the reserved bean liquid, and purée until smooth.

3. Combine the bread crumbs, Parmesan cheese, remaining rosemary, and remaining olive oil in a small bowl, and stir until well combined.

4. Place bean purée in an ovenproof bowl; top with the bread-crumb mixture. Transfer to oven; bake until golden brown, about 20 minutes. Serve hot.

FIT TO EAT RECIPE PER SERVING: 102 CALORIES, 6 G FAT, 0 MG CHOLESTEROL, 18 G CARBOHYDRATE, 342 MG SODIUM, 6 G PROTEIN, 6 G DIETARY FIBER

tzatziki

MAKES 1 QUART

This Middle Eastern condiment is often paired with spicy foods; yogurt tames the heat of chiles and spices.

- 3 *medium cucumbers, peeled, seeded, and cut into ½-inch chunks*
- 2 *teaspoons kosher salt*
- 2 *cups plain yogurt*
- 2 *teaspoons minced garlic*
- 2 *tablespoons minced fresh dill*
- 1 *tablespoon minced fresh mint*
- 1 *tablespoon extra-virgin olive oil*
- 1 *tablespoon fresh lemon juice*

In a colander, toss cucumbers and 1 teaspoon salt. Place colander in sink; let drain 20 to 30 minutes. Press cucumbers to extract the excess liquid. Transfer to a bowl; mix in yogurt, garlic, dill, mint, oil, lemon juice, and remaining salt. Chill about 1 hour for the flavors to blend; serve at room temperature.

almond skordalia

MAKES 2½ CUPS; SERVES 6 TO 8

This variation on the Greek dip, traditionally made with walnuts, is made with almonds. Bread is its basis, so make sure to use slices from a good-quality loaf. Serve with crisp vegetables such as bell peppers, fennel, and carrot strips.

- 10 *slices good-quality white bread, crusts removed*
- 1 *cup whole blanched almonds, chopped*
- 2 *large garlic cloves, minced*
- ¼ *cup plus 1 tablespoon fresh lemon juice*
- ¼ *cup extra-virgin olive oil*
- 2 *teaspoons kosher salt*
- ½ *cup Homemade Chicken Stock (page 624), or low-sodium store-bought broth, skimmed of fat*

1. Place the bread on a baking sheet to dry for 24 hours, or preheat the oven to 350°F and toast the bread on a baking sheet until lightly toasted, but not golden, about 5 minutes per side.

2. Place almonds and garlic in the bowl of a food processor; process until smooth, about 30 seconds.

3. Combine the lemon juice, oil, and salt. Drop the bread into a bowl of cool water, 1 slice at a time. When soaked, squeeze each slice between your palms, extracting half the water. Add the bread and the oil mixture to the almonds in the processor; process until smooth, about 20 seconds.

4. Transfer the skordalia to a bowl; cover and refrigerate 2 hours. To serve, bring to room temperature, and mix in the stock to thin as desired.

spicy squash dip

SERVES 8 TO 10

Serve this dip warm with Rosemary Flatbread (page 550). To toast seeds, see page 644. If using canned pumpkin, begin the recipe with step 2.

- 1 *3-pound butternut squash or 15-ounce can pumpkin purée*
- 1 *teaspoon whole cumin seeds, toasted*
- 1 *teaspoon whole mustard seeds, toasted*
- 1 *teaspoon whole coriander seeds, toasted*
- 2 *tablespoons extra-virgin olive oil*
- 1 *15-ounce can chickpeas, drained and rinsed*
- 1 *teaspoon kosher salt*
- ½ *teaspoon freshly ground black pepper*
- 2 *tablespoons fresh lemon juice*
- 1 *teaspoon fresh thyme leaves, plus sprigs for garnish*

1. If using squash, preheat the oven to 375°F. Cut the squash in half; remove seeds. Place the halves cut-side down on a parchment-lined baking sheet, and roast until very soft, about 1 hour. Let cool slightly, and scrape the flesh into a bowl. Set aside.

2. Grind the toasted cumin, mustard, and coriander finely in a spice grinder. Set aside.

3. Combine the squash or pumpkin, the mixed ground spices, olive oil, chickpeas, salt, pepper, lemon juice, and thyme leaves in a food processor. Process until smooth, about 30 seconds. Transfer to a serving dish, and garnish with thyme sprigs, if desired. Serve immediately or keep refrigerated, covered, for up to 3 days.

green olive and caper tapenade
MAKES ¾ CUP

- 1 cup (4½ ounces) green olives, pitted
- 5 anchovy fillets
- 3 tablespoons capers, drained
- 1 small garlic clove, peeled
- 2 teaspoons fresh lemon juice
  Freshly ground black pepper to taste

Place the ingredients in the bowl of a food processor. Pulse or grind until a coarse paste forms. Store in an airtight container, refrigerated, up to 1 week.

refreshing yogurt marinade
MAKES 3 CUPS

Chicken and seafood pair well with this sweet, tangy marinade. Don't leave the seafood in it for more than 2 hours or its texture will deteriorate.

- 1 mango, peeled, pit removed (see page 647), cut in medium pieces
- 2 cups plain yogurt
- 1 tablespoon honey
- 2 teaspoons dry hot mustard
- ¼ cup fresh mint leaves
- ½ teaspoon kosher salt
- ¼ teaspoon freshly ground black pepper

Combine the ingredients in the bowl of a food processor; process until smooth and flecked with the mint. Marinade may be made up to 1 day ahead and refrigerated in an airtight container.

FIT TO EAT RECIPE PER SERVING: 77 CALORIES, 0 G FAT, 2 MG CHOLESTEROL, 14 G CARBOHYDRATE, 236 MG SODIUM, 5 G PROTEIN, 0 G DIETARY FIBER

cherry preserves
MAKES 4 HALF-PINT JARS

YOU WILL NEED FOUR HALF-PINT CANNING JARS.

- 4 pounds fresh red or yellow cherries, unblemished, pitted
- 2¼ cups plus 2 tablespoons sugar
- 2 tablespoons fresh lemon juice

1. Sterilize the jars (see Safe Canning Procedures, page 622). Place four small plates in the freezer to prepare for the gel test.

2. Meanwhile, in a medium stockpot, combine cherries, ¼ cup sugar, and lemon juice; place over medium-high heat. Cook, stirring frequently, until sugar has dissolved, 2 to 3 minutes. Stir in one-third of the remaining sugar; cook, stirring, until it has dissolved, 1 to 2 minutes. Add sugar in two more batches, stirring until sugar has dissolved.

3. Cover; bring mixture to a boil. Cook, stirring frequently, 10 minutes. Clip a candy thermometer onto the saucepan; cook, stirring frequently, until temperature registers 220°F, 30 to 40 minutes, skimming any foam that rises to the surface.

4. With the temperature at 220°F, perform a gel test: Remove a plate from the freezer, and place a spoonful of the jam on it. Return plate to freezer; wait 1 minute. Remove plate from freezer; gently nudge the edge of the jam with one finger. If the jam is ready, it will wrinkle slightly when pushed. If it is not ready, it will be too thin to wrinkle. If the jam does not wrinkle on the first attempt, cook 2 or 3 minutes more, and repeat the gel test.

5. Fill the jars following the Safe Canning Procedures, page 622. Process the filled jars in boiling water for 10 minutes. Using tongs, transfer the jars to a wire rack to cool completely. Store the jam in a cool, dark place up to 1 year.

SOUR CHERRY VARIATION *To make sour cherry preserves, substitute 3 pounds of fresh sour cherries, and increase the sugar to 2½ cups. This will yield only three half-pint jars. You can also use frozen sour cherries: Use only 2 cups sugar, and, in step 2, add 1 cup of juice from the thawed cherries.*

three-fruit marmalade

MAKES FIVE 8-OUNCE JARS

Cut the citrus peel as thin or as thick as you like it in the marmalade.

- 1 grapefruit
- 1 orange
- 2 lemons
- 6¼ cups sugar

1. Sterilize the jars (see Safe Canning Procedures, page 622). Meanwhile, scrub the fruit, place in a large bowl, and cover with boiling water. Let stand 2 minutes, then drain. Remove the peel in thin slices with a zester, or cut off with a sharp knife into thicker pieces, as desired. Tie the peel in a piece of cheesecloth; set aside.

2. Chop the remaining pith and fruit into small pieces. You can do this in the bowl of a food processor, but be careful not to purée.

3. Combine the chopped fruit, cheesecloth bag, and 2 quarts water in a 4-quart stainless-steel pan. Cover and simmer 1½ hours over low heat, until reduced by almost half. Remove the cheesecloth bag, and set aside.

4. Strain the contents of the pan, pressing to extract the liquid. Discard solids, and return the liquid to the pan. Add the sugar, and dissolve over low heat. Cover and bring to a boil. Add the peel from the cheesecloth, and simmer, uncovered, over medium heat, 10 to 30 minutes, until the mixture reaches 221°F on a candy thermometer or falls in sheets from a spoon.

5. Fill jars, following the Safe Canning Procedures, page 622, and process for 20 minutes. Alternatively, prepare an ice-water bath, and transfer the mixture to a large bowl set over it to chill; store in an airtight container, refrigerated, up to 1 month.

LIME MARMALADE VARIATION *Substitute 9 limes for the grapefruit, orange, and lemons. Use the peel from 4 of the limes in the cheesecloth in step 1. Add the juice of 2 lemons with the fruit in step 3.*

applesauce

MAKES ABOUT 7 CUPS

Everything after the cinnamon is optional. If you want pink applesauce, don't peel the apples, then pass through a food mill to remove the skins. Homemade applesauce doesn't need any sugar, especially if you use the apple cider when cooking. It can be frozen, in airtight containers, up to 2 months.

- 18 McIntosh apples (about 6 pounds), peeled, cored, and quartered
- 1 cup apple cider
- 1 large cinnamon stick
- ½ vanilla bean, split lengthwise and scraped
- 1 teaspoon ground ginger
- ½ teaspoon ground cardamom
- ½ teaspoon ground nutmeg
- ½ teaspoon ground mace
- ½ cup sugar, or to taste
- 2 tablespoons fresh lemon juice

1. Combine apples, apple cider, cinnamon, vanilla bean and seed scrapings, the ginger, cardamom, nutmeg, mace, sugar, and lemon juice in a large heavy-bottomed wide saucepan.

2. Place the saucepan over medium heat, and cook, stirring often with a wooden spoon to prevent scorching, until the apples are broken down and saucy, 50 to 60 minutes. Mash any large pieces of apple with a large wooden spoon to help them break down. Season with more sugar and spices. Remove the apple mixture from the heat, and let stand to cool completely before serving, discarding the cinnamon stick and vanilla pod. The applesauce can also be stored in an airtight container for 2 to 3 days in the refrigerator.

assorted flavored butters

Make three different flavored butters, and spread on hot cornbread, toast, or dinner rolls.

  Kosher salt

 1 ounce mixed green herbs, such as tarragon, oregano, chives, basil, and flat-leaf parsley

 1½ pounds (6 sticks) unsalted butter, room temperature

  Freshly ground black pepper

 1½ tablespoons ground chili powder, such as arbol, ancho, or New Mexico

 1½ tablespoons curry powder

1. Cover and bring a small pot of salted water to a boil. Prepare an ice-water bath. Blanch herbs; using tongs, transfer to the ice bath to stop the cooking. Squeeze excess water from herbs; mince with a sharp knife. Transfer herbs to the bowl of a food processor, add ½ pound (2 sticks) of the butter, and process until well combined; season with salt and pepper. Transfer the herb butter to plastic wrap, pat into a log, and refrigerate or freeze until needed.

2. Divide remaining pound of butter between two bowls. Add chili powder to one bowl, curry powder to the other. Combine each thoroughly with a rubber spatula; season with salt. Wrap individually in plastic; refrigerate or freeze until needed.

maple butter

MAKES ABOUT 1 CUP

This butter is delicious spread over toast or on top of pancakes, waffles, and French toast.

 1 cup pure maple syrup

 1 2-inch-long cinnamon stick

 12 tablespoons (1½ sticks) unsalted butter, cut into pieces

1. Pour syrup into a saucepan; add cinnamon. Bring to a boil over medium-high heat. Clip on a candy thermometer. Cook until mixture is 240°F. (soft-ball stage), 10 to 15 minutes. Remove pan from heat; discard cinnamon stick. Stir in butter until melted.

2. Transfer mixture to the bowl of an electric mixer fitted with the paddle attachment. Beat, starting on low and increasing to high, until mixture is opaque and creamy, about 8 minutes. Store in an airtight container, refrigerated, up to 2 weeks. Do not freeze.

moroccan preserved lemons

MAKES 2 QUARTS

Lemons pickled in salt and lemon juice will keep for up to 6 months. Dice or cut the rind into matchsticks, and add to salads, pastas, and condiments.

 8 lemons, scrubbed

 ½ cup kosher salt

 2 1-inch cinnamon sticks

 ½ teaspoon whole black peppercorns

 6 dried bay leaves

 1 quart fresh lemon juice (about 24 lemons)

1. Cut each lemon lengthwise into quarters, but only two-thirds of the way through, so one end remains intact. Rub the insides with 1 to 2 teaspoons of salt. In 2 one-quart jars or 1 two-quart jar, layer the lemons, the remaining salt, the cinnamon sticks, peppercorns, and bay leaves. Pack the lemons as tightly as possible. Pour the lemon juice over the lemons until they are submerged. The lemons must be covered with the juice.

2. Close the jar or jars tightly. Place in a warm spot to ripen for at least 1 week before using. Gently shake the jars daily to redistribute the salt. Transfer the jar to the refrigerator. To use the preserved lemons, remove the amount needed from the jar, remove the flesh, and discard; rinse the rind under cold water to remove excess salt.

oven-dried tomatoes

MAKES 7 TO 8 DOZEN

You can oven-dry any tomato variety; each of the quantities given below generally fills one baking pan. In addition to the ingredients listed here, lemon zest, thyme, rosemary, red-pepper flakes, or cayenne can be sprinkled onto the tomatoes. For Silpats, nonstick baking mats, see Equipment Sources, page 650.

- 24 cherry tomatoes, cut in half
- 8 to 10 plum tomatoes, cut in half
- 8 to 10 yellow, orange, red, or green tomatoes, cut into ¼-inch-thick or thicker slices
- 1 tablespoon sugar

  Chopped fresh herbs, such as oregano, basil, or marjoram

  Kosher salt and freshly ground black pepper

1. Preheat the oven to 250°F. Line a baking pan with parchment paper; for very thinly sliced tomato chips, use a Silpat baking mat to keep them from sticking. Arrange the tomatoes, cut-sides up, on the pan, spaced ½ to 1 inch apart. Sprinkle with sugar and herbs; season with salt and pepper.

2. Transfer pan to oven; dry until juices have stopped running, edges are shriveled, and pieces have shrunken slightly; the timing will vary depending on the variety, ripeness, and desired degree of dryness, 1½ to 6 hours. Transfer to a wire rack to cool completely. Store in an airtight container, refrigerated, up to 3 days, or frozen up to 6 weeks.

OVEN-DRYING TOMATOES

If you use full, round tomatoes, slice them very thinly to make dried tomatoes that are as crisp as potato chips. Dried-tomato slices can be frozen for several months; thicker, juicier slices, enhanced with herbs, keep best when preserved in olive oil and refrigerated. After the tomatoes are gone, use the oil for marinades and vinaigrettes.

dried tomatoes in olive oil

MAKES 1 PINT JAR

- 16 dried plum-tomato halves (see Oven-Dried Tomatoes recipe, at left)
- 4 sprigs fresh rosemary
- 6 sprigs fresh thyme
- ½ cup extra-virgin olive oil, or more if needed

Using a long spoon or wooden skewer, arrange two layers of tomato halves in the bottom of a clean, dry, 1-pint glass jar. Insert a few sprigs of rosemary and thyme. Make more layers, using a spoon to pack the tomatoes tightly, until the jar has been filled to within ½ inch of the top. Add enough olive oil to completely cover the tomatoes and the herbs. Seal tightly, and store, refrigerated, up to 1 month.

oven-dried fruit

EACH QUANTITY BELOW FILLS ONE BAKING PAN

Any fruit to be dried should be ripe but still firm. Store the dried fruit in an airtight container, frozen, up to 6 weeks; warm the frozen fruit in a 200°F oven until soft, 5 to 15 minutes. For Silpats, nonstick baking mats, see Equipment Sources, page 650.

- 8 peaches, pitted, halved or quartered
- 12 to 14 plums, pitted, halved or quartered
- 10 to 11 apricots, pitted, halved or quartered
- 10 plumcots, pitted, halved or quartered
- 12 figs, stemmed, halved
- 2 small bunches seedless grapes, removed from stems
- 1 tablespoon sugar, or more to taste

1. Preheat the oven to 225°F. Line a baking pan with parchment paper (or a Silpat baking mat if you're drying figs). Arrange the fruit, cut-sides up, spaced ½ to 1 inch apart, on the pan. Sprinkle 1 tablespoon sugar over the fruit; depending on fruit's tartness, add more sugar.

2. Transfer the pan to the oven; dry until the fruit has shriveled, the edges have dried, and the centers are still juicy; timing will vary according to the variety of fruit, ripeness, and size, 1½ to 4 hours. If the juices start to run, baste with the juices every hour. Transfer the pan to a wire rack to cool; remove fruit from the pan while still warm.

oven-dried cherries

MAKES 4 CUPS

Toss these cherries into salads, or serve with a mild cheese.

- *1 pound red cherries, stemmed and pitted*
- *2 tablespoons balsamic vinegar*
- *2 tablespoons sugar*
- *1 pound yellow cherries, stemmed and pitted*

1. Preheat the oven to 300°F. Line two baking sheets with parchment paper, and set aside.

2. In a medium bowl, toss the red cherries with 1 tablespoon balsamic vinegar and 1 tablespoon sugar. In another bowl, toss the yellow cherries with the remaining tablespoon of balsamic vinegar and the remaining tablespoon sugar. Let the cherries stand 30 minutes.

3. Arrange the cherries cut-sides up on the baking sheets. Bake until the cherries are wrinkled but still moist, 30 to 40 minutes. Transfer the sheets to a wire rack to cool completely. Store the cherries in an airtight container, refrigerated, up to 1 week.

pear chips

MAKES 2 TO 2½ DOZEN

- *1 cup sugar*
- *5 unripe small pears, such as Seckel or Bosc*

1. Preheat the oven to 175°F. Line two baking pans with parchment paper; set aside. In a medium saucepan, combine the sugar and 1 cup water; bring to a boil. Boil, stirring occasionally, until the sugar has dissolved, about 8 minutes. Reduce heat to medium low; let simmer.

2. Using a mandoline, slice the pears lengthwise as thinly as possible; make sure that each slice remains intact and is uniform in thickness. Place in a single layer in the simmering syrup; cook for 1½ minutes. Using a slotted spoon, remove the slices, and place ¼ inch apart on the prepared baking pans. Cook all the pear slices.

3. Bake the pears until dry and crisp, without browning, about 3 hours; check regularly. Transfer to a wire rack to cool. Store in an airtight container for up to 2 days.

quick dill pickles

SERVES 4

These pickles will keep, refrigerated in an airtight container, for 3 to 5 days. If Kirby cucumbers are unavailable, English or other long seedless cucumbers may be substituted.

- *4 to 6 Kirby cucumbers*
- *1 small bunch fresh dill*
- *12 whole black peppercorns*
- *1 cup white-wine vinegar*
- *1 teaspoon kosher salt*
- *¼ cup sugar*
- *1 garlic clove, thinly sliced*

1. Cut the cucumbers into 1-inch-square chunks, and place in a heat-proof bowl with 12 to 15 sprigs of dill. Set aside.

2. Place the peppercorns, vinegar, salt, and sugar in a small saucepan over medium heat. Cook until the salt and sugar dissolve, 1 to 2 minutes. Add the garlic, cover, and bring to a boil. Remove from the heat, and pour hot mixture over the reserved cucumbers. Let stand 30 to 40 minutes, and serve.

pickled okra

MAKES 8 PINTS

- 2 *pounds tender okra*
- 1 *quart white vinegar*
- ¼ *cup plus 2 tablespoons kosher salt*
- 16 *small garlic cloves*
- 8 *small fresh hot red peppers*
- 1 *bunch fresh dill (about 24 sprigs)*
- ½ *cup whole yellow mustard seeds*

1. Rinse the okra; cut away any bruises or bad spots. Trim the stem ends, but do not remove the caps entirely.

2. Sterilize eight 1-pint canning jars (see Safe Canning Procedures, page 622).

3. Meanwhile, cover and bring the vinegar, 3 cups water, and the salt to a boil in a large pot.

4. Using stainless-steel tongs, remove the jars from the water, and set on a layer of clean towels. Evenly divide the garlic, peppers, dill sprigs, and mustard seeds among the jars. Pack tightly with the okra, alternating the direction of caps. Leave ¾ inch of space beneath the rim of the jar. Pour the hot liquid over the okra, covering it by ¼ inch and leaving ½ inch of space beneath the rim. Slide a clean chopstick or wooden skewer along the inside of each jar to release any air bubbles. Wipe the mouth of the jar with a clean, damp cloth. Place the hot lid on the jar; turn the screw band firmly without forcing.

5. Process the jars (see Safe Canning Procedures, page 622), adding enough hot water to cover by 2 inches, and boil for 10 minutes. Remove jars from the water bath; let stand on clean dish towels for 24 hours. Check cool jars for the slight indentation in the lids that indicates a vacuum seal. Jars that do not seal properly or that leak during processing should be stored in the refrigerator and the pickles consumed within 1 week. Allow sealed pickles to mellow in a cool, dry place for 6 to 8 weeks before serving. Store opened jars in the refrigerator.

pickled peppers

MAKES 2½ PINTS

Pickled peppers will keep up to 1 month.

- 1 *pound fresh jalapeño, serrano, or Hungarian wax peppers*
- 2 *cups cider vinegar*
- 2 *tablespoons kosher salt*
- 1½ *teaspoons sugar*
- 1½ *teaspoons whole black peppercorns*
- 6 *garlic cloves*
- 2 *sprigs fresh thyme*

1. Wash and dry the peppers, and slit each in two or three spots. In a small saucepan, cover and bring ½ cup water to a boil with the vinegar, salt, and sugar. Reduce heat to medium, and stir until the salt has dissolved. Set the vinegar-salt liquid aside.

2. Meanwhile, tightly pack the peppers into two 1¼-pint glass canning jars. Divide the peppercorns, garlic, and thyme between the jars. Pour the hot liquid into the jars, enough to cover the peppers. Close the jars tightly; let liquid cool to room temperature. Refrigerate 1 to 2 weeks for flavors to develop. Will keep, stored in the refrigerator, up to 4 weeks.

bread and butter pickled green tomatoes

MAKES 6 PINTS

Though the job is spread over 3 days, making this pickle is well worth the effort. See Food Sources, page 648, for pickling lime and blades of mace.

- 7 *pounds green tomatoes*
- 1 *cup pickling lime*
- 5 *pounds sugar*
- 1½ *quarts white vinegar*
- 1 *tablespoon whole cloves*
- 5 *small sticks cinnamon*
- 1 *tablespoon whole allspice*
- 1 *teaspoon whole celery seed*
- 2 *blades mace, optional*
- 1 *3-inch piece fresh ginger, sliced into ¼-inch rounds*

1. Wash the tomatoes thoroughly, and cut away any bruises or bad spots. Cut into ¼-inch-thick slices.

2. Combine 2 gallons water and the lime in a large nonreactive bowl; add tomatoes. Let soak 24 hours.

3. Drain the tomatoes, and cover with fresh water. Soak for 4 hours, changing the water every half hour. Rinse and drain well.

4. In a large nonreactive pot, combine the sugar and vinegar, and bring to a boil. Fold an 8 x 16-inch piece of cheesecloth in half to make a square; rinse with water and squeeze dry. Place the spices and ginger on the cloth; tie closed with one end of a 12-inch piece of kitchen twine. Tie a loop in the other end, and slip it over the handle of a wooden spoon. Suspend the spice bag in the syrup by placing the spoon across the top of the pot. Remove the syrup from the heat, add the tomatoes, and let sit overnight, covered with a clean dish towel.

5. Bring the tomatoes to a simmer, and cook, pushing them into the syrup occasionally, until translucent, about 35 minutes.

6. Meanwhile, sterilize 6 one-pint canning jars and lids; see the Safe Canning Procedures, page 622.

7. Using stainless-steel tongs, layer the hot tomatoes in the hot sterilized pint jars, leaving ¾ inch of space beneath the rim. Pour the hot syrup over the tomatoes, covering them by ¼ inch, leaving ½ inch of space beneath the rim. Slide a clean plastic chopstick or wooden skewer along the inside of each jar to release any air bubbles. Wipe the mouth of the jar with a clean, damp cloth. Place the hot lid on the jar; screw on the band firmly without forcing.

8. Process the jars in a water bath for 30 minutes. Using canning tongs, transfer the jars to a wire rack, or kitchen towels, to cool completely. Jars that don't seal properly or that leak during processing should be stored in the refrigerator and the pickles consumed within 1 week. The tomatoes can be served when cool but are more flavorful when allowed to mellow in a cool, dry place for 2 to 3 weeks.

rhubarb pickle

SERVES 12

It may be delicious in pies and cobblers, but rhubarb is never so good as it is pickled. Serve it with Fresh Ham 101 with Green-Herb Paste (page 242) for a spring supper.

- 2 cups apple-cider vinegar
- 1 tablespoon kosher salt
- 1½ cups sugar
- 1 teaspoon whole cloves
- 1 1½-inch piece fresh ginger, thinly sliced
- 4 small dried chile peppers
- 1 pound rhubarb, trimmed, cut into thin 5- to 7-inch batons

Combine vinegar, 1 tablespoon salt, and sugar in a nonreactive saucepan. Stir; set over medium heat; cook until salt and sugar have dissolved, about 5 minutes. Add cloves, ginger, and peppers. Cover. Bring to a boil over medium-high heat; cook 1 minute more. Pack rhubarb into a tall glass jar or a long plastic container. Pour hot liquid over rhubarb, completely covering it. Let cool; cover. Refrigerate 24 hours, and store, refrigerated, up to 1 week.

pickled peaches

MAKES 5 PINTS

Serve these with pork or chicken.

- 1   cup white vinegar
- 3   cups dry white wine
- ½   cup sugar
- 2   3-inch lengths fresh ginger,
      each cut into 5 thin slices
- 3   pounds (about 8) ripe peaches,
      cut into sixths
- 5   dried bay leaves

1. Wash five glass pint jars with lids in hot, soapy water, and rinse well. (You can use canning jars and lids, but you don't have to.)

2. Combine the vinegar, wine, sugar, and ginger in a saucepan, and bring to a boil.

3. Pack the jars with the peaches, leaving ¾ inch of space beneath the rim. Remove the ginger from the syrup; add to the jars along with the bay leaves.

4. Pour the hot liquid over peaches to completely cover, leaving ½ inch of space beneath the rim. Cover the jars, and let stand until cool. Peaches will keep in the refrigerator for up to 3 days.

SAFE CANNING PROCEDURES

Chutneys, jams, and pickles can be made and eaten right away or stored in the refrigerator for up to several weeks, but if you plan to give them as gifts, the only way to keep them at room temperature is to follow safe canning instructions. The United States Department of Agriculture offers a complete guide to home canning, which is available on the Internet. See www.uga.edu/nchfp.

1. Discard chipped or cracked jars. Wash the jars, lids, screw bands, canning tongs, ladle, and funnel in hot, soapy water; rinse well. Place the jars upright on a wire rack placed in a large pot, leaving at least an inch of space between the jars. Fill with hot water until the jars are submerged, and bring to a boil. Boil for 15 minutes. Turn off the heat; leave the jars in the water. Sterilize the lids according to manufacturer's instructions. Never reuse lids—the seals may not work a second time. Using a jar lifter or stainless-steel tongs, lift the jars from the pot, emptying the water back into the pot. Place the jars on a layer of clean dish towels.

2. Fill the jars. Place a stainless-steel canning funnel in the mouth of a jar, and fill with the mixture to a quarter inch from the rim. Remove the funnel, and run a small rubber spatula around the edges to release excess air bubbles. Clean the rim and threads of the

jar with a clean towel dipped in hot water. Use tongs to lift a prepared lid, and place it carefully on the rim of the jar. Screw on the band until it is secure but not too tight, or the air in the jars will not be able to escape and the jars will not be properly sealed.

3. Process the jars. After each jar is filled, use the canning tongs to place it back into the pot of water, keeping the jars an inch apart. When all of the jars have been filled and returned to the pot, cover and bring it back to a full boil. Process the jars according to recipe instructions. (At altitudes higher than 1,000 feet, longer processing times will be needed.)

4. Remove the jars. Transfer them from the water bath with the jar lifter, and transfer them to a wire rack, or clean dish towels, to cool for 24 hours. As the preserved food cools, a vacuum will form inside the jar, sealing it; sometimes a popping sound is heard. A slight indentation in the lid indicates the vacuum seal. The lid should not flex up and down when pressed firmly with a finger. Jars that do not seal properly or that leak during processing should be stored in the refrigerator and the mixture consumed within 1 to 2 weeks. (Jars may be reprocessed as well, with a fresh screw band.) Store jars in a cool, dry, dark place for up to 1 year.

basics

....

homemade chicken stock

MAKES 5 QUARTS

If you plan to use the stock for a specific recipe, begin making it at least 12 hours ahead of time, and refrigerate for 8 hours so the fat has a chance to collect on top and can be removed.

- 2 leeks, white and pale-green parts, cut into thirds, well washed (see page 646)
- 1 teaspoon whole black peppercorns
- 6 sprigs fresh dill or 2 teaspoons dried
- 6 sprigs fresh flat-leaf parsley
- 2 dried bay leaves
- 2 carrots, cut into thirds
- 2 celery stalks, cut into thirds
- 1 4-pound chicken, cut into 6 pieces
- 1½ pounds chicken wings
- 1½ pounds chicken backs
- 2 48-ounce cans (3 quarts) low-sodium chicken broth, skimmed of fat

1. Place the leeks, peppercorns, dill, parsley, bay leaves, carrots, celery, whole chicken, wings, and backs in a large stockpot. Add the chicken stock and 6 cups cold water, cover, and bring to a boil. Reduce to a very gentle simmer, and cook, uncovered, about 45 minutes. The liquid should just bubble up to the surface. A skin will form on the surface; skim it off with a slotted spoon, and discard, repeating as needed. After about 45 minutes, remove the whole chicken from the pot, and set it aside until it is cool enough to handle.

2. Remove the meat from the chicken bones, set the meat aside, and return the bones to the pot. Transfer the chicken meat to the refrigerator for another use; if you plan to use it for chicken noodle soup, shred the meat before refrigerating it.

3. Continue to simmer the stock mixture, on the lowest heat possible, for 3 hours, skimming foam from the top as needed. The chicken bones will begin to disintegrate. Add water if at any time the surface level drops below the bones.

4. Prepare an ice-water bath. Strain the stock through a fine sieve or a cheesecloth-lined strainer into a very large bowl. Discard the solids. Transfer the bowl to the ice-water bath; let the stock cool to room temperature.

5. Transfer the stock to airtight containers. Stock may be labeled at this point and refrigerated for 3 days or frozen for up to 4 months. If storing, leave the fat layer intact; it seals the stock.

ASIAN-FLAVORED CHICKEN STOCK *To make a stock that is excellent for Asian noodle soups, add one or more of the following ingredients to your stock while it is simmering: 2 stalks fresh lemongrass, 8 ounces shiitake mushrooms, 4 ounces thinly sliced fresh ginger, 10 fresh cilantro stems, 10 whole Szechuan peppercorns, 10 whole coriander seeds, 2 star anise. Or substitute 2 cups Japanese sake for the water.*

beef stock

MAKES 6 QUARTS

The butcher can cut veal bones into small pieces for you. If you want pieces of meat in your stock, see Beef Stock With Shredded Beef (opposite).

- 8 sprigs fresh flat-leaf parsley
- 6 sprigs fresh thyme or ¾ teaspoon dried
- 4 sprigs fresh rosemary or 2 teaspoons dried
- 2 dried bay leaves
- 1 tablespoon whole black peppercorns
- 1 pound beef-stew meat, cubed
- 5 pounds veal bones, cut into small pieces
- 1 large onion, unpeeled and quartered
- 2 large carrots, cut into thirds
- 2 celery stalks, cut into thirds
- 2 cups dry red wine

1. Preheat the oven to 450° F. Tie the parsley, thyme, rosemary, bay leaves, and peppercorns in a piece of cheesecloth to make a bouquet garni. Set aside.

2. Arrange the beef-stew meat, veal bones, onion, carrots, and celery in an even layer in a heavy roasting pan. Roast, turning every 20 minutes, until the vegetables and the bones are deep brown, about 1½ hours. Transfer the meat, bones, and vegetables to a large stockpot, and set aside. Pour off the fat from the roasting pan, and discard. Place the pan over high heat on the stove. Add the red wine, and stir, using a wooden spoon to loosen any browned bits from the bottom of the pan; boil until the wine is reduced by half, about 5 minutes. Pour the mixture into the stockpot.

3. Add 6 quarts cold water to the stockpot, or more if needed to cover bones. Do not use less water; cover and bring to a boil, then reduce to a very gentle simmer so that bubbles occasionally rise to the surface. Add the reserved bouquet garni. Skim the foam from the surface. Continue to simmer the stock over the lowest possible heat for 3 hours. A skin will form on the surface of the liquid; skim off with a slotted spoon. Repeat as needed. Add water if the surface level drops below the bones.

4. Prepare an ice-water bath. Strain the stock through a fine sieve, or a cheesecloth-lined strainer, into a large bowl. Discard the solids. Transfer the bowl to the ice-water bath, and let the stock cool to room temperature.

5. Transfer the stock to airtight containers. The stock may be labeled at this point and refrigerated for 3 days or frozen for up to 4 months. If using the stock for a recipe, refrigerate for at least 8 hours or overnight so the fat collects on the top and can be removed. If storing, leave the fat layer intact; it seals the stock.

beef stock with shredded beef
MAKES 2 QUARTS

Use this recipe for beef stock when you want to have shredded beef to use in the soup recipe. Most butchers carry beef shank, but short ribs are a good substitute.

- *3 pounds beef shank, cut into 1-inch pieces*
- *2 dried bay leaves*
- *1 onion, unpeeled and quartered*
- *1 celery stalk, cut into thirds*
- *2 carrots*
- *1 tablespoon whole black peppercorns*

1. Combine the beef shank, bay leaves, onion, celery, carrots, peppercorns, and 3½ quarts water in a 4-quart stockpot; cover and bring to a boil over medium-high heat. Reduce heat, and simmer, uncovered, for 2 hours, skimming occasionally to remove the foam as it rises to the top.

2. Prepare an ice-water bath. Strain the stock through a fine sieve or a cheesecloth-lined strainer into a large bowl. Let the stock cool slightly. Remove the meat from the bones; discard the bones and the vegetables. Transfer the stock to the ice-water bath. Shred the meat into small pieces, and reserve. Refrigerate stock, overnight if possible, and remove hardened fat with a spoon. The beef stock may be refrigerated, with shredded beef, up to 2 days or frozen for up to 4 months.

....

BEEF STOCK

The best beef stock starts with roasting the beef or veal bones in the oven, which turns them a dark brown that will provide the color for the rich stock and its complex, deep, meaty flavor. Quality like this can never be found in canned beef broth, which is generally watery and salty. An acceptable substitute for homemade broth is the high-quality frozen beef stock found in gourmet-food stores.

....

veal stock

MAKES ABOUT 5 QUARTS STOCK
OR 1 QUART DEMI-GLACE

This stock can be used at regular strength or reduced to a gel-like demi-glace.

- 4 sprigs fresh rosemary
- 8 sprigs fresh flat-leaf parsley
- 6 sprigs fresh thyme
- 2 dried bay leaves
- 1 tablespoon whole black peppercorns
- 1 pound veal-stew meat, cubed
- 7 pounds veal bones, such as necks,
     shanks, and knuckles, sawed or broken
     into 2-inch pieces
- 1 pound oxtail, optional
- 1 pig's foot, optional
- 2 large Spanish onions, unpeeled
     and quartered
- 3 large carrots, cut in half
- 3 celery stalks, cut in half
- 8 ounces mixed mushrooms, wiped
     clean, stems attached
- 1 head of garlic, cut in half widthwise
- 1 6-ounce can tomato paste
- 1 28-ounce can plum tomatoes,
     drained and quartered
- 2 cups dry red wine, such as a burgundy

1. Preheat the oven to 425°F. Tie rosemary, parsley, thyme, bay leaves, and peppercorns in a small piece of cheesecloth to make a bouquet garni; set aside.

2. Arrange the meat and veal bones (and oxtail or pig's foot, if using) in a single layer in a large heavy roasting pan, and place in the oven. Roast, turning several times, until they turn deep brown, about 1½ hours. Remove from oven, and place onions, carrots, celery, mushrooms, garlic, tomato paste, and chopped tomatoes on top of the bones. Reduce heat to 375°F, return pan to oven, and roast until vegetables are brown, about 45 minutes.

3. Transfer bones, meat, and vegetables to a 6-gallon stockpot; set aside. Discard the fat from the roasting pan; set the pan on the stove over high heat. Add wine, and stir, using a wooden spoon to loosen any browned bits from bottom of pan; boil until wine is reduced by half, about 5 minutes. Add to stockpot.

4. Add 8 quarts cold water to stockpot, just covering bones; cover, and bring to a boil. Reduce heat to a simmer; skim foam that rises to surface. Add bouquet garni. Cook 8 to 10 hours; skim frequently.

5. Prepare an ice-water bath. Strain stock through a fine sieve into a large bowl, and set in the ice-water bath. When cool, cover and refrigerate overnight.

6. Discard the layer of fat on stock. You should have about 5 quarts of stock. The stock can be refrigerated up to 3 days or frozen for up to 4 months.

FOR DEMI-GLACE *After step 6 above, transfer the veal stock to a smaller pot, bring to a boil, and reduce heat to medium high. Cook at a gentle boil, skimming frequently; reduce liquid to about 1 quart, about 2 hours 45 minutes. It will be dark and viscous. Pour into an 8-inch square pan, cover, and refrigerate overnight. Cut firm demi-glace with a knife into 1- to 2-inch squares; wrap each in plastic wrap, and place in a resealable freezer bag. Store in the freezer for up to 4 months.*

vegetable stock

MAKES 3 QUARTS

- 1 tablespoon unsalted butter
- 1 tablespoon olive oil
- 1 large onion, coarsely chopped
- 2 large carrots, coarsely chopped
- 2 parsnips, coarsely chopped
- 1 celery stalk, coarsely chopped
- 1 bunch (about 1½ pounds) red or green
     Swiss chard, cut into 1-inch pieces
     Several sprigs fresh thyme
     Several sprigs fresh flat-leaf parsley
- 1 dried bay leaf

1. In a medium stockpot, melt the butter and oil, stirring occasionally, over medium-low heat. Add the onion; cook until caramelized, 15 to 25 minutes. Add the carrots, parsnips, and celery, and cook until tender, about 20 minutes.

2. Add Swiss chard to vegetable mixture. Add 3½ quarts cold water, the thyme, parsley, and bay leaf. Cover and bring to a boil, reduce heat, and let simmer, uncovered, about 1 hour.

3. Remove from the heat, and strain the stock through a fine sieve or a cheesecloth-lined strainer, pressing on the vegetables to extract the juices. Discard the vegetables. The stock can be refrigerated for 3 to 4 days or frozen for up to 3 months.

court bouillon

MAKES 6 QUARTS

Court bouillon, the vegetable-and-herb broth traditionally used for poaching fish, imparts subtle flavor to the fish as it cooks. The bouillon can be made 2 or 3 days ahead. If preparing the fish the same day, make the bouillon right in the poacher.

- 1 bunch fresh thyme
- 1 bunch fresh flat-leaf parsley
- ½ teaspoon whole black peppercorns
- ½ teaspoon whole fennel seeds
- 1 750-ml bottle dry white wine
- 1 leek, white and pale-green parts, sliced into ¼-inch rounds, well washed (see page 646)
- 2 medium carrots, sliced into ¼-inch rounds
- 1 lemon, sliced into ¼-inch rounds
- 3 dried bay leaves
- 2 tablespoons kosher salt

Fit a 10-quart fish poacher with a rack in the bottom, and place the poacher over two burners on top of the stove (or use a large stockpot). Fill with 7 quarts water (about three-quarters full). Tie thyme, parsley, peppercorns, and fennel seeds together in a small piece of cheesecloth to make a bouquet garni, and place in poacher; add wine, leek, carrots, lemon, bay leaves, and salt. Cover, and bring to a simmer. Uncover; gently simmer for 30 minutes. Discard bouquet garni. Let bouillon cool to room temperature, about 1 hour. The bouillon can be refrigerated up to 1 week or frozen up to 3 months.

HOW TO MAKE FULL-FLAVORED STOCK

With a few simple ingredients, some basic kitchen equipment, and a little planning, wonderful stock is easy to make at home.

● *Use meat and bones to make a stock; if you use only bones, that's exactly what the stock will end up tasting like.*

● *The stockpot should be tall and narrow enough to keep the ingredients snug; too much space causes the flavorful liquid to evaporate rather than extracting the full flavor from the ingredients.*

● *Don't rush stock; it takes 3 to 4 hours to release all the flavor from the bones.*

● *Add enough cold water to cover ingredients by 1 or 2 inches—no more, or the stock may be too watery. Bring everything to a boil, then reduce the heat right away so the liquid barely simmers (use a metal trivet or a flame tamer). Letting the stock boil for too long can result in greasy, off flavors; all that churning makes the fat released from the bones and meat emulsify with the water.*

● *As the stock gently simmers, a thin skin of impurities will form on the surface. Skim this skin off with a slotted spoon, and discard. Skim the stock every 30 minutes. When the liquid falls below the level of the bones, add cold water.*

● *Strained and cooled, stock keeps in the refrigerator for 3 days and in the freezer for 3 to 4 months. Once it's refrigerated, a layer of fat develops on top of the stock; skim it off with a spoon, and discard. If you freeze the stock, leave the fat intact as a seal; remove it before using.*

fish stock

MAKES ABOUT 2½ QUARTS

Since this fish stock freezes well, double the recipe; use one batch, and freeze the second one for later use.

- 4 pounds heads and bones of non-oily fish, such as sole, flounder, snapper, or bass
- 2 dried bay leaves
- 8 sprigs fresh flat-leaf parsley
- 1 bunch fresh thyme
- ½ bunch fresh tarragon
- 1½ teaspoons whole fennel seeds
- 8 whole black peppercorns
- 3 tablespoons unsalted butter
- 1 large leek, white and pale-green parts, quartered and sliced ¼ inch thick, well washed (page 646)
- 1 medium onion, cut into ¼-inch dice
- 8 ounces white mushrooms, wiped clean, cut into ¼-inch dice
- 2 medium carrots, cut into ¼-inch dice
- 2 celery stalks, cut into ¼-inch dice
- ½ fennel bulb, cut into ¼-inch dice
- 1 cup dry white wine

1. Remove gills and any blood from fish heads; thoroughly wash bones, and cut them to fit in a 12-quart stockpot. Tie bay leaves, parsley, thyme, tarragon, fennel seeds, and peppercorns in a small piece of cheesecloth to make a bouquet garni; set aside.

2. Melt butter in the stockpot over medium heat; add the leek, onion, mushrooms, carrots, celery, and fennel, and cook until tender, 8 to 10 minutes. Increase the heat to medium high, and add the fish heads and bones. Cook, stirring, for 3 to 5 minutes. Add wine, bouquet garni, and 2½ quarts water, just covering the bones. Bring to a boil, reduce heat to low, skim, and let stock simmer for 25 minutes. Turn off heat; let sit for 10 minutes.

3. Prepare an ice-water bath. Strain the stock through a fine sieve into a large bowl; set the bowl in the ice bath to cool. Use the stock within 1 day, or freeze up to 3 months.

dashi

MAKES 3 CUPS

Dashi is a simple stock integral to Japanese cooking. The broth is used in both cold and hot soups and is delicious warm, all on its own. The ingredients may be found at an Asian grocer, or see Food Sources, page 648.

- 1 2-inch piece of kombu seaweed
- 2 tablespoons bonito flakes (fish flakes)
- 1 tablespoon plus 2 teaspoons soy sauce
- 1 tablespoon mirin
  Juice of ¼ lime

To make the dashi, bring 3 cups water to a boil in a small saucepan. Wipe off the kombu, add to the boiling water, and let boil for 3 minutes. Add the bonito flakes, remove from the heat, and let sit for 30 minutes. Strain, then add the soy sauce, mirin, and lime juice; serve hot or chilled. Dashi should be used within a few hours.

MEDITERRANEAN FISH STOCK

To infuse your fish stock with the flavors of the Mediterranean, add one or more of the following ingredients: ½ teaspoon crumbled saffron threads, 6 sun-dried tomatoes (not packed in oil), 1½ teaspoons sweet paprika, ½ teaspoon toasted fennel or cumin seeds, 3 garlic cloves, 20 shrimp shells, or the zest of 1 orange.

hollandaise sauce

MAKES 1 CUP

- 3 large egg yolks
- 1½ tablespoons fresh lemon juice
- 8 tablespoons (1 stick) unsalted butter, melted
  Kosher salt

1. In the top of a double boiler or in a large heat-proof bowl set over a saucepan of simmering water, whisk the egg yolks with 1½ tablespoons water, whisking vigorously, until the mixture thickens, about 4 minutes. Remove from the heat, and stir in the lemon juice.

2. Slowly whisk in the melted butter until thickened. Season with salt. Serve the sauce immediately, or keep warm over very gently simmering water, whisking occasionally.

dill bearnaise

MAKES 1 CUP

Try this sauce with poached eggs and smoked salmon.

- 2 tablespoons white-wine vinegar
- 2 tablespoons dry white wine
- 5 whole black peppercorns
- 1 shallot, minced
- 3 large egg yolks
- 12 tablespoons (1½ sticks) unsalted butter, cut in pieces
  Kosher salt
- 1 tablespoon finely snipped fresh dill

1. In a small saucepan, combine the vinegar, wine, peppercorns, and shallot. Place over medium-high heat; cook until almost all the liquid is evaporated, about 2 minutes. Add 2 tablespoons water; reduce the heat to low.

2. Add the yolks; whisk until the mixture is thickened, about 4 minutes. Remove from the heat; whisk in the butter until it's fully incorporated and the sauce thickens, about 3 minutes. Season with salt. Strain the sauce; discard the solids. Stir in the dill. Serve immediately, or keep warm over gently simmering water, whisking occasionally.

béchamel sauce

MAKES 1 QUART

- 4 tablespoons unsalted butter
- 1 tablespoon minced shallot
  Kosher salt and freshly ground white pepper
  Pinch of ground nutmeg
  Pinch of cayenne pepper
- ½ cup all-purpose flour
- 1 quart whole milk
- 1 dried bay leaf
- 1 cup grated Gruyère cheese (from 3 ounces)

1. In a large saucepan, heat the butter over medium heat. Add the shallot, and cook until translucent, without browning, 3 to 5 minutes. Season with salt, white pepper, nutmeg, and cayenne. Reduce heat to as low as possible.

2. Add the flour in thirds, whisking constantly. When fully incorporated, cook, whisking, without browning, until the sauce thickens, bubbles, and does not taste floury.

3. Meanwhile, heat the milk in a small saucepan over medium-high heat; bring to a boil, and immediately remove from the heat. Add the hot milk to the flour mixture, in thirds, whisking constantly. The texture should be thick with no lumps. Add bay leaf; continue to cook about 8 minutes over low heat.

4. Strain through a sieve; add the cheese while the béchamel is still hot. Season with salt and pepper. Once at room temperature, the sauce may be refrigerated, covered with plastic wrap placed directly on the surface of the sauce, in an airtight container for up to 3 days. Rewarm in the top of a double boiler over an inch of simmering water.

rémoulade sauce

MAKES ABOUT 2 CUPS

If you are concerned about raw eggs, use store-bought mayonnaise, and begin at step 3. The sauce can be made ahead and refrigerated in an airtight container for up to 2 days.

- 1 large whole egg
- 2 large egg yolks
- ½ teaspoon kosher salt
  Pinch of sugar
- ¼ teaspoon freshly ground black pepper
- ¾ cup extra-virgin olive oil
- 1 to 2 tablespoons fresh lemon juice
- ¾ cup canola oil
- 1 tablespoon capers, drained and chopped
- 2 teaspoons Dijon mustard
- 1 tablespoon chopped fresh flat-leaf parsley
- 1 tablespoon chopped fresh tarragon
- 1 tablespoon snipped chives
- 1 tablespoon minced shallot

1. Place egg, egg yolks, salt, sugar, and pepper in the bowl of a food processor. Process until blended.

2. With the machine running, slowly drizzle the olive oil through the feed tube. Add 1 tablespoon lemon juice, then slowly drizzle in the canola oil through the feed tube. Season with more lemon juice, salt, and pepper, if needed.

3. Stir in the capers, mustard, parsley, tarragon, chives, and shallot, and serve immediately.

vietnamese dipping sauce

MAKES 1½ CUPS

Known as "nuoc cham," this Vietnamese table sauce is used to season dumplings, soups, and noodle dishes.

- 1½ teaspoons minced garlic
- 1 teaspoon ground-chile paste
- 1 Thai bird chile or serrano pepper, chopped, optional
- ¼ cup Asian fish sauce (nam pla)
- 2 tablespoons fresh lime juice
- ¼ cup sugar
- 2 tablespoons grated carrots, for garnish

Using a mortar and pestle, pound the garlic, chile paste, and fresh chile into a paste (or mince together with a knife). Transfer to a bowl. Add the fish sauce, ⅔ cup hot water, the lime juice, and sugar. Whisk together until the sugar dissolves. Garnish with the carrots, and serve.

citrus dipping sauce

MAKES ABOUT 1 CUP

This refreshing sauce may be made up to 8 hours ahead and kept, refrigerated, in an airtight container.

- ⅓ cup fresh orange juice
- ⅓ cup fresh lime juice
- ¼ cup low-sodium soy sauce
- 1 tablespoon Chinese dark sesame oil
- ⅛ teaspoon freshly ground black pepper
- 2 scallions, white and green parts, thinly sliced

In a small bowl, whisk together the orange and lime juices, soy sauce, sesame oil, and pepper; add scallions. Serve.

perfect gravy

MAKES 3 CUPS

For the best poultry gravy, do not roast turkey or chicken in a nonstick roasting pan: It keeps the flavorful bits of meat and skin from cooking onto the pan.

>   *Giblets from a turkey or chicken: neck, heart, gizzard, and liver*
> 3½ *tablespoons unsalted butter*
> 2 *celery stalks, roughly chopped*
> 1 *carrot, roughly chopped*
> 1 *medium onion, roughly chopped*
> 1 *medium leek, white and green parts, roughly chopped, well washed (see page 646)*
> 6 *whole black peppercorns*
> 1 *dried bay leaf*
> 1½ *cups Madeira wine*
> 3 *tablespoons all-purpose flour*
> 2 *teaspoons minced fresh rosemary*
> ¾ *teaspoon kosher salt*
> ⅛ *teaspoon freshly ground black pepper*

1. Make the giblet broth while the turkey is roasting. Trim any fat or membrane from the giblets. The liver should not have the gallbladder, a small green sac, attached. If it is, trim it off, removing part of the liver if necessary. Do not pierce sac; it contains bitter liquid. Rinse the giblets, and pat dry.

2. In medium saucepan, melt 3 tablespoons butter over medium-high heat. Add vegetables. Cook, stirring, until slightly brown, 5 to 10 minutes. Reduce heat to medium; add the neck. Cook, stirring, until slightly brown, about 5 minutes. Add 1 quart water. Add the heart, gizzard, peppercorns, and bay leaf. Cover; bring to boil. Reduce heat to medium low; cook, uncovered, until broth is reduced to about 3 cups, 50 to 60 minutes. Set aside.

3. Meanwhile, chop the liver finely. Melt the remaining ½ tablespoon butter in a small skillet over medium-low heat. Add the liver; cook, stirring constantly, until the liver is fully cooked and no longer releases blood, 4 to 6 minutes. Add to the cooking giblet broth.

4. Transfer the roasted turkey to a large platter. Pour the juices from the pan into a gravy strainer. Set aside to separate, about 10 minutes.

5. Strain the reserved broth. Return to the saucepan, and warm over low heat. Place the roasting pan over medium-high heat. Pour the Madeira into a measuring cup, then into the pan, let bubble, and scrape the bottom and sides of the pan with a wooden spoon to loosen any browned bits.

6. Make a slurry: Place the flour in a glass jar with a tight-fitting lid. Ladle 1 cup of the broth into the jar. Shake until combined. Slowly pour into the roasting pan; stir to incorporate. Cook over medium heat, stirring until the flour is cooked, 2 to 3 minutes. Slowly stir in the remaining broth.

7. Raise heat to medium high. Add pan juices from the gravy strainer; add the dark drippings from the bottom into roasting pan. Discard the fat. Stir in rosemary. Season with salt and pepper. Cook 10 to 15 minutes to reduce and thicken. (For thicker gravy, add 1 more tablespoon of flour; reduce water to 2½ cups in step 2.) Strain liquid from pan through a very fine sieve. Season with salt and pepper. Keep warm in a heat-proof bowl over a pan of simmering water until ready to serve.

. . . .

PERFECT GRAVY EVERY TIME

To make gravy with a velvety texture and rich flavor:

● *Use every part of the bird, from the giblets to the crispy skin and caramelized juices in the bottom of the pan, which add both flavor and color to the gravy.*

● *Use a gravy strainer. This cup is fitted with a spout that feeds from the base. Because fat floats to the top of liquid, the spout pulls only the nonfatty juices into it.*

● *Eliminate lumps that form when flour is added to the roasting pan too quickly and not blended well: Mix flour and broth together before adding to the pan juices.*

. . . .

homemade mayonnaise

MAKES 2 1/2 CUPS

A food processor helps make homemade mayonnaise quickly, but a whisk works just as well. Martha prefers to use entire eggs, not just the yolks, for a lighter texture. Add the oil very slowly, literally drop by drop. This prevents the oil from overwhelming the egg yolks and produces a smooth, creamy spread. By varying the ingredients, you can create endless variations. Substitute a flavored vinegar such as tarragon or sherry for the lemon juice, or alter the flavor by trying different olive oils. Seasonings or chopped fresh herbs may be added to the mayonnaise after it is made.

- *1 cup light olive oil*
- *1 cup canola oil*
- *2 large eggs*
- *¼ teaspoon dry mustard*
- *¼ teaspoon kosher salt*
- *2 tablespoons fresh lemon juice*

1. Combine the oils in a large glass measuring cup. Place the eggs, mustard, and salt in the bowl of a food processor. Process until the mixture is foamy and pale, about 1½ minutes.

2. With the machine running, add the oil, drop by drop, through the feed tube, until the mixture starts to thicken (about ½ cup oil); do not stop the machine at this point or the mayonnaise may not come together. Add the remaining oil in a slow, steady stream. When all the oil has been incorporated, slowly add the lemon juice. The fresh mayonnaise can be kept, refrigerated in an airtight container, for up to 5 days.

· ·

CAUTION: RAW EGGS

Raw eggs should not be used in food prepared for pregnant women, babies, young children, the elderly, or anyone whose health is compromised.

· ·

garlic mayonnaise

MAKES 1 CUP

Good-quality prepared mayonnaise can also be used as a base: Whisk in mustard, lemon juice, and garlic.

- *2 teaspoons Dijon mustard*
- *1 large egg*
- *1 tablespoon fresh lemon juice*
- *1 teaspoon kosher salt*
- *1 cup canola oil*
- *1 large garlic clove, smashed to a paste*

In the bowl of a food processor, combine mustard, egg, lemon juice, and salt; process 5 seconds. With machine running, pour the oil through the feed tube in a slow, thin, steady stream; process until combined. Transfer to a bowl; stir in the garlic. Store in an airtight container, refrigerated, up to 3 days.

mint mayonnaise

MAKES ABOUT 1 CUP

Serve with small boiled red potatoes for dipping.

- *1 large egg*
- *1 teaspoon Dijon mustard*
- *2 tablespoons fresh lemon juice*
- *½ teaspoon kosher salt, plus more for seasoning*
- *1 cup canola or safflower oil*
- *1 small bunch fresh mint, 6 to 8 sprigs, coarsely chopped*
- *Freshly ground black pepper*

Place egg, mustard, lemon juice, and ½ teaspoon salt in a blender; pulse until well combined. With blender running, pour in the oil in a slow, steady stream until mixture is creamy. Pulse in mint until just combined. Season with salt and pepper. Serve immediately, or keep refrigerated for up to 3 days.

clarified butter

MAKES 1 ½ CUPS

1 pound (4 sticks) unsalted butter,
   cut in tablespoons

Place the butter in a small, deep saucepan over low heat. As the butter melts, three layers will develop: a bottom layer of milk solids; a middle layer of clear, yellow butter; and a top layer of milky foam. Allow it to gently simmer for 10 minutes to completely separate the layers. Remove from the heat, and let stand for 10 minutes, to allow the foam to solidify. With a spoon, carefully skim off the foam that rises to the surface, and discard. Carefully pour the clear, yellow butter off the milk solids at the bottom of the saucepan and into a glass jar. Discard the milk solids. Refrigerate the butter in an airtight container for up to 3 weeks, or freeze until needed.

fresh horseradish

MAKES 1 CUP

Fresh horseradish root is available in most large supermarkets.

1 14-ounce piece fresh horseradish
   root, peeled
½ tablespoon cider vinegar
1 teaspoon kosher salt
1 tablespoon sugar

Cut the horseradish root into ½-inch pieces. Place in the bowl of a food processor with the vinegar, salt, and sugar. Purée until finely minced and well combined, about 1 minute. Transfer to an airtight container, and refrigerate. The prepared horseradish will keep for up to 2 weeks.

chinese five-spice powder

MAKES ¼ CUP

Though available prepackaged, homemade five-spice powder is far more pungent and flavorful than store-bought. Rub it on fowl, fish, and meat.

10 whole star anise
 1 tablespoon whole Szechuan peppercorns
 1 cinnamon stick
 2 tablespoons whole fennel seeds
 ½ teaspoon whole cloves

1. Place all the ingredients in a small skillet over medium heat, and dry-roast, shaking pan often, until they give off an aroma, about 5 minutes.

2. Combine all the ingredients in a mortar or a spice grinder, and grind to a powder. Store in an airtight container in a cool, dark place.

curry powder

MAKES ¼ CUP

Homemade spice mixtures are more aromatic and flavorful than store-bought. Rub curry powder on poultry, lamb, and beef, or use it to flavor dips, marinades, and spreads. For curry leaves, see Food Sources, page 648.

 2 teaspoons whole coriander seeds
 1 teaspoon whole cumin seeds
 ½ teaspoon whole mustard seeds
 1 teaspoon whole fenugreek seeds
 4 small dried red chiles
 1 teaspoon whole black peppercorns
10 fresh or dried curry leaves, optional
 ½ teaspoon ground ginger
 1 teaspoon ground turmeric

Place all the seeds together in a small skillet over medium heat, and dry-roast, shaking the pan often, until they give off an aroma, about 5 minutes. Combine all the ingredients in a mortar or spice grinder, and grind to a powder. Store in an airtight container in a cool, dark place.

martha's perfect pâte brisée

MAKES TWO 8- TO 10-INCH SINGLE-CRUST PIES
OR ONE 8- TO 10-INCH DOUBLE-CRUST PIE

The pie dough may be made 1 day ahead and refrigerated, well wrapped in plastic, or frozen up to 1 month.

- 2½ cups all-purpose flour, plus more for dusting
- 1 teaspoon kosher salt
- 1 teaspoon sugar
- 1 cup (2 sticks) chilled unsalted butter, cut in pieces
- ¼ to ½ cup ice water

1. Place the flour, salt, and sugar in the bowl of a food processor, and process for a few seconds to combine. Add the butter pieces to the flour mixture, and process until the mixture resembles coarse meal, about 10 seconds. Add the ice water in a slow, steady stream, through the feed tube with the machine running, just until the dough holds together. Do not process for more than 30 seconds.

2. Turn the dough out onto a work surface. Divide into 2 equal pieces, and place on 2 separate sheets of plastic wrap. Flatten, and form two disks. Wrap, and refrigerate at least 1 hour before using.

large-quantity pâte brisée

MAKES FOUR 5-INCH PIES

This recipe make 1½ times Martha's Perfect Pâte Brisée (recipe above).

- 3¾ cups all-purpose flour
- 1½ teaspoons kosher salt
- 1½ teaspoons sugar
- 1½ cups (3 sticks) chilled unsalted butter, cut in pieces
- ½ to ¾ cup ice water

1. Place the flour, salt, and sugar in the bowl of a food processor, and process for a few seconds to combine. Add the butter pieces to the flour mixture, and process until the mixture resembles coarse meal, about 10 seconds. Add the ice water in a slow, steady stream, through the feed tube with the machine running, just until the dough holds together. Do not process for more than 30 seconds.

2. Turn the dough out onto a work surface. Divide into 2 equal pieces, and place on 2 separate sheets of plastic wrap. Flatten, and form two disks. Wrap, and refrigerate at least 1 hour before using.

PERFECT PIECRUST

- *Martha's Perfect Pâte Brisée will also make two 6½-inch double-crust pies: Divide dough into quarters and the filling in half; the baking time is the same.*

- *The amount of water that is required to hold pastry together will vary, depending on the humidity.*

- *Chilling the piecrust before it is baked helps it to keep its shape and gives it a professional look.*

- *Evenly brushing the egg wash over the piecrust results in an evenly browned crust.*

- *Martha likes to use glass pie plates so that she can see whether the bottom crust is done.*

- *Flour, cornstarch, or tapioca can be used to thicken a berry pie.*

- *A fruit filling is usually done when the juices are bubbling.*

- *Bake the pie with a baking sheet underneath the plate to catch overflow from the filling.*

pâte sucrée

This pastry dough may be stored in the freezer for up to 1 month. Defrost by refrigerating overnight or letting stand at room temperature for 1 hour.

- 2½ cups all-purpose flour
- 3 tablespoons sugar
- 1 cup (2 sticks) chilled unsalted butter, cut in pieces
- 2 large egg yolks
- ¼ cup ice water

1. Place the flour and sugar in the bowl of a food processor, and process for a few seconds to combine. Add the butter pieces to the flour mixture, and process until the mixture resembles coarse meal, about 10 seconds. In a small bowl, lightly beat the egg yolks and ice water. Add egg-water in a slow, steady stream through the feed tube, with the machine running, just until the dough holds together. Do not process for more than 30 seconds.

2. Turn the dough out onto a work surface. Divide into 2 equal pieces, and place on 2 sheets of plastic wrap. Flatten, and form two disks. Wrap, and refrigerate at least 1 hour before using.

chocolate crust

MAKES ONE 9-INCH CRUST

- 1¼ cups all-purpose flour
- 2 tablespoons unsweetened cocoa powder
- ⅓ cup sugar
- ½ teaspoon kosher salt
- 6 tablespoons chilled unsalted butter, cut in pieces
- 3 large egg yolks
- ½ teaspoon pure vanilla extract

1. Place the flour, cocoa powder, sugar, and salt in the bowl of a food processor, and process for a few seconds to combine. Add the butter pieces to the flour-cocoa mixture; process until mixture resembles coarse meal, about 10 seconds. Add egg yolks and vanilla in a slow, steady stream through feed tube, with machine running, just until dough holds together. Do not process for more than 30 seconds.

2. Turn the dough out onto a work surface. Form into a disk, wrap in plastic wrap, and chill at least 1 hour before using, or up to 2 days. The dough may be frozen for up to 2 months.

....

DECORATING TECHNIQUES

TO MAKE A CRIMPED EDGE, *line a pie plate with dough. Trim overhang to 1 inch. Using the thumb and forefinger of one hand, push with the thumb of the other hand, crimping; continue around crust. Use the tines of a fork to crimp a single-crust pie and to make a seal for a double crust.*

TO MAKE A BRAIDED EDGE, *cut 12-inch-long, ¼-inch-thick strips of dough; braid them. Brush the crust's edge or the bottom of the braids with water; gently press the braid around the pie plate's rim. Trim.*

TO BLIND BAKE THE CRUST *(prebaking the shell before adding filling), prick the bottom all over with a fork. Line the pastry with parchment paper; fill with pie weights or dried beans. For partially baked crusts, bake until the edges take on color, 15 to 18 minutes. To fully bake the crust, remove the weights and parchment; continue baking until golden brown all over, 8 to 10 minutes.*

TO MAKE DESIGNS ON THE CRUST, *use cookie and aspic cutters, then attach the cutouts to the crust with water.*

TO MAKE A LATTICE TOP, *roll out the crust. Using a fluted pastry wheel, make ½- to ¾-inch-wide strips, about 12 inches long. Lay strips, spaced 1 inch apart, across the filling. Fold back every other strip almost to the edge, then lay a strip perpendicular to them at the folds. Return the folded strips. Fold back the remaining strips; arrange another perpendicular strip. Continue until lattice is formed. Using a fork, seal the strips to the edge.*

FOR A SHINY CRUST, *brush it with a mixture of 1 egg and 2 tablespoons heavy cream.*

....

cookie crust

Fill this crust with Pastry Cream (page 639), top with fresh fruit, and serve.

- 1   cup (2 sticks) unsalted butter, room temperature
- 1   cup sugar
- 1½   tablespoons pure vanilla extract
- 4   large egg yolks
- 2¾   cups all-purpose flour
- ⅛   teaspoon kosher salt

1. In the bowl of an electric mixer fitted with the paddle attachment, cream the butter and sugar until light and fluffy, about 3 minutes. Add the vanilla and egg yolks, one at a time, beating well after each addition. Add the flour and salt; beat until just coming together but still crumbly.

2. Divide the dough in half. If using immediately, press half into a 9-inch tart pan; bake at 350°F until golden, about 30 minutes. Alternatively, wrap each half in plastic wrap; refrigerate until ready to use.

cream cheese dough

- 8   tablespoons (1 stick) unsalted butter, room temperature
- 1   cup sugar
- 1   large egg
- 3   ounces cream cheese (⅓ cup plus 1 tablespoon plus 1 teaspoon), room temperature
- 2   tablespoons buttermilk
- 1   teaspoon pure vanilla extract
- 3   cups all-purpose flour
- ¼   teaspoon baking soda
- 1   teaspoon baking powder
    Grated zest of 1 lemon
- ½   teaspoon kosher salt

1. In the bowl of an electric mixer fitted with the paddle attachment, combine the butter and the sugar. Beat on medium speed until light and fluffy, about 5 minutes. Add the egg to the sugar-butter mixture, and beat just until blended.

2. Add the cream cheese, buttermilk, and vanilla extract, and beat until well combined. Combine the flour, baking soda, baking powder, lemon zest, and salt, and add to the cream-cheese mixture. Beat until completely blended. Transfer the dough to a piece of plastic wrap, and, using your hands, press the dough into a 1-inch-thick disk, wrap well, and refrigerate for at least 1 hour before using. If preparing ahead of time, the dough can be stored at this point for up to 1 month in the freezer.

herbed pastry dough

This dough can be used for any savory tart.

- 1¼   cups all-purpose flour
- ½   teaspoon kosher salt
- 8   tablespoons (1 stick) chilled unsalted butter, cut in pieces
- 1   tablespoon fresh thyme or 1 teaspoon dried
- 1   small shallot, minced
- 3   tablespoons ice water

1. In the bowl of a food processor, combine the flour and salt. Add the butter; process for 10 seconds, or until the mixture resembles coarse meal. Add thyme and shallot; process a few seconds more.

2. With the machine running, add the water little by little, until the dough just holds together. Form into a flat disk, and wrap in plastic wrap. Chill until firm, at least 30 minutes.

puff pastry

This dough may be made in advance and frozen after the fourth turn for up to 2 months. The final two turns of the dough should be completed immediately before using.

- 2¾ cups all-purpose flour, plus more for dusting
- 1 cup plus 2 tablespoons cake flour (not self-rising)
- 1 teaspoon kosher salt
- 1 pound (4 sticks) very cold unsalted butter
- 1 tablespoon fresh lemon juice

1. Combine 2½ cups all-purpose flour, the cake flour, and salt in a medium bowl. Cut 1 stick butter into small pieces. Add with the lemon juice to the flour mixture; cut in the butter with a pastry cutter or two knives until the mixture resembles coarse meal. Gradually mix in up to 1 cup ice water, until the dough just comes together. Pat the dough into a 6-inch square; wrap in plastic. Chill 30 minutes.

2. Cut the remaining 3 sticks of butter into bits. Sprinkle with the remaining ¼ cup flour; mix together by rubbing against a cold work surface with the heel of your hand. Form into a 5½-inch square; wrap in plastic. Chill 15 minutes.

3. On a lightly floured surface, roll the chilled dough into a 6 x 18-inch rectangle with the short side facing you; place the chilled butter mixture in the center. Fold the top third of the dough over the butter mixture, and the bottom third of the dough over the top third. Seal the edges by pressing the dough with your fingers.

4. Turn the dough packet over so the overlapped section is on the bottom. Roll into a 6 x 18-inch rectangle (do not allow the butter to come through the dough). Fold in thirds, as before. Rotate 90° (one quarter turn); roll again into a 6 x 18-inch rectangle; fold in thirds. Press 2 fingers into the dough to indicate the completion of 2 turns. Wrap in plastic; chill 30 minutes.

5. Repeat the rolling-out process in step 4, rotating the dough 90° before beginning. Mark with 4 fingers, signifying the completion of 4 turns; chill 30 minutes. The dough may be wrapped and frozen at this point.

6. Remove the dough from refrigerator (if dough has been frozen, thaw overnight in the refrigerator). Give the dough its final 2 turns by repeating the rolling-out process in step 4, again rotating it 90°. before rolling it out. The dough should be used immediately after the sixth turn is completed.

quick puff pastry

- 1¾ cups all-purpose flour, plus more for dusting
- 2 cups cake flour (not self-rising)
- 1 teaspoon kosher salt
- 1 pound (4 sticks) chilled unsalted butter, cut in pieces
- 1 to 1¼ cups ice water
- 2 tablespoons fresh lemon juice

1. Sift together the all-purpose flour, cake flour, and salt into a large chilled bowl. Cut in the pieces of butter using a pastry knife until the butter is in very small lumps, about ½ inch in diameter.

2. Combine the ice water and the lemon juice, and stir into the flour mixture, a little at a time, pressing the dough together with your hands until it comes together.

3. Turn the dough out onto a well-floured surface, and roll it into a ½-inch-thick rough rectangle, approximately 12 x 18 inches. The dough will be very crumbly. Fold the bottom of the rectangle toward the center, then the top of the rectangle toward the center, overlapping the bottom third, like a letter, and give the dough a quarter turn to the right. Roll the dough into a large rectangle, ½ inch thick, and fold into thirds again. This completes the first double turn. Using a dry pastry brush, brush any excess flour from the dough. Repeat the rolling, folding, and turning process two more times to execute another double turn, refrigerating the dough for a few minutes if the butter becomes too warm. Wrap the dough in plastic wrap, and put in refrigerator to chill for 1 hour.

4. Remove the chilled dough from the refrigerator. Repeat the rolling, folding, and turning process again to execute one more double turn. There will be six turns in all. The dough needs to be rolled out to a ½-inch-thick rectangle each time. With each turn, the dough will become smoother and easier to handle. Store the dough, wrapped well in plastic, in the refrigerator for up to 2 days or in the freezer for 3 months.

choux pastry puffs

MAKES ABOUT 2½ DOZEN

Also called pâte à choux, this pastry is used to make cream puffs and profiteroles. Unfilled, cooked puffs may be made up to 3 weeks ahead and frozen in resealable plastic bags. When ready to use, defrost and warm in a 350°F oven for 3 minutes until crisp. Properly prepared choux pastry is slightly shiny and somewhat sticky. On humid days, you may need to reduce the number of eggs in order to achieve the right consistency. To test the pastry, run a wooden spoon down the middle of the dough; it should form a trough that quickly closes in on itself.

4 tablespoons unsalted butter, cut in pieces

Pinch of kosher salt

½ cup all-purpose flour

3 large whole eggs

1 large egg white

1. Preheat the oven to 375°F. Line a baking sheet with parchment paper; set aside. Combine the butter, salt, and ½ cup water in a small saucepan, and place over medium heat. Cook until the butter is melted and the water just comes to a boil.

2. Remove from heat, add flour, and stir rapidly with a wooden spoon. Return pan to heat; cook, stirring constantly, until the mixture comes together and pulls away from the sides of the saucepan as you stir, about 5 minutes. Remove the saucepan from the heat, and let cool for 5 minutes.

3. Add the eggs one at a time, beating vigorously until they are completely incorporated and the pastry is smooth. Transfer the pastry to a pastry bag fitted with a small coupler. Pipe about ½ tablespoon of the pastry into a mound on the prepared baking sheet; continue piping until all the pastry is used, spacing pastry about 1½ inches apart. Combine the egg white with 1 tablespoon water to make an egg wash, and brush the top of each mound with the egg wash. Smooth any rough spots on the top with the brush or a water-dampened finger. Bake until the puffs are golden brown all over, about 30 minutes. Remove from the oven, and transfer to a wire rack to cool completely.

DESSERT BASICS

sabayon

SERVES 12

This sabayon is lightened by the addition of chilled whipped cream at the end, which gives the sauce more volume. If you prefer a traditional sabayon (which will serve six people), omit the last step.

- 5 *large egg yolks*
   Pinch of kosher salt
- ¼ *cup plus 2 tablespoons sugar*
- 1 *cup Muscat de Beaumes-de-Venise, or other good-quality sweet dessert wine*
- ¾ *cup heavy cream*
- 2 *teaspoons fresh lemon juice*

1. Prepare an ice-water bath, and set aside. Fill a medium saucepan with 2 inches of water. Set over medium heat, and bring to simmer.

2. In a large stainless-steel bowl, whisk together the egg yolks, salt, and sugar until very pale. Add the Muscat; whisk to combine.

3. Transfer the yolk mixture to the top of a double boiler or a heat-proof bowl set over the pan of simmering water. Whisk together until the sabayon thickens and is fluffy and slightly stiff and has tripled in volume, about 6 minutes. The sabayon should begin to look satiny and start sticking to the bowl slightly. The air bubbles will become very fine, instead of large and loose. Remove the mixture from the heat, and immediately transfer to the ice-water bath. Whisk until chilled.

4. In a large bowl, whip the heavy cream until soft peaks form. Add the lemon juice, and whip until incorporated. Fold the whipped cream into the chilled sabayon. Serve the sauce on top of, or on the side of, the dessert.

pastry cream

MAKES 3 CUPS

This will fill two 9-inch tart shells, three 3 x 14-inch rectangles, or up to four dozen 3-inch tartlets. It can be made ahead and chilled for up to 3 days.

- 2 *large whole eggs*
- 2 *large egg yolks*
- ¾ *cup sugar*
- ¼ *cup plus 2 tablespoons cornstarch*
- 2 *cups milk*
- ½ *vanilla bean, split lengthwise and scraped or 1½ teaspoons pure vanilla extract*
- 3 *tablespoons unsalted butter, cut in tablespoons*

1. Combine the eggs, yolks, and ½ cup sugar in the bowl of an electric mixer fitted with the whisk attachment. Beat on medium-high speed until the mixture is pale yellow and thick, about 5 minutes. Turn off the machine. Sift in the cornstarch; beat on medium-low speed until combined, scraping down the sides of the bowl with a rubber spatula.

2. Prepare an ice-water bath; set aside. Combine the milk, the remaining ¼ cup of sugar, and the vanilla bean and seed scrapings in a medium saucepan, and bring to a boil. Remove from the heat, and discard the vanilla bean. Whisking constantly, slowly pour half of the hot milk mixture into the egg mixture; whisk until smooth. Pour the mixture back into the saucepan with the remaining hot milk. Set over medium heat, and whisk until the mixture reaches the consistency of pudding, 2 to 3 minutes.

3. Transfer the mixture to a large bowl. Add the butter 1 tablespoon at a time, stirring until melted and incorporated after each addition. Place the bowl over the ice bath, stirring occasionally, until chilled. Cover the surface of the pastry cream with plastic wrap to prevent a skin from forming; let chill overnight or at least 1½ hours before using.

cognac pastry cream

MAKES 3 1/3 CUPS

9   large egg yolks
¾   cup sugar
¼   cup plus 1½ teaspoons all-purpose flour
3   cups milk
¾   teaspoon pure vanilla extract
3   tablespoons cognac

1. In the bowl of an electric mixer fitted with the paddle attachment, combine the yolks and sugar, and beat on medium high until the mixture is pale yellow and thick, 2 to 3 minutes. Reduce speed to low, and add the flour; beat to combine.

2. Meanwhile, bring the milk just to a boil in a saucepan over medium-high heat. With machine running on medium low, slowly pour half the hot milk into the egg mixture to warm the yolks; beat until smooth. Pour mixture back into the saucepan over medium heat. Whisk until the mixture comes to a boil, 6 to 8 minutes. Transfer to a large bowl. Stir in the vanilla and cognac. Let cool. Cover the surface of the pastry cream with plastic wrap to prevent a skin from forming; place in the refrigerator to chill. The pastry cream will keep, tightly wrapped, for up to 3 days in the refrigerator.

lemon curd

MAKES 1 1/2 CUPS

This makes enough curd to fill a 6- or 7-inch double layer cake. It is delicious spread between the layers of a delicate chiffon cake or with sweet, fluffy meringue.

4   large egg yolks
2   large whole eggs
¾   cup sugar
½   cup fresh lemon juice
4   tablespoons unsalted butter, cut in pieces
    Grated zest of 2 lemons

1. Whisk together the egg yolks and the eggs in a medium bowl. Combine with the sugar and lemon juice in a small, heavy-bottomed saucepan. Cook over low heat, stirring constantly with a wooden spoon, until the mixture coats the back of a spoon, 8 to 10 minutes.

2. Remove the pan from the heat, and stir to cool slightly. If the mixture is at all lumpy, strain through a fine sieve into a medium bowl, and add the butter, a piece at a time, stirring until smooth. Stir in the zest. Cover surface with plastic wrap to prevent skin from forming. Let cool completely before using. Curd may be refrigerated for up to 4 days.

large-quantity lemon curd filling

MAKES 3 1/3 CUPS, ENOUGH TO FILL A 4-LAYER CAKE

This recipe makes a nice thick curd for filling layer cakes. It may be made 1 day ahead and refrigerated.

12   large egg yolks
     Grated zest of 2 lemons
1   cup fresh lemon juice (about 6 lemons)
1½   cups sugar
1   cup (2 sticks) chilled unsalted butter, cut in pieces

1. Combine yolks, lemon zest and juice, and sugar in a heavy-bottomed saucepan. Cook over low heat; stir constantly with a wooden spoon until the mixture coats the back of a spoon, 8 to 10 minutes.

2. Remove the saucepan from the heat. If the mixture is at all lumpy, strain through a fine sieve into a medium bowl. Add the butter, one piece at a time, stirring with a wooden spoon to incorporate into a smooth mixture. Transfer to a medium bowl, cover the surface with plastic wrap to prevent a skin from forming, and place in the refrigerator until firm and chilled, at least 1 hour.

lime curd

MAKES 3 CUPS

This recipe makes enough lime curd to fill two 9-inch tart shells, three 3 x 14-inch rectangles, or up to four dozen 3-inch tartlets. The curd can be refrigerated for up to 4 days.

- 8 *large egg yolks*
- 2 *large whole eggs*
- 2 *cups sugar*
- 1 *cup fresh lime juice, strained (about 10 limes)*
- 1 *cup (2 sticks) unsalted butter, cut in tablespoons*
- 2 *tablespoons grated lime zest, optional*

1. Whisk together the egg yolks and whole eggs in a nonreactive saucepan. Add the sugar and lime juice; whisk to combine.

2. Cook over low heat, stirring constantly with a wooden spoon, until the mixture thickens to almost puddinglike consistency, about 30 minutes. Remove from the heat; transfer to a heat-proof bowl. Stir in the butter one piece at a time, until fully incorporated. Stir in the lime zest, if using.

3. If not using immediately, cover the surface of the curd with plastic wrap to prevent a skin from forming, and refrigerate until ready to use.

caramel sauce two ways

Making caramel is actually quite simple. To make this sweet elixir at home, you can use one of two methods: dry or wet. The dry method includes placing the sugar directly in the pan and heating it until the sugar turns into a liquid and darkens. This method requires constant stirring, or the sugar can go from just melted to burned in an instant. The wet method is safer for those new to caramel-making. Sugar is combined with a liquid (usually water) and heated until the sugar dissolves. The risk of this method is recrystallization, which occurs when undissolved crystals of sugar are reintroduced to the sugar syrup (usually in the form of stray sugar crystals that have adhered to the side of the pan or on a stirring utensil). To avoid this, it is important not to stir the mixture once it is fully dissolved, but rather to swirl it in the pan and brush down the sides of the pan with a wet pastry brush. The caramel sauce may be kept, refrigerated in an airtight container, up to 1 week. Let the sauce return to room temperature before using; it may be gently warmed over very low heat in a small saucepan.

caramel sauce—dry method

MAKES 1 1/4 CUPS

- 1½ *cups sugar*
- 1 *vanilla bean, split lengthwise and scraped*

1. In a large heavy skillet, spread the sugar in an even layer over medium-high heat. Add the vanilla bean and seed scrapings. Without stirring, let cook until the outer edges of the sugar melt and begin to turn golden, about 5 minutes.

2. With a wooden spoon, slowly stir together the melted and unmelted sugar until all the sugar is melted, clear, and golden. At arm's length, carefully pour in 1 cup water while stirring rapidly. Continue stirring until the mixture has melted completely. Transfer to a bowl to cool, about 1 hour. Discard the vanilla pod. May be made 1 day ahead and kept at room temperature in an airtight container.

caramel sauce—wet method

MAKES 1 CUP

¾ cup boiling water
1 cup sugar
  Dash of pure vanilla extract
1 teaspoon cognac

Combine ¼ cup boiling water and sugar in a medium saucepan. Cook on high until sugar dissolves. Once dissolved, do not stir; let cook until caramel forms, brushing down sides of pan with a damp pastry brush as needed to keep crystals from forming, about 5 minutes. Remove from heat, and slowly whisk in remaining ½ cup boiling water at arm's length, being careful not to splatter the hot caramel. Remove from the heat, and stir in vanilla and cognac. Caramel sauce may be used warm or at room temperature.

....

MAKING CARAMEL

Caramel is sugar that has been taken just to the edge of burning. Caramel's color reveals the extent to which it is cooked. The palest form is just concentrated sugar syrup. The next stage is golden, followed by amber and dark. For most culinary purposes, amber is the color of choice for its deep golden hue and nutty, sweet flavor.

....

caramel bourbon vanilla sauce

MAKES 2 CUPS

2 cups sugar
1 cup heavy cream
1 vanilla bean, split lengthwise and scraped
2 teaspoons fresh lemon juice
2 tablespoons unsalted butter
1 tablespoon bourbon

1. Combine the sugar and ½ cup water in a 2-quart saucepan over medium heat. Without stirring, cook the mixture until dark amber in color, swirling the pan carefully while cooking, about 20 minutes.

2. Reduce the heat to low. Slowly add the cream, stirring with a wooden spoon. Scrape the vanilla seeds into the pan, and add the pod. Add the lemon juice, butter, and bourbon. Stir to combine.

3. Cover, and store, refrigerated, for up to 1 week. Bring the sauce to room temperature, or warm over low heat, and discard pod before using.

swiss meringue for pies

MAKES ENOUGH FOR HIGH TOPPING FOR ONE PIE OR LOW TOPPING FOR TWO PIES

This fluffy cooked meringue makes the best pie topping. It is easiest to beat the mixture with an electric mixer fitted with the whisk attachment.

7 large egg whites
¾ cup sugar
¼ teaspoon kosher salt

Combine the egg whites, sugar, and salt in a heatproof bowl. Set over a pan of simmering water; beat with a whisk until warm and the sugar is dissolved. Remove the bowl from the heat; beat until stiff peaks form. Use immediately.

swiss meringue

MAKES 4 CUPS

This meringue works well for piping shapes. Using the whisk attachment to beat egg whites in the final stage works best; warming the egg whites helps dissolve the sugar, giving the meringue greater volume.

- 4 *large egg whites, room temperature*
- 1 *cup sugar*
  Pinch of cream of tartar
- ½ *teaspoon pure vanilla extract*

1. Fill a medium saucepan one-quarter full with water. Set the saucepan over medium heat, and bring the water to a simmer.

2. Combine egg whites, sugar, and cream of tartar in the heat-proof bowl of an electric mixer; place over saucepan. Whisk constantly until the sugar is dissolved and the whites are warm to the touch, 3 to 3½ minutes. Test by rubbing mixture between your fingers to ensure that no sugar remains.

3. Attach the bowl to the electric mixer fitted with the whisk attachment, and beat, starting on low speed and gradually increasing to high until stiff, glossy peaks form, about 10 minutes. Add the vanilla, and mix until combined. Use the meringue according to the instructions in the recipes.

candied lemon, orange, or grapefruit peel

MAKES 1½ CUPS

You can use the same technique to make candied lemon or orange peel. The technique for candied grapefruit peel is slightly different (as detailed below) because more pith—the bitter white layer between the outer peel and the flesh of citrus fruit—must be removed.

- 8 *oranges, or 10 lemons, or 6 grapefruits*
- 6 *cups sugar, plus more for rolling*

1. Cut ends off each piece of fruit, and cut fruit in half lengthwise. Insert the tip of a knife carefully between fruit and pith about ½ inch deep, turn fruit on other end, and repeat, following the shape of fruit and keeping skin in one piece.

2. Using your fingers, gently pull the fruit away. Reserve the fruit for another use.

3. Place the citrus peel in a 6-quart pot, and fill with enough cold water to cover, about 3 quarts. Place the pot over medium heat; bring to a boil. Reduce the heat; simmer for the 20 minutes. Drain the citrus peel, and soak in cold water until cool enough to handle, about 5 minutes.

4. Using a melon baller, scrape the soft white pith from the peel, being careful not to tear or cut into the skin. If you're making candied grapefruit, after scraping the pith from the peel, simmer the peel for 20 minutes more, and repeat the technique to remove the remaining pith.

5. Slice each piece of peel into thin strips lengthwise, about ¼ inch wide if garnishing a cake or ⅜ inch wide if rolling in sugar.

6. Place 6 cups sugar in a saucepan with 3 cups water; stir to combine. Place the pan over medium heat, stirring occasionally until all the sugar has dissolved and syrup comes to a boil, about 8 minutes. Add the citrus strips to the boiling syrup; reduce heat to medium low. Using a pastry brush dipped in cold water, wash down any sugar crystals that form on the sides of the pan. Simmer the strips until they become translucent and the sugar syrup thickens, about 40 minutes. Allow the strips to cool in the syrup for 3 hours or overnight. When they have cooled, proceed to step 7, or store the strips in the syrup in an airtight container, refrigerated, for up to 3 weeks.

7. When the strips and syrup are cool, remove the strips with a slotted spoon. Using your fingers, wipe off the excess syrup, and roll the strips in sugar. Dry on racks.

NOTE *There are two variations of this method. In the first, use a vegetable peeler to remove only the outer skin from the fruit, and skip the first five steps. Slice the peels to the desired width, simmer in sugar syrup as in step 6, then follow the remaining step. This technique produces thin, translucent peels that make great garnishes for ice cream and cakes. The second variation results in wider, more opaque peels: After the outer skin has been removed from the fruit, slice the skin into strips of the desired thickness. Place the strips in the pot of boiling water for 1 minute, drain, and place in sugar syrup as in step 6; follow remaining step.*

lemon sugar
MAKES ABOUT 1 POUND

Because this sugar lasts so long, you can make it well in advance; you can also use this technique with other citrus fruit, such as limes or oranges.

Zest of 3 lemons
2 cups sugar

1. In the bowl of a food processor, combine the lemon zest and 1 cup sugar. Pulse until the zest has been finely ground, about 3 minutes.

2. Transfer the ground mixture to a medium bowl. Add the remaining cup sugar; toss to evenly mix.

3. Spread the lemon sugar on a baking pan, and let sit at room temperature until dry, about 1 hour. Store the sugar in an airtight container in a cool, dry place up to 1 month.

TECHNIQUES

TOASTING NUTS

Toasting not only crisps nuts; it also releases their essential oils, bringing out their fullest flavor. The easiest way to toast just about any kind of nuts is to place them on a single layer on a baking pan, and place in a 350° F oven until they are golden and aromatic, 8 to 12 minutes. Shake the pan halfway through baking to make sure the nuts toast evenly.

PEELING HAZELNUTS

Toasting hazelnuts brings out their fullest flavor and helps to loosen their bitter, papery skins, which are then removed. Preheat the oven to 350°F. Place the hazelnuts in a single layer in a baking pan; toast until the skins begin to split, about 10 minutes. Rub the warm nuts vigorously with a clean kitchen towel to remove the skins. Return to the pan; toast until fragrant and golden brown, 1 minute more. Let cool.

TOASTING SEEDS

Toasting whole seeds releases their flavor, adding a dimension to recipes that raw seeds do not. Although some recipes call for oil, we prefer to dry-toast the seeds, so no additional fat is added and the flavors of the toasted seeds remain clean and fresh.

To toast seeds, heat a heavy skillet, such as cast iron, over medium-low heat. Add the seeds, and shake the skillet gently to move the seeds around so they toast evenly and do not burn. Toast the seeds until they are aromatic and barely take on color. Allow them to cool slightly, and use as indicated in the recipe. Often, seeds are transferred to a spice grinder and pulsed into a fine powder.

PEELING FRESH CHESTNUTS

To peel fresh chestnuts, score the flat side on each with an "x." Simmer the chestnuts in water until the scored end on each begins to open, or roast on a baking pan in a 350°F oven until the shells begin to curl. Using a paring knife, remove the shells and skins while chestnuts are hot. Fresh chestnuts are available in the fall.

WORKING WITH FRESH AND DRIED PEPPERS

The complex flavor of peppers is released by using different cooking methods. The more you work with them, the more flavor and character they will add to your food. Fresh peppers can be either sweet (like bell peppers) or hot (like jalapeños), and come in a great range of colors. The smaller the pepper, the hotter it will be, so be careful. When chopping peppers, it is a good idea to wear plastic gloves, since the flesh and seeds can burn. The following preparations will make almost any dish more interesting.

ROASTING FRESH PEPPERS

Fresh large peppers, both hot and sweet, have a tough, transparent outer skin that should be removed unless they are served raw. The easiest way to loosen the skins is by charring them over a gas burner or under the broiler. Peppers may be roasted, peeled, seeded, and the ribs removed as described below 1 or 2 days in advance of their use in a recipe. Roasted peppers may be covered with olive oil and refrigerated for up to 1 week. Drain the olive oil from the peppers before using. If storing roasted peppers without oil, wrap them tightly in plastic wrap in an airtight container, and refrigerate for up to 3 days.

To roast fresh peppers: Place the peppers directly on the trivet of a gas-stove burner over high heat or on a grill. Just as each section turns puffy and black, turn the pepper with tongs to prevent overcooking. (If you don't have a gas stove, place the peppers on a baking pan, and broil in the oven, turning as each side becomes charred.) Transfer the peppers to a large bowl, and cover immediately with plastic wrap. The juices, which can be added to the liquid component of the recipe for deeper flavor, will collect in the bowl. Let the peppers sweat until they are cool enough to handle, approximately 15 minutes. The steam will help to loosen the skins. Transfer the pep-

pers to a work surface. (If you have sensitive skin, wear thin plastic gloves when handling the peppers.) Peel off the blackened skin and discard. There may be bits of charred skin that are not easily peeled away; it is fine to leave them. Refrain from rinsing the peeled peppers—it dilutes the smoky flavor of the charred peppers. Halve the peppers, and open them flat out on the work surface. Use the blade of a paring knife to remove the seeds and the hard seed cluster at the top. Remove the ribs. Slice each pepper according to recipe instructions.

TOASTING DRIED CHILES

Toasting dried chiles helps bring out their flavor and their heat. Place the chile peppers in a dry skillet over medium heat. Toast on both sides until slightly browned and aromatic. Remove from the heat, and allow to cool. Slit the chiles open, and discard the stems and seeds.

MAKING A PASTE FROM DRIED CHILES

Store dried chile peppers in a glass jar, out of the sun, or in a brown paper bag in the bottom of the refrigerator. Before using, rinse and pat each pepper dry.

1. Toast the peppers (see above).

2 . Transfer the peppers to a heat-proof bowl. Pour very hot water over the peppers to just cover. Let the peppers soak until they are softened and rehydrated, 20 to 30 minutes.

3. Strain the soaking liquid, and reserve it for cooking. Transfer peppers to a paper towel to dry.

4. Wear thin plastic gloves to handle all hot peppers. Cut open each pepper, lengthwise. Remove the seeds, veins, and stem from the inside of each pepper with a paring knife.

5. Scrape along the inside of each rehydrated pepper to remove the soft flesh. Place the flesh in a small dish, and mash it to form a soft paste for use in cooking. Use right away, or cover it with plastic wrap, and keep refrigerated. Use within 2 days.

ROASTING GARLIC

Roasting garlic turns its pungent flesh into a mildly sweet, buttery treat. Garlic heads differ greatly in size, but a medium-size head will yield about 2 tablespoons of purée.

To make roasted garlic, preheat the oven to 400°F. Cut about ½ inch from the top of a garlic head, just enough to expose the cloves. Place head of garlic in a small ovenproof baking dish, and drizzle it lightly with ½ teaspoon olive oil; cover with foil. Roast until soft and golden brown and the tip of a knife easily pierces the flesh, 30 to 45 minutes. Using either your hands or the dull edge of a large knife, squeeze the cloves out of their skins and into a small bowl. Discard the papery skins. Using a fork, mash the cloves together until smooth. Use the roasted garlic immediately, or store in an airtight container in the refrigerator for up to 3 days.

PURÉEING GARLIC

Separate the garlic cloves from 1 head of garlic, and peel them. Place the cloves in the bowl of a food processor. Process until chopped to the desired consistency, chunky or smooth. Transfer puréed garlic to an airtight glass or plastic jar, and cover with olive oil. This mixture will keep, refrigerated in an airtight container, for up to 1 week.

CARAMELIZING ONIONS

To make 1 cup of caramelized onions, heat 1 tablespoon butter and 1 tablespoon olive oil in a medium skillet over medium-low heat. Slice 2 medium onions (about 1½ pounds) into ⅛-inch rounds, add to pan, and cook until they begin to soften, stirring occasionally, about 15 minutes. Add 1 teaspoon sugar, ½ teaspoon salt, and ⅛ teaspoon pepper, raise heat slightly, and cook until golden brown, stirring occasionally, about 30 minutes. Serve warm.

CLEANING LEEKS

A member of the allium family, the leek is the restrained, shy relative of onions and garlic—far less pungent, but no less flavorful. Available year-round in most parts of the country, leeks vary enormously in size; the smaller the leek, the more tender the stalk. Before using, trim the tiny roots that hang off the root end, and trim the thick leaf end. Leeks grow into the soil, so they retain lots of dirt in their layers and leaves. Always wash them thoroughly before proceeding with a recipe.

The best way to ensure that every bit of dirt is washed from leeks is to cut them first into the size that is called for in the recipe. Generally they are halved lengthwise first, then sliced crosswise into ¼-inch-thick pieces. Transfer the leek pieces to a large bowl of cold water, stir, and let stand for 5 minutes to let any dirt and sand settle to the bottom. Lift the leeks out of the water using a slotted spoon, and drain them on paper towels.

FREEZING FRESH HERBS

Wash and pat dry fresh parsley or basil; remove the stems. Chop fine in the bowl of a food processor; slowly add olive oil until the mixture becomes a paste. Spoon the herb paste into the wells of a clean ice-cube tray and freeze. Transfer the frozen cubes to resealable plastic freezer bags, and use in tomato sauce, soups, or stews.

MAKING YOGURT CHEESE

Plain yogurt can undergo a delicious transformation overnight: It becomes yogurt cheese, which has the texture of soft cheese with yogurt's pleasant tang. To make it, wrap plain yogurt (low-fat is better than nonfat) in a double layer of cheesecloth, and suspend it over a bowl or sink, or simply place the yogurt in a cheesecloth-lined sieve or colander set over a bowl. Cover and refrigerate for at least 12 hours to let the whey drain out. The yogurt cheese will keep for 3 to 4 days, tightly wrapped, in the refrigerator. Serve it on toast, mixed with herbs as a dip, or spooned on a baked potato.

MAKING BREAD CRUMBS

Bread crumbs have two very appealing characteristics: They are simple to make, and they are an economical use of odds and ends of unsweetened breads. Keep fresh unused bread in a resealable plastic storage bag until you have a few handfuls' worth.

Bread crumbs can be either fresh or dried. For fresh, simply remove the crusts from the bread, place the bread in the bowl of a food processor, and process until fine. For dried bread crumbs, toast the bread in a 250°F oven until fully dried out, 12 to 15 minutes. Let the bread cool, and process until fine. Store in an airtight container in the refrigerator for up to 1 week or in the freezer up to 6 months. Never use stale bread to make bread crumbs: They will taste that way—stale. Bread crumbs can also be made from darker breads. These somewhat earthier crumbs add interesting flavor to gratins and breaded meats.

RECONSTITUTING DRIED MUSHROOMS

Dried mushrooms are essential in a well-stocked pantry. They should be stored in a cool, dry place and used within 6 months. To rehydrate, place the mushrooms in a heat-proof bowl, and cover with 1 inch of boiling water. Let stand for 20 minutes. The mushrooms should be soft and tender. Don't discard the soaking liquid; it is intensely flavorful and can be added to soups and sauces.

TOASTING SHREDDED COCONUT

Place the coconut in a single layer in a baking pan, and toast in a 350°F oven until lightly golden and aromatic, 6 to 8 minutes. Shake the pan halfway through baking to make sure the coconut toasts evenly.

PEELING AND PITTING MANGOS

The best way to determine whether a mango is ripe is to sniff the stem end; it should be fragrant and sweet-smelling. Choose mangos with taut skins that show some yellow and red and give slightly when pressed.

Using a sharp paring knife, cut a thin slice off the bottom of the mango to create a flat surface. Stand the mango on a cutting board, stem-side up. Beginning at the stem, run the knife to the bottom of the mango, following the contour of the fruit and trimming away the skin. Shaped like a flattened oval, the mango has two soft cheeks, which run from the top to the bottom of the fruit. To trim the fleshy cheeks away, place the knife at the top of the mango, slightly off center. Slice off one of the rounded cheeks in a clean, single cut, running the knife along the pit as you cut (some of the flesh will cling to the pit). Repeat on the other side.

PITTING AND SKINNING AVOCADOS

We all have to get our hands dirty at times, but not when it comes to skinning an avocado. Select avocados that are tender and slightly soft when pressed gently. If only firm avocados are available, buy them 3 days ahead so they have time to ripen. Cutting to the pit with an 8-inch chef's knife, slice all the way around the middle of the avocado. Twist the top half off. With a short, sharp, but careful chopping motion, embed the knife in the pit; remove the pit from the flesh. Scoop the flesh from the skin with a serving spoon.

food sources

ALMOND FLOUR A.L. Bazzini Company, Dean & DeLuca

AMARETTI COOKIES Dean & DeLuca, Salumeria Italiana

ANCHO CHILE PEPPERS, DRIED Kitchen/Market, Penzeys Spices

BACON, CORNCOB SMOKED North-country Smokehouse

BANH PHO RICE NOODLES Temple of Thai

BLACK CURRANT PURÉE The Perfect Purée of Napa Valley

BONITO FLAKES Chefshop.com

BRESAOLA Zingerman's Delicatessen

CARDAMOM PODS, GREEN Penzeys Spices

CARNAROLI RICE Salumeria Italiana

CAVIAR Russ & Daughters, Browne Trading Company

CHAMOMILE FLOWERS, DRIED Frontier Natural Products Co-op

CHILE PASTE Kitchen/Market

CHINESE FIVE-SPICE POWDER Penzeys Spices

CHIPOTLE CHILE PEPPERS, DRIED Kitchen/Market, Penzeys Spices

CITRIC ACID New York Cake & Baking Distributor

COCONUT, UNSWEETENED Uptown Whole Foods, Kitchen/Market

CORNICHONS Zingerman's Delicatessen

CRAB BOIL SEASONING CMC, Obrycki's Crab House and Seafood Restaurant

CRYSTAL SUGAR King Arthur Flour Baker's Catalog

CURRY LEAVES, DRIED AND FRESH Adriana's Caravan

DUMPLING WRAPPERS (SKINS) Katagiri & Co., Uwajimaya

ECHINACEA Frontier Natural Products Co-op

EDIBLE WAFER PAPER New York Cake & Baking Distributor

FENUGREEK Penzeys Spices

FOOD COLORING (GEL AND PASTE) New York Cake & Baking Distributor

FREGOLA PASTA (SARDINIAN PASTA) Dean & DeLuca

GALANGAL Penzeys Spices

GOLDENSEAL, DRIED Frontier Natural Products Co-op

GOOSE FAT Dean & DeLuca

GUAJILLO CHILES Kitchen/Market

HAM, COUNTRY CURED Basse's Choice

HARISSA Kitchen/Market

HERBAL TEAS, EASTERN AND FRENCH Takashimaya

ISRAELI COUSCOUS Kalustyan's

JUNIPER BERRIES Adriana's Caravan

KEY LIMES (FRESH) The Showcase of Citrus

KEY LIME JUICE The Showcase of Citrus

KOMBU SEAWEED Asian Food Grocer

LEMONS, PRESERVED (ALSO CALLED MOROCCAN PRESERVED LEMONS) Dean & DeLuca

LICORICE ROOT, DRIED Frontier Natural Products Co-op

MACE (BLADES) CMC Company

MANGOS, DRIED A.L. Bazzini Company

MASA HARINA, DRIED Kitchen/Market

MASCARPONE CHEESE Dean & DeLuca

MERINGUE POWDER New York Cake & Baking Distributor

MUSHROOMS, WILD; DRIED AND FRESH Urbani Truffles USA

MUSTARD SEEDS, BROWN AND BLACK Dean & DeLuca, Adriana's Caravan, Penzeys Spices

ORANGE-BLOSSOM WATER Kalustyan's

PAPRIKA, HOT Adriana's Caravan, Penzeys Spices

PARMA HAM, COOKED Dean & DeLuca

PEPPERMINT LEAVES, DRIED Frontier Natural Products Co-op

PEPPERS, DRIED CHILE (CASCABEL, PEQUIN, MORA) Kitchen/Market

PICKLING LIME Rafal Spice Company

PINK PEPPERCORNS Penzeys Spices

POMEGRANATE SEEDS, DRIED Adriana's Caravan

POMEGRANATE SYRUP Sultan's Delight

POPCORN RICE Uptown Whole Foods

RED CURRY Adriana's Caravan

RICE NOODLES, DRIED AND FLAT Temple of Thai

RUSTICHELLA D'ABRUZZO PASTA Dean & DeLuca

RYE FLOUR King Arthur Flour Baker's Catalog

SARDINIAN PASTA (FREGOLA PASTA) Dean & DeLuca

SAUSAGES Schaller and Weber, D'Artagnan

SEA SALT Zingerman's Delicatessen

SEASONED RICE VINEGAR Kalustyan's

SEMOLINA King Arthur Flour Baker's Catalog

SHRIMP, DRIED ImportFood.com

SLIPPERY ELM, DRIED Frontier Natural Products Co-op

SOMEN NOODLES Asian Food Grocer

SOPRESSATA Zingerman's Delicatessen

STONE-GROUND GRITS Hoppin' John's

SUGAR, AMBER King Arthur Flour Baker's Catalog

SUGAR, MAPLE Dean & DeLuca

SUGAR, NONMELTING King Arthur Flour Baker's Catalog

SUGAR, SANDING (WHITE AND COLORED) New York Cake & Baking Distributor

SUSHI RICE Uwajimaya

SZECHUAN PEPPERCORNS, WHOLE CMC Company

TORRONE igourmet.com

TRUFFLE OIL, WHITE AND BLACK Dean & DeLuca

VENISON D'Artagnan

ZAHTAR Sultan's Delight, Penzeys Spices

equipment sources

BAKING STONE Broadway Panhandler

BENCH SCRAPER Bridge Kitchenware, Broadway Panhandler

BROTFORMEN PANS King Arthur Flour Baker's Catalog

CAKE BOARDS Bridge Kitchenware, New York Cake & Baking Distributor

CHARLOTTE MOLD, 8 CUP Bridge Kitchenware

COOKIE CUTTERS (¾"–2½", VARIOUS SHAPES) New York Cake & Baking Distributor

CRÊPE PAN Bridge Kitchenware, Broadway Panhandler

DEEP-FRYING/CANDY THERMOMETER King Arthur Flour Baker's Catalog, Bridge Kitchenware

FISH GRILLING BASKET Broadway Panhandler

FISH SCALER Bridge Kitchenware

FLAN RING Bridge Kitchenware

FOOD MILL Bridge Kitchenware, Broadway Panhandler

HAM-SLICING KNIFE Bridge Kitchenware, Broadway Panhandler

ICE-CREAM MAKER Sur La Table

ICE-CREAM SCOOP (1¼") Bridge Kitchenware

INSTANT-READ THERMOMETER Bridge Kitchenware, Broadway Panhandler

JAPANESE MANDOLINE Broadway Panhandler

JAPANESE TURNING SLICER Katagiri & Co.

JELLY-ROLL PAN Bridge Kitchenware

LEAF-SHAPED CUTTER Bridge Kitchenware

METAL BAKING PAN AND RING Bridge Kitchenware

METAL PIE TIN Bridge Kitchenware

MINI CUPCAKE PAPERS New York Cake & Baking Distributor

MUFFIN TINS Bridge Kitchenware, Broadway Panhandler

PASTA MACHINE Bridge Kitchenware, Broadway Panhandler

PASTRY BAGS AND TIPS New York Cake & Baking Distributor, Bridge Kitchenware, Broadway Panhandler

PASTRY RING (2¾" X 2") Bridge Kitchenware

PETITS-FOURS CUPS Bridge Kitchenware, Broadway Panhandler

PIZZA PEEL Bridge Kitchenware, Broadway Panhandler

PIZZELLE IRON Bridge Kitchenware, Broadway Panhandler

POPOVER FRAMES Bridge Kitchenware

POTATO RICER Bridge Kitchenware, Broadway Panhandler

PUDDING MOLDS (5-CUP OVAL) Bridge Kitchenware, New York Cake & Baking Distributor

ROTATING CAKE STAND New York Cake & Baking Distributor

SALMON SLICING KNIFE Dean & DeLuca

SANDING SUGAR SET New York Cake & Baking Distributor

STEAMED PUDDING MOLDS/ BOWLS Bridge Kitchenware

STENCILS Martha by Mail

TART PAN (4" FLUTED, 10" HEART) New York Cake & Baking Distributor

TART RING, ROUND (9" X 1¾") New York Cake & Baking Distributor

TARTLET PAN WITH REMOVABLE BOTTOM (1" TO 4") New York Cake & Baking Distributor

TUBE PAN (10" HEART AND 7" ROUND) Bridge Kitchenware

WOODEN MALLETS Obrycki's Crab House and Seafood Restaurant, Broadway Panhandler

directory

ADRIANA'S CARAVAN
120 Coulter Avenue
#15/009
Ardmore, PA 19003
718-436-8565
800-316-0820
www.adrianascaravan.com

*Catalog available. Spices and
ethnic ingredients, including
tamarind concentrate, brown
and black mustard seeds, dried
pomegranate seeds, dried and
fresh curry leaves, Indian basmati rice, red curry paste, juniper berries, hot paprika, and
sea salt*

A.L. BAZZINI COMPANY
339 Greenwich Street
New York, NY 10013
212-334-1280
www.bazzininuts.com

*Catalog available. Nuts and
dried fruit, including toasted
hazelnuts, dried sour cherries,
dried apple slices, dried mangos, dried banana chips, almond flour, dried and peeled
chestnuts (seasonal), dried figs*

AMERICAN SPOON FOODS
P.O. Box 566
Petoskey, MI 49770
888-735-6700 (catalog)
800-222-5886 (customer service)
www.spoon.com

*Catalog available. Dried fruit,
including apple slices and sour
cherries*

ASIAN FOOD GROCER
131 W. Harris Avenue So.
San Francisco, CA 94080
888-482-2742
www.asianfoodgrocer.com

Dashi, komou seaweed

BASSE'S CHOICE
P.O. Box 250
Portsmouth, VA 23705
800-292-2773
www.smithfieldhams.com

*Country-cured ham: Genuine
Smithfield*

BRIDGE KITCHENWARE
711 3rd Avenue
New York, NY 10017
212-688-4220
800-274-3435 (outside New York)
www.bridgekitchenware.com

*Catalog $3 (applied to first
purchase). Deep-frying/candy
thermometer, food mill, potato
ricer, bench scraper, charlotte
mold, citrus zester, crêpe pans,
fish scaler, 10-inch heart-
shaped tube pan, jelly-roll pan,
muffin tins, leaf-shaped cutter,
metal baking pans, pasta ma-*
*chine, pastry ring, petits-fours
cups, pizza peel, Silpat baking
mat, steamed pudding
molds/bowls, pastry bags and
piping tips, ice-cream scoops,
ham-slicing knife, flan rings,
instant-read thermometer, pudding molds, popover frames,
pizzelle iron, cake boards,
metal pie tin*

BROADWAY PANHANDLER
65 E. 8th Street
New York, NY 10003
212-966-3434
www.broadwaypanhandler.com

*Citrus zester, fish grilling bas-
ket, food mill, pizzelle iron,
bench scraper, Japanese mandoline, wooden mallets, potato
ricer, crêpe pans, fish scaler,
ham-slicing knife, muffin tins,
pasta machine, petits-fours
cups, Silpat baking mat, pastry
bags and piping tips, instant-
read thermometer, pizza peel,
baking stone*

BROWNE TRADING COMPANY
800-944-7848
www.browne-trading.com

*Catalog available. Specialty
seafood, including smoked
salmon and caviar; squid ink
packets*

CHEFSHOP.COM
1415 Elliot Avenue W.
Seattle, WA 98119
800-596-0885
www.chefshop.com

Bonito flakes

CITARELLA
2135 Broadway
New York, NY 10023
212-874-0383
www.citarella.com

Shucked oysters

CMC COMPANY
401 Laura Drive #2
Danville, PA 17821
800-262-2780
www.thecmccompany.com

Specialty ethnic ingredients, including sambal, Morita chiles, crab boil, bladed mace, whole Szechuan peppercorns

D'ARTAGNAN
280 Wilson Avenue
Newark, NJ 07105
800-327-8246
www.dartagnan.com

Catalog available. Fresh game, foie gras, venison, and venison sausage

DEAN & DELUCA
560 Broadway
New York, NY 10012
800-999-0306
www.deandeluca.com

Catalog available. Mascarpone cheese, apple bacon, cooked Parma ham, brown mustard seeds, amaretti cookies, maple sugar, dried fennel branches, French green lentils, goose fat, salmon slicing knife, almond flour, dried porcini mushrooms, quatre épices, Rustichella D'Abruzzo pasta, white and black truffle oil, preserved lemons, Fregola pasta, dried figs, vacuum-packed chestnuts, sugar pumpkins (seasonal), meyer lemons, baby bok choy, kumquats

DIAMONDORGANICS.COM
272 Hwy 1
Moss Landing, CA 95039
888-674-2642
www.diamondorganics.com

Tatso, mizuna

FRIEDA'S INC.
4465 Corporate Center Drive
Los Alamitas, CA 90720
800-241-1771
www.friedas.com

Exotic and specialty produce, including sugarcane and Hungarian wax peppers

FRONTIER NATURAL PRODUCTS CO-OP
3021 78th Street
P.O. Box 299
Norway, IA 52318
800-669-3275
www.frontiercoop.com

Dried licorice root, dried peppermint leaves, dried goldenseal, echinacea, dried slippery elm, dried chamomile flowers, dried hibiscus flowers, dried verbena leaves

HARNEY & SONS
Box 665
Salisbury, CT 06068
888-427-6398
www.harney.com

Catalog available. A variety of imported teas

HOPPIN' JOHN'S
800-828-4412
www.hoppinjohns.com

Stone-ground grits

IMPORTFOOD.COM
P.O. Box 2054
Issaquah, WA 98027
888-618-8424
www.importfood.com

Dried shrimp

KALUSTYAN'S
123 Lexington Avenue
New York, NY 10016
212-685-3451
www.kalustyans.com

Israeli couscous, orange-blossom water, dried morels, wasabi paste, tandoori masala, seasoned rice vinegar

KATAGIRI & CO.
224 and 226 East 59th Street
New York, NY 10022
212-755-3566
212-838-5453
www.katagiri.com

Fresh shiso leaves, dumpling wrappers, Japanese turning slicer

KING ARTHUR FLOUR BAKER'S CATALOG
58 Billings Farm Rd.
White River Junction, VT 05001
800-827-6836
www.kingarthurflour.com

Catalog available. Extensive selection of supplies including nonmelting sugar, amber sugar, pearl sugar, semolina, cake flour, rye flour, brotformen pans, crystal sugar, deep-frying/candy thermometer

KITCHEN/MARKET
218 8th Avenue
New York NY 10011
888-468-4433
www.kitchenmarket.com

Catalog available. Dried ancho chile peppers, harissa, *guajillo chiles, achiote paste, dried pasilla chiles, Mexican oregano, black sesame seeds, morita powder, dried chipotle chile peppers, dried masa harina, chile paste, sesame chile oil, chipotle chiles in adobo, posole, unsweetened coconut, molcajete mortar and pestle, and dried peppers, such as cascabel, mora, and pequin*

MELISSA'S WORLD VARIETY PRODUCE INC.
P.O. Box 21127
Los Angeles, CA 90021
800-588-0151
www.melissas.com

Catalog available. Extensive variety of produce, including Asian produce, dried morels, dried porcini mushrooms, powdered wasabi (seasonal), kumquats (seasonal)

MURRAY'S CHEESE SHOP
254 Bleecker Street
New York, NY 10014
212-243-3289
888-692-4339
www.murrayscheese.com

Imported and domestic cheeses, including pecorino and taleggio

NEW YORK CAKE & BAKING DISTRIBUTOR
56 West 22nd Street, #1
New York, NY 10010
212-675-2253
800-942-2539
www.nycake.com

Baking and decorating supplies, including citric acid, anise extract, apricot extract, sanding sugar, gel and paste food coloring, meringue powder, edible wafer paper, paper candy cups, ice cream cup mold, fluted tart pan, tartlet pan with removable bottom, pudding mold (oval), tart ring, cake boards, metal baking rings, paper cupcake liners, pastry bags and piping tips, heart-shaped tart pan, rotating cake stand

NORTHCOUNTRY SMOKEHOUSE
471 Sullivan Street
Claremont, NH 03743
800-258-4304
www.ncsmokehouse.com

Corncob-smoked bacon

OBRYCKI'S CRAB HOUSE AND SEAFOOD RESTAURANT
1727 E. Pratt Street
Baltimore, MD 21231
410-732-6399
www.obryckis.com

Crab boil seasoning, wooden mallets

PENZEYS SPICES
P.O. Box 924
Brookfield, WI 53008
800-741-7787
www.penzeys.com

*Catalog available. Dried herbs
and spices, including pink peppercorns, galangal, long peppers, green cardamom pods,
brown mustard seeds, Chinese
five-spice powder, zahtar, fenugreek, paprika, dried ancho
chile peppers, dried chipotle
chile peppers, sesame seeds,
ancho chile powder*

PERFECT PURÉE OF NAPA VALLEY
2700 Napa Valley Corporate Drive
Suite L
Napa, CA 94558
800-556-3707
www.perfectpuree.com

*Black currant purée, passion
fruit concentrate purée*

RAFAL SPICE COMPANY
2521 Russell Street
Detroit, MI 48207
313-259-6373
800-228-4276
www.rafalspicecompany.com

Pickling lime

RUSS & DAUGHTERS
179 East Houston Street
New York, NY 10002
212-475-4880
800-787-7229
www.russanddaughters.com

*Assorted caviar and smoked
fish, including golden caviar;
candied fruits and glacé fruit*

SALUMERIA ITALIANA
Guy Martignetti
151 Richmond Street
Boston, MA 02109
800-400-5916
www.salumeriaitaliana.com

*Carnaroli rice, amaretti
cookies*

SCHALLER AND WEBER
1654 Second Avenue
New York, NY 10028
212-879-3047
www.schallerweber.com

*A variety of meats and
sausages, including white veal
sausage, smoked country
sausage, knackwurst*

THE SHOWCASE OF CITRUS
5010 Highway 27
Clermont, FL 34711
352-394-4377
www.showcaseofcitrus.com

*Fresh key limes (seasonal),
key lime juice*

SIMPLY NATURAL
Discount Natural Foods
146 Londonderry Turnpike #10
Hooksett, NH 03106
888-392-9237
www.simplynatural.biz

*Assorted grains, including
buckwheat kasha*

SULTAN'S DELIGHT
7128 5th Avenue
Brooklyn, NY 11209
800-852-5046
www.sultansdelight.com

Zahtar, pomegranate syrup

SUNRISE MART
494 Broome Street
2nd Floor
New York, NY 10013
212-219-0033

*Japanese specialty foods, in-
cluding dumpling wrappers,
pickled ginger, rice noodles,
fresh shiso leaves*

SUR LA TABLE
800-243-0852
www.surlatable.com

*Catalog available. Lussino
ice-cream maker*

TAKASHIMAYA
693 5th Avenue
New York, NY 10022
212-350-0100
800-753-2038

*Eastern and French herbal
teas, tea-related accessories,
Japanese kitchen utensils,
dried lavender*

TEMPLE OF THAI
14525 SW Millikan Way
RCM #10102
Beaverton, OR 97005
877-811-8773
templeofthai.com

*Asian rice noodles (bahn pho),
dried and flat rice noodles*

UPTOWN WHOLE FOODS
2421 Broadway
New York, NY 10024
212-874-4000

*Cracked wheat, Irish and Scot-
tish steel-cut oats, bulgur
wheat, unsweetened coconut,
millet, wheat flakes, popcorn
rice, grains*

URBANI TRUFFLES USA
Shore Pt., One Selleck Street
Norwalk, CT 06855
203-855-5766
877-482-7883
www.urbaniusa.com

*Catalog available. Fresh and
dried mushrooms, including
fresh chanterelles (seasonal),
fresh white and black truffles
(seasonal), truffle oil*

UWAJIMAYA
600 5th Avenue S.
Seattle, WA 98104
800-889-1928
www.uwajimaya.com

*Asian specialty foods, includ-
ing pickled ginger, miso paste,
sesame seeds, dumpling
wrappers, sushi rice, fresh
shiso leaves*

WELLFLEET OYSTER AND CLAM
P.O. Box 1439
60 Lewispain Way
Wellfleet, MA 02667
800-572-9227
wellfleetoysterandclam.com

*Quahog clams, oysters, and
other shellfish*

ZINGERMAN'S DELICATESSEN
422 Detroit Street
Ann Arbor, MI 48104
888-636-8162
www.zingermans.com

*Catalog available. Specialty
foods and delicacies, including
sweet sopressata, flaky sea
salt, cornichons, bresaola*

photograph credits

SANG AN 33

QUENTIN BACON 179

CHRISTOPHER BAKER 49

JOHN BLAIS 44 (right)

BEATRIZ DA COSTA 34, 44 (top and bottom left)

REED DAVIS 45, 47 (right), 51 (right), 54 (left), 187, 227, 255, 364

FORMULA Z/S 58 (top right)

DANA GALLAGHER 37 (right), 51 (left), 60, 234, 588

GENTL + HYERS 38 (right), 40, 62. 63, 184, 201

GRACE HUANG 53

KEN KOCHEY 46

MAURA MCEVOY 55 (left)

AMY NEUNSINGER 38 (left)

VICTORIA PEARSON 35, 42-43, 56

MARIA ROBLEDO 41, 54 (right), 55 (right), 57, 58 (bottom left and right), 59, 61 (left and right), 64, 325, 545

DAVID SAWYER 50, 197, 277, 291

VICTOR SCHRAGER 48

MATTHEW SEPTIMUS 523

PETRINA TINSLAY 52

SIMON WATSON 565

ANNA WILLIAMS 36, 37 (left), 39, 47 (left), 243, 556

index

Note: *Italicized* page numbers indicate photographs.